THE OXFORD HANDBOOK OF
INTERNATIONAL ENVIRONMENTAL LAW

THE OXFORD HANDBOOK OF

INTERNATIONAL ENVIRONMENTAL LAW

Second Edition

Edited by

LAVANYA RAJAMANI

and

JACQUELINE PEEL

OXFORD
UNIVERSITY PRESS

OXFORD
UNIVERSITY PRESS

Great Clarendon Street, Oxford, OX2 6DP,
United Kingdom

Oxford University Press is a department of the University of Oxford. It furthers the University's objective of excellence in research, scholarship, and education by publishing worldwide. Oxford is a registered trade mark of Oxford University Press in the UK and in certain other countries

First Edition published in 2007
Second Edition published in 2021

Published in the United States of America by Oxford University Press
198 Madison Avenue, New York, NY 10016, United States of America

British Library Cataloguing in Publication Data
Data available

Library of Congress Control Number: 2020952249

ISBN 978–0–19–884915–5

DOI: 10.1093/law/9780198849155.001.0001

Printed and bound by
CPI Group (UK) Ltd, Croydon, CR0 4YY

Preface

In almost a decade and a half, international environmental law has expanded and matured. But the question remains, 'Is International Environmental Law fit for purpose?', as Lavanya Rajamani and Jacqueline Peel point out in their introduction to this second edition of the Handbook of International Environmental Law. When the first edition of the handbook was published in 2007, international environmental law was still a relatively young field. Customary law and treaty law had been applied to selected conservation or pollution issues since the late nineteenth century. But it was not until after the 1972 Stockholm Conference on the Human Environment that modern international environmental law began to grow in earnest, with the 1992 Rio Conference on Environment and Development providing a significant impulse for its further development. Since 2007, international environmental law has acquired 'breadth, depth, nuance, complexity, and reach', as Lavanya and Jacqueline note in their introduction. 'Nevertheless, international environmental law's achievements in environmental terms' continue to be 'modest'.

Our goal in 2007 was to capture the distinctive debates, concepts, features, and approaches of what we concluded had emerged as a discrete field in international law. Rather than focus on the substantive content of the law, the first edition sought to provide an analytical map that we hoped would offer durable guidance and insight about international environmental law both as a subject area and as a discipline. The second edition has expanded the handbook's coverage. But while the number of chapters has grown, the basic approach remains the same: the second edition too is committed to providing durable analysis to assist readers in navigating, and reflecting on, the field. Indeed, taken together, the two editions of the handbook serve to illuminate the field's evolution from 2007 to the present. Against the backdrop of the fading of post-Cold War optimism and the onset of the backlash against multilateralism, international environmental law has both expanded and retreated, gained in strength while being diluted.

The new edition of the handbook examines the evolving range of conceptual and analytical approaches deployed to make sense of the pressures on, and trends in, the field. It highlights international environmental law's relatively constant conceptual pillars and reveals the shifts in the relative importance of approaches to normative development. While treaties, for example, remain central sites of normative development, the adoption of new treaties has slowed, and norm development activity has shifted to non-binding standard setting under the auspices of existing environmental agreements and by non-state actors. Also noteworthy is the increasing focus on procedural environmental law. This is seen both in treaty law, as exemplified by the largely procedural obligations of the Paris Agreement, as well as in the jurisprudence of the International Court of Justice, which has elaborated the duty of due diligence through procedural obligations of assessment, notification, and consultation.

In the first edition, we flagged the fact that international environmental problems are primarily caused by private conduct as a key trait, and challenge for, the field. The second edition is testament to the manifold ways in which international environmental law has come to embrace the important role of non-state actors, be it in approaches to governance, standard setting, or implementation. Similarly, while inter-state recourse to international courts, notwithstanding some up-tick, remains sporadic, individuals and civil society groups are bringing an ever-growing number of cases involving international environmental issues to national courts or human rights tribunals. The second edition tracks these developments in chapters examining the role of courts in normative development, inter-state dispute settlement, and, not least, in a new section on developments in national and regional courts.

The growth of international environmental law has caused it to be increasingly interwoven with other branches of international law. The first edition of the handbook devoted a single chapter to the relationship between international environmental law and other areas of international law. The second edition reflects the exponential developments since 2007, with eight chapters now devoted to the interplay between international environmental law and areas ranging from trade to human rights to armed conflict. Finally, the expansion and maturation of international environmental law as a discipline is also reflected in the diversity of scholars represented in this second edition of the handbook.

It is a real pleasure to hand over editorial responsibilities for the handbook to our good friends and colleagues, Lavanya and Jacqueline. We know from experience that editing the handbook is a daunting, even if intellectually fascinating, task. Anyone who knows Lavanya and Jacqueline will not be surprised that they have carried it out with their usual insight and grace. Congratulations on the publication of this second edition, which we are confident will enlighten generations of academics and practitioners.

Daniel Bodansky, Jutta Brunnée, and Ellen Hey
November 2020

Acknowledgements

THE four years it took us to steer this volume to completion—with sixty-seven chapters and seventy-five authors—have been eventful. Our knowledge of the dynamic field of international environmental law has grown exponentially thanks to the rich and scholarly contributions we received. We have acquired a new and useful set of managerial skills, and learned that academics take many routes to a scholarly contribution. We have made many new friends and deepened previous collaborations. And, we've incurred countless debts.

We are immensely grateful to the exceptional group of scholars and practitioners who contributed such insightful chapters to the second edition of the handbook. It has been a privilege for us to work with such a talented and genuinely nice group of international environmental lawyers.

A volume of this size and complexity, however, demands an immense 'back of house' effort from many people beyond the listed contributors. We are particularly grateful to Bhuvanyaa Vijay, who has been the organizational glue that held this vast project together and kept the manuscript on schedule. Her work ethic, copy-editing skills, and attention to detail are evident in the quality (and consistency) of the final manuscript. We could not have done this as seamlessly as we have without her. At Melbourne Law School, a special thank-you is also due to Rebekkah Markey-Towler, who assisted with the referencing effort for the introduction to the handbook.

We also recognize, with gratitude, the financial and other support offered to the project by our respective institutions, the Centre for Policy Research in New Delhi, Oxford University, and the University of Melbourne, which provided various grants and research assistance to facilitate the project. In particular, the University of Melbourne Law School supported the project through a Research Excellence grant (which allowed us to collaborate on the project in Melbourne and to employ, in conjunction with the Centre for Policy Research, the wonderful Bhuvanyaa) and via its Institute for International Law and the Humanities (IILAH), which loaned us time from Balawyn Jones to assist with the review of first chapter drafts.

At Oxford University Press there are also many in the publishing team to whom our gratitude is due. We would particularly like to thank Jack McNichol and Merel Alstein from OUP's legal team who, in addition to discharging all the usual publishing responsibilities efficiently, provided us with the right combination of encouragement, advice, and space to complete this project. The last year of the production process overlapped with the global pandemic but our remarkable team of contributors, assistants, publishers, and OUP's skilful production house in Chennai, kept the project on track. We are eternally grateful for the professionalism we have encountered through the entire project, and for the professional relationships that we have been fortunate to have built over this time.

Finally, we thank our families who are a source of endless support for our endeavours, and particularly our children who provide inspiration for our continuing efforts to improve environmental protections in international law.

Lavanya Rajamani and Jacqueline Peel
September 2020

Contents

PART III CONCEPTUAL PILLARS

PART IV NORMATIVE DEVELOPMENT

PART V SUBJECT MATTER

PART VI ACTORS

PART VII INTER-LINKAGES WITH OTHER REGIMES

PART IX INTERNATIONAL ENVIRONMENTAL LAW IN NATIONAL/REGIONAL COURTS

Table of Cases

AFRICAN COMMISSION ON HUMAN AND PEOPLE'S RIGHTS

AFRICAN COURT ON HUMAN AND PEOPLE'S RIGHTS

EUROPEAN COMMITTEE OF SOCIAL RIGHTS

EUROPEAN COURT OF HUMAN RIGHTS

EUROPEAN COURT OF JUSTICE

EUROPEAN PATENT OFFICE

INTER-AMERICAN COMMISSION ON HUMAN RIGHTS

INTER-AMERICAN COURT OF HUMAN RIGHTS

INTERNATIONAL CENTER FOR THE SETTLEMENT OF INVESTMENT DISPUTES

INTERNATIONAL COURT OF JUSTICE

INTERNATIONAL TRIBUNAL FOR THE LAW OF THE SEA

IRAN-US CLAIMS TRIBUNALS

OTHER AD-HOC ARBITRATION

PERMANENT COURT OF ARBITRATION

PERMANENT COURT OF INTERNATIONAL JUSTICE

REPORTS OF INTERNATIONAL ARBITRAL AWARDS

UN HUMAN RIGHTS COMMITTEE

WORLD TRADE ORGANIZATION

ARGENTINA

AUSTRALIA

BANGLADESH

BRAZIL

CANADA

CHILE

CHINA

COLOMBIA

COOK ISLANDS

FEDERATED STATES OF MICRONESIA

INDIA

ITALY

KENYA

NETHERLANDS

NEW ZEALAND

PAKISTAN

PAPUA NEW GUINEA

PHILIPPINES

REPUBLIC OF SOUTH AFRICA

UGANDA

UNITED KINGDOM

UNITED STATES

TABLE OF LEGISLATION

INTERNATIONAL INSTRUMENTS

INTERNATIONAL DOCUMENTS

CBD Documents

DECISIONS

ECOSOC Documents

FAO Documents

ICAO Documents

ILA Documents

ILC Documents

IMO Documents

IPCC Documents

OECD Documents

UNCC Documents

UNHRC and OHCHR Documents

RESOLUTIONS

UN Environment Documents

UNESCO Documents

UNFCCC Documents

DECISIONS

UNGA Documents

UNSC Documents

World Bank Documents

WTO Documents

Decisions and documents under various Conventions

EU LEGISLATION

Commission

Decisions and Directives

Regulations

Treaties

OTHER LEGISLATION

Argentina

Australia

Bangladesh

Bolivia

Brazil

Canada

China

Contributors

Natasha Affolder

Natasha Affolder is a Professor of Law at the Peter A Allard School of Law, University of British Columbia. Her research and teaching seek to illuminate the complexity of transnational environmental law and its practice.

Shawkat Alam

Shawkat Alam is a Professor of Law and Director of the Centre for Environmental Law at Macquarie University, Australia. He teaches and researches in the area of international law, with a focus on developing economies achieving sustainable development by examining international legal, institutional and policy frameworks.

Steinar Andresen

Steinar Andresen is a Research Professor at the Fridtjof Nansen Institute in Norway. He has published extensively internationally, particularly on global environmental governance.

J Michael Angstadt

J Michael Angstadt is an Assistant Professor of Environmental Studies at Colorado College. He researches how domestic legal systems interact with international environmental law and global environmental politics.

Harro van Asselt

Harro van Asselt is a Professor of Climate Law and Policy with the University of Eastern Finland Law School, a Research Fellow with the Copernicus Institute of Sustainable Development at Utrecht University, and Associate with the Stockholm Environment Institute. He has published widely on climate change law and policy and its interactions with other fields of law. He is also Editor of the *Review of European, Comparative and International Environmental Law* (RECIEL).

Sumudu Atapattu

Sumudu Atapattu is Director of Research Centers and International Programs at University of Wisconsin Law School, United States. She is affiliated faculty with Raoul Wallenberg Institute for Human Rights and Lead Counsel for Human Rights at CISDL. She has published widely on international environmental law, human rights and environment, climate change and human rights, and sustainable development.

Lisa Benjamin
Lisa Benjamin is an Assistant Professor at Lewis & Clark Law School. She has published extensively on international environmental law and climate law with a focus on developing countries and non-state actors. She is a member of the Compliance Committee (Facilitative Branch) of the UNFCCC.

Michele Betsill
Michele Betsill is a Professor of Political Science at Colorado State University and Associate Editor of the *Earth System Governance* journal. She is a leading scholar on non-state and sub-national actors in global environmental governance.

Daniel Bodansky
Daniel Bodansky is Regents' Professor of Law at the Sandra Day O'Connor College of Law, Arizona State University. He served as Climate Change Coordinator and Attorney-Adviser at the US State Department, and has published widely in the areas of public international law, international environmental law, and climate change law.

Alan Boyle
Alan Boyle is Emeritus Professor of Public International Law at the University of Edinburgh School of Law. His publications include *International Law and the Environment* (with Catherine Redgwell) (4th edn, 2021) and *The Making of International Law* (with Christine Chinkin). He is a barrister and practises international law from Essex Court Chambers, London.

Carl Bruch
Carl Bruch directs International Programs at the Environmental Law Institute and is the founding President of the Environmental Peacebuilding Association. He has helped many conflict-affected countries in Africa, the Americas, and Asia improve management of their environment and natural resources to support a sustainable peace.

Jutta Brunnée
Jutta Brunnée is Dean & James M. Tory Professor of Law; University Professor; Faculty of Law, University of Toronto. She was elected Fellow of the Royal Society of Canada in 2013 and Associate of the Institut de Droit International in 2017. In 2019, she delivered a course at the Hague Academy of International Law.

Laurence Boisson de Chazournes
Laurence Boisson de Chazournes is a Professor at the University of Geneva and Co-Director of the Geneva Center for International Dispute Settlement. She acts as arbitrator in investor-state disputes and has acted as Counsel in renowned international environmental law cases before the International Court of Justice (ICJ) and other dispute settlement fora.

Lynda Collins
Lynda Collins is a Full Professor with the Centre for Environmental Law & Global Sustainability at the University of Ottawa, Canada. She is an expert in rights-based approaches to environmental protection.

Philippe Cullet

Philippe Cullet is Professor of International and Environmental Law at SOAS University of London and a Senior Visiting Fellow at the Centre for Policy Research, New Delhi. He has published extensively on international and India's environmental law, natural resources law, water and sanitation law and policy, and socio-economic rights.

Cormac Cullinan

Cormac Cullinan practises as an environmental attorney in Cape Town, is a director of the Wild Law Institute, and is active in the global rights of Nature movement. His book *Wild Law: a Manifesto for Earth Justice* pioneered the Earth Jurisprudence approach based on principles formulated by Thomas Berry.

Meinhard Doelle

Meinhard Doelle is a Professor at the Schulich School of Law, Dalhousie University, Canada, and Chair, Marine Environmental Protection, at the World Maritime University. He is an associate with the Marine & Environmental Law Institute, and a senior fellow with CIGI. His teaching and publications have focused on climate change, energy, and environmental assessment law and governance.

David M Driesen

David M Driesen is Syracuse University's thirteenth University Professor. He has published numerous books and articles about law and economics, including extensive writing on instrument choice in environmental law.

John S Dryzek

John S Dryzek is Australian Research Council Laureate Fellow and Centenary Professor in the Centre for Deliberative Democracy and Global Governance at the University of Canberra, Australia. He is the author of a number of books on environmental politics and governance, climate change, and the Anthropocene.

Jeffrey L Dunoff

Jeffrey L Dunoff is the Laura H Carnell Professor of Law at Temple University Beasley School of Law. His research focuses on public international law; international regulatory regimes, including particularly international environmental and economic regimes; international courts and organizations; international legal theory; and interdisciplinary approaches to international law.

Pierre-Marie Dupuy

Pierre-Marie Dupuy is Emeritus Professor at the University of Paris (Panthéon-Assas) and at the Graduate Institute of International and Development Studies in Geneva. He delivered a General Course of International law at the Hague Academy of International Law in 2000 (vol 297, 2002). He has appeared before the ICJ in a number of inter-state cases, and he is an international arbitrator (ICSID, PCA, LCIA). He is a member of the IDI (Institut de droit international). In 2015, he was awarded the Manley Hudson Medal.

Jonas Ebbesson

Jonas Ebbesson is Professor of Environmental Law, former Dean, and Director of Stockholm Environmental Law and Policy Centre, at Stockholm University. He is also the Chair of the Compliance Committee of the UNECE Convention on Access to Information, Public Participation in Decision-making and Access to Justice in Environmental Matters (Aarhus Convention).

Adriana Fabra

Adriana Fabra is an expert in ocean law and policy. She has a long record of consultancy for non-profit organizations, most recently on fisheries-related issues for the Pew Charitable Trusts and the International MCS Network. She has combined research and policy advice with writing and teaching on a wide range of environmental matters.

Michael Faure

Michael Faure is a Professor of Comparative and International Environmental Law at Maastricht University and Director of the Maastricht European Institute of Transnational Legal Research (METRO). He is also a Professor of Comparative Private Law and Economics at the Erasmus School of Law (Rotterdam) and Academic Director of the European Doctorate in Law and Economics (EDLE).

Elizabeth Fisher

Elizabeth Fisher is Professor of Environmental Law, Corpus Christi College & Faculty of Law, University of Oxford.

Duncan French

Duncan French is Pro Vice Chancellor and Professor of International Law at the University of Lincoln in the United Kingdom. He has written widely on international environmental law, sustainable development, and general matters of public international law, including law of the sea and dispute settlement.

Shibani Ghosh

Shibani Ghosh is a Fellow, Centre for Policy Research, New Delhi and an Advocate-on-Record, Supreme Court of India. Her broad area of research is domestic environmental law and regulation. As a litigator, she is involved in several environmental cases before the Supreme Court of India and the National Green Tribunal.

Alexander Gillespie

Alexander Gillespie is a Professor at the School of Law, Waikato University, New Zealand. His areas of scholarship pertain to international and comparative environmental law; the laws of war; civil liberties; and a number of pressing issues of social concern. Alexander has published sixteen books. Those of most interest to this chapter are *International Environmental Law, Policy and Ethics*; and *The Long Road to Sustainability*.

Peter M Haas

Peter M Haas is a Professor of Political Science at the University of Massachusetts Amherst. He has had visiting positions at Yale University, Brown, Keio University, Oxford, and the Wissenschaftszentrum, Berlin. He has published extensively on international relations theory, constructivism, international environmental politics, global governance, and the science- policy interface. He is the recipient of the 2014 Distinguished Scholar Award of the International Studies Association Environmental Studies Section, and the 2015 University of Massachusetts Amherst Award for Outstanding Accomplishments in Research and Creative Activity.

Ellen Hey

Ellen Hey is Professor of Public International Law at Erasmus School of Law, Erasmus University, Rotterdam. She has worked for the Netherlands government, nongovernmental organizations, and international organizations (as a consultant), such as the European Union, the UN Food and Agriculture Organization, the UN Development Program, UN Environment, and the World Bank, and, inter alia several roles, has served as a member of the Aarhus Compliance Mechanism, as editor-in-chief of the Erasmus Law Review, and member of the editorial board of The Netherlands Yearbook of International Law. Her research interests include international institutional law, in particular the accountability of international organizations, and international natural resources law, including the law of the sea. Together with Professors Daniel Bodansky and Jutta Brunnée, she edited the first edition of The Oxford Handbook of International Environmental Law (OUP 2008).

Sam Johnston

Sam Johnston is a Senior Fellow at the Melbourne Law School; Project Manager, Baker & McKenzie Law for Development Initiative; International Lead Consultant, United Nations Development Programme; Consultant, UN Food and Agricultural Organisation; Indigenous Peoples Consultant, Green Climate Fund; Member of the Environmental and Social Safeguards (ESS) Experts Roster for the Green Climate Fund; Member of the Advisory Board of the Centre for Resources, Energy and Environmental Law, University of Melbourne; and Co-Chair of the Panel of Experts for the Benefit-sharing Fund of the International Treaty on Plant Genetic Resources for Food and Agriculture. He is also a qualified solicitor in Victoria, Australia.

Walter Kälin

Walter Kälin is Professor Emeritus of International and Constitutional Law at the Faculty of Law of the University of Bern, Switzerland and the present Envoy of the chair of the Platform on Disaster Displacement (formerly: The Nansen Initiative on Cross-Border Disaster-Displacement). He has published extensively on legal aspects of internal and cross-border displacement.

Natalie Klein

Natalie Klein is a Professor at UNSW Sydney's Faculty of Law, Australia. She previously served as Dean of Macquarie Law School and Acting Head of the Department for Policing, Intelligence and Counter-Terrorism at Macquarie University. Professor Klein's research focuses on law of the sea and international dispute settlement.

John H Knox

John H Knox is the Henry C Lauerman Professor of International Law at Wake Forest University, in North Carolina. From 2012 to 2018, he was the first United Nations Independent Expert, then the first Special Rapporteur, on human rights and the environment.

Louis J Kotzé

Louis J Kotzé is Research Professor of Law at North-West University, South Africa and Senior Visiting Professorial Fellow of Earth System Law at the University of Lincoln, United Kingdom. He has keen interests in global environmental constitutionalism, law and the Anthropocene, and Earth system law.

Peter Lawrence

Peter Lawrence is a Senior Lecturer, and co-convenor of the Climate Justice Network, Faculty of Law, College of Arts, Law and Education, University of Tasmania, Australia. He has published extensively in the field of international environmental law. Peter is a former diplomat with the Australian Department of Foreign Affairs and Trade and Senior Research Fellow, Earth System Governance Project.

Jolene Lin

Jolene Lin is Associate Professor and Director of the Asia Pacific Centre for Environmental Law at the Faculty of Law, National University of Singapore. She has published extensively on climate law, as well as environmental law in Asia.

Rowena Maguire

Rowena Maguire is an Associate Professor within the School of Law and a Domain Leader within the Institute for Future Environments at the Queensland University of Technology. She researches land-based environmental governance in the areas of forestry, agriculture, and waste, and focuses on gender and equity.

Sandrine Maljean-Dubois

Sandrine Maljean-Dubois is a researcher at the CNRS. She teaches international environmental law at the Faculty of Law and Political Sciences of Aix-Marseille University. She has published extensively on international environmental law, biodiversity, and climate change law as well as compliance mechanisms and the effectiveness of environmental law.

Thilo Marauhn

Thilo Marauhn is a Professor of Public Law and International Law at Justus Liebig University, Giessen, Germany. He also serves as head of the Research Group, Public International Law at the Peace Research Institute Frankfurt and is a Permanent Visiting Professor at the University of Lucerne, Switzerland. He has published widely on general international law and international environmental law.

Michael A Mehling

Michael A Mehling is a Professor at the University of Strathclyde Law School, and Deputy Director of the Center for Energy and Environmental Policy Research at the Massachusetts Institute of Technology. He is also the founding editor of the *Carbon & Climate Law Review*, the first academic journal dedicated to climate law and regulation.

Kate Miles

Kate Miles is a Fellow and Lecturer in Law, Gonville and Caius College, Cambridge, and a Fellow of the Lauterpacht Centre for International Law, University of Cambridge. She has published extensively on the interaction between international investment law and international environmental law.

Ronald B Mitchell

Ronald B Mitchell is a Professor of Political Science and Environmental Studies at the University of Oregon, United States. He has authored or co-authored four books, over twenty articles, and over thirty chapters on international environmental politics and international relations more generally.

Ginevra Le Moli

Ginevra Le Moli is Assistant Professor of Public International Law at the Grotius Center for International Legal Studies, University of Leiden (The Netherlands). She was previously a legal consultant for the UN OHCHR investigation teams for Syria and Yemen, for which she conducted several field missions.

Phoebe Okowa

Phoebe Okowa is Professor of Public International Law at Queen Mary, University of London. Educated at the University of Nairobi and Oxford, she previously taught at the University of Bristol and has held visiting appointments at the University of Lille and Stockholm. In 2011 and 2015 she was Global Visiting Professor at New York University, School of Law. She has published extensively on many topics in public international law including the interface between state responsibility and individual accountability for international crimes, unilateral and collective responses to protection of natural resources in conflict zones, and aspects of the protection of environment.

Hari M Osofsky

Hari M Osofsky is the Dean of Penn State Law and School of International Affairs, and also a Distinguished Professor of Law, Professor of International Affairs, and Professor of Geography at The Pennsylvania State University. Dean Osofsky's over fifty publications focus on improving governance and addressing injustice in energy and climate change regulation. Her scholarship includes books with Cambridge University Press on climate change litigation, textbooks on both energy and climate change law, and articles in leading law and geography journals.

Alice Palmer

Dr. Alice Palmer is a Senior Fellow at the Melbourne Law School. As a lawyer with the Foundation for International Environmental Law and Development (FIELD) in the United Kingdom, she assisted governments and non-governmental organizations in their work to implement international environmental law. Alice has published on international environmental law in national courts. Her research concerns the aesthetics of image in international environmental law.

Cymie R Payne

Cymie R Payne is Associate Professor of Law at Rutgers University, New Jersey. She has acted as expert and counsel before the International Court of Justice and the International Tribunal for the Law of the Sea.

Jacqueline Peel
Jacqueline Peel is a Professor of Law and Associate Director of the Centre for Resources, Energy and Environmental Law at the Melbourne Law School, Australia. She has published extensively on international environmental law and climate law, as well as the precautionary principle and the role of science in environmental regulation.

Anne Peters
Anne Peters is Director at the Max Planck Institute for Comparative Public Law and International Law Heidelberg, a Professor at the Universities of Heidelberg, Freie Universität Berlin, and Basel (Switzerland), and a William W Cook Global Law Professor at the University of Michigan.

Lavanya Rajamani
Lavanya Rajamani is Professor of International Environmental Law at the University of Oxford, Yamani Fellow in Public International Law at St Peter's College, Oxford, and a Coordinating Leading Author for the IPCC's Sixth Assessment Report. She has published extensively on international environmental law, in particular international climate change law, the intersections of climate change law with human rights, and on equity and differential treatment in international environmental law.

Catherine Redgwell
Catherine Redgwell is Chichele Professor of Public International Law, University Oxford, and Fellow of All Souls College. She has published extensively on international environmental law and international energy law and is currently co-director of two Oxford Martin School Research Programmes, on Sustainable Oceans and on the Future of Plastics.

Benjamin J Richardson
Benjamin J Richardson is a Professor of Environmental Law at the University of Tasmania, Australia, who specialises in corporate social responsibility, and environmental law philosophy and theory, and is active in community-based nature conservation.

Paul Rink
Paul Rink is a 2020–2021 Yale Law School Bernstein Fellow. His article on youth-driven climate change litigation received a medal from the International Sustainable Development Law Centre in the 2018 Climate Law and Governance Day essay competition. He has researched and written extensively on global environmental law and policy including as a chapter contributor for the 2019 publication *A Better Planet: 40 Big Ideas for a Sustainable Future.*

Beatriz Martinez Romera
Beatriz Martinez Romera is an Assistant Professor at the Center for International Law, Conflict and Crisis (CILCC), Faculty of Law, University of Copenhagen where she is involved in environmental and climate change research. Her research focuses on the international climate negotiations, and the regulatory processes at the International Civil Aviation Organization and the International Maritime Organization, as well as

developments at the EU level. She has published on ocean governance, environmental and climate-related regulation of the Arctic, and the aviation and maritime transport sectors.

Jacinta Ruru

Jacinta Ruru (Raukawa, Ngāti Ranginui) FRSNZ, is Professor of Law at the University of Otago where she also holds an inaugural Sesquicentennial Distinguished Chair. She is Co-Director of Ngā Pae o te Māramatanga New Zealand's Centre of Māori Research Excellence and has published extensively on Indigenous peoples' rights and interests to own, manage, and govern lands and waters.

Noah M Sachs

Noah M Sachs is a Professor at the University of Richmond School of Law and Director of the Robert R Merhige Jr Center for Environmental Studies. He has published extensively on international environmental law, climate change law, and regulation of toxic substances and hazardous waste.

Salman M A Salman

Salman M A Salman is the Editor-in-Chief of *Brill Research Perspectives in International Water Law* journal, a Fellow with the International Water Resources Association (IWRA), and a former World Bank Adviser on Water Law. He is the co-recipient of the IWRA Crystal Drop Award 2017, and has published extensively on water law issues.

Peter H Sand

Peter H Sand, former Legal Adviser/Environmental Affairs for several international organizations (FAO, IUCN, UNEP, UN/ECE, and World Bank), is with the Institute of International Law, University of Munich, Germany.

Werner Scholtz

Werner Scholtz is Professor of Global Environmental Law at the University of the Southampton, Southampton Law School, United Kingdom and Extraordinary Professor at the University of Western Cape, South Africa. He has published extensively on international environmental law, particularly on ecological sovereignty as well as on wildlife welfare.

Eloise Scotford

Eloise Scotford is Professor of Environmental Law in the Faculty of Laws, University College London. Her published research addresses international, European Union, UK, and Australian law, on various topics of environmental law, including the legal character of environmental principles, air quality law, climate change governance, waste law, and legislative processes as they relate to the environment.

Joanne Scott

Joanne Scott is a Professor of European Law at the European University Institute. She supervises doctoral students and undertakes research in EU law and environmental law. Her current research explores ways to reduce the EU's global environmental footprint. Her co-edited volume, *EU Law Beyond EU Borders*, was published by OUP in 2019.

Akiho Shibata

Akiho Shibata is a Professor of International Law and Director, Polar Cooperation Research Centre (PCRC), Graduate School of International Cooperation Studies (GSICS) at Kobe University, Japan. He has published extensively on sources of international law, the ICJ judgement on the *Whaling* case, and international law in polar regions, both in English and Japanese.

Beate Sjåfjell

Beate Sjåfjell is Professor Dr Juris at the Department of Private Law, Faculty of Law, University of Oslo. She is founder and head of the Oslo Faculty's Research Group Companies, Markets and Sustainability, which is now in its second period (2017–21), as well as several international networks and projects. Her main field is company law and corporate governance, concentrating on the regulation of business in the broader context of sustainability. Her notable publications include *The Greening of European Business Under EU Law* and *Creating Corporate Sustainability*.

Britta Sjöstedt

Britta Sjöstedt is a Senior Lecturer in Environmental Law at Lund University, Sweden and a founding board director of the Environmental Peacebuilding Association. Her current research interests focus mainly on environmental protection in times of armed conflict, environmental peacebuilding, and environmental security.

Tom Sparks

Tom Sparks is a Senior Research Fellow at the Max Planck Institute for Comparative Public Law and International Law in Heidelberg, Germany, where he works on questions of statehood and self-determination, international legal theory, and international environmental law.

Timothy Stephens

Timothy Stephens is Professor of International Law and Australian Research Council Future Fellow at the University of Sydney Law School, University of Sydney, Australia. He specializes in international environmental law, dispute settlement, and the law of the sea, and has published extensively on these topics.

Maria Antonia Tigre

Maria Antonia Tigre is an SJD Candidate at the Elisabeth Haub School of Law at Pace University. She has published on the legal aspects of environmental cooperation between the Amazon countries and is currently writing about gaps in international environmental law and the Global Pact for the Environment.

Robert R M Verchick

Robert R M Verchick holds the Gauthier-St Martin Chair in Environmental Law at Loyola University New Orleans. He is also a Senior Fellow in Disaster Resilience at Tulane University and President of the Center for Progressive Reform, a US policy institute focused on public health and environmental protection. He is the author of four books, including the award-winning, *Facing Catastrophe: Environmental Action for a Post-Katrina World.*

Jorge E Viñuales

Jorge E Viñuales is the Harold Samuel Professor of Law and Environmental Policy at the University of Cambridge, where he founded and directed the Cambridge Centre for Environment, Energy and Natural Resources Governance (C-EENRG).

Christina Voigt

Christina Voigt is Professor at the Department of Public and International Law, University of Oslo, Norway, and an expert in international environmental law. Her work is primarily on legal issues of climate change, environmental multilateralism, and sustainability. Since 2008, she has been Norway's lead legal negotiator in the UN climate negotiations, as well as REDD+ negotiator. Professor Voigt is the chair of the Climate Change Specialist Group of the IUCN World Commission on Environmental Law and a member of the IUCN Climate Change Task Force.

Jacob D Werksman

Jacob D Werksman is Principal Adviser to the Directorate General for Climate Action, European Commission, where his work focuses on the international dimensions of European climate policy. He is lead negotiator for the European Union in, among others, the UN climate change negotiations. He has published extensively on international environmental law and economic law.

Annecoos Wiersema

Annecoos Wiersema is a Professor of Law, Associate Dean of Academic Affairs, and Co-Director of the Environmental and Natural Resources Law Program at the University of Denver Sturm College of Law. Her research spans the field of international environmental law, with a particular focus on wildlife law.

David A Wirth

David A Wirth is Professor of Law and former Director of International Programs at Boston College Law School. He is former Attorney-Adviser for Oceans and International Environmental and Scientific Affairs in the Office of the Legal Adviser of the US State Department, where he had principal responsibility for all international environmental issues. He has taught, researched, and published extensively on international environmental law, climate, international trade and investment, and food law. Among numerous other honours, he has served as the first Fulbright Distinguished Chair in Sustainable Development at the Higher School of Economics in Moscow.

Margaret A Young

Margaret A Young is Professor at the Melbourne Law School, University of Melbourne, Australia. She was the inaugural research fellow in public international law at the Lauterpacht Centre for International Law and Pembroke College, University of Cambridge. Elected Fellow of the Australian Academy of Law in 2021, she currently serves as a member of the international expert group for the proposed 'Global Pact for the Environment'.

CHAPTER 1

INTERNATIONAL ENVIRONMENTAL LAW

Changing Context, Emerging Trends, and Expanding Frontiers

LAVANYA RAJAMANI AND JACQUELINE PEEL

I. INTRODUCTION

In recent years, global environmental harm—in particular, the prospect of profound and irreversible climate change—has occupied centre stage in popular and political consciousness, diplomatic efforts, and even cultural and artistic imagination. A pertinent example features on the front cover of this handbook, which shows the aftermath of unprecedented wildfires in the Australian Blue Mountains that attracted global attention and concern during the country's 'black summer' of 2019/2020.[1] Such events vividly demonstrate both the seemingly uncontrollable nature and the unparalleled scale of the environmental harms unleashed in what is often called the era of the Anthropocene.[2] They also bring into focus the crucial importance of efforts to regulate such harms.

[1] Labelled Australia's 'black summer' in keeping with naming fires based on the day or locality—Ash Wednesday 1983, Canberra bushfires 2003, and Black Saturday 2009: Scott Morrison, 'Speech Prime Minister: Condolence—Bushfires' (4 February 2020) <https://www.pm.gov.au/media/condolence-bushfires> accessed 23 September 2020. See also Lesley Hughes *et al*, *Summer of Crisis* (Climate Council of Australia 2020); Commonwealth Scientific and Industrial Research Organisation (CSIRO), *Climate and Disaster Resilience: Technical Report* (CSIRO 2020) 52.

[2] Coined in the 1980s by Eugene Stoermer and popularized around 2000 by Paul Crutzen, the term describes the current geological epoch, emphasizing the major and ongoing impacts of human activities on the Earth and atmosphere at all scales: Paul Crutzen and Eugene Stoermer, 'The "Anthropocene"'

International environmental law is the legal and regulatory framework devised by the community of sovereign states to address global environmental harms. It is a dynamic and rapidly evolving field of international law, which encompasses a wide range of ideological perspectives, draws on multidisciplinary insights, and features innovative legal tools to deal with a diverse array of complex environmental problems. These problems include some of the most significant challenges facing the global community, including the potential for runaway climate change, vanishing biodiversity, increasing freshwater scarcity, and severe degradation of marine resources and ocean ecosystems.

The first edition of the *Oxford Handbook of International Environmental Law*, edited by pioneering international environmental law scholars—Daniel Bodansky, Jutta Brunnée, and Ellen Hey—was published in 2008. At the time, international environmental law was a 'relatively new field'.[3] The editors and authors of the first edition mapped the field of international environmental law by taking stock of the major developments of the time. In the years that have elapsed since then, popular consciousness of global environmental harm and demand for effective legal intervention has grown in leaps and bounds. This has offered law-makers—in addition to a range of non-state actors—the opportunity to explore international law's potential in addressing such harms and to experiment with novel tools, techniques, and approaches to do so. However, in the process, the fundamental and seemingly rigid limits of international law have also become more apparent.

As the contributions to this second edition abundantly demonstrate, international environmental law has acquired further breadth, depth, nuance, complexity, and reach in the last decade. In particular, it is more deeply interconnected with policy and legal efforts in many other fields, including international trade and investment, human rights and migration, energy, disaster response, armed conflict, technology innovation, and intellectual property protection. In response to these shifts—some profound, others more subtle—as well as the growing maturity of international environmental law in the last decade, the second edition of the *Oxford Handbook of International Environmental Law* includes several new sections and chapters covering a wider landscape of issues than the first edition. The expansion of international environmental law has also led to the emergence of new scholars and voices in the field. Reflecting this, the second edition of the handbook incorporates a broader range of perspectives, covering more regions of the world, and reflecting greater gender balance and ethnic spread.

This introductory chapter to the second edition of the handbook explores and illustrates the ways in which international environmental law has evolved over the last decade (see Figure 1.1). It highlights how the field has adapted to a changing geo-political

Global Change Newsletter, 41 (2000): 17; Will Steffen *et al*, 'The Anthropocene: Conceptual and Historical Perspectives' *Philosophical Transactions of the Royal Society*, 369/1938 (2011): 842.

[3] Daniel Bodansky, Jutta Brunnée, and Ellen Hey, 'International Environmental Law: Mapping the Field' in Daniel Bodansky, Jutta Brunnée, and Ellen Hey (eds), *The Oxford Handbook of International Environmental Law* (1st edn, OUP 2008) 1, 2.

context, as well as to the possibilities and limits of global regulation in addressing the complex, polycentric, and intractable nature of environmental harms. It also explores the increasing activity at the interface of international environmental law with other fields of law and policy, expanding the sites at which international environmental law is made, applied, and implemented. The chapter concludes with reflections on the future of international environmental law in the context of the emerging understanding of the fundamental limits posed by the nature and operation of environmental law within the current architecture of international law and politics.

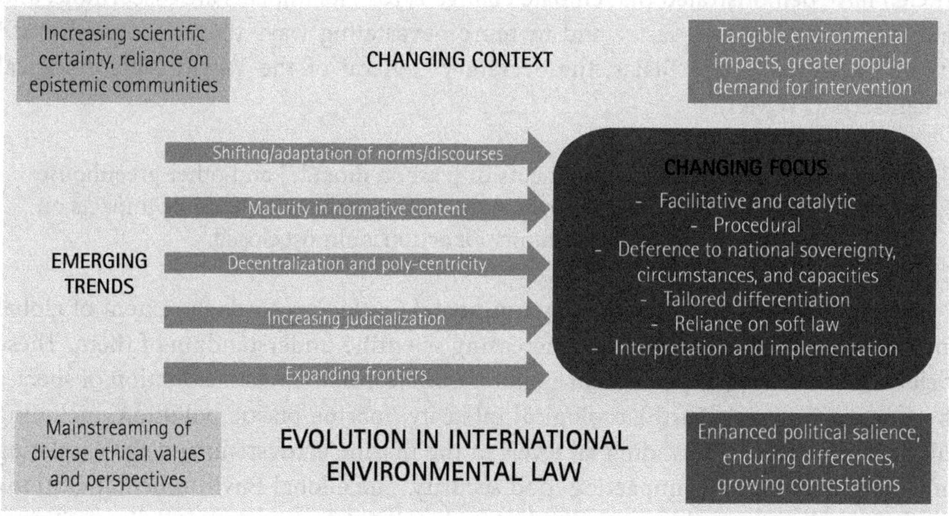

FIGURE 1.1 Evolution in international environmental law

II. THE CHANGING CONTEXT FOR INTERNATIONAL ENVIRONMENTAL LAW

The geo-political, social, economic, epistemic, and cultural context within which international environmental law operates today has altered in fundamental ways since the turn of the century.[4] In this section of the chapter, we trace these shifts in underlying scientific knowledge of global environmental harm; popular understanding of environmental problems and social activism to address them; the growth and 'mainstreaming' of diverse approaches and voices in international environmental law; and the increasing political salience of environmental issues.

[4] See Chapter 3, 'Origin and History', in this volume.

A. Growing Understanding, Tracking, and Documentation of Global Environmental Harm

Our understanding of global environmental harms—their causes, the interconnectedness of causes and harms, and their impacts on people and the planet—is now more sophisticated, complex, and nuanced. As one pertinent example, the science relating to climate change—characterized as the 'defining issue of our age'[5]—has advanced considerably. Successive reports of the Intergovernmental Panel on Climate Change (IPCC) have demonstrated that climate change is real, its impacts are discernible, and that it is occurring ever faster and in more devastating ways than once predicted.[6] In the words of Petteri Taalas, the Secretary-General of the World Meteorological Organization (WMO):

> The science is clear. Without rapid cuts in [carbon dioxide] and other greenhouse gases, climate change will have increasingly destructive and irreversible impacts on life on Earth. The window of opportunity for action is almost closed.[7]

In other areas, the 2019 Global Environmental Outlook records the extent of global environmental challenges and our increasing scientific understanding of them. These include the enduring impacts of air pollution on health; the mass extinction of species that is compromising Earth's ecological integrity; marine plastic pollution, including microplastics, that is pervading all levels of the marine ecosystem; and the escalating land degradation that is impacting food security. The Global Environmental Outlook report finds that the world is not on track to achieving the environmental dimensions of the United Nations' (UN) Sustainable Development Goals by 2030 or to delivering long-term sustainability by 2050.[8] Similarly, the 2020 Global Biodiversity Outlook, titled 'Humanity at Crossroads', finds that not only is the world unlikely to meet any of the

[5] Ban Ki-moon, 'Opening Remarks at 2014 Climate Summit' (23 September 2014) <https://www.un.org/sg/en/content/sg/speeches/2014-09-23/opening-remarks-2014-climate-summit> accessed 23 September 2020; and more recently, António Guterres, 'Remarks on Climate Change' (10 September 2018) <https://www.un.org/sg/en/content/sg/speeches/2018-09-10/remarks-climate-change> accessed 23 September 2020.

[6] See eg IPCC, *Global Warming of 1.5°C—Special Report* (2018) 4–12; IPCC, *Climate Change 2014: Synthesis Report* (2014) 4–16, 20; IPCC, *Climate Change 2007: Synthesis Report* (2007) 5–14; United Nations Environment Programme (UNEP), *Emissions Gap Report* (2019); World Meteorological Organisation (WMO), *United in Science 2020: A multi-organisation high-level compilation of the latest climate science information* (2020) <https://public.wmo.int/en/resources/united_in_science> accessed 23 September 2020; Chapters 29 and 15, 'Climate Change' and 'Science', in this volume.

[7] Quoted in UN Framework Convention on Climate Change (FCCC), 'WMO: Greenhouse Gas Levels in Atmosphere Reach New Record' (22 November 2018) <https://unfccc.int/news/wmo-greenhouse-gas-levels-in-atmosphere-reach-yet-another-high> accessed 23 September 2020.

[8] UNEP, 'GEO-6 key messages' <https://www.unenvironment.org/resources/assessment/geo-6-key-messages> accessed 23 September 2020; UNEP, *GEO-6: Healthy Planet, Healthy People* (2019).

Aichi Biodiversity Targets,[9] but also there are significantly worsening trends concerning the drivers of biodiversity loss and the current state of biodiversity.[10]

The central message across the slew of recent scientific reports is that current patterns of production and consumption, population growth, and technological development are unsustainable. In the absence of transformative change involving all states, every sector of the economy, and across the full gamut of stakeholders and actors, irreversible and unprecedented environmental harm will be unleashed on the planet, affecting human health, well-being, and even the long-term survival of humanity and the other species that inhabit Earth.

B. Increasing Reporting and Popularization of Global Environmental Harms

In keeping with the growing scientific understanding, tracking, and documentation of global environmental harm, in the last decade, there has been increased reporting and public discussion of such harm, triggered in part by the rapid expansion in internet penetration,[11] and rise in the use of social media.[12] Our senses are continually bombarded with arresting images of starving polar bears, melting glaciers, bleaching corals, massive storms and record flooding devastating communities, sinking islands, raging wildfires, and growing islands of ocean plastic. Like no other generation before us, we have had a profound impact on the environment, recognized in the characterization of the current epoch as that of the Anthropocene.[13] This acknowledgement, along with a renewed

[9] Set in 2010, the twenty Aichi Biodiversity Targets are structured around five strategic goals relating to the underlying causes of biodiversity loss, direct pressures on biodiversity, the status of biodiversity, enhancing the benefits to all from biodiversity, and enabling the implementation of the Strategic Plan for Biodiversity 2011–2020: Secretariat of the Convention on Biological Diversity (CBD), 'Aichi Biodiversity Targets' (18 September 2020) <https://www.cbd.int/sp/targets/> accessed 23 September 2020.

[10] Secretariat of the CBD, *Global Biodiversity Outlook 5* (2020) Summary for Policymakers, 10.

[11] Jessica Clement, 'Global number of internet users 2005–2019' *Statista* (7 January 2020) <https://www.statista.com/statistics/273018/number-of-internet-users-worldwide/> accessed 23 September 2020.

[12] Esteban Ortiz-Ospina, 'The rise of social media' *Our World in Data* (18 September 2019) <https://ourworldindata.org/rise-of-social-media> accessed 23 September 2020.

[13] In 2019, the Anthropocene Working Group voted in favour of designating the Anthropocene as a formal unit in the geological time scale and plan to formalize a proposal to the International Commission on Stratigraphy, the body overseeing the geological time scale: Working Group on the 'Anthropocene', 'Results of binding vote by AWG: Released 21st May 2019' *Subcommission on Quaternary Stratigraphy* <https://quaternary.stratigraphy.org/working-groups/anthropocene/> accessed 23 September 2020. For geological literature on the Anthropocene see eg Steffen *et al* (n 2); Will Steffen *et al*, 'Trajectories of the Earth System in the Anthropocene' *Proceedings of the United States of America*, 115/33 (2018): 8252; Jan Zalasiewicz *et al*, *The Anthropocene as a Geological Time Unit: A Guide to the Scientific Evidence and Current Debate* (CUP 2019). For legal perspectives see eg Nicholas Robinson, 'Fundamental Principles of Law for the Anthropocene' *Environmental Policy and Law*, 44/1–2 (2014): 13; Louis Kotzé (ed), *Environmental Law and Governance for the Anthropocene* (Hart Publishing 2017); Emily Webster and Laura Mai, 'Transnational Environmental Law in the Anthropocene' *Transnational Legal Theory*, 11/1–2 (2020): 1.

interest in addressing humanity's impacts on the planet, has fuelled multiple forms of social-ecological engagement, particularly transnational social movements, reactive advocacy and radical direct-action around global environmental issues. The Extinction Rebellion,[14] and school strikes,[15] offer excellent recent examples, while anti-whaling and energy-siting protests are of longer vintage.[16] It has also inspired a new wave of artistic expression through eco-art,[17] eco-poetry,[18] music,[19] and literature.[20] Indeed, Margaret Atwood, in the eerily prescient *MaddAdam Trilogy*, asks the ever-pressing questions at the core of our current environmental crisis:

> What if we continue down the road we're already on? How slippery is the slope? What are our saving graces? Who's got the will to stop us?[21]

C. Mainstreaming of Diverse Ethical Values, Approaches, and Perspectives

There is, in this context, a reckoning of the ethical values, approaches, choices, and conflicts at the heart of environmental discourses. Although international environmental law has always reflected a mix of anthropocentric and non-anthropocentric values, non-anthropocentric values are gaining ground. Eco-centric notions, such as biodiversity, ecosystem approaches, and rights of nature are increasingly referenced, even if only implicitly, across a wide range of international instruments.[22] These trends coalesce with the concept of Earth Jurisprudence—the eco-centric belief that our life, health, and well-being flow from the complex web of ecological and social relationships that constitute the Earth Community, and require humanity's harmonious coexistence

[14] Extinction Rebellion, 'About Us' <https://rebellion.global/about-us/> accessed 23 September 2020.

[15] Fridays for Future, 'Who we are' <https://fridaysforfuture.org/what-we-do/who-we-are/> accessed 23 September 2020.

[16] Chapter 38, 'Non-State Actors', in this volume.

[17] See eg the EcoArt Project that uses art to mobilize climate change action: EcoArt Project, 'Channeling the forces of art & design to inspire climate change action' <https://www.ecoartproject.org/#mission> accessed 23 September 2020.

[18] See eg the series published in *The Guardian* of twenty original poems on climate change: 'Keep it in the ground: a poem a day' *The Guardian* (20 November 2015) <https://www.theguardian.com/environment/series/keep-it-in-the-ground-a-poem-a-day> accessed 23 September 2020.

[19] Brett Milano, 'Don't Drink The Water: How The Environmental Movement Shaped Music' *uDiscover Music* (21 April 2020) <https://www.udiscovermusic.com/stories/environmental-movement-in-music/> accessed 23 September 2020.

[20] Adeline Johns-Putra, 'Climate Change in Literature and Literary Studies: From Cli-fi, Climate Change Theatre and Ecopoetry to Ecocriticism and Climate Change Criticism' *WIREs Climate Change* 7/2 (2016): 266.

[21] 'Perfect Storms: Writing Oryx and Crake' in Margaret Atwood, *Curious Pursuits: Occasional Writing* (Virago Press 2005) 321–323.

[22] Chapter 13, 'Ethical Considerations', in this volume; *Report of the United Nations Conference on Environment and Development* (UN 1993) vol I, annex I— 'Rio Declaration on Environment and Development', principle 7; 1992 UNFCCC, art 1.3; Decision COP V/ 6, 'Ecosystem Approach' (2000) UN Doc UNEP/CBD/COP/DEC/V/6.

within a healthy Earth community.[23] Earth jurisprudential ideas have been recognized in some international instruments and by national constitutions and courts that have in turn bestowed rights to rivers and mountains.[24] The growth of this approach, driven primarily by global civil society and Indigenous peoples,[25] reflects a broader trend towards mainstreaming diverse approaches and voices in international environmental law.

Among the approaches that have gathered traction, a notable one is the Global South Approach. This approach highlights both the exploitative colonial origins of international law and the disproportionate contribution of the industrialized countries to environmental harm. In this context, it seeks to advance principles and frameworks that recognize differential contributions to, and capacities in addressing, global environmental harm.[26] The centrality of differentiation and the principle of common but differentiated responsibilities in international environmental law indicates the success that this approach has had thus far.[27] Feminist Approaches to International Law have also made headway in this time, offering the international community a 'lens to examine the exploitation of nature and women, through analyses of power, social constructs, and inter-species relationships'.[28] Proponents of feminist approaches showcase the consistently undervalued yet pivotal contribution of women and children to the evolution of international environmental law, and spear-head efforts to embed gender within international environmental processes. International environmental law is increasingly gender-literate, and richer for these efforts.[29] These trends, signalling greater inclusion and sensitivity to diverse values, approaches, and perspectives in international environmental law, are likely to gather strength as societies face the consequences of the environmentally destructive trajectory that we are on.

At the opposite end of the spectrum, economic perspectives and actors—long-recognized as pivotal contributors to the shaping of international environmental law—are taking on new roles.[30] Concepts such as the 'circular economy', 'green growth', and 'product stewardship'[31] are melding with ideas of corporate social responsibility and environmentally sustainable investment practices to re-envision the role of the market and

[23] Chapter 14, 'Earth Jurisprudence', in this volume.

[24] See eg the rights of nature in the Constitution of the Republic of Ecuador 2008, preamble, arts 71–74; the Te Awa Tupua (Whanganui River Claims Settlement) Act 2017 (New Zealand) recognizing the Whanganui River as a legal person, s 14; and India's court ruling that the Ganges river has legal personhood: *Mohd. Salim v State of Uttarakhand & others* Writ Petition (PIL) No 126/2014 (Order of High Court of Uttarakhand, 20 March 2017). See Chapter 14, 'Earth Jurisprudence', in this volume.

[25] Chapter 42, 'Indigenous Peoples', in this volume. See also Chapter 2, 'Discourses', in this volume.

[26] Chapter 11, 'Global South Approaches', in this volume.

[27] Ibid; Chapter 19, 'Differentiation', in this volume.

[28] Chapter 12, 'Feminist Approaches', in this volume.

[29] Ibid; Rio Declaration (n 22) principle 20.

[30] See generally Chapters 10 and 41, 'Economics' and 'Business and Industry', in this volume.

[31] See eg Natalie Jones and Geert van Calster, 'Waste Regulation' in Emma Lees and Jorge Viñuales (eds), *The Oxford Handbook of Comparative Environmental Law* (OUP 2019) 607, 607–625; Alexander Gillespie, *Waste Policy: International Regulation, Comparative and Contextual Perspectives* (Edward Elgar 2015) 73, 73–85; Martijn Wilder and Lauren Drake, 'International Law and the Renewable Energy Sector' in Cinnamon Carlarne, Kevin Gray, and Richard Tarasofsky (eds), *The Oxford Handbook of International Climate Change Law* (OUP 2016) 357, 357–387.

the private sector in international environmental law. While such developments have not displaced a continuing strong adherence to conventional notions of the capitalist market economy in international law and politics, there is growing evidence of some 'greening' of business and industry, including a greater focus of global capital (investors and asset owners) on the unsustainability of 'business as usual' approaches.

D. Increasing Political Salience and Contestation

As the science has become more certain, the impacts more tangible, and the demand for action stronger, global environmental harm has garnered considerable political salience. The issue of climate change, in particular, has captured the political imagination in the last decade. More than 150 Heads of State and Government participated in the negotiations for the 2015 Paris Agreement, and successive UN Secretary-Generals have prioritized addressing climate change during their terms. This focus of states and intergovernmental organizations was paralleled by unprecedented levels of civil society and business involvement in the Paris negotiations.[32] Yet, the task of addressing climate change, and global environmental harm more generally, has also become infinitely more contentious and challenging in this time frame.

There have been fundamental shifts in states' political and economic power in the last few decades. Many large developing countries, in particular China, India, Brazil, and South Africa, have grown exponentially across this period, and are emerging as leaders and innovators in addressing environmental challenges. They are also, however, imposing more serious and sustained costs on the global environment than before. China, for instance, is the world's largest emitter of greenhouse gases (GHGs) today, having overtaken the United States several years ago.[33] The differences between and within the developed and developing country groupings have also increased, blurring the lines between these groups, and leading to demands that such categorizations of states be obliterated.[34]

Yet, there are persistent inequalities between those living in developed and developing countries,[35] and the situation of communities living in vulnerable small island states and least developed countries is worsening. Many developing countries

[32] Over 6,000 representatives of NGOs and business and approximately 2,800 press attended the Paris Conference: Daniel Bodansky, 'The Paris Climate Change Agreement: A New Hope?' *The American Journal of International Law*, 110/2 (2016): 288, 291. See also UNFCCC, 'Statistics on Participation and In-Session Engagement' <https://unfccc.int/process-and-meetings/parties-non-party-stakeholders/non-party-stakeholders/statistics-on-non-party-stakeholders/statistics-on-participation-and-in-session-engagement> accessed 25 February 2021.

[33] See the World Resource Institute's Climate Analysis Indicator Tool (CAIT), which compiles figures on global and national emissions: World Resource Institute (WRI), 'CAIT Climate Data Explorer' <https://cait.wri.org/> accessed 23 September 2020.

[34] Chapters 9 and 19, 'International Relations Theory' and 'Differentiation', in this volume.

[35] See Branko Milanovic, *The Haves and the Have-Nots: A Brief and Idiosyncratic History of Global Inequality* (Basic Books 2011) 115–119, finding that if country averages are broken down into actual incomes received by people in each country 'practically all people living in a richer country are better off than all people living in a poorer country' and that the 'poorest Americans are better off than two-thirds of the world population'.

have yet to lift their populations out of poverty and provide energy access and other life-sustaining services to all their citizens. An estimated 1.1 billion people, 14% of the world's population, do not have access to electricity,[36] and an estimated 700 million people, predominantly in sub-Saharan Africa, are projected to remain without electricity in 2040.[37] Such continuing differences between states, and their priorities, have fundamentally shaped the scope and nature of obligations negotiated in international environmental instruments.[38] Although many of these shifts in the political and economic power of states had begun to influence the negotiation of international environmental agreements in the early 2000s, they have had a more profound impact in the last decade.

Many states, both developed and developing, have been struggling with disruptive shifts in domestic politics, including moves towards populism, nationalism, protectionism, distrust of experts, and increased polarization, which have had an immediate impact on international environmental law. The turn to right-wing governments in some parts of the world, fostered by powerful fossil fuel and agri-business lobbies, has taken its toll on the environment. The US Obama administration, for instance, played a decisive role in negotiating the Paris Agreement and introducing numerous domestic climate regulations. However, the Trump administration later dismantled these regulations and withdrew from the Paris Agreement.[39] The Biden administration re-engaged with the Paris Agreement, but the four-year US absence had consequences for the regime. Although the Bolsonaro government in Brazil chose to stay in the Paris Agreement,[40] it has reportedly dismantled many of Brazil's environmental regulations,[41] and reignited the 'arc of fire' in the Amazon.[42] India's Modi government

[36] International Energy Agency (IEA), *Energy Access Outlook 2017: From Poverty to Prosperity* (2017) 40.

[37] IEA, *World Energy Outlook 2018* (2018) 27.

[38] See Chapters 29 and 33, 'Climate Change' and 'Hazardous Substances and Activities', in this volume.

[39] The United States announced its withdrawal from the Paris Agreement in June 2017: Donald Trump, 'Statement by President Trump on the Paris Climate Accord' *White House* (1 June 2017) <https://www.whitehouse.gov/the-press-office/2017/06/01/statement-president-trump-parisclimate-accord> accessed 23 September 2020.

[40] Rodrigo Viga Gaier, 'Brazil's Bolsonaro scraps pledge to quit Paris climate deal' *Reuters* (25 October 2018) <https://uk.reuters.com/article/uk-brazil-election/brazils-bolsonaro-scraps-pledge-to-quit-paris-climate-deal-idUKKCN1MZ1CR> accessed 23 September 2020; Lisa Viscidi and Nate Graham, 'Brazil was a global leader on climate change. Now it's a threat' *Foreign Policy* (4 January 2019) <https://foreignpolicy.com/2019/01/04/brazil-was-a-global-leader-on-climate-change-now-its-a-threat/> accessed 23 September 2020. In 2020 Brazil introduced a new first nationally determined contribution under the Paris Agreement that arguably reflects a downgrading of earlier commitments: see 'Brazil First NDC, Updated Submission' *UNFCCC* (8 December 2020) <https://www4.unfccc.int/sites/NDCStaging/Pages/Party.aspx?party=BRA> accessed 25 February 2021; Climate Action Tracker (CAT), 'Climate Target Update Tracker: Brazil' (9 December 2020) <https://climateactiontracker.org/climate-target-update-tracker/brazil/> accessed 25 February 2021.

[41] Oliver Stuenkel, 'International Pressure can save the Amazon from Bolsonaro' *Financial Times* (10 August 2020) <https://www.ft.com/content/0f97c674-b7aa-4ec4-8fa1-88b810bc3dc7> accessed 23 September 2020.

[42] Alexander Zaitchik, 'Rainforest on fire' *The Intercept* (6 July 2019) <https://theintercept.com/2019/07/06/brazil-amazon-rainforest-indigenous-conservation-agribusiness-ranching/> accessed 23 September 2020.

has also (notwithstanding a seemingly progressive stance on global environmental issues) weakened domestic environmental regulations, in particular relating to Environment Impact Assessment (EIA).[43]

Finally, and perhaps most tellingly, the seismic disruption caused by the COVID-19 pandemic in 2020—an omen of the nature and scale of disruption to be caused by climate change—is likely to have an enduring impact on international environmental law. The coronavirus crisis has underscored the profound consequences of biodiversity loss and ecosystem degradation for human health, well-being, and survival. It has exposed our systems' fragility, and demonstrated that abrupt change, whether related to pandemic disease or climate shifts, will affect the poor, marginalized, and vulnerable the most.[44] The response to the pandemic has accentuated some environmental concerns, such as plastic and other forms of waste, with a dramatic uptick in the use of single-use personal protective equipment.[45] And while the worldwide lockdowns in 2020, which confined people to their homes and shuttered businesses, resulted in a temporary downturn in energy demand and carbon dioxide (CO_2) emissions,[46] COVID-19 associated disruption could create a serious (and potentially fatal drag) on global efforts to address climate change.

The postponement of the 2020 annual climate negotiations by a year is merely the tip of the iceberg. The emissions decreases in 2020—occasioned by traumatic and drastic confinement measures rather than structural changes in the economic, transport, energy, or agricultural systems—were temporary. Meanwhile, the ambitious commitments, actions, policies, and measures needed to trigger and sustain emissions reductions in line with the Paris Agreement's 'well below 2°C' temperature limit grow ever further from reach.[47] Many nations are tackling the deepest recession they have faced in a generation. India's economy, for instance, shrank by 24% during the lockdown

[43] Haris Zargar, 'India's Modi dismantles environmental safeguards' *New Frame* (30 July 2020) <https://www.newframe.com/indias-modi-dismantles-environmental-safeguards/> accessed 23 September 2020. See generally Navroz Dubash and Shibani Ghosh, 'The Ecological Costs of doing Business: Environment, Energy and Climate Change' in Niraja Gopal Jayal (ed), *Re-forming India: the Nation Today* (Penguin 2019) 254.

[44] See eg the impact of COVID-19 related lockdowns on migrant workers in India: Sohini Sengupta and Manish Jha, 'Social Policy, COVID-19 and Impoverished Migrants: Challenges and Prospects in Locked Down India' *The International Journal of Community and Social Development*, 2/2 (2020): 152.

[45] Charlotte Edmond, 'How face masks, gloves and other coronavirus waste is polluting our ocean' *World Economic Forum* (11 June 2020) <https://www.weforum.org/agenda/2020/06/ppe-masks-gloves-coronavirus-ocean-pollution/> accessed 23 September 2020. See generally Chapter 31, 'The Protection of the Marine Environment: Pollution and Fisheries', in this volume. The Basel Convention Secretariat has advised that used PPE should be treated as hazardous waste and disposed of separately from household wastes. For further discussion of the 1989 Basel Convention, see Chapter 33, 'Hazardous Substances and Activities', in this volume.

[46] Researchers estimate that daily CO_2 emissions decreased by 17% in April 2020, and that annual emissions in 2020 are likely to reduce by 4 to 7%: Corinne Le Quéré *et al*, 'Temporary reduction in daily global CO2 emissions during the COVID-19 forced confinement' *Nature Climate Change*, 10 (2020): 647.

[47] CAT, 'Climate Target Update Tracker' <https://climateactiontracker.org/climate-target-update-tracker/> accessed 25 February 2021.

in 2020.[48] While momentum is gathering across the world for a 'green recovery' and to 'build back better',[49] whether states will, in the process of economic recovery, entrench the reliance on fossil-fuels,[50] or take the opportunity to transform their economies towards net zero emissions remains to be seen.

However, the coronavirus crisis showcased the ability of governments to intervene decisively, and at scale,[51] and our ability to make fundamental, if painful, behavioural shifts in response to a global crisis. The crisis has also mobilized a range of actors, including civil society, business interests, and investors, to step up interventions to hold national governments accountable for managing the recovery process and preparing for future systemic risk scenarios. These developments will hold us in good stead in managing the risks of future environmental disasters and integrating and re-evaluating disaster law in relation to environmental harms.[52]

III. EMERGING TRENDS IN INTERNATIONAL ENVIRONMENTAL LAW

It is against this ever-changing context that international environmental law is maturing and discovering its limits. In this section of the chapter, we discuss how international environmental law has adapted to this changing context and several discernible trends that have emerged as a consequence. These include shifts in norms and discourses of international environmental law; increasing maturity in the interpretation of the content of customary norms, principles, and techniques; a change in focus towards more facilitative and procedural modes and implementation over rule-making, with a concomitant nuancing of concepts of differentiation and an enhanced role for soft law; and greater diversification in the participating actors and sites of international environmental law activity, including a growing judicialization of the field.

[48] Jeffrey Gettleman, 'Coronavirus Crisis Shatters India's Big Dreams' *The New York Times* (5 September 2020) <https://www.nytimes.com/2020/09/05/world/asia/india-economy-coronavirus.html> accessed 23 September 2020. See also International Monetary Fund, *World Economic Outlook: A Long and Difficult Ascent* (2020) 21; World Bank, *Global Economic Prospects* (June 2020) 5.

[49] Cameron Hepburn *et al*, 'Will COVID-19 fiscal recovery packages accelerate or retard progress on climate change?' *Oxford Review of Economic Policy*, 36/1 (2020): 359.

[50] Mayank Aggarwal, 'India's plan to revive its flailing economy by boosting coal production is deeply flawed' *Scroll* (2 August 2020) <https://scroll.in/article/967951/indias-plan-to-revive-its-flailing-economy-by-boosting-coal-production-is-deeply-flawed> accessed 23 September 2020.

[51] Some governments, usually led by women, have acted more decisively and effectively than others: Supriya Garikipati and Uma Kambhampati, 'Leading the Fight Against the Pandemic: Does Gender 'Really' Matter?' *University of Reading*, Discussion Paper No 2020-13 (3 June 2020) <https://www.reading.ac.uk/web/files/economics/emdp202013.pdf> accessed 23 September 2020.

[52] See Chapter 47, 'Disaster', in this volume.

A. Discursive Dominance of the Discourse of Sustainable Development

Environmental ideas, norms and discourses, and the epistemic communities that generate them,[53] are shifting and adapting to the changing context within which international environmental law is set. The notion of 'planetary boundaries' has gained ground but is yet to be endorsed in international instruments.[54] Promethean discourses that deny the existence of such limits or believe that human ingenuity will find a way if there are limits, overlap with identity politics, and have adapted to current challenges. Their proponents place reliance on the redemptive power of technology, as for instance in the promotion of geo-engineering to resolve the climate crisis.[55] The discourse of sustainable development, which gained ground in the 1980s, assumes that environmental conservation and economic growth can be mutually reinforcing rather than conflicting values. It has the breadth, which other discourses lack, to consider social justice concerns across generations. And it has over time taken decisive hold of international environmental law, albeit with differing emphases at different points in time in the trajectory of the field's evolution. This is reflected in the UN Sustainable Development Goals[56] and 2030 Agenda,[57] which rely on the foundational notion of sustainable development while also attempting to give it more concrete form. Informal mechanisms, such as discourses, in general matter more in the international system since formal institutions are relatively weak and informal approaches provide options for coordination across actors.[58]

B. Increasing Maturity in the Content of International Environmental Law

1. *Developments in customary international law relating to the environment*

There is increasing maturity, borne in part of experimentation and innovation, in the content of international environmental law. Developments in customary international law have been important in particular sub-disciplines of international environmental law, such as international law governing watercourses,[59] as well as in respect of some

[53] See Chapter 40, 'Epistemic Communities', in this volume.

[54] See Chapter 2, 'Discourses', in this volume.

[55] Ibid.

[56] Division for Sustainable Development Goals (DSDG) in the United Nations Department of Economic and Social Affairs (UNDESA), 'The 17 Goals' <https://sdgs.un.org/goals> accessed 25 September 2020.

[57] United Nations General Assembly (UNGA) Res 70/1, 'Transforming our world: the 2030 Agenda for Sustainable Development' (21 October 2015) UN Doc A/RES/70/1.

[58] Chapter 2, 'Discourses', in this volume.

[59] Chapter 30, 'Freshwater Resources', in this volume.

foundational principles. For example, the harm prevention principle, 'central to the normative structure of customary international environmental law',[60] has evolved and been fleshed out in recent cases, including *Costa Rica v Nicaragua/Nicaragua v Costa Rica.*[61] Its core content has been clarified and consolidated, although ambiguities remain, in particular, relating to the relationship between its procedural and substantive aspects.

The harm prevention principle and the three related duties—the duty of due diligence and the procedural duties to conduct an EIA and to cooperate in good faith,[62] including through notification and consultation—are now recognized as comprising the core of customary environmental law which is 'finally coming out of the thick fog in which it was engulfed for decades'.[63] While custom has potential, as part of a 'legal toolkit', in curbing transboundary environmental impacts,[64] it is limited in addressing complex, polycentric, collective action environmental challenges, such as climate change, ozone depletion, and biodiversity loss, which are better addressed through multilateral environmental treaties.[65]

2. *Crystallization of principles of international environmental law*

The principles of international environmental law, particularly the principles of sustainable development, precaution, common but differentiated responsibilities, and inter- and intra-generational equity, are a fundamental part of the conceptual architecture of international environmental law.[66] They have been operationalized in numerous treaty regimes and have been referred to in several international judgements over the last decade.[67] In the process, these principles have begun to acquire concrete content. While interpretational ambiguities remain at the heart of these principles, there is greater clarity around the nature and sources of these ambiguities, and a growing appreciation of their potential benefits in providing flexibility and a capacity for the evolution of international environmental law.

The legal status of some of these principles, such as the principle of sustainable development, has crystallized,[68] while that of others, such as the precautionary principle, remains in the process of crystallization.[69] More broadly, there is a growing realization

[60] Chapter 16, 'Harm Prevention', in this volume.

[61] *Certain Activities Carried Out by Nicaragua in the Border Area (Costa Rica/Nicaragua)* and *Construction of a Road in Costa Rica along the San Juan River (Nicaragua/Costa Rica)* (Judgement) [2015] ICJ Rep 665. See generally discussion in Chapters 23 and 27, 'Customary International Law and the Environment' and 'Judicial Development', in this volume.

[62] On the duty of good faith, more generally, see Chapter 22, 'Good Faith', in this volume.

[63] Chapter 23, 'Customary International Law and the Environment', in this volume.

[64] Chapter 16, 'Harm Prevention', in this volume.

[65] See Chapter 24, 'Multilateral Environmental Treaty Making', in this volume.

[66] Philippe Sands and Jacqueline Peel, *Principles of International Environmental Law* (4th edn, CUP 2018) 197–251.

[67] See Chapters 17, 18, 19, and 20, 'Sustainable Development', 'Precaution', 'Differentiation', and 'Equity', in this volume.

[68] Chapter 17, 'Sustainable Development', in this volume.

[69] Chapter 18, 'Precaution', in this volume.

that the formal legal status of these principles is less critical than their operational significance. Principles, for all their inherent ambiguities, form a skeletal structure for the body of international environmental law. As such, they guide the interpretation of existing regimes and structure of new ones. The French proposal for a legally binding *Global Pact for the Environment*[70] was intended to strengthen the coherence and provide authoritative definitions of the core principles of international environmental law. However, its one-size-fits-all approach encountered fierce opposition.[71] It remains to be seen whether the interpretational ambiguities at the heart of these principles enable further dynamism, adaptability, and resilience in international environmental law, or pose fundamental challenges to its ongoing evolution and implementation.

3. *Expansion in the legal tool-kit*

Although far fewer multilateral environmental treaties were negotiated in the last decade than previous decades,[72] the ones that have, mark a step change from the earlier generation of such treaties in several respects. States have begun to experiment with a wider range of regulatory instruments,[73] including market-based ones, that embrace 'flexible market forces rather than legal coercion' under these treaties.[74] The 1997 Kyoto Protocol to the UNFCCC, containing market-based instruments, came into effect in 2005, and the full potential and limits of market-based instruments have become apparent in the last decade.[75] Recent measures adopted under International Civil Aviation Organization (ICAO) to address GHG emissions from the aviation industry include, for instance, a Carbon Offsetting and Reduction Scheme for International Aviation (CORSIA),[76] and the Paris Agreement also recognizes a role for markets in achieving global emissions reductions.[77] Although 'market approaches have firmly entered the canon of international environmental law', the challenges in negotiating the rules relating to markets under the Paris Agreement demonstrate that consensus on such approaches is still elusive.[78]

70 UNGA Res 72/277, 'Towards a Global Pact for the Environment' (14 May 2018) UN Doc A/RES/72/277.

71 See Chapter 5, 'Fragmentation', in this volume.

72 In keeping with a more general trend in international law of treaty stagnation: Joost Pauwelyn, Ramses Wessel, and Jan Wouters, 'When Structures Become Shackles: Stagnation and Dynamics in International Lawmaking' *European Journal of International Law*, 25/3 (2014): 733.

73 See Chapter 6, 'Instrument Choice', in this volume.

74 See Chapters 53 and 10, 'Market Mechanisms' and 'Economics', in this volume.

75 See Chapter 53, 'Market Mechanisms', in this volume.

76 ICAO Res A39-3, 'Consolidated Statement of Continuing ICAO Policies and Practices related to Environmental Protection—Global Market-based Measure (MBM) Scheme' (27 September–6 October 2016). See Chapter 34, 'Aviation and Maritime Transport', in this volume.

77 art 6. See Chapters 29 and 53, 'Climate Change' and 'Market Mechanisms', in this volume.

78 Chapter 53, 'Market Mechanisms', in this volume.

C. Shifting Focus of International Environmental Law

1. *Facilitative and catalytic*

More generally, environmental treaties have begun to focus on identifying objectives rather than prescribing how states are to achieve them.[79] Instruments negotiated in the last decade, notably the 2013 Minamata Convention on Mercury and the 2015 Paris Agreement, identify goals, and provide a menu of regulatory options, but are facilitative and catalytic rather than 'top down' and prescriptive, as many earlier instruments were.[80] Ongoing negotiations on protecting Biodiversity Beyond National Jurisdictions (BBNJ) reflect a similar approach.[81]

2. *Procedural 'turn'*

Relatedly, recent instruments signal a procedural turn in international environmental law. The Paris Agreement, for instance, creates a web of inter-locking procedural commitments requiring states to submit 'nationally determined contributions' (NDCs) to address climate change, as well as detailed information, subject to expert review, to clarify these contributions as well as to track the conduct of states in achieving their NDCs.[82] It does not, deliberately, create substantive obligations of result in relation to NDCs.[83]

This trend, some note, is reflective of a broader 'turn to transparency' in international law, a turn that reflects a recognition that transparency is a valuable and substantive goal in itself, and not just a means to other ends.[84] The successful implementation of the 1998 Aarhus Convention[85]—demonstrated via the numerous pieces of national legislation that have been introduced and implemented to enhance public participation in environmental decision-making, access to environmental information, and effective remedies—and the adoption of the 2018 Escazú Agreement[86] offer further evidence of this turn to transparency in international environmental law.[87] While these instruments are of limited geographical scope, they endorse the ongoing normative development of expanding participation in international law.[88]

The turn to procedure, in particular relating to transparency, is also reflected in the intersections of human rights law and international environmental law. The right of

[79] Chapter 6, 'Instrument Choice', in this volume.

[80] See Chapters 33 and 29, 'Hazardous Substances and Activities' and 'Climate Change', in this volume.

[81] See Chapter 31, 'The Protection of the Marine Environment: Pollution and Fisheries', in this volume.

[82] See Chapter 29, 'Climate Change', in this volume.

[83] Ibid.

[84] See Chapter 52, 'Transparency Procedures', in this volume.

[85] Convention on Access to Information, Public Participation in Decision-Making and Access to Justice in Environmental Matters.

[86] Regional Agreement on Access to Information, Public Participation and Justice in Environmental Matters in Latin America and the Caribbean.

[87] Ibid.

[88] See Chapter 21, 'Public Participation', in this volume.

individuals to access environmental information, although of recent vintage, has become quickly entrenched in international law.[89] Further, the emerging jurisprudence of human rights bodies suggests that while states are offered a wide margin of discretion in relation to the appropriate level of environmental protection they choose for themselves, they are subject to more specific procedural requirements.[90] These require states to conduct impact assessments for proposed activities that can cause environmental harm and violate human rights, to publicize environmental information, and to provide individuals access to judicial remedies.[91] The 2018 Framework Principles on Human Rights and the Environment, presented by the then Special Rapporteur on Human Rights and Environment, John Knox, highlights the procedural obligations of states in this regard.[92] The evolution of the customary international law principle of harm prevention, mentioned earlier, to provide increased clarity on the procedural obligations of states, also matches this trend.[93] While this turn to procedure, and particularly transparency, enhances governance, legitimacy, and democratic structures in international and national environmental decision-making,[94] it may also be a troubling sign insofar as it takes the place of, rather than complements, politically contentious substantive standard-setting in international environmental law.

3. *Greater deference to national sovereignty, circumstances, and capacities*

That the lack of political will for a substantive standard-setting role for international environmental law, may, at least in part, explain the turn to procedure in international environmental law—is supported by yet another general trend in recent international environmental instruments, namely, that of greater deference to national sovereignty, circumstances, and capacities. The paradigm shift in the climate change regime from legally binding obligations of result in the 1997 Kyoto Protocol to NDCs (subject to obligations of conduct alone) in the 2015 Paris Agreement is the sharpest example of this trend.[95] The Paris Agreement also includes a telling reference to 'in light of different national circumstances' in its invocation of the principle of common but differentiated responsibilities.[96]

[89] Chapters 52 and 21, 'Transparency Procedures' and 'Public Participation', in this volume.
[90] Chapter 45, 'Human Rights', in this volume.
[91] Ibid.
[92] United Nations Human Rights Council (OHCHR), 'Report of the Special Rapporteur on the issue of human rights obligations relating to the enjoyment of a safe, clean, healthy and sustainable environment' (24 January 2018) UN Doc A/HRC/37/59, and Chapter 45, 'Human Rights', in this volume.
[93] See Chapter 23, 'Customary International Law and the Environment', in this volume.
[94] Chapter 21, 'Public Participation', in this volume.
[95] Chapter 29, 'Climate Change', in this volume.
[96] Ibid; art 2.

In a similar vein to the Paris Agreement's use of NDCs, a 2019 ICAO resolution on climate change 'encourage[s]' states to submit 'voluntary action plans' on climate policies and measures, and to report on the 'basket of measures reflecting respective national capacities and circumstances'.[97] Unlike in international wildlife and biodiversity law, where the starting point is permanent sovereignty over natural resources,[98] in relation to global commons the starting point is 'common concern', and the related understanding that it generates obligations *erga omnes*. The move towards greater deference to state sovereignty and autonomy in this context is remarkable, but tracks with the changing geo-politics discussed earlier, and the need to appeal to political regimes that are inward-looking, nationalistic, and agnostic to international law.

4. *Tailored and nuanced differentiation*

Recent international environmental instruments, in line with the changing geo-politics, also reflect greater parity between states in relation to obligations, and capture greater nuance in the nature and extent of differentiation between and among developing countries and developed countries, than earlier instruments. The Minamata Convention contains uniform obligations for states. Unlike the Kyoto Protocol that contains different commitments for different categories of parties, the Paris Agreement tailors differentiation to the specificities of each of the areas of regulation—mitigation, adaptation, finance, technology, capacity-building, and transparency. This seems to depart from earlier expressions of differentiation in international environmental instruments, such as the 1987 Montreal Protocol, which more clearly recognized different starting points and contributions of states in respect of the problem of ozone depletion and provided for a system of continual adjustments and amendments to phase in developing country participation over time.[99] In effect, more recent shifts in the understanding of differentiation have resulted in different forms of differentiation in different areas and enhanced discretion for all. Efforts to circumscribe and nuance differential treatment in favour of developing countries are also evident in the CORSIA, negotiated under the auspices of ICAO.[100]

5. *Increased reliance on soft law*

These shifts in differentiation have often provoked greater resistance to hard law instruments and obligations. This has led, in part, to a proliferation of fine-grained distinctions in the forms of law generated by states, and a spectrum of 'bindingness' in relation to instruments and obligations. This is most evident in the Paris Agreement, the

97 ICAO Res A40-18, 'Consolidated statement of continuing ICAO policies and practices related to environmental protection—Climate change' (2019). See Chapter 34, 'Aviation and Maritime Transport', in this volume.

98 Chapter 32, 'Wildlife', in this volume.

99 Montreal Protocol on Substances that Deplete the Ozone Layer.

100 Chapter 34, 'Aviation and Maritime Transport', in this volume.

provisions of which blur the boundaries of law, soft law, and non-law, and between all of which there is dynamic interplay.[101]

More generally, soft law, at the core of international environmental law from the start (the 1972 Stockholm[102] and 1992 Rio Declarations[103] are obvious examples[104]) has further consolidated its hold on international environmental law. Soft law, which not only takes the form of resolutions and declarations, but also of decisions taken by conferences of parties (COPs) to multilateral environmental agreements (MEAs), as well as of private and quasi-private standards,[105] plays a central role in the day-to-day functioning of international environmental law.[106] Soft law is easier to arrive at, attracts wider participation, is more responsive to change, and can be immediately implemented.[107] In the context of increasing political contestation over global environmental issues, and wariness of legally binding instruments (with the attendant loss of sovereignty), soft law offers a less contentious alternative that is nevertheless responsive, and potentially as effective, if not more so, than hard law, in addressing certain environmental issues. Soft law, in any case, is the 'product of an increasingly sophisticated legal system',[108] and international environmental law is certainly that.

6. *Treaty-making to treaty interpretation and implementation*

While the decades between Stockholm and Rio witnessed robust growth in international environmental treaty-making,[109] even at the time the first edition of this handbook was published, this pace had slowed down. In the years that have elapsed since, multilateral environmental treaty-making at the global level has been limited to the Minamata Convention, the Paris Agreement, and the ongoing negotiations for the protection of BBNJ.[110] Some treaty-making activity has also been evident regionally, including conclusion of the Escazú Agreement and ongoing development of environmental protection rules within the European Union (EU).[111] Regional treaties, such as the 1992 UNECE (UN Economic Commission for Europe) Convention on the Protection and Use of Transboundary Watercourses and International Lakes (Helsinki Water Convention),

[101] See generally Lavanya Rajamani, *Innovation and Experimentation in the International Climate Change Regime* (vol 41, *Collected Courses of the Hague Academy of International Law (Recueil des Cours)*, Brill 2020); Lavanya Rajamani, 'The 2015 Paris Agreement: Interplay Between Hard, Soft and Non-Obligations' *Journal of Environmental Law*, 28/2 (2016): 337; Chapter 29, 'Climate Change', in this volume.

[102] UN, 'Report of the United Nations Conference on the Human Environment' (5-16 June 1972) UN Doc A/CONF.48/14/Rev.1, 3, ch 1—'Declaration of the United Nations Conference on the Human Environment'.

[103] Rio Declaration (n 22).

[104] Chapter 3, 'Origin and History', in this volume.

[105] Chapter 26, 'Private and Quasi-Private Standards', in this volume.

[106] Chapter 25, 'Soft Law', in this volume.

[107] Ibid.

[108] Ibid.

[109] Chapter 3, 'Origin and History', in this volume.

[110] Chapter 31, 'The Protection of the Marine Environment: Pollution and Fisheries', in this volume.

[111] Chapter 37, 'Regional Organizations: The European Union', in this volume.

have also expanded their potential reach by allowing accession by parties outside the region.[112] However, even at the regional level, only a handful of new treaties have emerged.

The focus of international efforts has shifted instead to implementing existing regimes, and addressing the regulatory overlaps, inconsistencies, and inefficiencies between and within regimes that flow from a congested legal field.[113] For example, in the area of transboundary air pollution regulation, the rapid development of new protocols to the 1979 Convention on Long-range Transboundary Air Pollution (LRTAP) that characterized the period from 1980 to 2000 has given way to refinement of existing protocols to extend their coverage.[114] The stagnation in treaty-making in this phase tracks with developments in international law more generally, but is also the result of ongoing normative development, albeit of soft law, under MEAs and regional environmental treaties, through COP decisions. Much of this normative development is directed at interpreting and implementing treaty requirements.

MEAs are often the outcome of consensus-based decision-making and they frequently represent high-level skeletal compromises that need to be fleshed out before they can be operationalized. These treaties also contain provisions that are drafted in a manner that is deliberately ambiguous to preserve the positions of all sides,[115] and often defer contentious issues to be resolved through seemingly less political subsequent rule-making. COPs, in this context, are tasked not just with overseeing the implementation of these treaties, but also with interpreting them, and resolving deferred issues. As such, these bodies, and processes to enhance coordination between them, have become an important element of the institutional architecture of international environmental law.[116]

MEAs contain a range of mechanisms to support and enhance implementation, including those offering financial support and assistance with capacity building and technology development and deployment.[117] Financial assistance, especially, has proven to be key not just in enhancing the implementation of treaty commitments, but also in bringing defaulting states back into compliance. The experience of the Montreal Multilateral Fund offers a useful example in this context.[118] Multilateral environmental

[112] Chapter 30, 'Freshwater Resources', in this volume. The amendment to the 1992 UNECE Helsinki Water Convention to allow accession by all UN Member States, even if not ECE members, came into force on 6 February 2013 and gives this treaty potentially global scope: Convention on the Protection and Use of Transboundary Watercourses and International Lakes as amended, along with Decision VI/3 clarifying the accession procedure <https://www.unece.org/env/water/text/text.html> accessed 25 September 2020.

[113] See Chapter 3, 'Origin and History', in this volume. See also Chapter 5, 'Fragmentation', in this volume.

[114] See Chapter 28, 'Transboundary Air Pollution', in this volume. For example, amendments to the 1999 Gothenburg Protocol to Abate Acidification, Eutrophication and Ground-level Ozone made in 2012 and in force from 7 October 2019 extend controls to fine particulate matter, including black carbon: <https://www.unece.org/env/lrtap/multi_h1.html> accessed 25 September 2020.

[115] Chapter 24, 'Multilateral Environmental Treaty Making', in this volume.

[116] See Chapter 36, 'International Institutions', in this volume.

[117] See Chapters 54 and 55, 'Financial Assistance' and 'Technology Assistance and Transfers', in this volume. Eg Paris Agreement, arts 9–11, 13.9, 13.10.

[118] See Chapter 54, 'Financial Assistance', in this volume.

funds, in particular those directed at addressing climate change, have multiplied over the last decade,[119] and expanded to include *sui generis* public-private mechanisms such as the Prototype Carbon Fund, and the Rainforest Trust Fund.[120] More broadly, in keeping with the increasing diversity of actors engaging with international environmental law, and the scale of the environmental challenge, private finance and enterprise play a far more decisive role than before. Technology assistance and transfers, albeit long recognized as central to implementation, have proven unequal to the task, mired as they are in conflicts over intellectual property rights.[121]

Many MEAs also rely on reporting, monitoring, and review mechanisms to strengthen implementation and identify potential cases of non-compliance. As discussed earlier, such mechanisms have come off the sidelines to occupy centre stage in international environmental law.[122] For instance, the 2015 Agreement's 'enhanced transparency framework', bolstered by detailed rules under the 2018 Paris Rulebook,[123] places significantly higher and more frequent informational demands on states than the 1992 UN Framework Convention on Climate Change. Indeed, the Agreement's design complements information flow with obligations of conduct in a bid to generate peer-to-peer assessments, mutual trust, and reciprocity, which in turn is expected to enhance ambition and implementation.[124]

Non-compliance procedures also play a key role in enhancing implementation. Non-compliance procedures in MEAs are typically facilitative.[125] The Kyoto Protocol's compliance committee, which performed both facilitative and enforcement functions, was the notable exception. Although the Kyoto Protocol's compliance committee proved to be effective in the performance of its enforcement function, the political calculus has since shifted towards more facilitative instruments, diffuse and contextual obligations and thus facilitative non-compliance procedures as well. The Montreal Protocol non-compliance procedure, which is largely facilitative, with some enforcement tools at its disposal, has emerged as the standard for environmental compliance systems.[126]

More broadly, the experience and scholarship on the effectiveness of international environmental instruments provides useful insights into causally-informed notions of compliance that can help determine if observed behavioural shifts can indeed be attributed to an agreement, and to carefully identify the conditions under which different regulatory approaches best foster an agreement's influence.[127] Studies of the

[119] Ibid.

[120] Ibid.

[121] Chapter 55, 'Technology Assistance and Transfers', in this volume. See also Chapter 48, 'Intellectual Property', in this volume.

[122] Chapter 52, 'Transparency Procedures', in this volume.

[123] The full set of decisions agreed to at the 24th COP to the UNFCCC is characterized as the 'Paris Rulebook' <https://unfccc.int/process-and-meetings/the-paris-agreement/paris-agreement-work-programme/katowice-climate-package> accessed 4 February 2020.

[124] Chapter 29, 'Climate Change', in this volume.

[125] Chapter 56, 'Non-Compliance Procedures', in this volume.

[126] Ibid.

[127] Chapter 51, 'Compliance Theory', in this volume.

effectiveness of MEAs over the last few decades suggest that although most international regimes have had some effect on the problems they address, they rarely, if ever, solve them.[128] In relation to effectiveness, the Montreal Protocol has emerged as the gold standard for MEAs, a status often attributed to the treaty's flexible processes for amendment and adjustment of its rules, as well as its well-functioning finance, technology transfer, and non-compliance mechanisms.[129] The existing climate change regime suffers in comparison, and the Paris Agreement is yet to be fully operationalized and tested.[130]

National implementation of international environmental law has also changed over time in response to the nature of instruments being negotiated and the actors involved. The characterization of implementation as a 'top down' imposition of law on a state is no longer accurate for agreements, such as the Paris Agreement, where contributions are 'nationally determined' and a wider set of actors are engaged in delivering on these contributions.[131] Where there are serious breaches of international environmental law, the law of state responsibility can hold states accountable and provide reparation for the damage that has occurred. However, this law is yet to be put to serious test by environmental claims, especially in the context of collective action problems like climate change and biodiversity loss.[132] This international accountability void is being met—most prominently in the climate context—through increased reference to international environmental law in domestic policy-making, including at sub-national levels,[133] and via arguments looking to states' obligations under MEAs in litigation before domestic courts.[134]

D. Increasing Resort to International Courts and Tribunals

In keeping with the rapid growth and proliferation of international environmental law, the turn of the century has marked the start of a phase of brisk growth in the judicialization of international environmental law.[135] International courts and tribunals, especially in the last two decades, have played an important role in the development of international environmental law by providing authoritative articulations of rules and principles, and in identifying standards and expectations associated with these rules and

[128] Chapter 57, 'Effectiveness', in this volume.

[129] See eg Chapters 54, 56, and 57, 'Financial Assistance', 'Non-Compliance Procedures', and 'Effectiveness', in this volume.

[130] Chapter 57, 'Effectiveness', in this volume.

[131] Chapter 59, 'National Implementation', in this volume.

[132] Chapter 58, 'International Environmental Responsibility and Liability', in this volume.

[133] Chapter 39, 'Sub-National Actors', in this volume.

[134] See eg Lennart Wegener, 'Can the Paris Agreement Help Climate Change Litigation and Vice Versa?' *Transnational Environmental Law*, 9/1 (2020): 17.

[135] Chapter 60, 'International Environmental Law Disputes before International Courts and Tribunals', in this volume.

principles.[136] They have been effective in some respects, for instance, in influencing state behaviour in relation to the obligation to perform transboundary EIAs, but less effective in others, for instance, in preventing harmful transboundary effects.[137] International environmental disputes have also contributed more broadly to the development of jurisprudence relating to state responsibility and the law of treaties.[138] Regional human rights courts have begun to weigh in on international environmental law, with some far-reaching recent decisions emerging from the Inter-American Court on Human Rights (IACtHR).[139] There is also increased use of investor–state arbitration as an environmental protection mechanism.[140] And, as noted above, a growing effort to seed and translate norms of international environmental law in domestic litigation.[141]

This trend towards increasing judicialization of environmental concerns is set to grow, particularly in the context of climate change, where the glacial pace of the negotiations relative to the narrow window of opportunity to address the problem has caused immense frustration. There are several cases in the pipeline, and in courts, national, regional, and international. Non-state actors are taking governments and corporate actors to court to force ambitious action. As laws and policies, both international and national, fall far short of what science dictates as necessary to address climate change, increasing recourse to litigation seems inevitable.[142]

E. Enhanced Decentralization and the Emergence of Polycentric Governance

The last decade has witnessed a dramatic uptick in actors, initiatives, and networks across and within states engaging with international environmental law. The business community, including multinational corporations, banks, investors, and insurers, is

[136] Ibid and Chapter 27, 'Judicial Development', in this volume.

[137] Chapter 27, 'Judicial Development', in this volume.

[138] Chapter 60, 'International Environmental Law Disputes before International Courts and Tribunals', in this volume.

[139] Chapter 27, 'Judicial Development', in this volume.

[140] Chapter 44, 'Investment', in this volume.

[141] See Part IX, 'International Environmental Law in National/Regional Courts', in this volume, covering the jurisdictions of Africa, China, EU/UK, India, Bangladesh, and Pakistan, North America, Oceania, and South America, for a range of examples.

[142] See eg Jacqueline Peel and Hari Osofsky, *Climate Change Litigation: Regulatory Pathways to Cleaner Energy* (CUP 2015); Jacqueline Peel and Hari Osofsky, 'A Rights Turn in Climate Change Litigation?' *Transnational Environmental Law*, 7/1 (2018): 37; Joana Setzer and Lisa Vanhala, 'Climate Change Litigation: A Review of Research on Courts and Litigants in Climate Governance' *WIREs Climate Change*, 10/3 (2019): 1; Joana Setzer and Rebecca Byrnes, 'Global Trends in Climate Change Litigation: 2020 Snapshot' *Grantham Research Institute on Climate Change and the Environment and Centre for Climate Change Economics and Policy, London School of Economics and Political Science* (3 July 2020); Jacqueline Peel and Jolene Lin, 'Transnational Climate Litigation: The Contribution of the Global South' *American Journal of International Law*, 113/4 (2019): 679.

more deeply and constructively engaged in international environmental law than at any period in the past.[143] Non-state and sub-national actors are both active participants in shaping international environmental regulation, and effective vehicles for its implementation.[144]

The Paris Climate Conference, for instance, launched the Global Climate Action portal to record efforts of non-state actors. It contains 27,000 commitments from over 10,000 cities, 4,000 companies, and 1,000 investors.[145] The most telling example of such non-state actor influence and reach is that notwithstanding the US decision under the Trump administration to withdraw from the Paris Agreement, many US states, cities, and businesses undertook to meet the country's pledged GHG mitigation targets.[146] The normative developments promoting public participation, referred to earlier, support such an expansive role for non-state actors.[147] While most pronounced in the climate change arena, these trends are also evident in other areas of international environmental activity, such as the emerging focus on marine plastic pollution, which is bringing together a coalition of international organizations, non-state actors, scientists, and investor groups to push for greater action.[148]

Needless to say, the growing role and significance of non-state and sub-state actors in international environmental law, has brought the role and continued salience of the state into question.[149] The role of states as 'authors and guardians of the law' has changed over time, yet states have remained crucial as 'addressees' of international environmental law.[150] They engage in cooperative law enforcement against each other and implement and enforce standards within their jurisdiction. Indeed, new forms of governance have arguably given the state a broader canvas to write on and a wider range of actors to influence.[151] Consistent with trends in domestic environmental governance, the shift in states' role is often one from 'rowing' to 'steering' developments.[152] The increasing autonomy offered to states in more recent multilateral environmental instruments also supports the argument that the state is as powerful and central as before, albeit in a changed context, and with more sophisticated demands placed on it.

The trend towards decentralization and enhanced polycentricity of international environmental law—both in relation to non-state and sub-national actors, as well as

[143] Chapter 41, 'Business and Industry', in this volume.

[144] Chapters 38 and 39, 'Non-State Actors' and 'Sub-National Actors', in this volume.

[145] 'Global Climate Action portal' <https://climateaction.unfccc.int/> accessed 23 September 2020.

[146] 'We are all still in' <https://www.wearestillin.com/> accessed 23 September 2020. See also Chapter 39, 'Sub-National Actors', in this volume.

[147] Chapter 21, 'Public Participation', in this volume.

[148] 'Global Partnership on Marine Litter' <https://www.unenvironment.org/gpml/> accessed 23 September 2020.

[149] Chapter 35, 'The State', in this volume.

[150] Ibid.

[151] Ibid.

[152] Neil Gunningham, 'Environment Law, Regulation and Governance: Shifting Architectures' *Journal of Environmental Law*, 21/2 (2009): 179.

the autonomy states have in newer, facilitative, 'bottom-up' forms of environmental governance—developed in part due to the gaps exposed in traditional environmental law, together with difficulties in shifting the entrenched positions of sovereign states. It has, in its wake, shrunk the space for international enforcement and expanded the scope for domestic law, litigation, and courts. This has also led to interesting discussions around the appropriate level of governance for addressing environmental issues,[153] and tensions and complementarities at the interface of international and domestic law.[154]

IV. EXPANDING FRONTIERS OF INTERNATIONAL ENVIRONMENTAL LAW

As international environmental law has grown in ambition and reach, it has encountered other specialized international law regimes. Some of these encounters have resulted in colliding 'objectives and values',[155] as, for instance, in relation to the legal frameworks governing trade, investment, energy, and intellectual property. Other encounters, as, for instance, with the legal frameworks governing human rights, migration, and disaster, have generated opportunities for convergence, complementarity, and integration. As this section of the chapter discusses, both sets of encounters—characterized by remarkable ingenuity and creative lawyering directed at rendering international law fit for environmental purpose—expand the frontiers of international environmental law and these other regimes.

States and dispute settlement bodies have sought over time to balance the needs of the environment with the demands of the multilateral trading system, with some success. However, since this balancing exercise is spear-headed by bodies such as the World Trade Organization dispute settlement mechanism, the balance is often struck in favour of trade over the environment.[156] This is particularly problematic in the context of the 'new generation' of trade disputes emerging in relation to governmental efforts to support low-carbon industries.[157]

Similar collisions of 'objectives and values' are evident in the context of investor–state arbitrations.[158] In this field too, rules of international investment law were at least initially prioritized over international and domestic environmental law and decision-making. The culture and context, however, is constantly shifting, and the demand for a more balanced approach, or even one that favours the environment, is growing quickly.

[153] See Chapter 4, 'Multilevel and Polycentric Governance', in this volume.

[154] See Part IX, 'International Environmental Law in National/Regional Courts', in this volume.

[155] Chapter 43, 'Trade', in this volume.

[156] Ibid.

[157] Ibid.

[158] Chapter 44, 'Investment', in this volume.

Early signs of responsiveness are evident in recent bilateral investment treaties (BITS) and foreign trade agreements (FTAs) that capture a more balanced version of the environment and investment nexus.[159] Moreover, arbitrators in investor–state arbitrations are also beginning to demonstrate some sensitivity to environmental concerns and familiarity with environmental rules. Nevertheless, this is still a work in progress, and if environmental harms, including climate change, are to be effectively addressed, trade, investment, and environmental rules need to be truly 'mutually supportive'.

International legal frameworks governing energy are also frequently at odds with international environmental law. Conventional energy that powered the twentieth century is a source of significant environmental harm. Although sustainable energy is expected to drive responses to such environmental harm, reliance on alternative energy sources, such as biofuels and wind, can have deleterious impacts on the environment, food security, and species protection. Yet, since international energy regulation is directed principally at facilitating energy activities and only incidentally at mitigating its negative transboundary effects, environmental risks, particularly fossil-fuel use, are largely unregulated at the international level.[160] This has led to increasing efforts to find synergies between energy and environmental objectives, as for instance, under the 1971 Ramsar Convention on Wetlands, and the 1972 World Heritage Convention.[161] This activity is likely to grow and become increasingly salient, as the impacts of climate change take hold and the demand for energy transition expands.

The legal framework governing intellectual property rights offers another source of potential tension with international environmental law. Technological innovation is key to combatting global environmental harm, and indeed is the dominant paradigm in Promethean environmental discourses. However, access to such technologies because of the intellectual property rights that attach to them is challenging and has been a site of conflict between developed and developing countries. There are efforts underway to increase public investment and foster cooperation in research and development, and experiment with technology patent pools, which could address the restrictions that intellectual property regimes pose to the availability and diffusion of existing and future technologies.[162] The demand for widespread diffusion of emergent green technologies—indeed their centrality given the seemingly impossible alternative of transitioning away from our capitalist structures and consumerist lifestyles—will require creative lawyering at the interface of international environmental law and the international law relating to intellectual property.

In other fields such as human rights, migration, and disaster, although 'objectives and values' often complement rather than collide with those in the environmental field, developments proceeded in siloed parallel for several decades. The primary points of intersection between human rights law and environmental law are concerning the

[159] Ibid.

[160] Chapter 49, 'Energy', in this volume.

[161] Ibid.

[162] Chapter 48, 'Intellectual Property', in this volume.

'human right to a healthy environment,' procedural rights relating to access to environmental information, public participation, and remedy, and the jurisprudence of regional and national courts that recognizes the human rights impacts of environmental harms.[163] There have been rapid developments along all three points of intersection, expanding the frontiers both of human rights law and international environmental law. The human right to a healthy environment, long featured in international soft law instruments, regional human rights instruments, and national constitutions and laws, is yet to be recognized as a legally binding right at the international level. However, the Paris Agreement contains a preambular reference to human rights, thus offering a hook for further integration of human rights concerns into environmental, in particular climate, discourses.

The 2017 draft Global Environmental Pact contained a clear articulation of a human right to a healthy environment,[164] and successive special rapporteurs on Human Rights and the Environment have proposed the adoption of such a right at the international level.[165] Procedural rights relating to the environment, as discussed earlier, are being increasingly recognized and respected. The jurisprudence of regional and national human rights bodies on environmental matters has increased exponentially, and as these bodies are exposed to environmental principles and sensibilities, they are tapping into a rich vein of cross-fertilization. Indeed, one of the most path-breaking decisions in international environmental law to emerge in recent times did so from a regional human rights body. In an advisory opinion, in response to a request from Colombia, the IACtHR went as far as to opine that the jurisdiction and responsibility of states under the 1969 American Convention on Human Rights extend to those outside their territory whose human rights have been violated by transboundary environmental harm originating from that state.[166] More broadly, there is evidence of 'converging trends towards greater uniformity and certainty' in understanding human rights in relation to environmental harms.[167]

This trend towards greater convergence and integration is also evident in relation to migration[168] and disasters.[169] Although historically international environmental law and the law relating to migration rarely intersected, growing understanding that

[163] Chapter 45, 'Human Rights', in this volume.

[164] Le Club des Juristes: International Group of Experts for the Pact, 'Draft Global Pact for the Environment by the IGEP' (La Sorbonne, 24 June 2017) <https://globalpactenvironment.org/uploads/EN.pdf> accessed 15 September 2020. See also UNGA Res 72/277 (n 70).

[165] Under Human Rights Council resolution 37/8, Special Rapporteur on Human Rights and the Environment, John Knox, recommended that the General Assembly recognize the human right to a safe, clean, healthy, and sustainable environment: UNGA, 'Human rights obligations relating to the enjoyment of a safe, clean, healthy and sustainable environment' (19 July 2018) UN Doc A/73/188. See also Chapter 45, 'Human Rights', in this volume.

[166] *State Obligations in Relation to the Environment* (Advisory Opinion) IACtHR (2017) OC-23/17 (State Obligations case) [77]–[78].

[167] Chapter 45, 'Human Rights', in this volume.

[168] Chapter 46, 'Migration', in this volume.

[169] See Chapter 47, 'Disaster', in this volume.

environmental factors drive forced and voluntary migration,[170] has led to increasing convergence in these two areas, in particular as applied to climate change. The UN climate change regime has, in the last decade, begun to engage with the human costs of climate impacts, including forced and voluntary migration caused by sudden-onset and slow-onset climate events, respectively.[171] Meanwhile, the legal framework for migration has also begun to address the humanitarian consequences of large scale climate-related displacement and migration, as in the Global Compact for Migration and the Sendai Framework.[172] The developments in the climate change and migration fields are converging towards an integrated 'law of environmental migration'.[173]

Similarly, as the scale and frequency of disasters caused by sudden-onset and slow-onset climatic events is becoming evident, the legal framework governing disasters is increasingly intersecting and converging with international environmental law.[174] However, such intersections are still in their infancy. While some principles of international environmental law, such as those relating to compensation, are widely reflected in disaster law, others, such as precaution, are absent.[175] The rising ecosystem-based disaster risk reduction (Eco-DRR) movement, as well as the demand for an effective international response to disaster migrants, suggests that there will be rapid developments at this interface as well.[176]

Finally, at the interface of international environmental law with armed conflict, there is also a pull towards integration. In addition to international humanitarian law, international criminal law, and international human rights law, norms of international environmental law are also beginning to shape the protection of the environment during conflict.[177]

International environmental law is increasingly encountering, enriching, and expanding other specialized bodies of international law from trade and investment, to human rights and armed conflict. In the process, international environmental law is expanding its frontiers, demonstrating maturity, and reflecting the real-world complexity in addressing 'super wicked' environmental challenges such as climate change.[178] International environmental law's increasing encounters with other regimes

[170] See Chapter 46, 'Migration', in this volume.

[171] Ibid. See also Paris Agreement; Decision 1/CP.16, 'The Cancun Agreements: Outcome of the work of the Ad Hoc Working Group on Long-term Cooperative Action under the Convention' (15 March 2011) UN Doc FCCC/CP/2010/7/Add.1, 2.

[172] Chapter 46, 'Migration', in this volume; 'Global Compact for safe, orderly and regular migration' (13 July 2018) <https://refugeesmigrants.un.org/sites/default/files/180713_agreed_outcome_global_compact_for_migration.pdf> accessed 25 September 2020; UNGA Res 69/283, 'Sendai Framework for Disaster Risk Reduction 2015–2030' (23 June 2015) UN Doc A/RES/69/283.

[173] Chapter 46, 'Migration', in this volume.

[174] Chapter 47, 'Disaster', in this volume.

[175] Ibid.

[176] Ibid.

[177] Chapter 50, 'Armed Conflict', in this volume.

[178] For 'super wicked' in the context of climate: Richard Lazarus, 'Super Wicked Problems and Climate Change: Restraining the Present to Liberate the Future' *Cornell Law Review*, 94/5 (2009): 1153. See also

have resulted in colliding 'objectives and values', exposed differing motivations, and unearthed new sites of conflict and contestation, but it has also presented valuable opportunities for accommodation and integration. It has, moreover, multiplied the sites at which international environmental law is made, interpreted, applied, and implemented. International environmental law is richer, and perhaps more effective as a result.

V. CONCLUSION: IS INTERNATIONAL ENVIRONMENTAL LAW FIT FOR PURPOSE?

The last decade has been a period of rapid, responsive change for international environmental law. The geo-political, social, economic, epistemic, and cultural context within which international environmental law is set has changed in fundamental ways, fostering legal experimentation and triggering an expansion in the scope, content, and reach of international environmental law. There is increasing maturity in the interpretation of the content of customary norms, principles, and techniques; a change in focus towards more facilitative and procedural modes and implementation over rule-making, with a concomitant nuancing of concepts of differentiation and an enhanced role for soft law; and greater diversification in the participating actors and sites of international environmental law activity, including a growing judicialization of the field. The frontiers of international environmental law are also expanding to accommodate, engage, and integrate with legal efforts in many other fields, reflecting gradual tailoring of the discipline to the nature of the problem it addresses—complex, polycentric, and intractable global environmental harms. International environmental lawyers, diplomats, and other stakeholders are demonstrating remarkable ingenuity, creativity, and passion in stretching international environmental law to its limits to address existential environmental harms.

Nevertheless, international environmental law's achievements in environmental terms are modest. Much of international environmental law's promise and potential has been explored in these last few decades, and it is fast approaching the limits of its ability to influence state behaviour. As developments in the climate change regime demonstrate, notwithstanding hair-raising twists and turns in response to geo-political shifts, and breath-taking legal experimentation and innovation,[179] the international community is still taking a collective leap of faith in the Paris Agreement, which may well

Daniel Bodansky, Jutta Brunnée, and Lavanya Rajamani, *International Climate Change Law* (OUP 2017) 2–4.

[179] Rajamani, 'Innovation and Experimentation' (n 101).

stop short of averting catastrophic climate change. The world has arrived at biosphere tipping points—the edge of a precipice, beyond which lies irreversible environmental harm that fundamentally compromises life support systems.[180] If the world is facing a state of 'planetary emergency,'[181] it does beg the question whether international environmental law is fit for purpose, and whether, for all its sophistication and maturity as a sub-discipline of international law, it is fundamentally limited. International environmental law, like other fields of international law, is hostage to national sovereignty, and political will and its limits are equally the limits of international law.

Daniel Bodansky, Jutta Brunnée, and Ellen Hey concluded their introduction to the first edition of the *Oxford Handbook of International Environmental Law* by posing the question 'Is international environmental law a distinct field?'[182] Concluding that it is a distinct and indeed sophisticated field of international law today, the introduction to the second edition instead concludes by posing the question 'Is international environmental law fit for purpose'? The third edition, it is hoped, will conclude that it is, and illustrate the ways in which it came to be so. Or if it does not, track the changes to new paradigms and approaches that better suit the complexity of environmental challenges in a world of planetary constraints.[183]

There are clear limits to what international environmental law—set squarely within the current architecture of international law and hostage to national will and power politics—can do and can be expected to do.[184] If international environmental law is to do more, it must move beyond the constraints of the current architecture and framing, and embrace a fundamental reconceptualization of existing models of governance, whether economic, political, social, or legal.[185] Such reconceptualization is already underway and is gaining ground, from the increasing traction that Earth jurisprudence has received,[186] to the judicial efforts to deterritorialize international environmental law.[187] At the scale required, fundamental realignments, demand imagination—imagination that is both outrageous, and fuelled by outrage. In its absence, humanity's answer to this poignant question posed by the Irish poet, Theo Dorgan will be one steeped in unrelenting regret and sadness.

[180] See the IPCC's finding that continued GHG emissions will cause 'further warming' and increase the likelihood of 'severe, pervasive and irreversible impacts': IPCC, *Climate Change 2014* (n 6) 7. See also the finding of 'robust differences' between limiting warming to 1.5°C and 2°C, with possible irreversible consequences at higher temperatures: IPCC, *Global Warming of 1.5°C* (n 6) 7–8. And further Timothy Lenton *et al*, 'Climate Tipping Points—Too Risky To Bet Against' *Nature*, 575 (2019): 592 <https://www.nature.com/articles/d41586-019-03595-0> accessed 25 September 2020.

[181] Lenton *et al*, ibid, 595.

[182] Bodansky, Brunnée, and Hey (n 3) 24.

[183] Duncan French and Louis Kotzé (eds), *Research Handbook on Law, Governance and Planetary Boundaries* (Edward Elgar 2021).

[184] See generally Chapter 8, 'Legal Imagination and Teaching', in this volume.

[185] See generally Chapter 7, 'Scholarship', in this volume.

[186] See Chapter 14, 'Earth Jurisprudence', in this volume.

[187] State Obligations case (n 166).

The Question

When the great ships come back, and come they will, when they stand in the sky all over the world, candescent suns by day, radiant cathedrals in the night, how shall we answer the question:

What have you done with what was given you, what have you done with the blue, beautiful world?

Theo Dorgan (2015)[188]

[188] Theo Dorgan, 'A climate change poem for today: The Question by Theo Dorgan' *The Guardian* (1 June 2015) <https://www.theguardian.com/environment/2015/jun/01/a-climate-change-poem-for-today-the-question-by-theo-dorgan> accessed 25 September 2020.

PART I

CONTEXT

CHAPTER 2

DISCOURSES

JOHN S DRYZEK

I. INTRODUCTION

DISCOURSES are kinds of intersubjective understanding that condition individual action and social outcomes in the international system no less than elsewhere. They have no formal existence resembling that of organizations, constitutions, laws, and treaties. However, they can be none the less effective in coordinating the behaviour of large numbers of actors, which is especially true in a political system as decentralized as the international one, where formal sources of order are weak. Even in the presence of laws and formal organizations, discourses constitute the 'software' that is important in explaining how institutions work.[1] It is impossible to understand international environmental law without coming to grips with the informal understandings that condition its creation and operation.

I begin by elaborating on the concept of discourse, then turn to how the main discourses of environmental concern can be mapped through reference to their reactions against an earlier industrialism. The bulk of this chapter examines the content, history, and impact of the discourses of environmental problem-solving, limits and survival, sustainability, and green radicalism, as well as old and new backlashes against environmentalism. Finally, I consider the importance of discourses in ordering international environmental affairs compared with other influences.

II. BASICS

A discourse is by definition composed of shared concepts, categories, and ideas that enable actors to understand situations. Thus any discourse will entail and include

[1] Vivien Schmidt, 'Discursive Institutionalism; The Explanatory Power of Ideas and Discourse' *Annual Review of Political Science*, 11 (2011): 303.

judgements, assumptions, capabilities, dispositions, and intentions, establishing the foundations for analysis, debates, agreements, and disagreements. Those who subscribe to a discourse will be able to put together pieces of information into coherent accounts organized around storylines in meaningful ways to fellow subscribers. Discourses establish meanings, identify agents in contrast to those who can only be the object of action, confirm relations between actors and other entities, set the boundaries for what is legitimate knowledge, and generate what is accepted as common sense.[2] Practices, as well as words, enter discourses, for social actions are always associated with language that establishes their meaning. Power is internal to discourses as they constitute norms and perceptions, serving some interests while squashing others. While discourses are often thought of as sources of order, discourses can also be disruptive: think of the recent role of authoritarian populism and American nationalism in disrupting the international system. An emphasis on the constitutive role of discourses is consistent with constructivism in international relations theory (though constructivists do not have to be discourse analysts).

Individuals are generally socialized into discourses rather than formally educated in them. In social life, discourses can come before subjects; that is, in large measure, individuals are the creations of the discourses in which they move. Discourses can be so ingrained that subjects are unaware of their presence. What an outsider can see as a discourse, an insider will often take for granted as the natural order of things. The dominant discourse relevant to environmental affairs before the 1960s—industrialism—had exactly this character, which long prevented conceptualization of 'the environment'. However, individuals can sometimes escape the terms of particular discourses; one aspect of modernization is the capacity of individuals to subject discourses to critical attention.

Discourses have origins that can be both multiple and complex. Sometimes they are an outgrowth of an ingrained social order (eg medieval discourses about sin and punishment). Sometimes skilled rhetoricians can bend established discourses in new directions (eg Pope Francis reoriented a religious discourse in environmental directions in his *Laudato Si* encyclical). A discourse may prove functional for a dominant economic system: Marxists often saw the discourse of liberal democracy in this light, as providing cover for the injustices of capitalism. There is no general theory of the origins of discourses; the best way to account for where they come from and how they change is to write their histories.

Industrialism constitutes the background against which environmental discourses develop, so let me turn to categorization and analysis of the major discourses of environmental concern, positioning them initially in terms of their departure from, and challenge to, industrialism.

[2] Jennifer Milliken, 'The Study of Discourse in International Relations: A Critique of Research and Methods' *European Journal of International Relations*, 5/2 (1999): 225.

III. MAPPING ENVIRONMENTAL DISCOURSES

The defining feature of industrialism is its dedication to growth in the amount of goods and services that society produces and in the human material well-being that results. Industrial society has witnessed diverse ideological currents, ranging from liberalism and fascism to conservatism, socialism, and Marxism. However, from the perspective of environmentalism, these ideologies can seem similar; however much this similarity might surprise their proponents. None was especially interested in the environment (setting aside some Nazi interest in Aryan nature). Even what we now recognize as environmental concerns were treated mainly as inputs to industrial processes, or at most a matter of public health. Consider, for example, the US Conservation Movement of the early twentieth century, led by Gifford Pinchot. This movement wanted resources such as minerals, timber, and fish to be used carefully rather than in a profligate free-for-all—to better support industrial growth. Industrialism does not have to require that particular resources be infinite. However, it must deny the existence of systemic limits to human economic activity, stemming, for example, from the finite character of the ecosystems in which society is embedded.

Industrialism was not vanquished by the rise of environmentalism that began in the 1960s, and persisted into the twenty-first century. When President Donald Trump announced withdrawal from the 2015 Paris Agreement on climate change in 2017, he said it was because the Agreement was bad for the US economy, mirroring George W Bush's withdrawal from the 1997 Kyoto Protocol on climate change in 2001. The international trade regime, for its part, has often ruled against environmental protection measures by interpreting them as simply 'restraints on trade'.

Environmental discourses can be positioned in terms of how they differ from the industrialism from which they depart—their dispute with industrialism generally being more pronounced than their engagement with each other. On one dimension, this departure can range from reformist to radical; on another, from prosaic to imaginative. Prosaic discourses accept as given the character of the game set by industrial society: environmental issues are principally conceptualized as difficulties run into by the industrial, political economy. The response required does not involve social transformation, though it can be substantial and indeed radical. For example, some environmentalists believe that economic growth must be curbed and perhaps even stopped, but at the same time want to manage this transition only by deploying instruments and institutions developed in industrialism: especially strong central administration guided by scientific expertise.

Imaginative departures from industrialism reconfigure the game, mainly by conceptualizing environmental issues as opportunities, not troubles. Notably, environmental values are not placed in opposition to economic values but in potential

Table 2.1 Classifying Environmental Discourses

	Reformist	Radical
Prosaic	Problem-solving	Limits and survival
Imaginative	Sustainability	Green Radicalism

complementarity. The environment can then be welcomed into cultural, social, and economic systems, not just seen as generating difficulties for these systems from the outside. While imaginative, the desired social change can range from the incremental and reformist to the extensive and radical. The two dimensions—reformist to radical and prosaic to imaginative can be combined to give four cells, presented in Table 2.1.[3]

Environmental Problem-Solving is prosaic and reformist, taking the political economy of industrial society as given, but requiring some policy changes to deal with environmental issues. Three main types of change are available, stressing respectively citizens organized into politics, consumers and producers organized into markets, and experts organized into governmental administration. The result is three discourses of environmental problem-solving: democratic pragmatism, economic rationalism, and administrative rationalism. There is room for dispute about the relative merits of these three discourses or their suitability for different purposes. Some want to curb pollution through administrative control, others by economic incentives.

Limits and Survival is prosaic and radical, arriving with a splash in the early 1970s. Especially influential was the 1972 report to the Club of Rome, 'The Limits to Growth'. Originally, the discourse charged that economic and population growth must at some point encounter limits given by the Earth's finite supply of natural resources and the ability of ecosystems to support agricultural and industrial activity and assimilate wastes. This discourse is radical in rejecting economic growth and in wanting experts to steer the global political economy. It is prosaic for it sees a simple conflict between economy and environment, and conceptualizes solutions in terms set in industrialism, involving control by elites, administrators, and scientists. More recently, the idea of planetary boundaries identifies nine boundaries whose transgression presages catastrophe.

Sustainability began in the 1970s, and was confirmed as the dominant discourse in global environmental politics by the Brundtland Report in 1987.[4] Sustainable development features imaginative dissolution of the clash between environment and

[3] This categorization is explored at greater length in John Dryzek, *The Politics of the Earth: Environmental Discourses* (3rd edn, OUP 2013).

[4] World Commission on Environment and Development (WCED), *Our Common Future* (OUP 1987).

economy that underlines discourses of problem-solving and limits alike. Growth and development became thought of in ways that undermined the limits discourse's predictions of overshoot and collapse; limits fade into the background (though they do not entirely disappear). With the urgency of limits having receded, sustainability discourse does not have to be radical (and with time, its centre of gravity becomes less radical). Also in the 1980s, a discourse of ecological modernization appears in Northern Europe. Ecological modernization, too, believes economic growth and environmental conversation can be complementary. While initially concerned mainly with re-engineering developed economies, ecological modernization eventually spread to other parts of the world. So far, its impact at the international level has been limited, and so I will not address it further here (though Hajer and Versteeg discern elements of ecological modernization in the establishment and operation of the 1992 United Nations Framework Convention on Climate Change (UNFCCC)[5]). Ecological modernization lacks the breadth of sustainable development that extends to social justice, the developing world, and global concerns. Their origins are different, with ecological modernization growing alongside public policy and corporate practice in Northern Europe.

Green Radicalism combines imagination and radicalism, rejecting both the fundamental structure of industrial society and how that society conceptualizes 'the environment'. Industrialism's conceptualizations are replaced by some very different ways of thinking about people, society, and humanity's position in the world. Green radical discourse has had many internal varieties: animal liberationists, more holistic ecological thinkers, deep ecologists, environmental justice advocates, lifestyle advocates, the environmentalism of the global poor, and wild lawyers.[6] Green radicals vary in their degree of ecocentrism, and the degree to which they might be willing to compromise ecological concerns for the sake of other values such as social justice. However, all these varieties have more similarities with each other than with either industrialism or the other three environmental discourses, especially when it comes to the need to move to a different kind of society that has ecological concerns at its core.

I will now take a closer look at the discourses I have enumerated, with special reference to how they manifest themselves in international environmental affairs, and to what effect.

[5] Maarten Hajer and Wytske Versteeg, 'Voices of Vulnerability: The Reconfiguration of Policy Discourses' in John Dryzek, Richard Norgaard, and David Schlosberg (eds), *The Oxford Handbook of Climate Change and Society* (OUP 2011) 82.

[6] See Chapter 14, 'Earth Jurisprudence', in this volume.

IV. THE MAJOR ENVIRONMENTAL DISCOURSES

A. Limits, Boundaries, and the Promethean Response

The heyday of the discourse of limits was the 1970s, otherwise known as the doomsday decade.[7] An earlier contribution came in Paul Ehrlich's 1968 declaration that the Earth was about to be hit by a 'population bomb', more devastating than nuclear weapons.[8] Other population biologists, such as Garrett Hardin, added their warnings to the debate. The 'Limits to Growth' forecasts received massive publicity, and the book sold over four million copies worldwide.[9] While the timetable was a little hazy, the book forecast that the world would hit absolute ecological limits at some point by the middle of the twenty-first century. Unless action could be taken to forestall matters, the consequence would be overshoot and collapse,[10] meaning economic crash and decimation of human numbers. The action seen as necessary was coordinated and global, to steer global systems away from uncontrolled economic and population growth.

Survivalism's impact has been limited. Occasionally figures in high places have endorsed survivalism, and this was especially true in the 1970s. Occasionally countries have followed population-control policies enforced in a heavy-handed fashion; the best example would be China. It is harder but not impossible to discern lasting impacts of the discourse on international regimes and institutions. Meadows, Meadows, Randers, and Behrens, in their 1992 follow-up to 'Limits to Growth,' themselves believe that the success of the 1987 Montreal Protocol for the Protection of the Ozone Layer demonstrates that at the all-important global level, we can indeed move 'back from beyond the limits'.[11] However, this claim is not especially plausible, given that cheap technological solutions were at hand for the ozone issue, with no suggestion in the Montreal Protocol that economic or population growth should be curbed or even redirected. According to Peter Haas, a united epistemic community of atmospheric scientists motivated global action, precisely as limits discourse would require; though there are competing accounts of the dynamics of the ozone issue (one of which I will discuss later).[12]

[7] For particularly gloomy prognostications, see Robert Heilbroner, *An Inquiry into the Human Prospect* (Norton 1974); William Ophuls, *Ecology and The Politics of Scarcity* (WH Freeman 1977).

[8] Paul Ehrlich, *The Population Bomb* (Ballantine Books 1968).

[9] Donella Meadows *et al*, *The Limits to Growth* (Universe Books 1972).

[10] William Catton, *Overshoot: The Ecological Basis of Revolutionary Change* (University of Illinois Press 1980).

[11] Donella Meadows, Dennis Meadows, and Jørgen Randers, *Beyond the Limits: Confronting Global Collapse, Envisioning a Sustainable Future* (Chelsea Green 1992) 141–160.

[12] Peter Haas, 'Banning Chlorofluorocarbons: Efforts to Protect Stratospheric Ozone' *International Organization*, 46/1 (1992): 187.

This mixed record does not mean the emphasis on global limits is wrong. If nothing else, by identifying some apocalyptic horizons, the discourse of limits and survival confirmed that the environment is perhaps the most important issue humanity confronts in the twenty-first century. It receives an echo in the work of those who seek an economy with no growth or de-growth.[13]

By the 2010s, the idea of planetary boundaries had largely displaced that of limits. Planetary boundaries specify the tolerable degree of stress on the planet's life support systems. There are nine of these judgement calls, including climate change, biosphere integrity, and ocean acidification.[14] Together they define a 'safe operating space' for humanity. The boundaries for climate change, biosphere integrity, and the nitrogen cycle have already been exceeded in the judgement of the scientists who advanced the concept. While pushed aggressively by the relevant scientific community, it has been hard to get planetary boundaries recognized in international agreements. Planetary boundaries appeared in the draft declaration of the 2012 UN Conference on Sustainable Development (Rio+20), but proved too controversial and were removed from the final draft. There was no reference to them in the 2015 Sustainable Development Goals (SDGs). Many scientists who have conceptualized planetary boundaries now speak of the 'Anthropocene' as an emerging epoch of human-induced instability in the Earth system. Planetary boundaries can be thought of as guidelines to maintain relatively stable Holocene conditions, and thus avoid the dire consequences of the Anthropocene. Planetary boundaries have been joined with social justice concerns in the 'Oxfam Doughnut' that locates a 'safe and just space for humanity'.[15]

The opposite of limits and boundaries is a Promethean discourse that simply denies the existence of ecological and resource limits, mainly because that no global scarcities have ever limited human economic activity, because human ingenuity always finds a way around them. However, the implicit assumption that such a happy situation can be projected indefinitely into the future should not be accepted uncritically. No evidence is capable of finally adjudicating the dispute between Prometheans and their opponents, short of global shortages and ecological collapse someday vindicating the idea that there are indeed global limits or boundaries. Prometheans adduce evidence from the past, concerning for example, trends that show resources are becoming less scarce with time (because their prices are falling), and that global indicators of well-being have been moving in positive directions. Their opponents can argue that even if trends currently look fine, eventually global limits will be hit, or the catastrophic consequences of boundary transgression will become apparent. The two discourses offer contending interpretations of the world and can be linked to different scientific paradigms. Limits discourses utilize

[13] Tim Jackson, *Prosperity Without Growth: Economics for a Finite Planet* (Earthscan 2009).

[14] Will Steffen *et al*, 'Planetary Boundaries: Guiding Human Development on a Changing Planet' *Science*, 347/6223 (2015): 736.

[15] Kate Raworth, *Doughnut Economics: Seven Ways to Think Like a 21st Century Economist* (Random House 2017).

population biology and ecology, planetary boundaries were formulated drawing on earth systems science, while Promethean discourse utilizes micro-economics. The economic connection provides the key mechanism for Prometheans: if resources become scarce, their price will rise, providing incentives to develop substitutes.

Promethean discourse is an extension of the exuberance of industrialism. The difference is that while industrialism took economic growth for granted as the highest good, Prometheans must articulate a defence of perpetual economic growth in light of the limits critique. In addition, the collective management of resources can be accommodated within industrialism, less easily in Promethean discourse, which is completely wedded to the market in a way industrialism is not.

Promethean discourse has been especially influential in the US presidencies of Ronald Reagan and George W Bush, and has a robust permanent presence in the US Senate. The leading Promethean publicist in the George W Bush era was Bjørn Lomborg, who had ties to the government of Denmark rather than the United States, though Republican congressional candidates were pointed in Lomborg's direction in the 2004 US election campaign.[16]

When it comes to international environmental affairs, the opposition of both the Reagan and GW Bush presidencies to coordinated global environmental protection (with the important exception of the 1987 Montreal Protocol) can be attributed to their domination by Promethean and industrialist discourse. So long as Promethean discourse has a hold on the Senate, the United States cannot ratify any global environmental treaty, which means that other forms of international agreement must be sought—helping to explain, for example, why the 2015 Paris Agreement contains no legally binding emissions reductions (though it does bind conduct). US disregard for the global environment peaked under President Donald Trump, who in 2017 announced that the United States would withdraw from the Paris Agreement.

It is tempting to see the Trump administration's assault on the environment (both domestically and internationally) as an extreme manifestation of Promethean discourse, but that would miss its key aspect. For Trump's core supporters and right-wing conservatives in the United States in general, hostility to environmentalism is a necessary affirmation of identity. Economics has nothing much to do with it; instead, what Kahan calls 'cultural cognition' is central.[17] This explains the enthusiasm for coal—long after it has become uneconomic compared to renewable energy. In Australia, extreme right-wing politicians organized in the Monash Forum propose government intervention and finance to build new coal-fired power stations and open new coal mines—because the market has determined that coal has no future. This kind of identity politics confirms the importance of discourses, because identity is a product of discourse—in this case, right-wing extremist discourse.

[16] Bjørn Lomborg, *The Skeptical Environmentalist: Measuring the Real State of the World* (CUP 2001).

[17] Dan Kahan, Hank Jenkins-Smith, and Donald Braman, 'Cultural Cognition of Scientific Consensus' *Journal of Risk Research*, 14/2 (2011): 147.

Promethean discourse has also received a twist from those who recognize the reality of challenges such as climate change—but believe technology offers solutions. This includes Lomborg himself, who argued that cost-benefit analysis shows the best response to climate change is geoengineering (through marine cloud whitening and the injection of sulphate aerosols into the atmosphere).[18] Promethean environmentalism is advanced by the Breakthrough Institute, for whom the appropriate response to the environmental crisis is the benign assertion of human control over the Earth system.[19]

B. Problem-Solving Discourses

The three discourses of environmental problem-solving are democratic pragmatism, economic rationalism, and administrative rationalism. All developed initially in the context of a liberal democratic state and capitalist economy. Thus, all three require modification in translation to the international level, because each assumes a state capable of organizing and implementing problem-solving activity in its territory. Of the three, administrative rationalism is particularly problematic in the absence of a sovereign state to organize the apex of any hierarchy of administrative authority. Hierarchical international organizations with some capacity to exercise binding authority are also in short supply. There is no World Environment Organization (WEO) analogous to the World Trade Organization (WTO), though it has its advocates.[20] Organizations such as the United Nations Environment Program have little implementation capacity of the sort that administrative rationalism requires. Transnational networks composed of administrators from different jurisdictions may exist, but they operate as networks, not as administrative hierarchies. Scientific assessments such as those of the Intergovernmental Panel on Climate Change rely on the mobilization of expertise, but there is no tight connection of expertise to any administrative hierarchy. Rationalistic policy analysis techniques such as cost-benefit analysis can be applied at the planetary scale, as the work of Lomborg and his associates shows, but any conclusions yielded by these techniques would enter a political process—not simply be adopted by the apex of an administrative hierarchy.

Democratic pragmatism fares somewhat better. Dealing in interactive problem-solving, it can more easily escape its origins in the liberal democratic state. Even in their domestic affairs, such states increasingly yield to networked problem-solving that involves interactions among government officials, interest organizations, corporations, labour unions, and political activists.[21] The term 'governance' is often used to describe

[18] Bjørn Lomborg, *Smart Solutions to Climate Change: Comparing Costs and Benefits* (CUP 2010).

[19] Breakthrough Institute, *An Ecomodernist Manifesto* (2015).

[20] Frank Biermann, 'The Case for a World Environment Organization' *Environment: Science and Policy for Sustainable Development*, 42/9 (2010): 22.

[21] R A W Rhodes, *Understanding Governance: Policy Networks, Governance, Reflexivity, and Accountability* (Open University Press 1997).

such activity. Given that 'governance without government' is a staple of international politics,[22] interactive democratic pragmatism is potentially at home here too. For example, transnational forest product certification is carried out by a network of stakeholders supporting the Forest Stewardship Council—engaged in a worldwide struggle against more Promethean approaches to forest resources.[23] Braithwaite and Drahos show how activists and non-governmental organizations (NGOs), along with government officials, can create a global web of business regulation—including environmental regulation.[24] The consultative dialogues leading up to the adoption of the 2015 SDGs are also consistent with a discourse of democratic pragmatism.

Economic rationalism can be defined in terms of its commitment to the deployment of market mechanisms to achieve public ends. Market-type instruments (tradeable permits to pollute or extract resources, green taxes, and so on) were endorsed in passing in the Brundtland Report. The stress on markets is consistent with the neoliberal discourse that dominates international economic affairs. The 1987 Montreal Protocol provides for limited international trade in quotas for chlorofluorocarbon emissions. Marketization is increasingly prominent in the global governance of climate change, beginning with the elaborate processes for emissions trading set up under the 1997 Kyoto Protocol.[25] Emissions trading and offset schemes are not necessarily by any formal governmental authority, as various networked and cooperative arrangements come into play, involving corporations and NGOs as well as governmental actors. Carbon traders are set up to make money from these sorts of schemes. There are some national and subnational carbon dioxide emissions trading schemes. Many countries (beginning with the four Nordic countries and the Netherlands) have adopted carbon taxes to reduce carbon dioxide emissions. Tradeable quotas can also be applied to natural resources such as fish.

However, there are limits to the degree to which economic rationalist instruments can be deployed in the absence of central government enforcement. This limit can be highlighted in the context of Anderson and Leal's suggestion that 'Whales can also be "branded" by genetic prints and tracked by satellite' in order to create secure property rights in an international market for whales.[26] Conservationists could buy whales to save them, whalers could buy whales to kill them, and the market would determine the optimal balance. The problem is that no international authority stands ready to enforce the property rights in question; certainly, the International Whaling Commission is not up to the task.

[22] James Rosenau and Ernst-Otto Czempiel (eds), *Governance Without Government: Order and Change in World Politics* (CUP 1992).

[23] Sandra Moog, André Spicer, and Steffen Böhm, 'The Politics of Multi-Stakeholder Initiatives: The Crisis of the Forest Stewardship Council' *Journal of Business Ethics*, 128/3 (2015): 469.

[24] John Braithwaite and Peter Drahos, *Global Business Regulation* (CUP 2000) 256–296.

[25] Peter Newell and Matthew Paterson, *Climate Capitalism: Global Warming and the Transformation of the Global Economy* (CUP 2010).

[26] Terry Anderson and Donald Leal, *Free Market Environmentalism* (Westview Press for the Pacific Research Institute for Public Policy 1991) 34.

In short: discourses of environmental problem-solving that have dominated environmental problem-solving within liberal democratic states over the past five decades have now made their way into international environmental affairs and multilateral environmental agreements. Let me now turn to the discourse that has in many ways defined international environmental affairs since the mid-1980s.

C. Sustainability

Sustainable development's discursive domination of the global environmental stage was confirmed in 1987 by Brundtland, and has persisted since then. The precise meaning of sustainable development remains a matter of some contention. Brundtland herself famously characterized the matter: 'Humanity has the ability to make development sustainable—to ensure that it meets the needs of the present without compromising the ability of future generations to meet their own needs.'[27] Subsequently, definitions have proliferated and been contested. But in many ways, that proliferation and contestation constitute the whole point: sustainable development is a discourse, not a concept, still less a scientific concept.[28] For the World Business Council on Sustainable Development, 'development' is closely linked to economic growth. Environmentalists might try to build a respect for intrinsic values in nature into the 'sustainable' aspect of the discourse, respect that is conspicuously missing in Brundtland. Developing country advocates would stress the need for global redistribution and highlight the needs of the poor.

Contestation over what sustainable development means is central to the discourse of sustainability, but the discourse has boundaries. A rejection of the four other discourses defines these. The older discourse of limits and survival is rejected because, while global ecological limits can still lurk in the background, they are treated as capable of being dealt with.[29] Green radicalism is rejected because no wholesale change in the basic structure of the international political economy is deemed necessary. Market liberalism and Promethean discourses are rejected because markets alone are thought incapable of achieving sustainability; instead, conscious, coordinated, collective action is required. More positively, sustainable development assumes that environmental conservation and economic growth can be mutually reinforcing rather than conflicting values.

The 1992 UN Conference on Environment and Development in Rio confirmed that sustainable development was now a discourse for North and South, rich and poor. In 2002, the World Summit on Sustainable Development (WSSD) in Johannesburg witnessed significant repositioning within the discourse. Rich states that once promoted environmental values now stressed development through economic globalization, and so bent sustainable development in the direction of industrialism. Third World

[27] WCED, *Our Common Future* (n 4) 8.

[28] See Chapter 17, 'Sustainable Development', in this volume.

[29] Oluf Langhelle, 'Why Ecological Modernization and Sustainable Development Should Not be Conflated' *Journal of Environmental Policy and Planning*, 2/4 (2000): 303.

governmental delegations showed new appreciation of their own environmental problems, rather than dismissing conservation as a luxury.[30] Corporations established a major role for business in producing solutions, very different from business's older image as a generator of environmental problems. Hundreds of business partnerships with NGOs and government were created at the Summit. On a sceptical view, this was 'the privatization of sustainable development',[31] transforming the discourse into commercial projects.[32] The 2012 UN Conference on Sustainable Development mainly confirmed these developments, producing little shift in the terms of the discourse. The World Business Council on Sustainable Development was dismayed by the lack of progress, its president declaring that it was now time for business to take the lead.[33]

New life was breathed into the discourse in the SDGs, adopted by the UN in 2015. The idea that the poverty-alleviation agenda of the Millennium Development Goals (MDGs) should be joined to sustainability concerns was the outcome of a successful political move initiated by Colombia at the 2012 Rio+20 Conference. The goals themselves defy easy summary; the extensive list of seventeen goals and 169 associated targets reflect a wide range of concerns and a wide range of options for what sustainable development might mean in national and local practice. One striking development is that, unlike the MDGs, they apply to all countries of the world, not just developing ones, thus confirming the global reach of the discourse. However, these goals put ecological concerns on par with economic and social goals—instead of treating a healthy Earth system as a prerequisite for achieving social and economic goals. They fail to say anything about addressing risks to the Earth system.[34]

Sustainable development pervades the discourse of international institutions, though its impact on multilateral environmental agreements remains patchy. The European Union (EU) has inserted sustainable development into its constituent treaties, and at most global summits shows far greater enthusiasm for sustainability than does the United States. The United States is unique in the degree to which sustainable development does not pervade environmental discourse, mainly because its environmental policy debates are stuck in a standoff between supporters and opponents of the regulatory systems established in the 1970s.[35] Some slight movement could be discerned with the Obama administration's interagency Partnership for Sustainable Communities

[30] Paul Wapner, 'World Summit on Sustainable Development: Toward a Post-Jo'burg Environmentalism' *Global Environmental Politics*, 3/1 (2003): 4–6.

[31] Ina von Frantzius, 'World Summit on Sustainable Development Johannesburg 2002: A Critical Assessment of the Outcomes' *Environmental Politics*, 13/2 (2004): 469.

[32] Wapner, 'World Summit' (n 30) 4.

[33] Jo Confino, 'Rio+20: WBCSD president says the future of the planet rests on business' *The Guardian* (22 June 2012) <https://www.theguardian.com/sustainable-business/rio-20-business-sustainable-development> accessed 14 October 2019.

[34] John Dryzek and Jonathan Pickering, *The Politics of the Anthropocene* (OUP 2019) 99.

[35] Gary Bryner, 'The United States: Sorry—Not Our Problem' in William Lafferty and James Meadowcroft (eds), *Implementing Sustainable Development: Strategies and Initiatives from High Consumption Societies* (OUP 2000) 277.

established in 2009, but perhaps more revealing is the delayed reaction of the Republican National Committee to Agenda 21 coming out of the 1992 Rio Conference: it took the Committee twenty years to notice Agenda 21's existence, and then to pass a motion in 2012 denouncing it as involving 'a socialist/communist redistribution of wealth' and 'extreme environmentalism'.[36]

If we were to look for sustainable development as an accomplished fact, where would we find it? The answer is undoubtedly: nowhere. Cross-national quantitative comparisons of environmental performance such as the Environmental Performance Index compiled by the Yale Center for Environmental Law and Policy and the Center for International Earth Science Information Network for the World Economic Forum show the top rankings dominated by wealthy West European countries.[37] These countries have outsourced much of their production and so embedded stress on ecosystems—and the Earth system as a whole—caused by their over-consumption to other parts of the world. Sustainable development cannot be conceptualized as a path taken by wealthy countries that others could follow, but rather should be thought of as a discourse that requires rethinking the development process.

D. Green Radicalism

Green radicalism can be defined in terms of its presumption that the liberal capitalist political economy cannot be sustained, and that intersecting concerns relating to social and environmental justice, conservation, and congenial human existence require fundamental structural transformation. The discourse is home to a wide variety of philosophical viewpoints, repertoires, and political movements. As befits a radical discourse, its origins lie in oppositional movements confronting governments, corporations, and other centres of power. However, there are times when aspects of green radicalism have been influential on these power centres, or have constituted countervailing power.

In common with many other social movement discourses, some of the impact of green radicalism is found in cultural change—in lifestyles and consumer behaviour. Wapner suggests that when it comes to international environmental affairs, 'NGO cultural politics may be more politically significant than NGO policy efforts'[38] (though, of course, not all NGO activities are radical). While cultural change might seem remote from law and institutions, it can also be thought of as an alternative to the more conventional political and legal route. One way of inducing behavioural change is through

[36] Republican National Committee, 'Resolution Exposing United Nations Agenda 21' (approved 13 January 2012) <https://www.defendruralamerica.com/files/20120113RNC_A21.pdf> accessed 14 October 2019.

[37] Yale Center for Environmental Law & Policy and Center for International Earth Science Information Network, *2018 Environmental Performance Index*, Policymakers' Summary.

[38] Paul Wapner, 'Horizontal Politics: Transnational Environmental Activism and Global Cultural Change' *Global Environmental Politics*, 2/2 (2002): 37, 51.

law, another is through culture. People can choose to recycle, conserve energy, install solar panels, boycott forest products from old-growth logging, and so on without laws requiring them to do so.

Green radical discourse has sometimes succeeded in provoking international institutions to the point where it at least merits a response, for example as one of the discourses present in the anti-corporate globalization movement. Initially derided as incoherent and contradictory, this movement at least forced global institutions such as the International Monetary Fund (IMF), World Bank, and WTO to take seriously some concerns they would have preferred to ignore.[39]

Green radicalism has influenced on environmental law at the national level.[40] In New Zealand, the Whanganui River and Mount Taranaki now have the status of legal subjects, as does the Ganges in India. Ecuador has embodied the rights of nature in its constitution, as Pachamama, or Mother Earth. In both New Zealand and Ecuador, Indigenous peoples have pushed these developments. International law has yet to catch up.

For the most part, green radical discourse is practised and cultivated in an oppositional public sphere.[41] Radical transnational movements include the Pesticides Action Network, La Via Campesina, and Climate Justice Now! The radical green public sphere is often highly visible at gatherings such as the Conference of the Parties of the UNFCCC, holding parallel forums (such as the Klimaforum in 2009 at Copenhagen). In 2010 the government of Bolivia hosted the World People's Summit on Climate Change and Mother Earth Rights. The World Social Forum is a radical gathering, meeting most years, that features environmental as well as social concerns.

The green public sphere is home to all kinds of creative and varied thinking, but only very occasionally is its influence felt in the dominant institutions of national and international society. Sometimes that influence affects the terms of discourse, as in the anti-corporate globalization case; or in establishing 'environmental justice' and 'climate justice' as principles that must be addressed, in international affairs no less than elsewhere. Sometimes influence comes with the threat of political instability that can accompany the discourse. At the national level, it was such a threat that led to the pioneering burst of environmental law and policy in the United States around 1970. President Nixon was keen to draw the nascent environmental movement away from the radicalism of the counterculture into the political mainstream—and succeeded brilliantly.[42] The results included laws such as the National Environmental Policy Act and institutions such as the federal Environmental Protection Agency.

[39] Joseph Stiglitz, *Globalization and its Discontents* (Norton 2002) 20.

[40] See Chapter 14, 'Earth Jurisprudence', in this volume.

[41] Douglas Torgerson, *The Promise of Green Politics: Environmentalism and the Public Sphere* (Duke University Press 1999).

[42] John Dryzek *et al*, *Green States and Social Movements: Environmentalism in the United States, United Kingdom, Germany, and Norway* (OUP 2003) 59.

V. THE RELATIVE IMPORTANCE OF DISCOURSES

International environmental affairs are, then, home to a constellation of discourses. How important are discourses in conditioning outcomes compared to other influences? This question can be hard to answer when discourses are entwined with these other influences. For example, the dominant discourse in the international political economy is neoliberalism. States generally abide by its prescriptions of free trade and capital mobility because they fear punishment by disinvestment and capital flight if they are (say) over-zealous in environmental regulation of business. However, in large measure, the punishment occurs because investors perceive such states as inhospitable. Moreover, investors perceive this because they, too, are under the sway of the discourse of market liberalism. So is the ultimate influence here rooted in the material facts of international markets, or the facts of discourse? The answer is 'both'. Discourses can provide the 'software' that makes international regimes work, while more formal organizations and rules provide the 'hardware'.

How then are we to demonstrate the importance of discourse? One way is to examine history and look for discourse shifts that are followed by changed outcomes. Litfin's study of 'ozone discourses' is exemplary.[43] Litfin argues that the 1987 Montreal Protocol was made possible by a widely-accepted shift to a 'discourse of precautionary action' that interpreted existing and still inconclusive scientific evidence in a new way. The idea of an 'ozone hole' as a piece of rhetoric that dramatized changed seasonal variations in ozone levels in Antarctic regions was crucial. The fact that discourse shift was followed by policy shift does not of itself prove that the discourse shift was crucial, and so Litfin has to disprove alternative explanations (eg one stressing the role of an epistemic community).

The ozone case reveals the conversion of important actors from one discourse to another in a short space of time. However, discourses can also undergo a slow shift in their content, whose consequences should be traceable. Consider, in this light, sustainable development. The discourse has its roots in the 1970s in challenges to conventional development models, pushed mainly by advocates for the poor and marginalized in the Third World, in opposition to transnational capitalism.[44] Brundtland in 1987 deradicalized the discourse somewhat by accepting the desirability of substantial global economic growth—while retaining concern for global redistribution. With time the discourse became still more business-friendly, furthered by the dominant role played by business at the 2002 WSSD. The idea of 'green growth' is advanced in the business-friendly side

[43] Karen Litfin, *Ozone Discourses: Science and Politics in Global Environmental Cooperation* (Columbia University Press 1994).

[44] David Carruthers, 'From Opposition to Orthodoxy: The Remaking of Sustainable Development' *Journal of Third World Studies*, 18 (2001): 93.

events at the annual Conference of the Parties of the UNFCCC, stressing the business opportunities linked to low-emission technologies.

Gradual change can also be played out in contests between discourses. Consider commercial whaling. The International Whaling Commission agreed upon a moratorium on commercial whaling starting in 1986—long after whaling ceased to make economic sense, and after evidence of severe depletion of whale stocks had accumulated for several decades. 1986 was a tipping point in the contest between an older industrialist discourse that saw whales as a natural resource, and an anti-whaling discourse with roots in green radicalism that had slowly emerged and come to dominate the global politics of whaling.[45] The moratorium was not the result of any material factors but rather of a discourse shift that involved the reconceptualization of whales as beautiful sentient creatures with intrinsic value. Discursive resistance can be found. Iceland, Norway, and Japan remained committed to an older industrialist treatment of whales as a source of useful products for human consumption (though they also had to add a 'culturalist' overlay to this commitment to make it more palatable internationally). In the whaling case, unlike sustainable development and market liberalism, there has been no rapprochement across competing discourses.

VI. CONCLUSION

Discourses pervade international environmental affairs no less than other social and political life realms. How important are they compared to other influences on collective outcomes? It is hard to generalize because discourses are bound up with regimes, other institutions, material forces, and non-linguistic practices. Indeed, such practices help constitute discourses, which are not just a matter of words. Often their influence is constitutive rather than causal: discourses constitute the subjective dispositions and capacities of actors. To the degree a discourse is pervasive in this constitutive sense, it may even go unnoticed as a set of background assumptions shared by all or most actors. The influence of discourses can be discerned only by writing histories of particular cases. However, in the end, there is one reason to expect discourses to be more consequential in the international system than in the internal affairs of states. Formal institutions are relatively weak in the international system, meaning coordination (and disruption) across actors has to be supplied by informal mechanisms such as discourses.

BIBLIOGRAPHY

John Dryzek, *The Politics of the Earth: Environmental Discourses* (3rd edn, OUP 2013)

[45] Charlotte Epstein, *The Power of Words in International Relations: Birth of an Anti-Whaling Discourse* (MIT Press 2008).

Charlotte Epstein, *The Power of Words in International Relations: Birth of an Anti-Whaling Discourse* (MIT Press 2008)

Maarten Hajer and Wytske Versteeg, 'Voices of Vulnerability: The Reconfiguration of Policy Discourses' in John Dryzek, Richard Norgaard, and David Schlosberg (eds), *The Oxford Handbook of Climate Change and Society* (OUP 2011) 82

Karen Litfin, *Ozone Discourses: Science and Politics in Global Environmental Cooperation* (Columbia University Press 1994)

CHAPTER 3

ORIGIN AND HISTORY

PETER H SAND

I. INTRODUCTION

'Environmental law has no history'—or so it would seem if the provocative opening statement of David Schorr's historiographic account[1] were to be taken at face value. It is, of course, true that the very term 'environmental law' etymologically did not come into use, in any language, until the mid-twentieth century. Yet it is equally true that specific components of the Earth's natural environment—land, freshwaters, oceans, biological and abiotic resources—have been a subject of human exploitation and attempts at societal management (including law) for ages, as documented in the burgeoning literature on 'environmental history', 'green imperialism', and the history of 'ecological economics'.

By the same token, the dearth of writings on the environmental dimension in histories of international law, in turn, may be more apparent than real. The focus of historical research on the emergence of environment-related legal concepts, principles, and institutions has primarily been on the study and comparison of developments at the level of national law. Even so, the interface with international law is easily documented—as in the preambles of many twentieth-century environmental treaties, which can be traced back to their domestic origins in nineteenth-century cultural romanticism. Simultaneously, in parallel and in close analogy to the development of concepts of 'vicinage' (*droit de voisinage*) in domestic real property law, the emergence of a body of rules of environmental 'neighbourliness' has long been observed in transfrontier relations between states.

It is important to keep in mind that the field is not confined to public international law but that it also encompasses 'transnational' administrative law and private international

[1] David Schorr, 'Historical Analysis in Environmental Law' in Markus Dubber and Christopher Tomlins (eds), *Oxford Handbook of Legal History* (OUP 2018) 1001. Along the same lines, see Éric Naim-Gesbert, 'Voir les choses à leur vrai début: de l'histoire en droit de l'environnement' *Revue Juridique de l'Environnement*, 44 (2019): 5, 7: 'Le droit de l'environnement a un passé sans histoire'.

law (conflict of laws); that is, the entire *corpus* of international law, public and private, relevant to environmental problems. Moreover, the continuous impact of domestic environmental law, public and private, on international law-making in this field as well as the related 'problem of scale'[2]—that is, the transferability of empirical generalizations and theoretical models from one level to another—makes comparative information and analysis indispensable.

Most narratives of the historical evolution of international environmental law distinguish three major 'periods', 'epochs' or 'phases':[3]

- the 'traditional era' until about 1970 (that is, preceding the 1972 United Nations Conference on the Human Environment in Stockholm);
- the 'modern era' from Stockholm to the 1992 UN Conference on Environment and Development in Rio de Janeiro (UNCED); and
- the 'post-modern era' from Rio onwards.

Any such periodization is, however, bound to remain approximate and potentially problematic. As pointed out by Martti Koskenniemi, the reality of international law is 'historically and synchronically discontinuous';[4] hence, contemporary law typically reflects traditional, modern, and post-modern elements alike.

II. THE TRADITIONAL ERA

The shared human use—and misuse—of the Earth's natural resources has been a subject of international law-making for centuries, both in a transboundary context across territorial jurisdictions and in the context of competing claims to resources in the global commons outside national jurisdiction.

A. Shared Transboundary Resources

The Musée du Louvre in Paris and the British Museum in London hold tangible evidence of the world's first known legal agreement on boundary water resources: viz, the Mesilim Treaty, concluded in the twenty-fifth century BC between the two Mesopotamian states of Lagash and Umma. The terms of the treaty have been preserved as cuneiform

[2] Oran Young, *The Institutional Dimensions of Environmental Change: Fit, Interplay, and Scale* (MIT Press 2002) 139.

[3] See eg Edith Brown Weiss, 'The Evolution of International Environmental Law' *Japanese Yearbook of International Law*, 54 (2011): 1.

[4] Martti Koskenniemi, 'Letter to the Editors of the Symposium on Methods in International Law' *American Journal of International Law*, 93/2 (1999): 351, 359.

inscriptions on limestone cones and the 'stele of the vultures' commemorating Lagash's victorious battle enforcing the treaty.

Mesilim (or *Mesalim*, born ca. 2600 BC) was the ruler of Kish, a kingdom further to the north of Lagash and Umma, which held a traditional 'hegemonic' position in the loose alliance of small adjoining Sumerian city-states in the region between the Tigris and Euphrates rivers, south of what was to become Babylon.[5] Because of the prevailing precarious rainfall conditions, the agricultural economy of the entire delta area has always been crucially dependent on irrigation, mainly from the 'great Tigris', through an elaborate system of canals and levees which inevitably require close inter-community cooperation. The geographic focus of the Lagash-Umma agreement, concluded under Mesilim's authority as external arbiter, was the fertile Gu-edena valley, irrigated by Tigris waters from a canal on the border between Umma and Lagash, with boundaries marked by stone steles.

Part of the treaty was a crop-sharing arrangement for a portion of boundary land downstream on Lagash territory that Umma cultivated under lease against payment of an annual rental fee. When Umma repeatedly refused to honour its accumulated tenancy debts, hostilities broke out, resulting in the partial destruction of the canal and in unilateral diversions of water upstream. In several successive military confrontations over the next forty years (the first known war in history that was, in essence, fought about water), Umma was ultimately defeated by Lagash and was forced to accept the reconstruction (and extension) of the canal and the reinstatement of the boundaries as originally drawn up by Mesilim.

Alas, the treaty so renewed and 'writ in stone', and the peace so re-established, does not seem to have survived for long and was eventually overtaken and mooted by external political events (the Akkadian-Sargonic invasions) in subsequent generations. Even so, the agreement remains a unique early attempt at resolving a dispute over boundary waters by formal reference to a superior spiritual order (in this case, the deities of both parties, repeatedly 'sworn to' in the text), and hence may indeed qualify as a precursor of international law in this field—a Sumerian version of *pacta sunt servanda* (agreements must be kept).

As early as 1430, the judicial resolution of intergovernmental disputes over shared water resources in Europe can be shown to have drawn on common Roman law sources going back to the sixth century AD. In fact, the circumstances of the Mesopotamian Lagash-Umma dispute were not fundamentally different from those of the *Lake Lanoux* controversy over a European boundary river some 4,000 years later: there, the waters from a lake high up in the French sector of the Eastern Pyrenees had long ensured the irrigation of farm areas on both sides of the Carol river along the Spanish border, on the basis of bilateral agreements dating back to the nineteenth century. When the French government announced plans for a new 'grand canal' to divert the Carol waters

[5] See Amnon Altman, 'Tracing the Earliest Recorded Concepts of International Law: The Early Dynastic Period in Southern Mesopotamia' *Journal of the History of International Law*, 6/2 (2004): 152, 157.

upstream, for agricultural and power production uses on its territory, a major dispute erupted which, after forty years of negotiations, was finally resolved by a historic arbitration in 1957.[6]

With regard to environmental quality, the 1909 Boundary Waters Treaty between Canada and the United States succeeded in prohibiting water pollution 'to the injury of health or property on the other side of the border',[7] an approach later extended to transboundary air pollution by the 1939–41 *Trail Smelter* arbitration.[8] Hunting and fishing in frontier sectors had already been addressed in bilateral agreements in continental Europe from the fourteenth century. The Convention concluded in 1781 between the King of France and the Prince-Bishop of Basel thus provided for the punishment of forest, hunting, and fishing delicts in the French-Swiss border area. In North America, the 1790 Treaty between the United States and the Creek Indian Nation prohibited unauthorized attempts by US citizens or inhabitants 'to hunt or destroy the game on the Creek lands'.[9] The 1856 Bayonne Boundary Treaty between France and Spain, which preceded the Lake Lanoux arbitration, had also aimed at 'preventing destruction of the fishery' (*prévenir la destruction du poisson*) in the Bidassoa River.[10] And although initial multilateral agreements regarding the Rhine and the Danube were mainly concerned with navigation uses, they were followed by several inland fishery conventions for the Rhine basin since 1869 and for the Danube basin since 1901.[11]

By contrast, early endeavours to secure binding multilateral agreements on terrestrial wildlife and wilderness resources ended in failure or near-failure: The first Convention on Wildlife Conservation in Africa, signed by several colonial powers in London on 19 May 1900, never entered into force for lack of ratifications; and its successor, the 1933 London Convention Relative to the Preservation of Fauna and Flora in their Natural State (also primarily covering colonial territories in Africa and Asia), lacked permanent institutional arrangements, and after unsuccessful attempts at the revision of the treaty in 1938 and 1953 eventually lapsed in the wake of decolonization. The Convention for the Protection of Birds Useful to Agriculture, signed in Paris on 19 March 1902, was ratified by a few European countries only and turned out to be ineffective in practice. The pioneering initiative by US President Theodore Roosevelt in January 1909 to convene a World Conservation Conference at The Hague, to be modelled after the Hague Peace Conferences, was abandoned in the face of domestic political opposition at the time.[12] While bilateral treaties for the protection of migratory birds and game mammals were subsequently concluded by the United States with Canada and Mexico, it took until 1940 for a multilateral conservation agreement to be reached in this field: the Convention

[6] *Lake Lanoux Arbitration (Spain/France)* (1957) 12 RIAA 281.

[7] art IV.

[8] *Trail Smelter Arbitration (United States/Canada)* (1938 and 1941) 3 RIAA 1905.

[9] art VII.

[10] art XXII.

[11] See Chapter 30, 'Freshwater Resources', in this volume.

[12] See Siegfried von Ciriacy-Wantrup, *Resource Conservation: Economics and Policies* (3rd edn, University of California Department of Agriculture 1968) 315.

on Nature Protection and Wildlife Preservation in the Western Hemisphere, under the auspices of the Organization of American States.

B. Resource-Sharing in Areas Beyond National Jurisdiction

Intergovernmental accords for the sharing of marine living resources date back at least as far as the British-Portuguese Treaty of 20 October 1353 on fishing rights in the North Atlantic;[13] and the history of bilateral and regional ocean fisheries agreements is well documented from the eighteenth century onwards. Other living resources outside national jurisdiction first became the subject of international litigation in the 1893 *Bering Sea Fur Seals* arbitration.[14] The dispute arose over the pelagic hunting of seals in the North Pacific by British-flag vessels beyond the territorial waters of the Pribilof Islands west of Alaska. Invoking the threat of extinction of the Pribilof population of fur seals, the US government justified its extraterritorial seizure of the foreign vessels concerned by claiming to have acted as 'trustee for the benefit of mankind'. Even though the arbitral tribunal rejected that claim, successive regional conventions for fur seal conservation eventually banned most pelagic sealing in the North Pacific.[15]

The first global whaling conventions and protocols concluded in 1931 and 1937/38 were essentially resource-sharing agreements for 'rational' economic exploitation. While their post-war successor, the 1946 International Convention for the Regulation of Whaling, echoed those concerns, its preamble recognized the growing threat of overfishing and 'the interest of the nations of the world in safeguarding for future generations' the remaining whale stocks. The next major step in international law-making for the global commons, the 1959 Antarctic Treaty, explicitly envisaged cooperative measures regarding 'preservation and conservation of living resources in Antarctica', followed—in the 'modern era' of international environmental law—by the 1972 Convention for the Conservation of Antarctic Seals, the 1980 Antarctic Marine Living Resources Convention, and the 1991 Madrid Protocol on Environmental Protection to the Antarctic Treaty. Efforts at extending this approach to other global *res communes* (under the label of 'common heritage of mankind') were only partly successful. The Antarctic experience did, however, serve as a precedent for the evolution of the international regime of natural resources in extraterrestrial space, under Article

[13] Latin text in Thomas Rymer (ed), *Foedera, conventiones, literae et cuiuscumque generis acta publica*, vol 5 (Néaulme 1704) 763.

[14] *Bering Sea Fur Seals Arbitration (United States/United Kingdom)* (1893) 28 RIAA 263; see John Moore (ed), *History and Digest of the International Arbitrations to which the United States has been a Party*, vol 1 (G.P.O. 1898) 755.

[15] 1911 Convention between the United States and Other Powers Providing for the Preservation and Protection of Fur Seals; 1942 Provisional Fur Seal Agreement between the US and Canada; 1957 Interim Convention between the US, Canada, Japan, and the USSR on Conservation of North Pacific Fur Seals, expired in 1984.

II of the 1967 Outer Space Treaty, and Article 11 of the 1979 Moon Agreement, and in the high seas area under Article 136 of the 1982 UN Convention on the Law of the Sea (UNCLOS).

C. Intergenerational Resource-Sharing?

To be sure, intergenerational responsibility for the conservation of natural resources has been acknowledged by lawyers since the seventeenth century: With regard to forest resources, John Evelyn pleaded in 1664 that 'man should perpetually be planting, so posterity might have trees fit for their service';[16] and in 1713, Hans Carl von Carlowitz advocated the sustainable use (*nachhaltende Nutzung*) of forests for the benefit of future generations (*denen Nachkommen zum Besten*).[17] It must be kept in mind, though, that their concern for forest conservation had very precise economic and strategic motivations: in the case of Carlowitz (manager of the Duke of Saxony's silver mines), the future supply of timber for mine construction and maintenance; and in Evelyn's book (commissioned by the British Royal Navy), long-term timber supplies for shipbuilding—paralleled in 1669 by Jean-Baptiste Colbert's re-organization of French forestry governance through his pioneering '*Ordonnance des eaux et forêts*'. There had indeed been ominous historical warning signals before: In particular, the decline of Venetian maritime dominance in the Mediterranean during the sixteenth and early seventeenth centuries was widely attributed to timber shortages in naval construction, caused by perpetual deforestation. In retrospect, therefore, the concept of long-term sustainability of resource use, now a mantra of modern international environmental law, may well be said to have its roots in mercantile economics and national geo-politics as early as four centuries ago. Its rationale at the time, however, was unabashedly utilitarian and anthropocentric, and quite unrelated to questions of 'eco-centric' environmental ethics.

That being said, there remains inter-temporal fiduciary accountability of each human generation for any depletion or deterioration of the Earth's common natural heritage to the detriment of future generations; viz, intergenerational equity. In present-day international environmental law doctrine, the issue is variously framed in terms of international 'public trusteeship', 'guardianship', 'custodianship', or 'stewardship'. However, its original formulation goes back to Karl Marx in 1865: 'Even society as a whole, a nation, or all contemporary societies taken together, are not owners of the Earth. They are merely its occupants, its users; and as diligent guardians (*boni patres familias*) must hand it down improved to subsequent generations.'[18]

[16] John Evelyn, *Sylva, or a Discourse of Forest-Trees, and the Propagation of Timber in His Majesty's Dominions* (Martyn & Allestry 1664).

[17] Hans Carl von Carlowitz, *Sylvicultura Oeconomica oder Hausswirtliche Nachricht und Naturmaessige Anweisung zur Wilden Baum-Zucht* (Braun 1713).

[18] Karl Marx, *Das Kapital*, in Friedrich Engels (ed), *Oekonomische Manuskripte 1863-1867*, reprinted in *Marx-Engels-Gesamtausgabe* vol II/4 (Dietz 1992) 718.

III. THE MODERN ERA

The beginning of 'modern' international environmental law is usually dated to 5 June 1972, the opening day of the first UN Conference on the Human Environment in Stockholm. Although the Stockholm Conference did not adopt any binding legal instrument of its own, the momentous preparatory process triggered four new global treaties: the 1972 World Heritage Convention (WHC), the 1972 London Dumping Convention, the 1973 Endangered Species Convention (CITES), and the 1979 Migratory Species Convention (CMS). It also led to the establishment of the United Nations Environment Programme (UNEP), as the first global intergovernmental institution in this field, which in turn then produced more than thirty multilateral (global and regional) legal agreements over the next two decades; and it generated one of the most influential and enduring international 'soft law' instruments, the 1972 Stockholm Declaration on the Human Environment.

A. The Challenge of Pluralism

One paradigmatic change initiated by the Stockholm Conference was the active participation of Third World countries, most of which had until then remained sceptical about global conservation accords, wary of the imposition of neo-colonial impediments to their legitimate aspirations of economic development.[19] A preparatory report for the conference (outcome of an expert seminar on 'Development and Environment' convened at Founex/Switzerland in June 1971) echoed these concerns, pointing out that environmental problems are caused both by development and by the lack of development; and in a memorable speech to the plenary on 14 June 1972, Indian Prime Minister Indira Gandhi provocatively asked the question: 'Are not poverty and need the greatest polluters?' It is no coincidence, therefore, that of the twenty-six 'principles' formulated in the Stockholm Declaration, no less than eleven emphasize the continuing special needs of the developing countries.

The most frequently-cited section of the Declaration is Principle 21, since incorporated in the preambles of numerous international conventions, and jurisprudentially recognized as 'part of the corpus of international law relating to the environment'.[20] It affirms, on the one hand, the sovereign right of states 'to exploit their own resources pursuant to their own environmental policies', thus restating the axiomatic concept of permanent sovereignty over natural resources proclaimed by the UN General Assembly since 1962. On the other hand, it balances and qualifies the concept by a duty to prevent

[19] See Chapter 11, 'Global South Approaches', in this volume.

[20] *Legality of the Threat or Use of Nuclear Weapons* (Advisory Opinion) [1996] ICJ Rep 226 [29] (Legality of Nuclear Weapons).

transboundary harm 'to the environment of other states or of areas beyond the limits of national jurisdiction', hence expanding the traditional focus of the *Trail Smelter* arbitration and its progeny.

B. Normative Innovation

The post-Stockholm era substantially broadened the international law-making agenda, from the classical risks of resource scarcity and extinction, to the new human-made risks of industrial pollution and resource degradation by hazardous substances or activities. Triggered by a series of eco-disasters (from the 1967 Torrey Canyon oil spill in the North Atlantic and the 1971 Minamata cases in Japan, to the accidents at Seveso in 1976, Bhopal in 1984, and Chernobyl in 1986), there now was a growing public awareness of environmental problems that had once seemed local, yet turned out to be globally shared—highlighted by seminal publications such as Rachel Carson's 1962 *Silent Spring* and the Club of Rome's 1972 *Limits to Growth*, and readily espoused by the civic protest movements of the late 1960s and early 1970s.

The spectrum of international regulation gradually expanded to include topics such as the transnational carriage of dangerous goods, and the production and use of potentially harmful chemicals entering international trade. At the same time, new regulatory and standard-setting functions for environmental matters were conferred on specialized intergovernmental institutions—either existing sectoral UN agencies like the International Atomic Energy Agency, International Maritime Organization (IMO), International Civil Aviation Organization (ICAO), International Labour Organization (ILO), Food and Agriculture Organization (FAO), and World Health Organization (WHO), or emergent autonomous or quasi-autonomous governance bodies (Conferences of the Parties, COPs) newly designated and empowered for the purpose.

The regulatory process so initiated inspired several genuine innovations in multilateral law-making techniques.[21] One of the most influential 'memes' introduced in the design of modern environmental agreements was the 'framework-protocols' construct first used in the 1976 Barcelona Convention for the Protection of the Mediterranean Sea Against Pollution, upon a proposal by Spain in 1974. Instead of the traditional model of a single 'one-off' treaty instrument, it envisaged the combination of a common framework text (basic normative and institutional principles) with an open series of separate specific protocols binding only those states willing and ready to take on further-reaching commitments. This flexible 'differential-speed' technique of treaty-making was subsequently replicated not only in twelve further regional seas conventions and over thirty protocols for marine environment protection adopted under UNEP auspices from 1978 onwards; but the 'framework-protocols' architecture has also been followed since by several other regional and global environmental agreements dealing with atmospheric,

[21] See Chapter 24, 'Multilateral Environmental Treaty Making', in this volume.

terrestrial, and biological resources, and in related fields such as the 2003 WHO Framework Convention on Tobacco.

Several of the new agreements also championed a subtle adjustment method which historically goes back to two of the oldest international organizations: Since the mid-nineteenth century, both the Universal Postal Union and the International Telegraphic Union (forerunner of today's International Telecommunication Union) have adopted technical rules by way of 'regulations' drafted and periodically revised by expert meetings rather than by plenipotentiary conferences, and which are then 'accepted' by the administrations of the member states without having to go through the cumbersome traditional ratification process to enter into force. The method was emulated in the twentieth century by several international fisheries commissions and by the 'technical annexes' of the ICAO and of the IMO, both of which now use it, inter alia, for their air pollution standards.[22] The rationale, of course, was to make the legal instruments concerned sufficiently flexible and adaptable to changing natural circumstances and to scientific/technological progress. The net outcome of this continuous adjustment process has been a gradual transition from quasi-contractual to quasi-legislative decision-making, and from static treaty instruments to dynamic international regimes.

Curiously, international adjudication or arbitration in environmental matters played no significant role during the two decades from Stockholm to Rio. Although most of the multilateral and bilateral agreements adopted during that period contain clauses for dispute settlement between states, including references to the International Court of Justice (ICJ) and elaborate arbitration procedures, those were virtually never used in practice. The main obstacle was a standard requirement making third-party adjudication dependent on 'common agreement' by the parties to a dispute unless a party expressly waives that condition. This restrictive requirement—as in the 1989 Basel Convention on Hazardous Wastes—goes back in substance to a clause first introduced by the US State Department (in the wake of the ICJ *Nicaragua* dispute) in the 1983 Cartagena Convention for Marine Environment Protection in the Caribbean Region, and reiterated in the 1985 Vienna Convention for the Protection of the Ozone Layer, over strong opposition by sixteen other western countries favouring easier access to arbitration or the ICJ. In practice therefore, transfrontier pollution disputes still had to be resolved by domestic court decisions relying on classic conflict-of-laws principles, albeit in conjunction with simultaneous diplomatic negotiations, as illustrated by the protracted *Scarlino Red Slicks (Montedison)* cases in the Mediterranean (1974–89) and the *Alsatian Potash (Chlorides)* cases in the Rhine river basin (1976–91).[23]

[22] See Chapter 34, 'Aviation and Maritime Transport', in this volume.

[23] *Italian Republic et al v Cefis, Montedison et al*, Pretura di Livorno 27 April 1974, and Tribunale di Livorno 7 July 1976 *Italian Yearbook of International Law*, 3 (1977): 294, 298; *Prud'hommie des Pêcheurs de Bastia v Montedison & SIBIT*, French Cour de Cassation 3 April 1978, and Tribunal de Grande Instance de Bastia 4 July 1985 *Foro Italiano* 112/IV (1987): 499; see also Chapter 27, 'Judicial Development' and Part IX, 'International Environmental Law in National/Regional Courts', in this volume.

C. Emergence of an International Environmental Law Discipline

Yet, at the same time, the 'greening' of international law and governance became something of a missionary goal and meta-narrative to an entire generation of dedicated 'environmentalists'. Professional networks of international environmental lawyers had come into existence, as part of a global 'epistemic community', mainly under the auspices of the International Union for Conservation of Nature and Natural Resources,[24] which had begun to play a pioneering role in the drafting of several regional and global environmental instruments, including the African Convention on the Conservation of Nature and Natural Resources in 1968; the WHC, CITES and CMS treaties in 1972–79; the revision of the 1971 Ramsar Convention on Wetlands of International Importance in 1982–87; and ultimately the Convention on Biological Diversity (CBD) in 1988–92. With courses on environmental law now part of the law school curriculum in a growing number of countries, international environmental law emerged as a 'distinct academic discipline'.[25]

There also was a rush of new initiatives for the international codification of trans-sectoral environmental law 'principles', including the 1974 OECD Principles concerning Transfrontier Pollution, the 1978 UNEP Principles on Shared Natural Resources, the 1982 World Charter for Nature, the 1982 Montreal Rules of International Law Applicable to Transfrontier Pollution proposed by the International Law Association, and the 1987 Legal Principles proposed by the World Commission for Environment and Development. The UN International Law Commission (ILC), the focus of whose work in this field had initially been on international water law, began to draft principles of responsibility and liability for environmental harm in 1978; and in 1991, the *Institut de Droit International*, in turn, embarked on the drafting of general principles and procedures for the implementation of international environmental law.

Much of the new body of international law so emerging consisted of 'vertical transplants' of concepts derived from national environmental law, such as the technique of 'environmental impact assessments', originally developed under the 1970 US National Environmental Policy Act, subsequently spread to other legal systems worldwide, incorporated in several multilateral treaties, and 'globalized' by international jurisprudence. Similarly, the 'precautionary approach' was first enacted as a rule of general environmental legislation in Sweden (1969) and Switzerland (1983), to guide administrative decision-making under conditions of uncertainty. Even though its interpretation and policy implications remain controversial, it has since been adopted in several

[24] See Chapter 40, 'Epistemic Communities', in this volume.

[25] As acknowledged in 1991 by the editors of the Harvard Law Review, 'Developments in the Law: International Environmental Law' *Harvard Law Review*, 104/7 (1991): 1484 (editor-in-chief of the review at the time was Barack Obama); see also Chapters 7 and 8, 'Scholarship' and 'Legal Imagination and Teaching', in this volume.

regional and global agreements, and codified as one of the key principles of the 1992 Rio Declaration on Environment and Development.

IV. THE POST-MODERN ERA

Inevitably perhaps, the proliferation of new multilateral environmental instruments and norms also raised new questions and expressions of alarm about 'treaty congestion', and about the effectiveness of the existing international legal structure in this field. With the state of the world's environment continuing to deteriorate, international environmental law as a 'mobilizing myth'[26] risked suffering a severe loss of credibility—a symptom typical of post-modernity.[27]

A. Coping with the Implementation Gap

The 1992 Rio Conference (UNCED), while adding yet another layer of global treaties, offered a historic opportunity for stocktaking. In March 1991, the UNCED Preparatory Committee had entrusted its Working Group III (on legal and institutional matters) with the task of preparing 'an annotated list of existing international agreements and international legal instruments in the environmental field, describing their purpose and scope, evaluating their effectiveness, and examining possible areas for the further development of international environmental law'.[28] The assessment produced under this mandate, analyzing 124 agreements on the basis of evaluation criteria laid down by the UNCED Preparatory Committee, was first in a series of similar 'effectiveness surveys' undertaken over the next decade; and the periodic follow-up reviews now built into several global and regional environmental agreements may indeed be considered among the important 'lessons learned' during the post-Stockholm era.

Not least as a result of UNCED's increased emphasis on effective treaty implementation, the range of reporting duties for contracting parties has tended to expand, from scientific monitoring of environmental data to 'compliance monitoring' of governmental action, in some cases backed up by external verification schemes. Historically, controls of compliance with agreed multilateral standards originated in the 1920s in the ILO, where they continue to ensure the application of global ILO conventions, inter alia for protecting the working environment. In agreements for ocean resource management

[26] René-Jean Dupuy (ed), *The Future of the International Law of the Environment* (Nijhoff 1985) 513.

[27] Jean-François Lyotard, *The Post-Modern Condition: A Report on Knowledge* (Manchester University Press 1984) xxiv.

[28] UNCED Preparatory Committee Decision 2/3, UN Doc A/46/48, 1, annex I (1991).

and conservation, compliance controls—including mutual observer, boarding, and inspection schemes—have also had a long-standing tradition.[29]

In the 1990s, a new variety of 'non-adversarial and non-confrontational' compliance controls began to make its appearance in the design of international environmental agreements, side by side with the existing (though notoriously un-used) dispute settlement clauses. In practice, non-compliance often does not flow from deliberate disregard, but from an ambiguity of norms or from limitations on implementation capacity, especially in developing countries. Hence the remedy advocated by proponents of a 'managerial' approach was a series of facilitations and incentives for voluntary compliance, ranging from temporary dispensations to technical-administrative assistance programmes. The pluralist North/South structure so emerging was first translated into permanent dualistic ('double-weighted') decision-making procedures in the Montreal Protocol's Multilateral Fund (established by the 1990 London Amendments), and in the World Bank's Global Environment Facility (GEF, established in 1991/1994). It was consolidated in Principle 7 of the 1992 Rio Declaration, under the terms of 'common but differentiated responsibility', restated in the 1992 UN Framework Convention on Climate Change Articles 3 and 4, and in the preambles of subsequent agreements such as the 2001 Stockholm Convention on Persistent Organic Pollutants and the 2013 Minamata Convention on Mercury.[30]

B. Civil Society Concerns

The UNCED is also credited with having ushered in a 'participatory revolution',[31] by opening international law-making processes to access by civil society. With over 1,400 non-governmental organizations registered as observers, it served as a precedent not only for reforms in UN accreditation rules, but it also inspired a whole range of new initiatives for increasing the role of individuals and non-governmental civic groups in the creation and operation of international environmental regimes. Among the most prominent examples is the establishment of the World Bank's Independent Inspection Panel in 1993.[32] The Panel was set up in the wake of public protests over environmental and human rights encroachments by large-scale Bank-funded development projects (such as the Narmada Dam in India), to hear and investigate complaints by affected community groups in project areas, regarding non-compliance by the responsible authorities with the Bank's applicable environmental and social standards. Since

[29] See Chapters 51, 52, and 56, 'Compliance Theory', 'Transparency Procedures', and 'Non-Compliance Procedures', in this volume.

[30] See Chapters 19, 54, and 55, 'Differentiation', 'Financial Assistance', and 'Technology Assistance and Transfers', in this volume.

[31] Kal Raustiala, 'The "Participatory Revolution" in International Environmental Law' *Harvard Environmental Law Review*, 21/2 (1997): 357. See Chapters 21 and 38, 'Public Participation' and 'Non-State Actors', in this volume.

[32] World Bank, IBRD Resolution 93-10 (22 September 1993).

1993, the Panel has considered over 120 requests, thirty-four of which have been fully investigated; and its operating procedures (updated in 2014) served as a model for similar complaint and review mechanisms in many other international institutions.

At a regional level, further symptoms of the rising demand for accountability and public participation were the 1998 Aarhus Convention (in the European/North American context), and the corresponding 2018 Escazú Regional Agreement in Latin America and the Caribbean. Most European countries had long clung to a centuries-old tradition of administrative secrecy (*arcana imperii*), denying public access to government files, including licensing data for environmentally hazardous activities. The one exception was Sweden: Starting with the Freedom of the Press Act of 1766, Swedish citizens had a general right of access to public data that is unmatched in any other legal system. Two centuries later, in North America, the 1966 US Freedom of Information Act (FOIA) and the 'toxics release inventory' (established under the 1986 US Emergency Planning and Community Right-to-Know Act) opened public access both to government-held and privately-held environmental risk information. After European Union (EU) Directive 90/313/EEC on Freedom of Access to Information on the Environment (modelled after FOIA), Europe gradually followed suit.[33] The Aarhus Compliance Committee (established in 2002) has since dealt with a total of some sixty-eight complaints from the public, for non-compliance with environmental treaty provisions by thirty-one states and the EU. 'Sunshine methods' of mandatory information disclosure thus came to be recognized as effective incentives for compliance with environmental treaties, and as a new 'third wave' of self-regulatory instruments of 'informational governance'.

C. The Quest for Synergy

With more than 1,300 multilateral and close to 3,000 bilateral environmental agreements currently recorded, international environmental law is of course prone to the risk of 'fragmentation' of contemporary international law which has figured prominently on the agenda of the ILC since 2002.[34] In the visionary words of Wilfred Jenks, 'conflict of law-making treaties ... must be accepted as being in certain circumstances an inevitable incident of growth'.[35] To cope with the problem of sectoral and/or geographical overlaps—both within the environmental law spectrum and at the interface with other regulatory regimes such as international economic law, human rights, and humanitarian law[36]—there have been several at rationalizing interaction, including ambitious

[33] See Peter Sand, 'The Right to Know: Freedom of Environmental Information in Comparative and International Law' *Tulane Journal of International and Comparative Law*, 20/1 (2011): 203.

[34] See Chapter 5, 'Fragmentation', in this volume.

[35] Wilfred Jenks, 'Conflict of Law-making Treaties' *British Yearbook of International Law*, 30 (1953): 401, 405.

[36] See Chapters 43–47, 'Trade', 'Investment', 'Human Rights', 'Migration', and 'Disaster', in this volume.

proposals for global reform.[37] The historical forerunner of regional synergies in the marine environment in particular was the International Council for the Exploration of the Sea established in 1902, which continues today to perform scientific advisory services for four different multilateral treaties, and which has been acclaimed as 'the oldest and most successful international agency connected with conservation'.[38]

Even though full-scale mergers of multilateral environmental agreements—as in the case of the 1992 Oslo-Paris Convention on the Protection of the Marine Environment of the North-East Atlantic—remain the exception, there are numerous examples of innovative arrangements for 'interplay' between treaty regimes, usually in the form of 'memoranda of understanding' (MOUs) between their respective governing bodies. Thematic 'clustering' has thus led to joint secretariat services and back-to-back COP meetings between three of the Geneva-based chemical-related conventions (since 2010), and to joint programming through liaison groups between seven biodiversity-related treaties. However, as it stands at present, the complex of (co-)existing global and regional environmental agreements hardly qualifies as a coherent international regime of its own. It may at best be described as a decentralized network, horizontally intertwined by administrative cooperation instruments to ensure a measure of normative compatibility.[39]

To some extent, judicial interpretation and review has served as a harmonizing factor. Compared to previous periods, 'an unparalleled growth in the environmental jurisprudence of international tribunals' has indeed been noted since the first decade of the new millennium.[40] Even though academic proposals for a specialized global environmental court were unsuccessful, and the designation of a special environmental chamber in the ICJ was discontinued in 2006, the sheer authority of ICJ pronouncements proved decisive in anointing some environmental rules as what is now widely considered customary international law.[41] Examples were the 1996 Advisory Opinion on the *Legality of Nuclear Weapons*, the 1997 *Gabčíkovo-Nagymoros* case,[42] the 2010 *Pulp Mills on the River Uruguay* case,[43] the 2014 *Antarctic Whaling* case,[44] and the 2015/2018 *Nicaragua Border Area* case.[45] A similar legitimizing effect appears to accrue to the environment-related

37 On the background of recent efforts towards a 'Global Pact for the Environment' (UNGA Res 72/277 of May 2018), see Yann Aguila and Jorge Viñuales (eds), *A Global Pact for the Environment: Legal Foundations* (CUP 2019).

38 Ciriacy-Wantrup (n 12) 307.

39 Young (n 2) 111.

40 Patricia Birnie, Alan Boyle, and Catherine Redgwell, *International Law and the Environment* (3rd edn, OUP 2009) 37; see also Chapters 27 and 60, 'Judicial Development' and 'International Environmental Law Disputes before International Courts and Tribunals', in this volume.

41 See Chapter 23, 'Customary International Law and the Environment', in this volume.

42 *The Gabčíkovo-Nagymaros Project (Hungary/Slovakia)* (Judgement) [1997] ICJ Rep 7.

43 *Pulp Mills on the River Uruguay (Argentina/Uruguay)* (Judgement) [2010] ICJ Rep 14.

44 *Whaling in the Antarctic (Australia/ Japan, New Zealand intervening)* (Judgement) [2014] ICJ Rep 226.

45 *Certain Activities Carried Out by Nicaragua in the Border Area (Costa Rica/Nicaragua)* and *Construction of a Road in Costa Rica along the San Juan River (Nicaragua/Costa Rica)* (Judgement) [2015]

decisions of other international judicial or quasi-judicial bodies, including the International Tribunal for the Law of the Sea (ITLOS), the Permanent Court of Arbitration (PCA), and the UN Compensation Commission, thereby associating them to the ongoing evolution of the nascent normative corpus of international environmental law.

V. CONCLUSION: BEYOND THE TERRITORIAL IMPERATIVE

A striking feature of traditional international environmental law was its territoriality, firmly grounded in the 'territorial obsession' of international lawyers diagnosed by Georges Scelle,[46] and culminating in the political topology of his declared adversary Carl Schmitt.[47] The 1939/1941 *Trail Smelter* awards had in fact been confined to environmental injury 'in or to the territory of another [state]'; and while the 1972 Stockholm Declaration extended the *Trail Smelter* rule to areas *outside* the geographical limits of any national jurisdiction, the spatial (transboundary) perspective still pervades the doctrinal discourse.[48]

One much-neglected aspect in this context has been the extraterritorial application of multilateral environmental agreements,[49] either by virtue of their sheer scope, as in the instruments adopted under the auspices of the 1959 Antarctic Treaty regime, and in instruments dealing with the Earth's upper atmosphere and outer space; or by specific jurisdictional provisions providing for application to 'activities beyond the limits of national jurisdiction', as in Article 4 of the CBD and Article I of the 2003 African Convention on the Conservation of Nature and Natural Resources (Maputo Convention). Nowhere is this 'deterritorialization' more visible than in global climate

ICJ Rep 665; *Certain Activities Carried Out by Nicaragua in the Border Area (Costa Rica/Nicaragua)* (Judgement of 2 February 2018 on Compensation owed by Nicaragua to Costa Rica) ICJ.

[46] Georges Scelle, 'Obsession du territoire: essai d'étude réaliste du droit international' in Frederik van Asbeck *et al* (eds), *Symbolae Verzijl* (Nijhoff 1958) 347; see also Dino Kritsiotis, 'Public International Law and Its Territorial Imperative' *Michigan Journal of International Law*, 30/3 (2009): 547.

[47] Carl Schmitt, *The Nomos of the Earth in the International Law of Jus Publicum Europaeum* (Telos Press 2003) 98 ('spatial context of all law'); see Oliver Simons, 'Carl Schmitt's Spatial Rhetoric' in Jens Meierhenrich and Oliver Simons (eds), *Oxford Handbook of Carl Schmitt* (OUP 2016) 776, 788.

[48] See Daniel Khan, 'Territory Taking Centre Stage in International Law: Some Preliminary Thoughts on the Rise of Territoriality to the Bedrock of Modern Statehood' in Pierre d'Argent (ed), *Droit des frontières internationales: The Law of International Borders* (Pedone 2016) 57.

[49] See Günther Handl, Joachim Zekoll, and Peer Zumbansen (eds), *Beyond Territoriality: Transnational Legal Authority in an Age of Globalization* (Nijhoff 2012); Markus Vordermayer, 'The Extraterritorial Application of Multilateral Environmental Agreements' *Harvard International Law Journal*, 59/1 (2018): 59.

change law, which in the wake of sea-level rise now faces the prospect of island states without territory.

Conversely, in common marine spaces beyond territorial waters, coastal states have continuously extended claims for national control ('sea-grab'), often under environmental labels—from Canada's successful 'custodial protection' claim to ice-covered coastal zones (100 miles, legitimated by UNCLOS Article 234), to creeping European claims of 'ecological protection zones' in the Mediterranean (out to approximately sixty miles since 2003–06), British claims for 'environment protection and preservation zones' surrounding overseas territories in the Indian Ocean and the Antarctic Southern Sea (200 miles since 2003–12), and US claims for 'marine national monuments expansion' of the country's Pacific territories (out to fifty miles since 2006, and to a full 200 miles since 2014).

The 'territorial temptation' in the ocean environment has its historical parallels in the international law of genetic resources: Whereas Article 1 of the International Undertaking on Plant Genetic Resources adopted by FAO in 1983 had still proclaimed 'the universally accepted principle that plant genetic resources are a heritage of mankind and consequently should be available without restriction', Article 15 of the 1992 CBD recognized 'the sovereign rights of States over their natural resources' and the 'authority to determine access to genetic resources' for the countries of (territorial) origin of such in-situ resources. This about-turn—largely motivated by the developing countries' legitimate fears of neo-colonial exploitation by multinational bio-pirates—has since been confirmed by Article 10 of the 2001 FAO International Treaty on Plant Genetic Resources for Food and Agriculture (ITPGRFA), which recognizes 'the sovereign rights of States over their own plant genetic resources'.

So is the pendulum swinging back to the other extreme—to that 'formidable defensive concept'of national territorial sovereignty?[50] True, the new treaty language seems to acknowledge that states can 'own' genetic resources in their territory, in the way in which the preamble of the WHC recognized cultural and natural heritage sites as 'property, to whatever people they may belong'. Yet the apparent analogy to private property rights is potentially misleading here: Just as the rights of coastal states in their 200-miles exclusive economic zones (EEZs) beyond territorial waters are qualified by specific duties owed to other states and to the international community,[51] the rights of 'countries of origin' over in-situ genetic resources are matched by specific conservation duties and by obligations to facilitate access for other parties to the CBD;[52] and by the multilateral system of access and benefit-sharing under the FAO Plant Gene Treaty.[53] A more appropriate analogy in both cases therefore, may be 'public trusteeship', for the benefit

[50] Philip Allott, 'International Law and International Revolution: Reconceiving the World' in David Freestone, Surya Subedi, and Scott Davidson (eds), *Contemporary Issues in International Law: A Collection of the Josephine Onoh Memorial Lectures* (Kluwer 2002) 77, 95.

[51] UNCLOS, arts 61–70.

[52] arts 5–15.

[53] art 10.

of present and future generations. The message then is simple: The sovereign rights of nation-states over certain common environmental resources are not proprietary, but *fiduciary*.[54] The challenge is to come up with mechanisms that will effectively monitor the performance of the trustees.

BIBLIOGRAPHY

Philip Allott, 'International Law and the Idea of History' *Journal of the History of International Law* 1/1 (1999): 1

David Christian, 'World Environmental History' in Jerry Bentley (ed), *Oxford Handbook of World History* (OUP 2011) 125

Martti Koskenniemi, 'Why History of International Law?' *Rechtsgeschichte: Journal of the Max Planck Institute for European Legal History*, 4 (2004): 61

Peter Sand (ed), *The History and Origin of International Environmental Law* (Edward Elgar 2015)

Jorge Viñuales, 'The Influence of Environmental Protection on the Fabric of International Law' in Riccardo Mazzeschi and Pasquale De Sena (eds), *Global Justice, Human Rights and the Modernization of International Law* (Springer International 2018) 255

[54] Birnie *et al* (n 40) 84; Peter Sand, 'The Rise of Public Trusteeship in International Environmental Law' *Environmental Policy and Law*, 44 (2014): 210, 213; see Marx (n 18); and cf. Robert Falkner and Barry Buzan, 'The Emergence of Environmental Stewardship as a Primary Institution of Global International Society' *European Journal of International Relations*, 25/1 (2019): 131.

CHAPTER 4

MULTILEVEL AND POLYCENTRIC GOVERNANCE

JEFFREY L DUNOFF

I. INTRODUCTION

In the face of intensifying environmental challenges, including species loss, climate change, and natural resource depletion, who should resolve contested issues of global environmental law and policy? Which bodies—local, national, regional, or global—possess the appropriate knowledge, technical capacities, and political legitimacy to manage the earth's limited resources? These and related questions regarding how environmental decisions get made and who makes them—that is, questions of *environmental governance*—lie at the heart of international environmental law and policy.

This chapter provides a synoptic overview of leading conceptual approaches to international environmental governance.[1] These approaches draw on arguments found in diverse literatures, including writings on fiscal federalism, the new institutionalism, international relations, and international law. It is not possible to do justice to these literatures or detail the important shifts in emphasis over time; instead I shall try to summarize and abstract many of the most recurrent and influential arguments, and provide illustrative examples.

To do so, this chapter proceeds as follows. Sections II, III, and IV map three broad approaches to conceptualizing international environmental governance. Section II reviews a prominent set of arguments in favour of decentralized environmental governance, and a competing set of claims in favour of greater centralization of governance authority. These approaches, in general, seek to produce the appropriate 'match'

[1] This chapter focuses on traditional, state-centric governance structures. While other actors play important roles and other governance structures are prominent in the environmental field, they are addressed comprehensively by other handbook chapters. See Chapters 38, 41, and 42, 'Non-State Actors', 'Business and Industry', and 'Indigenous Peoples', in this volume.

between the level or scope of governance and the level or scope of the relevant environmental issue.

Of course, to focus on whether responsibility over particular environmental issues should properly be vested at the local, national, regional, or global level seems to presuppose that there is a single 'best' or 'optimal' level of environmental governance. But substantive environmental problems do not necessarily correspond to political or jurisdictional borders, and public officials with authority over a particular policy domain are often located across several different levels of governance. Section III discusses 'multi-level governance' (MLG), an approach that does not view the allocation of authority among levels as mutually exclusive but rather explores how authority can be simultaneously exercised by multiple agents. In this context, researchers are less concerned with identifying *the* appropriate site of governance than with describing the *multiple* sources and levels of governance, and analyzing the accountability and effectiveness of this form of governance. In practice, MLG has a strong vertical focus, and has been fruitfully applied to analyse relationships among national, regional, and global environmental regimes.

Section IV discusses approaches that emphasize the horizontal sharing of governance authority. Across many issue areas, governance functions are shared among various bodies that typically have loose and non-hierarchical relations, raising concerns over coherence and coordination. These concerns are frequently addressed under the rubric of fragmentation,[2] and much attention is devoted to strategies for resolving inconsistencies and conflicts among rules emanating from different international legal regimes. The focus on rule and regime conflict is incomplete and potentially misleading, however, as conflicts are relatively rare. Section IV reviews several ways that actors from different regimes interact in ongoing patterns of regulatory cooperation and competition as they navigate or create shared regulatory space.

Having surveyed the leading literatures, Section V seeks to enlarge the intellectual tool-kit by briefly introducing strategies for advancing understanding of international environmental governance. First, I discuss comparative institutional analysis, which emphasizes that imperfections and biases are found in all governance institutions, and that the appropriate inquiry is to analyse the predictable shortcomings of any institution and compare any recommended approach to available alternatives. Next, I introduce a new conceptual framework that can be applied to international environmental governance debates by describing an underappreciated set of governance trade-offs among levels of participation, stringency of environmental obligations, and levels of compliance with environmental norms (the 'governance trilemma'). Finally, I briefly outline how emerging technologies of governance, including big data, can alter environmental governance. A short conclusion follows.

Presenting these different approaches in sequential order is intended as a useful heuristic, and not as an implicit evolutionary claim. Specifically, more recent approaches to

[2] See Chapter 5, 'Fragmentation', in this volume.

global environmental governance should not be understood as replacing or subsuming previous approaches. To the contrary, at least some of the approaches surveyed in this chapter not only coexist simultaneously, but can even complement and enrich each other. Indeed, one might even view the various iterations of arguments over global environmental governance as a set of separable but mutually reinforcing frames through which to approach many of the central challenges facing international environmental law that are explored throughout this handbook.

II. To Centralize or Not?

Following the 1972 Stockholm Conference on the Human Environment, international environmental law witnessed dramatic moves towards the centralization of authority at the national, regional, and international levels. During this time, many states created environmental ministries; regional treaties and regimes proliferated; and scores of important multilateral environmental agreements (MEAs) were concluded. The strong move towards greater centralization that marked international environmental governance for many years is no longer dominant. In part, this shift reflects organizational congestion and fatigue at the international level; concerns about effectiveness, as international policy-makers struggle to address problems of high political salience and great technical complexity; the rise of hybrid public-private bodies and transnational actors that constitute competing sources of governance; and a widespread populist backlash against international regimes and forms of global governance.

Regardless of shifts in prevailing political tendencies, however, diplomats, advocates, and scholars often invoke a recurrent set of arguments concerning the appropriate level of environmental governance. For ease of exposition, I first outline the most influential arguments commonly offered in support of decentralized environmental governance. In the aggregate, these arguments constitute a background presumption against centralization. I then discuss the most important arguments offered in favour of more centralized environmental governance.

A. Presumption Against Centralization

A variety of normative arguments are typically offered in support of less centralized forms of environmental governance. First, decentralized authority structures permit regulation to better reflect geographical variations in preferences for collective goods such as environmental quality and localized knowledge about how best to produce those goods. In particular, as policy priorities, resource levels, risk tolerance, and assimilative capacity diverge substantially across different geographic areas, tailoring environmental standards to local circumstances can increase aggregate social welfare. Moreover, noncentralized decision-making enables different jurisdictions to experiment with diverse policies and generate evidence about the effectiveness and administrative feasibility of alternative approaches. Other jurisdictions can learn from and then adopt, modify, or avoid these programmes.

Decentralization and experimentation permit different jurisdictions to compete with one another. Inter-jurisdictional competition encourages socially desirable levels of environmental protection in much the same way that competition in private markets is thought to produce socially desirable levels of goods and services. Competition is also said to promote efficient and effective regulation.

Finally, dispersal of regulatory authority promotes political participation and 'self-determination', as individuals can more easily and more meaningfully participate in smaller scale governance structures. Both individually and in the aggregate, these normative arguments are said to have a special force in the environmental realm, as natural environmental conditions, levels of economic development, and environmental values often vary widely across jurisdictions.

These arguments both contribute to, and are reinforced by, background norms in many political systems that favour decentralization of regulatory authority. In many federal systems, national constitutions provide that sub-national jurisdictions have authority over all matters not constitutionally delegated to the national government. In the European Union (EU), a similar commitment in favour of decentralized authority finds expression in the concept of 'subsidiarity'. As a result of these and similar norms in other legal systems, many debates over the appropriate level of environmental governance take place against a strong background presumption in favour of decentralization.

B. Arguments that Favour Centralization

A series of arguments are commonly deployed to counter the presumption against centralization. The general rhetorical structure of these arguments is to identify structural features of common fact patterns that render decentralized environmental governance insufficient and, therefore, by implication, require more centralized governance. Many of the arguments attempt to 'match' the scope or level of regulatory authority with the scope or level of the underlying environmental problem.

1. *Externalities*

The clearest justification for moving regulatory authority to a more centralized—that is, a hierarchically and vertically superior—level is found in the case of 'externalities' that originate in one jurisdiction but cause harm in another. The paradigmatic case involves pollution generated in jurisdiction A that travels downstream or downwind into jurisdiction B. Jurisdiction A may have insufficient incentive to regulate the polluting activity as it enjoys the full benefits of the activity and exports some or all of the resulting environmental harm. Jurisdiction B may have strong incentive to regulate, but lack authority to effectively regulate parties or activities in other jurisdictions.

Environmental spill-overs present a strong argument for moving environmental governance from a sub-national to a national level or from a national to a regional (or an international) level. Similar arguments support more centralized governance in cases of shared resources, such as migratory birds, or where a resource, such as a river, forms a boundary or flows between two jurisdictions. In these cases, the underlying goal is to match the scale of political governance to the physical scale of the externality.

2. *Game theoretic approaches*

A second conceptual approach shifts attention from static environments, where actors simply respond to events, to strategic environments, where actors understand that the consequences of their actions depend, in part, on what other actors do. In this context, scholars highlight a series of 'collective action' problems where parties might predictably fail to cooperate to produce optimal outcomes.

The most prominent of these problems is the Prisoner's Dilemma, which is often taken to teach that rational pursuit of individual self-interest can lead to collectively sub-optimal results. The Prisoner's Dilemma is thought to capture the incentives that individuals, firms, and states often face in international environmental affairs, and to illustrate the frequent divergence between individual and collective rationality in situations marked by interdependence.

The 'Tragedy of the Commons', extends the structure and logic of the two-player Prisoner's Dilemma to situations involving 'commons' resources and a large number of actors. The generalized idea is that when a resource is freely available to all, every actor has an incentive to maximize consumption of the resource, and no actor has an incentive to invest in the resource, even though the ultimate result may be the destruction of the resource itself.[3] The Prisoner's Dilemma and Tragedy of the Commons serve as starting points for much analysis of international environmental issues, and are thought to illustrate how self-interested actors predictably generate individually and collectively sub-optimal outcomes.

Yet there is also a second important message. While certain resource allocations seem capable of producing tragic outcomes, tragedy is not inevitable. Rather, shifting governance from the parties themselves to more centralized levels can improve the quantity and quality of information available to the parties, provide a set of stable expectations, and minimize the transaction costs associated with monitoring behaviour and enforcement mechanisms. In these ways, greater centralization assists parties to achieve mutually beneficial outcomes that otherwise likely would not occur.

3. *Regulatory competition*

A third approach highlights the possibility of regulatory competition among jurisdictions producing a 'race to the bottom'. One common version of this argument starts with the observation that firms operating in jurisdictions with lax environmental

[3] Garrett Hardin, 'The Tragedy of the Commons' *Science*, 162/3859 (1968): 1243.

standards will, other things being equal, enjoy a competitive advantage in global markets over firms operating in high-standard jurisdictions. This result will trigger political pressures for high-standard jurisdictions to lower their standards. However, if high-standard jurisdictions relax their environmental standards, low-standard jurisdictions will have an incentive to lower their standards even more; this act will trigger renewed downward pressures in high-standard jurisdictions, and so on. The resulting dynamic creates a 'race to the bottom'.

To break this dynamic, a high-standard jurisdiction might use tariffs, subsidies, or other trade-policy instruments to eliminate the market advantage that products from low-standard jurisdictions would otherwise enjoy. Such measures, however, may violate obligations found in trade liberalization agreements.[4] Moreover, the use of subsidies or other trade measures may prompt similar measures from other jurisdictions, thereby sparking yet another form of regulatory competition.

One common response to 'race to the bottom' dynamics is regulatory harmonization. Some harmonized standards establish minimum environmental norms that lower-level jurisdictions are free to surpass, while other harmonized standards serve as ceilings. In most instances, harmonized environmental standards are associated with the creation of a more centralized authority in national or supranational rules and bodies. Federal states such as the United States and regional entities such as the EU employ a variety of harmonization strategies in response to competitiveness concerns. On the international front, harmonization often occurs through MEAs that set out standards for all parties to meet.

Race to the bottom arguments have come under sharp challenge on both normative and positive grounds. As a normative matter, the argument that inter-jurisdictional competition will produce sub-optimal levels of environmental regulation is countered by those who claim that competition among jurisdictions for mobile firms will produce socially desirable levels of environmental protection in much the same way that competition in private markets generates socially optimal levels of goods and services. Critics also note that there is little empirical evidence that firms relocate to other jurisdictions to take advantage of lower environmental regulations,[5] and that within national and international contexts, jurisdictions with stronger environmental policies generally do not experience slower rates of economic growth than low-standard states.

Given the contested normative and empirical claims, perhaps the most enduring lesson from the regulatory competition literature is rooted in political economy:

> If the beneficiaries of environmental regulation are a politically weaker constituency than the beneficiaries of industrial growth, government will set environmental standards too low and over-invest in attracting industry. And if regulatees are

[4] See Chapter 43, 'Trade', in this volume.

[5] For a review of the empirical literature, see Organization for Economic Co-operation and Development, *Environmental Issues in Policy-Based Competition for Investment: A Literature Review* (4 April 2002) Doc ENV/EPOC/GSP(2001)11/Final.

politically weaker than environmentalists, environmental standards will be set too high. The moral of the state competition literature in the environmental context is simply that government competition is contingent on political forces.[6]

III. MULTILEVEL GOVERNANCE

Notwithstanding efforts to identify the optimal level of environmental governance, across a vast array of areas, responsibility for environmental issues has virtually always been, and continues to be, divided and shared among overlapping levels of governance. In response, much attention has been devoted to understanding and modelling how different governance levels connect and interact. The most influential of these efforts was an approach that conceptualized MLG. Multilevel governance, which first emerged in the field of European studies but was soon applied to other domains, including environmental law, is distinguished from the literature on centralization reviewed above by its focus on the overlaps and relationships among different governance units.

As this approach was refined and elaborated, scholars distinguished between two ideal types of MLG arrangements, often labelled 'Type I' and 'Type II'.[7] Type I MLG refers to 'general purpose' governance arrangements consisting of a limited number of levels. Type I jurisdictions have nonintersecting memberships, and are characterized by relatively stable, system-wide institutional architectures. The classic example would be a federal state. Type II MLG, in contrast, is characterized by jurisdictions that are task-specific, rather than general purpose; one might think of public authorities responsible for providing specialized services, such as electricity or water.

Each type of MLG uses a different strategy to balance the benefits of scale flexibility with the transaction costs of coordinating multiple actors. Type I MLG controls transaction costs by limiting the number of actors to be coordinated; typically there is a local, intermediate, and central unit. Type II MLG, on the other hand, does not limit the number of relevant actors. Rather, it constrains the number of interactions by limiting them to functionally distinct policy domains. Thus, Type II governance structures are designed to solve specific policy problems, such as managing a common pool resource or setting technical standards in a particular policy area.

Virtually all areas of international environmental law possess features of MLG. The standard treaty regime, consisting of regulatory standards set out in an international legal instrument, typically relies on national officials to ensure implementation and compliance at the domestic level. This structure has some features of 'Type I' MLG. More often, however, MLG on the international plane resembles 'Type II' MLG. Consider, by

[6] Daryl Levinson, 'Empire-Building Government in Constitutional law' *Harvard Law Review*, 118/3 (2005): 915, 947.

[7] Liesbet Hooghe and Gary Marks, 'Unraveling the Central State But How? Types of Multi-level Governance' *American Political Science Review*, 97/2 (2003): 233.

way of example, the international legal regime governing fisheries, which involves multiple multilateral, regional, and domestic actors. The underlying legal norms in this area are contained in the 1982 United Nations Convention on the Law of the Sea (UNCLOS), which requires parties to cooperate on necessary conservation measures, and provides that this cooperation is to occur through regional or sub-regional fisheries organizations, collectively known as Regional Fisheries Management Organizations (RFMOs).[8]

MLG is not always successful. For example, despite the establishment of numerous RFMOs, global fish stocks continued to decline. In response, governance activity shifted back to the international sphere. Among other actions, in 1993 states adopted the Agreement to Promote Compliance with International Conservation and Management Measures by Fishing Vessels on the High Seas; in 1995 a Food and Agriculture Organization (FAO) Code of Conduct for Responsible Fisheries was issued; and in 1995, states entered into the UN Fish Stocks Agreement (FSA). These instruments were intended, in part, to address various failures in RFMO governance and to enhance compliance with RFMO measures.

Although these instruments prompted several improvements in RFMO governance, dissatisfaction with regional efforts did not totally dissipate, and the interplay among regional and multilateral levels continued. For example, in 2006, a High Seas Task Force on Illegal, Unreported and Unregulated Fishing, hosted by the Organization for Economic Cooperation and Development (OECD), called for developing a model for improved RFMO governance and independent review of RFMO performance, and a UN review conference on the FSA called for strengthening RFMO mandates to implement modern approaches to fisheries management. Thereafter, many RFMOs undertook performance reviews and took steps to improve, inter alia, data collection, implementation, and compliance. This iterative process continues: in 2010 and 2016 UN reviews took place, recommendations were adopted, and implementation efforts followed.

MLG does not eliminate all conflict. Nonetheless, the focus on MLG usefully highlights jurisdictional overlap, fluidity, cooperation, and negotiation among actors at different governance levels, in striking contrast to the 'zero-sum' approach to the allocation of governance authority characteristic of the debates over more of less centralization reviewed above.

IV. FRAGMENTATION, POLYCENTRIC GOVERNANCE, AND REGIME INTERACTIONS

The MLG literature is primarily focused on relationships among actors located at different vertical levels of governance. In recent years, however, much attention has

[8] arts 117, 118.

been devoted to the horizontal relationships among actors in parallel international legal regimes.[9]

This literature starts with the observation that international law is the product of highly decentralized processes. Thus international legal norms often develop in specialized functional regimes, such as environment, human rights, or trade. In practice, specialized law-making, institution-building, and dispute resolution in any particular field tends to be relatively insulated from developments in adjoining fields. Moreover, each functionally differentiated area of law has its own treaties, principles, and institutions, and the values and interests advanced by any particular regime do not necessarily correspond with those advanced by other specialized regimes, raising the risk of gaps, inconsistencies, and conflicts. Conflicts can result when bodies from one specialized area of international law, such as trade, are asked to interpret or apply norms generated in other specialized areas, or when the same fact pattern is considered by multiple bodies that might apply inconsistent norms from different international legal regimes.

The spectre of regime conflict naturally leads to a conceptualization of regime interactions in terms of discrete disputes arising from specific events. This model, however, is dramatically incomplete; the overwhelming majority of regime interactions do not arise out of discrete transactions, or trigger high-profile conflicts. Rather, most regime interactions—including many forms of international environmental governance—occur in ongoing relationships among actors from different regimes. For ease of exposition, we can distinguish among 'regulatory', 'operational', and 'conceptual' regime interactions.

Regulatory interactions include a wide range of regulatory and administrative decisions that involve more than one international body. For example actors from a number of international bodies—including United Nations Environment Programme (UNEP), FAO, the World Health Organization (WHO), the International Labour Organization (ILO), and others—jointly created the Inter-Organization for the Sound Management of Chemicals, which generated a globally harmonized system for the classification and labelling of chemicals.[10] The Basel Secretariat, the International Maritime Organization, and ILO were centrally involved in efforts to negotiate a treaty on ship scrapping.[11] For years, actors from the 1973 Convention on International Trade in Endangered Species (CITES), UNCLOS, the FAO, the WTO, and RFMOs have engaged in ongoing efforts designed to produce rules to reduce fisheries subsidies.[12] As these examples suggest, actors from diverse international bodies frequently engage in

[9] See eg 'Report of the International Law Commission on the work of its fifty-second session' (2000) UN Doc A/55/10, 144.

[10] WHO, 'The Inter-Organization Programme for the Sound Management of Chemicals (IOMC)' <https://www.who.int/iomc/en/> accessed 14 October 2019.

[11] See eg Joint ILO/IMO/BC Working Group on Ship Scrapping, 'Outcome of the 2nd Session of the Joint Working Group' (1 September 2008) ILO/IMMO/BC WG 3/2/4.

[12] Margaret Young, *Trading Fish, Saving Fish: The Interaction between Regimes in International Law* (CUP 2011).

ongoing, collaborative interactions intended to produce legal norms across a wide range of international environmental issues.

Another form of governance occurs when actors from different international legal regimes engage in *operational interactions* in the environmental area. For example, the Global Environment Facility (GEF), began as a partnership among the World Bank, UNEP, and the United Nations Development Programme to fund efforts to fulfil global environmental objectives. It works with several MEA secretariats to mobilize financial support for projects that generate global environmental benefits. GEF decisions to fund certain activities and not others, and the conditions it imposes upon use of funds, is a form of international environmental governance.

Notably, many operational interactions involve efforts to implement and enforce international norms—efforts that, in turn, sometimes lead to creation or modification of international legal norms. Ongoing interactions between the World Customs Organization (WCO) and actors from various MEAs illustrate this dynamic. WCO developed and updates the Harmonized Commodity Description and Coding System (Harmonized System). Virtually every state uses this system as a basis for their customs tariffs and for the collection of trade statistics.[13]

The 1987 Montreal Protocol controls production and trade in ozone depleting substances (ODS). The treaty's effectiveness turns, in part, on the ability of customs officials to monitor lawful and control unlawful trade in ODS. However, when the Montreal Protocol came into force, the Harmonized System combined ODS and non-ozone-depleting substances in a single category. At the request of the Montreal Protocol parties, UNEP's Executive Director asked the WCO to create separate customs codes for ODS controlled by the Protocol. WCO initially resisted, but eventually created new codes, which greatly facilitated enforcement of the Protocol. Similarly, upon request, the Harmonized System has also been amended from time to time to reflect new subheadings for specific chemicals controlled under the 1998 Rotterdam Convention and for specific categories of waste controlled by the 1989 Basel Convention. In short, inter-regime operational partnerships are increasingly common across a range of issues. For the most part, however, these initiatives constitute sites of international governance that are 'hidden in plain sight', whose significance has been understudied and undertheorized.

Finally, actors from different functional international bodies collaborate to produce not only rules, but also knowledge. These *conceptual interactions* are often efforts to reconceptualize difficult or controversial policy domains. Thus, they are designed to offer new ways of understanding the world, as a precursor to acting in the world.

For example, the OECD, UNEP, and the World Bank have jointly undertaken research to identify how public and private actors can most effectively shift financial flows in infrastructure to produce low carbon emitting, highly resilient infrastructure.

[13] WCO, 'What is the Harmonized System (HS)?' <http://www.wcoomd.org/en/topics/nomenclature/overview/what-is-the-harmonized-system.aspx> accessed 14 October 2019.

In 2018, these organizations jointly authored a report that outlines a series of systemic conceptual and behavioural changes intended to produce a 'transformative agenda' on low-carbon, climate resilient investment.[14] Similarly, in 2009, UNEP and WTO jointly published a report addressing linkages between trade and climate change.[15] The report challenges conventional wisdom and argues that trade liberalization can have a positive effect on greenhouse gas emissions by, inter alia, accelerating the transfer of clean technologies. Notably, neither report purports to generate new rules. Rather, both are designed to introduce new concepts and to shift underlying debates; as the 2009 report states, its 'aim is to promote greater understanding of [the interaction between trade and climate change policies] and to assist policymakers in this complex policy area.'[16]

Note that unlike the litigations that are the focus of the fragmentation scholarship, conceptual interactions between different international organizations are not intended to settle jurisdictional boundaries, or to privilege or subordinate one norm or another. Rather, these conceptual interactions are intended to shape elite and public understandings of various international environmental issues. Shaping understandings is, perhaps, the most powerful form of governance available to international actors.

V. ADVANCING UNDERSTANDINGS OF GLOBAL ENVIRONMENTAL GOVERNANCE

The approaches reviewed above have framed much of the discourse to date over international environmental governance. This section, in contrast, is forward-looking and offers several strategies for advancing understandings of international environmental governance. Specifically, it introduces a new question to ask about any proposal for international environmental governance, presents a new conceptual framework that illuminates inevitable trade-offs in the institutional design of international environmental governances structures, and identifies several ways that new technologies promise to transform international environmental governance.

A. Comparative Institutional Analysis

The approaches surveyed above generally analyse one specific form of governance. For example, conventional analysis teaches that sub-national units will underregulate environmental spill-overs and externalities, and that states facing prisoner's dilemmas will reach sub-optimal results. These predictable governance failures are said to justify more

[14] OECD, *Financing Climate Futures: Rethinking Infrastructure* (2018).
[15] UNEP and WTO, *Trade and Climate Change* (2009).
[16] Ibid.

centralized governance structures. This argument, however, is not entirely persuasive unless it examines whether the alternative level of governance is subject to predictable failures of its own, which may be as great as or greater than the failures of the original form of governance.[17] In many instances, for example, a national legislature or international body may generate regulatory solutions worse than those produced by subnational or national jurisdictions.

The call for comparative analysis is, of course, not new. In fact, environmental scholarship has generated important insights through comparative analysis of the efficacy of different regulatory tools.[18] Yet most environmental scholarship to date has not made the analytic and conceptual shift from comparing the efficacy of various *regulatory mechanisms* to comparing the efficacy of various *governance structures*.[19] Moreover, to the extent that scholars have engaged in comparative institutional analysis, they have often focused primarily upon comparisons among governance mechanisms located on the same horizontal plane. In other words, they compare the relative strengths of, say, domestic legislatures and domestic courts to address an issue, or analyse whether a proposed World Environmental Organization would be more or less effective than an enhanced UNEP. Environmental governance scholarship to date has not sufficiently engaged in a comparative analysis of governance mechanisms on different vertical planes, such as a comparison of regional versus national governance.

Thus, conventional approaches, like those surveyed in Sections II, III, and IV, typically ignore the insight that all governance structures are subject to one or more 'failures'. For students of international environmental governance, the crucial question is not whether one particular governance structure is subject to predictable failures, but whether a proposed alternative structure, subject to its own predictable failures, would perform better. Environmental governance scholarship would benefit immensely from adding in this comparative inquiry to its traditional intellectual repertoire.

B. The Governance Trilemma

Much attention has been devoted to conceptualizing and measuring the effectiveness of international environmental regimes.[20] From a governance perspective, effectiveness can be broadly understood as a function of three factors. First is the level of the ambition of its substantive provisions; a pollution control treaty that calls for more stringent emission reductions will, *ceteris parabis*, be more effective than one that requires less stringent reductions. Second is the level of participation; a pollution control treaty with

[17] The seminal work developing this argument remains Neil Komesar, *Imperfect Alternatives: Choosing Institutions in Law, Economics, and Public Policy* (University of Chicago Press 1994).

[18] See Chapter 6, 'Instrument Choice', in this volume.

[19] For a notable exception, see Daniel Esty, 'Toward Optimal Environmental Governance' *NYU Law Review*, 74/6 (1999): 1495.

[20] Chapter 57, 'Effectiveness', in this volume.

more participants will be more effective, particularly if major polluters are parties.[21] And third is the level of compliance—low compliance with stringent standards is hardly a recipe for environmental success.

The governance trilemma is that governance systems face inevitable trade-offs regarding these three features, such that any given system can maximize two, but not all three, of these features. First, they can obtain high levels of compliance and a highly inclusive agreement, but at the cost of relatively low substantive ambition; these arrangements are sometimes known as 'broad but shallow'. Alternatively, a governance system can achieve high ambition and high levels of compliance, but only at the cost of reduced participation—a 'deep but narrow' arrangement.[22] Finally, they can have high levels of ambition, and large numbers of participants, but at the cost of relatively low levels of compliance.[23] This trilemma is captured graphically in Figure 4.1:

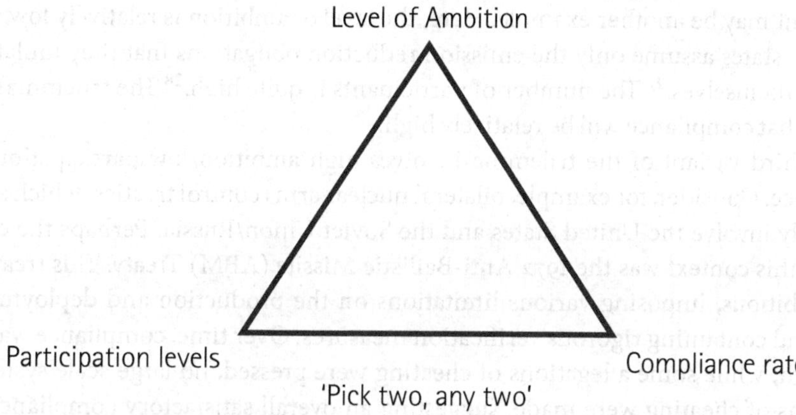

FIGURE 4.1 The governance trilemma

A few examples will help to illustrate the governance trilemma.

International humanitarian law (IHL) seeks to alleviate the effects of armed conflict. This ambitious body of law contains dense legal regimes governing air, land, and maritime warfare, the law of occupation, and the law of neutrality. Participation in the key IHL treaties, including the 1949 Geneva Conventions, is universal, or nearly so. With

[21] Many states join agreements that regulate behaviours that they do not, or only minimally, engage in, as evidenced in the many countries that are party to, but not significantly engaged in, the behaviours regulated by the 1946 International Convention for the Regulation of Whaling, the 2006 International Tropical Timber Agreement, or the 1987 Montreal Protocol on Substances That Deplete the Ozone Layer.

[22] See eg Daniel Bodansky, *The Art and Craft of International Environmental Law* (Harvard University Press 2010) 182–187.

[23] Using different terminology, the argument is explored in Scott Barrett, *Environment and Statecraft: The Strategy of Environmental Decision-Making* (OUP 2003); see also Daniel Bodansky, 'Legally Binding Versus Non-Legally Binding Instruments' in Scott Barrett *et al* (eds), *Towards a Workable and Effective Climate Regime* (CEPR Press 2015) 155 ('the effectiveness of an international regime is a function of three factors: (1) the ambition of its provisions; (2) the level of participation by states; and (3) the degree to which states comply').

high ambition and high participation, the trilemma suggests that compliance will lag; indeed, at a 2009 conference organized by the Swiss government, states 'identified compliance with IHL as one of the key challenges to the continued relevance of this body of law going forward'.[24] One need not go as far as the International Committee of the Red Cross (ICRC) President, who declared that '[i]nternational humanitarian law is flouted almost every day, in every conflict around the world',[25] to conclude that non-compliance is unacceptably high. IHL is a high ambition, high participation, low compliance regime.

An alternative approach to the trilemma is seen in regimes that are high in participation and compliance, but low in terms of ambition. Consider early international efforts to regulate whaling. For many years, virtually all whaling states were parties to the whaling treaties, but these treaties contained whale-catch quotas that roughly matched the demand of the whaling industry. Not surprisingly, compliance was 'nearly perfect, but only because the legal standard codified then-current behaviour'.[26] The 2015 Paris Agreement may be another example. Here, the level of ambition is relatively low, in the sense that states assume only the emission reduction obligations that they unilaterally select for themselves.[27] The number of participants is quite high.[28] The trilemma's logic suggests that compliance will be relatively high.

Yet a third variant of the trilemma involves high ambition/low participation/high compliance. Consider, for example, bilateral nuclear arms control treaties, which almost exclusively involve the United States and the Soviet Union/Russia. Perhaps the central treaty in this context was the 1972 Anti-Ballistic Missile (ABM) Treaty. This treaty was quite ambitious, imposing various limitations on the production and deployment of ABMs, and containing rigorous verification measures. Over time, compliance was relatively high; while some allegations of cheating were pressed, no large scale systematic allegations of cheating were made, suggesting an overall satisfactory compliance rate. The treaty was widely seen as successful during its nearly three decade duration.

The structural nature of the trade-offs associated with the trilemma can be seen in Table 4.1, on the next page.

Several observations are in order. First, many treaties and treaty regimes evolve over time. For example, the Montreal Protocol originally had only forty-six signatories; today it has 197 parties. In such circumstances, the trilemma should be understood in dynamic, rather than static terms.

Second, the trilemma does not suggest that states will *necessarily* maximize two out of the three desiderata of ambition, participation, and compliance. Rather, it suggests

[24] See ICRC, 'Strengthening Compliance with International Humanitarian Law—Concluding Report' (2015) 32IC/15/19.2.

[25] 'No agreement by States on mechanism to strengthen compliance with rules of war' *ICRC News Release* (10 December 2015).

[26] Kal Raustiala, 'Compliance & Effectiveness in International Regulatory Cooperation' *Case Western Reserve Journal of International Law*, 32/1 (2000): 387, 392.

[27] art 4.2.

[28] As of October 2019, 186 parties had ratified the treaty. See 'Paris Agreement—Status of Ratification' <https://unfccc.int/process/the-paris-agreement/status-of-ratification> accessed 14 October 2019.

Table 4.1 Structural trade-offs associated with the governance trilemma

	Ambition	Participation	Compliance
International Humanitarian Law	High	High	Low
Paris Agreement	Low	High	High (predicted)
Bilateral nuclear arms control (ABM, etc)	High	Low	High

that *at most* states can maximize two out of three. Any particular treaty can maximize one or none of these desiderata. The 1991 US Canada Air Quality Agreement required the United States only to make the emissions reductions already required under pre-existing domestic law.[29] In the language of the trilemma, this is a low ambition, low participation, and high compliance treaty.

Is it possible to 'solve' the trilemma? The Montreal Protocol mandates dramatic reductions in the production and consumption of chlorofluorocarbons (CFCs), has nearly universal membership, and it is celebrated as a resounding success. Is the Montreal Protocol a high ambition/high participation/high compliance treaty?

One important reason for the treaty's success was its use of differentiated commitments. Developing states were originally given a ten-year grace period, during which they would not have to meet the treaty's substantive obligations. Differentiated obligations permits states that are willing to take on more ambitious obligations to do so, but not at the cost of excluding less ambitious states from the treaty regime. Of course, this strategy can be seen as *reinforcing*, rather than repudiating, the basic logic of the trilemma, as the 'cost' of obtaining membership of less ambitious states is a watering down of the treaty's substantive ambitions.

The Montreal Protocol also illustrates a second strategy for ameliorating the trilemma, the possibility of 'side payments'. Treaty parties created a Multilateral Fund to offset developing states' cost of transition from ODS. Side payments can be made in issue areas that are closely related to issues addressed by a treaty, as in the Montreal Protocol context, or in unrelated issue areas. Side payments can shift the financial costs of treaty ambition to those better able to pay, and thereby help ameliorate the trilemma.

To summarize, those seeking to construct international environmental regimes invariably confront trade-offs between levels of ambition, number of participants, and rates of compliance. Appreciating the interactions and trade-offs among these three factors can produce a more robust and theoretically informed account of the institutional design of international environmental governance structures than that found in scholarship to date.

[29] Bodansky, *The Art and Craft of International Environmental Law* (n 22) 95.

C. New Technologies, New Governance, New Technologies of Governance

New technologies can enhance or undermine existing governance structures—and make possible new modes of governance. In the paragraphs that follow, I briefly discuss how technological developments can both assist the monitoring and enforcement of existing international legal norms and create new incentives for environmentally sustainable behaviour, and describe how new technologies can themselves create new technologies of governance.

New technologies, such as big data, can assist with more traditional monitoring and enforcement issues. State of the art technology permits officials to use vessel tracking data and machine learning to better identify vessels engaged in illegal, unreported, and unregulated (IUU) fishing. For example, Global Fishing Watch, an independent non-profit organization, hosts an online map that tracks global movements of commercial fishing vessels that is freely available to governments and individuals. The map can enable customs and law enforcement officials to accurately identify, track, and search vessels suspected of IUU activity.[30]

Cutting-edge technologies can be used to enhance other environmental regimes as well. For example, the Earth Bank of Codes is an effort to collect the genetic sequence of the natural world, register these on a public blockchain, and thereby make this information publicly accessible to scientists and innovators. The goal is to promote creation of new bioproducts, while at the same time reduce the level of bio-piracy and ensure the fair and equitable sharing of ensuing commercial benefits, all in furtherance of the provisions of the 2010 Nagoya Protocol to the 1992 Biodiversity Convention.[31]

New technologies can also make possible and incentivize new types of sustainable development. New types of financial technology, such as virtual currencies and mobile payment platforms, permit firms in developing states to offer home solar systems to off-grid, low-income customers, who make small daily payments using mobile money.[32] The system promises to provide renewable solar power to millions of customers who otherwise would use kerosene, or for whom power was historically not affordable. The firm M-KOPA already provides clean energy to three million people in East Africa.[33] Other firms seek to extend this model to other utilities like water and gas in developing states around the globe. The success of these initiatives will turn, in part, on national and regional regulation of the energy, telecom, and financial sectors, and on regional regulatory efforts to protect the integrity of systems and digital identities across borders.

Finally, big data, machine learning, artificial intelligence, and related technologies can facilitate the development of *new technologies of governance*. For example, Singapore and

[30] See <https://globalfishingwatch.org> accessed 14 October 2019.

[31] <https://www.earthbankofcodes.org> accessed 14 October 2019.

[32] UNEP, *Fintech and Sustainable Development: Assessing the Implications* (2016).

[33] <http://www.m-kopa.com/> accessed 14 October 2019.

other cities use real time data to 'govern' ground transportation. By using anonymized data from commuter fare cards, computers can identify patterns of traffic congestion and automatically re-route buses. Similarly, big data and machine learning can be used to collect comprehensive, aggregate, real-time traffic data to automatically adjust everything from the timing of traffic lights to road pricing systems to optimize traffic flows and reduce energy use. Policy-makers are already starting to identify how emerging smart technologies can likewise be used for governance functions in areas such as climate change, biodiversity and conservation, oceans, water security, clean air, disaster management, and other policy domains.[34]

V. CONCLUSION

Despite the volume and sophistication of writings on environmental governance, one should not view any of the arguments as presenting an algorithm capable of determining with precision the appropriate structure of environmental governance in any particular instance. Moreover, there is little reason to believe that structures that are effective at one time will be so at all times. New production and consumption patterns generate unexpected problems; novel technologies render one or another regulatory approach more effective; and governance structures that successfully addressed past problems may not be well-suited to new economic and social realities. International environmental governance has long been characterized by a wide variety of approaches, and will always be in a state of flux.

Nonetheless, scholarship addressing environmental governance can provide increasingly sophisticated analyses of the range of theoretical and practical questions raised when considering whether a specific governance structure is likely to be effective in particular contexts. More importantly, debates over governance properly focus our attention on the central issues underlying environmental law and policy, namely: who decides? Choices among alternative governance structures will often determine which environmental policies are pursued. Thus, decisions about governance structures can mark the difference between environmental improvement or harm and between success and failure in managing ecosystems and natural resources.

BIBLIOGRAPHY

Scott Barrett, *Environment and Statecraft: The Strategy of Environmental Decision-Making* (OUP 2003)

Daniel Bodansky, *The Art and Craft of International Environmental Law* (Harvard University Press 2010)

[34] UNEP (n 32).

Jeffrey Dunoff, 'Mapping the Hidden World of International Regulatory Cooperation' *Law & Contemporary Problems*, 78/4 (2015): 267

Liesbet Hooghe and Gary Marks, *Multi-Level Governance and European Integration* (Rowman & Littlefield 2001)

Neil Komesar, *Imperfect Alternatives: Choosing Institutions in Law, Economics, and Public Policy* (University of Chicago Press 1994)

Margaret Young, *Trading Fish, Saving Fish: The Interaction between Regimes in International Law* (Cambridge University Press 2011)

CHAPTER 5

FRAGMENTATION

MARGARET A YOUNG

I. INTRODUCTION—INTERNATIONAL ENVIRONMENTAL LAW OR INTERNATIONAL LAW

THIS chapter considers fragmentation within the field of 'international environmental law'—the diversification of specific treaties and institutions to deal with different ecological issues such as the protection of the atmosphere, the conservation of biological diversity, the regulation of hazardous substances, and so on—which this handbook helps us understand and navigate. Multilateral environment agreements (MEAs) covering specific issues and sectors now number in the hundreds, and at times their aims and methods may be in opposition, while gaps remain especially in implementation.[1] Initiatives to bring coherence to the field, such as a proposed 'Global Pact for the Environment', demand analysis. But it would be remiss not to also consider the fragmentation and diversification of international law *as a whole*.[2] There is long-standing scholarly engagement with the fragmentation of international law into largely self-contained 'regimes' such as trade, investment, the law of the sea, and human rights. Such regimes are of fundamental importance to the governance of environmental matters. Thus, relationships of cooperation or conflict within the system of public international law are vital to examine.

[1] See United Nations General Assembly (UNGA), 'Gaps in international environmental law and environment-related instruments: towards a global pact for the environment—Report of the Secretary-General' (30 November 2018) UN Doc A/73/419, 6–26.

[2] 'Fragmentation of International Law: Difficulties Arising from the Diversification and Expansion of International Law—Report of the Study Group of the International Law Commission finalized by Martti Koskenniemi' (13 April 2006) UN Doc A/CN.4./L.682 and Corr.1.

This chapter begins with a discussion of the functional conception of law-making within 'regimes', which has origins in both international relations and international law.[3] I argue that the governance of environmental matters does not always (or even most often) happen in the context of environmental treaties (such as the 1992 Convention on Biological Diversity (CBD)) and environmental institutions (such as the United Nations Environment Programme (UNEP)), but also within norms and institutions that are constituted to pursue other functions, such as trade liberalization or investment protection. Next, the chapter considers the relationships of conflict or interpretation that exist between relevant norms and institutions. It is important to include international adjudication in this analysis. The laws and principles that are currently grouped as 'international environmental law' suffer from weak enforcement vis-à-vis other norms within public international law. Though the International Court of Justice (ICJ) and the International Tribunal for the Law of the Sea (ITLOS) are increasingly dealing with inter-state environmental disputes, for example, these bodies do not have the busy dockets or enforcement powers that are enjoyed by trade panels, investment arbitrators, and other forums. The proliferation of international courts and tribunals thus has special salience for environmental matters. The final part of this chapter considers coordinating initiatives including the proposal for a Global Pact for the Environment.

II. REGIMES AND NON-REGIMES

While I endorse 'international environmental law' as apt for a book title, and as a description of the work of many professional specializations, I simultaneously hesitate at what might be missed when this short-hand term is used. In disputes relating to the environment, international jurisprudence refers to 'obligations of States to respect and protect the natural environment',[4] or 'existing international law relating to the protection and safeguarding of the environment'.[5] To point to the differences in these unwieldy descriptors is not to engage in lawyerly affectation. Rather, it serves to emphasize that while the grouping of a particular set of laws, institutions, and vocabularies provides important clarity and a sense of purpose, it also risks obscuring the general backdrop of public international law. The essential underpinning foundations such as *pacta sunt servanda*, and the customary international law that is not housed within a programme of an international organization but which nonetheless applies universally, are all part of public international law and, more often than not, relate to the

[3] See further Margaret Young, 'Introduction: The Productive Friction between Regimes' in Margaret Young (ed), *Regime Interaction in International Law: Facing Fragmentation* (CUP 2012) 1.

[4] *Request for an Examination of the Situation in Accordance with Paragraph 63 of the Court's Judgement of 20 December 1974 in the Nuclear Tests (New Zealand/France) Case* (Order) [1995] ICJ Rep 288 [64].

[5] *Legality of the Threat or Use of Nuclear Weapons* (Advisory Opinion) [1996] ICJ Rep 226 [33] (Legality of Nuclear Weapons).

environment.[6] The overarching norms were mostly developed with little regard to ecological limits,[7] and international lawyers must be ready to interrogate key concepts of sovereignty, development, and growth regardless of whether problems are to be solved within international environmental law or within a broader or different conception of inter-state relations. The same need for contextualization and caveats arises for international 'regimes'. The following sections discuss regimes, the organizational mandates of intergovernmental organizations, and the coexistence of multilateral, regional, and bilateral approaches to the environment.

A. Issue-Areas and the Boundaries between Them

Regimes are 'sets of norms, decision-making procedures and organizations coalescing around functional issue-areas and dominated by particular modes of behaviour, assumptions and biases'.[8] MEAs covering issues such as biodiversity and climate change fit well within a regime descriptor, given they are underpinned by treaties and institutions.[9] Soft law is more difficult to categorize, including the dominant instrument on reconciliations between the environment and development.[10] Other issue-areas lead to conceptions of 'non-regimes', as might be said to apply to global tropical forest protection, which notoriously failed to garner enough support for an international forest treaty.[11] Indeed, the issue of state-support is an important aspect of fragmentation: separate legal norms and institutions are often instigated by non-identical groupings of states, so that there is overlapping but not identical membership.[12] Specific obligations of states might conflict, or at least there will be uncertainty and confusion about expected roles and practices. Other times, the relevant intergovernmental organizations may

[6] See Chapter 23, 'Customary International Law and the Environment', in this volume.

[7] Usha Natarajan and Kishan Khoday, 'Locating Nature: Making and Unmaking International Law' *Leiden Journal of International Law*, 27/3 (2014): 573, 592.

[8] Young (ed), *Regime Interaction* (n 3) 11.

[9] Oran Young, 'The Politics of International Regime Formation: Managing Natural Resources and the Environment' *International Organization*, 43/3 (1989): 349; see Chapter 24, 'Multilateral Environmental Treaty Making', in this volume. In contrast to MEAs, efforts to restore damaged ecosystems are declared in soft law instruments: see eg Anastasia Telesetsky, An Cliquet, and Afshin Akhtar-Khavari, *Ecological Restoration in International Environmental Law* (Routledge 2017).

[10] *Report of the United Nations Conference on Environment and Development* (UN 1993) vol I, annex I; see Jorge Viñuales (ed), *The Rio Declaration on Environment and Development: A Commentary* (OUP 2015).

[11] See eg Radoslav Dimitrov *et al*, 'International Nonregimes: A Research Agenda' *International Studies Review*, 9/2 (2007): 230.

[12] See eg Toshiyuki Kono and Steven Van Uytsel, 'Intangible Cultural Heritage and the Convention on the Diversity of Cultural Expressions' in Toshiyuki Kono and Steven Van Uytsel (eds), *The UNESCO Convention on the Diversity of Cultural Expressions: A Tale of Fragmentation of International Law* (Intersentia 2012) 143.

have completely separate membership, as, for example, with rival multilateral and regional approaches to whaling.[13]

Examples of MEAs overlapping on environmental issues abound.[14] The objectives of the 1992 UN Framework Convention on Climate Change (UNFCCC) may be at odds with biodiversity conservation, though the protection of the environment is generally in the sights of the negotiators within relevant regimes.[15] In addition, regimes that were conceived with little regard to the environment have an important influence in environmental governance; these have been described as 'environment-related instruments' by the UN Secretary-General.[16] Environmental issues traverse international environmental law and environment-related instruments, with varying levels of attention and success at sustainability: whether fish can be both saved and traded occupies more than one regime;[17] climate change mitigation efforts also seek to safeguard human rights;[18] the governance of emissions from international aviation and maritime transport is still to meaningfully respond to the evidence of their environmental impact.[19]

The issue of framing and problem definition is not just about the interests of states. It also relates to particular professional sensibilities, biases, and modes of expertise. The example of the international transport of hazardous chemicals has been invoked by Martti Koskenniemi as an issue that could 'be conceptualised at least through half a dozen vocabularies accompanied by the same number of forms of expertise and types of preference: law of trade, law of transport, law of the environment, law of the sea, "chemical law", and the law of human rights'.[20] Energy production and consumption—a fundamental issue for the environment given climate change—has occupied the attention of regimes relating to climate change, trade, investment, and human rights. The experts

[13] See International Whaling Commission versus the North Atlantic Marine Mammal Commission (NAMMCO): Benedict Singleton, 'Clumsiness and Elegance in Environmental Management: Applying Cultural Theory to the History of Whaling' *Environmental Politics*, 25/3 (2016): 414, 424.

[14] Rüdiger Wolfrum and Nele Matz, *Conflicts in International Environmental Law* (Springer-Verlag 2003); Donald Anton, '"Treaty Congestion" in Contemporary International Environmental Law' in Shawkat Alam *et al* (eds), *Routledge Handbook of International Environmental Law* (Routledge 2013) 651.

[15] Harro van Asselt, *The Fragmentation of Global Climate Governance: Consequences and Management of Regime Interactions* (Edward Elgar 2012).

[16] UNGA, 'Gaps in international environmental law' (n 1) para 7 ('those international legal instruments that do not fall exclusively within the field of the environment or have as their primary objective the protection of the environment').

[17] Margaret Young, *Trading Fish, Saving Fish: The Interaction between Regimes in International Law* (CUP 2011).

[18] Stephen Humphreys, 'Introduction: Human Rights and Climate Change' in Stephen Humphreys (ed), *Human Rights and Climate Change* (CUP 2010).

[19] Beatriz Martinez Romera, *Regime Interaction and Climate Change: The Case of International Aviation and Maritime Transport* (Routledge 2018); Sophia Kopela, 'Climate Change, Regime Interaction, and the Principle of Common but Differentiated Responsibility: The Experience of the International Maritime Organization' *Yearbook of International Environmental Law*, 24/1 (2013): 70.

[20] Martti Koskenniemi, 'The Politics of International Law—20 Years Later' *European Journal of International Law*, 20/1 (2009): 7.

and actors within these regimes tend to view (and sometimes count) the production and consumption of oil, gas, and coal differently.[21] A socio-legal perspective attuned to legal pluralism, and especially the way in which 'global law' develops from globalization processes independently of the laws of the nation-states, highlights that regimes are sometimes disassociated from traditional public international law.[22] Regimes may involve private ordering operating transnationally, soft-law and informal rules,[23] and an incorporation of perspectives from groups that are marginalized within states such as Indigenous peoples.[24]

This serves to remind us that international regimes have distinctive ways of conceiving environmental problems and of finding solutions to them, often tied to a political, historical, and even temporal[25] context that demands scholarly engagement. Practical challenges arise for parties to treaties when issue-areas that relate to the environment are governed by more than one regime, especially when new scientific developments or major environmental crises expose deficiencies in a dominant regime. Such issues are becoming increasingly urgent given accelerating human pressures and unprecedented impacts:[26] as Tim Stephens shows, 'most environmental regimes are not (yet) remotely up to the task of maintaining Earth's main biogeophysical systems'.[27]

B. Organizational Mandates and the Boundaries between Them

Integral to the diverse approaches to environmental issues are international intergovernmental organizations and other institutions. Many of these are specifically mandated to address environmental issues, such as UNEP, the UN General Assembly, and a range

[21] See Margaret Young, 'Energy Transitions and Trade Law: Lessons from the Reform of Fisheries Subsidies' *International Environmental Agreements: Politics Law and Economics*, 17/3 (2017): 371.

[22] Gunther Teubner, '"Global Bukowina": Legal Pluralism in the World Society' in Gunther Teubner (ed), *Global Law Without a State* (Dartmouth 1996) 3; Andreas Fischer-Lescano and Gunther Teubner, 'Regime-Collisions: The Vain Search for Legal Unity in the Fragmentation of Global Law' *Michigan Journal of International Law*, 25/4 (2004): 999.

[23] See Chapter 26, 'Private and Quasi-Private Standards', in this volume. See generally Part IV, 'Normative Development', in this volume.

[24] As recognized within legal pluralism, Indigenous peoples may have legal and constitutionalist structures with varying degrees of recognition by the state: see Maureen Tehan *et al*, *The Impact of Climate Change Mitigation on Indigenous and Forest Communities: International, National and Local Law Perspectives on REDD+* (CUP 2017).

[25] Benjamin Richardson, *Time and Environmental Law: Telling Nature's Time* (CUP 2017).

[26] See *Global Environment Outlook—GEO-6: Healthy Planet, Healthy People* (UNEP 2019).

[27] Tim Stephens, 'Reimagining International Environmental Law in the Anthropocene' in Louis Kotzé (ed), *Environmental Law and Governance for the Anthropocene* (Hart Publishing 2017) 31.

of treaty-specific secretariats.[28] Yet the governance of environmental matters is also covered by 'non-environmental' frameworks and international regimes, meaning that secretariats within bodies such as the World Trade Organization (WTO) have significant roles.

There are two views on the coexistence of intergovernmental organizations in the context of fragmentation. On the first view, the principle of specialty of intergovernmental organizations leads to an a priori determination of competence for an international organization to address a particular policy issue.[29] This view curtails the work of an intergovernmental organization on environmental problems unless expressly mandated within constitutive documents. The second view exposes the principle of specialty as failing to recognize that 'complex problems have ramifications in many specialized directions'.[30] Instead of assuming a 'right' solution to environmental issues will be found when the correct decision-makers are in charge, this view is open to dynamic institutional engagement. Applying the latter view allows for a more flexible interpretation of the implied powers of intergovernmental organizations, not only in addressing environmental issues but in formally or informally cooperating with one another.[31]

The political and historical context is important to bear in mind when addressing implied or express mandates. It is also important for an evaluation of institutional effectiveness in international environmental law. For example, UNEP may seem to be on the periphery rather than in the centre of the UN system, both geographically (it is housed in Nairobi, Kenya) and status-wise (it is a programme rather than a specialized agency). There were important political and strategic reasons that led to the choice of venue for UNEP, including the laudable goal of better integration of developing countries into the UN system, but marginalization remains.[32] Potential for side-lining of international environmental law also occurs because of the uncertainty about the legal status of decisions of conferences of the parties to MEAs, which are not necessarily binding.[33] Such institutional issues are important when evaluating reform proposals, such as the Global Pact, discussed below in Section IV.

[28] See Chapter 36, 'International Institutions', in this volume.

[29] On this view, for example, the World Health Organization was not mandated to request an advisory opinion on nuclear weapons from the ICJ, given the mandate of the Security Council. See Legality of Nuclear Weapons case (n 5) [25].

[30] Legality of Nuclear Weapons case (n 5) (Dissenting Opinion of Judge Weeramantry) 151.

[31] Margaret Young, 'Protecting Endangered Marine Species: Collaboration between the Food and Agriculture Organization and the CITES Regime' *Melbourne Journal of International Law*, 11/2 (2010): 441.

[32] Maria Ivanova, 'UNEP in Global Environmental Governance: Design, Leadership, Location' *Global Environmental Politics*, 10/1 (2010): 30.

[33] See further n 53 and accompanying text.

C. Multilateralism, Regionalism, Bilateralism, and Unilateralism

Environmental issues are 'polycentric' in nature.[34] States cooperate on environmental issues through bilateral arrangements, regional approaches, and at the multilateral level.[35] Some regional groupings of states seek a special leadership role on environmental issues; the European Union (EU) is often seen as experimenting with policies that, if not universalized on merit, may nevertheless stimulate action elsewhere.[36] Even unilateral declarations may create obligations in international law, which has increasing relevance for international environmental law with the design of approaches such as the nationally determined contributions under the Paris Agreement.[37] Further complicating this picture is the emergence of sub-national actors, including provinces and cities, on the global stage.[38]

Analyzing the design and implementation of the resulting legal measures (and determining which ones will trump) requires an understanding of historical alliances, scale, geography, and other factors; lawyers need to be familiar with comparative methodologies and multidisciplinary approaches. Polycentricity presents particular challenges for international courts,[39] but also requires broader institutional engagement at the level of law-making and implementation.

III. FRAGMENTATION AND REGIME INTERACTION

The fragmentation of international law can promote diversity in approaches, experimentation and flexibility, but also uncertainty, confusion, and the entrenchment of power imbalances. The risks of the latter are particularly pronounced in contexts that relate to environmental degradation.[40] This section discusses the efforts of international lawyers

34 See Chapter 4, 'Multilevel and Polycentric Governance', in this volume.

35 See Chapter 37, 'Regional Organizations—The European Union', in this volume.

36 Joanne Scott and Lavanya Rajamani, 'EU Climate Change Unilateralism' *European Journal of International Law*, 23/2 (2012): 469.

37 Benoît Mayer, 'International Law Obligations Arising in relation to Nationally Determined Contributions' *Transnational Environmental Law* 7/2 (2018): 251; see also *Nuclear Tests (Australia/France)* (Judgement) [1974] ICJ Rep 253 [43].

38 Helmut Aust, 'The Shifting Role of Cities in the Global Climate Change Regime: From Paris to Pittsburgh and Back?' *Review of European, Comparative & International Environmental Law*, 28/1 (2019): 57.

39 See generally Tim Stephens, *International Courts and Environmental Protection* (CUP 2009) 95.

40 See UNGA, 'Gaps in international environmental law' (n 1) para 109.

to resolve relationships of conflict, especially through the work of the International Law Commission (ILC). The role of international adjudication is a major part of this discussion, especially given the lack of compulsory enforcement on environment matters vis-à-vis other regimes. The principal scholarly responses to fragmentation are constitutionalism and pluralism, and I place these responses in the context of environmental discourses.

A. Relationships of Conflict or Interpretation

Whether norms of public international law exist in a relationship of conflict or mutual supportiveness is a question with political dimensions. An intuition to interpret treaties so as to reduce the appearance of conflict usually modulates the weaker regime.[41] The tendency to downplay differences between international environmental law and human rights law has major consequences for conceptions of nature.[42] By contrast, states may have interests in creating treaty conflict.[43] This dynamic situation exposes fragmentation as an important rhetorical device,[44] but also a material consequence of differences in regime objectives, professional orientations, and structural biases.

The way in which the fragmentation of international law impacts the obligations of states can be understood pictorially with the following infographic (Figure 5.1), which was developed to help understand how UN climate mitigation strategies to 'reduce emissions from deforestation and forest degradation' (REDD+) impact indigenous and forest communities. The environmental context is not the focus of the present discussion; rather, Figure 5.1 demonstrates the way in which relevant treaties and instruments co-exist in relationships of conflict or interpretation.

The infographic shows how the countries receiving funds from the World Bank's Forest Carbon Partnership Facility (FCPF) or the UN programme (UNREDD) may also have participated in instruments such as the UN Declaration on the Rights of Indigenous Peoples (UNDRIP)[45] or ratified treaties such as the 1992 CBD, the 1973 Convention on the International Trade in Endangered Species of Wild Flora and Fauna (CITES), the 1989 International Labour Organization (ILO) Convention No 169, and the 2010 CBD Nagoya Protocol. These sources of law may overlap with the climate mitigation aims of REDD+, but they may sometimes operate in conflict: for example, the practice of

[41] Joost Pauwelyn, *Conflicts of Norms in Public International Law: How WTO Law Relates to Other Rules of International Law* (CUP 2003).

[42] Marie-Catherine Petersmann, 'Narcissus' Reflection in the Lake: Untold Narratives in Environmental Law beyond the Anthropocentric Frame' *Journal of Environmental Law*, 30/2 (2018): 235.

[43] Surabhi Ranganathan, *Strategically Created Treaty Conflicts and the Politics of International Law* (CUP 2014).

[44] Anne-Charlotte Martineau, 'The Rhetoric of Fragmentation: Fear and Faith in International Law' *Leiden Journal of International Law*, 22/1 (2009): 1.

[45] UNGA Res 61/295, 'United Nations Declaration on the Rights of Indigenous Peoples' (2 October 2007) UN Doc A/RES/61/295.

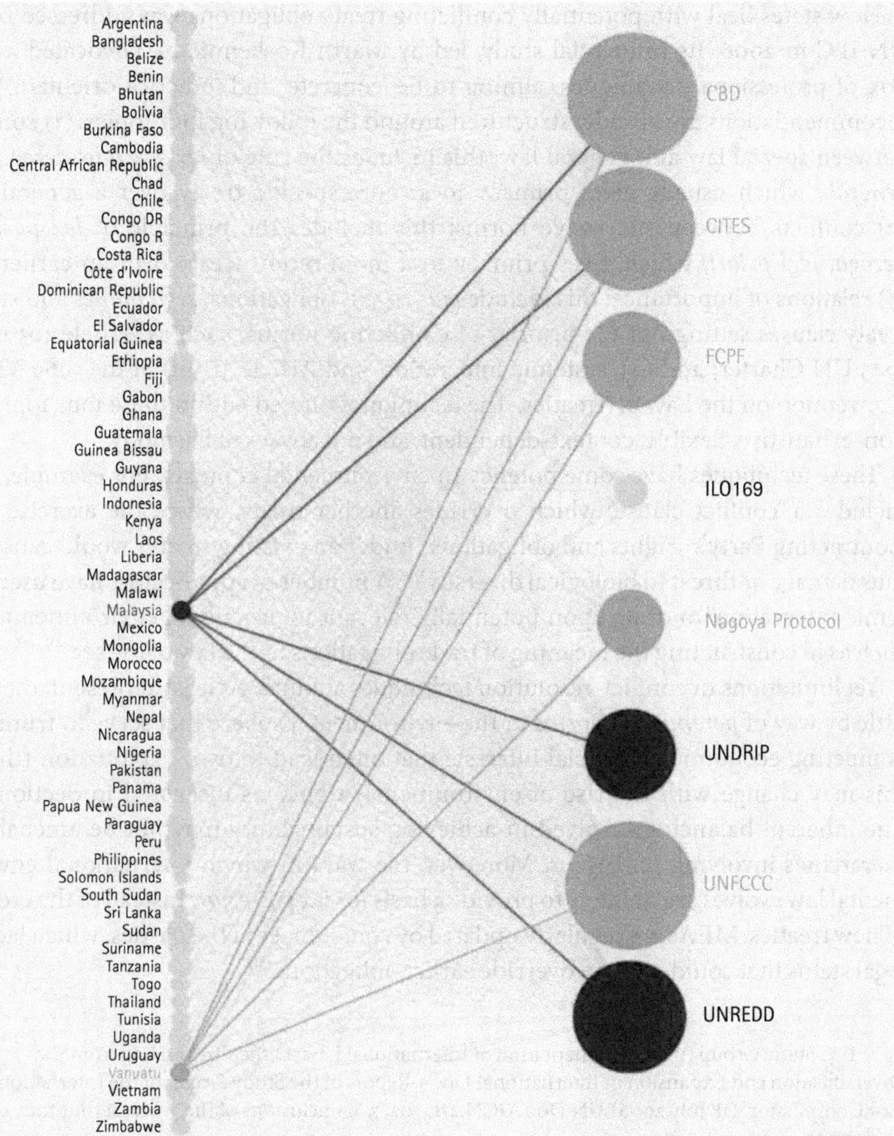

FIGURE 5.1 Infographic of international obligations of countries participating in forest carbon sequestration programs: Malaysia and Vanuatu

forest carbon sequestration may encourage fast-growing monocultures rather than the preservation of old-growth, biodiversity-enhancing forests, thus conflicting with the CBD. These relationships are highlighted by Figure 5.1's identification of Malaysia's and Vanuatu's[46] international obligations.

[46] First published in Tehan *et al* (n 24) 51.

How states deal with potentially conflicting treaty obligations was addressed by the UN ILC in 2006. Its influential study, led by Martti Koskenniemi, advocated a toolbox of professional techniques, aiming to be 'concrete' and 'practice-oriented'.[47] The recommendations are broadly structured around the following four topics: (1) conflicts between special law and general law: this includes the rule of *lex specialis derogat legi generali*, which usually gives primacy to a more specific treaty over a general one; (2) conflicts between successive norms: this includes the principle of *lex posterior derogat legi priori*, which gives primacy to a more recent treaty over an earlier one; (3) relations of importance: this includes *jus cogens* obligations, *erga omnes* and special treaty clauses setting out the priority of conflicting norms, such as Article 103 of the 1945 UN Charter; and (4) 'systemic integration' and Article 31.3(c) of the 1969 Vienna Convention on the Law of Treaties. The techniques offered within these four topics are non-exhaustive, flexible, context-dependent, and not always in harmony.

These techniques have some potency in environmental contexts. For example, CBD includes a 'conflict clause', which overrides another treaty 'where the exercise of [a Contracting Party's] rights and obligations [under an existing treaty] would cause serious damage or threat to biological diversity'.[48] A number of adjudicators have used 'systemic integration' to draw upon potentially relevant international environmental law, such as in constructing the meaning of trade obligations or the law of the sea.[49]

Yet limitations in conflict-resolution techniques abound. At least at present, there are little by way of *peremptory norms* in the environmental sphere that serve to trump the competing economic and social interests that often lead to over-exploitation (though this may change with the rise of environmental rights, as discussed in Section IV). The inherent balancing involved in achieving sustainability may not be amenable to hierarchies involving *jus cogens*. Moreover, the ways in which international environmental law evolves are unlikely to provide a basis for *lex posterior*. Instead of the creation of new treaties, MEAs are regularly updated by conferences of the parties, which lack the legal status that could serve to override earlier obligations.[50]

[47] ILC Study Group (n 2); 'Fragmentation of International Law: Difficulties arising from the Diversification and Expansion of International Law—Report of the Study Group of the International Law Commission' (18 July 2006) UN Doc A/CN.4/L.702, 7, 'Conclusions of the Work of the Study Group'.

[48] art 22.

[49] *United States—Import Prohibition of Certain Shrimp and Shrimp Products* (Appellate Body Report) [12 October 1998] WTO Doc WT/DS58/AB/R (Shrimp/Turtle case); *The MOX Plant (Ireland/United Kingdom)* (Provisional Measures, Order of 3 December 2001) [2001] ITLOS Rep 95; *Dispute Concerning Access to Information Under Article 9 of the OSPAR Convention (Ireland/United Kingdom)* (Final award of 2 July 2003) PCA Case no 2001-03, (2003) 42 ILM 1118; *MOX Plant Case (Ireland/United Kingdom)* (Order No 3 of 24 June 2003) PCA Case no 2002-01, (2003) 42 ILM 1187; see also Campbell McLachlan, 'The Principle of Systemic Integration and Article 31(3)(C) of the Vienna Convention' *International and Comparative Law Quarterly*, 54/2 (2005): 279; Nikolaos Lavranos, 'The OSPAR Convention, the Aarhus Convention and EC Law: Normative and Institutional Fragmentation on the Right of Access to Environmental Information' in Tomer Broude and Yuval Shany (eds), *Multi-Sourced Equivalent Norms in International Law* (Hart Publishing 2011) 143.

[50] See Margaret Young, 'Climate Change Law and Regime Interaction' *Carbon & Climate Law Review*, 5/2 (2011): 147.

Alternative approaches that emphasize institutional cooperation and coordination can be grouped as 'regime interaction'.[51] Examples of inter-organizational cooperation abound in the environmental context.[52] Indeed, the dominant approach in the forest carbon sequestration scenarios depicted in Figure 5.1 has been to address fragmentation through institutional coordinating and conflict-avoidance strategies. For example, states have sought to mediate REDD+'s relationship with other regimes through the setting of 'safeguards' at UNFCCC conferences of the parties which, though lacking legal status, are tied to the dispersal of REDD+ funds.[53] Rather than agreeing to an ex ante allocation of priorities, states and other actors seek to respond in a dynamic and experimental way to pluralism.

Regime interaction involves a range of actors besides states and intergovernmental organizations. Models of pluralist global governance depend upon an appropriate balance of 'top-down' and 'bottom-up'—that is, ensuring that a localized, contextualized implementation of rules is combined with peer-review and oversight.[54] Finding the balance in different environmental contexts, where expertise in green or brown environmental issues demands varying levels of historic engagement, scientific and technical prowess, and local experience, is a time-consuming and sensitive undertaking. An important element is the use of penalty defaults and enforcement mechanisms, which may or may not include international adjudication. While not fatal to effective governance,[55] it is undeniable that the differences in availability of compulsory dispute settlement in international law affect the environment in significant ways, as I next discuss.

B. The Role of International Adjudication

The proliferation of international court and tribunals, though useful in providing choice and diversity to states, can reduce coherence and convergence in international law,[56]

[51] See generally Young (ed), *Regime Interaction* (n 3).

[52] See eg reference to coordination among the 1989 Basel Convention on the Control of Transboundary Movements of Hazardous Wastes and Their Disposal, the 1998 Rotterdam Convention on the Prior Informed Consent Procedure for Certain Hazardous Chemicals and Pesticides in International Trade, and the 2001 Stockholm Convention on Persistent Organic Pollutants, in UNGA, 'Gaps in international environmental law' (n 1) para 70.

[53] Annalisa Savaresi, 'The Role of REDD in the Harmonisation of Overlapping International Obligations' in Erkki Hollo, Kati Kulovesi, and Michael Mehling (eds), *Climate Change and the Law* (Springer 2013) 391; Tehan *et al* (n 24) 329–345.

[54] See eg Gráinne de Búrca, Robert Keohane, and Charles Sabel, 'New Modes of Pluralist Global Governance' *New York University Journal of International Law and Policy*, 45/3 (2013): 723. See also Chapter 4, 'Multilevel and Polycentric Governance', in this volume.

[55] See especially alternative conceptions of compliance in Abram Chayes and Antonia Handler Chayes, *The New Sovereignty: Compliance with International Regulatory Agreements* (Harvard University Press 1995).

[56] Mads Adenas and Eirik Bjorge (eds), *A Farewell to Fragmentation: Reassertion and Convergence in International Law* (CUP 2015).

in particular in the environmental context. Where the 'environment' is conceived proactively, through MEAs and other protective principles, there is a lack of enforcement because there is no compulsory adjudication of disputes. But for international law that conceives of the 'environment' as an exploitable part of the permanent sovereignty of states, protective principles only arise in exception clauses that need to be invoked by defendant states in litigation to which they must compulsorily submit. So while the growth of regimes may promote adaptability and enforceability for states, a more fine-grained assessment recognizes that the goals and substance of those regimes may in fact run counter to environmental protection.

The imbalance of international law in jurisdictional terms—with most countries accepting compulsory dispute settlement by the WTO but not the ICJ[57]—is most prominent when trade panels and investment arbitrators adjudicate on important inter-state environmental disputes. These have included fisheries, genetically modified foods, renewable energy, atmospheric pollution, hazardous waste disposal, and animal welfare.[58] There is a risk that key principles of international environmental law are missed or misapplied by adjudicatory bodies attuned to other issues or rationalities.[59] It is important to consider whether this situation is 'by design'. It may be an unfortunate outcome of an otherwise benign set of processes whose tunnel vision rendered invisible environment concerns even as it achieved great success in focusing on economic growth. An alternative view recognizes that there are political, ethical, and social decisions that have been constantly made and remade in the sovereign concession to third party dispute settlement. Calls for a World Environment Organization have gone unheeded.[60]

That is not to say that there is an absence of international adjudication to defend the environment. The ICJ has built an important environmental jurisprudence,[61]

[57] Benedict Kingsbury, 'International Courts: Uneven Judicialisation in Global Order' in James Crawford and Martti Koskenniemi (eds), *The Cambridge Companion to International Law* (CUP 2012) 203.

[58] Shrimp/Turtle case (n 49); *Metalclad Corporation v The United Mexican States*, International Centre for Settlement of Investment Disputes Case No ARB(AF)/97/1, (2001) 40 ILM 36; *European Communities—Measures Affecting the Approval and Marketing of Biotech Products* (Panel Report) [29 September 2006] WTO Docs WT/DS291/R, WT/DS292/R, WT/DS293/R; *Brazil—Measures Affecting Imports of Retreaded Tyres* (Appellate Body Report) [3 December 2007] WTO Doc WT/DS332/AB/R; *European Communities—Measures Prohibiting the Importation and Marketing of Seal Products* (Appellate Body Report) [22 May 2014] WTO Doc WT/DS400/AB/R; *Canada—Measures Relating to the Feed-In Tariff Program* (Appellate Body Report) [6 May 2013] WTO Doc WT/DS426/AB/R; *India—Certain Measures Relating to Solar Cells and Solar Modules* (Appellate Body Report) [16 September 2016] WTO Doc WT/DS456/AB/R.

[59] Stephens, *International Courts* (n 39); Oren Perez, *Ecological Sensitivity and Global Legal Pluralism: Rethinking the Trade and Environment Conflict* (Hart Publishing 2004).

[60] UNGA, 'Gaps in international environmental law' (n 1) para 6.

[61] See eg *The Gabčíkovo-Nagymaros Project (Hungary/Slovakia)* (Judgement) [1997] ICJ Rep 7; *Pulp Mills on the River Uruguay (Argentina/Uruguay)* (Judgement) [2010] ICJ Rep 14; *Whaling in the Antarctic (Australia/ Japan, New Zealand intervening)* (Judgement) [2014] ICJ Rep 226 (Whaling in Antarctic case); *Certain Activities Carried Out by Nicaragua in the Border Area (Costa Rica/Nicaragua)* (Judgement of 2 February 2018 on Compensation owed by Nicaragua to Costa Rica) ICJ; see also, Chapter 27, 'Judicial Development', in this volume. For a comparison of ICJ, ITLOS, and WTO jurisprudence in cases

although this occurs in an ad hoc way, and includes the risk that states will withdraw their standing acceptance of the Court's jurisdiction if they disagree with the outcome.[62] ITLOS and other tribunals, by contrast, enjoy compulsory jurisdiction pursuant to the 1982 Law of the Sea Convention.[63] The contribution of these bodies to the development of environmental principles has grown in recent times,[64] including through the granting of provisional measures and advisory opinions,[65] and they may well be the forum of a much-anticipated, inter-state adjudication on climate change.[66]

C. Constitutionalism and Pluralism

Academic engagement with the fragmentation of international law has led to two main approaches: a constitutionalist conception, that seeks to identify unifying principles and instruments within the world order, and legal pluralism, that doubts that conflicting rationalities can ever cohere.[67] The difference between these two approaches can be overstated; indeed, the political contestations resulting from regime collisions may even found a kind of procedural constitutionalism.[68]

Within environmental discourses, the dominance of either approach is often a strategic choice. In a constitutionalist vein, dormant narratives provide a teleology for public international law. Like approaches that seek to 'mainstream' human rights,[69] threats to

involving environmental commons, see Margaret Young, 'International Adjudication and the Commons' *University of Hawaii Law Review*, 41/2 (2019): 353.

[62] See eg the US's withdrawal of the optional clause after *Military and Paramilitary Activities in and against Nicaragua (Nicaragua/US)* (Judgement) [1986] ICJ Rep 14; see also Japan's modification of its acceptance of the optional clause after the Whaling in Antarctic case (n 61): <https://www.icj-cij.org/en/declarations/jp>.

[63] UNCLOS, part XV.

[64] Most recently, *The South China Sea Arbitration (Philippines/China)* (Final award of 12 July 2016) PCA Case no 2013-19.

[65] *Southern Bluefin Tuna Cases (New Zealand/Japan; Australia/Japan)* (Provisional Measures, Order of 27 August 1999) [1999] ITLOS Rep 280; *Responsibilities and obligations of States sponsoring persons and entities with respect to activities in the Area* (Advisory opinion) [2011] ITLOS Rep 10; *Request for an advisory opinion submitted by the Sub-Regional Fisheries Commission (SRFC)* (Advisory opinion) [2015] ITLOS Rep 4.

[66] Philippe Sands, 'Climate Change and the Rule of Law: Adjudicating the Future in International Law' *Journal of Environmental Law*, 28/1 (2016): 19; Benoît Mayer, 'Climate Change Reparations and the Law and Practice of State Responsibility' *Asian Journal of International Law*, 7/1 (2017): 185.

[67] Martti Koskenniemi, 'The Fate of Public International Law: Between Technique and Politics' *Modern Law Review*, 70/1 (2007): 1; see also the literature discussed in Margaret Young, 'Fragmentation' (*Oxford Bibliographies*, 12 May 2017) <http://www.oxfordbibliographies.com/abstract/document/obo-9780199796953/obo-9780199796953-0113.xml> accessed 7 February 2019.

[68] Anne Peters, 'The Refinement of International Law: From Fragmentation to Regime Interaction and Politicization' *International Journal of Constitutional Law*, 15/3 (2017): 671.

[69] Ibid, 689.

the environment begin to shape the interpretation and core normative structures of public international law. For example, the recognition of a new geological epoch of the Anthropocene, which emphasizes the irreversible and geologically-detectable human destruction of planetary systems, has led to calls for a new framing of global constitutionalism and the 'environmental' rule of law.[70] Post-humanist conceptions of environmental law incorporate the needs of nonhumans as well as humans with radical consequences for methodologies and subjects.[71] Rights for nature have been established in domestic legal systems, including in domestic constitutions,[72] and are debated in international forums.[73] Creative rewriting of the judgements of courts and tribunals in the 'Wild Law Judgement Project' offer insightful accounts of how 'the earth' is missed in jurisprudence.[74] More broadly, earth-centred governance repositions planetary needs within international governance frameworks.[75]

There is much to be gained by devising an overriding environmentally-oriented goal for international law. However, as the literature on fragmentation demonstrates, the necessary conditions for constitutionalism may be absent in an unequal and unjust world. There are important reasons for the absence of a 'redemptive narrative' in public international law.[76] Indeed, the universalizing narratives of an earth-systems governance may elide the human needs of justice and fairness, especially for individuals in the global south.[77] The UNFCCC regime demonstrates the ongoing struggle to incorporate ethical and redistributive accounts for individuals and countries that did little to create global warming but that are most vulnerable to its effects, when the overriding impetus is an instrumentalist one.[78] The following section considers these issues in the context of current initiatives to better account for, and coordinate, ecological needs within public international law.

70 Louis Kotzé, 'Global Environmental Constitutionalism in the Anthropocene' in Kotzé (n 27) 189.

71 Andreas Philippopoulos-Mihalopoulos, 'Critical Environmental Law as Method in the Anthropocene' in Andreas Philippopoulos-Mihalopoulos and Victoria Brooks, *Research Methods in Environmental Law: A Handbook* (Edward Elgar 2017) 131.

72 See eg David Boyd, *The Rights of Nature: A Legal Revolution that Could Save the World* (ECW Press 2017).

73 John Knox, 'Report on the Issue of Human Rights Obligations Relating to the Enjoyment of a Safe, Clean, Healthy and Sustainable Environment' (2018) UN Doc A/HRC/37/59.

74 Nicole Rogers and Michelle Maloney (eds), *Law as if Earth Really Mattered* (Routledge 2017).

75 See also Chapter 14, 'Earth Jurisprudence', in this volume.

76 On the absence of a 'redemptive narrative', see Jeffrey Dunoff, 'A New Approach to Regime Interaction' in Young (ed), *Regime Interaction* (n 3) 136.

77 See eg Benoît Mayer, 'Climate Change and International Law in the Grim Days' *European Journal of International Law*, 24/3 (2013): 947.

78 Ibid. For other examples, see Shawkat Alam *et al* (eds), *International Environmental Law and the Global South* (CUP 2015); Cait Storr, 'Island and the South: Framing the Relationship between International Law and Environmental Crisis' *European Journal of International Law*, 27/2 (2016): 519.

IV. GLOBAL PACT FOR THE ENVIRONMENT

The Global Pact for the Environment is a proposed new treaty that, amongst other things, seeks to address the gaps within international environmental law.[79] A preliminary text was initiated by the France-based '*club des jurists*' and agreed by an international network of judges, lawyers, and academics in 2017.[80] The IGEP text is aimed at 'the growing threats to the environment and the need to act in an ambitious and concerted manner ... to better ensure its protection'.[81] An accompanying White Paper outlines the Pact's antecedents, which include the non-binding Rio Declaration on Environment and Development.[82] The impetus of the Global Pact was to create a binding treaty. It seeks to provide a framework that follows the existing international human rights covenants—on civil and political rights and on economic, social, and cultural rights—to promote a 'third generation' of fundamental rights.[83]

While developments in 2018 seemed to support prospects for a binding Global Pact,[84] in 2019 a working group at the UN preferred to seek a political declaration.[85] These discussions are occurring amidst alternative reform efforts before the UNGA that could include the development of an additional protocol to an existing treaty such as the International Covenant on Economic, Social, and Cultural Rights, a new international covenant on environmental rights, or a resolution on the right to a healthy environment.[86]

[79] See Le Club des Juristes: International Group of Experts for the Pact, 'Draft Global Pact for the Environment by the IGEP' (La Sorbonne, 24 June 2017) <https://globalpactenvironment.org/document/draft-global-pact-for-the-environment-by-the-igep/?lang=en> accessed 17 October 2019 (IGEP text); Le Club des Juristes, 'Toward a Global Pact for the Environment' (White Paper, September 2017); see also Yann Aguila and Jorge Viñuales, 'A Global Pact for the Environment: Conceptual Foundations' *Review of European, Comparative and International Environmental Law*, 28/1 (2019): 3.

[80] IGEP text (n 79). The author was a member of the international group of experts.

[81] Ibid, 1–2.

[82] Rio Declaration (n 10); Le Club des Juristes, 'White Paper' (n 79).

[83] The IGEP text (n 79) provides that 'Every person has the right to live in an ecologically sound environment adequate for their health, well-being, dignity, culture and fulfilment' (art 1). This differs from 'rights for nature' approaches; see also 'Statement by David R. Boyd, Special Rapporteur on human rights and the environment at the 73rd session of the General Assembly' *OHCHR* (25 October 2018).

[84] UNGA Res 72/277 'Towards a Global Pact for the Environment' (14 May 2018) UN Doc A/RES/72/277.

[85] See 3rd Substantive Session of the Ad Hoc Open Ended Working Group Towards a Global Pact for the Environment, United Nations at Nairobi, Kenya, 'Recommendations, as agreed by the Working Group' (22 May 2019) <http://hdl.handle.net/20.500.11822/28367> accessed 17 October 2019.

[86] Boyd (n 83); see also works initiated by civil society including the International Council of Environmental Law (ICEL) & IUCN Environmental Law Programme, *Draft International Covenant on Environment and Development: Implementing Sustainability* (5th edn, 2015) <https://portals.iucn.org/library/node/46647> and the Declaration on Human Rights and Climate Change: see Kirsten Davies *et al*, 'The Declaration on Human Rights and Climate Change: A New Legal Tool for Global Policy Change' *Journal of Human Rights and the Environment*, 8 (2017): 217.

The lens of fragmentation provides a useful perspective to assess these reform efforts. From the perspective of fragmentation *within* international environmental law, a 'one-size-fits-all' approach to environmental law lacks the nuance of tailor-made MEAs, and reduces the potential for more radical change.[87] From a broader perspective of fragmentation, however, the Global Pact could be highly beneficial.[88] Having regard to the hegemony of regimes outside of international environmental law,[89] a widely ratified treaty would provide clear direction for treaty-interpreters to achieve systemic integration, due both to its crystallization of custom and to its status as a binding treaty. For example, a binding obligation to promote patterns of consumption 'both sustainable and respectful of the environment'[90] could change the interpretative context of trade and investment agreements.[91]

Reducing the ecological blind spots of trade and investment panels is undeniably useful. Yet the broader institutional dimension of fragmentation is not necessarily addressed by the current draft Global Pact by the IGEP. In its current form, it is not designed to create a high-level environmental institution to adjudicate upon conflicts in interpretation and the imbalance described in Section III will not change. Thus, while the entrenchment of environmental rights offers a route for environmental protection to be achieved through adjudication by courts and tribunals, the implementation of such rights would mostly depend on domestic litigation.[92] The promise of a cohesive and unified approach to international environmental law would in this way be contingent on the arrangements within specific domestic constitutional orders. When bearing in mind the lessons of legal pluralism, this may well be appropriate, until one remembers the universal threats to the environment that are faced by all, and the yet unaccounted responsibility for environmental harm that is held by only some members of the global community.

V. CONCLUSION

It is trite to observe that the fragmentation of international law has consequences, some good and some bad. While diversity and difference may help promote local solutions

[87] Duncan French and Louis Kotzé, '"Towards a Global Pact for the Environment": International Environmental Law's Factual, Technical and (Unmentionable) Normative Gaps' *Review of European, Comparative and International Environmental Law*, 28/1 (2019): 25.

[88] Margaret Young, 'Global Pact for the Environment: Defragging International Law?' *EJIL: Talk!* (29 August 2018).

[89] Martti Koskenniemi, 'Hegemonic Regimes' in Young (ed), *Regime Interaction* (n 3) 305.

[90] IGEP text (n 79) art 3.

[91] This could conceivably change the outcome of the cases summarized above (n 58).

[92] See remarks of Lord Carnwath, Justice of the Supreme Court of the United Kingdom 'Climate Justice and the Global Pact' (Judicial Colloquium on Climate Change and the Law, Lahore, Pakistan, 26 February 2018).

and experimentation, the 'environment' is often left behind when the interests of states are shaped by, and pursued through, other regimes, whose functional orientation does not prioritize ecological concerns. Those other regimes have institutional strength and compulsory dispute settlement, while environmental principles are often scattered amongst custom and non-binding instruments.

Fragmentation within the field of international environmental law, which has garnered recent attention, must be understood in the context of the fragmentation of international law. The literature on regime interaction reminds us that existing legal boundaries (both normative and institutional) are not immutable or inevitable. Environmental governance does not always (or even most often) happen in the context of MEAs and environmental institutions but also in matters that are regulated by 'non-environmental' frameworks and international regimes. The division of organizational mandates, including within trade, investment, human rights, or other regimes, is due to particular political and historical circumstances. Critical engagement with these circumstances reduces the risk of path-dependency and ensures an openness and flexibility in dealing with environmental issues, especially in the present era of largescale crisis and change.

Fragmentation contains ongoing tensions between local-level governance and higher-level aspirations, which are often translated through debates over pluralism and constitutionalism. This creates special challenges for law, which must be both stable and adaptable, especially in the face of ecological needs. Thus, a common ground of contestation occurs when treaties are interpreted. A key question that emerges from environmental disputes is whether such treaties can be read as incorporating relevant rules of international environmental law or the subsequent practice of parties. The promise of a binding instrument in the form of the proposed Global Pact for the Environment could provide much needed integration of environmental issues in international law. Yet institutionally and conceptually, ongoing questions about whether international law can appropriately and justly recognize ecological limits remain unanswered.

BIBLIOGRAPHY

'Fragmentation of International Law: Difficulties Arising from the Diversification and Expansion of International Law—Report of the Study Group of the International Law Commission finalized by Martti Koskenniemi' (13 April 2006) UN Doc A/CN.4./L.682 and Corr.1

Le Club des Juristes: International Group of Experts for the Pact, 'Draft Global Pact for the Environment by the IGEP' (La Sorbonne, 24 June 2017)

UNGA, 'Gaps in International Environmental Law and Environment-Related Instruments: Towards a Global Pact for the Environment—Report of the Secretary-General' (30 November 2018) UN Doc A/73/419

Margaret Young (ed), *Regime Interaction in International Law: Facing Fragmentation* (CUP 2012)

CHAPTER 6

INSTRUMENT CHOICE

DAVID M DRIESEN

I. INTRODUCTION

This chapter addresses the problem of choosing environmental law instruments in international environmental law. Choosing the means of environmental protection contrasts with the problem of choosing the goals countries agree to when they seek to address international environmental problems. This chapter focuses on the means of environmental protection rather than its ends.

I use the term 'instrument choice' to refer to policy tools, rather than mere legal forms. One might view treaties and executive agreements as instruments of environmental protection whenever they address environmental matters. But the literature uses the term 'instrument choice' to refer to various kinds of policy devices that governments might adopt through treaties, executive agreements, or other legal forms.[1] I also do not address capacity-building, which figures in international environmental law, but not in any conventional account of instrument choice.

A country seeking to comply with a goal established under international environmental law can engage in instrument choice just as it would in seeking to comply with purely domestic environmental goals. While this chapter mentions some of the common domestic uses of instruments to contribute to the achievement of international environmental goals, it primarily addresses adoption or encouragement of particular instruments in international law itself—cases where parties to treaties agree to encourage or use a particular instrument.

This chapter begins with a discussion of the various environmental protection instruments, such as environmental benefit trading, pollution taxes, subsidies, and traditional regulation. It then suggests that, for the most part, international environmental

[1] See Jody Freeman and Charles Kolstad (eds), *Moving to Markets in Environmental Regulation: Lessons from Twenty Years of Experience* (OUP 2006); Jonathan Wiener, 'Global Environmental Regulation: Instrument Choice in Legal Context' *Yale Law Journal*, 108/1 (1999): 677.

law has left the choice between traditional regulation and market-based instruments to nation-states. Efforts to create new international environmental law focus more upon forging agreement about goals than on how to achieve goals, since states play such a huge role in implementation and countries can achieve any given goal in a variety of ways. But some devices, which some experts treat as environmental instruments—such as subsidies, liability, and trade sanctions—more often become part of international environmental law. The final section discusses the extent to which the desire for international environmental benefit trading has driven a departure from the norm of leaving the choice between market mechanisms and traditional standards to implementing polities.

II. INSTRUMENTS OF ENVIRONMENTAL PROTECTION: A TYPOLOGY

This section begins with a discussion of traditional standards. It continues by discussing the instruments most widely described as market-based instruments—environmental benefit trading, pollution taxes, and subsidies.[2] Finally, it will discuss devices that scholars sometimes describe as instruments of environmental protection that play a role in international environmental law.

A. Traditional Standards

Much of the literature refers to traditional standards as 'command-and-control' regulation.[3] The term 'command-and-control' regulation is pejorative and misleading.

Most traditional standards are performance standards.[4] They require a particular actor to achieve a specified level of environmental performance. For example, many countries require manufacturers of automobiles to make cars that meet a numerical standard for fuel efficiency, measured in litres-per-kilometre or miles-per-gallon. These standards, while adopted for domestic policy reasons initially, now play a role in most countries' efforts to reduce greenhouse gas (GHG) emissions under the global climate regime. Similarly, countries seeking to protect their fisheries will sometimes

[2] See David Driesen, 'Alternatives to Regulation? Market Mechanisms and the Environment' in Robert Baldwin, Martin Cave, and Martin Lodge (eds), *The Oxford Handbook of Regulation* (OUP 2010) 206–207.

[3] See David Driesen, 'Is Emissions Trading an Economic Incentive Program?: Replacing the Command and Control/Economic Incentive Dichotomy' *Washington and Lee Law Review*, 55/2 (1998): 289.

[4] Ibid, 297–299.

set Total Allowable Catch (TAC) limits for fishing boats—a performance standard for fishing boats.

Performance standards usually offer some flexibility in how regulated firms can meet the required level of performance.[5] So, for example, vehicle manufacturers can meet fuel efficiency standards by increasing gasoline-burning vehicles' efficiency, by manufacturing hybrid vehicles, or by creating vehicles that run on electricity only.

Sometimes, however, traditional standards take the form of a 'work practice standard'. Such standards require a particular action to reduce environmental impacts. For example, law in the United States on asbestos requires contractors to wet down asbestos when removing it from buildings to limit atmospheric emissions.[6] Usually, regulators rely on work practice standards when measurement difficulties make it impossible to enforce a performance standard.

The term 'command-and-control' regulation proves misleading, because it seems to describe only work practice standards, where the regulator specifies a required technological approach.[7] But the literature sometimes uses the term 'command-and-control' regulation to describe performance standards as well, where nobody commands a particular pollution control approach.[8] The term misleads by exaggerating traditional regulation's rigidity.

Another type of traditional standard bans a particular substance altogether. The international community strongly encouraged this approach for addressing stratospheric ozone depletion by phasing out ozone depleting substances (ODS) under the 1987 Montreal Protocol on Substances That Deplete the Ozone Layer and its successors. This approach, while rarely used, has some big advantages. It tends to reduce pollution in all relevant media. It proves relatively easy to enforce. And it strongly encourages innovation. But it disrupts existing practices dramatically and therefore often appears unattractive to regulators.

International law also sometimes employs media-specific prohibitions, which should be understood as a zero discharge limit (a performance standard) rather than as a ban of a substance. The 1996 Convention on the Prevention of Marine Pollution by Dumping of Wastes and Other Matter (London Convention), for example, generally prohibits dumping of a list of substances set out in annex I of the Convention.[9] These materials include industrial waste and very hazardous substances, like radioactive waste, mercury, and several heavy metals.[10] The London Convention also bans particular work practices, prohibiting incineration of industrial waste and sewage at sea.[11]

[5] Ibid, 302.

[6] *Adamo Wrecking v United States* 434 US 275, 287, 294–295 (1978).

[7] See Daniel Dudek and John Palmisano, 'Emissions Trading: Why is This Thoroughbred Hobbled' *Columbia Journal of Environmental Law*, 13/2 (1989): 217, 220; Robert Hahn and Gordon Hester, 'Where Did All the Markets Go: An Analysis of EPA's Emissions Trading Program' *Yale Journal on Regulation*, 6/1 (1989): 109, 109.

[8] See eg Robert Hahn and Robert Stavins, 'Incentive-Based Regulation: A New Era for an Old Idea?' *Ecology Law Quarterly*, 18/1 (1991): 1, 5.

[9] art IV.1(a); cf. art V.2.

[10] London Convention, annex I.

[11] See ibid, para 10.

Traditional standards can ease enforcement, but usually prove inefficient. Regulators may set a uniform standard for all the firms in an industry. But firms in the same industry frequently face widely varying pollution control costs. A uniform standard therefore generates very high control costs at some facilities. The regulator could achieve the same overall reduction in pollution at lower cost if she could reallocate control obligations to reflect differentials in marginal costs, requiring more reductions from facilities with relatively low marginal control costs and fewer reductions from facilities with relatively high marginal control costs. Unfortunately, regulators rarely have the detailed marginal cost information needed to facilitate such cost-effective tailoring.

B. Market-Based Instruments

Environmental benefit trading and pollution taxes solve this efficiency problem by creating greater flexibility for polluters for cost-effective actions. Commentators refer to at least these two instruments as 'market-based' instruments of environmental protection, which they usually contrast with 'command-and-control' regulation.[12] They also usually consider a subsidy a market-based instrument.[13]

Environmental benefit trading solves the efficiency problem by making the pollution control obligations created under a performance standard tradeable. So, for example, a regulator might require each polluter to reduce emissions by 100 tons a year. But she will allow a polluter with high control cost (Expensive) to make no reductions if the polluter pays somebody else with low control costs (Cheap) to make extra reductions in her stead. Thus, Expensive might forego local pollution control and instead pay Cheap for 100 tons of pollution reduction credit. Cheap might generate a 200 ton reduction in order to realize Cheap's 100 ton reduction obligation and produce 100 tons of credits to sell to Expensive. Polluters have an incentive, under such a programme, to reallocate their emission reduction obligations through trades among themselves in order to maximize abatement's cost-effectiveness. While this example features pollution reduction, in principle the same approach can apply to efforts to get at problems other than pollution. For example, fishermen might trade limits on the amount of fish they catch. I employ the term 'environmental benefit trading' rather than 'emissions trading' in this chapter, because the international law on trading contemplates trading of some environmental benefits not realized through emission reductions.

Pollution taxes, like trading, facilitate cost-effective abatement. For example, suppose that a regulator establishes a tax of $50 per ton of carbon dioxide. Polluters with

[12] See Kenneth Richards, 'Framing Environmental Policy Choice' *Duke Environmental Law and Policy Forum*, 10/2 (2000): 221, 231.

[13] See eg Hongli Feng *et al*, 'Subsidies! The Other Incentive-Based Instrument: The Case of the Conservation Reserve Program' in Freeman and Kolstad (n 1).

abatement costs of less than $50 per ton have an incentive to reduce their emissions and avoid paying the $50-per-ton tax on emissions. Polluters that face more than $50 per ton of control cost, however, would presumably pay the tax and not reduce emissions. Hence, in response to the tax, polluters would tend to abate in a cost-effective manner, doing so only when they have marginal control costs below the tax rate.

Many experts associate market-based measures with enhanced innovation.[14] With respect to emissions trading, however, the literature on innovation is divided.[15] Facilitating least-cost abatement can reduce incentives for high-cost innovation.[16] But high-cost innovation sometimes significantly advances technology and lowers long-term costs.[17] The small amount of empirical evidence on innovation suggests that traditional regulation produces more innovation than emissions trading.[18]

Subsidies for environmentally beneficial activity can also enhance efficiency. Many economists, however, express concerns that subsidies, while sometimes useful in helping establish new techniques, can remain in place long after the economic justification for them disappears.[19] Subsidies for research into new techniques for enhancing environmental protection prove less controversial.

The feed-in tariff subsidizes renewable energy in many developed countries by providing an above-market price for renewable energy, even though it does not usually meet the legal definition for a subsidy under EU law. It has sparked an increase in supply and a decrease in the price of renewable energy. Countries adopted this mechanism for domestic policy reasons, but it also helps them meet obligations to reduce GHG emissions under international law.

[14] See Bruce Ackerman and Richard Stewart, 'Reforming Environmental Law: the Democratic Case for Market Incentives' *Columbia Journal of Environmental Law*, 13/2 (1988): 171, 183; Dudek and Palmisano (n 7) 234–235; Hahn and Stavins (n 8) 13; Richard Stewart, 'Controlling Environmental Risks Through Economic Incentives' *Columbia Journal of Environmental Law*, 13/2 (1988): 153, 160.

[15] See David Driesen, 'Does Emissions Trading Encourage Innovation?' *Environmental Law Reporter (Environmental Law Institute)*, 33/1 (2003): 10094; Suzi Kerr and Richard Newell, 'Policy-Induced Technology Adoption: Evidence From the U.S. Lead Phasedown' *Journal of Industrial Economics*, 51/3 (2003): 317, 320; David Malueg, 'Emissions Credit Trading and the Incentive to Adopt New Abatement Technology' *Journal of Environmental Economics and Management*, 16/1 (1987) 52.

[16] Malueg (n 15); Driesen, 'Does Emissions Trading Encourage Innovation?' (n 15) 10095–10101.

[17] Driesen, 'Does Emissions Trading Encourage Innovation?' (n 15) 10097; Richard Newall *et al*, 'The Induced-Innovation Hypothesis and Energy-Saving Technological Change' *Quarterly Journal of Economics*, 114/3 (1999): 941.

[18] See Driesen, 'Does Emissions Trading Encourage Innovation?' (n 15) 10103-10105; David Driesen, 'Sustainable Development and Market Liberalism's Shotgun Wedding: Emissions Trading under the Kyoto Protocol' *Indiana Law Journal*, 83/1 (2008): 21, 40–44; David Popp, 'Pollution Control Innovation and the Clean Air Act of 1990' *Journal of Policy Analysis and Management*, 22/4 (2003): 641; Margaret Taylor, 'Innovation Under Cap-and-Trade Programs' *Proceedings of the National Academy of Sciences of the United States*, 109/13 (2012): 4804; Margaret Taylor, Edward Rubin, and David Hounshell, 'Regulation as the Mother of Invention: The Case of SO2 Control' *Law and Policy*, 27/2 (2005): 348, 370.

[19] Driesen, 'Alternatives to Regulation' (n 2) 207.

C. Other Instruments

While most of the literature focuses on market-based instruments and mentions 'command and control' regulation, other instruments exist. Scholars, however, have not agreed upon a typology of instruments.[20]

Some scholars refer to eco-labelling as a market-based instrument, because notifying purchasers of a product's environmental attributes might influence purchase decisions.[21] For example, the US Dolphin Protection Consumer Information Act of 1990 required labelling of tuna as 'dolphin-safe', partly to implement an international agreement on how to manage a tuna fishery.[22] This labelling requirement, along with other measures, caused a large decline in dolphin mortality.[23]

Eco-labelling also played a role in encouraging sustainable timber harvesting internationally. Because eco-labelling in this context stems from voluntary agreements among those concerned about forest management, one might debate whether this constitutes a use of labelling in international environmental *law*. But Errol Meidinger has suggested that these private arrangements do constitute law because of the somewhat coercive supply change pressures labelling creates to engage in sustainable forest management and the resemblance of the regimes' formulation of criteria to administrative rule-making.[24]

The literature sometimes refers to liability and trade restrictions as instruments of environmental protection.[25] One can debate whether either constitute environmental protection instruments. They might be more aptly considered enforcement mechanisms in some contexts.[26]

Trade restrictions play a prominent role in one of most successful and earliest global environmental agreements, the 1973 Convention on Trade in Endangered Species (CITES). CITES restricts trade in endangered species.[27] In some cases, these trade restrictions function as instruments of environmental protection by limiting the incentive to kill a species.[28] In other cases, they operate as enforcement mechanisms to

20 Richards (n 12) 230–231.

21 Driesen, 'Alternatives to Regulation' (n 2) 207.

22 See David Hunter, Jim Salzman, and Durwood Zaelke, *International Environmental Law and Policy* (Foundation Press 1998) 1030–1032.

23 See ibid, 1029–1033.

24 Errol Meidinger, 'The Administrative Law of Global Private-Public Regulation: The Case of Forestry' *European Journal of International Law*, 17/1 (2006): 47.

25 See eg Thomas Lunmark, 'International Law and the Environment by Patricia Birnie and Alan Boyle (book review)' *Ecology Law Quarterly*, 21/4 (1994): 1073, 1076.

26 See Chapter 58, 'International Environmental Responsibility and Liability', in this volume, which addresses liability. Hence, in this chapter, I only address trade restrictions.

27 art 2.1.

28 Charlene Daniel, 'Evaluating U.S. Endangering Species Legislation—The Endangered Species Act as an International Example: Can This Be Pulled Off—The Case of the Rhinoceros and Tiger' *William and Mary Environmental Law and Policy Review*, 23/2 (1999): 687.

encourage countries to comply with international law calling for national programmes to protect endangered species.[29]

Trade sanctions also played a role in perhaps the most successful international environmental agreement, the Montreal Protocol. The Montreal Protocol (as amended) only permits countries to sell ODS on international markets if they comply with the regimes' phase-out schedule.[30] They thus provide a powerful economic incentive for compliance. In this case, the trade sanctions function more as an enforcement tool than as a standalone environmental protection instrument.

Finally, trade restrictions play a role in the 1989 Basel Convention on the Control of Transboundary Movements of Hazardous Wastes and Their Disposal.[31] This agreement uses a trade restriction as an instrument of environmental protection by forbidding the shipment of waste from developed to developing countries.[32] It also uses restrictions on the trade of hazardous waste to enforce other obligations, such as the obligation to dispose of waste in an environmentally sound manner.[33] Similarly, it bans trade in hazardous waste with non-parties to the convention.[34]

Trade restrictions, whether considered an instrument or not, fell out of fashion in the mid-1990s. They do not figure in the global climate change regime or other recent environmental agreements. This change reflects hostility of the World Trade Organization towards trade restrictions as a means of environmental protection and growing assertiveness by developing countries—the targets of many trade restrictions.

III. THE ROLE OF INSTRUMENTAL AGNOSTICISM IN INTERNATIONAL ENVIRONMENTAL LAW

Countries frequently design international agreements to solve global or regional environmental problems. But most environmental problems stem from actions of private firms and individuals. And international institutions do not have the capacity to create and enforce requirements applicable to private parties. So, international environmental law necessarily relies on nation-states (and sub-national entities) to carry out most of the enforcement and implementation of international agreements.

The necessity for nation-state implementation suggests the desirability of leaving choices between market-based mechanisms and traditional standards out of

[29] Ibid.
[30] art 4.
[31] art 4.
[32] art 4.2(e).
[33] art 4.2(g).
[34] art 4.5.

international agreements, so that states can choose instruments compatible with their administrative capabilities and customs. This section will show that many international agreements have conformed to this suggestion, reflecting what one might call instrumental agnosticism.

A. International Agreements' Tendency to Include Goals and Procedures While Leaving Choices about the Role of Market-Based Instruments to Nation-States

Parties to international environmental treaty regimes often focus heavily on reaching agreement about environmental goals and procedures for further developing regimes, rather than on instrument selection. Usually, parties cannot even reach agreement on concrete goals when they start to tackle a new environmental problem, let alone reach agreement about instruments. Instead, they settle for a framework convention that features an agreement about abstract goals, such as promoting sustainable development, avoiding dangerous climate disruption, or protecting 'human health and the environment' against a particular hazard.[35] These framework conventions often create procedures for subsequent development of the treaty regime, including creation of institutions for further research and future decision-making.

If the regime proves successful, the parties eventually reach more concrete agreements about what they will do through protocols to the framework convention. These protocols commonly focus heavily on goals, but often feature more concrete goals than one finds in framework conventions.

Protocols establish goals for countries, not for individual firms. Traditionally, they have not focused heavily on the choice between market-based instruments and traditional standards or on the choice among instruments within these categories, because countries would choose instruments when they translate internationally agreed upon goals into concrete measures applicable to firms.

A good example of this agnosticism towards instrument choice comes from the Montreal Protocol itself (rather than the entire regime). The Montreal Protocol establishes quantitative limits on ODS at the country level through agreements to percentage reductions of consumption of ODS by particular dates (measured by production volumes minus exports plus imports).[36] The United States used performance standards, work practice standards, taxes, and trading to achieve these goals. Other countries likewise could use any instruments they would like to achieve the targets.

Yet the Montreal Protocol took at least a baby step towards internationalizing environmental instruments by authorizing trading among nations through an 'industrial

[35] See eg 1985 Vienna Convention for the Protection of the Ozone Layer, art 2.1; 1992 United Nations Framework Convention on Climate Change, art 2.

[36] arts 1.6, 2.1–2.4.

rationalization' provision. There is no evidence that any party made use of the international trading opportunity this created.

Regional air pollution control agreements even more strongly exhibit instrumental agnosticism. Commonly these agreements require particular levels of emissions reductions from the states agreeing to them. But they do not specify levels or techniques for particular emitting firms, leaving instrument choice to states.

Global international fisheries law also reflects instrumental agnosticism and the difficulty in agreeing upon concrete goals. The 1982 Law of the Sea Convention serves as a framework convention for fishing conservation (among other things). It requires coastal states to seek agreement on conservation measures.[37] The subsequent 1995 United Nations Fish Stock Agreement, which helps strengthen the role of Regional Fisheries Management Organizations (RFMOs) in managing international fisheries, studiously punts on the issue of instrument choice: requiring states to 'agree, as appropriate, on participatory rights such as allocation of allowable catch or levels of fishing effort'.[38] Many RFMOs establish Total Allowable Catch (TAC) quotas, which limit the amount of fish a state's fishermen may take collectively.[39] Others, however, do not.[40] Even when an RFMO executes an agreement on a catch share or level of effort, this may leave open choices from member states about what instruments to use in complying with the agreement. So, for example, a TAC may suggest that states should allocate catch shares to individual fishermen. But it does not rule out achieving the national TAC by limiting the fishing season or use of destructive fishing equipment. Nor does it speak to whether nations should make TACs tradeable among nations in those cases where they choose a TAC in a regional fisheries agreement. Parties often leave the choice between market-based and traditional regulation out of international agreements, treating such decisions as choices about how a country will comply with international obligations.

B. Trade Restrictions and Subsidies in International Law

A trade restriction, however, constitutes a measure that can only exist on the international level, since the term 'trade restriction' provides a shorthand for a limit on international trade. Accordingly, this measure plays a major role in international environmental law. CITES provides a prominent example of that. The CITES parties may use this as an instrument because of the inability of the international community to secure sufficient measures within many countries' borders to protect species valued by

[37] art 61.3.

[38] art 10(b).

[39] See Tore Henriksen and Alf Håkon Hoel, 'Determining Allocation: From Paper to Practice in the Distribution of Fishing Rights Between Countries' *Ocean Development and International Law*, 42/1 (2011): 66.

[40] Ibid.

the international community, in spite of the 1992 Convention on Biological Diversity, enacted in part to protect species.

Subsidies also perform a prominent role of international environmental law. Intragenerational equity considerations integral to the concept of sustainable development often lead to the conclusion that developed countries should subsidize green development in developing countries. For example, a global phase-out of ozone depleting chemicals would imply that developing countries lacking refrigeration and air conditioning in hot climates might have to pay more to make these services available to their citizens because of the problems developed countries had created by manufacturing and using ozone depleting chemicals, which have been used as refrigerants. Accordingly, the Montreal Protocol included an agreement that developed countries would pay 'all agreed incremental costs' of developing country compliance.[41] The United Nations Framework Convention on Climate Change includes a similar agreement with respect to costs necessary for developing country participation in the climate regime.[42] The parties to the global climate agreements eventually broadened the scope of funding to include adaptation to climate disruption.[43] Article 9 of the 2015 Paris Agreement reaffirms developed country commitment to aiding developing country mitigation and adaptation.[44]

IV. INTERNATIONALIZATION OF ENVIRONMENTAL BENEFIT TRADING

The 1997 Kyoto Protocol, however, internationalized instrument choice to a degree not seen before. The Kyoto Protocol contains numerous provisions addressing environmental benefit trading. This section explores some of the advantages and disadvantages of making instrument choice a part of international environmental law, instead of making it solely a matter of state choices about how to implement international agreements.

The Montreal Protocol example shows that one need not include trading in the international agreement in order to make emissions trading work. Anytime an international agreement requires states to achieve targets, they remain free to use a trading programme domestically to implement the target. With a trading programme on the national level, however, firms in a country choosing trading only trade with other firms in the same country.

[41] art 10.

[42] David Driesen, 'Free Lunch or Cheap Fix: Emissions Trading under the Kyoto Protocol' *Boston College Environmental Affairs Law Review*, 26/1 (1998): 1, 51.

[43] See Robert Verchick, *Adaptation, Economics, and Justices* in David Driesen (ed), *Economic Thought and U.S. Climate Change Policy* (MIT Press 2010) 280.

[44] art 9.

A major advantage of trading on the international level involves the potential for enhanced cost-effectiveness. In principle, international environmental benefit trading creates the potential to rely on the cheapest opportunities for progress anywhere in the world. Countries may sponsor projects in other countries in order to realize their targets at lower cost than would be possible through purely domestic abatement. Some countries have done this. But they have also delegated the capacity to trade to regulated firms. Under this approach, firms in one country can purchase credits from projects carried out in other countries as a substitute for compliance at their own firm.

On the other hand, international environmental benefit trading creates governance issues, because there is no international institution capable of monitoring international trading properly, especially among firms. And some have argued that institutional weakness in some countries makes trading a bad idea in some places.[45] To the extent they are right, a global environmental trading programme may work poorly, because it would include countries that suffer from a lack of capacity to monitor trading effectively.

The Kyoto Protocol authorized no fewer than three trading programmes. The first trading provision authorizes developed countries to trade their emission reduction obligations under the Kyoto Protocol among themselves.[46] This is the least problematic trading provision, because developed countries assumed caps on their emissions under the Kyoto Protocol. The second trading provision authorizes the Clean Development Mechanism (CDM), which involves trading between developed and developing countries.[47] The third provision, called the Joint Implementation provision (JI), authorizes trading between developed countries and countries in transition, mostly former members of the Soviet Union.[48] Experts refer to JI and CDM as 'project-based mechanisms' because they contemplate the generation of credits in countries that have no immediate emission reduction obligations through discrete projects undertaken to generate credits for sale to developed countries that have assumed emission caps under the Kyoto Protocol or firms with emission reduction obligations under a trading programme.

The Kyoto Protocol in a limited sense continues the tradition of leaving instrument choice to states. It does not *require* states to engage in environmental benefit trading. And in practice, countries implementing the Kyoto Protocol (and the subsequent Paris Agreement), whether they use trading or not, use a variety of other measures not mentioned in the treaties, such as pollution taxes, traditional regulation, feed-in tariffs, renewable portfolio standards, and energy efficiency standards.[49]

On the other hand, by including three trading mechanisms in the agreement, the international community sends a strong signal encouraging environmental benefit

[45] See eg Ruth Greenspan Bell, 'What to do About Climate Change' *Foreign Affairs*, 85/3 (2006): 105.

[46] art 16.

[47] art 12.

[48] art 6.

[49] David Driesen, 'Emissions Trading and Pollution Taxes: Playing "Nice" With Other Instruments' *Environmental Law*, 48/1 (2018): 29, 51–55.

trading as a mechanism for limiting global warming under the Kyoto Protocol, and it creates some institutional architecture to support international trading. To that extent, it internationalizes instrument choice. Yet, the Kyoto Protocol reflects some hesitance to wholeheartedly authorize broad international environmental benefit trading in a variety of ways, including a requirement that reductions realized abroad be 'supplemental' to a country's domestic compliance effort, suggesting a limit on the amount of credits traded.[50]

Because no international government exists, trading under the Kyoto Protocol has arisen from national and regional domestic decisions under the Kyoto regime. The European Union (EU) pioneered the development of trading called for in the Kyoto agreement by creating an 'emissions trading scheme' (ETS). This scheme places caps on the emissions of firms in the electric power industry and key industrial sectors.

The EU ETS has a rocky history, some of which stems from its international character.[51] Because the EU is not a country, it failed to establish caps for regulated facilities' GHG emissions in the first two phases of the ETS' implementation, leaving that task to its member states. The member states failed miserably at this task, causing a failure to realize significant emission reductions. The EU corrected this failure and took on the cap-setting task in subsequent phases.

Since the EU viewed itself as a strong supporter of the international regime, it weakened the ETS by incorporating the Kyoto Protocol's project-based mechanisms. The history of emissions trading demonstrates that successful trading requires that all trades take place between firms that have caps.[52] But the Kyoto Protocol's project-based mechanisms contemplated using offset credits from projects from uncapped sources of emissions (or even from projects enhancing carbon sinks). The United States had experimented with offset credits under the Clean Air Act in the 1980s and could not verify that this approach achieved required pollution control targets.[53] For technical reasons, realizing emission reductions in offset programmes is extraordinarily challenging.

But the Kyoto Protocol's project-based mechanisms made strong monitoring and enforcement in countries with weak governance structures potentially important to the successful operation of the EU ETS. To the extent that firms subject to the EU ETS relied on claims of emission reductions in developing countries and countries in transition to satisfy their obligations, actual compliance depended on accurate verification of the project-based credits in the regions where project developers generated the credits.

The international community recognized that governments in regions generating credits under the CDM and JI programmes often lacked adequate capacity to verify and monitor claims of emission reduction credits, so it created a complex institutional

[50] art 17; Driesen, 'Free Lunch or Cheap Fix' (n 42) 30–35.

[51] See eg Michael Grubb, Regina Betz, and Karsten Neuhoff (eds), *National Allocation Plans in the EU Emissions Trading Scheme: Lessons and Implications for Phase II* (Routledge 2007).

[52] David Driesen, 'Trading and its Limits' *Penn State Environmental Law Review*, 14/1 (2006): 169.

[53] See Driesen, 'Is Emissions Trading an Economic Incentive Program?' (n 3) 314–316.

architecture to overcome this barrier. It created international executive boards, consisting mostly of experts, to certify the bona fides of claimed project-based credits and a set of rules to encourage real additional credits.[54] Recognizing the need for adequate information to assess projects on the ground both before and after credit approval, the international community authorized 'designated operating authorities' to certify credits on the ground. Project sponsors would then pay these 'operating entities' (really consultants) to certify the projects.[55] Delegating this crucial task to private consultants circumvented reliance on weak governments but created a conflict of interest undermining the programme. Consultants paid by project developers have an interest in helping them claim credit for programmes that added nothing new or exaggerate the amount of emission reductions a project generates.[56]

Both of the project-based mechanisms suffered serious integrity problems, because this privatized structure did not provide an adequate substitute for having a strong governmental authority verify compliance under a cap. Accordingly, the EU has sharply curtailed its use of project-based credits.[57] The EU claims that it realized sufficient reductions within member states to make up for that problem. International environmental benefit trading can undermine the capacity of the most capable developed countries to generate real emission reductions, by allowing problems from the least capable countries to infect the programme.

Still, regional and national trading programmes have proliferated. All of them follow the flawed design suggested by the Kyoto architecture, even though, as a formal matter, countries remain free to reject offset credits and use a sounder design.[58] Countries and sub-national entities implementing these programmes have tried to contain the bad effects from offset credits by limiting their volume and enhancing monitoring protocols. Hence, international instrument choice has not only influenced national and regional instrument choices; it has also entrenched design fundamentals suggested by the international agreement.

54 David Freestone and Charlotte Streck (eds), *Legal Aspects of Implementing the Kyoto Protocol Mechanisms: Making Kyoto Work* (OUP 2005); David Driesen, 'Linkage and Multilevel Governance' *Duke Journal of International and Comparative Law*, 19/3 (2009): 389, 393; Decision 17/CP.7, 'Modalities and procedures for a clean development mechanism, as defined in Article 12 of the Kyoto Protocol' (21 January 2002) UN Doc FCCC/CP/2001/13/Add.2, 20; Decision 9/CMP.1, 'Guidelines for the implementation of Article 6 of the Kyoto Protocol' (30 March 2006) UN Doc FCCC/KP/CMP/2005/8/Add.2, 2.

55 Freestone and Streck (n 54) 198–202.

56 Driesen, 'Linkage and Multilevel Governance' (n 54) 394.

57 See Felix Ekardt and Anne-Katrin Exner, 'The Clean Development Mechanism as a Governance Problem' *Carbon and Climate Law Review*, 6/4 (2012): 396, 404; Council Directive 2009/29/EC Amending Directive 2003/87/EC, OJ 2009 L 140/63; Commission Regulation (EU) 550/211 of 7 June 2011 on Determining, Pursuant to Directive 2003/87/EC of the European Parliament and of the Council, Certain Restrictions Applicable to the Use of International Credits from Projects Involving Industrial Gases, OJ 2001 L 149/1, art 1.

58 See Jorgen Wettestad and Lars Gulbrandsen (eds), *The Evolution of Carbon Markets: Design and Diffusion* (Routledge 2018).

In spite of this failure of internationalization, national and regional governments remain captivated by the possibilities of broad international environmental benefit trading. Government officials have devoted significant resources to pursuing 'linkage', the idea of agreements linking together various national and regional emission-trading markets. But problems of harmonizing requirements and securing sufficiently robust monitoring in a broad international space have limited the success of these efforts.[59] The EU adopted a linking directive to take advantage of the project-based mechanisms, which led to some problems for its programme (as discussed above).[60] Norway and Switzerland linked to the EU ETS by basically adopting its provisions.[61] California helped create a Western Climate Initiative, hoping to link up trading programmes in a number of American States and Canadian provinces. Currently, concrete links within the Western Climate Initiative only exist between California and Quebec's trading programmes. These links have required extensive work on harmonizing programmes and it is not clear what if any benefits they have delivered, because the Quebec-California linkage is too new to generate useful data.[62]

The Paris Agreement contemplates some continuation of trading on the international level, but on a different basis in light of the different structure of the Paris Agreement.[63] Under the Kyoto Protocol, most countries have now made pledges to reduce emissions. Trading, therefore, creates a risk of double counting. Article 6 of the Paris Agreement authorizes the use of 'internationally transferred mitigation outcomes' to meet national pledges. It also authorizes creation of a mechanism to generate emission reductions, apparently in a similar vein to the CDM. The agreement recognizes the problem of double counting that can arise if two countries claim credit for a 'mitigation outcome' from a discrete project generating transferrable credits and therefore requires avoidance of double counting. Designing effective rules to prevent this will likely prove challenging because of the differences between the metrics and contents of national pledges and the possibility that Article 6 may still allow participation of sectors not subject to caps, which tend to make tracking demand shifts impossible.

As a technical matter, linkage among trading programmes will not contribute to the global effort to enhance the ambition of climate disruption policy, as called for in the Paris Agreement. Linking programmes lowers the price of meeting trading programmes' existing targets.[64] And unless done well, linking compromises achievement of those targets. It does nothing to enhance the targets themselves.

[59] See Augusta Wilson, 'Linking Across Borders: Opportunities and Obstacles for a Joint Regional Greenhouse Gas Initiative-Western Climate Initiative Market' *Columbia Journal of Environmental Law*, 43(S) (2018): 227, 228–230.

[60] Council Directive 2004/101/EC amending Directive 2003/87/EC, OJ 2004 L 338.

[61] See Dmitry Fedosov, 'Linking Carbon Markets: Developments and Implications' *Carbon and Climate Law Review*, 10/4 (2016): 202, 208.

[62] See Wilson (n 59) 237–241.

[63] art 6.

[64] See David Driesen and David Popp, 'Meaningful Technology Transfer for Climate Disruption' *Journal of International Affairs*, 64/1 (2010): 1.

While international environmental benefit trading has proven deeply problematic as a technical matter, especially in less developed countries, it may have realized important political benefits. At the time of the Kyoto Protocol's negotiation, developing countries refused to assume binding emission reduction obligations in light of developed countries' greater capacity and responsibility for the lion's share of historical GHG emissions. Jonathan Wiener argued shortly after the Kyoto Protocol's promulgation that the CDM enhances developing country participation.[65] In the run-up to the Paris Agreement, many developing countries with substantial GHG emissions agreed to assume voluntary emission reduction targets, a crucial step forward as the world cannot avoid dangerous climate disruption (the stated goal of the Framework Convention) without global participation. The experience of earning money as a host country for CDM projects and seeing that reductions are feasible may have played a role in persuading these countries to make pledges to reduce GHG emissions. In other words, the CDM may have politically supported new emission reductions even as it created an impediment to achievement of the first targets.

In other areas of international environmental law, scholars consider internationalization of instrument choice impracticable. In fisheries management, we have seen a lively debate about instrument choice, including some advocacy of making fishing quotas tradeable.[66] As a practical matter, regional fishing authorities, some of which are international, find it difficult to implement and enforce private property rights in fishing.[67] Still, a number of countries have adopted 'Individual Transferrable Quota' programmes, which make fishing rights tradeable.[68] But regional international bodies seeking to protect fisheries shared by several nations have generally not found Individual Transferrable Quotas practicable. The only case I could find of anything resembling international trading involved Japanese fishermen's leasing of Australian quotas for southern bluefin tuna.[69]

The Paris Agreement, however, takes a step back towards the instrument choice agnosticism found in fisheries agreements by coupling provisions for environmental trading with provisions recognizing the importance of 'non-market mechanism'.[70] It describes these mechanisms in very broad terms, thus leaving open a wide scope of instrument choice. It speaks of non-market mechanisms assisting in implementing

[65] See Wiener, 'Global Environmental Regulation' (n 1).

[66] See eg Jonathan Adler and Nathaniel Stewart, 'Catch Shares and the Future of Fishery Conservation' *UCLA Journal of Environmental Law and Policy*, 31/1 (2013): 150.

[67] See Katrina Miriam Wyman, 'The Property Rights Challenge in Marine Fisheries' *Arizona Law Review*, 50/2 (2008): 511, 528; Katrina Miriam Wyman, 'From Fir to Fish: Reconsidering the Evolution of Private Property' *NYU Law Review*, 80/1 (2005): 117.

[68] See Adler and Stewart (n 66) 173.

[69] Holly Doremus, 'Why International Catch Shares Won't Save Biodiversity' *Michigan Journal of Environmental and Administrative Law*, 2/2 (2013): 385, 424–425; see also Seth Korman, 'International Management of High Seas Fishery: Political and Property-Rights Solutions and the Atlantic Bluefin' *Virginia Journal of International Law*, 51/3 (2011): 697, 745.

[70] art 6.8.

nationally determined contributions, thus suggesting their use in mitigating climate disruption, presumably by reducing GHG emissions and perhaps by enhancing sinks.[71] But the next sentence links these non-market mechanisms not only to mitigation, but also to adaptation, finance, technology transfer, and capacity-building. It also calls for a 'framework for non-market approaches to sustainable development'.[72] Hence, the Paris Agreement, while continuing the Kyoto Protocol's effort to encourage international emissions trading, also recognizes and encourages use of non-market mechanisms.

V. CONCLUSION

For good reasons, much of international environmental law establishes goals for nations to pursue in order to reduce international environmental harms. Nations necessarily engage in instrument choice when they seek to meet these goals.

Countries can pursue common goals without agreement about the means of achieving these goals, and frequently do. But strong enforcement of international agreements may require trade sanctions, which some consider an environmental protection instrument. And many international environmental agreements use international subsidies to address intra-generational equity concerns.

Creating market-based instruments that operate between firms from different countries, such as international emissions trading, does require direct support from international law. Such instruments can enhance economic efficiency and international cooperation. But the international community struggles to make them work effectively given the administrative weakness of international institutions and many countries' governments.

So, instrument choice forms an essential part of nation-state implementation of international environmental law. International environmental instrument choice can sometimes be avoided, but sometimes fills a need or captures the imagination of state representatives trying to solve international environmental problems.

BIBLIOGRAPHY

Holly Doremus, 'Why International Catch Shares Won't Save Biodiversity' *Michigan Journal of Environmental and Administrative Law*, 2/2 (2013): 385

David Driesen, 'Free Lunch or Cheap Fix: Emissions Trading under the Kyoto Protocol' *Boston College Environmental Affairs Law Review*, 26/1 (1998): 1

David Driesen, 'Linkage and Multilevel Governance' *Duke Journal of International and Comparative Law*, 19/3 (2009): 389

[71] See ibid.

[72] See art 6.9.

Errol Meidinger, 'The Administrative Law of Global Private-Public Regulation: The Case of Forestry' *European Journal of International Law*, 17/1 (2006): 47
Jorgen Wettestad and Lars Gulbrandsen (eds), *The Evolution of Carbon Markets: Design and Diffusion* (Routledge 2018).
Jonathan Wiener, 'Global Environmental Regulation: Instrument Choice in Legal Context' *Yale Law Journal*, 108/1 (1999): 677

CHAPTER 7

SCHOLARSHIP

DUNCAN FRENCH AND LYNDA COLLINS

I. INTRODUCTION

In any comprehensive guide to international environmental law, analysis of the scholarship of this domain occupies a necessarily unique position. It is an opportunity for scholars of international environmental law to take a step back from the status quo and examine how we construct, describe, and interrogate the field. As with any legal discipline, scholarship is an essential element in the wider discourse, as the means of creating and promulgating knowledge, and yet it rarely is itself subject to analysis. However, scholarship, defined here as academic research and the ensuing publications written primarily—though increasingly not now exclusively—for an academic audience or for teaching purposes, is fundamental to the historical development and ongoing formulation of any sub-discipline.

Scholarship in international law has a particular resonance arising from Article 38.1(d) of the Statute of the International Court of Justice (ICJ), as a subsidiary source of international law. In other words, scholars of international environmental law have the opportunity to actively *create* law (if invariably as a 'subsidiary means'), particularly where there is a convergence of authoritative voices articulating a clear principle. In addition to this unique potential, scholarship is particularly valuable in international environmental law since the challenges of the global environmental crisis undoubtedly call for a profound reconceptualization of our collective systems of (economic, political, social, and legal) governance. Thus, the role of the visionary scholar is urgently needed in the realm of global environmental policy.

The purpose of this chapter is to consider the role of international environmental law scholarship in shaping the sub-discipline, to explore its limitations, and to reflect on the relationship between scholarship and praxis. We begin by defining the context, content, and key players in international environmental law scholarship. Next, we canvass major challenges in the area including: fragmentation; reactivity; under-represented voices and issues; and inter-disciplinarity. Finally, we elaborate the important dialectic between theory and practice in international environmental law, touching in particular on the role of international environmental law scholars in litigation, advocacy, and consultancy.

The general theme of the chapter is that international environmental law scholarship is a rich, maturing, and increasingly diverse body of work, and yet it lacks coherency in some important respects. The field is rapidly evolving as the global community confronts the unprecedented challenges of the Anthropocene era, and we view this chapter as a salutary opportunity to survey the 'state of the art' in international environmental law scholarship and to forecast possible directions for its future development.

II. WHAT IS (INTERNATIONAL) ENVIRONMENTAL LAW SCHOLARSHIP?

In seeking to answer the question what is international environmental law scholarship, several challenges confront us. First, it is not the purpose of this section to describe, either in whole or in part, the 'back catalogue' of such scholarship. Setting aside the enormity of the task, determining the outer contours of the discipline is itself hugely problematic. For instance, is a general edited collection of international law, with a contribution on multilateral environmental regimes, part of the scholarship? On one level—and arguably at its most important—it absolutely is. But, at another, this question highlights in a very simple way, the complexity of demarcation. More significantly, what of that scholarship which is not explicitly environmental at all, but has made an enduring impression on the discipline? HLA Hart's work on justice,[1] Koskenniemi's *From Apology to Utopia*,[2] and Franck's work on fairness[3] to name but three. These and other works would surely fall outside the accepted canon of environmental law under almost any definition but they have had enormous influence on numerous environmental law scholars, both consciously (and expressly) or (perhaps more often) implicitly.

Second, as the parenthesis in the section title highlights, international environmental law is the progeny of more than one discipline; and indeed its parentage would seem to be diverse. The obvious contenders are public international law and environmental law, but to restrict its normative source to those two areas would be to dull the incredibly rich material that—especially now—feeds into international environmental law. Again, even to try to list in a comprehensive way the other legal disciplines that contribute to international environmental law is a fool's errand. Nevertheless, one might mention human rights law, jurisprudence and legal theory, Indigenous law, private law, private

[1] HLA Hart, *The Concept of Law* (3rd edn, OUP 2012).

[2] Martti Koskenniemi, *From Apology to Utopia: The Structure of International Legal Argument* (CUP 2006).

[3] Thomas Franck, *Fairness in International Law and Institutions* (OUP 1998).

international law, European Union law, etc. Indeed, the list is almost endless and thus futile. International environmental law as a self-defined area of study is made richer, but also more porous, by interaction with other areas of law.

Third, this notion of interaction is hugely important. International environmental law is not simply a product of these legal disciplines, but itself contributes a richness to other areas of law. Unlike the traditional common law metaphor of the stream: ('common law and equity are two streams running alongside one another, but never mingling their waters'[4]), surely international environmental law—as with any other maturing area of legal scholarship—is more akin to Lord Diplock's updated analogy: 'If ... (the) ... fluvial metaphor is to be retained at all, the confluent streams of law and equity have surely mingled now'.[5] To attempt to disentangle scholarship into its component parts, while not wholly impossible, is both difficult and of questionable epistemological value.

Fourth, the previous paragraph purposely inserted the concept of maturity, reflecting the well-known accusation that environmental law scholarship is immature. In their pivotal article in *Journal of Environmental Law* in 2009, Fisher *et al* shine a spot light on the discipline and its scholars, noting: 'The stubborn persistence of this perception of enduring immaturity signifies the need for environmental lawyers to take a harder look at, and talk more about, what they do, how they do it and why they do it'.[6] They focus, specifically, on the lack of self-reflection in the methodology of such scholarship. International environmental law does not escape the critique; rather poetically they note that 'there is too much focus on identifying particular species of tree and not enough on analyzing how particular identified species interact with the rest of the "legal" ecosystem'.[7]

A fifth and final point is perhaps worth raising as a challenge in reflecting on international environmental law scholarship. It is the hegemonic dominance of English as a medium of communication. This 'Oxford Handbook' is in English; many of leading publishers publish almost exclusively in English; a large percentage of the journals, monographs, and edited collections in this—and in most other fields of international law—are printed in English. And this chapter on scholarship has invariably (though not exclusively) focused on that available in the English language. It runs counter to everything as liberal international lawyers we countenance: the plurality of legal forms, the rights of peoples, and indeed having access to material in language so as to give full effect to human rights. The pre-eminence of English is thus an unfortunate trait in any form of international law scholarship. And yet, we proceed.

This second section of the chapter is divided into four brief sections which attempt to accomplish the following: First, recognition of the plethora of international environmental law scholarship. Second, an acknowledgement that scholarship is not just the

[4] Walter Ashburner, *Principles of Equity* (2nd edn, Butterworths 1933) 18.

[5] *United Scientific Holdings Ltd v Burnley Borough Council* [1978] AC 925.

[6] Elizabeth Fisher *et al*, 'Maturity and Methodology: Starting a Debate about Environmental Law Scholarship' *Journal of Environmental Law*, 21/2 (2009): 214.

[7] Ibid, 241.

printed word but when scholars (and others) congregate into interest groups and legal societies. Third, the relationship between legal theory and environmental law scholarship. And fourth, the relationship between method and that same scholarship.

A. Plethora of Form and Content

As noted above, it is not the purpose or aim of this chapter to catalogue international environmental law scholarship, and any attempt to do so would invariably omit important pieces. Whether in the form of journals—print or electronic—or in the ever-expanding array of book length pieces, international environmental law holds its own against most other areas of public international law, perhaps with the exception of human rights. A quick perusal of any good academic library's journal list will identify well over a dozen journals dedicated to international environmental law, or where international environmental law forms a significant element. Of course, there are those which even by their title, are exclusively dedicated to the specific sub-discipline (ie 'Georgetown International Environmental Law Review', 'Yearbook of International Environmental Law') and others which recognize the multi-jurisdictional nature of the subject ('Review of European, Comparative and International Environmental Law') and there are those that intentionally eschew traditional jurisdictional nomenclatures (ie 'Transnational Environmental Law').

For others, a regional focus is their particular hook (ie 'Asia Pacific Journal of Environmental Law', 'Revue Africaine de Droit de l'Environnement') or, increasingly, a focus on one discrete aspect of the law (ie 'Climate Law', 'Carbon and Climate Law Review', 'Journal of Human Rights and Environment', 'Journal of International Wildlife Law and Policy'). Indeed, in the latter category, as well as climate change—for which there is an ever-expanding number of law reviews—another field worthy of particular mention is in the maritime field, which has also had a strong environmental flavour (ie 'International Journal of Maritime and Coastal Law', 'Journal of International Maritime Law'). And, of course, there are as many again—if not more so—'domestic' law environmental journals that will often include international environmental law papers, as well as an increasing willingness amongst most generalized journals—both international and national—to publish pieces on international environmental law. Any past anecdotes suggesting that environmental law was not worthy of serious scholarly attention would seem—now—to be largely a historical footnote. This is also true—if admittedly to varying degrees of acceptance and engagement—of interdisciplinary journals, such as 'Climate Policy', 'Environmental Values', and 'Global Environmental Politics'.

If the number of journals is of note, the other principal written forms—the monograph and edited collection—are voluminous. The breadth is only matched by the diversity of subject-matter, though as Section III will highlight, we identify numerous challenges in the scholarship, including how scholarship can be reactive to intergovernmental action, and fail to represent the full panoply of voices and issues within international environmental law. Nonetheless, even the briefest perusal of publishers' catalogues will testify the interest in—at least in the writing of—international environmental law. There is undoubtedly a dynamism at work here that is worth reflecting on. More academic interest in a subject generates academic teaching on that subject—as the latter often provides a firm base on which to exclude ourselves from teaching other (perceived as less desirable) subjects!—which in time will generate postgraduate studies and PhD students, which in turn will generate further publications and new scholars.

There is thus a strong link between Chapter 8 on the teaching of international environmental law and its legal scholarship, particularly when one considers the archetypal teaching tool; the textbook. There are several well-established textbooks in the area, each with their own particular structures and foci, though on the whole many follow a reasonably similar pattern; historical development, structure (including law-making and dispute settlement) and actors, elucidation of general principles, sector- or issue-specific chapters on the principal forms of environmental harm, liability, dispute settlement, and compliance. The other commonality is that they seemingly grow in page number as the discipline has become larger, and ever-more complex—the second edition of this handbook is a prime example. It would be churlish to criticize the significance of textbooks to the development of the discipline, and indeed in some cases, one can see a broader contribution to the law, through their inclusion in legal argumentation as 'teachings of the most highly qualified publicists'.[8] Nevertheless, most of these textbooks—for reasons of space if not perspective—invariably tell only part of the narrative; both third world and feminist critics have pointed out the risk of selectivity in such texts. More proactively, others have sought to fill the perceived gaps.[9]

But even with such (justified) criticism, the regularity of the new editions of many of these textbooks points to the fact that there is no doubt that international environmental law—as a civil movement, as a governmental exercise (both inter-governmentally and domestically), and as an academic opportunity—has reached the point of self-perpetuation. Of course, the popularity for a particular topic will wax and wane (as fashions and fads change) and yet the overall trajectory of student interest, and academic research in international environmental law continues on a generally upward movement. Nevertheless, this relationship between scholarship and praxis must not go unchallenged. As French and Rajamani have noted as regards climate change legal scholarship, but we would suggest holds good generally: 'how does one distinguish between scholarship from the law and practices it is assessing and evaluating?'[10]

Thus, contemporariness is both international environmental law's strength and a potential curse. To be too connected to the changing events of the day damns scholarship to an unduly speedy demise of limited lasting relevance—especially when one takes publishing timelines into account—and yet, scholarship that fails to connect at all

[8] ICJ Statute, art 38.1(d).

[9] See for instance, Shawkat Alam *et al* (eds), *International Environmental Law and the Global South* (CUP 2016).

[10] Duncan French and Lavanya Rajamani, 'Climate Change and International Environmental Law: Musings on a Journey to Somewhere' *Journal of Environmental Law*, 25/3 (2013): 459.

with the changing normative and political environment is surprisingly often regarded as of secondary importance. The *turn-to-now* in environmental law reveals a disjunction in the scholarship; as Richardson points out: 'Legal scholarship commonly rests on arguments about doctrinal and philosophical issues rather than addressing empirical questions about the impact or efficacy of governance.'[11]

Therefore in considering international environmental law scholarship, the quantity of that scholarship is not easily weighed. Indeed, in the modern social media age, tweets and blogs are a way of reaching a much wider audience, including policy-makers and the general public. Whether tweets can be viewed as scholarship is a debate for another occasion; blogs—often with references and endnotes—we feel most certainly can be. Yet the richness of all this scholarship will always lie in its content, its context, and the links it makes with other disciplines, both within legal scholarship but perhaps more importantly externally; with international relations, political science, economics, sociology, and of greatest challenge (and importance) the natural sciences. Volume of scholarship by itself is therefore a crude measure of the health of a discipline. And up to now, we have invariably implied that scholarship is an individual (or at best a co-authored) matter; but of course scholarship is much more than publication. Thus, in the next section we consider the role of interest groups and legal societies to the development of a broader, and more collective, scholarship.

B. Interest Groups and Legal Societies

The role of academic societies in the study, exposition, and further development of international law is long-standing and of significant pedigree. Though any list is going to be incomplete, mention might particularly be made of the International Law Association and *Institut de Droit International* (as two of the oldest such associations), as well as organizations such as the African Association of International Law, Latin American Society of International Law (ASIL), European Society of International Law (ESIL), Australian and New Zealand Society of International Law, Asian Society of International Law, American Society of International Law, British Institute of International and Comparative Law, Canadian Council on International Law, and a wide array of other national-based interest groups. Within these associations, environmental issues have gained increased prominence, often following developments at the intergovernmental level, notably the key foundational moments of the 1972 Stockholm Conference and the 1992 Rio Conference. For instance, within the International Law Association, there have been a wide array of past and present committees and study groups on environmental issues, including on coastal state jurisdiction over marine pollution, water resources law, transnational enforcement of environmental law, legal principles relating to climate change, due diligence, sustainable development, and ground water resources. Within

[11] Benjamin Richardson, *Time and Environmental Law: Telling Nature's Time* (CUP 2017) 42.

both ESIL and ASIL, there are for instance, special interest groups on international environmental law. The International Bar Association has also played a notable role in the study and promotion of international environmental law, with its section on Energy, Environment, Natural Resources and Infrastructure Law, and in particular the work of its Academy Advisory Group, which has produced several notable publications.

If the general associations have played an important role, specific mention must be given to those organizations, with a specific focus on the promotion of environmental law, with particular reference to the work of the International Union for Conservation of Nature (IUCN), and its World Commission on Environmental Law (WCEL). As is well-known, the IUCN has a particular place in the categorization of international organizations, open to both states and non-state participation. Its capacity, thus, to influence debate is arguably unparalleled. One of the principal mechanisms which the IUCN seeks to influence debate is through its commissions, the most important for the purpose of this chapter being WCEL. WCEL is a network of environmental law experts from all around the world which 'supports action by international governmental organisations, governments and non-governmental organisations to improve or develop legal and institutional infrastructure best attuned to natural resources conservation in the context of sustainable development'.[12]

One of the most prominent texts coming out of the WCEL, in cooperation with another network, the International Council of Environmental Law, is the Draft International Covenant on Environment and Development, now in its fifth iteration. Though never adopted by states, it has had a significant influence on debate and is in many ways the (fuller) precursor to the work of the *Le Club des Juristes* and their more recent proposal for a Global Pact for the Environment.[13] Presently being discussed within the UN system, the Global Pact underlines the importance of effective connections between the academy and government, in this case the support of the French government and, in particular, President Macron. Additional networks are emerging to propose legal responses to global environmental crisis, notably the Ecological Law and Governance Association, which was launched in October 2017.

Whether general or particular, such associations and networks often have (at least) two functions. First, they give meaningful effect to scholarship as a corporate exercise; to allow groups of similar-minded academics often to undertake detailed exposition of particular areas of the law. That in itself is a worthwhile exercise and the reports and other outputs created thereby undoubtedly add to the overall literature on a subject. Second, though not invariably the case, there can be a more normative outcome, with specific recommendations and actions aimed either at domestic implementation or future international negotiations. Space precludes detailed evaluation of the effectiveness or otherwise of such reports; and while there are undoubtedly examples of success, on the whole

[12] <https://www.iucn.org/commissions/commission-environmental-law/about> accessed 11 October 2018.

[13] <https://www.iucn.org/sites/dev/files/content/documents/draft-project-of-the-global-pact-for-the-environment.pdf> accessed 16 March 2019.

the duality of the nature and purpose of many of these interest groups can often complicate the specificity and external value of these outputs. Of course, where the purpose of the group is expressly to critique the law with no intention of developing a normative proposal, then its value is intrinsically achieved merely by the process of the collective discourse. Finally, separate mention should also be made, and for more than just completeness, of the work of United Nations Experts and Special Rapporteurs, especially the recent Special Rapporteurs on human rights and the environment,[14] both in how they have incorporated a broad range of academic work into their reports and how, more generally, academic debates have been mainstreamed into wider political discourse.

C. Relationship between Scholarship and Theory

There is an undoubted paradox in the relationship between international environmental law scholarship and its engagement with theory. As with general international law, the discipline is broad enough to allow a wide range of theoretical perspectives and viewpoints. This is both in terms of applying more generalized theory to the particularities of environmental law, and the elaboration of theoretical viewpoints embedded within and which have evolved from the development of international environmental law. Moreover, international environmental law benefits from the insights from, and is increasingly called to respond to, an array of insights from a wider set of disciplines; political and international relations, sociological, economic, and philosophical. So where is the paradox? As Mickelson notes in the first edition of this handbook, and to which we refer for further and more in-depth detail: 'Critical approaches have doubtless had some influence, but they have largely remained on the periphery of scholarly engagement'.[15] Though one can point to (in some cases many) examples, for instance, of Third World, feminist, Marxist, eco-radical, Indigenous, and other less mainstream positions, they are invariably counterpointed against the positivist and standard approaches, often reflected best in the key textbooks. Even where they are included in such texts, they will almost certainly follow, be secondary to, and separate from the dominant discourse.

One particular feature of international environmental law scholarship is the extent to which it attaches to weak, or more radical, eco-centric positions. It is widely recognized that much of international environmental law is deeply anthropocentric in both content and purpose; one distinguishing feature therefore is how far scholarship has responded to this ontological challenge. There are many different shades of 'eco law'; including wild law, deep ecological perspectives, commons perspectives, Earth jurisprudence, etc;[16]

[14] <https://www.ohchr.org/en/Issues/environment/SRenvironment/Pages/SRenvironmentIndex.aspx> accessed 16 March 2019.

[15] Daniel Bodansky, Jutta Brunnée, and Ellen Hey (eds), *The Oxford Handbook of International Environmental Law* (1st edn, OUP 2008) 289.

[16] See Chapter 14, 'Earth Jurisprudence', in this volume.

each with its own distinctive strands and adherents. Many have a strong ethical base, with a greater or lesser connection to the law as it presently stands. For some, environmental law is on a journey; transitioning from the exclusively instrumental to a biocentric standpoint. Others view environmental law as part of the problem; that it masks the dominant paradigm of global capitalism.

As other chapters in this handbook consider in depth the content of some of these 'alternative' theoretic positions, the purpose of this section is not to be explanatory but to reflect what we briefly consider to be the existence—yet also the side-lining—of alternative voices in this scholarship generally. One immediate issue relates to how (and what) international environmental law is taught, but this is not our principal focus. We want to ask a rather more difficult question; can a body of scholars (and scholarship) which, by its very purpose, is global and progressive withstand and embrace controversy and dissent? Does the invariable normative quality to international environmental law scholarship (note the absence of scholarship that promotes environmental destruction) allow for viewpoints and theoretical positions that deviate from the norm? And even if such diversity is permissible within the academy, does it survive when scholars begin to engage with external actors? Just as with human rights discourse, are there theoretical positions where one cannot go?

Certainly, the scope and extent of environmental crises worldwide militate strongly in favour of clear, persuasive, and normative scholarship in international environmental law. If, as scholars of international environmental law, we cannot collectively agree on the compelling moral/legal imperative to preserve the natural systems on which human (and non-human) lives depend, then our research might fairly be viewed as irrelevant at best or, at worst, self-indulgent. However, we believe there is ample scope for disagreement and diversity in our debates about *how* to achieve sustainability. Scholars from the developing world, for example, have had to remind developed world thinkers and activists repeatedly of the need to account for poverty alleviation in any path towards sustainability.[17] This kind of healthy tension within the field enriches international environmental law theory and ensures that it remains engaged with the real world we write and teach about. Similarly, the articulation of Indigenous legal principles, feminist analysis,[18] ecological law discourse, and intergenerational perspectives deepen our understanding of international environmental law at both theoretical and practical levels.

D. Relationship between Scholarship and Method

The question of method is something that international environmental lawyers have spent an insufficient time considering. As Fisher *et al* pointed out, until we acknowledge the methodological challenges of our discipline and begin to debate them, we will be

[17] See Chapter 11, 'Global South Approaches', in this volume.
[18] See Chapter 12, 'Feminist Approaches', in this volume.

stymied in our disciplinary endeavours.[19] Of course, much of the scholarship is doctrinal in nature; empirical research is rarely undertaken. And where it is, the rest of the academy seems to treat it with suspicion or mild curiosity. If one reviews the principal textbooks, for instance, there is almost no reference to empirical research; perhaps occasionally to quantitative analysis but almost never to qualitative research, notwithstanding the insights such research would bring. An exception to this general trend is the scholarship of rights-based approaches, which includes several rigorous empirical works.[20]

One interesting comparator is international economic law where, despite the existence of substantial doctrinal analysis, there would seem to be a broader acceptance of empirical research, admittedly usually of a quantitative rather than qualitative nature, but nevertheless a more integrated scholarship than would presently seem to exist in international environmental law. This may be because international economic law has more frankly embraced its inherently interdisciplinary nature. The relative paucity of empirical work in international environmental law could be addressed through increased inter-disciplinary collaborations. Since many legal academics are not trained in (qualitative or quantitative) empirical research, it may be useful for scholars of international environmental law to undertake joint projects with experts in the natural sciences, economics, or sociology (for example) in order to enrich the tool-kit of available methods.

There is a secondary issue which is also worth raising; and which the final section of this chapter picks up, namely who is our audience, and what are we writing for? These are separate questions but they are inter-related:

> [W]e spend very little time pondering who we are writing for. The specialist academic? The interested professor? The student? The practitioner? The policy-maker? It may be all or none of these depending partially on where we publish, but also what we write ... it would be naïve not to recognise the broadly informative function of [much of our] writing.[21]

Moreover scholarship is often dependent upon funding, especially if the project is collaborative, inter-disciplinary, and/or has transnational elements. These factors often not only allow such scholarship to proceed, but can—and we must emphasize the conditional nature of our argument here—drive its focus and direction. Thus, connecting this back to method, it should prompt us to ask what we want to achieve in our writing, for what purpose, and for what audience(s)? Only once those questions are answered, can we then decide the appropriate method to undertake the research. Perhaps the biggest

[19] Fisher *et al* (n 6) 228.

[20] See for instance, David Boyd, *The Environmental Rights Revolution: A Global Study of Constitutions, Human Rights, and the Environment* (UBC Press 2012) and Josh Gellers, *The Global Emergence of Constitutional Environmental Rights* (Routledge 2017) both of which employ rigorous statistical analysis.

[21] French and Rajamani (n 10) 460.

weakness at the moment is the paradigmatic view that doctrinal research can provide answers beyond its purview. Instinctively, we know this not to be true. Yet most of us are reluctant to change our method to answer our own questions. The fact that we are not—however challenging that would be—will impact the long-term value of what we are seeking to argue and critique. The first stage would be to recognize our limitations in this regard. And if we wish to speak beyond ourselves as a legal community, we should rightly expect scrutiny of not only *what* we think but *how* we got there.

III. CHALLENGES IN INTERNATIONAL ENVIRONMENTAL LAW SCHOLARSHIP

This section will explore in more depth some of the identified challenges in international environmental law scholarship, both in terms of its historical development and its ongoing elaboration. Four particular challenges are identified as exemplars: fragmentation; reactivity; under-represented voices and issues; and the sub-discipline's relationship with other fields (eg international relations, natural sciences).

A. Fragmentation

Fragmentation—the creation of de jure or de facto silos and specialisms—is a significant weakness in international environmental law. Such fragmentation is similarly a feature of its scholarship (and scholars), though with the acknowledged caveat that there are also, and always have been, instances of integrated scholarship. Such fragmentation can be seen at the meta-level between disciplines (eg environmental law *versus* the natural sciences that inform it); sub-disciplines (eg environmental law *versus* human rights, law of the sea, trade law, finance law, etc), and at the intra-discipline level. Within international environmental law itself, discrete areas of inquiry have developed that do not always integrate well with each other.

Thus, there are specialists in biodiversity law, water law, hazardous waste, civil liability for environmental harms, etc. Perhaps most notably, climate change—which is in fact the paradigmatic example of the inseparability of all areas of environmental policy—has gradually emerged as a discrete area of international environmental law scholarship (and practice). Even within the specialized field of international climate law, the various features of climate change policy are often considered in isolation (eg climate finance, mitigation, common but differentiated responsibilities). Fragmentation also occurs at the systemic level, that is, between international, regional, and national environmental law specialists. Scholars (and practitioners) working at these various levels do not always collaborate (or even communicate their respective findings) effectively, despite the obvious futility of developing policy for any one level in isolation.

B. Reactivity

International environmental law has historically been reactive to problems as they arise; rarely is law adopted prior to the identification of any discernible risk. More generally, customary international environmental law is focused on harm prevention and not the positive protection of the environment. Scholarship has historically followed this pattern, focusing primarily on previously identified problems. But more than this, scholarship is often 'reactive' to political and legal developments, focusing on rule and regime development, recent dispute settlement cases, etc. Scholarship that seeks to be proactive and to set out positive, normative, change has been generally less forthcoming. Further, international environmental law scholarship has tended to embrace the dominant intellectual paradigms underpinning this field itself, from resource extraction in the early twentieth century, to sustainable development in the 1990s and early 2000s.[22] It has less commonly challenged the foundational ideas driving international environmental law and policy, but this is changing.

More recently, some have suggested that the exigencies of the Anthropocene era require scholars of international environmental law to question and reconstruct our understandings of the very *raison d'être* of the field. Rather than focusing on empirical descriptions of current developments in the practice of international law, or discrete recommendations for improvements, international environmental law scholarship should explicitly embrace the goal of keeping human societies within planetary boundaries. This new, more radical scholarship of international environmental law in the Anthropocene calls on scholars to be thought leaders, tasked with imagining a new world order and mapping out the myriad ways to get there. This refreshing new vein within international environmental law scholarship seems to be gaining momentum as more scholars embrace the Anthropocene crisis as a starting point for their analysis of whatever environmental issue happens to be their particular focus.

C. Under-represented Voices and Issues

As with most disciplines, international environmental law scholarship has a mainstream and a periphery. There are thus both voices and issues that are under-represented. Most obviously, Indigenous voices are highly under-represented in international environmental law scholarship due to the multiple and serious structural barriers to Indigenous peoples entering the legal academy virtually anywhere around the world. Feminist voices are also marginal in the scholarship of international environmental law; indeed Linda Malone and Kang He observe that '[t]here is a resounding silence in legal scholarship

[22] Tim Stephens, 'What is the Point of International Environmental Law Scholarship in the Anthropocene?' in Ole Pedersen (ed), *Perspectives on Environmental Law Scholarship: Essays on Purpose, Shape and Direction* (CUP 2018) 121.

in the past decade on feminist reformulation of international environmental law generally'.[23] Similarly, while there is an important body of international environmental law emanating from the developing world, scholars from the developing world tend to receive less funding and attention than their counterparts in the developed world. There have, however, been significant attempts to mitigate structural disadvantages and increase production and dissemination of international environmental law scholarship from the developing world (eg the IUCN Academy of Environmental Law's sliding scale registration fees for its annual Colloquium).

There are also under-represented issues in the scholarship; just as biodiversity has its 'charismatic mega-fauna', international environmental law scholarship has its preferred topics and those that receive less attention. Climate change obviously belongs in the former category while topics such as land-based marine pollution, hazardous waste, and invasive species would fall into the latter. Focal points in the scholarship of international environmental law evolve with time. In addition to the key example of climate change, other relatively new areas of prominence in the field include rights-based approaches to environmental protection, Indigenous environmental law, and environmental law and governance for the Anthropocene era.

D. Connecting Law and Related Disciplines in International Environmental Scholarship

One of the principal challenges in international environmental law scholarship is how far, and to what extent, the legal literature effectively engages with other related disciplines, such as international relations and political science, economics, sociology, and the natural sciences. International environmental law scholarship has had a mixed relationship to such other disciplines, ranging from nominal to much fuller engagement. The uneasy marriage between law and science in international environmental law scholarship deserves particular mention. The natural sciences are evidently the bedrock of all environmental law practice and scholarship; the necessity, scope, and efficacy of international environmental law can only be evaluated on the basis of data generated by the natural sciences. Yet deep challenges exist in the inter-disciplinary dialogue between legal academics and scientists. First, there is very little cross-fertilization in graduate training in these two disciplines, with the result that many legal scholars have little scientific education (and the converse is also true). Second, law and science differ in many key aspects: they involve different conventions of communication, different values, different timelines, and different technical vocabularies. Third, there are relatively few

[23] Linda Malone and Kang He, 'Women and International Environmental Law' in *Essential Readings in Environmental Law* (IUCN Academy of Environmental Law) 3 <http://www.iucnael.org/en/documents/1126-women-international-env-law-essential-readings-in-environmental-law/file> accessed 11 October 2018.

academic venues to encourage inter-disciplinary collaboration between legal and scientific experts, such that it is possible to have a very successful career as a legal academic without having co-authored a single paper with a scientific colleague. The disciplinary divides are perhaps less pronounced as between law and other social sciences, but similar challenges remain.

IV. SCHOLARSHIP AND PRAXIS: LITIGATION, ADVOCACY, AND CONSULTANCY

Many academics are increasingly not confining their expertise to the classroom or within an academic paper but are utilizing their expertise in a wide range of fora and for a broad array of purposes, both voluntary and in an employed capacity. These roles can be ad hoc, acquired by word-of-mouth, sometimes through serendipity or as a consequence of a second career; that is, advocate, civil servant, consultant, arbitrator/judge, or member of such august bodies as the International Law Commission. It might be through civil society, international organizations, government—national or local—or as a commentator via the media. The ability to utilize one's expertise outside the academy is ever-increasing, and the forms and manner in which this can occur is largely determined by the individual academic's own personal preference for external engagement.

As a matter of course, such praxis is invariably commended as a form of outreach, though increasingly universities seek to quantify such activity in either pecuniary terms or by virtue of its 'value'. In the United Kingdom, for instance, the government-backed Research Excellence Framework (REF) has begun to measure impact, defined as 'an effect on, change or benefit to the economy, society, culture, public policy or services, health, the environment or quality of life, beyond academia'.[24] But, undoubtedly, one of the most high-profile uses of academic expertise is as part of litigation, either where an academic's work is cited to make, or to strengthen, an argument or where the academic herself is part of the litigation team. As is well-known, the International Court in its judgements traditionally does not refer to secondary literature, though individual judges in their separate and dissenting opinions might.[25] A particular example of the reliance on academic expertise within a litigation strategy can be seen in the pleadings of Nicaragua at the compensation stage of *Certain Activities carried out by Nicaragua in*

[24] <http://webarchive.nationalarchives.gov.uk/20180319120009/http://www.hefce.ac.uk/rsrch/REFimpact/> accessed 11 October 2018.

[25] See for instance, the Joint Separate Opinion of Judges Al-Khasawneh and Simma in *Pulp Mills on the River Uruguay (Argentina/Uruguay)* (Judgement) [2010] ICJ Rep 14 [110] in which they quoted, inter alia, Caroline Foster, *Science and the Precautionary Principle in International Courts: Expert Evidence, Burden of Proof and Finality* (CUP 2011).

the Border Area (Costa Rica/Nicaragua) where an annex is attached drafted in part by a named international environmental law professor.[26]

A further area where academics are increasingly drawn into praxis is the work of non-governmental organizations, government expert groups, in the work of MEAs (eg compliance/implementation committees), and in negotiation teams, again either on an ad hoc or on a more permanent basis. There is no doubt that such practical experience has a two-way benefit, of allowing academics to utilize their knowledge for real-time effect, but also to allow them to appreciate much more fully the complexities of how their knowledge of the law is utilized in such circumstances. Thus, to the extent that such experience will usually be a two-way process, it will be a positive and enriching opportunity. Certainly, the ability to then utilize that enhanced and practice-based knowledge both in the classroom and in one's scholarship cannot be underestimated; subject of course to any limitations of confidentiality.

Nevertheless, there are a number of pitfalls into which any academic can fall when engaging with such activity. This section limits itself to two examples. First, there is often a difference between what academics are permitted—and one would hope encouraged—to do under the guise of academic freedom as part of their scholarship (ie the luxury to think and write freely) and what academics might be asked, and required, to do in their practice. It may be purely a matter of elucidating the law in a less complex manner; but equally in some situations, it may be more challenging. For instance, adapting their academic writing to match the expectations of the 'consumers' of their knowledge (especially those in government) who will often demand less nuance and less critical insight. That dilemma—felt by almost every academic involved in external activity at some point—will be experienced in different ways and challenge each scholar very differently.

Secondly, and perhaps particularly for those academics involved in intergovernmental negotiations, there is the risk of being lost in the minutiae of negotiations at the expense of the broader context. This would seem particularly so where a multilateral regime has grown, fragmented, and itself become subject to individual specialisms. One might think here, for instance, of the climate change regime where one might reasonably talk of experts in emissions trading, carbon taxation, adaptation, and even on such specific areas as REDD+, carbon capture and storage, and carbon derivatives. To be clear, we are not questioning the importance of such fields of enquiry and expertise; we simply point out the risk for an academic who has to move between the narrow and the broad, as well as the positive and the analytical. Like all risks, it is about being self-reflective of the challenges. But once these and similar considerations have been taken into account, engaging beyond the academy can be a positive experience for any scholar.

[26] *Certain Activities Carried Out by Nicaragua in the Border Area (Costa Rica/Nicaragua)* (Counter-Memorial of Nicaragua on Compensation) (2 June 2017) ICJ, 99, annex 1: Cymie Payne and Robert Unsworth, *Report on Environmental Damage Valuation*, incorporated 26 May 2017; The judgement was issued on 2 February 2018. The written pleadings are available on the ICJ website <https://www.icj-cij.org/en/case/150> accessed 14 November 2019.

V. CONCLUSION

We offer the above brief foray into the scholarship of international environmental law in the hope that this self-reflexive analysis will assist international environmental law scholars to remain relevant in an era of unprecedented global environmental challenges (and opportunities). In our view, scholarship is not simply the *means* by which academic study is promulgated, but is itself an important *object* of enquiry. Scholarship raises its own particular challenges, but to a large part mirrors the developments within international environmental law itself. As international environmental law has grown and matured, so has the relevant research and theorizing. Cutting-edge scholars in this field are questioning the basic premises underlying existing regimes of international environmental law and are envisioning new paradigms for global environmental governance. While scholars in the physical sciences have identified solutions to many of the environmental problems we collectively face, it is widely recognized that the journey from environmental crisis to ecological sustainability is as much an intellectual, socio-cultural, and ethical process as a technical, scientific, or political one. For this reason, scholars of international environmental law have the potential to play an important role as intellectual catalysts for the necessary evolution in our global legal orders.

BIBLIOGRAPHY

Shawkat Alam *et al* (eds), *International Environmental Law and the Global South* (CUP 2016)

Elizabeth Fisher *et al*, 'Maturity and Methodology: Starting a Debate about Environmental Law Scholarship' *Journal of Environmental Law*, 21/2 (2009): 213

Linda Malone and Kang He, 'Women and International Environmental Law' in *Essential Readings in Environmental Law* (IUCN Academy of Environmental Law) <http://www.iucnael.org/en/documents/1126-women-international-env-law-essential-readings-in-environmental-law/file> accessed 11 October 2018

Benjamin Richardson, *Time and Environmental Law: Telling Nature's Time* (CUP 2017)

Tim Stephens, 'What is the Point of International Environmental Law Scholarship in the Anthropocene?' in Ole Pedersen (ed), *Perspectives on Environmental Law Scholarship: Essays on Purpose, Shape and Direction* (CUP 2018) 121

CHAPTER 8

LEGAL IMAGINATION AND TEACHING

ELIZABETH FISHER*

I. INTRODUCTION

RECENTLY, I reworked a chapter on international environmental law for a new edition of an environmental law textbook that I co-author.[1] The original chapter began by stating that while students often perceive that international environmental law can save the world, 'much is wrong with this perception'.[2] I then went on to chart the subject and its relationship to public international law. My constant theme was that students needed to lower their expectations about international environmental law and what it could do. My aim was to disenchant those who had an enchanted vision of the subject.

I could see I had been well-intentioned in my approach. As any teacher of international environmental law knows, students, and sometimes scholars, tend towards 'wishful thinking' when it comes to the potential of international environmental law. But what was confronting in what I had written was that in attempting to dissuade naïve optimism in the subject, I had failed to focus on the expertise needed to master it. While constantly underlining the legal difficulties of international environmental law, I had not provided any framework for helping students develop an understanding of the type of reasoning and associated legal skills it needed. Specifically, I had failed to explain how international environmental law requires legal imagination.[3] That is, it requires both an

* I would like to thank Sanja Bogojević, Steven Vaughan, and the editors of this handbook for comments on an earlier draft of this chapter.

[1] Elizabeth Fisher, Bettina Lange, and Eloise Scotford, *Environmental Law: Text, Cases and Materials* (OUP 2013) ch 5.

[2] Ibid, 169.

[3] I have touched on ideas of legal imagination and environmental law in Elizabeth Fisher, *Environmental Law: A Very Short Introduction* (OUP 2017) ch 5.

understanding of what law substantively is, and what it can be, both in terms of its limits, but also in its creative possibilities.

In this short contribution I argue that while dispelling wishful thinking is important in teaching and writing about international environmental law,[4] it is equally important to foster legal imagination. My structure is as follows. First, I consider three challenges in teaching international environmental law: the lack of intellectual baselines among students, scholars, and teachers; the legal complexity of the subject; and the 'hope' that is often placed in international environmental law. In Section II, I argue that responding to the third of these challenges means that the focus in much teaching in international environmental law has been to dissuade wishful thinking. In Section III, I show how the focus on wishful thinking has overlooked the importance of legal imagination in international environmental law. An important aspect of fostering legal imagination is to ground it in legal reality and this is explored in Section IV. Section V concludes.

Before starting let me make two points. First, I am acutely aware that in reading the above, you might have the image of me as a dour and humourless academic who thinks she knows better than her students (or anyone else for that matter). But the inspiration for this essay comes from what I see as the three-way disjunction between the hopes placed in international environmental law, the legal reality of the subject, and how it is taught. My argument is not that I know best, but that we need to put these disconnections front and centre when we teach international environmental law. Second, I see this chapter as starting a conversation. Environmental law scholarship has become a focus of scrutiny in recent years,[5] but besides a few early discussions, environmental law pedagogy has remained an underdiscussed topic.[6] But teaching is where we as scholars are likely to have the greatest impact. In particular, it is the forum in which we provide future practitioners with the intellectual tool-kit of international environmental law. By reflecting on the challenges of the subject, my aim is to encourage debate on how to further evolve international environmental law from its already solid basis. I suspect that many international environmental law teachers are already fostering legal imagination, and one hope I have is that this essay will encourage them to put pen to paper to describe what they are doing.

[4] For more detail on scholarship see Chapter 7, 'Scholarship', in this volume.

[5] Elizabeth Fisher *et al*, 'Maturity and Methodology: Starting a Debate about Environmental Law Scholarship' *Journal of Environmental Law*, 21/2 (2009): 213; Andreas Philippopoulos-Mihalopoulos and Victoria Brooks (eds), *Research Methods in Environmental Law* (Edward Elgar 2017); Ole Pedersen (ed), *Perspectives on Environmental Law Scholarship: Essays on Purpose, Shape and Direction* (CUP 2018); see also Chapter 7, 'Scholarship', in this volume.

[6] David Wirth, 'Teaching and Research in International Environmental Law' *Harvard Environmental Law Review*, 23 (1999): 423; Michael Kelly, 'Teaching International Environmental Law—Tools of The Trade: A Survey of Materials' *Stetson Law Review*, 28/4 (1999): 1197.

II. THREE CHALLENGES IN TEACHING INTERNATIONAL ENVIRONMENTAL LAW

International environmental law is a relatively 'new' area of legal study. But with that said, it now has all the features of an area of scholarly specialization—journals, textbooks, academic posts, and even an Oxford Handbook in its second edition. Most significantly, it is taught as a part of university degree courses. Teaching international environmental law is challenging. But before considering those challenges it is useful to say something about teaching more generally.

To teach a subject is to teach 'mastery of core concepts and skills'.[7] That requires the elucidation of the basic knowledge of a subject, the fostering of some essential legal skills, and providing some experience in it. After teaching a subject to someone, they should be able to know and understand things they did not know and understand before. Teaching, in this regard, should aid intellectual development[8] and the cultivating of expertise. Expertise is the development of knowledge, skills, and experience that others do not have. It is a mixture of both the explicit (easily transferrable knowledge) and the tacit (that gained through experience).[9]

For many core legal subjects the framework for teaching is established and there is general agreement over what the core concepts of the subject are. The fundamentals of contract law are one example. There may be different pedagogical approaches to those fundamentals (eg teaching the subject from a doctrinal or legal realist approach),[10] but there is general agreement on what should be covered.

The situation is different in regards to international environmental law. This is not just because the subject is new, but because there are three common challenges in teaching it, which mean that teaching the subject is difficult. I consider each in turn.

The first challenge relates to who is being taught international environmental law and who is teaching it. Lawyers and others come to the study of international environmental law through a range of different intellectual paths. Law students will usually study the subject as an option on a law degree. They may or may not study it alongside public international law and/or national environmental law. They also may not study it as part of their first degree, but rather as part of a masters degree. In that context they may study the subject alongside those who have studied law in other jurisdictions. International environmental law may also be offered up as a course on non-law courses as part of an interdisciplinary offering. Given the vast nature of international environmental law, it

[7] Michael Hunter Schwartz, Gerald Hess, and Sophie Sparrow, *What the Best Law Teachers Do* (Harvard University Press 2013) 26.

[8] Ibid, 26–29.

[9] Harry Collins, *Tacit and Explicit Knowledge* (University of Chicago Press 2010).

[10] Lawrence Friedman and Stewart Macaulay, 'Contract Law and Contract Teaching: Past, Present, and Future', *Wisconsin Law Review* (1967): 805.

is also inevitable that any specific international environmental law course may look at a specific area of international environmental law or it may be that on one degree there is a suite of different international environmental law courses on offer.

There are deliberately many 'mays' in the above paragraph. In teaching international environmental law or in writing a textbook on international environmental law there are many possibilities of who is being taught and what their legal skill set will be. Prior knowledge cannot be taken as a given.[11]

A similar, but not as pronounced a pattern is evident among those who teach and research international environmental law. Some are public international law scholars who have developed some form of specialization in international environmental law. But there are also those who have migrated into international environmental law (some permanently and some temporarily) after studying national and supranational regimes. Social science research also makes important contributions to international environmental law, particularly the field of international relations.[12] Furthermore, international environmental law is also often taught and researched by those who have practised, or are practising in international environmental law and associated fields.

Thus, few presumptions can also be made about the teachers and scholars of international environmental law. I could add that there are different ways to study and research international environmental law.[13] But methodological pluralism is not quite my focus here. This is because, as we shall see below, most textbooks of international environmental law embrace that pluralism. Rather my focus is upon the fact that in the teaching and research of international environmental law there is no intellectual baseline that is being worked from. There are no shared assumptions about what the starting points for teaching the subject are. As this is the case, the teaching of international environmental law as enabling the 'mastery of core concepts and skills' can require the teaching of many things.

The second challenge involved in teaching international environmental law is that international environmental law is a dynamic and legally complex subject. As Dupuy and Viñuales note, the 'specificities' of the subject create 'significant barriers to entry' for the newcomer to the subject.[14] In part this is a product of its relationship with its public international law roots. International environmental law is a form of public international law.[15] International environmental law law-making processes are public international law law-making processes. The basic starting point is the nature and limitations

[11] Note also the reluctance to impose prerequisites for taking a course in international environmental law, Kelly (n 6) 1199.

[12] For a discussion of international relationship contributions to public international law more generally, see Jeffrey Dunoff and Mark Pollack (eds), *Interdisciplinary Perspectives on International Law and International Relations: The State of the Art* (CUP 2013).

[13] Fisher, 'Maturity and Methodology' (n 5).

[14] Pierre-Marie Dupuy and Jorge Viñuales, *International Environmental Law* (2nd edn, CUP 2018) xviii.

[15] A state of affairs most obviously expressed in the title of Patricia Birnie, Alan Boyle, and Catherine Redgwell, *International Law and the Environment* (3rd edn, OUP 2009).

of public international law norms as the law between consenting sovereign states. But with that said, international environmental law is distinct from public international law. Not least because environmental issues highlight the limits of a body of law based on ideas of sovereignty. Moreover, it is arguable that international environmental law has reshaped understandings of what public international law is.[16]

Furthermore, international environmental law is a rich and diverse field of legal practice. Legal norms come in a variety of different forms and new agreements create new types of norms.[17] Multilateral environmental agreements construct a range of different autonomous institutional regimes.[18] Fragmentation is inevitable, as is the professional specialization in international environmental law that accompanies it.[19] The footpaths of custom are hard won but examples of custom can be found in international environmental law.[20] Hybrids of international environmental law that are grounded in both private and multilevel practices are emerging.[21] The law between sovereign states is being interweaved with law between a range of private actors and sub-national actors.[22]

The challenge of fostering expertise in this complex field of study is not made any easier by the lack of intellectual baselines among students. Nor is it made simpler by the third challenge in teaching international environmental law which is that many students and scholars have a sense of hope that international environmental law will achieve certain aims. This hope arises for a range of different valid reasons and is worth a study in its own right. What I want to note here is that anyone who has taught international environmental law will have had the experience of those who understand the subject as literally being about saving the world. This is particularly the case in relation to what is seen as the most global issue of them all—climate change. Indeed, it is not too far-fetched to say that this optimism is often the common denominator among students than any shared legal knowledge.

The ways in which international environmental law is perceived to save the world vary. For some it is an instrument to achieve particular ends. For others, it is a source of meta-authority. As Humphreys and Otomo note:

[16] Daniel Bodansky, *The Art and Craft of International Environmental Law* (Harvard University Press 2010) 29; Nico Krisch, 'The Decay of Consent: International Law in an Age of Global Public Goods' *American Journal of International Law*, 108/1 (2014): 1.

[17] Lavanya Rajamani, 'The 2015 Paris Agreement: Interplay Between Hard, Soft and Non-Obligations' *Journal of Environmental Law*, 28/2 (2016): 337.

[18] Robin Churchill and Geir Ulfstein, 'Autonomous Institutional Arrangements in Multilateral Environmental Agreements: A Little Noticed Phenomenon in International Law' *American Journal of International Law*, 94/4 (2000): 623.

[19] Cinnamon Carlarne, 'Good Climate Governance: Only a Fragmented System of International Law Away?' *Law and Policy*, 30/4 (2008): 450.

[20] *Pulp Mills on the River Uruguay (Argentina/Uruguay)* (Judgement) [2010] ICJ Rep 14.

[21] Lorraine Elliott, 'Cooperation on Transnational Environmental Crime: Institutional Complexity Matters' *Review of European, Comparative and International Environmental Law*, 26/2 (2017): 107.

[22] Veerle Heyvaert, *Transnational Environmental Regulation and Governance: Purpose, Strategies and Principles* (CUP 2018).

> [I]nternational environmental law, more than most bodies of law, has many of the trappings of a faith. It derives its effect largely from its affect: international environmental law stages a kind of global moral authority, premised on an aesthetic ideal and an ethical disquiet.[23]

Hope in international environmental law also derives from a frustration with national regimes or with politics more generally. These different forms of hope can lead to international environmental law being understood as a 'magic wand' that will provide the answer to vexed environmental problems.

III. WISHFUL THINKING

This confidence in international environmental law to solve environmental problems is a form of wishful thinking. The late Ursula Le Guin described wishful thinking in the context of fiction-writing as 'thinking cut loose from reality, a self-indulgence that is often merely childish, but may be dangerous ... Wishful thinking is Hitler's Thousand-Year Reich'.[24] These are strong words, and they highlight the fact that wishful thinking carries with it risks of not only misunderstanding international environmental law, or even making it ineffective, but also that utopianism can become a vehicle for dystopia.

Wishful thinking is not only a problem among international environmental law students, it haunts environmental law and public international law scholarship as well. Thinking cut free from legal reality, can result in scholars articulating a vision of international environmental law that is not legally possible to deliver. Principles are asserted to be customary even though there are no practices that fit commonly understood ideas of customary international law. Faith is placed in a treaty to coordinate and direct action across a multitude of sovereign states.

Wishful thinking manifests itself in a range of ways and for a range of reasons among students. One set of reasons for wishful thinking is the appeal of thinking of global environmental problems in global terms. If environmental problems such as climate change are 'whole earth' problems then it seems to follow that global responses are the answer. As Jasanoff notes:

> The picture of the earth hanging in space not only renders visible and immediate the object of environmentalists' concern, but it resonates with the themes of finiteness and fragility, and of human dependence on the biosphere, that have provided the chief impetus for environmental mobilization since the 1960s. It is as well a

[23] Stephen Humphreys and Yoriko Otomo, 'Theorizing International Environmental Law' in Anne Orford and Florian Hoffmann (eds), *The Oxford Handbook of the Theory of International Law* (OUP 2016) 799.

[24] Ursula Le Guin, 'Making up Stories' in Ursula Le Guin (ed), *Words Are My Matter: Writings About Life and Books 2000–2016* (Small Beer Press 2016) 108–109.

> deeply political image, subordinating as it does the notional boundaries of sovereign power in favour of swirling clouds that do not respect the lines configured by human conquest or legislation. It is in this respect a fitting emblem of western environmentalism's transnational ambitions.[25]

This form of imagery appears to catalyse global consensus about the nature of environmental problems and possible responses to them, which in turn reinforces the perceived desirability of global responses even if that consensus is in the softest of public international law terms.[26] Indeed, global thinking understands global responses as the *only* answer.[27] Fashionable holistic concepts such as the Anthropocene reinforce this. Again, climate change is a prime example of a problem that attracts such an approach. Such global thinking creates what Tsing has described as a 'dream space of the globe'[28] in which transformations are seen as possible. But therein lies the problem. It is only a 'dream space'.

Another reason for purposive thinking is it is a potential side product of specialization. As Koskenniemi states, 'the world of legal practice is being sliced up in institutional projects that cater for special audiences with special interests and special ethos. The point of creating such specialized institutions is precisely to affect the outcomes that are being produced in the international world'.[29] Such specialization also encourages what he describes as a 'managerial' mind-set in which the 'formal aspect of the legal craft' is 'often seen as an obstacle for effective action'.[30] Such thinking wants to realize ' "actors" … more or less unproblematic "interests" '.[31] To put the matter another way, the functionalist agenda of a subject can lead to hopeful assumptions that law can deliver on those functions. If international environmental law is about protecting the environment then that is what it is assumed to do.

This is not an exhaustive set of reasons. Poor scholarship can also contribute. In highlighting wishful thinking, I am not pretending to unearth something new. Teachers of international environmental law know wishful thinking all too well. The need to quash it is reflected in most international environmental law textbooks, which stress the legal complexity of international environmental law and its limits. Birnie, Boyle, and Redgwell on their first page state that the body of international environmental law that has emerged 'is neither primitive nor unsystematic, though unsurprisingly it has its

25 Sheila Jasanoff, 'Image and Imagination: The Formation of Global Environmental Consciousness' in Clark Miller and Paul Edwards (eds), *Changing the Atmosphere: Expert Knowledge and Environmental Governance* (MIT Press 2001) 309, 310.

26 A point well made by Eloise Scotford, *Environmental Principles and the Evolution of Environmental Law* (Hart Publishing 2017) 74.

27 Bruno Latour, *Down to Earth: Politics in a New Climatic Regime* (Polity Press 2018) 13.

28 Anna Lowenhaupt Tsing, *Frictions: An Ethnography of Global Connection* (Princeton University Press 2005) 86.

29 Martti Koskenniemi, 'The Politics of International Law—20 Years Later' *European Journal of International Law,* 20/1 (2009): 7, 9.

30 Martti Koskenniemi, *The Politics of International Law* (Hart Publishing 2011) 72.

31 Ibid.

weaknesses, as we will see'.[32] Sands and Peel frame the subject through a set of principles, but still explicitly recognize the limits of international environmental law.[33]

Textbooks chart the history of the subject so as to illustrate that the development of international environmental law has been far from smooth.[34] There is attention to formal legal-making processes, but also discussion of governance regimes. By the fifth page of her *Advanced Introduction to International Environmental Law*, Hey is making clear that a study of international environmental law cannot only focus on 'classic inter-state law'.[35] Textbook authors spill much ink getting students to have a tactile appreciation of different types of legal material. The first three hundred pages of Birnie, Boyle, and Redgwell are a case in point.[36] Principles are postulated, but there is no pretence that these provide neat answers. There is also no hiding the complexity of the subject behind neat schematas and over-generalizations.

In short, international environmental law texts are trying to discourage global and managerialist thinking. Indeed, what textbooks often do, like I did in the introduction to my international environmental law chapter is attempt to bring their reader back to earth. Bodansky, for example, at the start of *The Art and Craft of International Environmental Law*[37] begins with an anecdote about a discussion between him and an environmental organization campaigner, the point of which is that 'legal matters are rarely so simple' in international environmental law as the campaigner thought them.[38]

All this is good at responding to the second and third challenges in teaching international environmental law as outlined in the first section. Using one of these textbooks, there cannot be any doubt that international environmental law is complex and not a simple answer to environmental problems. It is also the case that nearly all these textbooks attempt to balance formalist and realist accounts of international environmental law. This is important to note because in discussing wishful thinking, scholars in international environmental law and public international law often perceive it as just about too great an emphasis on posited law.[39] Simpson notes that the latter has been classically understood as involving an 'entertaining and inconclusive conversation between a hopeful and self-righteous legalism and a self-assured dismissive realism'.[40] But textbooks, generally speaking, attempt to describe both the legal norms of international environmental law and how they work in practice. This is not just in relation to a general

[32] Birnie, Boyle, and Redgwell (n 15) 1.

[33] Philippe Sands and Jacqueline Peel, *Principles of International Environmental Law* (4th edn, CUP 2018) 11, 16–17.

[34] See eg Dupuy and Viñuales' discussion of the sustainable development 'snake' (n 14) 23.

[35] Ellen Hey, *Advanced Introduction to International Environmental Law* (Edward Elgar 2016) 5.

[36] Birnie, Boyle, and Redgwell (n 15).

[37] Bodansky (n 16) 1–4.

[38] Ibid, 3.

[39] Daniel Bodansky, 'Legal Realism and its Discontents' *Leiden Journal of International Law*, 28/2 (2015): 267.

[40] Gerry Simpson, 'On the Magic Mountain: Teaching Public International Law' *European Journal of International Law*, 10/1 (1999): 70, 71.

overview of the subject but also in regards to specific areas. Birnie, Boyle, and Redgwell highlight how an area such as the international regulation of toxic substances illustrates the 'importance of adequate institutional machinery for supervising implementation'.[41] Sands and Peel are clear-eyed in their discussion of the complex reality of different regulatory areas.[42]

Yet while these texts in their mixture of internal and external accounts of the law[43] are clearly responding to wishful thinking in international environmental law, that message can get a little lost. One reason is to do with the amount of material that any international environmental law text must cover. Thus as Bonilla Maldonado notes, some scholarly texts focus on providing a systematic discussion of materials which 'end up being excessively similar to the materials created by the legislature or the judiciary'.[44] This need to systematically describe is reinforced by the lack of an intellectual base line among students. Given this, much teaching of international environmental law ultimately has to focus on helping students understand the subject in a descriptive sense and nothing else. The 'mastery of core concepts' primarily becomes focused on charting the vast landscape of international environmental law.

There is of course nothing inherently wrong in this. The importance of providing a map for a landscape should not be under-estimated. But there are two potential problems that do emerge. The first is the one that I started this chapter with—that as a teacher of international environmental law, the pedagogical temptation is to teach cynicism as you map the subject.[45] Faced with students wanting to place their faith in international environmental law, instruction becomes an ongoing process of quashing those expectations. 'No, the Paris Agreement is not the "answer" to climate change.' 'Environmental principles are not automatically general principles of public international law.' 'Yes, I know states have ratified the treaty but that they are sovereign states and this is public international law.'

These are not very effective pedagogical responses however. Not only do such statements tend to be met by incredulous looks from students (and on occasion other scholars), they do little to help students 'master core concepts' so as to foster their legal expertise in regards to international environmental law. As Koskenniemi has argued, international law involves a dialectic between a commitment to it as an intellectual idea and a cynicism concerning its limits.[46] Focusing too much on addressing wishful thinking, results in too little being paid to the 'commitment' to legal ideas—that is the

[41] Birnie, Boyle, and Redgwell (n 15) 486.

[42] Sands and Peel (n 33).

[43] On this distinction see Christopher McCrudden, 'Legal Research and the Social Sciences' *Law Quarterly Review*, 122 (2006): 632.

[44] Daniel Bonilla Maldonado, 'Environmental Law Scholarship: Systemization, Reform, Explanation, and Understanding' in Pedersen (n 5) 45.

[45] On ideas of cynicism in public international law, see Martti Koskenniemi, 'Between Commitment and Cynicism: Outline for a Theory of International Law as Practice' in Jean d'Aspremont *et al* (eds), *International Law as a Profession* (CUP 2017).

[46] Ibid.

'wholesale, ultimately unreflective or sentimental "throwing-of-oneself" into one's work, an unthinking loyalty to one's profession, its constitutive goodness rules and traditions, as well as an unwavering belief in its intrinsic goodness'.[47]

IV. LEGAL IMAGINATION

It is at this point that is useful to return to Le Guin. In talking about wishful thinking in fiction writing, she was comparing it with imagination. In contrast to wishful thinking, 'imagination, even in its wildest flights, is not detached from reality: imagination acknowledges reality, starts from it, and returns to enrich it . . . Imagination is the Constitution of the United States'.[48] This may again read as exaggeration, but Le Guin is highlighting two important points.

The first is the idea of imagination. Imagination is important in legal thinking.[49] Law is abstract. What it is, and what it can be, depends on how lawyers think about formulating, applying, and enforcing the law. This is not an individual exercise of creativity, what it is acceptable to imagine about the law is about a 'common understanding which makes possible common social practices, and a widely shared sense of legitimacy'.[50] In fostering legal expertise, teachers of international environmental law are really fostering legal imagination. We are teaching what are, and what are not, shared understandings of international environmental law.[51]

Thus, textbooks such as Birnie, Boyle, and Redgwell, are getting students to think about different types of legal norms.[52] Likewise, in the wider literature there is an emphasis on getting readers to engage with the nature of the legal texts in international environmental law. Take for example the excellent article by Rajamani and Werksman examining the legal nature of Article 2 of the 2015 Paris Agreement.[53] In that article, by careful legal analysis they show the legal nature, legal potential, and legal limitations of Article 2. They show its symbolism, its operational implications, but also how it falls short of the 'existential aspirations of the most vulnerable countries that the goal represents'.[54] Or consider Boyle's remarks about the nature of international adjudication and its limits in international environmental law which makes clear the importance of

[47] Ibid, 40.

[48] Le Guin (n 24) 108–109.

[49] Martin Loughlin, 'The Constitutional Imagination' *Modern Law Review*, 78/1 (2015): 1.

[50] Charles Taylor, *A Secular Age* (Belknap Press 2007) 172 discussing the idea of social imaginaries.

[51] The importance of imagination can be seen in other disciplines. See eg Jens Beckert, *Imagined Futures: Fictional Expectations and Capitalist Dynamics* (Harvard University Press 2016).

[52] Birnie, Boyle, and Regdwell (n 15).

[53] Lavanya Rajamani and Jacob Werksman, 'The Legal Character and Operational Relevance of the Paris Agreement's Temperature Goal' *Philosophical Transactions of the Royal Society A*, 376 (2018): 20160458.

[54] Ibid, 12.

having a theory of international environmental law law-making and adjudication for understanding the role of courts in enforcing international environmental law norms.[55]

In these different texts we can see the emphasis on teaching what it is that you can and can't do with international environmental law. What is possible and what is not. What is a ridiculous argument and what has potential. All in all, we are in the realm of legal imagination. As Del Mar, one of the thoughtful scholars on the topic of legal imagination, notes:

> [I]magination plays an important and under-estimated role in legal reasoning by enabling and sustaining an inquiry into normative relevance, i.e. into what values and interests may be at stake in a particular case and in cases of that kind. Artefacts like metaphors, hypothetical scenarios and figuration are valuable for individual lawyers and judges, for scenes of interaction in courtrooms and for the resourcefulness of legal language over time.[56]

This comment may suggest that imagination is only for courtrooms. That is not the case. Del Mar has described legal imagination in the public international law context as 'an active and conscious mental process … which involves four different (though combinable) abilities: supposing, relating, image-making and/or perspective-taking'.[57] In teaching international environmental law, we are really teaching all these things. We need to teach supposition, because so much of international environmental law is directed towards understanding how international environmental law will operate in the future. We need to teach how things relate to each other, and how different perspectives operate.

As Del Mar stresses, public international law is full of metaphor and that metaphor is doing a lot of legal work.[58] Del Mar used the example of metaphor in customary international law, and this is an area where metaphor has been particularly significant.[59] But the role of metaphor can also can be seen in regards to other areas. Take for example, discussions around the legal norms in the Paris Agreement. By analyzing the variety of forms of the 'softness' of legal norms, an understanding of what international environmental law is, and what it can be can be, develops.[60] As Rajamani notes, the Agreement 'contains a carefully calibrated mix of hard, soft and non-obligations, the boundaries

[55] Alan Boyle, 'The Limits of Judicial Mechanisms for Developing and Enforcing International Environmental Norms: Remarks by Alan Boyle' *Proceedings of the ASIL Annual Meeting*, 109 (2015): 198.

[56] Maksymilian Del Mar, 'Educating the Legal Imagination' *Law and Method*, Special Issue on Active Learning and Teaching in Legal Education (2018): 16.

[57] Maksymilian Del Mar, 'Metaphor in International Law: Language, Imagination and Normative Inquiry' *Nordic Journal of International Law*, 86/2 (2017): 170, 174.

[58] Ibid, 183–184.

[59] See egVaughan Lowe, *International Law: A Very Short Introduction* (OUP 2015) 21 discussing the idea of custom as a footpath.

[60] Rajamani, 'Paris Agreement: Interplay' (n 17) and Jonathan Pickering *et al*, 'Global Climate Governance Between Hard and Soft Law: Can the Paris Agreement's "Crème Brûlée" Approach Enhance Ecological Reflexivity?' *Journal of Environmental Law*, 31/1 (2019): 1

between which are blurred. Each of these types of obligations plays a distinct and valuable role'.[61] Seeing this allows one to see what international environmental law is, and what it can be.

My overall point is that Koskenniemi's idea of 'commitment', in the teaching context at least, is better understood as less a commitment to law, but as a commitment to legal imagination. The focus in teaching international environmental law must be on teaching law, but in doing so the focus is on what is, and is not, possible to do with a body of law. Approaching the challenges of teaching in this way provides a different intellectual starting point. The first priority is not to dash student's expectations, but to introduce them to the lived existence of international environmental law. By that I don't mean just the politics of international environmental law (which is what legal realists focus on), but something far more multifaceted. This is because the actuality of international environmental law does not have a singular dimension.

V. LEGAL AND ENVIRONMENTAL REALITIES

That brings me to the other point that Le Guin makes about imagination—that it is grounded in reality. What distinguishes wishful thinking and imagination is this grounding. The important point about legal imagination is thus that any form of legal reasoning must relate to what actually exists—in terms of common understandings of legal norms and the contexts they operate in. And it is this which the different examples of scholarship I noted above are doing. Specifically, they are getting readers to pay careful attention to legal texts and the political realities of international relations.

Putting this type of work front and centre in the teaching of international environmental law is thus important. It is also not an easy feat given the first of the challenges highlighted in the first section—that students come to the study of international environmental law from a range of different intellectual backgrounds. But, what is interesting to note about some of the pieces cited above is that not all are written for legal audiences. The Rajamani and Werksman article is a prime example.[62] It is also the case that by clarifying what 'mastery of concepts' we are trying to foster in students, we can begin to meet the challenge more head on. As I suggested in the second section, there is a problem that the importance of focusing on the nature of legal norms can get rather lost in the perceived need to map international environmental law. By shifting our pedagogical priorities, we can perhaps begin to centre our attention more on fostering legal imagination. In doing that, the teaching needs of different groups of students might become more obvious.

[61] Rajamani, 'Paris Agreement: Interplay' (n 17) 358.
[62] Rajamani and Werksman (n 53).

Focusing directly on the legal realities of law is not enough however. The wishful thinking in regards to international environmental law is also wishful thinking in regards to the ease with which environmental problems can be solved. On this basis, the challenges in teaching international environmental law are not just problems of not understanding law, but also problems of not understanding how intractable environmental problems are and how that intractability resonates within legal thinking. Presuming that environmental problems are capable of managerial and global responses is due to thinking such problems are discrete and contained enough that they can yield to utopian and technical answers.[63]

Part of teaching the reality of international environmental law thus needs to be teaching the nature of environmental problems. Environmental problems are themselves socially and environmentally complex. While they may be global, environmental problems are inherently polycentric and multilevel.[64] They are also dynamic and the science in regards to them unsettled. As I have explained elsewhere, building on the work of Michel Callon,[65] environmental problems are 'hot situations' in which it is hard to provide an authoritative account of the facts, the relevant interests are by no means clear, and the socio-political controversies meaningful.[66] Getting your head around just how structurally significant these things are for law is not easy, but by showing that legal significance, the nature of international environmental law can be understood.

A fundamental starting point in international environmental law is thus showing how environmental problems are not always easy to identify and can be even more difficult to frame. Indeed, much of the work of law is in framing environmental problems so that responses can be developed in relation to them.[67] The 1992 Convention on Biological Diversity may by soft law, but it has a powerful role in making genetic diversity—a thing to identify and a thing to value. The Paris Agreement reframed inter-state cooperation in regards to climate change.[68] What these examples also highlight is the way in which the substance of international environmental law develops as a response to the nature of environmental problems. This is its legal reality—hot situations led to 'hot law'.[69]

But hot law is not something that is pulled out of the proverbial hat. It builds on, and evolves out of, the law that already exists. In the first instance that is public international law, but given the multilevel nature of environmental problems it also involves other

[63] Elizabeth Fisher, 'Imagining Technology and Environmental Law' in Roger Brownsword, Eloise Scotford, and Karen Yeung (eds), *Oxford Handbook of Law, Regulation and Technology* (OUP 2017).

[64] Elinor Ostrom, 'Polycentric Systems for Coping with Collective Action and Global Environmental Change' *Global Environmental Change*, 20/4 (2010): 550.

[65] Michel Callon, 'An Essay on Framing and Overflowing: Economic Externalities Revisited by Sociology' in Michel Callon (ed), *The Laws of the Markets* (New Jersey: Blackwell 1998) 260–261.

[66] Elizabeth Fisher, 'Environmental Law as "Hot" Law' *Journal of Environmental Law*, 25/3 (2013): 347.

[67] Sheila Jasanoff *et al*, 'Adjudicating the GM Food Wars: Science, Risk, and Democracy in World Trade Law' *Yale Journal of International Law*, 30 (2005): 1.

[68] Lavanya Rajamani, 'The Devilish Details: Key Legal Issues in the 2015 Climate Negotiations' *Modern Law Review*, 78/5 (2015): 826.

[69] Fisher, 'Hot Law' (n 66).

legal processes. It may involve states, but it also will involve a range of other actors. That is one of the reasons why in studying international environmental law there is a need to study different forms of international environmental law hybrids—whether multilevel[70] transnational,[71] or private actor based[72] in nature. Overall, by teaching the 'hot' reality of environmental problems, the importance of legal imagination can be reinforced. In covering these areas, it is not simply covering another subject area, but understanding what types of legal norms and legal reasoning are operating.

In saying all this I am not saying I have mastered international environmental law teaching (or international environmental law for that matter). Also remember that I offer up here a few reflections, rather than a template for teaching international environmental law. The revised international environmental law chapter for my co-authored textbook may be less cynical, but it could still do more to foster legal imagination.

My overall point is a more prosaic one—in teaching we should aim to use those approaches that foster the expertise needed for international environmental law. In doing that, we need to confront the series of disconnections involved in that process of teaching. All I have identified above is a set of starting points for doing that—the need to focus our efforts on teaching both legal imagination and legal realities. Such a starting point not only makes clear that international environmental law can never be a magic wand, but also the types of legal skills that are needed to understand it and practise it. What is perhaps more significant is that established divisions between legal formalism and legal realism are not what really haunts the subject. We also must be wary of too much cynicism.

VI. CONCLUSION

There are those who think teaching is for losers—on this basis it is for those who failed at practice, or as scholars, or just for those who can't 'do'. Textbook writing can often attract a similar critique. None of this is the case. Teaching is hard. Good teaching is even harder. Good textbook writing even harder still.[73] This is particularly so when it comes to international environmental law.

More importantly, teaching is fundamental to the future of law and the legal profession. This is particularly so when, as a form of expertise, law is a socialized form of

[70] Lorraine Elliott, 'Cooperation on Transnational Environmental Crime: Institutional Complexity Matters' *Review of European, Comparative and International Environmental Law*, 26/2 (2017): 107.

[71] Gregory Shaffer and Daniel Bodansky, 'Transnationalism, Unilateralism and International Law' *Transnational Environmental Law*, 1/1 (2012): 31.

[72] Joanne Scott *et al*, 'The Promise and Limits of Private Standards in Reducing Greenhouse Gas Emissions from Shipping' *Journal of Environmental Law*, 29/2 (2017): 231.

[73] Liz Fisher, Bettina Lange, and Eloise Scotford, 'The Glamour of Textbook Writing' (2017) <https://global.oup.com/uk/orc/law/environmental/fisher/resources/textbook-writing/> accessed 7 December 2018.

expertise—it depends not just on a single person—but the way in which the legal community interacts and operates.[74] The acquisition of expertise is a 'social process—a process of socialization into the practices of an expert group', and, as a result, individuals gain expertise by 'social immersion' in groups who possess an expertise.[75] That process of immersion begins as soon as a student enters an international environmental law classroom. In teaching international environmental law, we are teaching those processes of interaction, and in so doing we are helping our students to identify the concepts and skills they must master. We must teach legal substance and we must teach about the reality of the law. We must discourage wishful thinking, but more importantly we must foster legal imagination by grounding our analysis in the lived reality of international environmental law.

BIBLIOGRAPHY

Maksymilian Del Mar, 'Metaphor in International Law: Language, Imagination and Normative Inquiry' *Nordic Journal of International Law*, 86/2 (2017): 170

Elizabeth Fisher, *Environmental Law: A Very Short Introduction* (OUP 2017)

Elizabeth Fisher, Bettina Lange, and Eloise Scotford, *Environmental Law: Text, Cases and Materials* (2nd edn, OUP 2019) ch 12

Lavanya Rajamani and Jacob Werksman, 'The Legal Character and Operational Relevance of the Paris Agreement's Temperature Goal' *Philosophical Transactions of Royal Society A*, 376 (2018): 20160458

[74] Richard Sennett, *The Craftsman* (Allen Lane 2008).

[75] Harry Collins and Robert Evans, *Rethinking Expertise* (University of Chicago Press 2007) 3.

PART II

ANALYTICAL APPROACHES

CHAPTER 9

INTERNATIONAL RELATIONS THEORY

PETER LAWRENCE

I. INTRODUCTION

THE current fabric of international environmental law is clearly inadequate to address the global ecological crisis. Scientists point to planetary boundaries spanning not just climate—but also biological diversity—which have been crossed or will be in the near future.[1] However, the current international treaty regimes are deficient to meet this challenge. Moreover, in relation to significant environmental threats such as geo-engineering and plastics in the ocean, there is either a fragmentary or no international regime at all.

Understanding how international law works is a precondition for its reform. This makes international relations (IR) of vital importance to international environmental law (IEL). IR theory and empirical studies provide insights into how international environmental agreements may be modified to effectively address environmental threats. Key issues include whether sanctions are essential for compliance and effectiveness, and whether the choice of hard law rather than soft law makes a difference. Reform strategies either make explicit assumptions about how international law affects state behaviour, or such assumptions remain implicit. Either way, IR theory throws light on the relationship between international law and state behaviour.

This chapter proceeds on the basis that such assumptions should be brought out in the open and debated. Some have argued, however, that IR methodology should be kept away from international legal discourse as combining the two in interdisciplinary projects carries 'a serious risk of reproducing, or even strengthening, existing power

[1] Will Steffen *et al*, 'Planetary Boundaries: Guiding Human Development on a Changing Planet' *Science*, 347/6223 (2015): 1259855.

configurations'.[2] It is true that IEL and IR have distinct methodologies which should not be blurred. However, IR literature can shed light on issues related to the implementation and effectiveness of IEL which is critical to reform efforts.

Interdisciplinary work between international environmental lawyers and IR scholars has burgeoned only recently. The dominance of the 'realist school' of IR until the 1980s stymied such collaborative work. This flowed from the realist assumption that international law had no independent normative force on states, and was just an instrument of state power. In recent decades this picture has been shown to be simplistic, and a more sophisticated picture of the inter-relationship between law and power has emerged.[3]

The field of IR and IEL has become increasingly dense in terms of approaches. This chapter aims to introduce some (not all) of the key theories and suggest areas for future research.

The chapter is structured as follows. Section II explores the relationship between power and IEL. Section III deals with governance. Section IV deals with norms, legalization, and effectiveness, and the linkage between norms and discourses is also explored. Section V addresses legitimacy and democratization. Section VI examines how scientific knowledge can be incorporated into IEL. Section VII draws conclusions.

II. POWER AND HEGEMONY

IR Insight 1: International Environmental Law Reflects Relational Power—Both Material and Discursive

The concept of power is multidimensional. It involves not just the capacity to cause particular events, but also the capacity to maintain particular institutions and rules which favour particular interests.[4] Power has both a material dimension (eg military, economic) but also a discursive one,[5] including the capacity to influence through ideas, ideologies, or discourses.[6]

IR theorists have posed important questions about power and IEL. To what extent do multilateral environment agreements reflect particular power relations between states

[2] Jan Klabbers, 'The Relative Autonomy of International Law or The Forgotten Politics of Interdisciplinarity' *Journal of International Law and International Relations*, 1/1-2 (2004): 35, 35–36.

[3] Mark Klamberg, *Power and Law in International Society, International Relations as the Sociology of International Law* (Routledge 2015) 29.

[4] Shirley Scott, 'International Law as Ideology: Theorising The Relationship Between International Law and International Politics' *European Journal of International Law*, 5/3 (1994): 313, 315; Scott maintains that 'causation is the essence of all definitions of power'.

[5] Peter Newell, 'The Political Economy of Global Environmental Governance' *Review of International Studies*, 34/3 (2008): 507, 524.

[6] Maarten Hajer, *The Politics of Environmental Discourse: Ecological Modernization and the Policy Process* (OUP 1995).

and the power of non-state interests such as corporations? Do such agreements have any power to influence behaviour?

According to the 'realist' (and later 'neo-realist' versions) school of IR, states are the key players in international system (not international organizations or non-governmental organizations (NGOs)); states will only act out of narrow self-interest; and international law has no pull on state behaviour.[7] According to this approach, power politics determines outcomes, with international law, ethics, and justice pushed to the margins and only utilized when deemed necessary for the vital interests of state.[8] And states enter into—and comply—with treaties, only if the obligations accord with the particular states' self-interest.[9]

While this approach has some explanatory power, it fails to explain particular international events. This is reflected, for instance, in the negotiations for the 1995 Waigani South Pacific Convention on Nuclear and Hazardous Waste.[10] While some elements of these negotiations reflected power politics (eg the United States' insistence on transit passage for nuclear vessels through the South Pacific), other elements can only be understood through a justice framing entailing the position that it was unfair for wealthy countries to ship hazardous waste to vulnerable island states.[11] More fundamentally, the realist approach glosses over the extent to which international law plays a constitutive role in establishing the parameters within which states justify particular conduct. Reflecting this criticism, a number of scholars, including Wendt and Ruggie, have taken a 'constructivist' view which emphasizes the international system as a social structure involving social relationships.[12] While realists focus on material resources, constructivists emphasize social structures which include not only material resources, but also shared knowledge and practices.

The following case studies illustrate the interplay between material interests and discourses and ideas, in the process of making IEL.

The development of the global regime relating to plant genetic resources illustrates the importance of material economic power.[13] Prior to the 1980s, property rights did not extend to plant genetic resources (PGR), only to individual plants, so at this stage PGRs were

[7] See eg Hans Morgenthau, *Politics among Nations: The Struggle for Power and Peace* (4th edn, Alfred Knopf 1967).

[8] Klamberg (n 3) 38.

[9] Ibid.

[10] The author led the Australian delegation to the final negotiation session of the Convention to Ban the Importation into Forum Island Countries of Hazardous and Radioactive Wastes and to Control the Transboundary Movement and Management of Hazardous Wastes within the South Pacific Region.

[11] Peter Lawrence and David Hoogstraten, 'Protecting the South Pacific from Hazardous and Nuclear Waste Dumping: The Waigani Convention' *Review of European Community & International Environmental Law*, 7/3 (1998): 268.

[12] Alexander Wendt, 'Constructing International Politics' *International Security* 20/1 (1995): 71, 72–73; John Gerard Ruggie, *Constructing the World Policy: Essays on International Institutionalism* (Routledge 1998) 11; see also Christian Reus-Smit (ed), *The Politics of International Law* (CUP 2004).

[13] This case study relies on Kal Raustiala and David Victor, 'The Regime Complex for Plant Genetic Resources' *International Organization*, 58/2 (2004): 277.

considered the 'common heritage of mankind'. This changed owing to the development, initially in the United States, of genetic engineering and biotechnology. The companies involved in this process pushed for an extension of intellectual property protection to PGRs as they would then receive rewards for their investments. Internationally, this set of interests resonated with developing countries who asserted sovereignty over PGRs as a means of gaining a return for the exploitation of this resource. This set of interests played a decisive role in the extension of intellectual property rights to PGRs which found reflection in the 1994 World Trade Organisation (WTO) TRIPs agreement (Agreement on Trade-Related Aspects of Intellectual Property Rights) as well as the 1992 Convention on Biological Diversity (CBD) and the 2001 International Treaty on Plant Genetic Resources for Food and Agriculture Organisation treaty on PGRs.[14]

The content of IEL in this example reflects material interests in the form of economic power—evidenced both in corporations pursuing a return on their investments, and the economic interests of developing countries. Developing countries' interests were expressed through discourses emphasizing fairness and justice. Neo-realists and constructivists are likely to perceive the influence of these discourses differently. However, at a minimum, it is indisputable that the interplay between these discourses and material interests, accounts for the development of IEL in this field.

The relatively weak global regime for climate change partly reflects the continuing power of vested fossil-fuel related interests,[15] but also power expressed through discourses and ideologies. IR discourse analysis has explained the global climate regime in terms of 'discourses', defined as a 'shared way of apprehending the world' which 'rests on assumptions, judgements, and contentions'.[16] 'Discourse analysis' traces the process whereby particular discourses become 'authoritative', whereas others become 'discredited'.[17] Progress in developing the climate regime has been held back because of the dominance of discourses of economic growth and a 'Promethean discourse' involving a belief that the market will provide a technological fix.[18]

The climate negotiations have also been impacted by material or economic power in conjunction with the discourse of neoliberalism. Indeed, IEL can be understood in a historical context as involving the triumph of the discourse of neoliberalism. McGee and Steffeck demonstrate this in the climate context as involving the shift in the move from top-down regulatory approaches reflected in the 1997 Kyoto Protocol, to a voluntary 2009 Copenhagen pledge and review approach, which came to be reflected in the 2015 Paris Agreement's system of nationally determine contributions (NDCs).[19] The

[14] See Chapter 48, 'Intellectual Property', in this volume.

[15] David Ciplet, Timmons Roberts, and Mizan Khan, *Power in a Warming World: The New Global Politics of Climate Change and the Remaking of Environmental Inequality* (MIT Press 2015).

[16] John Dryzek, *The Politics of the Earth: Environmental Discourses* (1st edn, OUP 1997) 8.

[17] Hajer (n 6) 44.

[18] Hayley Stevenson and John Dryzek, *Democratizing Global Climate Governance* (CUP 2014).

[19] Jeffrey McGee and Jens Steffek, 'The Copenhagen Turn in Global Climate Governance and the Contentious History of Differentiation in International Law' *Journal of Environmental Law*, 28/1 (2016): 37;

push for injecting justice into the Paris Agreement framework is continuing, but in a different form, including in, for example the global stocktake which involves interpretation of references to equity in the Paris Agreement.[20]

In summary, IR theory and empirical studies demonstrate that the form and substance of IEL reflects both material/economic interests and discursive elements, including dominant discourses of growth and neoliberalism.

III. NORMS, LEGALIZATION, AND EFFECTIVENESS

IR Insight 2: IEL Contains a Spectrum of Soft to Hard Norms which Reflect Not Only Material Interests, but Shared Understandings and Discourses with Justice and Ethical Dimensions

Discourses, ideas, and ideologies may coalesce into 'norms'. Bodansky defines 'norms' as 'a community standard that aims to guide or influence the behaviour' of states, institutions, and private actors.[21] 'Normative' is used to refer to the ethical/justice-related underpinnings of such norms.

Applying Bodansky's definition, legal norms are a subset of the category of norms, the scope of which depends on one's theory of law. A strictly positivist approach would limit this subset, excluding for example non-binding 'soft law'. Recent IR scholarship has tended to analyse the full spectrum of legal/hard and soft/non-legal norms. This is, however, a recent phenomenon. The realist and neo-realist approaches which held sway until the 1980s, assumed that norms (whether legal or not) had no impact on state behaviour. With recent constructivist, regime theorist, and other challenges to realist accounts, the role of norms has come to be understood in a more nuanced fashion.[22] This shift in IR theory opened up the possibility of analyzing a broader range of questions related to the role of norms, including through interdisciplinary scholarship with international

the Copenhagen Accord is found at Decision 2/CP.15, 'Copenhagen Accord' (30 March 2010) UN Doc FCCC/CP/2009/11/Add.1, 4–9.

[20] See Chapter 20, 'Equity', in this volume; Peter Lawrence and Michael Reder, 'Equity and the Paris Agreement: Legal and Philosophical Perspectives' *Journal of Environmental Law*, 31/3 (2019): 511.

[21] Daniel Bodansky, *The Art and Craft of International Environmental Law* (Harvard University Press 2010) 87; cf. Martha Finnemore and Kathryn Sikkink, 'International Norm Dynamics and Political Change' *International Organization*, 52/4 (1998): 887, 891 who define a norm as 'a standard of appropriate behaviour for actors with a given identity'.

[22] See eg Martha Finnemore and Stephen Toope, 'Alternatives "Legalization": Richer Views of Law and Politics' *International Organization*, 55/3 (2001): 743.

lawyers. While international lawyers such as Henkin tended to assume that international law was complied with most of the time,[23] IR scholars insisted on the need for empirical demonstration of this. This opened up further research questions. These included, for instance: whether sanctions were indispensable for compliance with law; whether hard (binding) norms were more likely to be complied with than soft norms; whether this involved a trade-off in terms of maximizing participation; whether ethics influences norms, or were norms always rationalizations of state interest; and what role do non-state actors play in the evolution of norms?

Approaches to answering these questions reflected a range of theories, each built on assumptions about the behaviour of states. The constructivist approach challenged the realist and neo-realist view that state behaviour could always be attributed to material self-interest. Scholars such as Wendt pointed out that there were many norms at work in the international system that were uncontested and had become internalized, for example norms linked to sovereignty and non-intervention.[24] Furthermore, some norms (eg in relation to slavery) changed over time, and this change could not be explained just by material interests but also reflected changing notions of ethical conduct. While rationalist /realist approaches assumed that states made choices based on a cost benefit analysis, Wendt suggested, rather that states chose institutional designs 'on the basis of what is normatively appropriate'.[25] Wendt suggested there was a 'life-cycle of norms' involving 'norm entrepreneurs' who played a leadership role in persuading others to ascribe to the new norm. Once a minimum number of states ascribed to a new norm, there was a 'norm cascade' as the norm was rapidly adopted by a large number of states. Norms were linked to identity.[26] For example, liberal western states came to see their identity linked to equal voting rights for women from the early 1930s.[27]

However, this early scholarship on norms had its limitations. It manifest a pro-western bias with 'norm entrepreneurs' limited to western states. And it tended to treat 'norms' as unchanging over time. Recent IR literature has sought to overcome these deficiencies, through examining how non-western states are influencing norms,[28] the processes involved in both norm creation over time,[29] and resistance to norm creation.[30]

[23] Louis Henkin, *How Nations Behave: Law and Foreign Policy* (2nd edn, Columbia University Press 1979).

[24] Alexander Wendt, 'Driving with a Rearview Mirror: On the Rational Science of Institutional Design' *International Organization*, 55/4 (2001): 1019.

[25] Ibid, 1024.

[26] Ibid, 1025.

[27] Ibid, 1025.

[28] Amitav Acharya, 'Norm Subsidiarity and Regional Orders: Sovereignty, Regionalism, and Rulemaking in the Third World' *International Studies Quarterly*, 55/1 (2011): 95.

[29] See survey of the literature in Shirley Scott, 'Treaty-Making in International Organizations: International Relations Theory' in Simon Chesterman, David Malone, and Santiago Villalpando (eds), *The Oxford Handbook of United Nations Treaties* (OUP 2019) 2–4.

[30] Alan Bloomfield and Shirley Scott, *Norm Antipreneurs and the Politics of Resistance to Global Normative Change* (Routledge 2018).

The development of IEL can be described as the promulgation of norms in the shape of principles which have a strong ethical/justice dimension (eg sustainable development, common but differentiated responsibilities, polluter pays, precautionary principle and no harm principle). Sustainable development entails a concept of not only addressing north-south inequality but also intergenerational equity. The development of the climate regime can partly be explained as the result of contestation between these ethically-based concepts and dominant discourses on the one hand and vested interests on the other which have restrained the full embodiment of these principles in the regime. Stevenson and Dryzek, analyzing the climate regime in terms of the dominant discourses, found the negotiation process reflective of discourses which emphasized the compatibility between economic growth and environment protection (so-called 'ecological modernisation').[31]

IR empirical studies[32] suggest that global environment regimes will not be successful unless they embody overlapping understandings of 'fairness' in terms of the distribution of burdens between countries. Furthermore, such understandings require trust between the north and the south. Such trust is unlikely to be forthcoming until the considerable inequalities in the structure of the global economic system are addressed including, for example, the WTO rules relating to agricultural subsidies which ignore the interests of developing countries.[33] Breakey has argued that the key to the success of the Paris Agreement is an approach to negotiation that involves genuine moral discourse with states willing to make compromises for the greater good.[34] Such a move, he argues, may be spurred through self-interest as catastrophic climate events become more frequent. Recent IR empirical studies indicate that in the climate change negotiations, states have tended to support distributive principles of fairness which happen to align with their national self-interest.[35] This does not undermine the importance of norms in effective environmental treaty-making. To the contrary it demonstrates that without shared understandings of equity there may be no agreement, or no effective agreement.[36]

The constructivist approach has opened the door to a wider range of approaches to the study of norms in IEL.[37] This has included the process of so-called 'legalization'.

[31] Stevenson and Dryzek (n 18).

[32] See eg Cecilia Albin, *Justice and Fairness in International Negotiation* (CUP 2001).

[33] Kimberly Ann Elliot, 'The WTO, Agriculture, and Development: A Lost Cause' *Bridges Africa*, 7/1 (15 February 2018).

[34] Hugh Breakey, 'COP 20's Ethical Fallout: The Perils of Principles Without Dialogue' *Ethics, Policy & Environment*, 18/2 (2015): 155, 159; see an analysis of how this would play out in relation to equity in the Paris global stock take in Lawrence and Reder (n 20).

[35] Vegard Torstad and Hakon Saelen, 'Fairness in the Climate Negotiations: What Explains Variation in Parties' Expressed Conceptions' *Climate Policy*, 18/5 (2018): 1.

[36] Oran Young, 'Does Fairness Matter in International Environmental Governance? Creating an Effective and Equitable Climate Regime' in Todd Cherry, Jon Hovi, and David McEvoy (eds), *Toward a New Climate Agreement: Conflict, Resolution and Governance* (Taylor and Francis 2014).

[37] See Jutta Brunnée and Stephen Toope, 'International Law and Constructivism: Elements of an Interactional Theory of International Law' *Columbia Journal of Transnational Law*, 39/1 (2000): 18, 19; Brunnée and Toope's interactionist theory of international law strongly incorporates the constructivist approach.

Legalization was defined by Abbott *et al* as including three important dimensions: 1) obligation—whether hard or soft, 2) precision of obligation—was the norm in question sufficiently precise to make clear what conduct was compliant or not with the norm, and 3) delegation—was the norm linked to a third-party dispute resolution procedure, which would assist in making the norm more precise.[38] This framework enabled empirical research to determine the extent to which, for example, a particular environmental regime had progressed in relation to these criteria.[39]

A strength of this approach is that it enabled IEL to be analysed in its institutional setting, and to include a wider spectrum of actors, including NGOs and corporations. Valuable empirical studies have been made in relation to the use of soft law in the CBD[40] and in the Paris climate regime.[41]

A weakness of the 'legalization approach', however, is that it incorporates standards that may be relevant at the national level, but are inappropriate at the international level where a decentralized mode of law-making prevails. The assumption that imprecise rules would necessarily be less effective at the international level is questionable.[42] For example, the vague notion of 'equity' which is part of the Law of the Sea regime, has not prevented this regime in being highly successful in adjudicating maritime delimitation disputes.[43] Lack of precision in relation to the concept of common but differentiated obligations within the climate regime has not prevented this norm from having continuing influence within this regime, albeit in a new form.[44] Similarly, at the international level elaboration of vague standards in treaties tends to occur more often through the use of Conference of Party (COP) decisions, rather than third-party adjudication.[45]

[38] Kenneth Abbott *et al*, 'The Concept of Legalization' *International Organization*, 54/3 (2000): 401–419.

[39] See eg Sylvia Karlsson-Vinkhuyzen and Antto Vihma, 'Comparing the Legitimacy and Effectiveness of Global Hard and Soft Law: An Analytical Framework' *Regulation & Governance*, 3/4 (2009): 400.

[40] Stuart Harrop and Diana Prichard, 'A Hard Instrument Goes Soft: The Implications of the Convention on Biological Diversity's Current Trajectory' *Global Environmental Change* 21/2 (2011): 474.

[41] Jonathan Pickering *et al*, 'Global Climate Governance between Hard and Soft Law: Can the Paris Agreement's 'Crème Brûlée' Approach Enhance Ecological Reflexivity?' *Journal of Environmental Law*, 31/1 (2018): 1; Lavanya Rajamani, 'The 2015 Paris Agreement: Interplay Between Hard, Soft and Non-Obligations' *Journal of Environmental Law*, 28/2 (2016): 337.

[42] Brunnée and Toope (n 37).

[43] See eg *North Sea Continental Shelf (Germany/Denmark; Germany/Netherlands)* (Judgement) [1969] ICJ Rep 3.

[44] See Lavanya Rajamani, 'Ambition and Differentiation in the 2015 Paris Agreement: Interpretative Possibilities and Underlying Politics' *International and Comparative Law Quarterly*, 65/2 (2016): 493; see also Chapter 20, 'Equity', in this volume.

[45] See eg the analysis of the 1994 OECD–non-OECD Basel Convention ban which illustrates how COP decisions interpreting the relevant Basel Convention provisions have played an important role; James Crawford and Phillippe Sands, 'Article 11 Agreement and Basel Convention Export Ban' *ICME Newsletter*, 2 (1997): 1.

Empirical IR studies on the question of whether soft or hard obligations lead to stronger compliance have been equivocal.[46] Part of the problem is methodological. If a state is required by a treaty to undertake action which coincides with its interests then it can be difficult to demonstrate that the action is caused by the treaty obligation.[47] The category of soft treaty norms (non-binding norms within a treaty framework) remains relatively unexplored.[48] This is a key question in terms of the likely effectiveness of the Paris Agreement.

Norms, whether soft or hard, have the potential to change behaviour. IR studies have made an important contribution here, by analyzing the relationship between norms and effectiveness. Effectiveness may be defined narrowly in terms of the specified objectives of a particular environment agreement, or more expansively to include the extent to which the agreement solves the environmental problem in question.[49] If the agreement contains inadequate obligations, then notwithstanding full compliance it can remain ineffective.

In analyzing effectiveness, IR scholarship has demonstrated the wide spectrum of possibilities for behaviour to be modified through a particular regime. In spite of their non-legally binding status, norms may have impacts over time by changing behaviour in ways not captured by a narrow focus on compliance with international legal obligations. An example is the Paris Agreement, which arguably contains weak mitigation commitments, but which nevertheless may, through its overarching goal of moving to a net zero emissions global economy, catalyse ambitious action from NGOs, business, and other actors.[50]

In summary then, IR scholarship has made international environmental lawyers more attuned to the full spectrum of norms, in terms of their possible effectiveness, which is to be demonstrated empirically rather than held as a tenet of faith. Constructivist perspectives have demonstrated the extent to which norms are linked not only to material interests but also to discourses of ethics/justice, which change over time through processes of persuasion involving norm entrepreneurs. Discourse analysis of the climate regime has helped to explain its contours. IR studies have shown the crucial role of developing common understandings on what constitutes fairness as a precondition of agreement.

[46] See eg Joost Pauwelyn, Ramses Wessel, and Jan Wouters (eds), *Informal International Lawmaking* (OUP 2012); see Chapter 51, 'Compliance Theory', in this volume.

[47] 'Commentary and Conclusions' in Dinah Shelton (ed), *Commitment and Compliance: The Role of Non-binding Norms in the International Legal System* (OUP 2000) 449, 457.

[48] See Pickering *et al* (n 41); cf. Peter Lawrence and Daryl Wong, 'Soft Law in the Paris Climate Agreement: Strength or Weakness?' *Review of European, Comparative & International Environmental Law*, 26/3 (2017): 276.

[49] Oran Young (ed), *The Effectiveness of International Environment Agreements: Causal Connections and Behavioural Mechanisms* (MIT Press 2011).

[50] See Harro van Asselt, 'International Climate Change Law in a Bottom-up World' *Questions of International Law* 26 (2016): 5.

IV. GOVERNANCE

IR Insight 3: While States Continue to be Key, There Has Been a Shift Away from State Dominated Institutions to Sub-State and Non-State Actors, Constituting Both a Strength and Weakness

IR theory uses the language of 'governance' and 'regimes' when referring to the institutional context and broader set of practices which place IEL in its institutional setting. Has the increasing role of sub-state and non-state actors in global environmental governance shifted power away from the state to these other actors? To the extent there has been such a shift, does this enhance or limit the effectiveness of IEL? Does the Paris Agreement represent a shift from 'top-down' to 'bottom-up' regimes and what are the repercussions of this? To what extent is fragmentary governance in IEL, with a lack of coherence for example between trade and environment rules, hampering progress?

The Paris climate agreement has been portrayed as a shift from a 'top-down' architecture (involving the targets and timetables of the Kyoto Protocol) to a 'bottom-up' one where governments decide on their own level of greenhouse gas reductions.[51] An advantage of this bottom-up approach is that it has ensured broad participation. But at what cost? Currently, scientists estimate that the combined impact of NDCs, even if fully implemented, will push the planet well above the 1.5/2°C goal contained in the Paris Agreement.[52] A further concern is that the Paris Agreement only contains a soft managerial style non-compliance mechanism. While such a mechanism could potentially work in conjunction with NGO naming and shaming, NGOs are unlikely to be given a strong role in this mechanism.[53] Those of a more optimistic bent, hope that the global stock take process of ramping up emission reductions embedded in the Paris Agreement will provide a vehicle for increasing stringency of commitments. But this remains to be seen.

The Paris Agreement also represents a 'bottom-up' approach in the quantum shift in terms of participation and commitment by sub-state (eg cities) and non-state actors. Since COP 20, the United Nations Framework Convention on Climate Change (UNFCCC) Secretariat has coordinated the NAZCA (the Non-state Actor

[51] Jonathan Pickering, 'Top-Down Proposals for Sharing the Global Climate Policy Effort Fairly: Lost in Translation in a Bottom-Up World?' in Hugh Breakey, Vesselin Popovski, and Rowena Macguire (eds), *Ethical Values and the Integrity of the Climate Change Regime* (Ashgate 2015) 89.

[52] United Nations Environment Programme, *Emissions Gap Report* (2018).

[53] Harro van Asselt, 'The Role of Non-State Actors in Reviewing Ambition, Implementation, and Compliance under the Paris Agreement', *Climate Law*, 6/1 (2016): 91; for analysis of the pros and cons of developing various aspects of the climate regime inside and outside the Paris Agreement see Lawrence and Reder (n 20).

Zone for Climate Action) online portal which contains more than 12,500 individual commitments and initiatives undertaken by sub-national actors and firms.[54] These initiatives involve sub-state and non-state actors in norm setting. IR scholars have used the concept of 'orchestration' to explain the phenomenon.[55]

Orchestration refers to governments and international organizations convening groups of non-state or sub-state actors, and providing guidance on norm-setting pursued by these actors. Thus the NAZCA example above involved orchestration by the UNFCCC Secretariat. Van der Ven *et al* provide an interesting case study of the World Bank orchestrating a coalition of interested governments and industry players who worked together to ban the practice of flaring in oil exploration. These empirical studies suggest that care needs to be taken in assessing the extent to which there is a shift away from the power of the state in law-making in these new non-/sub-state networks. Van der Ven *et al* also demonstrate that overly narrow criteria can give a false impression of the effectiveness of such initiatives. The UK government introduced a, since abandoned, carbon footprint standard in conjunction with a coalition of industry partners. However, the project provided a model which was taken up by governments in France, Japan, and South Korea and also in an international ISO standard.[56]

The shift away from exclusive state-based law-making strengthens IEL in that the processes of norm development can continue despite intransigence by particular governments. Nevertheless, the increased role of non- and sub-state actors raises further complex questions, including issues about how to accurately measure the effectiveness of norms arising from these new processes. The Paris Agreement's incorporation of a 'bottom-up' approach is a strength in that it has facilitated broad participation. But it remains to be seen how effective this approach will prove to be.

V. LEGITIMACY AND DEMOCRATIZATION

IR Insight 4: Legitimacy of Law-Making Institutions and Norms Depends on Both Their Inclusiveness in Terms of Affected Interests and Their Effectiveness

The link between legitimacy and effectiveness was recognized early on by Max Weber who observed that the more an institution was perceived as legitimate, the more stable

[54] See Global Climate Action NAZCA <https://climateaction.unfccc.int/> accessed 23 December 2019.

[55] See eg Kenneth Abbott and Duncan Snidal, 'International Regulation Without International Government: Improving IO Performance through Orchestration' *Review of International Organizations*, 5/3 (2010): 315.

[56] Hamish van der Ven, Steven Bernstein, and Matthew Hoffmann, 'Valuing the Contributions of Nonstate and Subnational Actors to Climate Governance' *Global Environmental Politics*, 17/1 (2017): 1.

and effective it was likely to be.[57] In the more recent period, IR literature has enriched an understanding of the link between IEL and effectiveness. 'Legitimacy' refers to the justification for norms and rules and norm-making institutions.[58]

Bodansky identifies three categories of legitimacy comprising: (1) source-based legitimacy, (2) fairness of process in decision-making (process-based legitimacy), and (3) substantive value of the outcome (outcome-based legitimacy). Karlsson-Vinkhuyzen and Vihma[59] have developed an analytical framework for evaluating both norms and institutions based on governance literature for evaluating normative legitimacy, which further refines Bodansky's framework. Under their schema, source-based legitimacy, includes *expertise* (eg scientific input), *tradition* (history of addressing problems), and *discourses* (eg human rights). Process-based legitimacy refers to normative judgements about the fairness of decision-making processes. This can include, for example, government action through equal participation of states, supplemented by non-governmental participation. It also includes principles of accountability and transparency. Outcome-based legitimacy refers to the effectiveness of norms and institutions, the extent to which governance contributes to problem-solving, but also the extent to which outcomes meet the principles of distributive justice.[60]

In developing these criteria, Karlsson-Vinkhuyzen and Vihma follow those scholars (eg Young)[61] who think it necessary to combine in a holistic way, insights from the rational choice and constructivist paradigms (referred to above), as 'each paradigm has explanatory power for specific situations'.[62] Thus, rationalists have assumed that actors base their decisions on utilitarian calculations, and that compliance therefore depends on carrots and sticks. In contrast, constructivist scholars critique the rationalist approach for its overly narrow positivism and focus on legalization.[63] Under the constructivist paradigm the legitimacy of international norms has a strong link to both the construction of the identity of states and the ultimate effectiveness of such norms.[64]

A further issue is whether *democratic* values should be part of legitimacy criteria. Whether democratic values should be applied at the international level remains contested (cf. Held[65] and Dahl[66]). Most theories of democracy involve a concept

[57] Daniel Bodansky, 'The Legitimacy of International Governance: A Coming Challenge for International Environmental Law?' *American Journal of International Law*, 93/3 (1999): 596, 603.

[58] Ibid.

[59] Karlsson-Vinkhuyzen and Vihma (n 39).

[60] Ibid, 410–413. For application of this framework to mini-lateral climate fora, see Sylvia Karlsson-Vinkhuyzen and Jeff McGee, 'Legitimacy in an Era of Fragmentation: The Case of Global Climate Governance' *Global Environmental Politics*, 13/3 (2013): 56.

[61] Oran Young, *The Institutional Dimensions of Environmental Change: Fit, Interplay, and Scale* (MIT Press 2002).

[62] Karlsson-Vinkhuyzen and Vihma (n 39) 403.

[63] Ibid.

[64] Ibid, 403–404.

[65] David Held, *Democracy and the Global Order: From the Modern State to Cosmopolitan Governance* (Stanford University Press 1995).

[66] Robert Dahl, 'Can International Organisations Be Democratic? A Sceptic's View' in Ian Shapiro and Casiano Hacker-Cordón (eds), *Democracy's Edges* (CUP 1999) 19.

of inclusion, according to which those affected by a decision should have a say in the making of that decision.[67] A strong argument can be made that democratic legitimacy matters for the performance of global institutions and norms, both for intrinsic and instrumental reasons.[68] Indeed international instruments evidence strong support for the value of democracy both in itself and as a precondition for maximizing the fulfilment of human rights.[69] The intrinsic argument is that democratic values imply respect for persons inherent in procedural justice.[70] The instrumental argument is that inclusion can help ensure support for compliance with norms, as participation by actors in the development of norms increases the likelihood that the same actors will support compliance with the same norms.[71]

Until the Paris Agreement, gridlock in global climate negotiations prompted calls for inclusive or exclusive mini-lateralism entailing small groups of countries (eg the twenty highest emitters) pushing ahead to reduce greenhouse gas emissions, including on a regional basis. In spite of the conclusion of the Paris Agreement, issues around mini-lateralism are likely to again come to the fore. Given that the Paris Agreement is inadequate in terms of the current level of NDCs,[72] pressure is likely to mount on small groups of countries moving ahead in terms of deeper commitments but also possibly deciding to treat their NDCs as legally binding.[73] Such scenarios raise the issue of trade-offs between democratic legitimacy and effectiveness. There is a strong argument that such moves should be made in a manner that does not undermine the global UN regime, given the risk of free riding. Kuyper argues that more inclusive decision-making is likely to involve high-quality decision-making given the incorporation of a diversity of interests; it is also likely to maximize the likelihood of compliance with the norms which result from such processes.[74]

The shift towards hybrid forms of multilateralism with important roles for non- and sub-state actors, and governance based on orchestration raises challenging issues of legitimacy.[75] In the Paris climate regime, the plethora of public-private partnerships and

[67] Robert Goodin, 'Enfranchising All Affected Interests, and Its Alternatives' *Philosophy and Public Affairs*, 35/1 (2007): 40; this principle can also arguably be extended to proxy style representation of ecological systems; see Chapter 14, 'Earth Jurisprudence', in this volume.

[68] Klaus Dingwerth has developed criteria for democratic legitimacy which incorporates elements found across a wide spectrum of theories: inclusiveness or fair representation; democratic control (accountability and transparency) and deliberation. See Klaus Dingwerth, *The New Transnationalism: Transnational Governance and its Democratic Legitimacy* (Palgrave Macmillan 2007).

[69] See eg UNGA Res 55/2, 'United Nations Millennium Declaration' (18 September 2000) UN Doc A/RES/55/2, para 6 which states that '[d]emocratic and participatory governance based on the will of the people' best ensures 'dignity' and a range of human rights.

[70] Jonathan Kuyper, 'Gridlock in Global Climate Change Negotiations: Two Democratic Arguments against Minilateralism' in Aaron Maltais and Catriona McKinnon (eds), *The Ethics of Climate Governance* (Rowman and Littlefield 2015) 67.

[71] Ibid.

[72] Emissions Gap Report (n 52).

[73] See Lawrence and Wong (n 48).

[74] Kuyper (n 70).

[75] Karin Baeckstrand and Jonathan Kuyper, 'The Democratic Legitimacy of Orchestration: The UNFCCC, Non-State Actors, and Transnational Climate Governance' *Environmental Politics*, 26/4 (2017): 764.

other non-state commitments are extremely important. However, the lines of accountability in relation to these mechanisms are unclear. Many of the initiatives under the NAZCA, for example, lack quantifiable long-term goals and targets, and there is no mechanism to assess whether targets—where they are included—are achieved.[76] This is an important area of ongoing research, which needs to be extended to other areas.

In summary, IR scholarship has brought a more sophisticated understanding of the ways in which legitimacy operates in relation to IEL. Empirical studies such as those by Karlsson-Vinkhuyzen and Vihma demonstrate that it is crucial to investigate both output forms of legitimacy and process-based elements such as the fairness of decision-making. Such process-based criteria are integral to democratic legitimacy. While the application of such criteria at the international level remains contested, the powerful link between effectiveness and incorporation of affected interests in decision-making, provide ample grounds for democratic legitimacy criteria in relation to IEL processes.

VI. KNOWLEDGE

IR Insight 5: To Be Effective, Environment Agreements Need To Be Linked To Institutions which Ensure Scientific Knowledge Is Fed into Decision-Making Processes in a Manner which Ensures Credibility, Legitimacy and Saliency

The most successful global environmental regimes ensure the smooth transmission of scientific knowledge into policy-making processes, for example the scientific panels of the ozone and the 1973 CITES (Convention on International Trade in Endangered Species of Wild Fauna and Flora) regimes. But the climate regime has been less successful in the transmission of scientific knowledge, and an interesting question is the extent to which this is linked to its institutional arrangements. IR scholarship has focused on what type of institutional arrangements are likely to be most successful, including the issue of whether we need so-called 'boundary organizations' that mediate between scientific and policy-making communities.[77] Concepts of 'usable knowledge' seek to identify the preconditions for scientific knowledge being usable for policy-makers. Procedural justice issues relating to scientific policy inputs have also been raised.[78] Constructivist approaches have proved valuable in this area owing to their

[76] Ibid, 781.

[77] Rolf Lidskog and Göran Sundqvist, 'When Does Science Matter? International Relations Meets Science and Technology Studies' *Global Environmental Politics*, 15/1 (2015): 1.

[78] Chukwumerije Okereke, 'A Six-Component Model for Assessing Procedural Fairness in the Intergovernmental Panel on Climate Change (IPCC)' *Climate Change*, 145/3–4 (2017): 509.

sensitivity to institutional factors and the impact of ideas, which are not adequately reflected in approaches focused only on material interests.[79]

Scientific knowledge is more likely to have traction in the policy-making process if it meets the requirements of 'usable knowledge'. 'Usable knowledge' is knowledge: 1) grounded in robust science, 2) the result of legitimate processes, and with 3) strong saliency in addressing the needs of policy-makers in a timely fashion.[80] Haas provides an incisive critique of the Intergovernmental Panel on Climate Change, based on the concept of usable knowledge, pointing out that IPCC findings are not couched in terms that would map onto responsibilities for individual countries or components of countries. Moreover, its reports are not aligned with the timeframes of the UN climate negotiations.[81]

Haas has demonstrated that the relative success of environment regimes depends on so-called 'epistemic communities'—a community of like-minded government officials, international bureaucrats, scientists, and NGOs with shared goals.[82] Haas argues that such epistemic communities act as a conveyor belt between scientific knowledge and policy-makers.

In summary, IR scholarship in relation to the links between science and policy and law-making has given international environmental lawyers a better understanding of the preconditions for the effective transmission of science into global environment treaty regimes.

VII. CONCLUSION

This chapter has sought to demonstrate that IR scholarship has provided a series of important insights into IEL. These insights have included, first that IEL can be explained through the exercise of power, influenced by both material interests and discursive elements. Second, the full range of norms (from soft to hard) have influence within IEL, and these norms find expression in discourses with justice/ethical dimensions. The constructivist approach has demonstrated how norms can change over time through the persuasive efforts of 'norm entrepreneurs'. Third, there has been a decisive move away from the exclusive domination of the state in law-making processes. This represents a particular strength of IEL as norm-making processes can continue in spite of intransigence by states. However, measuring the effectiveness of such non- and sub-state

[79] Peter Haas, 'When does Power Listen to Truth? A Constructivist Approach to the Policy Process' *Journal of European Public Policy*, 11/4 (2004): 569, 586.

[80] Daniel Compagnon and Steve Bernstein, 'Non-Demarcated Spaces of Knowledge-Informed Policy Making: How Useful Is the Concept of Boundary Organisation in IR?' *Review of Policy Research*, 34/6 (2017): 812, 820.

[81] Haas (n 79) 583.

[82] Peter Haas, *Saving the Mediterranean* (Columbia University Press 1990); see Chapter 40, 'Epistemic Communities', in this volume.

initiatives remains challenging. Fourth, IR scholarship has focused on legitimacy which sheds light on a range of factors (including procedural fairness) which are key to effectiveness. Democratic legitimacy remains important not only in terms of the inherent value of inclusiveness, but also in terms of its correlation with high-quality decision-making. Finally, IR studies on scientific knowledge transmission have shed light on designing institutions to ensure effective transmission of scientific knowledge into environmental regimes.

As we enter the Anthropocene, with human beings permanently and irreversibly modifying Earth systems, a key question is whether this requires a dramatic rethink in terms of institutions and law-making.[83] Certainly there are powerful arguments to reform multilateral environment agreements by making them more responsive to ecological systems.[84] But reform efforts in this direction are likely to be complex as they risk unravelling sectoral agreements, some of which have been relatively successful.[85] In this context, there is a need for further IR studies which sharpen our knowledge of the interaction between power, norms, effectiveness, and compliance. More work is needed in comparing experience empirically across regimes. As we have seen, there are difficult methodological problems to be overcome in such analysis. Both IEL and IR need to retain their distinctive methodologies. But IR scholarship is vitally important in understanding how law works in its broader context and this understanding is a necessary precondition for reform.

BIBLIOGRAPHY

Peter Haas and Casey Stevens, 'Organised Science, Usable Knowledge and Multilateral Environmental Governance' in Rolf Lidskog and Göran Sundqvist (eds), *Governing the Air: The Dynamics of Science, Policy, and Citizen Interaction* (MIT Press 2011) 125

Mark Klamberg, *Power and Law in International Society: International Relations as the Sociology of International Law* (Routledge 2015)

Hayley Stevenson and John Dryzek, *Democratizing Global Climate Governance* (CUP 2014)

[83] John Dryzek, 'Institutions for the Anthropocene: Governance in a Changing Earth System' *British Journal of Political Science*, 46/4 (2015): 937.

[84] Tim Stephens, 'Reimagining International Environmental Law in the Anthropocene' in Louis Kotzé, *Environmental Law and Governance for the Anthropocene* (Hart Publishing 2017) 31.

[85] Frank Bierman, *Earth Systems Governance, World Politics and the Anthropocene* (MIT 2014) 91; see 'Task Force on Earth System Law' <https://www.earthsystemgovernance.org/research/taskforce-on-earth-system-law/> accessed 22 December 2019.

CHAPTER 10

ECONOMICS

MICHAEL FAURE

I. INTRODUCTION

The starting point for the economic approach to both domestic as well as international environmental law is that environmental problems (including but not limited to environmental pollution) constitute a market failure. Just like in the domestic context rational firms would, in the absence of law, have an incentive to externalize harm to society at large, in the international context states have an incentive to shift the polluting effects of economic activities to neighbouring states. That is why from this economic perspective, transboundary environmental pollution emerges. Moreover, global environmental quality is from an economic perspective a so-called public good from which all states will benefit. But since no state can exclude others from benefitting from this global environmental good there is a danger of so-called free-riding as a result of which this global public good (environmental quality) may be insufficiently produced.

These starting points, which will be further explained in Section II provide a basis for the emergence of international environmental law, more particularly treaty law. However, a classic paradigm in the so-called law and economics literature is the Coase Theorem, based on the work of Nobel Prize winner Ronald Coase.[1] This theorem holds that when bargaining between parties is possible, a market failure will be cured without the need for an intervention by law. Section III will therefore address the likelihood of Coasean solutions to emerge as a remedy to transboundary environmental pollution.[2] For a variety of reasons, ad hoc bargaining on transboundary pollution between states does not (always) lead to a cure for the market failure caused by transboundary pollution. That is why treaty law, which forms the core of international environmental law, has emerged. Yet, why states would bind themselves through treaties requires an

[1] Ronald Coase, 'The Problem of Social Cost' *Journal of Law and Economics*, 3 (1960): 1.

[2] See on this topic equally Chapter 4, 'Multilevel and Polycentric Governance', in this volume.

explanation. The traditional answer provided in the economic theory of international law is that states as rational actors would only conclude a treaty when it is in their self-interest to do so.[3] These and alternative reasons for states to conclude treaties will be addressed in Section IV. The likelihood of participation (and subsequent compliance) in a treaty is to a large extent determined by the specific treaty design, including the number of parties, the primary rule system, and the instruments used (Section V). Those elements will also have a crucial bearing on the effectiveness and compliance of treaties (Section VI).

II. INTERNALIZING EXTERNALITIES AND PROVIDING PUBLIC GOODS

What are the main economic justifications for the emergence of international environmental law? The economic analysis of environmental law starts by stating that beneficial activities of one actor (eg a firm) may produce negative consequences for others which are not felt by the firm. That is why they are referred to as an externality. Pollution is an example of such an externality. It is an example of a market failure as the firm will not take into account the polluting effects on third parties when deciding for example on whether or not to invest in pollution abatement.[4] Externalities do not only cause pollution problems for third party humans or communities; the impact could be transboundary in scope. From an economic perspective, the basic problem is that local industry, governed by local rules, exports environmental pollution to other legal jurisdictions downstream or downwind, leading to a de facto 'externalization of pollution problems'. Economists have often argued that the reasons for the transboundary character of environmental pollution problems are well-known: local politicians will not have incentives to act strongly against polluters who may be able to export large quantities of pollution outside the borders of the national territory. Thus, the pollution activity could result in 'local' socio-economic benefits for the upstream nation (increased tax revenues and job security) whereas the costs of the negative effects are exported to the neighbouring downstream countries.[5] Because politicians need to be re-elected by the citizens within their particular state, their primary concern may not be with the transboundary effect of pollution caused by factories within their nation.

[3] See in this respect especially the work by Jack Goldsmith and Eric Posner, *The Limits of International Law* (OUP 2005); Eric Posner and Alan Sykes, *Economic Foundations of International Law* (Harvard University Press 2013).

[4] See Scott Barrett, 'An Economic Theory of International Environmental Law' in Daniel Bodansky, Jutta Brunnée, and Ellen Hey (eds), *The Oxford Handbook of International Environmental Law* (1st edn, OUP 2008) 231, 239.

[5] Posner and Sykes (n 3) 226.

Seen in this context, it is unsurprising that such an externalization of pollution to other countries takes place.

Moreover, all states could benefit if each state would engage in pollution abatement, for example a reduction of greenhouse gas emissions to reduce climate change. This global environmental benefit can in economic terms be qualified as a public good: all benefit from it and the consumption of this benefit by each state does not diminish the amount available to others.[6] Public goods will, however, be undersupplied as a result of so-called free-riding behaviour: states benefit from the abatement measures taken by others, but do not want themselves to take the necessary measures. A result of this free-riding behaviour is that those public goods (like global environmental quality) may be undersupplied.[7] These two reasons combined—transboundary negative externalities and the under-provision of public goods—provide, from an economic perspective, the main justification for the emergence of international environmental law. However, before addressing the question why international environmental law, more particularly via treaties does emerge, we first have to take the analysis concerning the under-provision of global environmental public goods and free-riding behaviour one step further by introducing the prisoner's dilemma and by asking why bargaining such as suggested by the Coase Theorem could not solve the market failures related to transboundary environmental pollution.

III. PRISONER'S DILEMMA AND BARGAINING

A. Game Theory

In the previous version of this handbook, Barrett presented a general theory of international environmental law based on game theory.[8] Also in other studies the emergence of transboundary environmental pollution is analysed in terms of free-riding, connected to the prisoner's dilemma.[9] In essence the problem is that individual states may hope that others will take the necessary measures to reduce the sources of, for example, a transboundary pollution problem, and thus free-ride on those other states' efforts. In this situation mutual efforts (in the sense of investments in pollution reduction) may be in the interest of all states (in order to reduce the transboundary pollution), but the fear of absence of actions by one may lead parties to believe that they should

[6] Barrett (n 4) 238.

[7] Ibid.

[8] Barrett (n 4) 237–241.

[9] Michael Faure, 'Transboundary Pollution' in Roger Martella Jr. and Brett Grosko (eds), *International Environmental Law: The Practitioner's Guide to the Laws of the Planet* (American Bar Association 2014) 235–267.

not invest in prevention and could instead free-ride on the efforts of others. The goal of international environmental law should therefore be to correct the inter-state failures that result from this free-riding behaviour.[10] Still the question arises whether this strategic change in the incentive structure of states cannot be achieved via bargaining between the states.[11]

B. The Coase Theorem

Ronald Coase showed that the goal of correcting the market failure related to the negative externality caused by pollution should not necessarily be reached via the introduction of legal rules. If for example a factory causes pollution to victims and the pollution could be abated either by the installation of a filter or by the relocation of the victims, the lowest cost solution will always be implemented as long as parties can bargain. Even when the polluter (in the domestic context) would not be liable for the consequences of the harm, victims could pay the polluter to install the preventive measure (presuming that this is cheaper than the relocation of the victims). Posner and Sykes hold that this can apply in the transboundary pollution case as well: they argue that the focus in international environmental law has been too much on the prohibition of pollution generating activities that affect people in a foreign state as a violation of the sovereignty of the victim state. That is basically what was decided in the 1941 *Trail Smelter* arbitration. Posner and Sykes hold that it is not clear why the polluting state should give up the benefits of the polluting activity as these could potentially be larger than the damage to the neighbouring country.[12] They criticize the concept of sovereignty as it implies both that the polluting state has the legal right to engage in a polluting activity and that the victim state has the legal right to be free of its effects.[13] That was another important lesson from the Coase Theorem—harm has a reciprocal character. The question equally arises whether a correction of the market failure could be reached through bilateral negotiations between states for example resulting in an agreement on the installation of cost-effective preventive measures. In theory, for example, when only two states are involved, one upstream polluting state and one downstream victim state, bargaining should be possible, leading either the victim state paying the polluter state to install efficient pollution reduction mechanisms, or the polluting state taking those measures itself.

10 Barrett (n 4) 239.

11 For the sake of completeness, it should be mentioned that there are other games that may affect the states' incentives to invest in pollution prevention in different ways. For a more detailed overview see ibid, 239–241.

12 Posner and Sykes (n 3) 227–228.

13 Ibid.

C. Limits to Efficient Bargaining

However, in practice this type of efficient bargaining between states is rarely observed. A variety of reasons may explain this.

One problem is that a state is not necessarily the rational actor assumed to maximize its own utility according to the Coase theorem. States are represented by politicians who primarily seek re-election.[14] That may cause distortions as a result of which politicians may lack incentives to invest in solutions (eg investments in a water treatment plant) that would only provide benefits after their term in office.[15]

Another problem is that in some cases politicians may be insufficiently willing to represent the interests of a presumably (smaller number of) victims actually suffering the harm. As a result it is not easy to reach an internalization of transboundary externalities via bargaining. It is for that reason that from an economic perspective the transboundary character of externalities is an important reason for shifting powers to a higher level of government. That explains why larger or federal government entities such as the European Union (EU) or the United States often are awarded powers especially to deal with transboundary pollution problems. Likewise, the central goal of international treaties at the core of international environmental law is from this economic perspective the internalization of transboundary environmental externalities as that cannot always sufficiently be reached via ad hoc Coasean bargaining between states.

IV. WHY DO STATES CONCLUDE TREATIES?

We have so far established, based on the game theoretical approach, that a problem may arise since investing in the common public good may be in the interest of all, but because of the prisoner's dilemma there is a danger that these efficient investments are not made and that free-riding causes underinvestment in the public good. However, the literature indicates that states sign a spectacularly high number of environmental treaties. Barrett even indicated that environmental treaties far outnumber treaties in other domains like for example health law. Barrett refers to the conclusion of more than 300 multilateral environmental treaties.[16] Mitchell even refers to more than 700 multilateral environmental

[14] See Hans-Bernd Schäfer, 'Can Member State Liability for the Infringement of European Law Deter National Legislators?' in Thomas Eger and Hans-Bernd Schäfer (eds), *Research Handbook on the Economics of European Union Law* (Edward Elgar 2012) 82–94; also the school of Social Choice Theory expands the methods developed for the economic analysis of law to application in a political science context, with similar results.

[15] On similar problems with respect to the necessary investments in prevention of disasters see Ben Depoorter, 'Horizontal Political Externalities: The Supply and Demand of Disaster Management' *Duke Law Journal*, 56/1 (2006): 101.

[16] Barrett (n 4) 236.

agreements and over 1,500 bilateral.[17] That seems at first blush a paradox: after all, why would states voluntarily agree to international agreements for example to curb emissions (and potentially impose costs upon their domestic industry)? There are in fact two different views on this. The traditional economic approach[18] is that states will mainly conclude agreements and comply with those when it is in their self-interest.[19] States are from this perspective considered as rational, and motivated by self-interest.[20] The rational choice approach relies strongly on the principle of the sovereignty of states. In this approach, states are sovereign actors in the international arena, meaning that they are free to act as they find necessary, unrestricted by any external authority or rules. From this perspective governments only accept those international treaties that are in their own interest and a breach would be viewed as intentional. Towards the end of the 1990s, this traditional view of compliance problems was increasingly criticized in scholarly writings;[21] criticism that goes hand in hand with the so-called new approach to sovereignty. Some argue that states should no longer be seen as completely sovereign entities but as willing to accept limits on their original sovereign rights for the benefit of the environment, future generations, or the international community as a whole.[22] The international community is increasingly organized in *regimes*.[23] These regimes consist of frameworks with relatively well-developed sets of rules and norms on specific subjects. The development of regimes can be placed between the traditional concept of sovereignty, leaving the states unbound, and a comprehensive world order, placing the states within a new world governance. Examples of important regimes are the climate change regime, constructed around the 1992 UNFCCC (United Nations Framework Convention on Climate Change), the 1997 Kyoto Protocol and the 2015 Paris Agreement. With the development of these regimes, 'sovereignty no longer consists in the freedom of states to act independently, in their perceived self-interest, but in membership in reasonably good standing in the regimes that make up the substance of international life'.[24]

[17] Ronald Mitchell, 'Compliance Theory' in Bodansky, Brunnée, and Hey (n 4) 893.

[18] Strongly represented in the earlier mentioned works by Goldsmith and Posner (n 3) and Posner and Sykes (n 3).

[19] See in that respect also Andrew Guzman, 'A Compliance-Based Theory of International Law' *California Law Review*, 90 (2002): 1823.

[20] Barrett (n 4) 235; Mitchell (n 18) 902.

[21] This new approach is not followed by all scholars, however. See eg Goldsmith and Posner (n 3) who stress that states will mainly conclude agreements and comply when this is in their self-interest; see also Guzman (n 20).

[22] This new idea is probably best formulated by Abraham Chayes and Antonia Handler-Chayes, *The New Sovereignty: Compliance with International Regulatory Agreements* (Harvard University Press 1995), especially ch 1.

[23] Michael Faure and Jurgen Lefevere, 'Compliance with Global Environmental Policy: Climate Change and Ozone-Layer Cases' in Regina Axelrod and Stacy VanDeveer (eds), *The Global Environment: Institutions, Law, and Policy* (4th edn, Sage 2014) 110–132.

[24] Chayes and Handler-Chayes (n 23) 27.

States' interests are increasingly determined by their membership in, as well as good reputation under, these regimes.[25]

It is obvious that the question of why states engage in international environmental agreements cannot be separated from the next two issues to be discussed—treaty design (Section V) and compliance (Section VI). Logically, the more a state considers the primary rule system in the treaty as one with which it can easily comply (mostly because it will not require much behavioural change from domestic actors), the more likely it is to participate in and comply with the agreement. The three issues are hence inseparably connected.

V. TREATY PARTICIPATION AND DESIGN

A. State Characteristics

The characteristics of the countries involved in negotiating and adopting international environmental treaties will have an important impact on the likelihood of treaty adoption and of course on the probability of compliance as well. Barrett explains that the likelihood of participation (and compliance) is to a large extent dependent upon the number of participating states.[26] An important issue is that treaties often only enter into force after a threshold number of signatory countries have ratified it. Barrett explains this game theoretically by arguing that the gains from participation and compliance also increase when the number of participating states is larger. Therefore the determination level of the minimum participation is crucial and depends upon the incentives facing different countries.[27] The greater the number of countries that have ratified an accord, and the greater the extent of their implementation and compliance, the greater the probability of compliance by any individual country, because non-compliance would run counter to the international public opinion.

There is also a relationship between the area to be regulated in the environmental treaty and the number of countries that can be expected to comply. For example, the International Whaling Commission faces a trade-off between, on one hand, maintaining a moratorium on commercial whaling in a treaty that fewer countries have been willing to agree to and, on the other hand, allowing some commercial whaling in order to keep a larger number of countries within the scope of the treaty and thus achieve a higher compliance record.[28] Treaty making thus often requires a trade-off between the coverage of a

[25] The role of reputation in complying with international agreements is strongly stressed in the work of Andrew Guzman; see Andrew Guzman, 'The Design of International Agreements' *European Journal of International Law*, 16/4 (2005): 579; Andrew Guzman, *How International Law Works: A Rational Choice Theory* (OUP 2008) especially ch 3.

[26] Barrett (n 4) 247.

[27] Ibid, 248–249.

[28] Faure and Lefevere (n 24) 121–123.

treaty and the strength of the standards set in the treaty—where the effectiveness of the treaty will be determined by the interplay between the two.[29]

B. Primary Rule System

The likelihood that a country will participate in a treaty of course also depends on the actual contents of the particular international environmental agreement, in other words on the design of the treaty. Again, this is strongly linked to the probability of compliance.

A first important aspect in the design of the treaty system relates to whether it requires any behavioural change from domestic actors, and if so, what the costs of this change will be. It is easier for a state to participate in an agreement (and subsequently to comply) if the degree of behavioural change and the costs of this change are low. That partially explains the success of the 1987 Montreal Protocol. The Montreal Protocol requires behavioural changes mainly from the producers and corporate users of a limited number of very important but replaceable chemicals.

In a number of cases treaty rules require no change in behaviour of the industry in a specific country. This is often the case when industries are already meeting specific pollution standards (eg emissions). These industries may even lobby in favour of treaties that impose on their foreign competitors the standards that domestic industries have to comply with at the national level.[30] In such cases the industries already meeting the specific standard will readily comply, since the treaty merely erects a barrier to entry for the foreign competitors.

In some cases the treaties are clearly in the interest of industry for other reasons. One example is the treaties relating to liability for nuclear accidents and oil pollution. On paper these treaties serve the interests of victims, but, in fact, the contents are often such that the liability of operators is limited (eg through financial caps). The nuclear liability conventions that originated in the late 1950s came into being as a reaction to the growing nuclear industry's fear of unlimited liability.[31] Hence, compliance with the conventions, which included limited liability of nuclear operators, was relatively high.[32]

The likelihood of participation (and compliance) also depends on the level of detail or specificity in a treaty. States may in some cases be more willing to agree to participate by negotiating vague and ambitious rules. Specific obligations (such as emission reduction targets in the Kyoto Protocol) will be more difficult to agree to, since they not only

[29] See further on those issues Chapter 4, 'Multilevel and Polycentric Governance', in this volume.

[30] Examples of this can be found in European environmental law; see Michael Faure, 'Optimal Specificity in Environmental Standard-Setting' in Claudia Soares *et al* (eds), *Critical Issues in Environmental Taxation: International and Comparative Perspectives*, vol VIII (OUP 2010) 730–745.

[31] See the 1960 Convention on Third Party Liability in the Field of Nuclear Energy (Paris Convention); the 1977 Vienna Convention on Civil Liability for Nuclear Damage (Vienna Convention).

[32] For a critical discussion see Michael Faure, 'In the Aftermath of the Disaster: Liability and Compensation Mechanisms as Tools to Reduce Disaster Risks' *Stanford Journal of International Law*, 25/1 (2016): 117–119, 136–140.

require large behavioural changes, but also remove the excuse of inadvertence and misinterpretation in case of non-compliance. A so-called 'narrow but deep' treaty will often only attract the participation of a smaller fraction of countries; the larger the number of participants, unavoidably the shallower the agreement also becomes. Treaties that attract widespread participation are therefore often relatively weak.[33] A general formulation of the obligations is sometimes unavoidable simply because political consensus may not support more precision. Article 4.2(a) of the UNFCCC is an example of diplomatically formulated 'obligations'. In fact it is so vague that it is unclear whether it contains any specific obligation at all.

C. Instruments

From an economic perspective it is also important to verify which particular instruments of environmental law and policy are imposed by the treaty.[34]

1. *Liability rules*

An important instrument of environmental law is civil liability which is also considered to be a robust tool in correcting the problems of internalizing environmental externalities.[35] Under a regime of civil liability, courts can compel polluters to compensate victims by selecting specific rules. Choice of strict liability compels polluters to pay for damage done in all cases, without regard to efforts to avoid harm. Choice of the negligence rule compels polluters to pay if a certain level of care was not followed.

Liability rules could therefore play an important role in remedying transboundary environmental externalities and are to an important extent also used in international environmental agreements. A problem, however, relates to the fact that in this specific design the international conventions often include serious limits on the liability of, for example, a tanker owner or the licensee of a nuclear power plant as a result of which the incentive effects are relatively limited.

2. *Command and control*

Another type of regulatory instrument, also included in international conventions, is what is commonly described as command-and-control rules. Such a command-and-control technology requirement in fact prescribes specific conduct of the operator.[36]

[33] Barrett (n 4) 953.

[34] Space does not permit me to discuss all possible instruments; see generally on instrument choice in environmental policy, Richard Stewart, 'Instrument Choice' in Bodansky, Brunnée, and Hey (n 4) 147; Jonathan Wiener, 'Global Environmental Regulation: Instrument Choice in Legal Context' *Yale Law Journal*, 108 (1999): 677; see further on instrument choice also, Chapter 6, 'Instrument Choice', in this volume.

[35] For details see Steven Shavell, 'Liability for Accidents' in Mitchell Polinsky and Steven Shavell (eds), *Handbook of Law and Economics*, vol I (North-Holland 2007) 139.

[36] See Wiener (n 35) 706.

Command-and-control regulation may be more effective in setting standards than civil liability rules as civil liability requires an injury before enabling the creation of a standard and the necessary conditions for robustly functioning civil liability rules are often found to be lacking.[37] Command-and-control regulations, however, also do have their limits: they may be insufficiently dynamic and not quick to adapt to changing developments in technology. Nevertheless, some international environmental agreements describe particular technologies (such as the incorporation of segregated ballast tanks into oil tankers). However, in that particular case, the choice for a specific technology standard also promoted participation.[38]

3. *Market-based instruments*

Precisely because of those limits of command-and-control regulation, a different approach, advocated as early as in the 1920s by Pigou, is the use of financial instruments to internalize externalities. The most common market-based instrument is the use of Pigouvian taxes, but they are rarely, if ever, introduced in international environmental agreements. However, other market-based instruments have been introduced, more particularly in the climate change regime, where flexible and market-based instruments are popular. These mechanisms allow developed countries to meet their emission limitation targets by buying 'emission rights' from countries in which the marginal costs of emission reduction are lower, thus reducing the costs of compliance. The Kyoto Protocol's mechanisms are Joint Implementation (JI), the Clean Development Mechanism (CDM), and International Emissions Trading (IET). The CDM is the most interesting of these mechanisms: it allows developed countries to invest in emission reduction projects in a developing country and in return receive emission rights that they can use to comply with their emission limitation or reduction obligations. A well-implemented CDM project can thus help to provide financial aid and technologies to developing countries and hence also help remedy capacity problems, in addition to reducing the compliance costs for the developed country purchasing those emission rights.[39]

4. *Searching for smart instrument mixes*

If no one legal instrument can fully address the circumstances of a particular environmental problem, then what? Gunningham and Grabosky established in the influential

[37] In a nutshell, rules of civil liability are less likely to work as intended when parties face asymmetrical information on risks (creating strategic advantages), when parties face insolvency (reducing informational value of adjudicated damages), and when the threat of lawsuit is lacking or weak. The threat of lawsuits is weak when there is (i) a low probability of injury detection, (ii) a low probability of prosecution, or (iii) a low probability of enforced judgements.

[38] For details see Barrett (n 4) 254–256.

[39] For more in-depth background on the Kyoto Protocol mechanisms see Javier de Cendra de Larragan, 'The Kyoto Protocol, with a Special Focus on the Flexible Mechanisms' in Daniel Farber and Marjan Peeters (eds), *Climate Change Law* (Edward Elgar 2016) 227.

text, 'Smart Regulation' (1998), that all legal instruments have particular advantages and weaknesses; but they can be combined in bespoke arrangements.[40]

An important consideration in the 'choice of instrument' literature is therefore the type of policy instrument indicated under particular circumstances. The insight that no instrument alone can lead to optimal results also indicates that in most cases a combination of different instruments may be necessary to optimally internalize externalities. This has led to a growing literature on the search for smart mixes between different legal and policy instruments. The crucial question is how a variety of legal and policy instruments can be combined to optimally internalize environmental externalities.

VI. EFFECTIVENESS AND COMPLIANCE

We started this chapter by mentioning that from an economic perspective it is important that international environmental law is able to cure the market and state failure caused by transboundary environmental harm. That of course raises the question to what extent international environmental agreements are able to reach that goal. It concerns both the question of effectiveness of international environmental agreements and the relationship of compliance to effectiveness.[41]

A. Effectiveness

Effectiveness addresses the question of whether a treaty that is correctly complied with actually achieves its stated objectives, or whether the treaty actually helped to reach the environmental goal for which it was designed. It is this problem-solving effectiveness that is often used as a criterion to examine the results of a particular international environmental agreement. This notion of effectiveness comprises elements of several common conceptualizations of effectiveness, in particular effectiveness in terms of output and outcomes.[42] The output of a regulatory arrangement refers to the extent of compliance with legal obligations (*legal effectiveness*). Outcome refers to the ability of an international environmental agreement to induce states, private actors, and individuals to modify their behaviour (*behavioural effectiveness*). Problem-solving introduces a more dynamic perspective, in which effectiveness is not limited to pre-determined

[40] This choice of instruments is discussed in a detailed manner by Wiener (n 35) and may also lead to hybrid regulatory approaches; see Stewart (n 35) 154.

[41] As compliance theory will be discussed in Chapters 51 and 57, 'Compliance Theory' and 'Effectiveness', in this volume, we will only briefly touch upon those topics in this chapter, but cannot avoid them given their importance from an economic perspective.

[42] Joel Mintz, 'Assessing National Environmental Enforcement: Some Lessons from the United States Experience' *Georgetown International Environmental Law Review*, 26/1 (2013): 1.

goals but also includes overcoming negative side-effects or new problems that have emerged as a result of an international environmental agreement. Obviously, outputs, outcomes, and impacts are closely related. They may constitute 'three distinctive steps in a causal *chain* of events, where one serves as a starting point for analysing the subsequent stages'.[43]

B. Compliance

Compliance is generally defined as the extent to which the behaviour of a state—party to an international treaty—actually conforms to the conditions set out in the treaty. Mitchell rightly mentions that the notion of compliance as such is perhaps less useful than considering whether actors have behaved differently than they would have without agreement and why they have behaved as they have.[44]

The terms *compliance* and *effectiveness* are often used interchangeably but, in fact, have very distinct meanings. Compliance is in most cases a condition for effectiveness, if by effectiveness we mean the reaching of the treaty's goals. If a treaty is complied with, however, this does not automatically signify that it is effective in reaching the environmental goal for which it was originally designed. Effectiveness also depends on the treaty design, the instruments and goals contained in the treaty, as well as other external factors, such as changing political situations or even changing environmental conditions. Compliance is only a proxy for effectiveness; greater compliance will usually lead to environmental improvement, but whether this is actually the case will to a large extent depend on the contents of the treaty. If a treaty is badly drafted, non-compliance could even contribute to its effectiveness. For instance, this ironic result could be reached in a treaty that on paper protects the environment (or potential victims) but that, in fact, protects industrial operators, for example, by introducing financial caps on their liability and thus enabling them to continue their activities. One could argue that potential victims would be better off with non-compliance, but this is true only in cases where special interests (not primarily environmental concerns) dictated the contents of the treaty.

C. Why and When Do States Violate?

As such it may seem strange and (yet again) paradoxical that states on the one hand participate in a treaty (through ratification) but nevertheless do not comply. One would assume that states as rational actors would only take up obligations under a treaty if they know they can comply. There may, however, be a variety of reasons why states do sign,

[43] Arild Underdal, 'One Question, Two Answers', in Edward Miles *et al*, *Environmental Regime Effectiveness: Confronting Theory with Evidence* (MIT Press 2001) 3, 6.

[44] Mitchell (n 18) 895, 920–921.

but subsequently not comply.[45] A state may ratify an agreement because of international pressure or to serve domestic interests. Domestic interests, however, may also oppose compliance. Hence, it may well be in the state's interest to ratify the agreement but not comply. Moreover, compliance with international environmental agreements is seldom black-or-white: states may view most provisions of a treaty as being in their interest, and they may comply with those provisions but violate others.

As to why states do not comply there is again a difference between the traditional economic (rational actor) approach and the alternative (managerial) perspective on international environmental agreements. According to the rational actor approach states would only become parties to agreements that reflect their interests and with which they can comply.[46] As a result non-compliance was usually considered to be intentional. The managerial approach has, however, pointed at a number of (practical and other) obstacles, outside the direct will or control of the states that may make compliance difficult.[47] In some cases non-compliance is caused by inadvertence which can result from vague treaty obligations. Another source of non-compliance may be the incapacity of states to fulfil the treaty obligations owing to a lack of resources or technological abilities. The latter, especially, may play a large role with developing countries. Of course these reasons for non-compliance could also be taken into account in the treaty design ex ante in order to reduce the likelihood of non-compliance ex post.

D. Promoting Compliance

In considering how states can be brought to better comply with treaty obligations, one can again see the distinction between the more economic (rational actor) approach and the managerial perspective. According to the economic approach, as breach is considered intentional, enforcement measures should be severe and deterrent. States would only violate if it is in their interest and if the benefits of violation are higher than the costs.[48] In order to increase the costs, severe punishments and enforcement should be included in the treaty, not necessarily to be applied, but as a credible threat.[49] The goal of sanctions would not be to punish but to deter non-compliance.

The managerial approach argues that it is better to design treaties to address the problems that lead to non-compliance. For example, inadvertence could be remedied by drafting more specific and detailed obligations. Problems relating to lack of capacity may be prevented if the primary rules are designed to take into account the differing capacities of states. Treaty obligations can be differentiated based on the varying

45 See on the differences between the motives for participation and compliance, also in detail Barrett (n 4) 249–252.

46 Mitchell (n 18) 904.

47 For details see Barrett (n 4) 249–252; Mitchell (n 18).

48 Mitchell (n 18) 908–909.

49 Barrett (n 4) 952.

capacities of states, or resources or technologies can be transferred. This is, again, an example of a managerial approach; instead of blunt sanctions, instruments are developed in the treaty design stage that take into account the varying capacities of states and thus help to prevent non-compliance. The idea of differentiated standards according to states' capacities is predominant in the FCCC and its Kyoto Protocol.[50] Mitchell therefore mentions that in reality treaties make use both of mechanisms that correspond to the managerial view as well as of traditional sanctions to induce enforcement.[51]

Finally, it is important to point at the work of Andrew Guzman concerning compliance. Guzman mentions three factors that can increase the costs of violations and thus promote compliance: reputation, reciprocal non-compliance, and retaliation. Cooperative outcomes can thus be enhanced by increases in the costs of these factors.[52] The role of reputation of course also depends upon the international environment. The greater the number of countries that have ratified an accord, and the greater the extent of their implementation and compliance, the greater the probability of compliance by any individual country, because non-compliance would run counter to the international public opinion.[53]

BIBLIOGRAPHY

Scott Barrett, 'An Economic Theory of International Environmental Law' in Daniel Bodansky, Jutta Brunnée, and Ellen Hey (eds), *The Oxford Handbook of International Environmental Law* (1st edn, OUP 2008) 231

Andrew Guzman, *How International Law Works: A Rational Choice Theory* (OUP 2008)

Richard Stewart, 'Instrument Choice' in Daniel Bodansky, Jutta Brunnée, and Ellen Hey (eds), *The Oxford Handbook of International Environmental Law* (1st edn, OUP 2008) 147

Jonathan Wiener, 'Global Environmental Regulation: Instrument Choice in Legal Context' *Yale Law Journal*, 108 (1999): 677

50 For details see Benoît Mayer, *The International Law on Climate Change* (CUP 2018) 39–42; Tulla Honkonon, 'The CBDR and Climate Change' in Farber and Peeters (n 40) 142151; see also Philippe Sands and Jacqueline Peel, *Principles of International Environmental Law* (4th edn, CUP 2018) 307–317.

51 Mitchell (n 18) 911.

52 Guzman, *How International Law Works* (n 26) 175.

53 Faure and Lefevere (n 24) 122.

CHAPTER 11

GLOBAL SOUTH APPROACHES

SUMUDU ATAPATTU

I. INTRODUCTION

THE headline 'Billionaires Are the Leading Cause of Climate Change'[1] was striking. This media report published soon after the Intergovernmental Panel on Climate Change (IPCC) released its report 'Global Warming of 1.5°C',[2] noted that 'more than 70 percent of global emissions come from just 100 companies … The people who are actively cranking up the global thermostat and threatening to drown 20 percent of the global population are the billionaires in the boardrooms of these companies'.[3]

This narrative of the corporate world holding the rest of humanity to ransom, is perhaps to be expected in a world where just twenty-six people (billionaires) control as much wealth as 3.6 billion of the world's poorest people combined.[4] This astounding inequity is the result of centuries of colonial domination, subordination, racism, and plunder of resources of the colonized, coupled with laws and institutions that made such practices possible. The case of Nauru, discussed later, highlights these complexities.

As many international law principles were created at a time when most states were under colonial domination, southern states have consistently struggled to adopt principles that are conducive to them. The broad North-South debate does not mean that these issues affect people in these countries equally. In fact, different groups in both

[1] Luke Darby, 'Billionaires Are the Leading Cause of Climate Change' *GQ* (11 October 2018). More than 70% of the global greenhouse gas emissions come from just 100 companies; see Paul Griffin, 'The Carbon Majors Database: CDP Carbon Majors Report 2017' (Carbon Disclosure Project).

[2] See IPCC, *Global Warming of 1.5°C—Special Report* (2018) Summary for Policymakers.

[3] Darby (n 1).

[4] Max Lawson *et al*, *Public Good or Private Wealth?* (Oxfam 2019) 12. Oxfam calculations use wealth of the richest individuals from Forbes Billionaires listing and wealth of the bottom 50% from Credit Suisse Research Institute, 'Global Wealth Databook 2016'.

sets of countries are affected disproportionately by environmental issues. The environmental justice movement highlights these disparities. Similarly, adverse consequences of climate change disproportionately affect vulnerable groups including women.[5] Women constitute the majority of small farmers in many parts of Asia and Africa and with increasing droughts and severe weather events, their livelihoods and food security are affected. Similarly, traditional knowledge and access to genetic resources has caused injustice to Indigenous communities worldwide where multinational companies in the global North have developed 'new' products based on 'stolen' genetic material and traditional knowledge from Indigenous communities.[6] Southern countries, for their part, have been guilty of acting in disregard of the welfare of Indigenous and local communities. Examples include the REDD+ program[7] and Clean Development Mechanism projects[8] that have led to massive human rights violations. Genetically modified crops and other practices that put local farmers out of business,[9] and terminator technology have also led to exacerbating the plight of vulnerable communities.[10] Thus, the debate on the North-South divide should take these disparities into consideration.

This chapter discusses the global South approaches to international environmental law. It is divided into five sections. Section II discusses the colonial origins of international law while Section III traces the evolution of international environmental law and the North-South divide. Section IV discusses global South perspectives on international environmental law, including principles and frameworks adopted to address the North-South divide. Section V provides concluding thoughts on the potential and limits of these perspectives. This chapter argues that unless and until the neoliberal economic model based on capitalism is discarded in favour of a more ecologically friendly model that accommodates the needs of the global South, especially their vulnerable

[5] See United Nations Development Programme, *Human Development Report 2007/2008—Fighting Climate Change: Human Solidarity in a Divided World* (2007); Christian Nellemann, Ritu Verma, and Lawrence Hislop, *Women at the Frontline of Climate Change: Gender Risks and Hopes* (UNEP 2011).

[6] Craig Jacoby and Charles Weiss, 'Recognizing Property Rights in Traditional Biocultural Contribution' *Stanford Environmental Law Journal*, 16/1 (1997): 74, 89.

[7] See 'Forced Eviction by Kenya threatens indigenous communities' human rights and ancestral forests' (7 January 2014) <http://www.redd-monitor.org/2014/01/07/forced-eviction-by-kenya-threatens-indigenous-communities-human-rights-and-ancestral-forests/> accessed 15 November 2019; David Takacs, 'Forest Carbon (REDD+), Repairing International Trust, and Reciprocal Contractual Sovereignty' *Vermont Law Review*, 37 (2013): 653.

[8] See International Rivers, 'Submission regarding Human Rights to the CDM' (25 March 2013); Christina Voigt, 'The Deadlock of the Clean Development Mechanism: Caught between Sustainability, Environmental Integrity and Economic Efficiency' in Benjamin Richardson *et al* (eds), *Climate Law and Developing Countries: Legal and Policy Challenges for the World Economy* (Edward Elgar 2009) 235.

[9] See David Downes, 'New Diplomacy for the Biodiversity Trade: Biodiversity, Biotechnology, and Intellectual Property in the Convention on Biological Diversity' *Touro Journal of Transnational Law*, 4 (1993): 1; Food & Water Watch, 'How GMO Crops Hurt Farmers,' Fact Sheet (January 2015).

[10] Genetic Literacy Project, 'GMO FAQs: What's the Controversy Over 'Terminator' seeds?' <https://geneticliteracyproject.org/gmo-faq/whats-the-controversy-over-terminator-seeds/> accessed 24 January 2021.

communities, not only will current North-South tensions be exacerbated, the world will also speedily move towards environmental tipping points from which there is no hope of return.

In this chapter, the terms 'developed countries', 'Northern countries', or the 'Global North' refer to affluent industrialized nations, while the terms 'developing countries', 'Southern countries', or the 'Global South' refer to their less affluent counterparts.[11] While acknowledging that this is an oversimplification and that there are affluent people in the global South as well as poor, marginalized people in the global North, the global North/South nomenclature is useful to describe the broad divisions in the international community today.[12] It will not, however, engage in a debate on what the 'Third World' is[13] as the United Nations (UN) itself has moved away from this language.

This chapter acknowledges that the global power balance has shifted dramatically with the rise of China as a global power. Its unprecedented economic growth has come at a huge environmental cost. In addition to creating domestic pollution, China is now the highest emitter of greenhouse gases (GHGs) surpassing the United States in 2007.[14] India and Brazil have become major players at the global level especially with regard to climate negotiations.[15] The North-South debate should take cognizance of this emerging geo-political context and shifting power balances.

II. THE COLONIAL ORIGINS OF INTERNATIONAL LAW

This chapter is based on the premise that colonial history is '[a] formative element in the making of international law, including how particular doctrines and institutions of international law have been shaped by the colonial encounter',[16] and how power relations

[11] See Sumudu Atapattu and Carmen Gonzalez, 'North-South Divide in International Environmental Law: Framing the Issues' in Shawkat Alam *et al* (eds), *International Environmental Law and the Global South* (CUP 2015) 1, 10; Ruchi Anand, *International Environmental Justice: A North-South Dimension* (Ashgate 2004) 1.

[12] Within this broad distinction, there are many other categories: BASIC countries (Brazil, South Africa, India, and China), G-8, G-20, G-77, V-20, BRICs (Brazil, Russia, India and China), etc.

[13] See 'Introduction' in Richard Falk, Balakrishnan Rajagopal, and Jacqueline Stevens (eds), *International Law and the Third World: Reshaping Justice* (Routledge-Cavendish 2008) 3; cf. Obiora Okafor, 'Newness, Imperialism, and International Legal Reform in our Time: A TWAIL Perspective' *Osgoode Hall Law Journal*, 43 (2005): 171, 174 who argues that the debate about the existence of the Third World is wrongly framed.

[14] See Hannah Ritchie and Max Roser, 'CO_2 and Greenhouse Gas Emissions' *Our World in Data* (2019).

[15] See Rowena Maguire and Xiaoyi Jiang, 'Emerging Powerful Southern Voices: Role of BASIC Nations in Shaping Climate Change Mitigation Commitments' in Alam *et al* (n 11) 214.

[16] See Falk, Rajagopal, and Stevens (n 13) 3.

continue to produce outcomes that are harmful to the most disadvantaged peoples and countries.[17] Mainstream treatment of international law continues to ignore its colonial origins. This narrative resonates with the origins of international environmental law as well, explored in the next section.

As the colonial origins of international law are well-documented[18] only a brief overview is provided here. The origins of international law are firmly rooted in colonial history dating back several centuries when European countries engaged in a civilizing mission to Africa, Asia, and Latin America.[19] Colonial masters plundered the resources of the colonized to amass wealth for themselves in total disregard of the impact on the colonized people and their environment. While the colonial era is in theory over, former colonies continue to be underdeveloped, depend economically on the global North, and suffer disproportionately from the adverse impacts of environmental degradation.

After the First World War, scholars began denouncing international law for legitimizing colonial exploitation. The League of Nations adopted the Mandate system to lead to decolonization of 'backward people'. However, 'Third World sovereignty' differed from 'European sovereignty' and 'was created in a way that could continue to serve Western interests. Crudely put, an examination of the Mandate System illuminates the ways in which political sovereignty could be created to be completely consistent with economic subordination'.[20] The example of Nauru, discussed in Section IV, exemplifies this. Even though Australia agreed under the Trusteeship Agreement to '[t]ake into consideration customs and usages of the inhabitants of Nauru and respect the rights and safeguard the interests, both present and future',[21] not only did it decimate the environment, it believed that such behaviour was totally within its sovereign prerogative.

The Mandate system was replaced by the UN Trusteeship system and the Trusteeship Council was established to carry out its functions. The UN Charter stresses the sacred trust vested in the trustee to promote to the utmost, the well-being of the inhabitants of the trust territories.[22] The Trusteeship Council suspended its operations in November 1994, after the independence of Palau, the last remaining UN trust territory. Colonialism shaped not only the doctrines of international law but also its very foundations. Even though colonialism formally ended, it did not arguably result in the end of colonial relations. Rather, Third World societies believe that colonialism has merely been

[17] Ibid.

[18] See Antony Anghie, *Imperialism, Sovereignty and the Making of International Law* (CUP 2004).

[19] See Carmen Gonzalez, 'Environmental Justice, Human Rights, and the Global South' *Santa Clara Journal of International Law*, 13/1 (2015): 151.

[20] See Antony Anghie, 'The Evolution of International Law: Colonial and Postcolonial Realities' *Third World Quarterly*, 27/5 (2006): 739, 747.

[21] See Antony Anghie, 'The Heart of My Home: Colonialism, Environmental Damage, and the Nauru Case' *Harvard International Law Journal*, 34/2 (1993): 445.

[22] UN Charter, art 73.

replaced by neocolonialism as they continue to play a subordinate role in the international system, with rules of international economic law that disproportionately favour the global North ensuring that this subordinate role continues.[23] A good example is bilateral investment treaties that allow multinational companies, most of which are in the global North, to sue sovereign states, most of which are in the global South.[24]

Although colonialism is considered a thing of the past, the UN currently lists seventeen non-self-governing territories.[25] In its Declaration on the Granting of Independence to Colonial Countries and Peoples,[26] the UN General Assembly (UNGA) recognized the link between human rights and colonialism, declaring that the 'subjection of peoples to alien subjugation, domination and exploitation constitutes a denial of fundamental human rights, is contrary to the Charter of the United Nations and is an impediment to the promotion of world peace and co-operation.'[27]

Despite such laudable statements, international law has largely failed to account for its colonial past, to remedy the damage inflicted on former colonies, or to provide any reparations. This past continues to haunt international relations but the global North has generally ignored the colonial underpinnings of international law.[28] Given that decolonization results in a postcolonial state 'where the effects of colonialism have become an inextricable part of the culture and of its legal, educational, and political institutions,'[29] postcolonial theory[30] and TWAIL (Third World approaches to international law) are inextricably interlinked. The global South has pressed for the adoption of principles, frameworks, and alternative approaches to international law addressing the glaring disparities in the global community today.

[23] See Carmen Gonzalez, 'Global Justice in the Anthropocene' in Louis Kotze (ed), *Environmental Law and Governance for the Anthropocene* (Hart Publishing 2017) 223.

[24] See Shyami Puvimanasinghe, 'From a Divided Heritage to a Common Future? International Investment Law, Human Rights, and Sustainable Development' in Alam *et al* (n 11) 328.

[25] The UN and Decolonization, 'Non-Self-Governing Territories' <https://www.un.org/dppa/decolonization/en/nsgt> accessed 3 January 2020. The majority are under the authority of UK while three are under the authority of the US.

[26] UNGA Res 1514 (XV), 'Declaration on the granting of independence to colonial countries and peoples' (20 December 1960) UN Doc A/RES/1514(XV).

[27] Ibid, para 2. In its resolution on the Third International Decade for the Eradication of Colonialism the UNGA reiterated its determination to completely eradicate colonialism; see UNGA Res 65/19, 'Responsibility of States for internationally wrongful acts' (10 January 2011) UN Doc A/RES/65/19.

[28] See Alpana Roy, 'Postcolonial Theory and Law: A Critical Introduction' *Adelaide Law Review*, 29/1–2 (2008): 315, 318.

[29] Ibid, quoting Margaret Davies, *Asking the Law Question: The Dissolution of Legal Theory* (2nd edn, Law Book Company 2002) 278.

[30] While acknowledging the heterogeneity and interdisciplinary nature of the postcolonial theory; see also David Slater, *Geopolitics and the Post-colonial: Rethinking North-South Relations* (Blackwell Publishing 2004); Sally Merry, 'Colonial and Postcolonial Law' in Austin Sarat (ed), *The Blackwell Companion to Law and Society* (Blackwell Publishing 2004) 569.

III. EVOLUTION OF INTERNATIONAL ENVIRONMENTAL LAW AND THE NORTH-SOUTH DIVIDE

International environmental law is also grounded in colonialism. The European colonization of many parts of the world 'devastated Indigenous societies and wreaked havoc on the flora and fauna of the colonized territories' and paved the way for current social and economic inequality through slavery and indentured labour.[31]

Addressing poverty is a top priority for the global South,[32] but not by emulating the destructive developmental path of the global North. After decolonization when Southern states became the majority in the UNGA they sought to adopt resolutions that favoured them—these included permanent sovereignty over natural resources,[33] the common heritage of mankind,[34] the New International Economic Order,[35] the right to development,[36] and benefit sharing.[37] However, the adoption of these resolutions and principles did little to change the existing power asymmetry that favours the global North.[38] In addition, globalization with its structural adjustment policies and economic reforms[39] compounded inequities in the global South, and were reminiscent of the colonial era.[40]

From the start, divisions along North-South lines were evident. By the late 1960s, industrialized countries were beginning to feel the negative impacts of industrialization. For developing countries, improving the living standards of their people was the priority rather than protecting the environment.

It was against this backdrop that the 1972 Stockholm Conference on the Human Environment was held. The Indian Prime Minister, referring to India's long tradition

[31] See Gonzalez, 'Environmental Justice' (n 19) 159.

[32] As a result, some scholars distinguish between luxury emissions and subsistence emissions; see Henry Shue, *Climate Justice: Vulnerability and Protection* (OUP 2014) 47.

[33] UNGA Res 1803(XVII), 'Permanent sovereignty over natural resources' (14 December 1962) UN Doc A/RES/1803(XVII).

[34] David Hunter, James Salzman, and Durwood Zaelke, *International Environmental Law and Policy* (5th edn, Foundation Press 2015) 451.

[35] UNGA Res 3201 (S-VI), 'Declaration on the Establishment of a New International Economic Order' (1 May 1974) UN Doc A/RES/S-6/3201.

[36] UNGA Res 41/128, 'Declaration on the right to development' (4 December 1986) UN Doc A/RES/41/128, annex.

[37] See the 2010 Nagoya Protocol on Access to Genetic Resources <https://www.cbd.int/abs/doc/protocol/nagoya-protocol-en.pdf> accessed 3 January 2020.

[38] See Puvimanasinghe (n 24) 328.

[39] See Gonzalez, 'Global Justice' (n 23) 225.

[40] See Bhupinder Chimni, 'Third World Approaches to International Law: A Manifesto' *International Community Law Review*, 8/3 (2006): 3.

of forest and wildlife preservation, rejected the notion that environmental stewardship is a western idea.[41] She expressed concern about the assault on nature committed in the name of progress, and highlighted the environmental impacts of poverty.[42] Despite this, the portrayal of developing countries as unwilling participants in global environmental policy-making has been 'extraordinarily long-lasting and difficult to dislodge'.[43]

After the Stockholm Conference, in response to the global North's call for environmental protection, the global South prioritized economic development, arguing that since the North industrialized without any regard for the environment, their call was another form of oppression. To address this increasing polarization, the UNGA established the World Commission on Environment and Development (WCED) in 1983 to find ways to reconcile economic development with environmental protection. The Commission's report led to the adoption of the now famous definition of sustainable development.[44]

At the 1992 Rio Conference on Environment and Development, continuing North-South divisions were evident: over-consumption versus population growth; intergenerational equity versus intra-generational equity; environmental protection versus sustainable development; and funding.[45] At the 2012 Johannesburg Summit on Sustainable Development, the South sought action on poverty eradication and emphasized the need to implement existing treaties rather than adopt new ones.[46] Ten years later, the Rio+20 agenda was surprisingly unambitious with only two broad areas for action (green economy and institutional framework) and North-South divisions revolved around funding and technology transfer.[47] A major grievance of the South is over-consumption of world's natural resources by Northern countries,[48] leaving the Southern countries with much of the pollution to cope with and no room for GHG emissions needed for them to develop.[49] By redefining the global commons to include tropical forests and biodiversity, the North found another way to control the rich resources of the global South.[50]

[41] See Karin Mickelson, 'The Stockholm Conference and the Creation of South-North Divide in International Environmental Law and Policy' in Alam *et al* (n 11) 115.

[42] Ibid, 116.

[43] Ibid, 118.

[44] See World Commission on Environment and Development, *Our Common Future* (OUP 1987).

[45] Hunter, Salzman, and Zaelke (n 34) 152–153.

[46] Ibid, 180.

[47] See Thalif Deen, 'Q&A: North-South Divide Looms Heavily Over Rio+20 Summit' (30 May 2012).

[48] See Imrana Iqbal and Charles Pierson, 'A North-South Struggle: Political and Economic Obstacles to Sustainable Development' *Sustainable Development Law & Policy*, 16/2 (2017): 16.

[49] Ibid, 24.

[50] Ibid, 25.

Despite the near universal acceptance of sustainable development by the global community,[51] deep divisions along North-South lines continue. From the disposal of hazardous waste to climate change, and from ozone depletion to marine pollution, international environmental law is replete with examples of Northern countries imposing environmental externalities on Southern countries. Take for instance the practice of dumping hazardous waste generated in the global North on Southern countries, referred to as 'toxic colonialism'.[52] Even though the 1989 Basel Convention was adopted to regulate the transboundary movement of hazardous waste, the biggest generator of hazardous waste—the United States—has not ratified it, opting instead to regulate such shipments through bilateral treaties.[53] Meanwhile, African nations have banned hazardous waste originating from outside Africa.[54] Electronic waste is the newest form of waste to be exported to developing countries where they lack the facilities to safely dispose them or extract materials for recycling.[55]

Similarly, the dominant economic model has played a major role in creating the externalities that resulted in climate change. Those most affected by the adverse consequences of climate change are the least responsible for GHG emissions and least able to protect themselves.[56] As a result, many in the global South consider climate change as another form of colonialism,[57] and believe that the global North should take responsibility for causing climate change and compensate the global South for its consequences.[58] Meanwhile, the biggest emitter historically—the United States—has refused to shoulder a greater burden and to reduce its emissions. The former US President Trump formally withdrew from the Paris Agreement,[59] much to the dismay of the global community, but the decision was reversed by President Biden in early 2021.

[51] See Hunter, Salzman, and Zaelke (n 34) 145 who believe that this is partly due to its 'brilliant ambiguity'.

[52] See Anand (n 11) 62; Hunter, Salzman, and Zaelke (n 34) 956; Basel Action Network <https://www.ban.org/> accessed 3 January 2020.

[53] See Hunter, Salzman, and Zaelke (n 34) 962; Anand (n 11) ch 3.

[54] 1991 Bamako Convention on the Ban of the Import into Africa and the Control of Transboundary Movement and Management of Hazardous Wastes within Africa; see also Hunter, Salzman, and Zaelke (n 34) 973.

[55] See Hunter, Salzman, and Zaelke (n 34) 977.

[56] See Anand (n 11) 35; Zackary Stillings, 'Human Rights and the New Reality of climate Change: Adaptation's Limitations in Achieving Climate Justice' *Michigan Journal of International Law*, 35 (2014): 637; Margaux Hall and David Weiss, 'Avoiding Adaptation Apartheid: Climate Change Adaptation and Human Rights Law' *Yale Journal of International law*, 37 (2012): 309.

[57] See Martin Mahony and Georgina Endfield, *Climate and Colonialism* (Wiley Periodicals Inc 2018); Luisa Galvao, 'Confronting climate colonialism ahead of the Paris summit' *Friends of the Earth* (12 September 2015).

[58] See Atapattu and Gonzalez (n 11) 10.

[59] See Michael Shear, 'Trump Will Withdraw U.S. From Paris Climate Agreement' *New York Times* (1 June 2017).

IV. AN ALTERNATIVE APPROACH TO INTERNATIONAL LEGAL SCHOLARSHIP—THIRD WORLD APPROACHES TO INTERNATIONAL LAW (TWAIL)

One of the early critiques of the dominant international law paradigm came from the 'Third World Approaches to International Law' (TWAIL).[60] TWAIL challenges 'the hegemony of the dominant narrative of international law',[61] by writing the Third World's shared historical experiences into international thought and action, and focusing on substantive, rather than formal, equality of Third World people. Thus, one of the main objectives of TWAIL is to bring colonialism and the Eurocentric origins of international to the fore.[62] TWAIL seeks to bring Third World perspectives into the discourse of international law, including the voices of non-state actors, especially vulnerable groups such as Indigenous peoples and women. To what extent it has succeeded is debatable.[63] On that account, both mainstream international law and TWAIL scholarship seem to be lacking although the state-centric focus of international law seems to be slowly adjusting to the realities of other actors in the field.

The example of Nauru highlights the intersectional nature of the complex issues at play. Prior to the arrival of the Europeans, the people of Nauru had relied on the resources of the island including fishing for their subsistence. Phosphate was discovered on the island in 1900. Australia occupied the island during the First World War and administered it under the Mandate system until the outbreak of the Second World War. Australia mined approximately one third of the island's phosphate deposits while Nauru was under its administration. In 1947 Nauru was placed under the UN Trusteeship system. While Nauruans became involved in limited legislative actions, they were deprived of any right in the administration of the phosphate industry. Nauru finally gained full control over the phosphate industry in 1967 and became an independent

[60] See generally Chimni (n 40); Luis Eslava and Sundhya Pahuja, 'Beyond the (Post)Colonial: TWAIL and the Everyday Life of International Law' *Verfassung and Recht in Ubersee*, 45 (2012): 195; James Thuo Gathii, 'TWAIL: A Brief History of its Origins, its Decentralized Network, and a Tentative Bibliography' *Trade Law & Development*, 3/1 (2011): 26; Usha Natarajan, 'TWAIL and the Environment: The State of Nature, the Nature of the State, and the Arab Spring' *Oregon Review of International Law*, 14/1 (2012): 177; Okafor (n 13); Macau Mutua, 'What is TWAIL?' *ASIL Proceedings* (2000): 31; Sara Seck, 'Transnational Business and Environmental Harm: A TWAIL Analysis of Home State Obligations' *Trade Law & Development*, 3/1 (2011): 164.

[61] Gathii (n 60) 37.

[62] Within TWAIL, several other approaches have emerged—critical, feminist, post-modern, Lat-Crit, critical race theory, and critical legal studies—are some of them, see Okafor (n 13) 178.

[63] Ibid.

state in 1968. Nauru established a Commission of Inquiry into the Rehabilitation of the Worked-out Phosphate Lands of Nauru in 1986 which established that the three partner governments—Australia, New Zealand, and Britain—were responsible for the damage done to the lands prior to 1967.

In 1989, Nauru filed legal action against Australia in the International Court of Justice (ICJ) alleging that it had suffered damage as a result of Australia's actions under both the UN Trusteeship provisions and general principles of law, including self-determination, permanent sovereignty over natural resources, and abuse of rights. Nauru sought a declaration from the ICJ that Australia is bound to make reparation for the damage it had caused. Nauru drew attention to the plight of the people whose land had been transformed into a wasteland by mining and argued that the rehabilitation of the island is necessary for its survival. Rejecting Australia's preliminary objections, the ICJ held that it had jurisdiction to entertain Nauru's application.[64] Although the case was later settled, the ICJ showed willingness to adjudicate the dispute. This was the first time the court was confronted with a case that questioned the very foundations of international law challenging the fiduciary duty placed on the trustee, its destructive activities that decimated the land, and its failure to rehabilitate it. Thus, while colonial realities continue to shape international law, international law treats colonialism as peripheral to the discipline.

V. GLOBAL SOUTH PERSPECTIVES ON ENVIRONMENTAL LAW

A. Differential Treatment, and the Common But Differentiated Responsibility Principle

Over the years, the global South has pressed, with some success, to have the disparities in the global community reflected in international environmental law, in particular through the adoption of differential treatment in favour of developing countries. Examples include differential treatment under the GATT, and the principle of common but differentiated responsibility (CBDR) under international environmental law,[65] the latter adopted amidst intense North-South divisions.[66] The CBDR principle acknowledges that it is unfair to treat all states equally when their contribution to environmental damage as well as the impacts on them are unequal. It seeks to take this disparity into account when designing a legal regime but as the climate regime has shown,

[64] *Certain Phosphate Lands in Nauru, Preliminary Objections (Nauru/Australia)* (Judgement) [1992] ICJ Rep 240.

[65] See Lavanya Rajamani, *Differential Treatment in International Environmental Law* (OUP 2006).

[66] See Sumudu Atapattu, 'The Significance of International Environmental Law Principles in Reinforcing or Dismantling the North-South Divide' in Alam *et al* (n 11) 93.

this differentiation can be contentious, especially because of the complex alliances that states have formed.[67]

Suffice it to say in the context of this chapter that the biggest opposition to the adoption of this principle came from the United States[68] who even entered an interpretative statement to it when signing the Rio Declaration[69] which refers to the special leadership role of developed countries given their superior technical expertise, wealth, and industrial development. Far from acknowledging their responsibility for causing environmental damage this statement underscores their assumed superiority.[70] Southern countries not only had undergone decades of colonial rule but now have to bear a disproportionate burden of environmental degradation.

B. Intergenerational Equity

Intergenerational equity is central to many international environmental law principles including sustainable development. When this principle was being debated, Southern states argued that the inequity in the current generation should be addressed *before* equity between generations is addressed.[71] This led to the adoption of the *intra*-generational equity principle as an integral component of sustainable development.[72]

While together these principles have endeavoured to level the playing field for developing countries, it has been much harder to dislodge the attitude of Northern countries demonstrated by the 'interpretative statement' made to Principle 7 by the United States when signing the Rio Declaration.

C. Environmental Justice

Just as many environmental issues disproportionately affect the global South, many polluting activities affect poor and minority communities disproportionately at local and national levels. This realization gave birth to the environmental justice movement.[73] There are numerous examples of environmental injustices: Hurricane Katrina, Mossville case, Kivalina, Shishmarof, and Newtok[74] in Alaska, and Isle de Jean Charles, where the

[67] See Chapter 19, 'Differentiation', in this volume.

[68] *Report of the United Nations Conference on Environment and Development* (UN 1993) vol I, annex I—'Rio Declaration on Environment and Development', principle 7.

[69] Referred to in Hunter, Salzman, and Zaelke (n 34) 466.

[70] See Atapattu (n 66) 97.

[71] Ibid, 92.

[72] See Duncan French, 'Sustainable Development and the Instinctive Imperative of Justice in the Global Order' *Global Justice and Sustainable Development* (Martinus Nijhoff 2010) 8.

[73] Michael Gerrard and Sheila Foster (eds), *The Law of Environmental Justice: Theories and Procedures to Address Disproportionate Risks* (2nd edn, American Bar Association 2008).

[74] Brad Plumer, 'Impossible to Ignore: Why Alaska Is Crafting a Plan to Fight Climate Change' *New York Times* (15 May 2018).

entire island is being relocated to the mainland because of climate change.[75] While many of the environmental injustices are global in nature where the global South suffers disproportionately from externalities of activities originating from the global North, these examples show that there is essentially a 'South in the North' just as there is a 'North in the South' where the rich minority is essentially emulating the decadent lifestyle of their counterparts in the global North.

Scholars adopt various definitions of environmental justice.[76] This chapter adopts the four-part categorization of environmental justice proposed by Kuehn—distributive justice, procedural justice, corrective justice, and social justice—as this best suits our discussion.[77]

While the United States is often identified as the birthplace of the modern environmental justice movement, such struggles have taken place all over the world for decades.[78] In the United States it was a direct response to the practice of locating polluting and hazardous activities in low income and minority communities. Not surprisingly, the demands of the environmental justice movement overlapped with those of the Civil Rights Movement for racial justice. In October 1991, the People of Color held their first Environmental Leadership Summit and adopted 17 Principles of Environmental Justice.[79] It is a remarkable document for its vision and has since served as a defining document for the grassroots movement for environmental justice.[80] These principles reinforced the above four-fold characterization of environmental justice.[81] Despite the Executive Order on Environmental Justice issued in 1994, poor and minority communities continue to suffer disproportionately from polluting activities in the United States.[82] A case currently pending before the Inter-American Commission of Human Rights against the United States involves environmental justice and

[75] Michael Stein, 'How to Save a Town from Rising Waters' *Citylab* (24 January 2018).

[76] See Dinah Shelton, 'Describing the Elephant: International Justice and Environmental Law' in Jonas Ebbesson and Phoebe Okowa (eds), *Environmental Law and Justice in Context* (CUP 2009) 55, who equates it with Aesop's elephant where in Aesop's fable, several blind men who touch an elephant describe it in different ways depending on where they touch.

[77] See Robert Kuehn, 'A Taxonomy of Environmental Justice' *Environmental Law Reporter*, 30 (2000): 10681; Hari Osofsky, 'Learning from Environmental Justice: A New Model for International Environmental Rights' *Stanford Environmental Law Journal*, 24/1 (2005): 71, 89–90.

[78] See Usha Natarajan, 'Environmental Justice in the Global South' in Sumudu Atapattu, Carmen Gonzalez, and Sara Seck (eds), *Cambridge Handbook on Sustainable Development and Environmental Justice* (CUP 2021).

[79] People of Color Environmental Leadership Summit, 'Principles of Environmental Justice' (1991) <https://www.nrdc.org/sites/default/files/ej-principles.pdf> accessed 3 January 2020.

[80] Ibid.

[81] 'Federal Actions to Address Environmental Justice in Minority Populations and Low-income Populations', Executive Order 12898, 59 Fed Reg 7629 (11 February 1994) <https://www.archives.gov/files/federal-register/executive-orders/pdf/12898.pdf> accessed 3 January 2020.

[82] Carol Davenport and Campbell Robertson, 'Resettling the First American "Climate Refugees"' *New York Times* (2 May 2016).

environmental racism. In *Mossville Environmental Action Now v US*,[83] the petitioners alleged that the Mossville residents, who are predominately African American, are disproportionately affected by pollution—what they referred to as environmental racism—in breach of the American Declaration of the Rights and Duties of Man. They further alleged that the state is responsible for the violation of Mossville residents' rights to life, health, and private life guaranteed under the American Declaration. This is the first case that has been brought against the United States on the basis of environmental justice and environmental racism before an international forum. The Commission held the petition admissible.[84]

The practice of locating polluting industries in impoverished communities can be seen in other parts of the world too. Examples include La Oroya mine in Peru, dubbed as the most polluted place on Earth, Indigenous communities in Ecuador who continue to suffer from the environmental injustices caused by Chevron (Texaco was bought by Chevron), and Ogoni people in Nigeria who suffered severe environmental pollution and human rights abuse by Shell Oil.[85]

1. *Distributive justice*

Distributive justice requires the equal treatment of people, equal access to resources and amenities, and the equal distribution of benefits and burdens. Environmental justice advocates call for the *lowering* of environmental risks and not shifting the risks.[86] In some instances, however, differential treatment or affirmative action is necessary to address past injustices and level the playing field.[87] One of the contentions of the global South, in the context of the climate change issues, is that Northern countries have reaped the benefits of industrialization while externalizing the resulting pollution which resulted in climate change. While Southern countries need to raise the living standards of their people, this is no longer possible because there is no space available for their emissions. They thus argue that a distinction should be made between 'luxury emissions' and 'subsistence emissions'.[88]

2. *Procedural justice*

Procedural justice requires that relevant stakeholders and the affected public should have access to timely and relevant information, they must be given an opportunity to

[83] *Mossville Environmental Action Now v US* (2010) IAComHR, Report No 43/10, Case 242-05, OEA/Ser.LV/II.138, doc.47 [2]; see also Jeannine Cahill-Jackson, 'Mossville Environmental Action Now v. United States: Is a Solution to Environmental Injustice Unfolding?' *Pace International Law Review Online*, 3/6 (2012): 173, 174.

[84] See Sumudu Atapattu, 'Extractive Industries and Inequality: Intersections of Environmental Law, Human Rights and Environmental Justice' *Arizona State Law Journal*, 50/2 (2018): 431. A complaint is also pending before the UN Committee on Racial Discrimination.

[85] Ibid.

[86] See Kuehn (n 77).

[87] The CBDR is an example of such an attempt.

[88] See Shue (n 32).

participate in the decision-making process, and that they should have access to justice.[89] While procedural rights are the most developed in relation to environmental matters,[90] and form part of international human rights law, the colonial context is different. One of the main contentions of southern countries is that when many of the international law principles were created, they were not full-fledged members of the international community and hence, could not participate in their creation.

Since becoming independent states, southern countries have influenced the development of international law by adopting resolutions that favour them.[91] Despite their active involvement, their participation at international negotiations is hampered by lack of resources and technical expertise. While decolonization has given them the majority in many international fora, many developing countries cannot afford to send large delegations to multiple negotiations under various treaties.[92] The practice of weighted voting by international financial institutions which allocates votes proportionate to the contribution of countries to these institutions[93] favours rich and powerful states.[94]

The reaction of ALBA countries (Bolivarian Alliance of the Peoples of Latin America) to the Copenhagen Accord in 2009 highlights procedural injustices that can undermine global negotiations. There were high expectations that states will adopt a protocol to the UNFCCC to govern the post-2012 legal regime at the Copenhagen conference.[95] However, a handful of countries, headed by the United States, adopted a document without referring to the plenary derailing the COP process.[96] Not only did they adopt a document, they publicized it before the plenary had a chance even to read it. This infuriated many delegates who, in the end, refused to adopt the document as an official document of the UNFCCC (UN Framework Convention on Climate Change) process.[97] Most vocal were ALBA countries. They objected to the procedural irregularities in negotiating the Accord as well as its substantive inadequacies especially, adaptation finance for developing countries.[98]

[89] See Kuehn (n 77); see also Sumudu Atapattu and Andrea Schapper, *Human Rights and the Environment: Key Issues* (Routledge 2019) ch 6.

[90] See 1998 Aarhus Convention on Access to Information, Public Participation in Decision-Making and Access to Justice in Environmental Matters and 2018 Regional (Escazú) Agreement on Access to Information, Public Participation and Justice in Environmental Matters in Latin America and the Caribbean.

[91] Examples include the New International Economic Order, Permanent Sovereignty over Natural Resources, and the UN Declaration on the Right to Development (1986); see nn 33, 35–36.

[92] See Edward Goodwin, 'Delegate Preparation and Participation in Conferences of Parties to Environmental Treaties' in Malgosia Fitzmaurice and Duncan French (eds) *International Environmental Law and Governance* (Brill/Nijhoff 2015) 51.

[93] World Bank, 'Voting Powers' <https://www.worldbank.org/en/about/leadership/votingpowers> accessed 2 January 2020.

[94] See Gonzalez, 'Global Justice' (n 23) 231.

[95] See Lavanya Rajamani, 'The Making and Unmaking of the Copenhagen Accord' *The International and Comparative Law Quarterly*, 59/3 (2010): 824.

[96] Ibid, 825.

[97] Ibid, 826.

[98] Ibid.

The Venezuelan President, Hugo Chavez, a member of ALBA group, was highly critical of capitalism: 'Our problem is not just about climate, but about poverty, misery, unnecessary child deaths, discrimination and racism—all related to capitalism.'[99] Bolivia's President, Evo Morales, pointed out that there is a profound difference between a document drawn up by a handful of states and those who are fighting for humanity and the planet; moreover, limiting the temperature increase to 2^{0}C as 'safe' will be the end of existence for many island nations. Both leaders agreed that the process reflected a lack of political will by rich countries headed by the 'US Empire'.[100]

3. *Corrective justice*

Corrective justice requires that wrongdoers are punished, past wrongs are redressed, wrongful acts are discontinued, and victims are compensated.[101] In the environmental field this means that polluters are punished and are not allowed to reap the benefits of their wrongful acts. An ongoing struggle in this context relates to controlling the activities of multinational companies operating in the global South and ensuring that the victims of their polluting operations are compensated. From Bhopal in India to Chevron in Ecuador, from Rana Plaza in Bangladesh to La Oroya in Peru,[102] history is replete with examples of innocent victims being forced to bear their losses alone. Controlling activities of multinational companies has been one of the most challenging issues for international law. Many multinational corporations (MNCs) that have caused massive environmental degradation and engaged in horrific violations of human rights continue to operate with impunity. Moreover, they have created complex project finance structures that make it impossible to identify the responsible party.[103] Further, bilateral investment treaties authorize MNCs to sue defaulting *states*. In the dispute between Chevron and Ecuador where victims of Chevron's polluting activities are still awaiting redress, Ecuador had to pay USD 2.3 billion in damages for 'violating' the bilateral investment treaty with the United States.[104]

Another example of egregious inequity is that suffered by small island states, who without having contributed significantly to climate change, will suffer its worst impacts.[105] These islands are disappearing into the sea and their inhabitants are facing the possibility of becoming stateless and devoid of citizenship. No state in the global North has offered them any compensation or shelter (except New Zealand which is planning to expand its refugee law to include climate refugees).[106] While these countries

[99] 'COP15: An Insider's Report from the ALBA Delegation' *Venezuela Analysis* (23 December 2009).
[100] Ibid.
[101] See Kuehn (n 77).
[102] See Atapattu (n 84).
[103] See Shalanda Baker, 'Project Finance and Sustainable Development in the Global South' in Alam *et al* (n 11) 338.
[104] See Puvimanasinghe (n 24).
[105] See Randall Abate (ed), *Climate Justice: Case Studies in Global and Regional Governance Challenges* (Environmental Law Institute 2016) especially chs 11, 12, 13.
[106] See Jan Lee, 'New Zealand Creates First Climate Change Refugee Visa Program' *Triple Pundit* (31 January 2018).

fought to get 'loss and damage' included in the 2015 Paris Agreement,[107] Northern states ensured that the loss and damage mechanism will not lead to liability and compensation.[108] It is thus not surprising that the President of Uganda characterized climate change an 'act of aggression' by Northern countries.[109]

More generally, it is worth noting that none of the former colonies have received compensation for the plunder and pillage of their resources. Neither did the colonizers repair any environmental damage or apologize for destroying ancient cultures, decimating the environment, and for creating a vicious cycle of poverty and dependence that we see even today.

4. *Social justice*

The final component recognizes that environmental justice cannot be separated from other struggles for justice. It is closely related to the social pillar of sustainable development,[110] demonstrating that environmental justice cannot be separated from struggles for other forms of justice that often underlie the reasons for environmental problems. Focusing on distributive justice alone could neglect the social structures and agents that cause environmental problems.[111] This chapter showed that causes such as colonialism, racism, and marginalization underlie many of the environmental problems. These underlying structural issues that lead to environmental injustice must be addressed and while a holistic approach to these struggles and injustices is necessary, the wider focus can often seem overwhelming. Moreover, it could overlook other factors that contribute to these inequities such as the role played by the market[112] and the current neoliberal economic system based on capitalism.[113]

VI. CONCLUSION: POTENTIAL AND LIMITS OF GLOBAL SOUTH PERSPECTIVES

While the global South has succeeded in persuading the international community to adopt principles and frameworks favourable to them, northern countries have

[107] art 8.

[108] Decision 1/CP.21, 'Adoption of the Paris Agreement' (29 January 2016) UN Doc FCCC/CP/2015/10/Add.1; see Linda Siegele, 'Loss and Damage (Article 8)' in Daniel Klein *et al* (eds), *The Paris Agreement on Climate Change: Analysis and Commentary* (OUP 2017) 224.

[109] See Oli Brown and Alec Crawford, *Assessing the Security Implications of Climate Change for West Africa* (IISD 2008).

[110] *Report of World Summit on Sustainable Development* (UN 2002) ch I.1, annex—'Johannesburg Declaration on Sustainable Development'.

[111] See Sheila Foster, 'Justice From the Ground Up: Distributive Inequities, Grassroots Resistance, and the Transformative Politics of the Environmental Justice Movement' *California Law Review*, 86/4 (1998): 775.

[112] Kuehn (n 77) 10699.

[113] Gonzalez, 'Global Justice' (n 23).

consistently refused to accept responsibility for creating environmental hazards and externalizing polluting costs while reaping the benefits for themselves. The politics surrounding the CBDR principle reflects this.

In this chapter we discussed global South approaches to international environmental law and how international environmental law is also grounded in colonialism. Many environmental issues date back to practices originating from the colonial era, practices entrenched by the neoliberal economic system. Parallels can be drawn between the disproportionate impact of environmental degradation at the international level with the disproportionate impact of polluting activities on poor, minority communities at the national level. While the former can be traced to colonization, the latter stems from discriminatory practices based on slavery, racism, and other forms of marginalization.

Unless we succeed in changing the current economic and trade regimes that favour the global North and their consumerism, and the institutions that perpetuate these unsustainable lifestyles, North-South tensions will worsen. Humanity's greatest challenge—climate change—requires all states to cooperate and work together as no country, no matter how rich or powerful, will be able to insulate itself from the consequences of climate change. To expect to solve climate change by relying on the economic system that created it is not only short-sighted but also naive. Humanity has succeeded in getting a geologic epoch named after it—the Anthropocene[114]—because of the destruction it has caused. However, not all humanity participated equally in that destruction and we must acknowledge that unequal contribution when adopting laws and governance mechanisms to address these challenges.[115]

BIBLIOGRAPHY

Ruchi Anand, *International Environmental Justice: A North-South Dimension* (Ashgate 2004)

Antony Anghie, *Imperialism, Sovereignty and the Making of International Law* (CUP 2004)

Richard Falk, Balakrishnan Rajagopal, and Jacqueline Stevens, 'Reshaping Justice: International Law and the Third World: An Introduction' *Third World Quarterly*, 27/5 (2006): 711

Carmen Gonzalez, 'Environmental Justice, Human Rights, and the Global South' *Santa Clara Journal of International Law*, 13/1 (2015): 151

Shawkat Alam *et al* (eds), *International Environmental Law and the Global South* (CUP 2015)

[114] See Louis Kotze, 'Human Rights and the Environment in the Anthropocene' *The Anthropocene Review*, 1/3 (2014).

[115] See Louis Kotze, 'Rethinking Global Environmental Law and Governance in the Anthropocene' *Journal of Energy & Natural Resources Law*, 32/2 (2014): 121, 156—who points to the need to reimagine the legal and governance constructs but does not discuss this unequal contribution.

CHAPTER 12

FEMINIST APPROACHES

ROWENA MAGUIRE

I. INTRODUCTION

This chapter provides a brief overview of ecofeminist theory, charting its rise due to the perception of women having a closer relationship with nature, the retreat of ecofeminism when essentialist notions of women's connections to nature were challenged, followed by the subsequent re-framing of ecofeminism, in light of material and power relationships. One of the central tensions within ecofeminist literature is the rejection of arguments premised on women being inherently closer to nature due to their shared roles in biological reproduction, while also highlighting the significance of biological reproduction on women's subordination within society.[1] This inherent tension, along with other pressures, resulted in a period of stagnation of feminist considerations within International Environmental Law (IEL). More recently, scholars have defended ecofeminism, arguing that it provides a lens to examine the exploitation of nature and women, through analyses of power, social constructs, and inter-species relationships.[2] The chapter also examines the contribution of women in shaping IEL in pre- and post-UNCED (United Nations Conference on Environment and Development) periods. Finally, the chapter explores recent efforts to embed gender within IEL processes, through the adoption of Gender Action Plans in the 1994 UNCCD (UN Convention to Combat Desertification), the 1992 UNCBD (Convention on Biological Diversity), and UNFCCC (UN Framework Convention on Climate Change). The chapter shows that, while IEL is generally gender-blind, it is transitioning through a period of gender mainstreaming and the future of IEL is likely to be increasingly gender-literate.

[1] Cecile Jackson, 'Women/Nature or Gender/History? A Critique of Ecofeminist Development' *Journal of Peasant Studies*, 20/3 (2008): 389.

[2] Sherilyn MacGregor, 'Introduction' in Sherilyn MacGregor (ed), *Routledge Handbook of Gender and Environment* (Routledge 2017) 7.

II. RISE, RETREAT, AND REFRAMING OF ECOFEMINISM

A. Defining Ecofeminism

Ecofeminism is not a single theory but refers to a variety of scholarly works and activist movements which focus on gender and environment relationships. Karen Warren's commonly quoted and helpful definition provides that ecofeminism is the 'position that there are important connections between how one treats women, people of colour and the underclass on one hand, and how one treats the non-human natural environment'.[3] Ecofeminism has been developed by scholars and activists from the global North and global South, and has influenced the development of international environmental law. Notably, legal academics have been largely absent from the development of ecofeminist theories. Thus, this section draws upon work from the social sciences more broadly.

B. Rise and Retreat of Ecofeminism

Many of the early authors on ecofeminism were activists, as opposed to academics, who based their arguments around a shared biological connection between women and nature, and the oppression of both by man.[4] Ecofeminist thought emerged at the height of the Cold War and was supported by women involved in the radical environmental and anti-nuclear movements. During this period, ecofeminism became associated with the discourse of women as virtuous proponents against nuclear power and other environmentally destructive practices, due to their closer relationship with nature.[5] This argument was framed on the premise that women held an affinity with nature due to their biology, reproductive functions, or innate tendency towards nurturing.[6]

A French writer, Francoise d'Eaubonne, is widely recognized as first coining the term 'ecofeminism' in *Le Feminisme ou la Mort*.[7] In this book, d'Eaubonne argued that male control over production and women's sexuality causes the twin crises of environmental destruction, through excessive production, and overpopulation.[8] Echoing a similar argument, Ynestra King stated 'our present patriarchy enshrines together the hatred

[3] Karen Warren, 'Introduction' in Karen Warren (ed), *Ecofeminism: Women, Culture, Nature* (Indiana University Press 1997) xi.

[4] Mary Mellor, 'The Politics of Women and Nature: Affinity, Contingency or Material Relation?' *Journal of Political Ideologies*, 1/2 (1996): 147.

[5] Ibid.

[6] Raewyn Connell and Rebecca Pearse, *Gender in World Perspective* (3rd edn, Polity Press 2014) 103.

[7] Francoise d'Eaubonne, *Le Feminisme ou la Mort* (Pierre Horay 1974).

[8] MacGregor (n 2) 7.

of women and the hatred of nature. In defying this patriarchy, we are loyal to future generations, this planet, and to life itself'.[9]

In 1980, Carolyn Merchant published 'The Death of Nature, Women, Ecology and the Scientific Revolution',[10] which documented the male domination of western science and industrial progress, while identifying the voices of women silenced from mainstream history. The book traces the linkages between the shift from organic relationships with the natural world, based on meeting subsistence needs, to the end of feudalism, the rise of commercial and capitalist economies in the sixteenth century, and humans' manipulation of the natural world. She argues that men partake in the public sphere of commodification, while women dominate the domestic sphere of unpaid labour, and that it is the public sphere of production that alienates humans from nature, by transforming, degrading, and polluting ecosystems.[11]

Following the publication of 'The Death of Nature' in 1980, scholars believed that ecofeminism would become the third wave of feminism in Northern countries.[12] The first wave of feminism in Northern countries occurred during the early nineteenth and twentieth centuries and focused on issues of women's enfranchisement, with a primary focus on the right to vote and rights to property; while the second wave of feminism peaked in the 1960s and 1970s, and focused on issues of work and pay inequalities.[13] Ecofeminism failed to ascend as the third wave of feminism in the global North for a number of reasons, including: ecofeminism's racial divide; class issues; the dominance of white and middle-class women; the rise of structural post-modernist theory which rejected a stable nature/culture divide; and critique of the idea of universal feminine values.[14]

Scholars in the global South, however, continued exploring ecofeminism, including Vandana Shiva, who left a career as a nuclear physicist in order to campaign against ecologically destructive activities occurring in the global South under the banner of 'development'. Her book, *Staying Alive*,[15] attributes the process of maldevelopment to the growing environmental destruction in the global South. Maldevelopment is defined as the North's imperialist imposition of modernity and capitalist expansion on the global South, justified by ideologies of economic growth and scientific knowledge.[16] Shiva's

9 Ynestra King, 'The Ecofeminist Imperative' in Leonie Caldecott and Stephanie Leland (eds), *Reclaim The Earth: Women Speak Out for Life on Earth* (Women's Press 1983) 11; cited in Charis Thompson and Sherilyn MacGregor, 'The Death of Nature: Foundations of Ecological Feminist Thought' in MacGregor (n 2) 47.

10 Carolyn Merchant, *The Death of Nature: Women, Ecology and the Scientific Revolution* (Harper and Row 1980).

11 Connell and Pearse (n 6) 106.

12 Thompson and MacGregor (n 9) 45.

13 Rosi Braidotti *et al*, *Women and Sustainable Development: Towards a Theoretical Synthesis* (Zed Books 1994) 61–75.

14 Thompson and MacGregor (n 9) 47.

15 Vandana Shiva, *Staying Alive: Women, Ecology and Development* (Zed Books 1989).

16 Ibid, 214-215.

conceptualization of environmental justice adopts a feminist lens, as she argues that maldevelopment is violence against nature and women.

International environmental law was influenced by these ecofeminist discourses which resulted in the emergence of the Women, Environment, and Sustainable Development (WED) movement in the 1980s.[17] Vandana Shiva, Wangari Maathai from Kenya, Bella Abzug from America, and many others, laid the foreground for a materialist analysis of the links between women and nature.[18] WED was influential throughout the 1990s and 2000s in gender, livelihoods, and natural resource planning and development institutions. The WED movement was based on the narrative of a feminine subject in the global South, who was vulnerable to environmental degradation, but who was virtuous and had agency to effect environmental conservation. In application, it meant that women in the global South were seen as the most effective stakeholders in environmental and conservation projects, due to their material connections with nature and natural resources.[19] As Bernadette Resurrección explains, this framing had an untended consequence of adding 'environmental caretaker' to the already long list of women's caring roles and shifted responsibility for the emerging environmental crisis to women.[20]

C. Reframing Ecofeminism

Bina Agarwal's extremely influential article 'The Gender and Environmental Debate from India'[21] demonstrated that the environmental/women relationship is mediated through structures of class, caste, race, and ethnicity over time. This approach has elements of intersectoral and materiality theory. Agarwal proposes a new framework for examining the gender and environmental relationship called 'feminist environmentalism' which examines women's and men's relationship with nature based on their material interaction with the environment.[22] This framework examines the structures that influence women's and men's material relationships with the environment, including the gender/caste/race division of labour, property, and power. A gendered examination of material relationships with the environment requires consideration of the gendered inequity of: labour; property rights; decision-making authority; and participation in environmental governance frameworks.[23]

[17] Braidotti *et al* (n 13) 2.

[18] Bernadette Resurrección, 'Gender and Environment in the Global South: From "Women, Environment and Development" to "Feminist Political Ecology"' in MacGregor (n 2) 71.

[19] Ibid, 73; Seema Arora-Jonsson, 'Virtue and Vulnerability: Discourses on Women, Gender and Climate Change' *Global Environmental Change*, 21/2 (2011): 744.

[20] Rusurreción (n 18).

[21] Bina Agarwal, 'The Gender and Environment Debate: Lessons from India' *Feminist Studies*, 18/1 (1992): 119.

[22] Ibid, 126.

[23] Bina Agarwal, *Structures of Patriarchy: The State, the Community and the Household* (Zed Books 1998) 68–77.

With the rise of the climate crisis, Sherilyn MacGregor also sought to re-examine the gender and environment nexus by examining climate change politics and power structures. She argues that a sole focus on material and measurable conditions means that a deeper gender analysis, involving critical feminist theorizing of the discursive constructions that shape modern climate policies, is deficient from climate scholarship.[24] She identifies a tension between prioritizing the urgent needs of women vulnerable to climate change versus the longer-term political goal of ecofeminism, to challenge patriarchal discourses and structures. The majority of scholarship on gender and climate focuses on the one-dimensional vulnerable women in the global South, requiring support from UN institutions funded by the global North. MacGregor argues that this frames the gendered impacts of climate change as an issue for 'them' and not 'us'.[25]

MacGregor argues that there are two dominant discourses within the UNFCCC which have gendered implications: ecological modernization and environmental security. Economic modernization presents science and economics as the essential pillars of knowledge needed to address climate change. As MacGregor argues, 'Climate change is widely represented as a techno-scientific problem requiring technical solutions' and ecological modernization presents technological advancement as the solution to a better environment.[26] There is an unwillingness to accept that fundamental changes to the way in which we live our lives is necessary and a belief that technology will save us. The second discourse of environmental security uses Hobbesian predications that climate change will inevitably lead to conflict over scarce resources between and within states. In some circles, climate change is presented as a serious threat to national and global security. MacGregor argues that 'by securitising and militarising it, the environmental crisis becomes a problem that requires technical, diplomatic and military solutions, entirely consistent with hegemonic (hyper)masculinity'.[27]

III. GENDER AND PUBLIC INTERNATIONAL LAW

In 1991, Hilary Charlesworth, Christine Chinkin, and Shelley Wright published a pivotal article, 'Feminist Approaches to International Law'.[28] While this article does not explicitly focus on IEL, many of the critiques of Public International Law (PIL) correlate with the arguments of ecofeminists. Charlesworth *et al* assert '[A] feminist account of

[24] Sherilyn MacGregor, 'Gender and Climate Change: From Impacts to Discourses' *Journal of the Indian Ocean Region*, 6/2 (2010): 223, 226.

[25] Ibid.

[26] Ibid, 230.

[27] Ibid, 231.

[28] Hilary Charlesworth, Christine Chinkin, and Shelley Wright, 'Feminist Approaches to International Law' *The American Journal of International Law*, 85/4 (1991): 613.

international law suggests that we inhabit a world in which men of all nations have used the statist system to establish economic and nationalist priorities to serve male elites, while basic human, social and economic needs are not met'.[29] They argue that the international legal order is impervious to the voices of women due to the organizational and normative structures of PIL.

With respect to the organizational structures of PIL, they note that women are under-represented in national and global decision-making processes.[30] When this article was published, some studies suggested that it would take until 2021 to reach equal representation of women in UN positions. This timeframe was described as grotesque in 1991, however progress in 2019 suggests that the 50% target will not be met by 2021. Charlesworth *et al* argue that the normative development of PIL 'rests on and reproduces various dichotomies between the public and private spheres'.[31] The public/private divide described by these authors mirrors some of the arguments made by ecofeminists regarding the nature/culture divide discussed above. This is explained as '[T]he public realm of the work place, the law, economics, politics and intellectual and cultural life, where power and authority are exercised, is regarded as the natural province of men; while the private world of the home, the hearth and children is seen as the appropriate domain of women'.[32] They argue that PIL regulates the public realm, but largely ignores the private realm, which has the effect of erasing women's issues from the main agenda of PIL.

The authors offer a critique of the rights-based approach to resolving gender equality, arguing that the acquisition of legal rights is a simplistic means of addressing gender equality. Although the legal granting of rights is often assumed to have solved a power imbalance, rights on paper do not translate to rights in practice.[33] Furthermore, the authors argue that PIL prioritizes civil and political rights, which generally provide little benefit to women, while the major forms of gender-based oppression operate within the economic, social, and cultural realms, which are often interpreted as a lesser form of international right with increased barriers to implementation. The feminist approach to PIL, pioneered by Charlesworth, Chinkin, and Wright,[34] provides important insights into the gendered operation of international law, while being sensitive to the complexity

[29] Ibid, 615.

[30] Ibid, 622.

[31] Ibid, 625

[32] Ibid, 626.

[33] Ibid, 635.

[34] For further guidance on developing feminist research methods for PIL, see Hilary Charlesworth, 'Feminist Methods in International Law' *The American Journal of International Law*, 93/2 (1999): 379; Hilary Charlesworth and Christine Chinkin, *The Boundaries of International Law: A Feminist Analysis* (Manchester University Press 2000); Sari Kouvo and Zoe Pearson (eds), *Feminist Perspectives on Contemporary International Law: Between Resistance and Compliance?* (Hart Publishing 2011); Sue Rimmer and Kate Ogg (eds), *Research Handbook on Feminist Engagement with International Law* (Edward Elgar 2019).

of advocating for women at the global level, given the diverse material lives and priorities of women across the globe.

IV. GENDER AND IEL: DEVELOPMENTS PRIOR TO UNCED

Women who participated in global environmental negotiations came predominately from forestry and agricultural backgrounds, due to the gendered impacts of the dominant development model within these sectors. Within the forestry sector, the gendered divisions of labour meant that women required wood collection for cooking and heating, resulting in forest conservation projects having gendered impacts.[35] While in the agriculture sector, Ester Boserup's influential book, *Women's Role in Economic Development*,[36] demonstrated that the development process had segregated gender relations, by drawing men into initiatives aimed at modernizing agriculture and isolating women to subsistence agriculture, with no access to credits, training, and technology. Such interventions were highly gendered and shifted traditional gendered divisions of labour; herbicides overtook women's roles in weeding, and the introduction of new high-yield crop seeds dislocated women from their traditional role in seed selection. Modern farm technology meant the men focused on production for export, while women were left with marginal lands, unsuitable for cash crop production, to pursue traditional methods of household subsistence farming.[37] Boserup's work also importantly challenged the myth that family income was equally distributed to all household members. This finding remains relevant today when observing the flows of IEL finance from a gendered perspective.[38]

In the lead-up to the UNCED period, gender and environment campaigns generally involved a two-pronged approach of enhancing participation in official UN events, to increase the recognition of material interests of women, and hosting separate parallel events, where more radical feminist environmental visons were created. A timeline of

[35] The Oil Crisis of 1970 and large-scale drought in the Sahel prompted development planners to realize that the majority of the global South depend on wood fuel for their energy needs, due to the expense of other energy sources. Women, in their role as users of wood, were pressured to: a) reduce wood fuel consumption by introducing wood-saving stoves; and b) introduce large-scale afforestation to increase wood supply; see Braidotti *et al* (n 13) 84.

[36] Ester Boserup, *Women's Role in Economic Development* (Earthscan 1970).

[37] Braidotti *et al* (n 13) 79.

[38] For Agarwal the benefits of payment being made at the household level and individual payments for men and women, see Bina Agarwal, 'Gender and Forest Conservation: The Impact of Women's Participation in Community Forest Governance' *Ecological Economics*, 68 (2009): 2785. On the gendered implications of REDD+ finance flows, see Rowena Maguire, 'Benefit Sharing for Women under the REDD+ Mechanism: Implications for Women' in Matthew Rimmer (ed), *Intellectual Property and Clean Energy: The Paris Agreement and Climate Justice* (Springer 2018) 615.

notable events on women and environment, with the parallel NGO events indented, includes:

- **1984**—UNEP (UN Environment Programme) established Senior Women's Advisory Group on Sustainable Development. The group prepared the contribution on environment for the 1985 UN Conference on Women and Development.
  - 1984: Development with Women for a new Era (DAWN) meeting took place in India. Group of women from the global South had joined forces to criticize the western development model as well as the WED approach.[39]
- **1985:** UN Conference on Women and Development. The final conference document from the 1985 Event is the 'Nairobi Forward Looking Strategies for the Advancement of Women.'[40]
  - **1985:** Environmental Liaison Centre International hosts a parallel event on Women and the Environmental Crisis; led to the Plan of Action for Women, Environment and Development.[41]
- **1986:** UN Secretariat for the Advancement of Women appointed UNEP as leading agency on women and environment.
- **1987:** 'Our Common Future' report (Brundtland Report)[42] recognizes gendered implications of environmental regulation in Chapters, 5, 6, 7, and 9.
  - **1991:** Women's Environment and Development Organisation (WEDO) organized 'World Women's Congress for a Healthy Planet in Miami' to prepare for the Rio Earth Summit; led to creation of Women's Action Agenda 21. In Miami, environmental problems were summarized as wasteful overconsumption in the North, inappropriate development leading to debt and structural adjustment in the South, environmental damage, pollution and toxic wastes, population growth, creation of ecological refuges, and excessive war and military spending associated with environmental damage.[43]

[39] See Fatma Alloo *et al*, 'Rethinking Social Development: DAWN's Vision' *World Development*, 23/11 (1995): 2001. DAWN's alternative vision of development argued that 'The quality of social progress of a society, or a nation, should be judged by the absence of grinding and widespread poverty, the elimination of violence and conflict associated with injustice and deep inequality'.

[40] UN General Assembly (UNGA) Res 40/108, 'Implementation of the Nairobi Forward-looking Strategies for the Advancement of Women' (13 December 1985) UN Doc A/RES/40/108, paras 28, 224–227 and 292.

[41] See Braidotti *et al* (n 13) 86. This plan outlined how different organizations could contribute to awareness-raising; advocacy; strengthening women's leadership in environmental action; providing information to and educating the public; and networking and training.

[42] World Commission on Environment and Development, *Our Common Future* (OUP 1987).

[43] Braidotti *et al* (n 13) 102–103. Braidotti argued that the 'Miami Conference' was a major breakthrough because women across political, geographical, class, race, professional, and institutional divides developed the first participatory and democratic critique of development and collective position on the environmental crisis.

V. GENDER AND IEL: DEVELOPMENTS FROM UNCED

The central document concerning gender from the UNCED negotiations was Agenda 21, Chapter 24: Global Action for Women Towards Sustainable and Equitable Development.[44] The UNCED negotiations led to the: Rio Declaration,[45] Agenda 21,[46] UNFCCC, UNCBD, UNCCD, and the Non-Legally Binding Forest Principles.[47] All of these instruments, aside from the UNFCCC, provide some recognition of the implications of sustainable development for women, as captured in Table 12.1 below. Braidotti *et al*, write that in order to integrate gender into the UNCED instruments, it became strategically necessary to simplify women's message, which resulted in an essentialist position of women being propagated as the basis for a collective position.[48]

A. Feminist Critiques of Sustainable Development and the Green Economy

The Rio Declaration and Agenda 21 lay the foundations of IEL's governance around the concept of sustainable development. The UNCED instruments refer to the definition of sustainable development in 'Our Common Future' as 'development that meets the needs of the present without compromising the ability of future generations to meet their own needs'.[49] The concept is commonly conceived as containing three limbs: economic development, environmental protection, and social equity,[50] and the development of a green economy is proposed as the way to implement to sustainable development. Civil groups, including feminist groups, were critical of the damaging, unequal, and wasteful theory of 'economic growth as the key way to achieve gender equality and environmental sustainability' in the approach of the UNCED documents.[51] Susan Buckingham

[44] *Report of the United Nations Conference on Environment and Development* (UN 1993) vol I, annex II, 'Agenda 21', ch 24: 'Global Action for Women Towards Sustainable and Equitable Development'.

[45] *Report of the United Nations Conference on Environment and Development* (UN 1993) vol I, annex I, 'Rio Declaration on Environment and Development'.

[46] Agenda 21 (n 44).

[47] *Report of the United Nations Conference on Environment and Development* (UN 1993) vol I, annex III, 'Non-legally Binding Authoritative Statement of principles for a Global Consensus on the Management, Conservation and Sustainable Development of all Types of Forests'.

[48] Ibid.

[49] Our Common Future (n 42) 43.

[50] John Drexhage and Deborah Murphy, 'Sustainable Development: From Brundtland to Rio+20' (19 September 2010).

[51] Women's Major Group, 'From the Future We Want to the Future We Need: Women's Major Group Final Statement on the Outcomes of Rio+20' (24 June 2012) <https://www.wedo.org/wp-content/uploads/Womens-Major-Group-RIO+20_FINAL-STATEMENT_24-June-2012.pdf> accessed 14 May 2019.

Table 12.1 Multilateral Environmental Agreements (MEAs) from UNCED

MEA	References to Gender
Rio Declaration	*Principle 20* acknowledges women's vital role in environmental management and development and that full participation is therefore essential to achieve sustainable development.
Agenda 21	*Chapter 24*: Global Action for Women Towards Sustainable and Equitable Development
UNCBD	*Preamble*: affirms the vital role that women play in the conservation and sustainable use of biological diversity and the need for the full participation of women at all levels of policy-making and implementation for biological diversity conservation.
UNCCD	• *Prologue* stresses important role of women in regions affected by desertification/drought. • *Article 5(d)*: promote awareness and facilitate participation of local populations, women, and youth in efforts to combat desertification and mitigate effects of drought. • *Article 10.2(f)*: provide for effective participation at all levels of government processes for both women and men. • *Article 19.1(a)*: promote capacity building of local institutions to deal with desertification/drought through full participation of local people especially women and youth. • *Article 19.3(e)*: assess education needs in affected areas, develop school curricula and adult literacy programme for all, in particular girls and women on the identification, conservation, and sustainable use of natural resources. • *Annex I:* Regional Implementation for Africa, Article 2(c): increase participation of local communities including women farmers and delegation of more responsibility for management.
UNFCCC	No reference.

argues that action needs to be taken to prioritize quality of life issues, compared to the accumulation of resources, and that a redistribution of resources should be central to policy, rather than generating more growth.[52] Similarly, Kate Wilkinson maintains 'that the dominant social paradigm includes a belief that the primary goal for governments, after national defence, is to create conditions that increase commodity production and satisfy the materialist needs of citizens'.[53]

[52] Susan Buckingham, 'Ecofeminism in the Twenty-First Century' *The Geographical Journal*, 170/2 (2004): 146–148.

[53] Kate Wilkinson, 'Is this the Future We Want? An Ecofeminist Common on the UN Conference on Sustainable Development Outcome Document' in Kim Rubenstein and Katharine Young (eds), *The Public Law of Gender: From the Local to the Global* (CUP 2016) 541.

The follow-up meetings of Rio+10,[54] held in Johannesburg in 2002, and Rio+20,[55] held in Brazil in 2012, continued to pursue an economic growth model as the way to achieve sustainable development. The Women's Major Group's critique of the green economy raised concerns that it will be misused to green-wash existing unsustainable economic practice, which infringe on the rights of affected present and future generations, because it does not fundamentally question and transform the current economic paradigm.[56]

B. The Vision of Agenda 21: Chapter 24—Enhancing Women's Participation in IEL

'Chapter 24: Global Action for Women Towards Sustainable and Equitable Development' creates an ambitious set of objectives and activities to recognize and ensure women's participation in national ecosystem management and control of environmental degradation. Due to space constraints, two provisions are elaborated upon, as these provisions have been further developed within IEL.

Objective 2(d) calls for the establishment of mechanisms at the national, regional, and international levels to assess the implementation and impact of development and environmental policies and programmes on women and to ensure their contributions and benefits by 1995. This provision has taken far longer to implement within IEL; Gender Action Plans were introduced in the UNCBD in 2007, and the UNCCD and UNFCCC in 2017 (discussed below). As a result of this delayed implementation of gender mechanisms within IEL frameworks, national and sub-national environmental laws largely ignore issues of gender. Outcomes from UNCED laid the foundations of modern environmental law within states, and these regimes are based on the problematic norm of sustainable development. Accordingly, ecofeminist solutions, including reducing consumption, equitable redistribution of resources, and transference of military expenditure to environmental initiatives, are not a part of national environmental laws.

Activity 3(a) requires the introduction of 'measures to review policies and establish plans to increase the proportion of women involved as decision makers, planners, managers, scientists and technical advisers in the design, development and implementation of policies and programmes of sustainable development'. Both Objective 2(d), discussed above, and Activity 3(a) are initiatives commonly associated with the practice of 'gender mainstreaming'. One main theme emerging from feminist scholarship is the critique of gender mainstreaming for failing to challenge existing patriarchal power

54 *Report of World Summit on Sustainable Development* (UN 2002).

55 UN, 'Report of the United Nations Conference on Sustainable Development' (13 August 2012) UN Doc A/CONF. 216/16.

56 Women's Major Group (n 51).

struggles.[57] Consequently, gender concerns fall within a business-as-usual approach, while the more radical elements of ecofeminism, which seek to challenge the prioritization of economic growth, technological intervention, and scientific knowledge, are not addressed. A number of scholars, however, acknowledge the strategic and pragmatic basis for the practice of gender mainstreaming, on the basis that achieving some gender progress is better than no progress at all.[58]

In addition to strategizing ways to increase the quantity of women participating in IEL, attention must also be paid to improving the quality of such participation. While there is a need to have equal numbers of male and female decision-makers, this alone will not guarantee gender justice in an institution.[59] The Feminist Standpoint theory of Sandra Harding,[60] contends that those embedded in, and benefitting from, positions of power cannot readily see the consequences of this power and lack the epistemic privilege required to understand and properly address the imbalance.[61] There is a need to consider gender relationships as being underpinned by differential power relations and the privileging of some forms of knowledge and contribution over other forms.

C. Incorporation of Gender Within the UNCCD

The inclusion of gender within the UNCCD was reportedly less controversial, as this instrument was largely driven by the global South and perceived as a tool for local development, when compared with the other MEAs.[62] The UNCCD provides some insights as to how IEL can incorporate gender and shape domestic environmental law. While it has been praised for its textual references to gender, emphasis on local capacity-building and education, and its bottom-up approach, the resources to assist with implementing its provisions have been limited.[63] An examination of the Conference of the Parties (COP) decisions finds that issues concerning gender and women's role are largely rhetoric, operating in a vacuum of concrete action.[64] Participation rates of women

[57] Buckingham (n 52).

[58] Andrea Cornwall, Elizabeth Harrison, and Ann Whitehead, 'Gender Myths and Feminist Fables: The Struggle for Interpretive Power in Gender and Development' *Development and Change*, 38/1 (2007): 1, 13.

[59] Susan Buckingham, 'Gender and Climate Change Politics' in MacGregor (n 2) 389.

[60] Sandra Harding, *The Feminist Standpoint Theory Reader: Intellectual and Political Controversies* (Routledge 2003).

[61] Buckingham, 'Gender and Climate Change Politics' (n 59).

[62] Lorena Aguilar Revelo, 'Putting Words into Action: Analysis of the Status of Gender Mainstreaming in the Main Multilateral Environmental Agreements' (International Union for Conservation of Nature (IUCN) Global Gender Office, June 2008) 19.

[63] Phillipa Norman, 'Surfacing the Silent "Others": Women and the Environment' *New Zealand Journal of Environmental Law*, 19 (2015): 1.

[64] Friederike Knabe and Lene Poulsen, 'How the Convention to Combat Desertification and Drought has Promoted the Role of Women in Decision-Making' (IUCN, 18 May 2004).

in UNCCD COP practices peaked in 2013 at 25%,[65] but this figure remains far below 50% and is lower than women's participation rates in the UNCBD and UNFCCC. This demonstrates that mere textual references to women in an instrument will not promote gender balance unless mechanisms are implemented to give effect to the references. In 2017, a Gender Action Plan was adopted within the UNCCD, requiring parties to increase the participation and leadership of women at all levels of decision-making and local implementation, with the aim of reaching gender parity by 2030.

In addition to the gender balance, a key theme emerging from the UNCCD gender policies relates to women's land rights. This land-rights focus is unique to the UNCCD, as asserting rights to land in the UNCBD and UNFCCC would likely prove far more controversial, despite similar policy relevance in these domains. Sustainable Development Goal 5A also requires governments to 'undertake reforms to give women equal rights to economic resources, as well as access to ownership and control over land and other forms of property, financial services, inheritance and natural resources in accordance with national laws'. However, one of the key barriers for measuring progress on women's land rights is the lack of comparable and reliable data at the global level.[66]

D. Essentializing Women in the UNCBD

The framing of women's contributions in the UNCBD historically relied upon essentialist notions of women, framing women as being more connected with nature due to their roles in human reproduction and socially constructed gender roles, which saw them as custodians of seed selection, improvement, and storage.[67] Recognition of women's role in conserving and benefitting from biodiversity has largely arisen in connection with Article 8(j) of the UNCBD, which recognizes the integral role of indigenous and local communities in conserving biodiversity. Early decisions surrounding Article 8(j) and women were founded on encouraging women to participate in conservation activities, but were not concerned with promoting gender equality in terms of access to benefit sharing.[68]

Parties to the UNCBD are encouraged to embed gender within their National Strategies and Actions on Biodiversity (NBSAPs). A study conducted by IUCN in 2017, found that 56% of NBSAPs contained at least one reference to gender or women, with 37% framing women as stakeholders, 27% seeing women as beneficiaries, 17% referring to women as vulnerable, and 4% characterizing women as agents of change.[69] In 2007,

[65] UN Women and the Mary Robinson Foundation—Climate Justice, *The Full View: Ensuring a Comprehensive Approach to Achieve the Goal of Gender Balance in the UNFCC Process* (2016) 30.

[66] Cheryl Doss *et al*, 'Gender Inequalities in Ownership and Control of Land in Africa: Myth versus Reality' *International Food Policy Research Institute*, Discussion Paper 01308 (2013).

[67] Paola Deda and Renata Rubian, 'Women and Biodiversity: The Long Journey from Users to Policy-Makers' *Natural Resources Forum*, 28/3 (2004): 201–204.

[68] Revelo (n 62) 21.

[69] Barbara Clabots and Molly Gilligan, 'Gender and Biodiversity: Analysis of women and gender equality considerations in National Biodiversity Strategies and Actions Plans (NBSAPs)' (IUCN Global Gender Office, January 2017).

a Gender Plan of Action (GPoA) was introduced to integrate gender into all areas of work, by setting sixteen targets for parties and Secretariat to the Convention, which were updated in 2014 to update the targets for the years 2015–20. Participation rates of women in UNCBD COP meetings is roughly on par with UNFCCC participation rates, at approximately 35% in 2014.[70]

E. Journey of Gender in the UNFCCC: Silence on the Gender Action Plan

1. *Women's participation in the UNFCCC*

As discussed, the UNFCCC was the only instrument to emerge from the UNCED without mentioning women or considering gender issues. Some scholarship has considered the reasons underlying this, which can be summarized as: the domination of north/south tensions;[71] the technical nature of the negotiations effectively side-lining women's contributions;[72] and the characterization of climate change as a global and transboundary problem marginalizing issues of participation in favour of solving more pressing issues.[73]

Karen Morrow's analysis explores the timeline of women's rights to participate in the UNFCCC, which is founded upon Article 4.1(i): 'encourage the widest participation in this process, including that of non-governmental organisations.'[74] Women were not included as one of the Major Groups defined by Agenda 21,[75] and it took until 2014 for women's groups to be granted constituency at the Warsaw COP. Morrow contends that the Major Groups created at Agenda 21 resulted in the domination of hard science and economics within the UNFCCC at the expense of social factors.[76] She identifies three arguments to support women's participation within the UNFCCC: regime functionality; matter of principle; and representative role. First, with respect to regime functionality, Morrow suggests that gendered social roles mean that women have considerable practical insights into addressing the many manifestations of climate change and, practically, their engagement is necessary to implement climate change policy.[77] Second, Morrow argues that climate change is having, and will continue to have, disproportionate

[70] The Full View (n 65).

[71] Rowena Maguire, 'Gender, Climate Change and the United Nations Framework Convention on Climate Change' in Sue Harris Rimmer and Kate Ogg (eds), *Research Handbook on Feminist Engagement with International Law* (Edward Elgar 2019) 63.

[72] Buckingham, 'Gender and Climate Change Politics' (n 59) 390.

[73] Sherilyn MacGregor, 'Only Resist: Feminist Ecological Citizenship and the Post-Politics of Climate Change' *Hypatia*, 29/3 (2014): 617.

[74] Karen Morrow, 'Changing the Climate of Participation: The Gender Constituency in the Global Climate Change Regime' in MacGregor (n 2) 399.

[75] The major groups identified in Agenda 21 were: women; children and youth; Indigenous peoples; non-governmental organizations; local authorities; workers and trade unions; business and industry; scientific and technological community; and farmers.

[76] Morrow (n 74) 399.

[77] Ibid, 401.

impacts on those most vulnerable in society and that entrenched societal gender inequalities result in women being amongst those groups most disadvantaged by the impacts of climate change and least well-placed socially, legally, and economically to respond to them.[78] Third, gender mainstreaming is a principle of the UN due to Economic and Social Council (ECOSOC) 1997.[79]

2. *Gender within UNFCCC Instruments*

The first reference to gender within the UNFCCC occurred in 2001 within the Bali COP decision, which recognized the lack of women contributing to international climate policy.[80] This was reinforced in the Cancun Agreements, which called for gender balance in bodies established pursuant to the Convention and Protocol.[81] There are two key gender concepts presented by the UNFCCC: gender balance, which considers issues of representation, and gender-responsive climate policy, which considers issues around the design and implementation of climate policy.

In 2014 the Lima Work Programme on Gender was created with the aim of improving measures concerning women's representation on Convention bodies.[82] This decision calls for 'additional efforts' to ensure participation of women in the UNFCCC and requested the Secretariat to publish data on gender representation in its annual reports. The 2016 COP 22 decision from Marrakesh extended the Lima Work Programme on Gender for a further three years and encouraged parties not only to improve women's representation at international climate negotiations, but also to enable effective participation in UNFCCC meetings by enhancing the skills and capacity of female delegates.

The preamble to the 2015 Paris Agreement requires parties to consider the human rights implications of climate policy for 'indigenous peoples, local communities, migrants, children, persons with disabilities and people in vulnerable situations and the right to development, as well as gender equality, empowerment of women and intergenerational equity'. Gender receives two mentions in the operative provisions of the text, but these provisions are limited to the specific issues of adaptation and capacity building. Article 7.5 requires parties to 'acknowledge' that adaptation action should follow a 'country driven, gender responsive approach', while Article 11.2 requires gender-responsive capacity building initiatives.

[78] Ibid, 402.

[79] Ibid. Gender mainstreaming is 'the process of assessing the implications for women and men of any planned action, including legislation, policies or programmes in all areas and at all levels', with the ultimate goal of achieving gender equality; ECOSOC Resolution 1997/2: Agreed Conclusions (18 July 1997).

[80] Decision 36/CP.7, 'Improving the Participation of women in the representation of Parties in bodies established under the United Nations Framework Convention on Climate Change or the Kyoto Protocol' (9 December 2001) UN Doc FCCC/CP/2001/13/Add.4 (Bali COP Decision).

[81] Decision 1/CP.16 'The Cancun Agreements: Outcome of the work of the Ad Hoc Working Group on Long-term Cooperative Action under the Convention' (15 March 2011) UN Doc FCCC/CP/2010/7/Add.1 (Cancun Agreements LCA).

[82] See Table 12.2 for gender composition of UNFCCC bodies and party delegations.

The Gender Action Plan (GAP), adopted at COP 23 in 2017, sits under the Lima Work Programme on Gender and 'seeks to advance women's full, equal and meaningful participation and promote gender-responsive climate policy and the mainstreaming of a gender perspective in the implementation of the Convention and the work of the Parties, the secretariat, United Nations entities and all stakeholders at all levels'. It is noted that gender-responsive climate policy requires strengthening in all activities concerning adaptation, mitigation, and related means of implementation-finance, technology development, and transfer and capacity building.

Table 12.2 Gender composition of UNFCCC bodies and party delegations

	Representation of Women within UNFCCC Bodies	Proportion of Women in Party Delegations at the COP Negotiations	Women as heads of party delegations
2013 Report (of 2012 COP)[a]	Ranges from 11 to 52%	29.4%	n/a
2014 Report (of 2013 COP)[b]	Ranges from 10 to 43%	36%	n/a
2015 Report (of 2014 COP)[c]	Ranges from 6 to 40%	36%	26%
2016 Report (of 2015 COP)[d]	Ranges from 10 to 52%	32%	20%

[a]UNFCCC Secretariat, 'Report on Gender Composition' (27 August 2013) UN Doc FCCC/CP/2013/4.

[b]UNFCCC Secretariat, 'Report on Gender Composition' (28 October 2014) UN Doc FCCC/CP/2014/7.

[c]UNFCCC Secretariat, 'Report on Gender Composition' (21 September 2015) UN Doc FCCC/CP/2015/6.

[d]UNFCCC Secretariat, 'Report on Gender Composition' (19 September 2016) UN Doc FCCC/CP/2016/4.

VI. CONCLUSION

As Agarwal wrote in 1992, 'environmental and gender concerns taken together open up both the need for examining, and the possibility of throwing new light on, many long standing issues relating to development, redistribution, and institutional change'.[83] This chapter has traced the rise, retreat, and rethinking of ecofeminist theory, showing that current conceptions of ecofeminism offer critical perspectives into understanding the material relationship between women and nature, as well as offering insights into the types of knowledge privileged within IEL institutions. This chapter has shown that there are a range of practical and ethical reasons for embedding gender into IEL. Practically,

[83] Agarwal (n 21) 152.

women are necessary to ensuring that IEL is translated into discernible action on the ground. Socially constructed gender roles have meant that women have agency over decisions with respect to household consumption, energy, food, and water use. This does not mean that women should be charged with sole responsibility for solving environmental issues, but rather, that women should be listened to about ways in which laws and governments can assist them to transition to a more sustainable lifestyle.

There are two different pathways in which ecofeminism can influence IEL. First, ecofeminism highlights the importance of having women participate in formal governance mechanisms for environmental regulation. Referred to as gender mainstreaming, this process seeks to ensure that the material interests of women are accounted for in IEL. The second approach, which can accompany the first approach, is to challenge the dominant norms and solutions of IEL. This more radical approach would seek to redefine IEL, shifting from solutions premised on economic growth, to an approach requiring fundamental changes to the ways in which we live our lives, by reducing consumption and redistributing resources. This approach also aims to incorporate and prioritize a range of different knowledge into IEL mechanisms. IEL is currently in the early stages of gender mainstreaming, with the first approach outlined above being the dominant approach. The journey of gender mainstreaming may well open opportunities for the incorporation of more radical ecofeminist perspectives within IEL, but such changes will take time. Ecofeminism reminds us that humans have a duty to care for our shared environment, that the planet's resources are limited, and that techno-scientific progress alone will not solve our environmental crisis. Ultimately, humans need to change the way in which we live our lives and the way we value and interact with nature.

BIBLIOGRAPHY

Bina Agarwal, 'The Gender and Environment Debate: Lessons from India' *Feminist Studies*, 18/1 (1992): 119

Rosi Braidotti *et al*, *Women and Sustainable Development: Towards a Theoretical Synthesis* (Zed Books 1994)

Hilary Charlesworth, Christine Chinkin, and Shelley Wright, 'Feminist Approaches to International Law' *The American Journal of International Law*, 85/4 (1991): 613

Sherilyn MacGregor, 'Gender and Climate Change: From Impacts to Discourses' *Journal of the Indian Ocean Region*, 6/2 (2010): 223

CHAPTER 13

ETHICAL CONSIDERATIONS

ALEXANDER GILLESPIE*

I. INTRODUCTION

THE purpose of this chapter is to give the reader an overview of where some of the ethical debates in international environmental law are currently found.

II. ANTHROPOCENTRIC VALUES

Most of the values discussed in this chapter are anthropocentric in their origins. This view regards humanity as the centre of existence. The anthropocentric paradigm can be traced to the great philosophers of antiquity, such as Protagoras who proclaimed, 'Man is the measure of all things'.[1] Such views permeate the vast majority of cultural traditions. Subject to a few exceptions, this type of anthropocentric outlook that underpins the human relationship with the natural world, also manifests itself in international environmental law. For example, the 1972 Declaration of the United Nations Conference on the Human Environment reflected its anthropocentric basis in its title. Additionally, the Declaration emphasized (as Mao had done earlier) that 'of all things in the world, people are the most precious'.[2] In 1987 the World Commission on Environment and Development added that, 'Sustainable development ... is a process ... that is designed

* This chapter builds upon my earlier work in this area, which is contained in Alexander Gillespie, *International Environmental Law, Policy and Ethics* (2nd edn, OUP 2014).

[1] Protagoras, quoted in John Rodman, 'The Dolphin Papers' *The North American Review*, 259/1 (1974): 12, 16.

[2] UN, 'Report of the United Nations Conference on the Human Environment' (5–16 June 1972) UN Doc A/CONF.48/14/Rev.1, 3, ch 1, 'Declaration of the United Nations Conference on the Human Environment', para 7.

to enhance both current and future potential to meet human needs and aspirations'.[3] Likewise, the 1992 Rio Declaration on Environment and Development states, 'Human beings are at the centre of concerns for sustainable development'.[4]

Although this approach was broadly reiterated at the 2002 World Summit on Sustainable Development, it was notable that the 'representatives of the world' pledged their responsibility to, 'one another, to the greater community of life and to our children'.[5] The extension of ethical concern to the 'greater community of life' was a leap in the philosophical thinking of international environmental law, because it attempted to move the paradigm of what was important, and why, away from a sole focus on what is valuable to humanity.

Although the 2002 Declaration was a notable leap, the majority of philosophical discussions in this area continue to be dominated by anthropocentric justifications. That is, nations typically seek to protect the environment because of its anthropocentric value, not its value independent of humanity. The four common forms of arguments that follow exemplify this approach.

A. Self-interest

Although it is axiomatic it is useful to point out the obvious—that humanity exists because of the Earth, its ecosystems, and the species upon it—not the other way around. This has always been the way, and it is more than likely to continue to be the basis of our existence for thousands of years to come. From the food we eat to the purified air we breathe, biodiversity and ecosystems contribute both directly and indirectly to the success, if not the very existence, of humanity. The problem is, we often fail to practise adequate conservation and/or control the pollution that threatens to undermine the very physical basis upon which our existence is built. To prevent this from happening, it is suggested that we should protect the environment, because it is in our own self-interest.

The justification to protect the environment, because of its self-interest to humanity, can be traced to the Old Testament when God commanded Noah to take all the species that were available onto the ark.[6] However, God made it quite clear that the species were saved, inter alia, so that the chosen ones would inherit a 'land in which they would lack nothing'.[7] That is, God commanded that the species be conserved, for the benefit of humanity, not because they were valuable in themselves. Today, this is the most commonly

[3] World Commission on Environment and Development (WCED), *Our Common Future* (OUP 1987) 23, 46.

[4] *Report of the United Nations Conference on Environment and Development* (UN 1993) vol I, annex I, principle 1.

[5] *Report of World Summit on Sustainable Development* (UN 2002) 6, 'Plan of Implementation', para 8.

[6] Genesis 7:8–9.

[7] Deuteronomy 8:7–9. See also Genesis 9:1–3.

articulated argument, by which conservation is justified by reference to direct human benefit.

At the micro level, conservation of individual species is often justified along these lines. We want to conserve them because they might be valuable in medicine, as food, or perhaps as an indicator of environmental change, or they are a keystone species, upon which so many others depend. For example, when Mao Zedong declared a three-day war on songbirds and sparrows in 1958, claiming they consumed too much grain, so many were killed that the remnant populations could not control the proliferation of insects and plagues of locusts followed the year after.[8]

A variation on the theme, is that we want to conserve wildness because it is good for our mental well-being. The conservation of wilderness often falls into this approach, whereby areas free of human impact, from the mountains to the coastlines, are desired, as in such natural and empty spaces, we can reconcile and reconnect to the natural world. This approach mirrors the oft quoted dictum of Henry Thoreau that, 'in wilderness is the preservation of the world'.[9]

At the macro level, we fight pollution because it is bad for humans. The example of air pollution (globally, shortening the life expectancy of around three to five million people per year), to which regional air pollution conventions and now the Sustainable Development Goals aims by 2030 to substantially reduce the number of deaths and illnesses from, inter alia, air pollution, is strong here.[10] So too, the example of the ozone layer, to which humanity has collectively acted to stop the problems of skin cancer, cataracts, and reduced immune systems, all enhanced by a depleted ozone layer, is a good instance of the way self-interest can work in international environmental law. For as the 1987 Montreal Protocol recorded, from which one of the most effective international environmental agreements ever created was cast, 'world-wide emissions of certain substances can significantly deplete and otherwise modify the ozone layer in a manner that is likely to result in adverse effects on human health and the environment'.[11]

The best example of this self-interest thinking, hopefully, is climatic change. In this area, 'humanity is conducting an unintended, uncontrolled, globally pervasive experiment whose ultimate consequences could be second only to a global nuclear war'.[12] The boldness of this statement is supported by reports that suggest that depending on what pathway (as dependent on technology, demographic change, and economic development) was adopted, the world could warm between 1°C–4.8°C by 2100. These increases suggest severe, pervasive, and irreversible impacts for many people and ecosystems, with heatwaves occurring more often and lasting longer and extreme precipitation

[8] Timothy Beardsley, 'Enlightening Self Interest' *BioScience*, 57/7 (2007): 547.

[9] Henry Thoreau (1906), *Excursions and Poems* (Houghton Mifflin and Company 1978) 224.

[10] See *Ambient Air Pollution: A Global Assessment of Exposure and Burden of Disease* (WHO 2016) 15–19.

[11] Preamble.

[12] United Nations Environment Programme (UNEP), *Proceedings of the World Conference on the Changing Atmosphere* (CUP 1988) vii.

becoming more intense and frequent in many areas. Ecosystems will have to adapt to changing conditions, the ocean will continue to warm and acidify, and global mean sea level is likely to rise. The future impacts are likely, depending on how much the temperature rises, and where the human communities are, to range from moderate to extreme. In the worst case scenario, as with small island states, their very survival may be threatened.[13]

B. Culture

The ethical justifications surrounding debates on conservation, based upon cultural considerations, are some of the most prominent philosophical debates in international environmental law. This is not a surprise as from ancient times to modern day, cultural attitudes that link to the natural environment have been recognized as important. Consequently, it is suggested that to preserve the environment (or vice versa, with culture) is to preserve the natural expressions of the values of culture, history, and identity.[14]

The interlinking argument for the protection of the environment because of its cultural importance then becomes multifaceted, and ranges in conservation, from species to areas. Consider, in the United States, their Wild Horses and Burros Act mandated conservation because, 'Congress finds and declares that wild free roaming horses and burros are living symbols of the historic and pioneer spirit of the West ... they enrich the lives of the American people.'[15]

Such an approach, where conservation and culture overlap, is at the core of the 1972 World Heritage Convention (WHC) which recognized that, 'the deterioration or disappearance of any item of cultural or natural heritage constitutes a harmful impoverishment to all nations of the world.'[16] Consequently, the signatories recognized the importance of preserving 'exceptional combinations of natural and cultural elements.'[17] This type of understanding is mirrored in further conventions in 2003[18] and 2005.[19]

Where examples become more universal, and not nation-specific, is with Indigenous peoples. They are commonly perceived as having a strong connection with the natural world, and with it, good examples of sustainable practices. For example, at the Rio+20 conference in 2012, those attending, acknowledged, 'the natural and cultural diversity of

[13] The various reports were Intergovernmental Panel on Climate Change (IPCC), *Climate Change 2014: The Synthesis Report* (2014); IPCC, *Climate Change 2013: The Physical Science Basis* (2013); IPCC, *Climate Change 2007: The Scientific Basis* (2007); IPCC, *Climate Change 2001: The Scientific Basis* (2001).

[14] Manenti Claudia, 'Sustainability and Place Identity' *Procedia Engineering*, 21 (2011): 1104.

[15] The Wild Horses and Burros Act 16 USC, ss 1331–1340.

[16] Preamble.

[17] See Listing Criteria and art 4.

[18] The Convention for the Safeguarding of Intangible Cultural Heritage.

[19] The Convention on the Protection and Promotion of the Diversity of Cultural Expressions.

the world and recognize that all cultures and civilizations can contribute to sustainable development'.[20]

This recognition, and need to support Indigenous peoples' in general, and specifically, with regard to the preservation of their exemplars of sustainability, has been repeatedly endorsed since in statements, treaties (especially the 1992 Convention on Biological Diversity (CBD)),[21] and high level commitments, of which the 2007 Declaration on the Rights of Indigenous Peoples is most important. This Declaration emphasized that to achieve the desired goals for indigenous peoples, it is necessary to ensure that their distinctive spiritual relationships with traditionally owned or otherwise occupied and used lands, territories, waters, and coastal seas, and other resources is upheld.[22]

C. Economic Values

Sophisticated methods have been evolving over the last four decades which attempt to maximize, and display, the net economic value of the environment. This idea which began in 1910 with Gifford Pinchot[23] took over a century to be fully appreciated, before it was well articulated by Achim Steiner, the erstwhile Director of the UNEP when he suggested that 'green economics is the key to … sustainability'.[24] The key, for the World Bank, is that 'markets and governments [need] to price the environment appropriately'.[25] Thereafter, as the environmental economist David Pearce suggested, 'environmental concerns must be properly integrated into economic policy from the highest level to the most detailed level'.[26]

This type of thinking has been endorsed by numerous international environmental conventions, including the CBD,[27] UNESCO's Man and the Biosphere regime,[28] and the 1971 Ramsar Convention on Wetlands of International Importance. In relation to Ramsar, given the diversity of values of wetlands, the parties have consistently recommended that in cases of large scale wetland transformation, 'the decision is not

[20] UNGA RES 66/288, 'The Future We Want' (11 September 2012) UN Doc A/RES/66/288, annex, para 41.

[21] See arts 8(j), 10(c)–(d).

[22] UNGA RES 61/295, 'United Nations Declaration on the Rights of Indigenous Peoples' (2 October 2007) UN Doc A/RES/61/295, arts 24, 25.

[23] Gifford Pinchot, *The Fight for Conservation* (Harcout Brace 1910) 38–41.

[24] Steiner as noted in Fred Pearce, 'Earth Summit signals move to give nature a price tag' *New Scientist* (30 June 2012).

[25] World Bank, *World Development Report 1992: Development and the Environment* (OUP 1992) 71.

[26] David Pearce *et al*, *Blueprint for a Green Economy* (Earthscan 1989) xiv.

[27] art 11.

[28] UNESCO, 'The Seville Strategy for Biosphere Reserves' (1995) Objective I.1; UNESCO, 'International Co-ordinating Council of the Programme on Man and the Biosphere—Sixteenth session. Paris, 6–10 November 2000: Final Report' MAB Report Series No 68.

taken until an assessment of all the values involved has been made'.[29] The question of 'all values' was furthered when the Ramsar parties suggested that the quantification of both direct (monetary) and indirect (non-monetary) values of wetlands be fully taken into account in the planning and conservation of wetlands.[30]

In practice there is a need to develop a method whereby the economic value of parts of the natural world are clearly and robustly adduced and displayed. This task has been accomplished by a new form of economic equation that seeks to establish the 'Total Economic Value'. Total Economic Value consists of a total economic aggregate of three separate economic factors. These are consumptive or direct use value, non-consumptive or indirect use values, and existence and option values. Consumptive use values can be assigned prices through such mechanisms as estimating market value if the product were sold on the market, instead of being consumed. An exemplar of such non-consumptive values is eco-tourism, which can turn areas into high value money-making areas. For example, the top World Heritage sites draw over one million visitors and generate over USD one billion, per site, in revenue per year.[31]

Indirect use values correspond to the economic value of ecological functions (such as how much would it cost to clean the air, if forests were not doing the work for free). Option values relate to the amount that an individual would be willing to pay to conserve something for possible future use, and existence values relate to how much people are willing to pay for the existence of parts of the environment, irrespective of its other uses or values. When all three of these economic values are subsumed into the Total Economic Value, then economic logic should provide a strong justification for the conservation of the natural environment, in terms of either entire ecosystems, or individual species.[32]

When this type of accounting is done, it is possible to show that it makes good economic sense, prima facie, to conserve a number of species, ranging from the smallest, to the largest. Thus, it has been estimated that the economic value of the services offered by four insects in the United States in terms of dung burial, pest control, wildlife control, and pollination is worth over USD 157 billion each year. In this last service, bees are of particular interest, since one in every three human mouthfuls of food is linked to pollination by bees. Although this process could be done by humans, it would be much more expensive than ensuring that bee populations remain healthy.[33]

[29] Ramsar Convention, '1st Meeting of the Conference of the Contracting Parties' (1980) Recommendation 1.6 <https://www.ramsar.org/sites/default/files/documents/library/key_rec_1.06e.pdf> accessed 10 January 2020.

[30] 'Principles and guidelines for incorporating wetland issues into Integrated Coastal Zone Management (ICZM); adopted by Resolution VIII.4 (2002) of the Ramsar Convention', principle 2.

[31] Helen Hazen, 'Valuing Natural Heritage: Park Visitors' Values related to World Heritage Sites in the USA' *Current Issues in Tourism*, 12/2 (2009): 165–181.

[32] Nick Hanley, *Pricing Nature: Cost Benefit Analysis and Environmental Policy* (Edward Elgar 2009).

[33] *Rapid Assessment of Pollinators' Status* (FAO 2008) 7, 47; John Losey and Mace Vaughan, 'The Economic Value of Ecological Services Provided by Insects' *BioScience*, 56/4 (2006): 311.

Larger species can also have considerable economic worth. On average, a day tripper in the United States focused on birdwatching will spend somewhere between USD 32 and 142 in a local community. Gorilla watching operations generate over USD one million per year in tourist income per enterprise. Each lion in Kenya is thought to be worth USD 27,000 per year in tourism revenues. Each Hawksbill turtle in Hawaii is estimated to be worth USD 30,000 to the local resort economy. Shark watching in Palau, is now worth over USD eighteen million per year, while ray watching, globally, is worth over USD 140 million. However, the real stars, whales, are now engaged in an industry worth over USD two billion per year.[34]

The same logic applies to a number of different systems, such as with some types of tropical forests, wetlands or coral reefs and marine protected areas. And, with respect to most types of pollution control, of which climate change is the most obvious. This has been evident since the 2006 Report by Nicolas Stern on the 'Economics of Climate Change'. The report concluded that, depending on the level of impact of climate change, the economic costs could be twenty times higher than the costs of solving the problem. In particular, the report estimated that 1% of global GDP investing in combatting climate change over the next fifty years (to stabilize greenhouse gas concentrations) would be considerably lesser than the estimated potential cost of USD four trillion to the global economy, of doing nothing.[35]

D. Aesthetics

The aesthetic value of nature is a well-recognized justification for its protection for, as Holmes Rolston suggested, 'people are learning to respect natural things ... because we find a beauty we are unwilling to destroy'.[36] Conservation groups have long recognized this value. The most recent high-level support for aesthetic values came at the 2012 Earth Summit which reaffirmed, inter alia, 'the aesthetic values of biological diversity'.[37] There have been several similar affirmations in between.

This value of aesthetics is well recognized in the need to preserve landscapes and seascapes, the high value real estate in coastal areas, the prevention of oil spills which blight ecosystems, and the regulation of litter. People intuitively understand and value beauty. In terms of biodiversity, people already gravitate towards what they perceive to be attractive. Butterflies trump beetles. Marine mammals trump fish. Gorillas trump sheep.[38] Many conservation groups, aware of this bias, choose flagship ecosystems or

[34] Miko Maekawa *et al*, 'Mountain Gorilla Tourism Generating Wealth and Peace' *Natural Resources Forum*, 37/2 (2013): 127.

[35] See Nicholas Stern, 'The Economics of Climate Change' *The American Economic Review*, 98/2 (2008): 1.

[36] Holmes Rolston, 'Is There An Ecological Ethic?' *Ethics*, 85/2 (1975): 103.

[37] UNGA RES 66/288 (n 20) para 197.

[38] Jeffrey Skibins, 'Charisma and Conservation: Charismatic Megafauna's Influence on Safari and Zoo Tourists' Pro-Conservation Behaviors' *Biodiversity and Conservation*, 23/2 (2013): 17.

flagship species for their aesthetic value. In some instances, the conservation results have been spectacular. The foremost example of this involved the campaigns against seal hunting in the 1980s, that involved the clubbing to death of baby seals. Central to this media and image orientated campaign was the fact that, 'the seals were very young and very attractive; the killing took place in the open on the ice; and the killing was bloody and looked brutal'.[39]

The idea that protected areas may have a high aesthetic value is well recognized in the philosophical literature,[40] and in the preambles of a number of international agreements.[41] However, the WHC is the only convention to have developed a specific jurisprudence in this area. The launching point into the discussion of aesthetic values comes from the WHC appreciation of 'natural features consisting of physical and biological formations or groups of such formations, which are of outstanding universal value from the aesthetic ... point of view' and/or 'natural sites or precisely delineated natural areas of outstanding universal value from the point of view of ... natural beauty'.[42] This section of the WHC has been interpreted to allow for the inscription of sites that 'contain superlative natural phenomena or areas of exceptional natural beauty and aesthetic importance'.[43] For example, with the 2009 inscription of the Dolomites in Italy, they were noted as being among the most attractive mountain landscapes in the world, due to their spectacular vertical forms of pinnacles, spires, and towers, all set within a mosaic of colours of pale-coloured rock, forests, and meadows.[44]

E. Future Generations

The justification that we should pursue environmental goals so that we do not damage the chances or potential of future generations is the most commonly touted environmental value. The thinking behind this value is that our generation has benefitted from the efforts of the generations before us, and ideally, future generations should obtain a similar legacy from our generation. The problem is that this current generation is in the process of causing damage not just to itself, but also to future generations.[45]

[39] Canadian Royal Commission, *Seals and Sealing in Canada* (Government Printer 1986) vol I, 25–28; vol II, ch 9.

[40] William Godfrey-Smith, 'The Value of Wilderness' *Environmental Ethics* 1/4 (1979): 309.

[41] See Alexander Gillespie, *Protected Areas and International Environmental Law* (Martinus Nijhoff 2007) ch 4.

[42] art 2.

[43] UNESCO, 'Operational Guidelines for the Implementation of the World Heritage Convention' (July 2002) para 77(vii).

[44] UNESCO Decision 33 COM 8B.6, 'Natural properties—Properties deferred or referred back by previous sessions of the World Heritage Committee—The Dolomites (Italy)' WHC-09/33.COM/20 (20 July 2009).

[45] Pascal Lamy et al, *Now for the Long Term: The Report of the Oxford Martin Commission for Future Generations* (OUP 2013) 6.

Therefore, a number of scholars have argued for restraint on the part of those in the present. One of the first in this context, Gifford Pinchot proclaimed in the first decade of the twenty-first century,

> No generation can be allowed needlessly to damage or reduce the future general wealth and welfare by the way it uses or misuses any natural resource.[46]

In an international context, the idea of recording the interests of future generations became apparent with the conclusion of the Second World War. The opening paragraph of the United Nations Charter states, 'We, the peoples of the United Nations, determined to save succeeding generations from the scourge of war . . . '. This idea made its way to international environmental law by the 1970s with the 1972 Stockholm Declaration of the United Nations Conference of the Human Environment, which recognized that, 'man, . . . bears a solemn responsibility to protect and improve the environment for present and future generations'.[47]

The idea was repeated continually before the 1987 World Commission for Environment and Development famously defined the concept of sustainable development to mean that the present generation meets its own needs without compromising the ability of future generations to meet theirs.[48] Supplementary work, such as that undertaken by organizations like UNESCO in 1997, with their Declaration on the Responsibilities of the Present Generations Towards Future Generations, have further enhanced the understandings in this area.[49]

III. NON-ANTHROPOCENTRIC VALUES

Although anthropocentric values within international environmental law and policy are dominant, over the last two decades, the growth of non-anthropocentric values has also become obvious.

A. Sentience and Humane Considerations

Peter Singer is often credited with laying the intellectual foundations for the contemporary basis for the moral respect for animals. Singer's commitment is to the utilitarian

[46] Gifford Pinchot, 'What it all Means' in Ian Burton and Robert Kates (eds), *Readings in Resource Management and Conservation* (University of Chicago Press 1965) 255.
[47] Stockholm Declaration (n 2) principle 1.
[48] WCED, *Our Common Future* (n 3) 8, 40.
[49] UNESCO, 'Declaration on the Responsibilities of the Present Generations Towards Future Generations' (12 November 1997).

doctrine, according to which moral agents are expected to do those acts which, directly or indirectly, can reasonably be expected to yield the best consequences or lead to the greatest happiness. Conversely, moral agents should seek to minimize the occurrence of badness in the world.[50] The goal is to achieve the best balance of good over bad. To achieve this, all interests, no matter which entity they relate to, are meant to be taken into account. This is because every interest is just what it is, and counts for its own weight. Accordingly, as Jeremy Bentham suggested, 'the question is not can they reason? Nor can they talk? The question is can they suffer?'.[51]

When this focus upon sentience becomes the prism for ethical thinking about the environment, the goal becomes to reduce pain in all sentient creatures, irrespective of what species they are, or whether they are endangered, or not. In this area, although some have called for a 'Universal Declaration of the Rights of Animals',[52] this type of thinking is far beyond what is acceptable to most. Accordingly, the focus has been upon trying to create an enhanced moral status for particular animals, which may be considered the flagships, notably whales and great apes, perhaps the most charismatic of all species. However, despite their popularity, and their well-recognized importance, they do not have a right to life in international law.

For example, on whales, the question of their intelligence (or awareness, consciousness, and/or sentience) has become a foremost consideration for many at the International Whaling Commission since the mid-1970s. However, although many nations argue that whales are 'special', a blocking minority[53] dismiss these claims, especially at the generic level. The result is that there is no consensus on this approach at international law, and although whales are protected, it is for conservation, not because they possess qualities akin to humanity.[54]

Similarly, with the great apes, despite their striking similarities to humanity, impressive campaigns such as the Great Ape Project and high-level support from a number of prominent scientists and philosophers, who lobbied for the United Nations to endorse a 'Declaration on Great Apes', failed in their efforts. Thus, again, the protection of great apes is pursued for conservation. Accordingly, when the Gorilla Agreement (under the auspice of the 1979 Convention on Migratory Species (CMS)) was concluded in 2007, aside the central goal of preventing the extinction of the gorilla, their only moral recognition was the note in the preamble of the parties' awareness, 'of the exceptional significance of Great Apes for the natural and cultural heritage of humankind'.

50 Peter Singer, 'Utilitarianism and Vegetarianism' *Philosophy and Public Affairs*, 9/4 (1979): 325, 327.

51 Jeremy Bentham (1789), 'An Introduction to the Principles of Morals and Legislation' in *The Works of Jeremy Bentham* vol I (Russell & Russell 1962) 328.

52 The Universal Declaration of the Rights of Animals was adopted by the International League of the Rights of Animals on 21 September 1977, London. It is reprinted in Charles Magel, *Animal Rights* (Mansell 1989) appendix B.

53 IWC, *31st Report of the International Whaling Commission* (Cambridge 1981) 24.

54 Philippa Brakes, *Whales and Dolphins: Cognition, Culture, Conservation and Human Perceptions* (Arnold 2011): 1–18, 23–34, 49–65. See also the classic in this area—Joan McIntyre, *Mind In the Water* (Scribner 1974) 69–70.

International environmental law has been, however, more successful in the quest to reduce unnecessary pain when animals are killed.[55] This goal, to not cause unnecessary pain, is found in the 1973 Convention on International Trade in Endangered Species of Flora and Fauna (CITES)[56] and in the World Organisation for Animal Health (the OIE) Guidelines. The OIE Guidelines aim to reduce the amount of time animals spend on journeys and ensure animal welfare by buttressing each part of the journey by detailed management considerations.[57] The 1991 Madrid Protocol on Environmental Protection to the Antarctic Treaty is noteworthy. It requires that, 'all taking of native mammals and birds shall be done in the manner which involves the least degree of pain and suffering practicable'.[58]

Some methods of capture, such as leg-hold traps, cause so much unnecessary pain that they have been prohibited between countries which trade in the pelts of these animals. This is evident with agreements between Europe, Canada, Russia, and the United States. The 1998 Agreement on International Humane Trapping Standards (AIHTS) recalls 'their deep commitment to the development of international humane trapping standards'.[59] Similar obligations are also found in documents pertaining to the taking of seals[60] and birds. The 1950 International Convention for the Protection of Birds prohibits certain methods which would cause mass killing of birds 'or cause them unnecessary suffering'.[61] A more contemporary example involves the 2001 Agreement on the Conservation of Albatross and Petrels which mandates that, when dealing with albatrosses or petrels which could not be rescued, only 'humane killing, by duly authorized persons, to end the suffering of seriously injured or moribund albatrosses or petrels' would be permissible.[62] The importance of causing minimal pain, when releasing animals which have been unintentionally caught in nets, can be found in regimes dealing with turtles[63] and dolphins.[64]

The final example of humane killing objectives in international environmental law is the International Whaling Commission. In this forum, the objective to reduce both pain and time to death for hunted cetaceans goes back to the 1958 United Nations Conference on the Law of Sea which suggested that the killing of all marine life should be done with

[55] Gary Francione, 'Animal Welfare and the Moral Value of Nonhuman Animals' *Law, Culture and Humanities*, 6/1 (2010): 24–36.

[56] art III.4(b); see also arts III.5(c), III.2(c), IV.2(c), IV.5(b), IV.6(b), VIII.3.

[57] The OIE Guidelines can be found in the Report of the Fourth Meeting of the OIE Working Group on Animal Welfare (2005).

[58] arts 3.5, 3.6.

[59] preambular recital 1.

[60] 1957 Interim Convention on the Conservation of North Pacific Seals, art IX.3; 1972 Convention for the Conservation of Antarctic Seals, art 3.1, annex—s 7; 1990 Agreement on the Conservation of Seals in the Wadden Sea, art VI.2.

[61] art 5.

[62] art III.5; CMS, 'ACAP Action Plan' <https://www.cms.int/en/document/acap-action-plan> para 1.4.2.

[63] 1996 Inter-American Convention for the Protection and Conservation of Sea Turtles, art IV.2(h).

[64] 1998 Agreement on the International Dolphin Conservation Program, art 5(b), annex VIII.3(d).

the intention of sparing them suffering 'to the greatest extent possible'.[65] Since then, most of the countries within the International Whaling Commission have attempted to move towards more modern primary and secondary killing techniques that reduce the time to death for whales caught in either commercial or subsistent whaling operations. The exception is with indigenous hunting of cetaceans, to which modern humane standards do not apply, and traditional hunting methods can result in deaths closer to an average of about forty-five minutes, as opposed to about ninety seconds for commercial hunting.[66]

B. Existence Values

An alternate non-anthropocentric route for environmental thinking is, rather than thinking about sentience or the ability of something to feel pain, to value something because it is alive, an end in itself, and seeks to pursue that existence. This suggests that it is the goal of life, rather than the capacity to experience pleasure and pain, that should be the criterion of moral consideration. Therefore, the ethical focus should be located, in natural (as opposed to self-recreating machines), autonomous, regenerating individuals (as opposed to wholes, like ecosystems) which are alive, even if they are not conscious or cognizant of why they seek to exist. It is thus all living individuals which have an inherent value, independent of their instrumental value to humans.[67]

This type of thinking has had some impact in international environmental law, as it is now common to find documents which refer to the 'intrinsic' or 'inherent' value of life. For example, the preamble of the CBD recognized the 'intrinsic value of biological diversity' and in 2012, those present at the Rio+20 summit, reaffirmed the intrinsic value of biological diversity.[68] However, this affirmation that all life is valuable is as far as the progress goes when dealing with the topic of life, irrespective of its conservation status.

Conversely, there is a very clear ethic around 'life' considerations, when dealing with the species (as opposed to the individuals that make up the species) that are endangered and at risk of extinction. This recognition in international environmental law of the need to protect endangered species dates back to the turn of the twentieth century. For example, the 1900 Convention for the Preservation of Wild Animals, Birds and Fish in Africa had five schedules. Schedule I contained animals whose preservation was desired to ensure their usefulness or 'on account of their rarity and threatened extermination'. Such regional obligations, with the goal to prevent the extinction of species, continued to proliferate during the twentieth century, before being supplemented with dozens of

[65] See 'Resolutions adopted by the United Nations Conference on the Law of the Sea at Geneva, Switzerland from 24 February to 27 April 1958' UN Doc A/CONF.13/L.56.

[66] See Alexander Gillespie, *Whaling Diplomacy* (Edgar Ellen 2006) ch 8.

[67] Albert Schweitzer, *Civilisation and Ethics* (Adam and Charles Black 1929) 246.

[68] UNGA RES 66/288 (n 20) para 197.

species-specific conventions starting with seals in 1911,[69] birds from 1916,[70] whales from 1931,[71] fish (in general) from 1958,[72] polar bears from 1973,[73] turtles from the 1990s,[74] and so on.

These goals then overlapped with a series of international conventions, with the same goals. The most notable of these include the CITES which seeks to limit trade in any species which may 'endanger their survival',[75] and the CMS which seeks to conserve migratory species which have an unfavourable conservation status, with the parties specifically required to take action to avoid any migratory species becoming endangered.[76]

The CBD then went further, and from the turn of the twenty-first century began setting targets for all parties to prevent extinctions of biodiversity. These targets eventually evolved into the Millennium Development Goals (to achieve a significant reduction in biodiversity loss by 2010) before the 2012 Rio+20 Summit, reiterated the commitment to 'effectively reduce the rate of, halt and reverse the loss of biodiversity'.[77] Three years later, in the 2015 Sustainable Developments Goals, the international community agreed to take urgent and significant action to reduce the degradation of natural habitats, halt the loss of biodiversity and, by 2020, protect and prevent the extinction of threatened species.[78]

C. Ecosystem Values

The last non-anthropocentric way to think about environmental values is where the ecosystem is valued over all other considerations. What matters in this view, is not individuals, their sentience, or even the status of species populations, but only what is good for the ecosystem in its totality. To many theorists, moral considerations should reside, in the good of the whole, not the good of individuals. Aldo Leopold, commonly recognized as the founder of this 'land ethic' explained,

[69] The 1911 Convention Respecting Measures for the Preservation and Protection of the Fur Seals in the North Pacific Ocean.

[70] 1916 Migratory Bird Convention Between Canada and the United States, preamble, art IV.

[71] 1931 Regulation of Whaling Convention, art 4.

[72] 1958 Convention on Fishing and Conservation of the Living Resources of the High Seas, preamble, art 1; Even clearer rules were later expressed in the 1982 United Nations Convention on the Law of the Sea, arts 61, 118, 119.

[73] 1973 Agreement on the Conservation of Polar Bears, art II.

[74] See Alexander Gillespie, 'The Slow Swim From Extinction: Saving Turtles' *International Journal of Marine and Coastal Law*, 21/1 (2006): 57.

[75] preambular recital 1, art II.

[76] preambular recitals 1–3, art II.

[77] UNGA RES 66/288 (n 20) para 198.

[78] MDG, goal 7; SDG, goal 15.

> The effect on ecological systems is the decisive factor in the determination of the ethical quality of actions … A thing is right when it tends to preserve the integrity, stability and beauty of the biotic community. It is wrong when it tends otherwise.[79]

This type of thinking is becoming integrated into international environmental law. For example, the 2012 Earth Summit called for:

> holistic and integrated approaches to sustainable development that will guide humanity to live in harmony with nature and lead to efforts to restore the health and integrity of the Earth's ecosystem.[80]

A recognition of ecosystem types of approaches had been evident for over four decades at this point. The 1980 World Conservation Strategy worked around the central precept of the maintenance of 'essential ecological processes and life support systems'.[81] The preamble of the 1992 Rio Declaration noted 'the integral and interdependent nature of Earth, our home' and Principle 7 recognized the necessity to 'conserve, protect and restore the integrity of the Earth's ecosystem'.[82]

The conventions on protection of the ozone layer and the climate change are exemplars of this. The international community came together to protect 'the layer of atmospheric ozone above the planetary boundary layer',[83] and prevent or adapt to the adverse effects on 'the Earth's climate', respectively. The climate system, was defined to mean 'the totality of the atmosphere, hydrosphere, biosphere and geosphere and their interaction'.[84] To protect this critical ecosystem, most of the international community in the subsequent 2015 Paris Agreement agreed to limit temperature rise to 'well below 2°C above pre-industrial levels' and aspire to 1.5°C above pre-industrial levels 'recognizing that this would significantly reduce the risks and impacts of climate change'.[85]

Even in relation to regional air pollution, the trend, since the turn of the century, is that increasingly the impact upon the ecosystem, rather than the pollutant per se is the focus.[86] This flexible approach means that instead of requiring set percentage reduction in emissions, policy-makers set reduction targets based on the effects of pollutants on different environments, or the critical loads that they could cope with.

79 Aldo Leopold, *A Sand County Almanac* (OUP 1949) 224–225.

80 UNGA RES 66/288 (n 20) para 40.

81 UNGA RES 37/7, 'World Charter for Nature' (28 October 1982) UN Doc A/RES/37/7, preamble, general principle 1.

82 Rio Declaration (n 4).

83 1985 Vienna Convention for the Protection of the Ozone Layer, art 1.

84 1992 UN Framework Convention on Climate Change, arts 1, 2.

85 Paris Agreement, art 2(a).

86 Jean-Paul Hettelingh *et al*, 'Assessing Interim Objectives for Acidification, Eutrophication and Ground Level Ozone of the EU National Emissions Ceiling Directive' *Atmospheric Environment*, 75 (2013): 129.

The need to focus on the totality of ecosystems, is also recognized with particular types of ecosystems, such as forests (with their 'complex and unique ecological processes');[87] wetlands;[88] particular geographical areas, such as Antarctica;[89] and conventions which set out to conserve areas—such as the WHC (through which ecosystems of outstanding universal value are preserved). Conventions which focus on endangered species nearly always oblige the parties also to protect the habitat (and thus, ecosystems) of the species they focus upon. The CMS and the 1979 Convention on the Conservation of European Wildlife and Natural Habitats are good examples of this approach. Similar obligations to conserve related habitats have arisen in the context of international law, of which those related to fish—and the practice of bottom trawling, has become particularly notable.[90]

At a broader level, the CBD recognizes that all species and all protected areas must be seen within the ecosystem in which they occur, and not in isolation, or as its preamble notes, 'the fundamental requirement for the conservation of biological diversity is the in-situ conservation of ecosystems and natural habitats'. Given the importance of ecosystems, the parties to the CBD have developed, as a thematic and cross-cutting topic, the 'ecosystem approach'.[91] This ecosystem approach was subsequently endorsed by the international community at the 2002 World Summit on Sustainable Development.[92]

To meet this need to protect ecosystems and stop habitat loss the parties to the CBD agreed to a target of achieving by 2020 that 'at least 17% of terrestrial and inland water, and 10% of coastal and marine areas, especially areas of particular importance for biodiversity and ecosystem services, are conserved ... through effectively and equitably managed, ecologically representative and well-connected systems of protected areas and other effective area-based conservation measures'.[93] Only the 10% target for coastal and marine areas was incorporated into the Sustainable Development Goals in 2015.

IV. CONCLUSION

This chapter has discussed the dominant philosophical values currently operating within international environmental law. In doing so, it has sought to provide examples of where these values are to be found, and some of the debates associated with them.

[87] *Report of the United Nations Conference on Environment and Development* (UN 1993) vol I, annex III—'Non-legally Binding Authoritative Statement of principles for a Global Consensus on the Management, Conservation and Sustainable Development of all Types of Forests', preamble, art 3.

[88] Ramsar Convention, preamble.

[89] Madrid Protocol was built around the need to protect the 'Antarctic environment and dependent associated ecosystems' of which the signatories promised a 'comprehensive protection'; art 3.

[90] See FAO, *International Guidelines for the Management of Deep-sea Fisheries in the High Seas* (2008).

[91] See Decision COP V/6, 'Ecosystem Approach' (2000) UN Doc UNEP/CBD/COP/DEC/V/6.

[92] Plan of Implementation (n 5) para 44(e).

[93] Aichi Biodiversity Targets, 'Target 11' <https://www.cbd.int/sp/targets/rationale/target-11/> accessed 10 January 2020.

Collectively, international environmental law operates in a maze of anthropocentric and non-anthropocentric values. Often these values overlap both within and between regimes, and conflicts are relatively rare.

Although anthropocentric values are more common than non-anthropocentric ones, there is no one dominant philosophical value that towers above all others in international environmental law. Non-anthropocentric values are also becoming particularly noticeable across a large range of topics. Once more, there is no dominant non-anthropocentric value in this setting either. However, what is obvious in international environmental law is that the debates about the philosophical value of the environment are not novel. In the space of twenty years, debates which were once the exclusive province of philosophy journals have moved to the core of many of the most high-profiles international regimes which are seeking to resolve some of the most pressing difficulties of the twenty-first century. Now, it is up to the reader to find which value works best in the environmental challenge of their choosing.

BIBLIOGRAPHY

Alexander Gillespie, *International Environmental Law, Policy and Ethics* (OUP 2014)
Simon James, *Environmental Philosophy: An Introduction* (Wiley 2015)
Michael Zimmerman *et al* (eds), *Environmental Philosophy: From Animal Rights to Radical Ecology* (4th edn, Pearson 2004)

CHAPTER 14

EARTH JURISPRUDENCE

CORMAC CULLINAN

I. INTRODUCTION

EARTH jurisprudence is a philosophical approach to legal and governance systems at every level, rather than a theory of international environmental law. It refers to philosophies of law and governance which seek to guide humans to behave in ways that contribute to the integrity, healthy functioning, beauty, and ongoing evolution of the community of life known as 'Earth'.[1] This approach seeks to promote the flourishing of the Earth Community and a 'mutually enhancing human-Earth relationship',[2] rather than its subjugation and exploitation by humankind.

Section I of this chapter explains the worldview that informs Earth jurisprudence and Section II explains the essential concepts and principles that make this approach so distinctive. Section III tracks the emergence of Earth jurisprudence and the rights of Nature/Mother Earth within the international sphere while Sections IV (Implementation and Future Development) and V (Conclusion) evaluate how this approach may affect the development of international law.

The international legal system and the legal systems of almost all states reflect a deeply anthropocentric worldview.[3] Anthropocentrism provides the philosophical basis for societal systems (including legal systems) that seek to subjugate Nature to human will and to validate the right or entitlement of humans to exploit Earth.[4]

[1] In this chapter 'Earth', 'Mother Earth', 'Earth Community' (a term used to emphasize that the whole is created by the relationships between a myriad of beings), and 'Nature' are all capitalized to indicate that they are names which refer to a specific subject (ie they are being used as proper nouns) and are used interchangeably.

[2] Thomas Berry, *The Great Work: Our Way into the Future* (Bell Tower 1999) 61.

[3] See Chapter 13, 'Ethical Considerations', in this volume.

[4] The 'logic' of domination is a common thread that connects anthropocentrism (domination of Nature), patriarchy (domination of women), and racism. Crimes against humanity such as genocide

Earth jurisprudence on the other hand reflects integral and eco-centric worldviews that recognize the reality that humans are an integral and inseparable part of ordered ecological systems and that our life, health, and well-being flow from the complex web of ecological and social relationships that constitute the Earth Community.[5] Since human well-being is derived from the Earth Community, in the long term human societies will only be healthy and flourish if societal structures promote the harmonious coexistence of humans within a healthy Earth Community.[6] The idea that humans should strive to live in harmony with Nature is both ancient and pervasive, and was explicitly referred to in the 1982 World Charter for Nature.[7]

This perspective is consistent with the eco-centric approaches expressed in Aldo Leopold's land ethic[8] and in the principles of deep ecology.[9] Both share the ontological belief that any existential distinctions that can be made between humans and other-than-human Nature do not justify claims that humans have greater intrinsic value than other-than-human beings, and that the interests of the Earth Community as a whole must take precedence over those of individual beings.[10]

II. CONCEPTUAL FRAMEWORK

A. Great Jurisprudence

The 'Great Jurisprudence' refers to the inherent characteristics of the Universe which determine how it is structured or ordered, and how different aspects relate to one another and behave. It can be understood both as a term used to describe the set of fundamental relationships and principles that constitute the Earth Community and produce the order we observe in Nature, and as a logical premise for the development of Earth jurisprudences by human societies.[11]

and apartheid, and ecocide (which has been proposed for recognition in the 1998 Rome Statute that establishes the International Criminal Court) are extreme expressions of such domination.

[5] This worldview is apparent in the preamble to the 2010 Universal Declaration of the Rights of Mother Earth (UDRME); World People's Conference on Climate Change and the Rights of Mother Earth, 'Universal Declaration of the Rights of Mother Earth' (22 April 2010).

[6] The recognition in the UDRME of 'the right to integral health' (art 1.1(d)) is a reference to the idea that the health of an individual, and the health of the system which the individual is part of, are closely interrelated.

[7] UNGA RES 37/7, 'World Charter for Nature' (28 October 1982) UN Doc A/RES/37/7.

[8] Aldo Leopold, *A Sand County Almanac* (OUP 1949).

[9] The term 'deep ecology' was coined in 1973 by the Norwegian philosopher Arne Naess; see Arne Naess, 'The Shallow and the Deep, Long-Range Ecology Movement: A Summary' *Inquiry*, 16 (1973): 95.

[10] See Stan Rowe, 'Ecocentrism: The Chord that Harmonizes Humans and Earth' *The Trumpeter*, 11/2 (1994): 106–107.

[11] See Cormac Cullinan, *Wild Law: A Manifesto for Earth Justice* (2nd edn, Green Books 2011) ch 6, 'Respecting the Great Law'; Peter Burdon, 'The Great Jurisprudence' in Peter Burdon (ed), *Exploring Wild Law: The Philosophy of Earth Jurisprudence* (Wakefield Press 2011).

The fundamental relationships and principles that constitute the Earth Community include a priori characteristics, principles, or 'laws of Nature' that influence the functioning of the Earth system. These apply regardless of whether or not we know of or can prove their existence. However, we can infer the existence of the fundamental principles which constitute the Great Jurisprudence from our observations of order in the Universe in the same way as Albert Einstein inferred the 'cosmological principle' in 1931. The cosmological principle states that when viewed on a sufficiently large scale, the properties of the Universe look the same from every point within it, and consequently the same physical laws apply throughout. Although Einstein could not prove empirically that the laws of physics are the same everywhere in the Universe, based on the available empirical evidence, this principle seems to be a reasonable assumption. In the same way, our knowledge of the cosmos and the Earth Community provides a basis for articulating the ordering principles that would explain our observations. These can then be used to inform the design of human governance systems.

For example, the structure of molecules of greenhouse gases (GHGs) and how they interact with infrared radiation from the sun (which are aspects of the Great Jurisprudence) make it inevitable that increasing atmospheric concentrations of GHGs above a certain level will destabilize the climate. Anthropocentric legal systems are inevitably ineffective in maintaining a stable climate because they are not designed to align with the parameters established by the Great Jurisprudence (eg by defining human activities that risk causing climate change as unlawful). Since humankind can neither alter the content of the Great Jurisprudence nor avoid the consequences of exceeding its homeostatic parameters, the Great Jurisprudence can be characterized as universally-binding and self-enforcing.

B. Earth Jurisprudences

Earth jurisprudence may be characterized as a holistic, integral, or systemic approach because it views human governance systems within the context of natural systems of order. Consequently it seeks to balance human rights and freedoms with responsibilities to contribute to maintaining and enhancing the integrity, functioning, and well-being of Earth. It prioritizes the good of the global community of life over specific human interests (including the interests of states) but with the understanding that this will benefit humankind because human well-being is derived from natural systems and cannot be sustained at their expense.

The diversity of human cultures and the ecosystems within which they exist must inevitably produce a range of Earth jurisprudences—each aligned with the Great Jurisprudence but adapted to the specific conditions under which it was developed. Each variant of Earth jurisprudence will reflect a particular human community's understanding of how to regulate itself as part of the Earth Community and can be understood as a bio-culturally specific philosophy of eco-centric governance.[12] Nevertheless the intercultural cross-pollination of ideas through initiatives like the UDRME is contributing to

[12] Some scholars prefer the term 'Ecological jurisprudence' to 'Earth jurisprudence' because it transcends the planetary boundaries of the latter; see Alessandro Pelizzon, 'Earth laws, Rights of Nature

the emergence of a common global concept of Earth jurisprudence which unifies these diverse jurisprudences.[13]

1. *Principles of Earth jurisprudence*

Although Earth jurisprudence will vary between cultures and contexts, each variant is likely:

- to reflect a recognition that the Universe, rather than any human institution, is the source of the inherent fundamental rights held by all members of the Earth Community;
- to recognize that by virtue of their existence, all members of the Earth Community have the fundamental right to exist and to be free to play their unique role within that community;
- to treat these inherent, fundamental rights as inalienable (ie human law cannot validly circumscribe or abrogate them);
- to regard human acts or laws that unjustifiably prevent other-than-human members of the Earth Community from fulfilling their unique roles within that community or infringe these fundamental rights as inherently illegitimate and 'unlawful' because they violate the fundamental relationships and principles that constitute the Earth Community;
- to condone or condemn human conduct on the basis of whether or not the conduct strengthens or weakens the bonds that constitute the Earth Community;
- to decide between competing rights on the basis of what is best for Earth as a whole and thereby contribute to maintaining a dynamic balance between the rights of humans and those of other members of the Earth Community; and
- to provide effective legal remedies for human acts that violate fundamental rights and to apply restorative justice to strengthen damaged bonds rather than punishment (retribution).

2. *Applying Earth jurisprudences*

The Earth jurisprudence of a particular human society or community may be expressed in many forms, including in ethics, religious beliefs, laws, economic and political systems, societal institutions, and policies and practices. This is particularly evident in the cultures of Indigenous peoples who maintain intimate relationships with Nature and whose laws reflect their understanding of the cosmos as sacred.[14]

and Legal Pluralism' in Peter Burdon and Michelle Maloney (eds), *Wild Law: In Practice* (Routledge 2014) 176–177. Since the Great Jurisprudence is universal, there is no reason that this approach cannot be applied beyond Earth, for example in the field of space law.

[13] The UDRME is discussed in Section III.A.

[14] Indigenous laws and legal traditions are often referred to as 'chthonic' from the Greek word meaning 'of, or relating to Earth'. Chthonic law is inextricably interwoven with, and inseparable from, all aspects of the lives of Indigenous peoples and can only be understood within the context of their

Laws that reflect Earth jurisprudence have been characterized as 'Earth' or 'wild'[15] laws and may be either what Weston and Bollier term 'Vernacular Law' or 'State Law'.[16] Wild laws are laws that regulate humans in ways that foster intimate relationships between humans and other beings and create freedom for all members of the Earth Community to express themselves and to play their part within that community. For example, a law that recognizes that an other-than-human being has legal rights, could be characterized as wild law. On the other hand most environmental laws seek only to limit the worst excesses of exploitation and to preserve representative examples of ecosystems and species, and have little or no effect on the perspectives, values, and systems that drive ecological degradation.

The difference between most contemporary laws (including environmental laws) and wild laws is analogous to Václav Havel's distinction between the aims of post-totalitarian systems and the aims of life itself. The former demands 'conformity, uniformity and discipline' whereas 'life, in its essence, moves towards plurality, diversity, independent self-constitution and self-organisation, in short, towards the fulfilment of its own freedom'.[17] In this sense wild laws are laws that promote life.

3. *Rights of Nature*

Many different legal techniques can be used to give effect to Earth jurisprudence, one of which is the recognition of the rights of Nature or Mother Earth. This involves: (a) expanding the class of legal/ juristic persons to include all members of the Earth Community which have come into being as a consequence of the creation and evolution of this planet (ie what may be termed 'ecological beings'); (b) recognizing that all ecological beings have inherent and inalienable fundamental rights analogous to human rights; (c) prohibiting human beings and human institutions (including artificial juristic persons such as corporations and governments) from infringing upon the rights of other ecological beings without adequate justification; (d) imposing duties on human beings to seek to live harmoniously within the Earth Community; and (e) establishing enforcement mechanisms.

4. *Legal personality*

International law and many legal systems recognize the creation of 'legal persona' or 'juristic personality' as the alter ego of an entity (typically an intangible institution such

worldview and beliefs. This description was proposed in Edward Goldsmith, *The Way: An Ecological World View* (Rider 1992) and later popularized in Patrick Glenn, *Legal Traditions of the World* (5th edn, OUP 2014).

[15] 'Wild' in this context refers to the mysterious creative force that flows through and connects everything and drives evolutionary processes.

[16] Burns Weston and David Bollier, *Green Governance: Ecological Survival, Human Rights, and the Law of the Commons* (CUP 2013) 104–111.

[17] Václav Havel, The Power of the Powerless Open Letters: Selected Writings 1965–1990 (Vintage 1992) 134–135.

as a corporation or state). This 'legal fiction' is employed to enable that entity to participate in the legal system in a manner analogous to how human beings (or 'natural persons') participate. It makes that entity 'visible' to the legal system as a legal subject capable of holding rights, being owed duties, and litigating in its own name.

This technique has now been used in the constitutions of Ecuador and Bolivia,[18] national legislation,[19] and by national courts[20] to recognize specific ecological beings as having legal personality. In principle, all ecological entities or 'beings', both individually and collectively (eg as the Earth Community) should be recognized as having legal personality as envisaged in the UDRME.[21]

5. *Legal rights and duties*

Rights of Nature advocates argue that if legal systems recognize that human beings have inherent, inalienable human rights simply by virtue of their existence, they should also recognize analogous rights for all beings that constitute the Earth Community.[22] Only recognizing human rights promotes ecological imbalance but if the rights of all are recognized, legal systems can be used to promote ecological health by resolving conflicts between humans and other aspects of Nature according to the best interests of the Earth Community as a whole.

These rights are conceived of as being inherent, inalienable, limited, and differentiated in the sense that some are common to all beings while others are specific to a particular species or kind. They are limited by the rights of other beings to the extent necessary to maintain the integrity, balance, and health of the communities within which that being exists.[23] The universal rights common to all beings are conceived of as including the right to exist, to habitat or a place to be, and to participate in the evolution of the Earth Community.[24]

Using the language of rights in relation to Nature is an effective means of exposing and challenging the anthropocentric framing of most legal systems because it requires expanding the concepts of legal persons who may hold rights to include other ecological

[18] eg the rights of Nature, or 'Pacha Mama' are recognized in the Constitution of Ecuador, 2008 (preamble, arts 71–74) and in the *Constitucion Del Estado Plurinacional de Bolivia*, 2008 (arts 33–34).

[19] eg New Zealand has passed the Te Urewera Act 51 of 2014 and the Te Awa Tupua (Whanganui River Claims Settlement) Act 7 of 2017 which recognize the former Te Urewera national park and the Whanganui River respectively, as legal persons.

[20] See eg Corte Constitucional, Decision T-622 (10 November 2016) (Colombia) in which the Colombian Constitution Court recognized the Atrato River as a legal person; *Mohd. Salim v State of Uttarakhand & Others* (20 March 2017) Uttarakhand High Court (India) PIL 126/2014 in which an Indian court recognized the Ganges and Yamuna rivers and their tributaries as having legal personality.

[21] arts 4.1, art 1.5.

[22] See eg Evo Morales Ayma *et al*, *The Rights of Nature: The Case for a Universal Declaration of the Rights of Mother Earth* (The Council of Canadians, Fundación Pachamama, and Global Exchange 2011).

[23] The UDRME provides in art 1.7 that any conflict between rights must be resolved in a way that maintains the integrity, balance, and health of Mother Earth.

[24] Thomas Berry, *Evening Thoughts: Reflecting on Earth as Sacred Community* (Sierra Club Books 2006) 107–112, appendix 2—'Ten Principles for Jurisprudence Revision'.

beings. However it also serves the vital function of creating corresponding duties on humans to respect, protect, and enforce the rights of other beings.[25] In order to do so, human governance systems will have to be transformed to ensure that they take account of the individual and collective interests of other beings, and of the Earth Community as whole.

III. EMERGENCE OF EARTH JURISPRUDENCE IN INTERNATIONAL LAW

Earth jurisprudence and the rights of Nature are emergent, rather than established approaches within the sphere of international law and governance. The idea of rights of Nature has emerged independently in different parts of the world but its current profile within the international sphere is largely due to it being championed by the Bolivarian Alliance for the Peoples of Our America (ALBA).[26]

Rights of Nature were propelled onto the international stage in September 2008 when a referendum in Ecuador approved a new constitution that committed both the state and peoples of Ecuador to achieving well-being for all by living in harmony with Nature.[27] The Constitution provides for the recognition and enforcement of the rights of Nature as one of the principal means of guiding people to live in harmony with Nature.[28]

On 22 April 2009, the United Nations General Assembly (UNGA) adopted a resolution proposed by Bolivia proclaiming 22 April as 'International Mother Earth Day'[29] and Bolivian President Evo Morales Ayma called upon member states to begin developing a 'Declaration on the Rights of Mother Earth'. A Declaration that, among other rights, would enshrine the right to life for all living things; the right for Mother Earth to live free of contamination and pollution; and the right to harmony and balance among and between all things.[30]

[25] Earth jurisprudence does not propose that other beings owe such duties to human beings as this would give rise to unhelpful absurdities in implementation.

[26] The member countries of ALBA as of December 2019 are: Antigua and Barbuda, Cuba, Dominica, Grenada, Nicaragua, Saint Kitts and Nevis, Saint Lucia, Saint Vincent and the Grenadines, and Venezuela. Three former members have withdrawn: Honduras (on 16 December 2009), Ecuador (23 August 2018), and Bolivia (15 November 2019). Haiti, Iran, and Syria have observer status.

[27] The preamble to the Constitution explicitly refers to the intention of the people of Ecuador 'to build a new order of cohabitation for citizens, in its diversity and in harmony with nature, to achieve well being' (which is defined by using both the Spanish term 'el buen vivir' and the Indigenous Quichwa term 'sumak kawsay'); see art 275.

[28] The fundamental rights of Nature are set out in ch 7 of the Constitution which provides that: 'Nature or Pachamama, where life is reproduced and exists, has the right to exist, persist, maintain and regenerate its vital cycles, structure, functions and its processes in evolution'; see art 72.

[29] UNGA RES 63/278, 'International Mother Earth Day' (1 May 2009) UN Doc A/RES/63/278.

[30] UN, 'General Assembly proclaims 22 April 'International Mother Earth Day' adopting by consensus Bolivia-led resolution' (22 April 2009) GA/10823.

Later that year a summit of the nine ALBA-TCP states[31] adopted a 'Special Declaration for a Universal Declaration of Mother Earth Rights'[32] which succinctly expressed the rationale for the international recognition of the rights of Nature. The declaration argues that because human and other natural beings are part of an interdependent Earth system (Mother Earth), the full protection of human rights cannot be achieved without living together in harmony and balance, which requires humans to recognize, respect, and defend the rights of other beings and of Mother Earth as a whole.

A. Universal Declaration of the Rights of Mother Earth

After the failure of the 2009 meeting of the Conference of the Parties (COP) of the 1992 United Nations Framework Convention on Climate Change (UNFCCC) in Copenhagen, the Bolivian President convened a 'World People's Conference on Climate Change and the Rights of Mother Earth' from 19 to 22 April 2010.[33] The Conference proclaimed the UDRME on 22 April 2010 and called on the UNGA to adopt it.

The Preamble and first article of the UDRME express the integral worldview discussed in Section I.B. 'Mother Earth' is referred to as a self-regulating, indivisible living community of interrelated and interdependent beings that sustains, contains, and reproduces all beings.[34]

1. *Rights recognized in UDRME*

The UDRME recognizes that Mother Earth and all beings are entitled to all the inherent and inalienable rights recognized in the Declaration, that all beings (including human beings) have rights which are specific to their species or kind and appropriate for their role and function within the communities within which they exist. The rights of each being are limited by the rights of other beings and any conflict between their rights must be resolved in a way that maintains the integrity, balance, and health of Mother Earth.[35]

Some of the fundamental rights common to all beings are set out in Article 2.[36] They include: the right to life and to exist; the right to continue their vital cycles and processes

[31] Venezuela, Cuba, Bolivia, Nicaragua, Commonwealth of Dominica, Antigua and Barbuda, Ecuador, Saint Vincent and the Grenadines, and Santa Lucia.

[32] The special declaration was made in Cochabamba, Bolivia on 17 October 2009; see 'Letter dated 23 October 2009 from the Permanent Representative of the Bolivarian Republic of Venezuela to the United Nations addressed to the Secretary-General' (28 October 2009) UN Doc A/C.2/64/9.

[33] More than 30,000 delegates from social movements and organizations from 140 countries participated in the conference.

[34] art 4.1 states that: 'The term "being" includes ecosystems, natural communities, species and all other natural entities which exist as part of Mother Earth.'

[35] art 1.7.

[36] art 4.2 states that: 'Nothing in this Declaration restricts the recognition of other inherent rights of all beings or specified beings.'

free from human disruptions; the right to integral health; and the right to full and prompt restoration if human activities violate any of these rights.

Most of the UDRME is devoted to setting out the obligations of human beings and human institutions to other beings (Article 3). The fundamental obligation is that every human being is responsible for respecting and living in harmony with Mother Earth.[37] A further twelve specific duties are imposed on human beings, all states, and all public and private institutions. These include the obligations: to act in accordance with, and promote the full implementation and enforcement of, the rights and obligations recognized in the Declaration; to establish and apply effective norms and laws for the defence, protection, and conservation of those rights; to guarantee that the damages caused by human violations of the rights recognized in the Declaration are rectified and that those responsible are held accountable for restoring the integrity and health of Mother Earth; and to promote economic systems that are in harmony with Mother Earth and in accordance with the rights recognized in the Declaration.

2. *Implications for human rights*

The UDRME provides a context for the 1948 Universal Declaration of Human Rights, which from an Earth jurisprudence perspective is a species-specific articulation of rights. Neither instrument is legally binding in the conventional sense that it is directly enforceable in a court of law. However both claim universal validity and application within domestic and international law on the basis that they articulate inherent rights and duties that arise from the fact of existence rather than from agreements between states (treaties), state practice or legislation.

Climate change has made the connection between the legal protection of the environment and human rights abundantly clear since it threatens many human rights including the rights to water, food, and life. The UDRME articulates specific human duties to respect, protect, conserve, and restore the integrity of vital ecological cycles and processes, and to take proactive measures to reform legal and economic systems to ensure that they function in ways that are in harmony with Nature. If these duties were implemented, the root causes of ecological destruction would be severed and ecological restoration would become central to human societies.

3. *Influence of UDRME*

Although the UDRME has not been adopted by the UNGA, its adoption by a peoples' world conference imbued it with a high degree of legitimacy and effectively created a common manifesto for global civil society to promote Earth jurisprudence. The establishment in 2010 of the Global Alliance for the Rights of Nature (GARN)[38] has been particularly important in popularizing the UDRME and Earth jurisprudence generally.

[37] art 3.1.

[38] GARN was established in 2010 to facilitate global collaboration between civil society organizations and indigenous and local communities who advocate implementation of the UDRME; see <http://therightsofnature.org/> accessed 13 January 2019.

One of the notable successes of GARN has been the establishment of an International Rights of Nature Tribunal to investigate and rule on any serious violation of the rights, or breach of the duties, established by the UDRME.[39] The Tribunal contributes to the on-going development of Earth jurisprudence by interpreting and applying the rights and duties in the UDRME in specific circumstances.

The UDRME has no formal status under international law and few states have endorsed it. Consequently, it can be understood as an example of 'Vernacular Law', which is described by Weston and Bollier as 'unofficial law' that 'originates in the informal, unofficial zones of society and is a source of moral legitimacy and power in its own right'.[40]

B. Application to Climate Change

The UDRME has also been used in UNFCCC negotiations both as a means of advocating the fundamental systemic or structural change which many believe is necessary to address climate change successfully, and as an aspect of an emerging vision of ecologically benign forms of post-capitalist civilizations. This is particularly evident in the submissions regarding a shared vision for long-term cooperative action that were made to the UNFCCC Ad-Hoc Working Group on Long-Term Cooperative Action (AWG LCA). Bolivia submitted the outcomes of the People's World Conference, including the UDRME to the AWG LCA arguing that: 'A shared vision for a long-term cooperative action requires the recognition of the rights of not only the human beings, but also of the rights of Mother Earth and of all its beings' and consequently it was essential for the UN to develop a Universal Declaration of Mother Earth's Rights.[41]

The 2010 official submission of Venezuela, Cuba, Bolivia, Ecuador, and Nicaragua to AWG LCA stated bluntly that: 'Humanity is at the crossroads—to continue on the way of capitalism, predation and death, or take the way of harmony with nature and respect for life'.[42] Following in the same vein, twenty states[43] submitted a draft decision on a shared vision which stated in the preamble that 'in order to achieve a just balance among

[39] The Tribunal was formally constituted on 4 December 2015 by civil society organizations signing a 'Peoples' Tribunal Convention' in Paris, and by the adoption of the statutes of the Tribunal; see <http://therightsofnature.org/rights-of-nature-tribunal-paris/> accessed 13 January 2019.

[40] Weston and Bollier (n 16) 104, argue that the self-organizing and self-governing of the internet is a contemporary example of the emergence of Vernacular Law to govern a commons (106).

[41] 'Shared vision for a long-term a cooperative action—The need of a Universal Mother Earth's Rights Declaration' <https://unfccc.int/files/kyoto_protocol/application/pdf/bolivia110909.pdf> accessed 13 January 2019.

[42] 'Official Submission of the Bolivarian Republic of Venezuela on behalf of Cuba, Bolivia, Ecuador and Nicaragua (ALBA-PTT Member States to the UNFCC Ad-Hoc Working Group on Long-Term Cooperative Action)' (26 April 2010).

[43] Argentina, Bolivia, Democratic Republic of the Congo, China, Dominica, Ecuador, Egypt, El Salvador, India, Iran, Iraq, Kuwait, Malaysia, Mali, Pakistan, Philippines, Saudi Arabia, Sri Lanka, Sudan, and Thailand.

the economic, social and environmental needs of present and future generations, it is necessary to promote harmony with nature in a holistic and integrated approach to sustainable development and lead to efforts to restore the health and integrity of the Mother Earth ecosystem.'[44]

Neither international nor domestic environmental law has been effective in bringing about the structural changes to the legal, economic, and other societal systems that incentivize and legitimize activities that emit large quantities of GHGs or in compelling the dramatic and swift reductions in atmospheric GHG concentrations necessary to stabilize the climate. Earth jurisprudence speaks directly to these fundamental deficits by proposing that societies re-orient their entire governance systems towards ensuring that humans play a mutually beneficial role within the Earth Community, and restore the damage they have caused. For example if the UDRME were implemented, every person, state, and public or private institution that had made a significant contribution to GHG emissions would be required to help reduce GHG levels to pre-industrial levels in order to restore the integrity and health of Mother Earth.[45] States would be required to promote economic systems that are consistent with the rights of Nature, to take effective measures to prevent human activities from disrupting the climate and to restore climatic stability, and to empower individuals and institutions to defend Nature's rights.[46]

C. United Nations Harmony with Nature Programme

The 1982 World Charter for Nature was the first UN resolution to use the term 'living in harmony with Nature'. Today the United Nations Harmony with Nature Programme plays an extremely important role in both developing and disseminating Earth jurisprudence ideas at the international level.[47] The Programme has convened an annual Interactive Dialogue of the General Assembly on Harmony with Nature to commemorate International Mother Earth Day since 2011 and in 2016 conducted a virtual dialogue with experts from around the world that established a Harmony with Nature Knowledge Network. The Secretary General has produced a series of annual reports on the subject which track the development and implementation of measures to promote living in harmony with Nature throughout the world.[48]

[44] 'Proposal on draft decisions submitted by the Plurinational State of Bolivia' (9 December 2010) UN Doc FCCC/AWGLCA/2010/CRP.4.

[45] UDRME, art 3.2(f).

[46] arts 3.2(h)–(i), 3.2(l).

[47] <http://www.harmonywithnatureun.org/> accessed 31 December 2019. The 2018 Harmony with Nature Report of the Secretary General stated that: 'The United Nations is committed to remaining conversant with recent and forthcoming transformations and actions in law, policy, education and public engagement with regard to Earth jurisprudence and with the increasing number of declarations, statements and calls to restore a respectful relationship with the Earth'; UNGA, 'Harmony with Nature—Report of the Secretary General' (23 July 2018) UN Doc A/73/221, para 104.

[48] See <http://www.harmonywithnatureun.org/unDocs/> accessed 13 January 2019.

The preamble to the first UNGA resolution on the subject stated 'Convinced that humanity can and should live in harmony with nature' and then invited submissions of views, experiences, and proposals on the issue of promoting life in harmony with Nature.[49] The discussions of this question through the dialogues and knowledge networks convened by this Programme have covered an enormously wide scope, and have demonstrated the growing global recognition of the need to move away from an anthropocentric worldview and to create societies that embrace an Earth-centered worldview and respect Nature.[50] The aspiration to live in harmony with Nature is becoming increasingly visible in other UN documents such as the 2030 Agenda for Sustainable Development.[51]

IV. IMPLEMENTATION AND FUTURE DEVELOPMENT

A. Implementation

The growing number of domestic laws, policies, and judicial decisions that reflect the influence of Earth jurisprudence recorded by the UN Harmony with Nature Programme are evidence that this philosophy is gaining significant traction globally.[52] Perhaps more significantly, this approach is contributing to the emergence of a widely-shared norm that human beings should treat other species and aspects of Nature as subjects with intrinsic rights that humans must respect and protect. As Weston and Bollier point out, if the disjuncture between socially negotiated norms, values, principles, and rules embodied in what they term 'Vernacular Law', and State Law becomes too great, dramatic 'corrections' of State Law can occur. For example, in 1215 the English aristocracy forced King John to accept the Magna Carta which restricted his powers, and in 1217 his son King Henry III adopted the complementary Charter of the Forest, which formally

[49] UNGA RES 64/196, 'Harmony with Nature' (12 February 2010) UN Doc A/RES/64/196.

[50] The UN Programme has adopted an expansive view of Earth jurisprudence and the 2016 virtual dialogue explored its implications in eight areas: 1. Earth-centred Law; 2. Ecological Economics; 3. Education; 4. Holistic Science (includes Biology, Chemistry, Cosmo-visions, Geology, Physics, Holistic Food Systems including Fisheries and Water) and Holistic Medicine; 5. Humanities (includes Anthropology, Linguistics, Psychology, and Sociology); 6. Philosophy and Ethics; 7. The Arts, Media, Design, and Architecture; and, 8. Theology and Spirituality.

[51] UNGA RES 70/1, 'Transforming our World: The 2030 Agenda for Sustainable Development' (21 October 2015) UN Doc A/RES/70/1 states: 'We are determined to ensure that all human beings can enjoy prosperous and fulfilling lives and that economic, social and technological progress occurs in harmony with nature.'

[52] 'Rights of Nature Law, Policy and Education' <http://www.harmonywithnatureun.org/rightsOfNature> accessed 30 July 2019

recognized the Vernacular Law that already governed the use of forests by commoners for subsistence purposes.[53]

B. Transformative and Disruptive Potential

Proponents of Earth jurisprudence argue that a fundamental transformation of anthropocentric legal systems is both necessary and urgent to enable societies to adapt to and survive the huge environmental challenges of the twenty-first century.[54] In their view, applying an Earth jurisprudence approach within societies that prioritize economic growth will progressively transform their legal, political, and economic systems as well as the worldview which those systems reflect. Civil society organizations and social movements throughout the world, many of which are members of GARN, have embraced the transformative potential of this approach.

Earth jurisprudence also has the potential to be a significant disruptor of the current international law system because it calls into question the very nature and purpose of international law as currently understood.[55] For example, international law is currently conceived of as law created by the express or tacit consent of states, to regulate relationships between states (and to a lesser degree, with international organizations). However, Earth jurisprudence posits the existence of fundamental a priori principles or 'rules' that apply to humans and the institutions that they have created, such as states, regardless of whether or not they consent to them. Consequently, human beings and institutions, whether local, national, or international, would all be subject to the same fundamental duties to respect the rights of ecological beings.

As discussed below, applying an Earth jurisprudence approach will require reconceptualizing many of the fundamental concepts and doctrines of public international law. Others, like the precautionary principle, are potentially compatible with this approach.

C. Sources of Law

The Statute of the International Court of Justice identifies three principal sources of international law (ie international treaties between states, customary international law derived from the practice of states; and general principles of law recognized by civilized

[53] Weston and Bollier (n 16) 107.

[54] See eg Berry, *Evening Thoughts* (n 24) ch 9, 'Legal Conditions for Earth Survival'; Cullinan (n 11) ch 5, 'The Conceit of Law'.

[55] The term 'disruptor' is used here to mean something that prevents a system or process from continuing as usual or as expected. The term has long been used in biology (eg hormone disruptors) but is increasingly used to refer to innovations which enable goods or services to be offered far better that can be done employing traditional business methods.

nations) and two 'subsidiary means for the determination of rules of law' (ie judicial decisions and the writings of 'the most highly qualified publicists').[56]

However from an Earth jurisprudence perspective, as Berry pointed out 'the Universe is the primary law-giver'[57] and consequently the Great Jurisprudence would be the primary source of law. This raises two fundamental questions: 'How do we identify the content of the Great Jurisprudence?' and 'How do we give effect to the Great Jurisprudence in law?'. The fields of physics, chemistry, mathematics, biology, and ecology help us answer the first question by contributing to our (limited) understanding of the Great Jurisprudence, particularly in relation to the physical functioning of the Universe. Indigenous knowledge systems can also play an important role in this regard. For example they all insist on the vital importance of non-tangible, spiritual dimensions of Earth and of respect for the sacred aspects which lie beyond the boundaries of science.

There will inevitably be many ways of translating the Great Jurisprudence into the legal philosophies, laws, and governance institutions of different cultures, within different ecosystems. For example Ecuador has used its Constitution to establish well-being through living in harmony with Nature as an overarching societal goal. Indigenous peoples often use myths and rituals to transmit ethics and rules of ecologically appropriate behaviour such as respect for other beings and the principle of reciprocity, that is, all who receive must give. Indigenous cultures that have lived more or less harmoniously with other beings over long periods of time are a particularly important source of inspiration and guidance. Colonial cultures have long denigrated such Indigenous cultures as primitive, and 'uncivilized'. Ironically, from an Earth Jurisprudence perspective it is the general principles of law recognized by such 'uncivilized nations' rather than those of 'civilized nations' that are potentially rich sources of law.

D. Permanent State Sovereignty Over Natural Resources

The doctrine of permanent sovereignty over natural resources (PSNR) recognizes that all states have the inalienable right to dispose of their natural wealth and resources in accordance with their national interests[58] and is one of the most fundamental doctrines in international environmental law.[59] From an ecological perspective the PSNR doctrine is problematic for several reasons. First it legitimizes and entrenches exploitation

[56] ICJ Statute, art 38.

[57] Berry, *The Great Work* (n 2) 64.

[58] See eg the preamble to UNGA RES 1803/(XVII), 'Permanent Sovereignty over Natural Resources' (14 December 1962) UN Doc A/RES/1803(XVII).

[59] The concept of 'permanent sovereignty over natural resources' was first proposed by Chile in 1952, and has since been recognized and developed in a series of UNGA Res (eg Res 1803/(XVII) of 14 December 1962, 2158/(XXI) of 25 November 1966, 2386/(XXIII) of 19 November 1968, 2625/(XXV) of 24 October 1970, 2692/(XXV) of 11 December 1970 and 3016/(XXVII) of 18 December 1972, and Security Council Res 330/(1973) of 21 March 1973). It has also been repeatedly reaffirmed in many international treaties and non-binding instruments, including principle 21 of the 1972 Stockholm Declaration.

as the dominant mode of human-Earth relationship. Secondly, it fragments responsibility for protecting Earth. Each state determines how much environmental degradation is permissible within its jurisdiction and in the absence of voluntarily assumed treaty obligations, does not have a legal duty to contribute to the health of ecosystems beyond its borders, or to the biosphere as whole. This makes it is very difficult for humanity to respond effectively to the most pervasive and serious forms of environmental degradation (eg climate change, and the global decline in biodiversity, fish stocks, indigenous forests, and freshwater). Thirdly, since treaties are negotiated by representatives of states seeking to protect their national self-interest, treaty obligations often reflect the lowest common denominator and are too weak to be effective.

From an Earth jurisprudence perspective, even in the absence of a treaty, states have a duty to establish national laws and political and economic systems that ensure that human beings and their institutions (including corporations) fulfil their fundamental duties in relation to other beings and the Earth Community as a whole. As more and more people suffer the consequences of ecological devastation and become acutely aware of the value of healthy ecosystems, public pressure on states to transform dysfunctional governance systems along the lines envisaged in the UDRME, is likely to intensify.

E. Institutions

Implementing Earth jurisprudence also requires developing new forms of institutions designed to fulfil different purposes, at every level of society. For example, judicial bodies will require knowledge of the Great Jurisprudence and the expertise to judge whether or not an infringement on the rights of other-than-human beings is so severe that the healthy functioning of ecosystems are being impaired. Countries like Ecuador, which have recognized the rights of Nature, are now wrestling with these challenges. Global civil society is playing an important role in pioneering proto-types of such institutions, such as the International Tribunal for the Rights of Nature established by the Global Alliance for the Rights of Nature.[60]

V. CONCLUSION

Earth jurisprudence burst onto the international political arena in a remarkably short period between late 2008 and 2010. In September 2008 the Ecuadorian Constitution was adopted, on 22 December 2009 the rights of Mother Earth was put on the agenda of the UNGA for the first time. By early 2010 the UDRME which articulates the central principles of Earth jurisprudence had been proposed for adoption by the UN. The

60 See <http://therightsofnature.org/rights-of-nature-tribunal/> accessed 13 January 2019.

application of Earth jurisprudence by local communities, legislatures, and courts in various countries has accelerated and this approach is gaining traction in many areas of the world.

The emergence of Earth jurisprudence is an aspect of a wider global cultural shift in our understanding of the Universe and the place and role of humanity within the ecological systems of Earth. It reflects changing cultural norms in the face of new realities, particularly climate change and the catastrophic collapse in populations of other species. There is also a growing appreciation that under these conditions most governance systems will hasten the collapse of the societies that developed them and are accordingly maladaptive from an evolutionary perspective.

Although a few states have played a leadership role within the UN and international fora, the adoption of this approach is being driven primarily by global civil society and Indigenous peoples. This trend can be expected to gather strength as societies face the increasingly extreme consequences of exploiting Earth instead of seeking harmonious coexistence with other beings.

BIBLIOGRAPHY

Thomas Berry, *The Great Work: Our Way into the Future* (Bell Tower 1999)

Thomas Berry, *Evening Thoughts: Reflecting on Earth as Sacred Community* (Sierra Club Books 2006)

Peter Burdon (ed), *Exploring Wild Law: The Philosophy of Earth Jurisprudence* (Wakefield Press 2011)

Peter Burdon and Michelle Maloney (eds), *Wild Law: In Practice* (Routledge 2014)

Cormac Cullinan, *Wild Law: A Manifesto for Earth Justice* (2nd edn, Green Books 2011)

Alessandro Pelizzon, 'Can You Hear the Rivers Sing? Legal Personhood, Ontology, and the Nitty Gritty of Governance' *Ecology Law Quarterly*, 45/4 (2019): 787

CHAPTER 15

THE ROLE OF SCIENCE

SAM JOHNSTON

I. INTRODUCTION

SCIENCE has a crucial and multifaceted role in international environmental law, identifying and framing its challenges, threats, and problems. The political momentum to develop international environmental law initially relies heavily on the ability to show that the lack of action by the international community is likely to result in significant adverse effects. The persistence of sceptical views about the science of climate change illustrates the chilling effect that scientific uncertainty may have on developments of international environmental law.[1]

The role of science in international environmental law has been the subject of vigorous debate, focusing around competing claims concerning the need for action in almost every area of environmental regulation, such as climate change, restrictions on use of areas or resources such as fisheries, and restrictions on 'dangerous' substances such as genetically modified organisms (GMOs).[2] The developing jurisprudence on the role of science in international environmental law articulated by various international tribunals such as the International Court of Justice (ICJ) highlights the important role that science plays in this field.[3]

This chapter considers how science has influenced international environmental law and in turn, how international environmental law has contributed to the promotion of science. The term 'science' is used in this chapter in a broad way. It is more than just the

[1] See Steinar Andresen and Jon Birger Skjærseth, 'Science and Technology: From Agenda Setting to Implementation' in Daniel Bodansky, Jutta Brunnée, and Ellen Hey (eds), *The Oxford Handbook of International Environmental Law* (1st edn, OUP 2008) 182.

[2] Jacqueline Peel, *Science and Risk Regulation in International Law* (CUP 2010).

[3] Tracey Kanhanga, 'Scientific Uncertainties: a Nightmare for Environmental Adjudicators' in Christina Voigt (ed), *International Judicial Practice on the Environment: Questions of Legitimacy* (1st edn, CUP 2019) 121. See also Chapter 27, 'Judicial Development', in this volume, where judicial decisions under international environmental law are dealt with in more detail.

study of the natural or physical world, but also includes the study of social, cultural, and economic facts.

The chapter begins with a short history of science in international environmental law. Next, it considers important aspects of the relationship between international environmental law and science—the role that science plays in the development of international environmental law, that international environmental law plays in promoting science and, in managing threats posed by science. It concludes with some observations about future challenges.

II. THE HISTORY OF SCIENCE IN INTERNATIONAL ENVIRONMENTAL LAW

Science has long been an important factor in international environmental law with its origins going back as far as international environmental law itself.[4] An early important manifestation of science in modern international environmental law is the role it played in the United Nations Convention on the Law of the Sea (UNCLOS), negotiated throughout the 1970s and finally concluded in 1982.[5] A principal aim of this treaty was the promotion of science. The preamble of UNCLOS makes it clear that one of its key purposes is to 'promote the peaceful uses of the seas and oceans ... and the study, protection and preservation of the marine environment'. The discovery of manganese nodules in the deep seabed was a catalyst for the establishment of the legal regime governing the area.[6] Marine science provides essential data for the implementation of many of the key developments and features of UNCLOS, such as the fishery regime's key concepts of maximum sustainable yield and total allowable catch, as well as boundary limits and the identification of the outer limits of the continental shelf beyond 200 nautical miles.

The rising importance of science in international environmental law in the 1980s is further illustrated by the rapid response to the scientific discovery of the damage being done to the ozone layer, resulting in the adoption of the 1985 Vienna Convention for the Protection of the Ozone Layer and its 1987 Montreal Protocol on Substances That Deplete the Ozone Layer.[7] Both treaties have been universally ratified and are widely recognized as the most successful examples of the use of a treaty in order to respond to scientific challenges.[8]

[4] Philippe Sands and Jacqueline Peel, *Principles of International Environmental Law* (4th edn, CUP 2018) ch 2, 'History', 21.

[5] Donald Rothwell and Tim Stephens, *The International Law of the Sea* (2nd edn, Hart Publishing 2016) 10.

[6] Ibid, 120.

[7] David Hunter, James Salzman, and Durwood Zaelke, *International Environmental Law and Policy* (4th edn, Foundation Press 2011) ch 10, 'Ozone Depletion', s III, 566–605.

[8] Ibid.

In 1992, Agenda 21 of the United Nations Conference on Environment and Development (UNCED) confirmed the status of the scientific community as one of the nine 'major groups' which were to be consulted with regard to sustainable development issues.

UNCED also brought about the adoption of three key treaties, the 1992 Convention on Biological Diversity (CBD), the 1992 United Nations Framework Convention on Climate Change (UNFCCC), and the 1994 Convention to Combat Desertification—collectively known as the Rio Conventions—that were all fundamentally shaped by science and contain important provisions for using and promoting science to develop each treaty.

Climate change is perhaps the most important issue on the agenda of the UN that has been influenced by, and in turn has influenced, science. The process of negotiations was from the very beginning significantly influenced by the contribution from science. The five assessment reports of the Intergovernmental Panel on Climate Change (IPCC) benefit from the contributions of thousands of scientists from all regions and have become an important basis for intergovernmental negotiations on the UNFCCC. The international authority of the IPCC in this field has also been recognized through its receipt of the Nobel Peace Prize in 2007.[9]

The Intergovernmental Platform on Biodiversity and Ecosystem Services (IPBES),[10] founded in 2010 after years of negotiations, is modelled on the IPCC. IPBES provides a platform for interaction and cooperation among more than forty science organizations, UN programmes, specialized agencies, and several important UN treaty bodies, such as those established under the CBD and 1979 Convention on the Conservation of Migratory Species of Wild Animals (CMS). It aims to provide international environmental law with: scientific information; assessments of the interrelationship between biodiversity and ecosystem functions; and to indicate capacities and activities which can contribute to strengthening the networks between sciences and global policy-making.

Science and technology feature prominently in the Sustainable Development Goals (SDGs). Among 169 targets, fifteen targets explicitly refer to 'science' and another thirty-four targets relate to issues that are largely technologically or scientifically oriented. There are also significant scientific and technological dimensions to the other remaining 121 targets. The forty-eight targets that are most closely related to science and technology relate to three goals: (a) developing science and technology; (b) promoting access to science and technology; and (c) global effective innovation systems. The UN General Assembly launched the UN inter-agency task team on science, technology, and innovation for the SDGs to 'promote coordination, coherence and cooperation within the United Nations system on science, technology and innovation-related matters, enhancing synergy and efficiency, in particular to enhance capacity-building initiatives'. The Global Sustainable Development Report aims to strengthen the science-policy

[9] 'The Nobel Peace Prize 2007' <https://www.nobelprize.org/prizes/peace/2007/summary/> accessed 23 September 2019.

[10] <https://www.ipbes.net/> accessed 27 August 2019.

interface and provide a strong evidence-based instrument to support policy-makers to achieve the SDGs.[11]

III. INTERNATIONAL ENVIRONMENTAL LAW AND SCIENCE

Comprehensively detailing such a wide-ranging relationship as the one between science and international environmental law is not possible within the confines of this chapter. There are, however, a number of recognized aspects to this relationship that illustrate systemic issues and challenges that international environmental law faces in using and contributing to science, namely: the role that science plays in the development of international environmental law, the role of international environmental law in promoting science, and the role of international environmental law in managing threats posed by science.

A. The Role that Science Plays in the Development and Implementation of International Environmental Law

Science contributes to successfully developing international environmental law in a number of ways. Laws based on scientific facts tend to be more successful as they can more effectively identify and respond to real issues and problems.[12] Science has an important facilitative effect on legal development. Science is used to identify a problem, develop a common starting point, and narrow the scope of the negotiations and law.[13] Science helps with developments by identifying potential solutions and provides states multiple ways of complying with commitments.[14] Science also helps facilitate action by allowing states and other law-makers to reframe questions of burden and equity. For example, policy-makers may claim that science demonstrates the need for an unpopular decision that will entail short-term cost for long-term gains.[15] As a result, much of international environmental law is developed in response to new science and shaped fundamentally by science.

[11] *Global Sustainable Development Report 2019: The Future is Now—Science for Achieving Sustainable Development* (United Nations 2019).

[12] Timothy Meyer, 'Institutions and Expertise: The Role of Science in Climate Change Lawmaking' in Cinnamon Carlarne, Kevin Gray, and Richard Tarasofsky (eds), *The Oxford Handbook of International Climate Change Law* (OUP 2016) 442.

[13] Ibid.

[14] Ibid.

[15] Ibid.

Consequently, international environmental law has developed considerable sophistication in ensuring that science is delivered in a useful manner to the legal-making processes and that it is used appropriately. The range of mechanisms is as numerous as the fora that develop law. Framework conventions with various types of amendment procedures, standing or permanent subsidiary bodies of the plenary/scientific advisory bodies, assessment processes, periodic reporting, relationships with scientific organizations, clearing house mechanisms, intersessional platforms, rosters of experts, and science expertise on the delegations are some of the more common and important techniques.

Over recent years even dispute settlement processes have become a mechanism for including science in international environmental law, with decisions such as the ICJ's decision in the *Whaling* case,[16] the International Tribunal for the Law of the Sea's *Bluefin Tuna* case,[17] or the Advisory Opinion on *Responsibilities and obligations of States sponsoring persons and entities with respect to activities in the Area*[18] and the *South China Seas* case recently before the Permanent Court of Arbitration,[19] being examples where the relevant court closely examined the science associated with the matter, based their decisions on that science, and thereby supported science in the process.[20]

An important and instructive area where science has played a crucial role in developing international environmental law is the regime for the protection of the atmosphere. Science played an important role in each of the key developments of this regime such as the *Trail Smelter* case,[21] the 1979 Convention on Long-Range Transboundary Air Pollution (LRTAP), the ozone regime, and the UNFCCC. The latter two are considered next.

1. *Ozone regime*

The multilateral environmental agreements (MEAs) addressing the protection of the ozone layer are widely recognized as the most successful examples of international environmental law responding to science. However, the success of this response belies the controversy and complexity surrounding the issue at the time of the negotiation of the regime in the 1980s which included: scientific uncertainty; no concrete evidence of harmful effects; potentially high costs; widespread use of ozone-depleting substances

[16] *Whaling in the Antarctic (Australia/ Japan, New Zealand intervening)* (Judgement) [2014] ICJ Rep 226; Margaret Young and Sebastián Rioseco Sullivan, 'Evolution Through the Duty to Cooperate: Implications of the *Whaling* Case at the International Court of Justice' *Melbourne Journal of International Law*, 16 (2015): 311.

[17] *Southern Bluefin Tuna Cases (New Zealand/Japan; Australia/Japan)* (Award on Jurisdiction and Admissibility, Decision of 4 August 2000) 23 RIAA 1.

[18] (Advisory Opinion) [2011] ITLOS Rep 10.

[19] *The South China Sea Arbitration (Philippines/China)* (Final award of 12 July 2016) PCA Case no 2013-19.

[20] Kanhanga (n 3).

[21] *Trail Smelter Arbitration (United States/Canada)* (1938 and 1941) 3 RIAA 1905.

(ODSs); the opposition of some of the largest companies in the world; unequal contribution and capacity; and a global problem that required global participation.[22]

The regime centres around the 1985 Vienna Convention and the 1987 Montreal Protocol, mentioned above. Both treaties have been universally ratified, the first treaties to reach universal participation in the history of the UN.

The assessment panels, established by Article 6 of the Montreal Protocol, have been the main mechanism for incorporating science into the regime. The panels carry out a periodic assessment every four years. The first was published in 1989 and the latest in 2014. The Scientific Assessment Panel (SAP), made up of hundreds of top scientists from around the world, assesses the status of the depletion of the ozone layer and relevant atmospheric science issues. Any emerging scientific issues of importance are brought to the attention of the parties by the SAP co-chairs for consideration at the meetings of the parties.

The Vienna Convention contained no commitments to reduce the use of ODSs. The Montreal Protocol only contained limited commitments. However, from 1990 there was a rapid increase in the commitments of parties. These were developed through five amendments to the Protocol (adopted in London (1990), Copenhagen (1992), Montreal (1997), Beijing (1999), and Kigali (2016)) and thirteen adjustments of the annexes of the Protocol.[23] Amendments require ratification by a particular number of parties before they enter into force; adjustments enter into force automatically unless a party expressly notifies it is opting out. This regime, adapted and strengthened through its amendment and adjustment procedures to meet scientific challenges, has led to the phase-out of 99% of ODSs and the first signs of recovery of the ozone layer.[24]

The framework approach and its flexible opt-in and opt-out mechanisms of adjustment represents an important technique for incorporating science rapidly into the usually slow and cumbersome MEA process.

Another important lesson of the Montreal Protocol is the role of the scientists, and, over time, diplomats who develop a high level of expertise through their active involvement in the process. The emergence of an epistemic community of atmospheric scientists and expert diplomats played a primary role in gathering information, disseminating it to governments and ODS manufacturers, and helping them formulate international, domestic, and industry policies regarding ODS consumption and production.[25] This core group has been widely recognized as contributing to the timing and stringency of ODS regulations through a combination of strategies ranging from the

[22] Richard Benedick, *Ozone Diplomacy: New Directions in Safeguarding the Planet* (Harvard University Press 1991) xii, an insider's account of the negotiations of the Montreal Protocol; see also the 2nd edn, 1998.

[23] UNEP, Ozone Secretariat, *Handbook for the Montreal Protocol on Substances that Deplete the Ozone Layer* (12th edn, 2018).

[24] 'Ozone on track to heal completely in our lifetime, UN environment agency declares on World Day' *UN News* (16 September 2019) <https://news.un.org/en/story/2019/09/1046452> accessed 14 October 2019.

[25] See Chapter 40, 'Epistemic Communities', in this volume.

persuasion of individuals and the capture of the negotiating process. They also ensured that the underlying science was known to, and influenced, the policy-making process. By influencing the actions of the United States and DuPont, the largest producer of ODS, the epistemic community developed the political context or enabling environment of the negotiations.[26]

2. *UNFCCC*

Science has played a key role in identifying, shaping, and influencing the effort to tackle climate change—which is widely recognized as one of the greatest threats to peace, security, and development.[27]

The UNFCCC, its 1997 Kyoto Protocol, and 2015 Paris Agreement identify the need for an effective and progressive response to the urgent threat of climate change on the basis of the best available scientific knowledge. For example, the UNFCCC calls on parties to promote and cooperate in research, systematic observation, and the development of data archives, including through exchange of information; to support programmes, networks, and organizations; and improve the capacities of developing countries.[28]

Through their national communications, parties report on their national and cooperative research activities and their contributions to climate science, as well as emerging research needs and priorities.

The IPCC has been the most important and influential direct mechanism for the incorporation of science in the UNFCCC regime. It has a well-established role in the UNFCCC process in communicating scientific information through its assessment reports, special reports, and technical papers.[29] The IPCC predates the UNFCCC and is an independent body founded under the auspices of the World Meteorological Organization and the United Nations Environment Programme (UNEP). It assesses the scientific literature and provides vital scientific information to the UNFCCC process.

Article 21.2 of the UNFCCC provides that the secretariat 'will cooperate closely with the Intergovernmental Panel on Climate Change to ensure that the Panel can respond to the need for objective scientific and technical advice'. Cooperation with the IPCC has been further defined and strengthened by several decisions of the Conference of Parties (COP). In 1995, COP 1 invited the Subsidiary Bodies (SBs), in particular the Subsidiary Body for Scientific and Technological Advice (SBSTA), to submit proposals for future cooperation with the IPCC.[30] This resulted in a Joint Working Group (JWG) of the SBSTA and the IPCC, established the same year. This informal group meets regularly to ensure coordination and exchange information on the activities of the two bodies. The

[26] Peter Haas, 'Epistemic Communities and Policy Knowledge' in Neil Smelser and Paul Bates (eds), *International Encyclopedia of the Social and Behavioural Sciences* (Elsevier 2001) 11578.

[27] Sands and Peel (n 4) ch 8, 'Climate Change', 295.

[28] arts 4.1(g)–(h), 5.

[29] UNFCCC, 'Cooperation with the IPCC' <https://unfccc.int/topics/science/workstreams/cooperation-with-the-ipcc> accessed 27 August 2019.

[30] Decision 6/CP.1, 'The subsidiary bodies established by the Convention' (6 June 1995) UN Doc FCCC/CP/1995/7/Add.1, 21.

JWG is composed of the chairs of the SBSTA and IPCC, other presiding officers of the Convention and IPCC, and members of the secretariats.

The IPCC is best known for its comprehensive assessment reports, which are widely recognized as the most credible sources of information on climate change. The First Assessment Report in 1990 helped launch negotiations on the Convention.[31] The 1995 Second Assessment Report, in particular its statement that 'the balance of evidence suggests ... a discernible human influence on global climate', stimulated many governments into intensifying negotiations on what was to become the Kyoto Protocol.[32] The Fourth Assessment Report (AR4), released in 2007, provided the scientific foundation for the Marrakech Accords which were critical to operationalizing the Kyoto Protocol.[33] The Fifth Assessment Report, finalized in 2014, informed the negotiations and policy formulation towards the Paris Agreement.[34] The sixth assessment due in 2020 is seen as a critical input to the review and development of parties' commitments under the Paris Agreement.

The IPCC also produces shorter special reports and technical papers on specific issues, a number of them at the request of the COP or the SBSTA. For example, in 2000 the IPCC issued a Special Report on Land Use, Land-Use Change and Forestry (LULUCF), which provided the basis for the negotiations on the rules for the LULUCF sector under the Kyoto Protocol[35] and the IPCC's Special Report on *Global Warming of 1.5°C*[36] mandated by the COP of the UNFCCC[37] is seen as a crucial input to implementing the Paris Agreement.

Science has also played an important facilitative role in the UNFCCC. An early example is consideration of the Brazilian proposal on historic responsibility in the negotiations for the Kyoto Protocol by the SBSTA, which resulted in the proposal being given serious consideration through a largely scientific and technical examination, whilst at the same time allowing the negotiations for the Protocol to progress.[38]

3. *The influence of science on international environmental law*

Assessing the influence of science on international environmental law in general, and MEAs in particular, is a challenging task. It is an issue that political scientists and international relations scholars have been researching and analyzing for decades, addressing

[31] UNFCCC, 'Background—Cooperation with the IPCC' https://unfccc.int/topics/science/workstreams/cooperation-with-the-ipcc/background-cooperation-with-the-ipcc accessed 27 August 2019.

[32] Ibid.

[33] Ibid.

[34] Ibid.

[35] Ibid.

[36] IPCC, *Global warming of 1.5°C—Special Report* (2018).

[37] Decision 1/CP.21, 'Adoption of the Paris Agreement' (29 January 2016) UN Doc FCCC/CP/2015/10/Add.1, 2.

[38] Emilio La Rovere, Laura Valente de Macedo, and Kevin Baumert, 'The Brazilian Proposal on Relative Responsibility for Global Warming' in Kevin Baumert *et al* (eds), *Building on the Kyoto Protocol: Options for Protecting the Climate* (World Resources Institute 2002) 157.

topics such as 'when does power listen to truth'.[39] Scholars are increasingly sceptical about the influence that science has on the policy-making process, whether scientists are capable of developing truth, and whether power ever listens to them anyway. The lack of progress on emission cuts under the UNFCCC despite the increasingly clear and certain science about the causes and effects of climate change is an important and contemporary example of this lack of influence. Indeed, many scholars seem surprised by the occasions when science does have a demonstrable impact on the policy-making process.

Part of the problem is that international environmental law addresses issues that are inherently political or economic in nature and there are few, if any, examples in which science is the overriding or predominant influence. Even with the ozone regime, it is hard to assess the extent to which governments were influenced by the science or the lobbying by big chemical companies whose patents over ODS were expiring, whose markets were diminishing through domestic regulatory action in the United States and who had an interest in phasing-out old ODS technology to speed up the introduction of a new and more profitable generation of ODS technology. The interests of these companies were therefore very much aligned with the rapid development of the treaty.[40]

Further complicating any assessment is the experience where conclusive science has not been a necessary condition for significant developments in international environmental law. The decision of the 1987 North Sea Conference to adopt very stringent and ambitious targets to reduce pollution, even though the scientific message was very far from conclusive, on the basis of the precautionary principle, is an important example.[41] The 1982 International Whaling Commission (IWC) moratorium on commercial whaling, even though its Scientific Committee gave no such recommendation, is another.[42]

Nevertheless, it is clear from the experience that an important issue is the institutional relationship between the law-making process and the relevant scientific advisory mechanism. Each MEA has a different structure, even closely related treaties such as the atmospheric treaties differ in structure. Whereas under the Montreal Protocol the main assessment processes are established as part of the Protocol itself, in the UNFCCC they are independent.

Science generated by the MEA is controlled by governments and therefore relevant to the treaty, but it is viewed as being less independent, credible, and authoritative. Integrity is seen as being important to ensure that the scientific input is objective.

[39] Aaron Wildavsky, *Speaking Truth to Power: The Art and Craft of Policy Analysis* (Little, Brown 1979); Peter Haas, *Epistemic Communities, Constructivism, and International Environmental Politics* (Routledge 2015).

[40] Hunter, Salzman, and Zaelke (n 7) 1053.

[41] David Freestone and Tony IJlstra, 'The North Sea: Perspectives on Regional Environmental Cooperation' in special issue of *International Journal of Coastal and Estuarine Law* (Graham and Trotman 1990).

[42] Meyer (n 12) 442.

A direct link between the legal and scientific process is necessary so that scientists are aware of the needs of law-makers. This link is also important to ensure that the enabling or receiving environment—the MEA—is not only aware of the science but has a responsibility to respond to the science. The lack of influence UNEP's 1995 Global Biodiversity Assessment[43] had on the CBD is a stark example of the importance of this responsibility to respond.

The IPCC has been criticized along both these lines, with some questioning the legitimacy of the IPCC process and others the relevance and impact.[44] A reflection of this is the increasing difficulty with which reports of the IPCC are received by the COP of the UNFCCC. For example, at COP 24 there was a protracted negotiation about whether to 'note' or 'welcome' the IPCC's Special Report on Global Warming of 1.5°C which could not be resolved and was deferred to later meetings of the Subsidiary Bodies of the UNFCCC.[45] The increasingly political nature of the delegations and process of adopting the final summary of IPCC assessments—known as the Summary for Policy Makers—is a further manifestation of the tensions around these issues for the UNFCCC.

Independence and relevance serve different functions for different states. For many countries, the independence of science is a feature that boosts its credibility and utility. Other countries tend to perceive so-called 'independent science' to be science done by and for the countries that commissioned it. The more marginal their role in science, the more critical they tend to be of science. These perceptions are amplified by politicization of science in many countries recently, especially in the United States, the United Kingdom, and Australia.

An important example of these tensions can be seen even in preeminent international scientific processes such as the IPCC, which relies predominantly on English language sources. Other science or what the IPCC calls 'marginalised knowledge systems', which even includes Spanish and French climate change science and knowledge, let alone more marginalized knowledge such as Indigenous peoples' knowledge systems, are not adequately represented or reflected in the IPCC's work. As a result, over recent years there has been increasing criticism about the authority and credibility of IPCC work and serious, although relatively unsuccessful, attempts by the IPCC to develop mechanisms to access these 'marginalised knowledge systems'.[46]

IPBES has put an enormous amount of effort into drawing on a wide range of knowledge systems, in particular Indigenous peoples' knowledge systems, but so far the

[43] Vernon Heywood *et al*, *Global Biodiversity Assessment* (CUP 1995).

[44] Peter Haas and Casey Stevens, 'Organized Science, Usable Knowledge, and Multilateral Environmental Governance' in Rolf Lidskog and Göran Sundqvist (eds), *Governing the Air: The Dynamics of Science, Policy, and Citizen Interaction* (MIT Press 2011) 125.

[45] See 'Summary of the Katowice Climate Change Conference: 2-15 December 2018' *Earth Negotiations Bulletin*, 12/747 (2018).

[46] James Ford *et al*, 'Including Indigenous Knowledge and Experience in IPCC Assessment Reports' *Nature Climate Change*, 6 (2016): 349.

results have been disappointing.[47] For example, there has only been superficial inclusion of and references to the traditional knowledge of Indigenous people.

Another aspect of the problems faced in broadening knowledge systems is that the social, economic, and legal sciences tend to be more qualitative, subjective, and value-laden, thereby undermining the acceptability or 'credibility' of those sciences. Problems over the objectivity of risk-assessment processes—addressed in Section III.C of this chapter—illustrate the limitations of science when addressing more value-laden issues such as precaution. As a result, serious questions have been raised about the neutrality of all science.

In this age of fake news and alternative facts, achieving scientific consensus is increasingly challenging. Smoking and tobacco control, climate change, and GMOs, provide examples in which progress in the negotiation, conclusion, or implementation of international law has been slowed, even stymied, by subjective or biased science.[48]

The UNFCCC commitments are to a significant extent technologically and scientifically neutral, allowing states to choose their pathways and the technologies they encourage or deploy to achieve their commitments. This allows parties to choose contested and less proven technologies to implement their commitments such as carbon capture and storage or geo-engineering, despite the scientific uncertainties as to the impacts and consequences of these technologies. There is a tendency among some states to favour such scientific and technological solutions, as they are less demanding in terms of transformational changes. Their vociferous support for dubious technologies supported by questionable science further politicizes the neutrality of science in general.

Another issue is the increasing complexity of the range of issues and actors involved in international environmental law. For example, at COP 24, there were over 1,200 different organizations registered.[49] These included lobby groups, think tanks, companies, industry umbrellas, radical activists, and religious groups. The UNFCCC receives all their input without making any meaningful assessment of their expertise or qualification. In this more complex diverse world, science is being crowded out and losing its influence.

In conclusion, science has played a significant catalytic role in much of international environmental law. The ozone regime is widely recognized as a success and has many lessons for other MEAs. The UNFCCC is widely recognized as the most important example of an MEA shaped by science. Yet as science becomes more successful and influential it is increasingly scrutinized, more politicized, and less certain. And as MEAs and international environmental law become more open and complex, science is increasingly becoming less influential.

47 See eg Ehsan Masood, 'The Battle for the Soul of Biodiversity' *Nature*, 560 (2018): 423.

48 Kevin Trenberth, 'More Knowledge, Less Certainty' *Nature Climate Change*, 1 (2010): 20.

49 UNFCCC, COP 24, 'Provisional list of registered participants' (2018) COP24.PLOP.

B. The Role of International Environmental Law in Promoting Science

International environmental law has many principles and MEAs with specific provisions calling for better access for developing state parties to science, the promotion of science, research, and development. Agenda 21 identifies scientific community as a major stakeholder.[50] As mentioned above, the SDGs extensively refer to science and every MEA adopted since UNCLOS contains provisions on science. Typically the relevant instrument calls for science and technology needs assessments, provision of capacity-building and calls on parties to exchange information, cooperate, and assist one another with resources and expertise.[51]

Cutting-edge approaches are moving to a more dynamic arrangement geared towards: fostering public-private partnerships; promoting innovation; catalyzing the use of technology road-maps or action plans; responding to developing country requests on matters related to technology transfer; and facilitating joint research and development activities.[52]

Few, if any, of the MEAs provide resources for the implementation of these provisions. Consequently, their impact on the work of the science is limited, with domestic priorities and budgets being much more important.

One important contribution, albeit not well acknowledged, is the extent to which meetings of MEAs and other international environmental law meetings such as Rio+20, UNGA, or the Global Platform for Disaster Risk Reduction provide important venues for scientific exchange and collaboration. As mentioned before, the UNFCCC COPs have become important scientific conferences in their own right with many technical expert meetings being held as part of these meetings.[53]

One area of science in which international environmental law has played an important role is managing global commons for peaceful purposes. Scientific research is an important peaceful activity of the global commons, such as the high seas and the so-called 'Area' (ie the seabed and ocean floor beyond the limits of national jurisdiction), outer space, and the polar regions. UNCLOS, the Antarctic Treaty System,[54] the treaties dealing with space—in particular the 1967 Outer Space Treaty and the 1979 Agreement Governing the Activities of States on the Moon and Other Celestial Bodies, and the 2001 International Treaty on Plant Genetic Resources for Food and Agriculture (ITPGRFA),

[50] *Report of the United Nations Conference on Environment and Development* (UN 1993) vol I, annex II, 'Agenda 21', ch 31: 'Scientific and technological community', 403.

[51] See eg CBD, arts 12, 17, 18.

[52] See 'Technology Mechanism of the UNFCCC' <https://unfccc.int/ttclear/support/technology-mechanism.html> accessed 27 August 2019.

[53] UNFCCC, 'Technical Expert Meetings' <http://unfccc.int/resource/climateaction2020/tep/technical-expert-meetings/index.html> accessed 27 August 2019.

[54] The central instrument in the Antarctic Treaty System is the 1959 Antarctic Treaty.

have provided the framework to support and promote science in relation to these global commons. This has been done in the face of intense political tensions between key states, representing an important achievement for science.

As these areas become more accessible, commercial, economically valuable, and important to security issues, international environmental law and the legal principles that have supported scientific research in these areas will become increasingly important and will be subject to greater scrutiny. A key legal tension emerging from this relationship is balancing the need for retaining and promoting the free access to science and information that underpins the traditional approach, with the increasing need to share benefits equitably in the face of rising commercialization.

For example, the use of outer space has until recently been restricted to government-sponsored exploration. This is changing with the emergence of private satellites, paying tourists, and the mining of helium or plutonium from asteroids or the moon. Indeed, there are now so many satellites using outer space that there are serious concerns about space debris and challenges with regard to the allocation of orbits. The general regime is based upon free use and a prohibition of claims to sovereignty by individual states. However, increasing private sector interest is creating a need for these basic principles to be developed.[55]

The ITPGRFA does the same for plant genetic resources covered by it. An increasing proportion of these genetic resources have been subject to various forms of ownership, as a result of advances in science, technology, and the expansion of property rights, particularly plant variety rights and patents supported by developments under the International Union for the Protection of New Varieties of Plants and the World Trade Organization's (WTO) trade-related intellectual property agreements. As a response to this privatization, international environmental law has tried to maintain the public nature and open access of plant genetic resources, which is particularly important for food security. The centre of these efforts is the ITPGRFA that recognizes that plant genetic resources for food and agriculture are the 'common concern of all countries' and establishes a multilateral system for sixty-four of the most important crops, included in Annex I of the ITPGRFA. Under this multilateral system, pursuant to Article 11.2, parties agree to provide each other with facilitated access to the listed plant genetic resources that are 'under the management and control' of national governments and 'in the public domain', for the purposes of training, research, and breeding for food and agriculture.[56] The effectiveness of this system is important to maintaining global food security and obviously for science as well. It is also being considered as an important

[55] Gbenga Oduntan, 'Aspects of the International Legal Regime concerning Privatization and Commercialization of Space Activities' *Georgetown Journal of International Affairs*, 17/1 (2016): 79.

[56] See FAO, ITPGRFA, 'List of Press Dossiers' <http://www.fao.org/plant-treaty/news/press-dossier/en/> accessed 27 August 2019.

model for other types of global commons genetic resources under threat such as those of the high seas or Antarctica.

UNCLOS ensures that the high seas and the seabed beyond national jurisdictions or deep seabed (the Area) are managed for peaceful purposes, including the practice of science. UNCLOS also recognizes marine scientific research as a freedom of the high seas in Part XIII and contains provisions protecting this freedom in the exclusive economic zone (EEZ) and continental shelf.[57] Historically marine scientific research was akin to a freedom of the high seas. Part XIII of UNCLOS changed this significantly due to pressure from developing countries in the negotiations. Part XIII balances the freedom of marine scientific research and the recognition of the interests of coastal states, with the freedom being seen as a prerequisite to developing marine scientific research.

This balance is an evolving and dynamic one. 'Marine scientific research' is not defined in the Convention, despite a number of proposals that were made for a definition during the negotiations for UNCLOS. Without any guidelines or definition, it is often difficult to distinguish marine scientific research from exploration of natural resources in practice.[58] The distinction between marine scientific research and other activities also remains unclear. This ambiguity has been the source of dispute with regard to coastal state jurisdiction over marine-survey activities in the EEZ, in particular between China and the United States.[59] The legality of hydrographic and military-survey activity in the EEZ of another state is a particularly contentious issue. Whilst the United States advocates the freedom of such surveys in the EEZ of a third state as marine scientific research, China takes the position that they are entitled to regulate these activities.[60] So far, the question remains open.

Another example of this problem is whether geo-engineering experiments involving the fertilization of the sea with iron to increase plankton and thereby increase absorption of carbon dioxide by the ocean is marine scientific research or rather an activity that involves depositing material covered by the London Dumping Convention. Parties have responded to this by developing amendments to the London Protocol, which outline in some detail what is 'research' and what is a 'prohibited activity', with the distinction essentially being drawn between pure research which is allowed and applied or commercial science which is prohibited.[61]

These types of legal tensions around marine scientific research are escalating and threaten to undermine its role, the ability of UNCLOS to promote science and, ultimately, UNCLOS itself.

57 See eg art 246.

58 Rothwell and Stephens (n 5) 324.

59 Ibid, 330.

60 Ibid.

61 IMO, 'Marine geoengineering: Guidance and Amendments under the London Convention/Protocol' <http://www.imo.org/en/OurWork/Environment/LCLP/EmergingIssues/geoengineering/Pages/default.aspx> accessed 27 August 2019.

C. The Role of International Environmental Law in Managing Threats Posed by Science

An important role of international environmental law is to manage the threats posed by dangerous substances. Science also has a pivotal role in determining what is 'dangerous' and what measures are legal (reasonable or precautionary[62]).

Important international environmental law examples of this role include: the 1994 Nuclear Safety Convention; the 1989 Basel Convention on the Control of Transboundary Movements of Hazardous Wastes and Their Disposal, the 1998 Rotterdam Convention on the Prior Informed Consent Procedure for Certain Hazardous Chemicals and Pesticides in International Trade, and the 2001 Stockholm Convention on Persistent Organic Pollutants addressing hazardous substances; and the 2000 Cartagena Protocol on Biosafety, the 1951 International Plant Protection Convention and the FAO's *Codex Alimentarius*[63] in the field of biosafety.

The approaches adopted for each of these areas are highly technical, usually centred around the provision of prior informed consent by the receiving country and involving both a heavy reliance on science as a key way of assessing the risk.

The Cartagena Protocol on Biosafety illustrates these points. Article 15 of the Protocol requires that decisions regarding the import of Living Modified Organisms (LMOs) for intentional introduction into the environment be taken in accordance with a risk assessment. Annex III provides more detailed guidance on the application of risk assessments, including some general principles such as the need for them to be carried out in a scientifically sound and transparent manner, taking into account expert advice and relevant international guidelines. Articles 10 and 11 also provide that when making a decision as to whether to allow import of an LMO, 'Lack of scientific certainty due to insufficient relevant scientific information and knowledge regarding the extent of the potential adverse effects of a living modified organism … taking also into account risks to human health, shall not prevent that Party from taking a decision.'[64]

A critical aspect of the relationship between science and policy-makers is how a decision can be simultaneously based on risk assessment and precaution.[65] A source of confusion about the compatibility of risk assessment and precaution is the misunderstanding that decisions based on risk assessment cannot reflect value judgements. Decision-makers inevitably base their decisions in part on their values or risk attitudes, or those of the constituencies they represent. Two different decision-makers, faced with

[62] See Chapter 18, 'Precaution', in this volume.

[63] 'Codex Alimentarius—International Food Standards' <http://www.fao.org/fao-who-codexalimentarius/en/> accessed 2 October 2019.

[64] Ryan Hill, Sam Johnston, and Cyrie Sendashongam, 'Risk Assessment and Precaution in the Biosafety Protocol' *Review of European, Comparative & International Environmental Law*, 13/3 (2004): 263.

[65] See Chapter 18, 'Precaution', in this volume.

the same decision, may make different choices because one is less willing than the other to accept the risks.[66]

Differences were clearly evident during the negotiations of the Protocol and the WTO *GMO* case,[67] where the governance cultures of the opposing groups contributed significantly to different understandings of the need for, and the role of, the Protocol. On the one hand, the Miami Group (comprising the United States, Canada, Argentina, Australia, Uruguay, and Chile) believed that the precautionary approach might not lead to decisions based on sound science. They were concerned that it could be applied in an arbitrary manner and could lead to distortions of trade. On the other hand, the EU and other governments could not understand the reluctance of the Miami Group to accept rules which would allow a prudent approach to this new technology. These different views were in part a reflection of the different cultures of risk assessment that existed in each country. For example, the type of risk assessment favoured by the United States is a highly formalized and adversarial method that is to the greatest possible extent based on quantitative data. This process has evolved in response to a regulatory environment in which decisions based on ambiguous scientific findings are liable to be contested in court. Most other countries do not have such a complex and adversarial system of governance.[68]

It is important that international environmental law and governments recognize such differences as legitimate. Insistence upon, or careless translation of, one approach to risk management will not resolve deep-seated cultural differences regarding risk management of new technologies. In fact, attempts to harmonize these differences out of existence are liable to be resisted as attacks on types of governance rather than a dispute about science.

IV. CONCLUSION

This chapter has considered how science has influenced international environmental law and in turn, how international environmental law has contributed to the promotion of science.

The history of this relationship reveals a growing influence of science and in turn increasing tendency for law-making processes to respond to science and engage scientists. This partnership centres around the issues described in Section III, namely—scientific influence in the law-making process, promoting science, and managing the threats posed by science.

[66] Ibid.

[67] *European Communities—Measures Affecting the Approval and Marketing of Biotech Products* (Panel Report) [29 September 2006] WTO Docs WT/DS291/R, WT/DS292/R, WT/DS293/R.

[68] Hill, Johnston, and Sendashongam (n 64).

Science will also play an important role in developing international environmental law to respond to new and emerging areas such as protecting biodiversity of the high seas,[69] managing new technologies like nanotechnologies or synthetic biology,[70] new forms of pollution such as microplastics[71] or space debris[72] and managing new uses of the environment, such as deep seabed or outer-space tourism.[73]

To ensure that science maintains its role and influence, international environmental law will need to respond to the challenges highlighted in this chapter such as—resolving the tensions that exist between pure and applied science, maintaining science's role as a peaceful activity in the global commons, ensuring that scientific input is not lost among the increasing complex and crowded nature of law-making, ensuring that science is more inclusive, holistic, and balanced, and improving its relevance whilst retaining its credibility.

An emerging issue highlighted in this chapter is the increasing politicization of science and the need to understand the limitations of science. It is ironic that science has never before been so necessary, while being so contested. Failures of science in predicting and managing threats from climate change, GMOs, and nuclear disasters have revealed the uncertainties underlying much of science and reinforces the critical role that social, economic, and institutional expectations play. Recognizing that science is not neutral or objective is an important step in addressing the key shortcomings facing the role of science in international environmental law. Determining what measures need to be taken to balance social and economic influences is another important side of this challenge. Reconciling these challenges will be increasingly important in all areas where international environmental law and science intersect.

BIBLIOGRAPHY

Harriet Harden-Davies, 'The Next Wave of Science Diplomacy: Marine Biodiversity Beyond National Jurisdiction' *ICES Journal of Marine Science*, 75/1 (2018): 426

Tracey Kanhanga, 'Scientific Uncertainties: a Nightmare for Environmental Adjudicators' in Christina Voigt (ed), *International Judicial Practice on the Environment: Questions of Legitimacy* (1st edn, CUP 2019) 121

[69] See UN, 'Intergovernmental Conference on Marine Biodiversity of Areas beyond National Jurisdiction' <https://www.un.org/bbnj/> accessed 27 August 2019.

[70] Elen Stokes and Diana Bowman, 'Looking Back to the Future of Regulating New Technologies: The Cases of Nanotechnologies and Synthetic Biology' *European Journal of Risk Regulation*, 3/2 (2012): 235.

[71] Laura Green, 'Global Marine Plastic Waste and the Newly Recommended Amendment to the Basel Convention: a Bandage or a Bandaid?' *Blog of the European Journal of International Law* (2018).

[72] Lawrence Li, 'Space Debris Mitigation as an International Law Obligation' *International Community Law Review*, 17/3 (2015): 297.

[73] Dirk Spennemann, 'Extreme Cultural Tourism: From Antarctica to the Moon' *Annals of Tourism Research*, 34/4 (2007): 898.

Timothy Meyer, 'Institutions and Expertise: The Role of Science in Climate Change Lawmaking' in Cinnamon Carlarne, Kevin Gray, and Richard Tarasofsky (eds), *The Oxford Handbook of International Climate Change Law* (OUP 2016) 442

New Frontiers in Science Diplomacy: Navigating the Changing Balance of Power (The Royal Society 2010)

Jacqueline Peel, *Science and Risk Regulation in International Law* (CUP 2010)

PART III

CONCEPTUAL PILLARS

CHAPTER 16

HARM PREVENTION

JUTTA BRUNNÉE

I. INTRODUCTION

INTERNATIONAL environmental law originates from and revolves around the harm prevention rule. As a practical matter, it is difficult to argue with the proposition that the prevention of harm should be the primary objective of international environmental law. However, it is important to appreciate that the harm prevention rule finds its conceptual origins not in the protection of the environment, but in the mutual limitation of sovereign rights to the use and enjoyment of territory. Only gradually did its focus expand from transboundary interferences to impacts on areas beyond the jurisdiction of states, and from harm to sovereign rights to harm to the environment. And yet, state-centrism constrains the operation of the harm prevention rule to this day. Furthermore, notwithstanding the rule's status as general international law and its centrality in the field, ambiguities and conceptual puzzles obscure its apparently straightforward message.

In this chapter, I focus on three points of contention, each related to the role of due diligence in harm prevention, and each highlighted by recent judicial engagements with the harm prevention rule. First, it is generally accepted that a state's obligation to prevent environmental harm is not absolute, but requires due diligence in the face of risk of significant harm. However, it is unclear whether a failure to act diligently to avert harm on its own—absent actual harm—can amount to a breach of the harm prevention rule. Second, the relationship between the procedural and substantive dimensions of the harm prevention rule remains ambiguous. Third, there is some uncertainty as to where the line runs between the harm prevention obligation and the precautionary principle, given the focus of both notions on risk.

As I will go on to show, these inter-related conceptual questions affect the harm prevention rule's function as a reference point for international environmental law. For example, whether or not a breach of the rule presupposes causation of significant harm has important implications for both the application of the law of state responsibility and the rule's potential as a basis for recourse to judicial processes. In turn, the harm prevention rule's due diligence nature and its transboundary impact focus help illuminate the emergence, and distinctive features, of treaty-based approaches to regional and global environmental concerns.

In exploring the development and traits of the harm prevention rule, I show that, notwithstanding the conceptual puzzles, the harm prevention rule is the normative cornerstone of international environmental law, both customary and treaty-based.

II. CONCEPTUAL QUESTIONS

A. Status as General International Law

Commentators generally trace the harm prevention rule in international environmental law back to the 1941 arbitral award in the *Trail Smelter* case. The tribunal held that:

> … no State has the right to use or permit the use of its territory in such a manner as to cause injury by fumes in or to the territory of another or the properties or persons therein, when the case is of serious consequence and the injury is established by clear and convincing evidence.[1]

The *Trail Smelter* award marked the first time that an international tribunal articulated the harm prevention rule in relation to transboundary pollution.[2] In so doing, the tribunal built upon broader principles pertaining to a state's duty 'to respect other States and their territory',[3] and upon earlier arbitral awards that had confirmed states' attendant duties.[4] These duties, in turn, harken back to the conceptual necessity of balancing between the rights of sovereign equals,[5] as well as to principles such as *sic*

[1] *Trail Smelter Arbitration (United States/Canada)* (1938 and 1941) 3 RIAA 1905 (Trail Smelter case) 1965.

[2] See eg Leslie-Anne Duvic-Paoli, *The Prevention Principle in International Environmental Law* (CUP 2018) 146–147; Duncan French, 'Trail Smelter (United States of America/Canada) (1938 and 1941)' in Eirik Bjorge and Cameron Miles (eds), *Landmark Cases in Public International Law* (Hart Publishing 2017) 159, 159–160; Timothy Stephens, *International Courts and Environmental Protection* (CUP 2009) 123.

[3] See Trail Smelter case (n 1) 1963.

[4] See *Alabama claims of the United States of America against Great Britain* (Award rendered on 14 September 1872 by the tribunal of arbitration established by Article I of the Treaty of Washington of 8 May 1871) 29 RIAA 125 (Alabama Arbitration). This is referred to in Trail Smelter case (n 1); see also *British Property in Spanish Morocco (Spain/UK)* (1925) 2 RIAA 615 (British property case); *Island of Palmas Case (The Netherlands/US)* (1928) 2 RIAA 829.

[5] See eg Günther Handl, 'Territorial Sovereignty and the Problem of Transnational Pollution' *American Journal of International Law*, 69/1 (1975): 50, 56.

utere tuo ut alienum non laedas (use your own property in such a manner as not to injure that of another), abuse of rights, and good neighbourliness.[6]

Today, it is beyond doubt that the harm prevention rule is binding under general international law. The International Court of Justice (ICJ) first engaged with states' duties to protect within their territories the rights of other states in the *Corfu Channel* case.[7] However, only in 1996, in *Legality of the Threat or Use of Nuclear Weapons*, did the court confirm that the harm prevention rule is 'part of the international law relating to the environment', and applicable to environmental impacts both in other states and in 'areas beyond the limits of national jurisdiction'.[8] The ICJ reiterated this conclusion in the *Gabčíkovo-Nagymaros* case,[9] the *Pulp Mills* case,[10] and in the *Costa Rica v Nicaragua/ Nicaragua v Costa Rica* cases.[11]

The affirmation of the harm prevention rule by the ICJ followed the accelerating development of international environmental law that began in the 1970s. The perhaps most influential restatement of the rule is found in Principle 21 of the 1972 Stockholm Declaration on the Human Environment. It stipulates that states have 'the sovereign right to exploit their own resources pursuant to their own environmental policies, and the responsibility to ensure that activities within their jurisdiction or control do not cause damage to the environment of other States or of areas beyond the limits of national jurisdiction'.[12] The phrasing of Principle 21, reaffirmed in the 1992 Rio Declaration on Environment and Development,[13] and in a series of multilateral environmental agreements (MEAs),[14] highlighted that harm prevention duties extend also to global commons.[15] Furthermore, although Principle 21 did not stipulate a particular threshold

[6] See Duvic-Paoli (n 2) 16–17; Jelena Bäumler, *Das Schädigungsverbot im Völkerrecht* (Springer Verlag 2017) 18–21.

[7] *Corfu Channel case (UK/Albania)* (Judgement) [1949] ICJ Rep 4 (Corfu Channel case).

[8] *Legality of the Threat or Use of Nuclear Weapons* (Advisory Opinion) [1996] ICJ Rep 226 (Legality of Nuclear Weapons case) 242.

[9] *The Gabčíkovo-Nagymaros Project (Hungary/Slovakia)* (Judgement) [1997] ICJ Rep 7 (Gabčíkovo-Nagymaros case) 41.

[10] *Pulp Mills on the River Uruguay (Argentina/Uruguay)* (Judgement) [2010] ICJ Rep 14 (Pulp Mills case) 55–56, 78.

[11] *Certain Activities Carried Out by Nicaragua in the Border Area (Costa Rica/Nicaragua)* and *Construction of a Road in Costa Rica along the San Juan River (Nicaragua/Costa Rica)* (Judgement) [2015] ICJ Rep 665 (Certain Activities case) 705–707.

[12] United Nations, 'Report of the United Nations Conference on the Human Environment' (5-16 June 1972) UN Doc A/CONF.48/14/Rev.1, 3, ch 1—'Declaration of the United Nations Conference on the Human Environment'.

[13] *Report of the United Nations Conference on Environment and Development* (UN 1993) vol I, annex I, principle 2. Principle 2 here restates principle 21 of Stockholm Declaration, but clarifies that states have the right to exploit their resources 'pursuant to their own environmental *and developmental* policies' (emphasis added).

[14] See Malgosia Fitzmaurice, 'Legitimacy of International Environmental Law—The Sovereign States Overwhelmed by Obligations: Responsibility to React to Problems Beyond National Jurisdiction?' *Zeitschrift für ausländisches öffentliches Recht und Völkerrecht*, 77/2 (2017): 339, 342.

[15] Patricia Birnie, Alan Boyle, and Catherine Redgwell, *International Law and the Environment* (3rd edn, OUP 2009) 145 (speaking of obligations that, in this context, operate *erga omnes*).

of harm, it is accepted today that the rule focuses on 'significant' harm—harm that is more than 'detectable', but not necessarily 'serious' or 'substantial'.[16] According to the ICJ, the 'principle of prevention, as a customary rule, has its origins in the due diligence required of a State in its territory'.[17] It is difficult to overstate the importance of the harm prevention rule's status as a rule of general international law, such that *all* states are required to avert significant transboundary environmental harm, wherever it may occur. Equally important is the rule's due diligence nature, to the implications of which I turn below.

Before I do, I should note that I deliberately speak of the 'harm prevention' rule throughout this discussion. Some commentators argue that an older 'no harm' rule, focused on assigning responsibility for harm, came to be complemented by a harm prevention principle specific to international environmental law.[18] To be sure, the older cases, including the *Trail Smelter* case, revolved around instances of actual harm, prompting much of the early scholarly debate to focus on questions of state responsibility.[19] Nonetheless, as I suggest below, the older case law bears out that the 'no harm' rule always implied a duty to act diligently to prevent harm from occurring in the first place. Over time, as environmental problems became more pressing and the need for proactive approaches better understood, this preventive dimension assumed increasing importance in the environmental context. The harm prevention rule in international environmental law thus represents a shift in emphasis, not a rule that is separate from a 'no harm' rule.[20] This is not to say that the general rule and the one that operates in international environmental law are identical. The most significant difference is the focus of the latter on *environmental* harm, including in particular harm to areas beyond state jurisdiction.[21]

[16] See 'Report of the International Law Commission on the work of its fifty-third session' (2001) UN Doc A/56/10, ch V.E—'Draft articles on prevention of transboundary harm from hazardous activities' 148, 152; Pulp Mills case (n 10) 83; Certain Activities case (n 11) 706–707, 720; Ulrich Beyerlin and Thilo Marauhn, *International Environmental Law* (Hart Publishing 2011) 41.

[17] Pulp Mills case (n 10) 55–56; Certain Activities case (n 11) (invoking, in both cases, its judgement in the *Corfu Channel* case).

[18] See Duvic-Paoli (n 2) 21–24, ch 2; Leslie-Anne Duvic-Paoli and Jorge Viñuales, 'Principle 2: Prevention' in Jorge Viñuales (ed), *The Rio Declaration on Environment and Development: A Commentary* (OUP 2015) 108; Philippe Sands and Jacqueline Peel, *Principles of International Environmental Law* (4th edn, CUP 2018) 206–213 (distinguishing a 'responsibility not to cause and environmental damage' and a 'principle of preventive action').

[19] But see also Alan Boyle, 'State Responsibility and International Liability for Injurious Consequences of Acts Not Prohibited by International Law: A Necessary Distinction?' *International and Comparative Law Quarterly*, 39/1 (1990): 1, 18 (noting that the *Trail Smelter* case too had a preventive dimension, focused on 'the control and regulation of the future operation of the smelter').

[20] See also Alexander Proelβ, 'Prinzipien des Internationalen Umweltrechts' in Alexander Proelβ (ed), *Internationales Umweltrecht* (De Gruyter 2017) 69, 83; Birnie *et al* (n 15) 143–150; Benoît Mayer, *The International Law of Climate Change* (CUP 2018) 67–69.

[21] Note that in the Trail Smelter case (n 1) the focus was still squarely on 'injury . . . in or the territory of another [state] or the properties or persons therein'.

B. The Role of Due Diligence

1. *Harm prevention and the due diligence standard*

When the ICJ, in its *Pulp Mills* decision, held that the harm prevention rule is intertwined with 'the due diligence required of a State in its territory',[22] it confirmed a long-standing view in the international environmental law literature.[23] The *Trail Smelter* decision did not explicitly address the standard of conduct required in harm prevention,[24] nor did the Stockholm and Rio Declarations several decades later.[25] However, as we have seen, these articulations of the environmental harm prevention duty built on broader principles that encumber territorial sovereignty.[26] It is directly relevant, therefore, that in the *Corfu Channel* case, the ICJ confirmed that states' general duty to avert harm to the rights of other states was not absolute, but contingent on what they knew or should have known about risks emanating from their territories.[27] The court considered this proposition to be a 'general and well-recognized principle'.[28] And, indeed, the idea that states owe one another not harm prevention as such but due diligence had already found expression in earlier cases revolving around duties in relation to potentially harmful conduct by various actors within a state's territory.[29] The fact that the potentially harmful conduct frequently is not state conduct but conduct of private actors within a state's territory is, of course, one of the defining traits of international environmental law.[30] In more than one sense, then, a consistent line runs from these early cases to the *Pulp Mills* ruling, where the ICJ invoked precisely its decision in the *Corfu Channel* case to anchor the environmental harm prevention rule in the due diligence incumbent upon states under general international law.

In *Pulp Mills*, as well as in its subsequent decision in the *Costa Rica v Nicaragua/ Nicaragua v Costa Rica* cases, the ICJ expanded on what due diligence requires of states

[22] Pulp Mills case (n 10).

[23] See eg Kerryn Anne Brent, 'The Certain Activities Case: What Implications for the No-Harm Rule?' *Asia Pacific Journal of Environmental Law*, 20/1 (2017): 28, 34; Beyerlin and Marauhn (n 16) 42; Günther Handl, 'Transboundary Impacts' in Daniel Bodansky, Jutta Brunnée, and Ellen Hey (eds), *The Oxford Handbook of International Environmental Law* (1st edn, OUP 2008) 531, 538; Birnie *et al* (n 15) 143, 217–219.

[24] See French (n 2) 172–175.

[25] But see eg *Responsibilities and obligations of States sponsoring persons and entities with respect to activities in the Area* (Advisory Opinion) [2011] ITLOS Rep 10 (Responsibilities in the Area case) [110]–[112] (noting that obligations 'to ensure' in international law tend to be understood as due diligence obligations).

[26] See nn 3–6 and accompanying text.

[27] Corfu Channel case (n 7) 22.

[28] Ibid.

[29] See eg Alabama Arbitration (n 4); British property case (n 4) 644–645; see discussion in Awalou Ouedraogo, 'La due diligence en droit international: de la règle de la neutralité au principe général' *Revue générale de droit*, 42/2 (2012): 641, 645–646.

[30] See Daniel Bodansky, Jutta Brunnée, and Ellen Hey, 'International Environmental Law: Mapping the Field' in Bodansky *et al*, *Handbook of IEL* (n 23) 1, 6–7.

in the harm prevention context. According to the court, states are 'obliged to use all the means at [their] disposal in order to avoid' transboundary harm from activities occurring in their territories or under their jurisdiction.'[31] More specifically, due diligence 'entails not only the adoption of appropriate rules and measures, but also a certain level of vigilance in their enforcement and the exercise of administrative control applicable to public and private operators, such as the monitoring of activities undertaken by such operators.'[32] In other words, due diligence has substantive as well as procedural aspects. Due diligence is also an inherently contextual standard. What is reasonable and appropriate depends in part on the risks of harm that attach to a given activity. The required level of care may also change over time, as risks or technological and regulatory standards evolve, and may differ as between economically and technologically advanced countries and countries with capacity limitations.[33]

The International Law Commission's (ILC) 2001 Draft Articles on Prevention of Transboundary Harm from Hazardous Activities constitute the most detailed effort to date to tease out the implications of the harm prevention rule and its attendant due diligence requirements.[34] The Draft Articles underscore the role of due diligence in 'the phase prior to the situation where significant harm ... might actually occur.'[35] They also highlight a crucially important point that follows from the very idea of harm prevention: the attendant due diligence obligations are triggered not by significant harm, but when activities entail a risk of such harm.[36] The ICJ appears to agree. In *Costa Rica v Nicaragua/Nicaragua v Costa Rica*, the court observed that 'to fulfil its obligation to exercise due diligence in preventing significant transboundary environmental harm, a State must, before embarking on an activity having the potential adversely to affect the environment of another State, ascertain if there is a risk of significant transboundary harm.'[37]

2. *Procedure and substance*

International environmental lawyers, and textbooks in the field, routinely distinguish between 'substantive' and 'procedural' obligations.[38] Substantive rules set out standards that states' actions or conduct must meet, the obligation to prevent serious transboundary environmental harm being one example. Procedural obligations include the duties to notify, warn, inform, or consult states potentially affected by transboundary

[31] Pulp Mills case (n 10) 55–56.

[32] Ibid, 79.

[33] See ILC draft articles on prevention (n 16) 154–155, commentary to art 3, paras 11, 17; Responsibilities in the Area case (n 25) [117]; Birnie *et al* (n 15) 148–149.

[34] ILC draft articles on prevention (n 16).

[35] Ibid, 148, general commentary, para 1.

[36] Ibid, 149, 155 (arts 1–3). For a discussion, see Birnie *et al* (n 15) 143–152.

[37] Certain Activities case (n 11) 706.

[38] See eg Pierre-Marie Dupuy and Jorge Viñuales, *International Environmental Law* (1st edn, CUP 2015) 54; Beyerlin and Marauhn (n 16) 41–45; Birnie *et al* (n 15) 137, 164–184.

impacts, and to undertake (transboundary) environmental impact assessments (EIA).[39] The ICJ, in its *Pulp Mills* and *Costa Rica v Nicaragua/Nicaragua v Costa Rica* decisions, followed this categorization, in each case beginning the assessment of state conduct in relation to procedural obligations and then turning to substance.[40]

In teaching and writing about international environmental law over the years, I had always proceeded from the premise that, legally, these procedural obligations are both an element of the harm prevention duty and independent of it as customary rules in their own right.[41] This conclusion seemed obvious, because states do not owe an absolute duty to prevent significant transboundary environmental harm, but a duty to take diligent measures to avoid such harm. Thus, in addition to taking appropriate regulatory and policy measures, states must undertake EIAs and notify, inform, or consult with potentially affected states, as the case may be. In short, while due diligence is 'substantive' in the sense that it functions as the standard of conduct of the harm prevention rule, it actually gives rise to substantive and procedural requirements. The ICJ says as much in *Pulp Mills*, not only tracing the harm prevention rule back to the due diligence required of states, but also confirming that due diligence entails substantive and procedural duties.[42] The court makes the point perhaps most explicitly in *Costa Rica v Nicaragua/Nicaragua v Costa Rica*, when it observes in relation to EIA that:

> [T]o fulfil its obligation to exercise due diligence in preventing significant transboundary environmental harm, a State must, before embarking on an activity having the potential adversely to affect the environment of another State, ascertain if there is a risk of significant transboundary harm, which would trigger the requirement to carry out an environmental impact assessment.[43]

Yet, notwithstanding its conclusion that a state would not act diligently if it failed to take the appropriate procedural steps, the ICJ proceeded to hold in both *Pulp Mills* and *Costa Rica v Nicaragua/Nicaragua v Costa Rica* that, absent actual transboundary harm, no substantive breach had occurred.[44] The court has been roundly criticized in the literature for this approach to the harm prevention rule.[45] Indeed, strongly worded

[39] See Jutta Brunnée, 'Procedure and Substance in International Environmental Law: Confused at a Higher Level?' *ESIL Reflections*, 5/6 (2016) <http://esil-sedi.eu/?p=1344> accessed 22 February 2019.

[40] See Pulp Mills case (n 10) ss III ('The Alleged Breach of Procedural Obligations'); IV ('Substantive Obligations'); Certain Activities case (n 11) 705–710 (procedural obligations), 710–712 (substantive obligations), 719–726 (procedural obligations), 726–737 (substantive obligations).

[41] See also Birnie *et al* (n 15) 141, 147–150.

[42] Pulp Mills case (n 10) 79.

[43] Certain Activities case (n 11) 706–707 (going on to note that, should an EIA confirm there is a risk of significant transboundary harm, 'the State planning to undertake the activity *is required, in conformity with its due diligence obligation, to notify and consult in good faith with the potentially affected State*') (all emphases added).

[44] See Pulp Mills case (n 10) 101; Certain Activities case (n 11) 736–737.

[45] See eg Proelβ (n 20) 83; Sandrine Maljean-Dubois and Vanessa Richard, 'The International Court of Justice's Judgement of 20 April 2010 in the Pulp Mills on the River Uruguay (Argentina v. Uruguay)

separate opinions in both decisions reveal that the court itself was divided on the issue, and on the relationship between the procedural and substantive aspects of the harm prevention rule.[46]

One could read the court's decisions in the two cases as illustrating that the connections between procedure and substance, and the core notion of due diligence, are far less settled than one might have assumed.[47] One might go further, however, and conclude that the court's approach sidesteps the full implications of the harm prevention rule in international environmental law.[48] After all, it is not primarily an obligation not to cause harm, but an obligation to take diligent steps to prevent harm. It is, in other words, an obligation of conduct.[49] As such, whether harm results or not, the rule is violated when a state's conduct falls short of what due diligence requires. Furthermore, this result should obtain even if the due diligence failures are procedural in nature.[50] While it may seem counterintuitive at first glance to suggest that a procedural failure might suffice to breach a substantive obligation, this is precisely what the harm prevention rule entails. This result is entirely consistent with the importance of prevention in environmental protection and, in turn, with the crucial role that procedural duties play in enabling harm prevention.[51] These duties are central to the shift in international environmental law from the older, relatively amorphous, 'negative' duty to avoid harm to the modern 'positive' duty to take concrete steps to protect the environment.[52]

3. *Prevention and precaution*

A third area of ambiguity revolves around the boundary between the harm prevention rule and the precautionary principle. Notionally, the harm prevention rule applies when a risk of significant harm is foreseeable. By contrast, the precautionary principle is triggered even when there is some uncertainty as to the existence of a risk of serious or irreversible harm.[53] But in practice, and even conceptually, it is difficult to draw a clear

case' in Paula Almeida and Jean-Marc Sorel (eds), *Latin America and the International Court of Justice: Contributions to International Law* (Routledge 2017) 309.

46 See eg Pulp Mills case (n 10) (Joint Dissenting Opinion Al-Khasawneh & Simma) 120 (regretting that the ICJ missed an 'opportunity to clarify the relationship between procedural and substantive obligations'); and see Certain Activities case (n 11) (Separate Opinion of Judge Donoghue) [9] (noting that 'a failure to exercise due diligence to prevent significant transboundary harm can engage the responsibility of the State of origin even in the absence of material damage to potentially affected States').

47 See Brunnée, 'Procedure and Substance' (n 39).

48 See also Brent (n 23) 56.

49 See also Responsibilities in the Area case (n 25) [110]; Certain Activities case (n 11) (Separate Opinion of Judge Donoghue) [9]; ILC draft articles on prevention (n 16) 154; Birnie *et al* (n 15) 143; Proelβ (n 20) 77; Pierre-Marie Dupuy, 'Reviewing the Difficulties of Codification: On Ago's Classification of Obligations of Means and Obligations of Result in Relation to State Responsibility' *European Journal of International Law*, 10/2 (1999): 375, 379.

50 See also Birnie *et al* (n 15) 177.

51 See also Maljean-Dubois and Richard (n 45).

52 See also French (n 2) 181.

53 See Duvic-Paoli (n 2) 265–266.

line between prevention and precaution. For example, in defining the risk that triggers the harm prevention rule, the ILC's Draft Articles on Prevention stipulate a range from 'a high probability of causing significant transboundary harm' to 'a low probability of causing disastrous transboundary harm'.[54] In its commentary, the ILC observes that the duty to act diligently in harm prevention 'could involve ... such measures as are appropriate by way of abundant caution, even if full scientific certainty does not exist, to avoid or prevent serious or irreversible damage'.[55] In so doing, the ILC invokes the most common formulation of the precautionary principle, found in Principle 15 of the Rio Declaration.[56]

The 2011 Advisory Opinion of the Seabed Chamber of the International Tribunal on the Law of the Sea (ITLOS) on *Responsibilities in the Area* appears to build on the ILC's approach and locates the ultimately fluid line between prevention and precaution in the notion of due diligence.[57] The ITLOS Chamber emphasizes the contextual nature of the due diligence standard, which it considers may differ inter alia in light of the risks involved in a given activity.[58] The implication is that due diligence provides a bridge between the duty to prevent environmental harm and the proposition that, even in the absence of 'full scientific certainty', states must take precautionary measures to 'prevent environmental degradation'.[59] According to the Chamber, 'the precautionary approach is ... an integral part of the general obligation of due diligence'.[60] The due diligence obligation, which requires states 'to take all appropriate measures to prevent damage', therefore 'applies in situations where scientific evidence concerning the scope and potential negative impact of the activity in question is insufficient but where there are plausible indications of potential risks'.[61] The Chamber concludes that a state 'would not meet its obligation of due diligence if it disregarded those risks'.[62]

While this perspective seems sensible in many respects, it remains to be seen whether its fluid approach to prevention and precaution, in addition to finding the support of expert bodies,[63] will be more widely embraced in international practice. The perhaps most significant implication of this approach to prevention and precaution is the increased importance that it accords to procedural obligations, including in particular EIA obligations, and the lowering of thresholds that it entails for the triggering of these obligations. The ICJ has remained cautious. It did not pick up on the approach, let alone

54 ILC draft articles on prevention (n 16) art 2(a).
55 Ibid, 155, commentary on art 3, para 14.
56 Ibid; and see Rio Declaration (n 13) principle 15.
57 Responsibilities in the Area case (n 25) [116].
58 Ibid [117].
59 See Rio Declaration (n 13) principle 15.
60 Responsibilities in the Area case (n 25) [131].
61 Ibid.
62 Ibid.
63 See eg International Law Association (ILA), 'Report of the seventy-fifth conference held at Washington' (2014) 22, 'ILA Legal Principles relating to Climate Change', principles 7A, 7B; commentary (supporting the approach).

the ITLOS Chamber's Advisory Opinion, in its discussion in *Costa Rica v Nicaragua/Nicaragua v Costa Rica* of due diligence and of the risk threshold necessary to trigger the EIA obligation.[64]

III. THE HARM PREVENTION RULE AS A REFERENCE POINT FOR INTERNATIONAL ENVIRONMENTAL LAW

The conceptual questions explored in Section II shape the harm prevention rule's implications for the functioning of international environmental law. For example, whether or not a breach of the rule presupposes causation of harm affects the application of the law of state responsibility and the recourse to judicial processes. In turn, the harm prevention rule's due diligence nature and its enduring transboundary impact focus provide a frame of reference for the distinctive features of treaty-based approaches to international environmental concerns.

A. The Law of State Responsibility

The law of state responsibility is triggered by breaches of a rule of international law.[65] In international environmental law, recourse to the law of state responsibility is most likely to follow from a breach of the harm prevention rule or one of the associated procedural obligations. That is because the harm prevention rule is uncontested as a rule of general international law, such that any state that is exposed to a risk of significant transboundary harm that emanates from activities in another state can invoke the rule against that state.[66] The attendant procedural obligations will tend to play a central role in this context. They are relevant in assessing whether the state in question made diligent efforts to prevent transboundary harm. Furthermore, it is likely to be considerably easier to establish that required procedural steps were not taken than it would be to show that regulatory or oversight measures were inadequate. It is not surprising, therefore, that the recent ICJ cases on transboundary environmental impacts revolved around the harm prevention rule and, more specifically, the attendant procedural requirements, such as EIA, notification, and consultation.

64 See Certain Activities case (n 11) 705–707, 719–722.

65 'Report of the International Law Commission on the work of its fifty-third session' (2001) UN Doc A/56/10, ch IV.E—'Draft Articles on Responsibility of States for Internationally Wrongful Acts, with commentaries', arts 1, 2.

66 See ibid, art 42 (on invocation of responsibility).

At first glance, one might assume that state responsibility for a breach of the harm prevention rule would presuppose proof of the causation of significant transboundary environmental harm, making it a legal long shot. Indeed, it could be quite difficult to establish the causal links between activities in one state and particular harm in another, especially when the states concerned are not immediate neighbours. But, as suggested in Section II.B.2, successful invocation of the harm prevention rule does not in fact require proof of actual or future harm.[67] Since the harm prevention rule is not an obligation of result but rather an obligation of conduct, a breach occurs when the relevant state's conduct falls short of what due diligence required.[68] Hence, a plaintiff state must establish a risk of significant transboundary harm and show that the other state failed to take the preventive steps appropriate in light of that risk. In other words, the harm prevention rule and the related procedural obligations are potentially powerful legal tools. They can help ensure that states take the concrete steps that transboundary harm prevention requires in practice.

Furthermore, the harm prevention rule could be consequential even in relation to complex problems such as climate change.[69] In invoking the rule, an island or coastal state would not need to show a causal link between another state's emissions and actual or imminent damage to it from sea level rise. It would need to show risk and lack of diligent preventive measures.[70] Using the ILC's risk spectrum from 'high probability of significant harm' to 'low probability of disastrous harm' as a yardstick,[71] it should not be difficult to establish the requisite risk. Indeed, we now live in a world of high probability of disastrous climate harm,[72] certainly as far as small island nations are concerned.

What would be gained by deploying the law of state responsibility in this way? Perhaps counterintuitively, the primary objective of this approach would not be compensation for harm, but confirmation and concretization of what diligence requires of states in the context of climate change.[73] The consequences that the law of state responsibility would attach to a breach of the harm prevention rule explain why. Only if a state

[67] See nn 36, 49, and accompanying text.

[68] See ILC draft articles on prevention (n 16) 154 ('It is the conduct of the State of origin that will determine whether the State has complied with its [due diligence] obligation'); see also Dupuy, 'Reviewing the Difficulties of Codification' (n 49); Ilias Plakokefalos, 'Prevention Obligations in International Environmental Law' (2012) *Yearbook of International Environmental Law*, 23/1 (2012): 3, 31–32.

[69] See Jutta Brunnée, 'International Environmental Law and Community Interests: Procedural Aspects' in Eyal Benvenisti and Georg Nolte (eds), *Community Interests Across International Law* (OUP 2018) 151; Brent (n 23) 29–30.

[70] See Daniel Bodansky, Jutta Brunnée, and Lavanya Rajamani, *International Climate Change Law* (OUP 2017) 45, 48–49.

[71] ILC draft articles on prevention (n 16) art 2(a).

[72] See Intergovernmental Panel on Climate Change (IPCC), *Global warming of 1.5°C—Special Report* (2018) Summary for Policymakers.

[73] Bodansky *et al*, *ICCL* (n 70); René Lefeber, 'Climate Change and State Responsibility' in Rosemary Rayfuse and Shirley Scott (eds), *International Law in the Era of Climate Change* (Edward Elgar 2012) 321, 341.

can show that another state's lack of diligent preventive action resulted in the specific harm it suffers would compensation be a possible remedy.[74] By contrast, the most likely legal consequence of a failure to exercise diligence, absent proof of harm, would be the obligation to cease the internationally wrongful act, and thus to comply with the duty to take appropriate preventive measures.[75] Given the difficulties of establishing causation, for the purposes of general international law, the development of more specific criteria for climate diligence, therefore, may well be the most valuable result of an invocation of the law of state responsibility.[76]

Lest I be accused of undue optimism as to the potential of the harm prevention rule, a few caveats are in order. First, so far the ICJ has been unwilling to fully embrace the preventive logic of the harm rule.[77] The *Pulp Mills* and *Costa Rica v Nicaragua/Nicaragua v Costa Rica* decisions suggest that the ICJ distinguishes between the duty to take diligent steps to *prevent* significant transboundary harm, which it then deals with under the rubric of separate procedural obligations, and the duty to take diligent steps not to *cause* harm, which it considers cannot be violated simply by a failure to act diligently.[78] It appears, then, as if the ICJ considers significant harm to be an element of the primary rule, rather than a factor that is relevant in determining the legal consequences of and remedies for a breach. Second, the flipside of the proposition that harm prevention entails a duty to act diligently is that, even when significant harm results, the rule will not be violated as long as a state can show that it has exercised due diligence.[79] Third, to date, the harm prevention rule at custom has been deployed only in cases involving immediately neighbouring states. Although the notion of transboundary harm prevention should encompass any inter-state situation,[80] it has not been invoked in relation to risks of long-range or diffuse impacts.[81] The least developed part of the harm prevention rule concerns impacts beyond the jurisdiction of states. Yes, states are obligated to prevent harm to areas beyond national jurisdiction, but is that obligation owed *erga omnes*, such that 'all States can be held to have a legal interest' in compliance with it?[82] Clear state practice in relation to the commons dimension of the harm prevention rule is lacking. The ILC's Draft Articles on Prevention, for their part, are explicitly limited to

[74] See generally Sands and Peel (n 18) 749–750.

[75] See Lefeber (n 73); Philippe Sands, 'Climate Change and the Rule of Law: Adjudicating the Future in International Law' *Journal of Environmental Law*, 28/1 (2016): 19, 31.

[76] See also Daniel Bodansky, 'The Role of the International Court of Justice in Addressing Climate Change: Some Preliminary Reflections' *Arizona State Law Journal* 49/3 (2017) 689, 709, 712.

[77] See also Brent (n 23) 56.

[78] Brunnée, 'Procedure and Substance' (n 39).

[79] See Bodansky *et al*, *ICCL* (n 70) 45–46.

[80] See ILC draft articles on prevention (n 16) 152, art 2(c).

[81] However, Legality of Nuclear Weapons case (n 8) did involve such a context, suggesting that the harm prevention rule could be invoked by affected states in comparable circumstances.

[82] *Barcelona Traction, Light and Power Company, Limited (Belgium/Spain) (New Application: 1962)* (Judgement) [1970] ICJ Rep 3 [33]; but see also [91] (requiring a concrete treaty mechanism to provide standing). For a discussion, see Bodansky *et al*, *ICCL* (n 70) 49–51.

'harm caused in the territory of or in other places under the jurisdiction or control of a State other than the State of origin'.[83]

B. Judicial Processes

When it comes to the avenues for giving legal effect to international environmental protection goals, states must contend not only with the parameters provided by the harm prevention rule and the law of state responsibility, but also with the procedural rules that constrain recourse to international courts and tribunals. For present purposes, suffice it to focus on the ICJ as a court of general jurisdiction. Contentious cases are contingent on the consent of the states concerned.[84] So far, this precondition has been met primarily in cases involving neighbouring states, accounting for the ICJ's case law on the harm prevention rule. In line with the uncertainties surrounding the *erga omnes* effect of the harm prevention rule, the ICJ has not pronounced itself on that aspect of the rule. It remains unclear, therefore, whether and under what circumstances a state would have standing under general international law to invoke the harm prevention rule in relation to risks to or impacts on a commons.[85]

Some commentators rightly suggest that, outside of the transboundary context narrowly conceived, an Advisory Opinion may be a more promising option for deploying the harm prevention rule, giving the ICJ an opportunity to 'perform its most important role ... , namely to clarify and elaborate the relevant norms of general international law'.[86] Standing issues would not arise in this context, and it would be possible to frame the question put to the court in such a way as to sidestep the question of the role of harm in the primary rule, and the need to prove causation. The focus could be squarely on what the harm prevention rule requires of states, including what due diligence entails in relation to global issues such as climate change. But the route to an Advisory Opinion is constrained by its own procedural requirements. Specifically, the request for an Advisory Opinion must be made by an organ of the United Nations,[87] most commonly the General Assembly. While it has been possible to carefully craft questions so as to secure the required majority of votes even for highly contentious issues, the ICJ has not yet the opportunity to offer an Advisory Opinion squarely focused on the harm prevention rule.[88] An initiative by Palau to ask the court to opine on states' legal responsibility to ensure that any activities on their territory that emit greenhouse gases do not harm other

[83] ILC draft articles on prevention (n 16) art 2(c).
[84] ICJ Statute, art 36.
[85] See Brunnée, 'Community Interests' (n 69) 161–162.
[86] See Bodansky, 'Role of ICJ' (n 76) 712; Sands (n 75).
[87] UN Charter, art 96; see also art 18.3 (requiring a majority vote).
[88] In the context of Legality of Nuclear Weapons case (n 8) the harm prevention rule was relevant only as one of several considerations that might constrain the legality of states' recourse to nuclear weapons.

states was abandoned in the face of resistance from key countries.[89] It is worth noting that Palau had framed the proposed question in terms of the inter-state aspect of the harm prevention rule, not the commons aspect, a choice that underscores the enduringly state-centric practice relating to the rule.

C. Treaty-Based Approaches

So far, I have made the case that the harm prevention rule is not only the core rule of customary international environmental law, but also provides a potentially promising legal tool-kit for states in curbing transboundary environmental impacts. But for all its potential, today's complex regional and global environmental problems exceed the capacity of the rule. Multifaceted collective action challenges that implicate multiple states with widely ranging priorities and capabilities cannot be solved on the basis of a rule that remains predominantly focused on inter-state impacts. Furthermore, notwithstanding the importance of the due diligence standard as a background rule of conduct in general international law, such an open-textured standard cannot support the finely calibrated responses required to deal with large-scale problems like long-range transboundary air pollution, ozone depletion, or climate change. The parameters of the harm prevention rule illustrate, therefore, why treaty-based approaches were needed to address the vast majority of international environmental concerns today. It is in this sense that the harm prevention rule provides a reference point not only for general international law, but also for MEAs.

Treaty-based approaches typically invoke the harm prevention rule in general international law as a background norm,[90] but also provide tailored substantive and procedural duties to advance parties' collective harm prevention goals. For example, MEAs can enshrine specific information gathering, risk assessment, information exchange, and consultative duties.[91] These procedural requirements, which elaborate upon states' procedural obligations under general international law, help prepare the ground for and further develop substantive standard setting. While, at customary law, much of the substance of harm prevention is furnished by the requirements that flow from the due diligence standard, in the treaty context dedicated procedures exist for the elaboration of highly specific substantive standards.[92] For the most part, the substantive standards generated under the auspices of MEAs, such as emission standards or reduction targets, provide obligations of result.[93] Thus, whether or not a party acted diligently in meeting

[89] See Aaron Korman and Giselle Barcia, 'Rethinking Climate Change: Towards an International Court of Justice Advisory Opinion' *Yale Journal of International Law Online*, 37 (Spring 2012): 35; Stuart Beck and Elizabeth Burleson, 'Inside the System, Outside the Box: Palau's Pursuit of Climate Justice and Security at the United Nations' *Transnational Environmental Law* 3/1 (2014): 17, 26.

[90] See Fitzmaurice (n 14).

[91] See Brunnée, 'Community Interests' (n 69) 167–168.

[92] Ibid, 168–170.

[93] See eg Bodansky *et al*, *ICCL* (n 70) 172 (commenting on obligations of result in the Kyoto Protocol); Mayer (n 20) 115. But note also that the Paris Agreement, to the extent that it does provide substantive

the standard will be irrelevant in assessing its compliance with its commitments. Finally, MEAs can also provide for mechanisms that are animated by the collective interest of all treaty parties in promoting the widest possible compliance with treaty commitments.[94] The enforcement of the harm prevention rule at customary law, by virtue of the parameters and constraints explored in the preceding sections, is bound to be highly selective. By contrast, treaty-based compliance mechanisms can be designed with a view to systematic performance assessment, while also enabling accommodation of and assistance to states with capacity limitations.

IV. CONCLUSION

The harm prevention rule is the normative cornerstone of international environmental law. It serves as a reference point for international environmental law in a number of interrelated ways. First, it is the point of origin of international environmental law. Second, notwithstanding the ambiguities that obscure its full preventive potential, the harm prevention rule is central to the normative structure of customary international environmental law. It provides the yardstick for a range of procedural obligations, whether these are understood as independently existing rules of customary law or as anchored in the rule's due diligence standard. Third, the harm prevention rule should be understood as an obligation of conduct that requires states to exercise due diligence in the face of risks of significant transboundary environmental harm. Fourth, conceiving of the rule in this way reveals that it provides a potentially strong basis for the invocation of the law of state responsibility and recourse to international courts and tribunals, at least in the context of inter-state impacts. Fifth, the potential of the harm prevention rule is more limited in relation to environmental harm beyond the limits of national jurisdiction and in the context of complex, polycentric environmental problems. Finally, the harm prevention rule has nonetheless served as a baseline for multilateral approaches to international environmental protection, and its inherent constraints help illuminate many of the key features of contemporary environmental agreements.

BIBLIOGRAPHY

Leslie-Anne Duvic-Paoli, *The Prevention Principle in International Environmental Law* (CUP 2018)

Kerryn Anne Brent, 'The Certain Activities Case: What Implications for the No-Harm Rule?' *Asia Pacific Journal of Environmental Law*, 20/1 (2017): 28

requirements, casts them as obligations of conduct. See Christina Voigt, 'The Paris Agreement: What is the Standard of Conduct for Parties?' *Questions of International Law, Zoom-In*, *26* (24 March 2016): 20.

[94] See Brunnée, 'Community Interests' (n 69) 170–172.

Jutta Brunnée, *Procedure and Substance in International Environmental Law* (vol 40, Collected Courses of the Hague Academy of International Law (*Recueil des Cours*), Brill 2020)

Duncan French, 'Trail Smelter (United States of America/Canada) (1938 and 1941)' in Eirik Bjorge and Cameron Miles (eds), *Landmark Cases in Public International Law* (Hart 2017) 159

René Lefeber, 'Climate Change and State Responsibility' in Rosemary Rayfuse and Shirley Scott (eds), *International Law in the Era of Climate Change* (Edward Elgar 2012) 321

CHAPTER 17

SUSTAINABLE DEVELOPMENT

JORGE E VIÑUALES

I. INTRODUCTION

SUSTAINABLE development is the main concept underpinning our policy response to the environmental crisis the world faces. As such, it is pervasive in all sorts of documents, writings, and discourse, including legal ones and, within the latter, international legal instruments.[1] Its ubiquitous character is only matched by its vagueness; and its vagueness is a deliberate choice driven by its function, which is to rally rather than to divide.[2]

This chapter examines the concept of sustainable development specifically from the perspective of international law. It investigates three main aspects: (1) the conceptual history of sustainable development; (2) the legal meaning attached to this concept; and, on the basis of these two aspects, also (3) the nature, functions, and practical operation of sustainable development in international legal practice. The emphasis is placed on (2) and (3) because (1) is examined in detail elsewhere in this volume.[3]

One major challenge that must be overcome when writing about sustainable development is the conceptual fog coating a large part of the work in this area. This is partly due to the deliberate vagueness of the concept, which lends itself to far too many (mis-)interpretations. To navigate this difficulty, one must strike a balance amongst three competing considerations, namely the conceptual aspects of sustainable development (which sometimes misrepresent its legal use), the actual practice in the use of this concept (which is sometimes incoherent and difficult to conceptualize clearly), and

[1] See the Bibliography at the end of the chapter.

[2] See Jorge Viñuales, 'The Rise and Fall of Sustainable Development' *Review of European, Comparative and International Environmental Law*, 22/1 (2013): 3.

[3] See Chapter 2, 'Origin and History', in this volume.

its inherent ethical dimension (which requires a view of what sustainable development 'should' be). I cannot claim that this chapter solves this set of equations, but they have been specifically taken into account. The balance struck in this chapter prioritizes actual practice, with the normative dimension and the conceptual clarity coming in the second and third place, respectively. This will become clearer as the discussion unfolds.

II. THE CONCEPT OF SUSTAINABLE DEVELOPMENT IN HISTORICAL PERSPECTIVE

Historically, the concept of 'sustainable development' is a newcomer. Although it was in use already in 1980,[4] it was only brought to the centre stage of global environmental governance much later, between 1987 and 1992. This period saw the transformation of sustainable development from a policy proposal made in the influential report of the Brundtland Commission, 'Our Common Future',[5] into the conceptual epicentre of global environmental governance, at the 1992 Rio Conference. The Rio Conference and, particularly, the Rio Declaration,[6] brought the concept of sustainable development to the forefront, as the embodiment of a compromise between two—still—competing considerations: development (whether economic or social) and environmental protection.

Before 1992, the tension between these two considerations had received less consensual articulations. The first such attempt was made at a meeting held in Founex, one year before the 1972 Stockholm Conference. At Founex, a fragile conceptual truce was reached between development and environment, whereby the primary environmental responsibility of developing and newly independent countries was deemed to be development.[7] As Indira Gandhi, then India's Prime Minister, put it in her address at Stockholm: '[a]re not poverty and need the greatest polluters? … The environment cannot be improved in conditions of poverty'.[8]

The Founex approach was not the only solution to the environment-development equation considered in the early years of global environmental governance. Other concepts were proposed, each representing a deeper strand of thought, including the

[4] IUCN, UNEP, and WWF, *World Conservation Strategy: Living Resource Conservation for Sustainable Development* (1980).

[5] World Commission on Environment and Development, *Our Common Future* (OUP 1987).

[6] *Report of the United Nations Conference on Environment and Development* (UN 1993) vol I, annex I.

[7] 'The Founex Report on Development and Environment' (4–12 June 1971) paras 1.4, 1.5.

[8] Indira Gandhi, 'Man and Environment', Plenary Session of United Nations Conference on Human Environment Stockholm (14 June 1972).

concepts of 'de-growth',[9] 'eco-development',[10] and even the 'green economy', which was first launched in the 1980s[11] and made a comeback after the 2008 economic crisis. These concepts and their associated programmes can be organized along a spectrum ranging from de-growth, which questioned the very idea of growth and development, to the green economy, which essentially presented environmental policy as the best industrial policy approach to achieve prosperity. Concepts such as eco-development, which came to represent the Founex approach, and sustainable development, were somewhere between the two poles of the spectrum. Thus, from the standpoint of conceptual history, sustainable development was but one contender among several others until the Brundtland Commission selected it and the Rio Conference 'crowned' it.

As a conceptual synthesis, sustainable development offered two major advantages. First, it was less associated with a specific stance or country group than 'eco-development' or the 'green economy'. Secondly, the very vagueness of the concept made it malleable enough to rally all countries to the cause right after the end of the Cold War, in what appeared to be a unique window for global normative re-organization. A quarter of a century after the 1992 Rio Conference, one can better appreciate the merits and the shortcomings of such a conceptual bet. The bet indeed paid off as far as normative development is concerned. Since the 1990s, virtually all countries have rallied behind the concept of sustainable development and that, in turn, has facilitated the adoption of several treaty regimes bringing together developed and developing countries. Yet, that convening power was premised on the 'original sin' of sustainable development: its deliberate vagueness. Such vagueness has become a major obstacle in attempts to go beyond the mere adoption of new law and into its effective implementation.

The conceptual evolution of global environmental governance, and the place of sustainable development within it, are summarized graphically in Figure 17.1.[12] This graphic representation draws a line that starts with a view of nature as a 'natural resource' to be exploited for the benefit of each state, epitomized by UN General Assembly Resolution 1803(XVII) on 'Permanent Sovereignty over Natural Resources',[13] and ends with our current horizon, the sustainable development goals (SDGs) adopted in 2015 as the core of the 2030 Agenda for Sustainable Development.[14] The integrated and participative

[9] For founding works see Nicholas Georgescu-Roegen, *The Entropy Law and the Economic Process* (Harvard University Press 1971); Nicholas Georgescu-Roegen, *Demain la décroissance: entropie-écologie-économie, préface et présentation d'Ivo Rens et Jacques Grinevald* (Favre 1979).

[10] See Koula Mellos, *Perspectives on Ecology: A Critical Essay* (Palgrave Macmillan 1988) ch 3; for a founding work see Ignacy Sachs, *Stratégies de l'écodéveloppement* (Editions économie humanisme, 1980).

[11] See David Pearce, Anil Markandya, and Edward Barbier, *Blueprint for a Green Economy* (Earthscan 1989).

[12] Viñuales, 'Rise and Fall' (n 2).

[13] UNGA RES 1803/27, 'Permanent Sovereignty over Natural Resources' (14 December 1962) UN Doc A/RES/1803/XVII.

[14] UNGA RES 70/1, 'Transforming our World: The 2030 Agenda for Sustainable Development' (21 October 2015) UN Doc A/RES/70/1.

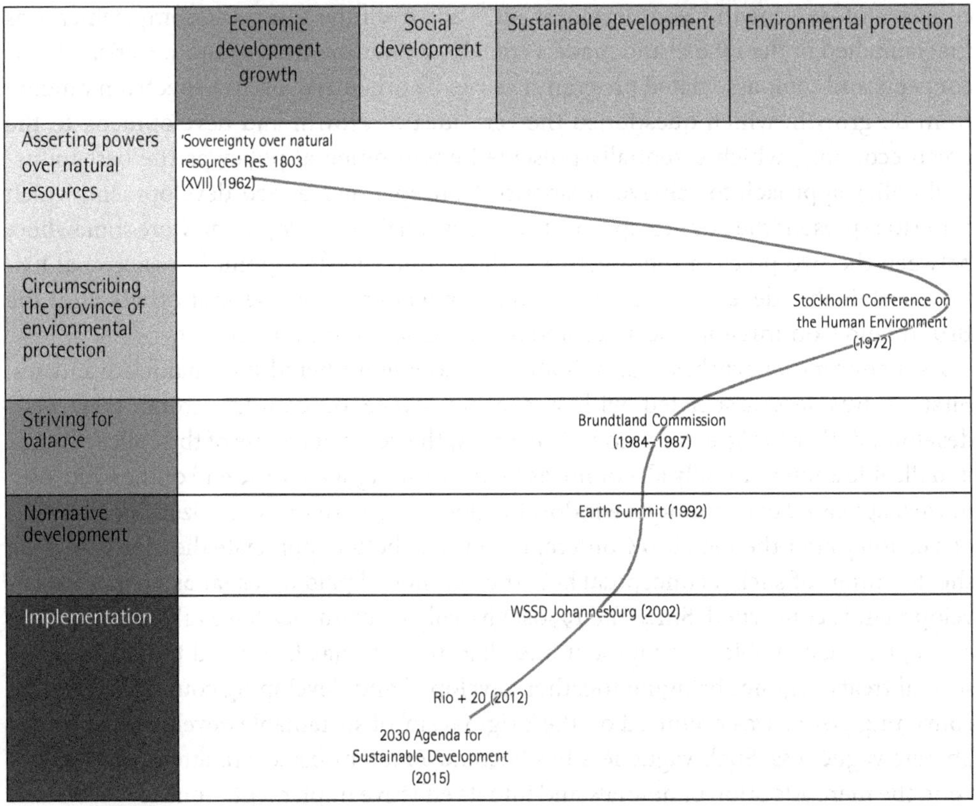

FIGURE 17.1 The conceptual evolution of sustainable development

nature of the SDGs must certainly be praised. 'Development' no longer refers to the situation of 'developing' countries but, as presently understood, it also encompasses 'growth' and it is hence applicable also to developed countries. In other words, 'development' now means prosperity. The SDGs provide a momentous and, in practice, influential guide for action for all countries. But at no point in the entire strategy is environmental protection clearly and unambiguously prioritized over economic and social development. This is the broad context in which international environmental law must operate and where the legal concept of sustainable development 'should' be understood.

III. 'SUSTAINABLE' DEVELOPMENT FROM A LEGAL STANDPOINT

The determination of the legal content of the concept of sustainable development presupposes two premises, which, in turn, can only be derived from an analysis of practice. The first premise is that sustainable development is not only a concept but also a 'norm' and, more specifically, a norm of international law. The second is that the legal content of such a norm can be sufficiently ascertained.

The first premise can be derived from a simple observation, namely that the concept of sustainable development has been referred to in legal practice, not only in policy instruments[15] but also in treaties[16] and judicial decisions.[17] Such references are not merely descriptive, as could be the reference to a certain fact or set of facts (eg development disparities or an emergency situation); they refer to sustainable development as a norm, understood as a prescriptive or permissive proposition which entails legal effects (prescribes or permits the operation of other interlocked norms).[18] I will investigate the nature, identity (across legal sources), and operation of such a norm in Section IV. For now, it is sufficient to observe that sustainable development is not merely a concept, such as de-growth, eco-development, or the green economy, but a normative concept.

The second premise assumes the first but goes a step further. It holds that, as a norm, sustainable development has distinctive or identifiable content. The ascertainment of this content involves two separate inquiries. First, one must determine the content of this norm in a discursive context where there are competing accounts of it. Secondly, and most importantly, one must identify the process or method followed to determine the content of the norm. Different processes are likely to lead not only to different

[15] Rio Declaration (n 6); *Report of the United Nations Conference on Environment and Development* (UN 1993) vol I, annex II, 'Agenda 21'; *Report of World Summit on Sustainable Development* (UN 2002) 1, 'Political Declaration' and 6, 'Plan of Implementation'; UNGA RES 66/288, 'The Future We Want' (11 September 2012) UN Doc A/RES/66/288; 2030 Agenda (n 14).

[16] See Section IV.B.2.

[17] See in chronological order *The Gabčíkovo-Nagymaros Project (Hungary/Slovakia)* (Judgement) [1997] ICJ Rep 7 (Gabčíkovo-Nagymaros case) [140]; *United States—Import Prohibition of Certain Shrimp and Shrimp Products* (Appellate Body Report) [12 October 1998] WTO Doc WT/DS58/AB/R (Shrimp/Turtle case) [131], [153]; *Social and Economic Rights Action Center (SERAC) and the Center for Economic and Social Rights (CESR) v Nigeria*, African Commission on Human Rights and Peoples' Rights (2001) Communication no 155/96 (Ogoni case) [52]; *Hatton v UK* (Judgement) Grand Chamber ECtHR (8 July 2003) Application no 36022/97; *Hatton v UK* (Joint Dissenting Opinion of Judges Costa, Ress, Turmen, Zupancic, and Steiner) [1]; *Award in the Arbitration regarding the Iron Rhine ('Ijzeren Rijn') Railway between the Kingdom of Belgium and the Kingdom of the Netherlands* (2005) 27 RIAA 35 (Iron Rhine Railway case) [57]–[59]; *Pulp Mills on the River Uruguay (Argentina/Uruguay)* (Provisional Measures, Order of 13 July 2006) [2006] ICJ Rep 133 [80]; *Pulp Mills on the River Uruguay (Argentina/Uruguay)* (Judgement) [2010] ICJ Rep 14 (Pulp Mills case) [75]–[77], [177]; *Award in the Arbitration regarding the Indus Waters Kishenganga between Pakistan and India* (Partial Award of 18 February 2013) 31 RIAA 1 (Indus Waters Kishenganga case) [448]–[452]; *China—Measures Related to the Exportation of Various Raw Materials* (Appellate Body Report) [30 January 2012] WTO Doc WT/DS394/AB/R (China—Raw Materials case) [306]; *China—Measures Related to the Exportation of Rare Earths, Tungsten, and Molybdenum* (Panel Report) [26 March 2014] WTO Doc WT/DS431-3/R (China—Rare Earths case) [7.263]; *State Obligations in Relation to the Environment* (Advisory Opinion) IACtHR (2017) OC-23/17 (State Obligations case) [52]–[55].

[18] For a clarification of the set of propositions that can be described as norms see Georg von Wright, *Norm and Action: A Logical Enquiry* (Routledge and Kegan Paul 1963) 1.

contents but also to different normative implications. For this reason, the second inquiry is more fundamental than the first and, as noted earlier, I shall prioritize actual practice over both moral preference and conceptual clarity. Thus characterized, the second inquiry consists of reviewing actual practice to determine the content of 'sustainable development' as a norm and, first and foremost, the 'practice' on the basis of which one can assert that sustainable development is not a mere concept, but a norm. To remove any major ambiguities, I will rely primarily on treaties in force and, above all, the case law explicitly referring to 'sustainable development'.

Relying on such a body of practice, 'sustainable' development means: (i) development which, as a necessary procedural step, 'takes into account' environmental protection (integration); and (ii) which does so in a way that is consistent with the environmental treaty obligations undertaken by a country or, at the very least, with the core content of customary international environmental law applicable to all countries (ie the prevention principle, integrating the duty of due diligence in the context of environmental protection, as further expressed in procedural form by the duty to co-operate and the duty to conduct an environmental impact assessment (EIA)).[19] This understanding is suggested by the first judicial recognition, in explicit terms, of the 'concept of sustainable development' by the International Court of Justice (ICJ) in the case concerning the *Gabčíkovo-Nagymaros Project*.[20]

The procedural step of 'tak[ing] into consideration' new environmental norms is often called 'integration'. There is ample support for integration in the case law[21] and this requirement is seen as a step towards the achievement of sustainable development.[22] But this step is not sufficient to determine the content of 'sustainable' development as such. For development to be 'sustainable': 'new norms and standards ... set forth in a great number of instruments' have to be given 'proper weight'.[23] Those norms and standards encompass both treaties and a range of other instruments codifying general international law. The relevant treaties involve many multilateral environmental treaties (MEAs) with almost universal participation but also regional and bilateral treaties.[24] But the minimal core content of the concept is the one recognized in general international

[19] See Chapter 23, 'Customary International Law and the Environment', in this volume.

[20] Gabčíkovo-Nagymaros case (n 17) [140] (italics added).

[21] See Shrimp/Turtle case (n 17) [131], [153]; *S.D. Myers Inc. v Canada* (Partial Award) NAFTA Arbitration (UNCITRAL Rules) (13 November 2000) [247]; Hatton v UK (Judgement) (n 17) [128]; Iron Rhine Railway case (n 17) [59]; Pulp Mills case (n 17) [177]; Indus Waters Kishenganga case (n 17) [449]; China—Raw Materials case (n 17) [306]; China—Rare Earths case (n 17) [7.263]; State Obligations case (n 17) [52].

[22] See Virginie Barral, 'Sustainable Development in International Law: Nature and Operation of an Evolutive Legal Norm' *European Journal of International Law*, 23/2 (2012): 377, 381; Pierre-Marie Dupuy, 'Où en est le droit international de l'environnement à la fin du siècle?' *Revue générale de droit international public*, 101/4 (1997): 873, 891.

[23] Gabčíkovo-Nagymaros case (n 17) [140].

[24] For examples of integration of environmental protection by reference to standards not included in the treaties at stake in the dispute see Iron Rhine Railway case (n 17) [59]; Pulp Mills case (n 17) [75]–[77]; Indus Waters Kishenganga case (n 17) [451].

law. To determine such content, a finer-grained analysis is necessary to distill from other judicial decisions what the inquiries conducted by different international courts and tribunals regarding this issue converge on.

A close examination of the relatively limited set of decisions that makes explicit and unambiguous reference to 'sustainable development' supports the proposition that 'sustainable' development means development in accordance with customary international environmental law. In the case concerning the *Iron Rhine Railway*, the tribunal specifically discussed the *Gabčíkovo-Nagymaros* case and concluded that 'where development may cause significant harm to the environment there is a duty to prevent, or at least mitigate, such harm (see paragraph 222). This duty, in the opinion of the Tribunal, has now become a principle of general international law'.[25] Paragraph 222 of the award explicitly refers to the prevention principle, recognized as a customary norm in the ICJ's *Advisory Opinion on the Legality of Nuclear Weapons*.[26] In the *Pulp Mills* case, the ICJ reasoned that the need to integrate economic and environmental considerations embodied in the concept of sustainable development was achieved *in casu* 'through the performance of both the procedural and the substantive obligations laid down by the [applicable river treaty]'.[27] In turn, these obligations were presented as specific treaty applications of core customary norms.[28] Such understanding has been subsequently confirmed in at least three other cases decided in different fora.[29]

The evidence discussed so far demonstrates that sustainable development is indeed a norm and that its content must be determined by reference to the evolving treaty and customary law of environmental protection. This conclusion has three important implications. First, despite the contribution of some earlier studies to the conceptual clarification of sustainable development,[30] they do not represent accurate statements of the content of sustainable development in positive international law. Their contribution, and perhaps their fundamental purpose, lies in an attempt at formulating what sustainable development 'should' be (moral preference) and at clarifying how it inter-relates

[25] Iron Rhine Railway case (n 17) [57]–[59], [222].

[26] *Legality of the Threat or Use of Nuclear Weapons* (Advisory Opinion) [1996] ICJ Rep 226 [29].

[27] Pulp Mills case (n 17) [75]–[77].

[28] Ibid [101] (referring to the prevention principle), [204] (recognizing for the first time the customary requirement to conduct an environmental impact assessment), and [77], [102], [144]–[146] (referring to the duty of cooperation).

[29] Indus Waters Kishenganga case (n 17) [450] (expressly stating that 'sustainable development' is translated through the duty to conduct an environmental impact assessment and the duty of vigilance and prevention); China—Rare Earths case (n 17) [7.110]–[7.111], [7.260]–[7.265] (referring to the principle of sustainable development as requiring prevention of environmental harm); State Obligations case (n 17) [55] (stating that, as a result of the interconnection between sustainable development and human rights, the principles of general international environmental law can be relied upon to determine the scope of the human rights guaranteed by the ACHR).

[30] See UN Commission on Sustainable Development, 'Report of the Expert Group Meeting on Identification of Principles of International Law for Sustainable Development' (26–28 September 1995); 'ILA New Delhi Declaration of Principles of International Law Relating to Sustainable Development' (6 April 2002); Michael Decleris, *The Law of Sustainable Development: General Principles* (European Commission 2000).

with a range of other principles (conceptual clarity). Secondly, treaty and customary law do evolve and, over time, that evolution will place increasingly stringent conditions for development to be genuinely 'sustainable'. Thirdly, as discussed next, sustainable development is a peculiar type of norm, a 'normative concept', which cannot perform some functions unless it is decomposed into more specific norms.

IV. THE OPERATION OF SUSTAINABLE DEVELOPMENT IN LEGAL PRACTICE

A. The Nature of Sustainable Development as a Norm

When the ICJ first recognized the 'concept' of sustainable development, Judge Weeramantry appended a Separate Opinion dissenting with the majority on this point and calling for its recognition as a 'principle'.[31] This dissension epitomizes a broader debate in the scholarship as to the nature of 'sustainable development'.[32]

Here again, my focus will be on actual practice rather than on normative stances or attempts at conceptual clarification. For present purposes, it will suffice to make three observations. First, from the perspective of general international law, particular weight must be given to the position of the majority of the ICJ, which has confirmed the characterization of 'sustainable development' as a 'concept' in a subsequent decision.[33] Secondly, the reservations expressed by Judge Weeramantry must be situated in their historical context. What he seemed to fear was a characterization that would deprive 'sustainable development' of 'normative value'. Yet, with the benefit of hindsight, such 'normative value' has indeed been ascribed to the concept. As noted earlier, unlike 'eco-development', the 'green economy' or 'de-growth', 'sustainable development' is not a mere concept, but a normative concept. Thirdly, as discussed in more detail in the next section, using different terms such as a 'concept' or a 'principle' to characterize 'sustainable development' is only relevant if such characterization carries different legal consequences.

The third observation raises an additional point. It assumes an analytical cartography of consequences or functions. These cartographies can be built in such a way as to reach a pre-determined conclusion driven by an end purpose (reflecting practice, asserting a moral preference, or enhancing conceptual clarity). That may well be an unavoidable feature of any account, but at the very least one must state explicitly the approach selected. My priority in this chapter is accuracy from a practitioner's perspective. The approach followed in the next section thus endeavours to provide an accurate

[31] Gabčíkovo-Nagymaros case (n 17) (Separate Opinion of Vice-President Weeramantry) 88.

[32] See the Bibliography at the end of the chapter.

[33] Pulp Mills case (n 17) [75]–[77].

reflection of legal practice. It relies on an analytical cartography under which whether a norm is a 'concept' or a 'principle' depends upon the function it performs in practice. In this account, the main difference between 'concepts' and 'principles' is that, unlike the former, the latter can perform a 'decision-making' function, that is, operate as a primary rule of obligation governing the conduct of states and on the basis of which a case can be decided. From this perspective, 'sustainable development' is a concept. This will become clearer in the following discussion.

B. Functions of Sustainable Development as a Norm

1. *Analytical distinctions*

In order to map the operation of sustainable development in legal practice, it is necessary to follow a clear methodology that sets both the reach and the limits of the inquiry. In this section, I rely on a methodology that I developed in some of my earlier work.[34]

This methodology is based on a distinction between three main functions. First, a norm may perform an 'architectural function' in that it may shape, at least partly, a treaty (or a section thereof), a legally-linked set of treaties or, more generally, a policy instrument (eg an agenda). I will call 'normative impact' the extent to which the concept of sustainable development has performed an architectural function. Given the nature of sustainable development, the normative impact can be expected to be vast. But, in my discussion, I will only include a sub-set of instruments selected on the basis of their importance (only major instruments, both binding and non-binding) and their representative character (only instruments adopted in or after the 1992 Rio Conference). Secondly, a norm may perform an 'interpretive function' in that it is relied upon to clarify another norm, or to update its content (a peculiar form of clarification involving an intertemporal element), or to reconcile competing norms or the values underpinning them (another peculiar type of clarification seeking to harmonize different legally protected interests). Thirdly, a norm may perform a 'decision-making function' when it can be relied upon, as such and without reference to related but more specific norms, as a primary rule of obligation defining a conduct to decide a case. I will call 'jurisprudential relevance' the extent to which a norm can perform interpretive and decision-making functions.

As I shall endeavour to show, the concept of sustainable development performs only architectural and interpretive functions. So far, it has not performed a decision-making function in international adjudication and that is possibly an inherent rather than a merely practical limitation. Indeed, to the extent that the 'sustainable' component is defined by reference to treaty norms, it is not the concept of sustainable development as

[34] See Jorge Viñuales, 'The Rio Declaration on Environment and Development: Preliminary Study' in Jorge Viñuales (ed), *The Rio Declaration on Environment and Development: A Commentary* (OUP 2015) 20.

such which is used to decide the case but the relevant treaty norm. As for cases where the 'sustainable' component is defined by reference to customary norms, so far in all relevant cases the controlling norm was one of the expressions of the concept of sustainable development (ie the prevention principle, the duty to cooperate, and the duty to conduct an environmental impact assessment). Even if other possible expressions of the concept of sustainable development are considered, such as the procedural requirement to 'take into account' environmental protection or to interpret existing norms in the light of environmental standards, the decision-making function would be performed by a standalone principle (eg the principle of integration or, more likely, a specific application of systemic integration or intertemporal law) or the function itself would be different (an 'interpretive' rather than a 'decision-making' function).

2. *Normative impact*

The normative impact of the concept of sustainable development can be assessed at different degrees of specificity. At a rather general level, references to 'sustainable development' appear in a number of important instruments, including non-binding policy instruments,[35] environmental agreements,[36] and even agreements focusing on other matters.[37] Of particular note, at this first level, are the references to 'sustainable development' in the 1992 Rio Declaration,[38] the 1995 Marrakesh Agreement establishing the World Trade Organization (WTO), the 1992 UNFCCC (United Nations Framework Convention on Climate Change), and, more recently, the 2030 Agenda for Sustainable Development and 2015 Paris Agreement. Yet, this level is too general to ascertain whether the concept of sustainable development has indeed played an 'architectural function'.

At a second and more specific level, it appears that the concept of sustainable development has indeed performed an architectural function in the design of some important action plans, particularly Agenda 21 (1992), the 2002 Johannesburg Plan of Implementation, the 2012 Outcome document of the Rio+20 Summit and, above all, the 2030 Agenda for Sustainable Development (2015). The latter is noteworthy for its attempt at integrating the economic, social, and environmental dimensions of development.[39] Yet, the integrative dimension is only one aspect of the legal concept of

[35] See policy instruments detailed in n 15.

[36] 1992 UNFCCC, art 3.4; 1997 Kyoto Protocol, arts 2.1, 10 (chapeau), 12.2; 2015 Paris Agreement, preamble, arts 2.1, 4.1, 6.1, 6.2, 6.4, 6.8, 6.9, 7.1, 8.1, 10.5; 1992 Convention on Biological Diversity, art 8(e) (otherwise reference to 'sustainable use'); 2000 Cartagena Protocol on Biosafety, preamble (mutually supportive); 2010 Nagoya Protocol, preamble; 1994 UNCCD, preamble, arts 1(b), 5(b), 9.1, 18.1, annex I – art 6, annex II – art 3.1, annex III – art 2(c), annex V – art 2(i); 1995 Straddling Fish Stocks Agreement, art 24.1; 1997 UN Convention on Law of Non-Navigational Uses of International Watercourses, art 24.2(a); 1998 Rotterdam Convention, preamble; 1999 Protocol on Water and Health to the 1992 Convention on Transboundary Watercourses and International Lakes, preamble, arts 1, 4.4(c); 2001 Stockholm Convention on Persistent Organic Pollutants, art 7.3.

[37] See in particular 1995 Marrakesh Agreement establishing the World Trade Organization, preamble.

[38] See Rio Declaration (n 6) principles 4, 8.

[39] 2030 Agenda (n 14) para 55.

sustainable development. The other aspects, whether formulated in treaty or customary norms, are less present in the SDGs. Very few agreements and legal norms are explicitly referred to in the SDGs, in relation to economic development (eg the WTO, particularly the TRIPs Agreement[40]), social development (eg human rights[41] or the WHO Framework Convention on Tobacco Control[42]) and environmental protection (eg the UNFCCC,[43] UNCLOS,[44] and international agreements of public access to information[45]). But this may be explained by the fact that neither the SDGs nor the wider 2030 Agenda are intended to be legal instruments or to emphasize legal standards.

To find a clearer influence on the shaping of legal instruments, one must look beyond these policy instruments and track specific sections or even provisions of certain agreements. This third level of inquiry is much more specific and, within the limits of this chapter, it can only be illustrated. I will take two examples. The first concerns the 'sustainable development' provisions and chapters included in a growing number of bilateral and regional trade agreements concluded by the European Union (EU) since 2007,[46] following the mandate given in the 2006 Global Europe Communication[47] and the 2006 Renewed Sustainable Development Strategy (SDS).[48] Such provisions/chapters have been included in the EU economic partnership agreements with CARIFORUM states,[49] South Korea, Central America, Colombia, and Peru. As a general matter, they contain a reference to sustainable development as part of the 'context and objectives', which is then fleshed out by provisions on the right to regulate, the role of MEAs, the obligation not to lower environmental regulation to attract trade and investment, the promotion of green trade and investment, cooperation and implementation mechanisms, among others.[50] The second illustration is provided by the shaping of two specific 'market mechanisms',

[40] Ibid, SDG 3, target 3(b), referring to the 1994 Agreement on Trade-Related Aspects of Intellectual Property Trade.

[41] Ibid, SDG 4, target 4.7, referring to human rights indistinctly.

[42] Ibid, SDG 3, target 3(a), referring to the 2003 World Health Organization Framework Convention on Tobacco Control.

[43] Ibid, SDG 13, target 13(a), referring to 1992 UNFCCC.

[44] Ibid, SDG 14, target 14(c), referring to the 1982 UNCLOS (United Nations Convention on the Law of the Sea).

[45] Ibid, SDG 16, target 16.10 referring to instruments on public participation indistinctly.

[46] Rok Želc, 'Environmental Integration in EU Trade Policy: The Generalised System of Preferences, Trade Sustainability Impact Assessments and Free Trade Agreements' in Elisa Morgera (ed), *The External Environmental Policy of the European Union: EU and International Law Perspectives* (CUP 2012) 174–203.

[47] Commission of the European Countries, 'Global Europe: Competing in the world: A contribution to the EU's Growth and Jobs Strategy' (4 October 2006) COM(2006) 567.

[48] EU Council, 'Review of the EU Sustainable Development Strategy (EU SDS)—Renewed Strategy' (26 June 2006) 21 <http://register.consilium.europa.eu/doc/srv?l=EN&f=ST%2010917%202006%20 INIT> accessed 16 December 2019.

[49] The Forum of Caribbean States (CARIFORUM) brings together the following countries: Antigua and Barbuda, The Bahamas, Barbados, Belize, Cuba, Dominica, Dominican Republic, Grenada, Guyana, Haiti, Jamaica, St. Kitts and Nevis, Saint Lucia, St. Vincent and the Grenadines, Suriname, and Trinidad and Tobago.

[50] Želc (n 46) 195–200.

respectively in Article 12 of the Kyoto Protocol (the 'Clean Development Mechanism') and in Article 6.4 of the Paris Agreement (often called 'Sustainable Development Mechanism'). In both cases, the purpose of the mechanism is to conduct, in more efficient terms, mitigation projects while at the same time contributing to the development of the country hosting the project. The CDM operated for several years, raising problems such as the concentration of projects in some emerging economies, the perverse incentives to maintain certain sectors only to profit from the carbon credits (technically 'certified emission reductions') resulting from them or, more generally, matters of environmental integrity. Thus, one should not overstate its achievements. Whether these challenges are inherent to the vagueness of the concept of sustainable development is unclear. The failure so far[51] to reach agreement on the specifics of the SDM suggests that the ability of the concept of sustainable development to genuinely perform an architectural function and shape a legal mechanism is limited by its vagueness.

3. *Jurisprudential relevance*

The legal concept of sustainable development has played a significant role in international adjudication, but only from the perspective of its 'interpretive function'. As noted earlier, a norm may perform such a function when it is used to clarify or update another norm or to conciliate competing norms or the values underpinning them. The concept of sustainable development has explicitly performed this function in a number of cases. In what follows, I provide some illustrations relying on those cases where 'sustainable development' is expressly mentioned as part of the legal reasoning of an international court or tribunal. I must note, however, that the legal 'concept', 'objective', or 'notion' relied upon is, in some cases, enshrined in a treaty rather than directly derived from customary international law.

The basis for the analysis is provided by the aforementioned excerpt of the ICJ judgement in the *Gabčíkovo-Nagymaros* case, where the court noted, by reference to environmental norms, that they had 'to be taken into consideration, and … given proper weight, not only when States contemplate new activities but also when continuing with activities begun in the past'.[52] *In casu*, there was an explicit provision in the applicable treaty allowing for the application of new norms. In order to fully understand the reach of this statement, it is therefore useful to see its operation in some other cases. In some cases, the 'objective' of sustainable development expressly mentioned in the preamble of the 1995 Marrakesh Agreement establishing the WTO has been relied upon to interpret certain terms in a legally-linked treaty, namely the 1994 GATT and, more specifically, its Article XX. Thus, in *Shrimp/Turtle*, the WTO Appellate Body reasoned that the terms 'exhaustible natural resources' in Article XX(g) of the GATT had to 'be read by a treaty interpreter in the light of contemporary concerns of the community of nations about the protection and conservation of the environment'[53] and, in this light,

[51] Decision 8/CMA.1, 'Matters relating to Article 6 of the Paris Agreement and paragraphs 36–40 of decision 1/CP.21' (19 March 2019) UN Doc FCCC/PA/CMA/2018/3/Add.1.

[52] Gabčíkovo-Nagymaros case (n 17) [140].

[53] Shrimp/Turtle case (n 17) [129].

they included not only mineral but also living resources, such as turtles. Similarly, in *China—Raw Materials*, after referring to the 'objective of sustainable development' the Appellate Body stated that it understood 'the WTO Agreement, as a whole, to reflect the balance struck by WTO Members between trade and non-trade-related concerns'[54] but then concluded that such considerations could not change the content of China's Accession Protocol. A more detailed discussion of this question was provided in *China—Rare Earths*, where the Panel made an explicit reference to the 'principle' of sustainable development as embodied in Principles 2 (prevention) and 4 (integration) of the Rio Declaration.[55] The reference to the Rio Declaration to support reasoning under the WTO Agreement is noteworthy.

Other adjudicative bodies have made reference to sustainable development or, at least, to integration, even in the absence of a specific treaty basis. In *S.D. Myers v Canada*, an investment arbitration tribunal operating under Chapter 11 of the 1992 NAFTA (North American Free Trade Agreement) relied on the Rio Declaration to consider, as part of the principles relevant to interpret Article 1102 of the NAFTA (non-discrimination), the idea that 'environmental protection and economic development can and should be mutually supportive'.[56] In *Hatton v UK*, a dissenting opinion signed by five judges relied on two non-binding instruments, Principle 1 of the 1972 Stockholm Declaration and Article 37 of the European Union's Charter of Fundamental Rights (which expressly refers to sustainable development), to conclude that Article 8 of the 1950 European Convention on Human Rights should have been interpreted to accord more protection to the environment.[57] Although less clear, the role of sustainable development in the *Ogoni* case before the African Commission also deserves mention. The Commission reasoned that Article 24 of the 1981 African Charter on Human and Peoples' Rights (the collective right to a generally satisfactory environment) required Nigeria 'to take reasonable and other measures ... to secure an ecologically sustainable development and use of natural resources'.[58]

But these decisions do not provide a concrete and clear basis to understand the type of interpretive function performed by the concept of sustainable development. In order to reach that higher level of specificity, one must rely on three other decisions[59] where (i) the concept of sustainable development was specifically referred to, (ii) without any express basis in the applicable treaty, and (iii) with a sufficiently elaborate reasoning to understand the implications of interpreting a norm in the light of this concept.

In the *Iron Rhine* case, the arbitral tribunal had to consider whether to take into account environmental protection considerations in interpreting a treaty between Belgium and the Netherlands dating back to 1839. The tribunal expressly framed its

54 China—Raw Materials case (n 17) [306].
55 China—Rare Earths case (n 17) [7.263].
56 Myers case (n 21) [247].
57 Hatton v UK (Joint Dissenting Opinion) (n 17).
58 Ogoni case (n 17) [52].
59 Iron Rhine Railway case (n 17); Indus Waters Kishenganga case (n 17); State Obligations case (n 17).

analysis as a matter of 'inter-temporality in the interpretation of treaty provisions'.[60] Its reasoning sheds light on the three questions identified above. Indeed, it expressly relies on 'the concept of sustainable development' (by reference to the ICJ) as it arises from general international law and, importantly, it does so with two specific consequences. First, sustainable development is used to interpret and, more specifically, to update a treaty that makes no mention of sustainable development and, given its date of conclusion, could not possibly imply any such consideration. Secondly, the specific consequence of interpreting this treaty in the light of the concept of sustainable development is the applicability of the prevention principle, which is mentioned in the first sentence and further specified in paragraph 222 of the award. Thus, the concept of sustainable development is not only a matter of systemic integration (as in the *Shrimp/Turtle* case) but also, explicitly, one of intertemporal law. This conclusion is confirmed by the reasoning of the tribunal in the *Indus Water Kishenganga* case.[61]

In both hypotheses (systemic integration and intertemporal law), the specific result is the need to interpret the relevant norm (eg a treaty) in the light *not of the concept of sustainable development as such* but of the more specific norms that embody the 'sustainable' aspect of sustainable development. In the *Iron Rhine* case, the tribunal made this point explicitly.[62] Similarly, in the *Indus Water Kishenganga* case, the arbitral tribunal noted that what it called (relying however on the ICJ) the 'principle' of sustainable development 'translate[d]' into the duties to conduct an EIA and, more generally, to prevent environmental harm.[63] The same conclusion can be reached by reference to the *Advisory Opinion of the ICtHR on the relations between environmental protection and human rights*. The court noted indeed that '[a]s a consequence of the close connection between environmental protection, sustainable development and human rights', which it also characterized as the 'interdependence and indivisibility between human rights and environmental protection', the court could 'make use of the principles, rights and obligations of international environmental law, which as part of the international *corpus juris* contribute in a decisive manner to set the scope of the obligations arising from the American Convention in this area'.[64]

The latter point is also relevant to the assessment of the 'decision-making function' of the concept of sustainable development. I noted earlier that, so far, the concept has not performed a decision-making function and it is doubtful that it could do so. In the cases reviewed, the concept of sustainable development is relevant but somewhat removed from the primary norm governing the conduct of the state. The specific operation of the concept is to require a certain approach to interpretation (whether in the form of systemic integration or intertemporal law) and thereby to render applicable, for

[60] Iron Rhine Railway case (n 17) [57]–[59].
[61] Indus Waters Kishenganga case (n 17) [452].
[62] Iron Rhine Railway case (n 17) [222].
[63] Indus Waters Kishenganga case (n 17) [450].
[64] State Obligations case (n 17) [55] (my translation from the Spanish original).

interpretation purposes, the specific primary rules of obligation (prevention, cooperation, EIA) defining the 'sustainable' aspect of sustainable development.

Such norms can perform an interpretive function but also, quite clearly, a decision-making function. Several examples of the latter, both old and new, can be identified such as the *Trail Smelter* arbitration,[65] the *Costa Rica/Nicaragua* case,[66] or the *South China Sea* arbitration.[67] Even when the concept of sustainable development may appear to have a permissive effect, as suggested by a passage of the Panel Report in *China—Rare Earths*, it does not operate as a standalone primary norm. It is, in fact, the underlying primary rule (interpreted in the light of a norm such as the prevention principle) which remains controlling.[68] For these reasons, following my previous observations in Section IV.A, sustainable development must be considered a normative 'concept', rather than a 'principle'.

V. 'SUSTAINABLE' VS 'DEVELOPMENT'

The analysis of the history and legal expression of the concept of sustainable development conducted in this chapter shows that over the last half of a century, there has been a deliberate effort to reconcile, conceptually and legally, the terms of the environment-development equation. As noted earlier, the very concept of the sustainable development was selected to draw a veil over these differences and rally all countries to the cause. But this approach has not solved the equation. The tension between these two competing terms remains.

From the first Founex meeting in June 1971, we have certainly made progress in understanding the scale and seriousness of the problem we face. Certain concepts, such as those of 'Planetary boundaries'[69] or the 'Anthropocene',[70] have been developed to convey the unprecedented magnitude of the crisis. However, the crisis is not being successfully tackled. The reason is that we are still not ready to prioritize the environment over prosperity. This problem is not merely expressed but indeed embodied in the concept of 'sustainable development'.

This conclusion emerges from the reliance on the economic theory of externalities. An externality is the effect of a transaction on those not participating in it (third parties). If such effects are harmful, we speak of 'negative externalities'. Environmental

[65] *Trail Smelter Arbitration (United States/Canada)* (1938 and 1941) 3 RIAA 1905, 1965 (no harm).

[66] *Certain Activities Carried Out by Nicaragua in the Border Area (Costa Rica/Nicaragua)* and *Construction of a Road in Costa Rica along the San Juan River (Nicaragua/Costa Rica)* (Judgement) [2015] ICJ Rep 665 [162] (duty to conduct an EIA).

[67] *The South China Sea Arbitration (Philippines/China)* (Final award of 12 July 2016) PCA Case no 2013-19 [941], [964], [966] (prevention).

[68] China—Rare Earths case (n 17) [7.110]–[7.111].

[69] See Johan Rockström *et al*, 'A Safe Operating Space for Humanity' *Nature*, 461/7263 (2009): 472.

[70] See Paul Crutzen, 'Geology of Mankind' *Nature*, 415/6867 (2002): 23.

degradation, even on the scale of climate change, massive species extinction, or, all together, the Anthropocene epoch where humans are the defining geological force, are still seen as mere negative externalities of a transaction or, more specifically, a body of transactions that today is called 'development'. International law, much like law in general, first organizes the legal aspects of the transaction (eg through sovereign prerogatives, investment law, trade law, etc) and only then places an additional layer of regulation dealing with the negative environmental externalities. What we call international environmental law is, with rare exceptions (eg the moratorium of commercial whaling), the law of externalities, and it is becoming even more so due to the excessive reliance on market mechanisms. This external layer is only allowed to interfere with the underlying transaction up to a certain point beyond which the legal organization of the transaction prevails. The *India—Solar Cells* case epitomizes this problem.[71] The local content requirements introduced by India were certainly illegal under international trade law. Yet, if we are realistic about tackling climate change, India must move massively into renewable energy, and we cannot politically expect that the massive transfer of public resources involved in a feed-in-tariff scheme will be operated with no economic benefit for the local industry.

The illegality of India's scheme is but one illustration of a much wider and deeper phenomenon. International law and, as I have written elsewhere,[72] law in general are built upon an asymmetry whereby productive transactions are first organized and only later is an additional layer of law introduced to tackle the externality, within clearly defined limits. We have grown so used to this asymmetry that we no longer see it. It is at the heart of all instruments that call for 'development' (organization of the transaction) to be 'sustainable' (additional layer to tackle the 'externality'). At the margin, 'sustainable' will no longer be able to accommodate 'development' and, under the current thinking, development is organized so as to prevail.

There have been a few rare occasions in history when the outrage arising from certain transactions of massive economic importance led to their outright banning. The banning of slavery was one such example. In an attempt to keep the legal recognition of the transaction, there were efforts to improve the lives of slaves (tackling merely the 'externality'), while keeping them legally subjected. In the absence of such wide-ranging prohibition (eg a legally mandated phase-out of fossil-fuels), another possibility may be that, in a display of Schumpeterian creative destruction, some new technological choices may diffuse in time to render our current pathways to development uncompetitive and obsolete.[73] This appears to be the hope of political decision-makers today. It is a bet, based on the egoism and lack of courage of the political class but also of all of us who timidly exercise our political rights; and the stakes have never been higher.

[71] See *India—Certain Measures Relating to Solar Cells and Solar Modules* (Appellate Body Report) [16 September 2016] WTO Doc WT/DS456/AB/R.

[72] See Jorge Viñuales, *The Organisation of the Anthropocene: In Our Hands?* (Brill 2018).

[73] See Jean-François Mercure *et al*, 'Macroeconomic Impact of Stranded Fossil-Fuel Assets' *Nature Climate Change*, 8/7 (2018): 588.

BIBLIOGRAPHY

Virginie Barral, *Le développement durable en droit international* (LGDJ 2015)

Pierre-Marie Dupuy and Virginie Barral, 'Principle 4: Sustainable Development through Integration' in Jorge Viñuales (ed), *The Rio Declaration on Environment and Development: A Commentary* (OUP 2015) 157

Francesco Francioni, 'Sviluppo sostenibile e principi di diritto internazionale nell'ambiente' in *SIDI, Il principio dello sviluppo sostenibile nel diritto internazionale ed europeo dell'ambiente* (XI Convegno 2007) 41

Katja Gehne, *Nachhaltige Entwicklung als Rechtsprinzip* (Mohr Siebeck 2011)

Vaughan Lowe, 'Sustainable Development and Unsustainable Arguments' in Alan Boyle and David Freestone (eds), *International Law and Sustainable Development* (OUP 1999) 19

José Juste Ruiz, Valentín Franch, and Francisco Coutinho (eds), *Desarrollo Sostenible y Derecho Internacional* (Tirant 2018)

Phillipe Sands, 'International Law in the Field of Sustainable Development' *British Yearbook of International Law*, 65/1 (1994): 303

Nico Schrijver, 'The Evolution of Sustainable Development in International Law' *Le Recueil des Cours de l'Académie de Droit International de La Haye*, 329 (2007): 217

CHAPTER 18

PRECAUTION

JACQUELINE PEEL*

I. INTRODUCTION

THE concept of precaution in international environmental law concerns anticipatory action in response to scientifically uncertain threats of environmental harm. Its most frequently referenced formulation—in Principle 15 of the Rio Declaration on Environment and Development—expresses precaution in the following terms:

> In order to protect the environment, the precautionary approach shall be widely applied by States according to their capabilities. Where there are threats of serious or irreversible damage, lack of full scientific certainty shall not be used as a reason for postponing cost-effective measures to prevent environmental degradation.[1]

Precaution is often characterized as one of the most important innovations of international environmental law. This is because it stands in opposition to the idea—previously widely-accepted—that measures to address environmental threats ought only to be adopted where there exists firm scientific evidence establishing a likelihood of harm.[2] The Rio Declaration's endorsement of precaution in Principle 15 thus introduced to international environmental law a new discourse over the appropriate evidentiary

* This chapter draws on the following previously published works: Philippe Sands and Jacqueline Peel, *Principles of International Environmental Law* (4th edn, CUP 2018) 229–240; Jacqueline Peel, *The Precautionary Principle in Practice: Environmental Decision-making and Scientific Uncertainty* (Federation Press 2005); Jacqueline Peel, 'Precaution: A Matter of Principle, Approach or Process?' *Melbourne Journal of International Law*, 5/2 (2004): 483.

[1] *Report of the United Nations Conference on Environment and Development* (UN 1993) vol I, annex I, principle 15.

[2] Philippe Sands and Jacqueline Peel, *Principles of International Environmental Law* (4th edn, CUP 2018) 230.

foundations of global environmental regulation.[3] While the notion of acting to prevent environmental harm before it materializes has since achieved broad international policy consensus,[4] precaution continues to generate disagreement over its meaning and effect, including the extent of scientific evidence and uncertainty that is required to justify environmentally protective measures.[5] Reflecting these complexities, precaution has spawned a vast legal (and extra-legal) scholarship,[6] as well as significant jurisprudence in the field of international environmental law.[7]

In the available space it is not possible to capture fully the diverse insights on the concept of precaution found in scholarship and practice. Instead, the chapter focuses on four key questions (and attendant debates) regarding precaution that have been critical in understanding its role in international environmental law. These are:

1. The meaning of precaution as a conceptual pillar of international environmental law;
2. The legal status of precaution as a principle of international environmental law;
3. The formulation and understanding of precaution evident from international environmental treaties and case law; and
4. The consequences of applying precaution in decision-making concerning threats of environmental damage.

II. PRECAUTION AS A CONCEPTUAL PILLAR

The concept of precaution seeks to guide the development and application of international environmental law where there is scientific uncertainty. Although debates over the value of precaution in international environmental law continue (with critics seeing it as placing an unnecessary burden on technological development, leading to over-regulation of insignificant environmental risks despite the cost implications),[8] its place as one of the conceptual pillars of the field is now well-established.

[3] Jacqueline Peel, 'Changing Conceptions of Environmental Risk' in Jorge Viñuales (ed), *The Rio Declaration on Environment and Development: A Commentary* (OUP 2015) 75.

[4] Owen McIntyre and Thomas Mosedale, 'The Precautionary Principle as a Norm of Customary International Law' *Journal of Environmental Law*, 9/2 (1997): 221.

[5] See Section II.A.

[6] Key scholarly references are indicated in the Bibliography at the end of this chapter.

[7] Summarized in Section IV.

[8] Kenneth Foster, 'The Precautionary Principle—Common Sense or Environmental Extremism?' *IEEE Technology and Society Magazine*, 21/4 (2002): 8. For a strong critique see Cass Sunstein, *Laws of Fear: Beyond the Precautionary Principle* (CUP 2005).

A. Scientific Uncertainty Over Threats of Harm

The core requirements for invocation of precaution—as reflected in international definitions such as that of Principle 15 of the Rio Declaration—are 'threats of serious or irreversible damage' and 'lack of full scientific certainty'. Where these circumstances arise, precaution provides a justification for action to prevent potential environmental degradation.

While each of the elements of 'threats of … damage' and 'lack of full scientific certainty' may seem straightforward, their interpretation and application in practice has proved more complex. Taken at its most general level, precaution means that states agree to act with caution and foresight when taking decisions about activities that may have adverse environmental impacts.[9] A more focused interpretation requires activities and substances, which may pose environmental threats, to be regulated, and possibly prohibited, even if no conclusive or overwhelming evidence is available regarding the harm or likely harm they may cause to the environment.[10] Although Principle 15 uses mandatory language to describe the need for precaution (lack of full scientific certainty 'shall not be used' as a reason to prevent action), this does not resolve questions over the level of scientific uncertainty sufficient to override arguments for postponing measures, as well as the significance of environmental harms that must be at stake.

It has been suggested in the literature on precaution that the reference to 'full scientific certainty' does not justify its application in the case of *any* uncertainty; something more than 'mere speculation' is required.[11] Indeed, reaching 100% certainty would be beyond the capacity of the science, which is premised on an experimental method that always admits of some potential that observed results are the consequence of chance.[12] Hence, even in the case of well-characterized phenomena and settled theories, some level of scientific uncertainty technically remains.[13]

By the same token, limiting the application of precaution to circumstances where environmental risks are well understood would deny its function to anticipate environmental damage before it becomes fully apparent and too late to prevent. This is the basis for use of the term 'threats of … damage', which connotes the potential for harm rather than a probability of its occurrence.[14]

9 Sands and Peel (n 2) 234.

10 Ibid.

11 Kenisha Garnett and David Parsons, 'Multi-Case Review of the Application of the Precautionary Principle in European Union Law and Case Law' *Risk Analysis*, 37/3 (2017): 502.

12 Peter Riggs, *Whys and Ways of Science: Introducing Philosophical and Sociological Theories of Science* (Melbourne University Press 1992).

13 See further Chapter 15, 'Role of Science', in this volume.

14 Garnett and Parsons (n 11) 503.

Many, albeit by no means all, formulations of precaution qualify the types of threats of damage that justify precautionary action with terms such as 'serious', 'irreversible', or 'significant'.[15] This suggests that the threatened harm must be perceived as carrying with it particularly undesirable consequences, although scientific uncertainty may remain over the actual nature or extent of these consequences.

Principle 15, and a number of other formulations of precaution in international environmental law, also indicate a concern that measures taken to prevent uncertain but serious threats should not ignore cost implications. For instance, both Principle 15 and Article 3.3 of the 1992 United Nations Framework Convention on Climate Change (UNFCCC) refer to '*cost-effective* measures to prevent environmental degradation'. This is generally interpreted to mean that where alternative measures are available to achieve a given environmental objective, the least cost option should be preferred.[16]

Uncertainty in science can arise from a variety of sources, including gaps in knowledge (epistemic uncertainty), inaccurate or inadequate models, theories and methods (methodological uncertainty), or vagueness, context dependence, ambiguity, indeterminacy of theoretical terms, and under-specificity in natural and scientific language (linguistic uncertainty).[17] How significant these sources of uncertainty are for decision-making can often only be judged in light of the particular threats of environmental damage at issue in any case. For example, the international community may have a lower tolerance for uncertainty where there are threats of catastrophic or irreversible harm, but a higher tolerance where threats are less serious, potentially reversible, or offset by other benefits. Such preferences may also reflect cultural orientations to risk in different societies.[18] These factors point to the importance in understanding and applying precaution as part of a holistic assessment of threats and uncertainty. An approach that separates out questions of whether there is a threat of damage and what level of uncertainty exists runs the risk of missing the important interconnections between these concepts. It can also lead to an over-emphasis on the need for 'sufficient' or 'plausible'

[15] See the table in Section III.A.

[16] Mark Geistfeld, 'Implementing the Precautionary Principle' *Environmental Law Reporter*, 31 (2001): 11326, 11327. The principle is generally seen as standing in opposition to cost-benefit analysis although some have proposed approaches for reconciling the two: see David Driesen, 'Cost-Benefit Analysis and the Precautionary Principle: Can they be Reconciled?' *Michigan State Law Review* (2013): 771.

[17] For examples of taxonomies of scientific uncertainty see Helen Regan, Mark Colyvan, and Mark Burgman, 'A Taxonomy and Treatment of Uncertainty for Ecology and Conservation Biology' *Ecological Applications*, 12/2 (2002): 618; Brian Wynne, 'Uncertainty and Environmental Learning: Reconceiving Science and Policy in the Preventative Paradigm' *Global Environmental Change*, 2 (1992): 111; Vern Walker, 'The Siren Songs of Science: Toward a Taxonomy of Scientific Uncertainty for Decisionmakers' *Connecticut Law Review*, 23 (1991): 567.

[18] Ortwin Renn and Bernd Rohrmann, 'Cross-Cultural Risk Perception: State and Challenges' in Ortwin Renn and Bernd Rohrmann (eds), *Cross-Cultural Risk Perception* (Springer 2000) 211.

scientific evidence to establish threats that ignores how uncertainties may compromise the availability and adequacy of such knowledge.[19]

B. Precaution vs Prevention

In thinking about the meaning and operation of precaution in international environmental law, it is useful to draw a distinction between this concept and prevention. The prevention principle concerns measures to prevent or minimize risks of significant transboundary environmental harm.[20] Like precaution, the prevention principle requires action to be taken at an early stage and, if possible, before damage has actually occurred.

Whereas prevention applies to known risks of harm, however, precaution allows anticipatory action to address uncertain threats of damage. Several treaties on freshwater or marine pollution, for example, adopt a preventative approach in the face of well-known risks of pollution from certain substances and hazardous chemicals.[21] Although the probability of a pollution event occurring and the extent of its consequences cannot be precisely known in advance, preventive measures seek to remove the risk or at least minimize it to acceptable levels. By contrast, precaution is applied in circumstances where the nature, extent and/or consequences of a particular threat are scientifically uncertain but enough is known to indicate that a course of cautious and forward-thinking action is warranted.

Over time as scientific knowledge of a particular problem improves, the basis for international environmental action may shift from a precautionary to a preventative footing. This is arguably the situation that now exists in respect of anthropogenic climate change caused by emissions of greenhouse gases. Action pursuant to the UNFCCC was first taken on a precautionary basis, but as scientific understanding of the mechanisms and impacts of climate change has improved, many of the risks are now well-known and require action on a preventative rather than a precautionary basis.[22] This is not to say there is no remaining room for precaution in the climate change regime; in the case of some mooted technological 'solutions', such as geo-engineering, considerable uncertainty exists regarding their environmental impacts, justifying a precautionary approach.[23]

[19] Jacqueline Peel, 'When (Scientific) Rationality Rules: (Mis)Application of the Precautionary Principle in Australian Mobile Phone Tower Cases' *Journal of Environmental Law*, 19/1 (2007): 103.

[20] See Chapter 16, 'Harm Prevention', in this volume.

[21] See Chapters 30 and 31, 'Freshwater Resources' and 'Marine Environment: Pollution and Fisheries', in this volume.

[22] International Law Association (ILA), 'Report of the seventy-fifth conference held at Washington' (2014) 22, 'ILA Legal Principles relating to Climate Change', draft article 7B(3).

[23] Ralph Bodle, 'Geoengineering and International Law: The Search for Common Legal Ground' *Tulsa Law Review*, 46 (2013): 305.

III. PRECAUTION AS A PRINCIPLE OF INTERNATIONAL ENVIRONMENTAL LAW

In international environmental law, the precautionary principle is the legal manifestation of the concept of precaution. The principle is of relatively recent origin, only emerging in international legal instruments in the mid-1980s, although it previously featured as a principle in domestic legal systems, most notably those of Sweden and West Germany.[24] In the period since, the precautionary principle (or the precautionary approach)[25] has been adopted in many international environmental law instruments and treaties. While the formulation of the precautionary principle across these various instruments differs, the language of Principle 15 of the Rio Declaration attracts broad support.[26] Hence, the Declaration's articulation of precaution is often regarded as a pivotal point in acceptance of the principle in international environmental law.[27]

A. Incorporation of Precaution in International Environmental Law Instruments

The emergence of the precautionary principle in international environmental law was heralded by treaty language departing from the previously conventional regulatory approach, which insisted on the existence of probative scientific evidence of a hazard in order to establish a basis for preventive measures.[28] The first reference to precaution in an environmental treaty came with the 1985 Vienna Ozone Convention, which referred in the preamble to parties' recognition of 'precautionary measures' for controlling ozone depleting substances taken at the national and international levels.[29] In the subsequent 1987 Montreal Protocol, parties declared their determination to 'protect the ozone

[24] Staffan Westerlund, 'Legal Antipollution Standards in Sweden' *Scandinavian Studies in Law*, 25 (1981): 223; Sonja Boehmer-Christiansen, 'The Precautionary Principle in Germany—Enabling Government' in Timothy O'Riordan and James Cameron (eds), *Interpreting the Precautionary Principle* (Earthsea 1994) 31. On the domestic implementation of the precautionary principle, see further Chapter 59, 'National Implementation' and Part IX, 'International Environmental Law in National and Regional Courts', in this volume.

[25] See Section III.B.

[26] Sands and Peel (n 2) 230.

[27] Alexandre Kiss, 'The Rio Declaration on Environment and Development' in Luigi Campiglio (ed), *The Environment After Rio: International Law and Economics* (Martinus Nijhoff 1994) 55; James Cameron and Juli Abouchar, 'The Status of the Precautionary Principle in International Law' in David Freestone and Ellen Hey (eds), *The Precautionary Principle and International Law: The Challenge of Implementation* (Kluwer Law 1996) 29, 30.

[28] Sands and Peel (n 2) 230.

[29] preambular recital 5.

layer by taking precautionary measures to control equitably total global emissions of substances that deplete it'.[30]

Incorporation of the precautionary principle in international instruments applicable to other environmental issues followed, with a particular focus on the marine environment. For instance, the Ministerial Declaration of the Second North Sea Conference in 1987 accepted that 'in order to protect the North Sea from possibly damaging effects of the most dangerous substances, a precautionary approach is necessary'.[31] A more general application of the principle, linked to sustainable development, emerged in the 1990 Bergen Ministerial Declaration on Sustainable Development in the United Nations Economic Commission for Europe (UNECE) Region. This Declaration provided that '[i]n order to achieve sustainable development, policies must be based on the precautionary principle',[32] paving the way for the 1992 Rio Declaration's inclusion of precaution as part of the international agenda on the integration of environment and development. The Rio Declaration principles have since been affirmed on numerous occasions, including by the 2012 UN Conference on Sustainable Development (Rio+20) and the accompanying 2030 Agenda for Sustainable Development.[33]

Since the Rio Declaration, many environmental treaties—of both global and regional application—have adopted the precautionary principle or its underlying rationale. As Table 18.1 illustrates, however, there is considerable variation in the formulation of the principle across different environmental treaties.[34]

Lack of consistency in the formulation of the precautionary principle adopted in international environmental treaties contributes to continuing debate over its international legal status. Formulations differ as to the nature of the threatened environmental harm, the extent of scientific uncertainty surrounding any such threat, whether precautionary action is mandatory or merely desirable, and the relevance of cost considerations. At one end of the spectrum, treaties such as the 1991 Bamako Convention and 1992 OSPAR Convention adopt a permissive approach to application of the precautionary principle, allowing invocation where harm to human health or the environment 'may' be caused or there are 'reasonable grounds for concern' but 'no conclusive evidence of a causal relationship between the inputs and the effects'. By contrast, in treaties where the inclusion of precaution was more controversial, such as the UNFCCC and POPs Convention, the formulation adopted is more circumscribed. This is evident in the UNFCCC, which places limits on the application of the precautionary principle through requiring a threat

[30] preambular recital 8.

[31] Ministerial Declaration of the Second International Conference on the Protection of the North Sea (25 November 1987) 27 ILM 835 (1988), para VII.

[32] (16 May 1990) IPE (I/B/16_05_90) para 7.

[33] UNGA RES 66/288, 'The Future We Want' (11 September 2012) UN Doc A/RES/66/288, annex, para 15; UNGA RES 70/1, 'Transforming our World: The 2030 Agenda for Sustainable Development' (21 October 2015) UN Doc A/RES/70/1, Declaration, para 12.

[34] This table presents a selection of treaties only. More comprehensive assessments have been undertaken by authors considering the customary law status of the principle: n 41.

Table 18.1 Formulation of precautionary principle in international environmental treaties

Treaty	Formulation of precaution
1991 Bamako Convention, art 4.3(f)	… the preventive, precautionary approach to pollution which entails, *inter alia*, preventing the release into the environment of substances which may cause harm to humans or the environment without waiting for scientific proof regarding such harm.
1992 Convention on Biological Diversity, preamble	Where there is a threat of significant reduction or loss of biological diversity, lack of full scientific certainty should not be used as a reason for postponing measures to avoid or minimise such a threat.
1992 UNFCCC, art 3.3	The Parties should take precautionary measures to anticipate, prevent or minimize the causes of climate change and mitigate its adverse effects. Where there are threats of serious or irreversible damage, lack of full scientific certainty should not be used as a reason for postponing such measures, taking into account that policies and measures to deal with climate change should be cost-effective so as to ensure global benefits at the lowest possible cost.
1992 OSPAR Convention, art 2.2(a)	The Contracting Parties shall apply … the precautionary principle, by virtue of which preventive measures are to be taken when there are reasonable grounds for concern that substances or energy introduced, directly or indirectly, into the marine environment may bring about hazards to human health, harm living resources and marine ecosystems, damage amenities or interfere with other legitimate uses of the sea, even when there is no conclusive evidence of a causal relationship between the inputs and the effects.
1994 Energy Charter Treaty, art 19	In its policies and actions each Contracting Party shall strive to take precautionary measures to prevent or minimise environmental degradation.
1995 Fish Stocks Agreement, art 6	1. States shall apply the precautionary approach widely to conservation, management and exploitation of straddling fish stocks and highly migratory fish stocks in order to protect the living marine resources and preserve the marine environment. 2. States shall be more cautious when information is uncertain, unreliable or inadequate. The absence of adequate scientific information shall not be used as a reason for postponing or failing to take conservation and management measures.
1996 Protocol to the 1972 London Dumping Convention, art. (1)	In implementing this Protocol, Contracting Parties shall apply a precautionary approach to environmental protection from dumping of wastes or other matter whereby appropriate preventative measures are taken when there is reason to believe that wastes or other matter introduced into the marine environment are likely to cause harm even when there is no conclusive evidence to prove a causal relation between inputs and their effects.

(*Continued*)

Table 18.1 Continued

Treaty	Formulation of precaution
2000 Biosafety Protocol, art 10.6	Lack of scientific certainty due to insufficient relevant scientific information and knowledge regarding the extent of the potential adverse effects of a living modified organism on the conservation and sustainable use of biological diversity in the Party of import, taking also into account risks to human health, shall not prevent that Party from taking a decision, as appropriate, with regard to the import of the living modified organism in question ... in order to avoid or minimize such potential adverse effects.
2001 POPs Convention, arts 1, 8.9	Mindful of the precautionary approach as set forth in Principle 15 of the Rio Declaration on Environment and Development, the objective of this Convention is to protect human health and the environment from persistent organic pollutants. The Conference of the Parties, taking due account of the recommendations of the [POPs] Committee, including any scientific uncertainty, shall decide, in a precautionary manner, whether to list the chemical, and specify its related control measures, in Annexes A, B and/or C.
2002 Northeast Pacific Convention, art 5.6(a)	In order to protect the environment and contribute to the sustainable management, protection and conservation of the marine environment of the region, the Contracting Parties shall: (a) Apply, in accordance with their capacity, the precautionary principle, by virtue of which, when confronted with serious or irreversible threats to the environment, the absence of complete scientific certainty should not serve as a pretext for delaying the adoption of effective measures to prevent environmental degradation, because of the costs involved.
2003 Antigua Convention (Inter-American Tropical Tuna Commission), art IV	1. The members of the Commission, directly and through the Commission, shall apply the precautionary approach ... for the conservation, management and sustainable use of fish stocks covered by this Convention. 2. In particular, the members of the Commission shall be more cautious when information is uncertain, unreliable or inadequate. The absence of adequate scientific information shall not be used as a reason for postponing or failing to take conservation and management measures.
2017 Draft Global Pact for the Environment, art 6	Where there is a risk of serious or irreversible damage, lack of scientific certainty shall not be used as a reason for postponing the adoption of effective and proportionate measures to prevent environmental degradation.

of 'serious or irreversible damage', and by linking the commitment to an encouragement ('should', not 'shall') to take measures that are 'cost effective'.[35]

While the precautionary principle was extensively included in environmental treaties concluded throughout the 1990s and into the first decade of the twenty-first century,

35 Sands and Peel (n 2) 232.

it has been notably absent from more recent instruments such as the 2013 Minamata Mercury Convention and the 2015 Paris Agreement. The latter refers obliquely to the precautionary principle in the preamble through text indicating parties are 'guided by [the UNFCCC's] principles', which include precaution.[36] The preamble to the Minamata Convention also takes this approach, '[r]ecalling the United Nations Conference on Sustainable Development's reaffirmation of the principles of the Rio Declaration on Environment and Development'.[37] However, there are no references to precaution in the substantive provisions of the Convention; instead Article 16 on health aspects speaks of 'science-based' guidelines and preventative programmes.[38]

An exception to this trend is the draft Global Pact for the Environment, which includes a restatement of the precautionary principle as part of its aim 'to adopt a common position and principles that will inspire and guide the efforts of all to protect and preserve the environment'.[39] Nonetheless, differences in formulation of precaution between the draft Pact and other environmental treaties may only serve to increase confusion over its content and meaning.[40]

Based on this state practice, international law scholars and courts have reached different conclusions as to whether the precautionary principle has crystallized as a norm of customary international law.[41] In any event, the diversity of situations to which the precautionary principle may apply suggests that 'the precise consequences of its application in any given case' will vary depending on the nature of the threats at issue and the degree of scientific uncertainty surrounding those threats.[42] Indeed, some scholars have suggested that the debate over the customary law status of the principle is

[36] preambular recital 3.

[37] preambular recital 4.

[38] arts 16.1(a), (b).

[39] Le Club des Juristes: International Group of Experts for the Pact, 'Draft Global Pact for the Environment by the IGEP' (La Sorbonne, 24 June 2017) <https://globalpactenvironment.org/document/draft-global-pact-for-the-environment-by-the-igep/?lang=en> accessed 17 October 2019, preamble, art 6. On 10 May 2018, the UNGA adopted Res 72/277, 'Towards a Global Pact for the Environment' as the first step in negotiations to consider the feasibility of an international instrument on this topic. For discussion of the Pact see Yann Aguila and Jorge Viñuales, 'A Global Pact for the Environment: Conceptual Foundations' *Review of European, Comparative & International Environmental Law*, 28/1 (2019): 3.

[40] Susan Biniaz, '10 Questions to Ask about the Proposed "Global Pact for the Environment"' *Sabin Center for Climate Change Law, Columbia Law School* (August 2017) <http://columbiaclimatelaw.com/files/2017/08/Biniaz-2017-08-Global-Pact-for-the-Environment.pdf> accessed 21 December 2019.

[41] See eg McIntyre and Mosedale (n 4); Arie Trouwborst, 'The Precautionary Principle in General International Law: Combating the Babylonian Confusion' *Review of European, Comparative and International Environmental Law*, 16/2 (2007): 185. For a more sceptical view, see Daniel Bodansky, 'Law: Scientific Uncertainty and the Precautionary Principle' *Environment*, 33/7 (1991):4. For the different positions reached by courts see Aguila and Viñuales (n 39) 6.

[42] Sands and Peel (n 2) 239–240.

a distraction and efforts should instead focus on translating it from vague declaratory formulations into concrete treaty provisions and actions.[43]

B. Approach vs Principle

Contributing to uncertainty over the international legal status and meaning of precaution is debate over whether it is a 'principle' or merely an 'approach'. This debate centres on questions of whether precaution has recognized legal effects or is merely aspirational, whether it prescribes outcomes or simply guides the decision-making process. Principle 15 of the Rio Declaration provides no resolution in this regard. Although it is a 'principle' of the Declaration, the opening sentence refers to wide application of 'the precautionary approach' in order to protect the environment. In international environmental treaties, both formulations—principle and approach—are used, sometimes in preambular statements and sometimes in binding articles, and often interchangeably, raising the question whether the distinction is just a semantic one.[44]

On one view—put forward particularly by the United States—precaution is an 'approach' the content of which may vary from context to context.[45] By contrast, the European Union (EU) has argued on a number of occasions in international disputes that precaution is a 'principle' and, moreover, one that is already 'a general customary rule of international law or at least a general principle of law'.[46] Moreover, under EU environmental law, precaution is a core principle enshrined in Article 191.2 of the Consolidated Treaty on the Functioning of the EU. Other states have taken the middle road seeing the 'precautionary approach' as an emerging 'principle of international law'.[47]

One way of reading the trans-Atlantic precautionary-approach-versus-principle debate is as a reflection of different cultural tolerances of risk and uncertainty between the two regions over particular environmental threats.[48] For their part, developing countries have not engaged in disputes over whether precaution is an approach or principle with the same fervour as their Northern hemisphere counterparts. Even highly precautionary treaties applicable in developing country regions, such as the Bamako Convention, nonetheless refer to the 'precautionary approach'.

[43] Daniel Bodansky, 'Customary (and Not so Customary) International Environmental Law' *Indiana Global Legal Studies Journal*, 3/1 (1995): 105.

[44] Jacqueline Peel, 'Precaution—A Matter of Principle, Approach or Process?' *Melbourne Journal of International Law*, 5/2 (2004): 483.

[45] *European Communities—Measures Concerning Meat and Meat Products (Hormones)* (Appellate Body Report) [16 January 1998] WTO Docs WT/DS26/AB/R and WT/DS48/AB/R (Hormones case) [43]. The US stated that the SPS Agreement, at issue in the case, recognized a precautionary approach (in art 5.7) so there was no need to invoke a 'precautionary principle' to be risk-averse.

[46] Ibid [16].

[47] This was the Canadian argument in Hormones case, ibid [60].

[48] David Vogel, *The Politics of Precaution: Regulating Health, Safety, and Environmental Risks in Europe and the United States* (Princeton University Press 2012).

IV. PRECAUTION IN THE INTERNATIONAL JURISPRUDENCE

Precaution has been frequently raised in international environmental disputes where states have differing views of the importance of action to address uncertain threats of harm. Judicial practice regarding precaution has helped flesh out the requirements for application of the principle in international environmental law,[49] although international courts and tribunals are yet to issue a definitive statement on its international legal status.

The precautionary principle was first raised before the International Court of Justice (ICJ) in New Zealand's 1995 request concerning the resumption of French nuclear testing.[50] Although the ICJ's order did not refer to these arguments,[51] Judge Weeramantry's dissent noted that the principle had 'evolved to meet [the] evidentiary difficulty caused by the fact [that] information required to prove a proposition' may be 'in the hands of the party causing or threatening the damage', and that it was 'gaining increasing support as part of the international law of the environment'.[52]

In the *Gabčíkovo-Nagymaros Project* case, the precautionary principle was once again invoked but not addressed by the ICJ, notwithstanding acknowledged uncertainties over future harm to freshwater supplies and biodiversity threatened by the parties' joint dam project. The court rejected Hungary's defence of necessity as a justification for breaching treaty obligations owed to Slovakia, holding that uncertainties in the available scientific evidence 'could not, alone, establish the objective existence of a "peril" in the sense of a component element of a state of necessity'.[53] Although the decision was criticized by some commentators as a 'missed opportunity',[54] the absence of a precautionary approach may have reflected the ICJ's concern with the application of the law as it stood in 1989 when the precautionary principle had not yet emerged and could not realistically be applied as general international law.

The same could not be said in regard to the *Pulp Mills* case, decided in 2010. In this decision, the ICJ noted the relevance of 'a precautionary approach' in the interpretation and application of an environmental treaty—in that instance, the 1975 Uruguay River

[49] See further Chapters 27 and 58, 'Judicial Development' and 'International Environmental Responsibility and Liability', in this volume.

[50] *Request for an Examination of the Situation in Accordance with Paragraph 63 of the Court's Judgement of 20 December 1974 in the Nuclear Tests (New Zealand v France) Case*, Application instituting proceedings (21 August 1995) [105].

[51] *Request for an Examination of the Situation in Accordance with Paragraph 63 of the Court's Judgement of 20 December 1974 in the Nuclear Tests (New Zealand/France) Case* (Order) [1995] ICJ Rep 288.

[52] Ibid (Dissenting Opinion of Judge Weeramantry) 342.

[53] *The Gabčíkovo-Nagymaros Project (Hungary/Slovakia)* (Judgement) [1997] ICJ Rep 7, 42.

[54] Afshin A-Khavari and Donald Rothwell, 'The ICJ and the *Danube Dam* Case: A Missed Opportunity for International Environmental Law?' *Melbourne University Law Review*, 22 (1998): 507.

Statute. However, it rejected the implication that the principle 'operates as a reversal of the burden of proof'.[55] This statement recognized that the precautionary principle plays a role in international environmental law, albeit in a limited way.

The approach of the International Tribunal for the Law of the Sea (ITLOS) in interpreting the precautionary principle has been markedly more liberal than that of the ICJ. In the *Southern Bluefin Tuna* cases—in response to Australia and New Zealand's request that the tribunal order 'that the parties act consistently with the precautionary principle in fishing for southern bluefin tuna pending a final settlement of the dispute'[56]—ITLOS found that there was 'scientific uncertainty regarding measures to be taken to conserve the stock of southern bluefin tuna' and that the parties should 'act with prudence and caution to ensure that effective conservation measures are taken to prevent serious harm to the stock of southern bluefin tuna'.[57] As Judge Treves noted in his Separate Opinion, while the tribunal's order to the parties to refrain from conducting experimental fishing programmes did not mention the precautionary principle, it reflected a precautionary approach.[58]

Arguments over the need to apply a precautionary approach were also before ITLOS in 2001, in the *MOX Plant* case.[59] Ireland invoked the principle at the provisional measures phase in support of its claim that the United Kingdom had the burden of demonstrating that no harm to the Irish Sea would arise from discharges and other consequences of the operation of the MOX plant, and to inform the assessment by the tribunal of the urgency of the measures sought.[60] ITLOS did not grant the Irish request for suspension of the MOX plant operations. Instead, again referencing considerations of 'prudence and caution', it ordered the parties to cooperate and enter into consultations to exchange further information on possible consequences for the Irish Sea arising out of the commissioning of the MOX plant and to devise, as appropriate, measures to prevent pollution of the marine environment which might result from its operation.[61]

In its *Advisory Opinion on Responsibilities and Obligations in the Area*, the ITLOS Seabed Disputes Chamber noted that, under UNCLOS and related instruments, states sponsoring activities for prospecting and exploration for polymetallic nodules and polymetallic sulphides in the Area had 'the obligation to apply a precautionary approach'.[62] Additionally, the Chamber characterized this approach as 'an integral part of the general

[55] *Pulp Mills on the River Uruguay (Argentina/Uruguay)* (Judgement) [2010] ICJ Rep 14 (Pulp Mills case) 61.

[56] *Southern Bluefin Tuna Cases (New Zealand/Japan; Australia/Japan)* (Provisional Measures, Order of 27 August 1999) [1999] ITLOS Rep 280, 288–289.

[57] Ibid, 296.

[58] Ibid (Separate Opinion of Judge Treves) 318.

[59] *The MOX Plant case (Ireland/United Kingdom)* (Provisional Measures, Order of 3 December 2001) [2001] ITLOS Rep 95.

[60] Ibid, 108–109.

[61] Ibid, 110. See also *Land Reclamation in and around the Straits of Johor (Malaysia/Singapore)* (Provisional Measures, Order of 8 October 2003) [2003] ITLOS Rep 10, 26.

[62] *Responsibilities and obligations of States sponsoring persons and entities with respect to activities in the Area* (Advisory opinion) [2011] ITLOS Rep 10 (Responsibilities in the Area case) 44.

obligation of due diligence of sponsoring States' applicable even outside the scope of the Regulations.[63] The Advisory Opinion provided guidance for interpretation of precaution, finding it applied 'in situations where scientific evidence concerning the scope and potential negative impact of the activity in question is insufficient but where there are plausible indications of potential risks'.[64] While the Chamber did not definitively rule on the international legal status of precaution, it noted that the precautionary approach has been incorporated into numerous international treaties and other instruments that reflect Principle 15 of the Rio Declaration, and that this has 'initiated a trend towards making this approach part of customary international law'.[65]

A more cautious approach to precaution is evident in the rulings of panels and the Appellate Body in the World Trade Organization (WTO) dispute settlement system. In 1998, in the *Hormones* case, the European Community invoked the principle as the basis of a prohibition on imports of US and Canadian meat produced with artificial hormones, given uncertain health impacts. The Appellate Body, however, ruled that the precautionary principle did not override express provisions of the Sanitary and Phytosanitary (SPS) Agreement, although it considered that precaution was reflected in the preamble to, and Articles 3.3 and 5.7 of, the SPS Agreement, noting that this did not exhaust the relevance of the principle.[66] Nonetheless, the Appellate Body found it 'unnecessary, and probably imprudent' to take a position on the customary law status of the precautionary principle.[67] Nearly a decade later, in the *Biotech Products* case, a WTO panel reiterated this view, stating that the legal status of the precautionary principle was 'unsettled' and since it did not need to take a position on whether or not the principle was a recognized principle of international law it would 'refrain from expressing a view on this issue'.[68]

Precaution has also been raised before human rights courts and commissions. In *San Mateo de Huanchor v Peru*, the Inter-American Commission on Human Rights adopted precautionary measures requiring an environmental impact assessment for the removal of sludge.[69] In *Tătar v Romania*, the European Court of Human Rights (ECtHR) acknowledged 'the importance of the precautionary principle' and invoked it in support of its finding that Article 8 of the 1950 European Convention on Human Rights (ECHR) had been violated.[70] In a more recent Advisory Opinion on human rights and the environment issued in November 2017, the Inter-American Court of Human Rights noted that although the status of the precautionary principle in international law may be contested, there was sufficient evidence to conclude that the principle was relevant

63 Ibid, 75.

64 Ibid, 47.

65 Ibid.

66 Hormones case (n 45) 48.

67 Ibid, 47–48.

68 *European Communities—Measures Affecting the Approval and Marketing of Biotech Products* (Panel Report) [29 September 2006] WTO Docs WT/DS291/R, WT/DS292/R, WT/DS293/R, 340–341.

69 (15 October 2004) IACtHR, 504/03, Report No 69/04, OEA/Ser.L/V/II.122 Doc. 5 rev.1, 487.

70 (27 January 2009) ECtHR, 67021/01 (in French).

in determining whether a state had complied with its duties under the 1969 American Convention.[71] The court found that obligations stemming from the rights to life and personal integrity in the American Convention required state parties to act in keeping with the precautionary principle to protect those rights in the event of possible serious and irreversible damage to the environment, even in the absence of scientific certainty.[72] This jurisprudence, along with that of the WTO under the SPS Agreement, reflects the extent to which the precautionary principle in international law has expanded to cover issues of human health and well-being impacted by environmental degradation in addition to 'pure' environmental damage.

V. IMPLEMENTING PRECAUTION

Formulations of precaution in international environmental law direct the adoption of 'precautionary measures' (or at least that such measures should not be postponed where the principle applies). However, international environmental law is generally not prescriptive as to the particular measures that should be applied to implement the precautionary principle. A range of measures might therefore be considered precautionary in different circumstances, depending on the nature of the threatened harm and level of prevailing scientific uncertainty.

Arguably, in assessing what precautionary measures should be adopted, other principles of international environmental law—such as the principle of common but differentiated responsibilities—will also be relevant.[73] Principle 15 of the Rio Declaration notably refers to wide application of the precautionary approach by states 'according to their capabilities'. This may mean that states with a higher level of technical and financial capacity are expected to take more stringent precautionary measures to prevent the realization of uncertain environmental risks than countries that lack such resources.[74]

The types of measures that may be taken to implement the precautionary principle range from prohibitions or bans on products that are seen as necessary to prevent serious, but scientifically unproven, dangers to softer measures such as consultation and prior environmental impact assessment before carrying out potentially harmful activities. In a number of domestic environmental systems, approaches such as adaptive management—a continual process of experimentation with an activity and modification

[71] Maria Banda, 'Inter-American Court of Human Rights' Advisory Opinion on the Environment and Human Rights' *American Society of International Law Insights*, 22/6 (2018).

[72] *State Obligations in Relation to the Environment* (Advisory Opinion) IACtHR (2017) OC-23/17 [180].

[73] See further Chapter 19, 'Differentiation', in this volume.

[74] Responsibilities in the Area case (n 62) 46, 54.

in response to feedback on its effects—have gained popularity as means for implementing the precautionary principle.[75]

Although the terminology of 'adaptive management' is not found in international environmental law, several treaties embrace a similar approach. For example, the 2001 Stockholm POPs Convention calls for an ongoing process of review by the POPs committee to identify further chemicals for listing, with the Conference of the Parties then directed to decide on listing in light of those recommendations 'in a precautionary manner'.[76] The 2003 Antigua Tuna Convention provides that '[w]here the status of target stocks or non-target or associated or dependent species is of concern', the Inter-American Tropical Tuna Commission shall 'subject such stocks and species to enhanced monitoring in order to review their status and the efficacy of conservation and management measures' and 'revise those measures regularly in the light of new scientific information available'.[77]

In international environmental disputes, one specific application of precaution that has been argued for in cases such as *MOX Plant* is reversal of the burden of proof. If adopted, this application of precaution would result in the state wishing to carry out an activity having to prove that its actions would not adversely or significantly affect the environment before being permitted to release potentially polluting substances or carry out a proposed activity. This interpretation could also require national or international regulatory action where the available scientific evidence suggests that lack of action may result in serious or irreversible harm to the environment, or where there are divergent views on the risks of action. However, at least in the context of international disputes, the ICJ has suggested that precaution does not operate as a blanket justification for reversal of the burden of proof.[78]

VI. CONCLUSION

Precaution is one of the most important conceptual pillars of international environmental law because it attempts to respond to the limits of scientific knowledge and put in place measures that will anticipate and ultimately prevent the materialization of environmental threats. In this sense, precaution stands as a challenge to the largely reactive approach of the majority of international environmental law. As a departure from traditional regulatory approaches that require firm scientific evidence of harm before acting, it is perhaps unsurprising that controversy has attended the interpretation and application of precaution in international environmental law. At a deeper level, these

[75] Jan McDonald and Megan Styles, 'Legal Strategies for Adaptive Management under Climate Change' *Journal of Environmental Law*, 26/1 (2014): 25.

[76] art 8.9.

[77] art IV.

[78] Pulp Mills case (n 55) 71.

differences over precaution—including its status in international law, whether it is a principle or approach, and what implementing measures it requires—reflect different societal tolerances of uncertainty in relation to different types of environmental threats.

Current state practice, as reflected in international environmental instruments and arguments put before courts and tribunals in international disputes, demonstrates that, at the very least, precaution makes an important contribution to the interpretation of international law in a manner that enhances the protection of the environment in cases of scientific uncertainty as to the impacts of potentially harmful activities. As these threats grow in their seriousness and unpredictability—as in the case of the potential for planetary tipping points and runaway climate change—the importance of an international legal approach that can act in anticipation of environmental damage is only likely to increase.

BIBLIOGRAPHY

David Freestone and Ellen Hey (eds), *The Precautionary Principle and International Law: The Challenge of Implementation* (Kluwer Law 1996)

Nicolas de Sadeleer, *Environmental Principles: from Political Slogans to Legal Rules* (OUP 2002)

Annecoos Wiersema, 'The Precautionary Principle in Environmental Governance' in Douglas Fisher (ed), *Research Handbook on Fundamental Concepts of Environmental Law* (Elgar 2016) 449

CHAPTER 19

DIFFERENTIATION

PHILIPPE CULLET

I. INTRODUCTION

DIFFERENTIAL treatment between different groups of countries constitutes one of the bases of international environmental law. Such differentiation between the global South (South) and the global North (North) is firmly anchored in the structure of international environmental law that cannot be understood without reference to the various measures taken to reflect the situation of developing and least developed countries.

Differential treatment is one of the main instruments that exist in international environmental law to foster equity. It builds on ideas of global distributive justice and helps to rebalance some of the most visible inequalities arising between formally equal states of very different size, power, and natural resource endowments.[1] The principle that reflects differential treatment in international environmental law is that of common but differentiated responsibilities (CBDR). CBDR has been repeatedly endorsed since the 1990s, including, in the United Nations (UN) summit for the adoption of the post-2015 development agenda.[2] This confirms the central position of differentiation and the intrinsic link between equity and existing international environmental law. This is not surprising in a context where more than thirty years after the release of the Brundtland Commission report,[3] states have neither tackled inequality nor poverty. In such a situation, differentiation is and will remain necessary for the majority of countries of the South for decades to come.

The chapter begins with a discussion of the conceptual bases for and development of differential treatment. This confirms the significance of the break proposed to the traditional international legal framework and explains the continuing opposition

[1] See references in the Bibliography.

[2] UNGA Res 70/1, 'Transforming our World: The 2030 Agenda for Sustainable Development' (21 October 2015) UN Doc A/RES/70/1, Declaration, para 12.

[3] World Commission on Environment and Development, *Our Common Future* (OUP 1987).

to differential treatment by some countries. This chapter then highlights the various manifestations of differential treatment in international environmental law and shows that differential treatment pervades the whole field. While debates tend to focus specifically on the presence or absence of CBDR, this section shows that the reality is much more complex, and that differentiation arises in many forms and places. The section that follows examines some of the critiques of differentiation and the forms of differential treatment that have evolved over the past couple of decades. The final section moves on to consider the need for differentiation in the context of ongoing inequalities, and for a broader conceptual framework that better reflects the complexity of international society.

II. CONCEPTUAL BASES AND DEVELOPMENT OF DIFFERENTIATION

A. Conceptual Bases

Differentiation is a relatively novel phenomenon in international law. Its development is directly linked to the rapid increase in the number of states following decolonization that fundamentally changed the nature of the 'international community'.[4] Indeed, countries newly recognized as states often shared a common past of colonial exploitation and a relatively similar socio-economic profile, very different from other countries having been recognized as states for much longer.

The development of differentiation can be explained from two different perspectives. First, differential treatment is based on a recognition that deep inequalities must be addressed to legitimize the international legal order. Equity is at the root of measures that seek to foster substantive equality in a world structured around formal equality.[5] Second, differentiation is the product of the convergence of different interests in international negotiations that offer a basis for diverging from the usual reciprocity of obligations.[6] In international environmental law, differential treatment reflects equity considerations, as well as the necessity for the North to offer suitable conditions to countries of the South to entice them to join environmental regimes on issues of global importance.[7]

[4] Dino Kritsiotis, 'Imagining the International Community' *European Journal of International Law*, 13/4 (2002): 961.

[5] On equity see Chapter 20, 'Equity', in this volume.

[6] See Philippe Cullet, 'Differential Treatment in International Law: Towards a New Paradigm of Inter-State Relations' *European Journal of International Law*, 10/3 (1999): 549, 551.

[7] See Anne Gallagher, 'The "New" Montreal Protocol and the Future of International Law for the Protection of the Global Environment' *Houston Journal of International* Law, 14 (1992): 267, 311.

Structurally, differential treatment constitutes a recognition of the limits of a system based on the fiction of legal equality between states, which are not otherwise equal in practice. This fiction is at the root of the traditional structure of international law based on reciprocity of commitments by all state parties to a given treaty.[8] Differentiation thus implies rethinking the structure of these rules and moving away from the idea of strict reciprocity.[9] The rationale for introducing non-reciprocal norms is to foster a reduction in inequality, prevent an increase in inequality, and more generally ensure results that are more just than without differentiation.

Differential treatment seeks to foster substantive equality where formal equality does not lead to adequate results. Different conceptions of justice can provide a justification for differential treatment in international environmental law. The first is corrective justice that leads to a focus on the differential historical contributions of states to environmental degradation. The most debated case in this context is climate change since there is a direct correlation between greenhouse gas emissions over the past couple of centuries and present levels of per capita economic development.[10] Yet, while differential treatment may be given strong roots in corrective justice, the North has rejected an understanding of the principle of CBDR that includes an historical dimension.[11]

The second conception of justice at the root of differentiation is distributive justice. This focuses on the need to address existing inequalities in human development. In a context where the legal framework equates justice with formal equality, distributive justice reminds us that equality of opportunities is not sufficient, and that equality of results matters.[12] Consequently, like cases should be treated alike and dissimilarly situated people should be treated dissimilarly.[13] In the Aristotelian formulation, dissimilar situations need to be addressed in ways that take into account existing differences,[14] something that has been accepted for decades in international law.[15] Internationally, in view of prevailing inequalities, it is imperative to take measures to address such inequalities. Yet, measures taken to address them, such as economic redistribution of resources has remained contentious in the North that has been shying

[8] Daniel Magraw, 'Legal Treatment of Developing Countries: Differential, Contextual and Absolute Norms' *Colorado Journal of International Environmental Law & Policy*, 1/1 (1990): 69.

[9] See Emmanuel Decaux, *La réciprocité en droit international* (Librairie générale de droit et de jurisprudence 1980).

[10] Concerning corrective justice, see Eric Posner and Cass Sunstein, 'Climate Change Justice' *Georgetown Law Journal*, 96 (2008): 1565.

[11] Kristin Bartenstein, 'De Stockholm à Copenhague—Genèse et évolution des responsabilités communes mais différenciées dans le droit international de l'environnement' *McGill Law Journal*, 56/1 (2010): 177, 187.

[12] See Francis Fukuyama, *The Origins of Political Order—From Prehuman Times to the French Revolution* (Profile Books 2012).

[13] HLA Hart, *The Concept of Law* (2nd edn, Clarendon 1994) 159.

[14] Aristotle, *The Nicomachean Ethics* (translated by David Ross, revised by John Ackrill and Jamies Urmson, OUP 1991).

[15] *South West Africa, Second Phase (Ethiopia/South Africa; Liberia/South Africa)* (Judgement) [1966] ICJ Rep 6 (Dissenting Opinion of Judge Tanaka) 306.

away from recognizing any entitlement linked to justice claims for such redistribution.[16] Indeed, even Rawls whose theory of justice had given a more humane touch to liberal philosophy,[17] finds that once the duty of assistance at the international level is satisfied and all people have working liberal or decent governments, 'there is again no reason to narrow the gap between the average wealth of different peoples'.[18] Stone argues in a similar manner when he queries in the context of an environmental discussion why redistribution should be based on 'exempting the Poor from efficient environmental and resource standards—giving them a "right to pollute"—rather than through a more straightforward step-up in aid and development assistance?'[19]

The points made by Rawls and Stone do not address the need for the international legal framework to retain or gain legitimacy in the eyes of the majority of the world's countries and people. Asserting that inequalities need no further attention once a framework of formal legal equality has been established, is an inappropriate way to address the world's reality. Success should be measured by the way in which desired environmental and social outcomes are reached.[20] In this context, differential treatment offers a basis to reach fair outcomes in the context of significant inequalities among states. This must be expressed first of all through measures of intra-generational equity. At the same time, the needs of future generations must also be taken into account through measures of intergenerational equity.[21]

B. Development

The first step in the development of differential treatment in international law came through the consideration of equity as a relevant factor in the application of reciprocal rules by international tribunals. This gave judges some flexibility in the interpretation of rules to ensure a just and fair result.[22] Judicial equity is premised on the need to ensure that legally correct decisions are not regarded as unjust.[23] It provides an important tool to address individual cases but does not offer a solution where structural inequalities

[16] See Duncan French, 'Global Justice and the (Ir)relevance of Indeterminacy' *Chinese Journal of International Law*, 8/3 (2009): 593, 608.

[17] John Rawls, *A Theory of Justice* (Clarendon 1972).

[18] John Rawls, *The Law of Peoples* (Harvard University Press 1999) 114.

[19] Christopher Stone, 'Common but Differentiated Responsibilities in International Law' *American Journal of International Law*, 98/2 (2004): 276, 293–294.

[20] Daniel Bodansky, 'The Legitimacy of International Governance: A Coming Challenge for International Environmental Law?' *American Journal of International Law*, 93/3 (1999): 596, 611.

[21] See Halina Ward, 'Beyond the Short Term: Legal and Institutional Space for Future Generations in Global Governance' *Yearbook of International Environmental Law*, 22/1 (2011): 3.

[22] See Anastasios Gourgourinis, 'Delineating the Normativity of Equity in International Law' *International Community Law Review*, 11/3 (2009): 327.

[23] See Michael Akehurst, 'Equity and General Principles of Law' *International and Comparative Law Quarterly*, 25/4 (1976): 801.

among formally equal states imply that the application of reciprocal norms is likely to lead to results considered generally illegitimate by a majority of states.

It is such concerns about the legitimacy of reciprocal rules that led to the introduction of preferential treatment in the years following decolonization. The lack of adequacy between legal and economic equality led to calls for special measures to assist developing countries to allow them to overcome their difficult colonial legacy.[24] Measures were, for instance, taken in the context of the 1947 General Agreement on Tariffs and Trade (GATT).[25] The high point of the push for preferential treatment was attained in the call for a New International Economic Order (NIEO) in the 1970s.[26] This ebbed rapidly and by the time the World Trade Organization (WTO) was set up in 1995, trade rules were largely premised on abandoning preferential treatment in favour of a return to reciprocity.[27]

The decline of preferences in international economic law was largely parallel to the development of differential treatment in international environmental law. Both preferential and differential treatment are based on the idea that reciprocity of obligations is not necessarily the best way to structure legal obligations among very different states. At the same time, differential treatment is distinct insofar as it relies less on unilateral claims of the South to redistribution than preferential treatment.

Differential treatment in international environmental law grew in part around the distinct interests of the South and North that were brought together by a combination of factors. On the one hand, the South showed limited interest in some proposed global environmental regimes in a context where these did not coincide with their own domestic environmental or development priorities. On the other hand, the North found itself in the position of seeking to adopt measures to address global problems that had been mostly caused by industrial development in the North. The South reacted by articulating equity claims that were relatively similar to the ones made relatively unsuccessfully in international economic law.[28] Yet, in this case, they found themselves in a stronger bargaining position, as confirmed in the case of the 1987 Montreal Protocol where India and China managed to premise their ratification on additional funds.[29] This explains in part the rapid development of the various forms of differential treatment that exist today in international environmental law.

[24] Ahmed Mahiou, 'Le droit au développement' in International Law Commission (ed), *International Law on the Eve of the 21st Century* (UN 1997) 217.

[25] arts XXXVI.3, XXXVI.8.

[26] UNGA RES 3201(S-VI), 'Declaration on the Establishment of a New International Economic Order' (1 May 1974) UN Doc A/RES/3201(S-VI).

[27] See Anastasios Gourgourinis, 'Common but Differentiated Responsibilities in Transnational Climate Change Governance and the WTO' in Panagiotis Delimatsis (ed), *Research Handbook on Climate Change and Trade Law* (Edward Elgar 2016) 31, 40.

[28] See Jerzy Makarczyk, *Principles of a New International Economic Order* (Nijhoff 1988).

[29] Gallagher (n 7) 301.

III. MANIFESTATIONS OF DIFFERENTIATION IN INTERNATIONAL ENVIRONMENTAL LAW

A. Differentiation and the Principle of Common But Differentiated Responsibilities (CBDR)

Equity concerns have been reflected in international environmental law since the 1970s. The 1972 Stockholm Declaration included references to equity, including a recognition of the importance of intergenerational equity, linking 'under-development' and the necessity to provide financial and technical aid, and calling on the North to ensure that environmental technologies should be made available to developing countries on terms which would encourage their wide dissemination without constituting an economic burden on the South.[30]

By the Earth Summit in 1992, references to differentiation had become much more specific. The Rio Declaration linked the realization of the right to development to equitably meeting the needs of present and future generations, and recognized the necessity to give special priority to least developed countries and the most environmentally vulnerable countries.[31] Crucially, it included principle 7 that has become the central principle reflecting the need for differentiation in international environmental law. It has since then been integrated directly and indirectly in a variety of legal instruments. This includes restatements in preambles, including in the 2001 Stockholm and 2013 Minamata conventions, as well as in programmatic instruments.[32] It has also been integrated in treaty provisions, notably in the 1992 UNFCCC under a formulation that links CBDR and 'respective capabilities'.[33] In some other cases, there may be no restatement of the principle verbatim but some provisions directly reflect it, as exemplified in situations where developing countries' implementation of their commitments is made conditional on developed countries' effective implementation of their own financial and technology transfer commitments.[34] In some instances, the principle of CBDR has also been used to guide judicial reasoning, as was the case in the WTO *Shrimp/ Turtle* dispute.[35]

[30] UN, 'Report of the United Nations Conference on the Human Environment' (5–16 June 1972) UN Doc A/CONF.48/14/Rev.1, 3, ch 1—'Declaration of the United Nations Conference on the Human Environment', principles 2, 9, 20.

[31] *Report of the United Nations Conference on Environment and Development* (UN 1993) vol I, annex I, principles 2, 6.

[32] UNGA Res 70/1 (n 2) Declaration, para 12.

[33] art 3.

[34] 1992 Convention on Biological Diversity (CBD), art 20.4; 2001 Stockholm Convention, art 13.4.

[35] *US—Import Prohibition of Certain Shrimp and Shrimp Products—Recourse to Article 21.5 by Malaysia* (Panel Report) [15 June 2001] WTO Doc WT/DS58/RW [7.2].

On the whole, CBDR is well-enshrined in the structure of international environmental law. There is, however, no specific reference to a necessity to differentiate at the level of legal commitments in the basic principles of international environmental law. Thus, while principle 7 recognizes differences between the North and the South, such as in terms of contributions to environmental degradation, it does not go as far as imposing legal obligations of redistribution on the North. Indeed, the United States specifically indicated that it did not believe principle 7 could be interpreted as creating any obligation or liability for the North.[36] Commentators often take a similar line and argue against the existence of binding commitments of differentiation to be borne by the North.[37]

B. Differential Norms

Differentiation has been introduced in different ways in international environmental treaties to reflect the different situation of countries of the South and North. At the level of treaty norms, the most frequent form of differentiation is contextualization. In this case, a typical binding reciprocal obligation may be qualified by a clause, such as 'in accordance with its particular conditions and capabilities'.[38] This reflects a desire to highlight the seriousness of the commitment and a recognition that member states do not have the same capacity to implement their obligations. This contextualization is a recurring feature in environmental agreements.

Differentiation is also enshrined in the obligations themselves, such as in the case where different groups of states take on different commitments. The 1997 Kyoto Protocol where only the North took on greenhouse gas emission reduction commitments is an example.[39] In the case of the 1994 Desertification Convention, differentiation is implemented in such a way that some commitments are only borne by the North.[40]

Overall, differentiation has been organized around groups of states, mostly developed and developing countries. This has been a compromise from the start since two large groups of states cannot effectively capture the diversity of situations within each of them. At the same time, it made negotiations slightly easier by structuring obligations around a well-known categorization, albeit one that is built around an economic development classification rather than an environmental one. In this context, the Paris Agreement breaks new ground insofar as it introduces individual differentiation in an international environmental legal instrument. Here, Nationally Determined Contributions (NDCs)

[36] *Report of the United Nations Conference on Environment and Development* (UN 1993) vol IV.

[37] See Jean-Maurice Arbour, 'La normativité du principe des responsabilités communes mais différenciées' *Cahiers de Droit*, 55/1 (2014): 33, 37; Thomas Deleuil, 'The Common but Differentiated Responsibilities Principle' *Review of European Community and International Environmental Law*, 21/3 (2012): 271; Stone (n 19) 299.

[38] CBD, art 6.

[39] art 3.

[40] art 6.

introduce self-differentiation whereby each country determines its own level of ambition.[41] In addition, differentiation emerges from individual commitments rather than through collective bargaining. This can be seen as responding to the long-standing call for more granular differentiation that is able to distinguish, for instance, the situation of a landlocked least developed country with that of a BASIC country.[42] At the same time, it can be criticized for restricting the ambition of the international community in tackling crucial environmental issues, since self-differentiation essentially reflects the inability to agree on binding targets at the international level.

Differential commitments introduced above are among the most significant ways in which traditional international law is challenged by the principle of CBDR. At the same time, in a number of treaties, alternative ways of reflecting CBDR have been found. Delayed implementation of certain commitments by developing countries is one of the techniques used in this context. For instance, the 1987 Montreal Protocol offered developing countries with a sufficiently low level of consumption of the controlled substances a ten-year grace period.[43] Delayed implementation ensures that the same environmental standards apply to all countries but reflects the fact that some countries need a longer adaptation period. This is also linked directly to financial and technology transfer commitments highlighted in the next section.

C. Differentiation at the Implementation Level

Differential norms reflect the need to provide developing countries leeway in terms of their commitments in environmental agreements, whether because of their diminished responsibility in causing the problem or limited capacity to address it. This led to the development of new forms of differentiation wherein all countries take similar commitments but developing countries have their compliance subsidized through implementation aid and technology transfer.

This has in fact become one of the most visible forms of differentiation.[44] Most treaties adopted since the early 1990s include provisions concerning implementation aid and technology transfer.[45] This was linked to the progressive recognition that a growing number of treaties with an increasing number of parties did not necessarily translate into effective implementation, in part because many states did not have the necessary

[41] 2015 Paris Agreement, art 4.2; See also Lavanya Rajamani, 'Ambition and Differentiation in the 2015 Paris Agreement: Interpretative Possibilities and Underlying Politics' *International and Comparative Law Quarterly*, 65/2 (2016): 493; Christina Voigt and Felipe Ferreira, '"Dynamic Differentiation": The Principles of CBDR-RC, Progression and Highest Possible Ambition in the Paris Agreement' *Transnational Environmental Law*, 5/2 (2016): 285.

[42] Brazil, South Africa, India, and China.

[43] art 5; see also Stockholm Convention, art 4.7.

[44] See Sophie Lavallée, 'Responsabilités communes mais différenciées et protection internationale de l'environnement: une assistance financière en quête de solidarité?' *Cahiers de Droit*, 55/1 (2014): 139.

[45] See eg CBD, art 20; Minamata Convention, art 14.

financial, technological, or administrative capacity. The response was to include an aid component to environmental treaties.

IV. CRITICISMS OF DIFFERENTIATION AND PROGRESSIVE EVOLUTION

A. Critiques

Differential treatment has been subjected to various forms of criticism, ranging from conceptual to practical aspects. The first criticism has been that differentiation affects the very structure of international law because it threatens the binding character of legal norms.[46] This is particularly targeted at contextual norms that are said to dilute the certainty offered by reciprocal rules. Indeed, contextualization is specifically meant to provide a degree of flexibility in the implementation of international commitments. This criticism is, however, not necessarily specific to differential norms, as international environmental agreements are regularly accused of being soft because the provisions they contain are drafted in relatively open-ended terms. While stricter environmental norms would be advantageous for the environment, the reality of international environmental law where enforcement options are limited and implementation depends in large part on states' willingness to comply makes the usefulness of the comparison with other branches of international law, such as trade law, unhelpful.

Differential treatment has also been criticized for weakening the environmental content of international agreements because it allows the South to do less than the North on internationally agreed commitments. More specifically, it has been suggested that differential treatment does not necessarily provide the basis for agreements favourable to sustainable development.[47] In this way, it is the presence of differentiation that is seen as the root cause of the dilution of environmental measures. Differentiation thus appears to be a factor limiting the potential ideal environmental outcome or a factor that needs to be constrained to ensure it does not affect the environmental goals of a treaty.

In fact, differentiation is an intrinsic part of the concept of sustainable development, as reflected, for instance, in the Rio Declaration. In other words, there cannot be sustainable development at the international level without differentiation, something that international environmental treaties have confirmed over the past few decades. An (environmentally) successful treaty is one whose environmental obligations are differentiated. In fact, differentiation is at the root of the consensus position that is

[46] Cf. Günther Handl, 'Environmental Security and Global Change: The Challenge to International Law' *Yearbook of International Environmental Law*, 1/1 (1990): 3, 9.

[47] Cf. Yves Le Bouthillier, 'Des constats et des questions sur le principe des responsabilités communes mais différenciées' *Cahiers de Droit*, 55/1 (2014): 315, 317–318.

reflected in the final negotiated text. As a result, it does not affect the environmental content of a treaty but is an intrinsic part of its development. Indeed, none of the main international treaties adopted since the 1980s would have been widely ratified if they did not include a differential component.[48] In other words, differential treatment needs to be seen against the baseline of the absence of agreement rather than against the ideal treaty that would do all that could be expected in environmental terms. There is in any case no ideal treaty since all environmental treaties are based on a compromise between conservation and use.

B. Evolving Differential Techniques

Differentiation has been strongly linked with measures benefitting the South as a single category of 'developing' countries. This remains the central modus operandi of environmental agreements. At the same time, the limitation of this division has been addressed to a certain extent in some contexts.

First, a limited number of environmental factors have been taken into account in framing contextual norms. This includes vulnerability in the UNFCCC, which acts as a subsidiary category within the broader group of developing countries.[49] The Convention uses this categorization to single out 'particularly vulnerable' developing countries in terms of the obligation put on developed countries to assist in meeting the costs of adaptation to the adverse effects of climate change.[50] In addition, the Convention also recognizes that certain groups of developing countries have special needs and singles out, for instance, the needs and concerns of small-island countries, countries with low-lying coastal areas, countries with areas prone to natural disasters or areas prone to desertification.[51] At the same time, the climate change example confirms that introducing environmental factors as a basis for differential measures does not guarantee fair results. Indeed, one of the few provisions of the FCCC specifically mentioning vulnerability singles out developing countries 'with economies that are vulnerable to the adverse effects of the implementation of measures to respond to climate change' and further specifies that this applies in particular to countries highly dependent on production, processing, and export, and/or consumption of fossil-fuels.[52] This seems to give OPEC (Organization of the Petroleum Exporting Countries) countries that are quite economically resilient a similar claim to vulnerability as low-lying and other small island countries directly affected by sea-level and is thus suspect in terms of fairness.

48 Gallagher (n 7) 356.
49 art 3.2.
50 art 4.4.
51 art 4.8.
52 art 4.10.

Secondly, environmental factors have been used in setting up voting mechanisms, as in the case of the 2006 International Tropical Timber Agreement where countries are grouped according to their importance in the production and the use of timber, with exporters and importers each holding 1,000 votes.[53] Among the producers, 40% of the votes are distributed equally among Africa, Asia-Pacific, and Latin America, and then redistributed equally among each producing member in the region; 30% of the votes are distributed in accordance with the respective shares of the total tropical forest resources of all producing members. Finally, the remaining 30% is allocated in proportion to the producing members' respective shares in tropical timber trade.[54] This arrangement is significant not only because it gives equal power to producing and consuming nations but also because it specifically allocates part of the voting power in accordance with producing countries' respective shares of forest resources.

Another example is the decision-making structure of the regime for the exploitation of deep seabed minerals put in place under the 1982 Law of the Sea Convention (UNCLOS). The composition of the Council, which is the executive organ of the Authority, reflects partly the share of exploitable minerals consumed by each country, the importance of investments made for the conduct of activities in the Area, the importance of these minerals as export products, the necessity to take into account the situation of developing countries, and partly the principle of equitable geographical representation.[55]

Thirdly, it is possible to consider doing away with categories altogether and differentiate on an individual basis since there is a relatively small number of states overall. This is what the UN has been doing for many years in assessing member states' contributions to the organization according to a scale of assessment where each state is classified mainly according to its capacity to pay.[56] This has not been implemented in environmental agreements but self-differentiation under the Paris Agreement could be seen as a step towards a new type of differential norms. In fact, some commentators have positively assessed the weak form of differentiation enshrined in the NDCs as a move ahead of a 'bipolar, rigid and static type of differentiation' in the Kyoto Protocol.[57] This is certainly the first time that a major environmental agreement does this and it reflects a lack of ambition by negotiating states rather than a step forward in terms of the measures proposed. It may be that the same will be repeated in a context where there seems to be limited appetite at the international level for strong environmental measures and where any agreement ends up being identified as successful in the face of the no-agreement

[53] art 10.

[54] Ibid.

[55] 1982 Agreement Relating to the Implementation of Part XI of UNCLOS, art 3.15.

[56] UNGA RES 73/271, 'Scale of Assessments for the Apportionment of the Expenses of the United Nations' (22 December 2018) UN Doc A/RES/73/271.

[57] Sandrine Maljean-Dubois, 'The Paris Agreement: A New Step in the Gradual Evolution of Differential Treatment in the Climate Regime?' *Review of European, Comparative and International Environmental Law*, 25/2 (2016): 151, 154.

option. At the same time, ambition-less environmental regulation is not an option in a world facing an environmental crisis that may end up destroying the very bases of human civilization. Negotiated differentiation thus remains a central part of any future answers to this mounting challenge.

Overall, the past decade has witnessed a weakening of the willingness of states negotiating multilateral environmental agreements to grant the South the kind of preferential measures granted in earlier decades. This is no doubt linked in part to the fast rising economic and political clout of a limited number of large developing countries. This is in particular the case of China that is still classified as a developing country but is at the same time the world's worst contributor to greenhouse gas emissions and one of the largest economies. This explains the growing unwillingness of the North to grant concessions to all developing countries indiscriminately and is reflected, for instance, in self-differentiation in the Paris Agreement. At the same time, while the situation of large and economically successful countries grabs the headlines, this does not reflect the reality of the majority of developing countries whose relative position has not significantly improved over the past few decades. In addition, fast economic growth does not necessarily translate in significant human development gains for the majority of poor people in those countries. As a result, it remains and will remain extremely difficult for the North to reject the principle of CBDR for many years. This is reflected in the re-assertion of the principle in various soft law instruments, as well as new conventions like the Minamata Convention.

V. ONGOING NEED FOR DIFFERENTIATION

A. Need to Maintain Some Form of Differentiation

Differential treatment has often been seen as an acceptable mechanism to redress inequalities, but only for a limited period of time since the aim is to ensure the swift return to a legal order based on legal equality and reciprocal obligations.[58] The rapid economic growth of BASIC countries since the beginning of the century has unsurprisingly led to calls for restricting or abolishing differential treatment based on the argument that these countries are now resilient enough and must bear the burden of their fast-increasing contribution to environmental degradation.[59]

Yet, the majority of countries of the South, in particular least developed countries, are comparatively no better off than they were at the beginning of the 1990s. A longer

[58] See Yoshiro Matsui, 'Some Aspects of the Principle of "Common but Differentiated Responsibilities"' *International Environmental Agreements: Politics, Law and Economics*, 2/2 (2002): 151.

[59] Cf. John Copeland Nagle, 'How Much Should China Pollute?' *Vermont Journal of Environmental Law*, 12 (2011): 591.

term comparison confirms this point. Thus, the share of world GDP of sub-Saharan Africa may have grown from barely 1% in the early 1970s to nearly 2% in 2017 but this remains abysmally low.[60] In terms of the Human Development Index (HDI), there has thankfully been a faster progression of the HDI in countries at the bottom of the scale. Yet, while countries with low human development saw their HDI increase from 0.345 in 1980 to 0.504 in 2017, countries with very high human development also saw their HDI increase significantly from 0.757 to 0.894 during the same period.[61]

There is thus neither reason to celebrate the progression witnessed in the South over the past few decades nor reason to be concerned by a situation where inequalities between the North and the South would be so reduced that the basis for differential treatment would be redundant. The idea that differentiation must be dynamically interpreted is a valid proposition,[62] but this must take place in a context where structural inequalities show signs of decreasing significantly. At present, the moral imperative for differential treatment remains as strong as it was a couple of decades ago. In fact, the need to 'combat inequalities' is one of the specific commitments taken by the UN summit for the adoption of the post-2015 development agenda.[63] Overall, inequalities in levels of human development between the North and South have only diminished to a limited extent over the past couple of decades, particularly between the North and small developing and least developing countries. This clearly confirms the relevance of differentiation.

Beyond the principled justification for differentiation, there are also strong pragmatic reasons that confirm the continued relevance of differential treatment. International environmental law is different from, for instance, international trade law in that its effectiveness depends not on the extent of enforcement against defaulting states but rather on the extent to which states willingly comply with the norms they adopt. The introduction of non-compliance procedures is a testament to this approach that prods states into compliance rather than punishes them for non-compliance. Differential treatment is part of this culture of incentives that seeks to ensure participation of all states regardless of their contribution to environmental harm and to provide a framework that facilitates implementation of commitments taken by all states, including those with limited administrative, financial, or technical capacity.

[60] Economic Commission for Africa, 'Africa in the Global Economy: Issues of Trade and Development for Africa' (2000); World Bank, 'World Development Indicators—2017 figures' <http://wdi.worldbank.org/table/WV.1> accessed 16 December 2019.

[61] *Human Development Report 2014—Sustaining Human Progress: Reducing Vulnerabilities and Building Resilience* (UNDP 2014) 167; *Human Development Indices and Indicators—2018 Statistical Update* (UNDP 2018) 29.

[62] Cf. Sandrine Maljean-Dubois and Pilar Moraga Sariego, 'Le principe des responsabilités communes mais différenciées dans le régime international du climat' *Cahiers de Droit*, 55/1 (2014): 83, 104.

[63] UNGA RES 70/1 (n 2) Declaration, para 3.

B. Broadening the Bases for and Forms of Differentiation

Differentiation has been based primarily on a simple categorization framed around economic factors. Initially, the developed and developing country dichotomy was used for convenience's sake and because in some cases there was a strong correlation between levels of economic development and contribution to environmental damage. This was, for instance, the case in relation to generation of hazardous wastes and contribution to greenhouse gas emissions. Yet, this is problematic because economic development tends to overshadow environmental debates. This has been confirmed in the case of the evolving understanding of sustainable development meant to provide a balance between environmental, social, and economic elements where economic growth has progressively become more important, as reflected in the introduction of the concept of green economy at the Rio+20 summit. As long as differentiation is structured around economic categories, this will contribute to undermining the environmental content of the measures taken. It is thus crucial to rethink the categories in environmental terms. Even if the ranking may not be significantly different, it will make a qualitative difference by giving more weight to environmental factors.

There is thus a need to move towards differentiation based primarily on an environmental and social assessment that will identify countries' vulnerability and resilience to environmental problems. This will have several advantages. First, it will help bring back the environmental agenda to the centre of environmental treaties. This is, for instance, a concern in the climate change regime where debates have focused on the extent to which countries should be allowed to pollute the atmosphere. This is inappropriate and climate change legal instruments should rather use the precautionary principle as a basis for differentiated obligations to take precautionary measures to mitigate and adapt to climate change. This would have the advantage of building obligations around each country reducing its impact on the global environment rather than on a grandfathering basis.

Second, using social and environmental indicators as the basis for differentiation will provide a much better basis for differentiating between countries. There is, for instance, little in common between China and Malawi in terms of their respective responsibilities to causing global environmental harm, their resilience to harm, and their capacity to address the consequences of environmental harm. Similarly, while Fiji is, like China, a country with high human development,[64] its contribution and needs in the face of climate change and sea-level rise as a small-island state is not at all comparable to China's.

Differential treatment also needs to be adapted to the nature of the environmental challenges we face. At present, it is organized around a territorial understanding of the world that reflects the structure of international law around sovereign legal entities. A complete rethink is needed that will take us beyond the idea of ownership of environmental resources by individual states to an understanding of certain resources being in

[64] UNDP, 'Human Development Indices' (n 61) 27.

the custody of the whole of humankind.[65] Under 'common heritage' status,[66] resources must be managed jointly and the benefits of their conservation and use must also be enjoyed jointly, in a manner that transcends national self-interest. The principle of common heritage is an appropriate basis for addressing global environmental issues from a redistributive perspective. Starting points could be made with resources that are already under some form of joint management, such as Antarctic water resources.[67]

VI. CONCLUSION

Differential treatment is a central conceptual pillar of international environmental law. This is reflected in the fact that all multilateral environmental agreements have a strong South-North dimension structured around the different situations, responsibilities, and capabilities of the two groups of states. The principle of CBDR may not have become a principle of customary international law in itself but the equity dimension of international environmental law constitutes an intrinsic part of this branch of international law. This is why debates concerning the impacts of differential treatment on the certainty of the legal order are not helpful insofar as they distract us from the centrality of equity in international environmental law. The question is not whether international law is threatened by non-reciprocity but rather whether international environmental law would ever have acquired its breadth and depth without differentiation. The answer is clearly negative since it is an inseparable part of the deals made by negotiators when adopting new legal instruments and central to implementation and compliance, for instance.

At the same time, there has been increasing resistance to differentiation, particularly in view of the fact that some countries still classified as developing countries in environmental agreements are now among the main contributors to the environmental problems that multilateral agreements address. This explains the weakening of differentiation in the Paris Agreement.[68] At the same time, the Paris Agreement also confirms that differentiation cannot be set aside, even if a distinct version of the principle has to be introduced.[69] Indeed, in this case, differentiation remains central, for instance, at the level of implementation.

[65] Thomas Franck, 'Fairness in the International Legal and Institutional System' *Recueil des Cours*, 240 (1993): 9, 92.

[66] See Stephen Stec, 'Humanitarian Limits to Sovereignty: Common Concern and Common Heritage Approaches to Natural Resources and Environment' *International Community Law Review*, 12/3 (2010): 361.

[67] See Jochen Sohnle, 'Le principe des responsabilités communes mais différenciées dans les instruments conventionnels relatifs aux eaux douces internationales – Cherchez l'intrus!' *Cahiers de Droit*, 55/1 (2014): 221, 251.

[68] Maljean-Dubois (n 57).

[69] Rajamani (n 41) 509.

Overall, the continuing inequalities among countries that have structured international relations since decolonization still constitute the basis for any further law-making because the structural gap between the majority of developing countries and developed countries remains immense. The socio-economic gaps will not be bridged for another few decades at least. As a result, even if equity measures are assumed to be temporary until such time as inequalities have disappeared, they will remain a central part of international environmental law for the foreseeable future.[70] This is in fact called for by the broader principle of solidarity among states that requires states to take measures to address inequalities, including through differentiation.[71] This was confirmed in 2015 in the context of the adoption of the development agenda that calls for a global partnership for sustainable development 'based on a spirit of strengthened global solidarity'.[72] It is within this context that differentiation constitutes one of important tools for addressing the shortcomings of a system based on formal equality and to bring about substantive equality.

BIBLIOGRAPHY

Philippe Cullet, *Differential Treatment in International Environmental Law* (Ashgate 2003)
Thomas Franck, *Fairness in International Law and Institutions* (Clarendon 1995)
Tuula Honkonen, *The Common but Differentiated Responsibility Principle in Multilateral Environmental Agreements* (Kluwer Law International 2009)
Lavanya Rajamani, *Differential Treatment in International Environmental Law* (OUP 2006)

[70] Cf. Kristin Bartenstein, 'L'opérationnalisation du principe des responsabilités communes mais différenciées repensée: plaidoyer pour une démarche ancrée dans l'équité' *Cahiers de Droit*, 55/1 (2014): 113, 127.

[71] Cf. Ronald St John McDonald, 'The Principle of Solidarity in Public International Law' in Christian Dominicé *et al* (eds), *Etudes de droit international en l'honneur de Pierre Lalive* (Helbing 1993) 275.

[72] UNGA RES 70/1 (n 2) section 'Partnership'.

CHAPTER 20

EQUITY

WERNER SCHOLTZ

I. INTRODUCTION

EQUITY remains a pivotal concept in international environmental law.[1] First, states share scarce natural resources, such as international rivers, which invoke the need for the equitable allocation of resources. Furthermore, the world is still characterized by wealth disparities between states that have different capabilities and historical contributions pertaining to global environmental degradation as well as environmental problems of a differential nature.[2] Thus, it is important to assign differential obligations to states to respond to environmental degradation. The adherence of international law to formal equality[3] and reciprocal obligations in the context of a world of disparity is not conducive to solving global environmental degradation, which requires the global participation of states in accordance with differential capabilities and responsibilities.[4] Hence, equity as distributive justice constitutes a vital response to the particular nature of the aforementioned key issues. Equity must remedy the adherence to the formal equality of states in order to pursue a global solution to the particular challenges posed by shared resources and environmental degradation.

This chapter critically analyses the notion of equity in international environmental law. The first part of the discussion focuses on the meaning of equity in international law and briefly reflects on familiar examples of the manifestation of equity in international

[1] Dinah Shelton, 'Equity' in Daniel Bodansky, Jutta Brunnée, and Ellen Hey (eds), *The Oxford Handbook of International Environmental Law* (1st edn, OUP 2008) 652.

[2] Ruchi Anand, *International Environmental Justice: A North-South dimension* (Routledge 2004) 3; John Ntambirweki, 'The Developing Countries in the Evolution of an International Environmental Law' *Hastings International and Comparative Law Review*, 14/4 (1991): 905.

[3] United Nations (UN) Charter, art 2.1.

[4] For a discussion on formal equality see Gerry Simpson, *Great Powers and Outlaw States: Unequal Sovereigns in the International Legal Order* (CUP 2004) 39. See also Chapter 19, 'Differentiation', in this volume.

environmental law treaties. The prominence of intergenerational and intra-generational equity in international environmental law warrants a subsequent critical analysis of the content, legal status, and relationship between these forms of equity. This discussion indicates that although the two components of equity may prima facie be in conflict, they constitute important complementary aspects of sustainable development. This chapter concludes with a call for the progressive development of aspects of intra-generational and intergenerational equity that may have profound consequences for international environmental law.

II. EQUITY IN INTERNATIONAL LAW

A. Meaning of Equity

What is the meaning of equity in international environmental law? It is important to understand the relationship between justice and equity, as the International Court of Justice (ICJ) observed, 'Equity as a legal concept is a direct emanation from the idea of justice'.[5] As such, one approach to appraise justice is to investigate equity in international law.[6] Equity (and justice) have, however, acquired distinct meanings and is void of a universal and precise meaning.[7] Thomas Franck is of the view that equity is included in the concept of fairness, which has procedural and substantive aspects. The procedural aspect relates to taking the right process in reaching decisions, whereas the substantive component is concerned with the pursuit of distributive justice.[8] These aspects of fairness are inter-related as fairer proceedings may result in fairer results.[9] Equity has manifested in different forms in international law. Article 38.2 of the ICJ Statute allows cases to be decided *ex aequo et bono* (fair and good) if the parties agree. Furthermore, equity *praeter legem* (equity apart from the law) enables a judge to respond to lacunae by filling in gaps in existing norms; equity *contra legem* (equity contrary to a legal obligation) allows for a derogation from law whereas equity *infra legem* (equity under the law) allows a judge with a certain amount of discretion to apply the law to individual cases with different circumstances.[10] Continental shelf allocation has invited the application of equitable principles in international law, in order to reach decisions in the *North Sea Continental Shelf* cases.[11]

[5] *Continental Shelf (Tunisia/Libyan Arab Jamahiriya)* (Judgement) [1982] ICJ Rep 18 [71].
[6] Thomas Franck, *Fairness in International Law and Institutions* (OUP 1995) 47.
[7] Anand (n 2) 122.
[8] Franck (n 6) 7.
[9] Ibid.
[10] Vaughn Lowe, 'The Role of Equity in International Law' *Australian Yearbook of International Law,* 12 (1988): 54, 56.
[11] *North Sea Continental Shelf (Germany/Denmark; Germany/Netherlands)* (Judgement) [1969] ICJ Rep 3.

Equity plays an important role in international environmental law and several treaties contain references to equity and/or equitable principles. One of the most important applications of equity in modern international law remains the development of equitable standards for the allocation and sharing of resource benefits, which require the application of distributive justice. For example, Article 5.1 of the 1997 UN Convention on the Law of Non-Navigational Use of International Watercourses requires states to utilize international watercourses in an equitable and reasonable manner.[12] Article 6 identifies a non-exhaustive list of factors which may be used to determine what constitutes reasonable and equitable utilization in individual cases. The factors do not provide an indication of their priority, which causes uncertainty in relation to the application of the principle.

The use thereof must also be consistent with the adequate protection of the watercourse. This implies that uses which could harm the watercourse could have an influence on the determination of equitability. Although Article 10.1 affirms that no use of an international watercourse has priority over any other uses, special regard is to be given to the 'requirements of vital human needs' under Article 10.2. The adoption of General Comment 15 on the Right to Water by the UN Committee on Economic, Social, and Cultural Rights (UNCESCR)[13] which calls on states to ensure inter alia an adequate supply of drinking water as well as water for sanitation and nutrition, may have an impact on the weight of the factors as the aforementioned may be indicative of vital human needs.[14] Conflicting uses could therefore not be in adherence to the principle of equitable and reasonable utilization. It is not only the human rights framework that has an influence on the notion of equitable allocation, but also the important position accorded to sustainable development as well as environmental protection.[15]

Equity also plays an important role in the conservation and management of global resources. The 1982 UN Convention on the Law of the Sea (UNCLOS) contains numerous references to this concept. For example, the preamble refers to 'the equitable and efficient utilization' of the ocean's resources and the 'equitable sharing of profits' is applicable in relation to the mineral exploitation of the deep seabed.[16]

An eminent example of the equitable sharing of benefits derived from the exploitation of natural resources may be found in the 1992 Convention on Biological Diversity (CBD). Article 1 includes 'the fair and equitable sharing of the benefits arising out of the utilization of genetic resources' as one of the three objectives of the CBD.[17] The

[12] See also 1992 UNECE Helsinki Water Convention, art 2.2.

[13] UNCESCR, 'General Comment No. 15 (2002): The right to water' (20 January 2003) UN Doc E/C.12/2002/11.

[14] See Christina Leb, *Cooperation in the Law of Transboundary Water Resources* (CUP 2013) 201.

[15] *Pulp Mills on the River Uruguay (Argentina/Uruguay)* (Provisional Measures, Order of 13 July 2006) [2006] ICJ Rep 133 [80]; *The Gabčíkovo-Nagymaros Project (Hungary/Slovakia)* (Judgement) [1997] ICJ Rep 7 (Gabčíkovo-Nagymaros case) [112], [140]; Owen Mcintyre, *Environmental Protection of International Watercourses under International Law* (Ashgate 2007).

[16] arts 140, 155.2, 160.2, 173.2. Other examples of equity can be found in arts 69, 70, 82.4.

[17] See also arts 8(j), 15, 19.

CBD (as well as its 2010 Nagoya Protocol on Access to Genetic Resources and the Fair and Equitable Sharing of Benefits Arising from their Utilization) attempts to link intra-generational equity (equitable access and benefit sharing) with the attainment of intergenerational equity (the other objectives of sustainable use and conservation of biodiversity as reflected in Article 1).[18]

Equity is also prominent in relation to rules that deal with the common heritage of mankind.[19] One of the constituent elements of this notion is that benefits arising from the exploitation and use of the common heritage areas must be shared by all. Furthermore, the area must be preserved for the benefit of future generations. The common heritage of mankind may be traced back to a 'radical' version of this notion, which was a central pillar of the New International Economic Order (NIEO). The benefits from the exploitation of resources, in particular the deep seabed, should have accrued to mankind, although preferential treatment would have been extended to developing countries.[20]

The calls for an NIEO in international law is an interesting example of advocacy for an international system based on equity and a strong form of distributive justice. The NIEO was a response to the manner in which developing states perceived the existence of inequity in international law and the need to realize material equity through economic independence subsequent to decolonization.[21]

This is evident from the principles included in the Declaration on the NIEO.[22] The Declaration includes principles related to equity, such as common interest[23] and co-operation among states,[24] permanent sovereignty,[25] an embodiment of solidarity,[26] as well as preferential treatment.[27]

Developing countries used their numerical majority in the General Assembly to adopt resolutions as the basis for the promotion of an NIEO. Developed countries, in general, rejected the non-binding resolutions which they perceived as an arbitrary imposition of non-binding, or so-called 'soft law', obligations. This triggered a divisive debate on the nature and scope of soft law in international law.[28] Ultimately, the absence of

[18] For a discussion see Virginie Barral, 'Sustainable Development and Equity in Biodiversity Conservation' in Elisa Morgera and Jona Razzaque (eds), *Biodiversity and Nature Protection Law* (Edward Elgar 2017) 59–69.

[19] Christopher Joyner, 'Legal Implications of the Concept of the Common Heritage of Mankind' *International and Comparative Law Quarterly*, 35/1 (1986): 190.

[20] Ram Anand, *Origin and Development of the Law of the Sea* (Marthinus Nijhoff 1983) 205.

[21] See also Chapters 11 and 19, 'Global South Approaches' and 'Differentiation', in this volume.

[22] UNGA Res 3201(S-VI), 'Declaration on the Establishment of a New International Economic Order' (1 May 1974) UN Doc A/RES/3201(S-VI); see also ILA, 'Report of the Sixty-Second Conference Held at Seoul' (24–30 August 1986).

[23] preamble.

[24] preamble, ch 1, and arts 4, 8, 9, 11, 12, 13, 17, 19, 23.

[25] art 2.

[26] art 18.

[27] art 19.

[28] Isabella Dunn, *The Right to Development and International Economic Law. Legal and Moral Dimensions* (Hart Publishing 2012) 138–140. See also Chapter 25, 'Soft Law', in this volume.

bargaining power on the side of the developing world resulted in the obsoleteness of the NIEO in international law.[29]

However, the promotion of equity *via* the pursuit of an NIEO did have an impact on subsequent developments in international environmental law. The preamble of the NIEO Declaration already hinted at the temporal aspects of equity in 1974 through a reference to the acceleration of 'economic and social development and peace and justice for present and future generations'. The consideration of the temporal aspects of equity alludes to the dilemma of 'Reconciling the claims of present generations against claims of future generations'.[30] Falk is of the opinion that: 'For centuries, relations among territorially bounded sovereign entities called "states" (spatial communities) preoccupied discussions of world order. More recently, this spatial focus has been attenuated by a rising concern about grievances from the past and worries about the life circumstances of future generations . . . '.[31] The reflection on the relationship between present and future generations finds expression in intergenerational and intra-generational equity in international environmental law, which constitute the core understanding of sustainable development as reflected in the Brundtland definition.[32] Developing states ultimately supplemented their calls for equity with the contentious right to development, which was the precursor of sustainable development.[33]

III. INTERGENERATIONAL AND INTRA-GENERATIONAL EQUITY IN INTERNATIONAL ENVIRONMENTAL LAW

A. Intergenerational Equity

A major development in international environmental law is the emergence of the concept of intergenerational equity. Intergenerational equity primarily entails two aspects: The present residents of the earth hold the earth in trust for future generations and at the same time the present generation is entitled to reap benefits from it. The notion of holding natural resources in trusteeship for the benefit of future generations

[29] Philippe Cullet, 'Differential Treatment in International Law: Towards a New Paradigm of Inter-state Relations' *European Journal of International Law*, 10/3 (1999): 549, 566.

[30] Richard Falk, 'The Pursuit of International Justice: Present Dilemmas and An Imagined Future' *Journal of International Affairs*, 52/2 (1999): 409, 433.

[31] Ibid.

[32] World Commission on Environment and Development, *Our Common Future* (OUP 1987) ('Brundtland Report').

[33] Karin Arts and Atabongawung Tamo, 'The Right to Development in International Law: New Momentum Thirty Years Down the Line?' *Netherlands Yearbook of International Law*, 63/3 (2016): 221–249.

already found application in the *Pacific Fur Seals* arbitration.[34] *In Fairness to Future Generations*, authored by Edith Brown Weiss, remains the foremost scholarly analysis of intergenerational equity in international environmental law.[35] The basic proposition of Weiss's proposal is that each generation is both a custodian or a trustee of the planet for future generations as well as a beneficiary of its fruits.

The following four criteria should guide the developments of principles of intergenerational equity: (i) the promotion of equality among generations which implies that they neither authorize the present generation to exploit resources to the exclusion of future generations, nor impose unreasonable burdens on it to meet future demands that are indeterminate; (ii) the principles 'should not require one generation to predict the values of future generations' but rather allow for flexibility in the pursuit of the objectives of future generations; (iii) the application of principles to foreseeable situations should be reasonably clear; and (iv) principles should be shared by 'different cultural traditions and be generally acceptable to different economic and political systems'.[36] Three basic principles of intergenerational equity may accordingly be distinguished.[37] The first, 'conservation of options', requires each generation to conserve the diversity of the natural and cultural resource base so that it does not unduly restrict options for future generations. The second, 'conservation of quality' requires each generation to maintain the quality of the planet so that it is passed on in the same condition as it was received so as to enable future generations to enjoy a quality of life comparable to that of the previous generation. The third, 'conservation of access', requires each generation to provide its members with equitable rights of access to the legacy of past generations and in addition should conserve this access for the future.

Various soft law legal instruments affirm the importance of intergenerational equity. Principle 1 of the 1972 Stockholm Declaration, for instance, reads that: 'Man ... bears a solemn responsibility to protect and improve the environment for present and future generations'.[38] The preamble of the 1982 UN World Charter for Nature also links the conservation of natural resources with the 'interests of present and future generations'.[39] The 1997 UNESCO Declaration on the Responsibilities of the Present Generations towards Future Generations, for instance, affirms that 'the present generations have the

[34] Phillipe Sands and Jacqueline Peel, *Principles of International Environmental Law* (4th edn, CUP 2018) 220.

[35] See Edith Weiss, *In Fairness to Future Generations: International Law, Common Patrimony, and Intergenerational Equity* (Transnational Publishers 1989); Paul Baressi, 'Beyond Fairness to Future Generations: An Intragenerational Alternative to Intergenerational Equity in the International Environmental Arena' *Tulane Environmental Law Journal*, 11/1 (1997): 59.

[36] Weiss (n 35) 38.

[37] Ibid. A recent exposition of the elements indicates a shift from the usage of conservation to 'comparable'. See Edith Weiss, 'Intergenerational Equity' in Rüdiger Wolfrum (ed), *Max Planck Encyclopedia of Public International Law* (OUP 2013) para 7.

[38] UN, 'Report of the United Nations Conference on the Human Environment' (5–16 June 1972) UN Doc A/CONF.48/14/Rev.1, 3, ch 1—'Declaration of the United Nations Conference on the Human Environment'.

[39] UNGA Res 37/7, 'World Charter for Nature' (28 October 1982) UN Doc A/RES/37/7.

responsibility to bequeath to future generations an Earth which will not one day be irreversibly damaged by human activity'.[40] The 1993 Vienna Declaration and Programme of Action adopted by the World Conference on Human Rights links the right to development with the needs of present and future generations.[41] The World Commission for Environment and Development (WCED) defined the concept of sustainable development via a reference to intergenerational equity.[42] Principle 3 of the Rio Declaration indicates that the right to development 'must be fulfilled so as to equitably meet developmental and environmental needs of present and future generations'.[43] In addition to the references to intergenerational equity in non-binding international documents, a number of international treaties also include this notion. Examples include the preambles of the 1946 International Convention for the Regulation of Whaling, the CBD, the 2015 Paris Agreement; Article 3 of the 1992 UN Framework Convention on Climate Change (UNFCCC) as well as Article 4 of the 1972 World Heritage Convention. At the domestic level, the importance of equity has also been confirmed. Exemplary is section 24(b) of the Constitution of the Republic of South Africa, 1996 which states that 'Everyone has the right to have the environment protected ... for the benefit of present and future generations'.

The inclusion of intergenerational equity in international documents points to an affirmation and acceptance thereof but does not necessarily provide a clear indication of its normative value. Intergenerational equity is frequently viewed as an important aspect of sustainable development.[44] It does not establish a binding legal rule but rather constitutes a principle, in the broad sense, to be taken into account.[45] As such it is a guiding principle for decision-making in international environmental law.[46] The ICJ has also referred to intergenerational equity. The court noted the importance of taking cognizance of the unique characteristics of nuclear weapons, in particular the danger that it poses for future generations in the *Advisory Opinion on the Legality of the Threat or Use of Nuclear Weapons* case.[47] This sentiment in relation to future generations was reiterated in the *Gabcíkovo-Nagymaros* case.[48] In the delimitation case of *Denmark v Norway*, Judge Weeramantry stated in his Separate Opinion that 'respect for these elemental constituents of the inheritance of succeeding generations dictated rules and attitudes

[40] UNESCO, 'Declaration on the Responsibilities of the Present Generations towards Future Generations' (12 November 1997) art 4.

[41] para 11.

[42] Brundtland Report (n 32).

[43] *Report of the United Nations Conference on Environment and Development* (UN 1993) vol I, annex I.

[44] Sands and Peel (n 34) 218.

[45] See Alan Boyle, 'Some Reflections on Relationship of Treaties and Soft Law' *International and Comparative Law Quarterly*, 48/4 (1999): 901, 908–909.

[46] Catherine Redgwell, 'Principles and Emerging Norms in International Law: Intra- and Intergenerational Equity' in Cinnamon Carlarne, Kevin Gray, and Richard Tarasofsky (eds), *The Oxford Handbook of International Climate Change Law* (OUP 2016) 199.

[47] *Legality of the Threat or Use of Nuclear Weapons* (Advisory Opinion) [1996] ICJ Rep 226 (Legality of Nuclear Weapons case) [35].

[48] Ibid [29]. This statement was reaffirmed in Gabčíkovo-Nagymaros case (n 15) [53].

based upon a concept of an equitable sharing which was both horizontal in regard to the present generation and vertical for the benefit of generations yet to come'.[49] In spite of these explicit references, the ICJ has been reluctant to elaborate on the notion or to use it as a legal basis to resolve a matter. However, Judge Weeramantry, in his dissenting opinion, referred to intergenerational equity in the *Nuclear Test* case of 1995 as 'an important and rapidly developing principle of contemporary environmental law'.[50] In his dissent to the Advisory Opinion, Weeramantry seems to consider intergenerational equity as more than a guiding principle as 'the rights of future generations have passed the stage when they were merely an embryonic right struggling for recognition. They have woven themselves into international law through major treaties, through juristic opinion and through general principles of law recognized by civilised nations'.[51] Judge Trindade echoed this sentiment in his separate opinion in the *Pulp Mills* case as he stated that the 'acknowledgement of intergenerational equity forms part of conventional wisdom in International Environmental Law'.[52]

At the national level the *Minors Oposa* case is best known for its recognition of the interests of future generations.[53] In this case the Supreme Court of the Philippines granted standing to a group of children on their own behalf and as representatives of future generations. The class action was concerned with an application to cancel timber licence agreements that contributed to excessive deforestation. The Supreme Court made it clear that standing to sue on behalf of future generations was based on intergenerational responsibility as far as the right to a 'balanced and healthful ecology' is concerned. This case serves as a landmark decision which links intergenerational equity, standing, and a constitutional environmental right. The *Goa Mining* case represents another progressive foreign jurisdiction decision that provides some insights concerning the implementation of intergenerational equity in the context of iron ore mining in India.[54] In this case the Supreme Court of India established an expert committee to conduct an environmental impact assessment study in order to determine a maximum limit for the annual excavation of iron ore in the state of Goa. This was to be done keeping in mind the principles of sustainable development and intergenerational equity.[55] The

[49] *Maritime Delimitation in the Area between Greenland and Jan Mayen (Denmark/Norway)* (Separate Opinion of Judge Weeramantry) [1993] ICJ Rep 211 [242].

[50] *Request for an Examination of the Situation in Accordance with Paragraph 63 of the Court's Judgement of 20 December 1974 in the Nuclear Tests (New Zealand/France) Case* (Dissenting opinion of Judge Weeramantry) [1995] ICJ Rep 317, 341.

[51] Legality of Nuclear Weapons case (n 47) (Dissenting Opinion of Judge Weeramantry) 429, 455.

[52] *Pulp Mills on the River Uruguay (Argentina/Uruguay)* (Separate opinion of Judge Cançado Trindade) [2010] ICJ Rep 135 [122].

[53] *Juan Oposal, et al v the Honorable Fulgencio Factoran Jr., Secretary of the Department of the Environment and Natural Resources et al*, G R No. 101083, 30 July 1993. For a discussions see Antonio La Viña, 'The Right to a Sound Environment in the Philippines: The Significance of the Minors Oposa Case' *Review of European, Comparative & International Environmental Law* 3/4 (1994): 246.

[54] *Goa Foundation v Union of India & others*, WP(C) 435 of 2012.

[55] Ibid [8], [56].

expert committee recommended an annual excavation of twenty million tons per annum.[56] Furthermore, the expert committee recommended the establishment of the Goa Iron Ore Permanent Fund, which is a 'permanent fund for inter-generational equity and sustainability of mining for all times' to be financed by the imposition of a 10% levy of the sale value of iron ore.[57] Hence, the aforementioned recommendations formed part of the declaratory order of the Supreme Court.[58] The cap of twenty million tons per annum was ordered in the interests of sustainable development and intergenerational equity.[59] This decision indicates how intergenerational equity may be translated into practical measures. The ceiling on the excavation of iron ore allows for availability of a natural resource for future generations and also limits environmental damage. The establishment of the permanent fund may ensure that future generations benefit from current mining operations.

The anonymous nature of future generations, however, complicates the determination and enforcement of their interests, but doesn't make it necessarily impossible. A number of proposals exist in order to ensure that the interests of future generations are considered, which include institutional proposals such as the establishment of a guardian *ad litem* or ombudsman for future generations.[60] In August 2013 the UN Secretary-General submitted his report on 'Intergenerational Solidarity and the Needs of Future Generations', which analysed institutional mechanisms concerning future generations. The four proposed options are: the establishment of a 'High Commissioner for Future Generations', a 'Special Envoy of the Secretary-General on Future Generations', a recurring agenda item to be discussed by the High Political Forum, and inter-agency coordination to promote intergenerational solidarity within the UN System through the Chief Executives Board (CEB) and its mechanisms.[61] Lawrence recently proposed key principles which could serve as criteria to assess whether an international climate change regime adheres to the requirements of intergenerational justice.[62] This may contribute to the clarification of an abstract concept and increase its utility. It is interesting to note that 'core human rights essential for human dignity' is considered to be one of the principles.

Intergenerational equity has also attracted its fair share of scholarly critique.[63] The relational aspect of intergenerational equity, which implies a connection between humans

[56] Ibid [11].

[57] Ibid [62], [70].

[58] Ibid [62], [70].

[59] Ibid [71].

[60] Edith Weiss, 'Implementing Intergenerational Equity' in Malgosia Fitzmaurice, David Ong, and Panos Merkouris (eds), *Research Handbook on International Environmental Law* (Edward Elgar 2010) 100, 110.

[61] UNGA, 'Intergenerational Solidarity and the Needs of Future Generations—Report of the Secretary-General' (15 August 2013) UN Doc A/68/322.

[62] Peter Lawrence, *Justice For Future Generations: Climate Change and International Law* (Edward Elgar 2014) 92.

[63] See eg Anthony D'Amato, 'Do We Owe a Duty to Future Generations to Preserve the Global Environment?' *American Journal of International Law*, 84/1 (1990): 190; Lothar Gündling, 'Our Responsibility to Future Generations' *American Journal of International Law*, 84/1 (1990): 207.

and the natural system, as well as the partnership between generations in a 'community of generations' is criticized as being overly anthropocentric. Humans are the only beings that are included in the community of generations. Humans, 'as the most sentient beings', have a special responsibility to protect the environment and do not have a right to destroy it.[64] The partnership between the community of generations and the environment is a skewed partnership where humans reap benefits from the environment in accordance with their generational interests and values. D'Amato's critical analysis of intergenerational equity already hinted at this flaw in 1990. His appraisal of Brown Weiss's arguments suggests that obligations to future generations are actually grounded in the international human rights framework as 'future generations also have a human right—the right to inherit an environment no worse than the one we enjoy'.[65] He, however, points to the fact that human rights are 'species chauvinist', which is problematic as it excludes other beings from consideration in an instrumentalist manner. Thus, an expansion of the purview of future generations is required in order to escape the constraints of the overtly anthropocentric and instrumentalist nature of intergenerational equity.[66]

The rights discourse in relation to future generations has also received the support of Judge Weeramantry in his dissenting opinion in the *Legality of Nuclear Weapons* case where he advocated for the recognition of the rights for future generations as indicated above. This issue should be viewed in the context of the linkage between human rights and environmental protection. Thus, this makes it possible to extend a human right to future generations as beneficiaries in order to cater for their well-being. One such proposal advocates the adoption of a domestic environmental constitutional provision that applies to present and future generations.[67] At an international level, the issue of an international environmental right has been debated, but at the time of writing this has not materialized.[68] It is not implausible to consider that such a provision may extend an environmental right to future generations. However, currently the feasibility of an adoption of such a right is slim. The inclusion of environmental rights for future generations in domestic constitutions (in the context of environmental constitutionalism)[69] could bolster the emergence of a framework of rights for future generations. As one commentator aptly notes, 'environmental rights mirror the connectedness through

[64] Edith Weiss, 'Our Rights and Obligations to Future Generations for the Environment' *American Journal of International Law*, 84/1 (1990): 198, 199.

[65] D'Amato (n 63) 195.

[66] Kyle Ash, 'Why Managing Biodiversity Will Fail: An Alternative Approach to Sustainable Exploitation for International Law' *Animal Law Review*, 13 (2009): 209. See also Chapters 13 and 14, 'Ethics' and 'Earth Jurisprudence', in this volume.

[67] Burns Weston and Tracy Bach, 'Recalibrating the Law of Humans with the Laws of Nature: Climate Change, Human Rights, and Intergenerational Justice' *Vermont Law School Research Paper No #10-06* (2009) <https://papers.ssrn.com/sol3/papers.cfm?abstract_id=1443243> accessed 15 October 2018.

[68] Louis Kotzé, 'In Search of a Right to a Healthy Environment in International Law' in John Knox and Ramin Pejan (eds), *Human Rights and a Healthy Environment* (CUP 2018) 163.

[69] James May and Erin Daly (eds), *Environmental Constitutionalism* (Edward Elgar 2015).

both space and time that characterises both constitutions and time itself'.[70] Even the absence of an explicit reference to future generations might contribute to the protection of the human rights of prospective generations as an environmental right or other derivative rights could result in the intertemporal protection of the environment. Adherence to environmental rights of future generations therefore, through the implementation of current measures, benefits both current and future generations and lends support to the fact that constitutional environmental rights in this sense may be conducive to the protection of the environmental interests of a temporal community of generations.

This statement does not ignore the importance of other human rights, such as the right to life, which also support the right to a healthy environment. These rights apply irrespective of the fact that some individuals are born at a later stage. The protection of these rights requires a continuous transgenerational application. The enforcement of the rights of future generations in terms of the international human rights framework may be impeded by doctrinal obstacles, such as difficulties relating to standing, establishment of causation, and attribution of responsibility for extraterritorial harms.[71]

A major point of critique concerning intergenerational equity relates to the relationship between current and future generations. It is possible that the interests of current and future generations may be in conflict. Molinari's analysis of the preparatory work concerning Principle 3 of the Rio Declaration, points to an initial emphasis placed on current generations (and as such the right to development) vis-a-vis future generations.[72] However, she argues that the initial emphasis on the development of current generations has yielded to a focus on the temporal dimension of the interests of future generations. Thus, the manner in which Principle 3 echoed the hope of developing nations for an NIEO, as epitomized by the right to development, lost ground to the temporal focus of this principle.[73] This deference to the interests of future generations is evident in the focus of scholars on intergenerational equity rather than the interests of current generations. This approach subordinates intra-generational equity to the temporal aspect of equity and accords too much weight to the interests of future generations.

Critique concerning the anonymous nature of future generations and the vagueness surrounding this concept also affirms the overt focus on future justice without responding to the historical responsibility of developed states for injustices of the past.[74] As such the argument is that equity is not merely an abstract concept but should be implemented among (current) individuals or groups.[75] Future generations represent

[70] Richard Hiskes, 'With Apologies to the Future: Environmental Human Rights and the Politics of Communal Responsibility' *The International Journal of Human Rights*, 21/9 (2017): 1401, 1409.

[71] Lawrence (n 62) 145.

[72] Claire Molinari, 'From a Right to Development to Intergenerational Equity' in Jorge Viñuales (ed), *The Rio Declaration on Environment and Development: A Commentary* (OUP 2015) 139, 141.

[73] Ibid, 143–144.

[74] Graham Mayeda, 'Where Should Johannesburg Take Us? Ethical and Legal Approaches to Sustainable Development in the Context of International Environmental Law' *Colorado Journal of International Environmental Law and Policy*, 15/1 (2004): 29, 48.

[75] Ibid, 42.

an abstract group, which could hamper the pursuit of concrete redistributive equity. Furthermore, intergenerational equity invokes the need to make assumptions about what future generations will value.[76] In order to make these assumptions we will use our present values to determine the interests of future generations. Values of current generations may not aspire to equity, which implies that the determination of the interests of future generations may be marred by values that perpetuate inequity.

It is imperative to recognize the importance of the interests of current generations and the need to address development as this will also contribute to a more equitable future for coming generations. The temporal aspect of intergenerational equity serves as an important constraint on the actions of current generations in recognition of the existence of ecological boundaries. It is, however, not necessary to elevate the dichotomy between current and future generations as two opposing and diverging entities. Current and future generations form part of a community of generations that spans over several generations. Different generations in the community of generations have intertwined interests and aspirations, which are also interwoven with the interests of other entities in the environment.[77]

B. Intra-generational Equity

The discussion thus far clearly indicates that intergenerational equity cannot be viewed in isolation from intra-generational equity, which is the other side of the sustainable development 'coin'. It is important to ensure that intra-generational is not merely relegated to a secondary component of equity. Intergenerational and intra-generational equity constitute the core of sustainable development and should be pursued simultaneously.

Principle 5 of the Rio Declaration reflects 'an intragenerational equity value' of the Rio Declaration as it focuses on 'eradicating poverty as an indispensable requirement for sustainable development'.[78]

The recognition of the importance of intra-generational equity in the pursuit of sustainable development underscores the importance of distributive justice among states and groups of people as 'wealthier countries and communities, which will benefit from protecting the general planetary for future generations, to contribute to the costs incurred by poor countries and communities in protecting these resources … '.[79] This idea is reminiscent of the demands for an NIEO, which preceded the emergence of sustainable development and its ancillary revival of NIEO principles[80] in the form of the

[76] Ibid, 48.

[77] Epigenetics may serve as an example of the manner in which preceding generations have an influence on subsequent generations. For a discussion see Robert Feil and Mario Fraga, 'Epigenetics and the Environment: Emerging Patterns and Implications' *Nature Reviews Genetics*, 13/2 (2012): 97.

[78] Takhima Karimova and Christopher Golay, 'Principle 5: Poverty Eradication' in Viñuales (n 72) 182.

[79] Ibid, 28.

[80] Kamal Hossain, 'General Principles, the Charter of Economic Rights and Duties of States, and the NIEO' in Kamal Hossain (ed), *Legal Aspects of the New International Economic Order* (Frances Pinter Ltd 1980) 2.

UNCED principles.[81] It is especially the principles of differential treatment (referred to as preferential treatment in the NIEO) and solidarity that warrant a discussion due to their relevance in the climate change regime.

Differential treatment is aimed at substantive equality as it allows for a divergence from reciprocal obligations in order to accommodate the existence of factors, such as differences in economic development or capacities to address a specific environmental problem.[82] The moral principle of solidarity finds practical application through differential treatment provisions. Solidarity is aimed at the promotion of equity as states should not take into consideration only their own interests in shaping their international interests but also those of other states and/or the interests of the community. Solidarity recognizes the inequalities that exist among states and the need for a differential burden in order to realize common objectives.[83]

The principle which clearly reflects the essence of differential treatment in international environmental law is the principle of common but differentiated responsibility (CBDR).[84] This principle entails two main elements.[85] Firstly, it concerns the common responsibility of states for the protection of the environment. Secondly, it concerns the acknowledgement of, for instance, the differential contributions of states to an environmental problem and the respective capabilities to respond to a problem. The differential responsibility is translated into differential obligations for states. Cullet considers CBDR as a 'manifestation of equity' since the acknowledgement of the inequalities among countries provides the basis for redistributive measures pursuant to distributive justice.[86] In terms of climate change, Article 3.1 of the UNFCCC first articulated the common but differentiated responsibilities and respective capabilities principle (CBDRRC) and linked this principle with equity as Article 3.1 stated that 'The Parties should protect the climate system for the benefit of present and future generations of humankind, on the basis of equity and in accordance with their common but differentiated responsibilities and respective capabilities'. Hence, the UNFCCC reflects the CBDRRC principle through a categorical differentiation and diffusion of obligations between Annex I and non-Annex I countries.[87] The Paris Agreement contains numerous references to equity and the CBDRRC principle. For example, the preamble

[81] Werner Scholtz, 'A Sustainable and Equitable Legal Order' in Jamie Benedickson *et al* (eds), *Environmental Law and Sustainability after Rio* (Edward Elgar 2011) 119, 121–123.

[82] See Chapter 19, 'Differentiation', in this volume.

[83] Rüdiger Wolfrum, 'Solidarity amongst States: An Emerging Structural Principle of International Law' in Pierre-Marie Dupuy *et al* (eds), *Völkerrecht als Wertordnung. Festschrift für Christian Tomuschat* (N.P. Engel Verlag 1995) 1087–1101; UNGA Res 3281-XXIX, 'Charter of Economic Rights and Duties of States' (12 December 1974) UN Doc A/RES/29/3281, art 18.

[84] Cullet, 'Paradigm of Inter-state Relations' (n 29) 577.

[85] For a discussion see Christopher Stone, 'Common but Differentiated Responsibilities in International Law' *American Journal of International Law*, 98/2 (2004): 276.

[86] Phillippe Cullet, 'Principle 7: Common but Differentiated Responsibilities' in Viñuales (n 72) 229, 231.

[87] See arts 4.2–4.4; art 4.1 establishes common obligations.

mentions that the Convention will be 'guided by its principles, including the principle of equity and common but differentiated responsibilities and respective capabilities'. Furthermore, the preamble emphasizes 'the intrinsic relationship that climate change actions, responses and impacts have with equitable access to sustainable development and eradication of poverty'. Article 2.2 tweaks the CBDRRC principle as reflected in the UNFCCC as it states that the Paris Agreement will be implemented on the basis of equity and the principle of CBDRRC 'in the light of different national circumstances'. The Paris Agreement is replete with further references to equity, CBDRRC, and different national circumstances or different national capacities.[88] The version of equity and CBDRRC in the Paris Agreement differs from the binary approach of the 1997 Kyoto Protocol as it requires all parties to prepare and implement nationally determined contributions (NDCs).[89] Rajamani therefore argues that the Paris Agreement contains a 'distinct rather than a derivative version' of the notions of equity and the CBDRRC in the UNFCCC.[90] Thus, the CBDRRC principle in the Paris Agreement does not apply in a static manner but is more evolutionary and open to change.[91] The Paris Agreement includes various differential treatment provisions which reflect notions of equity.[92] However, these provisions are generally non-binding obligations.[93] As such, the argument may be made that the Paris Agreement reflects a weaker form of CBDRRC and also intra-generational equity (in the sense of burden-sharing as well as distributive justice). The weaker nature of intra-generational equity may also be seen in the recognition of poverty eradication as merely a part of the context for action.[94] However, Lawrence and Reder argue that the understanding of equity and CBDR should not be constrained to notions of justice as burden-sharing, but should be understood through the lens of the Aristotelian tradition of equity, which is known as 'epiekeia'. They indicate that an understanding of CBDR and equity approached in this way 'involves not only a distributional justice imperative, but also the requirement that actors should not act based on their narrow self-interests, but ... in a morally good way, reflecting requirements of the greater public good'.[95] Hence, they argue that this approach is reflected in Article 2.2

[88] arts 4.1, 4.3, 4.4, 4.19, 13.1, 14.1, 15.2.

[89] art 3.

[90] Lavanya Rajamani, 'Ambition and Differentiation in the 2015 Paris Agreement: Interpretative Possibilities and Underlying Politics' *International and Comparative Law Quarterly*, 65/2 (2016): 493, 509.

[91] See Christina Voigt and Felipe Ferreira, 'Differentiation in the Paris Agreement' *Climate Law*, 6 (2016): 58; Sandrine Maljean-Dubois, 'The Paris Agreement: A New Step in the Gradual Evolution of Differential Treatment in the Climate Regime?' *Review of European, Comparative and International Environmental Law*, 25/2 (2016): 151.

[92] Examples include arts 4.1, 4.4, 9.1, 9.3.

[93] An exception is art 9.1, although this provision does not provide a detailed account of the content of the obligation.

[94] arts 2.1, 4.1, 6.8.

[95] Peter Lawrence and Michael Reder, 'Equity and the Paris Agreement: Legal and Philosophical Perspectives' *Journal of Environmental Law*, 31/3 (2019): 511.

of the Paris Agreement which states that it 'will be implemented to reflect equity and the principle of common but differentiated responsibilities and respective capabilities, in the light of different national circumstances'. The indeterminate nature of the provision has the potential to create binding legal obligations for parties. The focus on the implementation of the agreement (which should reflect equity) implies that states will implement the agreement in order to reflect equity based on solidarity reminiscent of 'epiekeia'.

IV. CONCLUDING REMARKS

Equity, in particular the pursuit of fairness, remains a key concept in international environmental law due to the specific nature of the issues that require attention in a context of different capabilities and respective responsibilities. Equity allows for a fair and cooperative basis for the allocation of shared resources, the equitable conservation and management of global resources, as well as the fair sharing of benefits arising from the utilization of natural resources between developing and developed states. Equity ultimately morphed into the principles of intra-generational and intergenerational equity in international environmental law in order to give recognition to the need to address poverty and its dire consequences, within a temporal context that acknowledges the generational consequences of environmental degradation associated with unconstrained development. The existence of intra-generational equity ensures that the pursuit of equity is not merely a focus on justice *in abstracto*, whereas the focus on the temporal aspect of intergenerational equity guarantees that the pursuit of current equity pays heed to future interests and ecological boundaries in the context of a community of interwoven and interdependent generations. The progressive development of intergenerational and intra-generational equity should continue as several questions remain. Further research needs to clarify the link between the utilization of human rights for future generations, as well as an expansive and more inclusive reading of intergenerational equity which includes the interests of non-human entities in an integrative manner. The pursuit of such a future research agenda will ensure true inclusive fairness and justice for human and non-human current and future generations.

BIBLIOGRAPHY

Thomas Franck, *Fairness in International Law and Institutions* (OUP 1995)

Peter Lawrence, *Justice For Future Generations: Climate Change and International Law* (Edward Elgar 2014)

Catherine Redgwell, 'Principles and Emerging Norms in International Law: Intra- and Intergenerational Equity' in Cinnamon Carlarne, Kevin Gray, and Richard Tarasofsky (eds), *The Oxford Handbook of International Climate Change Law* (OUP 2016) 186–201

Dinah Shelton, 'Equity' in Daniel Bodansky, Jutta Brunnée, and Ellen Hey (eds), *The Oxford Handbook of International Environmental Law* (1st edn, OUP 2008) 640–662

Jorge Viñuales (ed), *The Rio Declaration on Environment and Development: A Commentary* (OUP 2015)

Edith Weiss, *In Fairness to Future Generations: International Law, Common Patrimony, and Intergenerational Equity* (Transnational Publishers 1989)

CHAPTER 21

PUBLIC PARTICIPATION

JONAS EBBESSON

I. INTRODUCTION

Few areas of international law have developed so rapidly as that on public participation in environmental matters. With some exceptions, this notion hardly existed in international law until the early 1990s. The development since then stems from two disciplines of international law, namely, environmental law and human rights law. It pertains to public participation in decision-making at the national as well as international level, and involves several elements of multilevel governance. One important feature for this legal development, and also for the continuing vitality of the discourse, is the possibility in some environmental and human rights regimes for members of the public to access independent international review mechanisms. These bodies take the form of courts, committees, or commissions, with the mandate of examining whether state parties live up to their international obligations of ensuring participatory rights in their national jurisdictions.

Section II outlines key concepts and contexts in relation to public participation. Sections III and IV address public participation in national and international decision-making, respectively. As reflected in these two sections and in the conclusions, the link between the participatory opportunities at these two levels is essential.

II. CONCEPTS, CONTEXTS, AND SCALES

A. Concepts: Scope and Rationale of Public Participation

Public participation in environmental matters refers to the rights and opportunities for members of the public to engage in a wide range of environmental decision-making.

This includes decisions to permit new installations or activities with adverse environmental or health impact, approve environmental impact assessments, adopt various forms of plans, protect areas, and species, allow the marketing of chemicals or products with genetically modified organisms, and allocate emission trading units. *The related right, to access to information* not only facilitates meaningful participation in environmental decision-making, but it also enables members of the public to continuously assess matters that affect their living environment. *Access to justice* refers to the right to have decisions, acts, and omissions by the public administration and by private actors reviewed legally. It thus provides a means to make sure public authorities apply the law correctly and to keep them accountable. To different degrees, such participatory rights may give members of the public opportunities to:

- increase their general awareness;
- express their views;
- influence and engage in decision-, law- and policy-making on matters relating to the environment;
- trigger reviews of administrative decisions, acts, and omissions by public authorities;
- challenge acts by private actors;
- have existing laws enforced; and
- enjoy these rights and opportunities without being discriminated against, penalized, persecuted, or harassed.

In legal contexts, 'the public' is often defined negatively as encompassing almost all actors *outside* the public—governmental—administration. This includes individuals, groups, non-governmental organizations (NGOs), social movements, academia, Indigenous peoples, and local communities, who are not affiliated with the government or public administration. In most cases, however, the private corporate sector, when acting commercially, but not necessarily when organized in lobby groups, is excluded from the concept of 'the public' and is recognized as a separate category of stakeholders.

The legal development in support of public participation is usually motivated by factors relating to *legitimacy and democratic decision-making*. Having a say in the decision-making does not imply a veto for members of the public. Nevertheless, the trust in public authorities and the acceptance of decisions are enhanced if members of the public can voice their views in the development, application, implementation, and enforcement of legal norms and policies.

Participatory rights in environmental matters, as developed in international law, closely relate to *human rights* law. They draw on concepts already recognized in international human rights law, such as the generally acknowledged right to political participation, and the right to a fair trial,[1] while adapting and developing them to the specific features of environmental problems and contexts.

[1] Universal Declaration of Human Rights (UDHR), arts 10, 19; 1966 International Covenant on Civil and Political Rights (ICCPR), arts 14, 25; 1969 American Convention on Human Rights (ACHR), arts 8,

Public participation is also motivated by *straightforward environmental arguments*. Governments and public authorities sometimes fail to consider essential environmental concerns when seeking to realize different, often conflicting interests. Moreover, environmental authorities are not always able to act when environmental laws are not complied with (they may be understaffed or blocked, for political reasons). In these cases, allowing members of the public to initiate proceedings and invoke acknowledged environmental concerns, which otherwise risk being ignored, may lead to better decisions and more effective enforcement of existing laws. Public participation also provides opportunities to determine and question what constitutes a health or environmental problem in the first place. Finally, participatory procedures promote communication, exchanges of 'second thoughts', and reflections among those involved, and thinking of alternatives, which are essential elements in any sustainable development policy.

In light of the huge number of environmental and human rights activists and defenders being threatened, harassed, and penalized—many even killed—increasing attention has been paid to ensuring that states protect members of the public when enjoying their participatory rights.[2] This obligation is set out in bold provisions in the two most advanced treaty regimes on participatory rights in environmental matters, namely, the 1998 Aarhus Convention,[3] and the 2018 Escazú Agreement.[4]

Such a case was examined by the Aarhus Convention Compliance Committee, in *ACCC/C/2014/102 (Belarus)*, where activists opposing a planned nuclear power plant had been arrested, detained, fined, and subject to prolonged documents checks. The Committee found that Belarus had failed to comply with the Convention, emphasized the seriousness of its findings, and stated that '[i]f members of the public are penalized, harassed or persecuted for exercising their rights under the Convention, it puts in grave jeopardy the implementation of the Convention as a whole by the Party concerned'.[5]

The link between participatory rights in environmental matters and the protection and respect of established human rights is obvious. This explains why the protection from threats, harassment, and intimations when engaging in environmental matters has also been highlighted in international human rights contexts.[6]

23; 1981 African Charter on Human and People's Rights, art 13; 1950 European Convention on Human Rights (ECHR), art 6.

[2] See United Nations (UN) Environment, 'Promoting Greater Protection for Environmental Defenders—Policy' <https://wedocs.unep.org/handle/20.500.11822/22769> accessed 17 December 2019.

[3] art 3.8.

[4] art 9.

[5] UN Economic Commission for Europe (UNECE), 'Findings and recommendations with regard to communication ACCC/C/2014/102 concerning compliance by Belarus' (24 July 2017) UN Doc ECE/MP.PP/C.1/2017/19, para 110.

[6] See UN Human Rights Council (HRC), 'Resolution adopted by the Human Rights Council on 24 March 2017–34/20. Human rights and the environment' (6 April 2017) UN Doc A/HRC/RES/34/20; UNHRC, 'Report of the Special Rapporteur on the issue of human rights obligations relating to the enjoyment of a safe, clean, healthy and sustainable environment' (24 January 2018) UN Doc A/HRC/37/59.

B. Contexts: Legal Foundations and Development

The development of norms promoting public participation in national and international environmental decision-making reflects a move of expanding the involvement of non-state actors in decision-making procedures. This does not mean that public institutions have surrendered their decision-making and law-making powers. It is not a zero-sum game, and, as already pointed out, public participation can even help make governmental decisions more effective by enhancing the legitimacy and acceptability of decisions taken.

The development of international norms and policies regarding public participation in *domestic* environmental decision-making can be traced to before the 1990s. However, Principle 10 of the Rio Declaration, adopted at the 1992 UN Conference on Environment and Development (UNCED), has been particularly influential in this development by reflecting a level of international consensus of policy formation. It provides that:

> Environmental issues are best handled with the participation of all concerned citizens, at the relevant level. At the national level, each individual shall have appropriate *access to information* concerning the environment that is held by public authorities, including information on hazardous materials and activities in their communities, and the opportunity to *participate in decision-making processes.* States shall facilitate and encourage public awareness and participation by making information widely available. Effective *access to judicial and administrative proceedings,* including *redress* and *remedy,* shall be provided [emphasis added].

These matters belong to what traditionally was considered to be within a state's sovereignty. As such—with the exception of international human rights law—they remained outside the scope of international law. Today, however, many states have expanded the participatory rights for individuals and NGOs of their own accord, and, increasingly, international law is also imposing duties on states to develop participatory processes.

The outcomes from UNCED[7] and subsequent UN conferences, that is, 2002 World Summit on Sustainable Development (WSSD)[8] and 2012 UN Conference for Sustainable development (UNCSD, Rio+20),[9] all refer to good governance, Principle 10, and public participation. Moreover, while essentially *no* environmental treaty of global reach adopted before UNCED contains provisions in support of public participation, just about *all* global environmental treaties adopted at or after UNCED support, to varying degrees, public access to information or public participation.

In addition to these important, yet rather vague, treaty provisions, international human rights treaties and instruments of global scope support participatory rights.

[7] *Report of the United Nations Conference on Environment and Development* (UN 1993) vol I, annex I—'Rio Declaration', annex II—'Agenda 21'.

[8] *Report of World Summit on Sustainable Development* (UN 2002) 6, 'Plan of Implementation'.

[9] UNGA Res 66/288, 'The Future We Want' (11 September 2012) UN Doc A/Res/66/288.

These treaties, jurisprudence, and other indications are supportive of a global development of a duty under *general international law* to provide for public participation or consultation, in particular where harmful activities entail risks of significant transboundary harm.

The direct legal reflection of Rio Principle 10 is even more apparent in developments at the *regional* level. For Europe, the Caucasus and Central Asia, the Americas, and Africa, this is seen in both environmental treaties with particular focus on participatory rights and the jurisprudence developed in the respective human rights regime, where existing provisions have been interpreted and construed so as to recognize participatory rights in environmental contexts. The situation is different in most parts of Asia and the Pacific where there is little development of regional international law on the matter, neither through environmental treaties nor human rights regimes.

The development of a duty under *general international law* in relation to participation and consultation is also supported by intergovernmental policy documents, declarations, decisions, recommendations, guidelines, and action plans. The legal relevance of these documents differs. Yet, they all provide fragments of a *normative pattern*, which can be fully depicted only if these documents are studied together with relevant global and regional treaty regimes and jurisprudence; see Section III.[10]

While cases of public participation in environmental matters at the *international* level are seen already in the second half of the nineteenth and beginning of the twentieth centuries, the rules and regulations on the participation of non-state actors date back only to the 1970s. Most international environmental regimes, whether regional or global in scope, now have accreditation processes and regulations concerning the participation of non-state actors; see Section IV.

C. Scales: Participatory Rights and Social-Ecological Settings

International law and policies on public participation in environmental decision-making apply to a continuum of scales, ranging from local to global settings. These scales and settings refer to the *factual, social-ecological contexts* as well as to the *legal contexts*, and they involve public participation in national, international, and multilevel environments. A relevant factor, therefore, is whether the different legal approaches, concepts, and principles for public participation match the scales and scope of social-ecological contexts.

10 Jonas Ebbesson, 'Principle 10: Public Participation' in Jorge Viñuales (ed), *The Rio Declaration on Environment and Development: A Commentary* (OUP 2015) 287.

One such case, where the social-ecological contexts challenge the legal concepts and approaches, refers to who is considered to be concerned about the decision-making.[11] Contrary to the reference in Principle 10 of the Rio Declaration to the 'concerned citizens', in many contexts, appropriate public participation requires procedures which provide for participation not only by citizens, but also by the public across state borders; it may be equally or more affected than the public in the territory of the activity, installation, or plan in question.

A common approach to take the transboundary dimensions into account is to *prohibit discrimination and provide for equal access* in environmental decision-making on the basis of nationality, residence, or place of harm. This approach is reflected in several environmental treaties and other documents.[12] As set out by the International Law Commission (ILC):

> Unless the States concerned have agreed otherwise for the protection of the interests of persons, natural or juridical, who may be or are exposed to the risk of significant transboundary harm as a result of an activity within the scope of the present articles, a State shall not discriminate on the basis of nationality or residence or place where the injury might occur, in granting to such persons, in accordance with its legal system, access to judicial or other procedures to seek protection or other appropriate redress.[13]

The logic of non-discrimination is to ignore state borders. Accordingly, when a state makes a decision, for instance issues a permit or adopts a spatial plan, that may cause transboundary effects, it must not apply its criteria for participation and standing to appeal, or its applicable remedies, less favourably to those affected on the other side of the state borders.

The merit of non-discrimination in environmental decision-making is that it reflects the real world where pollution and threats to human health and the environment do not stop at state borders. Still, the transboundary rights based on the non-discrimination principle just reflect those of the state responsible for the decision-making process, whether generous or restrictive on public participation. Hence, ignoring state borders in decision-making does not necessarily ensure participatory rights.

[11] Jonas Ebbesson and Carl Folke, 'Matching Scales of Law with Social-Ecological Contexts to Promote Resilience' in Ahjond Garmestani and Craig Allen (eds), *Social-Ecological Resilience and Law* (Columbia University Press 2014) 265.

[12] 1974 Nordic Environmental Protection Convention; OECD, 'Recommendation of the Council for the Implementation of a Regime of Equal Right of Access and Non-Discrimination in Relation to Transfrontier Pollution' (17 May 1977) OECD/LEGAL/0152; 1991 Espoo Convention; Aarhus Convention; Escazú Agreement; 1997 UN Convention on the Law of Non-Navigational Uses of International Watercourses.

[13] 'Report of the International Law Commission on the work of its fifty-third session' (2001) UN Doc A/56/10, ch V—'International Liability for Injurious Consequences Arising out of Acts not Prohibited by International Law (Prevention of Transboundary Harm from Hazardous Activities)' 147, art 15.

The more ambitious approach in international law, therefore, is to *also* define minimum requirements for public participation to be implemented in national laws. In some regimes this means that, when the scale of the social-ecological contexts stretches across state borders, then so do the legal notions—as with *the public concerned* in the Aarhus Convention.

In *ACCC/C/2013/91 (UK)*, a German citizen alleged that the United Kingdom did not comply with the Convention because it did not provide the German public with opportunities to participate in a transboundary environmental impact assessment procedure concerning the proposed construction of two nuclear reactors in the United Kingdom. The Aarhus Convention Compliance Committee held that in determining 'the public concerned' in cases of 'ultra-hazardous activities', the magnitude of effects must be considered, and that the possible adverse effects in case of an accident can reach 'far beyond State borders and over vast areas and regions'. It considered that 'it is therefore important to secure public participation appropriate to that activity with respect to these areas and regions both within and beyond the State borders of the Party concerned' and that 'the public in Germany, including the communicant, are also part of the public concerned'. The Committee found that the United Kingdom had failed to comply with the Convention by 'not ensuring that the public concerned in Germany had a reasonable chance to learn about the proposed activity and the opportunities for the public to participate in the respective decision-making' and by not providing for notification outside its territory in its legislation.[14]

In other cases, like ozone layer depletion and climate change, the geographical distance between the harmful activity or installation and those affected can be even longer. While the transboundary dimension of public participation is clearly recognized in international law, it has not yet been established who may enjoy participatory rights in cases of global scale and planetary dimensions. In light of the increasing volume of climate change litigation this aspect will become increasingly relevant.

III. DECISION-MAKING IN NATIONAL CONTEXTS

Below, after briefly describing a few environmental treaties, I explore the jurisprudence of human rights regimes providing for participatory rights in environmental matters. To get a full picture for each region, one needs to consider all the applicable law, that is, global and regional, and environmental treaties and human rights regimes. It is also

[14] UNECE, 'Findings and recommendations with regard to communication ACCC/C/2013/91 concerning compliance by the United Kingdom of Great Britain and Northern Ireland' (24 July 2017) UN Doc ECE/MP.PP/C.1/2017/14.

necessary to check and compare the institutional setting of each treaty regime, in particular the system for reviewing compliance and implementation.

A. Basis for Public Participation in Environmental Treaties

As mentioned, there is some support for access to information or public participation in decision-making in nearly *all* global environmental treaties adopted at or after 1992 UNCED. These treaties—for example, the 1992 (UN Framework Convention on Climate Change with the 2015 Paris Agreement, the 1994 Desertification Convention, the 2001 Stockholm Convention, the 1992 Convention on Biological Diversity with the 2000 Cartagena and 2010 Nagoya Protocols, and the 2013 Minamata Convention—contain provisions for public awareness and participation, and the dissemination of information. In general terms, they aim to improve public engagement in environmental decision-making or access to environmental information.

The ILC Draft Articles on Prevention reflect this development as a matter of global law:

> States concerned shall, by such means as are appropriate, provide the public likely to be affected by an activity within the scope of the present articles with relevant information relating to the activity, the risks involved and the harm which might result and ascertain their views.[15]

The provision correctly conceives of access to information as closely related to public participation. Also of global relevance and far more specific in defining public participation in environmental matters, yet not a treaty, are the 2010 UNEP Bali Guidelines,[16] which draw on the Aarhus Convention.

Even though global agreements should be interpreted in light of the Rio Declaration and other policy documents, and may become the starting points for more progressive norms on public participation and access to information in the future, they currently are not reflecting the rights-based approach that is being developed in some regions.

The Aarhus Convention, administered by the UNECE, and applicable to Europe, the Caucasus region, and Central Asia, is the most advanced treaty providing for access to information, public participation in decision-making, and access to justice in environmental matters. By establishing minimum *rights* for members of the public in these three respects, the Aarhus Convention goes further than merely prescribing

[15] ILC Report of 53rd session (n 13) ch V.E—'Draft articles on prevention of transboundary harm from hazardous activities' 147, art 13.

[16] UNEP, 'Guidelines for the Development of National Legislation on Access to Information, Public Participation and Access to Justice in Environmental Matters' (26 February 2010).

non-discrimination. It also recognizes that environmental NGOs have a sufficient interest to take part in decision-making and submit complaints to legal review. It requires decision-making procedures to be transparent and include opportunities to submit comments and opinions at an early stage in the process. It also requires due account to be taken of the outcome of the participatory procedures.[17]

The right to access to environmental information means that all environmental information should be publicly available on request, unless refusal to disclose information is justified on any of the listed grounds. To make this right more useful, the Convention parties must also keep and update 'an adequate flow' of environmental information.[18]

Access to justice means a right to access to a court or court-like body to challenge decisions concerning requests for information and public participation with respect to specific activities and installations. However, the Aarhus Convention goes further by requiring access to justice, through judiciary or administrative procedures, to *all* acts and omissions by private persons and public authorities which contravene provisions of its national law relating to the environment. All these procedures for access to justice must provide adequate and effective remedies, and be fair, equitable, timely, and not prohibitively expensive.[19]

The Aarhus Convention deviates from international human rights law by relaxing the distinction between private and public matters. It promotes wider access to justice to members of the public, for example, by providing for legal review of decisions in cases where this would not necessarily follow from the human rights regimes. It also grants access to justice and thus a right to act on behalf of public interests to environmental associations.

The input of the Aarhus Convention on legal discourse, development, and compliance by the parties also depends on institutional factors. In particular, its system of an impartial and independent body, the Aarhus Convention Compliance Committee. Its review of compliance and implementation by the parties makes it more difficult for parties to silently get away with self-serving interpretations of the Convention.

Other regional UNECE environmental conventions, applicable in parallel to the Aarhus Convention, set out more narrowly defined provisions for access to information and participatory structures in decision-making with respect to environmental impact assessments, water issues, and industrial accidents.[20]

The Escazú Agreement, administered by ECLAC (Economic Commission for Latin America and the Caribbean) and applicable to Latin America and the Caribbean, is heavily influenced by and follows the structure of the Aarhus Convention, although it more explicitly links the obligations of the parties to the *rights* of the public. Thus,

17 arts 6–8.

18 arts 4–5.

19 art 9.

20 Espoo Convention, arts 3, 6; 1992 Convention on the Transboundary Effects of Industrial Accidents, art 9; 1999 Protocol on Water and Health to 1992 Convention on Protection and Use of Transboundary Watercourses and International Lakes, arts 5, 9, 10.

the parties 'guarantee' minimum rights for the public to access to information, participation in decision-making, and access to justice. It also relates the participatory elements to a broader range of principles and concepts intended to guide implementation by the parties, such as non-discrimination, non-regression (that is not to reduce the rights), prevention, precaution, and intergenerational equity.[21] Moreover, the Escazú Agreement places greater emphasis on persons and groups in vulnerable situations and on Indigenous peoples than the Aarhus Convention.

The Escazú Agreement also obliges the parties to guarantee the public's rights of access to information on request, subject to possible grounds for refusal, and to guarantee that relevant environmental information is indeed generated, collected, and disseminated. Public participation shall be provided for in decision-making processes for granting permits to projects and activities that may have a significant impact on the environment, and promoted for decision-making on land-use planning, policies, strategies, plans and programmes, and regulations. Here too, the right of access to justice applies to requests for environmental information, the participatory rights set out in the Agreement, and to any other decision, act, or omission that could adversely affect the environment or violate laws and regulations related to the environment.[22]

In North America, where the Escazú Agreement does not apply, the 1993 North American Agreement on Environmental Cooperation (NAAEC) provides for public participation in environmental matters. By comparison, the minimum standards for public participation in decision-making and access to information in the NAAEC are less ambitious than in the Aarhus Convention and Escazú Agreement. However, the approach to access to justice in the NAAEC is broader in scope. The parties are obliged generally to ensure judicial and administrative enforcement proceedings, whereby violations of domestic environmental laws can be sanctioned and remedied, and to ensure due process and private remedies for suing private actors, requesting governmental action, and seeking injunctions.[23]

There is no African treaty that corresponds to the Aarhus Convention, but the 2003 Revised African Convention on the Conservation of Nature and Natural Resources, applicable to almost one third of African states, clearly reflects Rio Principle 10. Although far less detailed than the Aarhus Convention and the Escazú Agreement, it sets out boldly that parties shall adopt legislative and regulatory measures to ensure dissemination of environmental information, access of the public to such information, participation of the public in decision-making, and access to justice in environmental matters. In addition, in transboundary contexts, each party is required to ensure equal access to administrative and judicial procedures to those affected as to nationals or residents of the party of origin.[24]

[21] arts 3–4.
[22] arts 5–8.
[23] arts 5–7.
[24] art 16.

For most parts of Asia and the Pacific, despite significant developments for public participation in some national contexts, there is essentially no regional international law on public participation. Yet, some international policy measures have been taken, which add modest support for public participation to the rather weak provisions of the global environmental treaties, and the developments of national systems.[25]

B. Basis for Public Participation in Human Rights Regimes

In addition to the support for participatory rights of global scope in the 1948 UDHR, the 1966 ICCPR, and the 1966 International Covenant on Economic, Social and Cultural Rights, significant developments to this end have taken place in regional human rights law.[26] These developments reflect the regional asymmetry of the environmental agreements promoting participatory rights.

In the ECHR, the jurisprudence on participatory rights in environmental matters is established mainly on the right to life, right to respect for privacy and family life, and the right to a fair trial.[27] The European Court of Human Rights (ECtHR) has ruled that a state violates the fundamental right to respect for privacy and family life if it fails to provide essential information about hazardous activities that enables members of the public to assess the risks they and their families might run.[28] Clearly inspired by the Aarhus Convention, the Court has construed the right to respect for privacy and family life as providing for a right of members of the public to participate in decision-making processes concerning environmental matter.[29] Access to justice in environmental matters, including access to effective remedies,[30] obviously draws on the right to a fair trial.[31] Nevertheless, the right to appeal cases where interests or comments have not been given sufficient weight in the environmental decision-making process is also part of the right to private and family life.[32]

In the ACHR, the jurisprudence providing for participatory rights mainly builds on the right to property. According to the Inter-American Court of Human Rights (IACtHR) and Commission of Human Rights (IAComHR), states must

[25] Ben Boer, 'Environmental Law and Human Rights in the Asia-Pacific' in Ben Boer (ed), *Environmental Law Dimensions of Human Rights* (OUP 2015) 135–179.

[26] Alan Boyle, 'Human Rights and the Environment: Where next?' in Boer (n 25) 201–239.

[27] Ibid.

[28] Cf. ECHR, art 8. *Guerra and Others v Italy* (19 February 1998) ECtHR, 116/1996/735/932.

[29] *Taskin and Ors v Turkey* (10 November 2004) ECtHR, 46117/99; *Tatar v Romania* (27 January 2009) ECtHR, 67021/01.

[30] *Kyrtatos v Greece* (22 May 2003) ECtHR, 41666/98; *Okyay and Other v Turkey* (12 July 2005) ECtHR, 36220/97.

[31] See *Karin Andersson et al v Sweden* (25 September 2014) ECtHR, 29878/09.

[32] Taskin case (n 29); *Giacomelli v Italy* (2 November 2006) ECtHR, 59909/00; Tatar case (n 29).

ensure effective participation of members of the community concerned, including by accepting and disseminating information, when concessions are granted for the exploitation and extraction of natural resources within territories of tribal communities.[33] In addition, states must ensure the right to access to information in relation to possible damage to the environment; ensure the right to participate in decision-making and in the issuing of policies that may affect the environment, as established through the right to participate in government; and ensure access to justice regarding the protection of the environment.[34] States are also obliged to take affirmative steps to ensure that the remedies are effective in establishing possible violations and in providing redress.[35]

For Africa, the African Charter on Human and Peoples' Rights has been far more important for promoting public participation than the 2003 African Nature Conservation Convention. Contrary to the European and Inter-American Conventions, the African Charter sets out a right to a satisfactory environment. This right and the provision on the right to best attainable state of health have been interpreted as obliging states to monitor threatened environments, require environmental and social impact studies, provide relevant information to the communities exposed to hazardous materials and activities,[36] and ensure meaningful opportunities for individuals to participate in the decision-making affecting their communities.[37] Lack of opportunities for such participation has also been found to violate the right to health and the right to a satisfactory environment.[38] In the jurisprudence under the African Charter, participatory rights have been considered both as individual and collective rights.[39] There is yet little, if any, jurisprudence under the African Charter on access to justice in environmental matters.

Again, the situation is different for most parts of Asia and the Pacific, where no effective international human rights regime has been established in addition to the applicable regimes of global reach.

[33] *Case of the Saramaka People v Suriname* (Judgement of 28 November 2007 on Merits, Reparations and Costs) IACtHR Ser C No 172 [133]; *Maya Indigenous Communities of the Toledo District, Belize*, IAComHR (12 October 2004) Report No 40/04, Case 12.053.

[34] *State Obligations in Relation to the Environment* (Advisory Opinion) IACtHR (2017) OC-23/17.

[35] Maya Indigenous Communities case (n 33); see also *Claude-Reyes and Others v Chile* (Judgement of 19 September 2006 on Merits, Reparations and Costs) IACtHR Series C No 151.

[36] *Social and Economic Rights Action Center (SERAC) and the Center for Economic and Social Rights (CESR) v Nigeria*, African Commission on Human and Peoples' Rights (AComHPR) (2001) Communication No 155/96 (Ogoni case).

[37] *Centre for Minority Rights Development (Kenya) and Minority Rights Group (on behalf of Endorois Welfare Council) v Kenya*, AComHPR (2009) Communication No 276/03; *African Commission on Human and Peoples' Rights v Kenya*, ACtHPR (26 May 2017) No 006/2012.

[38] Ogoni case (n 36).

[39] Endorois Welfare Council case (n 37); African Commission v Kenya case (n 37).

IV. DECISION-MAKING IN INTERNATIONAL CONTEXTS

A. Public Participation

When participating at international meetings, NGOs may influence the decision-making by invoking public interests in parallel to the governments themselves and bringing attention to issues and arguments that would otherwise be ignored. They may also influence the development and implementation of environmental laws and policies by pushing the agenda, providing expertise, lobbying, and monitoring. In performing these functions, NGOs act as 'whistle-blowers' by demanding attention for urgent concerns and as 'watch-dogs' by, for example, pressuring governments to implement international commitments. In yet other cases, NGOs may challenge decisions in review procedures.

Most UN bodies active in environmental matters have adopted accreditation programmes that apply to NGOs. Within the UN system, the legal basis for public participation is found in the mandate given to the Economic and Social Council (ECOSOC) to provide for 'consultative arrangements' with NGOs.[40] NGOs fulfilling the ECOSOC criteria may attain different consultative status, depending on the purpose and scope of the organization.[41] The numerous NGOs with such status serve as technical experts and advisers, take part in the implementation of programmes, and provide interventions, statements, and proposals for new initiatives. These organizations are generally invited to attend international conferences organized by the UN, but other NGOs may also be admitted.

Other international organizations, with differing degrees of engagement in environmental and health matters, such as the World Trade Organization (WTO), the Organisation for Economic Cooperation and Development (OECD), the Council of Europe, the European Union (EU), and the Organization of American States (OAS), also have schemes for NGO accreditation.

Most multilateral environmental agreements (MEAs) adopted after the mid-1980s provide for the participation of NGOs, qualified as competent in the subject matter of the respective agreement, at conferences of the parties, unless a minority of the parties present—at least one-third—objects. Even where an MEA or the constitutive document of an international organization does not provide for admitting NGOs as observers, the parties or members are rarely barred from deciding to establish

[40] Cf. UN Charter, art 71, according to which the ECOSOC 'may make suitable arrangements for consultations with non-governmental organizations concerned with matters within its competence'.

[41] ECOSOC Res 1996/31, 'Consultative relationship between the United Nations and non-governmental organizations' (25 July 1996).

participatory arrangements (eg the 1971 Ramsar Convention and the International Whaling Commission).

In general, accreditation entails the right to observe meetings and to submit documents, proposals, and petitions for consideration by the parties. In most environmental regimes, NGOs are given the right to address the meeting. Some regimes also entitle NGOs to participate in meetings of committees or expert groups or to nominate candidates. So, accreditation usually entails more opportunities than mere passive observation.

In addition to providing for NGO participation through accreditation, some treaty secretariats and international institutions have established various forms of communication centres, discussion forums, dialogue routines, or procedures that allow for members of the public to submit comments and views about a convention and its implementation.

The Aarhus Convention parties 'shall' and the Escazú Agreement parties 'may' promote the application of the treaties' principles on public participation in international forums.[42] Still, it is difficult to observe a trend in promoting public participation in international forums through operative policies, regulations, or guidelines of international organizations and treaty regimes.

B. Access to Justice

A special form of participatory rights at the international level is the ability to trigger independent reviews of states' performance. Except for the human rights courts, mentioned above, there is still no international court readily available for recourse by individuals or NGOs when states violate international norms on the protection of health and the environment.

However, other forms of international review mechanisms, available for the public, are slowly being established. One of the few global environmental agreements which provide for a review system accessible for international and accredited national NGOs is the 1979 Convention on Migratory Species (CMS). This system was set up in 2017,[43] inspired by some regional arrangements. The review of 'implementation matters', based on information submitted to the secretariat, for instance by NGOs, is carried out by the Standing Committee of the Convention, with the support of the Scientific Council. Various measures of a supportive, non-adversarial, and facilitative nature, including requesting an implementation plan, may be taken once an 'implementation matter' has been identified and the party has not addressed the matter within a reasonable time frame. It is also possible to issue a caution or warning to the party concerned. It is too

[42] Aarhus Convention, art 3.7; Escazú Agreement, art 4.10.

[43] UN Environment—CMS, 'Establishment of a Review Mechanism and a National Legislation Programme (Adopted by the Conference of the Parties at its 12th Meeting, Manila, October 2017)' UNEP/CMS/Resolution 12.9.

early yet to evaluate the effectiveness of this system, but it will likely provide for a more transparent and thorough review of the parties' compliance with the Convention.

Quite a few regional review mechanisms are available for the public, among them the Standing Committee of the 1979 Convention on the Conservation of European Wildlife and Natural Habitats (Bern Convention), the Council of the Commission for Environmental Cooperation (CEC) of the NAAEC, the Aarhus Convention Compliance Committee, and the Compliance Committees for the 2003 PRTR (Pollutant Release and Transfer Registers) Protocol to the Aarhus Convention and the Protocol on Water and Health to the Convention on the Protection and Use of Transboundary Watercourses and International Lakes. In addition, both the Escazú Agreement and the Revised African Nature Conservation Convention provide for the establishment of review bodies, but no such committees have yet been set up (these two treaties entered into force in April 2021 and July 2016, respectively).

The different review bodies have different objectives. The review procedures of the CMS, Bern Convention, Aarhus Convention, PRTR Protocol, and Water and Health Protocol are established to promote compliance with the international law standards set out by the treaties, whereas the NAAEC procedure is primarily intended to ensure enforcement of national environmental protection standards. A common feature of these regimes is that they all allow for triggering by non-state actors and for submitting *amicus curiae* briefs in the fact-finding phase. Still, the review bodies differ considerably in terms of structure, degree of independence, judicial properties, and remedies. In no case is the international review body competent to take decisions that are legally binding on the parties. However, in some of the regimes, the committees can adopt independent findings of non-compliance and they may in some cases recommend measures to be taken by the non-compliant state in order to bring it into compliance. The legal authority of such findings and recommendations increases if somehow endorsed by the parties to the treaty regime. Given certain circumstances—for instance, in cases of serious or consistent non-compliance—these review bodies may also recommend that the conference of the parties adopt measures against the non-compliant state.[44] While none of the review bodies is judicial in a strict sense, the NAAEC has a more politicized structure than the other review bodies.

The effectiveness and relevance of these mechanisms depends on several factors, for example, the legal basis, the rules of procedure, the institutional structures, the degree of integrity and independence, how they are engaged, and the extent of discretion they exercise in interpreting and applying the rules concerned. Given the lack of enforcement powers against a failing party, the impact of the decisions and findings resides in the authoritative interpretation of the treaty and in the authority of the review body itself. Such decisions and findings by international review bodies exert legal and political

[44] See UNECE—Aarhus Convention, 'Decision I/7—Review of Compliance, adopted at the first meeting of the Parties held in Lucca, Italy on 21–23 October 2002' (2 April 2004) UN Doc ECE/MP.PP/2/Add.8, para 37.

pressure on the failing state to comply with applicable rules and standards. They may also be used by non-state actors in domestic procedures.

V. CONCLUSIONS

The development of international rules for public participation in environmental matters has significantly changed the image of international environmental law. It is no longer limited to defining precautionary or other measures to reduce pollution levels or protect nature. It is also concerned with governance, legitimacy, and democratic structures in international and national decision-making.

Even though the provisions for public participation in globally applicable MEAs remain vague, there is emerging consensus in the desired policy direction. They endorse, rather than preclude, the ongoing normative development that expands participatory elements in decision-making. The described regional regimes with more substantial provisions both link into and complement these global agreements.

The treaties applicable to Latin America, the Caribbean, and Africa show that, even outside Europe and North America, public participation in environmental decision-making is not perceived as a national concern only. There are also other signs of increasing interest in participatory structures of environmental decision-making in most parts of the world. In the regions mentioned above, as well as in the Asia-Pacific, NGO activism is increasing, domestic measures are being developed for public participation, and intergovernmental meetings have been held to promote public engagement.

Irrespective of the level at which norms on public participation are developed, one central concern is to ensure that these arrangements do not result merely in *pro forma* participation. Access to information, participation in decision-making, and access to justice in national contexts represent fundamental values related to democracy. However, since they also serve to legitimize governmental decisions, there is always the risk that governments may abuse them, without providing members of the public with meaningful ways to voice their concerns and have these concerns taken into account. At the national level, transparency in public administration as well as the division of governmental power between the executive and the judiciary go a long way towards providing a safeguard against such abuse. The international participatory and review procedures that have been adopted within the framework of environmental agreements provide further safeguards. However, this still depends on the extent to which the review body is able to assert its discretionary powers and thus establish a degree of independence. Independence of review bodies, national and international, is crucial to avoid *pro forma* participation and will play a key role in determining whether the participatory structures can increase the effectiveness of environmental law, enhance legitimacy, and improve the protection of health and the environment.

BIBLIOGRAPHY

Ben Boer (ed), *Environmental Law Dimensions of Human Rights* (OUP 2015)

Steve Charnovitz, 'Two Centuries of Participation: NGOs and International Governance' *Michigan Journal of International Law*, 18/2 (1997): 184

Leslie-Anne Duvic-Paoli, 'The Status of the Right to Public Participation in International Environmental Law: An Analysis of the Jurisprudence' *Yearbook of International Environmental Law*, 23/1 (2012): 80

Jonas Ebbesson, 'The Notion of Public Participation in International Environmental Law' *Yearbook of International Environmental Law*, 8/1 (1997): 51.

Jonas Ebbesson, 'Principle 10: Public Participation' in Jorge Viñuales (ed), *The Rio Declaration on Environment and Development: A Commentary* (OUP 2015) 287

Elena Fasoli and Alistair McGlone, 'The Non-Compliance Mechanism Under the Aarhus Convention as "Soft" Enforcement of International Environmental Law: Not So Soft After All!' *Netherlands International Law Review*, 65/1 (2018): 27

Stephen Stec and Jerzy Jendroska, 'The Escazú Agreement and the Regional Approach to Rio Principle 10: Process, Innovation, and Shortcomings' *Journal of Environmental Law*, 31/3 (2019): 533

UNECE, *The Aarhus Convention: An Implementation Guide* (UN 2014)

Donald Zillman, Alastair Lucas, and George Pring (eds), *Human Rights in Natural Resource Development—Public Participation in the Sustainable Development of Mining and Energy Resources* (OUP 2002)

CHAPTER 22

GOOD FAITH

AKIHO SHIBATA

I. INTRODUCTION

THE principle of good faith has been declared by the International Court of Justice (ICJ) as 'a well-established principle of international law',[1] and, through judicial pronouncements and state practice, it has come to acquire concrete legal content.[2] The principle of good faith is closely linked to the concept of legal security. It provides certainty and foreseeability in society, and as such is fundamental and necessary to any legal system.[3] Good faith is a general principle of any legal system[4] whose main normative content is the protection of legitimate expectations based on some deliberate course of conduct.[5] Though it may 'not (be) in itself a source of obligation',[6] the principle of good faith is necessary to the operation of the whole international legal order.[7]

[1] *Land and Maritime Boundary, Preliminary Objections (Cameroon/Nigeria)* (Judgement) [1998] ICJ Rep 275 [38].

[2] See generally Robert Kolb, *Good Faith in International Law* (Hart Publishing 2017); Andrew Mitchell, Muthucumaraswamy Sornarajah, and Tania Voon (eds), *Good Faith and International Economic Law* (OUP 2015); Markus Kotzur, 'Good Faith (Bona fide)' in Rüdiger Wolfrum (ed), *Max Planck Encyclopedia of Public International Law* (OUP 2009); Anthony D'Amato, 'Good Faith' in Rudolf Bernhardt (ed), *Encyclopedia of Public International Law*, Instalment 7 (North-Holland 1984) 108; Elisabeth Zoller, *La bonne foi en droit international public* (Pedone 1977).

[3] Kolb (n 2) 23–31.

[4] ICJ Statute, art 38.1(c); see Malcolm Shaw, *International Law* (8th edn, CUP 2017) 77–78.

[5] Kolb (n 2) 23–28.

[6] *Border and Transborder Armed Actions, Jurisdiction and Admissibility (Nicaragua/Honduras)* (Judgement) [1998] ICJ Rep 69 [94].

[7] Michael Virally, 'Review Essay: Good Faith in Public International Law' *American Journal of International Law*, 77/1 (1983): 130, 133. Recently, in *The South China Sea Arbitration (Philippines/China)* (Final award of 12 July 2016) PCA Case no 2013-19 (South China Sea case) [1170], [1171], the arbitral tribunal constituted under annex VII to the 1982 UNCLOS declared that 'a duty to refrain from aggravating or extending a dispute during settlement proceedings' is 'inherent in the central role of good faith in the international legal relations between States'.

This chapter examines the role that the principle of good faith could play, first, in general international law relating to the environment, focusing on three broad areas of environmental treaty performance, environmental cooperation, and due diligence. The 2015 *Chagos Marine Protected Area* arbitral award exemplifies how the principle of good faith could have practical impacts in structuring a reasoning at the level of general law. The chapter then examines the more concrete role that the principle of good faith could play within multilateral environmental agreements (MEAs) as special legal regimes. The 2014 *Whaling in the Antarctic* judgement is pivotal in pronouncing the strengthened good faith obligation to cooperate amongst the regime members as well as with the regime institutions. The chapter then analyses two concrete contexts within which the principle of good faith could be engaged to perform specific normative functions in the operation of MEAs, namely in non-compliance and 'pledge and review' mechanisms. The final section summarizes the findings of the sections that precede it.

II. GOOD FAITH IN INTERNATIONAL ENVIRONMENTAL LAW

A. International Environmental Law as International Law of Cooperation

In the famous *Nuclear Tests* cases, the ICJ, highlighting the fact that '[t]rust and confidence are inherent in international co-operation, in particular in an age when this co-operation in many fields is becoming increasingly essential', declared:[8]

> One of the basic principles governing the creation and performance of legal obligations, whatever their source, is the principle of good faith.

The very nature of international environmental law which requires cooperation[9] signifies the important role that the principle of good faith plays in its general legal structure and in deriving, articulating, and interpreting its specific rules and procedures. As far back as in 1957, in response to the Spanish lack of confidence in the French assurance that they would maintain the legal regime regarding the utilization of Lake's shared resources, the *Lake Lanoux* arbitral tribunal said that bad faith of the French authority

[8] *Nuclear Tests (Australia/France)* (Judgement) [1974] ICJ Rep 253 [46]; *Nuclear Tests (New Zealand/France)* (Judgement) [1974] ICJ Rep 457 [49] (combined—Nuclear Tests cases).

[9] Philippe Sands and Jacqueline Peel, *Principles of International Environmental Law* (4th edn, CUP 2018) 3–6, 10–11; Rüdiger Wolfrum, 'Cooperation, International Law of' in Rüdiger Wolfrum (ed), *Max Planck Encyclopedia of Public International Law* (OUP 2010); Alan Boyle, 'The Principle of Co-operation: The Environment' in Vaughan Lowe and Colin Warbrick (eds), *The United Nations and the Principles of International Law: Essays in Memory of Michael Akehurst* (Routledge 1994) 120–136.

cannot be presumed.[10] In international law generally and in international environmental law in particular, a presumption of good faith (or absence of bad faith) plays an important role in interpreting and representing legally relevant facts, including the behaviour of states.[11]

Article 2, paragraph 2 of the United Nations (UN) Charter requires its members to 'fulfil in good faith the obligations assumed by them in accordance with the present Charter'.[12] The sense of the good faith requirement here is explained as fulfilling an obligation according to the spirit of the undertaking and not merely with regard to the letter.[13] Thus, the principle of good faith can be considered as a legal standard that enables reference to normal or expected social behaviour, incorporating socially shared values, conceptions, and expectations into the operation of legal norms.[14] This aspect of good faith will have significant legal consequences in environmental regimes established by MEAs, where their members come together with the common aims to be achieved collectively and continuously interact and deepen the dialogue within institutional settings, the outcome of such 'socialization' of regime members being expressed in consensus resolutions.

Finally, good faith and equity[15] have similar functions in calling for considerations of fairness, justice, and reasonableness. The ICJ based the concepts of acquiescence and estoppel on fundamental principles of both good faith and equity.[16] However, there are differences: equity designates the conditions for deriving the justice of the particular case, by focusing on individual facts of the case. Good faith, on its part, is centred on the softening of the socially unwelcome consequences of an excessive preponderance given to the will of one subject, by protecting the legitimate expectations of other subjects.[17]

Under general international law relating to the environment, good faith has been engaged in the following ways: (1) states parties to environmental treaties must perform their obligations in good faith; (2) states must cooperate in good faith for the protection and sustainable use of the environment; and (3) states must act diligently in good faith to prevent harm to the environment. The *Chagos Marine Protected Area* case illustrates the practical legal implications the principle of good faith may have in structuring a legal logic, and articulating and interpreting relevant international environmental rules and principles, and thus will be discussed separately.

[10] *Lake Lanoux Arbitration (Spain/France)* (1957) 12 RIAA 281 [9].

[11] Kolb (n 2) 15–21. The South China Sea case (n 7) [704]–[705] arbitral award, while accepting the good faith claims asserted by China as to its rights within certain waters in the South China Sea, indicated that 'in the case of attempts by one State to induce another to relinquish its rights through repeated statements, veiled threats, or diplomatic coercion' it may amount to claiming rights in bad faith.

[12] See Gillian White, 'The Principe of Good Faith' in Lowe and Warbrick (n 9) 230–255.

[13] Jörg Müller and Robert Kolb, 'Article 2(2)' in Bruno Simma (ed), *The Charter of the United Nations: A Commentary*, vol I (2nd edn, OUP 2002) 91–101.

[14] Kolb (n 2) 22–23.

[15] See Chapter 20, 'Equity', in this volume.

[16] *Delimitation of the Maritime Boundary in the Gulf of Maine Area (Canada/United States)* (Judgement) [1984] ICJ Rep 246 (Gulf of Maine case) [130].

[17] Kolb (n 2) 35–37.

B. Good Faith Performance of Environmental Treaties

The requirement that parties must perform their obligations in good faith is an application of the principle of *pact sunt servanda* to MEAs.[18] As early as 1910, the arbitral tribunal on the *North Atlantic Coast Fisheries* case declared that the obligation to execute the Treaty in good faith involves regulations which are 'appropriate or necessary for the protection and preservation of such fisheries', 'desirable or necessary on grounds of public order and morals without unnecessarily interfering with the fisheries itself', and 'equitable and fair ... not so framed as to give unfairly an advantage to (one or the other)'.[19]

It is important to note that the treaty as a whole needs to be performed in good faith, including obligations ensuing both from the provisions relating to the institutional and procedural mechanisms constituting the treaty and the substantive norms contained in it.[20] MEAs have distinctive institutional mechanisms for monitoring and reviewing the performance of member states' obligations in light of the substantive norms as well as the overarching object and purpose of the treaties. Moreover, based on such reviews, MEAs develop further norms. It is the totality and the integrity of the MEAs that must be observed in good faith. As to the good faith observance of treaties, the ICJ in its *Gabčikovo-Nagymaros Project* case pronounced as follows:[21]

> [I]t is the purpose of the treaty, and the intentions of the parties in concluding it, which should prevail over its literal application. The principle of good faith obliges the Parties to apply it in a reasonable way and in such a manner that its purpose can be realised.

C. Environmental Cooperation in Good Faith

Principles 7 and 27 of the 1992 Rio Declaration on Environment and Development[22] state respectively that 'States shall cooperate in a spirit of global partnership to conserve, protect and restore the health and integrity of the Earth's ecosystem', and that they 'shall co-operate in good faith and in a spirit of partnership in the fulfilment of the principles embodied in this Declaration and in the further development of international law in the field of sustainable development'. Article 4 of the International Law Commission (ILC)'s 2001 Draft Articles on Prevention of Transboundary Harm[23]

[18] This principle is contained in art 26 of the 1969 Vienna Convention on the Law of Treaties which reads: 'Every treaty in force ... must be performed by (the parties) in good faith'.

[19] *The North Atlantic Coast Fisheries Case (Great Britain/US)* (7 September 1910) 11 RIAA 167, 189.

[20] Jean Salmon, 'Article 26: Pacta sunt servanda' in Olivier Corten and Pierre Klein (eds), *The Vienna Conventions on the Law of Treaties: A Commentary*, vol I (OUP 2011) 677–681.

[21] *The Gabčikovo-Nagymaros Project (Hungary/Slovakia)* (Judgement) [1997] ICJ Rep 7 [142].

[22] *Report of the United Nations Conference on Environment and Development* (UN 1993) vol I, annex I.

[23] 'Report of the International Law Commission on the work of its fifty-third session' (2001) UN Doc A/56/10, ch V.E—'Draft articles on prevention of transboundary harm from hazardous activities' 148.

provides that 'States concerned shall cooperate in good faith and, as necessary, seek the assistance of one or more competent international organisations in preventing significant transboundary harm or at any event in minimising the risk thereof'. Draft Article 8 of the 2014 International Law Association (ILA)'s Legal Principles relating to Climate Change provides, in paragraph 1 that: 'States shall cooperate with each other and competent international organisations in good faith to address climate change and its adverse effects'.[24] Commentaries to those provision[25] as well as judicial pronouncements[26] reaffirm that cooperation in good faith in relations between states is recognized as a general principle of international law and is applicable to cooperation regarding protection, conservation, and sustainable use of the environment, as well as prevention of harm to the environment.

Article 8 of 1997 UN Convention on the Law of the Non-navigational Uses of International Watercourses provides insights into the specific content of such a good faith obligation to cooperate. While stating the general obligation to cooperate in good faith in order to attain optimal utilization and adequate protection of an international watercourse (paragraph 1), paragraph 2 provides that: 'In determining the manner of such cooperation, watercourse States may consider the establishment of joint mechanisms or commissions, as deemed necessary by them, to facilitate cooperation on relevant measures and procedures'. In other words, the precise manner of cooperation as well as relevant measures and procedures to facilitate such cooperation are to be worked out in specific regimes that address particular issues or areas of environmental problems. According to the ICJ's *Pulp Mills* judgement, such a treaty-based 'mechanism of cooperation between States is governed by the principle of good faith', and the good faith performance of a treaty 'applies to all obligations established by a treaty, including procedural obligations which are essential to cooperation between States'.[27] Thus, within such cooperative environmental regimes, the good faith obligations of their members will have more concrete and strengthened normative effects, as we will see in Section III.

The principle of good faith is an integral part of procedural obligations to consult and negotiate,[28] and thus plays a key role in the obligations to consult and negotiate on appropriate measures to prevent and address environmental harm. This is reflected in

[24] International Law Association (ILA), 'Report of the seventy-fifth conference held at Washington' (2014) 22, 'ILA Legal Principles relating to Climate Change', 25.

[25] ILC draft articles on prevention (n 23) 155–156; Peter Sand, 'Chapter 31: Principle 27 Cooperation in Spirit of Global Partnership' in Jorge Viñuales (ed), *The Rio Declaration on Environment and Development: A Commentary* (OUP 2015) 617; ILA climate change legal principles (n 24) 361–366.

[26] *The MOX Plant case (Ireland/United Kingdom)* (Provisional Measures, Order of 3 December 2001) [2001] ITLOS Rep 95 [82]: 'the duty to cooperate is a fundamental principle in the prevention of pollution of the marine environment under Part XII of the Convention and general international law'. See other cases mentioned in Sands and Peel (n 9) 216–217.

[27] *Pulp Mills on the River Uruguay (Argentina/Uruguay)* (Judgement) [2010] ICJ Rep 14 (Pulp Mills case) [145]. It is important to note that the court when pronouncing these statements was referring to general 'requirements of international law'.

[28] ILC draft articles on prevention (n 23) 160–161, commentary to art 9; Gulf of Maine case (n 16) [87], [112].

Principle 19 of the Rio Declaration, which provides that 'States shall consult with those (potentially affected) States (regarding activities that may have a significant adverse transboundary environmental effect) at an early stage and in good faith.'[29] In addition, Principle 7 of the 1978 UNEP (UN Environment Programme) Environmental Law Guidelines and Principles on Shared Natural Resources provides for exchange of information and notification based on the principle of good faith.[30] Article 3 of 1997 UN Watercourses Convention provides that 'watercourse States shall consult with a view to negotiating in good faith for the purpose of concluding a watercourse agreement or agreements'. ICJ in its *North Sea Continental Shelf* cases declared that those required negotiations in good faith must be 'meaningful, which will not be the case when either of them insists upon its own position without contemplating any modification of it'.[31]

D. Due Diligence and Good Faith

Under general international law, states are obliged to use all the means at their disposal in order to prevent activities within their jurisdiction or control causing significant damage to the environment of other states or areas beyond the limits of national jurisdiction.[32] According to the court, 'the principle of prevention, as a customary rule, has its origins in the due diligence that is required of a State in its territory'.[33] It has been argued that this due diligence implies an obligation to act rationally and in good faith.[34] The International Tribunal for the Law of the Sea (ITLOS) in its *Sub-Regional Fisheries Commission* Advisory Opinion of 2 April 2015 stated that the obligation to 'seek to agree' under UNCLOS Article 63.1 (on straddling stocks), and the obligation to cooperate under Article 64.1 (on highly migratory species) are 'due diligence' obligations which require the states concerned to consult with one another in good faith, pursuant to Article 300 of UNCLOS. Such consultation in good faith required by the due

[29] Rio Declaration (n 22).

[30] American Society of International Law, 'United Nations Environment Program: Governing Council Approval Of The Report of the Intergovernmental Working Group of Experts on Natural Resources Shared by two or more States' *International Legal Materials*, 17/5 (1978): 1091–1099.

[31] *North Sea Continental Shelf (Germany/Denmark; Germany/Netherlands)* (Judgement) [1969] ICJ Rep 3 [85(a)].

[32] See Chapter 16, 'Harm Prevention', in this volume; UN, 'Report of the United Nations Conference on the Human Environment' (5–16 June 1972) UN Doc A/CONF.48/14/Rev.1, 3, ch 1—'Declaration of the United Nations Conference on the Human Environment', principle 21; Rio Declaration (n 22) principle 2; *Legality of the Threat or Use of Nuclear Weapons* (Advisory Opinion) [1996] ICJ Rep 226 [29]; Pierre-Marie Dupuy and Jorge Viñuales, 'The Principles of International Environmental Law' in Pierre-Marie Dupuy and Jorge Viñuales, *International Environmental Law* (2nd edn, CUP 2018) 66–73, 'The Principle of Prevention'.

[33] Pulp Mills case (n 27) [101]; *Responsibilities and obligations of States sponsoring persons and entities with respect to activities in the Area* (Advisory Opinion) [2011] ITLOS Rep 10 [115]–[120]; Leslie-Anne Duvic Paoli and Jorge Viñuales, 'Principle 2: Prevention', in Viñuales (ed), *Commentary* (n 25) 118–119.

[34] Joanna Kulesza, *Due Diligence in International Law* (Brill 2016) 104.

diligence obligation, according to the Tribunal, 'should be meaningful in the sense that substantial effort should be made by all States concerned, with a view to adopting effective measures necessary to coordinate and ensure the conservation and development of shared stocks'.[35]

The international jurisprudence, including the *Sub-Regional Fisheries Commission* Advisory opinion, has not yet directly linked the due diligence obligation with the good faith principle.[36] However, arguably since a principal element of good faith is to protect the legitimate expectations of the community arising from the actual behaviour of states, there is potential for good faith to exert its unique normative influence in articulating and applying due diligence obligations to prevent environmental damage.

For example, in its elaborate reference to due diligence obligations, the court in its *Pulp Mills* judgement stated[37] that the due diligence obligation to protect and preserve the river's water and its ecological balance must 'be interpreted in accordance with a practice, which in recent years has gained so much acceptance among States'. This practice is the undertaking of an environmental impact assessment where there is a risk of significant adverse impact on shared resources. In light of such behaviour of states, establishing the expectation among the international community that a similar practice would be followed, the court then went on to say that 'due diligence, and the duty of vigilance and prevention which it implies, would not be considered to have been exercised' if such an assessment was not undertaken. Of course, the court pronounced that such practice 'may now be considered a requirement under general international law'. However, the rule the court applied was the due diligence obligation of prevention interpreted in light of the community's expectation that, in the specific circumstance of the case, a prior environmental impact assessment would be conducted. This line of reasoning captures the essence of good faith which is to protect the legitimate expectations of the community arising from the behaviour of states.

E. Good Faith in Action: *Chagos Marine Protected Area* Arbitration (2015)

The principle of good faith has practical implications in structuring a reasoning, and interpreting and applying relevant provisions pertaining to international environmental

[35] *Request for an advisory opinion submitted by the Sub-Regional Fisheries Commission (SRFC)* (Advisory opinion) [2015] ITLOS Rep 4 [210].

[36] In the South China Sea case (n 7) [725], [744] the Philippines argued that pursuant to art 56 of UNCLOS, states have an obligation, acting in good faith, to take the measures necessary to prevent their nationals from exploiting the living resources in the EEZ of another state party. In response, avoiding an explicit reference to good faith, the arbitral tribunal, interpreting art 62.4 of UNCLOS, concluded that 'anything less than due diligence by a State in preventing its nationals from unlawfully fishing in the exclusive economic zone of another would fall short of the regard due pursuant to Article 58 (3) of the Convention'.

[37] Pulp Mills case (n 27) [204].

law. The award rendered in 2015 by the Arbitral Tribunal constituted under Annex VII of UNCLOS in the matters of the *Chagos Marine Protected Area* is a case in point. The principle of good faith played a critical role in the Tribunal's determination that the United Kingdom breached its obligations towards Mauritius under Articles 2.3, 56.2, and 194.4 of UNCLOS by establishing the marine protected area (MPA) surrounding the Chagos Archipelago.[38]

First, the rule of estoppel, based on the principle of good faith, was determinative in recognizing the legally binding force of the so-called Lancaster House Undertakings. The Tribunal noted that the rule of estoppel 'stems from the general requirement that States act in their mutual relations in good faith and is designed to protect the legitimate expectation of a State that acts in reliance upon the representations of another'.[39] Based on the United Kingdom's repeated reaffirmation of the Undertakings and the Mauritius' reliance upon it, the Tribunal held that the United Kingdom is 'estopped from denying the binding effect of these commitments, which the Tribunal treat as binding on the United Kingdom'.[40]

Second, the Tribunal considered that Article 2.3 of UNCLOS requires the sovereignty of the coastal state over its territorial sea to be exercised in accordance with general rules of international law, and such general international law, in turn, requires the coastal state, in this case the United Kingdom, 'to act in good faith in relations with Mauritius, including with respect to the (Lancaster House) undertakings'.[41] Noting the binding effect of the Undertakings, in which fishing rights of Mauritius in the territorial sea of Chagos Archipelago are recognized, the Tribunal concluded that 'Article 2(3) requires the United Kingdom to exercise good faith with respect to Mauritius' rights in the territorial sea'.[42] It further elaborated that such an obligation is, 'for all intents and purposes, equivalent' to due regard obligations of coastal states under Article 56.2 of UNCLOS with respect to EEZ.[43]

Finally, the Tribunal considered that 'the United Kingdom's obligation to act in good faith and to have "due regard" to Mauritius' rights and interests arising out of the Lancaster House Undertakings, as reaffirmed after 1968, entails, at least, both consultation and a balancing exercise with its own rights and interests'.[44] The Tribunal recognized the fact that United Kingdom's statements and conduct 'created reasonable expectation on the part of Mauritius that there would be further opportunities to respond and exchange views'. However, 'this expectation was frustrated when the United Kingdom declared the MPA on 1 April 2010'.[45] Thus, the Tribunal interpreted Article

[38] *Chagos Marine Protected Area Arbitration (Mauritius/UK)* (2015) 31 RIAA 359 [547].

[39] Ibid [435]. On the distinction between estoppel and the doctrine on binding unilateral acts, see ibid [446]–[447].

[40] Ibid [448].

[41] Ibid [517].

[42] Ibid [520].

[43] Ibid.

[44] Ibid [534].

[45] Ibid.

2.3, through the principle of good faith, to include an obligation on the part of coastal state (UK) to consult and balance the rights and interests of other state (Mauritius). Then the Tribunal found that such good faith consultation had not been conducted because Mauritius' expectation of further exchanges of views was frustrated by the United Kingdom's declaration.

III. CONCRETE ROLE OF GOOD FAITH IN ENVIRONMENTAL REGIMES

A. The Implication of the *Whaling* Judgement

International environmental regimes are characterized by their far-reaching requirements on all the regime members to achieve and maintain a certain factual situation or condition, necessitating constant monitoring and supervision to ensure that the prescribed standards are being met.[46] This is the obligation incumbent upon *a member of a regime* as pronounced by the ICJ in its 1980 advisory opinion in the *Interpretation of the Agreement between the WHO and Egypt*. The court stated that 'the very fact of Egypt's membership of the Organisation entails certain mutual obligations of co-operation and good faith incumbent upon Egypt and the Organisation', and as a result the '*special legal regime* of mutual rights and obligations' has been created based on 'the legal relationship between Egypt and the Organisation . . . , the *very essence of which is a body of mutual obligations of cooperation and good faith*'.[47]

The court in its *Whaling in the Antarctic* judgement strengthened this obligation incumbent upon the regime members to cooperate in good faith to include the 'duty to cooperate with the [treaty's main organs such as] IWC and the Scientific Committee' and the consequent 'obligation to give due regard to such recommendations'.[48] These strengthened good faith obligations of cooperation imposed on the regime's members do not by themselves make the normative content of the relevant recommendations legally binding on them *qua* state parties to the Convention. However, the court, in the *Whaling* judgement, did not deny the potential legal effect of those recommendations

[46] Shinya Murase' 'Perspectives from International Economic Law on Transnational Environmental Issues' *Recueil des cours* 253 (1995): 283, 413–422.

[47] *Interpretation of the Agreement of 25 March 1951 between the WHO and Egypt* (Advisory Opinion) [1980] ICJ Rep 73 [43] (emphasis added by the author).

[48] *Whaling in the Antarctic (Australia/ Japan, New Zealand intervening)* (Judgement) [2014] ICJ Rep 226 (Whaling in Antarctic case) [83], [137], [240]. Although the court did not make a reference to the WHO Advisory Opinion, New Zealand in its written observation did refer to it in its argument for the duty to cooperate and to give due regard to the recommendations of the International Whaling Commission (IWC); Whaling in Antarctic case, ibid, Written Observations of New Zealand (4 April 2013) [96].

qua members of the regime, through the obligation imposed on them to give due regard to those non-binding recommendations.

Previously, a similar reasoning founded on good faith had been suggested by a renowned legal expert in relation to UN General Assembly resolutions. Judge Sir Hersch Lauterpacht, in his separate opinion in the *Voting Procedure* Advisory Opinion case, argued that UN members are bound to give due consideration in good faith to General Assembly recommendations, and by declining to act upon a series of recommendations adopted by overwhelming majority, a member may be found to be overstepping 'the imperceptible line between impropriety and illegality, between discretion and arbitrariness'.[49] The court's *Whaling* judgement, while not explicitly referring to good faith (although extensively argued by New Zealand[50]), has confirmed the duty of regime members to consider and act upon those non-binding recommendations by transforming the 'imperceptible line' into an objective standard of review established by those recommendations.[51] Arguably this line of reasoning based on the strengthened duty to cooperate in good faith within regimes enabled the court to take into account all those binding and non-binding instruments and practices adopted within the regime as a whole, and to evaluate the good faith behaviour of its member in relation to the dynamically perceived regime.[52]

B. Good Faith in Implementation of, and Compliance with, Environmental Regimes

States' implementation of and compliance with specific obligations within environmental regimes must be evaluated in a broader context of members' constructive contribution to the promotion and maintenance of the *raison d'être* of the regimes themselves. This is the essence of good faith performance by the members of environmental regimes, and this good faith requirement leads to certain flexibilities in addressing compliance problems, taking into account the specific status of the member in light of the regime's aim.

[49] *Voting Procedure on Questions relating to Reports and Petitions concerning the Territory of South West Africa* (Advisory Opinion) [1955] ICJ Rep 67 (Separate Opinion of Judge Lauterpacht) 119-120.

[50] Written Observations of New Zealand (n 48) [12], [45], [68], [96], [105], [109], [114].

[51] See eg Shotaro Hamamoto, 'From the Requirement of Reasonableness to a 'Comply and Explain' Rule: The Standard of Review in the Whaling Judgment' in Malgosia Fitzmaurice and Dai Tamada (eds), *Whaling in the Antarctic: Significance and Implications of the ICJ Judgment* (Brill 2016) 38–52.

[52] Akiho Shibata, 'ICRW as an Evolving Instrument: Potential Broader Implications of the Whaling Judgment' *Japanese Yearbook of International Law*, 58 (2015): 298, 306–309. In this line of reasoning, one should also be mindful of art 65 of UNCLOS which requires, in the case of cetaceans, the cooperation 'through the appropriate international organizations for their conservation, management and study'. The court in its judgement did not explicitly mention art 65, but New Zealand did in its written observation; see Written Observations of New Zealand (n 48) [97].

Under the Montreal Protocol Non-Compliance Procedure, it is only after a party makes 'its best, *bona fide* efforts' to comply with its obligations under the 1987 Protocol that the party may submit its compliance difficulties to the Implementation Committee and remain eligible for assistance, including financial assistance provided by the Multilateral Fund.[53]

Under the practice of the 1997 Kyoto Protocol's Compliance Committee, some parties undergoing the process of transition to a market economy have requested the application of 'a *bona fide* principle' to their cases of non-compliance. The 1992 UN Framework Convention on Climate Change (UNFCCC) Article 4.6 allows for 'a certain degree of flexibility' to those parties undergoing the process of transition to a market economy in the implementation of their commitments under the Convention. Explicitly basing its argument on 'a *bona fide* principle', one of these parties requested the interpretation and application by the Enforcement Branch of the Compliance Committee of specific provisions under the Kyoto Protocol to be more considerate of its specific circumstances in light of the flexible and evolutionary nature of the regime as a whole.[54] Another party called for 'the acknowledgment that, in certain circumstances, countries facing economic hardship and/or institutional, organizational, administrative or technical difficulties shall be given by the Compliance Committee the required leeway to adapt in consideration of their degree of development and of challenges faced in their implementing the Convention and subsequent acts'.[55] The Enforcement Branch accepted the argument that the good faith efforts by the relevant parties to comply with their obligations would be *sine qua non* for such acknowledgement, and found such good faith efforts by those parties. However, in this specific case, the Enforcement Branch noted the fact that the such 'flexibility' could only be allowed by the decision of the Conference of the Parties serving as the meeting of the parties to the Kyoto Protocol, and, lacking such decision in the present case, the Branch could not defer a decision or the application of consequences.[56]

Thus, the principle of good faith by demarcating the flexibility allowed to parties could play a role in the implementation of environmental regimes. It allows both the subjective element of a member's 'good will' and the objective element of the regime's

[53] Decision IV/5 (Montreal Protocol), 'Non-compliance procedure' (23 November 1992) UN Doc UNEP/OzL.Pro.4/15' as amended by Decision X/10, 'Review of the non-compliance procedure' (23 November 1998) UN Doc UNEP/OzL.Pro.10/9 [4], [7]. For the practice of Implementation Committee and its relation to Multilateral Fund under the Montreal Protocol, see Osamu Yoshida, *The International Legal Regime for the Protection of the Stratospheric Ozone Layer* (2nd edn, Brill 2019) 263–281, 322–333.

[54] See UNFCC, 'Appeal by Croatia against a final decision of the Enforcement Branch of the Compliance Committee' (19 February 2010) UN Doc FCCC/KP/CMP/2010/2, para 8 (later withdrawn, UN Doc FCCC/KP/CMP/2011/2 (4 August 2011)). See the argument on 'flexibilization of the legal system' in Robert Kolb, 'Principles as Sources of International Law (With Special Reference to Good Faith)' *Netherlands International Law Review*, 53/1 (2006): 1, 28–29.

[55] UNFCC, 'Further Written Submission from Ukraine' (28 September 2011) UN Doc FCCC/KP/CC-2011-2-8/Ukraine/EB, para 26.

[56] UNFCCC, 'Enforcement Branch of the Compliance Committee—Final Decision (Party concerned—Ukraine)' (12 October 2011) UN Doc FCCC/KP/CC-2011-2-9/Ukraine/EB, paras 5–6.

object and purpose to be taken into account. Importantly, in the context of environmental regimes, the legal evaluation of such good faith efforts by relevant parties in light of the regime's object and purpose shall be effectuated by a subsidiary body of the regime, often constituted by experts serving in their personal capacity.[57]

C. Good Faith in 'Pledge and Review' Environmental Regimes

Based on the principle of good faith, the ICJ in its *Nuclear Tests* judgements, read together with its judgement in the *Burkina Faso/Mali Frontier Dispute* case, has recognized that a unilateral declaration can create legal obligations (1) if it is made publicly, (2) with an intent to be bound by it,[58] and (3) when there are no other suitable means to bind the state under the circumstances.[59] These strict conditions are most relevant when a state unilaterally undertakes an obligation towards the international community as a whole (obligation *erga omnes*). For example, a statement by Japan regarding its withdrawal from International Convention for the Regulation of Whaling (ICRW) included a declaration that: 'From July 2019, after the withdrawal comes into effect on June 30, Japan ... will cease the take of whales in the Antarctic Ocean/Southern Hemisphere.'[60] Even under such strict conditions, considering the global nature of many of the current environmental problems, the legal potential of unilateral declarations, particularly made by influential states, to forge the development of international environmental law should not be underestimated.

Arguably, the principle of good faith will have strengthened (that is, under less strict conditions than those pronounced by the ICJ) potential to provide legal effect to unilateral pledges that are made within institutional frameworks established by environmental regimes. In the context of the UNFCCC and commenting on the original 'pledge and review' proposal by Japan in 1991,[61] Atsuko Kanehara suggested the possibility of making those pledges legally binding through legal and institutional mechanisms. More precisely, she argued that the intent of the pledging party to be bound could be

[57] Under the transparency framework of the Paris Agreement, the application of flexibilities for developing countries is 'self-determined', and the technical expert review teams do not have the authority to review such application; Decision 18/CMA.1, 'Modalities, procedures and guidelines for the transparency framework for action and support referred to in Article 13 of the Paris Agreement' (19 March 2019) UN Doc FCCC/PA/CMA/2018/3/Add.2, annex, para 6.

[58] Nuclear Tests cases (n 8) [42]–[45] (Australia/France), [45]–[48] (New Zealand/France).

[59] *Frontier Dispute (Burkina Faso/Republic of Mali)* [1986] ICJ Rep 554 [39]–[40]. See also ILC, 'Guiding Principles applicable to unilateral declarations of States capable of creating legal obligations, with commentaries thereto' (2006) 369.

[60] 'Statement of the Chief Cabinet Secretary of Japan' (26 December 2018) <https://japan.kantei.go.jp/98_abe/decisions/2018/_00008.html> accessed 1 July 2019.

[61] 'Japan: Informal paper on pledge and review process as a possible mechanism to implement commitments defined on the basis of the convention' (submitted 20 June 1991) UN Doc A/AC.237/Misc.1/Add.7.

clarified through the pledging procedure, and the binding force of those pledges could be formally recognized through international review processes after certifying that their substantive contents accord with the purpose of the Convention.[62] Here, Kanehara implicitly applies a strengthened version of the good faith principle by proactively establishing the expectation amongst the regime members on the action (pledge) by one of its members through formalized and transparent procedures.

Under the 2015 Paris Agreement, the nationally determined contributions (NDCs) are self-determined commitments by its parties, and, from the texts and their *travaux prepartoires*, it is difficult to claim parties have intended to be bound by the substantive content of their NDCs. However, according to Rajamani and Brunnée, interpreting the Paris Agreement in its totality and integrally, its Article 4, by requiring each of its parties to maintain its NDC that 'it intends to achieve', establishes 'a good faith expectation that Parties plan to deliver on their NDCs'.[63] As potential legal effects of such expectation being established amongst the regime members, 'the Paris Agreement seeks to discipline state autonomy by ... imposing certain obligations, albeit of conduct, on state behaviour in relation to these NDCs'.[64] One of these derivative obligations within the transparency framework established by the Agreement, according to Rajamani and Brunnée, is the party's requirement to explain the reasons if it fails to achieve its NDC.[65]

The 2018 Paris Rulebook's provisions relating to the transparency framework[66] oblige each party to identify indicators to track progress towards achievements of its NDC (paragraph 65) and to provide an assessment of whether it has achieved the targets for NDC based on the relevant information (paragraph 70). Against such information, the Technical Expert Review, although it shall not review the adequacy or appropriateness of a party's NDC (paragraph 149(b)), will consider the party's implementation and achievement of its NDC (paragraph 146(b)). In such consideration, 'the Party concerned shall cooperate with the technical expert review team ... and make every reasonable effort to respond to all questions and provide additional clarifying information and comments ... in a timely manner' (paragraph 165). Thus, the party that declared its intention to achieve its NDC is under an obligation to explain its efforts to achieve it, which presumably will include reasons for dragging behind or even failing to meet its NDC. Arguably, this obligation to explain the reasons for failing to achieve NDC, despite the fact that the NDC itself is not legally binding, could be derived from the regime member's good faith obligation to cooperate with the institutional review processes established by the Paris Agreement.

62 Atsuko Kanehara, 'The Significance of the Japanese Proposal of Pledge and Review Process in Growing International Environmental Law' *Japanese Annual of International Law*, 35 (1992): 1, 26.

63 Lavanya Rajamani and Jutta Brunnée, 'Legality of Downgrading Nationally Determined Contribution under the Paris Agreement: Lessons from the US Disengagement' *Journal of Environmental Law*, 29/3 (2017): 537, 541–542.

64 Ibid, 547.

65 Ibid, 542. See also Benoît Mayer, 'International Law Obligations arising in relation to Nationally Determined Contributions' *Transnational Environmental Law*, 7/2 (2018): 251–275.

66 Decision 18/CMA.1 (n 57).

Under the pledge and review type of environmental regimes, and against the backdrop of the strengthened good faith obligation to cooperate with the regime's institutions, the regime members may find themselves in a new legal setting where their non-legally binding pledges are used to benchmark their good faith efforts to achieve the common objective of the regime. Moreover, those members might be required to explain in an open and international context the reasons for not meeting their pledges. Considering the inherently cooperative nature of all environmental regimes, this legal requirement to engage with the international institutions and to explain the reasons for non-compliance in a transparent manner would arguably generate a stronger compliance-pull on those pledges than formally designating them as legally binding.

IV. CONCLUSION

Forty-five years ago, the *Nuclear Tests* judgements declared that trust and confidence are inherent in international cooperation. And, the principle of good faith legally underpins trust and confidence in the international legal system by protecting the legitimate expectations of the community based on the deliberate conduct of states. As a relatively new branch of international law, international environmental law relies heavily for its legitimacy and effectiveness on this principle. For example, it may provide the legal foundation for unilateral declarations made by influential states to terminate environmentally harmful conduct to be legally binding *erga omnes*. By incorporating socially shared values and expectations of the time in the performance of an environmental treaty, the principle of good faith allows the courts to apply the treaty in such a manner that its purpose can be realized, rather than restricting the courts to its literal application. The principle of good faith is an integral part of environmental procedural obligations to consult and negotiate, as it provides a yardstick in evaluating the appropriateness and timeliness of the measures taken by the relevant states during such processes. Today, the socially expected level of due diligence and vigilance required under international environmental law of harm prevention may be dictated through the application of the principle of good faith.

In MEAs all parties have explicitly agreed to the object and purpose of the treaty and have the shared expectation that those objectives will be achieved through their collective and concerted actions. The trust and confidence amongst the treaty parties is thus stronger. This legal setting is characterized in the ICJ *1980 WHO/Egypt* Advisory Opinion as a special legal regime, where its membership entails certain obligations of cooperation and good faith. The 2014 *Whaling* judgement is pivotal in strengthening the good faith obligation of cooperation amongst the regime members, which now includes the duty to cooperate with the regime institutions. Further, the *Whaling* judgement recognized the obligation to give due regard to non-binding recommendations adopted by such institutions, including those adopted by majority voting. Against this backdrop, there are now certain environmental regimes where the principle of good faith is applied by the international mechanisms comprising such regimes, namely the compliance committees and pledge and review mechanisms.

Thus, the strengthening normative role of the principle of good faith in both general international environmental law and treaty-based environmental regimes over the last half a century reflects the deepening sense of solidarity amongst the nations of the international community to tackle worsening environmental and ecological degradation of the Earth. A few governments, albeit of economic giants, cannot overturn this long, sustained trend of the development of international environmental law based on good faith.

BIBLIOGRAPHY

Robert Kolb, *Good Faith in International Law* (Hart Publishing 2017)

Shinya Murase, 'Perspectives from International Economic Law on Transnational Environmental Issues' *Recueil des cours* 253 (1995): 283

Lavanya Rajamani and Jutta Brunnée, 'Legality of Downgrading Nationally Determined Contribution under the Paris Agreement: Lessons from the US Disengagement' *Journal of Environmental Law*, 29/3 (2017): 537

Akiho Shibata, 'ICRW as an Evolving Instrument: Potential Broader Implications of the Whaling Judgment' *Japanese Yearbook of International Law*, 58 (2015): 298

Rüdiger Wolfrum, 'Cooperation, International Law of' in Rüdiger Wolfrum (ed), *Max Planck Encyclopedia of Public International Law* (OUP 2010)

PART IV

NORMATIVE DEVELOPMENT

CHAPTER 23

CUSTOMARY INTERNATIONAL LAW AND THE ENVIRONMENT

PIERRE-MARIE DUPUY, GINEVRA LE MOLI, AND JORGE E VIÑUALES

I. INTRODUCTION

DESPITE the large number of environmental agreements at all levels, the role of customary international law remains key in practice.[1] First, many treaties in force remain largely unimplemented.[2] Secondly, treaties only bind those states parties to them, and that introduces sometimes important variations in the scope of environmental agreements.[3] Thirdly, there is at present no treaty formulating binding overarching

[1] See United Nations General Assembly (UNGA), 'Gaps in international environmental law and environment-related instruments: towards a global pact for the environment – Report of the Secretary-General' (30 November 2018) UN Doc A/73/419. On environmental protection in general international law see Pierre-Marie Dupuy, 'Overview of Existing Customary Legal Regime Regarding International Pollution' in Daniel Magraw (ed), *International Law and Pollution* (University of Pennsylvania Press 1991) 61–89; Pierre-Marie Dupuy, 'Où en est le droit international de l'environnement à la fin du siècle?' *Revue générale de droit international public*, 101/4 (1997): 873; Jorge Viñuales, 'The Contribution of the International Court of Justice to the Development of International Environmental Law' *Fordham International Law Journal*, 32/1 (2008): 232; Pierre-Marie Dupuy, 'Formation of Customary International Law and General Principles' in Daniel Bodansky, Jutta Brunnée, and Ellen Hey (eds), *The Oxford Handbook of International Environmental Law* (1st edn, OUP 2008) 449, 66; Jorge Viñuales (ed), *The Rio Declaration on Environment and Development: A Commentary* (OUP 2015); Jorge Viñuales, 'La Protección Ambiental en el Derecho Consuetudinario Internacional' *Revista Española de Derecho Internacional*, 69/2 (2017): 71. These writings have all informed the present chapter. However, due to space constraints, in what follows we will refer mainly to primary sources.

[2] See *Global Environment Outlook—GEO 5: Environment for the Future We Want* (UNEP 2012) chs 2–6.

[3] For example, the US is not a party to several important multilateral environmental agreements.

principles interweaving sectorial environmental agreements. As a result, it is often necessary to revert to customary norms when difficulties of interpretation or implementation arise. Fourthly, custom is important to mediate between a range of environmental and non-environmental interests (eg trade, human rights, investment, armed action) governed by different treaties.[4] Finally, custom plays an important role in cases concerning a disputed area[5] or where there is no applicable treaty.[6]

In this context, this chapter examines two main questions. Section II analyses the process of custom formation with reference to environmental norms in order to show both the 'banality' and the peculiarities of this process. Section III focuses on the content of customary international environmental law as recognized in the case law.

II. FORMATION OF CUSTOMARY INTERNATIONAL ENVIRONMENTAL LAW

A. The 'Banality' of Custom in International Environmental Law

The formation of customary international law and its consolidation as a rule of positive international law are two sides of the same coin. The concept of 'custom' refers both to the law-making process and to its end result—a legally binding norm.

Yet, it is often problematic to capture both sides of the coin, formation and formulation. The identification of the materials reflecting the practice and the *opinio juris* necessary to show the emergence of custom—for example, treaties, soft law instruments, case law, opinions of scholars, etc—may indeed introduce a trade-off. On the one hand, the documentary basis evidencing the formation process must be sufficiently abundant, which encourages reference to a wide range of materials. On the other hand, however, relying of a wide range of materials may blur the contours of the specific norm for which authority is sought. In the environmental context, there is no better illustration than the fluctuation characterizing both the formation and the content of the precautionary

[4] See eg *United States (US)—Import Prohibition of Certain Shrimp and Shrimp Products* (Appellate Body Report) [12 October 1998] WTO Doc WT/DS58/AB/R (Shrimp/Turtle case) [114], [129]; *Tatar v Romania* (27 January 2009) ECtHR, 67021/01 [120]; *S.D. Myers Inc. v Canada* (Partial Award) NAFTA Arbitration (UNCITRAL Rules) (13 November 2000) [247]; *Legality of the Threat or Use of Nuclear Weapons* (Advisory Opinion) [1996] ICJ Rep 226 (Legality of Nuclear Weapons case) [29]–[33].

[5] *Dispute Concerning Delimitation of the Maritime Boundary between Ghana and Côte d'Ivoire in the Atlantic Ocean* (Provisional Measures, Order of 25 April 2015) [2015] ITLOS Rep 146 (Ghana/Côte d'Ivoire case) [68]–[73]; *The South China Sea Arbitration (Philippines/China)* (Final award of 12 July 2016) PCA Case no 2013-19 (South China Sea case) [940]–[948].

[6] *Certain Activities Carried Out by Nicaragua in the Border Area (Costa Rica/Nicaragua)* and *Construction of a Road in Costa Rica along the San Juan River (Nicaragua/Costa Rica)* (Judgement) [2015] ICJ Rep 665 (Certain Activities case) [107].

principle/approach/criterion.[7] But the challenge is not exclusive to environmental norms. In the classic *Asylum* case,[8] Colombia faced exactly this trade-off in trying to ascertain the existence of a customary right to unilaterally qualify the offence of the asylum-seeker with effect for both Colombia and Peru.

In the context of international environmental law, this difficulty is exacerbated by the fact that commentators sometimes overstate their case by citing the largest possible number of opinions, treaties, and recommendations in order to convince themselves that the recognition of the binding character of a norm is not just a moral imperative but an observable fact. Yet, the materials thus gathered yield an unclear picture. The prevention principle may be presented as a 'principle of sustainable development'[9] or as 'precaution',[10] or a range of 'principles' with limited connection with actual practice may be formulated in a declaration.[11] Whereas academic commentary may help to elucidate the existence of custom, it cannot substitute itself for actual 'practice'. Understanding which environmental norms have genuinely become customary norms is therefore a painstaking exercise to find one's way through the thick fog of diverging views, activist stances, and, sometimes, ill-considered conclusions.

Even the well-known theory of the 'two elements' of state practice and *opinio juris*, which taken together are necessary and sufficient for the creation of a custom, represents an overly simplistic explanation of a complex social process.[12] A customary norm emerges from a mixture of state practice, *opinio juris*, and express or tacit expression of consent. While, in theory, a state's persistent objection to a custom could arguably prevent such a rule from becoming binding upon that state, this has not been the case in practice, even where more than one state has objected to a norm. For instance, in the early 1980s some major flag states resisted the creation of the exclusive economic zone (EEZ), even though it was already recognized as part of customary international law well before the entry into force of the UNCLOS (UN Convention on the Law of the Sea).[13] In fact, a state's behaviour rarely remains coherent enough in the long term to achieve the theoretical result of not being bound by the rule.[14]

It has also been argued that the process of formation of customary international environmental law is unique because of its reliance on negotiations undertaken within

[7] See Chapter 18, 'Precaution', in this volume.

[8] *Asylum case (Colombia/Peru)* (Judgement) [1950] ICJ Rep 266, 277.

[9] *Award in the Arbitration regarding the Iron Rhine ('Ijzeren Rijn') Railway between the Kingdom of Belgium and the Kingdom of the Netherlands* (2005) 27 RIAA 35 (Iron Rhine Railway case) [59].

[10] Jean-Marie Henckaerts and Louise Doswald-Beck, *Customary International Humanitarian Law* (CUP 2009) Rule 44.

[11] 'ILA New Delhi Declaration of Principles of International Law Relating to Sustainable Development' (6 April 2002).

[12] Pierre-Marie Dupuy, 'L'unité de l'ordre juridique international: Cours général de droit international public' *Recueil des cours*, 297 (2002): 9, 157–179.

[13] Part VI. On the example of the EEZ see Jonathan Charney, 'The Persistent Objector Rule and the Development of Customary International Law' *British Yearbook of International Law*, 56/1 (1985): 11, 11–13.

[14] Dupuy, 'L'unité de l'ordre juridique international' (n 12) 174 ff.

the framework of international organizations and on an ever-increasing body of soft law instruments. Historically, 'soft law' was used in this field more than in some others. Softness here refers not only to the nature of the relevant instruments (recommendations or declarations) but also, at times, to their content (guidelines or standards), even if they are incorporated in binding instruments (treaties).[15] However, the growing importance of 'soft law' in the 1960s and 1970s could also be observed in other contexts, such as the law of decolonization[16] or the norms dealing with permanent sovereignty over natural resources.[17] The fact that some environmental norms, such as the prevention principle, may have received their accepted formulation in soft law instruments such as the 1972 Stockholm and 1992 Rio Declarations does not affect the nature of the law-making process.

It remains difficult, sometimes impossible, to determine exactly when a particular rule has moved from the status of a mere statement in a soft law instrument to that of a binding customary norm independent from such instrument, but authoritatively stated therein. A relevant consideration is the process by which the norm has been generated, which may be more or less 'disciplined' as a result of institutionalized diplomacy, thereby offering a more detailed cartography of the statements and *opinio juris* of states at different stages of the negotiations. Another factor is the changing political assessment of states regarding the authority of the norm produced by this process. This authority depends upon the belief of states that the norm has become binding. In turn, this belief may result from the perception that it has become too costly, politically, to challenge the binding character of the norm. Such shifts in the practice of states tend to be noticeable, either because they are expressly emphasized by state representatives or because the absence of active objection is conspicuous. More often than not, however, the moment of 'transition' will be retrospectively set by a body, for example an intergovernmental conference, a body of an international organization, or an international tribunal, as having taken place at some point in the past. But, again, environmental custom is no different in this regard than other norms of general international law.

[15] Pierre-Marie Dupuy, 'Soft Law and the International Law of the Environment' *Michigan Journal of International Law*, 12/2 (1991): 420; see also Chapter 25, 'Soft Law', in this volume.

[16] UNGA RES 1514/(XV), 'Declaration on the granting of independence to colonial countries and peoples' (14 December 1960) UN Doc A/RES/1514(XV); UNGA RES 1541/(XV), 'Principles which should guide Members in determining whether or not an obligation exists to transmit the information called for under Article 73e of the Charter (15 December 1960) UN Doc A/RES/1541(XV); UNGA RES 2625/(XXV), 'Declaration on Principles of International Law concerning Friendly Relations and Co-operation among States in accordance with the Charter of the United Nations' (24 October 1970) UN Doc A/RES/2625(XXV); *Western Sahara* (Advisory Opinion) [1975] ICJ Rep 12 [57]–[58].

[17] UNGA RES 523/(VI), 'Integrated economic development and commercial agreements' (12 January 1952) UN Doc A/RES/523(VI); UNGA RES 1314/(XIII), 'Recommendations concerning international respect for the rights of peoples and nations to self-determinations (12 December 1958) UN Doc A/RES/1314(XIII); UNGA RES 1803/(XVII), 'Permanent Sovereignty over Natural Resources' (14 December 1962) UN Doc A/RES/1803(XVII); *Kuwait v The American Independent Oil Company (AMINOIL)* 21 ILM 976 [90.2], [143].

The 'banality' of the process of formation of customary environmental norms does not mean that this process may not present some peculiarities. One prominent feature of international environmental law is the need for constant adjustment of some broadly defined norms, such as the prevention principle, by reference to technical standards reflecting evolving scientific understanding. This is important because the level of 'due diligence' required by the principle is thus allowed to evolve without the need for a new assessment of the customary grounding of the principle. Formation and formulation remain two sides of the same coin, but formulation evolves as standards change over time. Often, the relevant standards are adopted by a competent international organization, for example the regulations adopted by the International Seabed Authority with regard to the standard of environmental protection that must be ensured by entities conducting activities in the Area.[18] These evolving standards may also arise from the amendment of the annexes of multilateral environmental agreements. For example, the appendices of the 1973 Convention on the International Trade of Endangered Species (CITES),[19] which may be amended by a qualified majority of states present and voting, have been relied upon in international adjudication to interpret the content of both treaty and customary norms.[20]

However, what the two foregoing illustrations suggest is not a difference of nature in the processes of formation of environmental custom but some theoretical and practical challenges in its ascertainment. As discussed next, customary environmental law presents some difficulties with respect to the relationship between (i) treaties and custom, (ii) soft law and custom, and (iii) general principles, normative concepts, and custom.

B. Peculiarities of Customary International Environmental Law

1. *Relationship between treaties and custom*

One defining feature of international environmental law is the conclusion of hundreds of treaties on a range of sectoral areas, such as the marine environment, international watercourses, transboundary air pollution, ozone depletion, climate change, the protection of species, spaces or biodiversity, or, still, the regulation of dangerous substances and activities.[21] From the standpoint of custom formation, the adoption of these treaties presents a difficult—yet classic—ambiguity. On the one hand, those in favour of protecting the will of the state argue that if a treaty has been negotiated as a *lex specialis*,

[18] *Responsibilities and obligations of States sponsoring persons and entities with respect to activities in the Area* (Advisory Opinion) [2011] ITLOS Rep 10 (Responsibilities in the Area case) [131]–[135].

[19] Appendices I, II, III.

[20] See Shrimp/Turtle case (n 4) [130]; South China Sea case (n 5) [947]–[948].

[21] Pierre-Marie Dupuy and Jorge Viñuales, *International Environmental Law* (2nd edn, CUP 2018) chs 4–7.

it is precisely because the parties thought it necessary to explicitly set out the rules that would be binding upon them. The treaty thus provides evidence of the absence of any general custom or principle in the field. Others instead will rely on the same treaties as evidence of state practice underlying of a customary norm.

The possibility that a treaty may generate a customary norm was expressly recognized by the International Court of Justice (ICJ) in the *North Sea Continental Shelf* case, in 1969.[22] The court identified the conditions for a treaty provision to become a norm of customary international law. The treaty provision at stake must be 'of a fundamentally norm-creating character', and benefit from 'widespread and representative participation' including that of 'States whose interests [are] specially affected'.[23] Legally speaking, the migration of an obligation from the restricted scope of a treaty, limited to a particular group of states, to that of general international law is neither theoretically nor technically impossible. This issue was further considered by the court several times, most prominently, in the *Nicaragua* case,[24] when the ICJ reiterated that customary norms may emerge which are identical to, and coexist with, treaty obligations.[25]

Yet, eager commentators cannot simply solve the problem of establishing a customary environmental norm by merely citing a sufficient number of treaties. In fact, even the fulfilment of the criteria laid down by the court in 1969 is insufficient for this purpose. Other contextual conditions, including political ones, must be met, the balance and combination of which can hardly be given definitive formulation.

2. *Relationship between 'soft law' and custom*

The notion of 'soft law' has been a decisive factor in the rapid development of new norms and principles over the past fifty years in international environmental law. The 1972 Stockholm Declaration[26] initiated a process of normative development that was expanded and consolidated at the 1992 Rio Conference, with the adoption of the Rio Declaration.[27] Since then, the focus has been on organizing the implementation of existing law, most notably through the adoption of Sustainable Development Goals (SDGs) in 2015.[28]

[22] *North Sea Continental Shelf (Germany/Denmark; Germany/Netherlands)* (Judgement) [1969] ICJ Rep 3 (North Sea case) [71].

[23] Ibid [72]–[73].

[24] *Military and Paramilitary Activities in and against Nicaragua (Nicaragua/US)* (Judgement) [1986] ICJ Rep 14 (Nicaragua case).

[25] Ibid [175].

[26] United Nations, 'Report of the United Nations Conference on the Human Environment' (5–16 June 1972) UN Doc A/CONF.48/14/Rev.1, 3, ch 1—'Declaration of the United Nations Conference on the Human Environment'; see Louis Sohn, 'The Stockholm Declaration on the Human Environment' *Harvard International Law Journal*, 14/3 (1973): 423.

[27] *Report of the United Nations Conference on Environment and Development* (UN 1993) vol I, annex I; see Jorge Viñuales, 'The Rio Declaration on Environment and Development: Preliminary Study' in Viñuales (ed), *Commentary* (n 1) 1–64.

[28] UNGA RES 70/1, 'Transforming our World: The 2030 Agenda for Sustainable Development' (21 October 2015) UN Doc A/RES/70/1.

These soft law instruments are but some prominent examples of a heterogenous body of non-binding instruments with different origins and implications. Within this body, one must distinguish those adopted by experts acting in their personal capacity from those negotiated by states. Unlike the latter, the former cannot be relied upon to establish the existence of custom. This said, they may have a profound normative impact, as illustrated by the ILA's 1966 Helsinki Rules on International Rivers,[29] which are at the roots of both the 1997 UN Convention on the Law of the Non-Navigational Uses of International Watercourses and, more generally, of the customary norms in this field.[30] Regarding the resolutions adopted by state delegations, they provide better evidence of the expression of a potential *opinio juris*. It is indeed possible to consider them as indications of how the law may evolve, since national delegations negotiate them while continuously weighing their normative potential. On the other hand, resolutions adopted by experts enjoy a sort of residual legitimacy since they reflect primarily the experts' contribution to the rationalization and clarification of international law. In sum, resolutions adopted by states indicate how international law *may* evolve, whereas those adopted by experts indicate how international law *should* evolve.

Here again, the long-standing debate as to whether the accumulation of programmatic soft law instruments may help in the emergence of a binding norm is not specific to international environmental law. The problem lies, here as elsewhere, with the alas frequent discrepancy between what states say and do. Expressions of *opinio juris* that are not sufficiently sustained by practice do not take us particularly far in terms of customary law.[31] Faced, then, with diverse and inconsistent practice in terms of preventing the pollution of a shared natural resource, for example, the question is whether it is nevertheless possible to ascertain the existence of a positive rule of customary international law. In *Nicaragua*, the ICJ observed that it is sufficient for the conduct of states 'in general, [to] be consistent with such rules' as long as inconsistencies are treated as deviations or breaches.[32] Recently, the ILC has shed light on the process of custom formation in a manner that, aside from a misguided reference to the persistent objector theory, is an accurate representation of how this process is understood.[33]

3. *Relationship between general principles, normative concepts, and custom*

Another issue is the confusion that may arise from the terminology used to refer to certain norms of customary environmental law. References to a 'principle' (eg the

[29] International Law Association (ILA), 'Report of the fifty-second conference held at Helsinki from 14–20 August 1966' (1967) 477, 'Helsinki Rules on the Uses of the Waters of International Rivers'.

[30] See Slavko Bogdanović (ed), *International Law of Water Resources, Contribution of the International Law Association (1954–2000)* (Kluwer 2001).

[31] Nicaragua case (n 24) [184].

[32] Ibid [186].

[33] International Law Commission (ILC), 'Identification of Customary International Law—Text of the draft conclusions as adopted by the Drafting Committee on second reading' (17 May 2018) UN Doc A/CN.4/L.908.

prevention principle) or a 'concept' (eg the concept of sustainable development) may introduce some hesitation as to whether such norms are based on 'custom' or on some other source of international law. Yet, these hesitations can be easily dissipated.

Consider, for example, the prevention principle. References to its statement in the *Trail Smelter*[34] arbitration overlook the fact that, in this case, the arbitral tribunal relied on the domestic judicial practice of Switzerland and the United States in disputes among 'quasi sovereign' states, which was possible because Article VI of the choice-of-law clause in the *compromis*. The initial recognition of this principle by the ICJ, in the *Corfu Channel* case,[35] kept the ambiguity in referring to 'certain general and well-recognized principles'.[36] Yet, subsequently the ICJ made abundantly clear that it is a customary norm.[37] Thus, despite terminological variations, the norm derives its legally binding character from the custom formation process.

As for the nature of normative concepts, again, the use of the term 'concept' is not intended to indicate the source that underpins the norm but only its broad formulation. Normative concepts can and do rest on customary law. The best example is the 'concept' of 'sustainable development'.[38] As such, this concept is more of a *Weltanschauung*, implying a programme of action rather than a general principle in itself. Nevertheless, its legal authority depends on its recognition as a binding norm at the international level. Sustainable development as a concept may perform different functions, such as the interpretation of certain norms. However, due to its broad formulation, it is unable to perform a 'decision-making' function, unlike several other principles such as prevention.[39]

III. ENVIRONMENTAL PROTECTION IN GENERAL INTERNATIONAL LAW

A. Out of the Fog

A large part of the academic work devoted to customary international environmental law rehearses theoretical arguments without genuinely engaging with the simpler—but much harder—question of what norms have reached customary status and what is their specific content. That is partly justified by the thick fog that has engulfed this issue for years. Yet, the fog is slowly dissipating.

[34] *Trail Smelter Arbitration (US/Canada)* (1938 and 1941) 3 RIAA 1905 (Trail Smelter case) 1965.

[35] *Corfu Channel case (UK/Albania)* (Judgement) [1949] ICJ Rep 4.

[36] Ibid, 22.

[37] See Section III.B.

[38] *The Gabčíkovo-Nagymaros Project (Hungary/Slovakia)* (Judgement) [1997] ICJ Rep 7 (Gabčíkovo-Nagymaros case) [140].

[39] Dupuy and Viñuales (n 21) ch 3. See further Chapter 17, 'Sustainable Development', in this volume.

In 2015, the ICJ made a significant contribution to this question. In a single paragraph of its judgement in *Costa Rica/Nicaragua*, it summarized the core of customary international environmental law:

> to fulfil its obligation to *exercise due diligence in preventing significant transboundary environmental harm*, a State must, before embarking on an activity having the potential adversely to affect the environment of another State, *ascertain if there is a risk of significant transboundary harm, which would trigger the requirement to carry out an environmental impact assessment* ... If the environmental impact assessment confirms that there is a risk of significant transboundary harm, the State planning to undertake the activity is required, in conformity with its due diligence obligation, *to notify and consult in good faith* with the potentially affected State, where that is necessary to determine the appropriate measures to prevent or mitigate that risk.[40]

This clarification effort has great merits as well as some problems. As a general matter, the customary international law of environmental protection is not limited to those customary norms with specific environmental content, such as the norms identified in the excerpt reproduced above.[41]

There is a significant portion of customary law that is not specific to environmental protection but has considerable relevance for it. The most prominent examples include the law of state responsibility for internationally wrongful acts,[42] certain norms that confer a status over a resource or an area,[43] several human rights provisions,[44] or the recognition of obligations *erga omnes*.[45] Although no environmental norm is, at present, considered to be a peremptory norm or *jus cogens*,[46] the *erga omnes* character at least of the prevention principle now seems well established.[47] Such character opens the possibilities contemplated in the law of state responsibility, specifically the right of states to invoke the responsibility of other states for breach of the prevention principle, whether the former are 'injured States' or states 'other than injured States'.[48]

This non-specifically environmental body of norms is no less important than some specifically environmental norms, but it is discussed elsewhere in this volume.

40 Certain Activities case (n 6) [104] (italics added).

41 This basic point was clearly perceived early on. See Ian Brownlie, 'A Survey of International Customary Rules of Environmental Protection' *Natural Resources Journal*, 13/2 (1973): 179.

42 See Pierre-Marie Dupuy, *La responsabilité internationale des Etats pour les dommages d'origine technologique et industrielle* (Pédone 1976).

43 See Jutta Brunnée, 'Common Areas, Common Heritage, and Common Concern' in Bodansky, Brunnée, and Hey (n 1) 552–573.

44 See Chapter 45, 'Human Rights', in this volume.

45 See Viñuales, 'Contribution of ICJ' (n 1) 235–244 (discussing the 'first wave' of ICJ cases).

46 *Award in the Arbitration regarding the Indus Waters Kishenganga between Pakistan and India* (Final Award of 20 December 2013) 31 RIAA 309 (Indus Waters Kishenganga case) [110]–[111].

47 Responsibilities in the Area case (n 18) [180].

48 Ibid.

B. The Prevention Principle and the Duty of Due Diligence

The prevention principle is the cornerstone of international environmental law. Its customary grounding is widely recognized in the case law,[49] and in many ways it embodies the historical continuity from the early years of international environmental law to our present understanding. Its own transformation from a horizontal 'private law' logic to a vertical 'public law' logic emphasizing the protection of the environment per se can be used as a proxy for the wider transformation of international environmental law. In this transformation, the older 'duty of due diligence'[50] played a key role, which has been authoritatively recognized by the ICJ[51] and the Seabed Chamber of the International Tribunal for the Law of the Sea (ITLOS).[52] Before undertaking the analysis of the prevention principle as a customary norm, it is therefore necessary to clarify how it interlocks with the duty of due diligence.

These two norms largely overlap, but not entirely. The first difference stems from the broader scope of the duty of due diligence, which applies to several types of harm and risk other than 'environmental' harm or risk thereof. The second difference is that the prevention principle concerns only harm of a certain magnitude ('material' harm[53] or 'significant' harm[54]) or risk of thereof.[55] By contrast, the duty of due diligence is not thus limited. Hence, action/inaction that results in harm or risk to the environment that is below the threshold of significance required for a breach of the prevention principle remains governed by the duty of due diligence. For example, a state may be required, under the duty of due diligence, to take precautionary measures, even in the absence of scientific certainty as to the existence of risk of significant harm.[56] Aside from these two differences, the two norms converge to such a degree that, in the environmental context, due diligence operates as a component of the prevention principle.

[49] Legality of Nuclear Weapons case (n 4) [29]; Gabčíkovo-Nagymaros case (n 38) [140]; *Pulp Mills on the River Uruguay (Argentina/Uruguay)* (Judgement) [2010] ICJ Rep 14 (Pulp Mills case) [101]; Certain Activities case (n 6) [104], [118]; Iron Rhine Railway case (n 9) [59], [222]; Indus Waters Kishenganga case (n 46) (Partial Award of 18 February 2013) [448]-[451]; Ghana/Côte d'Ivoire case (n 5) [71]; South China Sea case (n 5) [941]. See generally Leslie-Anne Duvic Paoli and Jorge Viñuales, 'Principle 2: Prevention' in Viñuales (ed), *Commentary* (n 1) 107–138; Leslie-Anne Duvic Paoli, *The Prevention Principle in International Environmental Law* (CUP 2018).

[50] *Alabama claims of the United States of America against Great Britain* (Award rendered on 14 September 1872 by the tribunal of arbitration established by Article I of the Treaty of Washington of 8 May 1871) 29 RIAA 125 (Alabama Arbitration) 130–132.

[51] Pulp Mills case (n 49) [101].

[52] Responsibilities in the Area case (n 18) [125]–[135], particularly [131], [135].

[53] Trail Smelter case (n 34) 1980.

[54] See 'Report of the International Law Commission on the work of its fifty-third session' (2001) UN Doc A/56/10, ch V.E—'Draft articles on prevention of transboundary harm from hazardous activities' art 2(a); Pulp Mills case (n 49) [101].

[55] ILC draft articles on prevention (n 54) art 3.

[56] See Responsibilities in the Area case (n 18) [125]–[135], particularly [131], [135].

The most representative formulation of the prevention principle as a customary norm is that of Principle 2 of the Rio Declaration:

> States have ... the sovereign right to exploit their own resources ... and the responsibility to ensure that activities within their jurisdiction or control do not cause damage to the environment of other States or of areas beyond the limits of national jurisdiction.

This formulation includes the three main components of the principle, that is, the underlying right to exploit natural resources, the duty not to cause harm to the environment of other states, and the duty not to cause harm to the environment beyond national jurisdiction. But it omits two important components of the principle, namely the characterization of the harm as 'significant' and the requirement to minimize 'risk' thereof, which implies that the principle may be breached even in the absence of harm. These two components are found in the 2001 ILC draft articles on prevention,[57] and they partly reflect the articulation between the prevention principle and the duty of due diligence. Yet, the draft articles have their own shortcomings, including a narrow spatial scope limited to 'transboundary' harm,[58] which recalls the aforementioned horizontal logic, and a potentially confusing sequence between prevention, the duty to conduct an EIA, and the duty to cooperate.[59]

Moreover, the Rio Declaration and the draft articles remain unclear on three key aspects of the customary norm. First, its *applicability* irrespective of the powers exercised by a state over a given area, which could potentially include a state's own territory or areas where it exercises sovereign powers over the exploitation of natural resources.[60] Second, the *level of diligence* required from the state of origin, which depends on the gravity of the outcome that may result from negligence,[61] the capabilities of the state of origin,[62] and the historical moment at which diligence is assessed.[63] The latter is noteworthy because it provides a direct entry point into the content of the customary norm to a range of soft law 'standards', which reflect the state of science and technology. Third, the requirement to exercise due diligence goes beyond the adoption of suitable measures and includes the need to ensure that they are *effectively implemented*.[64] However, diligence in

[57] ILC draft articles on prevention (n 54) arts 2(a), 3.

[58] Ibid, art 2(c).

[59] Ibid, arts 7, 8, applied in Certain Activities case (n 6) [104].

[60] See Ghana/Côte d'Ivoire case (n 5) [68]–[73]; *Request for an advisory opinion submitted by the Sub-Regional Fisheries Commission (SRFC)* (Advisory Opinion) [2015] ITLOS Rep 4 (Request submitted by SRFC case) [111], [120]; South China Sea case (n 5) [927].

[61] See Alabama Arbitration (n 50) 129; Responsibilities in the Area case (n 18) [117]. This is acknowledged in the commentary to art 3 of the ILC draft articles on prevention (n 54) when it is stated that 'degree of care required is proportional to the degree of risk involved in the business' (para 18).

[62] See Responsibilities in the Area case (n 18) [158]–[159]. The commentary to art 3 of the ILC draft articles on prevention (n 54) also reflects this criterion, para 13.

[63] Responsibilities in the Area case (n 18) [117].

[64] Pulp Mills case (n 49) [197]; Responsibilities in the Area case (n 18) [115], [239]; ILC draft articles on prevention (n 54) commentary to art 3, para 10.

ensuring implementation does not mean 'strict liability'. In the absence of fault, the mere occurrence of harm does not amount to a breach. This conclusion was reached in the *Alabama* arbitration in connection with some specific vessels[65] as well as, in 2016, in the *South China Sea* arbitration, with respect to some specific instances of environmental damage.[66]

The prevention principle has many conceptual implications, some of which have been legally recognized. A sub-set of the latter concerns two procedural duties specifically recognized as separate norms of customary international law, namely the duty to conduct an EIA and the duty to cooperate.

C. The Duty to Conduct an Environmental Impact Assessment (EIA)

The origins of the duty to conduct an EIA lay in the 1969 NEPA in the United States.[67] The technique then spread around the world becoming one of the most representative regulatory tools in comparative environmental law.[68] At the international level,[69] it was first incorporated in treaties in 1991 such as the Espoo Convention[70] and the Madrid Protocol on the Antarctic Environment,[71] and formulated in Principle 17 of the Rio Declaration:

> Environmental impact assessment, as a national instrument, shall be undertaken for proposed activities that are likely to have a significant adverse impact on the environment and are subject to a decision of a competent national authority.

The ICJ first recognized this duty as part of general international law in the *Pulp Mills* case,[72] and then confirmed its stance in 2015 in the *Costa Rica/Nicaragua* case.[73] As with the prevention principle, the formulation in Principle 17 of the Rio Declaration calls for some additional comment on its content, spatial scope of application, and interaction with other norms, particularly the prevention principle and the duty to cooperate.

[65] Alabama Arbitration (n 50) 132 (discussion relating to the vessel 'Retribution').

[66] South China Sea case (n 5) [972]–[975]; see further Pulp Mills case (n 49) [187]; Responsibilities in the Area case (n 18) [110]; ILC draft articles on prevention (n 54) commentary to art 3, para 7.

[67] National Environmental Policy Act, 42 USC, ch 55.

[68] Nicholas Robinson, 'EIA Abroad: The Comparative and Transnational Experience' in Stephen Hildebrand and Johnnie Cannon (eds), *Environmental Analysis: The NEPA Experience* (Lewis Publishers 1993) 679–702.

[69] See Neil Craik, 'Principle 17: Environmental Impact Assessment' in Viñuales (ed), *Commentary* (n 1) 451–470.

[70] Espoo Convention, appendix III, para 1.

[71] art 8.

[72] Pulp Mills case (n 49) [204].

[73] Certain Activities case (n 6) [104].

The content of the norm is the most complex part. First, some minimal content was identified at the time the norm was recognized, such as a focus on 'activities' (rather than on policies or plans),[74] the need to conduct the EIA 'prior' to the approval decision of the competent authority and to monitor impact throughout the life of the project,[75] and the characterization of the level of 'risk' at stake. On the latter issue, the English, French, and Spanish versions do not use equivalent language. The English version of Principle 17 as well as the draft articles on prevention refer to 'significant adverse impact', which may suggest that what is targeted is the risk of 'significant' environmental harm covered by the prevention principle. This is also the terminology used by the ICJ in the English version of its judgement in the *Pulp Mills* case. Yet, the terms used in the French and Spanish versions differ from those used for the prevention principle. Principle 17 refers to '*effets nocifs importants*' (by contrast with the French version of the draft articles on prevention, which define the harm linked to prevention as '*significatif*') and the ICJ speaks of '*impact préjudiciable important*'[76] or '*risque de dommage transfrontière important*'.[77] The Spanish version of Principle 17 uses the adjective '*considerable*' to qualify the risk of harm, whereas the term used to characterize the harm targeted by the prevention principle in the draft articles is '*sensible*'. These ambiguities suggest that the duty to conduct an EIA has its own trigger. Significant harm or risk thereof activates the prevention principle but something more is needed to trigger the duty to conduct an EIA. A second source of complexity regarding the content relates to the somewhat elliptical statement of the ICJ that the content of the EIA is 'for each State to determine in its domestic legislation'.[78] This assertion is disconcerting because for a customary norm to emerge a sufficiently uniform body of practice is needed and, if there is practice, there must be some minimum content.

Regarding the spatial scope of application of the norm, the ICJ recognized it in a 'transboundary context', particularly on a 'shared resource'.[79] But the formulation of Principle 17 refers generally to 'activities that are likely to have a significant adverse impact on the environment', without any specific spatial limitation, and the application of the duty to activities in areas beyond national jurisdiction has been expressly recognized in the case law.[80]

Concerning the interactions between the duty to conduct an EIA and other related norms, we must emphasize the problem introduced by the sequential interpretation of the duties to conduct an EIA and to notify and consult. In *Costa Rica/Nicaragua*, the ICJ considered that the latter are only triggered once the risk of significant transboundary harm has been confirmed—unilaterally—by an EIA in the state of origin, the contents

74 Craik, 'Principle 17' (n 69) 456.
75 Pulp Mills case (n 49) [205].
76 Ibid [204].
77 Certain Activities case (n 6) [104].
78 Ibid.
79 Pulp Mills case (n 49) [204]–[205]; Certain Activities case (n 6) [104].
80 Responsibilities in the Area case (n 18) [145], [148]; South China Sea case (n 5) [947]–[948].

of which are also defined unilaterally. The ICJ seems to have followed the sequence in Articles 7 and 8 of the draft articles on prevention, but this is a narrow and problematic reading of this instrument. First, as a general matter, such an understanding places too much power in the hands of the state that has an interest in developing the activity. It gives this state the unilateral power to decide whether to conduct the EIA, to define the EIA's content, and to conduct it. Second, it overlooks the fact that, by necessity, such unilateral powers are inconsistent with the existence of a right, correlative to the duty to conduct the EIA, for the state affected to require this procedure on the basis of its own assessment of the risk. Third, it is difficult to see how the procedural step of notification could be conditioned upon the unilateral conduct of an EIA given that Article 4 of the draft articles on prevention generally require concerned states to cooperate, and this duty is part of general international law. How could such cooperation take place in good faith if the affected state is not made aware, by notification, of the proposed activity, before the EIA has been conducted. Fourth, Article 9 of the draft articles, which relates to 'consultations', is broad and encompasses situations where no EIA and/or notification has taken place. The commentary refers to consultations following notification as one among several other situations where consultations may take place[81] and, like Article 4, it emphasizes the customary duty to cooperate in good faith.[82] Finally, the status of certain shared resources such as international watercourses specifically require cooperation among the watercourse states as an integral part of the equitable and reasonable utilization principle.[83] It is only within this broader context that the conduct of an EIA and the duty of notification must be read.[84]

The position of the ICJ in *Costa Rica/Nicaragua* on the sequence of the duties arising from general international law must therefore be nuanced. It must be interpreted not as a normative sequence between the duties of EIA and cooperation in general but only as a logical—descriptive—sequence between the conduct of the EIA and communication of the relevant information through notification.

D. The Duty to Cooperate

The duty to cooperate is not limited to the environmental context; it has a much broader scope of application.[85] In the environmental context, two main strands of the duty can

[81] ILC draft articles on prevention (n 54) commentary to art 9, para 4.

[82] Ibid.

[83] 1997 UN Convention on Law of Non-Navigational Uses of International Watercourses, arts 5.2, 8, 9.

[84] Ibid, art 12.

[85] See general description in *Obligation to Negotiate Access to the Pacific Ocean (Bolivia/Chile)* (Judgement) [1 October 2018] (Access to Pacific Ocean case) [87]; see UNGA RES 2625/(XXV) (n 16); North Sea case (n 22) [85]; Legality of Nuclear Weapons case (n 4) [98]–[103]; Gabčíkovo-Nagymaros case (n 38); Pulp Mills case (n 49) [77], [102], [144]–[146]; Certain Activities case (n 6) [104], [106]; Request submitted by SRFC case (n 60) [139]–[140]; Ghana/Côte d'Ivoire case (n 5) [73]; South China Sea case (n 5) [946], [184]–[985].

be identified. The first, which enjoys wide recognition in general international law, is the duty to cooperate in a transboundary context. Aspects of this duty are formulated in Rio Principles 19 and 18 and more generally recognized in the case law.[86] The second strand is cooperation 'in a spirit of global partnership',[87] and it remains conceptual except in those cases where it has been fleshed out in treaty processes, such as the establishment of a Conference of the Parties or other bodies of global cooperation.

For present purposes, the starting-point of our analysis is the formulation of the duty in Rio Principle 19:

> States shall provide prior and timely notification and relevant information to potentially affected States on activities that may have a significant adverse transboundary environmental effect and shall consult with those States at an early stage and in good faith.[88]

The trigger of the duty to cooperate remains unsettled. This is not immediately apparent in the English formulation of Principle 19, which uses the term 'significant', much like the prevention principle. Yet, the French formulation uses a terminology ('*effets transfrontières sérieusement nocifs sur l'environnement*') which is closer to the '*effets nocifs importants*' required under Principle 17. In the French version of its judgement in the *Costa Rica/Nicaragua* case, the ICJ relied on a slightly reformulated version of the terminology of Principle 17 as the trigger of the duties to notify and consult (referring to '*risque de dommage transfrontière important*').[89] Reliance on the trigger of Principle 17 does not necessarily mean that the duty to cooperate, including notification and consultation, may not be triggered earlier when there are other elements suggesting the existence of risk, even if not yet ascertained through an EIA. The key issue here is therefore not the EIA itself but the existence of risk. This is expressly contemplated in Articles 4, 9, and 12 of the draft articles on prevention. The commentary to Article 4 observes that the state affected 'may know better than anybody else' about the possible impacts.[90] It has indeed been long held that the assessment of transboundary impact of an activity cannot be under the exclusive remit of the state of origin.[91]

The duty to cooperate includes the procedural duties to notify and consult, but also other forms of cooperation, such as the possibility to request the assistance of a relevant international organization,[92] regular exchange of information on a shared resource,[93] consultations in the absence of notification,[94] etc. Thus, the duty to cooperate is not

86 South China Sea case (n 5) [946], [984]–[985].

87 See Rio Declaration (n 27) principles 7, 27.

88 See Laurence Boisson de Chazournes and Komlan Sangbana, 'Principle 19: Notification and consultation on activities with transboundary impact' in Viñuales (ed), *Commentary* (n 1) 492–507.

89 Certain Activities case (n 6) [104], [108], [168].

90 ILC draft articles on prevention (n 54) commentary to art 4, para 1.

91 *Lake Lanoux Arbitration (Spain/France)* (1957) 12 RIAA 281 (Lake Lanoux case) [21].

92 ILC draft articles on prevention (n 54) commentary to art 4, paras 5, 6.

93 Ibid, art 12.

94 Ibid, art 11.

limited to the duties to notify and consult. With respect to notification, its purpose is to sufficiently and officially inform the affected states of the situation in order to enable cooperation.[95] For this reason, the duty is not met by the mere fact that the information is publicly available[96] or that the notification has been made by a private entity.[97] The addressees of the notification include the authorities of the affected state, which are in charge of conducting the consultations, but also, potentially, a relevant international organization.[98] The moment and content of the notification must be adequate to pursue the consultations usefully and in good faith.[99]

As for the consultation process, states must genuinely consult with each other in good faith.[100] Although the requirement to consult does not amount to conditioning the activity to the consent of the affected state, it does have some important practical consequences. While the consultations are ongoing, it is a breach of the duty to cooperate to grant approval to the activity in question.[101] Moreover, the purpose of the consultations is not entirely open-ended. Article 9 of the draft articles on prevention specifies that consultations shall be conducted 'with a view to achieving acceptable solutions'. This can be interpreted as an obligation to cooperate 'to achieve a precise result',[102] although the result is broadly defined. All in all, given the temporal extension, the bilateral nature and the precise result aimed by the consultations, this duty can be considered the core of the duty to cooperate in an environmental context, as well as a clear expression of the due diligence required by the prevention principle.

IV. CONCLUDING OBSERVATIONS

The analysis in this chapter has shown that, despite some peculiarities, the process of formation of customary norms of environmental protection is rather banal, in that it unfolds much like the process of customary law formation in general.

The development of such process has resulted in the emergence of a close-knit core of customary norms consisting of one principle (prevention) and three related duties, namely, the duty of due diligence as the heart of the prevention principle and the procedural duties to conduct an EIA and to cooperate in good faith, including through notification and consultation. The interconnections among these norms are complex and cannot be reduced to a mere sequence. This customary core finds expression mainly

95 Pulp Mills case (n 49) [113]—[115].

96 *Certain Questions of Mutual Assistance in Criminal Matters (Djibouti/France)* (Judgement) [2008] ICJ Rep 177 [150].

97 Pulp Mills case (n 49) [110].

98 Ibid [90], [119], [121].

99 Ibid [120].

100 Lake Lanoux case (n 91) [22].

101 Pulp Mills case (n 49) [144].

102 Legality of Nuclear Weapons case (n 4) [99]; Access to Pacific Ocean case (n 85) [87].

in Principles 2, 17, 19, and 18 of the 1992 Rio Declaration, as well as in some other *loci* reflecting general international law, such as the ILC codification efforts and a growing body of case law. Thus, it appears that customary international environmental law is finally coming out of the thick fog in which it was engulfed for decades. Commentators should take note of this important development and endeavour to further consolidate and clarify these norms.

Indeed, general international law has a distinctive role to play alongside treaties. As far as environmental protection is concerned, it will serve inter alia to provide discipline to the pervading promise of sustainable development.[103] No development can be genuinely sustainable if, at the very least, the core customary environmental norms are not fully met.

BIBLIOGRAPHY

Pierre-Marie Dupuy, 'Soft Law and the International Law of the Environment' *Michigan Journal of International Law*, 12/2 (1991): 420

Pierre-Marie Dupuy, 'Où en est le droit international de l'environnement à la fin du siècle?' *Revue générale de droit international public*, 101/4 (1997): 873

Pierre-Marie Dupuy and Jorge Viñuales, *International Environmental Law* (2nd edn, CUP 2018)

Leslie-Anne Duvic-Paoli, *The Prevention Principle in International Environmental Law* (CUP 2018)

Jorge Viñuales (ed), *The Rio Declaration on Environment and Development: A Commentary* (OUP 2015)

Jorge Viñuales, 'La Protección Ambiental en el Derecho Consuetudinario Internacional' *Revista Española de Derecho Internacional*, 69/2 (2017): 71

103 See Chapter 17, 'Sustainable Development', in this volume.

CHAPTER 24

MULTILATERAL ENVIRONMENTAL TREATY MAKING

DANIEL BODANSKY

I. INTRODUCTION

FROM its inception, international environmental law has consisted primarily of treaties and other forms of negotiated instruments.[1] Negotiated instruments offer several advantages over more informal mechanisms of international cooperation:

- They enable states to address issues in a purposive, rational manner.
- They promote reciprocity by allowing states to delineate precisely what each party is expected to do.
- They provide greater certainty about the applicable norms than non-treaty sources of international law, because of their canonical form.
- Finally, they allow states to tailor a regime's institutional arrangements and mechanisms to fit the particular problem.

Traditionally, treaties were comparatively static arrangements, memorializing the rights and duties of the parties as agreed at a particular point in time. Today, environmental agreements are usually dynamic arrangements, establishing ongoing regulatory processes.[2] The result is that, in most environmental regimes, the treaty text itself represents just the tip of the normative iceberg. Most norms are adopted through more

[1] This chapter is adapted and updated from Daniel Bodansky, *The Art and Craft of International Environmental Law* (Harvard University Press 2010) ch 8, 'Negotiating Agreements'.

[2] See generally Thomas Gehring, *Dynamic International Regimes: Institutions for International Environmental Governance* (Peter Lang 1994).

flexible techniques, which allow international environmental law to respond quickly to the emergence of new problems and new knowledge.

Section II of this chapter introduces the basic types of international instruments. Section III analyses why states negotiate and accept them. Section IV describes the process by which agreements are created, from the inception of negotiations to the adoption and entry into force of the resulting instrument. Finally, Section V explores various design issues in developing international environmental agreements. Although Section II briefly discusses non-binding instruments, including those involving non-state actors, the chapter focuses on legal agreements among states—that is, treaties.

II. CATEGORIZING INTERNATIONAL INSTRUMENTS: SOME INITIAL DISTINCTIONS

Negotiated instruments vary along many dimensions. Some address a wide subject area such as biodiversity; others are very specific, focusing on a particular problem such as mercury, polar bears, or wetlands. Some are global and others regional or bilateral. Some are written, others unwritten.

In classifying international instruments, four distinctions are of particular importance: (1) whether a negotiated instrument is legal or non-legal in form; (2) whether it is between states or involves other actors, such as business or environmental NGOs; (3) whether it is contractual or legislative in character; and (4) whether it is constitutive or regulatory in function.

A. Legal Form

Negotiations can lead to the adoption of legally binding agreements or non-legal instruments such as declarations, resolutions, codes of conduct, or guidelines. Prominent examples of non-legal instruments include the 1972 Stockholm Declaration on the Human Environment and the 1992 Rio Declaration on Environment and Development.[3] As the 2015 Paris Agreement illustrates, negotiated instruments can also have a hybrid character, through the inclusion of non-binding provisions in a legally binding agreement.[4]

Although making an instrument legally binding is often seen as an unqualified good, non-binding instruments have several advantages over treaties and do not necessarily

[3] See Chapter 25, 'Soft Law', in this volume.

[4] Daniel Bodansky, 'The Legal Character of the Paris Agreement' *Review of European, Comparative and International Environmental Law*, 25/2 (2016): 142.

represent a second-best outcome.[5] They can take effect more quickly than treaties because they do not require ratification. They are easier to negotiate because they represent a weaker level of commitment. And they give states a way to test more ambitious approaches without fully committing—a feature that is particularly attractive when uncertainties are high.

Generally, legally binding instruments between states are referred to as treaties, but they can also be called protocols, conventions, charters, agreements, or accords. What matters is not an instrument's title, but whether states intend the instrument to create legal rights and obligations. Occasionally, parties include an express statement about the legal character of an instrument, generally when they do not intend to create legal obligations and want to prevent any inference to the contrary.[6] But, in most cases, the parties' intent must be inferred from the instrument's context and content. For example, treaties include 'final clauses' relating to ratification, entry into force, and other legal formalities, whereas non-legal instruments do not.[7]

B. Parties: State and Non-State Actors

Traditionally, international environmental instruments have been among states. In some cases, non-state actors have played a role in their development, implementation, and administration. But only states have been allowed to join treaties as parties. During the Paris Agreement negotiations, some commentators suggested opening up the agreement to non-state actors (including sub-national governments), given their importance in combating climate change.[8] But these proposals did not make their way into the treaty. Although the Paris outcome recognizes the contributions of non-state actors,[9] it took the familiar form of an inter-state agreement.

In contrast to treaties, non-binding environmental instruments often involve non-state actors as parties. These reflect virtually every conceivable configuration of participants: international organization (IO)-government, IO-IO, government-industry,

[5] Dinah Shelton (ed), *Commitment and Compliance: The Role of Non-Binding Norms in the International Legal System* (OUP 2003).

[6] See eg *Report of the United Nations Conference on Environment and Development* (UN 1993) vol I, annex III, 'Non-legally Binding Authoritative Statement of Principles for a Global Consensus on the Management, Conservation and Sustainable Development of All Types of Forests'.

[7] Anthony Aust, *Modern Treaty Law and Practice* (3rd edn, CUP 2013).

[8] Yale Center for Environmental Law and Policy, 'Building Toward Breakthrough: Energizing the Paris 2015 Climate Negotiations and Post-Paris Action Agenda through Broader Engagement' (Yale Climate Change Dialogue White Paper, July 2015).

[9] Decision 1/CP.21, 'Adoption of the Paris Agreement' (29 January 2016) UN Doc FCCC/CP/2015/10/Add.1, 2, paras 117–122, 133–136.

non-governmental organization (NGO)-industry, and intra-industry.[10] For example, industry has worked with NGOs to develop non-binding codes of conduct such as the Code of Conduct on Sustainable Forestry developed by the Forest Stewardship Council. These international instruments do not have any formal status under international law, but nevertheless can play an important role in addressing environmental problems.

C. Contractual vs Legislative

To some degree, treaties can be understood as contracts between states. Although treaty and contract law differ in non-trivial respects,[11] they are alike in many ways: both treaties and contracts depend on consent; both define reciprocal obligations among the parties; both establish a fundamental obligation to comply; and both have similar grounds for invalidity (fraud, duress, impossibility, and so forth).

Treaties, however, can also have a legislative dimension. They often establish general rules of an ongoing nature rather than providing for a single transaction between the parties. Moreover, multilateral agreements that address public goods problems such as ozone depletion and climate change do not simply create obligations owed on a reciprocal basis between particular states, they create obligations owed to the community of states as a whole—what international law terms *obligations erga omnes*—and typically provide for some collective decision-making and control.

D. Constitutive vs Regulatory Instruments

International environmental agreements can serve two quite different functions. First, they can play a regulatory function, setting forth primary rules of conduct—for example, rules about how oil tankers are designed or how much oil they can discharge. Second, treaties can play a constitutive role, establishing an ongoing system of governance to address a particular issue area. Most international environmental agreements contain a mix of regulatory and constitutive elements. They not only impose obligations, they also create institutions, define their powers and decision-making rules, establish procedures to adopt and amend substantive regulatory rules, and provide methods for resolving disputes.

[10] Kenneth Abbott and Duncan Snidal, 'The Governance Triangle: Regulatory Standards Institutions and the Shadow of the State' in Walter Mattli and Ngaire Woods (eds), *The Politics of Global Regulation* (Princeton University Press 2009) 44.

[11] Evangelos Raftopoulos, *The Inadequacy of the Contractual Analogy in the Law of Treaties* (Hellenic Institute of International and Foreign Law 1990).

III. WHY DO STATES NEGOTIATE AND ACCEPT INTERNATIONAL AGREEMENTS?

Treaties represent self-limitations by states. Why do states accept these limitations on sovereignty? Why do they make commitments?[12]

A. Instrumental Factors

A common way to answer this question is in terms of costs and benefits. A state will enter into an agreement when it thinks that the benefits of doing so exceed the costs, and not otherwise. On this instrumental view, we would expect international agreements to be possible only when they leave all sides better off—that is, when they provide what economists call a Pareto improvement.

Consider a simple case involving a pollution externality. Two states each produce fumes that cross the international border into the other. Each has an environmental interest in getting the other to stop and an economic interest in continuing its own polluting behaviour. Assuming the former outweighs the latter, each should be willing to incur costly measures to reduce its own pollution, in exchange for the benefit it would receive from reciprocal action by the other side.[13] States with high environmental vulnerability and low abatement costs should readily agree to a treaty; those with lower ecological vulnerability and higher abatement costs should be reluctant, absent side payments from the victim state.[14]

Decisions about whether to participate in an international environmental agreement implicate other interests as well. On the plus side, international environmental agreements can further a state's foreign policy and security interests. For example, participation in an environmental agreement may help promote friendly relations with a state's neighbours by resolving environmental disputes; enhance a state's reputation internationally as a good global citizen; or promote stability and prevent conflict by reducing environmental stresses in other countries. On the minus side, international environmental agreements can affect a state's competitiveness. Moreover, since agreements have an ongoing character, they impose sovereignty costs on the participating states, by limiting their freedom of action.

12 See Chapters 4 and 10, 'Multilevel and Polycentric Governance' and 'Economics', in this volume.

13 The range of possible agreements that would leave both sides better off is usually referred to as the 'contract zone' or 'zone of agreement'; see generally Howard Raiffa, *The Art and Science of Negotiation: How to Resolve Conflicts and Get the Best Out of Bargaining* (Harvard University Press 1982).

14 Detlef Sprinz and Tapani Vaahtoranta, 'The Interest-Based Explanation of International Environmental Policy' *International Organization*, 48/1 (1994): 77.

B. Non-Instrumental Factors

Normative factors can also shape how states behave, influencing them to join agreements even when they might seem better off staying out. For example, government decision-makers might believe that their state has a moral responsibility to its neighbours to conserve shared resources or to future generations to prevent the loss of biodiversity or dangerous climate change.

In addition, a country's position in international negotiations often reflects domestic political factors. Decisions by states about whether to join an international agreement may hinge as much (if not more) on the distribution of costs and benefits domestically as on general calculations of 'national interest'. If the winners have more influence in the national political system than the losers, then a state is likely to join, and vice versa. Moreover, the limits on sovereignty imposed by the agreement help the beneficiaries lock in their gains by limiting the ability of states to backslide even if their influence should wane. In this way, international agreements help one group bind others, or one generation or government bind its successors.[15]

Finally, in some cases, government actors may accept a treaty (or treaty decisions) in response to pressure from other (typically more powerful) states. For example, the United States' threats in the 1970s to adopt oil tanker standards unilaterally spurred other states to agree to international standards in the 1973 International Convention for the Prevention of Pollution from Ships (MARPOL).[16] Similarly, US pressure in the late 1970s and early 1980s led first to the adoption of the moratorium on commercial whaling by the International Whaling Commission and then to acceptance of that decision by Japan and most other whaling countries.

IV. STEPS IN THE TREATY-MAKING PROCESS

The process by which international agreements are developed unfolds in several steps.

A. Initiation of Negotiations

The first step in the treaty-making process is the decision to initiate negotiations. This involves two primary issues: first, the choice of negotiating forum, and second, the

[15] On pre-commitment theory see Steven Ratner, 'Precommitment Theory and International Law: Starting a Conversation' *Texas Law Review*, 81/7 (2003): 2055.

[16] R Michael M'Gonigle and Mark Zacher, *Pollution, Politics, and International Law: Tankers at Sea* (University of California Press 1979).

adoption of a negotiating mandate. The choice of negotiating forum, though often the product of happenstance rather than conscious deliberation, can be extremely consequential. It may influence which domestic agencies have the lead in the negotiations, who represents each country, the general orientation of the agreement, and even which countries may take part in the negotiations, if an organization is not universal in membership. For example, the decision to negotiate the 1992 United Nations Framework Convention on Climate Change (FCCC) under the auspices of the UN General Assembly meant that the negotiations were open to every UN member state and were conducted, for many small developing countries, by their UN missions, rather than by more specialized ministries or departments.

The decision to authorize a negotiation may give a more or less specific mandate to the negotiators, addressing issues such as the scope of the negotiations, the legal status of the intended outcome, the types of provisions to include, and the target completion date.[17] Because the mandate shapes the ultimate agreement, it often involves hard-fought negotiations. In the mandate for the 1997 Kyoto Protocol negotiations, for example, developing countries insisted on a provision that expressly excluded them from any new commitments, thus effectively settling a central issue before the negotiations even began.[18] By contrast, developed countries proved more successful in negotiating the Paris Agreement mandate (the 'Durban Platform'), which launched a process to develop an agreement 'applicable to all Parties' and did not make any reference to differentiation between developed and developing country commitments.[19]

B. Negotiations

Although every negotiation has its own dynamic, they often follow a similar pattern. At first, little progress is apparent, as countries debate procedural issues and endlessly repeat their initial positions rather than seeking compromise formulations. Though frustrating to those hoping for rapid progress, this sparring process allows countries to voice their views and concerns, to learn about and gauge the strength of other states' views, and to send up trial balloons. Real negotiations, however, begin only in the final months (or even hours) before the negotiations are scheduled to conclude, when governments realize that they need to compromise if they wish to avoid failure.

[17] Susan Biniaz, 'A Beginner's Guide to Negotiating Mandates' (Sabin Center for Climate Change Law, 12 April 2018) <http://blogs.law.columbia.edu/climatechange/2018/04/12/setting-the-table-for-an-international-environmental-agreement-a-beginners-guide-to-negotiating-mandates> accessed 24 October 2018.

[18] Decision 1/CP.1, 'The Berlin Mandate: Review of the adequacy of Article 4, paragraph 2(a) and (b), of the Convention, including proposals related to a protocol and decisions on follow-up' (6 June 1995) UN Doc FCCC/CP/1995/7/Add.1, 4.

[19] Decision 1/CP.17, 'Establishment of an Ad Hoc Working Group on the Durban Platform for Enhanced Action' (11 December 2011) UN Doc FCCC/CP/2011/9/Add.1, 2, para 2.

With almost 200 states now comprising the international community, international law-making has become increasingly complex and unwieldy. To simplify the negotiating task, the closing stages of a negotiation typically involve only a small number of key delegations. In addition, states generally negotiate as part of a larger group rather than individually. Some groups are not negotiation specific—for example, regional groups or the so-called Group of 77 (G77), which comprises all of the 'developing' states. Other groups reflect common interests and positions regarding a particular issue or issue-area. Examples include states with large shipping industries in negotiations on vessel-source pollution standards; conservation-minded countries in the 1973 CITES negotiations; and so forth. Coalitions are particularly useful for small countries, which have greater influence collectively than individually. But even a superpower like the United States usually finds it useful to participate in coalitions of like-minded states. For example, in the climate negotiations, it has operated as part of the 'Umbrella Group', a loose coalition of non-EU industrialized states.[20]

When a negotiation proceeds under the auspices of an existing international organization, the organization's secretariat often prepares the initial negotiating draft, either internally or with the assistance of outside experts. But when an issue is politically sensitive, states usually seek to retain control and insist that the treaty text emerge through a bottom-up, inductive process, starting with proposals by states of possible provisions, which are eventually combined (often by the negotiating chair) into a composite text.

Although the rules of procedure of most negotiating groups provide for voting if agreement is not possible, in practice consensus decision-making prevails. This was not always the case. In the 1970s, when a smaller community of states negotiated MARPOL, they resolved many difficult issues through voting. Today, with many more states participating in international negotiations, the trust necessary for voting to be acceptable is less common; hence the strong preference for consensus. In this context, consensus does not mean unanimity, but rather the absence of formal objection.[21] In contrast to voting, where there are winners and losers, the objective of consensus-based negotiations is to address objections and find common ground. That is why the outcomes of consensus decision-making often represent a least common denominator or paper over differences through formulations that preserve the positions of all sides, are deliberately ambiguous, or defer issues to a future date.[22]

International environmental law places a good deal of emphasis on participation and transparency, but the actual practice of negotiations has moved in the opposite direction. Back in the 1950s and 1960s, verbatim records were often kept of negotiating

[20] See Daniel Bodansky, Jutta Brunnée, and Lavanya Rajamani, *International Climate Change Law* (OUP 2017) 81–82.

[21] Dapo Akande, 'What Is the Meaning of "Consensus" in International Decision Making?' *EJIL: Talk!* (8 April 2013).

[22] Susan Biniaz, 'Comma but Differentiated Responsibilities: Punctuation and 30 Other Ways Negotiators Have Resolved Issues in the International Climate Change Regime' *Michigan Journal of Environmental and Administrative Law*, 6/1 (2016): 37.

sessions and votes recorded. Today, most of the business of negotiations takes place, not in public sessions, but in off-the-record meetings of contact groups or 'friends of the chair'. Official reports say little more than that a meeting was held. As a result, accounts by participants or observers have become a key source of information about what transpired: who proposed what provisions, for what reasons, and with what results.

C. Adoption, Signature, Ratification, and Entry into Force

At the end of a negotiation, a treaty must be adopted, signed, and, in most cases, ratified, before it can enter into force. In the case of bilateral agreements, signature of an agreement may both conclude the negotiations and bring the treaty into effect. Usually, however, the conclusion of treaty negotiations is a multistep process. First, the negotiating body adopts the treaty, thereby finalizing the treaty text and ending the negotiations. Next, the treaty is opened for signature, a step signifying a state's preliminary support for the agreement. For states that wish to become bound—a decision that may require legislative approval—consent to a treaty is given by means of ratification (if a state has previously signed the treaty) or accession (if it has not). Finally, enough states must consent in order to satisfy the agreement's entry-into-force provision.

V. DESIGN ISSUES

The development of an international agreement raises numerous design issues. Some are familiar, such as:

- What objective and commitments should an agreement contain? The answer, of course, depends on the nature of the problem. The Convention on International Trade in Endangered Species (CITES) uses a permitting system; MARPOL establishes requirements for the construction and design of oil tankers; and the 1987 Montreal Protocol on Substances that Deplete the Ozone Layer limits the consumption and production of ozone-depleting substances.
- What institutions should the treaty establish? Some of the most common are a conference of the parties (COP), secretariat, financial mechanism, scientific body, and compliance committee.
- How should the treaty promote implementation and effectiveness? What reporting requirements, monitoring programmes, and/or review processes should it establish to generate information about treaty compliance and effectiveness? And how should it respond to cases of non-compliance?[23]

[23] See Chapters 52 and 56, 'Transparency Procedures' and 'Non-Compliance Procedures', in this volume.

In addition, treaty design involves several critical, but less familiar, issues, which have begun to receive greater attention:

- First, the breadth or scope of a treaty, both in terms of membership and subject matter.[24]
- Second, the depth of a treaty—the degree to which it requires states to depart from business as usual.
- Third, how the treaty promotes participation.
- Fourth, strategies for building a treaty regime over time.
- Fifth, the treaty's ability to respond flexibly to new information and changed circumstances.[25]

A. Breadth

1. *Who may participate in a treaty regime?*

Who should be allowed (or entitled) to participate in an international agreement on climate change, whaling, or Antarctica? Treaties answer this question in many ways. Some are open to any state, making them potentially global in scope. Others set geographic limits on participation—for example, on a regional basis. And others define membership along functional grounds.

One approach to the issue of membership is to say that any state with an interest in an issue has a right to participate in the decision-making process. The 1995 UN Fish Stocks Agreement, for example, provides that regional fisheries treaties should be open to any state with a 'real interest' in the fishery concerned.[26] But what constitutes a 'real interest'? Many view Antarctica as part of the global commons and therefore of concern to all states. The 1959 Antarctic Treaty, however, requires a state to 'demonstrate its interest' in Antarctica through substantial research activity, in order to fully participate in the regime.[27] In contrast, the 1946 International Convention for the Regulation of Whaling recognizes the 'interest of the nations of the world in safeguarding for future generations the great natural resources represented by the whale stocks'.[28] This reflects

[24] For a negotiation theory analysis of the problem of breadth see James Sebenius, 'Negotiation Arithmetic: Adding and Subtracting Issues and Parties' *International Organization*, 37/2 (1983): 281; see also Scott Barrett, *Environment and Statecraft: The Strategy of Environmental Treaty-Making* (OUP 2005) 153–158.

[25] See generally Barbara Koremenos, Charles Lipson, and Duncan Snidal (eds), *The Rational Design of International Institutions* (CUP 2001); Andrew Guzman, 'The Design of International Agreements' *European Journal of International Law*, 16/4 (2005): 579.

[26] art 8.

[27] art IX(2) (limiting full participation to states that demonstrate their interest in Antarctica 'by conducting substantial research activity there').

[28] preambular recital 2.

a much broader view that recognizes the interest of the international community as a whole in the 'existence value' of whales.

The pragmatic issues regarding the scope of participation are also closely balanced. On the one hand, broad participation brings important environmental and economic benefits. *Ceteris paribus*, it reduces leakage of pollution from participating to non-participating states, reduces competitiveness effects, and brings greater environmental effectiveness. But broader participation comes at a price: the greater the number of countries involved, the more difficult it is to negotiate and sustain cooperation. Thus, limiting membership to a smaller club, with shared values and interests, may sometimes allow greater progress.

2. *What are the minimum participation requirements?*

A treaty's minimum participation requirements are defined by its entry-into-force provision. In the case of regulatory treaties, minimum participation requirements serve to ensure a sufficient level of reciprocity. This does not require universal participation, just enough so that the participating states are better off cooperating with each other than not. In cases where some states contribute significantly more to an environmental problem than others, entry-into-force requirements may be formulated not simply as a minimum number of states, but also as a variable that reflects the magnitude of different states' contribution to the problem. The Kyoto Protocol, for example, required ratification by fifty-five states representing 55% of developed country greenhouse gas emissions,[29] while MARPOL required ratification by fifteen states representing at least 50% of global shipping tonnage.[30] Such entry-into-force requirements help ensure reciprocity by requiring participation by states that account for a significant share of the problem.

In contrast to regulatory treaties, constitutive treaties do not impose costly requirements. Therefore, in deciding whether to join, states do not need to worry about ensuring reciprocity. Instead, entry-into-force requirements reflect a different concern—political credibility. Constitutive agreements aim to establish a governance structure for a given issue. To be credible, these governance arrangements need a critical mass of participants. For example, a framework convention on climate change that had only five participating states would not be credible. Moreover, to the extent that states like to be charter members of a regime, so that they have a say in the start-up decisions about rules of procedure, financial arrangements, and so forth, then a lax entry-into-force requirement can undermine this incentive to join by allowing a treaty to come into force quickly, with only a few participants.

[29] art 25.1.
[30] art 15.1.

3. *Substantive scope*

International agreements also vary widely in their substantive scope. Both comprehensive and narrowly focused agreements have their pros and cons. Comprehensive agreements allow states to take account of the interdependent nature of environmental problems and to address them in a holistic manner, making appropriate trade-offs and issue-linkages. In contrast, more narrowly focused agreements create the potential for fragmentation, duplication of effort, and even conflict. But narrowly focused agreements also have a significant, compensatory advantage: they allow states to target problems and develop specific, meaningful responses.

B. Depth

A second issue in treaty design is depth, which is a function of two variables—stringency and strength. The stringency of a commitment is the 'extent to which it requires states to depart from what they would have done in its absence'.[31] In contrast, strength measures the intensity of a commitment. Both stringency and strength raise an agreement's costs, but they do so in different ways: stringency increases the expected costs of compliance, while strength increases the potential costs of non-compliance. The more stringent a commitment, the bigger the required changes in behaviour and the more costly compliance becomes. In contrast, the more intense the commitment, the bigger the limits to sovereignty and the higher the costs if a state fails to comply. Design elements that limit the strength of an agreement's commitments represent, in essence, risk management strategies, preserving more of a state's freedom of action in case an agreement does not work out as expected.[32]

Constitutive agreements are by their nature shallow; they aim to establish a general system of governance and impose few, if any, stringent requirements. In contrast, regulatory agreements vary widely in their stringency. The 1985 Sulphur Protocol's requirement that states reduce their SO_2 emissions by 30% is an example of a shallow commitment, since emissions were already coming down for other reasons.[33] In contrast, the decision of the Montreal Protocol parties to eliminate the use of methyl bromide was quite stringent, given its widespread use as a fumigant to control agricultural pests.

A number of treaty design features affect the stringency of its commitments:

- *Flexible/contextual commitments*—Typically, the more flexible the treaty commitment, the lower its sovereignty and compliance costs. Some agreements

[31] George Downs, David Rocke, and Peter Barsoom, 'Is the Good News about Compliance Good News about Cooperation?' *International Organization*, 50/3 (1996): 379, 383.

[32] See generally Richard Bilder, *Managing the Risks of International Agreement* (University of Wisconsin Press 1981).

[33] art 2.

include commitments that allow parties to choose among a menu of options.[34] Some contain commitments with qualifiers like 'as far as possible', 'as appropriate', or 'taking into account national circumstances', which give parties considerable discretion in deciding the appropriate level of protection.[35] At the far extreme, the Paris Agreement on climate change allows parties to self-determine their mitigation commitments.[36]

- *Differential standards*—Treaties can also differentiate the stringency of the commitments for different categories of countries, establishing more stringent commitments for some countries than others.[37]
- *Reservations/exemptions*—Rather than establish differential standards directly, a treaty can allow states to differentiate their obligations unilaterally through reservations or exemptions. Few multilateral environmental agreements allow reservations to the treaty itself, since reservations would undermine a treaty's constitutive functions.[38] But some agreements allow states to exempt themselves from particular regulatory requirements.[39]

States also can use many design elements to calibrate the strength of an agreement, including:

- *Legal bindingness*—All other things being equal, a legally binding obligation represents a stronger commitment than a non-binding pledge. First, it signals a greater intensity and seriousness of intent, and hence has greater credibility. Second, in countries that require legislative approval of treaties, legal agreements require greater domestic buy-in than non-binding agreements, making them more resistant to backsliding. Finally, legally binding provisions can potentially be enforced judicially. As the Paris Agreement illustrates, legal bindingness has two components: first, the legal form of the overall instrument (ie whether it is a treaty); second, the legal character of each component provision (ie whether it is mandatory ('shall'), hortatory ('should'), expectational ('will'), or permissive ('may')). Distinguishing these two components of legal bindingness was critical to the adoption of the Paris Agreement. Some states were able to accept it as a treaty, precisely because key provisions were not formulated as legally binding obligations.[40]

[34] See eg 2013 Minamata Convention, arts 4.2, 8.5, 9.5.

[35] See eg 1992 Biodiversity Convention, arts 5, 6(b), 7, 8, 9, 10, 11, 13(b), 14; Paris Agreement, arts 4.14, 5.1, 7, 12.

[36] art 4.2.

[37] See Chapter 19, 'Differentiation', in this volume.

[38] See Maurice Mendelson, 'Reservations to the Constitutions of International Organizations' *British Yearbook of International Law*, 45 (1971): 137 (reservations generally not allowed for constitutional agreements).

[39] See eg 2001 Stockholm Convention, art 4; Minamata Convention, art 6.

[40] Lavanya Rajamani, 'The 2015 Paris Agreement: Interplay between Hard, Soft, and Non-Obligations' *Journal of Environmental Law*, 28/2 (2016): 337.

- *Precision*—A second element of a commitment's strength is its precision. *Ceteris paribus*, more precise norms constrain states more tightly than vague ones, by making violations more apparent. Compare, for example, a requirement to reduce emissions by 20% with a requirement to reduce emissions 'significantly'.
- *Opt-out clauses*—Multilateral environmental agreements that establish ongoing regulatory systems create special sovereignty risks because of the danger that the regulatory regime will adopt decisions with which a state disagrees. Most environmental agreements lessen this risk by allowing states to opt out of future decisions with which they disagree.
- *Duration*—The longer an agreement's duration, the greater its strength. An agreement that lasts only a few years or allows states to withdraw limits sovereignty costs much less than an agreement of indefinite duration.[41] For this reason, most if not all environmental agreements give parties the right to exit after the expiration of some minimum period of time, usually simply by providing notice.[42]
- *International review and enforcement*—Finally, treaties that provide for international review and enforcement reflect a stronger level of commitment than those that do not. They raise the costs of non-compliance by increasing the likelihood of detection and some kind of international response.

C. Promoting Participation

Participation in international environmental regimes is driven by many exogenous factors—for example, dramatic events like oil spills that raise public awareness and increase domestic pressure to join a treaty; domestic political factors such as elections, which bring a new political party to power; technological developments that reduce the costs of complying with a treaty's requirements; or external inducements or pressure. But a treaty can also seek to encourage greater participation endogenously, through design elements that lower the costs of participation or raise the costs of non-participation.

One common way to conceptualize the problem of participation is in terms of a trade-off between the breadth of an international agreement and its depth: the more a treaty demands of states, the fewer will be willing to join; the more the treaty aspires to broad participation, the less ambitious it can be. States are reluctant to join deep agreements because the benefits of the bargain are too uncertain to incur the costs. By comparison, shallow agreements involve less risk, increasing their attractiveness. Other states are likely to comply because the costs of doing so are low, so the agreement is likely to

[41] As Helfer notes, exit clauses 'function as an insurance policy, providing a hedge against uncertainty that allows a state to renounce its commitments if the anticipated benefits of cooperation turn out to be overblown'; Laurence Helfer, 'Exiting Treaties' *Virginia Law Review*, 91/7 (2005): 1579, 1591.

[42] See eg Paris Agreement, art 28 (allowing a party to withdraw by giving one year's notice, at any time after three years from date of agreement's entry into force, ie 4 November 2019). On 1 June 2017, President Trump announced his intent to exercise the US' right to withdraw. Reversing this, on 20 January 2021, President Biden accepted the Paris Agreement on behalf of the US.

deliver the benefits it promises. But even if other states fail to comply and a state receives no benefit from joining the agreement, at least it has not lost very much either.

International agreements seek to encourage participation through a variety of design elements that we considered earlier, which loosen either the stringency or the strength of commitments.[43] Some of these elements make an agreement shallower for the parties in general—for example, flexible and contextual standards, which qualify commitments with phrases such as 'to the extent possible' or 'as the circumstances permit'; self-determined commitments; non-legal form; weak review mechanisms; and opt-out and withdrawal provisions. Others aim to encourage participation by a particular group or category of countries, by establishing differential (asymmetrical) standards. For example, a number of agreements, including the Montreal Protocol and the UNFCCC, contain differential standards for developing countries. In addition, some agreements create special deals for individual countries to address their particular national circumstances.[44]

International environmental agreements can also encourage participation by directly subsidizing the costs of joining. China and India, for example, were persuaded to join the Montreal Protocol only on the condition that developed countries establish a Multilateral Fund to provide developing countries with assistance to comply with the treaty. In essence, states with a strong interest in the treaty assumed a greater commitment themselves in order to lower the costs for other states.

Conversely, an agreement can encourage participation by raising the costs of staying out. Although international environmental law relies more heavily on carrots than on sticks, several agreements use trade measures to encourage participation. For example, the Montreal Protocol prohibits trade with non-parties of ozone-depleting substances and products containing these substances.[45]

D. Building a Treaty Regime Over Time

The trade-offs between breadth and depth suggest two general strategies for promoting stronger international cooperation over time:

- First, proceed in an incremental fashion, beginning with relatively modest commitments, in order to encourage participation, and then ratchet up the level of ambition.

[43] See Susan Biniaz, 'Join the Party: 25+ Ways to Promote Participation in Multilateral Environmental Agreements' (Sabin Center for Climate Change Law, March 2018) <https://columbiaclimatelaw.com/files/2018/03/Susan-Biniaz-2018-Join-the-Parties-FINAL-.pdf> accessed 25 October 2018.

[44] See eg Montreal Protocol, art 2.6 (grandfathering facilities under construction by the Soviet Union).

[45] art 4.

- Second, aim high from the outset, through a coalition of the willing, and then try to broaden the agreement by attracting more participants.[46]

Most international environmental regimes have adopted the first strategy, starting with relatively modest agreements that are broad but shallow, and then progressively deepening them. This deepening can involve either the strength or the stringency of the regime. The evolution from non-binding to binding instruments illustrates the former. In regulating trade in chemicals and pesticides, for example, states initially negotiated two non-binding instruments—the 1985 FAO Code of Conduct on the Distribution and Use of Pesticides and the 1987 London Guidelines for the Exchange of Information on Chemicals in International Trade. These non-binding instruments then became the basis for the 1998 Rotterdam Convention on the Prior Informed Consent Procedure for Certain Hazardous Chemicals and Pesticides in International Trade. Alternatively, the deepening of a treaty regime can involve the stringency of its commitments. An example is the framework convention-protocol approach, which has been used to address acid rain, ozone depletion, and climate change.[47] Initially, states negotiate a framework convention that establishes the regime's governance structure, but contains very lax commitments. Then, protocols are negotiated that elaborate more stringent commitments. This approach allows states to address a problem in a step-by-step manner rather than all at once. States are generally willing to join framework conventions because they do not contain stringent obligations. But framework conventions can create positive feedback loops by reducing uncertainties, providing an ongoing forum for negotiation, serving as a focal point for international public opinion, and building trust among participants.

Rather than start broad and deepen, a treaty regime can instead start with a comparatively deep agreement among like-minded states and then attempt to add new members and new subject areas. This approach has several potential benefits. First, the initial group is able to design the agreement the way it likes, rather than weakening the agreement to satisfy a wider group of states. Second, the comparatively small membership makes the decision-making process more manageable and improves the quality of the likely results. The regime grows in membership not through compromise but by proving that it works.

[46] See Daniel Bodansky and Elliot Diringer, *The Evolution of Multilateral Regimes: Implications for Climate Change* (Pew Center on Global Climate Change 2010)

[47] For an analysis and critique of the framework convention-protocol approach see George Downs, Kyle Danish, and Peter Barsoom, 'The Transformational Model of International Regime Design: Triumph of Hope or Experience?' *Columbia Journal of Transnational Law*, 38/3 (2000): 465.

E. Ensuring Agreements Stay Up to Date

Regardless of which development path is chosen, environmental agreements have an unusual need for flexibility in order to take account of developments in our scientific understanding of environmental problems as well as the changing nature of the problems themselves. Species that were once abundant become threatened from overhunting or habitat loss; chemicals that were once deemed safe are revealed as dangerous; and technologies emerge that pose new risks. In the case of the 1987 Montreal Protocol, knowledge of the problem changed so quickly that, according to a knowledgeable observer, '[t]he [CFC]-reduction rates agreed … in September 1987 were already obsolete by the time the protocol entered into force' in 1989.[48] In order to avoid obsolescence, international agreements need to be able to respond flexibly both to new information and to new problems.

International environmental agreements use three design elements to help keep up to date. First, they establish institutional arrangements—most importantly, regular meetings of the parties—that keep the spotlight on an issue and allow parties to take decisions to elaborate, supplement, or amend the treaty.

Second, some agreements provide for periodic reviews, which require parties to consider on a regular basis the agreements' adequacy and what additional steps are needed. The Montreal Protocol, for example, provides for quadrennial assessments of its control measures, based on the 'available scientific, environmental, technical, and economic information'.[49]

Third, most international environmental agreements segregate their detailed regulatory provisions, which are likely to require periodic updating and revision, by putting them in an annex or schedule that can be amended more easily than the rest of the agreement, without requiring the affirmative consent of each state in order to be bound. For example, the detailed regulations on whaling adopted by the International Whaling Commission—establishing catch limits, equipment requirements, open and closed seasons, and so forth—are included in a schedule to the Whaling Convention, which can be amended by a three-quarters majority vote.[50] In essence, these flexible amendment procedures vest environmental treaty institutions with ongoing regulatory authority. To reconcile this authority with state sovereignty and the consensual basis of international environmental law, environmental agreements generally give states the right to opt out of regulatory decisions with which they disagree. This right is included in most flexible amendment procedures.[51] It ensures that a state is not bound to an amendment unless it tacitly consents, by not objecting. Environmental agreements also generally require

[48] Peter Sand, *Lessons Learned in Global Environmental Governance* (World Resources Institute 1992) 15.

[49] art 6.

[50] art III(2).

[51] The Montreal Protocol's adjustment process and the specialized procedures established by regional fisheries management treaties are exceptions.

that amendments to technical annexes have a scientific basis. The 2001 Stockholm Convention on Persistent Organic Pollutants (POPs) tries to institutionalize the role of science by requiring a detailed scientific assessment in order to add new chemicals.[52]

VI. CONCLUSION

Despite the dynamism of treaty law, some argue that consensually based negotiations will ultimately prove too weak to address environmental problems such as climate change or loss of biodiversity. In their view, stronger, non-consensual decision-making methods will be required.[53] From a political standpoint, such a development seems unlikely. Perhaps more interestingly, it would also raise serious issues of legitimacy.[54] Domestically, democracy serves as the touchstone of legitimacy. Democratic decision-making, in which the minority accepts the will of the majority, depends on a sense of community, which has yet to develop internationally. Unless some other basis of legitimacy can be found, negotiated agreements based on state consent are likely to remain a central feature of the international law-making process.

BIBLIOGRAPHY

Scott Barrett, *Environment and Statecraft: The Strategy of Environmental Treaty-Making* (OUP 2003)

Pamela Chasek, *Earth Negotiations: Analyzing Thirty Years of Environmental Diplomacy* (United Nations University Press 2001)

Thomas Gehring, *Dynamic International Regimes: Institutions for International Environmental Governance* (Peter Lang 1994)

Barbara Koremenos, Charles Lipson, and Duncan Snidal (eds), *The Rational Design of International Institutions* (CUP 2001)

[52] art 8.

[53] See eg Geoffrey Palmer, 'New Ways to Make International Environmental Law' *American Journal of International Law*, 86/2 (1992): 259.

[54] Daniel Bodansky, 'The Legitimacy of International Governance: A Coming Challenge for International Environmental Law?' *American Journal of International Law*, 93/3 (1999): 596.

CHAPTER 25

SOFT LAW

ALAN BOYLE

I. WHY SOFT LAW?

MODERN international environmental law is the product of an essentially legislative process involving international organizations, conference diplomacy, codification and progressive development, international courts, and a relatively subtle interplay of multilateral treaties, non-binding instruments ('soft law'), and customary international law.[1] Soft law is often misunderstood, but evidence of its importance as an element in international law-making is abundant. The United Nations (UN) has pioneered its use through the adoption of non-binding General Assembly (UNGA) resolutions and declarations which, inter alia, interpret and amplify the UN Charter.[2] Among the most important of these is the 1948 Universal Declaration of Human Rights (UDHR). The key human rights instruments nearly all began in soft law form but are now incorporated in the multilateral treaties which today form the corpus of international human rights law. UN declarations have played a similarly formative role in the development of international environmental law, most notably the 1992 Rio Declaration on Environment and Development. Even though it is not a treaty, the Rio Declaration remains the most authoritative general statement of the core rules and principles of international environmental law, comparable in its legal status to the 1948 UDHR.

From a law-making perspective the term 'soft law' is normally a convenient description for a variety of non-legally binding but normatively worded instruments used

[1] See Daniel Bodansky, *The Art and Craft of International Environmental Law* (Harvard University Press 2010); see generally Alan Boyle and Christine Chinkin, *The Making of International Law* (OUP 2007).

[2] See in particular Blaine Sloan, 'General Assembly Resolutions Revisited' *British Yearbook of International Law*, 58/1 (1987): 39; Alan Boyle, 'The Choice of a Treaty: Hard Law versus Soft Law' in David Malone, Simon Chesterman, and Santiago Villalpando (eds), *Oxford Handbook of United Nations Treaties* (OUP 2018) 101.

in contemporary international relations by states and international organizations.[3] In addition to inter-state conference declarations and UNGA resolutions, the concept also extends to the codes of conduct, guidelines, and resolutions adopted by UN programmes, specialized agencies, and other international treaty bodies, including UN Environment Programme (UNEP), International Maritime Organization (IMO), International Atomic Energy Agency (IAEA), Food and Agriculture Organization (FAO), and the International Whaling Commission (IWC). Like UNGA resolutions these soft law instruments are not sources of law in the sense used by Article 38.1 of the Statute of the International Court of Justice (ICJ), but they are usually negotiated and drafted with care, sometimes in great detail, and are intended in many cases to have normative significance despite their non-binding, non-treaty form. There is at least an element of good faith commitment,[4] an expectation that they will be adhered to if possible, and in many cases, a desire to influence the development of state practice, or the interpretation and application of a treaty. Non-binding soft law can be contrasted with hard law, which is always binding. Seen from this angle, the legal form is decisive: customary international law and treaties which have entered into force are by definition hard law. But the key point is that custom, treaties, and soft law cannot be viewed in isolation: they interact to form a complex regulatory system that has to be capable of sometimes rapid evolution as the science, the policies, and the priorities of governments evolve and change.

Soft law has become a significant part of this evolutionary system of environmental law-making for three main reasons. First, it may be easier to reach agreement when the form is non-binding. It enables states to endorse commitments that otherwise they would not, or to formulate them in a more precise and detailed form that could not at that point be agreed in a treaty. The soft law approach thus allows states to tackle a problem collectively at a time when they do not want to shackle their freedom of action too firmly. On environmental matters this might be because scientific evidence is not

[3] See especially Richard Baxter, 'International Law in "Her Infinite Variety"' *International and Comparative Law Quarterly*, 29/4 (1980) 549; Mauro Barrelli, 'The Role of Soft Law in the International Legal System' *International and Comparative Law Quarterly*, 58/4 (2009): 957; Hartmut Hillgenberg, 'A Fresh Look at Soft Law' *European Journal of International Law*, 10/3 (1999): 499; Pierre-Marie Dupuy, 'Soft Law and the International Law of the Environment' *Michigan Journal of International Law*, 12/2 (1991): 420; Christine Chinkin, 'The Challenge of Soft Law: Development and Change in International Law' *International and Comparative Law Quarterly*, 38/4 (1989): 850; Dinah Shelton (ed), *Commitment and Compliance: The Role of Non-binding Norms in the International Legal System* (OUP 2000). For more sceptical views see Prosper Weil, 'Towards Relative Normativity in International Law' *The American Journal of International Law*, 77/3 (1983): 413; Jan Klabbers, 'The Redundancy of Soft Law' *Nordic Journal of International Law*, 65/2 (1996): 167; Jean d'Aspremont, 'Softness in International Law: A Self-Serving Quest for New Materials' *European Journal of International Law*, 19/5 (2008): 1075.

[4] *Voting Procedure on Questions relating to Reports and Petitions concerning the Territory of South West Africa* (Advisory Opinion) [1955] ICJ Rep 67 (Separate Opinion of Judge Lauterpacht) 118; see also Michel Virally, 'Valeur juridique des recommandations' *Annuaire Français de Droit International*, 2 (1956): 85–91.

conclusive or complete, but nonetheless a precautionary approach is required, or because the economic costs are uncertain or potentially over-burdensome. With soft law the commitments undertaken by states and the legal consequences of any non-compliance are more limited than they would be when a binding treaty is adopted. Soft law has thus been a useful instrument for gradually developing the law in relatively new fields such as environmental protection. This helps explain why in its early years UNEP made extensive use of soft law instruments. To take one of many examples, its guidelines on environmental impact assessment (EIA) have influenced national law, treaties, the International Law Commission (ILC), and the ICJ, and thereby stimulated the widespread and consistent state practice which has established transboundary EIA as 'a requirement under general international law'.[5] Although not all 'soft' instruments necessarily lend themselves to becoming 'hard' law, the very existence of such an instrument encourages the trend towards hardening the international legal order. Once the principles are accepted by states in soft law form, it becomes easier to incorporate them in a treaty when the need arises.[6]

Secondly, soft law instruments will normally be easier to supplement, amend, or replace than treaties, since all that is required is the adoption of a new resolution by the relevant international institution. Treaties take time to replace or amend, and the attempt to do so can result in an awkward and overlapping network of old and new obligations between different sets of parties. The important point is that soft law is often relied upon to provide the detailed technical rules and standards required to implement international regulatory regimes concerned with safety, pollution, resource conservation, and so on.[7] Because they are normally based on expert advice and may need to change frequently to reflect changes in policy or in the underlying science, there is little point putting these rules and standards into the text of a treaty which would soon require successive amendments. Soft law resolutions cannot change the object and purpose of a treaty nor can they formally amend it,[8] but provided they are adopted by consensus, soft law resolutions may constitute either a subsequent agreement on interpretation of a treaty, or subsequent practice, pursuant to Articles 31.3(a) and (b) of the 1969 Vienna Convention on the Law of Treaties (VCLT).[9] If the parties wish to add to or change their previous interpretation or practice they are free to do so by the simple expedient of adopting another resolution.

[5] *Pulp Mills on the River Uruguay (Argentina/Uruguay)* (Judgement) [2010] ICJ Rep 14 (Pulp Mills case) [204].

[6] See Section II.

[7] Paolo Contini and Philippe Sands, 'Methods to Expedite Environment Protection: International Ecostandards' *American Journal of International Law*, 66/1 (1972): 37; Daniel Bodansky, 'Rules vs Standards in International Environmental Law' *Proc American Society of International Law*, 98 (2004): 275.

[8] *Whaling in the Antarctic (Australia/ Japan, New Zealand intervening)* (Judgement) [2014] ICJ Rep 226 (Whaling in Antarctic case) [56].

[9] Ibid [46], [83]. See Section II.

Thirdly, it may be easier for some states to adhere to non-binding instruments because they can avoid the domestic treaty ratification process, and perhaps escape democratic accountability for the policy to which they have agreed. In this context the benefits of soft law are essentially domestic and constitutional in character. Of course, this very feature may make it comparably harder to implement such policies if public funding, legislation, or public support are necessary. A new government may also find it easier to repudiate soft law commitments, so other governments may wish to be careful about relying on them.

What all of this suggests is that the non-binding form of an instrument is of relatively limited relevance in the context of international law-making. Treaties do not generate or codify customary law because of their binding form but because they either influence state practice and provide evidence of *opinio juris* for new or emerging rules, or because they are good evidence of what the existing law is.[10] In many cases this is no different from the potential effect of non-binding soft law instruments. Both treaties and soft law instruments can be vehicles for focusing consensus on rules and principles, and for mobilizing a consistent, general response on the part of states. Depending upon what is involved, treaties may be more effective than soft law instruments for this purpose because they indicate a stronger commitment to the rules and principles in question and to that extent they may carry greater weight than a soft law instrument, but the assumption that they are necessarily more authoritative is misplaced.

To take the obvious environmental example, the 1992 Rio Declaration on Environment and Development codifies existing international law and seeks to develop new law.[11] It is not obvious that a treaty with the same provisions would carry greater weight or achieve its objectives any more successfully. On the contrary, it is quite possible that such a treaty would, years later, still have far from universal participation, whereas the 1992 Declaration secured immediate consensus support, with such authority as that implies. This does not mean that the Rio Declaration itself is binding law. Its value, like certain other soft law declarations, is evidential: it tells us what states believe the law to be in certain cases, or in others what they would like it to become or how they want it to develop. The Declaration's legal significance can therefore only be properly appreciated in conjunction with an examination of the pre-existing customary and treaty law, and the subsequent development of state practice, further treaties, protocols, regulations, and judicial decisions.

[10] See especially *North Sea Continental Shelf (Germany/Denmark; Germany/Netherlands)* (Judgement) [1969] ICJ Rep 3 (North Sea case); *Military and Paramilitary Activities in and against Nicaragua (Nicaragua/United States)* (Judgement) [1986] ICJ Rep 14 (Nicaragua case); *Continental Shelf (Libyan Arab Jamahiriya/Malta)* (Judgement) [1985] ICJ Rep 13 (Libya/Malta case).

[11] See generally Jorge Viñuales (ed), *The Rio Declaration on Environment and Development: A Commentary* (OUP 2015).

Two factors have given the Rio Declaration significant authority and influence in the articulation and development of contemporary international law relating to the environment. First, many of its carefully drafted terms are capable of being, and were intended to be, norm creating or to lay down the parameters for further development of the law.[12] These commitments were reaffirmed by the Rio+20 Conference and the UNGA in 2012.[13] Second, the Declaration's twenty-seven principles represent a 'package deal', negotiated by consensus, rather like the 1982 UN Convention on the Law of the Sea (UNCLOS), and must be read as a whole.[14] Some of its provisions thus reflect the interests of developed states, while others were more strongly supported by developing states. For the first time it was possible to point to a truly international agreement on some core principles of law and policy concerning environmental protection, sustainable development, and their inter-relationship. These principles have clearly influenced the subsequent development of the customary and conventional law of the environment.[15] Many of the Rio principles have been referred to by the ILC in support of the draft articles relating to transboundary harm,[16] and the Declaration appears to be one of the 'great number of instruments' setting out norms of international environmental law to which the ICJ referred in the *Gabčíkovo-Nagymaros case*,[17] and on which the court also relied explicitly in its *Nuclear Weapons* Advisory Opinion.[18]

[12] See *Report of the United Nations Conference on Environment and Development* (UN 1993); UNGA RES 47/191, 'Institutional arrangements to follow up the UNCED' (29 January 1993) UN Doc A/RES/47/191; UNGA RES 48/190, 'Dissemination of the principles of the Rio Declaration on Environment and Development' (20 January 1994) UN Doc A/RES/48/190.

[13] See UNGA RES 66/288, 'The Future We Want' (11 September 2012) UN Doc A/Res/66/288, annex.

[14] Ileana Porras, 'The Rio Declaration: A New Basis for International Cooperation' in Philippe Sands (ed), *Greening International Law* (Earthscan 1993) 20.

[15] See Alan Boyle and Catherine Redgwell, *International Law and the Environment* (4th edn, OUP 2020) ch 3.

[16] 'Report of the International Law Commission on the work of its fifty-third session' (2001) UN Doc A/56/10, ch V.E—'Draft articles on prevention of transboundary harm from hazardous activities—text with commentaries thereto' 148; 'Report of the International Law Commission on the work of its fifty-eight session' (2006) UN Doc A/61/10, ch V.E—'Draft principles on the allocation of loss in the case of transboundary harm arising out of hazardous activities' 106. These draw upon *Report of the United Nations Conference on Environment and Development* (UN 1993) vol I, annex I, principles 2, 7, 10, 11, 13, 15, 16, 17, 18, 19.

[17] *The Gabčíkovo-Nagymaros Project (Hungary/Slovakia)* (Judgement) [1997] ICJ Rep 7 (Gabčíkovo-Nagymaros case) [140].

[18] *Legality of the Threat or Use of Nuclear Weapons* (Advisory Opinion) [1996] ICJ Rep 226 (Legality of Nuclear Weapons case) [29]–[30]; see also *Request for an Examination of the Situation in Accordance with Paragraph 63 of the Court's Judgment of 20 December 1974 in the Nuclear Tests (New Zealand/France) Case* (Order) [1995] ICJ Rep 288 (Dissenting Opinion of Judges Weeramantry and Palmer) 317, 381; *Award in the Arbitration regarding the Iron Rhine ('Ijzeren Rijn') Railway between the Kingdom of Belgium and the Kingdom of the Netherlands* (2005) 27 RIAA 35 [59]; *Award in the Arbitration regarding the Indus Waters Kishenganga between Pakistan and India* (Partial Award of 18 February 2013) 31 RIAA 1 [449].

II. SOFT LAW AS PART OF THE MULTILATERAL TREATY-MAKING PROCESS

States and international organizations adopt soft law instruments for a variety of reasons. Some are the first step in a negotiating process eventually leading to conclusion of a multilateral treaty: UN soft law initiated a process of international law-making on outer space, the deep seabed, and climate change, inter alia.[19] IAEA Guidelines[20] formed the basis for the rapid adoption of the 1986 Convention on Early Notification of a Nuclear Accident following the Chernobyl accident; UNEP Guidelines on Environmental Impact Assessment[21] were substantially incorporated in the 1991 Espoo Convention on EIA in a Transboundary Context; and UNEP's Guidelines on Land-based Sources of Marine Pollution,[22] provided a model for regional treaties.[23]

More often non-binding soft law instruments adopted by treaty bodies and international organizations provide the detailed rules and technical standards required for implementation by the parties to a multilateral treaty and thereby ensure a common understanding of what that treaty requires. These internationally agreed standards are essential in giving content to the overly-general and open-textured terms of framework treaties.[24] The detailed rules can easily be changed or strengthened as scientific understanding develops or as political priorities change.

The ILC commentary to what is now Article 31.3(a) of VCLT notes simply that '... an agreement as to the interpretation of a provision reached after the conclusion of the treaty represents an authentic interpretation by the parties which must be read into the treaty for purposes of its interpretation'.[25] That agreement does not have to be binding so it can cover soft law instruments, including decisions of treaty parties, where

[19] UNGA RES 1962(XVIII), 'Declaration of Legal Principles Governing the Activities of States in the Exploration and Use of Outer Space' (13 December 1963) UN Doc A/RES/1962(XVIII); UNGA RES 2749(XXV), 'Declaration of Principles Governing the Sea Bed and Ocean Floor and Subsoil Thereof Beyond the Limits of National Jurisdiction' (17 December 1970) UN Doc A/RES/2749(XXV); UNGA RES 43/53, 'Protection of Global Climate for Present and Future Generations of Mankind' (6 December 1988) UN Doc A/RES/43/53.

[20] IAEA, 'Guidelines on Reportable Events, Integrated Planning and Information Exchange in a Transboundary Release of Radioactive Materials' (1985) UN Doc IAEA/INFCIRC/321.

[21] UNEP, 'Goals and Principles of Environmental Impact Assessment' (16 January 1987) adopted by UNEP Governing Council, Decision 14/25, 'Environmental impact assessment' (17 June 1987).

[22] UNEP, 'Montreal Guidelines for the Protection of the Marine Environment against Pollution from Land-based Sources' (1985) adopted by UNEP Governing Council, Decision 13/18(II) (24 May 1985).

[23] See eg 1990 Kuwait Protocol for the Protection of the Marine Environment Against Marine Pollution from Land-based Sources.

[24] Contini and Sands (n 7); Bodansky, 'Rules vs Standards' (n 7).

[25] 'The Law of Treaties' in Arthur Watts (ed), *The International Law Commission 1949–1998*, vol II (OUP 1999) 689, commentary to art 27, para 14. See also ILC, 'Subsequent agreements and subsequent practice in relation to the interpretation of treaties' (6 June 2016) UN Doc A/CN.4/L.874.

appropriate.[26] This is where UNEP soft law has been an important law-making tool. In the *Pulp Mills* case the ICJ noted that the UNEP Goals and Principles on EIA constitute guidance issued by an 'international technical body' and therefore have to be taken into account under Article 41 of the Statute of the River Uruguay.[27] The parties also relied on WHO standards for air and water pollution. These are also not binding on states, but as the ICJ indicated they are 'to be taken into account by the State so that the domestic rules and regulations and the measures it adopts are compatible with those guidelines and recommendations'.[28]

Nuclear safety standards adopted by the IAEA serve much the same purpose. As a general rule the 1956 IAEA Statute confers no binding force on any of the Safety Standards adopted by IAEA. Nevertheless, despite their non-binding character, IAEA health and safety standards have made a significant contribution to controlling the risks of nuclear energy. They reflect a large measure of expert technical consensus, and it is for this reason, rather than their legal status, that they have been influential and serve as important guidelines for most states in regulating their nuclear facilities. They have resulted in an appreciable degree of harmonization of national law and practice.[29] The 1994 Convention on Nuclear Safety and the 1997 Joint Convention on the Safety of Spent Fuel and Radioactive Waste Management have also incorporated as binding obligations the main elements of IAEA's fundamental safety standards for nuclear installations, radioactive-waste management, and radiation protection, and most of its Code of Practice on the Transboundary Movement of Radioactive Waste.[30] Moreover, those remaining IAEA standards which retain a soft law status may still be relevant when determining how the basic obligations of states parties to these agreements are to be implemented. The preamble to the Nuclear Safety Convention recognizes that internationally formulated safety guidelines 'can provide guidance on contemporary means of achieving a high level of safety'. IAEA guidelines would be the obvious starting point for determining what constituted the 'appropriate steps' with regard to safety controls required by Articles 10–19 of the Convention.[31]

The FAO has similarly made use of a mixture of hard and soft law instruments to promote implementation of the 1982 UNCLOS. The 1993 Agreement to Promote Compliance with Conservation Measures on the High Seas is a binding treaty, but it forms an integral part of the non-binding 1995 Code of Conduct on Responsible

[26] See *Kasikili/Sedudu Island (Botswana/Namibia)* (Judgement) [1999] ICJ Rep 1045 [47]–[51]; case law cited at [50]; see also 'Report of the International Law Commission on the work of its sixty-third session' (2011) UN Doc A/66/10, 281–284, 'Preliminary conclusions by the Chairman of the Study Group on the subject of Treaties over Time'.

[27] See Pulp Mills case (n 5) [205].

[28] Ibid [62], [197].

[29] Paul Szasz, *The Law and Practices of the IAEA* (IAEA 1970) 673, 682 ff; Peter Cameron, Leigh Hancher, and Wolfgang Kuehn (eds), *Nuclear Energy Law after Chernobyl* (Graham and Trotman 1988) 4, 159 ff.

[30] See Boyle and Redgwell, *International Law and the Environment* (n 15) ch 9, s 2.2.

[31] Ibid.

Fishing, which itself is further implemented by other soft law instruments. These include the 2001 Plan of Action on Illegal, Unreported and Unregulated (IUU) Fishing, the 2003 Guidelines on the Ecosystem Approach to Fisheries, and the 2008 Guidelines for the Management of Deep-Sea Fisheries, which address the protection of vulnerable marine ecosystems from the destruction caused by bottom trawling. The choice of soft law instruments can partly be explained by the opposition of some states to binding agreements. Another reason, however, is that they are aimed at regional fisheries organizations and the fishing industry as well as states and contain some elements which are unlikely to find their way into treaty form.

Negotiated in the same manner as treaties, and adopted by consensus in the FAO,[32] these non-binding 'voluntary instruments' reiterate, interpret, and amplify relevant provisions of UNCLOS and the 1995 Fish Stocks Agreement. They also seek to promote implementation of elements of the Fish Stocks Agreement by non-parties. The scope of the Code of Conduct is broader than either of these treaties, however. It contains some elements which are unlikely to find their way into a binding agreement, and others which could not be agreed on as part of the UN Fish Stocks Agreement. The 1993 Agreement and the 1995 Code of Conduct were negotiated in parallel with the Fish Stocks Agreement, and all three 'can be viewed as a package of measures that reinforce and complement each other'.[33]

These examples all point to the conclusion that the non-binding force of soft law can be overstated. In many of the above examples states are not free to disregard applicable soft law instruments: even when not incorporated directly into a treaty, they may represent an agreed understanding of its terms. Thus, although these instruments are not in legally binding form, their interaction with related treaties may transform them into something that is binding.

III. SOFT LAW AND CUSTOMARY LAW

Non-binding instruments may also serve law-making purposes if they generate widespread and consistent state practice and/or provide evidence of *opinio juris* in support of a customary rule.[34] Whether they do so will depend on various factors which must be assessed in each case. Chinkin notes that widespread acceptance of soft law instruments will tend to legitimize conduct and make the legality of opposing positions harder to sustain.[35] Brownlie refers in this context to the 'decisive catalytic effect' of certain UNGA

32 However some states expressed significant reservations when adopting the 2001 Plan of Action on IUU Fishing; see FAO, 'Report of the Committee on Fisheries on its 24th session' (2001).

33 Gerald Moore, 'The Code of Conduct for Responsible Fisheries' in Ellen Hey (ed), *Developments in International Fisheries Law* (Brill 1999) 91–92.

34 See eg Nicaragua case (n 10); Legality of Nuclear Weapons case (n 18); *Western Sahara* (Advisory Opinion) [1975] ICJ Rep 12 (Sahara case).

35 Chinkin, 'Challenge of Soft Law' (n 3) 866.

resolutions on the evolution of customary international law.[36] A potentially law-making resolution or declaration need not necessarily proclaim rights or principles *as law*, but as with treaties, the wording must be 'of a fundamentally norm-creating character such as could be regarded as forming the basis of a general rule of law'.[37] The context within which soft law instruments are negotiated and the accompanying statements of delegations will also be relevant if assessing the *opinio juris* of states.[38] Lastly, the degree of support is significant. A resolution adopted by consensus or by unanimous vote will necessarily carry more weight than one supported only by a majority of states.[39] Resolutions opposed by even a small number of states may have no law-making effect if those states are the ones most immediately affected.[40] The attempt by the UNGA in the 1970s to change the law on expropriation of foreign investments is a well-known example of the inability of majorities of states to legislate for minorities in this fashion.[41] The UNGA's ban on deep seabed mining outside the framework of UNCLOS is another. In this case, the minority of objecting states established their own parallel regime, until eventually a compromise agreement was reached.[42]

The adoption of non-binding resolutions or declarations can also lead to changes in the existing customary law, in some cases quite quickly. The termination of driftnet fishing on the high seas is a good example of the successful use of UNGA resolutions in this way.[43] Although the resolutions themselves have no legal force, and do not make 'instant' law, the widespread opposition to such fishing has been effective in pressuring the small number of states involved to comply with the resolutions and phase out the use of driftnets. Such changes in the law can of course only come about as a result of changes in practice by those states most closely involved. Moreover, even states which initially voted against such resolutions may eventually conform to the general will. The initial opposition of colonial powers to UN resolutions on self-determination soon faded, and

[36] Ian Brownlie, 'The Legal Status of Natural Resources' *Recueil des Cours*, 162 (1980): 261.

[37] North Sea case (n 10) [72].

[38] See eg Libya/Malta case (n 10) [43]–[44], [49], [58] where the court draws upon the negotiating record of the 3rd UN Conference on the Law of the Sea.

[39] Whaling in Antarctic case (n 8) [46], [83].

[40] See on this point the cautionary dissent of Vice-President Schwebel in Legality of Nuclear Weapons case (n 18) 319 noting that: 'If a resolution purports to be declaratory of international law, if it is adopted unanimously (or virtually so, qualitatively as well as quantitatively) or by consensus, and if it corresponds to State practice, it may be declaratory of international law'.

[41] See UNGA RES 3281/XXIX, 'Charter of Economic Rights and Duties of States' (12 December 1974) UN Doc A/RES/29/3281; *Texaco Overseas Petroleum Co* v *Libyan Arab Republic* 53 ILR (1977) 422 [80]–[91]. 120 states voted for the resolution, six voted against, ten abstained.

[42] UNGA RES 2749(XXV) (n 19) was adopted by 108 votes in favour with fourteen abstentions.

[43] UNGA RES 44/225 and UNGA RES 46/215, 'Large-scale pelagic drift-net fishing and its impact on the living marine resources of the world's oceans and seas' (22 December 1989) and (20 December 1991) UN Docs A/RES/44/225 and A/RES/46/215; see other instruments collected in Ellen Hey *et al*, *Legislative Study 47: The Regulation of Driftnet Fishing on the High Seas: Legal Issues* (FAO 1991). See Stuart Kaye, *International Fisheries Management* (Kluwer Law International 2001) 188–194.

as the *Western Sahara* and *East Timor* cases show,[44] former colonial states have become the principal advocates of self-determination for their former colonies.

Why use non-binding resolutions for such purposes? Negotiating a global treaty on driftnets would have taken as long or longer; it would not have entered into force until there were enough ratifications, and if the relevant states failed to become parties they would not be bound anyway. In the latter case the law would not change unless these states changed their practice, which is no less true of the non-binding resolutions adopted by UNGA. In such cases, if the consensus for a change in practice is strong enough, a treaty is not necessary. If it is not strong enough a treaty will not necessarily strengthen it. If the weakness of soft law is that states are not obliged to comply, the same is no less true of an unratified or poorly ratified treaty. Whether a treaty changes the customary law will still depend on how far it influences the practice of non-party states, rather than on its binding force.

IV. TREATIES AS SOFT LAW

The point was made many years ago by the late Judge Baxter that some treaty provisions are soft in the sense that they impose no real obligations on the parties.[45] Here it is the *formulation* of the provision which is decisive in determining whether it is hard or soft, not its form as a treaty or binding instrument. Though formally binding, the vagueness, indeterminacy, or generality of treaty provisions may deprive them of the character of 'hard law' in any meaningful sense. The 2015 Paris Agreement is arguably an example. Although unquestionably a treaty in force between its parties, some authors have queried whether the terms of the Agreement impose any real commitments.[46] While seeking to hold global temperature increases to 'well below' 2°C, state parties are merely required to 'prepare, communicate and maintain successive nationally determined contributions' to reducing greenhouse gas emissions.[47] Parties are thus expected to 'prepare' some level of contribution to ensuring that greenhouse gas emissions peak as soon as possible and thereafter reduce rapidly so as to stabilize in the second half of the century.[48] The precise contribution for each party has not been agreed but will be determined unilaterally by each party in accordance with its capabilities. The understanding is that these reductions (known as Nationally Determined Contributions

[44] Sahara case (n 34); *East Timor (Portugal/Australia)* [1995] ICJ Rep 90.

[45] Baxter (n 3).

[46] Daniel Bodansky, 'The Paris Climate Change Agreement: A New Hope?' *American Journal of International Law*, 110/2 (2016): 306; Daniel Bodansky, 'The Legal Character of the Paris Agreement' *Review of European, Comparative and International Environmental Law*, 25/2 (2016): 142; Lavanya Rajamani, 'The 2015 Paris Agreement: Interplay Between Hard, Soft and Non-Obligations' *Journal of Environmental Law*, 28/2 (2016): 337.

[47] arts 3, 4; see also art 5 on conservation of carbon sinks (ie forests).

[48] art 4.

(NDCs)) are to increase progressively, insofar as each country's circumstances allow, 'on the basis of equity, and in the context of sustainable development and efforts to eradicate poverty'.[49] Given this wording Bodansky concludes that 'The Paris Agreement does not require parties to implement their NDCs; instead it simply requires parties to pursue domestic mitigation measures, an obligation they already have under the UNFCCC'.[50] Other views on the interpretation of this agreement are possible, however, and it remains to be seen whether Paris really is as weak as Bodansky suggests.

So-called framework treaties which lay down broad principles for the development of environmental regimes may fall into the same category of 'soft' treaty. The 1992 UN Framework Convention on Climate Change provides a good example. The 'principles' found in Article 3 are arguably the most important 'law' in the whole agreement because they prescribe how the regime for regulating climate change is subsequently to be developed by the parties. It is worth quoting elements of this provision:

> In their actions to achieve the objective of the Convention and to implement its provisions, the parties shall be guided, *inter alia*, by the following:
>
> 1. The Parties should protect the climate system ... in accordance with their common but differentiated responsibilities ...
> 3. The Parties should take precautionary measures ...
> 4. The Parties have a right to, and should promote, sustainable development ...

All of these principles are open-textured in the sense that their content is undefined and they leave much room for interpretation and elaboration. They are not expressed in obligatory terms: the use of 'should' qualifies their application, despite the obligatory wording of the chapeau sentence. They are not at all like rules requiring states to conduct an EIA, or to take measures to prevent harm to other states.

Despite all these limitations, Article 3 is relevant to interpretation and implementation of the Convention as well as creating expectations concerning matters which must be taken into account in good faith in the negotiation of further instruments. In the context of a dynamic and evolutionary regulatory regime, Article 3 has the important merit of providing some predictability regarding the parameters within which the parties are required to work towards the objective of the Convention. They are not faced with a completely blank sheet of paper when entering subsequent negotiations or when the Conference of the Parties takes decisions under the various articles empowering it to do so. Thus, it is significant that the relevance of Article 3 was reiterated in the mandate for negotiation of the 1997 Kyoto Protocol,[51] and is referred to in the preamble to

[49] arts 3, 4.3.

[50] Bodansky, 'Legal Character' (n 46) 150.

[51] Decision 1/CP.1, 'The Berlin Mandate: Review of the adequacy of Article 4, paragraph 2(a) and (b), of the Convention, including proposals related to a protocol and decisions on follow-up' (6 June 1995) UN Doc FCCC/CP/1995/7/Add.1.

the Protocol and the Paris Agreement. As we shall see in the following section, sustainable development, intergenerational equity, and the precautionary principle are all more convincingly seen not as binding obligations which must be complied with, but as principles, considerations or objectives to be taken account of—their wording may be soft, but they still have some legal significance.

V. SOFT LAW GENERAL PRINCIPLES

International courts have of course always had the power under Article 38.1(c) of the ICJ Statute to refer to general principles of law. In most cases this entails borrowing by analogy from common elements of national law, such as non-discrimination or the right to a fair hearing.[52] In essence, resort to general principles of this kind is judge-made law.

However, it is also possible for states to adopt general principles not derived from national law with the intention that courts and states should apply them when relevant. Such general principles do not have to create rules of customary law to have legal effect. Rather, their importance derives principally from the influence they can exert on the interpretation, application, and development of other rules of law. Article 31.3(c) of the VCLT requires other rules of international law to be taken into account when interpreting a treaty. This provision appears to include reference to general principles as an aid to treaty interpretation.[53] Soft law declarations such as the 1992 Rio Declaration or the 1948 UDHR will thus have to be taken into account insofar as they articulate general principles agreed by consensus. That is why in the *Pulp Mills* case the ICJ accepted that 'a precautionary approach may be relevant to the interpretation and application of the provisions of the [River Uruguay] Statute'.[54]

The point is not confined to treaty interpretation, however. A general principle of this kind may also influence the interpretation and application of customary law. The precautionary approach is a common feature of almost all the Rio and post-Rio global environmental agreements. Some writers and governments have argued that it is a rule of customary international law, but international courts and most governments have been

[52] *South West Africa, Second Phase (Ethiopia/South Africa; Liberia/South Africa)* (Judgement) [1966] ICJ Rep 6 (Dissenting Opinion of Judge Tanaka) 294–301; *Golder v UK* (1975) ECtHR, Ser A No 18 [10]–[36] but cf. Dissenting Opinion of Judge Fitzmaurice [18]–[46], [48]; see generally Antonio Cassese, *International Law in a Divided World* (OUP 1986) 170–174; Bin Cheng, 'United Nations Resolutions on Outer Space: "Instant" Customary Law?' *Indian Journal of International Law*, 5 (1965): 23; Wolfgang Friedmann, 'The Uses of General Principles in the Development of International Law' *American Journal of International Law*, 57/2 (1963): 279.

[53] Thus in *Golder* the ECtHR referred to access to a court as a 'general principle of law' when interpreting art 6 of the 1950 European Convention on Human Rights (ECHR). See generally Campbell McLachlan, 'The Principle of Systemic Integration and Article 31(3)(c) of the Vienna Convention' *International and Comparative Law Quarterly*, 54/2 (2005): 279.

[54] Pulp Mills case (n 5) [164]; see also Responsibilities in the Area case (n 58) [131].

noticeably hesitant to accept this characterization.[55] If, alternatively, the precautionary approach is viewed simply as a general principle of law then its subsequent use by national and international courts and by international organizations is easier to explain. The ILC special rapporteur on transboundary harm concluded that the precautionary approach is already a component of customary rules on prevention of harm and EIA, 'and could not be divorced therefrom'.[56]

It follows that the transformative importance of the precautionary approach as a general principle is that it redefines existing rules of international law on control of environmental risks and conservation of natural resources and brings them into play at an earlier stage than before. No longer is it necessary to prove that harm is likely before requiring that preventive measures be taken. Evidence that such harm may be possible will be enough to trigger an obligation or to empower states to act.[57] To that extent the precautionary approach has redefined the applicable customary international law on prevention of harm.[58]

Much the same could be said of sustainable development, on which the parties in *Pulp Mills* also relied. Lowe makes the essential point with great clarity:[59]

> Sustainable development can properly claim a normative status as an element of the process of judicial reasoning. It is a meta-principle, acting upon other rules and principles—a legal concept exercising a kind of interstitial normativity, pushing and pulling the boundaries of true primary norms when they threaten to overlap or conflict with each other.

In the case law sustainable development thus becomes a mediating principle between the right to development and the duty to control sources of environmental harm.[60] Modifying norms or principles need not impose obligations or regulate conduct, they do not depend on state practice, and they do not need the same clarity or precision as

[55] See eg *EC—Measures Concerning Meat and Meat Products (Hormones)* (Appellate Body Report) [16 January 1998] WTO Docs WT/DS26/AB/R and WT/DS48/AB/R [120]-[125]; *Southern Bluefin Tuna Cases (New Zealand/Japan; Australia/Japan)* (Provisional Measures, Order of 27 August 1999) [1999] ITLOS Rep 280 [77]–[79]; Pulp Mills case (n 5) [164]. See Chapter 18, 'Precaution', in this volume.

[56] 'Report of the International Law Commission on the work of its fifty-second session' (2000) UN Doc A/55/10, para 716; see also Chapter 18, 'Precaution', in this volume.

[57] See *Pfizer Animal Health v Council of the EU* (2002) II ECR 3305 [135]–[173].

[58] *Responsibilities and obligations of States sponsoring persons and entities with respect to activities in the Area* (Advisory Opinion) [2011] ITLOS Rep 10 (Responsibilities in the Area case) [131].

[59] Vaughan Lowe, 'Sustainable Development and Unsustainable Arguments' in Alan Boyle and David Freestone (eds), *International Law and Sustainable Development: Past Achievements and Future Challenges* (OUP 2012) 31; see also Chapter 17, 'Sustainable Development', in this volume.

[60] See the ICJ's references to sustainable development in the Gabčíkovo-Nagymaros case (n 17) [140]; Pulp Mills case (n 5) (Provisional Measures, Order of 13 July 2006) [2006] ICJ Rep 113 [80]; Pulp Mills case (n 5) [177], [184]; see Virginie Barral, 'Sustainable Development in International Law: Nature and Operation of an Evolutive Legal Norm' *European Journal of International Law*, 23/2 (2012): 377; see also Chapter 17, 'Sustainable Development', in this volume.

rules. What gives general principles of this kind their authority and legitimacy is simply the endorsement of states—*opinio juris* in other words.[61]

Such principles have legal significance in much the same way that Dworkin uses the idea of constitutional principles.[62] They lay down parameters which affect the way courts decide cases or how an international institution exercises its discretionary powers. They can set limits, or provide guidance, or determine how conflicts between other rules or principles will be resolved. They may lack the supposedly harder edge of a 'rule' or 'obligation', but they should not be confused with 'non-binding' or emerging law. That is perhaps the most important lesson to be drawn from the ICJ's references to sustainable development in the *Gabcikovo-Nagymaros* and *Pulp Mills* cases. Even if sustainable development is not in the nature of a legal obligation, it does represent a policy goal or principle that can influence the outcome of litigation and the practice of states and international organizations, and it may lead to significant changes and developments in the existing law.[63]

These examples show that subtle changes in the existing law and in existing treaties may come about through reliance on such general principles. In any system of law the ability to make changes on a systemic basis is important. How else could this be done in international law? New *rules* of customary law are not appropriate to the elaboration of general principles of this kind and could not be created quickly enough; moreover, a treaty endorsing the precautionary principle or sustainable development would only bind the parties. A binding resolution of the UN Security Council may be a possible option, but only where questions of international peace and security are at stake. Thus the consensus endorsement by states of a general principle enshrined in a soft law declaration is an entirely sensible solution to such law-making challenges.

VI. CONCLUSIONS

This short survey points to several conclusions. First, the functions of soft law in the international legal system are diverse, but it would be wrong to see the choice of instrument—treaty or soft law—in either/or terms. It is inconceivable that modern treaty regimes or international organizations such as the UN could function successfully

[61] Lowe (n 59) 33, dispenses even with *opinio juris*, but unless such norms emerge from thin air at the whim of judges the endorsement of states must be a necessary element. All the norms Lowe relies on do in fact have such endorsement.

[62] Ronald Dworkin, *Taking Rights Seriously* (Harvard University Press 1977). This argument is developed by Philippe Sands, 'International Law in the Field of Sustainable Development' in Winfried Lang (ed), *Sustainable Development and International Law* (Martinus Nijhoff 1995) 53.

[63] See eg the inclusion of provisions on sustainable use or sustainable development in the 1994 Marrakesh Agreement establishing the World Trade Organization, the 1995 UN Fish Stocks Agreement, and the 1997 UN Convention on International Watercourses.

without resort to soft law. Soft law has perhaps been more significant in the evolution of newer areas of international law, such as human rights, outer space, and environmental protection, and rather less important in international economic law, international criminal law, or the law of the sea, where the legal foundations already existed. That tells us only that soft law is in some instances a necessary law-making tool, a means to an end. It does not tell us that these areas of international law are in some sense 'softer' than others.

Second, in deciding whether to use a treaty or a soft law instrument, or both, much will depend on what is proposed and the context. Treaties may carry greater weight than soft law instruments insofar as they become part of national law on ratification, or because they indicate a stronger commitment to the norms and principles in question. A treaty gives each party a credible assurance that its terms will be complied with in good faith and that some remedy exists if they are not.[64] Litigation, resort to non-compliance procedures, state responsibility, termination or suspension of the treaty, and countermeasures are all potentially available when one party breaches its treaty obligations. Soft law provides no such assurance for other interested states unless some form of non-compliance procedure has been specifically agreed.[65] A multilateral treaty serves above all to stabilize the policies and principles it promotes across the community of states; soft law will not necessarily achieve that objective. Thus the argument for using a treaty is strongest when binding commitments are necessarily required or where an existing treaty regime has to be changed or replaced.

Finally, choosing soft law forms over treaties does not diminish the need for negotiation or consensus. On the contrary, while treaties, protocols, or implementing agreements may limp into force with only partial participation, adopting soft law principles without consensus support has little if any impact on the law-making process. That is why they are rarely the product of majority voting. It is also why the voting record for UNGA resolutions matters.

Whether soft law instruments have the same effect as a treaty, or any legal effect at all, will depend on the particular instrument and its relationship to customary international law and to specific treaties. But we should not assume that rules adopted in soft law form are necessarily soft in their legal effects. Soft law is not the meaningless paradox portrayed in some of the literature.[66] It is the product of an increasingly sophisticated legal system. It needs to be understood, not simply dismissed as something that cannot fit a particular theory of law.

[64] Kenneth Abbott and Duncan Snidal, 'Hard and Soft Law in International Governance' *International Organisation*, 54/3 (2000): 421–427; Kal Raustiala, 'Form and Substance in International Agreements' *American Journal of International Law*, 99/3 (2005): 581; Andrew Guzman, 'The Design of International Agreements' *European Journal of International Law*, 16/4 (2005): 579.

[65] There are examples, see Shelton (n 3).

[66] See eg Jean d'Aspremont (n 3) who argues that soft law is the brainchild of 'Anglo-Saxon' lawyers who do not understand the 'theory of the legal act'; see also Klabbers (n 3).

BIBLIOGRAPHY

Richard Baxter, 'International Law in "Her Infinite Variety"' *International and Comparative Law Quarterly*, 29/4 (1980): 549

Alan Boyle and Christine Chinkin, *The Making of International Law* (OUP 2007) ch 5

Campbell McLachlan, 'The Principle of Systemic Integration and Article 31(3)(c) of the Vienna Convention' *International and Comparative Law Quarterly*, 54/2 (2005): 279

Lavanya Rajamani, 'The 2015 Paris Agreement: Interplay Between Hard, Soft and Non-Obligations' *Journal of Environmental Law*, 28/2 (2016): 337

Jorge Viñuales (ed), *The Rio Declaration on Environment and Development: A Commentary* (OUP 2015)

CHAPTER 26

PRIVATE AND QUASI-PRIVATE STANDARDS

JOANNE SCOTT*

I. INTRODUCTION

THE products in my local supermarket are adorned with a multitude of different labels, many of which have an environmental dimension. Organic; Fairtrade; Rainforest Alliance; hazardous chemicals warnings; Orang Utan Coffee Project, and so the list could go on. This supermarket is committed to cutting carbon and to the responsible sourcing of soya, fish, palm oil, timber, paper, and cotton.[1] While some of the labels are mandated by government (including European Union (EU)) regulation,[2] most of them are voluntary in that they are not mandated by law. The labels are attached to demonstrate a product's compliance with private or quasi-private standards that take the product 'beyond compliance' with the law.[3] While some of the labels attest to product quality, most concern the manner in which the product was harvested or produced.

This chapter examines the concept of private and quasi-private standards in the environmental domain. While many of these standards involve the labelling of compliant products, others do not. The chapter begins by defining the concept of private and quasi-private standards (Section I) and examines their rise (Section II) and the reasons for this (Section III). Although it may at first glance appear counter intuitive to include a chapter

* Thanks to Kim Bouwer and Yoshiko Naiki for their helpful comments on an earlier draft.

1 For details see <https://www.waitrose.com/home/inspiration/about_waitrose/the_waitrose_way/responsible_fishing.html> accessed 31 December 2019.

2 An example of this are the hazardous chemicals labelling requirements in Regulation (EC) No 1272/2008 of 16 December 2008 on Classification, Labelling and Packaging of Substances and Mixtures, amending and repealing Directives 67/548/EEC and 1999/45/EC, and amending Regulation (EC) No 1907/2006, OJ 2008 L 353/1.

3 Neil Gunningham, Robert Kagan, and Dorothy Thornton, 'Social License and Environmental Protection: Why Businesses go Beyond Compliance?' *Law & Social Inquiry*, 29 (2004): 307.

on private standards in a handbook on international environmental law, it will become clear that these standards interact with international law in a variety of important ways (Section IV). The chapter concludes by exploring the effectiveness (Section V) and legitimacy (Section VI) of private and quasi-private standards.

II. THE CONCEPT OF PRIVATE AND QUASI-PRIVATE STANDARDS

It is necessary to begin by defining the concept of a standard. A standard is understood here as a document that lays down rules, guidelines, principles, or characteristics for common and repeated use with which compliance is not mandatory.[4] A standard may relate to products or related processes and production methods or to other activities with the potential to damage the environment including transport.

A standard is considered to be private when the document in question is adopted by one or more non-governmental entities, including for example firms, non-governmental organizations (NGOs), and trade unions. Private standards may be firm- or sector-specific, or they may focus on a particular commodity such as sugar, palm oil, or soy.

The concept of a quasi-private standard is less clear and needs to be carefully defined.[5] For the purpose of this chapter three kinds of standards are considered to be quasi-private standards.

First, where the adoption of standards requires the consent of both governmental and non-governmental entities, they are considered to be quasi-private standards. This would include the standards adopted by the International Standardization Organization (ISO) because the national standards bodies that vote on the adoption of standards within this are drawn from both the state and private sector.[6] Individuals

[4] This draws on but adapts the definition of a standard included in annex 1.2 of the 1994 Agreement on Technical Barriers to Trade (TBT) adopted 15 April 1994, entered into force 1 January 1995) 1868 UNTS 120 (TBT). The definition has much in common with the definition laid down by the International Standardization Organization (ISO) which refers to 'documented agreements containing technical specifications or other precise criteria to be used consistently as rules, guidelines or definitions of characteristics, to ensure that materials, products, processes and services are fit for their purpose'. For a list of different definitions used by different organizations see World Trade Organization (WTO), Committee on Sanitary and Phytosanitary Measures (SPS), 'Existing Definitions of Private Standards in Other International Organisations' (18 June 2014) G/SPS/GEN/1334.

[5] In relation to quasi-private standards, it will sometimes be important to consider whether the standard can be attributed to the state on the basis that there has been 'sufficient governmental involvement with it'; see *Japan—Measures Affecting Consumer Photographic Film and Paper* (Panel Report) [31 March 1998] WTO Doc WT/DS44/R [10.56].

[6] See 'ISO Membership Manual' <https://www.iso.org/files/live/sites/isoorg/files/store/en/PUB100399.pdf> accessed 31 December 2019; see also Tim Büthe and Walter Mattli, *The New Global Rulers: The Privatization of Regulation in the World Economy* (Princeton University Press 2011).

from government bodies participate as experts and not as representatives of their governments.

Second, to the extent that standards adopted by private entities are based upon standards previously elaborated by states or international organizations, they are considered to be quasi-private standards.

Third, this chapter draws upon Jessica Green's distinction between 'entrepreneurial' and 'delegated' private authority.[7] Green considers non-state actors to be exercising entrepreneurial private authority when they act on their own initiative, and delegated private authority when they exercise powers that have been delegated to them by states acting collectively, including within an international organization.[8] Where standards are adopted as a result of delegated private authority, they are considered to be quasi-private standards because in this situation private actors are exercising governmental power.

This chapter refers to private standards rather than private and quasi-private standards, except where it intends to make a distinction between the two. The definition of private and quasi-private standards relied upon here is capacious. It includes corporate codes of conduct, certification systems, environmental management systems, and procedural standards for monitoring and reporting environmental performance. Nonetheless, the definition only includes the standard-setting function of private actors and does not include many of their other governance functions such as the provision of expertise, lobbying, or education. Also, for standards to be considered private or quasi-private standards, private entities must play a formal as opposed to a merely consultative or advisory role in their adoption.

It is challenging to write succinctly about the nature and role of private standards. This is because of the diversity of form that such standards take and the consequent segmentation of academic literature which often focuses on a sub-set of this broad phenomenon. While this chapter provides a general overview of this topic, it is important to distinguish between different kinds of private standards as the discussion proceeds.

Before leaving the issue of definitions behind, it is useful to reflect on the relationship between standards and the closely related concept of 'indicators'. Indicators are used to rank the performance of different entities or products 'through a process that simplifies raw data about a complex social phenomenon'.[9] While standards often adopt a binary approach that assesses compliance versus non-compliance, indicators recognize different levels or degrees of compliance.[10] Many indicators have been developed by non-governmental entities in the environmental sphere.

[7] Jessica Green, *Rethinking Private Authority* (Princeton University Press 2014).

[8] This chapter uses the terms 'non-governmental' and 'non-state' interchangeably.

[9] Kevin Davies, Benedict Kingsbury, and Sally Merry, 'Indicators as a Technology of Global Governance' *Law & Society Review*, 46/1 (2012): 71, 73–74.

[10] Although it has also been recognized that standards can move away from a binary approach; see Simon Bush and Peter Oosterveer, 'Vertically Differentiating Environmental Standards: The Case of the Marine Stewardship Council' *Sustainability*, 7/2 (2015): 1861.

It has been suggested that indicators are 'standard-setting instruments' because they embody standards which serve as benchmarks for evaluating performance. They are said to 'blend' standard-setting with evaluation of performance.[11] Indicators may use existing standards or involve the development of new standards. Sometimes indicators only embody procedural as opposed to substantive standards, because ranking is determined on the basis of a simple comparison of performance between units without reference to any substantive 'rules, guidelines or characteristics for common or repeated use'. Even here, indicators generally embody procedural standards because they identify what is to be measured and establish modalities for how to measure, monitor, verify, and report upon the performance of different units.[12]

III. THE PROLIFERATION OF PRIVATE STANDARDS

Abbott and Snidal have tracked the evolution of different kinds of 'regulatory standard-setting' within the framework of their famous governance triangle.[13] This triangle recognizes the regulatory function of states, civil society organizations, and firms, acting separately or together. Abbott and Snidal identify a rise in private standards since 1985 and a marked increase in quasi-private standards involving both state and non-state actors since 1994.[14]

Their findings are broadly consistent with those of other authors who have identified a rise in private standards since the 1990s. David Vogel has developed the concept of 'civil regulations' and has concluded that there was a rapid increase in the emergence of these starting in the 1990s.[15] He defines civil regulations as those that 'employ private, non-state, or market-based, regulatory frameworks to govern multinational firms and global supply networks'.[16]

Jessica Green has tracked the emergence of entrepreneurial private authority in the environmental domain from 1954 to 2009.[17] Although she regards the concepts

[11] See Davies, Kingsbury, and Merry (n 9) 83.

[12] Take the example of RightShip's Greenhouse Gas Rating for ships, which awards an A–G rating to a vessel depending on how its performance compares to the average performance of ships of a similar size and type. RightShip has, however, also elaborated a Ratings Methodology which specifies how performance is to be measured; see <https://www.rightship.com/sustainability/ghg-rating-methodology/> accessed 31 December 2019.

[13] Kenneth Abbott and Duncan Snidal, 'The Governance Triangle: Regulatory Standards Institutions and the Shadow of the State' in Walter Mattli and Ngaire Woods (eds), *The Politics of Global Regulation* (Princeton University Press 2009) 44.

[14] Ibid, fig 2(a)–(c). They only identify one example of a quasi-private standard before 1994, namely the International Labour Organisation Declaration on Multinational Enterprises dating from 1977.

[15] David Vogel, 'The Private Regulation of Global Corporate Conduct' in Mattli and Woods (n 13) 151.

[16] Ibid, 152–153.

[17] See Green (n 7) ch 3.

of entrepreneurial private authority, private standards, and civil regulation to be coterminus,[18] she endorses a conception of civil regulation than is narrower than Vogel. She expressly excludes first-party schemes,[19] and is only concerned with *transnational* civil regulations.[20] Nonetheless she, like Vogel, finds that there has been an increase in entrepreneurial private authority since 1990 and a particularly rapid rise since the turn of the century.[21]

IV. EXPLAINING THE EMERGENCE OF PRIVATE STANDARDS

There is a large and rich body of academic literature that explores the reasons for the emergence of private standards. This includes a number of accounts that aim to distill conclusions that are valid across different sectors. Perhaps the best account of this kind is a multi-author report examining the roles and limitations of sustainability certification (the 'Towards Sustainability' report).[22] This report was prepared by a steering committee with diverse membership which included leading academics and members drawn from business and NGOs.[23] Among other topics, it seeks to identify the principal 'drivers' which motivate different actors.[24]

For example civil society actors use private standards as a tool to accomplish both their 'substantive' (eg environmental protection) and 'survival' (eg fundraising or membership) goals.[25] Governments rely upon them to achieve public policy objectives when they are unwilling or unable to use traditional command-and-control regulation, including when they recognize that private standards can offer advantages such as flexibility.[26] They also rely upon them as a tool to uphold values and fulfil their missions,

[18] Ibid, 82.

[19] Ibid. That is to say, schemes in which the standard-setter is also responsible for verifying compliance with the standards.

[20] Ibid, 87. Civil regulations are considered to be transnational if they function in at least two countries.

[21] Ibid, 92. She identifies twelve examples before 1990, thirty-eight from 1990 to 1999, and sixty-nine from 2000 to 2009.

[22] Steering Committee of the State-of-Knowledge Assessment of Standards and Certification, *Toward Sustainability: The Roles and Limitations of Certification* (RESOLVE 2012). The Executive Summary (ES) is available separately at <https://www.resolve.ngo/docs/toward-sustainability-executive-summary.pdf> accessed 31 December 2019.

[23] The group included Michael Vandenbergh, a Law Professor from Vanderbilt University.

[24] See 'Toward Sustainability' report (n 22). This report is concerned with private, voluntary sustainability standards and certification. Standards are described as 'a defined set of social, environmental and/or economic criteria' and certification as 'a means of providing assurance that products or services comply' with the standards (ibid, 6). The establishment of the Forest Stewardship Council in 1993 is exemplary of the kind of standards/certification they have in mind.

[25] Ibid, ch 2, s A.

[26] Ibid, ch 2, s B.

and where recourse to them is better aligned with existing social values and norms. For companies, a multitude of different reasons drives engagement with private standards. This includes supply-side pressures such as security of supply, efficiency, traceability, or cost reduction, as well as external drivers such as buyer, civil society, regulatory, and investor pressures and incentives.[27]

The 'Toward Sustainability' report offers a particularly rich and nuanced account of the reasons for the emergence of private standards, four of which are highlighted here. First, the report is unusually attentive to the important role that 'regulatory incentives' play in driving the emergence of private standards. It argues that private standards may be used as a tool to pre-empt regulation, to decrease the costs of complying with regulation, to ensure regulatory consistency, to create barriers that deter the entry of new market participants, and to reduce tortious liability.[28]

Second, while the report accepts that consumer demand for certified products may 'in some cases [be] a driver of business behavior',[29] it emphasizes that there is wide variation in the willingness of consumers to pay for environmentally friendly products.[30] It concludes that 'consumer demand alone is unlikely to support a large-scale shift towards the use of certification and labeling systems, especially in product categories outside of organic agriculture'.[31]

Third, while the report acknowledges the key importance of utilitarian considerations in driving different actors' engagement with private standards, it also lays emphasis on the role played by norms. For example, personal, societal, and industry norms are identified as an internal driver of business engagement with private standards.[32] This emphasis upon norms is consistent with earlier writings by one of the authors of the report (Cashore).

In an important article,[33] Bernstein and Cashore argue that global norms played a role in the rise of private standards. For example, 'sovereignty norms' are viewed as facilitating such standards because they provide an alternative to intergovernmental agreements which are frequently thwarted due to concerns about sovereignty.[34] Also, shifting global environmental norms played a role because this resulted in a greater acceptance of market mechanisms.[35] Less intuitively, they contend that growing support for norms favouring greater democratization of global governance lent support

[27] Ibid, ch 2, s C.
[28] Ibid, 49.
[29] Ibid.
[30] Ibid, 50.
[31] Ibid.
[32] Ibid, 48.
[33] Steven Bernstein and Benjamin Cashore, 'Can Non-State Global Governance Be Legitimate? An Analytical Framework' *Regulation & Governance*, 1/4 (2007): 347. In this article, the authors are concerned exclusively with what they call 'non-state market driven governance systems'. These governance systems rely on private standards and certification.
[34] Ibid, 352.
[35] Ibid.

to private standards, because many of these standards were generated through open, transparent, and accountable multi-stakeholder processes.[36] They also suggest that the 'neoliberal normative environment' of the 1980s and 1990s led to the creation of a trade regime which imposed relatively greater constraints on government regulation as compared to private standards.[37]

Bernstein and Cashore also identify opportunities for the emergence of shared norms about appropriate ways of doing business as the 'life-cycle' of private standards moves from the initiation phase, to building support and towards achieving political legitimacy.[38] This is aided by opportunities for discussion, debate, and learning among stakeholders which may in turn be facilitated by the creation of multi-stakeholder institutions. Overall, they argue that a utilitarian logic of consequences is not sufficient to explain the lifecycle of private standards and that a logic of appropriateness, shaped by global norms and emerging shared norms, also plays an important role.

Finally, the 'Toward Sustainability' report paints a picture which is appropriately dynamic in which both the strategic calculations of actors and their norms and values are susceptible to influence and change. Civil society organizations, governments, and businesses are not just driven towards engagement with private standards but play multi-faceted roles that drive forward the emergence of private standards.[39] This dynamic quality also emerges clearly from Mattli and Wood's framework for explaining the emergence (or absence) of public interest regulation, including private standards.[40] They emphasize the importance of events in generating 'demonstration effects' that reveal the calamitous effects of regulatory failures, thereby fuelling demand for standards.[41] They also provide a taxonomy of 'entrepreneurs of regulatory change', including non-governmental entrepreneurs, pubic officials as entrepreneurs and private-sector entrepreneurs.[42] They include in the latter category 'corporate consumers', 'corporations at risk', 'corporate newcomers' and 'corporate levelers of the playing field'.[43] This taxonomy provides further insights into the kind of material incentives that businesses may have to support the adoption of private standards.

The findings set out in the 'Toward Sustainability' report overlap in important ways with other efforts to explain the emergence and rise of private standards. For example, Jessica Green has developed a synthetic supply-and-demand framework in the environmental domain.[44] As in the 'Toward Sustainability' report, she places emphasis upon

[36] Ibid, 353.
[37] Ibid, 354.
[38] Ibid, eg diagram on 356.
[39] See 'Toward Sustainability' report (n 22) ch 2, which sets out the different roles played the key actors.
[40] Walter Mattli and Ngaire Woods, 'In Whose Benefit? Explaining Regulatory Change in World Politics' in Mattli and (n 13) 1.
[41] Ibid.
[42] Ibid.
[43] Ibid.
[44] See Green (n 7) 39–45.

the importance of expertise in facilitating the supply of private standards by private actors.[45] She also acknowledges that business demand for private standards is driven by an expectation that they will secure benefits as a result. She places particular emphasis upon the capacity of private standards to reduce transaction costs, to solve coordination problems by enhancing credibility of commitments, to confer first mover advantage, and to improve reputation.[46]

V. THE ROLE OF INTERNATIONAL ORGANIZATIONS AND INTERNATIONAL LAW IN RELATION TO PRIVATE STANDARDS

Considerable attention has been paid to the relationship between private standards and the public authority of the state.[47] There is also growing interest in the relationship between private standards and international organizations/international law.[48] It is to this theme that this chapter now turns. As a preliminary matter, it is important to stress that 'public and private authority are not "zero-sum"'.[49] Rather, as Green has illuminated, there has been an increase in global environmental governance as well as a diversification of the kinds of actors involved.[50] The number of multilateral environmental agreements (MEAs) doubled from 1990 to 2010 and there was a 60% increase in bilateral environmental agreements during this period.[51]

International organizations and international law interact with private standards in a wide variety of different ways. At least outside of the WTO context,[52] there is a need for further research on this topic to improve our understanding. Four key aspects of this relationship are identified and discussed below.

45 Ibid, 44–45.

46 Ibid, 41.

47 See 'Toward Sustainability' report (n 22) ch 2, s B.

48 See for a recent example Markos Karavias, 'Interactions Between International Law and Private Fisheries Certification' *Transnational Environmental Law*, 7/1 (2018): 165.

49 See Green (n 7) 163.

50 Ibid.

51 Ibid.

52 Ming Du, 'WTO Regulation of Transnational Private Authority in Global Governance' *International & Comparative Law Quarterly*, 67/4 (2018): 867.

A. International Organizations Delegate Authority to Adopt Quasi-Private Standards to Private Actors

As noted earlier, Jessica Green coined the term 'delegated private authority' to describe situations in which international treaties, or post-treaty decisions, delegate governance functions to private actors.[53] Rule-making is included amongst the governance functions that she examines. Green's definition of rule-making is broad and while it would include standard setting, it also covers activities that go beyond this.[54] She distinguishes between delegation that is embedded in treaties and post-treaty delegation (eg through a decision adopted by the Conference of the Parties). She observes that both kinds of delegation are 'a largely modern phenomenon' but that the number of policy functions delegated has increased at a rate that is consistent with the overall rise in MEAs.[55] Whereas 9% of rule-making functions were delegated to private actors from 1857 to 2002, 23% were delegated from 1946 to 2008. In relation to rule-making, delegated authority is always shared between private actors and states/international organizations. Delegation to private actors is much more common at the post-treaty stage. Given the relative ease of reversing post-treaty delegation, this is consistent with Green's argument that states are reluctant to delegate in circumstances that entail high sovereignty costs.[56]

B. International Law Enhances the Authority of Private or Quasi-Private Standards

Article 2.4 of the WTO's Agreement on Technical Barriers to Trade (TBT) requires members to base their regulations on international standards other than when these standards would be an ineffective or inappropriate means to fulfil the member's legitimate objectives.[57] For this purpose, international standards are those adopted by a '[b]ody or system whose membership is open to the relevant bodies of at least all Members'.[58] This would include ISO standards because this organization is open to the national standards bodies of all countries.

[53] Green (n 7) ch 2.

[54] Ibid, 63: 'creating administrative rules, filling in gaps, or interpreting extant rules, as well as matters of procedure and voting'.

[55] Ibid, 71, 75.

[56] Ibid, 75.

[57] See also art 2.5 which creates a rebuttable presumption that national measures that are in accordance with international standards do not create an unnecessary obstacle to international trade.

[58] See annex 1.4.

C. International Organizations Serve as a Meta-Regulator Vis-À-Vis Private or Quasi-Private Standards

For the purposes of this discussion, the concept of meta-regulation can be taken to refer to situations in which the standard-setting activities of private actors are subject to constraints or guidance formulated by an external actor, including an international organization. It is different from delegation which describes the situation in which a state or intergovernmental authority confers power rather than oversees the exercise of power.

The TBT Agreement offers a compelling example in that it imposes an obligation on WTO members to perform a meta-regulatory function vis-à-vis private standard setting bodies ('standards about setting standards'[59]). Members are required to take such reasonable measures that are available to them to ensure that non-governmental standardizing bodies within their territories comply with the Code of Good Practice for the Preparation, Adoption and Application of Standards that is included in Annex 3 of the TBT Agreement, and to desist from taking measures which, directly or indirectly, have the effect of encouraging or requiring such bodies to act in a manner that is inconsistent with this Code.[60] This Code includes both substantive and procedural requirements which reflect the obligations that attach to WTO members under the TBT Agreement. Standardizing bodies, including non-governmental standardizing bodies, may also choose voluntarily to accept this Code.[61]

There are other examples of international organizations performing a meta-regulatory function vis-à-vis private standards in the environmental domain, as well as instances of regional organizations such as the EU performing a function of this kind. The example of EU meta-regulation of private sustainability standards for biofuels has become quite well known.[62]

[59] See Green (n 7) 90.

[60] See art 4.

[61] For a list of bodies that have done so see the 'WTO ISO Standards Information Gateway' <https://tbtcode.iso.org/sites/wto-tbt/list-of-standardizing-bodies.html> accessed 31 December 2019. While eighty-one non-governmental standardizing bodies have currently accepted the Code, the vast majority of these are the national standards bodies of members that participate in ISO activities.

[62] Directive 2009/28/EC of 23 April 2009 on the promotion of the use of energy from renewable sources and amending and subsequently repealing Directives 2001/77/EC and 2003/30/EC, OJ 2009 L 140; see also Yoshiko Naiki, 'Trade and Bioenergy: Explaining and Assessing the Regime Complex for Sustainable Bioenergy' *European Journal of International Law*, 27/1 (2016): 129; Jolene Lin, 'Governing Biofuels: A Principal-Agent Analysis of the European Union Biofuels Certification Regime and the Clean Development Mechanism' *Journal of Environmental* Law, 24/1 (2012): 43.

D. There is Substantive Borrowing between Private Standards and International Law and Vice Versa

In her exploration of entrepreneurial private authority, Green testifies to the changing nature of private standard setting in the environmental domain by observing that an increasing number of private standards repackage existing standards to a certain degree.[63] While Green's main focus in terms of interactions between standards is on interactions between different private standards, she does suggest that in relation to carbon offsetting, private standards have been 'very cognizant' of existing international rules under and pursuant to the Kyoto Protocol.[64] 'As a result', she argues, 'there is a high degree of recognition of public rules by private ones' and '77 percent of privately created offset standards recognize rules created under the [Clean Development Mechanism]'.[65]

It is of course clear that the relationship between international law and private standards will vary significantly according to context, and understanding this relationship requires a close examination of the scope and content of the relevant norms. My colleagues and I found evidence of a relationship between international law and private standards in our study concerning the regulation of greenhouse gas (GHG) emissions from shipping.[66] For example, in its methodology for measuring GHG emissions from ships, RightShip draws upon the Energy Efficiency Design Index that was developed by the International Maritime Organization.[67]

In his recent study of the relationship between private standards and international law in the governance of fisheries sustainability, Karavias identifies examples of substantive borrowing in both directions.[68] On the one hand, the private standards adopted by the Marine Stewardship Council are modelled on the Food and Agricultural Organization's (FAO) 1995 Code of Good Practice for Responsible Fisheries and also require compliance with international law. This relationship between private standards and international law is reinforced by the meta-regulation adopted by the FAO which in laying down minimum requirements for eco-labelling and certification schemes for marine capture fisheries suggests that these should be consistent with 1982 UNCLOS (United Nations Convention on the Law of the Sea), the 1995 Fish Stocks Agreement, and the FAO's Code of Good Practice for Responsible Fisheries. On the other hand, Karavias shows how private standards can serve as a model and as guidelines for international

[63] See Green (n 7) 93–94, who distinguishes between *de novo* and amended standards.

[64] Ibid, 101.

[65] Ibid, 101–102.

[66] Joanne Scott *et al*, 'The Promise and Limits of Private Standards to Reduce Greenhouse Gas Emissions from Shipping' *Journal of Environmental* Law, 29/2 (2017): 231.

[67] IMO Res MEPC.203(62), 'Amendments to the annex of the protocol of 1997 to amend the international convention for the prevention of pollution from ships, 1973, as modified by the protocol of 1978 relating thereto (Inclusion of regulations on energy efficiency for ships in MARPOL Annex VI)' (15 July 2011); see <https://site.rightship.com/sustainability/ghg-rating-methodology/≥ for RightShip's methodology.

[68] See Karavias (n 48).

law.[69] For example, the harvest control rules established by the Indian Ocean Tuna Commission incorporate 'reference points' contained in the private standards adopted by the Marine Stewardship Council.[70]

VI. APPRAISING THE EFFECTIVENESS OF PRIVATE STANDARDS IN THE ENVIRONMENTAL DOMAIN?

Drawing on existing literature including hundreds of case studies, together with commissioned studies and stakeholder interviews, the 2012 'Toward Sustainability' report appraised the impacts of private standards and certification.[71] It examined the ecological, social, and economic impacts in four sectors: agriculture, forestry, fisheries, and aquaculture. Within the concept of ecological impacts, it included ecosystem integrity, biodiversity, and pollution/waste to air, water, and soil.[72] The report reached a broadly positive, though heavily qualified, conclusion.

On the positive side, it observed that 'there is reasonable evidence that certification has had positive impacts on the environment in particular cases'.[73] This includes direct impacts on the behaviour of certified enterprises and indirect impacts on the behaviour of other actors as a result of demonstration effects, enhanced institutional capacity, and the realization of synergies between private standards and other forms of governance, including governmental regulation.[74] The report considers that indirect impacts are 'substantial' and 'probably greater' than direct impacts.[75]

The qualifications to this broadly positive conclusion noted in the 'Toward Sustainability' report are many and varied. The evidence base is relatively new and there are gaps in it, including in relation to the durability of impacts. It is difficult to generalize about impacts, to extrapolate from case studies and 'clear attribution of on-the-ground

[69] Ibid, ss 4.3, 4.4.

[70] Ibid, 179.

[71] 'Toward Sustainability' report (n 22) 57: The concept of impacts is defined as 'changes in the quality and resilience of ecosystems, changes in resource efficiency and livelihoods, and changes in social welfare within the workplace and wider community'; see also for an important recent contribution to this discussion Tim Bartley, *Rights Without Rules: Land, Labor and Private Authority in the Global Economy* (OUP 2018) who emphasizes the crucial role of domestic governance arrangements; see also Committee on Sustainability Assessment, 'The COSA Measuring Sustainability Report: Coffee and Cocoa in Twelve Countries' (2014).

[72] 'Toward Sustainability' report (n 22) 62–66.

[73] Ibid, 66.

[74] Ibid, Executive Summary, 6–12.

[75] Ibid, 8.

impacts is rare'.[76] The report also notes that it is methodologically challenging to take steps to improve the evidence base.

Despite these qualifications, the 'Toward Sustainability' report goes on to make a series of recommendations to the principal actors involved in certification. For certification organizations the key recommendations address four key themes, giving an insight into the deficiencies that the authors perceive and the steps that should be taken to address these. Their recommendations relate to the importance of improving the evidence base as we are promoting, learning, and continuously improving; fostering buy-in, including from small- and medium- sized enterprises; ensuring system integrity, for example through a strong monitoring and enforcement system; and stimulating impact and the potential for transformative change by designing systems to interact with government regulators and other sustainability tools. This last point is of critical importance for the authors of the report who recognize that while certification systems can create performance improvement incentives for 'top performers', governments will often need to step in to help improve the performance of 'low' and 'middle performers'.[77] The report also recognizes that it may sometimes be appropriate for governments to encourage harmonization among different standards or to develop governmental standards where a proliferation of private standards leads to consumer confusion and/or 'greenwashing'.[78]

Elsewhere in the 'Toward Sustainability' report, the authors stress that over the next forty years consumption will grow fastest in the global South and that the impact of private standards and certification will depend upon the emergence of a large market for certified products in countries such as China, Brazil, Chile, India, Indonesia, and Russia.[79]

A follow-up to the 'Toward Sustainability' report was published in 2018 which focused specifically on evaluating the ecological impacts of private standards and certification systems.[80] This noted that the intervening years had seen the emergence of a considerable body of new evidence on this topic as demand for evidence about impacts has increased.[81] This increasing demand is reflected in the activities of the non-governmental meta-regulator of private standards, ISEAL (International Social and Environmental Accreditation and Labelling Alliance), which has adopted a Code of

[76] Ibid, 60.

[77] See Green (n 7); 'Toward Sustainability' report (n 22) 104, and Executive Summary, 11.

[78] 'Toward Sustainability' report (n 22) 105.

[79] Ibid, 94. Philip Schleifer and Yixian Sun, 'Emerging Markets and Private Governance: The Political Economy of Sustainable Palm Oil in China and India' *Review of International Political* Economy, 25/2 (2018): 190.

[80] Kristin Komives *et al*, 'Conservation impacts of voluntary sustainability standards: How has our understanding changed since the 2012 publication of 'Toward sustainability: The roles and limitations of certification'?' (Meridien Institute 2018). This looked at the same sectors, namely agriculture, forestry, fisheries, and aquaculture. Recall the broader definition of impacts in the 'Toward Sustainability' report (n 22).

[81] 'Toward Sustainability' report (n 22) 7, 11.

Good Practice on 'Impacts'.[82] Although the team responsible for preparing this follow-up report had access to a vastly enriched evidence base regarding the effectiveness of private standards, they adopted strict criteria for including evidence within the report.[83]

In contrast to the 'Toward Sustainability' report, the follow-up report does not provide us with accessible summary conclusions about the impact of private standards. Reflecting improvements in the evidence base, the authors present the results by 'outcome' rather than by sector. For example, in relation to forestry, they include outcomes relating to forest cover change, forest quality, and conservation of important areas, air quality, carbon emissions, and biodiversity.[84] While this renders their findings rich and nuanced, it also makes them harder to communicate in an accessible form. It is for this reason that the authors developed a template for communicating their findings in relation to specific outcomes. This distinguishes between impacts that are 'negative', 'no difference', and 'positive' and grades the studies in which the evidence is found as 'suggestive only', 'less conclusive', 'conclusive', and 'most conclusive'.[85]

The key messages of this follow-up report are more sobering than of the initial 'Toward Sustainability' report. It identifies a number of remaining key deficits in the evidence base including 'missing sharp conclusions about performance'.[86] In relation to this, it notes that '[m]any of the studies we reviewed for this report did not find any significant difference between certified and noncertified operations, or in pre- and post- certification outcomes'.[87] The three key takeaways highlighted by the authors of this report are also salutary. While it is important not to lose sight of conclusions emerging in the strongest studies, including those that identify indirect as opposed to direct benefits, it is equally important to be 'realistic about what we can expect from research and humble about what we can claim to know'.[88] The report also observes the existence of an evidence deficit in relation to identifying 'determinants of performance' of private standards,[89] and emphasizes the limited capacity of supply-chain interventions to achieve landscape or seascape-level conservation outcomes such as deforestation or habitat or water quality.[90] Thus, collaborative efforts 'that seek to use the strength of different organisations' are necessary to leverage positive impacts at a broader scale.[91] This question of scale is especially important considering that the efficiency improvements incentivized by private standards can easily be offset by increasing

[82] ISEAL Alliance, 'Assessing the Impacts of Social and Environmental Standards System: ISEAL Code of Good Practice' (version 2, December 2014) <https://www.isealalliance.org/get-involved/resources/iseal-codes-good-practice> accessed 31 December 2019.

[83] See Komives (n 80) 8–9, annexes 1, 2.

[84] Ibid, 21–22.

[85] Ibid, 52, 54.

[86] Ibid, 30.

[87] Ibid.

[88] Ibid, 35.

[89] Some of the literature discussed earlier can help in understanding the determinants of the impact of private standards; see eg Vogel (n 15); Mattli and Woods (n 13).

[90] See Komives (n 80) 6, 35.

[91] Ibid.

overall demand for goods or services,[92] or by indirect effects which arise when standards contribute to the displacement of harmful activities from certified to non-certified sites.[93]

VII. THE LEGITIMACY OF PRIVATE STANDARDS

In 2008, Allen Buchanan and Robert Keohane published an article entitled 'The Legitimacy of Global Governance Institutions'.[94] Although this article addresses the question of the legitimacy of multilateral organizations such as the WTO or the International Criminal Court, it provides an analytical framework which is also useful in thinking about private standards. There are three primary reasons for this.

First, Buchanan and Keohane draw a distinction between a 'normative' and a 'sociological' conception of legitimacy. Whereas the former is concerned with an organization's 'right to rule', the latter is concerned with beliefs about an organization's right to rule.[95] Each of these two conceptions of legitimacy is at play in the literature regarding private standards. For example, some authors explore the normative legitimacy of private standards from the point of view of theories of democratic legitimacy including deliberative democracy. Bernstein and Cashore, by contrast, adopt a sociological conception of legitimacy because they view 'political legitimacy' as arising when stakeholders come together in a political community that grants a market-driven system of private governance, the authority to govern.[96]

Second, in considering what is at stake when it comes to the legitimacy of multilateral institutions, Buchanan and Keohane's account can also help us to understand why we should be concerned about the legitimacy of private standards. This is partly because standard-setting bodies exercise significant power. Like governments and multilateral institutions, 'they issue rules ... and claim the authority to do so'.[97] While these rules

[92] This point emerged clearly in our study on the role of private standards in reducing GHG emissions from shipping because private standards govern the carbon intensity of shipping rather than the sector's cumulative emissions; see Scott *et al* (n 66).

[93] See eg in relation to palm oil including as a result of indirect land use change, Justis von Geibler, 'Market-Based Governance for Sustainability in Value Chains: Conditions for Successful Standard Setting in the Palm Oil Sector' *Journal of Cleaner Production*, 56/1 (2013): 39.

[94] Allen Buchanan and Robert Keohane, 'The Legitimacy of Global Governance Institutions' *Ethics & International Affairs*, 20/4 (2006): 405.

[95] Ibid.

[96] See Bernstein and Cashore (n 33) 361. Schleifer discusses attempts to develop 'cross-cutting' approaches that overcome this distinction between normative and sociological approaches to legitimacy; see Philip Schleifer, 'Varieties of Multi-Stakeholder Governance: Selecting Legitimation Strategies in Transnational Sustainability Politics' *Globalizations*, 16/1 (2019): 50.

[97] See Buchanan and Keohane (n 94) 406.

are non-binding, significant sanctions, understood mainly in terms of deprivation of market access, can attach in the case of non-compliance.[98] Moreover, private standard-setting bodies 'constrain the choices facing societies ... and impose burdens as well as benefits'.[99] Like other forms of regulation, standards embody trade-offs between different values and distribute burdens and benefits between individuals and groups. The extent to which standard-setting bodies exercise power is of course a question of degree.

Third, Buchanan and Keohane's conception of normative legitimacy provides an excellent starting point in developing a framework for assessing the legitimacy of private standard-setting bodies.[100] They argue in favour of a conception of legitimacy that is both dynamic and relational. To achieve this, an institution is required to permit external actors to contest and an institution's 'most basic features' including its goals and accountability framework.[101] This requires that the institution in question be imbued with an adequate 'epistemic-deliberative' quality,[102] including an openness to external as well as internal contestation regarding the terms of its accountability, transparency, and sources of 'public justification'.[103] Buchanan and Keohane argue that this epistemic-deliberative quality can serve as a proxy for assessing fulfilment of key moral attributes in conditions of limited knowledge, moral disagreement, and uncertainty,[104] and that it can serve to protect fundamental democratic values whilst accepting that global governance institutions cannot be held to the same standard of democratic legitimacy as states.[105]

Assessment of the normative legitimacy of private standards is aided by increasing availability of information. The International Trade Centre's 'Sustainability Map' is illustrative of this trend.[106] This includes information about the requirements included in standards and the processes followed by standard-setting bodies, including private and international bodies. This captures one element of Buchanan and Keohane's dynamic and relational framework for normative legitimacy, due to the inclusion of information

[98] See Matteo Fiorini *et al*, 'Institutional Design of Voluntary Sustainability Standards: Evidence from a New Database' *Development Policy Review*, 57/2 (2018): 193 where it is noted that voluntary standards often become de facto mandatory because of the threat of exclusion from global value chains.

[99] See Buchanan and Keohane (n 94) 407.

[100] The one element of their conception that does not travel well from multilateral institutions to private standard setting is the requirement of state consent and so this will not be included in the discussion here.

[101] See Buchanan and Keohane (n 94) 433.

[102] Ibid, 425.

[103] Ibid, 426–429.

[104] Ibid, 428. They identify three criteria: minimum moral integrity (respect for human rights), minimum institutional integrity (congruence between an institution's performance and proclaimed goals/procedures) and comparative benefit (the institution provides benefits that cannot otherwise be obtained subject to feasibility, costs and moral acceptability).

[105] Ibid, 433–434.

[106] For access to the database see <https://www.sustainabilitymap.org/home> accessed 3 January 2020; see also Fiorni *et al* (n 98).

about the existence of clear procedures to continuously improve the standards. It also contains information about which meta-regulatory requirements a standard-setting institution has signed up to, including those promulgated by ISEAL.[107] Nonetheless, the database does not contain information about transparency or opportunities for external actors to contest the standards and/or procedures and to receive a reasoned response. This would be a useful next step.

VIII. CONCLUSION

This chapter has explored the concept of private and quasi-private standards which take a bewildering myriad of different forms. Standards of this kind would not score highly on an index of 'legalization' due to their non-binding quality[108] and they do not constitute a recognized source of public international law.[109] There are those, however, who are asking whether in our world of global legal pluralism we may need a new conception of law. For example, Roger Cotterrell has proposed a provisional understanding of law as 'institutionalised doctrine', embodying both norms, including standards, together with institutionalized practices for their creation, interpretation, and enforcement.[110] There is a danger that without a broader conception of law, international lawyers will be forced into the straightjacket of appraising the relevance of private standards not by reference to their proliferation, functions, and legitimacy, but exclusively by reference to their interactions with 'proper' international law.

BIBLIOGRAPHY

Tim Bartley, *Rights without Rules: Land, Labor and Private Authority in the Global Economy* (OUP 2018)

Steven Bernstein and Benjamin Cashore, 'Can Non-State Global Governance Be Legitimate? An Analytical Framework' *Regulation & Governance*, 1/4 (2007): 347

[107] Besides its Impacts Code, the private meta-regulator ISEAL has a Standard-setting Code of Good Practice which includes ten credibility principles such as improvement, engagement and transparency; see <https://www.isealalliance.org/get-involved/resources/iseal-codes-good-practice> accessed 31 December 2019.

[108] Kenneth Abbott *et al*, 'The Concept of Legalization' *International Organization*, 54/3 (2000): 401; for a critique see eg Martha Finnemore and Stephen Toope, 'Alternatives to "Legalization": Richer Views of Law and Politics' *International Organization*, 55/3 (2001): 743.

[109] ICJ Statute, art 38.

[110] Roger Cotterrell, 'A Concept of Law for Global Legal Pluralism' in Sean Donlan and Lukas Urscheler (eds), *Concepts of Law: Comparative, Jurisprudential and Social Science Perspectives* (Ashgate 2014) ch 12. By institutionalized, he means 'relatively stable, recognised, established processes or agencies existing for the purpose of creating (including changing), interpreting and enforcing doctrine'; see also William Twining, *Globalisation and Legal Theory* (CUP 2008).

Jessica Green, *Rethinking Private Authority* (Princeton University Press 2014)
Errol Meidinger, 'The Administrative Law of Global Private-Public Regulation: The Case of Forestry' *European Journal of International Law*, 17/1 (2006): 47
Steering Committee of the State-of-Knowledge Assessment of Standards and Certification, *Toward Sustainability: The Roles and Limitations of Certification* (RESOLVE 2012)

CHAPTER 27

JUDICIAL DEVELOPMENT

CYMIE R PAYNE

I. INTRODUCTION

JUDICIAL decisions are a 'subsidiary means for the determination of rules of law' according to Article 38.1 of the Statute of the International Court of Justice (ICJ), coming after treaties, custom, and general principles of law. This casts international judges as bit players in developing international environmental law, but that seemingly small role can be consequential. The most powerful effect of international court and tribunal (ICT) decisions is to shape states' future actions, including the behaviour of states that were not parties to the litigation that engendered the decision. Changing state behaviour to prevent environmental harm from occurring in the first place is a superior outcome to attempting to restore damage, so an ICT judgement that exercises a strong normative influence can be effective in providing environmental quality.

International judicial bodies' primary role with respect to the environment is to resolve disputes by deciding contentious cases, and to guide the application of international law by issuing Advisory Opinions. States directly comply with their legal duty by acknowledging and remedying their past wrongs.

States also conform their behaviour to judicial rulings in less obvious, traceable ways. ICTs influence global governance broadly when they create and alter normative expectations.[1] ICTs can influence the development of international environmental law by providing an authoritative articulation of a legal rule or principle. Some cases become widely cited—for example, the ICJ *Pulp Mills* case is frequently referenced as authority for the legal requirement to conduct an environmental impact assessment (EIA) and the *Trail Smelter* arbitration for the principle that a state may not allow its territory

[1] Armin von Bogdandy and Ingo Venzke, 'Beyond Dispute: International Judicial Institutions as Lawmakers' *German Law Journal*, 12/5 (2011): 979.

to be used for activities that cause transboundary environmental harm.[2] Statements by highly visible ICTs simplify the difficulty of identifying a 'correct' rule. They are also accepted as the *opinio juris* needed to construct customary law. The commentary to the International Law Commission's (ILC) 'Articles on the Responsibility of States for Internationally Wrongful Acts' (2001) illustrates this process, by tracing the state practice and ICT judgements underlying the Articles. This recognized role of judicial opinions gives them great weight in forming customary law.

Cases that develop cross-cutting norms, like the precautionary principle, will affect a wide range of subjects, while many disputes that ICTs settle have comparatively narrow normative effect. Boundary determinations, for example, are frequently brought before the ICJ and the International Tribunal for the Law of the Sea (ITLOS), often because the land or sea territory in question contains valuable natural resources, such as fish or oil.[3] These judgements 'require precision, completeness and finality in their settlement';[4] but generally they contribute to the development of rules related to the very specific subject matter of delimitation.[5]

This chapter looks at the development of legal norms for governing Earth's environment through ICT judgements, describing the range of courts available, the remedies that they can offer, the capacity of ICTs to handle environmental problems, and problems that challenge their effectiveness in the overarching objective of providing a high degree of environmental quality. It does this while recognizing that courts and law are but one part of the system of governance, technology, politics, and economics that shapes human interactions with the environment.

II. THE MODERN JUDICIAL ORDER AND ENVIRONMENTAL LAW

The ability of ICTs to affect norms depends on their effectiveness, activities, and position in international environmental governance, which in turn are functions of their structure. A court that is not respected, that is rarely used, or that has a narrow jurisdiction can be expected to have limited influence. ICTs are numerous, but relatively

[2] *Trail Smelter Arbitration (United States/Canada)* (1938 and 1941) 3 RIAA 1905 (Trail Smelter case); *Pulp Mills on the River Uruguay (Argentina/Uruguay)* (Judgement) [2010] ICJ Rep 14 (Pulp Mills case).

[3] *The South China Sea Arbitration (Philippines/China)* (Final award of 12 July 2016) PCA Case no 2013-19 [3] (South China Sea case); *Legal Consequences of the Separation of the Chagos Archipelago from Mauritius in 1965* (Request for Advisory Opinion) [2017] ICJ.

[4] Hugh Thirlway, 'Territorial Disputes and Their Resolution in the Recent Jurisprudence of the International Court of Justice' *Leiden Journal of International Law*, 31 (2018): 117, 119.

[5] Ibid, 126; *Territorial and Maritime Dispute between Nicaragua and Honduras in the Caribbean Sea (Nicaragua/Honduras)* (Judgement) [2007] ICJ Rep 659 [145].

Table 27.1 Selected International Courts

Global		*Regional*	
ICJ	International Court of Justice	**IACtHR**	Inter-American Court of Human Rights
ITLOS	International Tribunal for the Law of the Sea	**ECtHR**	European Court of Human Rights
WTO-DSB	World Trade Organization Dispute Settlement Body	**ECOWAS** Court of Justice	Economic Community of West African States Court of Justice
ICC	International Criminal Court		
Arbitral Facilities		*Ad Hoc Tribunal*	
PCA	Permanent Court of Arbitration	**UNCC**	United Nations Compensation Commission
ICSID	International Center for the Settlement of Investment Disputes		

few have extensive authority to shape law and politics for a wide range of global actors.[6] Those that do include the ICJ, ITLOS, IACtHR, and a handful of other courts and arbitral tribunals. Characteristics that make them influential include: users representing the most active stakeholders in environmental issues; broad subject-matter competence that can reach novel environmental issues; and applicable law that includes important multilateral environmental agreements and customary international law. The environmental docket puts demands on ICTs to reinterpret doctrine and to develop their procedures: so far, the response has been incremental, not revolutionary. No fish has attempted to bring a complaint to an ICT, no major development projects have so far been halted in their tracks, and scientists have not been brought into the process on a regular basis.

A. Nature and Scope of Environmental Cases

The nature of environmental claims that ICTs address expanded from disputes over the allocation of natural resources like water, fish, and fur seals to a much broader

[6] Karen Alter, Laurence Helfer, and Mikael Madsen (eds), *International Court Authority* (OUP 2018) 10–11.

docket.[7] Cases now address: transboundary pollution prevention,[8] ecological damage,[9] endangered species,[10] regulatory challenges by investors or trade partners,[11] human rights,[12] environmental quality conflicts with other treaty commitments,[13] and military damage to the environment,[14] including testing, use, and elimination of nuclear weapons.[15] Some important topics are still outside the scope of ICTs. For example, states unsuccessfully sought an Advisory Opinion on climate change from the ICJ.[16]

A legal system accustomed to disputes located within sovereign territory is adapting to transboundary environmental conflicts. Natural resources that are market commodities, such as timber and minerals, are usual subjects for international law. But damage to the environment in and of itself—such as wildlife and planetary systems, biodiversity, and cultural elements—requires different procedural and substantive rules. To address these novel subjects of international law, the ICJ recognized, for example, that ecosystem services like carbon sequestration have value under international law (though the court did not rely on the ecosystem services approach to monetize the value of compensation).[17] This is a notable development of the ICJ's jurisprudence from its first environmental case, the dispute over the *Gabčíkovo-Nagymaros Project*, where it

[7] *Bering Sea Fur Seals Arbitration (US/United Kingdom)* (1893) 28 RIAA 263.

[8] Trail Smelter case (n 2).

[9] Ibid; Pulp Mills case (n 2); *Certain Activities Carried Out by Nicaragua in the Border Area (Costa Rica/Nicaragua)* and *Construction of a Road in Costa Rica along the San Juan River (Nicaragua/Costa Rica)* (Judgement) [2015] ICJ Rep 665 (Certain Activities case (Judgement)) [118].

[10] *Whaling in the Antarctic (Australia/ Japan, New Zealand intervening)* (Judgement) [2014] ICJ Rep 226 (Whaling in Antarctic case).

[11] *US—Import Prohibition of Certain Shrimp and Shrimp Products* (Appellate Body Report) [12 October 1998] WTO Doc WT/DS58/AB/R (Shrimp/Turtle case) [152]–[154]; *Burlington Resources Inc. v Republic of Ecuador* (Decision on Counterclaims) ICSID Case No ARB/08/5 (2017).

[12] *State Obligations in Relation to the Environment* (Advisory Opinion) IACtHR (2017) OC-23/17.

[13] *The Gabčíkovo-Nagymaros Project (Hungary/Slovakia)* (Judgement) [1997] ICJ Rep 7 (Gabčíkovo-Nagymaros case).

[14] UNCC, Governing Council, 'Report and Recommendations Made by the Panel of Commissioners Concerning the Fifth Instalment of "F4" Claims' (2005) UN Doc S/AC.26/2005/10; *Armed Activities on the Territory of the Congo (Congo/Uganda)* (Judgement) [2005] ICJ Rep 168.

[15] *Nuclear Tests (Australia/France)* (Judgement) [1974] ICJ Rep 253 (Nuclear Tests (Australia/France) case); *Legality of the Threat or Use of Nuclear Weapons* (Advisory Opinion) [1996] ICJ Rep 226 (Legality of Nuclear Weapons case); *Obligations concerning Negotiations relating to Cessation of the Nuclear Arms Race and to Nuclear Disarmament (Marshall Islands/UK)* (Preliminary Objections, Judgement) [2016] ICJ Rep 833 (Obligations concerning Negotiations case).

[16] 'Statement by The Honorable Johnson Toribiong, President of the Republic of Palau, to the 66th Regular Session of the United Nations General Assembly' *Palau Mission to the United Nations* (22 September 2011) <http://gadebate.un.org/sites/default/files/gastatements/66/PW_en.pdf> accessed 8 February 2019.

[17] *Certain Activities Carried Out by Nicaragua in the Border Area (Costa Rica/Nicaragua)* (Judgement of 2 February 2018 on Compensation owed by Nicaragua to Costa Rica) ICJ (Certain activities case (Compensation Owed)) [76], [85].

acknowledged that new environmental norms existed without weighing them as a factor to release Hungary from its treaty obligation to construct a hydropower facility on the Danube River.[18]

B. Effectiveness of ICTs

The ability of ICTs to influence state behaviour has varied, with signal success in influencing the obligation to perform transboundary EIAs,[19] mixed results with preventing harmful transboundary effects,[20] and notable failure in restraining the development of nuclear weapons.[21] Alter *et al* describe five categories of ICT—de facto authority (recognizing a compliance obligation and engaging in meaningful conduct to give effect to the court's ruling): no authority; narrow authority affecting the parties; intermediate authority reaching 'similarly situated litigants and compliance partners'; extensive authority that is accepted by an even larger group of relevant actors; and popular authority acknowledged more widely by the general public.[22] This framework is appropriate for evaluating the role of ICTs in developing international environmental law and is informally used here.

Compliance with ICT decisions, even by powerful states, is generally good,[23] although not perfect.[24] Some claim ICTs are ineffective because they lack force to compel compliance with their decisions; notwithstanding that, for example, the UN Security Council can enforce ICJ judgements and decisions of the World Trade Organization's Dispute Settlement Body (WTO-DSB) can be enforced with trade sanctions.[25] ICT compliance dependency is not so different from national courts, which rely on the executive and legislative branches of government to implement their judgements and to reflect their influence on public norms.

[18] Gabčíkovo-Nagymaros case (n 13) [112].

[19] Pulp Mills case (n 2) [204].

[20] Pulp Mills case (n 2) [215]–[216] (the pulp mills were constructed despite some transboundary effects on Argentina).

[21] *Nuclear Tests (New Zealand/France)* (Judgement) [1974] ICJ Rep 457 [65]; Nuclear Tests (Australia/France) case (n 15) [63]; *Request for an Examination of the Situation in Accordance with Paragraph 63 of the Court's Judgment of 20 December 1974 in the Nuclear Tests (New Zealand/France) Case* (Order) [1995] ICJ Rep 288 (Request for an Examination case) [64]–[66]; Obligations concerning Negotiations case (n 15) [57]–[58].

[22] Alter *et al* (n 6) 33, 436.

[23] Karen Alter, 'Agents or Trustees? International Courts in their Political Context' *European Journal of International Relations*, 14/1 (2008): 33.

[24] For example, China's rejection of the South China Sea arbitration; South China Sea case (n 3) [1140].

[25] Alexandra Huneeus, 'Compliance with Judgments and Decisions' in Cesare Romano, Karen Alter, and Yuval Shany (eds), *The Oxford Handbook of International Adjudication* (OUP 2014) 438; UN Charter, art 94.2.

C. Remedies Available

Traditional remedies for breach of an international obligation—cessation, non-repetition, and reparations—have been adapted to address natural resource damage.[26] The most significant shift is ICT recognition of non-market environmental damage as a harm under international law, whereas, traditionally, only natural resources and real estate valued by markets were considered subjects of international liability.[27]

Declaratory remedies—Statements that a party to a dispute was in the wrong are fairly common, such as in the *Pulp Mills* case where the ICJ declaration that Uruguay breached its procedural obligations under the 1975 Statute of the River Uruguay constituted satisfaction.[28] But in the nuclear claims cases, where the court's declaration would have had weightier effect, the ICJ declined to provide the remedy sought.[29]

Restitution—ICTs are often reluctant to order states to undertake specific actions as a remedy,[30] but there are exceptions. The ICJ has often rejected provisional measure requests to halt a construction project that might harm another state.[31] An important counter-example is ITLOS's provisional measures order in the *Southern Bluefin Tuna* case, where the tribunal ordered all parties to refrain from 'experimental' tuna fishing in excess of their annual allocations without the agreement of the other parties;[32] but there the tuna fishing was in areas beyond jurisdiction of the respondent state.

Reparations and natural resource damages—The ICJ first addressed remedies for harm to the environment as such in its *Certain Activities-Valuation* decision. There, it found that full reparation can require compensation for 'damage caused to the environment, in and of itself', which might include costs of restoration and loss of environmental goods and services in the period prior to recovery.[33] Older civil liability conventions

[26] See Chapter 58, 'International Environmental Responsibility and Liability', in this volume.

[27] See eg Marjorie Whiteman, *Damages in International Law* (US Government Printing Office 1943) vol 2, 1458 ('the value of the felled trees and of the wood carried away' awarded in First World War cases, *Héritiers Gény* and *Alfred et Pierre Gény*).

[28] Pulp Mills case (n 2) [282].

[29] See eg Obligations concerning Negotiations case (n 15) [57]–[59]; *Obligations concerning Negotiations relating to Cessation of the Nuclear Arms Race and to Nuclear Disarmament (Marshall Islands/India)* (Jurisdiction and Admissibility, Judgement) [2016] ICJ Rep 255 [56], [21] (no jurisdiction for claims against China, the Democratic People's Republic of Korea, France, Israel, Russia and the US).

[30] Certain activities case (Compensation Owed) (n 17) [31].

[31] Pulp Mills case (n 2) (request to halt construction of pulp mills); *Passage through the Great Belt (Finland/Denmark)* (Provisional Measures, Order of 29 July 1991) [1991] ICJ Rep 12 (request to halt construction of high-level suspension bridge that would permanently close the Baltic for deep draught vessels of a certain size) [6], [38]; cf. *Award in the Arbitration regarding the Iron Rhine ('Ijzeren Rijn') Railway between the Kingdom of Belgium and the Kingdom of the Netherlands* (2005) 27 RIAA 35 (Iron Rhine Railway case).

[32] *Southern Bluefin Tuna Cases (New Zealand/Japan; Australia/Japan)* (Provisional Measures, Order of 27 August 1999) [1999] ITLOS Rep 280 [90] (Southern Bluefin Tuna cases—Provisional Measures).

[33] Certain activities case (Compensation Owed) (n 17) [41]–[42].

only compensate 'reasonable measures of reinstatement actually undertaken or to be undertaken'.[34] Heightened attention to restoring ecological functions has led to including both restoration of the damaged environment and, where the recovery of the damaged site will be long or permanently delayed, compensatory restoration 'not of the same but of similar level of resources and/or services, including, as appropriate, at another site',[35] known as 'complementary restoration'. For a war-time oil spill, the UNCC ordered 'reasonable' restoration including: 1) active remediation to accelerate weathering of oil, restoration of natural intertidal topography, and revegetation; 2) natural recovery (ie no action) where active remediation could cause negative impacts; and 3) shoreline preserves to compensate lost ecological services during the recovery period.[36]

Financial compensation could enrich the plaintiff without ecological restoration if the injured state chooses not to undertake the necessary measures. This would be inconsistent with the underlying theory of actual restoration of an essential common interest. Legislative regimes require the remedy to result in restoration.[37] The UNCC, similarly, required that award funds 'only be used for reasonable projects' by paying successful claimants' awards in instalments 'upon satisfactory completion of the environmental projects'.[38] The civil liability conventions that define compensable harm as 'reasonable measures of reinstatement actually undertaken or to be undertaken'[39] achieve the same result. Basing compensation on actual restoration also allows the ICT to establish the quantum of compensation more accurately, whether it is high or low.[40]

34 Edward Brans, 'Estimating Damages under the 2004 EC Directive on Environmental Liability' in Frank Maes (ed), *Marine Resource Damage Assessment, Liability and Compensation for Environmental Damage* (Springer 2005) 3, 23 (1989 Convention on Civil Liability for Damage Caused during Carriage of Dangerous Goods by Road, Rail and Inland Navigation Vessels, 1996 International Convention on Liability and Compensation for Damage in Connection with the Carriage of Hazardous and Noxious Substances by Sea, 1999 Protocol to the 1989 Basel Convention, and 2001 Bunker Fuel Oil Pollution Damage Convention).

35 Convention on Biological Diversity (CBD), 'Liability and Redress' (20 March 2008) UNEP/CBD/COP/9/20/Add.1, para 117.

36 UNCC, Governing Council, 'Report and Recommendations Made by the Panel of Commissioners Concerning the Third Instalment of 'F4' Claims' (2003) UN Doc S/AC.26/2003/31, 52–54; UNCC, 'Fifth Instalment' (n 14) 104.

37 European Commission, 'Report from the Commission to the Council and the European Parliament under Article 18(2) of Directive 2004/35/EC on environmental liability with regard to the prevention and remedying of environmental damage' (14 April 2016) COM(2016) 204; Oil Pollution Act 1990 (US) s 2701 et seq.

38 UNCC, Governing Council, 'Decision concerning follow-up programme for environmental claims awards' (8 December 2005) UN Doc S/AC.26/Dec.258.

39 Protocol of 1992 to amend the International Convention on Civil Liability for Oil Pollution Damage of 1969 (CLC), arts I(6), III.

40 Certain activities case (Compensation Owed) (n 17) [41]–[43], [157]; UNCC, 'Fifth Instalment' (n 14).

D. Science Before International Courts and Tribunals

An ICT's ability to manage science and technology elements of a case can be dispositive, particularly in the ICT's findings of significant harm. ICTs recognize that how they deal with scientific uncertainty can negate substantive conservation duties.[41] As with any other fact finding, the judge must scrutinize, understand, and weigh the evidence before her. Relevant information will always be presented by the parties in their pleadings, and for some advocates, this aspect of adversarial litigation suffices. ICTs appear to agree on the principle of transparency, but they have not arrived at a standard procedure for using court-appointed experts to assist in their understanding of complex and recondite information.

Courts may take judicial notice of facts. In *Serap v Nigeria*, the ECOWAS Court of Justice decided that the Nigerian government failed to regulate the Niger Delta's oil industry and thereby violated the inhabitants' human rights on the basis of 'facts on which there is agreement among the parties or those on which one of the parties does not raise objection while in a position to do so' and 'public knowledge' about the effects of oil spills.[42]

Relying on the adversarial process to bring out dispositive evidence, an ICT might detail a procedure for parties to each present their experts' written and oral testimony. In its *Antarctic Whaling* case, the parties' scientific experts presented oral testimony with cross-examination and questions from the bench, all webcast live from the court.[43] This followed harsh criticism from ICJ judges and outside commentators for using unacknowledged 'phantom experts' in the *Pulp Mills* case.[44]

Most ICTs have the authority to appoint their own experts.[45] The WTO panel in the *Hormones* dispute asked experts to assess the scientific evidence regarding heath risk from animal growth hormones in meat.[46] To assist its verification of massive and varied

[41] See Chapter 15, 'The Role of Science' and Part IX, 'International Environmental Law in International Courts and Tribunals', in this volume; Caroline Foster, *Science and the Precautionary Principle in International Courts and Tribunals: Expert Evidence, Burden of Proof and Finality* (CUP 2011).

[42] (Judgement) [2012] The Court of Justice of the Economic Community of West African States (ECOWAS) ECW/CCJ/JUD/18/12 [94] [96].

[43] Whaling in Antarctic case (n 10); see also Southern Bluefin Tuna cases—Provisional Measures (n 32) [25].

[44] Pulp Mills case (n 2) (Joint Dissenting Opinion of Judges Al-Khasawneh and Simma) [2]; Pulp Mills case (n 2) (Declaration of Judge Yusuf) [13].

[45] *Corfu Channel case (UK/Albania)* (Order) [1948] ICJ Rep 124–126 (appointing experts); *Corfu Channel case (UK/Albania)* (Order) [1949] ICJ Rep 237–238 (expert compensation assessment); *Delimitation of the Maritime Boundary in the Gulf of Maine Area (Canada/US)* (Order) [1984] ICJ Rep 165, 166 (appointing expert); see also *The Factory at Chorzów (Germany/Poland)* (Judgement) [1928] PCIJ (ser A) 51–52 (expert fixed the amount of compensation); ICJ Statute, art 50 and the ICJ Rules, rule 67; cf *Certain Activities Carried Out by Nicaragua in the Border Area (Costa Rica/Nicaragua)* and *Construction of a Road in Costa Rica along the San Juan River (Nicaragua/Costa Rica)* (Provisional Measures, Order of 22 November 2013) [2013] ICJ Rep 354 [54] (directing Costa Rica to consult with the secretariat of the Ramsar Convention).

[46] *European Communities—Measures Concerning Meat and Meat Products (Hormones)—Complaint by the United States* (Report of the Panel) [18 August 1997] WTO Doc WT/DS26/R/USA [1.1], [2.26],

scientific and technical evidence submitted by the parties, the UNCC appointed multi-disciplinary teams of independent experts.[47] ICTs are usually courts of first and last instance that could benefit from using court-appointed special masters to provide some of the fact-finding functions of a trial court.[48]

It has been suggested that environmental cases should be decided by scientifically trained judges. This would underscore the *lex specialis* nature of international environmental law. UNCLOS (UN Convention on the Law of the Sea) negotiators considered using special procedures instead of a single tribunal for technical and scientific disputes arising from the fisheries, pollution, scientific research, and transfer of technology provisions of UNCLOS but chose to grant general competence to ITLOS. Here and elsewhere the judicial enterprise has acknowledged that such a degree of specialization is simply not practical.

III. JURISPRUDENCE

Legal rules and principles develop through leading decisions of various courts, reinforced by their adoption, interpretation, and application by other ICTs. Relatively new environmental law principles that have not emerged as binding rules of law, much less as peremptory norms (*jus cogens*), may be used as interpretive devices or otherwise be taken into account by an ICT.

A. Environmental Obligations

1. *No harm—prevention—due diligence*

Through a series of cases, chiefly at the ICJ, environmental obligations evolved into a coherent series of inquiries and actions that are required of states to prevent transboundary environmental harm. ICTs recognized that states have a customary international law obligation 'to ensure that activities within their jurisdiction and control respect the environment of other States or of areas beyond national control'[49] ('prevention'), which is a consequence of the more general customary rule that 'no State has the right to use

[6.1], [6.5], [8.7]–[8.8]; *EC—Measures Concerning Meat and Meat Products (Hormones)* (Appellate Body Report) [16 January 1998] WTO Docs WT/DS26/AB/R and WT/DS48/AB/R [148].

[47] UNCC, 'Third Instalment' (n 36) 52–54.

[48] Cymie Payne, 'Mastering the Evidence: Improving Fact Finding by International Courts' *Environmental Law*, 41/4 (2011): 1191.

[49] Legality of Nuclear Weapons case (n 15); Gabčíkovo-Nagymaros case (n 13) [41], [53] (quoting the Legality of Nuclear Weapons case (n 15)).

or permit the use of its territory in such a manner as to cause injury ... to the territory of another'[50] ('no harm'). ICTs interpreted these as obligations of conduct, not absolute obligations of result.[51] That the state's 'no harm' obligation is subject to a due diligence standard is inferred as a general principle from the ICJ's early *Corfu Channel* case and developed in *Pulp Mills*.[52] ITLOS's Seabed Disputes Chamber explained that due diligence is an objective standard and that states must adopt appropriate rules and measures, and a 'certain level of vigilance in their enforcement and the exercise of administrative control'.[53] When a state is informed of non-compliance, it is then obliged 'to investigate the matter and, if appropriate, take any action necessary to remedy the situation as well as inform the reporting State of that action'.[54] 'Significant harm' is the threshold, for that is most often used in treaties and judgements applying the 'no harm' rule.[55]

2. *Environmental impact assessment*

Flowing from the due diligence obligation of prevention, the ICJ explained, there is an obligation to conduct an environmental impact assessment (EIA) 'where there is a risk that [a] proposed industrial activity may have a significant adverse impact in a transboundary context, in particular, on a shared resource'.[56] The ICJ seemed to derive EIA as 'a requirement under general international law' from widespread municipal law practice and the UN Environment Programme (UNEP) Goals and Principles.[57]

If an EIA indicates that there is a risk of significant transboundary harm, the state with jurisdiction and control over the activity 'is required, in conformity with its due diligence obligation, to notify and consult in good faith with the potentially affected State, where that is necessary to determine the appropriate measures to prevent or mitigate that risk'.[58]

[50] Trail Smelter case (n 2) 1965; see also *Lake Lanoux Arbitration (Spain/France)* (1957) 12 RIAA 281 (Lake Lanoux case); *Corfu Channel case (UK/Albania)* (Order) [1948] ICJ Rep 124–126 (appointing experts); *Corfu Channel case (UK/Albania)* (Order) [1949] ICJ Rep 237–238 (expert compensation assessment); Iron Rhine Railway case (n 31) [59].

[51] See Chapter 16, 'Prevention', in this volume.

[52] See Duncan French and Tim Stephens, 'ILA Study Group on Due Diligence in International Law—First Report' (7 March 2014); see also South China Sea case (n 3).

[53] *Responsibilities and obligations of States sponsoring persons and entities with respect to activities in the Area* (Advisory Opinion) [2011] ITLOS Rep 10 (Responsibilities in the Area case) [117]–[120].

[54] South China Sea case (n 3) [944], quoting *Request for an advisory opinion submitted by the Sub-Regional Fisheries Commission (SRFC)* (Advisory Opinion) [2015] ITLOS Rep 4 [139].

[55] Iron Rhine Railway case (n 31) [59]; cf Trail Smelter case (n 2) 1965 ('serious consequence').

[56] Pulp Mills case (n 2) [204]; Certain Activities case (Judgement) (n 9) [104]; Request for an Examination case (n 21) [5]; Gabčíkovo-Nagymaros case (n 13) (Separate Opinion of Vice-President Weeramantry) [1997] ICJ Rep 88.

[57] Pulp Mills case (n 2) [204].

[58] Certain Activities case (Judgement) (n 9) [104]; Lake Lanoux case (n 50) 15–16; *Corfu Channel case (UK/Albania)* (Judgement) [1949] ICJ Rep 4, 14, 22.

3. *Polluter pays*

A state may, therefore, go forward with a project over another state's objections, but it may be liable under the 'polluter pays' principle if transboundary harm does ensue. Thus, the *Trail Smelter* arbitral award resulted in a payment of compensation for agricultural harm caused by the smelter.[59]

This principle has advanced more rapidly through treaty than judicial opinions, with varying results. The civil liability conventions designed to spread the risk of tankering petroleum products provide compensation, but limit environmental recoveries to reasonable reinstatement measures that will enhance the speed of natural recovery after an oil spill, with caps on total compensation per incident.[60] In particular, compensatory restoration for interim environmental losses are not allowed under those conventions, although it may be under customary international law. ICTs have not yet found that the polluter pays in the context of climate change.[61] Ecuador's successful counter-claims against a mining company for pollution it caused at various sites provided a rare example of the polluter pays principle being applied in relation to foreign investors in the field of investor-state arbitration.[62]

4. *Conservation and environmental protection*

There is a tension between the apparent view of courts, that they cannot veto a state's projects, and ICTs' occasional finding that states have an affirmative duty of conservation and environmental protection. The duty may be found in a particular treaty. For example, ITLOS stated as a legal basis for its Provisional Measures Order in *Southern Bluefin Tuna* that the 'conservation of the living resources of the sea is an element in the protection and preservation of the marine environment', an obligation found in Article 192 of UNCLOS.[63]

5. *Cooperation*

The duty to cooperate for the purpose of pollution prevention and conservation of nature addresses the need for states to act together to govern environmental systems that are inherently transboundary. The duty to cooperate reinforces the obligations to notify, consult, and perform EIAs,[64] and it may also entail recognition of rights to participate. It is an obligation found in many treaties, including UNCLOS and its implementing

[59] Trail Smelter case (n 2) 1965–1966, 1974–1978.

[60] 1992 CLC.

[61] See David Hunter, 'The Implications of Climate Change Litigation for International Environmental Law-Making' in Hari Osofsky and Wil Burns (eds), *Adjudicating Climate Control: Sub-National and Supra-National Approaches* (CUP 2009) 128–130.

[62] Burlington Resources case (n 11) [74], [159].

[63] Southern Bluefin Tuna cases—Provisional Measures (n 32) [70], cited in South China Sea case (n 3) [959].

[64] *Dispute regarding Navigational and Related Rights (Costa Rica/Nicaragua)* (Judgement) [2009] ICJ Rep 213 [97].

instrument, the 1995 Fish Stocks Agreement, and has also been characterized as 'a fundamental principle in ... general international law' by ITLOS and arbitral tribunals.[65] It is invoked when affirmative steps are required to implement the object and purpose of a treaty, and to suggest that a treaty party should take account of a regime in which it participates, even on points of disagreement where it is not legally bound.

B. Environmental Rights

While the right to a healthy, functioning environment has been slow to become rooted in international law, there are numerous rights related to the environment that have been recognized by ICTs, often by finding that they are necessary to the enjoyment of the rights to life and health.[66] As Dinah Shelton demonstrated, the IACtHR and the Inter-American Commission on Human Rights have been instrumental in 'articulat[ing] a broad range of state obligations to maintain the environment at a quality that permits the enjoyment of other guaranteed rights'.[67] They include the human right to environment, the right to participation, intergenerational equity, Indigenous rights, and international community interests in the sense of obligations *erga omnes* that may include common concern, common interest, and common heritage. Environmental rights may be held by states, communities, or individuals. In contrast to these public rights, rights of natural and juridical persons as foreign investors protected by investment treaties must also be taken into consideration by international environmental law.

1. *Human right to a healthy environment*

The broadest affirmation of a fundamental right to a healthy environment came from the IACtHR. Its Advisory Opinion on 'State obligations in relation to the environment in the context of the protection and guarantee of the rights to life and to personal integrity', characterized the right to a healthy environment as a human right; recognized environmental harm, without a demonstration of specific harm to identifiable humans, as an independent legal interest; and took an 'effects' based approach that applies even beyond the state's territory.[68] Where there is a causal link between such harm and the action or omission of the state, the state will owe prompt, adequate, and effective reparations.[69]

65 *The MOX Plant case (Ireland/United Kingdom)* (Provisional Measures, Order of 3 December 2001) [2001] ITLOS Rep 95 [82].

66 See Chapter 45, 'Human Rights', in this volume.

67 Dinah Shelton, 'Environmental Rights and Brazil's Obligations in the Inter-American Human Rights System' *George Washington International Law Review*, 40 (2009): 733, 738.

68 State Obligations in Relation to the Environment (n 12) (referring to, inter alia, Trail Smelter case (n 2)); see Maria Banda, 'Inter-American Court of Human Rights' Advisory Opinion on the Environment and Human Rights' *American Society of International Law Insights*, 22/6 (2018).

69 State Obligations in Relation to the Environment (n 12) [103].

2. *Procedural rights*

The ECtHR presents a different picture; with an unusually large number of cases dealing with environmental subject matter,[70] it focuses on procedural rights rather than substantive rights. Claimants rely on their civil and political rights, grounded in the 1966 UN International Covenants on Civil and Political Rights (ICCPR), and on Economic, Social and Cultural Rights (ESCR),[71] the ECtHR's constitutive instrument: the 1950 European Convention on Human Rights (ECHR), and the 1998 Aarhus Convention.

3. *Common concern—common interest—common heritage of humankind*

The struggle to find legal rules to address planetary scale environmental governance reveals the poor fit between the sovereignty system and the physical world shared transnationally. Multilateral treaties, rather than bilateral dispute settlement mechanisms, have characterized global commons.[72] Biodiversity, climate, and other natural systems that transcend national boundaries have been characterized as 'common concerns' of humankind in the 1992 CBD.[73] UNCLOS defines seabed resources in areas beyond national jurisdiction as 'common heritage of humankind'; it defines some other resources as subject to capture under the 'freedom of the high seas'.[74] The principle of 'common interest of humankind' was proposed for a treaty on conservation and sustainable use of marine biological diversity in areas beyond national jurisdiction (BBNJ);[75] it is undefined in international law, though the phrase 'common interest' is frequently used for its ordinary meaning. ICTs have made limited contributions to interpreting these terms,

[70] A Non-Exhaustive List of Environmental-Related Cases in Human Rights Courts provided to participants at the Pluricourts conference on 'The Legitimate Role(s) of Human Rights Courts in Environmental Disputes' identified fifty-five cases of the ECtHR dealing with environmental subject matter, as compared to nineteen cases at the Inter-American Commission on Human Rights, ten cases each at the IACtHR and the Human Rights Committee, four cases at the African Commission on Human and Peoples' Rights, and one at the Court of Justice of the Economic Community of West African States; see University of Oslo, 'The Legitimate Role(s) of Human Rights Courts in Environmental Disputes' (8–9 September 2014).

[71] UN General Assembly (UNGA) Res 41/128, 'Declaration on the Right to Development' (4 December 1986) UN Doc A/RES/41/128 (specifically referencing art 2, s 3); *Report of the United Nations Conference on Environment and Development* (UN 1993) vol I, annex I (specifically referencing principle 3); UNGA Res 55/2, 'Vienna Declaration and Programme of Action' (25 June 1993) UN Doc A/RES/55/2.

[72] See Jutta Brunnée, 'Common Areas, Common Heritage, and Common Concern' in Daniel Bodansky, Jutta Brunnée, and Ellen Hey (eds), *The Oxford Handbook of International Environmental Law* (1st edn, OUP 2008) 550.

[73] Judge Weeramantry discussed biodiversity-protection measures that, in his view, the ICJ should have considered as a matter of common concern in his dissenting opinion in *Kasikili/Sedudu Island (Botswana/Namibia)* (Judgement) [1999] ICJ Rep 1045 [84].

[74] arts 1, 136, 137.

[75] First session of the Intergovernmental Conference on the negotiation of an international instrument on BBNJ: Item 6 (4 September 2018) <http://statements.unmeetings.org/media2/19408115/201894-item-6-chinese-statement-english-revised-3-.pdf> accessed 8 February 2019.

defining rights and duties in the commons, or addressing the procedural issues that are inherent in the concept of global commons.

4. *Rights holders*

States are normally the subjects of international law, but there are exceptions. Human rights courts allow individuals, communities, and Indigenous groups to bring claims against states. Through investment treaties, states grant special access rights to international arbitration to foreign investors. There is an open question whether the international community as a whole can act as a rights holder where an obligation is owed *erga omnes*. Two aspects to this question are: Can a non-state entity, such as an intergovernmental or non-governmental organization, enforce such rights? And, can a state which does not have a special, individualized injury enforce such rights?

ICTs flirted with the concept of international community rights, first in the ICJ's *Barcelona Traction* case.[76] Legal standing, the requirement that a party have a sufficient stake in the outcome of a case to bring it to a court, is a potential barrier for litigating interests of the international community, as well as obligations *erga omnes* and interpretation of multilateral agreements; issues raised by the *Nuclear Negotiations* case.[77] ITLOS's Seabed Disputes Chamber observed that a legal obligation can be 'owed to the international community as a whole'[78] and suggested 'the [International Seabed] Authority, entities engaged in deep seabed mining, other users of the sea, and coastal States' all might be claimants for reparations if mining harmed the environment.[79] Here, the Chamber appeared to recognize legal interests that include but transcend those of states. It suggested that either the International Seabed Authority might be able to act '"on behalf" of [hu]mankind' or any state party might be able to bring a claim 'in light of the *erga omnes* character of the obligations relating to preservation of the environment of the high seas and in the Area.'[80] The question of who may hold and enforce rights is squarely raised, but not resolved in these cases.

5. *Extraterritorial enforcement*

Another aspect of this question, a state's right to enforce its national environmental protection laws in areas beyond national jurisdiction, is yet to be tested. In the *Fisheries Jurisdiction* case, the ICJ did not reach a decision about whether Canada could enforce its fisheries regulations against Spanish boats fishing in the high seas.[81] The influence of evolving environmental norms on trade law is evident in the shift from the *Tuna/*

[76] *Barcelona Traction, Light and Power Company, Limited (Belgium/Spain) (New Application: 1962)* (Judgement) [1970] ICJ Rep 3 [33].

[77] Obligations concerning Negotiations case (n 15) (Declaration of Judge Xue) [8]–[9]; (Dissenting Opinion of Judge Crawford) [20]–[21], [29]–[30].

[78] Ibid.

[79] Responsibilities in the Area case (n 53) [179]; See also ITLOS Statute, arts 20–22; Request for an Examination case (n 21) 6.

[80] Responsibilities in the Area case (n 53) [180].

[81] *(Spain/Canada)* (Judgement) [1998] ICJ Rep 432 [89].

Dolphin decisions, where trade restrictions adopted to prohibit a method of catching tuna that harmed dolphins in a location beyond the sanctioning state's jurisdiction were a violation of the GATT.[82] The *Shrimp/Turtle* decision explained that the GATT 'must be read by a treaty interpreter in the light of contemporary concerns of the community of nations about the protection and conservation of the environment'.[83] Relying on a mention of sustainable development in the 1994 WTO Agreement preamble, it reinterpreted the same GATT provision and allowed a US law prohibiting shrimp imports from countries where turtle excluder devices in shrimp traps are not required.[84] However, the WTO Appellate Body specifically refrained from ruling on the existence, nature, or extent of a limitation on exterritoriality, simply finding 'a sufficient nexus between the migratory and endangered marine populations involved and the United States' for purposes of the exception.[85]

C. Interpretive Principles: Precautionary Principle and Sustainable Development

Both precaution and sustainable development are referred to regularly by ICTs. They also share a certain ambiguity in their definition.

The precautionary principle is more richly developed in national law and the writings of distinguished publicists than in ICT jurisprudence.[86] Based in conventional wisdom, translated from the German legal principle *Vorsorgeprinzip*,[87] the precautionary principle advises that, where an activity may cause some level of harm, but uncertainty about the risk exists, decisions about the activity should protect human health and the environment. Litigating parties have argued that ICTs should use the precautionary principle to shift the burden of proof. Others have urged its use to encourage caution in environmental decision-making. Some have 'in cases of doubt ... adopted the most protective standard in conformity with the principles of precaution and *in dubio pro natura*'.[88] ICTs have, in general, taken the view that at most it is an 'approach' that might be used as one of many factors in a court's weighing of facts and law.[89] Consistent with

[82] *US—Restrictions on Imports of Tuna* (Panel Report) [3 September 1991] 30 ILM 1594; *US—Restrictions on Imports of Tuna* (Panel Report) [16 June 1994] 33 ILM 839.

[83] Shrimp/Turtle case (n 11) [129].

[84] Ibid [2], [152]–[154]; 1994 Marrakesh Agreement.

[85] Shrimp/Turtle case (n 11) [133].

[86] See Chapter 18, 'Precaution', in this volume; Whaling in Antarctic case (n 10) (Separate Opinion of Judge Cançado Trindade) [2014] ICJ Rep 348 [60]–[71]; Patricia Birnie, Alan Boyle, and Catherine Redgwell, *International Law and the Environment* (3rd edn, OUP 2009) 163.

[87] Konrad von Moltke, *The Vorsorgeprinzip in West German environmental policy* (Institute for European Environmental Policy 1987).

[88] Burlington Resources case (n 11) [343].

[89] Pulp Mills case (n 2) [164]; Responsibilities in the Area case (n 53) [126], [135].

European Union (EU) legislative practice, the ECtHR applies the precautionary principle.[90] In contrast to the BBNJ negotiators' frequent reference to the *Pulp Mills* case as authority for the duty to perform an EIA, *Trail Smelter* for the 'no harm' principle, and the *Responsibilities in the Area* Advisory Opinion for the obligation of due diligence, ICT jurisprudence was not identified as a source of law for the precautionary principle.[91]

Sustainable development calls for consideration of environmental, social, and economic aspects of development activities, and has been widely referenced in ICT decisions.[92] Some judges considered that it does not provide a rule of decision that a court might apply to determine the outcome of a case.[93] In contrast, Judge Weeramantry wrote that it could reconcile the right to development and the right to environmental protection.[94] The striking result in the WTO *Shrimp/Turtle* dispute was based in part on the Appellate Body's interpretive use of sustainable development.[95] The *Iron Rhine* arbitral tribunal considered it an emerging principle that could be taken into account as a relevant rule of international law applicable in the relations between the parties.[96] A barrier to sustainable development becoming a useful rule is the divergence in ICTs' interpretation of what it requires and the resulting lack of justiciable standards.[97]

D. Law of War, Pillage

ICTs contributed to the recognition that environmental damage related to armed conflict can violate international law, an area where treaties lagged. The ICJ advised that states must consider the environment in making assessments of military necessity and proportionality for actions during armed conflict.[98] Severe intentional and collateral environmental damage inflicted by the 1990–91 Gulf War led the UN Security Council to

[90] *Tatar v Romania* (27 January 2009) ECtHR, 67021/01: *Affaire Tătar c. Roumanie* (Requête no 67021/01) ECHR 2009 ('le principe de précaution a été introduit par le Traité de Maastricht' ie the precautionary principle was introduced by the Treaty of Maastricht).

[91] 'Revised draft text of an agreement under the United Nations Convention on the Law of the Sea on the conservation and sustainable use of marine biological diversity of areas beyond national jurisdiction—Note by the President' (27 November 2019) 8–10, 29.

[92] See Chapter 17, 'Sustainable Development', in this volume; cf. ILC, 'Preliminary report on the protection of the environment in relation to armed conflicts' (5 May–6 June and 7 July–8 August 2014)) UN Doc A/CN4/674; Pulp Mills case (n 2) [177].

[93] Gabčíkovo-Nagymaros case (n 13) (Dissenting Opinion of Judge Oda) [1997] ICJ Rep 153 [14].

[94] Gabčíkovo-Nagymaros case (n 13) (Separate Opinion of Vice-President Weeramantry) [1997] ICJ Rep 88–89.

[95] Shrimp/Turtle case (n 11) [153], [168].

[96] Iron Rhine Railway case (n 31) [58]–[59].

[97] Birnie *et al* (n 86) 125–126.

[98] Legality of Nuclear Weapons case (n 15) [30]; see ILC, 'Second report on the protection of the environment in relation to armed conflicts' (4 May–5 June and 6 July–7 August 2015) UN Doc A/CN.4/685 [101]–[104].

explicitly include environmental damage in the mandate of the reparations commission it created.[99] The commission awarded USD 5.4 billion for environmental response, remediation, restoration, compensatory, and public health damage resulting from breach of customary law and UN Charter prohibitions on aggressive war.[100] Subsequently, the ICJ found that Ugandan Defence Forces' looting, plundering, and exploitation of natural resources in the Democratic Republic of Congo violated the law of war;[101] and, as the occupying power, Uganda was responsible for environmental damage caused both by its defence forces and private individuals.[102]

IV. LIMITS OF JUDICIAL MECHANISMS

The argument that ICTs extend their influence beyond the cases before them to the development of international environmental law itself depends on acceptance of ICT authority, legitimacy, and relevance by affected states. There are reasons to question the extent of these essential conditions. ICTs suffered, in the early twenty-first century, from some states' mistrust and rejection of their authority as actors that are external to the national legal order.[103] Global societies may not favour the global norms that ICTs develop, for historical reasons or because they value individualism and contract-based governance.[104]

Yet there is still a pull towards the attraction of universal norms. The Global Pact for the Environment project reflects this—at once a recognition of the need for shared goals and rules to regulate planetary, transboundary issues like climate change and biodiversity, and a desire for authority stated with simplicity and clarity.[105]

[99] See Chapter 50, 'Armed Conflict', in this volume; Cymie Payne and Peter Sand (eds), *Gulf War Reparations and the UN Compensation Commission: Environmental Liability* (OUP 2011); ILC Preliminary Report (n 92) [4].

[100] UNCC, 'Fifth Instalment' (n 14); see also *Eritrea-Ethiopia Claims Commission* (Ethiopia's Damages Claims, Final Award of 17 August 2009) 26 RIAA 631 [284]–[288], [308], [421]–[425].

[101] Armed Activities case (n 14) [245].

[102] Ibid [250].

[103] Alter *et al* (n 6) 435.

[104] Armin von Bogdandy and Sergio Dellavolle, 'Universalism Renewed: Habermas' Theory of International Order in Light of Competing Paradigms' *German Law Journal*, 10 (2009): 10; cf Elinor Ostrom, 'A Polycentric Approach for Coping with Climate Change' *World Bank Policy Research Working Paper No. 5095* (1 October 2009) 39 <https://openknowledge.worldbank.org/handle/10986/4287> accessed 8 February 2019.

[105] Cymie Payne, 'A Global Pact for the Environment' *ASIL Insights*, 22/12 (2018).

V. CONCLUSION

ICTs may be able to—and it may be right to expect them to—adopt an environmental jurisprudence fully equipped with fact-finding and administrative apparatus, and guided by an evolutionary interpretive approach that is capable of acknowledging twenty-first century science while remaining responsibly tethered to rational and consistent legality.

Extremely complicated and large-scale problems like climate change have not yet come before the ICTs in contentious cases. The rapid loss of biodiversity has hardly been touched by ICTs. It has been raised by parties in several cases before the ICJ, including the *Whaling* case. In the *Pulp Mills* case, the court found that it had no jurisdiction to apply, as Argentina argued, the 1973 Convention on International Trade in Endangered Species, the 1971 Ramsar Convention on Wetlands or the 1992 CBD.[106]

The future development of international environmental law through ICT jurisprudence may be narrowed in contentious cases where jurisdiction is treaty-based, as the climate and biodiversity fields seem to suggest. Yet, even if there is a trend for international agreements to use non-compliance procedures and to avoid binding third-party dispute settlement, there is still wide scope for ICTs to apply customary international law and general principles, to interpret a potentially broader range of sources in cases brought by *compromis*, and to address the environmental aspects of cases that are not framed solely in environmental terms. Of the sources of international environmental law, ICTs remain unique in their ability to ground legal rules in factual contexts, to respond to new information and developments in national law, and to offer clearly articulated statements of what the law is that can readily be located and understood by a wide constituency.

BIBLIOGRAPHY

Karen Alter, Laurence Helfer, and Mikael Madsen, *International Court Authority* (OUP 2018)

Armin von Bogdandy and Ingo Venzke, 'Beyond Dispute: International Judicial Institutions as Lawmakers' *German Law Journal*, 12/5 (2011): 979

Jutta Brunnée, 'Common Areas, Common Heritage, and Common Concern' in Daniel Bodansky, Jutta Brunnée, and Ellen Hey (eds), *The Oxford Handbook of International Environmental Law* (1st edn, OUP 2008) 550

Martha Finnemore and Kathryn Sikkink, 'International Norm Dynamics and Political Change' *International Organization*, 52/4 (1998): 887, 891–892

Caroline Foster, *Science and the Precautionary Principle in International Courts and Tribunals* (CUP 2011)

Tim Stephens, *International Courts and Environmental Protection* (CUP 2009)

Hanqin Xue, *Transboundary Damage in International Law* (CUP 2003)

106 Pulp Mills case (n 2) [56]–[63].

PART V

SUBJECT MATTER

CHAPTER 28

TRANSBOUNDARY AIR POLLUTION

PHOEBE OKOWA

I. INTRODUCTION

THERE are well-documented dangers of air pollution from industrial activities, stationary vehicles, atmospheric nuclear tests, as well as radioactive accidents.[1] A body of state practice has developed, although primarily in Europe and North America, in response to these dangers. This practice has considerable provenance. Trans-frontier air pollution problems have long been at issue between neighbouring states, especially where industrial activities are located in border areas. Such air pollution lends itself readily to resolution within the framework of legal rules, since the pollutants typically emanate from a discrete industrial plant in the territory of one state and cause reasonably identifiable damage in the territory of another.[2]

In the classic *Trail Smelter* arbitration between Canada and the United States both the source of harm and the receptors were clearly identified.[3] The tribunal famously pronounced that

> under the principles of international law ... no State has the right to use or permit the use of its territory in such a manner as to cause injury by fumes or to the territory of

[1] Rachel Rothschild, *Poisonous Skies: Acid Rain and the Globalization of Pollution* (University of Chicago Press 2018); Sweden Royal Ministry of Agriculture, *Air pollution across national boundaries: the impact on the environment of sulfur in air and precipitation—Sweden's case study for the United Nations Conference on the Human Environment* (Norstedt 1971).

[2] Andrew Hurrell and Benedict Kingsbury (eds), *International Politics of the Environment* (OUP 1992).

[3] *Trail Smelter Arbitration (United States/Canada)* (1938 and 1941) 3 RIAA 1905; Trail Smelter's lasting legacy was surely bound to be marginal if it could not be relied on to provide a dependable set of precepts for resolving the seemingly insurmountable difficulties presented by acid rain.

> another or the property of persons therein, when the case is of serious consequence and the injury is established by clear and convincing evidence.[4]

The dispute nevertheless remains one of the few cases of transboundary air pollution to have been resolved through the medium of litigation. Curiously, far from endorsing the *Trail Smelter* model, the subsequent air pollution treaties, such as the 1979 United Nations Economic Commission for Europe (UNECE) Convention on Long-Range Transboundary Air Pollution (LRTAP), eschewed any firm commitment to the liability model as a method of resolving these disputes.[5] In the decades since *Trail Smelter*, a direct causal nexus of the kind present in that case has been impossible to establish. The complex atmospheric processes that pollutants undergo effectively acted as a barrier to any reliable determination of the causes and effects of pollution. Further, emerging problems of transboundary air pollution involve a multiplicity of states, intractable evidential problems, and delayed manifestation of harm attributable to pollutants. Both litigation and uncoordinated unilateral efforts are likely to be ineffectual in this context. Thus, states have explored a range of multilateral cooperative arrangements, including bilateral and regional treaties, discussed in this chapter, to address transboundary air pollution.

The following section of this chapter discusses the causes of transboundary air pollution, noting that much of our experience and knowledge comes from the context of the global North, with far less known about problems of transboundary air pollution across Africa, Asia, and Latin America. The chapter then discusses the role of customary law rules in the field before turning to a discussion of the main treaty regimes addressing transboundary air pollution in Europe and North America, as well as the more recent 2002 Association of South East Asian Nations (ASEAN) Transboundary Haze Pollution Agreement. As yet, there is no global treaty addressing air pollution and this seems unlikely to emerge. The chapter concludes that further regulation will likely come through regional efforts, as well as intersection with the climate regime.

II. Causes of Transboundary Air Pollution

Industrial growth, the multiplication of human populations, and increased fossil-fuel consumption have led to a considerable increase in the amount of pollutants released into the atmosphere. In fact, there is today little dissent from the view that the main pollutants responsible for long-range transboundary air pollution are man-made sources of oxides of sulphur and nitrogen. The main sources of sulphur oxides are the

4 Ibid.

5 The possibility of liability was expressly excluded in a footnote to LRTAP, art 8.

burning of fossil-fuels in power plants and smelting processes that refine non-ferrous metal ores such as nickel, copper, lead, and zinc. Other emission sources are fuel combustion by industrial, commercial, and residential users. Many of the activities that give rise to long-range pollutants are routine beneficial activities that are indispensable to modern life. They include ordinary industrial processes, transportation, and even residential heating. The oxides of nitrogen are mainly caused by fuel combustion from stationary energy and transportation sectors.

A distinctive feature of long-range transboundary air pollution is the general inability to trace the precise sources of pollutants that eventually cause damage. This is largely due to the fact that owing to the large number of possible sources in different states, as well complex chemical processes that pollutants undergo before eventually causing damage, the determination of a cause and effect relationship is in most cases elusive. Although the level of emissions contributed by particular states can now be measured using monitoring techniques, these are, in almost all cases, estimates dependent on data supplied by states and other variables such as weather patterns. The precise contribution of individual states to the problem remains unclear. By contrast, the behaviour of long-range pollutants, notably their transportation over long distances, chemical transformation, interaction with other pollutants, and subsequent deposition, is well documented. Indeed, air pollution monitoring programmes in Europe, such as the European Monitoring and Evaluation Programme (EMEP), have been able to point out that the problem of transboundary air pollution is a regional one, in which all European states are both exporters and importers of pollutants. This provided a strong scientific foundation for the policy work that informed the air pollution treaty regimes adopted under the auspices of the UNECE.[6] A similar relationship exists between Canada and the United States.

Although a large measure of scientific uncertainty remains as to the precise effects of transboundary air pollutants, there is a credible body of scientific opinion that these pollutants cause considerable damage to forests, the aquatic environment, buildings, and increasingly human health. In Europe, transboundary air pollution was largely regarded as responsible for the acidification of freshwater lakes, damaging aquatic life, most notably in the decline of fish populations, and damage to flora and fauna resulting in a general decline in species diversity. In the period immediately preceding the adoption of the 1979 LRTAP, a survey concluded that in most countries of central Europe, air pollution is the major destabilizing factor of forest health.[7] Other less publicized cases of possible effects of air pollution include corrosion of and discoloration of buildings, acute respiratory stress in cattle, and some damage to agriculture. The World Health Organization (WHO) has also consistently emphasized the devastating effects of air pollution on human health and singled it out as the greatest

[6] Johan Sliggers and Willem Kakebeeke (eds), *Clearing the Sir: 25 Years of the Convention on Long-range Transboundary Air Pollution* (United Nations 2004) 31.

[7] Tanja Sanders, Alexa Michel, and Marco Ferretti, *30 Years of Monitoring the Effects of Long-Range Transboundary Air Pollution on Forests in Europe and Beyond* (UNECE/ICP Forests 2016) 5.

environmental risk to human health and one of the main avoidable causes of death and disease globally, with an estimated seven million premature deaths across the world attributed to indoor and outdoor pollution.[8]

There is still insufficient knowledge on the sources and pathways of air pollution in much of Africa, Asia, and South America. Africa, in particular, has virtually no reliable air quality information data, significantly limiting the development of mitigation strategies.[9] As Rana Roy has cogently argued, in the absence of a comprehensive understanding of the contribution of different sources of air pollutants, it is difficult to have consensus on what are likely to be appropriate remedial measures in regions outside of Europe and North America.[10]

There is also the related problem of prioritizing air pollution as a source of environmental harm in the global South given other environmental concerns such as lack of sanitation and water pollution. By the time the LRTAP was adopted in 1979, many other environmental harms had been reduced in Europe and North America making possible a singular focus on air pollution.[11] Although the literature on air pollution has largely used the 1979 Convention and its protocols as a point of departure, it is thus profoundly problematic to use them as a template for developing regulatory regimes for the less developed regions of Africa or Asia. The practice under the LRTAP was developed and effectively implemented under very different set of socio-economic and political circumstances. In addition, the European experience was almost entirely based on the effect of air pollution on ecosystems—principally acidification of lakes and forests—yet in the new cases of air pollution in Africa and Asia, the effects of air pollution on health have assumed a particular significance, and this arguably ought to influence the legal regime.[12]

Although industrial progress in large parts of Asia, Africa, and Latin America has given rise to serious concerns about questions of air pollution, which are increasingly being dealt with in multilateral forums, there is still very little conscious effort on the part of governments to regulate the problem in binding treaty instruments.[13] According to a recent study, 92% of Asia and the Pacific's population—about four million people—are exposed to levels of air pollution that pose a significant risk to their health.[14] Coal burning remains a significant contributor to regional air pollution, with high levels of

[8] WHO, 'Healthy environments for healthier populations: Why do they matter, and what can we do?' (2019) UN Doc WHO/CED/PHE/DO/19.01.

[9] AirVisual, '2018 World Air Quality Report: Region and City PM2.5 Ranking', 17 <https://www.airvisual.com/world-most-polluted-cities/world-air-quality-report-2018-en.pdf> accessed 2 January 2020.

[10] Rana Roy, *The Cost of Air Pollution in Africa* (OECD Publishing 2016) 43.

[11] UNECE, 'Protecting the Air We Breathe: 40 Years of Cooperation Under the Convention on Long-Range Transboundary Air Pollution' (September 2019) 2.

[12] UNEP, *Towards a Pollution Free Planet: Background Report* (2017) 14–16, 77.

[13] UNEP, *Air Pollution in Asia and the Pacific: Science-Based Solutions* (2019) 133.

[14] Ibid, 2.

coal production and consumption in mainland China and Mongolia in particular. The emissions from human activity have been aggravated by seasonal dust storms, which are prevalent in the region. According to a recent study, out of 100 most polluted cities in the world, fifty are in India, China, Pakistan, and Bangladesh.[15] Some air pollutants, such as black carbon, methane, and ground ozone are also climate change pollutants and several are therefore also the subject matter of regulation in the climate change regime considered in Chapter 29. Clearly, to the extent that these regions have made commitments under the climate change regimes, some of the air pollution problems will be indirectly addressed through them.

III. CONTENT OF CUSTOMARY LAW

Notwithstanding the proliferation of a large number of legal instruments regulating transboundary air pollution, discussed further in the following section, the restraints imposed by customary law are of a continuing relevance for a number of reasons. First, the obligations under treaty instruments are very general and, in many cases, indeterminate as they do not impose hard obligations. Many of the standards in the treaty regimes, such as due diligence and the polluter pays principle, are defined by way of *renvoi* to customary law and only make sense when considered in light of custom.[16] Second, the norms and standards contained in treaty instruments are concerned with the prevention of pollution, and in general they do not regulate issues of responsibility for damage that might arise in the event of non-compliance. Customary law thus provides a residual backup for those situations not covered by treaties, including historic pollution or where the treaties have failed to stop pollution.

Of significance, is the fact that treaties remain consensual obligations, binding only on those states that have affirmatively accepted them. Many states that currently contribute to atmospheric pollution have either opted out or are at present not bound by treaty regimes. Furthermore, there is considerable support for the view that the performance and interpretation of treaties are subject to emergent standards of conduct in the international community. This rule, which finds expression in Article 31.3(c) of the 1969 Vienna Convention on the Law of Treaties is particularly significant in the field of transboundary air pollution where applicable standards and best practice are constantly changing to take account of developments in scientific knowledge. The content of the relevant customary law rules is given extensive treatment in Chapter 16.

[15] 2018 World Air Quality Report (n 9) 17.

[16] Ibid, para 197.

IV. TREATY REGIMES REGULATING TRANSBOUNDARY AIR POLLUTION

A. LRTAP and its Protocols

While the European and North American experience of transboundary air pollution occurred under such different socio-economic and political circumstances that it cannot be applied without significant qualification to the new problems of air pollution in Africa and Asia, that body of rules developed under the auspices of the UNECE and their institutional framework still merit close attention. They have stood the test of time and been singularly successful in reducing the problem of transboundary air pollution in Europe.[17] Moreover the Executive Body of the LRTAP continues to play an important facilitating role in furthering inter-regional information sharing and cooperation.[18] When other regions adopt regulatory frameworks, it is very likely that they will follow the UNECE institutional model; specifically the detailed rules on technical infrastructure, emission inventories, modelling, and tools for risk assessment.

The most significant legal framework for the regulation of transboundary air pollution to date is that contained in the 1979 LRTAP. Eight Protocols to the Convention provide in detail both the institutional and substantive framework for achieving the Convention's obligations. The Convention could also be seen as a prototype of how to arrive at consensus in the face of scientific uncertainty, diverging priorities between states at different stages of economic development, and accordingly, different development priorities. The eight Protocols to the Convention provided the opportunity for on-going dialogue and occasion to adapt the provisions in the face of changing scientific evidence on both the nature and effects of pollutants.[19]

This framework Convention was negotiated under the auspices of the UNECE, a geo-political grouping of states in Europe, North America, as well as Eastern Europe, the Caucasus, and Central Asia. The original participants were confined to Northern Europe and North America, although since 2011 there have been concerted efforts to involve other European States with qualified success.[20] The Convention outlines a set of agreed general principles as well as mechanisms for negotiating more specific and concrete standards for the abatement of transboundary air pollution. The Protocols to the Convention lay down relatively specific standards for the control of the emissions

[17] UNECE, 'Protecting the Air we Breathe' (n 11); Peringe Grennfelt *et al*, 'Acid Rain and Air Pollution: 50 years of Progress in Environmental Science and Policy' *Ambio*, 49 (2020): 849.

[18] LRTAP, 'Report of the Executive Body on its thirty-eight session' (22 February 2019) UN Doc ECE/EB.AIR/142.

[19] Adam Byrne, 'Trouble in the Air: Recent Developments Under the 1979 Convention on Long-Range Transboundary Air Pollution' *Review of European Comparative and International Environmental Law*, 26/3 (2017): 210.

[20] Ibid, 216.

of sulphur, nitrogen, and volatile organic compounds. Thus, while the Convention sets broad goals for reducing transboundary pollution, the Protocols address specific sources of pollutants and lay down concrete remedial measures, as well as establishing an institutional framework for gathering scientific information and monitoring the Convention's achievements.[21]

1. *The LRTAP*

Although the idea of a Convention to control transboundary air pollution had been put forward by Scandinavian countries at the Stockholm Conference, a more direct impetus can be traced to the Conference on Security and Co-operation in Europe which took place between July 1973 and August 1975.[22] The final Act of the Conference reiterated a commitment to the prevention of pollution beyond national limits. The Convention was adopted by thirty-two states at a high-level meeting in November 1979 and entered into force on 19 March 1983.

According to Article 1(b), the Convention is directed at the regulation of:

> air pollution whose physical origin is situated wholly or in part within the area under the national jurisdiction of another state and which has adverse effects in the area under the jurisdiction of another state at such a distance that it is not generally possible to distinguish the contribution of individual emission sources or groups of sources.

This broad definition extends from trans-frontier pollutants of the kind at issue in the *Trail Smelter* case where the source of the pollutant and harm are clearly identifiable, to situations where the distances involved and the multiplicity of sources at stake make it virtually impossible to identify the contribution of individual sources. This comprehensive definition would make it equally applicable to nuclear pollution, but it is clear from the negotiating history and the debates that preceded the adoption of the Convention, that it was directed at the main transboundary air pollutants that were responsible for acid rain, specifically nitrogen and sulphur oxides.

Three key articles contain substantive obligations of means. In each case, a state party is required to achieve reduction in the level of emissions but is left a wide margin of appreciation as to the exact modalities of doing so. The parties are only required to 'endeavor to limit and as far as possible gradually reduce pollution'.[23] Under Article 3, parties were expected to realize their obligations through processes of information exchange, consultation, research, and monitoring of air pollutants. The due diligence expectations are reaffirmed in Article 6 where parties are exhorted to develop the best policies and strategies in combatting air pollution and to employ the best available

[21] Protocol to the 1979 LRTAP on Long-term Financing of the Co-operative Programme for Monitoring and Evaluation of the Long-range Transmission of Air Pollutants in Europe (EMEP).

[22] UNECE, 'Protecting the Air we Breathe' (n 11) 2, 8.

[23] LRTAP, art 2.

technology. The qualification in these terms means that the provisions only require the states parties to exercise due diligence and to that extent mirror an emerging principle of customary law, under which states are only responsible if they fail to take all practical and necessary measures to prevent pollution.[24] The interpretation of the 1979 ECE treaty in its context, and in light of its object and purpose as required by Article 31 of the Vienna Convention, militates against any conclusion that the treaty is a political statement devoid of legal effect. The apparently weak provisions were the result of a necessary compromise during the negotiations between states who did not want to accept stringent commitments.

Three further reasons may explain the underlying weaknesses of the Convention. First, the scientific uncertainty surrounding the causes and effects of transboundary air pollution at the time made many states reluctant to accept concrete commitments. Second, a number of less-developed European states, such as Ireland, Greece, and Portugal, were not prepared to accept stringent anti-pollution measures that would have significantly hampered their industrial development. Third, it is generally accepted that a certain amount of flexibility is required in formulating environmental obligations.[25] While the setting of specific goals such as ambient air quality standards or acceptable critical loads of pollutants that can be tolerated by the environment may be a more effective means of realizing environmental objectives, changing scientific evidence as to the nature of pollutants and their effects means that fixed obligations concerning emission levels quickly become outdated. This is in line with the general approach in environmental treaties which invariably starts with a framework Convention, which may then be followed with more specific obligations in an Annex or a Protocol, in light of new evidence and advances in technology.[26]

Those doubting the legal quality of the commitments in the 1979 CLRTAP cite the footnote to Article 8 of the Convention which—as highlighted earlier—expressly provides that the Convention does not contain a rule on state liability as to damage. It is true that the negotiating history was strongly influenced by a desire to reduce pollution through cooperation rather than the imposition of liability. But there is nothing to suggest that the intention was to exclude the application of the regime of state responsibility, or the normal remedies for breach of international law altogether.[27]

2. *The 1985 and 1994 Sulphur Protocols*

At the time of the adoption of the LRTAP, acidification of lakes was the main problem that the signatory states aimed to tackle, and priority was attached to the abatement of pollutants caused by sulphur compounds.[28] Two subsequent ministerial conferences strongly urged the adoption of more concrete measures to curb the ever-increasing

[24] See Chapter 16, 'Harm Prevention', in this volume.

[25] See also Chapter 24, 'Multilateral Environmental Treaty-Making', in this volume.

[26] Ibid.

[27] See Chapter 58, 'International Responsibility and Liability', in this volume.

[28] UNECE, 'Protecting the Air we Breathe' (n 11) 5.

effects of acidification. As a result, the 1985 Protocol was adopted under the auspices of the executive body in accordance with Article 10 of the LRTAP.[29]

The Protocol's key provision is found in Article 2. It required the states parties to reduce their national annual sulphur emissions or their transboundary fluxes by at least 30% by 1993 using the 1980 levels as basis for calculation of reductions. This arrangement enabled the many states that were unable to ratify the Protocol initially to do so at a later date when domestic circumstances permitted. In effect the Protocol imposed a moratorium on further increases in emissions. Each state party was left a wide margin of discretion on the implementation of the obligation. However, the target of 30% was criticized as too modest, and unlikely to have any real impact on the acidification of lakes and forests across Europe.

By introducing a flat rate for emissions, the Convention also failed to take into account variations in emission levels and effects between different countries. It was for this reason that the less developed states of Europe at the time, notably Ireland, Greece, and Portugal refused to ratify the Protocol. These states argued that their own contributions to sulphur emissions were minimal and that further reductions on their part were unwarranted. A 30% reduction was nevertheless adopted as an acceptable compromise since those ratifying the Protocol were not prepared to accept more stringent commitments. Many states including those with significant emission levels, such as the United Kingdom and the United States, nevertheless failed to ratify the Protocol. They were concerned that the decision to base the reduction of emissions on the 1980 levels ignored the very significant strides they had made in reducing emission levels since that date. Others felt that a reduction of 30% was too onerous and failed to take into account the technological challenges they would encounter in meeting these obligations.

It is significant that although there was already a marked downward trend in sulphur emissions, the commitment in the Protocol gave legal force to this trend, and effectively acted as a barrier against the resumption of increased emissions in the event of changed economic circumstances. The Protocol can be hailed as a success as the parties were able to achieve the 30% reduction target and a 50% reduction overall in the emission of sulphur oxides.

The 1985 Sulphur Protocol was replaced by a new Protocol in 1994.[30] The 1994 Protocol avoids many of the shortcomings of the previous Protocol by adopting a flexible range of measures for pollution reduction. In particular, the flat rate of emission reduction has been replaced by a set of varied, flexible targets, taking into account the different levels of state contributions to the sulphur problem. In each case, there is a conscious attempt to base the obligations of the parties on sound environmental principles. The main obligation of the parties is in Article 2 and requires them not to exceed identified critical loads. A further Annex to the 1994 Protocol specifies the levels and timing of reductions to be achieved by each of the parties annually.[31] These levels have been calibrated to take

[29] 1985 Protocol to the 1979 LRTAP on the Reduction of Sulphur Emissions or their Transboundary Fluxes by at Least 30 per cent.

[30] 1994 Protocol to the 1979 LRTAP on Further Reduction of Sulphur Emissions (Sulphur Protocol).

[31] See Sulphur Protocol, annexes IV, V.

into account the different state contributions, as well the different effects of pollutants in contributing states.

Apart from targets, the 1994 Protocol exhorts parties to employ both economic incentives and disincentives, energy efficiency strategies, and best available technologies.[32] Although the effectiveness of these extra-legal strategies has been known for some time, their formal inclusion in the Protocol underscored their importance as a means of realizing the parties' formal commitments. Some of the strategies designed to enhance the effectiveness of the Protocol included ongoing monitoring and reporting of emissions and their effects on the environment.[33] This periodic review was intended to provide a baseline for the ongoing adjustment of the parties' commitments, and for the overall evaluation of the Convention and its Protocols. In addition, an Implementation Committee is established under Article 7 and is tasked with monitoring reports and making recommendations on necessary measures for achieving full compliance.

3. *The 1988 NOX Protocol*

In 1988, a nitrogen oxides protocol to the Convention was adopted at Sofia.[34] Under the Protocol, the parties undertook to stabilize their nitrogen oxide emissions. Specifically, pursuant to Article 2.1, the parties agreed to control or reduce nitrogen oxide or their transboundary fluxes at or to the level of national annual emissions or transboundary fluxes of the calendar year 1987 by 14 December 1994.

Article 2 may be characterized as an obligation of result. The parties are left a wide margin of appreciation as to the exact modalities of achieving compliance. The parties also agree in Article 2.2 to progressively reduce emissions from new as well as existing stationary and automobile sources of nitrogen pollutants. The obligation here, like those under the Sulphur Protocols, may be characterized as requiring the exercise of due diligence. Although the parties are under a duty to apply national emission standards to new mobile and stationary sources, this is only insofar as such measures are economically and technologically feasible. However, the state party is not the final arbiter of the economic feasibility or otherwise of the measures required under the Convention; the appropriateness of the measures adopted may be scrutinized by the executive body. The Protocols allow states parties to it to select a year prior to 1987 as the reference point for the stabilization of emissions. This flexible element allows parties whose emissions have declined as a result of reduced economic activities to select a year during which their emissions were at their highest. In this way the obligation is not too onerous should the state in question resume a high level of economic activity.

Articles 6 and 7 of the Protocol require the parties to initiate a number of measures, including national programs and policies with a view to reducing the emissions of nitrogen oxides. In particular, Article 6 requires the parties to identify the effects of

[32] arts 2, 3.

[33] Sulphur Protocol, arts 5, 6, annex IV s VI.

[34] 1988 Protocol to the 1979 LRTAP concerning the Control of Emissions of Nitrogen oxides or their Transboundary Fluxes.

nitrogen emissions on humans, plant, and animal life, waters, soils, and materials as well as the geographical distribution of such pollutants.

These articles also leave the states parties free to determine the precise method for implementing the obligations assumed. Despite the general flexibility in the Protocol's provisions, a 1996 survey indicated that most parties to the Protocol had achieved its goals, and overall compliance with the Protocol has resulted in reduction in the level of emissions. For instance, eighteen of the twenty-five parties to the Protocol had stabilized their NO_X emissions at the 1987 level by 1990, and by 1993 all parties had reduced NO_X emissions by 6%.

4. *The 1991 Protocol on Volatile Organic Compounds*

This Protocol addresses the contribution to the formation of tropospheric ozone of volatile organic compounds (VOCs) and nitrogen oxides, which are transported across international boundaries affecting air quality in neighbouring states.[35] The focus like the previous Protocols is on Europe and North America. The broad aim of the Protocol as set out in the preamble is to control and reduce national annual emissions of VOCs and the resulting secondary photochemical oxidant products. Specific reduction percentages to be achieved by the parties were set out in subsequent provisions,[36] and are intended to reduce transboundary fluxes of VOCs and the resulting secondary photochemical oxidant products. Parties were encouraged to develop strategies that would give priority to substances that had the highest amount of photochemical ozone creation potential.[37] In other respects, the protocol mirrors its predecessors by providing for information exchange and periodic reporting on implementation measures.

5. *The 1998 Heavy Metals and POPs Protocols*

Although most heavy metals released into the air from industrial activities and power stations are deposited locally, a significant number of very small particles are transported over longer distances. In 1998 two further protocols to the LRTAP Convention addressed pollution from heavy metals,[38] and persistent organic pollutants (POPs).[39] The aim of the first Protocol is to reduce emissions from heavy metals caused by anthropogenic activities and that are capable of long range transboundary atmospheric transport with serious consequences for human health and the environment.[40] The Heavy Metals Protocol set reduction targets for cadmium, lead, and mercury emissions as well as emission limit values.[41] It also required the parties to apply the best available technology to all existing and new sources of heavy metals.

[35] 1991 Protocol to the 1979 LRTAP concerning the Control of Emissions of Volatile Organic Compounds or their Transboundary Fluxes (VOCs Protocol).

[36] Ibid, art 2.

[37] art 2.4.

[38] 1998 Protocol to the 1979 LRTAP on Heavy Metals.

[39] 1998 Protocol to the 1979 LRTAP on Persistent Organic Pollutants. This Protocol is addressed in Chapter 33, 'Hazardous Substances and Activities', in this volume.

[40] art 2.

[41] annex I.

The Heavy Metals Protocol was amended in 2012.[42] The amendments required parties to observe more stringent emission limits as well as including new emission sources. Annex III of the Protocol contains a list of the best available technology to be deployed; Annex IV and V contain specific emission limit values to be respected by the parties. Transparent record keeping is mandatory, and the parties are required to keep up to date registers on cadmium, lead, and mercury emission levels. Metal emission levels are to be reported at periodic intervals and the implementation committee is mandated to carry out inspections to verify the parties' compliance record.

6. *The 1999 Gothenburg Protocol on Acidification, Eutrophication and Ground-Level Ozone*

In 1999 a further Protocol to the Convention was adopted to abate acidification, eutrophication, and ground level ozone.[43] Unlike the previous protocols, which had addressed a single pollutant, the Gothenburg Protocol is a multi-pollutant protocol setting limits in one instrument for sulphur, nitrogen oxides, volatile organic compounds, and ammonia which had to be met by a set date in 2010 and beyond. It is particularly significant that Eastern European countries, Caucasus, and Central Asian countries that had largely stayed away from the pollution specific protocols have now been able to take part in this multi-pollutant protocol, in large part as result of a decision taken in 2011 to initiate a coordinating group to encourage participation beyond Western Europe and North America.[44] Although they are not formally parties, the process for dialogue is now in place with a view to achieving their participation. In 2012 the parties adopted further reduction targets to be met by the parties in 2020.[45] The technical annexes to the Protocol were also substantially revised to include new reduction targets for processing plants, factories, mobile machines, and vehicles and were further extended to include black carbon. Furthermore, the European Union (EU), unilaterally assumed more onerous obligations for its members by way of implementing the Protocol's amendments. In order to facilitate compliance with these enhanced

[42] Decision 2012/5, 'Amendment of the text of and Annexes other than III and VII to the 1998 Protocol on Heavy Metals' and Decision 2012/6, 'Amendment of annex III to the 1998 Protocol on Heavy Metals' (13 December 2012) UN Doc ECE/EB.Air/113/Add.1.

[43] 1999 Protocol to the 1979 LRTAP to Abate Acidification, Eutrophication and Ground-level Ozone.

[44] Decision 2010/17, 'Establishment of a coordinating Group on the Promotion of Actions Towards Implementation of the Convention in Eastern Europe, the Caucaus and Central Asia' (24 February 2011) UN Doc ECE/EB.AIR/106/Add.1.

[45] Implemented in the European Union through Directive 2016/2284/EU of the European Parliament and of the Council of 14 December 2016 on the reduction of national emissions of certain atmospheric pollutants, amending Directive 2003/35/EC and repealing Directive 2001/81/EC [2016] OJ L 344/1 and Directive 2015/2193/EU of the European Parliament and of the Council of 25 November 2015 on the limitation of emissions of certain pollutants into the air from medium combustion plants [2015] OJ L 313/1. The emission targets set in the Directives go much further than the formal requirements of the Protocol.

obligations, flexible transitional arrangements were offered to new parties with a final implementation deadline in 2030.[46]

B. The 1991 US-Canada Air Quality Agreement

This agreement was the result of several years of bilateral negotiations between the United States and Canada.[47] Its preamble reaffirms the basic principle of state responsibility for environmental damage as provided for in Principle 21 of the Stockholm Declaration. It can therefore be argued that, like the 1979 LRTAP, the intention was to create a practical mechanism for implementing the pre-existing duties of the parties under general international law. The treaty lays down specific targets and schedules to be observed by the two countries in their efforts to regulate transboundary air pollution. The basic substantive obligation of the parties is to be found in Article 2(a) which requires the parties to establish emission limitation objectives and specific programmes for their implementation. The specific objectives for sulphur and nitrogen oxides are set out in an Annex to the Convention.

The most significant feature of this agreement is its provisions on the monitoring of compliance. The implementation of the Convention is entrusted to a bilateral Air Quality Committee established under Article VII and the International Joint Commission. In 2000, an Ozone Annex was added to the US-Canada Agreement, committing both parties to reduce emissions of nitrogen oxides and volatile organic compounds, the precursor pollutants responsible for ground level ozone.[48]

Other bilateral agreements of relevance in the region include those regulating air pollution emissions between Mexico and the United States.[49]

C. 2002 ASEAN Agreement on Transboundary Haze Pollution

This agreement, negotiated under the auspices of the ASEAN, creates a national and international framework for tackling transboundary haze caused by land and or forest

[46] 1999 Gothenburg Protocol, as amended on 4 May 2012, art 3 bis.

[47] Agreement Between The Government of Canada and The Government of The United States of America on Air Quality Canada and United States of America Quality (adopted and entered into force 13 March 1991) 1852 UNTS 80.

[48] Government of Canada, 'Canada-US air quality agreement: ozone annex' <https://www.canada.ca/en/environment-climate-change/services/air-pollution/publications/canada-united-states-quality-agreement-ozone-annex.html> accessed 2 January 2020.

[49] Agreement on Co-operation Between the United States of America and the United Mexican States Regarding Transboundary Air Pollution Caused by Copper Smelters Along Their Common Border (1987) 26 ILM 15; see also Agreement of Co-operation Regarding International Transport of Urban Air Pollution (1990) 30 ILM 29, annex V.

fires.[50] In part, it builds on the 1995 ASEAN Co-operation Plan on transboundary pollution, which had called on parties to regulate transboundary atmospheric pollution and to establish procedures and mechanisms for cooperation among ASEAN member states to prevent, reduce, and mitigate the effects of haze and forest fires.[51] As of September 2014, all ten ASEAN Countries had ratified the Haze Agreement.

The treaty has created a framework for dialogue on the problem of haze. It has nevertheless encountered problems, not least the fact that Indonesia, the single biggest contributor to the haze problem, was the last to ratify the Convention. The key substantive obligations are contained in Articles 3 (on principles), 4 (on general obligations), and Articles 5, 6, 7, 8, and 9 (monitoring, assessment, prevention, and response). In accordance with these provisions, the parties undertake in the spirit of solidarity and partnership and in accordance with their respective needs, capabilities, and situations to cooperate and coordinate action in order to prevent and monitor transboundary haze. They are also required to take legal, administrative, and other implementing measures as required by the agreement.

The measures anticipated include precautionary measures;[52] exchange of information;[53] and cooperation in matters relating to transboundary haze pollution.[54] Institutionally, the coordinating work is to be undertaken under the auspices of the ASEAN Coordinating Centre for Transboundary Haze Pollution established under Article 5. In Article 9, the parties agree to undertake measures to prevent and control activities related to land and/or forest fires that may lead to transboundary haze. There are further extensive obligations on exchange of information and coordination of assistance.[55] Like the LRTAP, the task of implementing compliance with the Convention, including the amendment of its provisions, is entrusted to the Conference of the Parties (COP).

In 2016, an ASEAN Haze Free Roadmap was adopted at the 12th COP meeting.[56] This roadmap serves as a strategic framework for the implementation of the obligation to control transboundary haze in the ASEAN region and to create a haze-free region by 2020. Nevertheless, there are no mandatory air quality standards or emission reduction strategies, and governments remain free to decide on whatever measures they regard as

[50] ASEAN Agreement on Transboundary Haze Pollution (adopted in Kuala Lumpur on 10 June 2002, entered into force 25 November 2003) <https://haze.asean.org/?wpfb_dl=32> accessed 4 February 2020; Laely Nurhidayah *et al*, 'Regional Environmental Governance: An Evaluation of the ASEAN Legal Framework for Addressing Transboundary Haze Pollution' *Australian Journal of Asian Law*, 15/1 (2014): 1–7 (art 6).

[51] Ibid, preamble.

[52] art 3.

[53] art 4.

[54] Ibid.

[55] arts 12, 13, 16.

[56] ASEAN Haze Action Online, 'Roadmap on ASEAN Cooperation towards Transboundary Haze Pollution Control with Means of Implementation' <https://haze.asean.org/haze-free-roadmap/> accessed 2 January 2020.

appropriate in light of their national priorities.[57] Moreover, China, a highly polluting country and a non-member of ASEAN, is not bound by these commitments and is projected to increase its emissions. Furthermore, ASEAN member Indonesia, although bound by the Convention, has not made significant progress in reducing haze.[58]

D. Global Initiatives—UN Environment

There is at present no global treaty on air pollution and there is little evidence that states are likely to adopt one in the near future. The legislative arena described above thus largely consists of a patchwork of regional instruments which are broadly directory but do not contain hard obligations. The UN has, in the context of its sustainable development work, prioritized improving air quality and recognized that the abatement of air pollution is important to achieving sustainable development goals.[59] In 2017, the Assembly of the UN Environment called on member states to take action across sectors to reduce all forms of air pollution.[60] The resolution further called on member states to establish relevant systems to monitor air pollution, in order to be well informed of the state of air quality and sources of pollution in affected areas.[61] The resolution urges states to put in place policies and measures to prevent and reduce air pollution from significant sources. States are further encouraged to integrate these policies as far as possible into the national development agenda.

The most progressive aspect of this resolution is the call on parties to share knowledge, in the context of existing and future regional cooperation agreements, such as those under the UNECE, the Asia Pacific Clean Air partnership, and the Africa Sustainable Transport forum. Other provisions call on states, and financial and private sector institutions in a position to do so, to contribute technical and financial support towards regional and national initiatives to address air pollution. States are further urged to support developing countries in expanding the use of cleaner fuels for cooking so as to prevent and reduce air pollution. All states are required to increase public awareness on the dangers associated with air pollution and what can be done to mitigate their effects.

The measures in the resolution are modest both in the scale of their ambition and the demands they make on states. It is nevertheless encouraging that action required to tackle climate change is closely intertwined with air pollution since the sources of pollutants and greenhouse gases broadly overlap. The policies adopted to achieve

[57] Fadhilah Ghani *et al*, 'Review on ASEAN Transboundary Haze Agreement 2002: Problems and Solutions' *Journal of Humanities, Languages, Culture and Business*, 1/1 (2017): 153.

[58] Yenni Kwok, 'The Southeast Asian Haze is back and Worse may follow' *Time* (30 July 2013); 'Indonesian govt rapped over lack of action on haze' *Today* (18 September 2019).

[59] UNEP Environment Assembly, 'Preventing and reducing air pollution to improve air quality globally' (4–6 December 2017) UN Doc UNEP/EA.3/Res.8.

[60] Ibid, art 1.

[61] Ibid, art 1(a).

sustainable growth have the capacity to reduce both air pollution and carbon dioxide emissions.

V. CONCLUSION

At present a major focus of the international arena is on climate change and the greenhouse gases contributing to it. However, it would be premature to argue that the regulation of transboundary air pollution as a discrete phenomenon has been displaced by the rapid evolution of the climate change regime. Climate change remains a monumental project and it is difficult to predict with certainty just how effective the measures adopted will be in reducing greenhouse gases but specifically also in relation to transboundary air pollution. Yet, it is also clear that a degree of coordination and in some cases even integration between the two regimes will be necessary since climate change mitigation actions can help reduce air pollution and clean air measures may also reduce greenhouse gas emissions leading to reductions in global warming.

In the short-to-medium term, it is likely to be easier to develop regional strategies on air pollution between a smaller group of states than through global initiatives. The UNECE LRTAP and its Protocols have stood the test of time and it seems likely that states will continue to favour cooperation rather than the imposition of delictual responsibility for resulting harm. The customary law of state responsibility will continue to play an important role in cases of historic pollution but also as a reminder to states that any harm occurring as a result of their failure to implement obligations may entail liability. The cooperative model under the LRTAP and its protocols cannot, however, be applied without modification to the newer air pollution problems in Africa, Latin America, and Asia. The application of this particular model will require considerable adjustment to address the very different manifestations of transboundary air pollution in the global South and the need to integrate air pollution abatement strategies with other sustainable development goals.

BIBLIOGRAPHY

Frank Biermann, *Saving the Atmosphere: International Law, Developing Countries and Air Pollution* (Peter Lang 1995)

Adam Byrne, 'The 1979 Convention on Long-Range Transboundary Air Pollution: Assessing its Effectiveness as a Multilateral Environmental Regime after 35 Years' *Journal of Transnational Environmental Law*, 4/1 (2015): 37

Adam Byrne, 'Trouble in the Air: Recent Developments under the 1979 Convention on Long-Range Transboundary Air Pollution' *Review of European Comparative and International Environmental Law*, 26/3 (2017): 210

Laura Henry, Jasper Kim, and Dongho Lee, 'From Smelter Fumes to Silk Winds: Exploring Legal Responses to Transboundary Air Pollution over Korea' *Washington University Global Studies Law Review*, 11/3 (2012): 565

Phoebe Okowa, *State Responsibility for Transboundary Air Pollution in International Law* (OUP 2000)

Peter Sand, 'Regional Approaches to Transboundary Air Pollution' in John Helm (ed), *Energy: Production, Consumption and Consequences* (National Academy Press 1990) 246

CHAPTER 29

CLIMATE CHANGE

LAVANYA RAJAMANI AND JACOB D WERKSMAN

I. INTRODUCTION

WHILE the field of international environmental law has grown substantially in the last few decades, climate change law has evolved the most dramatically.[1] From relative obscurity in the late 1980s, when the negotiations for a United Nations Framework Convention on Climate Change (UNFCCC) were first launched,[2] to the rise and fall of the 1997 Kyoto Protocol, and the successful conclusion of the 2015 Paris Agreement, the annual UN Climate Change Conferences that host these treaties now typically attract more than 30,000 participants and dozens of heads of state and government. This evolution tracks an increase in the certainty of the science underpinning climate change and the political salience, public consciousness, and media attention to its impacts. Increasingly, domestic legislatures and courts have begun developing climate law in response to or ahead of what these treaties require. However, despite decades of intensive intergovernmental climate negotiations, emissions of greenhouse gases (GHGs) and global average temperatures continue to rise. The complex, polycentric, and seemingly intractable nature of the climate change policy challenge has made it difficult to translate growing awareness into ambitious international obligations and decisive and effective domestic action.

This chapter provides an overview of international regulatory efforts to address climate change. It focuses on the UN climate change regime, that comprises the 1992 UNFCCC, the Kyoto Protocol, the Paris Agreement, and decisions of parties under these instruments. The universe of climate change law extends well beyond the UN

[1] This chapter builds on earlier work, in particular, Lavanya Rajamani, *Innovation and Experimentation in the International Climate Change Regime* (vol 41, *Collected Courses of the Hague Academy of International Law (Recueil des Cours)*, Brill 2020).

[2] UNGA Res 45/212, 'Protection of global climate for present and future generations of mankind' (21 December 1990) UN Doc A/RES/45/212.

climate change regime. There are rules and principles of general international law, such as the harm prevention principle, due diligence, and state responsibility, that apply to climate change.[3] There are treaty regimes and institutions, including those addressing other areas of international environmental law or other fields of international law, that intersect with, complement, and function to implement the UN climate change regime.[4] There are also a multiplicity of rules, regulations, and institutions at the regional, sub-regional, and national levels that directly or indirectly address climate change, many of which have been put in place in response to the UN treaties. It is beyond the scope of this chapter to explore the entire universe of climate change law, but if read in conjunction with other chapters of this handbook that address specific aspects, a fuller picture emerges.

This chapter begins by exploring the scientific context, political challenges, key drivers, and milestones in the evolution of the UN climate change regime. It then outlines the central objectives, principles, commitments, and institutions in each of the three legally binding treaties in the regime, with a focus on the logic underpinning these treaties, the evolution of this logic, and on how the regime is expected to function in the future. Finally, the chapter explores the influence and reach of the UN climate change regime beyond states and concludes with observations on how the regime can be made more effective.

II. CONTEXT: SCIENCE, POLITICS, DRIVERS, AND MILESTONES

A. Science and Politics

The Intergovernmental Panel on Climate Change (IPCC) has, through successive reports over the last three decades, imparted increasing certainty to the science of climate change. The IPCC finds that the warming of the climate system is 'unequivocal',[5] and that human activities have already caused 'approximately 1.0°C of global warming above pre-industrial levels'.[6] Recent data from the United States' National Aeronautics and Space Administration (NASA) and the National Oceanic and Atmospheric Administration (NOAA) indicates a consistent and incontrovertible warming trend. The past five years, collectively, have been the warmest years in modern record, with twenty of the warmest years occurring over the past twenty-two years.[7] Emissions of

[3] Chapters 16 and 58, 'Harm Prevention' and 'International Environmental Responsibility and Liability', this volume.

[4] See Parts V and VII, 'Subject Matter' and 'Inter-Linkages with Other Regimes', in this volume.

[5] IPCC, *Climate Change 2014: Synthesis Report* (2014) Summary for Policymakers, 2, SPM 1.1.

[6] IPCC, *Global Warming of 1.5°C—Special Report* (2018) Summary for Policymakers, 4, para A.1.

[7] Sean Potter, '2018 Fourth Warmest Year in Continued Warming Trend, according to NASA, NOAA' *NASA* (6 February 2019).

carbon dioxide (CO_2) and other GHGs into the atmosphere are also at record levels.[8] The annual global average CO2 concentration at Earth's surface is higher than it has been in 800,000 years.[9] According to the IPCC, many of these changes are 'unprecedented over decades to millennia',[10] and 'have caused impacts on natural and human systems on all continents and across the oceans'.[11] The IPCC predicts that continued emission of GHGs will cause 'further warming' and increase the likelihood of 'severe, pervasive and irreversible impacts'.[12]

Successive IPCC reports, and the rapidly increasing certainty in climate science, have provided the context and impetus for the negotiation of the three treaties that comprise the UN climate change regime. Science has proven influential in bringing and keeping states at the negotiating table, but it has not been determinative of the content and ambition of these treaties.[13]

In part, this is because of the political challenges at the heart of the climate change problem, in particular the issue of equity. In 1992, the UNFCCC recognized the vast disparities in wealth, GHG emissions profiles, and vulnerabilities among states by grouping its parties into 'developed' and 'developing' countries. While much has changed since then, those countries categorized as developed have at present emitted about 2.3 times the historic CO_2 emissions of those categorized as developing.[14] However, present annual CO_2 emissions from developing countries are 60% of the total global CO_2 emissions,[15] and emissions from large developing countries are now higher in absolute and per capita terms than some developed countries.[16] Per capita emissions in many developing countries, however, continue to be low. Looking at historical, current, and future emissions, equity in climate change requires leadership from developed countries as well as significant efforts from developing countries—neither of which has proven easy to secure. Another equity issue at the heart of the climate change problem is the mismatch between those that have contributed the most to climate change, and those—such as the small island states—that have negligible GHG emissions but are at the frontlines of climate impacts.

At the domestic level, the causes of and solutions to climate change engage every aspect of domestic policy and thus are inextricably linked to domestic politics. Domestic politics in every state are shaped by numerous context-specific factors and

[8] WMO and Global Atmosphere Watch, 'The State of Greenhouse Gases in the Atmosphere Based on Global Observations through 2017' *WMO Greenhouse Gas Bulletin*, 14 (2018).

[9] See also Jessica Blunden and Derek Arndt (eds), 'State of the Climate in 2018' *Special Supplement to the Bulletin of the American Meteorological Society*, 100/9 (2019).

[10] IPCC, *Climate Change 2013: The Physical Science Basis* (2013) 4.

[11] Climate Change 2014 (n 5) 6, SPM 1.3.

[12] Ibid, 8, SPM 2.

[13] See generally Chapter 15, 'Role of Science', in this volume.

[14] World Resources Institute (WRI)—CAIT Climate Data Explorer, 'Cumulative Total CO_2 Emissions Excluding Land-Use Change and Forestry from 1850 to selected years—2014'.

[15] Ibid.

[16] See IPCC, *Climate Change 2014: Mitigation of Climate Change* (2014) 125–130.

actors, and few countries have prioritized the need to take action on climate change. Dependence on a fossil-fuel-driven economy, often cloaked in climate scepticism or denialism, continues to shape the policies of many countries. Domestic priorities are often strongly influenced by the need to promote a 'just transition' for all sectors of the society. For poorer countries, any policies to promote a low emissions economy must be reconciled with the political priorities of economic development, poverty eradication, and ensuring universal access to affordable and reliable energy. The fundamental transformations required to address climate change are only possible if there is a long-term political vision that includes sharing the societal and economic costs and benefits. Short-term election cycles in most states rarely lead to long-term vision aimed at large scale transformations.

Albeit politically challenging, if the ambitious goals set by the international treaties described below are to be met, climate change must be decisively addressed as a matter of urgency. There is a rapidly closing window of opportunity for averting climate change before a 'global cascade of tipping points' triggers irreversible ecosystem impacts, and leads to a 'a new, less habitable, "hothouse" climate state'.[17]

B. Drivers and Milestones

The climate change treaties have taken shape in the context of states' differing views on how best to set targets and other commitments in a fair and effective manner. At least three broad issues affect the architecture of these instruments. First, whether they should reflect a 'top-down' approach (through which states negotiate multilateral rules applicable to all parties), or a 'bottom-up' approach (which leaves parties the discretion to determine how they will meet the treaty's goals) or a hybrid of the two; secondly, the legal form of instruments and the legal character of commitments within them; and, thirdly, the nature and extent of differentiation in favour of developing countries in these instruments, including through more flexible commitments and financial support.

The three treaties in the UN climate change regime contain different regulatory approaches across these three dimensions. The UNFCCC—negotiated at a time when the science was not as clear or certain as it is now, and political will and salience was muted—reflects a 'framework' approach incorporating broad principles, soft obligations, and strong differentiation. It addresses not only the need to cut emissions (mitigation), but also to prepare for the predicted impacts of climate change (adaptation) and to support developing countries through the 'means of implementation' (finance, technology transfer, and capacity building). It also established the institutional architecture necessary for the regime to function, and negotiations to proceed, in

[17] Timothy Lenton *et al*, 'Climate Tipping Points—Too Risky To Bet Against' *Nature* (27 November 2019).

particular the Conference of the Parties (COP), the Subsidiary Bodies, and the financial mechanism.

The Kyoto Protocol advances the broad framework of the UNFCCC along several dimensions. The Kyoto Protocol was negotiated in the context of increasing scientific certainty, and a preparedness, at least among developed countries, to undertake mitigation commitments. It contains internationally negotiated legally binding GHG emissions budgets for developed countries set within a common time frame, and market mechanisms to reduce the costs of compliance, and backed by a compliance system. However, the Kyoto Protocol, both because of the prescriptive nature of the targets it contains as well as the extent of differentiation it reflects in favour of developing countries, was rejected by the United States in 2001.[18] In the wake of the United States' rejection, the costs of compliance, both political and financial, with the Protocol increased. The Protocol entered into force only in 2005, eight years after its adoption. It also lost its key constituents over time. The Kyoto Protocol's first commitment period running from 2008 to 2012 covered 24% of 2010 global emissions.[19] The 2012 Doha Amendment to the Kyoto Protocol contains a second commitment period running from 2013 to 2020, which covers only a fraction of global emissions. Several developed country Kyoto Protocol parties opted out, including Canada, Japan, and Russia.[20]

After the Kyoto Protocol entered into force, a progressive alliance of developed and developing countries began to explore ways of extending GHG mitigation commitments globally, including to developing countries and to the United States. Some developing countries, particularly those with large and growing emissions, strenuously resisted the extension of GHG mitigation commitments to them. The United States, the European Union (EU), and some vulnerable developing countries called for greater symmetry between developed and developing countries in relation to mitigation commitments—a dynamic which eventually led to 'nationally determined contributions' for all countries in the 2015 Paris Agreement. The first evidence of this 'paradigm shift'[21] emerged in the 2009 Copenhagen Accord. The Copenhagen Accord introduced a process for the pledging and review of voluntary 'nationally appropriate mitigation actions' from all parties for the period 2012–20. This step was significant because it opened the door for self-selected GHG mitigation targets and actions.[22] It also introduced the expectation

[18] The White House: President George W Bush, Office of the Press Secretary, 'Text of a Letter from the President to Senators Hagel, Helms, Craig, and Roberts' (13 March 2001).

[19] Igor Shishlov, Romain Morel, and Valentin Bellassen, 'Compliance of the Parties to the Kyoto Protocol in the First Commitment Period' *Climate Policy*, 16/6 (2016): 768.

[20] Australia, New Zealand, EU-28, Iceland, Norway, and Switzerland account for less than 11% of 2014 global GHG emissions, excluding land use, land-use change, and forestry (LULUCF), in the second commitment period. See Climate Watch—Data for Climate Action, 'Data Explorer' <https://www.climatewatchdata.org/> accessed 4 February 2020.

[21] Daniel Bodansky, 'The Paris Climate Change Agreement: A New Hope?' *American Journal of International Law*, 110/2 (2016): 289.

[22] Decision 2/CP.15, 'Copenhagen Accord' (30 March 2010) UN Doc FCCC/CP/2009/11/Add.1, 4, paras 4–5.

that all parties—developed and developing—undertake some form of commitment in relation to GHG mitigation targets and actions, and so began the gradual process of diluting the contentious Kyoto-style differentiation that contained GHG mitigation targets only for developed countries. Most parties continued to feel that a purely voluntary system of pledge and review was an inadequate response to climate change and in Durban, 2011, the COP agreed to launch the four-year negotiating process towards 'a protocol, another legal instrument or an agreed outcome with legal force under the Convention applicable to all Parties'.[23] This led to the Paris Agreement that reflects the hybrid approach described above.

C. A 'Nested' Regime

The relationship between these three treaties and the states that are parties to them is complex and dynamic. The UNFCCC is a 'framework' treaty, and the Kyoto Protocol is a protocol to the Convention adopted under its Article 17. The Paris Agreement is a *sui generis* legal instrument adopted 'under the Convention' but without reference to the forms of related legal instruments provided for under the Convention (amendments and protocols[24]). Together they comprise a 'nested' regime, in which the parties to each instrument rely on most of the same institutions, including the governing body of the COP, to serve all three instruments. All parties to Kyoto and Paris must be a party to the UNFCCC, but not all parties to the Convention have joined or remained as parties to the Kyoto Protocol and Paris Agreement. While some parties maintain that the UNFCCC, its provisions, and principles continue to bind all parties in the same manner as they did prior to the entry into force of Paris, others consider Paris to have 'updated' and refined key provisions. Although the Doha Amendment to the Kyoto Protocol has entered into force, the Protocol has begun to lose relevance since 2020 when its second commitment period came to an end. However, if a party to the Convention is outside the Paris Agreement, the legal and institutional relationship between the Convention and the Agreement will remain complex.

The Paris Agreement continues the process begun under the Convention and the Protocol of establishing 'constituted bodies' with specific responsibilities for implementing the regime. These include committees, bodies, mechanisms, and boards of limited membership, through which individuals, elected by the parties, carry out analysis and produce reports that provide the basis of decisions of the governing bodies and thus a source of state practice and interpretation of treaty provisions. Because the treaties' governing bodies have never adopted voting rules and operate by consensus,

[23] Decision 1/CP.17, 'Establishment of an Ad Hoc Working Group on a Durban Platform for Enhanced Action, 2011' (15 March 2012) UN Doc FCCC/CP/2011/9/Add.1, 2, para 2.

[24] UNFCCC, arts 15, 17.

the limited membership and, in some cases, rules of procedure, that apply for the constituted bodies may lead to more effective regime decision-making over time.

III. 1992 UNFCCC

The UNFCCC identifies an objective, introduces general principles, imposes a basic set of commitments, and establishes a skeletal institutional framework. Building on this, the Kyoto Protocol and the Paris Agreement, as 'related legal instrument[s]',[25] introduce specific, targeted measures reflecting different approaches to global climate regulation.

A. Objective

Article 2 identifies the 'ultimate objective' of the UNFCCC and any related instruments as 'stabilization of the greenhouse gas concentrations in the atmosphere at a level that would prevent dangerous anthropogenic interference with the climate system'. It does not indicate what this level is, implicitly leaving this to subsequent negotiation. Both the Kyoto Protocol and the Paris Agreement advance parties' understanding of how to achieve the Convention's objective.

B. Principles

Article 3 of the UNFCCC, entitled 'Principles',[26] calls for, among other things, consideration for the 'specific needs and special circumstances' of the particularly vulnerable;[27] precautionary measures to anticipate, prevent, or minimize the causes of climate change and to mitigate its effects;[28] the promotion of sustainable development;[29] and cooperation to promote a 'supportive and open international economic system'.[30] The principle that has fundamentally shaped the climate change regime and been shaped by it—is the principle of common but differentiated responsibilities, and respective capabilities (CBDRRC).[31] This principle, the basis for differential treatment in the climate change

[25] The UNFCCC recognizes that parties may adopt a 'related legal instrument', to which the provisions relating to the objective (art 2), the COP (art 7.2), and settlement of disputes (art 14.8) apply.

[26] Daniel Bodansky, 'The United Nations Framework Convention on Climate Change: A Commentary' *Yale Journal of International Law*, 18 (1993): 451, 502, fn 308.

[27] art 3.2.

[28] art 3.3.

[29] art 3.4.

[30] art 3.5.

[31] art 3.1; Paris Agreement, preambular recital 3, arts 2.2, 4.3, 4.19.

regime, has been interpreted and operationalized in distinct ways in the Kyoto Protocol and the Paris Agreement, discussed below, and its precise contours are a work in progress.[32]

C. Commitments

The UNFCCC requires all parties to develop national inventories of GHG emissions,[33] formulate policies and measures to limit GHG emissions,[34] and submit national communications containing information relating to their national inventories, and steps taken or envisaged to implement the Convention.[35] All parties are also required to 'cooperate' in relation to adaptation to the impacts of climate change,[36] technology development, application and transfer, conservation and enhancement of sinks of GHGs,[37] scientific and technological research,[38] and education, training, and public awareness.[39]

The UNFCCC requires developed countries listed in Annex I[40] to take policies and measures on GHG mitigation 'with the aim of returning individually or jointly' to their 1990 levels of GHGs[41] by 'the end of the present decade', that is, by 2000. A subset of these developed countries listed in Annex II have additional commitments to provide 'new and additional financial resources to meet the agreed full costs incurred by developing country Parties' in complying with the reporting requirements, and to 'meet the agreed full incremental costs' of developing countries in implementing emissions reduction measures.[42] Annex II parties also commit to assist particularly vulnerable developing country parties in 'meeting costs of adaptation' to the adverse effects of climate change. Over the years, numerous UNFCCC funds have been set up to support developing countries, especially the least developed among them, with the 1995 Global Environment Facility (GEF)[43] and the 2010 Green Climate Fund as the most significant.[44]

32 See further Rajamani (n 1) ch 4; Christina Voigt and Felipe Ferreira, 'Differentiation in the Paris Agreement' *Climate Law*, 6/1–2 (2016): 58; see also Chapter 19, 'Differentiation', in this volume.
33 art 4.1(a).
34 art 4.1(b).
35 art 12.
36 art 4.1(e).
37 art 4.1(d).
38 art 5.
39 art 6.
40 Parties listed in annex I correspond to the list of OECD (Organisation of Economic Co-operation and Development) members in 1992.
41 arts 4.2(a)–(b).
42 arts 4.4, 4.5.
43 <https://www.thegef.org/> accessed 4 February 2020.
44 <https://www.greenclimate.fund/> accessed 4 February 2020.

IV. THE 1997 KYOTO PROTOCOL

A. Principles

The Kyoto Protocol seeks to advance the climate change regime in line with the ultimate objective of the UNFCCC,[45] and its key principles.[46] Thus, although the Kyoto Protocol contains only one explicit reference to the CBDRRC principle, it has been characterized as the 'clearest attempt to transform, activate and operationalize CBDR from a legal concept into a policy instrument'.[47] The Kyoto Protocol differentiates between Annex I (developed) and non-Annex I (developing) countries, limiting GHG mitigation targets and timetables to Annex I countries.[48] Since emission targets apply only to Annex I parties, the provisions of the Protocol designed to monitor compliance with the targets are limited to Annex I parties,[49] and its compliance procedure is tailored to the differentiated obligations of parties.[50]

B. Commitments

The Kyoto Protocol establishes quantified and timebound GHG mitigation obligations, collective and individual, for developed countries,[51] backed by procedural obligations in relation to reporting and review,[52] and a compliance system.[53] Specifically, the Protocol requires developed countries listed in its Annex B to reduce their overall emissions of a basket of GHGs[54] 'by at least 5 percent below 1990 levels in the commitment period 2008 to 2012', and it identifies individual targets for each country towards this aim, which range from limits of 8% below 1990 levels (the EU and its member states) to 10% above 1990 levels (Iceland). These individual targets are legally binding, quantitative, absolute, and economy-wide. The individual targets were based on national offers and

45 Kyoto Protocol, preambular recital 2.

46 Ibid, preambular recital 3.

47 Remarks by Christopher Joyner, 'Common but Differentiated Responsibilities' *American Society of International Law Proceedings*, 96 (2002): 358.

48 art 3.

49 arts 5, 7, 8.

50 See Decision 27/CMP.1, 'Procedures and mechanisms relating to compliance under the Kyoto Protocol' (30 March 2006) UN Doc FCCC/KP/CMP/2005/8/Add.3, 92.

51 art 3.

52 arts 5, 7, 8. Elaborated through a series of decisions taken by the COP; see Decisions 2-24/CP.7, 'The Marrakesh Accords' (21 January 2002) UN Doc FCCC/CP/2001/13/Add.1-3.

53 art 18; Decision 27/CMP.1 (n 50).

54 These gases are listed in Annex A of the Kyoto Protocol and include carbon dioxide, methane, nitrous oxide, hydrofluorocarbons, perflourocarbons, and sulphur hexafluoride. Both the Convention and the Protocol exclude from their scope GHGs 'not controlled by the Montreal Protocol'.

ultimately agreed to by each respective party, but they were internationally negotiated, and in several instances reflected a shift from the party's initial offer. Once agreed, these targets were inscribed in the Kyoto Protocol, and became legally binding, and backed by compliance consequences. These are obligations of result. To reduce the costs of implementing these targets the Protocol permits parties to use market mechanisms, but only when in compliance with strict rules.

C. Market Mechanisms

The Kyoto Protocol's three market mechanisms[55] are the Clean Development Mechanism (CDM), Joint Implementation (JI), and Emissions Trading.[56] Of these the CDM and JI are project-based mechanisms—the CDM between developed and developing countries, and the JI between developed countries. These three market mechanisms were, at the time, an innovation designed to allow countries to meet their commitments cost effectively. They triggered the establishment of emissions trading systems around the world, most notably in the EU,[57] and gave rise to subsequent efforts to link different trading systems. Although cost effective, in practice, it is unclear to what extent these mechanisms foster environmental integrity. The project-based mechanisms—JI and CDM—have been beset by concerns about the extent to which the emissions credits they have generated are 'additional'[58] to that which would have occurred in the absence of the project. And, there is limited evidence that the CDM, intended to help developing countries achieve 'sustainable development',[59] has done so, given difficulties in defining, implementing, and securing sustainable development.[60] Moreover the vast majority of CDM projects have been hosted by a handful of countries, so the benefits, if any, are concentrated in large developing countries. Nearly 50% of projects are located in China, followed by India with over 20%.[61] It is worth noting that at the end of the Protocol's first compliance assessment period, parties were in compliance with their Kyoto targets, albeit in some instances through the use of carbon markets.[62]

55 See further Chapter 53, 'Market Mechanisms', in this volume.

56 arts 6, 12, 17.

57 EU Emissions Trading System <https://ec.europa.eu/clima/policies/ets_en> accessed 4 February 2020.

58 arts 6.1(b), 12.5(c).

59 art 12.2.

60 See further Daniel Bodansky, Jutta Brunnée, and Lavanya Rajamani, *International Climate Change Law* (OUP 2017) ch 6.

61 UNFCCC, 'Distribution of Registered Projects by Host Party' <https://cdm.unfccc.int/Statistics/Public/files/201912/proj_reg_byHost.pdf> accessed 4 February 2020.

62 Shishlov, Morel, and Bellassen (n 19).

V. 2015 PARIS AGREEMENT AND 2018 RULEBOOK

The Paris Agreement, like the Kyoto Protocol, is in pursuit of the objective of the Convention and is guided by its principles. It was adopted in 2015, entered into force rapidly in 2016, and came into full operation when its parties' nationally determined contributions took effect in 2020. It essentially takes over from the Kyoto Protocol as the source of specific commitments for the climate regime. While amendments to the Paris Agreement are possible, unlike the Convention and the Protocol, the Paris Agreement is built on the assumption that no additional treaty negotiations or legally binding instruments are necessary to achieve its ambitious goals.

A. Purpose

Paris Agreement Article 2.1 identifies the purpose of the Agreement as '[h]olding the increase in the global average temperature to well below 2°C above pre-industrial levels and pursuing efforts to limit the temperature increase to 1.5°C above pre-industrial levels'. The Paris Agreement builds on the UNFCCC objective by setting out, in terms of avoided temperature rise, what is 'dangerous' and by implying the level at which concentrations of GHGs in the atmosphere must be stabilized.[63] In order to achieve the long-term temperature goal, Article 4.1 requires parties to 'aim' to reach global peaking of GHG emissions as soon as possible, and to undertake 'rapid reductions' thereafter so as to achieve a balance between GHG emissions by sources and removals by sinks—popularly characterized as 'climate' or 'carbon' neutrality—in the second half of this century. Reaching the Agreement's temperature goal will require reductions in emissions far more rapid than represented by parties' current targets.[64] The temperature goal will, through the Agreement's five-year ambition cycle (discussed in Section V.C.), and the commitment by parties to communicate a target every five years in response to that cycle, provide an overall policy direction for the regime. The Paris Agreement's temperature goal is complemented by 'long term goals' for adaptation and resilience, and for financial flows to be reoriented, consistent with mitigation and adaptation objectives.[65] While these finance and adaptation goals are qualitative in nature, the global stocktake will focus on all three goals. The long-term temperature goals and the 'pathways' they generate could provide a quantified sense of the level of resources necessary to meet the goals.

[63] Jacob Werksman and Lavanya Rajamani, 'The Legal Character and Operational Relevance of the Paris Agreement's Temperature Goal' *Philosophical Transactions A*, 376 (2018): 2160458.

[64] UN Environment Programme (UNEP), *Emissions Gap Report* (2019).

[65] art 2.1.

B. Principles

The Paris Agreement introduced an important new qualification to the articulation of the UNFCCC's CBDRRC principle—'in the light of different national circumstances'[66]—which represents a compromise between the United States and China,[67] and arguably introduces dynamism in the interpretation of the CBDRRC principle. This shift in the articulation of the CBDRRC principle is reflected in the forms of differentiation now emerging in the climate change regime. The Paris Agreement and the 2018 Rulebook[68] evidence a decisive turn from prescriptive differentiation that matches categories of parties (based on the UNFCCC and Kyoto Annexes) to categories of commitments, towards tailored and nuanced differentiation. Different forms of differentiation are in evidence in different issue areas—from self-differentiation in relation to mitigation, to differentiation based on capacities in relation to transparency.[69] The Paris Agreement also side-steps the use of Annexes, which had proven controversial due to their static nature, as a method of distinguishing between categories of parties.

C. Commitments

The Paris Agreement contains a set of interlocking procedural obligations for all parties, the most significant of which is the obligation to communicate a 'nationally determined contribution' (NDC)[70] every five years,[71] accompanied by information that enhances its clarity, transparency, and understanding,[72] and to account for it.[73] Parties' contributions are 'nationally determined' rather than internationally negotiated, and not subject to obligations of result. Parties are obliged to *submit* NDCs but not to *achieve* their targets or objectives. Parties are obliged, however, to participate in what has come to be characterized as an 'ambition cycle'. The ambition cycle comprises several elements. Parties are obliged to provide information to track progress in implementing and achieving their NDCs, as part of an enhanced transparency framework.[74] Such

[66] arts 2.2, 4.3, 4.19.

[67] The White House, Office of the Press Secretary, 'US-China Joint Announcement on Climate Change, Beijing, China, 12 November 2014' (11 November 2014) para 2.

[68] The full set of decisions agreed to at the 24th COP to the UNFCCC is characterized as the 'Paris Rulebook' <https://unfccc.int/process-and-meetings/the-paris-agreement/paris-agreement-work-programme/katowice-climate-package> accessed 4 February 2020.

[69] See further Lavanya Rajamani, 'Ambition and Differentiation in the 2015 Paris Agreement: Interpretative Possibilities and Underlying Politics' *International and Comparative Law Quarterly*, 65/2 (2016): 493.

[70] art 4.2.

[71] art 4.9.

[72] art 4.8.

[73] art 4.13.

[74] art 13.7; Decision 18/CMA.1, 'Modalities, procedures and guidelines for the transparency framework for action and support referred to in Article 13 of the Paris Agreement' (19 March 2019) UN Doc FCCC/PA/CMA/2018/3/Add.2, 18.

information flows into a 'global stocktake' scheduled every five years,[75] and also into a facilitative implementation and compliance mechanism.[76] Although parties' contributions are nationally determined, there are normative expectations attached to these NDCs. Parties are expected to ensure that every successive NDC represents a 'progression' on its last, its 'highest possible ambition' and its 'common but differentiated responsibilities and respective capabilities', 'in light of different national circumstances'.[77] Developed countries are also expected to put forward NDCs that reflect their leadership role in the climate regime.[78]

The Paris Agreement significantly elaborates the Convention's provisions on adaptation. It establishes a 'global goal' to strengthen resilience and reduce vulnerability to climate change and provides parties with multiple modalities, including through their NDCs, to communicate how they intend to contribute to achieving this goal.[79] The Paris Agreement also codifies work begun under the Convention on 'loss and damage'—the adverse effects of climate change including extreme weather events and slow onset events such as sea level rise and desertification. Under Article 8 of the Agreement, parties commit to work together to avert, minimize, and address these effects, including through the work of a constituted body. Parties recognized the importance of loss and damage in this article on the understanding, expressed in a parallel COP decision, that Article 8 'does not involve or provide a basis for any liability or compensation'.[80]

In relation to the provision and mobilization of climate finance, the Paris Agreement follows the UNFCCC template with developed countries taking the lead.[81] The decision accompanying the Paris Agreement reflects an agreement to continue the collective developed countries' goal of mobilizing through 2025 USD 100 billion per year from public and private sources to support developing countries in the context of meaningful mitigation actions and transparency on implementation. Parties also agreed to set before 2025, a 'new collective quantified goal' from this USD 100 billion floor.[82] This collective mobilization goal for the post-2025 period is not restricted to developed countries.[83]

The Paris Rulebook adopted at the 2018 Katowice climate conference, comprises various modalities, procedures, and guidelines that elaborate the parties' obligations under the Paris Agreement, and flesh out the Agreement's procedures and mechanisms,

[75] art 14; Decision 19/CMA.1, 'Matters relating to Article 14 of the Paris Agreement and paragraphs 99–101 of decision 1/CP.21' (19 March 2019) UN Doc FCCC/PA/CMA/2018/3/Add.2, 53.

[76] art 15; Decision 20/CMA.1, 'Modalities and procedures for the effective operation of the committee to facilitate implementation and promote compliance referred to in Article 15, paragraph 2, of the Paris Agreement' (19 March 2019) UN Doc FCCC/PA/CMA/2018/3/Add.2, 59.

[77] art 4.3.

[78] art 4.4.

[79] art 7.

[80] Decision 1/CP.21, 'Adoption of the Paris Agreement' (29 January 2016) UN Doc FCCC/CP/2015/10/Add.1, para 51.

[81] art 9.

[82] Decision 1/CP.21 (n 80) para 53.

[83] Ibid.

including the transparency framework, the global stocktake, and the implementation and compliance mechanism.

The beating heart of the Paris Agreement is its enhanced transparency framework. Although the Paris Agreement offers parties considerable flexibility in determining the content of their NDCs, it seeks to restrain and direct the discretion they have, and generate the necessary pressure to ratchet up their NDCs by, inter alia, requiring parties to provide information to enhance the clarity, transparency, and understanding of their NDCs,[84] as well as track progress in implementing and achieving their NDCs.[85] The discretion parties have is reflected in the NDCs submitted thus far in which there are several types of targets, including absolute economy-wide GHG mitigation targets, targets reflecting a deviation from 'business as usual' emissions growth, sectoral targets, emissions intensity targets, and policies and actions. There are also differences in the reference points for the targets captured in the NDCs as well as in the scope and coverage of GHGs. While all parties must report every two years on their national inventories of GHG emissions, some parties have chosen 'non-GHG' elements of their NDCs, including targets to increase deployment of renewable energy. At the insistence of oil exporting developing countries, the Agreement also provides that parties may commit to emissions reductions as 'co-benefits resulting from Parties' adaptation actions and/or economic diversification plans'.[86] Such differences make it challenging to aggregate and compare the efforts of parties.

The Paris Rulebook provides a detailed list of informational elements to accompany NDCs,[87] and requires parties to identify indicators to assess their progress towards achievement of their NDCs.[88] The Rulebook is deferential, like the Paris Agreement, to 'national determination'. Thus, for instance, parties are required to provide the listed information only 'as applicable' to their NDC.[89] The Rules also permit parties to choose their own qualitative or quantitative indicators to track progress towards implementation and achievement of their NDCs.[90] The rules indicate, but do not prescribe, a list of illustrative indicators that a party 'could include, as appropriate'.[91] The underlying logic and expectation of these requirements is that they will help drive ambitious NDCs, as well as instill accountability for their implementation. The process of collating the required information is expected to build a party's capacity to generate

[84] art 4.8.

[85] art 13.7

[86] art 4.7.

[87] Decision 4/CMA.1, 'Further guidance in relation to the mitigation section of decision 1/CP. 21' (19 March 2019) UN Doc FCCC/PA/CMA/2018/3/Add.1, 6, para 7.

[88] Ibid, annex I.

[89] Decision 4/CMA.1 (n 87) para 7.

[90] Decision 18/CMA.1 (n 74) annex, para 65.

[91] Ibid, annex, para 66; see generally Jolene Lin and Alexander Zahar (eds), *Climate Law*, 9/1–2 (2019) (Special Issue on the Paris Rulebook); Lavanya Rajamani and Daniel Bodansky, 'The Paris Rulebook: Balancing Prescriptiveness with Flexibility' *International and Comparative Law Quarterly*, 68/4 (2019): 1023.

relevant data, encourage consultations with stakeholders, and generate robust analysis that strengthens the evidence-base for future NDCs. Further, in providing detailed information relating to their NDCs, parties are in effect opening up their NDC and its implementation to formal and informal peer review, scrutiny by non-state actors, and assessments by epistemic communities.[92]

The Paris Agreement, and the Rulebook, also enhance the level and quality of transparency on finance. The Paris Agreement obliges developed countries to biennially communicate 'indicative quantitative and qualitative information' in relation to provision and mobilization of finance.[93] The Rulebook reiterates this obligation, and recommends that parties submit specific listed types of information.[94] 'Other Parties' (understood as China and the Gulf countries that provide 'South-South' assistance), are encouraged to provide or continue to provide such resources and to communicate information on these resources biennially.[95] This information will feed into the global stocktake of collective progress.[96]

The transparency framework, with regard to mitigation and the provision of support, is backed by a three-part accountability system: (1) an expert review process with the purpose of 'tracking progress towards achieving' NDCs, and a mandate to 'identify areas of improvement'; (2) a multilateral consideration or peer review process that will consider each Party's respective 'implementation and achievement' of its NDC; and (3) a mechanism to facilitate implementation and compliance with (all provisions) of the Agreement, under a Standing Committee of experts that will operate in a 'facilitative, non-intrusive, non-punitive manner, respectful of national sovereignty, and avoid placing undue burden on Parties'. Together, these procedures provide an evidence base of whether parties are performing against their commitments and create regular moments of institutionalised political accountability for progress at the international and domestic level.

D. Market Mechanisms

Article 6 of the Paris Agreement builds on the experience of the Kyoto Protocol by recognizing that some parties may choose to cooperate in implementing their NDCs through international carbon markets. Unlike Kyoto, Paris does not create a common unit for international emissions trading but instead provides that such trading must allow for higher ambition in mitigation and adaptation, and promote sustainable

92 See generally Chapter 40, 'Epistemic Communities', in this volume.

93 art 9.5.

94 Decision 12/CMA.1, 'Identification of the information to be provided by Parties in accordance with Article 9, paragraph 5, of the Paris Agreement' (19 March 2019) UN Doc FCCC/PA/CMA/2018/3/Add.1, 35.

95 arts 9.2, 9.5.

96 art 9.6.

development and environmental integrity. Rules to ensure that more than one party does not use the same unit to demonstrate compliance with its NDC[97] ('double counting') are under negotiation.

Like the Kyoto Protocol, the Paris Agreement establishes a mechanism for the international certification of emissions reductions generated by activities hosted in one party for use by that party or traded internationally for use by any other party towards achieving its NDC. Unlike the Kyoto Protocol's CDM, activities certified under the Paris mechanism can be hosted by any party (including developed country parties). How this mechanism will operate and how parties will account for the transfer and use of these units are under negotiation.

VI. INCREASING REACH AND INFLUENCE OF THE UN CLIMATE CHANGE REGIME

The UN climate regime, by itself, is not adequate to the onerous task of addressing climate change within the narrow window of opportunity left to avert the most dangerous climate impacts. In particular, given the direction it has taken towards national determination and flexibility, there is little prospect that the regime by itself can ensure that parties' commitments are ratcheted up over time to the level necessary to meet the 'well below 2°C' temperature goal. The UN climate regime, however, is more than the sum of its parts.

In addition to its directive role in relation to states, the UN climate regime offers a useful hook for national courts, tribunals, and bodies to peg efforts to compel more ambitious national action. The most successful case thus far is *Urgenda Foundation v The State of Netherlands* in which the Dutch Supreme Court, finding the Dutch government's current efforts to be less than its fair share to meet the goals of the international climate regime, ordered the Dutch government to ensure that Dutch GHG emissions are at least 25% below 1990 levels by the year 2020.[98] In the United Kingdom, the group 'Plan B' sought a review of the United Kingdom's 2050 target to bring it in line with the goals of the Paris Agreement.[99] Although the case was dismissed on appeal, the UK Climate

[97] Including in relation to units that have been used for other international purposes, such as for compliance with the carbon offset scheme being developed by the International Civil Aviation Organization.

[98] *The State of the Netherlands (Ministry of Economic Affairs and Climate Policy) v Stichting Urgenda* (Judgement of 20 December 2019) No 19/00135, ECLI:NL:HR:2019:2007 (Supreme Court of the Netherlands).

[99] *The Queen on the Application of Plan B. Earth v The Secretary of State for Business and Energy and Industrial Strategy* (Order of 22 January 2019) No C1/2018/1750 (EWCA Civ).

Change Committee commenced a review of the 2050 target thereafter, and in 2019 announced a 2050 net zero emissions target.[100]

The UN climate regime has also provided impetus for cases against fossil-fuel companies for their role in causing dangerous climate change. In a case brought by Greenpeace and others against fifty large fossil-fuel companies, characterized as the 'Carbon Majors', before the Philippines Human Rights Commission,[101] the Commission found that the 'Carbon Majors' played a clear role in anthropogenic climate change and could be held liable for its impacts.[102] In a similar vein, a German court is currently hearing a case brought by a Peruvian farmer against the energy company, RWE, the second largest producer of GHGs in Europe, for damage caused to his Andean home, as a result of climate change.[103] And a French court is hearing a case brought by civil society groups and local authorities against the energy company, 'Total', for its failure to align its actions to the goals of the Paris Agreement.[104] These cases, whether or not successful in courts, have catalyzed climate ambition in some countries, and more broadly help steer the public conversation on climate ambition.

The UN climate change regime is also beginning to influence and shape international finance flows. For instance, the World Bank's 2018 Environmental and Social Standards requires borrowers to estimate gross GHG emissions for World Bank financed projects, in accordance with rules established under the international climate agreements, and to choose alternatives with lower carbon emissions.[105] Even private finance flows are increasingly influenced by voluntary carbon disclosure requirements.[106]

And, finally, the UN climate regime is also playing a catalytic and facilitative role in relation to sub-state and non-state actors.[107] Non-state actors are engaged in a wide range of voluntary climate actions. To record, recognize, and incentivize such non-state actor contributions, the UNFCCC Secretariat, Peru, and France launched the Global Climate Action portal in 2014. This portal records climate actions, with entries from more than 10,700 cities from 191 countries, 4,549 companies, 1,149 investors, and 1,983 organizations to date.[108] In 2015, parties began appointing

[100] Megan Darby, 'UK unveils 2050 net zero carbon target, in a first for a major economy' *Climate Change News* (11 June 2019).

[101] Greenpeace, Petition Requesting for Investigation of the Responsibility of the Carbon Majors for Human Rights Violations or Threats of Violations resulting from the Impacts of Climate Change <https://climatecasechart.com/non-us-case/in-re-greenpeace-southeast-asia-et-al/> accessed 4 February 2020.

[102] Isabella Kaminski, 'Carbon majors can be held liable for human rights violations, Philippines Commission rules' *Climate Liability News* (9 December 2019).

[103] 'Peruvian farmer takes on German energy giant RWE' *Deutsche Welle* (6 December 2019).

[104] 'French climate alliance takes legal action against Total' *AP News* (28 January 2020).

[105] The World Bank, 'Environmental and Social Framework' (2017) 15, 'Standard 1. Assessment and Management of Environmental and Social Risks and Impacts'.

[106] See <https://www.cdp.net/en> accessed 4 February 2020.

[107] See Thomas Hale, '"All Hands on Deck": The Paris Agreement and Nonstate Climate Action' *Global Environmental Politics*, 16/3 (2016): 12.

[108] See <https://climateaction.unfccc.int/> accessed 16 April 2021.

climate champions to connect the work of governments with that of non-state actors.[109]

Non-state climate actions complement, bolster, and strengthen NDCs. Indeed, some estimate that their actions could be instrumental in bridging the emissions gap to 2°C pathways.[110] Non-state climate actions could also take the place of state action, where the prevailing political forces are aligned against meaningful state action. For instance, the 'we are still in' coalition of American leaders—mayors, county executives, governors, tribal leaders, college and university leaders, businesses, faith groups, and investors—pledged to meet the US NDC, even in the face of the announced withdrawal of the US from the Paris Agreement in 2017.[111]

Non-state actors play a crucial role in the emerging climate change regime, as they can help review, demand, and ultimately compel governments to undertake adequate climate actions, something the climate change regime, as currently designed, cannot do. The climate change regime plays a synergistic role, however, as its transparency requirements provide these groups with considerable information for use in their public awareness campaigns. Further, it allows domestic groups to leverage the international regime, in particular its temperature goal, to galvanize domestic action.

VII. CONCLUSION: THE EFFECTIVENESS AND FUTURE OF THE UN CLIMATE REGIME

The future of the UN climate regime, and the fate of the ecosystems and species that have evolved on the planet as we know it, hang in the balance. Although the Paris Agreement entered into force in record time, at least some geo-political forces that led to its conclusion, have changed since, reflected in particular in the withdrawal, albeit temporary, of the United States from the Paris Agreement, and the rise of climate-agnostic political leadership in Brazil. Parties concluded most of the rules to operationalise the Paris Agreement in 2018, amidst considerable political uncertainty, but the rules to operationalize markets under Article 6 of the Paris Agreement are yet to be finalized. And, the COVID-19 pandemic has affected both the pace of the negotiations as well as the ability of states, given the economic downturn it triggered, to respond to the climate crisis.

The Paris Agreement relies for its effectiveness on voluntary upward movement of NDCs over time—a gradual bridging of the gap between the aggregate effect of the current NDCs and that needed to put the world on a pathway to meeting the goals of the Paris Agreement. The UNEP Emissions Gap Report 2019 finds that '[c]ountries must

[109] UNFCCC, 'Meet the Champions' <https://unfccc.int/climate-action/marrakech-partnership/actors/meet-the-champions> accessed 4 February 2020.

[110] UNEP, *Emissions Gap Report* (2018) XIX–XXI, para 5.

[111] See <https://www.wearestillin.com/> accessed 4 February 2020. See generally Chapter 39, 'Sub-National Actors', in this volume.

increase their NDC ambitions threefold to achieve the well below 2°C goal and more than fivefold to achieve the 1.5°C goal.'[112] This gap in mitigation ambition is matched by gaps in adaptation, and support as well, with some estimating the climate financing need as USD 1.5 trillion annually, only a fraction of which is now in place.[113] And, gaps in mitigation will have a direct effect on the extent of the adaptation challenge, which has largely been left to national governments, many under-resourced, to address.

The Paris Agreement, given its regulatory approach, and the politics that necessitated that approach, cannot by itself bridge these gaps, or meet its long-term goals. Many regimes and actors play a critical complementary role. Treaties such as the 1987 Montreal Protocol, and institutions such as the International Civil Aviation Organization (ICAO) are playing an important role in reducing GHGs. Actors other than states—among others, cities, mayors, national courts, business, industry, universities, civil society organizations, epistemic communities, youth groups—are generating considerable demand for as well as delivering climate action and ambition. There is also increasing decentralization, fostered by the Paris Agreement's architecture, and mainstreaming of climate factors into regional and national planning and implementation.

Ultimately however the scale of the challenge—requiring 'rapid and far-reaching transitions' across the global economy 'unprecedented in terms of scale'—and the magnitude of the emissions gap is such that bridging it may well require use of 'carbon dioxide removal' or negative emissions technologies such as solar radiation management and ocean fertilization.[114] Indeed, the IPCC's 1.5°C report assumes this for many of its scenarios. These technologies are inadequately governed under international law, and untouched by the climate change regime. The scale of the challenge also requires dramatic shifts in political will, in particular among major emitters such as the United States and Brazil. Whether this will occur in time to capture the narrow window of opportunity for effective climate action remains to be seen. The Paris Agreement represents an anthropogenic response in the Anthropocene era, in which the human species is determining not just its own future but the future of all species. The potential of this latest international legal instrument to address this challenge is fragile and as yet untested.

BIBLIOGRAPHY

Daniel Bodansky, Jutta Brunnée, and Lavanya Rajamani, *International Climate Change Law* (OUP 2017)

Cinnamon Carlarne, Kevin Gray, and Richard Tarasofsky (eds), *The Oxford Handbook of International Climate Change Law* (OUP 2016)

[112] 2019 Emissions Gap Report (n 64) X.

[113] UNFCCC, 'Bridging climate ambition and finance gaps' *UN Climate Press Release* (13 November 2017).

[114] IPCC, *Global Warming of 1.5°C* (n 6) Summary for Policymakers, SPMs C.2, C.3.

Daniel Klein *et al* (eds), *The Paris Agreement on Climate Change: Analysis and Commentary* (OUP 2017)

Lavanya Rajamani, *Innovation and Experimentation in the International Climate Change Regime* (vol 41, *Collected Courses of the Hague Academy of International Law (Recueil des Cours)*, Brill 2020)

Rosemary Rayfuse and Shirley Scott (eds), *International Law in the Era of Climate Change* (Edward Elgar 2012)

CHAPTER 30

FRESHWATER RESOURCES

SALMAN M A SALMAN

I. INTRODUCTION

WATER is a scarce and finite resource, without an alternative, and upon which there is total dependence for survival. Scarcity is evidenced by the fact that only about 2.5% of the water on planet earth is fresh, and less than one-third of that amount is actually available for human use.[1] The challenges facing this scarce and finite amount of water are enormous, with population growth topping the list. The world population grew from 1.6 billion to 6.1 billion during the last century, and surpassed 7.8 billion in 2020. The figure is expected to reach nine billion people by 2050,[2] competing over the same finite amount of water. Hydrological variability, environmental degradation, and climate change are other challenges to water resources, compounded by spatial and temporal variations in water availability.

While the world's population more than tripled during the last century, the aggregate use of water has increased six-fold. These increases have come at high environmental cost. Half the world's rivers and lakes are seriously polluted, 50% of the world's wetlands have disappeared in the last century,[3] and some important rivers do not flow to the sea. Similarly, many of the most important groundwater aquifers are being over-mined, with

[1] Edith Brown Weiss, 'The Coming Water Crisis: A Common Concern of Humankind' *Transnational Environmental Law*, 1/1 (2012):154.

[2] The World Bank, 'World Development Indicators' <https://data.worldbank.org/data-catalog/world-development-indicators> accessed 26 December 2019.

[3] WWF, 'Half of the world's wetlands have disappeared since 1900!' (2 February 2018) <https://wwf.panda.org/?322330/Half-of-the-worlds-wetlands-have-disappeared-since-1900> accessed 28 December 2019. Recent reports indicate that up to 87% of the global wetland resource has been lost since 1700; see Ramsar Convention on Wetlands, 'Global Wetland Outlook: State of the World's Wetlands and their Services to People' (2018) 19; see also 'Groundwater Depletion Stresses Majority of World's Largest Aquifers' (16 June 2015) <https://www.circleofblue.org/2015/world/groundwater-depletion-stresses-majority-of-worlds-largest-aquifers/> accessed 26 December 2019.

water tables already very deep and dropping by metres every year. It should be recalled that close to 300 river basins are shared by two or more states.[4] As noted by the World Commission on Dams, 'these basins cover about 45% of the earth's land surface, account for about 80% of global river flow, and affect about 40% of the world's population'.[5] However, most of these basins are without agreements regulating their management, use, or protection. In the few cases where agreements exist, most of them are not inclusive of all the riparians to that basin.

Moreover, shared watercourses have remained, until very recently, without a global treaty governing their use and protection. As such, the legal regime for shared watercourses is based in large part on customary international law, evidenced by the evolution of rules and principles derived from the practice of states and patterns of treaty principles over many centuries. In addition, there is the work of two scholarly non-governmental organizations—the Institute of International Law (IDI),[6] and the International Law Association (ILA),[7] on shared watercourses. Moreover, a number of decisions by judicial and arbitral tribunals have contributed to the emergence of customary international law principles in this field.

Codification of international water law began only in 1970. On 8 December of that year, the UN General Assembly (UNGA) adopted Resolution 2669 (XXV) asking the International Law Commission (ILC) to start work on a draft convention on the law of the non-navigational uses of international watercourses. The ILC started its work at its twenty-third session in December 1971. After close to a quarter of a century, five rapporteurs, and fifteen reports, the ILC completed its work, adopted the draft United Nations Convention on the Law of the Non-Navigational Uses of International Watercourses (Watercourses Convention), and recommended it to the UNGA in June 1994.[8] It took three more years of deliberations by the UNGA's legal drafting committee, the 'Sixth Committee', acting as a 'Working Group of the Whole', in two contentious sessions, before the UNGA itself finally adopted the Watercourses Convention and opened it for signature on 21 May 1997.[9] It was only in August 2014 that the Convention

[4] William Cosgrove and Frank Rijsberman, *World Water Vision: Making Water Everybody's Business* (Earthscan 2000) 43.

[5] World Commission on Dams, *Dams and Development: A New Framework for Decision-making* (Earthscan 2000) 15.

[6] IDI was established in 1873, and consists of selected invited members. Its objective is 'to promote the progress of international law'; see <http://www.idi-iil.org/en/a-propos/> accessed 26 December 2019.

[7] The ILA was founded in 1873. However, membership of the Association is open to all international lawyers, and is not by invitation. Its objectives are 'the study, clarification and development of international law'; see <http://www.ila-hq.org/> accessed 26 December 2019; see also Slavko Bogdanović, *International Law of Water Resources: Contribution of the International Law Association* (Kluwer Law International 2001).

[8] See *Yearbook of the International Law Commission—1994*, vol II, part 2 (UN 1997) 88.

[9] The Convention is annexed to UNGA Res 51/229, 'Convention on the law of the nonnavigational uses of international watercourses' (8 July 1997) UN Doc A/RES/51/229; it was adopted by a vote of 103 for, and three against (Burundi, China, and Turkey) with twenty-seven abstentions.

entered into force and effect, more than seventeen years after its adoption by the UNGA, and close to forty-five years after adoption of Resolution 2669.[10]

In parallel, the United Nations Economic Commission for Europe (UNECE) Convention on the Protection and Use of Transboundary Watercourses and International Lakes (Water Convention) was adopted in 1992, and entered into force in 1996.[11] In 2003, seven years after entry into force, the Water Convention was amended to allow accession by non-ECE countries. The amendment entered into force on 6 February 2013, ten years later, allowing the regional Water Convention to become a global treaty to which all UN member states can accede. Thus far, Chad, Senegal, and Ghana are the only three non-ECE countries that have become members of the Water Convention. Indeed, Chad and Ghana are the only two countries outside the ECE region that are members of both Conventions; Senegal is not yet a party to the Watercourses Convention.[12] Hence, the world community moved within a short period of time from complete reliance on customary international water law principles to two global treaties on shared watercourses, an unusual situation in the field of international law.

The purpose of this chapter is to trace the evolution of the legal regime for environmental protection of shared watercourses, and to analyse and compare the environmental provisions of these two global Conventions. The chapter will also attempt to discern the influence of the two Conventions on the environmental provisions of subsequent regional and bilateral treaties.

II. EVOLUTION OF CUSTOMARY INTERNATIONAL WATER LAW

The preamble to the Watercourses Convention recalled 'the existing bilateral and multilateral agreements regarding the non-navigational uses of international watercourses'. It also acknowledged 'the valuable contribution of international organizations, both governmental and non-governmental, to the codification and progressive development of international law in this field'. Indeed, the work of the IDI and ILA was influenced by, and has also influenced, bilateral and regional treaties. In addition, decisions by judicial and arbitral tribunals have also contributed to the emergence of customary international environmental law principles on shared watercourses.

[10] As of March 2021, the Watercourses Convention has thirty-seven parties; see Salman M A Salman, 'Entry into Force of the UN Watercourses Convention: Why Should It Matter?' *International Journal of Water Resources Development*, 31/1 (2015): 4.

[11] The UNECE encompasses Europe, Central Asia, North America, and Israel.

[12] As of March 2021, the Water Convention has forty-four parties.

A. Contribution of Non-Governmental International Organizations

Work by the IDI on shared watercourses started relatively earlier than the ILA. The first instrument issued by the IDI was the 1911 Madrid Declaration.[13] The Declaration forbade emptying of injurious matters, such as from factories, into international rivers, thus addressing the issue of pollution of shared watercourses. This obligation against causing pollution was elaborated and refined by the IDI in later resolutions, particularly the 1961 Salzburg Resolution,[14] and the 1979 Athens Resolution on the Environment.[15]

Similarly, starting in 1954, the ILA issued a number of statements and rules on shared rivers. These statements are based on the principle of equitable and reasonable utilization which was elaborated in the ILA's Helsinki Rules in 1966. The Helsinki Rules also addressed the issue of pollution of international watercourses, defining water pollution to refer 'to any detrimental change resulting from human conduct in the natural composition, content or quality of the waters of an international drainage basin'.[16] The Rules require each basin state to take all reasonable measures to abate existing water pollution, and to prevent any new form of water pollution, or any increase in the degree of existing pollution in an international drainage basin which would cause substantial injury in the territory of a co-basin state.

The Helsinki Rules were based mainly on the principle of equitable and reasonable utilization, and included no reference to the obligation against causing harm.[17] Although declarations and resolutions of the IDI and ILA have no legally binding force, the Helsinki Rules remained—until the adoption of the Watercourses Convention thirty years later—the single, most authoritative, widely quoted and relied-upon set of rules for regulating the uses and protection of international watercourses. Professor Bourne noted in this regard that the Helsinki Rules were soon accepted by the international community as customary international law.[18]

As indicated above, while the IDI emphasized the obligation against causing harm, the ILA embraced the principle of equitable utilization. Nevertheless, both organizations

[13] 'International Regulations Regarding the Use of International Watercourses for Purposes Other than Navigation, 1911' *Annuaire de l'Institut de Droit International* 24 (1911): 365.

[14] 'Resolution on the Utilization of Non-Maritime International Waters (Except for Navigation)' *Annuaire de l'Institut de Droit International*, 49 (1961): 370.

[15] 'Resolution on The Pollution of Rivers and Lakes and International Law' *Annuaire de l'Institut de Droit International*, 58 (1979): 196.

[16] ILA, 'Report of the fifty-second conference held at Helsinki from 14-20 August 1966' (1967) 477, 'Helsinki Rules on the Uses of the Waters of International Rivers', art IX.

[17] For a detailed account of the work of the ILA in this field see Charles Bourne, 'The International Law Association's Contribution to International Water Resources Law' *Natural Resources Journal*, 36/2 (1996): 155.

[18] Ibid, 215; see also Slavko Bogdanović, 'The International Law Association Helsinki Rules—Contribution to International Water Law' *Brill Research Perspectives in International Water Law* 3/4 (2018) 1.

adopted broad principles for protection of the environment of shared watercourses, and have thus made major contributions in this field.

B. Contribution of Bilateral and Regional Treaties and Soft Law Instruments

Bilateral and multilateral treaties dealing with the environmental aspects of international rivers can also be traced to the beginning of last century. As early as 1909, the United States and Canada agreed, as part of the treaty relating to their boundary waters, that such waters and the waters flowing across their boundaries shall not be polluted on either side to the injury of health or property of the other.[19]

The 1923 Geneva Convention Relating to the Development of Hydraulic Power Affecting More Than One State dealt with the right of any riparian state to carry out on its territory any operations for the development of hydraulic power subject to 'the limits of international law'.[20] Such limits have been interpreted to mean the obligation of the state not to cause significant harm to other states, as elaborated twenty-six years later by the International Court of Justice (ICJ) in the *Corfu Channel* case.[21]

In 1950, the International Commission for the Protection of the Rhine (ICPR) was formed by Germany, France, Luxembourg, the Netherlands, and Switzerland to control pollution of the River through their cooperative action.[22] A series of agreements aimed at protecting the Rhine followed, including the 1976 Convention for the Protection of the Rhine Against Chemical Pollution.

Outside Europe and North America, the Amazonian Cooperation Treaty was concluded in 1978 by the eight riparian states of the Amazon river (Bolivia, Brazil, Colombia, Ecuador, Guyana, Peru, Suriname, and Venezuela) with the overall objective of emphasizing the necessity of maintaining a balance between economic growth and conservation of the environment.

In addition to these agreements, mention should also be made of the contribution of soft law instruments on the protection of the environment of freshwater resources issued at international conferences. The 1972 UN Stockholm Conference on the

[19] Treaty Relating to the Boundary Waters and Questions Arising Along the Boundary Between the United States and Canada, art 2.

[20] art 1.

[21] *Corfu Channel case (UK/Albania)* (Judgement) [1949] ICJ Rep 4, 22 where the court stated that it is 'every State's obligation not to allow knowingly its territory to be used for acts contrary to the rights of other States'.

[22] For the history of the Rhine Commission see Götz Reichert, 'Transboundary Water Cooperation in Europe—A Successful Multidimensional Regime?' *Brill Research Perspectives in International Water Law*, 1/1 (2016) 1.

Human Environment identified water as one of the natural resources that needed to be safeguarded 'for the benefit of the present and future generations through careful management and planning'.[23]

Twenty years later, the UN Conference on Environment and Development was held in Rio de Janeiro, Brazil, in June 1992 (the Rio Summit). Agenda 21 of the Rio Summit Program of Action for Sustainable Development included a separate chapter (Chapter 18) on freshwater resources. The overall objective of the Program was 'to satisfy the fresh water needs of all countries for their sustainable development'. Realizing the potential effects of such a statement on the environment, the Program added, 'Water resources have to be protected, taking into account the functioning of aquatic ecosystems and the perenniality of the resources, in order to satisfy and reconcile needs for water in human activities'.[24]

C. Contribution of Judicial and Arbitral Decisions

In addition to the above, decisions by judicial and arbitral tribunals have also contributed to the evolution of customary international water law. In 1941, the Arbitration Tribunal in the *Trail Smelter* dispute between the United States and Canada concluded that 'no state has the right to use or permit the use of its territory in such a manner as to cause injury by fumes in or to the territory of another or the properties or persons therein'.[25] This rule was soon extended and applied to shared watercourses.

In 1957 the Arbitration Tribunal in the *Lake Lanoux* case ruled that France was entitled to use the waters of Lake Lanoux, which it shares with Spain, but could not ignore Spain's interests; and that Spain was entitled to demand that Spanish rights be respected, and its interests be taken into account.[26]

Clearly, the work of the ILC on the Watercourses Convention, as well as the UNECE work on the Water Convention, both grew out of rich historical traditions, including a considerable body of customary international law in the field of shared watercourses and their environment.[27]

[23] UN, 'Report of the United Nations Conference on the Human Environment' (5–16 June 1972) UN Doc A/CONF.48/14/Rev.1, 3, ch 1—'Declaration of the United Nations Conference on the Human Environment'.

[24] *Report of the United Nations Conference on Environment and Development* (UN 1993) vol I, annex II, 'Agenda 21'.

[25] *Trail Smelter Arbitration (US/Canada)* (1938 and 1941) 3 RIAA 1905, 1965.

[26] *Lake Lanoux Arbitration (Spain/France)* (1957) 12 RIAA 281.

[27] See Stephen McCaffrey, *The Law of International Watercourses: Non-Navigational Uses* (2nd edn, OUP 2007).

III. ENVIRONMENTAL PROVISIONS OF THE WATERCOURSES CONVENTION

A. The Principle of Equitable Utilization and the No Harm Rule

The environmental provisions of the Watercourses Convention must be seen against the backdrop of the larger debate on the relationship between the no harm rule, a cornerstone principle of international environmental law,[28] and the principle of equitable and reasonable utilization, which has played a central role in the law on international freshwater resources. It should be noted, in this context, that lower riparians tend to favour the no harm rule as they see it as protecting existing uses against impacts resulting from activities undertaken by upstream states. Conversely, upper riparians tend to favour the equitable utilization principle, because they believe it provides more scope for states to utilize their share of the watercourse for activities that may impact on downstream states.

Agreement on which rule takes priority had thus proven difficult, and the issue occupied the ILC throughout its work on the topic. After the ILC completed its work, the resulting draft articles were considered by the Sixth Committee. The compromise regarding the relationship between the two principles, now contained in Article 5 (equitable and reasonable utilization and participation) and Article 7 (obligation not to cause significant harm), requires the state that causes significant harm to take measures to eliminate or mitigate such harm 'having due regard to' the principle of equitable and reasonable utilization. As Lucius Caflisch noted:

> The new formula was considered by a number of lower riparians to be sufficiently neutral not to suggest a subordination of the no-harm rule to the principle of equitable and reasonable utilization. A number of upper riparians thought just the contrary, namely that, that formula was strong enough to support the idea of such a subordination.[29]

Despite the adoption of the Convention by a large majority with this compromise language, the issue seems far from resolved for some states on both sides of the debate. It is noteworthy that the three countries that voted against the Convention (Burundi, China, and Turkey) and some of those that abstained, such as Bolivia, Ethiopia, Mali, and Tanzania, are upper riparian states. Still, a number of downstream states, such as

[28] See Chapter 16, 'Harm Prevention', in this volume.

[29] See Lucius Caflisch, 'Regulation of the Uses of International Watercourses' in Salman M A Salman and Boisson de Chazournes (eds), *International Watercourses—Enhancing Cooperation and Managing Conflict* (World Bank Technical Paper No 414, 1998) 15.

Egypt, France, Pakistan, and Peru, also abstained. The perception by some upstream riparians that the Convention is biased in favour of downstream riparians, and vice versa, still lingers in the minds of a number of riparians, despite the entry into force of the Convention in 2014.

Nevertheless, a close reading of Articles 5, 6, and 7 would lead to the conclusion that the Convention has indeed subordinated the obligation not to cause significant harm to the principle of equitable and reasonable utilization. Some of the factors for determining equitable and reasonable utilization under Article 6 (namely existing and potential uses, and the effects of the uses of the watercourse by one state on other states) relate to the causing of harm. Moreover, Article 7 on the obligation not to cause significant harm is qualified by Articles 5 and 6, and further stipulates that the causing of harm may be tolerated in certain cases, such as when the possibility of compensation may be considered.

It should be pointed out in this regard that it is now widely acknowledged that harm is actually a two-way matter with regards to the issue of quantitative allocation of the waters of shared rivers. Just as upstream riparians can harm downstream ones through storage, diversion, and use of the waters of the shared rivers, downstream riparians can also harm upstream riparians by foreclosing their future uses of the shared waters through the prior use of, and the claiming of rights to such water, and invoking the no harm obligation.[30]

Hence, the no harm obligation has been subordinated to the principle of equitable and reasonable utilization, and the obligation applies to both downstream as well as upstream riparians.

B. Protection, Preservation, and Management of Watercourses Ecosystems

As stated above, the general rule laid down in Article 7 of the Watercourses Convention regarding the obligation not to cause significant harm applies both to the quantity and quality of the waters of the international watercourse, and is a basic principle of customary law. The causing of harm could result from a decrease in the flow of the quantity of waters, as well as from adversely affecting the quality of such waters and the environment of the watercourse itself. The Watercourses Convention addresses these environmental issues in Articles 20 to 23 of Part IV on 'Protection, Preservation and Management'.

[30] For a detailed analysis of this matter, see Salman M A Salman, 'The Obligation Against Causing Harm' in Boisson de Chazournes *et al* (eds), *The UN Convention on the Law of the Non-Navigational Uses of International Watercourses: A Commentary* (OUP 2018) 115; see also Salman M A Salman, 'Downstream Riparians Can also Harm Upstream Riparians: The Concept of Foreclosure of Future Uses' *Water International*, 35/4 (2010): 350.

Article 20 requires the watercourse states individually, and, where appropriate, jointly, to protect and preserve the ecosystems of the international watercourse. The obligation is broad because it relates to the entire ecosystems of the watercourse. Such ecosystems go beyond water, and include the fauna and flora, as well as the land contiguous to the watercourse, which should be used in a manner that would not harm the watercourse. The concept of the ecosystem, as noted by one expert, 'is and should be a broad one, its main function in ecological thought being to emphasize obligatory relationships, interdependence and causal relationships'.[31]

Article 21 requires watercourse states to prevent, reduce, and control pollution that may cause significant harm to other watercourse states or to their environment, including harm to human health or safety, to the use of the waters for any beneficial purposes, or to the living resources of the watercourse. The article also obliges the watercourse states to consult with each other with the view to arriving at mutually agreeable measures and methods to prevent, reduce, and control pollution. Consultation would cover matters such as setting water quality objectives and criteria, establishing techniques and practices to address pollution from point and non-point sources, and establishing lists of substances the introduction of which into the watercourse is to be prohibited, limited, investigated, or monitored. Pollution is defined under Article 21 to mean any detrimental alteration in the composition or quality of the waters of an international watercourse that results directly or indirectly from human conduct.

Article 22 requires watercourse states to take all measures necessary to prevent the introduction into an international watercourse of alien or new species that may have effects detrimental to the ecosystem of the watercourse, resulting in significant harm to other watercourse states.

Finally, marine environmental protection is dealt with under Article 23. This article obliges watercourse states to take all measures with respect to an international watercourse that are necessary to protect and preserve the marine environment, including estuaries, taking into account generally accepted international rules and standards.

A number of observations can be made with regards to these four articles outlining the environmental obligations of the watercourse states.

First, whereas the obligation to protect and preserve the ecosystems of the international watercourse under Article 20 is unqualified, the obligations with regard to pollution, introduction of alien species, and protection of the marine environment in Articles 21, 22, and 23, respectively, are qualified in different respects. Articles 21 and 22 establish 'significant harm' as the threshold, whereas under Article 23, the watercourse states are required to take into account generally accepted international rules and standards. A Statement of Understanding issued by the Sixth Committee, convening as the Working Group of the Whole, clarified that the term 'significant' is not used in

[31] Professor Odum, quoted in David Hunter *et al*, *International Environmental Law and Policy* (Foundation Press 1998) 842.

the Convention in the sense of 'substantial', and that while the effect 'must be capable of being established by objective evidence and not be trivial in nature, it need not rise to the level of being substantial'. Another Statement of Understanding clarified that Articles 21, 22, and 23 'impose a due diligence standard on watercourse States'.[32] It is widely agreed that the obligation under Article 20 is also of due diligence character, and thus is qualified, at least in this sense.[33]

Second, Articles 20, 21, and 23 require action by the watercourse states individually and, only where appropriate, jointly. As such, there is no obligation for collective action. The Watercourses Convention does not require establishment of joint management mechanisms. Rather, it obliges watercourse states, at the request of any of them, 'to enter into consultations concerning the management of an international watercourse, which may include the establishment of a joint management mechanism'.[34]

Third, Article 23 on protection and preservation of the marine environment extends the possibility of cooperation to other states that do not share the watercourse. This is important, and necessary, given that acts by either group of states could adversely affect the other, or the marine environment.

It can accordingly be concluded that the Watercourses Convention has contributed substantially to the international environmental regime of shared watercourses through codification of some basic customary principles. Moreover, the Convention has had considerable influence in subsequent watercourses agreements, such as the 2000 Revised Protocol on Shared Watercourses in the Southern African Development Community (SADC),[35] and the 1995 Agreement on the Cooperation and Sustainable Development of the Mekong River Basin, discussed later in this chapter.

The influence and relevance of the Watercourses Convention has also been underscored by the ICJ in the *Gabcikovo-Nagymaros* case, decided in September 1997, four months after adoption of the Convention by the UNGA.[36] The case provided an opportunity for the ICJ to address a wide range of international legal issues, including the law of treaties, state responsibility, environmental law, and the concept of sustainable development, as well as international watercourses.

With regards to international watercourses in particular, the ICJ quoted from a decision of the Permanent Court of International Justice that the 'community of interest

[32] Due diligence has been defined as 'the diligence to be expected from a good government, i.e. from a government mindful of its international obligations'; see Pierre-Marie Dupuy, 'Due Diligence in International Law of Liability' in *Legal Aspects of Transfrontier Pollution* (OECD 1977) 369.

[33] See Malgosia Fitzmaurice, 'General Principles Governing the Cooperation between States in Relation to Non-Navigational Uses of International Watercourses' *Yearbook of International Environmental Law*, 14 (2003): 3.

[34] art 8.2.

[35] The 2000 Protocol revised and replaced the 1995 SADC Protocol on Shared Watercourses, specifically to make the Revised Protocol consistent with the Watercourses Convention.

[36] *The Gabčíkovo-Nagymaros Project (Hungary/Slovakia)* (Judgement) [1997] ICJ Rep 7 (Gabčíkovo-Nagymaros case).

in a navigable river becomes the basis of a common legal right, the essential features of which are the perfect equality of all riparian States in the uses of the whole course of the river and the exclusion of any preferential privilege of one riparian State in relation to the others'.[37] In this connection, the ICJ added that modern development of international law has strengthened this principle for non-navigational uses of international watercourses as well, 'as evidenced by the adoption of the Convention of 21 May 1997 on the Law of the Non-Navigational Uses of International Watercourses by the United Nations General Assembly'.[38] Furthermore, the ICJ emphasized the concept of equitable and reasonable utilization when it directed that 'the multi-purpose programme, in the form a co-ordinated single unit, for the use, development and protection of the watercourse is implemented in an equitable and reasonable manner'.[39]

The ICJ reconfirmed this approach in 2010 in the *Pulp Mills* case between Argentina and Uruguay.[40] Commenting on the River Uruguay Statute 1975 which both parties relied on, the ICJ opined that the Statute 'embodies the interconnectedness between equitable and reasonable utilization of a shared resource and the balance between economic development and environmental protection that is the essence of sustainable development'.[41]

In both cases, the ICJ confirmed that equitable and reasonable utilization is indeed the guiding principle of international water law which has to be balanced by environmental protection.

IV. ENVIRONMENTAL PROVISIONS OF THE WATER CONVENTION

It should be stated at the outset that the environmental provisions of the Water Convention are more elaborate in scope when compared with the provisions of the Watercourses Convention. This is due, as discussed in Section V, to the original regional nature of the Water Convention, as compared with the global one of the Watercourses Convention.

Article 3 of the Water Convention obliges the parties to take all appropriate measures to prevent, control, and reduce any transboundary impact. It goes on to require the parties to take all appropriate measures to prevent, control, and reduce pollution of waters causing or likely to cause transboundary impact, and to ensure that transboundary waters are used with the aim of ecologically sound and rational water

[37] See *Case relating to the Territorial Jurisdiction of International Commission of the River Oder (United Kingdom et al/Poland)* (Judgement of 10 September 1929) PCIJ Rep Series A, No 23, 27.

[38] Gabčíkovo-Nagymaros case (n 36) [85].

[39] Ibid [150].

[40] *Pulp Mills on the River Uruguay (Argentina/Uruguay)* (Judgement) [2010] ICJ Rep 14, 226.

[41] Ibid [177].

management, and environmental protection. The Water Convention lays down three principles to guide the parties when taking those measures.

The first is the precautionary principle. The principle directs that action to avoid the potential transboundary impact of the release of hazardous substances should not be postponed on the ground that scientific research has not fully proven a causal link between those substances, on the one hand, and the potential transboundary impact, on the other hand.

The second is the polluter pays principle; and the third is the sustainability principle. Under the last principle, water resources should be managed so that the needs of the present generations are met without compromising the ability of future generations to meet their own needs.

It is noteworthy that the Watercourses Convention does not include an explicit reference to either of the first two principles. A reference to sustainability is included in the preamble; as well as in Article 5 on equitable and reasonable utilization. Article 5 requires using and developing the international watercourse 'with a view to attaining optimal and sustainable utilization thereof'.

The Water Convention defines transboundary impact to mean any significant adverse effect on the environment of one state resulting from a change in the conditions of transboundary waters caused by human activity, the physical origin of which is situated wholly or in part within an area under the jurisdiction of another party.[42] The definition goes on to state that such effects on the environment include effects on human health and safety, flora, fauna, soil, air, water, climate, landscape, and historical monuments or other physical structures or the interaction among these factors. They also include effects on the cultural heritage or socio-economic conditions resulting from alterations to those factors.

Furthermore, the Water Convention requires the parties to develop, adopt, and implement legal measures to ensure, inter alia, prior licensing of waste water discharges, limits of waste water discharges based on best available technology, biological treatment for waste water, application of environmental impact assessment and other means of assessment, and minimization of accidental pollution. It also requires exchange of data and information between the parties to cover, inter alia, the environmental conditions of the transboundary waters, emission and monitoring data, and measures taken or planned to be taken to prevent, control, or reduce transboundary impact.[43]

Thus, while the Water Convention revolves around the notion of transboundary impact, and includes an elaborate definition for this term, the Watercourses Convention is crafted around the principle of equitable and reasonable utilization, to be balanced by environmental protection.

[42] See art 1.2.

[43] Attila Tanzi *et al* (eds), *The UNECE Convention on the Protection and Use of Transboundary Watercourses and International Lakes: Its Contribution to International Water Cooperation* (Brill Nijhoff 2015).

V. Comparison of the Environmental Provisions of the Two Conventions

The above discussion shows that the environmental provisions of the Water Convention are more elaborate and comprehensive than those of the Watercourses Convention, and accordingly, it is more protective of the environment. This should be expected, given the global nature of the Watercourses Convention, which dictated taking into account the regional variations and standards on environmental issues. On the other hand, the Water Convention has been adopted in a regional setting, where the environmental standards of the parties are close to each other, and where action by one state could easily affect the environment of other states.

Moreover, the Watercourses Convention is a framework convention, which is to be complemented by agreements among/between the different riparian states. Although this could also be said of the Water Convention, the latter provides more minimum standards and guidelines than the Watercourses Convention.

It should also be noted that while the Water Convention pays more attention to the qualitative aspects of the shared watercourses, the Watercourses Convention is more concerned with the quantitative sharing and use of such waters. This is apparent from the subordination by the Watercourses Convention of the obligation not to cause significant harm to the principle of equitable and reasonable utilization, on the one hand, and the detailed annexes to the Water Convention dealing with water quality objectives and criteria, best environmental practice, and best available technology, on the other hand.

Because it started as a regional treaty, the Water Convention entered into force relatively quickly, four years after its adoption.[44] Following the quick entry into force of the Convention, the parties decided in 2003, as discussed earlier, to amend its provisions to allow countries outside the UNECE region to accede. This amendment has particular relevance and importance to the countries that share borders with the ECE countries, and could also play a role in exporting UNECE standards to other regions of the world.

VI. Influence on Subsequent Bilateral and Multilateral Treaties

A number of bilateral and multilateral treaties have been concluded subsequent to the adoption of the two Conventions. One such treaty is the 'Great Lakes—St. Lawrence River Basin Sustainable Water Resources Agreement' concluded in December 2005 by

[44] It is worth noting in this context that the non-regional members of the UNECE—the US, Canada, and Israel—are not parties to the Water Convention, or to the Watercourses Convention.

the states and provinces sharing the basin.[45] This is indeed an interesting development, given that all the previous agreements on the Great Lakes have been concluded by the United States and Canada, and not their states and provinces. The Agreement requires that lasting economic development be balanced with sustainable water use to ensure that waters are managed responsibly. In this regard the Agreement requires that regional goals and objectives for water conservation and efficiency be developed and reviewed every five years by the Regional Body established under it. Clearly, this Agreement lays down more stringent environmental standards than the previous agreements.

Similarly, the multilateral and bilateral agreements on shared watercourses in Europe that have been entered into after conclusion of the Water Convention apply even more stringent environmental standards than the latter. The Water Convention itself states that its provisions shall not affect the rights of the parties, individually or jointly, to adopt and implement more stringent measures than those set forth in the Convention.[46]

The Convention on Cooperation for the Protection and Sustainable Use of the River Danube that was concluded in 1994, two years after the UNECE Convention was adopted, is an example. Although the Danube Convention sets sustainable development and environmental protection of the Danube as the main objectives of the Convention, it goes beyond the general obligation of preventing, controlling, and reducing transboundary impact. Article 5 of the Danube Convention requires the contracting parties to develop, adopt, and implement legal, administrative, and technical measures to ensure efficient water quality protection and sustainable water use, and thereby also prevent, control, and reduce transboundary impact.

Due regard is paid by the Danube Convention to the protection of the Black Sea and its marine environment from pollution loads from sources in the catchment area of the Danube. The Danube Convention also includes an Annex containing a list of industrial sectors and industries, as well as an additional list of hazardous substances and groups of substances, the discharge of which from point and non-point sources is prevented or considerably reduced. To keep the list current with advances in science and technology, the Convention entrusts the International Commission for the Protection of the Danube with the task of updating the list.

Clearly, the Danube Convention has adapted the environmental provisions of the Water Convention to a specific watercourse context, and has indeed gone beyond the environmental requirements set forth in that Convention.

The 1999 Convention on the Protection of the Rhine also goes beyond requiring the parties to be guided by the precautionary, polluter-pays, and sustainable development principles, which are also set forth in the Water Convention. In addition, the Rhine

[45] Those states are Illinois, Indiana, Michigan, Minnesota, New York, Ohio, Pennsylvania, and Wisconsin in the US, and the Provinces of Ontario and Quebec in Canada. The Agreement is available at <https://docs.ontario.ca/documents/2700/200040.pdf> accessed 26 December 2019.

[46] See art 2.8.

Convention calls for the parties to be guided, inter alia, by the principle of preventive action, the principle of rectification as a priority at source, and application and development of the state of the art and best environmental practice. A number of aims are spelt out in the Rhine Convention. Such aims include conserving, improving, and restoring the most natural habitats possible for wild fauna and flora in the water, on the river bed and banks, and in adjacent areas, and improving living conditions for fish and restoring their free migration. They also include restoring the North Sea in conjunction with the other actions taken to protect it. Indeed, the Rhine can be said to be one of the first watercourses where detailed attention has been paid to the environment, and arguably one of the most environmentally protected watercourses in the world.

The number of multilateral and bilateral agreements dealing with the environment of international watercourses outside Europe and North America has increased considerably in recent years. One regional instrument that has addressed environmental issues in detail is the Revised Protocol on Shared Watercourses in the Southern African Development Community (SADC) which was concluded in August 2000. Article 4.2 on 'Environmental Protection and Preservation' consists of four parts reproducing, in more or less the same wording and order, the four articles of the UN Watercourses Convention dealing with the environment (discussed in Section III).[47]

Similarly, the Agreement on the Cooperation and Sustainable Development of the Mekong River Basin, concluded in April 1995, includes two articles which capture some of the basic environmental provisions for shared watercourses. Article 3 states the agreement of the parties to protect the environment, natural resources, aquatic life and conditions, and ecological balance of the Mekong River from pollution or other harmful effects resulting from any development plans and uses of water and related sources in the basin.[48]

The instruments discussed above present wide-ranging approaches to environmental protection of international watercourses. While the Watercourses Convention and some regional agreements provided the basic requirements for protecting the environment of the shared watercourses, the Water Convention and the other multilateral instruments in Europe and North America have gone a long way towards such protection. Yet, all these instruments incorporate both established principles of international environmental law such as the obligation to reduce and control pollution, as well as other emerging principles that include the obligation to protect and preserve the ecosystems of the international watercourse.

[47] Salman M A Salman, 'Legal Regime for Use and Protection of International Watercourses in the Southern African Development Community: Evolution and Context' *Natural Resources Journal*, 41/4 (2001): 981.

[48] Rémy Kinna and Alistair Rieu-Clarke, 'The Governance Regime of the Mekong River Basin: Can the Global Water Conventions Strengthen the 1995 Mekong Agreement?' *Brill Research Perspectives in International Water Law*, 2/1 (2017) 1.

VII. CONCLUSION

As discussed throughout this chapter, the environmental legal regime for shared watercourses has been based, in large part, until late last century, on customary international law, derived from the practice of states, and patterns of treaty principles over many centuries. With the entry into force of the Watercourses Convention in 2014, and of the amendment to the Water Convention in 2016, the world community moved, within two years, from a no treaty position, to two global treaties in the field of international water law.

The differences in regional standards and practices were one major complicating factor in the lengthy negotiations of the first global treaty—the Watercourses Convention. Accordingly, the Watercourses Convention could only be expected to reflect the minimum standards that could be agreed upon by these different regions/states of the world. On the other hand, the Water Convention incorporated the already existing and advanced, as well as the emerging, ECE region environmental standards.

Yet, despite this distinction between the two instruments, it is widely agreed that the two treaties are compatible, and they actually complement each other by virtue of their positive synergies and effects.[49]

Indeed, subsequent regional and bilateral agreements on shared watercourses have borrowed heavily from the environmental provisions of these two treaties, testifying to, and confirming their immediate and extensive influence, as well as the growing global consensus to respect and protect the environment and ecosystems of shared watercourses. The overarching obligation of states to ensure that activities within their jurisdiction respect the environment of other states, pronounced by the ICJ in the *Gabcikovo-Nagymaros* case, will keep developing with more advances in scientific knowledge of the ecosystems of shared watercourses. In turn, developments and advances in this scientific field will lead, by necessity, to more elaborate, advanced, and stringent agreements on the environmental protection of shared watercourses.

BIBLIOGRAPHY

Charles Bourne, 'The International Law Association's Contribution to International Water Resources Law' *Natural Resources Journal*, 36/2 (1996): 155

Pierre-Marie Dupuy, *Due Diligence in International Law of Liability, in Legal Aspects of Transfrontier Pollution* (OECD 1977)

Stephen McCaffrey, *The Law of International Watercourses: Non-Navigational Uses* (2nd edn, OUP 2007)

[49] See Steve McCaffrey, 'The 1997 UN Convention: Compatibility and Complementarity' in Tanzi *et al* (n 43) 58.

Salman M A Salman, 'Entry into Force of the UN Watercourses Convention: Why Should It Matter?' *International Journal of Water Resources Development*, 31/1 (2015): 4

Salman M A Salman, 'The Obligation Against Causing Harm' in Boisson de Chazournes *et al* (eds), *The UN Convention on the Law of the Non-Navigational Uses of International Watercourses: A Commentary* (OUP 2018) ch 6

Attila Tanzi *et al* (eds), *The UNECE Convention on the Protection and Use of Transboundary Watercourses and International Lakes: Its Contribution to International Water Cooperation* (Brill Nijhoff 2015)

CHAPTER 31

THE PROTECTION OF THE MARINE ENVIRONMENT

Pollution and Fisheries

ADRIANA FABRA

I. INTRODUCTION

OCEANS cover about 70% of the Earth's surface and make up more than 97% of the biosphere. They nurture life and shape the planet's weather and climate. Oceans create more than half of our oxygen and provide vital sources of protein, energy, and minerals. They provide food for a billion people and are also a source of income and livelihood for millions. However, oceans are under stress.

Current scientific literature acknowledges the existence of a complex set of interactions between humans and the marine environment. The principal threats and stressors include: overfishing, habitat loss, pollution, introduction of invasive species, and climate change.[1] The 2019 report of the Intergovernmental Panel on Climate Change (IPCC) on the ocean and cryosphere provides overwhelming evidence that global warming is resulting in a warmer, more acidic, and less productive ocean, with increasing sea level rise and extreme weather conditions, which will have further

[1] FAO, *The State of World Fisheries and Aquaculture: Meeting the Sustainable Development Goals* (2018) 6, 39; Alex Rogers and Dan Laffoley, 'Introduction to the special issue—The Global State of the Ocean; Interactions Between Stresses, Impacts and Some Potential Solutions—Synthesis papers from the International Programme on the State of the Ocean 2011 and 2012 Workshops' *Marine Pollution Bulletin*, 74/2 (2013): 491; United Nations Environment Programme (UNEP), 'Global Synthesis, A Report from the Regional Seas Conventions and Action Plans for the Marine Biodiversity Assessment and Outlook Series' (2010) 9.

negative consequences for ecosystems and people.[2] The cumulative effects of multiple ocean stressors, including fishing pressures and rising water temperatures, will force harmful changes that may not be reversible.[3]

Against this background, there is a scientific recognition that ocean problems cannot be tackled in a piecemeal fashion. The 2016 United Nations (UN) World Ocean Assessment acknowledges that 'the ocean is a complex set of systems that are all interconnected' and emphasizes the need to manage human activities that affect the ocean in an integrated manner.[4] The notion of 'integrated management' presents formidable practical challenges, requiring changes to current governance models and rules to bring together pollution prevention, fisheries management, and species and habitat protection. The 'ecosystem approach' is central to integrated management.[5]

Following an introduction on the role of the 1982 UN Law of the Sea Convention (UNCLOS) as the framework legal instrument on the oceans, this chapter discusses global and regional treaty requirements, soft law instruments, and case law concerning the protection of the marine environment from various sources of pollution, and the conservation of marine living resources, with a focus on fisheries, and the protection of marine biodiversity.[6]

II. LAW OF THE SEA CONVENTION AND OCEAN GOVERNANCE

The UNCLOS is one of the most significant international law instruments of all time and is at the core of today's governance of the oceans. UNCLOS is a product of the time when it was negotiated, which brought together a desire to provide global stability to competing jurisdictional claims over the oceans and devise solutions to rapidly increasing rates of marine pollution—all this in the framework of postcolonial demands by developing countries.

UNCLOS built upon the efforts to clarify jurisdiction over ocean spaces and ocean use that had resulted in the Geneva Conventions of 1958. It also built on the 1954 Oil

[2] H-O Pörtner *et al*, *IPCC Special Report on the Ocean and Cryosphere in a Changing Climate* (IPCC 2019).

[3] 'Pollution in the Open Oceans 2009–2013' (2015) GESAMP Reports and Studies No 91, 54–55.

[4] 'Summary of the first global integrated marine assessment' (22 July 2015) UN Doc A/70/112, 13; see <http://www.worldoceanassessment.org> accessed 31 December 2019.

[5] See its definition in the 1992 Convention on Biological Diversity (CBD), Decision V/6, 'Ecosystem approach' (26 May 2000) UN Doc UNEP/CBD/COP/5/23, 103, annex, s A.

[6] The conservation of threatened or endangered species, and the protection of marine ecosystems, essential for the conservation of all marine life and biodiversity, are addressed in Section V of this chapter and Chapter 32, 'Wildlife', in this volume.

Pollution Convention, and echoed principles of equitable exploitation and conservation of marine living resources emanating from case law at the time, such as the *Fisheries Jurisdiction* cases.[7] On jurisdictional matters, UNCLOS made a significant leap forward, rapidly establishing new concepts such as that of a 200 nautical-mile Exclusive Economic Zone (EEZ) and designing a radically new system to manage shared resources of the seabed, under the notion of the 'common heritage of mankind'.

However, technological changes and increased or unforeseen sources of pollution and habitat destruction have exposed some of the Convention's limitations, which derive from a fragmented perspective of the marine environment, and a failure to address the interaction between different ocean uses and marine stressors and provide rules on the conservation of marine biological diversity. Already in 1992, before UNCLOS entered into force, Agenda 21 acknowledged that the Convention provided the 'international basis' for the protection and sustainable development of the marine and coastal environment and its resources, but it also recognized that it was necessary to take 'new approaches to marine and coastal area management and development … that are integrated in content and are precautionary and anticipatory in ambit'.[8] In 2002, the WSSD Plan of Implementation emphasized the need to implement an ecosystem approach and promote 'integrated, multidisciplinary and multisectoral coastal and ocean development'.[9]

Despite its limitations, UNCLOS has continued to be the pillar on which later agreements, which incorporate the precautionary principle or the ecosystem approach, are based. Recent developments indicate that it also has the potential to provide a framework for yet another leap forward in ocean governance, as shown by the beginning of negotiations for an international legally binding instrument on the conservation and sustainable use of marine biological diversity of areas beyond national jurisdiction.[10] Moreover, its provisions on marine pollution have started to be interpreted extensively by international tribunals, recognizing that they also apply to activities not directly related to the prevention of pollution, such as the establishment of a marine protected area (*Chagos Marine Protected Area* arbitration) and the protection of fragile ecosystems from damaging fishing activities (*South China Sea* arbitration).[11]

[7] See eg *Fisheries Jurisdiction (Germany/Zeeland)* (Judgement) [1974] ICJ Rep 175 [64].

[8] *Report of the United Nations Conference on Environment and Development* (UN 1993) vol I, annex II, 'Agenda 21', para 17.1.

[9] *Report of World Summit on Sustainable Development* (UN 2002) 6, 'Plan of Implementation', paras 30 et seq.

[10] UNGA Res 72/249, 'International legally binding instrument under the United Nations Convention on the Law of the Sea on the conservation and sustainable use of marine biological diversity of areas beyond national jurisdiction' (19 January 2018) UN Doc A/RES/72/249.

[11] *Chagos Marine Protected Area Arbitration (Mauritius/UK)* (2015) 31 RIAA 359 (Chagos Marine case) [320], [538]; *The South China Sea Arbitration (Philippines/China)* (Final award of 12 July 2016) PCA Case no 2013-19 (South China Sea case) [945], [940]–[941], [956], [959].

III. PREVENTION OF MARINE POLLUTION

The principal cause of marine pollution is land-based activities, including intensive human settlement of coastal zones, which has resulted in destruction of habitats, eutrophication from nutrients and sewage, and changes in sediment flows due to hydrological changes.[12] Other sources of pollution include microbial contamination from untreated human sewage, the progressive build-up of chlorinated hydrocarbons, and the accumulation of tar on beaches from oil spills. In the open ocean, inputs of carbon dioxide and nitrogen through the atmosphere and of solid debris such as plastics in the water column and on the seabed are matters of special concern, as are the threats of exploration and extraction of minerals and hydrocarbons on or within the deep-ocean seabed.[13]

The development of rules to combat and prevent marine pollution began in the 1950s to address, mainly, concerns related to oil pollution from vessels. Efforts to regulate sources of marine pollution intensified rapidly, and particularly every time a notorious oil spill occurred, such as after the accidents of the Torrey Canyon in 1967, the Amoco Cadiz in 1978, and the Exxon Valdez in 1989. Marine pollution was a central issue in the 1972 Stockholm Conference and the Stockholm Declaration called on states to 'take all possible steps to prevent pollution of the seas by substances that are liable to create hazards to human health, to harm living resources and marine life, to damage amenities or to interfere with other legitimate uses of the sea'.[14] UNCLOS responded to this call.

A. UNCLOS Provisions on Marine Pollution

Part XII of UNCLOS regulates the 'protection and preservation of the marine environment'. Despite this general title, these measures were drafted to address marine pollution. The majority of measures in Part XII are considered by many states to reflect applicable principles or rules of customary law.[15] They pursue the prevention, reduction, and control of marine pollution and, to this end, UNCLOS establishes rules on information, scientific research, monitoring, environmental assessment, enforcement, and liability. In addition, principles and rules on environmental protection may also be found throughout the Convention, for example, when setting rights and obligations of

[12] 'The State of the Marine Environment' (1990) GESAMP Reports and Studies No 39.

[13] GESAMP, 'Pollution in Open Oceans' (n 3) 55.

[14] UN, 'Report of the United Nations Conference on the Human Environment' (5–16 June 1972) UN Doc A/CONF.48/14/Rev.1, 3, ch 1—'Declaration of the United Nations Conference on the Human Environment', principle 8.

[15] Philippe Sands and Jacqueline Peel, *Principles of International Environmental Law* (4th edn, CUP 2018) 462.

the coastal state in its territorial waters and in the EEZ.[16] The Convention establishes the primary obligation of all states 'to protect and preserve the marine environment', further distinguishing between the duty to protect the environment and the responsibility not to cause damage by pollution to other states and their environment.[17]

Article 194.3 of UNCLOS addresses specific sources of pollution: land-based activities, seabed activities, activities in the 'Area', dumping, vessels, and the atmosphere.[18] Article 194.4 limits the exercise of states' rights and obligations to prevent marine pollution, so that they cannot unjustifiably interfere with the rights of other states, and Article 194.5 requires special protection of rare or fragile ecosystems as well as the habitat of depleted, threatened, or endangered species and other forms of marine life. Recent decisions by arbitral tribunals consider that Article 194 is 'not limited to measures aimed strictly at controlling pollution and extends to measures focussed primarily on conservation and the preservation of ecosystems',[19] and clarify that the obligations it creates involve 'ensuring activities within their jurisdiction and control do not harm the marine environment', which is to be understood as an obligation of conduct requiring 'due diligence'.[20]

After the adoption of UNCLOS, international rules for the protection of the marine environment developed rapidly, both at global and regional levels. Global rules have focused, in particular, on pollution from vessels, including dumping at sea, while regional agreements have played an important role in the prevention of pollution from land-based sources. The articulation of a regional response to marine pollution has led to a robust system of regional treaties, institutions, and action plans that have resulted not only in a reduction of pollution levels for several substances but has also brought greater regional cooperation beyond strict pollution prevention, favouring a more integrated approach to marine protection.

B. Regional Arrangements

The UN Environment Programme (UNEP) Regional Seas Programme followed the 1972 Stockholm Conference and the creation of UNEP. It began with the establishment of the Mediterranean Action Plan and currently covers fourteen regional areas all over the world, comprising more than forty framework Conventions and Protocols. Each regional arrangement has its own Action Plan,[21] and ten regions are the subject of binding international agreements.[22]

16 See eg arts 21.1(f), 42.1(b), 54, 56.1(b)(iii), 56.2.

17 arts 192, 194.1, 194.2.

18 arts 194.3, 207–212.

19 Chagos Marine case (n 11) [538]; South China Sea case (n 11) [945].

20 South China Sea case (n 11) [944].

21 Mediterranean (1975, revised in 1995), ROPME Sea Area (1978), Wider Caribbean (1981), East Asian (1981), South-East Pacific (1981), Red Sea and Gulf of Aden (1982, revised in 1995), South Pacific (1982, revised in 2000), Western Africa (1981), Eastern Africa (1982), North-West Pacific (1994), South Asian Seas (1995), Black Sea (1996, revised in 2009), and North-East Pacific (2002).

22 The only regions without a framework convention are the Northwest Pacific, the South Asian Seas, and the East Asian Seas.

The ten regional seas framework conventions have a similar content and structure.[23] With some differences, most framework conventions establish obligations to combat pollution from different sources, including dumping from ships and aircraft, from exploration and exploitation of the territorial sea and/or continental shelf and/or seabed, and from land-based sources, as well as to cooperate in dealing with pollution emergencies. Although all framework conventions emphasize the prevention of marine pollution, most of them also contain at least one provision establishing the need for the conservation of marine habitats and species. Some require the establishment of specially protected areas, and others the conservation of biological diversity, or the protection of marine living resources.

Beyond the UNEP sphere, two influential systems were developed for the North Atlantic and Baltic Sea. Based on agreements from the 1970s, the 1992 OSPAR Convention for the North Atlantic and the 1992 Helsinki Convention for the Baltic brought a more integrated approach to marine protection. These Conventions incorporated many of the principles that emerged during the UNCED (UN Conference on Environment and Development) process, such as the precautionary principle, the polluter pays principle, the concept of best available techniques, and the ecosystem approach. Both regimes have adopted action plans aimed at reducing pollution (from radioactive and other hazardous substances, shipping, dredging, as well as noise pollution and marine litter), conserving biodiversity, and protecting endangered species through the establishment of marine protected areas and direct protection measures.[24] They also have specific plans related to fisheries conservation.

A distinct regime was also established for Antarctica, with the signing of the Antarctic Treaty in 1959, which preserved this area for peaceful and scientific uses. In 1991, states signed the Protocol on Environmental Protection, which designates Antarctica as a natural reserve and, notably, prohibits mining.

C. Global Rules to Combat Marine Pollution

Regional and global rules are generally complementary, although some aspects we find only, or better regulated, at the regional level. This section of the chapter provides an overview of some of the key global instruments to prevent marine pollution. In this context, the International Maritime Organization (IMO) plays a particularly important role. It acts as Secretariat to many of these agreements and implementing measures

[23] Sands and Peel (n 15) ch 11, 'Oceans, Seas and Marine Living Resources', contributed by Adriana Fabra.

[24] 'Strategy of the OSPAR Commission for the Protection of the Marine Environment of the North-East Atlantic 2010–2020 (OSPAR Agreement 2010–3)'; 'HELCOM Baltic Sea Action Plan 2007–2021' adopted on 15 November 2007 by the HELCOM Extraordinary Ministerial Meeting.

are adopted through its bodies, particularly the Marine Environment Protection Committee (MEPC).

1. *Pollution by dumping*

Pollution by dumping refers to the deliberate disposal of waste and other matter from non-land based sources, such as vessels or aircraft. While this source of pollution now raises fewer concerns than when the first agreements were developed in the 1970s, there is evidence of illegal dumping taking place today, including of radioactive waste.[25] This environmental hazard is addressed by UNCLOS, the 1972 London Convention and its 1996 Protocol, and the majority of regional agreements mentioned above, some of which have been complemented by specific Protocols on dumping.

In addition to the general obligations in UNCLOS,[26] the international regime to prevent pollution by dumping adopts a two-track approach: the 1972 London Convention[27] and the 1996 Protocol to this Convention. Both agreements are in force and, while the 1996 Protocol supersedes the Convention for those states that have ratified it, the London Convention remains in force for nearly as many states. The 1996 Protocol provides a stricter approach to dumping, prohibiting all forms of dumping except for some listed substances, which are subject to permits. By contrast, the 1972 Convention takes the reverse approach, establishing three categories of waste that are subject to different obligations and permits. Implementation of both instruments is poor, particularly because some of the world's largest economies have not become party to either agreement, and little is known with respect to dumping under their control.[28]

2. *Pollution from vessels*

The main international convention regulating pollution from vessels is the International Convention for the Prevention of Pollution from Ships, often referred to as MARPOL 73/78. The 1973 Convention (MARPOL 73), which replaced the 1954 Oil Pollution Convention, was modified by the 1978 Protocol (MARPOL 78) before the parent Convention entered into force.[29] The detailed rules on pollution from ships are set out in six Annexes to the Convention, and further clarifications and amendments to various

[25] World Ocean Assessment (n 4) 35.

[26] See eg arts 210, 216.

[27] art III.3.

[28] World Ocean Assessment (n 4) 35.

[29] Before MARPOL 1973 entered into force, it was recognized that the provisions of annex II would be difficult for even the most economically advanced states to comply with. MARPOL 1978 was therefore negotiated and adopted to establish a new instrument which provided that the new Convention comprised the 1978 Protocol and its annex *and* MARPOL 1973 as amended by MARPOL 1978, and that the provisions of MARPOL 1973 and MARPOL 1978 should be 'read and interpreted together as one single instrument': MARPOL 1978, art 1. MARPOL 1978 delayed the implementation of annex II and amended one of the provisions concerning the communication of information: MARPOL 1978, arts II,

provisions of MARPOL 73/78 have been adopted by the IMO MEPC. Overall, this regime provides some of the most precise and comprehensive measures in any international environmental agreement and has proven to respond flexibly to evolving needs in the shipping world. Possibly as a result of its measures, in the past forty years the number of oil spills has steadily decreased.[30]

MARPOL 73/78 covers both intentional and unintentional discharges from ships but excludes dumping and releases from the exploration and exploitation of the seabed. Of special interest today are new measures adopted to reduce the emissions of ozone-depleting substances and greenhouse gases.[31] Another important development in the framework of pollution prevention and the IMO is the entry into force in 2017 of the International Code for Ships Operating in Polar Waters (the Polar Code), after twenty years of negotiations.[32] Although it does not cover all vessels and all sources of pollution, it establishes discharge limits stricter than those set in MARPOL.[33]

A second generation of IMO agreements control different sources of pollution from ships: the 2001 International Convention on the Control of Harmful Anti-Fouling Systems on Ships (AFS), the 2004 International Convention for the Control and Management of Ships' Ballast Water and Sediments, the 2007 Nairobi International Convention on the Removal of Wrecks, and the 2009 Hong Kong International Convention for the Safe and Environmentally Sound Recycling of Ships. All these agreements are in force, except for the Hong Kong Convention. Instruments on safety at sea, of which the 1974 International Convention for the Safety of Life at Sea (SOLAS) is the most important example, are also relevant to the protection of the marine environment.

3. *Pollution from seabed activities*

Mining in the seabed has been an ongoing practice for several decades, but in recent years marine mining has become a matter of greater concern, particularly in the deep-seabed. Some estimates indicate that by 2020 5% of the world's minerals may come from the ocean floors, and this could rise to 10% by 2030.[34] The risks for the marine environment of deep-seabed mining, in particular, are not yet well known, but assessments indicate that removal of parts of the sea floor might result in disturbances to the benthic

III. 154 states, which represent more than 99% of the world's ship tonnage, are party to MARPOL 73/78 including annexes I and II.

[30] World Ocean Assessment (n 4) 37.

[31] Protocol of 1997 to amend MARPOL 73, as modified by MARPOL 78 (annex VI—Regulations for the Prevention of Air Pollution from Ships) regulations 12–15; IMO, 'Third IMO Greenhouse Gas Study 2014' (2015).

[32] 2014 International Code for Ships Operating in Polar Waters (Polar Code).

[33] See Polar Code, part II-A, ch 1 on oil pollution, ch 2 on noxious liquid substances, ch 3 on packaged harmful substances, ch 4 on sewage pollution, ch 5 on garbage.

[34] European Union, *Blue Growth—Opportunities for Marine and Maritime Sustainable Growth* (Publications Office of the European Union 2012) 10.

layer, toxic levels of contaminants in the water column, and sediment plumes from tailings.[35]

UNCLOS establishes a basic framework of general rights and obligations of coastal states, which includes the duty to prevent, reduce, and control pollution from seabed activities.[36] In 2015, in the *Arctic Sunrise* case, which concerned the arrest of Greenpeace activists by authorities of the Russian Federation as they protested against oil drilling, the arbitral tribunal ruled that certain UNCLOS provisions regulating the coastal state's rights regarding marine living resources also extended to 'non-living' resources in the seabed.[37]

For seabed activities outside areas of national jurisdiction, UNCLOS set a new regime in its Part XI, establishing the notion of 'the Area', administered by the International Seabed Authority (ISBA). These provisions were subsequently complemented by the 1994 Agreement Relating to the Implementation of Part XI of the Convention. Since 2000, the Authority has entered into fifteen-year contracts with twenty-one contractors for exploration of polymetallic nodules, polymetallic sulphides, and cobalt-rich ferromanganese crusts.[38] In parallel, it has developed specific rules and procedures on prospecting, exploration, and exploitation of marine minerals in the Area, a compendium which constitutes the so-called 'Mining Code'.[39]

Through its bodies, the Authority has the obligation to prevent and control pollution and protect and conserve the natural resources, and prevent damage to the flora and fauna of the marine environment.[40] Such environmental standards were the object of an Advisory Opinion, in 2011, by the Seabed Disputes Chamber of ITLOS. This Opinion provided clarification on the content of the obligations of states sponsoring activities in the Area, outlining their marked environmental character.[41] Unanimously, the Chamber determined that sponsoring states have a general obligation of 'due diligence',

[35] Kathryn Miller *et al*, 'An Overview of Seabed Mining Including the Current State of Development, Environmental Impacts, and Knowledge Gaps' *Frontiers in Marine Science*, 4 (2018): 418; GESAMP, 'Pollution in Open Oceans' (n 3) 51–52.

[36] See eg arts 208, 214.

[37] *The 'Arctic Sunrise' Case (Netherlands/Russia)* (Provisional Measures, Order of 22 November 2013) [2013] ITLOS Rep 230.

[38] See <https://www.isa.org.jm/deep-seabed-minerals-contractors> accessed 28 October 2018.

[39] ISBA Council, 'Decision relating to amendments to the Regulations on Prospecting and Exploration for Polymetallic Nodules in the Area and related matters' (22 July 2013) ISBA/19/C/17; ISBA Assembly, 'Decision relating to the regulations on prospecting and exploration for polymetallic sulphides in the Area' (15 November 2010) ISBA/16/A/12/Rev.1; ISBA Assembly, 'Decision relating to the Regulations on Prospecting and Exploration for Cobalt-rich Ferromanganese Crusts in the Area' (22 October 2012) ISBA/18/A/11; see also <https://www.isa.org.jm/mining-code> accessed 1 January 2020.

[40] art 145; see also UNCLOS, annex III, art 17.1(b)(xii) enabling the Authority to adopt minimum standards and practices, including those relating to conservation of resources and protection of the marine environment; 1994 Agreement on Part XI of UNCLOS, annex, s 1, para 5(g) requiring the Authority to concentrate on the adoption of rules, regulations, and procedures incorporating applicable standards for the protection and preservation of the marine environment.

[41] *Responsibilities and obligations of States sponsoring persons and entities with respect to activities in the Area* (Advisory Opinion) [2011] ITLOS Rep 10.

understood as an obligation 'of conduct', of which the precautionary approach is an integral part.[42] The Chamber also considered that the obligation to apply 'best environmental practices' should be mandatory under all regulations, and that the obligation to conduct an environmental impact assessment was 'a general obligation under customary law'.[43]

IV. CONSERVATION OF MARINE LIVING RESOURCES

The oceans are inhabited by a myriad of creatures and international law has provided measures for the protection or conservation of only some of them.[44] Some of the first international environmental agreements were aimed at the preservation of marine mammals, such as seals or whales, and other threatened creatures. Later on, states saw the need to regulate access to fisheries, especially as these resources started to become scarcer. Chapter 32 in this volume provides an overview of international law concerned with protected marine wildlife. This section focuses on international measures aimed at fisheries management.

The Food and Agriculture Organization of the United Nations (FAO) estimates that the annual take of fisheries from the oceans is occurring at a rate that goes far beyond sustainable levels.[45] The development and use of new technologies and fishing practices, the over-capitalization of fishing fleets, the continued use of destructive practices, such as bottom-trawling or dynamiting, and growing demand for fisheries resources for human consumption and animal feed, all put an increased strain on the ability of ocean resources to sustain and replenish.[46]

The main objective of international fisheries law is the establishment of a framework for international cooperation towards the management and conservation of fisheries and marine living resources, where the definition of jurisdictional rights over different maritime areas is entrenched. The terms and content of such cooperation has evolved over time, resulting in the extension of the rights of coastal states, a reduction in the area of the high seas where there is a general right for all states to fish, and the development

[42] On the duty of 'due diligence' as obligation of conduct, ibid [110]–[116]; on the implementation of the precautionary approach, mandatory under the Nodules Regulations and the Sulphides Regulations, ibid [131]–[135].

[43] Ibid [135]–[137].

[44] See generally FAO FishFinder <https://www.fao.org/fishery/fishfinder/about/en> accessed 1 January 2020; Jesse Ausubel, Darlene Crist, and Paul Waggoner, *First Census of Marine Life 2010, Highlights of a Decade of Discovery* (2010) and *First Census of Marine Life 2010, Scientific Results to Support the Sustainable Use and Conservation of Marine Life: Summary for Policymakers* (2010) 3; see also World Register of Marine Species <https://www.marinespecies.org> accessed 1 January 2020.

[45] FAO, State of World Fisheries and Aquaculture (n 1) 6, 39.

[46] See Daniel Pauly *et al*, 'Fishing Down Marine Food Webs' *Science*, 279/5352 (1998): 860.

of obligations for fishing nations to manage resources jointly. The solutions offered by international law provide a framework in which to manage shared resources while balancing sovereign rights, but overall have not succeeded in reversing the drivers conducive to unsustainable fishing practices.

A. UNCLOS Provisions on Fisheries Management

UNCLOS, in contrast to its approach to the regulation of the protection and preservation of the marine environment in Part XII, does not regulate marine living resources comprehensively in a single section of the Convention. Instead, it includes provisions on the conservation and sustainable use of marine living resources in the framework of states' rights and obligations in different jurisdictional areas: in territorial waters, in archipelagic waters, on the continental shelf, in the EEZ, and on the high seas. UNCLOS also includes special rules for stocks that move across the jurisdictions of two or more states, such as highly migratory, anadromous and catadromous species, and also for marine mammals.

Succinctly, UNCLOS recognizes full sovereignty of the coastal state over fisheries within its territory and does not set any obligation for it to ensure the conservation of resources therein.[47] On the high seas, UNCLOS maintains the recognition of freedom of all states to fish, with the requirement that states must have due regard to the rights of other states and adopt measures for the conservation of the living resources of the high seas. There is a general duty to cooperate with other states for the conservation of resources.[48]

The most significant innovation brought about by UNCLOS concerns the recognition of the exclusive sovereign rights of the coastal state to exploit living and non-living resources in the EEZ. Subject to its right to determine the total allowable catch, the coastal state must ensure that living resources are not endangered by over-exploitation, taking into account the best scientific evidence available.[49] These measures must also take into consideration the need to keep associate or dependent species above a level at which they would be seriously threatened.[50] Coastal states must promote the 'optimum utilisation' of living resources, and give other states access to the surplus of the allowable catch they cannot harvest themselves, taking into account all relevant factors, including the economic needs of the coastal state.[51] They also have the duty to cooperate with other states, particularly concerning straddling and highly migratory fish stocks.[52] The need

[47] Parts II, IV.

[48] arts 117–118.

[49] arts 61.1, 61.2.

[50] art 61.4.

[51] arts 62.1–62.3.

[52] arts 63–64.

for implementation of these obligations with regard to straddling and highly migratory species resulted in the adoption of the 1995 Fish Stocks Agreement.

B. The 1995 Fish Stocks Agreement

In 1992, before UNCLOS entered into force, Agenda 21 identified significant problems in the management of fisheries, which had not been addressed by the Convention.[53] To address these problems, which more than twenty-five years later remain alarmingly contemporary, Agenda 21 recommended a number of actions, including the negotiation of an international agreement to promote the effective implementation of UNCLOS on the issue of straddling and highly migratory fish stocks.[54] In a relatively short time, the 1995 Fish Stocks Agreement was adopted.

The 1995 Agreement applies to the conservation and management of straddling fish stocks and highly migratory fish stocks in areas beyond national jurisdiction, although coastal states must also apply the Agreement's core principles within their jurisdiction.[55] Among its most innovative provisions, it establishes the obligation to apply the precautionary and the ecosystem approaches, minimize pollution, waste, discards, and catch of non-target species, protect biodiversity in the marine environment, eliminate overfishing and excess fishing capacity, and enforce conservation and management measures through effective monitoring, control, and surveillance.[56] These core provisions have influenced subsequently adopted agreements.

The 1995 Agreement envisages a significant role for sub-regional and regional fisheries organizations and arrangements in facilitating cooperation by states in the development and enforcement of conservation and management measures for straddling and highly migratory stocks.[57] Where a regional fisheries management organization (RFMO) is competent to establish conservation and management measures for a particular stock, states fishing for those stocks are required to join the organization, or agree to apply its measures, in order to be permitted to continue to fish for the stock.[58] This far-reaching provision has the consequence, in effect, of departing from traditional high seas fisheries freedoms, even for those states that are not parties to regional agreements. This is precisely one of the provisions that has prevented some states from joining the Agreement.

On this basis, a large body of RFMOs has emerged in the past decades. Today, they are the primary actors in the international management of shared resources, covering most ocean areas and most exploited species. However, significant gaps in regulation remain,

[53] Agenda 21 (n 8) para 17.45.
[54] Ibid, para 17.49(e).
[55] art 3.
[56] art 5; see also art 6 on the precautionary approach.
[57] arts 8–10.
[58] arts 8.4, 17; see also Part IV—'Non-Members and Non-Participants'.

leaving areas such as the South-West Atlantic unregulated, and species such as sharks and rays often excluded from management measures. Notably, the Arctic is one of the regions with a patchy and under-regulated regime.[59]

C. The FAO and International Law on Fisheries

The FAO is the only UN specialized agency with a mandate to promote the conservation of natural resources. With more than 190 members, it has assisted in developing and supporting the implementation of international agreements in the field of fisheries, such as the 1993 Agreement to Promote Compliance with International Conservation and Management Measures by Fishing Vessels on the High Seas (1993 Compliance Agreement) and the 2009 Agreement on Port State Measures to Prevent, Deter and Eliminate Illegal, Unreported and Unregulated Fishing (2009 Port State Measures Agreement or PSMA). Some non-binding instruments developed in the framework of the FAO have had remarkable influence in guiding current policies and rules on international fisheries, such as the 1995 Code of Conduct for Responsible Fisheries.[60]

1. *Flag state obligations and the Compliance Agreement*

The 1993 Compliance Agreement was adopted to respond to the failure by some flag states to ensure compliance with measures for the conservation of living resources on the high seas.[61] The Agreement has received few ratifications, and did not enter into force until ten years after its conclusion.[62] It has been criticized for setting excessively broad obligations and being applicable only to fisheries on the high seas and to vessels twenty-four metres or greater. In 2014, to address flag state responsibility in the context of efforts to combat illegal, unreported, and unregulated (IUU) fishing, the FAO adopted the Voluntary Guidelines for Flag State Performance.[63]

2. *IUU fishing and the 2009 Agreement on Port State Measures*

In the late 1990s, fishing in violation of applicable rules, in areas or for species not regulated, became an issue of high concern. This led the FAO to adopt in 2001 the

[59] In 2015, a non-binding declaration was adopted to prevent unregulated commercial fishing in the Central Arctic Ocean; see 'Declaration concerning the prevention of unregulated high seas fishing in the Central Arctic Ocean' <https://www.regjeringen.no/globalassets/departementene/ud/vedlegg/folkerett/declaration-on-arctic-fisheries-16-july-2015.pdf> accessed 19 July 2019.

[60] See <https://www.fao.org/fi/agreem/codecond/ficonde.asp> accessed 1 January 2020. The Code has led to the adoption of International Plans of Action on seabirds, on sharks, on IUU fishing, and on fishing capacity, as well as guidelines on a wide range of issues, including by-catch, deep-sea fisheries, and flag state performance.

[61] UNCLOS, art 94.

[62] Approved on 24 November 1993 by FAO Res 15/93, at the 27th FAO Conference; entered into force 24 April 2003. As of December 2019, it had been accepted by forty-one states and the EU.

[63] Text of Guidelines available at FAO Doc COFI/2014/4.2/Rev.1, appendix 2, para 2.

International Plan of Action to prevent, deter, and eliminate IUU fishing, which has informed the current international response to this problem. In this framework, and considering challenges to ensure flag state responsibility, the international community focused on strengthening the role of port states. In 2009, the FAO adopted the PSMA, which entered into force in 2016.[64]

The sovereign rights of the port state over its ports are undisputed, but the singular contribution of the PSMA is its establishment of port state *obligations*. Under the PSMA, the port state can be required to deny access to port to vessels for which there is sufficient proof of engagement in IUU fishing and/or to carry out vessel inspections.[65] The PSMA introduces, for the first time, a definition of IUU fishing in a binding agreement of a global nature.[66]

IUU fishing was the object of the first Advisory Opinion issued by the International Tribunal on the Law of the Sea (ITLOS) in full.[67] This Opinion was requested by a West African fisheries management organization concerned about the high level of IUU fishing occurring in its region. The Tribunal explained the responsibilities of coastal and flag states in the face of IUU fishing: while for activities occurring within a state's EEZ primary responsibility rests with the coastal state, 'flag States are obliged to take the necessary measures to ensure that their nationals and vessels flying their flag are not engaged in IUU fishing activities'.[68] ITLOS clarified, referring to the previous opinion of the Seabed Disputes Chamber of 2011, that the obligation of the flag state is one of 'due diligence' not one 'of result', concluding that it is an obligation 'to deploy adequate means, to exercise best possible efforts, to do the utmost' to prevent IUU fishing by ships flying its flag.[69]

D. The UNGA and Destructive Fishing Practices

International law has regulated the means of fishing since the early nineteenth century. Today, technological innovations permit fishing on a large and indiscriminate scale, affecting species and ocean areas previously out of range. Among these practices, noteworthy are driftnets that involve the use of a large net with heavy weights, which is

64 Agreement on Port State Measures to Prevent, Deter and Eliminate Illegal, Unreported and Unregulated Fishing, approved on 22 November 2009 by FAO Res 12/2009, at the 36th FAO Conference under art XIV(1) of the FAO Constitution.

65 See in particular arts 9, 11, 12.

66 It incorporates the definition of the 2001 FAO International Plan of Action to Prevent, Deter and Eliminate Illegal, Unreported and Unregulated Fishing (IPOA-IUU).

67 *Request for an advisory opinion submitted by the Sub-Regional Fisheries Commission (SRFC)* (Advisory Opinion) [2015] ITLOS Rep 4.

68 Ibid [124].

69 Ibid [129]. This view was later on endorsed in the arbitral award in South China Sea case (n 11) [743]–[744].

dragged across the sea, scooping up everything in its path, from the targeted fish to ancient corals and other wildlife.[70] Driftnets can be up to thirty miles wide and sweep the high seas taking with them high rates of incidental catch such as dolphins, turtles, and sea birds, and bottom trawling. Other destructive practices, such as 'propeller chopping' for the harvesting of giant clams, which breaks through coral reefs, have been found by international tribunals to violate Articles 192 and 194.5 of UNCLOS on the protection of the marine environment.[71]

These practices have received minimal regulation by international treaties.[72] However, the UN General Assembly (UNGA) has taken up both issues and adopted Resolutions that, on the basis of a precautionary approach, have been influential in restricting these activities. On driftnets, UNGA Resolution 46/215 of 1991 called for a global moratorium by December 1992 on all large-scale pelagic driftnet fishing on the high seas.[73] Since 1991, the UNGA has reaffirmed its call on an almost yearly basis, and there is widespread support of its clear provisions that may now be considered sufficient to ground a rule of customary international law.[74] With regard to bottom trawling, the UNGA adopted in 2006 Resolution 61/105 by consensus and set time-bound and concrete objectives for states, and particularly for RFMOs, to implement measures in accordance with the precautionary approach, the ecosystem approach, and international law.[75] These resolutions have had a noticeable impact on the development of measures to protect deep-sea ecosystems, particularly vulnerable marine ecosystems, and to regulate bottom fishing. A number of RFMOs have taken measures in line with these resolutions.[76]

70 FAO, 'Deep-sea Fisheries in the High Seas: Ensuring sustainable use of marine resources and the protection of vulnerable marine ecosystems' (2009) 2.

71 South China Sea case (n 11) [848]–[851], [965]–[966], [1203.B(12)(b)].

72 See eg on driftnet fishing 1989 Convention for the Prohibition of Fishing with Long Driftnets in the South Pacific Wellington (adopted 23 November 1989, entered into force 17 May 199) 29 ILM 1454; on bottom trawling see references to UNCLOS, the Fish Stocks Agreement and CBD in Sands and Peel (n 15) 555–556.

73 UNGA Res 46/215, 'Large-scale pelagic drift-net fishing and its impact on the living marine resources of the world's oceans and seas' (20 December 1991) UN Doc A/RES/46/215.

74 Agenda 21 declares that 'states should fully implement' Res 46/215; see Agenda 21 (n 8) para 17.54.

75 UNGA Res 61/105, 'Sustainable Fisheries' (6 March 2007) UN Doc A/RES/61/105, paras 83, 84–89; see also UNGA Res 64/72, 'Sustainable Fisheries' (19 March 2010) UN Doc A/RES/64/72, paras 119–120, and UNGA Res 66/68 'Sustainable Fisheries' (28 March 2012) UN Doc A/RES/66/68.

76 Matthew Gianni *et al*, 'How much longer will it take? A ten-year review of the implementation of United Nations General Assembly resolutions 61/105, 64/72 and 66/68 on the management of bottom fisheries in areas beyond national jurisdiction' (2016) <https://www.savethehighseas.org/wp-content/uploads/2016/07/DSCC-Review-2016_Launch-29-July.pdf> accessed 10 January 2020.

V. CONSERVATION OF MARINE BIODIVERSITY

The conservation of marine biodiversity and ecosystems is intimately related to the prevention of marine pollution and the sustainable management of marine living resources. Success in pollution abatement and sustainable fisheries practices can ensure that marine ecosystems and biodiversity remain healthy. At the same time, international environmental law has recognized the conservation of marine biodiversity as a regulatory goal in and of itself.

After UNCED, and as reflected in the WSSD Plan of Implementation, Rio+20 Summit outcome, and the Sustainable Development Goals, international arrangements progressively began to introduce an ecosystem approach to their regimes, and therefore to consider the impacts that different activities had on oceans as a whole. This allowed greater linkage between efforts to abate pollution and measures to manage living resources sustainably and, more generally, to 'conserve biological diversity' in the sense called for by the Convention on Biological Diversity (CBD).

The following sections provide an overview of the international legal framework relevant to the conservation of marine biodiversity, highlight current practice on key management tools, particularly marine protected areas (MPAs), and describe the main elements of a future international agreement on the conservation of biological diversity in areas beyond national jurisdiction. The latter aims to respond to regulatory gaps concerning the exploitation of marine genetic resources, conservation through area-based management tools, and implementing mechanisms, such as environmental impact assessments (EIA), capacity-building, and technology transfer.

A. International Law and the Protection of Marine Biodiversity

1. *UNCLOS*

Under UNCLOS, 'states have the obligation to protect and preserve the marine environment'. This obligation is established in Article 192, which opens Part XII on 'Protection and Preservation of the Marine Environment'. As acknowledged by international courts and tribunals, this obligation is not limited to the duties to combat pollution set out in Part XII. ITLOS has recognized the conservation of the living resources of the sea as 'an element in the protection and preservation of the marine environment'.[77] In 2015, in the

[77] *Southern Bluefin Tuna Cases (New Zealand/Japan; Australia/Japan)* (Provisional Measures, Order of 27 August 1999) [1999] ITLOS Rep 280 [70].

Chagos Marine Protected Area case, the Arbitral Tribunal found that Article 194, under Part XII, 'is not limited to measures aimed strictly at controlling pollution and extends to measures focused primarily on conservation and the preservation of ecosystems'.[78]

In 2016, the arbitral award in the *South China Sea* case made significant findings when considering damage to marine biodiversity and ecosystems as a result of destructive fishing practices and direct habitat destruction. These included:

- Reiteration that the general obligation under Article 192 of UNCLOS applies both in and beyond national jurisdiction and includes a positive obligation to take active measures to protect the marine environment and a negative obligation to refrain from causing damage.[79]
- Confirmation that Part XII of UNCLOS is not solely concerned with controlling marine pollution. It extends to the conservation of living resources, the protection of fragile ecosystems, as established in Article 194.5, and the prevention of harvesting of endangered species, as informed by the 1973 Convention on International Trade in Endangered Species of Wild Fauna and Flora (CITES).[80]
- Affirmation, as established also by ITLOS in its Advisory Opinion on *IUU Fishing*, that the exercise of these obligations includes a duty of 'due diligence', where it is not possible to adopt measures to prevent damage to the marine environment.
- Emphasizing the importance for states to cooperate, including in the context of states bordering semi-enclosed seas, and to conduct assessments under Article 206.

Other international rules established in UNCLOS take due regard of the impact of certain activities on marine species and ecosystems. With respect to activities to exploit resources of the seabed in areas beyond national jurisdiction ('the Area'), UNCLOS requires the International Seabed Authority to take measures for 'the protection and conservation of the natural resources of the Area and the prevention of damage to the flora and fauna of the marine environment'.[81] Regarding fisheries, UNCLOS requires states, when determining conservation and management measures, to 'take into consideration the effects on species associated with or dependent upon harvested species' and to consider a number of other factors, such as 'fishing patterns [and] the interdependence of stocks'.[82] The 1995 Fish Stocks Agreement expressly incorporates ecosystem and precautionary approaches and establishes the duty of coastal states and states fishing on the high seas to 'protect biodiversity in the marine environment'.[83]

78 Chagos Marine case (n 11) [537]–[538].
79 South China Sea case (n 11) [940]–[941], also recalling Advisory Opinion on IUU Fishing (n 67).
80 South China Sea case (n 11) [956], [959].
81 art 145.
82 art 61.
83 art 5.

2. *Convention on Biological Diversity*

The provisions of the CBD also extend to marine biodiversity, although they have to be implemented consistently with the obligations of states under UNCLOS.[84] Since the first Conference of the Parties (COP) to the CBD, marine issues have consistently been part of its agenda. In 1995, parties adopted the Jakarta Mandate on Marine and Coastal Biological Diversity.[85] In 2010, they adopted the Aichi Targets for 2011–20, including Targets 6, 10, and 11, which are relevant to marine biodiversity.[86] According to these targets, by 2020 fish should be harvested with no significant adverse impacts on threatened species and vulnerable ecosystems, and 10% of marine areas should be effectively protected.[87] These and other targets have not yet been met.

The CBD COP has also taken decisions on a number of ocean-related issues, including: decisions relating to the conservation and sustainable use of deep seabed genetic resources beyond the limits of national jurisdiction;[88] implementation of integrated marine and coastal area management;[89] sustainable fisheries;[90] and impacts of noise pollution and acidification.[91] A significant number of decisions have concerned the establishment of marine protected areas, discussed further in the following sub-section.[92]

B. Marine Protected Areas

There is no single definition of a 'marine protected area' (MPA) in international law. A commonly accepted notion is provided by the CBD, which is area-based.[93] However, the notion of an MPA can encompass other forms of protection, such as spatial and temporal closures established for fisheries management, or the protection of the water column, vertically, instead of over a horizontally defined area.

[84] art 22.

[85] Decision II/10, 'Conservation and Sustainable Use of Marine and Coastal Biodiversity' (17 November 1995) UN Doc UNEP/CBD/COP/DEC/2/10.

[86] Decision X/2, 'The Strategic Plan for Biodiversity 2011–2020 and the Aichi Biodiversity Targets' (29 October 2010) UN Doc UNEP/CBD/COP/DEC/X/2.

[87] Ibid, Targets 6, 11.

[88] Decision VIII/21, 'Marine and coastal biological diversity: Conservation and sustainable use of deep seabed genetic resources beyond the limits of national jurisdiction' (15 June 2006) UN Doc UNEP/CBD/COP/DEC/VIII/21.

[89] Decision VIII/22, 'Marine and coastal biological diversity: Enhancing the implementation of integrated marine and coastal area management' (15 June 2006) UN Doc UNEP/CBD/COP/DEC/VIII/22.

[90] Decision XI/18, 'Marine and coastal biodiversity: Sustainable fisheries and addressing adverse impacts of human activities, voluntary guidelines for environmental assessment, and marine spatial planning' (5 December 2012) UN Doc UNEP/CBD/COP/DEC/XI/18.

[91] Decision XI/23, 'Biological diversity of inland water ecosystems' (5 December 2012) UN Doc UNEP/CBD/COP/DEC/XI/23.

[92] Decision VIII/24, 'Protected Areas' (15 June 2006) UN Doc UNEP/CBD/COP/DEC/VIII/24.

[93] art 2; Decision VII/5, 'Marine and coastal biological diversity' (13 April 2004) UN Doc UNEP/CBD/COP/DEC/VII/5.

Support for establishing MPAs stems from reasons similar to those that justify terrestrial protected areas. If properly designed and managed, MPAs can help protect, recover, and maintain fish stocks, ecosystem resilience, habitat structure, and biological diversity. The 2002 Johannesburg Plan of Implementation called upon states to establish MPAs 'consistent with international law and based on scientific information', and to achieve representative networks of MPAs by 2012.[94] This objective was reiterated by the COP to the CBD until the formulation of the 2010 Aichi Biodiversity Targets.[95] Sustainable Development Goal 14 restated the objective to protect 10% of coastal and marine areas by 2020.[96]

In 2018, about 16.8% of the world's EEZs were under nationally designated protected areas, and 1.2% of the high seas were protected. Overall, according to 2018 data, between 7.3%[97] and 5.3%[98] of the world's ocean is under some form of protection. This is still distant from the goal to protect, by 2020, 10% of the ocean. Nonetheless, in the last decade, the area covered by MPAs has almost doubled, particularly since 2016 when some very large areas were designated, notably the Papahānaumokuākea Marine National Monument within the EEZ of the United States, the Pitcairn Islands Marine Reserve, and the Marae Moana Marine Park in the Cook Islands. Just these three MPAs cover more than four million square kilometres. On the high seas, the Ross Sea MPA is the largest in the world, with a 72% 'no-take' zone.[99]

The regulation of MPAs under international law differs for areas established under national jurisdiction, namely, within a state's EEZ, and for areas beyond national jurisdiction. A number of regional agreements foresee the establishment of MPAs both under state jurisdiction and on the high seas.[100]

1. *Marine protected areas under national jurisdiction*

UNCLOS does not refer expressly to MPAs as a means to protect and preserve the marine environment or conserve marine living resources. However, a coastal state may designate MPAs within its territorial sea, as part of its sovereign rights established in Part II, or within its EEZ, in the exercise of its rights and obligations to conserve and manage natural resources established in Part V of the Convention. However, the right

[94] Plan of Implementation (n 9) para 32(c).

[95] Decisions VII/5 (n 93) and VII/28, 'Protected areas (Articles 8 (a) to (e))' (13 April 2004) UN Doc UNEP/CBD/COP/DEC/VII/28; Decision VIII/24 (n 92); Decision IX/18, 'Protected Areas' (9 October 2008) UN Doc UNEP/CBD/COP/DEC/IX/18; Aichi Biodiversity Targets adopted as part of Strategic Plan for Biodiversity 2011–2020, Decision X/2 (n 86).

[96] UNGA Res 70/1, 'Transforming our World: The 2030 Agenda for Sustainable Development' (21 October 2015) UN Doc A/RES/70/1.

[97] See *Protected Planet Report: Tracking Progress Towards Global Targets for Protected Areas* (UNEP 2018) 6; see also 'World Database on Protected Areas' <https://www.protectedplanet.net/> accessed 14 May 2020. This database indicates that there are around 16,928 designated MPAs in the world.

[98] 'Atlas of Marine Protection' <https://www.mpatlas.org/map/mpas/> accessed 14 May 2020.

[99] Commission for the Conservation of Antarctica Marine Living Resources, 'Report of the Thirty-Fifth Meeting of the Commission' (17–28 October 2016) para 8.37.

[100] See eg the network of MPAs under the 1976 Barcelona and 1992 OSPAR Conventions.

to so designate is subject to the requirements of UNCLOS, and a coastal state must have due regard to the rights and duties of other states.[101]

The *Chagos Arbitration* case brought by Mauritius against the United Kingdom concerned Mauritius' claim of sovereignty over the Chagos Archipelago, which in colonial times had been under British rule. The Arbitral Tribunal ruled that the United Kingdom had not lawfully established an MPA in Chagos. The Tribunal considered that setting up an MPA would be a measure foreseen by Article 194 for the conservation and preservation of ecosystems,[102] and that doing so could potentially justify the infringement of fishing rights of other states, whether on the high seas or in an EEZ.[103] However, in that case, such justification would have required significant engagement with Mauritius 'to explain the need for the measure and to explore less restrictive alternatives', and this had not occurred.[104]

2. *MPAs in areas beyond national jurisdiction*

The establishment of MPAs on the high seas is at the core of ongoing negotiations to draft an international and legally binding instrument to protect marine biodiversity in Areas Beyond National Jurisdiction, described further in Section V.D. However, high seas MPAs are not a new concept and where global or regional organizations have had the competence and consensus to establish protected areas they have already done so. This is the case for areas safeguarded under the scope of RFMOs,[105] regional seas agreements,[106] and global organizations such as the International Whaling Commission,[107] and the IMO.[108]

However, greater complexity arises when different international bodies and individual state interests need to converge and protect a specific geographical area. As a result, there are few multisectoral, high seas MPAs. OSPAR has led on efforts at this level and designated seven MPAs in areas beyond national jurisdiction. It has sought to establish cooperation arrangements with other organizations with competence over the area, such as the IMO or the International Seabed Authority, which so far have materialized

[101] art 56.2.

[102] Chagos Marine case (n 11) [538].

[103] On the need to balance rights, the Tribunal made similar findings for art 56.2, on the rights of the coastal state on the EEZ, which are considered to be 'functionally equivalent' to those set in art 194.4; ibid [540].

[104] Ibid [541].

[105] For example, NEAFC has closed 'vulnerable marine ecosystems' to bottom fisheries in the high seas of the Northeast Atlantic since 2009.

[106] See eg the Pelagos Sanctuary for the Conservation of Marine Mammals, of a transboundary nature, established in 2001 by the parties to the Barcelona Convention.

[107] The Indian Ocean Sanctuary was established in 1979 and covers the whole of the Indian Ocean south to 55°S; the Southern Ocean Sanctuary was adopted in 1994.

[108] The IMO has designated Particularly Sensitive Sea Areas since 1990, where special protective measures are applied. In 2005, the IMO adopted revised Guidelines for the Identification and Designation of Particularly Sensitive Sea Areas; see IMO Res A.982(24), 'Revised Guidelines for the Identification and Designation of Particularly Sensitive Sea Areas' (6 February 2006).

in a cooperation arrangement with the North East Atlantic Fisheries Commission (NEAFC).[109] Despite such progress, OSPAR itself acknowledges that its network of MPAs cannot yet be regarded as 'well-managed'.[110] This is not an isolated case: the designation of an MPA is not sufficient to ensure its protection.

C. Protection of Vulnerable Marine Ecosystems: The Deep-Sea

Beyond the establishment of MPAs, there are other forms of protection of 'rare or fragile ecosystems as well as the habitat of depleted, threatened or endangered species and other forms of marine life', as called for by UNCLOS. The deep-sea is one such ecosystem, which has received protection from destructive fishing practices thanks to the combined use of area-based management tools and the regulation of bottom fisheries. UN General Assembly (UNGA) resolutions have played a decisive role in safeguarding the deep-sea and its resources.

In 2004, the UNGA called on fishing nations and RFMOs to take urgent action to protect vulnerable marine ecosystems (VMEs) from destructive fishing practices, including bottom trawling, in areas beyond national jurisdiction.[111] In 2006, the COP to the CBD expressed its 'deep concern' over the threats to marine biodiversity beyond national jurisdiction, in particular to seamounts, cold water coral reefs, and hydrothermal vents.[112] The UNGA followed, adopting Resolution 61/105, which set time-bound and concrete objectives for states, and for RFMOs with competence, to regulate bottom fisheries. In particular, RFMOs were required to assess adverse impacts on VMEs, identify such VMEs and, where necessary, close such areas to bottom fishing until measures are in place to prevent adverse impacts.[113] In 2009, the UNGA adopted Resolution 64/72, which called for the better implementation of Resolution 61/105 and introduced some additional requirements.[114] Since then, and with the support of the FAO, including the 2009 International Guidelines for the Management of Deep-Sea Fisheries in the High Seas,[115] RFMOs in particular have made significant progress in the protection of VMEs.[116]

109 OSPAR Agreement 2014-09.

110 OSPAR, '2014 Status Report on the OSPAR Network of Marine Protected Areas' (2014) 5, 38; '2018 Status Report on the OSPAR Network of Marine Protected Areas' (2018) 46–48.

111 UNGA Res 59/25, 'Sustainable fisheries' (17 January 2005) UN Doc A/RES/59/25.

112 Decision VIII/24 (n 92).

113 UNGA Res 61/105 (n 75) para 83; see also paras 84–89.

114 UNGA Res 64/72 (n 75) paras 119–120; see also UNGA Res 66/68 (n 75).

115 See FAO, *International Guidelines for the Management of Deep-sea Fisheries in the High Seas* (2008).

116 Anthony Thompson *et al*, 'Vulnerable Marine Ecosystems: Processes and Practices in the High Seas' (FAO Fisheries and Aquaculture Technical Paper No 595, 2016); see also VME database <https://www.fao.org/in-action/vulnerable-marine-ecosystems/about-vme-database/en/> accessed 15 May 2020.

D. Conservation and Sustainable Use of Marine Biodiversity of Areas Beyond National Jurisdiction (BBNJ)

Despite singular initiatives to protect fragile ecosystems and threatened species described above, the conservation of marine biological diversity in areas beyond national jurisdiction requires a global and integrated response. Previous sections have provided an overview of the current international legal framework to address different ocean uses and responses to a wide range of challenges that span from pollution prevention to the extraction of living and non-living marine resources, including genetic resources. However, continued destruction of marine habitats and biodiversity loss indicate that, so far, international law has not been able to provide the common goals, principles, multisectoral coordination, geographic coverage, and accountability frameworks needed to ensure comprehensive conservation and enforcement.[117]

For more than ten years, efforts have been directed at providing an adequate international legal framework to conserve high seas biodiversity. Following several calls for action and negotiations at the international level since 2004,[118] the UNGA agreed to develop 'an internationally legally binding instrument under [UNCLOS] on the conservation and sustainable use of marine biological diversity of areas beyond national jurisdiction.'[119] Due regard was to be taken of other international agreements, particularly the CBD, which defines biodiversity and aims to promote its conservation, the sustainable use of its components, and the fair and equitable sharing of the benefits arising from the use of genetic resources, and the 2010 Nagoya Protocol on Access to Genetic Resources and the Fair and Equitable Sharing of Benefits Arising from their Utilization, which applies to genetic resources and to traditional knowledge within the scope of the Convention.

Formal negotiations for such an agreement were launched by the UNGA in 2017,[120] with a mandate to develop a 'package deal' focusing on four elements:

- Marine genetic resources, including the sharing of any benefits from their exploitation (MGRs);
- Area-based management tools, including marine protected areas (ABMTs);

[117] Kristina Gjerde *et al*, 'Protecting Earth's Last Conservation Frontier: Scientific, Management and Legal Priorities for MPAs Beyond National Boundaries' *Aquatic Conservation*, 26/2 (2016): 45, 47–48; Kristina Gjerde, *Regulatory and Governance Gaps in the International Regime for the Conservation and Sustainable Use of Marine Biodiversity in Areas Beyond National Jurisdiction* (IUCN 2008).

[118] UNGA Res 59/24, 'Oceans and the law of the sea' (4 February 2005) UN Doc A/RES/59/24, para 73; UNGA Res 66/288, 'The Future We Want' (11 September 2012) UN Doc A/Res/66/288, para 162.

[119] UNGA Res 69/292, 'Development of an international legally binding instrument under the United Nations Convention on the Law of the Sea on the conservation and sustainable use of marine biological diversity of areas beyond national jurisdiction' (6 July 2015) UN Doc A/RES/69/292.

[120] UNGA Res 72/249 (n 10).

- Environmental impact assessments (EIAs); and
- Capacity-building and the transfer of marine technology (CB&TT).[121]

The Intergovernmental Conference (IGC) on the Conservation and Sustainable Use of Marine Biodiversity of Areas Beyond National Jurisdiction held three sessions between 2018 and 2019. The fourth and final session, scheduled for early 2020, was postponed due to the COVID-19 crisis. At the third IGC, states negotiated on the basis of a 'zero draft'. Outcomes of such text negotiations are reflected in the revised draft prepared for the fourth IGC.[122]

The draft text of the Agreement develops provisions for the package deal elements mentioned above, but also introduces general principles, definitions, and cross-cutting issues such as institutional arrangements. While the Agreement presents an adequate architecture, much of its effectiveness will depend on giving effective and agile powers to the COP, and setting arrangements that ensure transparency, information-sharing, and state accountability. A much-debated structural element in the Agreement concerns its relationship with other relevant international legal instruments. As mentioned above, effective coordination among all instruments and bodies impacting high seas biodiversity is essential in a new regime for areas beyond national jurisdiction. The current text indicates that the new instrument 'should not undermine the existing relevant legal instruments and frameworks and relevant global, regional and sectoral bodies'. As indicated by some commentators, if this provision is to stay, the treaty should ensure that existing agreements are implemented in light of the new Agreement's objective.[123]

Regarding the elements of the package deal, on MGRs there are substantial issues pending, mainly related to the applicable overarching principles, including the predominance of the common heritage of mankind notion versus the freedom of the high seas. Under the former, there would be oversight on access to MGRs and standardized, mandatory, and monetary benefit-sharing. Under the freedom of the high seas approach, parties would favour unimpeded access to MGRs and the sharing of benefits on a

[121] UNGA, 'Letter dated 30 June 2011 from the Co-Chairs of the Ad Hoc Open-ended Informal Working Group to the President of the General Assembly' (30 June 2011) UN Doc A/66/119.

[122] UNGA, 'Revised draft text of an agreement under the United Nations Convention on the Law of the Sea on the conservation and sustainable use of marine biological diversity of areas beyond national jurisdiction—Note by the President' (18 November 2019) UN Doc A/CONF.232/2020/3. The IGC President compiled textual proposals submitted by delegations by 20 February 2020, for consideration at the fourth session of IGC. See all conference documents at <https://www.un.org/bbnj/> accessed 15 May 2020.

[123] Ibid, art 4; See Klaudija Kremers *et al*, 'A Preliminary Analysis of the Draft High Seas Biodiversity Treaty' *IDDRI* (2020): 6; 'Summary of the Third Session of the Intergovernmental Conference (IGC) on the Conservation and Sustainable Use of Marine Biodiversity of Areas Beyond National Jurisdiction: 19-30 August 2019' *Earth Negotiations Bulletin*, 25/218 (2019). On legal considerations see Glen Wright *et al*, 'The Long and Winding Road: Negotiating a Treaty for the Conservation and Sustainable Use of Marine Biodiversity in Areas Beyond National Jurisdiction' *IDDRI* (2018); David Freestone, *Conserving Biodiversity in Areas Beyond National Jurisdiction* (Brill 2019).

voluntary basis. The issue of whether MGRs refer only to *in situ* resources, or also those *ex situ*, has not been resolved.[124]

On ABMTs, states are called to cooperate for the establishment of new protected areas or in regard to areas already under some form of protection. However, fundamental elements are pending agreement, including the objective of establishing a comprehensive system of area-based management tools; the role of relevant global, regional, and sectoral bodies, including on information sharing and monitoring; and standards and criteria for the establishment of ABMTs.[125]

Regarding EIAs, the treaty will develop rules on strategic environmental assessments and on cumulative impacts in the conduct of EIAs.[126] It is far from clear what may be the minimum standards for conducting EIAs, although the latest draft foresees that EIAs will be mandatory for areas that are 'ecologically or biologically significant or vulnerable'.[127] On capacity-building and technology transfer, further work is still needed on whether capacity-building is to be voluntary, or also mandatory; who should benefit; and on whether the COP should have a determining role in elaborating relevant modalities.[128]

VI. CONCLUSION

International law for the protection of the oceans and its resources covers large substantive areas of regulation, principally measures against pollution and for fisheries management. Steps have also been taken to regulate the protection of marine species and habitats as a result of increased awareness about their vulnerability. UNCLOS, although fragmented and incomplete, has proven to be sufficiently flexible to allow important developments in ocean law in the past few decades. However, these developments have not prevented the further deterioration of the oceans, the over-exploitation or depletion of marine species, and the destruction of natural marine habitats. This situation may require states to review current practices and search for new solutions.

First steps could be taken by incorporating, and effectively implementing, principles of modern ocean governance, such as the precautionary approach and the ecosystem approach, more broadly than they have been up until now, particularly by RFMOs. This could be coupled with an improvement in compliance and greater accountability of states, which so far have faced limited accountability for their failures. However, a greater change is needed; one that involves rethinking the entire regime for the protection of the oceans. The current focus on high seas governance is important to respond to regulatory

124 See 'Revised draft text' (n 122) arts 7–13.

125 Ibid, arts 14–21; Kremers *et al* (n 123) 8–9.

126 'Revised draft text' (n 122) arts 28 and 25, respectively.

127 Ibid, arts 27 and 24, 29, 30.

128 Ibid, Part V.

gaps, particularly concerning the protection of marine biodiversity beyond areas of national jurisdiction, but change must take place also within national jurisdictions. A connecting thread needs to be woven through all previously disconnected areas of regulation, overcoming some of the initial fragmentation and effectively balancing sovereign rights with the common interest of mankind to protect and preserve the marine environment.

BIBLIOGRAPHY

William Burke, *The New International Law of Fisheries: UNCLOS 1982 and Beyond* (Clarendon Press 1994)

Thomas Burns, 'Marine Pollution' in *The Wiley-Blackwell Encyclopedia of Globalization* (2016)

Daud Hassan and Saiful Karim, *International Marine Environmental Law and Policy* (Routledge 2018)

Philippe Sands and Jacqueline Peel (with Adriana Fabra and Ruth MacKenzie), *Principles of International Environmental Law* (4th edn, CUP 2018) ch 11

Yoshifumi Tanaka, *The International Law of the Sea* (CUP 2015)

CHAPTER 32

WILDLIFE

ANNECOOS WIERSEMA

I. INTRODUCTION

INTERNATIONAL wildlife law is concerned with conserving and avoiding the extinction of species of wild animals and plants. Wildlife—living animals and plants that are not human and are not domesticated—is at risk in the Anthropocene. The most recent global assessment report on biodiversity and ecosystem services produced by the Intergovernmental Science-Policy Platform on Biodiversity and Ecosystem Services (IPBES) estimates that 'of an estimated 8 million animal and plant species (75% of which are insects), around 1 million are threatened with extinction', many 'within decades'.[1]

As a whole, the most significant threats to species are over-exploitation and agriculture.[2] Additional threats come from invasive species, pollution, and habitat disturbance, and—increasingly—climate change.[3] Many of these threats stem from a combination of national and international drivers. For example, global demand for palm oil creates incentives to increase palm oil plantations, which in turn destroys critical habitat for orangutans. However, decisions about land use and the use of natural resources traditionally fall within the domestic jurisdiction of sovereign states. As a result of this dynamic, the scope and substance of international wildlife law are strongly influenced by the question of when international law is considered to have a role to play in wildlife conservation.

This chapter begins with a discussion of the themes and principles that shape international wildlife law. It then discusses certain international regimes that focus on particular species, before discussing examples of ecosystem-based regimes and regimes

[1] IPBES, *Global Assessment Report on Biodiversity and Ecosystem Services* (2019) Summary for Policy Makers, 14.

[2] Sean Maxwell *et al*, 'The Ravages of Guns, Nets and Bulldozers' *Nature*, 536 (2016): 143, 144.

[3] Ibid.

with a more regional focus. The chapter concludes with brief thoughts on the most significant issues facing global wildlife conservation.

II. THEMES AND PRINCIPLES

International wildlife law shares attributes with other fields of international environmental law, but also has certain particular attributes. In particular, the degree to which treaties affecting wildlife conservation impose strict or flexible obligations on their member states is often a product of a variety of factors, for example: how specific the scope of the treaty is, whether the treaty primarily focuses on individual species or on ecosystem and habitat protection, and whether the treaty targets primarily domestic or primarily international activities or species. This section of the chapter discusses these themes and principles, beginning with a discussion of the various justifications invoked for wildlife conservation.

A. Justifications for Wildlife Conservation

It is always easier to justify protecting something when it has direct implications for human well-being.[4] While certain environmental problems, like pollution and climate change, directly affect human health and well-being, the loss of biodiversity and wildlife species do not appear, at first sight, to affect humans directly. Nevertheless, utilitarian reasons for protection can be invoked, particularly when it comes to the need to protect biodiversity. First, biodiversity and the interactions among species give the planet natural capital.[5] Second, each component of biodiversity may provide some direct benefit to humans, for example, in the form of a cure to a disease. Yet we do not have enough information to know which species are important to save for these direct benefits to accrue. Not only do we not know which species potentially provide cures or other benefits, but also we do not know how the loss of other species in an ecosystem may affect the directly beneficial species. As a result, the potential for direct benefit can provide a justification to protect all components of global biodiversity. Other anthropocentric reasons for protecting wildlife include its value to scientists for study, aesthetic value, existence value, and cultural value.

Beyond anthropocentric justifications for protection, some people would invoke the intrinsic value of wildlife's survival for itself and not for the benefit of humans.[6] These arguments could take the form of justifying the survival of species, but not specifically

[4] See Chapter 13, 'Ethical Considerations', in this volume.

[5] Robert Costanza *et al*, 'The Value of the World's Ecosystem Services and Natural Capital' *Nature*, 387 (1997): 253, 254.

[6] See Chapter 14, 'Earth Jurisprudence', in this volume.

opposing the killing of individual animals. Alternatively, notions of intrinsic value can be placed within an animal-rights framework that urges the protection of the life of individual animals. These two approaches, although both based on rationales beyond anthropocentric justifications, are not always consistent.

Once we acknowledge how connected wildlife species are with each other and that humans are part of those connections, the distinctions among these justifications can seem less significant. The baseline approach of international wildlife law acknowledges a range of justifications and at its core is about avoiding extinction. However, the different justifications and the values they embody can have a significant impact on the details of which species we give most attention to, how to conserve species, how to balance competing interests, and who should answer these questions. Thus, many of the most contentious disputes in international wildlife law stem in part from differences in how various constituencies answer those questions. For example, while many conservationists are willing to allow the use of wildlife for human benefit as long as it is sustainable for that species—sustainable utilization—some animal rights perspectives object to use for some or all animal species. Further, some commentators are warier about whether commodification of wildlife, particularly animals, should be the norm because of concerns about whether the use can be truly sustainable or because of moral concerns about use of animals.

B. Permanent Sovereignty Over Natural Resources

One of the most significant and firmly established principles in international law is the principle of permanent sovereignty over natural resources: the principle that sovereign states have the authority to make decisions regarding natural resources within their borders. While treaties can erode that fundamental principle, the reality is that international wildlife treaties take permanent sovereignty as a starting principle.

The scope of international wildlife law is affected by this principle because there is a relationship between how much an agreement calls for specific actions and contains hard obligations, and the subject matter of the agreements. The less a treaty focuses on internal land use decisions, the more likely it is to have strong and specific requirements. For example, species that migrate or are traded across international borders trigger international law because their protection cannot be achieved by an individual state. For those species, treaties may contain specific and firm requirements, as with the restriction on 'taking' species protected under Appendix I of the 1979 Convention on Migratory Species (CMS) and the strict obligations placed on member states of the 1973 Convention on International Trade of Endangered Species of Wild Fauna and Flora (CITES). In the case of the 1992 Convention on Biological Diversity (CBD), by contrast, the goal is to conserve biodiversity, primarily *in situ*, meaning 'within ecosystems and natural habitats'.[7] This implicates species that do not cross borders and, in its approach, also implicates the kinds of land use decisions that would typically be made within

[7] art 2.

states. The obligations under the CBD are, accordingly, vague and modified by phrases such as 'as far as possible and as appropriate'. Similarly, the 1971 Ramsar Convention on Wetlands of International Importance focuses on the conservation of wetlands within the jurisdiction of states and, in turn, contains only broad obligations that are largely procedural in nature.

The principle of permanent sovereignty over natural resources also raises another important issue, namely who should be the decision-maker regarding the protection of species. To the extent that the conservation of wildlife species is, at minimum, the common concern of humankind, the international community at large has an interest in protection, triggering a role for international law. But to the extent that those species or individual animals and plants do not migrate or cross international borders, they would fall within the natural resources of the country they live in. Thus, with permanent sovereignty over natural resources, there is a stronger claim for decision-making to lie with range states—states where the species live. International cooperation is then only deemed necessary to ensure that the efforts of the range state are effective, as stated in the preambles to many wildlife treaties.

C. Species and Ecosystem Perspectives

International wildlife law can also be shaped by whether it takes a species-by-species approach or a more holistic approach focused on conserving habitat and ecosystem processes. Ecologists focus on processes and the connections among species as the keys to understanding ecosystems. In turn, they have urged that the focus of conservationists and managers should similarly be on the connections among species rather than individual species in isolation. On this view, any attempt to conserve species without reference to these connections and, correspondingly to habitat, would be extremely limited in its effectiveness. Nevertheless, treaties vary in whether they take a species-specific approach or an ecosystem approach. Both have a role to play, given that threats come from different sources. As with the other principles and themes, the choice to use a species-centred or ecosystem-oriented approach in an instrument seems to correlate with the hardness or softness of the commitments contained in that instrument. Where the Ramsar Convention contains soft obligations with procedural reporting requirements to back them up, CITES has hard obligations triggered when a species is listed.

D. Uncertainty, Precaution, and Adaptive Management

As with other environmental problems, uncertainty abounds with regard to wildlife and wildlife conservation. Ecological systems are complex, nonlinear, and dynamic.[8] These uncertainties are exacerbated by climate change, with current and projected impacts

[8] Crawford Holling, 'What Barriers? What Bridges?' in Lance Gunderson *et al* (eds), *Barriers and Bridges to the Renewal of Ecosystems and Institutions* (Columbia University Press 1995) 19.

on every aspect of biodiversity and inevitable accompanying effects on processes and connections among living organisms. With or without the effects of climate change, uncertainty with regard to wildlife comes from four sources: current data gaps, historical data gaps, variables and complexity, and indeterminacy.[9]

Current data gaps exist because scientists and policy-makers simply do not know enough about every species. That in turn means they do not know all the ways those species interact: the processes and connections that are key to understanding biological systems. This is not just a problem affecting the most hidden or uncharismatic species, although it does particularly affect them. Current data gaps exist for some of the most prominent species as well, including the African elephant and polar bears.

Historical data gaps also lead to uncertainty because they can make it hard to determine how a species is changing—for example, in number, range, and behaviour. Historical data gaps affect, therefore, the interpretation of current data.[10] Although this should change gradually over time as data is collected going forward, the starting point for the data collection will not change except in certain circumstances where fossil records can provide information.

Even with concerted efforts to fill in data gaps, the variables at play and the complexity of ecological systems means that those studying a system are unlikely to gain a full understanding of how any single variable will respond.[11] Modelling is critical for navigating complexity and can significantly help with predictions to aid management decisions. However, models will always be based on assumptions and therefore cannot make predictions with absolute certainty.

Further, the fourth source of uncertainty—indeterminacy—exacerbates the uncertainty stemming from variability and complexity. If ecological systems do not have a fixed state of equilibrium with, for example, some fixed population number for a species, a conservationist's task is harder than the already difficult task of trying to maintain a particular state of equilibrium. Instead, a conservationist may be faced with managing the evolution of a system—something that may become increasingly necessary in the face of climate change where it will likely be impossible to maintain every species in its current situation. Alternatively, a conservationist may have to choose among different options, resulting in the need for value-based decision-making.

In international environmental law, the precautionary principle or approach has come to be the primary means by which this uncertainty is addressed, allowing for conservation action even before full scientific certainty.[12] Application of the principle

[9] Annecoos Wiersema, 'Uncertainty, Precaution, and Adaptive Management in Wildlife Trade' *Michigan Journal of International Law*, 36/3 (2015): 375, 378–383.

[10] Ibid, 381.

[11] M Henry Stevens, *A Primer of Ecology with R* (Springer 2009) 4; Jacqueline Peel, *The Precautionary Principle in Practice: Environmental Decision-Making and Scientific Uncertainty* (Federation Press 2005) 37.

[12] *Report of the United Nations Conference on Environment and Development* (UN 1993) vol I, annex I—'Rio Declaration on Environment and Development'.

is contentious and not without difficulty.[13] For implementation in the face of uncertainty, scientists and policy-makers have developed a management approach to deal with uncertainty, known as adaptive management. This allows managers to approach conservation with some experimentation in mind, monitor what is happening, and revise their goals or means accordingly. Although most international wildlife treaties were agreed on without explicit provision for adaptive management, their institutional structure, discussed next, allows for some provision for adaptation and input from scientific authorities, and adaptive management approaches have become important for the implementation of many international wildlife treaties.

E. Institutional Arrangements and Participants

International wildlife law is made up of a few global and broadly applicable agreements and many regional agreements, as well as agreements that focus on one species or a set of related species. A species or region may be governed by several different treaty regimes. This chapter will focus primarily on the global and broadly applicable agreements. Nevertheless, it is worth noting a few common features to wildlife-focused agreements.[14]

Standing in the shadow of permanent sovereignty over natural resources and incomplete information, these treaties tend to leave out much detail of implementation. However, the treaty creates an institutional structure, consisting of committees and standing bodies—often a Secretariat—that play a critical role in developing interpretations, establishing guidelines for implementation, and making assessments of the status of particular species. These committees are often populated by technical and scientific experts drawn from the parties. They are often important drivers for the effectiveness of the treaty. However, when the stakes are high and the scientists are less independent of the states, these committees can become too politicized. The work of these committees often feeds into the regular meetings of the parties to the treaties: Conferences of the Parties (COPs) and Meetings of the Parties (MOPs). The outcomes of COPs and MOPs have a significant impact on the direction and interpretation of the treaty.[15]

The work of secretariats and technical committees brings in experts from around the world, allowing for participation beyond the state representatives who attend the regular COPs and MOPs. This work is also facilitated by non-governmental organizations (NGOs), which can usually attend and participate in meetings, but cannot vote. NGOs perform a variety of functions: lobbyists, capacity-builders, and information providers.[16] For CITES, the work of the NGO TRAFFIC is critical to understanding legal and illegal

[13] For a full discussion see Chapter 18, 'Precaution', in this volume.

[14] See Chapter 24, 'Multilateral Environmental Treaty Making', in this volume.

[15] Annecoos Wiersema, 'The New International Law-Makers? Conferences of the Parties to Multilateral Environmental Agreements' *Michigan Journal of International Law*, 31/1 (2009): 237–246.

[16] Anne-Marie Slaughter, 'International Law and International Relations' *Recueil Des Cours*, 285/9 (2000): 96.

trade in species. Some NGOs have formal partnerships with treaties, such as BirdLife International, Wetlands International, and the World Wildlife Fund (WWF) with the Ramsar Convention. Further, many NGOs provide support and resources within countries to further conservation. They may also use that support to promote their own values, which can be contentious.

III. SPECIES-CENTRED APPROACHES

Species-centred approaches range from treaty regimes that focus on particular groups of species, to ones that focus on species within a particular region, to ones that can apply to any species falling within their scope. They operate by identifying individual species for particular conservation action, rather than identifying relevant habitat to achieve beneficial conservation outcomes. There are many treaties that focus on a particular species or group of species. This section of the chapter discusses only the most prominent and global species-centred regimes.

A. Trade in Endangered Species

For many species, unsustainable demand has led historically to significant reduction in populations, leading in some cases to a significant threat of extinction. To address this threat, the international community adopted CITES in the early 1970s. It has been widely adopted, with 183 parties, and is often regarded as the cornerstone of international wildlife law even though its scope is limited to addressing threats to species from international trade.

CITES regulates—and sometimes severely curtails—trade in species threatened by international trade. To do this, the treaty requires states to set up Scientific and Management Authorities to implement a permitting system that depends on a listing system with three Appendices. Species are listed according to whether, and how much, they are threatened by international trade. Once listed, trade in a species is regulated by the text of CITES. Parties seeking to trade with non-parties must essentially abide by the terms of the treaty as well, so that if enough countries are party to the treaty, there is little incentive for states to decide to stay outside the treaty regime.[17] Listing on the two most significant Appendices, Appendices I and II, occurs by a vote of the parties requiring a two-thirds majority of the parties present and voting.[18] That listing is then binding on every party regardless of how they voted. States may enter reservations to a particular listing. However, due to the non-party provisions referred to, a state will still

[17] art 10.

[18] art 15.

be governed by the requirements of the treaty unless the state it is trading with is either a non-party or has also entered a reservation to a particular listing.

Appendix I listing is for 'all species threatened with extinction which are or may be affected by trade'.[19] Once listed on Appendix I, that species can only be traded internationally if both an export permit and an import permit are issued.[20] For the export permit, the Scientific Authority in the exporting state must advise that the trade 'will not be detrimental to the survival of that species'.[21] The importing state's Scientific Authority must advise—for the import permit—that the import 'will be for purposes that are not detrimental to the survival of the species involved'.[22] These are non-detriment findings (NDFs), an important aspect of CITES. Import permits have an additional requirement. The Management Authority of the importing state must be satisfied that the Appendix I-listed specimen 'is not to be used for primarily commercial purposes'.[23] This amounts to an almost complete ban on commercial trade in that species, although there are exceptions in the text of the treaty for captive-bred species, scientific exchange, and exchange among zoos and similar organizations.[24] Nevertheless, the commercial trade in a specimen of a species listed on Appendix I is prohibited by the treaty.

The Appendix II listing is for 'all species which although not necessarily now threatened with extinction may become so unless trade in specimens of such species is subject to strict regulation in order to avoid utilization incompatible with their survival'.[25] In addition, this includes non-threatened species whose listing is necessary to ensure that trade in specimens of threatened species listed on Appendix II 'may be brought under effective control'.[26] This allows, therefore, for listing of lookalike species to protect the threatened species.

Appendix II listing is intended to result in regulated international trade rather than a ban on commercial trade, hopefully allowing sufficient regulation to ensure the species is not over-exploited. Import permits are not required and therefore the prohibition on commercial trade does not apply to these species. As an export permit is still required, an NDF is still required.[27] Countries can also put stricter provisions in place in their domestic law, which can be contentious if it is inconsistent with range state preferences.[28]

Much of the attention surrounding negotiations under CITES is focused on the most charismatic and iconic species: elephants, rhinoceros, lions, tigers, and sharks. Although CITES is often discussed as a trade ban treaty, the vast majority of its species are listed on Appendix II and, on Appendix II, the vast majority of species are plants.

19 art 2.1.
20 arts 3.2, 3.
21 art 3.2(a).
22 Ibid.
23 arts 3.2(d), 3.3(c).
24 art 7.
25 art 2.2(a).
26 art 2.2(b).
27 art 4.2(a).
28 art 14.1.

Empirically, it is difficult to know how much the existence of CITES has made a difference to illegal trade in pure enforcement terms and there is some debate about the treaty's effectiveness.[29] In addition, debates have arisen due to disagreements about whether the approach CITES takes helps or may even hurt the species it is seeking to protect.[30] Some critics of CITES argue that regulated trade can help species and also allow local communities to benefit economically from sustainable utilization of those species. However, while sustainable utilization can be consistent with CITES, it is not always easy to know when that utilization will be sustainable for the species and whether demand can be sufficiently controlled to ensure that permitting trade does not result in over-consumption and increased killing. In addition, some people oppose utilization for certain species, for example elephants, even if they would not oppose it for other animals or for plants. This is an area riven by both uncertainty and fundamental value disagreements.[31] Although listing decisions are meant to be driven by science, rather than politics or values, different positions on the role of trade in conservation inform the outcomes of many voting decisions and CITES COPs are extremely political.

B. Migratory Species

Migratory species are obvious candidates for the invocation of international law because, by definition, more than one state will encounter a particular migratory species. The Convention on the Conservation of Migratory Species of Wild Animals, known as the Convention on Migratory Species (CMS) or the Bonn Convention, was concluded in 1979 and entered into force in 1983. As its name suggests, it applies only to migratory species, defined in the treaty to cover species 'a significant proportion of whose members cyclically and predictably cross one or more national jurisdictional boundaries'.[32] Its definition includes 'the entire population or any geographically separate part of the population of any species or lower taxon of wild animals' and the parties have interpreted this somewhat broadly.[33]

Like many wildlife conservation instruments, the CMS relies on a listing system. However, the Appendices in the CMS operate differently from each other and are not incompatible. A species can, therefore, be listed on one or both depending on the level of

[29] Cf. Geoffrey Wandesforde-Smith, 'Looking for Law in All the Wrong Places? Dying Elephants, Evolving Treaties, and Empty Threats' *Journal of International Wildlife and Policy*, 19/4 (2016): 365; Annecoos Wiersema, 'CITES and the Whole Chain Approach to Combating Illegal Wildlife Trade' *Journal of International Wildlife Law & Policy*, 20/3–4 (2017): 207.

[30] Michael Bowman, 'A Tale of Two CITES: Divergent Perspectives upon the Effectiveness of the Wildlife Trade Convention' *Review of European Community & International Environmental Law*, 22/3 (2013): 228.

[31] Annecoos Wiersema, 'Uncertainty and Markets for Endangered Species under CITES' *Review of European, Comparative & International Environmental Law*, 22 (2013): 239.

[32] art 1.1.

[33] Ibid.

threat they are facing and what conservation instruments they may need.[34] Whereas the CITES Appendices discussed above operate along one axis in terms of extent of regulation and address only the level and type of trade allowed, Appendix I and Appendix II of the CMS operate in different jurisdictional ways. Appendix I specifies the obligations of range states internally for the species and Appendix II provides for further international cooperation.[35]

Appendix I is for 'migratory species which are endangered', meaning that the species is 'in danger of extinction throughout all or a significant portion of its range'.[36] For these species, range states shall 'endeavour' to take conservation actions to limit harm and to restore habitat.[37] More forcefully, these range states 'shall' prohibit 'the taking of animals belonging to such species', except in certain narrow circumstances.[38] 'Taking' is defined in the treaty as 'hunting, fishing, capturing, harassing, deliberate killing, or attempting to engage in any such conduct'.[39] Although these provisions are stricter than for Appendix II-listed species, the only truly concrete requirement is the prohibition on taking. The other obligations for Appendix I-listed species are less well-defined and modified by the phrases 'to the extent feasible and appropriate', 'where feasible and appropriate', and 'as appropriate'.[40] They therefore leave a great deal of discretion to the range state itself—consistent with the focus on deference to state action encompassed by the principle of permanent sovereignty over natural resources discussed above. Even migratory species are always within the jurisdiction of a particular state and deference to that state then plays a role.

Appendix II is for those migratory species that 'have an unfavourable conservation status', defined as the absence of any one of four factors that encompass the long-term: population viability of the species, reductions or likely reductions in the range of the species, the sufficiency of habitat to maintain the population, and a reference to historic levels of the species as a baseline against which to measure the distribution and abundance of the species.[41] Species to be included on Appendix II also have another criterion to meet: that they 'would significantly benefit from the international co-operation that could be achieved by an international agreement'.

This international component is important because species listed on Appendix II are not subject to a specific set of provisions listed in the treaty text but, rather, are to become the subject of further international agreement. For Appendix II-listed species, the CMS provides for two different types of international agreement.[42] Alternative actions include the development of a Memorandum of Understanding (MOU) or an Action

[34] art 4.2.
[35] arts 3.4, 3.5, 4.3.
[36] arts 3.1, 1.1(e).
[37] art 3.4.
[38] art 3.5.
[39] art 1.1(i).
[40] art 3.4.
[41] arts 1.1(c)–(d).
[42] arts 4.3, 4.4.

Plan. Parties do not need to be a member of the CMS to be a member of one of the treaties negotiated pursuant to the CMS. Since the CMS came into force, the parties have negotiated four treaties under Article 4.3 of the CMS and three agreements under Article 4.4, as well as nineteen MOUs and four special species initiatives. Some of these subsidiary agreements have provided opportunity for innovative treaty-making and implementation, and they can serve to supplement both the CMS and other treaties.[43]

C. Whales

The 1946 International Convention for the Regulation of Whaling (ICRW) takes the species-specific approach further by focusing on a particular set of species, whales. The conservation of whale populations is primarily governed by the ICRW, which entered into force in 1948 with just whaling states as parties. It now has eighty-nine member states, including many non-whaling states. The ICRW was negotiated after prior attempts to address the impacts of whaling on whale populations had failed, with some populations in severe decline at the time of the ICRW's agreement. It is a product of this history and its time, with a preamble that notes that the parties decided 'to conclude a convention to provide for the proper conservation of whale stocks and thus make possible the orderly development of the whaling industry'.[44] Thus, conservation under the ICRW was not about opposition to whaling *per se*, but about ensuring enough whales could survive so that whaling could continue. The treaty text does not determine how much whaling is permissible but assigns this task to the International Whaling Commission (IWC). The IWC is made up of representatives of member states, with each state having one vote.

In its early years, the ICRW did not appear to have much impact on whale populations as it consistently set whaling quotas too high. As some states experienced domestic pressure against whaling and stopped whaling, they started to push against commercial whaling. States opposed to commercial whaling also encouraged participation by new members, primarily developing countries, to oppose commercial whaling, thereby shifting the balance of power. In 1982, after a few failed attempts, the parties voted to place a moratorium on commercial whaling.[45] Some whaling states left the treaty or entered a reservation. Iceland and Norway currently have reservations and continue to whale commercially without violating the treaty. However, Japan, which is also in favour

[43] Richard Caddell, 'International Law and the Protection of Migratory Wildlife: An Appraisal of Twenty-Five Years of the Bonn Convention' *Colorado Journal of International Environmental Law and Policy*, 16/1 (2005): 113; Melissa Lewis, 'Migratory Waterbird Conservation at the Flyway Level: Distilling the Added Value of AEWA in Relation to the Ramsar Convention' *Pace Environmental Law Review*, 34 (2016): 1.

[44] Preamble.

[45] Patricia Birnie, 'The Role of Developing Countries in Nudging the International Whaling Commission from Regulating Whaling to Encouraging Nonconsumptive Uses of Whales' *Ecology Law Quarterly*, 12/4 (1985): 964.

of commercial whaling, opted to stay within the treaty and rely on an exception within the ICRW for whaling for scientific purposes rather than ostensibly undertake commercial whaling. Whether Japan will remain a party to the treaty going forward remains an open question.

Under Article VIII of the ICRW, a member state 'may grant to any of its nationals a special permit authorizing that national to kill, take and treat whales for purposes of scientific research'.[46] Japan relied on this provision for a number of years before Australia, with New Zealand intervening, had a case heard and decided before the International Court of Justice (ICJ) for breach of the treaty.[47] This chapter focuses on two issues of particular interest to international wildlife law: how the ICJ navigated competing values relating to whaling in determining the purpose of the ICRW, and the role of a scientific organization, the IWC, established under the treaty.

On the question of the purpose of the ICRW, the ICJ noted that the preamble and treaty refer to both conservation and whaling and that even if, over time, the international community may have come to adopt a more conservation-oriented approach to whales, this was not part of the treaty text. With regard to the IWC, the ICJ observed both that the recommendations of the IWC were not binding, nor were they irrelevant. The parties have a duty to cooperate with the IWC and should pay 'due regard' to their recommendations.[48] In addition, the ICJ noted that 'when they are adopted by consensus or by a unanimous vote, [these recommendations] may be relevant for the interpretation of the Convention or its Schedule'.[49] These aspects of the ICJ's decision are significant for international wildlife law where, as described above, much of the work under a treaty regime is done by committees charged with performing certain tasks by the treaty text, or by COPs and MOPs. The ICJ acknowledged that the authority granted to the IWC made the Convention an 'evolving instrument'.[50] Yet it did not recognize the IWC's work as binding on the parties or the Court.

The functioning of the IWC reflects a significant problem in international wildlife law, namely that even bodies that are intended to focus on the science are often highly politicized. The IWC itself is a notoriously politicized body, with distrust and stark disagreements among parties.[51] These disagreements are often fuelled by different opinions on whether whaling should occur at all, but play out using scientific data and a decision-making body that is meant to be guided by science. Some commentators have advocated changes that would allow independent scientists a voice distinct from states'

[46] art 8.

[47] *Whaling in the Antarctic (Australia/ Japan, New Zealand intervening)* (Judgement) [2014] ICJ Rep 226 (Whaling in Antarctic case); for a discussion of this case see Chapter 27, 'Judicial Development', in this volume.

[48] Whaling in Antarctic case (n 47) [83].

[49] Ibid [46].

[50] Ibid [45].

[51] Richard Caddell, 'Science Friction: Antarctic Research Whaling and the International Court of Justice' *Journal of Environmental Law*, 26/2 (2014): 331.

positions.[52] Where things currently stand, however, agreement on the science may be impossible given deep disagreements on values.

IV. ECOSYSTEM AND HABITAT-BASED APPROACHES

International wildlife law is also made up of agreements that take an ecosystem or habitat-based approach. Sometimes these have the specific goal of protecting wildlife or, more broadly, biodiversity. At other times, the focus of the agreement or international law does not specifically target the conservation of wildlife, but this may be a beneficial side-effect. The broadest of these is the CBD, which is discussed first before turning to more specific agreements for wetlands, protected areas, and forests.

A. Biodiversity

In 1992, the same year the international community tackled climate change with a broad multilateral treaty, it also tackled biodiversity. The CBD is a treaty with wide-ranging scope. Rather than focusing on the protection of specific species or habitats, its organizing principle is diversity, defined as meaning 'the variability among living organisms from all sources including, *inter alia*, terrestrial, marine and other aquatic ecosystems and the ecological complexes of which they are part'.[53] Every scale is relevant: 'this includes diversity within species, between species and of ecosystems'.[54] Further, the definitions make clear that genetic diversity is a relevant aspect of this goal of diversity. Indeed, in Article 1, the CBD states that its objectives are 'the conservation of biological diversity, the sustainable use of its components and the fair and equitable sharing of the benefits arising out of the utilization of genetic resources, including by appropriate access to genetic resources and by appropriate transfer of relevant technologies'.[55] Thus, from the outset, the CBD is less focused on the protection of individual species of wildlife, than on the maintenance of genetic diversity in part as a resource. It is in keeping with this approach that, despite important provisions on *in situ* conservation discussed below, the two protocols that have been developed to date

[52] William de la Mare *et al*, 'Applying Scientific Principles in International Law on Whaling' *Science*, 345 (2015): 1125, 1126.

[53] art 2.

[54] Ibid.

[55] art 1.

under the framework of the CBD focus on genetic resources in various ways: the 2000 Cartagena Protocol on Biosafety and the 2010 Nagoya Protocol on Benefit-Sharing.[56]

The CBD is sometimes dismissed because it contains language that limits the obligations of the parties with modifiers like 'as far as possible and as appropriate'.[57] It leaves a great deal of discretion to the parties and contains very few concrete obligations. In Article 3, it sets out the 'principle' that states have 'the sovereign right to exploit their own resources pursuant to their own environmental policies'. The treaty demonstrates the trade-offs that appear in international environmental law generally, and international wildlife law more specifically, as described above: the broader in scope a treaty is, the softer its obligations are likely to be, and the more a treaty focuses on internal land use, the more deference it will give to national sovereignty. The CBD has even been viewed by some commentators as soft law because its obligations are imprecise and the COPs have done little or nothing to harden them.[58] In trade tribunals, the CBD and its Biosafety Protocol have not had enough force to counter states' trade treaty responsibilities.[59]

For the purposes of this chapter, however, the treaty text and subsequent actions developed by the parties have both done some important work in advancing ecosystem approaches to conservation. In its treaty text, the CBD begins the work of focusing on ecosystem protection as the means of conserving biodiversity. In particular, the main means for conservation of diversity is to be through *in situ* conservation. Article 8 sets out a number of ways to achieve this, with all the caveats of the 'as far as possible and as appropriate' language. For parties, this includes directions to establish 'a system of protected areas or areas where special measures need to be taken to conserve biological diversity' and to '[p]romote the protection of ecosystems, natural habitats and the maintenance of viable populations of species in natural surroundings'. The CBD also says that parties shall limit activities—including introduction of alien species—that could put those things at risk.[60] In Article 9, where the CBD discusses *ex situ* conservation, it does so with the preface that this conservation is 'predominantly for the purpose of complementing *in situ* measures'.

The CBD's COPs have also been important in promoting the ecosystem approach to conservation of biological diversity and providing support and resources for that. In 1995, the parties adopted the ecosystem approach as 'the primary framework of action

[56] See Chapters 42 and 48, 'Indigenous Peoples' and 'Intellectual Property', in this volume for discussion of the Nagoya Protocol.

[57] arts 5, 6(b), 7–11, 14.

[58] Stuart Harrop and Diana Pritchard, 'A Hard Instrument Goes Soft: The Implications of the Convention on Biological Diversity's Current Trajectory' *Global Environmental Change*, 21/2 (2011): 474; Elisa Morgera and Elsa Tsioumani, 'Yesterday, Today, and Tomorrow: Looking Afresh at the Convention on Biological Diversity' *Yearbook of International Environmental Law*, 21/1 (2010): 3.

[59] For discussion of the *Biotech* dispute in the World Trade Organization (WTO), in which the European Union (EU) raised arguments based on the CBD and Biosafety Protocol see Chapter 43, 'Trade', in this volume.

[60] art 8.

to be taken under the Convention'.[61] Under Article 2, 'ecosystem' is defined as 'a dynamic complex of plant, animal and micro-organism communities and their non-living environment interacting as a functional unit'. The ecosystem approach has been described as a 'strategy for the integrated management of land, water and living resources that promotes conservation and sustainable use in an equitable way', which will allow a balance of the three objectives of the Convention: conservation, sustainable use, and the fair and equitable sharing of benefits arising out of the use of genetic resources.[62]

At COP 9, the role of the ecosystem approach was reiterated as key to achieving the Millennium Development Goals, but the parties also recognized the difficulties of implementation, the need for flexibility in how it is applied, and the fact that it has not been fully implemented by the parties.[63] The parties noted that '[t]he application of the ecosystem approach should be regarded as a process where learning by doing is the priority need at present'.[64] Since then, a number of resources for practitioners have been developed to allow implementation of the ecosystem approach and shared knowledge, with an Ecosystem Approach Sourcebook that includes a website and a case study database.[65]

The work of the parties under the CBD has given rise to some key developments that have influenced international wildlife law more broadly. In 2010, at the tenth COP, the parties adopted the Strategic Plan for Biodiversity 2011–20 and the Aichi Targets.[66] These were intended to guide not only work under the CBD, but also the entire United Nations (UN) system. Other conventions, including wildlife conventions, have taken note of the approach of the Aichi Targets, and given them influence over the work of those conventions. There are twenty Aichi Targets, grouped under five Strategic Goals that highlight the main themes of the CBD convention text: (A) addressing the underlying causes of biodiversity loss and integrating biodiversity concerns into decision-making; (B) reducing direct pressures on biodiversity and promoting sustainable use; (C) safeguarding ecosystems, species, and genetic diversity as a means to enhance biodiversity; (D) enhancing benefits to all people from biodiversity and ecosystem services; and (E) improving the processes for implementation with participatory planning, knowledge management, and capacity building.[67] As of 5 March 2020,

[61] Decision II/8, 'Preliminary consideration of components of biological diversity particularly under threat and action which could be taken under the Convention' (17 November 1995).

[62] 'Recommendations adopted by the Subsidiary Body on Scientific, Technical and Technical Advice at its fifth meeting' (25 February 2000) UN Doc UNEP/CBD/COP/5/3, Annex I, Recommendation V/10—'Ecosystem approach: further conceptual elaboration'.

[63] Decision IX/7, 'Ecosystem Approach' (9 October 2008) UN Doc UNEP/CBD/COP/DEC/IX/7.

[64] Ibid, para (b).

[65] See CBD, 'Ecosystem Approach Sourcebook' <http://www.cbd.int/ecosystem/sourcebook> accessed 16 May 2020.

[66] Decision X/2, 'The Strategic Plan for Biodiversity 2011–2020 and the Aichi Biodiversity Targets' (29 October 2010) UN Doc UNEP/CBD/COP/DEC/X/2.

[67] Ibid, annex, Section IV; see also CBD, 'Aichi Biodiversity Targets' <https://www.cbd.int/sp/targets/> accessed 16 May 2020.

in accordance with Target 17, 191 out of 196 parties had adopted a national biodiversity strategy and action plan that incorporates at least one of the Aichi Targets.

All of these goals reflect key attributes of international environmental law, including a focus on integrated decision-making processes to enhance protection with tools like environmental impact assessment (EIA). Of particular note is the emphasis in Goal B on promoting sustainable use. As discussed above in relation to CITES, the question of sustainable use has become somewhat contentious in international wildlife law. The targets under Goal B of the Aichi Targets do not enter this fray explicitly, focusing instead on sustainable management of fisheries, agriculture, and forestry. However, the overall goal of sustainable use has influenced the debate among parties in forums like the CITES COPs.

Because of the soft imperatives of the CBD and the fact that most of its implementation happens within the borders of countries and often at very localized levels within countries, its influence is diffuse and it is hard to identify specific impacts outside of the more concrete focus of its two protocols. However, in developing targets relating to biodiversity, promoting an ecosystem approach and sustainable use, and promoting planning tools, the CBD has shaped the conversation across international environmental law, and within international wildlife law specifically. For parties with the political will to implement the CBD for the protection of wildlife, it can add support. For parties without that political will, however, it does not provide strong imperatives.

B. Wetlands

The Ramsar Convention has always had a focus on habitat, even though the original impetus for its adoption was concern about individual species of waterfowl. Parties have two different types of obligation. First, they are to designate wetlands of international importance for inclusion in the Convention's List. The criteria for this designation have evolved over the years and reflect concern about both ecosystem protection and individual species protection. For wetlands on the List, parties are to formulate and implement their national wetlands planning 'so as to promote the conservation of the wetlands included in the List'.[68] In addition, parties are to promote 'as far as possible the wise use of wetlands in their territory', an obligation that extends to all wetlands and not just wetlands included in the List.[69]

With its emphasis on protection and wise use of wetlands, it is unsurprising that the Ramsar Convention has relatively soft obligations, focusing on exhortations to plan and stay informed. The treaty operates primarily by having stronger procedural obligations, relying on reporting and its accompanying potential for shaming to promote compliance. Despite its limited substantive obligations, the Ramsar Convention's institutions,

[68] art 2.
[69] art 3.

most notably the Scientific and Technical Review Panel, have been at the forefront of trying to grapple with how to promote conservation while acknowledging the role of humans in wetlands and the complexity of ecological systems.

C. Protected Areas

The 1972 World Heritage Convention (WHC) has 193 states parties, and is therefore a universally adopted treaty. It is focused on protecting cultural and natural heritage and establishes a scheme for states to delineate the sites on its territory that meet the treaty's definitions of cultural and natural heritage. For the purposes of this chapter, the most significant is the definition of 'natural heritage'.[70] This definition specifically includes 'geological and physiographical formations and precisely delineated areas which constitute the habitat of threatened species of animals and plants of outstanding universal value from the point of view of science or conservation'.[71] While this definition is somewhat narrow with regard to the wildlife that will fall within it—threatened and of outstanding universal value—the definition of 'natural heritage' also includes natural features 'of outstanding universal value from the aesthetic or scientific point of view' and sites 'of outstanding universal value from the point of view of science, conservation or natural beauty', which could further encompass wildlife.

The WHC's approach is consistent with the overall approach of international wildlife law, deferring to states when it comes to land management. As Article 4 states, each state party 'recognizes that the duty of ensuring the identification, protection, conservation, presentation and transmission to future generations of the cultural and natural heritage . . . situated in its territory, belongs primarily to that State'.[72]

D. Forests

Forests provide important habitat for wildlife. They also affect climate change; it has been estimated that 24% of anthropocentric greenhouse gas emissions are generated from agriculture, forestry, and other land uses (AFOLU).[73] The international community has relied exclusively on soft law instruments to address forest conservation. The hardest set of international rules that could affect forest conservation has come instead through the climate change regime in the form of REDD+, which stands for 'reducing emissions from deforestation and forest degradation, and the role of conservation, sustainable management of forests and enhancement of forest carbon stocks in developing

[70] art 2.

[71] art 2.2.

[72] art 4.

[73] Intergovernmental Panel on Climate Change (IPCC), *Climate Change 2014: Synthesis Report* (2014) 46.

countries'.[74] The REDD+ programme is intended to allow for states to earn credit for activities that conserve forests and thereby reduce emissions. These credits could then be used to meet any mitigation targets under the international climate change regime.

Policy-makers and advocates working on biodiversity and forest conservation believe that REDD+ provides an opportunity to capture funding and support for that conservation by linking it directly to climate change mitigation. It seems like a win-win, with biodiversity a co-benefit of reducing greenhouse gas emissions by reducing deforestation and forest degradation. Nevertheless, it comes with some risk. Mitigation and biodiversity protection are not always aligned.[75] For example, single-species plantations of trees can reduce greenhouse gas emissions and even absorb greenhouse gases but are generally not beneficial to biodiversity conservation. To ensure that biodiversity and other important interests are not harmed by the REDD+ programme, the parties have adopted 'safeguards'.[76] In addition, they have adopted various procedural mechanisms, including reporting, to ensure that the safeguards are accounted for in REDD+ projects. Implementation of REDD+ will ultimately fall to the states, with some potential oversight at the international level either through treaty institutions or private oversight bodies. It remains to be seen how much it will contribute to biodiversity conservation.

V. REGIONAL AGREEMENTS

In addition to the multilateral treaties already discussed, regional agreements can also play a significant role in conservation, as is evident from the agreements negotiated pursuant to the CMS. They may be species-specific or may target habitat. They can cover a range of countries, for example Europe or Central America, or can be site-specific, as with trans-frontier agreements for the management of a park. Such agreements can be critically important not only for beginning the process of cooperation, but also for ensuring ongoing communication and sharing of expertise among states engaged in a common conservation endeavour so that management can further, rather than impede, conservation action.

[74] Decision 4/CP.15, 'Methodological guidance for activities relating to reducing emissions from deforestation and forest degradation and the role of conservation, sustainable management of forests and enhancement of forest carbon stocks in developing countries' (30 March 2010) UN Doc FCCC/CP/2009/11/Add.1, 11.

[75] Imke Sagemüller, 'Forest Sinks Under the United Nations Framework Convention on Climate Change and the Kyoto Protocol: Opportunity or Risk for Biodiversity?' *Columbia Journal of Environmental Law*, 31 (2006): 189; Annalisa Savaresi, 'Reducing Emissions from Deforestation in Developing Countries Under the UNFCCC: Caveats and Opportunities for Biodiversity' *Yearbook of International Environmental Law*, 21/1 (2010): 81.

[76] Decision 1/CP.16, 'The Cancun Agreements: Outcome of the Work of the Ad Hoc Working Group on Long-Term Cooperative Action under the Convention' (15 March 2011) UN Doc FCCC/CP/2010/7/Add.1, 12, 26.

The polar regions provide a particular example. They are both home to many species. For the Antarctic, where claims by individual states to jurisdiction are currently frozen by the 1959 Antarctic Treaty,[77] states have negotiated important binding agreements to help conserve terrestrial and marine species, including the 1980 Convention on the Conservation of Antarctic Marine Living Resources and the 1991 Madrid Protocol on Environmental Protection to the Antarctic Treaty. Protection for the Arctic Region is complicated by the fact that much of its territory falls within the jurisdiction of individual states. Some species-specific treaties apply to the Arctic, for example for polar bears.[78] Beyond such agreements, the international activity related to the Arctic is almost entirely in the form of soft law. Nevertheless, cooperation on the protection of species and biodiversity is increasing, largely through the Arctic Council.[79]

VI. CONCLUSION AND NEXT STEPS

Wildlife is under severe threat and will only face greater challenges with climate change. Yet conservation is rarely given the resources and attention needed for it to be effective. In addition, fundamental disagreements across several fault lines can lead to politicized decision-making, while concerns about intrusion into national sovereignty limit the scope and force of international wildlife law. Disputes are often configured as pitting the global North against the global South, preservationists against conservationists, and animal rights perspectives against sustainable utilization perspectives. Yet the future of international wildlife law and effective global conservation depends on its participants breaking free from polarized rhetoric to find solutions to difficult problems.

Along these lines, commentators are bringing ethics into questions of conservation. This work may begin to break down the traditional barrier between conservation and animal rights and allow ethical concerns to influence conservation decision-making, for example, on questions related to captive breeding of certain species for hunting. A second important area for research that could bring multiple stakeholders to the table is work on human-wildlife conflict. Understanding conservation practices that enable humans and wildlife to coexist has the potential to relieve pressure on wild species from local communities who may currently view those species as dangerous or damaging to their economic interests, as when elephants destroy crops or leopards feed on cattle. Such work cannot resolve all disagreement, but it can help to continue a problem-solving approach to conserving wildlife and the planet's biodiversity, drawing on international law where it can facilitate conservation.

[77] art 4.

[78] eg 1973 Agreement on the Conservation of Polar Bears.

[79] Michael Bowman, Peter Davies, and Catherine Redgwell, *Lyster's International Wildlife Law* (2nd edn, CUP 2010) 355.

BIBLIOGRAPHY

Michael Bowman, Peter Davies, and Catherine Redgwell, *Lyster's International Wildlife Law* (2nd edn, CUP 2010)

IPBES, *Global Assessment Report on Biodiversity and Ecosystem Services* (2019)

Annecoos Wiersema, 'Uncertainty, Precaution, and Adaptive Management in Wildlife Trade' *Michigan Journal of International Law*, 36/3 (2015): 375

CHAPTER 33

HAZARDOUS SUBSTANCES AND ACTIVITIES

DAVID A WIRTH AND NOAH M SACHS

I. INTRODUCTION

THE modern world is built on synthetic and naturally occurring chemicals that are used to produce almost everything humans use, including pharmaceuticals, electronics, automobiles, fabrics, and construction materials. Companies may manufacture toxic chemicals as useful products with commercial applications, and they may also generate hazardous substances as by-products of manufacturing. Once released into the environment, the chemicals can be transported over long distances through air and water, raising issues of international law.

For humans, chemicals may present risks of cancer, birth defects, genetic mutations, nerve damage, hormone disruption, and a wide array of other adverse health effects. Chemicals may also harm plants and animals. Pesticides, for example, can cause species loss through concentration of the chemicals in animal tissues that are consumed at higher levels on the food chain.

This chapter analyses the enormous scope of international instruments addressing hazardous substances and activities by assessing both the regulatory junctures and the specific strategies that governments rely upon to reduce risk. It begins with the challenge of identifying which substances are hazardous to human health or the environment (risk assessment) and then discusses the major treaties that regulate chemical hazards (risk management). This chapter discusses treaties and other international instruments governing chemical production, use, labelling, and disposal as well as those governing industrial accidents. It concludes with a discussion of instruments designed to promote pollution prevention and toxics use reduction.

II. HAZARD IDENTIFICATION AND TESTING

One of the first questions that regulators encounter in crafting public policies for toxic substances is how to identify the substances that will be subject to regulation. Because of the wide variety of toxic substances and exposures, the decision on which substances to regulate is largely a social policy determination involving the application of judgement and values. In making the distinction between 'toxic' or 'hazardous' substances[1] that warrant policy interventions and the remainder that do not, regulators must first gather basic empirical toxicity data. Of the tens of millions of known chemical substances, about 100,000 are utilized in industrial processes. Of those, very few have been thoroughly tested for human toxicity or adverse environmental impacts.

The criteria justifying testing and specific testing protocols are mostly a matter of domestic law rather than international law. In 2016, the United States overhauled its law governing chemical testing, the Toxic Substances Control Act (TSCA), strengthening the authority of the federal government to require manufacturers to test chemicals. The pace is slow, however. TSCA required the Environmental Protection Agency to evaluate the risk of only twenty high priority substances by 2020.

In the European Union (EU), chemical testing is conducted under a 2007 regulation called Registration, Evaluation, and Authorization of Chemicals (REACH). Under REACH, the EU established a mission-specific supranational authority, the European Chemicals Agency (ECHA), to compile testing data. As of 2020, the ECHA had flagged approximately 300 substances for further review and evaluation. In both the United States and the EU, chemical testing is usually conducted by manufacturers, under protocols developed by governments, rather than conducted by governmental authorities themselves.

A. OECD Harmonization Initiatives

International coordination of chemical testing has significant benefits. It can reduce redundant or contradictory requirements from one state to another and reduce deaths of laboratory animals. Divergent municipal testing requirements, on the other hand, can sometimes impede global trade. Based on these considerations, the Organization for Economic Cooperation and Development (OECD) has been actively involved for several decades in harmonizing national policies for testing chemicals. These harmonization efforts have been largely non-binding, as there is no compulsory international

[1] For the purposes of this chapter, the terms 'toxic' and 'hazardous' are used interchangeably in a non-technical sense to identify situations characterized by a heightened risk of injury, disease, or death from exposure to a substance. Further elaboration as to specific risks in a variety of contexts is set out in the discussion of legal instruments later in this chapter.

instrument that mandates chemical testing, establishes testing protocols, or requires mutual recognition.

Building on prior efforts, the OECD harmonization initiative reached an important milestone with its Screening Information Data Set programme, which was first set out in a 1991 undertaking on cooperative investigation and risk reduction of existing chemicals. Under this programme, OECD member states have tested and shared basic toxicity information for more than 1,200 high production volume chemicals. The data include the results of tests for physico-chemical properties, environmental fate, environmental effects, and health effects. As with other testing programmes, the principal goal is to assure adequate characterization of a substance to determine appropriate regulation for that chemical. Since the 1980s, the OECD has also had a programme to encourage the mutual recognition of chemical test data by OECD member states, an initiative that has now been extended to non-members as well.[2]

In 2018, the OECD adopted a Decision-Recommendation on the Co-operative Investigation and Risk Reduction of Chemicals,[3] which replaced the 1991 effort. The 2018 Decision-Recommendation reiterates the importance of harmonizing testing protocols and sharing of data and also recommends 'concerted activities' by OECD members to reduce chemical risks. The recommended activities include traditional command-and-control regulation as well as non-regulatory efforts, such as use of environmentally preferable production techniques, product labelling, and economic incentives.

Within the OECD, efforts at harmonizing toxicity testing have been largely non-binding, and testing regimes remain based in municipal law rather than international law. States have opted for this modest, primarily voluntary approach to chemical testing because of their concerns over sovereignty, protection of domestic industry, and protection of confidential business information.[4]

B. Initiatives in the United Nations System

In 1995, following a recommendation in Agenda 21, several intergovernmental organizations established the Inter-Organization Program for the Sound Management of Chemicals (IOMC). The World Health Organisation (WHO) provides secretariat

[2] See eg 'Decision Concerning the Mutual Acceptance of Data in the Assessment of Chemicals' OECD Doc C(81)30, as amended by OECD Doc C(97)186; 'Decision-Recommendation on Compliance with Principles of Good Laboratory Practice' OECD Doc C(89)87, as amended by OECD Doc C(95)8; 'Decision Concerning the Adherence of Non-Member Countries to the Council Acts Related to the Mutual Acceptance of Data in the Assessment of Chemicals' OECD Doc C(97)114.

[3] 'Decision-Recommendation on the Co-operative Investigation and Risk Reduction of Chemicals' OECD Doc C(2018)51.

[4] The International Agency for Research on Cancer (IARC), a component of the World Health Organization (WHO), publishes a series of monographs, in which more than 1,000 chemical agents have been evaluated. Unlike the OECD, the IARC is primarily a scientific research organization and not a forum for harmonizing national policies.

services. The OECD, Food and Agriculture Organization (FAO), the International Labour Organization (ILO), UNEP (now UN Environment), United Nations Industrial Development Organization (UNIDO), and United Nations Institute for Training and Research (UNITAR) are participating organizations that provide resources, while the United Nations Development Programme (UNDP) and the World Bank participate as observers. Unlike the OECD's work on chemicals, the efforts of the IOMC are potentially global in reach.

The IOMC coordinates international assessment of chemical risks; harmonization of classification and labelling of chemicals; information exchange on chemicals and chemical risks; establishment of risk reduction programmes; strengthening of municipal capabilities and capacities for management of chemicals; and prevention of illegal international traffic in toxic and dangerous products. In 2001, the IOMC facilitated the establishment of a globally harmonized system for the classification and labelling of chemicals, and it implemented a non-binding prior informed consent procedure similar to the legally binding 1998 Rotterdam Convention (Section VI). It has assisted states in developing national implementation plans under the 2001 Stockholm POPs (persistent organic pollutants) Convention (Section III) and has assisted African states with the management and disposal of pesticides.

The IOMC's most far-reaching effort to date is the Strategic Approach to International Chemicals Management (SAICM). Launched in 2006, SAICM outlines a framework for chemical risk management under five main themes: risk reduction, knowledge and information, governance, capacity-building and technical cooperation, and illegal international traffic. Relying mainly on voluntary action, the SAICM adopted a Global Plan of Action in 2006 containing a menu of work areas and activities for each of the five themes. The Global Plan of Action also contains targets, timetables, and indicators of progress for each theme. Despite missing a prior target to assure that every country will produce and use chemicals in ways that minimize significant adverse impacts on the environment and human health by 2020, SAICM has recently reaffirmed its fundamental analytical approach.[5]

III. CONDITIONS OF PRODUCTION AND USE

Another regulatory strategy for addressing toxic chemical risks is to establish conditions to reduce hazards from the production and use of chemicals. Regulators may prescribe product or production standards as requirements for governmental pre-market approval or licensing of the substance. For example, both the EU's REACH regulation and the US TSCA (Section II) authorize imposing conditions of use on a chemical. The EU's

[5] SAICM, 'Lessons from the past to inform SAICM and the Sound Management of Chemicals and Waste Beyond 2020' (2020).

Seveso III Directive (Section V) likewise relies on this regulatory approach. In some cases, a government may phase out or ban a substance if it concludes that the environmental and public health risks of the substance are unacceptable.

A. Stockholm POPs Convention

Persistent organic pollutants (POPs) are a global threat because they damage human health and remain in the environment for long periods before decomposing. These chemicals, such as PCBs (Polychlorinated biphenyls) and DDT (Dichloro-diphenyl-trichloroethane), are dangerous at the local level and also end up widely distributed geographically, often far from the place of manufacture or release. They accumulate in the fatty tissue of living organisms and therefore concentrate at higher levels of the food chain. The Stockholm Convention on Persistent Organic Pollutants addresses the risk from POPs through both phase-outs and bans, initially targeting a 'Dirty Dozen' list of pesticides and industrial chemicals which originated from a global NGO campaign.

The Stockholm Convention goes further than other treaties governing toxic chemicals (Section VI) in directly limiting production and release of certain chemicals at the domestic level, whether those substances are involved in international trade or not. It is an example of global harmonization of municipal policies on conditions of use, in some cases by eliminating use of a substance altogether.

The Convention initially targeted nine chemicals and categories of chemicals for limitation: the pesticides aldrin, chlordane, dieldrin, endrin, heptachlor, mirex, and toxaphene; and the chemicals hexachlorobenzene and PCBs. The Agreement also strictly limits the use of DDT to controlling disease-carrying insects and requires governments to limit unintentional releases of PCBs, hexachlorobenzene, dioxins, and furans.

As a dynamic instrument, the Stockholm Convention contains a process by which the parties can regulate new substances as the need arises. That mechanism expressly states that decisions to list new chemicals should be taken on the basis of a precautionary approach.[6] Many of the original Dirty Dozen chemicals were already banned in major industrialized states under domestic law, which explains widespread support for the treaty. Since 2001, however, listing additional substances under the treaty has been more controversial. Nonetheless, since the treaty entered into force, the parties have added sixteen substances to the list of chemicals governed by the Convention.

The Global Environment Facility (GEF) serves as the funding mechanism for the Stockholm Convention, as well as other major multilateral environmental agreements including the Minamata Convention (Section VIII). The GEF has financed national implementation plans for the management of POPs, and a majority of the parties have implemented legal and administrative efforts to control the original Dirty Dozen

[6] See Chapter 18, 'Precaution', in this volume.

chemicals.[7] As a result, the concentration of the twelve original POPs has decreased or remained low in both air samples and in human tissues.[8] However, the growing number of POPs governed by the Stockholm Convention places additional pressures on governments because it is difficult to monitor chemical concentrations in the environment comprehensively. Environmental monitoring is often not comparable across states, inhibiting evaluation of the Convention's effectiveness.

B. Multilaterally-Agreed Standards for Pesticides and Other Toxics

The international community has also implemented standards for the production and use of chemicals through non-binding mechanisms. The best known voluntary instrument is the FAO Code of Conduct on the Distribution and Use of Pesticides, first adopted in 1985. The Code of Conduct was revised in 2013 to include provisions on vector control and pesticides intended to protect public health, while the original Code focused only on agricultural pesticides. The FAO Code of Conduct has become the internationally accepted standard for labelling, packaging, storing, using, and disposing of pesticides.

The OECD has established a broader set of non-binding guidelines, the Guidelines for Multinational Enterprises, which include standards for pesticides and also apply to a larger set of business activities that might cause environmental damage. The Guidelines, for example, include measures to reduce toxic chemical releases and risks from operations involving hazardous substances.[9] Consistent with the non-binding format, the FAO Code of Conduct and the OECD Guidelines are addressed not only to municipal governments but also to local officials, industry, workers, consumers, non-governmental organizations (NGOs), and the general public.

IV. REGULATION OF POLLUTANT RELEASES

Regulating the conditions under which pesticides and other toxic substances should be used is an effective strategy to reduce risks, but mainly addresses risks to workers and immediate users of chemicals. Many of the risks from toxic substances fall, however, on a wider population who may be exposed when the substances are released into the environment. Policies are needed to protect the public and the environment from harmful

[7] See 'Effectiveness Evaluation of the Stockholm Convention on Persistent Organic Pollutants Pursuant to Article 16' (10 November 2016) UN Doc UNEP/POPS/COP.8/22/Add.1, para 36.

[8] See 'Second Global Monitoring Report' (23 January 2017) UN Doc UNEP/POPS/COP.8/INF/38 21, 26.

[9] OECD, *Guidelines for Multinational Enterprises* (2000).

levels of pollutants released as by-products of industrial activities or electricity generation. Water and air pollution are the best known examples of these chemical releases.

A. Examples from Domestic and Supranational Law

There are several policies for regulating such releases that are evident in domestic law and the law of the EU. One approach is to establish a numerical limit on emissions from particular facilities. The quantitative limit usually reflects the emissions that facilities can achieve by application of 'best' pollution control technology or 'maximum' available control. This approach ensures that each facility is achieving the maximum possible reduction in pollution releases. One drawback to this approach is that it may be difficult to correlate the regulatory standard to real-world exposures. If there are enough sources, then even stringent emissions limitations on each source may still result in unacceptable ambient concentrations of a toxic pollutant.

Another approach is to establish limitations on environmental exposures directly. This strategy is typically articulated as an upper limit on ambient concentrations of a toxic substance. While this approach seeks directly to limit exposures, it faces many conceptual and practical difficulties. A regulatory authority must establish an 'acceptable' concentration or level of exposure, which may be politically controversial or scientifically difficult. Ultimately, the ambient exposure limitation must be implemented by reductions in emissions from sources, a process that requires complicated extrapolations or modelling to correlate source emissions with environmental concentrations. Regulators must implement extensive monitoring, moreover, to assure that the regulatory targets are actually achieved.

B. ECE Protocols on Toxic Air Pollution

The regional Convention on Long-Range Transboundary Air Pollution (LRTAP) was concluded in 1979 under the auspices of the UN Economic Commission for Europe (ECE), whose membership includes European states, all the states of the former Soviet Union including Central Asia, Canada, and the United States. The LRTAP regime is a 'framework' convention that anticipates the subsequent adoption of ancillary agreements or 'protocols'.[10]

LRTAP Convention parties have adopted several protocols governing specific air toxics. A protocol on POPs, adopted in 1998, addresses POPs in regional air pollution in a manner that is complementary to the globally-applicable Stockholm Convention. The protocol, which governs sixteen POPs, eliminates the production and use of some

[10] See Chapter 28, 'Transboundary Air Pollution', in this volume.

substances, restricts the uses of others, establishes emissions limitations, and specifies waste management practices.

The Protocol on Heavy Metals, also adopted in 1998, governs an additional category of hazardous air pollutants and addresses three toxics specifically: cadmium, lead, and mercury. This instrument relies primarily on an emissions reduction strategy for achieving its policy goals. The Agreement requires parties to reduce emissions of those three heavy metals by reference to a base year, an international regulatory technique frequently encountered in the regulation of toxics. The instrument also specifies numerical technology-based emissions limitations and target dates for new and existing stationary sources in eleven enumerated categories. The Agreement likewise sets out technology- and process- based emissions limitations for major industrial categories, including iron and steel, non-ferrous metals, power generation, road transport, and waste incineration.

V. HAZARDOUS PROCESSES AND INDUSTRIAL ACCIDENTS

Another regulatory strategy for controlling risks from toxic chemicals is to establish safety standards and design requirements for industrial facilities. Several major industrial accidents in the latter part of the twentieth century highlighted the need for this approach. In 1976, a factory in the Italian town of Seveso released a cloud of dioxin, requiring the evacuation of more than 600 people and the treatment of several times that many for dioxin poisoning. In 1984, a pesticide plant in Bhopal, India operated by a subsidiary of Union Carbide, a United States-based corporation, released methyl isocyanate, killing nearly 4,000 people. In 1986, water used to combat a fire at the Sandoz Chemical Company plant near Basel, Switzerland resulted in the release of mercury compounds, pesticides, and other agricultural chemicals into the Rhine River. These chemicals spread downstream to Germany, France, and the Netherlands, causing a massive fish die-off.

To reduce the risk of such industrial accidents, regulators have established design requirements for manufacturing facilities and standards for specific manufacturing processes and for chemical storage. They have also encouraged shifts to less toxic materials in manufacturing processes.

The EU's Seveso Directive, the first and most influential instrument in the field, was adopted in 1982 and was most recently amended in 2012 (Seveso III).[11] The Seveso III Directive addresses both the storage of hazardous substances in industrial installations and hazardous processes themselves. Under the directive, operators of industrial

[11] Directive 2012/18/EU of the European Parliament and of the Council of 4 July 2012 on the control of major-accident hazards involving dangerous substances, amending and subsequently repealing Council Directive 96/82/EC Text with EEA relevance, OJ 2012 L 197/1.

establishments must notify the competent national authority and establish a major accident prevention policy. In addition, operators of the most dangerous installations must file a safety report, a safety management system, and an emergency plan.

A. ECE Convention on the Transboundary Effects of Industrial Accidents

The Convention on the Transboundary Effects of Industrial Accidents, negotiated and adopted in 1992 under the auspices of the ECE, is a multilateral effort similar to the Seveso Directives, but addressed more generally to Europe, Central Asia, and North America. Like the Seveso Directives, the Convention aims to reduce the likelihood of industrial accidents and mitigate the effects of those that do occur. The Convention promotes international cooperation among the parties before, during, and after an industrial accident.

The Convention obliges parties first to identify hazardous operations within their borders that could have transboundary effects in the event of an accident. After identification, parties must inform the other parties that could be affected and consult with them. The Convention directs that new installations be sited in areas where the risks are minimized and requires parties to analyse potential transboundary effects of industrial facilities. Parties must ensure that operators of facilities prepare on-site and off-site contingency plans for accidents. In situations in which several parties to the Convention might be affected by a hazardous operation, it specifies that they work together. The Convention additionally articulates standards for public disclosure and administrative and judicial remedies in the event of an accident.

If an industrial accident occurs, it requires that parties provide early notice to any affected parties. The parties have established the UNECE Industrial Accident Notification System for this purpose. Additionally, parties must take action to minimize transboundary effects after an accident. Each party to the Convention must designate a competent authority as a focal point for communication and action with respect to the Convention's obligations.[12]

B. Multilaterally-Agreed Good Practice Standards for Industrial Accidents

As in other areas of international chemicals law, industrial accidents have been addressed through non-binding measures. For example, the OECD Working Group on

12 ILO Convention No 174 on the Prevention of Major Industrial Accidents adopts an analogous approach at the global level.

Chemical Accidents has adopted Guiding Principles for Chemical Accident Prevention, Preparedness, and Response.[13] The Principles address planning, construction, management, operation, and review of the safety performance of industrial installations employing hazardous processes. The Principles also apply to industrial accident response, clean-up, and investigation.

The OECD Guidelines for Multinational Enterprises specify that private entities addressed by the instrument should maintain contingency plans to prevent and control accidents and emergencies, report accidents immediately to public authorities, and educate workers in the proper handling of hazardous materials so as to avoid accidents. A companion guidance document on Safety Performance Indicators is intended to help governments and industry reduce the risk of industrial accidents as well as their effects.[14]

VI. INTERNATIONAL TRADE IN HAZARDOUS SUBSTANCES, PRODUCTS, AND WASTE

It is often difficult for governments to take action to abate toxic risks that emanate from abroad. Therefore, the point at which something—a bulk shipment of a chemical, a finished product, or hazardous waste—crosses a national border assumes great importance as a regulatory juncture to reduce toxic risks. For this reason, many international instruments regulate the transboundary trade in hazardous substances and hazardous waste.

Such regulatory interventions raise significant North-South equity issues.[15] After banning or severely restricting toxic substances to protect health and the environment within their territories, industrialized states have in some cases continued to allow those same substances to be exported. In response, developing states have objected to a 'double standard' in which private enterprises in the industrialized world may profit at the expense of poorer states. Developing countries may not have the technical capacity, resources, or governmental infrastructure to control the entry of these substances into their territory or to regulate their domestic use. They sometimes charge that they are the 'dumping ground' for the toxic detritus of the North. When developed and developing states come together to negotiate treaties regarding trade in toxic substances, the negotiations often involve tense arguments about equity and morality.

[13] OECD, *Guiding Principles for Chemical Accident Prevention, Preparedness, and Response* (2003).

[14] OECD, *Guidance on Safety Performance Indicators* (OECD 2008).

[15] See Chapter 11, 'Global South Approaches', in this volume.

A. Basel and Bamako Conventions

The 1989 Basel Convention on the Control of Transboundary Movements of Hazardous Wastes and Their Disposal was the first potentially universal, binding instrument addressing international trade in wastes. It has since matured into the principal multilateral instrument governing international trade and standards for disposal of both hazardous wastes and municipal trash, including an amendment specifically addressing plastics adopted in May 2019.

Among parties to the Agreement, the core regulatory approach of the Basel Convention is the establishment of a 'prior informed consent' (PIC) regime. Any party to the Convention may choose to ban the importation of hazardous or other wastes. If a party allows imports, then the government of the state of export must assure prior notification of the governments of the receiving state and any transit states in advance of a waste shipment. The shipment may not commence until the government of the proposed state of import has given its consent in writing. Based on the written consent of relevant states of import, states of export may allow exporters to use a 'general' notification procedure for up to one year for multiple shipments of the same types of wastes.

With respect to states not party to that instrument, the Convention establishes a limited ban. Specifically, the Convention prohibits exports from parties to non-parties and limits transboundary movements of wastes, both imports and exports, only to those states that are parties to the Convention. However, if a party has entered into a bilateral agreement on waste shipments with a non-party pursuant to Article 11 of the Convention, and the provisions of that bilateral agreement are 'not less environmentally sound' than the requirements of the Convention itself, then the trade can take place.

The third Conference of the Parties to the Convention, held in Geneva in September 1995, adopted an amendment to the Agreement, the so-called 'Basel Ban Amendment',[16] that imposes a wider ban on waste shipments, which entered into force in December 2019 after considerable delay. Specifically, the amendment bans *all* shipments of hazardous waste from wealthy countries, mostly OECD members listed in a new Annex VII of the Convention, to states not on that list. In the case of shipments of waste intended for recycling or recovery, the amendment imposes a phase-out of such shipments from states listed in Annex VII to destinations outside that group.

Critics of the Basel Ban Amendment argue that it is paternalistic and environmentally counterproductive because it may limit recycling and the development of developing economies' capacities to manage hazardous wastes. There is also concern the Ban Amendment could limit the ability of developing economies to choose for themselves what types of waste they want to import.

[16] Basel Convention, Decision III/1, 'Amendment to the Convention' (22 September 1995) UN Doc UNEP/CHW.3/35.

Even before the Basel Convention was adopted, many negotiating states charged that it was not sufficiently rigorous and served to perpetuate the global waste trade. African states expressed concern over the Basel Convention's failure to impose a ban on transboundary movements of hazardous and other wastes, and no sub-Saharan African country signed the Convention at the time of its adoption. Under the auspices of the Organization of African Unity, now the African Union, those states in 1991 adopted a stronger regional agreement, the Bamako Convention on the Ban of the Import into Africa and the Control of Transboundary Movement and Management of Hazardous Wastes within Africa. The Bamako Convention imposes a total ban on imports of hazardous waste into Africa and creates a PIC procedure for trade in such wastes within Africa.

B. Rotterdam Convention

The 1998 Rotterdam Convention on the Prior Informed Consent Procedure for Certain Hazardous Chemicals and Pesticides in International Trade establishes a legally binding PIC regime for international shipments of hazardous chemicals and pesticides. The Rotterdam Convention applies to goods in the form of useful chemicals in international commerce, in contrast with the Basel Convention, which applies to presumptively harmful wastes or 'bads'. As with the Basel Convention, the principal motivation for the Agreement was to assist developing economies that might have limited regulatory capacity or difficulty controlling imports to implement their own domestic environmental and public health policies.

The Rotterdam Convention applies to pesticides and industrial chemicals that parties have domestically banned or severely restricted for health or environmental reasons. The parties have also added additional chemicals for inclusion in the PIC procedure. The Convention requires that any import ban be universal and non-discriminatory. That is, a party cannot refuse to import a chemical from another party while continuing to permit domestic production, or allow imports from other parties or from non-parties.

With respect to the covered substances, the Convention requires the formal, written consent of the government of the state of import before export may take place. In response to a notification from the Convention secretariat, a state of import that is a party to the Convention may decide to allow importation of the chemical, to prohibit importation, or to allow importation subject to specified conditions. Alternatively, the Convention provides that states of import may provide an interim response.

Like the Stockholm POPs Convention, the Rotterdam Convention contains a mechanism for subsequent additions to the list of covered substances. At the time it was adopted, the Rotterdam Convention's requirements applied to twenty-two pesticides and five industrial chemicals, now increased to thirty-five pesticides and sixteen industrial chemicals. The Convention also contains provisions for exchange of information concerning potentially hazardous chemicals, and establishes channels for providing technical assistance to developing economies to manage toxic chemicals and pesticides.

VII. DISPOSAL OF TOXIC WASTE

The lifecycle of a hazardous substance may result in release to the environment, typically to air or water, at which juncture regulatory requirements such as emissions limitations may apply. Alternatively, a particular toxic substance may ultimately find its way into industrial waste as a component of the detritus remaining at the conclusion of a manufacturing process. Similarly, household or consumer products consisting of or containing hazardous materials may enter the waste stream. As with releases of toxics to the environment, the treatment, storage, and disposal of hazardous waste presents risks to public health and the environment that have been addressed by regulatory policies.

A. Basel Convention Disposal Requirements

The Basel Convention requires that parties manage and dispose of hazardous wastes and other wastes under the rubric of Environmentally Sound Management (ESM). In order to ensure that the wastes are disposed of under ESM principles, the parties must take all practical steps to ensure that hazardous wastes or other wastes are managed in a manner which will protect human health and the environment. The states of export and import must understand the hazards of the particular wastes they are dealing with and communicate that information among private parties and public authorities involved in management or disposal of the chemical waste. For specific chemicals, such as POPs and mercury, ESM standards are detailed in technical guidelines issued under the Basel Convention.[17]

Notably, the Basel Convention states that the state of export has the ultimate responsibility to ensure that the disposal is performed consistent with ESM criteria. That is, the consent of the state of import to import the waste, standing alone, is insufficient to satisfy the treaty, and the state of export bears responsibility for ensuring ESM disposal within the state of import. Undercover research by the Basel Action Network and other NGOs has shown, however, that a large portion of international hazardous waste shipments are not disposed of pursuant to ESM standards and that national import bans are widely flouted.

[17] See Basel Convention, Latest Technical Guidelines <http://www.basel.int/Implementation/Publications/LatestTechnicalGuidelines/tabid/5875/Default.aspx#> accessed 2 January 2020 (listing technical guidelines for specific chemicals).

B. IAEA Agreements and Standards

Nuclear safety, along with technology transfer and verification, is one of the three pillars of the International Atomic Energy Agency (IAEA). After the Chernobyl accident, four binding multilateral agreements in the area of nuclear safety were adopted under IAEA auspices. One of those agreements, the 1997 Joint Convention on the Safety of Spent Fuel Management and on the Safety of Radioactive Waste Management, is the first binding international agreement to address management and storage of radioactive waste and spent fuel.

The Joint Convention requires parties to establish and maintain a legislative and regulatory framework to govern the safety of spent fuel and radioactive waste management through a system of facility licensing. The Agreement sets out standards for siting, design, construction, operation, closure, and safety assessment of spent fuel management and radioactive waste management facilities. Both existing and proposed facilities are covered by the Joint Convention, which also articulates general requirements for safe operation. Additionally, the Joint Convention sets out a regime of notification and consent for transboundary movements of radioactive waste based on the 1990 IAEA Code of Practice on the International Transboundary Movement of Radioactive Waste.

Other IAEA agreements are designed to further the goal of nuclear safety. The 1986 Convention on Early Notification of a Nuclear Accident and the 1986 Convention on Assistance in the Case of Nuclear Accident or Radiological Emergency are intended to facilitate international preparedness for and responses to nuclear and radiological emergencies. The 1994 Convention on Nuclear Safety obliges parties to operate nuclear power plants consistent with high standards of safety. It requires each party to develop and enforce safety standards, but it does not actually prescribe the standards. Consequently, there is no internationally binding instrument that sets minimum safety standards for nuclear reactors.

The IAEA has also adopted hundreds of safety standards, which are not binding on IAEA member countries, intended in part to serve as models of good practice for states in crafting their own legislation and regulations. These safety standards are further categorized as fundamental principles, mandatory requirements, and recommended guidance. Published IAEA standards in the area of radioactive waste management include those addressing classification of radioactive waste, predisposal management of radioactive waste, and management of radioactive waste from medicine, industry, research, agriculture, and education.[18]

[18] <https://www.iaea.org/resources/safety-standards> accessed 2 January 2020.

VIII. INTEGRATED APPROACHES TO POLLUTION PREVENTION

In recent years, governments have increasingly focused on pollution prevention and toxics use reduction because of the difficulty of managing hazardous substances and products once they have been produced. This approach necessarily targets the entire product lifecycle, from making better design choices to using different materials, improving recyclability, and minimizing waste. The US state of Massachusetts was a leader in promoting the reduction of toxics use. The 1989 Toxics Use Reduction Act[19] encourages reductions in use of approximately 1,400 chemicals by setting out specific, numerical reduction targets by comparison with a reference baseline. The EU's 2010 Industrial Emissions directive adopted a similar approach for certain volatile organic compounds. It allows member states to require that facilities adopt toxics use reduction plans as an alternative to end-of-pipe emissions limitations.[20]

A. Minamata Convention

The 2013 Minamata Convention on Mercury, the most recent global treaty addressing toxic chemicals, relies heavily on an integrated approach to reduce pollution. Unlike many of the other multilateral instruments analysed in this chapter, the Minamata Convention addresses toxic substances containing only one element, but in a holistic manner specifically crafted to address those specific risks. The Convention is named after the town of Minamata, Japan, where industrial wastewater containing mercury poisoned thousands of people in 1956.

Mercury is a highly toxic heavy metal associated with severe risks to the environment and human health by damaging the central nervous system, thyroid, kidneys, lungs, immune system, eyes, gums, and skin. There is no safe level of mercury exposure. Mercury is globally transported through air and water, and in its organic form of methylmercury, it accumulates in the food chain. It can damage human health and the environment in areas of the world, such as the Arctic, that are far from emissions sources. Consequently, it is difficult for one state independently to control the transboundary effects of mercury.

The Minamata Convention takes an integrated approach to controlling mercury from various sources, rejecting an alternative approach in which each party must achieve a certain numeric reduction in mercury emissions. The integrated approach requires parties to implement policies and measures to control mercury throughout its lifecycle,

[19] Toxic Use Reduction Act of 1989, Mass Gen L ch 21I, ss 1–23.

[20] Directive 2010/75/EU of 24 November 2010 on industrial emissions (integrated pollution prevention and control) Text with EEA relevance, OJ 2010 L 334/17, art 59.

including reductions across various products, processes, and industries where mercury is used, released, or emitted. For example, the Convention prohibits any new mercury mines and requires existing mines to be phased out within fifteen years. It also requires the progressive elimination of products that use mercury, such as measuring devices and batteries.

The Convention targets certain mercury-intensive industries. It requires a phase-out of mercury use in chlor-alkali production, the elimination of mercury in artisanal and small scale gold mining, and a significant reduction in mercury in PVC (polyvinyl chloride) and polyurethane manufacturing. For dental amalgam, which enters the environment through flushing down drains or cremation of human remains, the Convention requires parties to reduce emissions by selecting at least two measures from a list of nine options.

The largest source of mercury emissions is the combustion of coal, and reducing emissions from that source proved to be controversial. Parties must require that new sources of mercury emissions to the air, such as coal-fired power plants, install pollution controls within five years. For existing sources of emissions, however, parties are given ten years within which they must require pollution controls. These existing sources include coal-fired power plants as well as industrial boilers, certain smelters, cement plants, and waste incinerators.

The Minamata Convention is widely considered to be a landmark achievement in international environmental law because it addresses all the principal sources of a single toxic substance in the environment, and more than 100 states are now parties. Because it takes decades for mercury to cycle through the environment, however, ambient concentrations of mercury are not expected to decrease significantly until the latter half of this century.

B. OECD Recommendation on Pollution Prevention

The OECD in 1990 adopted a non-binding recommendation on Integrated Pollution Prevention and Control.[21] The recommendation contains an Appendix entitled 'Guidance on Integrated Pollution Prevention and Control' which identifies basic principles, including consideration of the entire life cycle of substances and products; anticipation of environmental effects in a variety of environmental media, including consideration of multiple pathways to exposure and movement through the environment; and minimization of waste. The recommendation also identifies the desirability of zero- or low-waste technology, recycling, and alternative manufacturing strategies designed to reduce the use of toxic substances. The form of this instrument, a non-binding recommendation adopted by wealthier industrialized countries, is perhaps

[21] 'Recommendation of the Council on Integrated Pollution Prevention and Control' OECD Doc C(90)164.

indicative of the emerging nature of pollution prevention as a regulatory strategy on the international level.

IX. OTHER RELATED POLICIES

There are several other legal approaches in international environmental law that are relevant to controlling toxic substances. Most of these are procedural in nature and apply to toxic chemical risks as well as to other public health and environmental hazards.

A. Right to Know

One public policy approach to reducing risks from hazardous substances and activities is to inform the public of the release of potentially toxic substances, the presence of potentially dangerous activities, or the nature or magnitude of associated risks. Public information approaches can complement other substantive regulatory approaches, such as those related to industrial accidents. Provision of information can also comprise a complete public policy in itself. Governments can design policies to allow consumers, workers, and members of the public to make informed choices about the products they purchase and risks in their communities, and information disclosure can often prompt industry to voluntarily reduce risks.

The 2003 Kyiv Protocol on Pollutant Release and Transfer Registers, a protocol to the 1998 Aarhus Convention on Access to Information, Public Participation in Decision-Making and Access to Justice in Environmental Matters, is the only legally binding instrument on pollutant release and transfer registers. The Kyiv Protocol requires that parties establish registers to track industrial toxic emissions into air and water as well as off-site transfers of waste. The national registers must be searchable by location and facility and must be publicly accessible. The protocol also mandates that parties require facility operators to submit information, at least annually, on the names and amounts of chemicals released or transferred off-site.

B. Environmental Impact Assessment

Environmental impact assessment (EIA) is a component of a planning process through which environmental considerations are integrated into governmental decision-making. A process-oriented technique distinct from substantive environmental standards and requirements, EIA facilitates informed decision-making through thorough scrutiny of anticipated environmental effects. Decision-makers can use this information to assess whether projects should go forward and whether they can be modified to mitigate adverse environmental effects.

While not confined to the field of toxics, EIA is useful for identifying and analyzing potential adverse effects from hazardous substances and activities. For example, an EIA could project the potential effects of toxic emissions from a new facility on the environment and public health. It might characterize populations that would be exposed to emissions, identify mechanisms to lower exposures, and model expected impacts. Several international instruments encourage or mandate the application of the EIA methodology at the municipal level. Examples include the 1991 ECE Convention on Environmental Impact Assessment in a Transboundary Context (Espoo Convention) and the IAEA Joint Convention. The 2003 Protocol to the Espoo Convention on Strategic Environmental Assessment to the Convention on Environmental Impact Assessment in a Transboundary Context provides for strategic environmental impact assessment (SEA), expanding the methodology from the discrete project level to programmatic and policy initiatives.

X. CONCLUSION

Presently there is no single, overarching international framework for addressing environmental and public health risks from hazardous substances and activities. Public policy has been implemented at the national, supranational, regional, and global levels, sometimes simultaneously, with considerable interaction among various settings. Like-minded countries, such as members of the OECD, may coordinate policies among themselves, or a universal strategy such as that found in the Stockholm POPs Convention may be adopted. International instruments, as in the case of the Basel and Rotterdam Conventions, may be consciously targeted to address equity and informed consent issues.

From the perspective of international policy, this multiplicity of efforts and approaches is beneficial. Governments face many difficulties in effectively reducing risks from hazardous substances at the domestic and supranational levels, and the impediments are even more imposing at the international level. The wider the array of options, the greater the potential for creatively meeting new challenges. Given the scope of the problem, humankind can hardly afford to ignore any realistic options to reduce health and environmental risks from toxic chemicals and hazardous processes.

BIBLIOGRAPHY

Lucas Bergkamp *et al* (eds), *Elgar Encyclopedia of Environmental Law, Volume XI: Chemicals and the Law* (Edward Elgar 2022) (forthcoming)

Alexander Gillespie, *Waste Policy: International Regulation, Comparative and Contextual Perspectives* (Edward Elgar 2015)

Shunmugam Jayakumar *et al* (eds), *Transboundary Pollution: Evolving Issues of International Law and Policy* (NUS Centre for International Law & Edward Elgar 2015)

Katharina Kummer, *International Management of Hazardous Wastes: The Basel Convention and Related Legal Rules* (OUP 2000)

Philip Wexler et al (eds), *Chemicals, Environment, Health: A Global Management Perspective* (CRC Press 2011)

CHAPTER 34

AVIATION AND MARITIME TRANSPORT

BEATRIZ MARTINEZ ROMERA

I. INTRODUCTION

INTERNATIONAL transport of both freight and passengers has grown exponentially over the last fifty years,[1] with further increases projected in the coming decades.[2] This increase in the volume and frequency of international transport exacerbates existing environmental concerns and creates new ones. The impacts of aviation on the environment include noise and air pollution, and the effects of maritime transport on the environment include both marine and air pollution, ranging from oil spills to discharge operations, invasive species, and ship dismantling. Crucially, in recent years, the increasing contribution of aviation and maritime transport to climate change has turned the spotlight on the regulation of greenhouse gas (GHG) emissions.

This chapter provides an overview of the leading environmental issues relating to aviation and maritime transport and the key international legal and regulatory frameworks and tools to address them. After this introductory section, the chapter is divided into four sections. Section II summarizes the international legal regimes involved in aviation and maritime transport environmental governance. Sections III and IV delve into the specific regulation of different environmental matters. Section V concludes with a summary of the key issues and pathways for the sustainable future of these sectors.

[1] OECD, *Globalisation, Transport and the Environment* (2010) 14.

[2] International Air Transport Association (IATA), 'Annual Review 2019', 37 <https://www.iata.org/en/publications/annual-review/> accessed 11 February 2020.

II. AVIATION AND MARITIME TRANSPORT ENVIRONMENTAL GOVERNANCE

The environmental regulation of aviation and maritime transport activities is orchestrated primarily under the auspices of the International Civil Aviation Organization (ICAO) and the International Maritime Organization (IMO), two United Nations (UN) specialized agencies[3] dealing with all aspects of aviation and maritime transport, respectively. However, the environmental governance of aviation and maritime transport also encompasses actors, processes, and instruments outside these regimes, and interactions with other treaty-based regimes.[4]

The Convention on International Civil Aviation (Chicago Convention)[5] was adopted, and the ICAO created, in 1944. This Convention stands as 'the backbone of the international legal regulation of civil aviation'[6] charging ICAO 'to develop the principles and techniques of international air navigation and to foster the planning and development of international air transport'.[7] Environmental aims have been included in ICAO's work and its strategic objectives.[8] In fostering the sustainable development of air transport, the ICAO seeks to ensure full respect for rights, fair opportunities, and non-discrimination between countries.[9]

The Convention on the International Maritime Organization (IMO Convention)[10] establishing the IMO, was adopted in 1948.[11] It aims to provide a machinery for co-operation in the regulation of ships engaged in international trade, encouraging and facilitating the general adoption of the highest practicable standards, including for the prevention and control of marine pollution from ships,[12] and the removal of 'discriminatory action and unnecessary restrictions'.[13] IMO also aims to serve as a forum for the exchange of information among governments and for the consideration of matters

3 'Draft Agreement between UN and ICAO' (30 September 1946) A/106; UN Economic and Social Council Res 165(VII), 'Draft Agreement between UN and IMCO (IMO)' (27 August 1948); these agreements were signed pursuant to ch IX of UN Charter.

4 See eg Beatriz Romera, *Regime Interaction and Climate Change: The Case of International Aviation and Maritime Transport* (Routledge 2018).

5 As amended by ICAO Doc 7300/9 (2006).

6 Michael Milde, 'Future Perspective of Air Law' in Karl-Heinz Böckstiegel *et al*, *Perspectives of Air Law, Space Law, and International Business Law for the Next Century* (C. Heymanns 1996) 13–18.

7 art 44.

8 ICAO Council, 'Strategic objectives of ICAO for 2005–2010—Consolidated vision and mission statement' (adopted 17 December 2004).

9 art 44.

10 Amended and renamed Convention on the International Maritime Organization via 14 November 1975 amendment, which entered into force on 22 May 1982.

11 Until 1982 the IMO was named Inter-governmental Maritime Consultative Organization (IMCO).

12 Mentions of marine pollution and the environment were included in the 1975 and 1977 amendments.

13 arts 1(a), 1(b).

concerning shipping and the effect of shipping on the marine environment referred to it by any organ or specialized agency of the United Nations (UN).[14]

Both the ICAO and IMO share characteristics, such as quasi-universal country participation and comparable functioning structures based on three main organs: Council, Assembly, and a Secretariat. Here, while all members are represented in the respective ICAO and IMO Assemblies, the Council in both organizations has limited participation and is dominated by countries with major stakes. A third element in common relates to the strong influence exerted by the industry in shaping regulatory outcomes.

The environmental governance of maritime transport encompasses, as explored earlier in this volume,[15] a relationship with the 1982 UN Convention on the Law of the Sea (UNCLOS), which plays a role in the regulation of pollution from ships due to the general framework for jurisdictional and enforcement rights and obligations of states, and the provisions on environmental protection contained in Part XII, in particular Article 211.[16] In addition, UNCLOS establishes duties for parties to follow and apply IMO rules and standards.[17]

III. INTERNATIONAL ENVIRONMENTAL LAW AND AVIATION

A. Aviation and the Environment: Noise and Air Quality

Although over time the ICAO has increasingly acknowledged the role of aviation in environmental quality,[18] in the last two decades, the focus of environmental concerns at the ICAO has heavily shifted from local noise and air pollution to the global atmospheric impacts of aviation, most notably how to address GHG emissions from the sector.

The main instrument for environmental regulation of the sector is the ICAO's Standards and Recommended Practices (SARPS)[19] for Environmental Protection launched in 1971 as Annex 16 of the Chicago Convention.[20] SARPs on aircraft noise and

[14] arts 1(c), 1(d), 1(e).

[15] See Chapter 31, 'The Protection of the Marine Environment: Pollution and Fisheries', in this volume.

[16] Part XII—Protection and Preservation of the Marine Environment (arts 192–237).

[17] The IMO is 'the competent international organization', referred to in UNCLOS arts 21, 210, 211, 217.

[18] Acknowledged by the Assembly in ICAO Assembly Res A18-11, 'ICAO Position at the International Conference on the Problems of the Human Environment (Stockholm, June 1972)' (1971) Doc 8958, 36, clause 2; development of the Action Program Regarding the Environment; establishment of the Committee on Aviation Environmental Protection (CAEP) in 1983.

[19] Chicago Convention, ch VI—International standards and recommended practices; see Thomas Buergenthal, *Law-making in the International Civil Aviation Organization* (1st edn, Syracuse University Press 1969).

[20] ICAO Assembly Res A16-3, 'Aircraft Noise in the Vicinity of Airports' (1968) Doc 8779, 30, which initiated work on Annex 16 calling for a conference on aircraft noise.

air quality were adopted and first considered, respectively, that year.[21] Today, Annex 16 comprises three volumes, which are devoted to aircraft noise (Volume I), aircraft engine emissions (Volume II), and CO_2 certification requirements (Volume III).

The ICAO's efforts on policies to limit the number of people affected by significant aircraft noise[22] focus mostly on reducing noise at source through aircraft noise certification standards[23] aiming to incorporate noise reduction technology in aircraft design. These certifications attesting the noise of a given aircraft are granted by the state of registry of the airplane or helicopter, and must be carried on board. Certifications are mutually recognized by states, if they comply with the minimum requirements (maximum noise limits)[24] established by the ICAO SARPs.[25] Noise monitoring measures, airport noise assessment, and the Guidance on the Balanced Approach to Aircraft Noise Management[26] were also adopted to tackle noise in the affected vicinities. SARPs on noise pollution are continuously updated[27] for future aircraft in line with new noise reduction technologies, and with regard to the interactions and trade-offs with reducing the fuel burn and emissions standards.[28]

Despite the progress achieved in the last few decades, environmental noise is still a cause of public concern[29] and one of the main challenges for this sector.[30] Indeed, several claims related to environmental noise from airports and aircraft have been put forward in different jurisdictions[31] and before the European Court of Human Rights (ECtHR).[32] These concerns are often raised in the context of expanding existing or building new airports.

[21] ICAO Assembly Res A18-11 (n 18).

[22] See eg World Health Organization, *Burden of Disease from Environmental Noise: Quantification of Healthy Life Years Lost in Europe* (2011).

[23] Other policies in this area include airport planning and community engagement.

[24] Vol I contains chapters with different aircraft categories according to parameters such as year, type, and weight of the aircraft and maximum noise emission level set for each category.

[25] Chicago Convention, annex 16, vol I, part II.

[26] ICAO Assembly Res 33-7, 'Consolidated statement of continuing ICAO policies and practices related to environmental protection' (2001); ICAO, 'Guidance on the Balanced Approach to Aircraft Noise Management' (2nd edn, 2008) Doc 9829/AN.415.

[27] The latest version of vol I is 8th edn, 2017.

[28] *Report by the Second CAEP Noise Technology Independent Expert Panel: Novel Aircraft—Noise Technology Review and Medium- and Long- Term Noise Reduction Goals*, Doc 10017 (ICAO 2014).

[29] See James Lees, Cait Hewitt, and Tim Johnson, 'Aircraft Noise and Public Health: The Evidence is Loud and Clear' (Aviation Environment Federation 2016).

[30] Mathias Basner *et al*, 'Aviation Noise Impacts: State of the Science' *Noise & Health*, 19/87 (2017): 41.

[31] Ricarda Bennett, 'Airport Noise Litigation: Case Law Review' *Journal of Air Law and Commerce*, 47/3 (1982): 449.

[32] Claims based on violation of art 8 of the 1950 European Convention on Human Rights (ECHR) include *Powell and Rayner v United Kingdom* (Judgement) ECtHR (21 February 1990) Application no 9310/81; *Hatton v UK* (Judgement) Grand Chamber ECtHR (8 July 2003) Application no 36022/97. See ECtHR, 'Guide on Article 8 of the Convention—Right to respect for private and family life' (August 2019); Laura Cristiana, 'Air Traffic and Aircraft Noise Pollution in the ECHR's Case Law' *The Aviation & Space Journal*, XVI/1 (2017): 47.

An emerging area of noise regulation includes upcoming certifications for supersonic aeroplanes, currently under consideration at CAEP.[33] However, while the potential of supersonic aviation will require attention, the steep upswing of aviation activities, and associated noise impact on populations, would require states to develop stringent standards for traditional subsonic aircraft.

The second set of environmental problems stemming from aviation activities relates to air quality.[34] Regulatory efforts here focus on the emissions of pollutants released by engine-powered aircraft during landing and take-off,[35] where engine certification schemes granted by the state of registry are the main tool for local air quality control.[36] In 1997, the Circular on Control of Aircraft Engine Emissions paved the way for the inclusion of vented fuel, smoke, and certain gaseous emissions in Annex 16.[37] Building on this, the engine certification standards for the diverse type of aircraft in Volume II of the Annex set a limit on the emissions of gaseous pollutants, namely unburned hydrocarbons, oxides of nitrogen and carbon monoxide, and smoke.[38] Volume II also contains provisions regarding vented fuel.[39] To promote the uniform implementation of Volume II, CAEP has developed a manual to guide certificating authorities on the procedures deemed acceptable for demonstrating compliance with the standards.[40] As with other SARPs, emissions standards are regularly updated. Standards for particulate matter, mainly consisting of soot or black carbon emissions, were added in January 2020.

Although the ICAO's regulation has significantly reduced emissions affecting air quality near airports, the forecast growth in aviation volume is likely to trump these improvements. This also holds true in relation to global air quality and the impact of aviation on ozone,[41] areas of interaction not fully understood.[42]

[33] ICAO, 'Environmental Report Aviation and Environment: Destination Green—The Next Chapter' (2019) 81–84.

[34] See Mauro Masiol and Roy Harrison, 'Aircraft Engine Exhaust Emissions and Other Airport-Related Contributions to Ambient Air Pollution: A Review' *Atmospheric Environment*, 95 (2014): 409.

[35] Emissions considered by the ICAO's standards are those released below 915 metres of altitude, however the control of emissions here could have a positive spill-over for atmospheric pollution, specifically for ozone depleting substances. Nonetheless, as with regards to air quality, the non-landing and take-off cycle emissions are considered to have a negligible effect on air quality, even in areas with heavy air traffic; see Huikyo Lee *et al*, 'Impacts of Aircraft Emissions on the Air Quality Near the Ground' *Atmospheric Chemistry and Physics*, 13/1 (2013): 689.

[36] Other policies' scope relate to emissions from airport sources, such as airport traffic, ground service equipment, and de-icing procedures.

[37] ICAO Circular No 134, 'Control of Aircraft Engine Emissions' (1997).

[38] Chicago Convention, annex 16, vol II, part III.

[39] Ibid, part II.

[40] *Environmental Technical Manual—Volume 2—Procedures for the Emissions Certification of Aircraft Engines*, Doc 9501 (2nd edn, ICAO 2014).

[41] Sebastian Eastham and Steven Barrett, 'Aviation-Attributable Ozone as a Driver for Changes in Mortality Related to Air Quality and Skin Cancer' *Atmospheric Environment*, 144 (2016): 17.

[42] Masiol and Harrison (n 34).

B. Aviation and Climate Change

GHG emissions from aviation account for around 2% of global GHG emissions[43] and are forecast to grow exponentially by an estimated 300–700% by 2050[44] due to high levels of sustained energy demand in the sector arising from increased air travel, which is projected to double by 2035.[45] CO_2 emitted by aircraft engines is the biggest contributor to aviation's impact on climate change. However, research suggests that this impact is greater when considering non-CO_2 emissions, namely nitrogen oxides (NOx), water vapour, sulphur (SOx), and soot particles, and the formation of condensation trails.[46]

The climate change regime has struggled to regulate international aviation (and maritime transport) GHG emissions.[47] Although discussed by the Intergovernmental Negotiating Committee for a Framework Convention on Climate Change,[48] and subsequently under the 1992 UNFCCC (UN Framework Convention on Climate Change) umbrella, there have been limited meaningful outcomes. UNFCCC reporting obligations[49] make a crucial distinction between domestic and international aviation. Emissions from domestic aviation are included in country parties' inventories under national totals, and international aviation emissions are reported separately, that is, decoupled from countries' responsibilities.[50] In turn, the Kyoto Protocol excluded international aviation emissions from its targets in 1997 and acknowledged the role of the ICAO as the venue for negotiating measures.[51] Nonetheless, discussions on how

[43] Joyce Penner *et al*, Aviation and the Global Atmosphere (CUP 1999) 185; David Lee *et al*, 'Transport Impacts on Atmosphere and Climate: Aviation' *Atmospheric Environment*, 44 (2010): 4678; see also David Lee *et al*, 'Aviation and Global Climate Change in the 21st Century' *Atmospheric Environment*, 43 (2009): 3520.

[44] This figure comes from the ICAO, and other studies have shown similar trends, see eg Bethan Owen *et al*, 'Flying into the Future: Aviation Emissions Scenarios to 2050' *Environmental Science & Technology*, 44/7 (2010): 2255; and more recently see Brandon Graver, Kevin Zhang, and Dan Rutherford, 'CO2 Emissions from Commercial Aviation, 2018' *The International Council on Clean Transportation: Working Paper 2019-16* (2019).

[45] IATA, '20 Year Forecast Report' <https://www.iata.org/en/publications/store/20-year-passenger-forecast> accessed 11 February 2020. The growth is mainly driven by increasing demand in the Asia-Pacific region.

[46] Lee, 'Transport Impacts' (n 43); Lee, 'Aviation and Global Climate Change' (n 43); Owen (n 44); these studies suggested a contribution to global warming of between 3.5–4.9% to the global total.

[47] Chapter 29, 'Climate Change', in this volume.

[48] UNGA, 'Matters relating to commitments: Methodologies for calculations/inventories of emissions and removals of greenhouse gases—Note by the secretariat' (15 July 1993) UN Doc A/AC.237/34.

[49] UNFCCC, arts 4.1(a), 12; 1997 Kyoto Protocol, art 7.

[50] For reporting purposes, international aviation emissions are calculated on the basis of the country where the fuel is sold; see Farhana Yamin and Joanna Depledge, *The International Climate Change Regime: A Guide to Rules, Institutions and Procedures* (CUP 2004) 85–89.

[51] Kyoto Protocol, art 2.2 states that '[T]he Parties included in Annex I shall pursue limitation or reduction of emissions of greenhouse gases not controlled by the Montreal Protocol from aviation and marine bunker fuels, working through the International Civil Aviation Organization and the International Maritime Organization, respectively'.

to address emissions from international aviation continued under the climate regime, not only with the work of the SBSTA (Subsidiary Body for Scientific and Technological Advice) in improving inventories[52] but also under the mandate of the Ad Hoc Working Group on Long-term Cooperative Action[53] and the Ad Hoc Working Group on the Durban Platform for Enhanced Action (ADP).[54] Although international aviation was included in the negotiating draft agreement prepared by ADP and presented to the COP 21 for adoption,[55] the clause did not make it to the final text of the 2015 Paris Agreement.[56] Disagreements leading to the omission of aviation in the Paris Agreement coalesced, primarily, around the divergent understandings of parties on the application of CBDRRC (common but differentiated responsibilities and respective capabilities) to international aviation,[57] in particular, due to the principles of non-discrimination and equal opportunities enshrined in the Chicago Convention,[58] and to concerns over potential distortion of competition.

Since the adoption of the Kyoto Protocol, the ICAO has been increasingly accepted as the forum for the regulation of climate-related aviation impacts by UNFCCC parties. Beyond commissioning reports and task groups to advance discussions on different aspects of the problem,[59] the ICAO adopted a Programme of Action in 2010,[60] which included an aspirational goal to achieve carbon neutral growth in the sector from 2020 onwards. To achieve this goal, a 'basket of measures' have been adopted, including technical and operational measures, the advance of alternative fuels, and the establishment

[52] Decision 4/CP.1, 'Methodological Issues' (6 June 1995) UN Doc FCCC/CP/1995/7/Add.1, para 1(f); see also Decision 2/CP.3, 'Methodological Issues Related to the Kyoto Protocol' (25 March 1998) UN Doc FCCC/CP/1997/7/Add.1, which recalls that aviation emissions are not to be included in national totals according to the IPCC guidelines and urges the SBSTA to elaborate on the inclusion of these emissions in the parties' inventories.

[53] Decision 1/CP.13, 'Bali Action Plan' (14 March 2008) UN Doc FCCC/CP/2007/6/Add.1, para 1(b)(iv).

[54] Decision 2/CP.17, 'Outcome of the Work of the Ad Hoc Working Group on Long-term Cooperative Action under the Convention' (15 March 2012) UN Doc FCCC/CP/2011/9/Add.1, para 78.

[55] UNFCCC, 'Draft Agreement and Draft Decision on Workstreams 1 and 2 of the Ad Hoc Working Group on the Durban Platform for Enhanced Action' (3 December 2015) para 20; 'Draft Agreement and Draft Decision on Workstreams 1 and 2 of the Ad Hoc Working Group on the Durban Platform for Enhanced Action' (4 December 2015) para 20; 'Paris Outcome—Revised Draft Conclusions Proposed by the Co-Chairs' (5 December 2015) UN Doc FCCC/ADP/2015/L.6/Rev.1, para 20.

[56] On the consequences of this omission see Beatriz Romera, 'The Paris Agreement and the Regulation of International Bunker Fuels' *Review of European Comparative & International Environmental Law*, 25/2 (2016): 215.

[57] On CBDR and aviation see Beatriz Romera and Harro van Asselt, 'The International Regulation of Aviation Emissions: Putting Differential Treatment into Practice' *Journal of Environmental Law*, 27/2 (2015): 259.

[58] Chicago Convention, preamble, arts 11, 44(f), 44(g).

[59] Since 1998 the ICAO has included GHG emissions in its work.

[60] ICAO Assembly Res A37-19, 'Consolidated Statement of Continuing ICAO Policies and Practices Related to Environmental Protection—Climate Change' (2010).

of a global market-based measure (MBM) for international aviation. Crucially, in 2013, the ICAO Assembly agreed develop an MBM,[61] which was finally adopted in 2016.[62]

The Carbon Offsetting and Reduction Scheme for International Aviation (CORSIA) aims to stabilize the sectors' emissions by addressing any increase above 2020 levels through offsetting.[63] The cap-and-offset scheme requires airlines operating in the routes covered (exceptions are granted for certain flights, volumes, and routes) to buy carbon credits to compensate for their growth in CO_2 emissions above 2020 levels.[64] The scheme's coverage is based on routes and the scheme applies equally to all air carriers on a route by route basis, with emissions allocated to air carriers, not to countries for a given flight stage. However, to reach an agreement to adopt CORSIA, differential treatment in favour of developing countries needed to be incorporated. In this connection, Least Developed Countries, Small Island Developing States and landlocked Developing Countries are exempted from the scheme and invited to join CORSIA voluntarily.[65]

The scheme is envisioned to be deployed in three implementation phases. The first two phases (a pilot phase from 2021 to 2023 and a first phase from 2023 to 2026) are voluntary for all states. After 2027, when the second phase (2027–35) starts, the scheme becomes mandatory for all states above the threshold of 0.5% of total revenue tonne kilometres.[66] The ICAO's country members are responsible for monitoring, reporting, and verifying the emissions data and related offsets for its aircraft operators of flights covered by the scheme. From 1 January 2019, all carriers are required to report their CO_2 emissions on an annual basis. CORSIA is currently under development at the ICAO and a crucial issue to be determined is the eligibility criteria of the offset credits, which will largely determine the environmental effectiveness of the scheme.[67] Notably, sustainable aviation fuels have received much attention in the ICAO and support from the industry,[68] and they might be used for compliance with CORSIA[69] under certain conditions (eg a 10%

[61] ICAO Assembly Res A38-18, 'Consolidated Statement of Continuing ICAO Policies and Practices Related to Environmental Protection—Climate Change' (2013) 18–24.

[62] ICAO Assembly Res A39-3, 'Consolidated statement of continuing ICAO policies and practices related to environmental protection—Global Market-based Measure (MBM) scheme' (2016); see further Ruwantissa Abeyratne, 'Outcome of the 39th Session of the International Civil Aviation Organization Assembly' *Air and Space Law*, 42/1 (2017): 13.

[63] ICAO Assembly Res A39-3 (n 62) para 3.

[64] Offset costs are likely be embedded as an additional fuel cost for airlines.

[65] ICAO Assembly Res A39-3 (n 62) paras 9, 10.

[66] Ibid, para 9.

[67] Carsten Warnecke *et al*, 'Robust Eligibility Criteria Essential for New Global Scheme to Offset Aviation Emissions' *Nature Climate Change*, 9/3 (2019): 218.

[68] IATA, 'Aim for 1 Billion Passengers to Fly on Sustainable Fuel Flights by 2025' (26 February 2018) <https://www.iata.org/pressroom/pr/Pages/2018-02-26-01.aspx> accessed 30 December 2019.

[69] ICAO, '2019 Environmental Report' (n 33) 188–191.

minimum GHG reduction and not made from biomass obtained from land with high carbon stock value). However, the potential of sustainable aviation fuels is contested.[70]

Other climate-related measures adopted in the ICAO include a CO_2 certification standard for aircraft,[71] which became part of Volume III to Annex 16 of the Chicago Convention. The standard applies to new aircraft from 2020, and to aircraft already in production as of 2023. Additional measures include establishing State Action Plans on mitigation activities, the enhancement of capacity-building and assistance, and a mechanism to facilitate access to financial resources for climate purposes.[72]

The ICAO has failed to adopt a carbon target in line with the Paris Agreement goals.[73] Existing policies at the ICAO, namely the CO_2 standard for new aircraft and CORSIA, have raised criticism, and more comprehensive approaches have been suggested.[74] Current measures are deemed insufficient to reduce international aviation emissions meaningfully,[75] which will mean that by 2050 aviation would have consumed 12% of the global carbon budget in a 1.5°C scenario.[76]

Under these circumstances, ambitious countries might seek to complement international efforts with unilateral action.[77] Most notably, the European Union (EU) passed legislation in 2008 to include aviation (all flights arriving or departing from an aerodrome in EU territory) in the EU Emissions Trading Scheme (ETS).[78] The measure faced political, commercial, and legal opposition ending with international flights being temporarily waived from compliance.[79] Here, questions arise about the coexistence

[70] Mark Staples *et al*, 'Aviation CO2 Emissions Reductions from the Use of Alternative Jet Fuels' *Energy Policy*, 114 (2018): 342.

[71] Adopted in 2013, amended in 2017.

[72] ICAO Assembly Res A38-18 (n 61) paras 11–15, 33(e).

[73] Discussions to set a long-term aspirational goal for the sector are on the agenda of the ICAO Assembly; see Working Paper A40-WP/58 <https://www.icao.int/Meetings/A40/Documents/WP/wp_058_en.pdf> accessed 30 December 2019.

[74] Chris Lyle, 'Beyond the ICAO CORSIA: Towards a More Climatically Effective Strategy for Mitigation of Civil-Aviation Emissions' *Climate Law*, 8/1–2 (2018): 104.

[75] Nik Pavlenko, 'ICAO CORSIA Scheme Provides a Weak Nudge for In-Sector Carbon Reductions' *International Council on Clean Transportation* (6 August 2018); Brandon Graver and Dan Rutherford, 'U.S. Passenger Jets Under ICAO's CO2 Standard, 2018–2038' *International Council on Clean Transportation* (2 October 2018).

[76] Roz Pidcock and Sophie Yeo 'Analysis: Aviation Could Consume a Quarter of 1.5C Carbon Budget by 2050' *Carbon Brief* (8 August 2016) and the figure would double if compliance with existing measures fails.

[77] Some countries are introducing carbon taxes for aviation, like Sweden or the Netherlands. China might include aviation in its emissions trading system.

[78] Directive 2008/101/EC of 19 November 2008 amending Directive 2003/87/EC so as to include aviation activities in the scheme for greenhouse gas emission allowance trading within the Community, OJ 2009 L 8/3.

[79] Decision 377/2013/EU of 24 April 2013 derogating temporarily from Directive 2003/87/EC establishing a scheme for greenhouse gas emission allowance trading within the Community, OJ 2013 L 113/1.

of the EU scheme with CORSIA.[80] Additionally, a new regulatory frontier relates to the non-CO_2 impacts of aviation. For example, the 2018 amendment of the EU ETS[81] envisages that 'before 1 January 2020, the Commission shall present an updated analysis of the non-CO_2 effects of aviation, accompanied, where appropriate, by a proposal on how best to address those effects'.

IV. INTERNATIONAL ENVIRONMENTAL LAW AND MARITIME TRANSPORT

A. Maritime Transport and the Environment

Chapter 31 in this volume analyses the general legal and regulatory framework for protecting the marine environment and introduces the main instruments regulating pollution from vessels.[82] Building on that, this chapter examines some of the key legal instruments dealing with the prevention of maritime transport environmental impact.

Shipping poses several threats to the environment both through accidents at sea involving spills of oil and other substances, and in the normal operation of vessels. In preventing pollution from ships, regulations focusing on ship safety standards are relevant, such as the 1974 Safety of Life at Sea Convention, which not only aims to protect human lives, but also extends to environmental protection. In regulating pollution from vessels, there are four main regulatory frameworks,[83] regarding the prevention and control of pollution from ships (MARPOL73/78),[84] dumping of waste,[85] invasive species carried in ballast water,[86] and environmental pollution from ship-breaking.[87]

[80] Uwe Erling, 'How to Reconcile the European Union Emissions Trading System (EU ETS) for Aviation with the Carbon Offsetting and Reduction Scheme for International Aviation (CORSIA)?' *Journal of Air Space Law*, 43/4–5 (2018): 371.

[81] Directive (EU) 2018/410 of 14 March 2018 amending Directive 2003/87/EC to enhance cost-effective emission reductions and low-carbon investments, and Decision (EU) 2015/1814, OJ 2018 L 76/3.

[82] Chapter 31, 'The Protection of the Marine Environment: Pollution and Fisheries', in this volume.

[83] Other instruments include the International Convention on the Control of Harmful Anti-Fouling Systems on Ships (2001) and the International Convention on the Removal of Wrecks (2007).

[84] 1973 International Convention for the Prevention of Pollution from Ships (MARPOL 73) as modified by the Protocol of 1978 (MARPOL 78). The Convention and the Protocol were merged into one legal instrument. The Protocol came after a series of disasters that proved a lack of uniform application of MARPOL 73. See further in Douglas Brubaker, *Marine Pollution and International Law: Principles and Practice* (Belhaven Press 1993) 122–129.

[85] 1972 London Convention on the Prevention of Marine Pollution by Dumping of Wastes and Other Matter and the 1996 Protocol to the London Convention.

[86] 2004 International Convention for the Control and Management of Ships' Ballast Water and Sediments.

[87] 2009 Hong Kong International Convention for the Safe and Environmentally Sound Recycling of Ships.

MARPOL aims to eliminate all types of pollution[88] caused by ship operations and to minimize discharges,[89] through detailed technical regulation incorporated in its annexes.[90] However, not all the annexes have the same weight since only Annexes I and II dealing with the prevention of pollution by oil and the control of pollution by noxious liquid substances, respectively, are obligatory for all parties to the MARPOL Convention. Annex III on the prevention of pollution by harmful substances in packaged form, Annex IV on the prevention of pollution from sewage from ships, Annex V on the prevention of pollution by garbage from ships, and Annex VI on the prevention of air pollution from ships are optional for the parties. However, these standards are generally accepted and might be regarded as prescriptive for flag states under Article 211 of the UNCLOS.[91]

MARPOL addresses both accidental and non-accidental pollution. A vital element in preventing accidental oil pollution incorporated in MARPOL is the double-hull requirements adopted in 1993.[92] After the Erika oil spill in 1999, parties agreed to a stricter timetable for the phasing-out of single-hull tankers, and this now includes a ban on the carriage of heavy grade oil in certain single-hull tankers.

The prevention of air pollution from ships was first considered in 1991.[93] Annex VI on air pollution was adopted in 1997[94] to 'preserve the marine environment through the complete elimination of pollution by oil and other harmful substances and the minimization of accidental discharge of such substances'.[95] In particular, limits on sulphur oxide (SO_x) and nitrogen oxide (NO_x) emissions, and a prohibition on deliberate release of emissions of ozone depleting substances, were adopted. In addition, Annex VI introduces emission control areas (ECAs) with tighter requirements. A significant revision of Annex VI was agreed in 2008,[96] and progressively Annex VI has been incorporating new substances,[97] including GHGs. Revised MARPOL Annex VI establishes that ships constructed on or after certain years (2000, 2011, and 2016) must comply with three different NO_x limits (Tier I, II, and III), depending on certain

[88] Except waste dumping, which is covered under the London Convention on Dumping and its Protocol.

[89] Preamble.

[90] Revisions to MARPOL are carried out by the adoption of resolutions at the Marine Environmental Protection Committee (MEPC) of the IMO.

[91] See Patricia Birnie, Alan Boyle, and Catherine Redgwell, *International Law and the Environment* (3rd edn, OUP 2009) 404.

[92] Annex I, regulations 19–21.

[93] IMO Res A.719(17), 'Prevention of Air Pollution from Ships' (6 November 1991).

[94] Protocol of 1997 to amend MARPOL 73, as modified by MARPOL 78 (annex VI—Regulations for the Prevention of Air Pollution from Ships).

[95] MARPOL, art 1.

[96] IMO, 'Revised MARPOL Annex VI: regulations for the prevention of air pollution from ships and NOx technical code 2008' (2009).

[97] Colin de la Rue and Charles Anderson, *Shipping and the Environment: Law and Practice* (2nd edn, Informa Law 2009) 840–847.

conditions, and with a lower emission limit in the ECAs.[98] The control of NO_x emissions is achieved through the Engine International Air Pollution Prevention Certificate.

Another major development is the lowering of the maximum content of sulphur in marine fuels to 0.50%.[99] While a noteworthy environmental improvement, this poses a significant operational burden on the industry, risking severe enforcement complications since entering into force in 2020.[100]

In relation to MARPOL, the Polar Code seeks to prevent vessel pollution from ships operating in polar waters (Antarctica and the Arctic) through mandatory requirements and recommendations.[101] The Polar Code enhances the requirements already applicable to ships under MARPOL, such as more ambitious mandatory operational discharges. In addition, the Polar Code confirms the prohibition of carrying or using heavy grade oils in the Antarctica,[102] and encourages parties not to use or carry heavy fuel oil in the Arctic.

The incineration and dumping at sea of hazardous materials and waste falls outside the scope of MARPOL, and is covered by the 1972 London Dumping Convention and its 1996 Protocol. Dumping is defined as 'any deliberate disposal into the sea of wastes or other matter from vessels, aircraft, platforms or other man-made structures'.[103] The Protocol applies the precautionary approach to environmental protection from dumping[104] and the polluter pays principle,[105] and states that parties should not allow the transfer of pollution and environmental damage.[106] The Protocol prohibits all dumping of waste, with limited exceptions that can be accepted through a permit system, under certain conditions and strict control.[107] The Protocol was amended in 2009 to include CO_2,[108] which is allowed to be stored in the sub-seabed.[109]

98 MARPOL annex VI, regulations 13.8, 5.3.2; NOx Technical Code (n 96).

99 MARPOL annex VI, regulation 14—Sulphur Oxides and Particulate Matter. The limit was 3.5% and 0.5% for ECAs before the 2008 Revision.

100 Jesper Fanø, 'Enforcement of the 2020 Sulphur Limit for Marine Fuels: Restrictions and Possibilities for Port States to Impose Fines Under UNCLOS' *Review of European, Comparative and International Environmental Law*, 28/3 (2019): 278

101 2014 International Code for Ships Operating in Polar Waters (Polar Code), part II.

102 IMO Res MEPC.189(60), 'Amendments to the annex of the protocol of 1978 relating to the international convention for the prevention of pollution from ships, 1973' (26 March 2010) which added a new ch 9 to MARPOL annex I dealing with special requirements for the use or carriage of oils in the Antarctica area.

103 art 3.1(a).

104 art 3.1.

105 art 3.2.

106 art 3.3.

107 art 4, annex 1. The exception includes: dredged material; sewage sludge; fish waste; vessels, platforms or other man-made structures; inert, inorganic geological material; organic material of natural origin; bulky items; CO_2 storage in sub-seabed geological formations.

108 IMO Res LP.3(4) 'On the amendment to article 6 of the London Protocol' (30 October 2009).

109 See Chapter 31, 'The Protection of the Marine Environment: Pollution and Fisheries', in this volume.

The 2004 Ballast Water Management Convention is the third relevant treaty.[110] It takes a precautionary approach to the problem of the biological materials carried and discharged through ships' ballast water operations, which is a leading source of invasive aquatic species. Due to the enlargement of ship sizes and the speeding up of shipping voyages, greater quantities of ballast water are transported faster to different parts of the world, causing a significant transfer of alien species. To avoid this transfer, the Convention, which builds on the IMO's Guidelines for the control and management of ships' ballast water,[111] requires all ships to implement a Ballast Water Management Plan. Ships must carry a record book on board and must perform ballast operations according to the standards under the Convention, including ballast water treatment system. New guidelines and procedures for uniform implementation of the Convention have been adopted,[112] and the guidelines for approval of ballast water management systems converted into a mandatory code in 2018.[113]

An array of instruments (including IMO recommendations) are relevant for controlling ship-breaking activities. Most notably, the 2009 Hong Kong Convention for the Safe and Environmentally Sound Recycling of Ships, which aims to prevent, minimize, reduce, and eliminate accidents and injuries on human health and environmental impact caused by ship recycling.[114] In 2018, the global merchant fleet accounted for around 52,000 ships,[115] of which, approximately, 750 were dismantled. 78% of the ship-breaking worldwide takes place under the 'beaching method', which causes severe pollution.[116] The dismantling of end-of-life vessels releases materials such as oil, asbestos, toxic chemicals, and heavy metals into the environment.[117] The Hong Kong Convention provides for establishing ship recycling facilities, inspection of ships, and sanctions for violations of the Convention.[118] However, since the Convention is not yet in force, the interplay with the 1989 Basel Convention,[119] which enjoys wide ratification, is pertinent here,[120] given that the ships fall under the definition of waste of Article 2.[121]

110 On implementation challenges see Stephan Gollasch and Matej David, 'Ballast Water Management Convention Implementation Challenges' *Ocean Yearbook*, 32/1 (2018): 456.

111 IMO Res A.868(20), 'Guidelines for the control and management of ships' ballast water to minimize the transfer of harmful aquatic organisms and pathogens' (27 November 1997).

112 A total of fourteen guidelines ranging from sampling to reception facilities; see 'Guidelines and Guidance Documents Related to the Implementation of the International Convention for the Control and Management of Ships' Ballast Water and Sediments' (2004).

113 IMO Res MEPC.300(72) 'Code for approval of ballast water management systems' (13 April 2018).

114 art 1.

115 UN Conference on Trade and Development (UNCTAD), *Review of Maritime Transport 2019*, 37.

116 European Commission, 'Ship Recycling: Reducing Human and Environmental Impacts' *Science for Environment Policy*, 55 (June 2016): 3; Beaching occurs mostly in India, Bangladesh, Pakistan, and China.

117 See European Commission and Science for Environment Policy, 'Ship recycling: reducing human and environmental impacts' Thematic Issue 55 (June 2016).

118 art 10.

119 See also Chapter 33, 'Hazardous Substances and Activities', in this volume.

120 Center for International Environmental Law, 'Shipbreaking and the Basel Convention: Analysis of the Level of Control Established under the Hong Kong Convention' (2011).

121 Basel Convention, Decision VII/26, 'Environmentally sound management of ship dismantling' (25 January 2005) UN Doc UNEP/CHW.7/33.

B. Maritime Transport and Climate Change

GHG emissions from international maritime transport account for around 2–3% of the global total, and are forecast to increase between 50% and 250% by 2050.[122] Moreover, the contribution of shipping to climate change will intensify as 'regional' climate change[123] opens up routes in the Arctic.

Like aviation, the regulation of GHG emissions emanating from maritime transport has been part of the negotiating agenda of the UNFCCC since the inception of the regime.[124] Parties agreed to a similar distinction between domestic and international maritime transport in relation to their reporting obligations, and the sector, like aviation, is excluded from the Kyoto Protocol, and not referenced in the Paris Agreement.[125]

In 1997, parties to MARPOL adopted a resolution recognizing the adverse impact of CO_2 emissions from shipping on the environment, and requesting the IMO to study the climate challenge. However, it was not until 2003 that the MEPC was tasked with identifying and developing the mechanisms needed to achieve limitations or reductions of GHG emissions from ships.[126] In 2011, chapter four on 'Regulations on Energy Efficiency for Ships' was added to MARPOL Annex VI, with mandatory energy efficiency requirements for ships.[127] The Energy Efficiency Design Index (EEDI) covers all new ships from 2013 and aims to promote innovation and reduce consumption through an energy-efficiency design standard.[128] Since the EEDI is based on performance, the way in which the target should be achieved is largely left to the industry. In 2019, amendments to strengthen EEDI were approved.[129] In addition, in 2011, an operational measure applying to all ships (Ship Energy Efficiency Management Plan) was agreed upon. SEEMP sets a mechanism for monitoring ship and fleet energy efficiency and a voluntary Energy Efficiency Operational Indicator (EEOI) as a monitoring tool.[130]

122 IMO, 'Third IMO Greenhouse Gas Study 2014' (2015).

123 Black carbon particles, emitted by ships burning heavy fuel oil in the Arctic, are potent short-lived pollutants that absorb sunlight and trap heat in the atmosphere, accelerating global warming in the Arctic region.

124 Farhana Yamin and Joanna Depledge, *The International Climate Change Regime: a Guide to Rules, Institutions and Procedures* (CUP 2004).

125 See Section III.B in this chapter.

126 IMO Res A.963(23), 'IMO Policies and Practices Related to the Reduction of Greenhouse Gas Emissions from Ships' (2004).

127 IMO Res MEPC.203(62), 'Amendments to the annex of the protocol of 1997 to amend the international convention for the prevention of pollution from ships, 1973, as modified by the protocol of 1978 relating thereto (Inclusion of regulations on energy efficiency for ships in MARPOL Annex VI)' (15 July 2011).

128 Minimum energy efficiency level per capacity mile for different ship type and size segments.

129 At the 74th session of MEPC in May 2019; see IMO, 'UN agency pushes forward on shipping emissions reduction' (20 May 2019).

130 Andreas Chrysostomou and Eivind Vågslid, 'Climate Change: A Challenge for IMO Too' in Regina Asariotis and Hassiba Benamara (eds), *Maritime Transport and the Climate Change Challenge* (Earthscan 2012) 75, 91–95.

In including EEDI and SEEMP in MARPOL Annex VI, many developing countries raised concerns about the absence of differentiation in favour of developing countries,[131] in relation to capacity-building, technical assistance, and transfer of technology. These concerns echoed a long-standing debate on how to apply CBDRRC at the IMO, in particular for MBMs. Contrary to the climate regime, the IMO Convention,[132] the IMO treaties, and the IMO practice build on the principle of non-discriminatory regulation of all ships and the principle of no-more-favourable treatment of ships.[133] Here, the system of ship registries with increasing foreign-flagging and flag-jumping practices poses challenges in differentiating between countries.[134] Whereas a resolution providing a framework for the promotion of technical cooperation and the transfer of technology for the measures included in Annex VI was adopted in 2013,[135] there were irreconcilable views on the application of differentiation to potential MBMs, so discussions were suspended.

In 2015 discussions reopened with a proposal to set a global CO_2 target,[136] and after the adoption of the Paris Agreement, the IMO approved a Roadmap for GHG emissions.[137] Thereafter, a mandatory Data Collection System for recording and reporting data on fuel consumption was adopted via MARPOL Annex VI,[138] which requires ships of 5,000 gross tonnage and above to collect data on fuel oil consumption and distance. This mechanism is regarded as a first step towards establishing further measures such as MBMs.

Crucially, in 2018, an Initial Strategy on GHG emissions was adopted,[139] aiming to set an overall vision for decarbonizing the sector consistent with the Paris Agreement goals. This vision is understood as requiring a peaking of GHG emissions from international shipping as soon as possible, and achieving reductions by at least 50% by 2050, from 2008 levels. The specific measures to achieve this target, and its consequences for

[131] 'Report of the Marine Environment Protection Committee on its 62nd Session' (26 July 2011) MEPC 62/24; China, Saudi Arabia, and South Africa opposed a regulation on GHGs with no consideration of the CBDRRC principle so the measures were adopted by resorting to a vote.

[132] art 1(b).

[133] Chrysostomou and Vågslid (n 130) 81.

[134] Less than 25% of the world's fleet is flagged in the country the vessel is from.

[135] IMO Res MEPC.229(65), 'Promotion of Technical Co-Operation and Transfer of Technology Relating to the Improvement of Energy Efficiency of Ships' (17 May 2013) annex 4.

[136] IMO, 'Reduction of GHG Emissions from Ships: Setting a reduction target and agreeing associated measures for international shipping' (20 March 2015) MEPC 68/5/1.

[137] Roadmap for developing a comprehensive IMO Strategy on reduction of GHG emissions from ships was approved at MEPC 70.

[138] IMO Res MEPC.278(70), 'Amendments to MARPOL Annex VI (Data collection system for fuel oil consumption of ships)' (28 October 2016). The measure followed the adoption of a Monitoring, Reporting and Verification System in the EU; see 'Regulation (EU) 2015/757 of 29 April 2015 on the monitoring, reporting and verification of carbon dioxide emissions from maritime transport, and amending Directive 2009/16/EC' OJ 2015 L 123/55.

[139] IMO Res MEPC.304(72), 'Initial IMO Strategy on Reduction of GHG Emissions from Ships' (13 April 2018).

international shipping, are still under discussion, in particular with regard to the potential short-, mid-, and long-term measures.[140]

To advance the climate agenda at the IMO, a Fourth IMO GHG Study has been commissioned, and two resolutions have been adopted to encourage voluntary cooperation between ports and the shipping industry, and to establish a multi-donor trust fund to provide financial support for technical cooperation and capacity-building activities aimed at the implementation of the GHG Strategy.[141]

V. CONCLUSIONS: TOWARDS SUSTAINABLE AVIATION AND MARITIME TRANSPORT

There are a range of instruments regulating the environmental impact of aviation and maritime transport, but the predicted exponential growth in international aviation and maritime transport activities is likely to require significantly more stringent environmental measures, as well as regulation of new technologies and developments. The ICAO and IMO have been able to rise to the challenge in some respects, but two major challenges remain largely unaddressed, namely: the dismantling of ships and GHG emissions for both sectors.

In particular, the IMO is yet to develop meaningful measures to tackle the contribution of shipping to climate change, and the ICAO will need to elaborate on CORSIA's ambition. In working towards these pressing and core tasks, interaction with the Paris Agreement, including the application of CBDRRC and coherence with the long-term temperature goal, will be crucial. Here, the forecast contribution of the sectors to climate change in the forthcoming decades is likely to lend gravitas to domestic and regional action, if significant ambition is not reached at the multilateral level.

BIBLIOGRAPHY

Meinhard Doelle and Aldo Chircop, 'Decarbonizing International Shipping: An Appraisal of the IMO's Initial Strategy' *Review of European, Comparative and International Environmental Law* 28/3 (2019): 268

[140] Meinhard Doelle and Aldo Chircop, 'Decarbonizing International Shipping: An Appraisal of the IMO's Initial Strategy' *Review of European, Comparative and International Environmental Law*, 28/3 (2019): 268.

[141] IMO Res MEPC.323(74), 'Invitation to member states to encourage voluntary cooperation between the port and shipping sectors to contribute to reducing GHG emissions from ships' (17 May 2019).

Jesper Fanø, 'Enforcement of the 2020 Sulphur Limit for Marine Fuels: Restrictions and Possibilities for Port States to Impose Fines Under UNCLOS' *Review of European, Comparative and International Environmental Law*, 28/3 (2019): 278

Stephan Gollasch and Matej David, 'Ballast Water Management Convention Implementation Challenges' *Ocean Yearbook*, 32/1 (2018): 456

Beatriz Romera, *Regime Interaction and Climate Change: The Case of International Aviation and Maritime Transport* (Routledge 2018)

PART VI

ACTORS

CHAPTER 35

THE STATE

THILO MARAUHN

I. INTRODUCTION

SINCE the early days of modern public international law, the state has been its most important subject. However, today, the state is neither the sole, nor necessarily the primary, actor in international (environmental) relations. In recent years, the role of the state and, notably, the ability of the state to address environmental risks and threats, have come under scrutiny. While the role of state in norm making remains important—albeit with varying degrees of intensity and normativity—commentators have argued that there are major weaknesses in the ability and willingness of states to implement and enforce such norms. This so-called implementation deficit,[1] both at the national and at the international levels, has long been recognized and discussed. As a consequence, the traditional reliance on national implementation has been questioned[2]—stimulating fundamental debates about the state as an actor in international environmental relations.

The role of the state is also increasingly questioned from the perspective of legal and political theory.[3] Although a growing literature claims the demise of the

[1] Michael Bothe, 'Vollzugsdefizit im Völkerrecht—Überlegungen zu 30 Jahren Umweltrecht' in Hans Cremer, Thomas Giegerich, and Dagmar Richter (eds), *Tradition und Weltoffenheit des Rechts* (Springer 2002) 83.

[2] Daniel Cole and Peter Grossman, 'When Is Command-and-Control Efficient? Institutions, Technology, and the Comparative Efficiency of Alternative Regulatory Regimes for Environmental Protection' *Wisconsin Law Review* (1999): 887; cf. Rena Steinzor, 'Reinventing Environmental Regulation: The Dangerous Journey from Command to Self-Control' *Harvard Environmental Law* Review, 22/1 (1998): 103.

[3] Christian Kreuder-Sonnen and Bernhard Zangl, 'Which Post-Westphalia? International Organizations between Constitutionalism and Authoritarianism' *European Journal of International Relations*, 21/3 (2015): 568; José-Manuel Barreto, '*Cerberus*: Rethinking Grotius and the Westphalian System' in Martti Koskenniemi *et al* (eds), *International Law and Empire: Historical Explorations* (OUP 2016) 149.

state,[4] these claims should be treated with caution. As a descriptive matter, the state is much less in decline than is often claimed. From a normative perspective, the demise of the state may destabilize the international legal order and entail more problems than benefits. Simply put, if a state's administrative capacity breaks down, there is no adequate replacement for it. It is against this background that initiatives such as the New Partnership for Africa's Development have actually called for strengthening and reconstructing statehood.[5] In other words, the state remains a truly important actor in international relations. This chapter thus addresses the changing role of the state rather than its demise.

Historically, states were reluctant to accept environmental responsibility, and once they did, it took them a while to move from standard setting towards implementation. Today, states have to find their place within a complex environmental governance structure. Due to the perceived inadequacy of pure command-and-control strategies, questions of instrument choice and incentive-based techniques of environmental governance,[6] have also influenced the role of the state. While negative incentives come close to command-and-control strategies, the spectrum of positive incentives ('carrots') offers a much broader perspective on steering the behaviour of individuals, groups (including private corporations), and states. Carrots are more acceptable than sticks, enabling the state to expand the scope of environmental governance while, at the same time, relying upon a broader variety of means. These shifts are crucial given the need for states to position themselves between the conflicting trends of privatization and internationalization of environmental policies.[7]

The starting point for this chapter is the Westphalian notion of states' unimpaired freedom of action, increasingly revealed as a 'myth'. The chapter then considers ideas of contemporary statehood—an element of a global system of environmental governance. Contemporary statehood and its relevance for international environmental law can best be illuminated by focusing on the roles assumed by states as authors, addressees, and guardians of international law. The final sections of the chapter discuss the changing role of states in light of ongoing transformations in the international legal system, including the growing plurality of actors, norms, and institutions, as well as the growth of inter-linked networks of states and other actors.

[4] Eric Ip, 'Globalization and the Future of the Law of the Sovereign State' *International Journal of Constitutional Law*, 8/3 (2010): 636.

[5] Chinedu Ezetah, 'Legitimate Governance and Statehood in Africa: Beyond the Failed State and Colonial Self-Determination' in Edward Kofi (ed), *Legitimate Governance in Africa* (Kluwer Law International 1999) 419.

[6] See Chapter 6, 'Instrument Choice', in this volume.

[7] Keith Maskus and Jerome Reichman, 'The Globalization of Private Knowledge Goods and the Privatization of Global Public Goods' *Journal of International Economic Law*, 7/2 (2004): 279; Michael Zürn, *Regieren jenseits des Nationslstaats* (Suhrkamp 1998).

II. WESTPHALIAN MYTH OF UNIMPAIRED FREEDOM OF ACTION

States have long been considered to have more or less unimpaired freedom of action and inaction, a notion often said to be grounded in the so-called Westphalian system. This historical explanation, however, is questionable since territoriality and sovereignty can be traced further back in history than the political system established on the basis of the Westphalian peace.[8] In addition, the concept of territorial sovereignty remains elusive. In their environmental relations, states have never enjoyed absolute territorial integrity or sovereignty. Rather, coexistence and cooperation have always been hallmarks of environmental sovereignty, and the idea of the Westphalian system is misinterpreted and over-estimated, de facto and de jure.[9]

As one of the conceptual and definitional elements of statehood, territory is invariably taken into account in inter-state relations. However, notwithstanding the legal characteristics of territorial sovereignty in principle, states have to cope with the fact that the environment, and natural resources, do not necessarily conform to agreed territorial boundaries. In the past, transboundary issues primarily focused on rivers and lakes. Today, concerns relating to resources such as air, the global climate, marine biodiversity beyond areas of national jurisdiction, and groundwater have made it clear that it is impossible to construct a 'hermetically sealed' sphere of sovereignty. Sovereignty over such resources can only be a claim, never a fact.

Nevertheless, the claim has remained important in international environmental law. In order to become operational, sovereignty must be split up into freedom of action, which is mostly characterized as territorial sovereignty, and the protection of territory against outside interference, which is mainly considered in terms of territorial integrity. These concepts are still relevant today although, in light of the numerous rules that have been developed and agreed upon in international environmental law, they are less central than in earlier times.[10]

While international environmental agreements came to the fore only after the Second World War,[11] treaties dealing with the shared utilization of natural resources have been concluded from the second half of the nineteenth century onwards. Most of the early treaties were bilateral, addressing surface water, fisheries, and even the protection of

[8] For a balanced assessment see Heinhard Steiger, 'Der Westfälische Frieden—Grundgesetz für Europa?' in Heinz Duchhardt (ed), *Der Westfälische Friede* (Oldenbourg 1998) 33; see also Rainer Grote, 'Westphalian System' in Rüdiger Wolfrum (ed), *Max Planck Encyclopedia of Public International Law* (OUP 2006) para 8.

[9] Andreas Osiander, 'Sovereignty, International Relations, and the Westphalian Myth' *International Organisation*, 55/2 (2001): 251.

[10] Duncan French, 'A Reappraisal of Sovereignty in the Light of Global Environmental Concerns' *Legal Studies*, 21/3 (2001): 376.

[11] See Chapter 3, 'Origin and History', in this volume.

birds. Some of the agreements that were concluded during the first half of the twentieth century pursue ecological, as opposed to merely resource conservation or sharing, objectives.

These agreements illustrate that states deployed the concept of sovereignty as a claim, but adopted a pragmatic approach in light of shared natural resources. While this pragmatism did not prevent conflicts, perhaps in distinction to other fields of international law, the environmental context has always led states to seek cooperation with each other. Arguably, the fact that a resource transcends political boundaries stimulated legal cooperation. In short, the Westphalian system of absolute sovereignty and integrity could never be fully operationalized with respect to transboundary natural resources.[12]

This is further illustrated by the early arbitral awards in international environmental relations, including the *Bering Sea Fur Seals* arbitration,[13] the *Trail Smelter* arbitration,[14] and the *Lake Lanoux* arbitration[15]—the cases that tend to be cited to show the Westphalian roots of international environmental law. The 1893 *Bering Sea Fur Seals* case arose out of the decline in seals because of over-exploitation on the high seas. The Arbitral Tribunal rejected the position of the United States, which sought to rely upon its territorial jurisdiction to protect seals against being taken on the high seas, but recognized the need for conservation to prevent over-exploitation and the decline of a hunted species. According to the arbitral award in the *Trail Smelter* case, 'under the principles of international law ... no State has the right to use or permit the use of its territory in such a manner as to cause injury by fumes in or to the territory of another, of the properties or persons therein, when the case is of serious consequences and the injury is established by clear and convincing evidence'.[16] The Arbitral Tribunal in the *Lake Lanoux* case concluded that prior consultation and negotiation were required not only by the treaty but more generally by customary law.[17]

In all three cases states sought to balance their mutual interests rather than the interests of the ecosystem. However, states were seeking compromise and cooperation, which can best be illustrated by the fact that the nine-point plan for conservation adopted by the Arbitral Tribunal in the *Bering Sea Fur Seals* case still serves as a model for fisheries commissions today.[18] Thus, arguably Westphalian sovereignty has been,

[12] With regard to international watercourses see Stephen McCaffrey, *The Law of International Watercourses* (3rd edn, OUP 2019) 111 et seq.

[13] *Bering Sea Fur Seals Arbitration (US/United Kingdom)* (1893) 28 RIAA 263.

[14] *Trail Smelter Arbitration (United States/Canada)* (1938 and 1941) 3 RIAA 1905 (Trail Smelter case).

[15] *Lake Lanoux Arbitration (Spain/France)* (1957) 12 RIAA 281.

[16] See Trail Smelter case (n 14).

[17] Astrid Epiney, 'Lac Lanoux Arbitration' in Rüdiger Wolfrum (ed), *Max Planck Encyclopedia of Public International Law* (OUP 2006) para 13.

[18] Francisco Vicuña, 'From the Bering Sea Fur-Seals Case to the 1999 Southern Bluefin Tuna Cases: A Century of Efforts at Conservation of the Living Resources of the High Seas' *Yearbook of International Environmental Law*, 10/1 (1999): 40–47.

and is of, limited relevance for international environmental law and its significance continues to be over-estimated.[19]

Arguably, the growing efforts to address global environmental problems, in particular through treaty practice since 1972, have led to changing perceptions of sovereignty.[20] The Stockholm Conference marked the beginning of the development of new multilateral environmental agreements (MEAs) covering different subject areas.[21] However, notwithstanding the 1974 Helsinki Convention on the Protection of the Marine Environment of the Baltic Sea Area,[22] the Cold War political environment did not allow for a more ambitious 'all embracing' international environmental agreement instead of many sectoral treaties.[23] The end of the Cold War, leading to a period of enhanced globalization,[24] raised new—somewhat idealistic—hopes for an increased cooperation among states and multilateralism, not least due to growing awareness of environmental threats, which eventually allowed for the adoption of the Rio Conventions in 1992.[25] Furthermore, non-state actors, especially non-governmental organizations (NGOs) gained more recognition in the international arena. The 1992 Rio Conference generated considerable momentum to the involvement of non-state actors in decision-making processes and to the development of legally non-binding norms in the field of environmental protection.

Whether the resulting hopes were short-lived is questionable. It is noteworthy that the end of the Cold War in 1989/1990 and the Srebrenica massacre of 1995[26] had implications on international law-making in general. While between 1950 and 2000 around thirty-five new multilateral treaties were concluded in each decade, the ten years between 2000 and 2010 are marked by a gradual decline to only twenty new multilateral

[19] Olufemi Elias, 'Regionalism in International Law-Making and the Westphalian Legacy' in Christopher Harding (ed), *Renegotiating Westphalia* (Martinus Nijhoff 1999) 25.

[20] Edith Weiss, 'The Evolution of International Environmental Law' *Japanese Yearbook of International Law*, 54 (2011): 1, 8.

[21] Pierre-Marie Dupuy and Jorge Viñuales, *International Environmental Law* (2nd edn, CUP 2018) 11 et seq.

[22] Tuomas Räsänen and Simo Laakkonen, 'Cold War and the Environment: The Role of Finland in International Environmental Politics in the Baltic Sea Region' *Ambio*, 36/2–3 (2007): 229.

[23] Yann Aguila and Jorge Viñuales, 'A Global Pact for the Environment: Conceptual foundations' *Review of European, Comparative and International Environmental Law*, 28/1 (2019): 1, 2; Richard Tucker, 'The International Environmental Movement and the Cold War' in Richard Immerman and Petra Goedde (eds), *The Oxford Handbook of the Cold War* (OUP 2013) 565.

[24] Jost Delbruck, 'Prospects for a "World (Internal) Law"?: Legal Development in a Changing International System' *Indiana Journal of Global Legal Studies*, 9/2 (2002): 401, 408.

[25] Carl Bruch *et al*, 'International Law, Natural Resources and Post-conflict Peacebuilding: From Rio to Rio+20 and Beyond' *Review of European, Comparative and International Environmental Law*, 12/1 (2012): 44. The three Rio Conventions are the 1992 Convention on Biological Diversity (CBD), the 1992 United Nations Framework Convention on Climate Change (UNFCCC), and the 1994 United Nations Convention to Combat Desertification.

[26] Thilo Marauhn, 'The International Rule of Law in Light of Legitimacy Claims' in Heike Krieger, Georg Nolte, and Andreas Zimmermann (eds), *The International Rule of Law—Rise or Decline?* (OUP 2019) 277, 278.

treaties deposited with the UN Secretary-General.[27] Between 2010 and 2018, there have been only three new MEAs concluded at the global level that deserve to be mentioned in this context: the 2010 Nagoya Protocol on Access and Benefit-sharing, the 2013 Minamata Convention on Mercury, and the 2015 Paris Agreement on Climate Change. Developments since 2001 demonstrate a return to unilateralism in inter-state relations, as exemplified by the US retreat from the Kyoto Protocol and its temporary retreat from the Paris Agreement under the Trump Administration. Nevertheless, cooperation remains a leading concept as evident from the Paris Agreement that affirms the importance of 'cooperation at all levels' and, unlike the UNFCCC, does not contain any reference to state sovereignty.[28]

III. CONTEMPORARY STATEHOOD

The basic criteria of statehood reflected in state practice, doctrine, and pertinent legal documents have remained more or less unchanged: people, territory, and government. The need for an effective government has been discussed in light of the phenomenon of state failure, and the territorial element in the context of climate-induced sea level rise.[29] An effective government is indispensable to the implementation of international environmental agreements.

International environmental obligations—while formally addressed to the state—are, in substance, often primarily concerned with the behaviour of non-state actors, in particular, private entities, including individuals, corporations, and similar types of actors. International environmental law, however, rarely addresses private individuals and entities directly. Usually, it requires states to adopt implementing legislation, which then will address the behaviour of private actors. In this respect, the state is indispensable as a legislator and enforcement agency for international environmental law. Thus arguably, sovereignty is not an end in itself but rather a tool for the development and implementation of international environmental law.

This section focuses on statehood as an element of a global system of environmental governance, which replaces a status-oriented approach with an action-oriented one. Governance refers to processes and systems that make an organization or a society work. Global governance consequently may be described as 'a continuing process through which conflicting or diverse interests may be accommodated and co-operative action

[27] Joost Pauwelyn, Ramses Wessel, and Jan Wouters, 'When Structures Become Shackles: Stagnation and Dynamics in International Lawmaking' *European Journal of International Law*, 25/3 (2014): 734.

[28] María Carazo, 'Contextual Provisions (Preamble and Article 1)' in Daniel Klein *et al* (eds), *The Paris Agreement on Climate Change: Analysis and Commentary* (OUP 2017) 107, 119.

[29] With regard to the latter see International Law Association Sydney Conference, 'International Law and Sea Level Rise' (2018).

may be taken. It includes formal institutions and regimes empowered to enforce compliance, as well as informal arrangements.'[30] International environmental governance, in turn, includes the development of common interests of states and related institutions.[31] The effective steering capacity of international environmental law depends on the proper combination of various levels and techniques of governance.[32]

While international governance structures have been established—including international organizations with secretariats, compliance committees, numerous other organs, and a broad range of other non-state actors[33]—the actual functioning of the system depends on the activities performed at the national level. The international level will only be able to govern successfully if states participate in these systems and, adopt and enforce national implementing legislation. Contemporary statehood and its relevance for international environmental law can best be illuminated by focusing on the roles assumed by states as authors, addressees, and guardians of the law.

A. States as Authors of International Environmental Law

Within the decentralized system of international law, states are still the primary authors of international environmental law.[34] Treaties are normally adopted and ratified by states; customary international environmental law[35] is based on state practice and *opinio juris* as derived from official statements; and even general principles of international environmental law are developed on the basis of principles of national environmental law—that is, they are ultimately state-authored provisions.[36]

The role of states as authors of the law, however, has changed over time. While the final decision within law-making processes still rests with states, they have lost relative importance in the process of law-making. Many MEAs have been drafted under the auspices of international organizations.[37] Furthermore, the participation of NGOs and other non-state actors[38] in international environmental conferences has influenced the substance of the law. For instance, while the impact of NGOs on the outcome of the

[30] Commission on Global Governance, *Our Global Neighbourhood* (OUP 1995) 2–3.

[31] Ulrich Beyerlin, 'State Community Interests and Institution-Building in International Environmental Law' *ZaöRV*, 56/3 (1996): 602.

[32] See Chapter 4, 'Multilevel and Polycentric Governance', in this volume.

[33] With regard to the Paris Agreement see Harro van Asselt, 'The Role of Non-State Actors in Reviewing Ambition, Implementation, and Compliance under the Paris Agreement' *Climate Law*, 6/1–2 (2016): 91.

[34] See Chapter 24, 'Multilateral Environmental Treaty Making', in this volume.

[35] See Chapter 23, 'Customary International Law and the Environment', in this volume.

[36] Duncan Hollis, 'Why State Consent Still Matters: Non-State Actors, Treaties, and the Changing Sources of International Law' *Berkeley Journal of International Law*, 23 (2005): 137.

[37] Julia Sommer, 'Environmental Law Making by International Organisations' *ZaöRV*, 56/3 (1996): 628.

[38] See Chapter 38, 'Non-State Actors', in this volume.

Kyoto negotiations was weak,[39] NGOs played a role in including the reference to the 1.5°C temperature limit in the Paris Agreement.[40]

In addition, the resolutions of international organizations and the declarations adopted by global conferences have changed the law-making process.[41] Although non-binding, such documents have contributed to the development of international environmental law. Resolutions adopted by the statutory bodies of the United Nations Environment Programme (UNEP), the Food and Agriculture Organization (FAO), the International Maritime Organization (IMO), the International Atomic Energy Agency (IAEA), and by treaty bodies—such as the Conference of the Parties to the 1973 Convention on International Trade in Endangered Species adopting quota systems which had the effect of an 'informal amendment' to the treaty[42]—have invited states to act on the basis of the principles embodied therein, thus developing a significant law-making effect without, however, depriving states of their final say in the law-making process.

The continued relevance of states as authors of international environmental law remains legitimate for at least two reasons.[43] First, states enjoy comprehensive legitimacy as actors in public international law. Second, states still bear primary responsibility as addressees of those rules and—insofar as the behaviour of non-governmental actors and private individuals is concerned—they remain the primary implementing agents of such rules. In a decentralized legal system, making the law without paying tribute to those most affected by the law will deprive the law of its effectiveness. If international environmental law is designed to have an effect 'on the ground', then it must accommodate the interests of states. This is best done at the stage of law-making.

B. States as Addressees of International Environmental Law

Even though international environmental governance impacts private actors, these actors are rarely directly addressed by international law. Consequently, states have at least three different types of obligations: obligations to refrain, obligations to prevent, and obligations to preserve.

[39] Michele Betsill, 'Environmental NGOs and the Kyoto Protocol Negotiations: 1995 to 1997' in Michele Betsill and Elisabeth Corell (eds), *NGO Diplomacy: The Influence of Non-Governmental Organizations in International Environmental Negotiations* (MIT Press 2008) 43, 58.

[40] Lavanya Rajamani and Emmanuel Guérin, 'Central Concepts in the Paris Agreement and How They Evolved' in Klein *et al* (n 28) 74–75.

[41] See Chapters 24 and 36, 'Multilateral Environmental Treaty Making' and 'International Institutions', in this volume.

[42] Karen Scott, 'The Dynamic Evolution of International Environmental Law' *Victoria University of Wellington Law Review*, 49/4 (2018): 607, 613.

[43] Daniel Bodansky, 'The Legitimacy of International Governance: A Coming Challenge for International Environmental Law?' *American Journal of International Law*, 93/3 (1999): 596.

While obligations to refrain from conduct harmful to the environment are a feature of municipal environmental law addressed to private entities, similar obligations are included in international agreements, although directed towards states. International environmental law includes obligations to refrain from transboundary environmental harm, from polluting transboundary watercourses, from dumping hazardous waste on land or at sea, from releasing particular substances into the atmosphere, from destroying ecosystems or biodiversity, and so forth, even though these obligations must be implemented domestically to have an impact on the behaviour of non-state actors.

Obligations to prevent include the adoption of legislation, the establishment of an administrative infrastructure (such as licensing systems and supervisory bodies), and sometimes even the enforcement of criminal law, which necessitates governmental action.

The third category of obligations addressed towards states, the obligation to preserve, may require more in terms of the state's own conduct or in relation to activities of non-state actors under its jurisdiction. For example, the preservation of the marine environment may require improvements of water quality in coastal areas, or the protection of the Earth's climate may require measures of reforestation under the implementation mechanism of the climate change regime.[44]

C. States as Guardians of International Environmental Law

States act as guardians of international environmental law, traditionally, in the context of law enforcement, with an initiating role in connection with compliance control procedures. The traditional international law-enforcement perspective still focuses on state responsibility for breaches of international law, and the resulting secondary obligations (normally an obligation to make reparations). There seems to be widespread agreement, however, on the limited effectiveness of the state responsibility regime in environmental matters.[45] As the examples of the Chernobyl accident, the Sandoz chemical spill, and the salination of the Rhine illustrate, even when the facts and causal links are clear, there may be no recourse to the law of state responsibility. Retorsions and reprisals are not an option in the case of common goods and, thus, fail to meet the needs of international environmental law.

Arguably thus the role of states has changed most significantly where they act as guardians of the law. In light of the ineffectiveness of traditional international law-enforcement mechanisms, new compliance control mechanisms have been developed with a less dominant role for states.[46] Since collective, rather than unilateral,

[44] See Chapter 29, 'Climate Change', in this volume.

[45] See Chapter 58, 'International Responsibility and Liability', in this volume.

[46] See Chapter 56, 'Non-Compliance Procedures', in this volume.

enforcement cooperation rather than confrontation, prevention rather than repression, and compliance assistance rather than sanctions, have become the characteristics of the 'enforcement' of international environmental law, the contribution of states to this system has become largely, though not exclusively, procedural. They may initiate the procedure, provide relevant data for the assessment of their own or another party's compliance, and participate in decision-making in the event of non-compliance.[47]

IV. ONGOING TRANSFORMATION OF THE INTERNATIONAL LEGAL SYSTEM

Changes in the international legal system in the second half of the twentieth century also prompted changes in the role of the state in international environmental law. In particular, such systemic changes unleashed the potential of non-state actors within international environmental regimes to develop their own ideas on change and improvement. This section picks up on two developments—the growing plurality of actors and regimes—as a consequence of which state-to-state networks have been partially replaced by inter-linked networks of states and other actors.

A. Growing Plurality of Actors

Until the early 1970s, states were the authors, addressees, and enforcers of the limited rules of international environmental law that existed. However, the establishment of international environmental regimes led over time to a progressive institutionalization of international environmental law and thus to the gradual rise of a new type of international actor. Although attempts at institutionalizing international environmental protection had begun in the nineteenth century, the major impetus for developments in this field arose from the 1972 Stockholm Conference which led to the establishment of UNEP, and several other international environmental institutions. Today, there is a proliferation of international environmental regimes and institutions that raises issues of coherence and fragmentation. Attempts to cluster such regimes and institutions around either UNEP or the former Commission on Sustainable Development (CSD), have so far been unsuccessful.[48] Indeed, as in international law in general,[49] there are tendencies towards a fragmentation of international environmental law.

[47] Thilo Marauhn, 'Towards a Procedural Law of Compliance Control in International Environmental Relations' *ZaöRV*, 56/3 (1996): 696.

[48] Niko Urho *et al* (eds), *International Environmental Governance: Accomplishments and Way Forward* (Nordic Council of Ministers 2019) 83 et seq.

[49] Matthew Craven, 'Unity, Diversity and the Fragmentation of International Law' *Finnish Yearbook of International Law*, 14 (2003): 3.

In addition to international organizations, NGOs and other non-state actors have also played an increasingly prominent role. Indeed, international environmental law has granted NGOs varying degrees of legal status, in contrast to general international law, where the status of NGOs is less certain. Moreover, in light of their considerable—positive and negative—impacts on environmental protection, the role of commercial actors, including national and, in particular, transnational corporations, is also relevant.[50]

Finally, the role of the individual in international environmental law must also be considered. Although, no universal instrument yet recognizes a human right to a healthy environment, the national law of many countries and some regional instruments do.[51] In any case, judges have extended other well-established human rights to address environmental considerations.[52]

The complexity of international environmental relations arising out of the plurality of actors is thus of a dual nature, best described by reference to the notions of internationalization and privatization. Internationalization refers to the increasing number of government-based actors beyond the state, such as regional and universal (intergovernmental) organizations, while privatization refers to the increasing number of non-governmental actors at the local, national, regional, and international levels, reflecting the environmental concerns of civil society and the business community. While both these categories of actors are non-state, they differ, in that intergovernmental organizations can be more easily considered to be instrumental for state or public interests, whereas NGOs focus on private interests, notwithstanding their claim to be representing public interests.

B. Growing Plurality of Regimes

Another important development since 1972 has been the increasing number of international regimes. States have not only moved from bilateralism in environmental law to multilateralism, but they have also negotiated a broad variety and large number of international environmental agreements. The sheer number of such agreements, while impressive, has also given rise to various problems with repercussions for the role of the state.

First, many regimes are sectoral, addressing a particular environmental problem, a particular source of pollution, or a particular part of the environment. This approach is often mirrored at the national level by implementation measures within the branch of government that is tasked with a given sector. Different branches of government may then have to address conflicts arising out of different environmental regimes.

50 See Chapter 41, 'Business and Industry', in this volume.

51 'Report of the Special Rapporteur on the issue of human rights obligations relating to the enjoyment of a safe, clean, healthy and sustainable environment' (24 January 2018) UN Doc A/HRC/37/59.

52 See Chapter 45, 'Human Rights', in this volume.

Some international instruments have moved towards integrated pollution control and integrated environmental protection to alleviate such problems.

Second, the proliferation of environmental regimes has increased the administrative burden on states in particular in relation to reporting obligations,[53] and compliance procedures.[54]

Third, the growing number of regimes has given rise to a sprawling international and quasi-international bureaucracy, that places a burden on traditional statehood and governance. In certain respects, the displacement of national with international bureaucracies may contribute to better protection of the global environment. However, this leaves open the question of the appropriate level of governance of environmental problems.

It is also noteworthy that states are increasingly reluctant to conclude legally binding treaties, and binding provisions within them, as evidenced in the 2015 Paris Agreement that although legally binding, includes provisions that raise serious doubts as to their effectiveness and legally binding character.[55] It seems that states prefer to adopt soft law instruments though the 2013 Minamata Convention is an exception to this trend. Recent developments, such as a so-called 'Global Pact for the Environment'[56] show that there is a trend in international law favouring a multilayered approach with potentially negative effects: the adoption of (legally non-binding) instruments reproducing or rephrasing legally binding norms may weaken international law by undermining the content of binding norms.[57]

Arguably political agreement and environmental governance at the global level have not yet been achieved—they are not even in sight. The development of international environmental law still largely follows the traditional patterns of consent-based treaty-making. There is limited secondary 'legislation' by international environmental institutions and there is no global environmental agency to coordinate or oversee treaty implementation. UNEP's powers are limited, and its potential has not been realized.

Although international environmental law has developed concepts that reflect the global nature of certain environmental problems—global commons, common interest, common concern, and common heritage—it is doubtful whether they truly develop new legal coordinates or point towards a new level of law-making and law-enforcement.

[53] See Chapter 52, 'Transparency Procedures (Monitoring, Reporting, Verification)', in this volume.

[54] See Chapter 56, 'Non-Compliance Procedures', in this volume.

[55] Ayse-Martina Böhringer, 'Das neue Pariser Klimaübereinkommen: Eine Kompromisslösung mit Symbolkraft und Verhaltenssteuerungspotential' *ZaöRV*, 76/3 (2016): 753, 779 et seq; Lavanya Rajamani, 'The 2015 Paris Agreement: Interplay between Hard, Soft and Non-Obligations' *Journal of Environmental Law*, 28/2 (2016): 337.

[56] United Nations General Assembly (UNGA) Res 72/277, 'Towards a Pact for the Global Environment' (10 May 2018) UN Doc A/RES/72/277.

[57] Aria Gavouneli, 'Legislating by Compacts?—The Legal Nature of the Global Compacts' *EJIL: Talk!* (28 February 2019).

C. From State-to-State Networks Towards Inter-Linked Networks

It is possible to distinguish relations between states, between states and international organizations, and between non-state actors and states. While inter-state relations remain central to international environmental law, the overall trend favours replacing state-to-state networks with inter-linked networks.

1. *Linking with non-state actors*

International environmental law has primarily developed on the basis of inter-state relations. It is principally based on treaties and customary international law, both typical modes of inter-state legal regulation. Approaches to treaty-making, such as the framework convention and protocol approach, have made law-making quicker and more responsive,[58] but have not led to major changes in legal form or a shift towards secondary law-making by international bodies. In relation to the substance of the rules of international environmental law, the conceptual framework of inter-state relations plays an increasingly limited role. Similarly, the law of state responsibility, a tool to enforce standards in international law, is based on the elements of an internationally wrongful act committed by the state, a subject of international law. However, notwithstanding a large body of literature on state responsibility in the environmental context and many international efforts to develop responsibility and liability regimes in this area,[59] virtually no environmental disputes have been resolved on the basis of the law of state responsibility.

There are also issue areas where the substance of international environmental law goes beyond inter-state relations. For example, climate change goes far beyond inter-state conflicts of interest since the resource in question and the effects of environmentally harmful activities are not limited to a particular state. Interestingly, the decision adopting the Paris Agreement, in a shift from the traditional approach, assigns an active role to non-state actors in global climate governance. For instance, private actors are encouraged to register their voluntary climate actions on the 'Non-State Actor Zone for Climate Action'.[60] In addition, it is difficult to establish a clear causal nexus between specific polluters and atmospheric degradation. The so-called greenhouse effect is both complex and truly global. In contrast, traditional inter-state relations are reflected in other agreements, as in the context of biodiversity where the concepts of access to genetic resources and benefit sharing have led to rights and obligations of a reciprocal nature.[61]

[58] See Chapter 24, 'Multilateral Environmental Treaty Making', in this volume.

[59] See Chapter 58, 'International Responsibility and Liability', in this volume.

[60] Sander Chan, Clara Brandi, and Steffen Bauer, 'Aligning Transnational Climate Action with International Climate Governance: The Road from Paris' *Review of European, Comparative and International Environmental Law*, 25/2 (2016): 238, 241.

[61] Thilo Marauhn, 'Die Erhaltung der Biologischen Vielfalt und die nachhaltige Nutzung ihrer Bestandteile' in Klaus Lange (ed), *Nachhaltigkeit im Recht* (Nomos Verlag 2003) 87.

There are a range of relevant specialized UN agencies, either focused on environmental concerns directly, such as the UNEP, or by extension from their mandates, such as the FAO, the UN Educational, Scientific, and Cultural Organization (UNESCO), the World Health Organization (WHO), the World Meteorological Organization (WMO), the IMO, and the IAEA. MEAs have created secretariats to administer the implementation of environmental treaties, as well as an extensive network of supervisory bodies, conferences of the parties, commissions, and working groups. As a result there are a variety of institutions involved in some aspect of global environmental governance, giving rise to growing problems of coordination and consistency within the system.[62]

States have not transferred sovereign powers to these international institutions but relied upon them as forums for law-making, where their decisions normally remain subject to the approval by states parties. Some transfers of responsibilities have occurred in the context of technical monitoring,[63] and, to a limited extent, in the context of supervisory bodies, such as treaty-based compliance or implementation committees. These latter bodies are authorized to receive and evaluate reports submitted by state parties, and they may even propose certain consequences in case of non-compliance. However, the final determinations of non-compliance and decisions on response measures generally remain political decisions taken by states, which confirms that there has been limited transfer of responsibility to international environmental institutions. Instead, states have made use of international institutions as providers of legal and technical expertise. Notably, developing states have turned to international (environmental) institutions for assistance with capacity-building and training.[64] However, the task of facilitating such assistance has now largely moved to the UN Development Programme, the World Bank, and regional development banks.[65]

The relationship between states and NGOs is ambivalent. NGOs are normally established according to municipal law and are thus at least partially dependent upon acceptance by states. While they often claim to act in the common interest of societies, they usually provide a voice to particular groups within society. Many intergovernmental organizations grant NGOs some status in their fields of activity, allowing them to observe international law-making processes, make submissions, or even participate in non-compliance procedures.[66] NGOs can complement or contribute to governmental activities with regard to the environment. The relationship between states and NGOs thus deserves further reflection, in particular, when states are trying to identify areas of common concern and common interests.

[62] See Chapter 36, 'International Institutions', in this volume.

[63] For example in the case of the European Evaluation and Monitoring Network under the LRTAP Convention.

[64] Daniel Navid, 'Compliance Assistance in International Environmental Law: Capacity-Building, Transfer of Finance and Technology' *ZaöRV*, 56/3 (1996): 810.

[65] See Chapters 54 and 55, 'Financial Assistance' and 'Technology Assistance and Transfers', in this volume.

[66] Farhana Yamin, 'NGOs and International Environmental Law' *Review of European, Comparative and International Environmental Law*, 10/2 (2001): 149.

Transnational corporations (TNCs) also have particular relevance in international environmental relations.[67] While TNCs are in part subject to the laws of their home country and their host country, their economic power tends to have an impact on states. Through the emergence of *lex mercatoria*[68] and the use of commercial arbitration, TNCs have contributed to the development of law not outside the reach of governmental control but with a life of its own. This phenomenon has given rise to concerns with regard to labour standards and other regulatory issues.[69] High profile events, such as the Bhopal disaster in India[70] and *The Social and Economic Rights Action Centre and the Centre for Economic and Social Rights v Nigeria* case,[71] continue to press the question of how to control the activities of transnational corporations if the host state is not capable and the home state not willing to act. Overall, while the rise of TNCs may not affect the formal powers of states, it impacts their ability to make international environmental law applicable to corporations and to enforce it within the municipal system.

While primarily a subject of domestic law, the individual has gained a greater role in international environmental law, particularly in the context of environment-related human rights law. Individuals also play a role as members of NGOs that are active at the international or national levels in pressing for the development or implementation of international environmental law, and as claimants under municipal environmental law helping to enforce it. Other opportunities to enhance implementation of environmental standards have been provided by the World Bank Inspection Panel,[72] which gives individuals and groups of individuals some voice with regard—among others—to environmental consequences of development projects. However, these developments do not fundamentally change the role of the state in international law.

2. *Cross-cutting relationships and 'new' networks*

In addition to these links between state and non-state actors, the emergence of cross-cutting relationships and 'new' networks have implications for states. The state is not a homogenous actor. It needs organs to act and organs ultimately comprise individuals. While such individuals are bound by governmental policies, they establish networks

[67] See Chapter 41, 'Business and Industry', in this volume.

[68] Peer Zumbansen, 'Lex mercatoria: Zum Geltungsanspruch transnationalen Rechts' *Rabels Zeitschrift für ausländisches und internationales Privatrecht*, 67/4 (2003): 637.

[69] Janelle Diller, 'Social Conduct in Transnational Enterprise Operations: The Role of the International Labour Organization' in Roger Blanpain (ed), *Multinational Enterprises and the Social Challenges of the Twenty-First Century* (Kluwer Law International 2000) 17.

[70] Kenneth McCallion, 'Institutional and Procedural Aspects of Mass Claims Litigation and Settlement: The Exxon Valdez and Bhopal Gas Disaster Cases' in International Bureau of the Permanent Court of Arbitration, *Institutional and Procedural Aspects of Mass Claims Settlement Systems* (Kluwer Law International 2000) 43.

[71] *Social and Economic Rights Action Center (SERAC) and the Center for Economic and Social Rights (CESR) v Nigeria*, African Commission on Human Rights and Peoples' Rights (2001) Communication No 155/96, text reprinted in (2003) 10 IHRR 282.

[72] Alix Gualtieri, 'The Environmental Accountability of the World Bank to Non-State Actors: Insights from the Inspection Panel' *British Yearbook of International Law*, 72/1 (2001): 213.

among themselves. For example, emerging epistemic communities have an impact on governmental activities.[73] Cross-cutting relationships thus have to be scrutinized carefully. While a detailed analysis cannot be provided in this chapter, some aspects are highlighted.

From a legal perspective, it is difficult to assess the effect of inter-personal interactions and mechanisms, and their impact on international environmental law. Social network analysis[74] has emerged as a key tool in modern organizational studies to do so. It focuses on the social structure between actors, both individuals and organizations, and highlights the ways in which they are interconnected. Law-related social network analysis can demonstrate that such networks operate at many levels, within corporations as well as NGOs, among both categories of non-state actors, within governments, among government departments, within international organizations, and between these different levels. In practical terms, social network analysis may play a decisive role in clarifying how problems are solved, how organizations are run, and to what degree particular actors manage to achieve their goals. This type of information is particularly important in the context of international environmental relations because of the variety of actors and individuals involved. Above all, knowledge about environment-related international networks is important in order to develop international environmental regimes that are effective in a dual sense. They effectively address a particular environmental problem, and their implementation and compliance instruments are adequate to meet the objectives of the regime.[75]

Interestingly, highly specialized governmental officials and their counterparts within international organizations as well as other types of non-state actors tend to share similar approaches to the issues they deal with. For instance, Public Private Partnerships, that is, voluntary agreements between governments and the private sector beyond the nation state, serve as tools for participating in cooperative relationships towards common goals.[76] Although their outcomes may remain modest, they can contribute to international environmental governance by providing expertise and enforcement capacity.[77] This commonality often serves as an incentive to maintain contact with each other across the boundaries of their respective political frameworks. Such sharing of approaches creates valuable channels for information flow, the possibility of discussing new perspectives, and an informal basis for the development of common ideas and positions. Epistemic communities that have developed over time may agree on how to address particular environmental problems, even though governmental and other

[73] See Chapter 40, 'Epistemic Communities', in this volume.

[74] John Scott, *Social Network Analysis: A Handbook* (Sage Publications 2000).

[75] For a European perspective, see Karl-Heinz Ladeur, 'The New European Agencies: The European Environment Agency and Prospects for a European Network of Environmental Administrations' *European University Institute working papers* (1996).

[76] Ulrich Beyerlin and Thilo Marauhn, *International Environmental Law* (Hart Publishing 2011) 308 et seq.

[77] Axel Marx, 'Public-Private Partnerships for Sustainable Development: Exploring their Design and its Impact on Effectiveness' *Sustainability*, 11 (2019): 1.

actors have difficulty in reaching agreement. It is against this background that epistemic communities have contributed to the development of international environmental law.[78] Epistemic communities can both weaken and strengthen the role of the state in international environmental law.

From the perspective of states, overlapping networks can be useful in several respects. They provide sources of information, and they facilitate communication between various types of actors. In addition, overlapping networks have the potential to provide synergies when implementing international environmental regimes. At the same time, there are potential downsides. For example, overlapping networks may blur the lines of accountability and responsibility because they cut across traditional categories of actors. Also, they contribute to the development of communities, the legitimacy of which is limited to the expertise of participating individuals. These ambivalent tendencies have to be borne in mind when taking a closer view on contemporary statehood, and the roles assumed by states in contemporary international environmental law.

The role of states must be contrasted with the comparative advantages of non-state actors. International organizations bundle national interests, balance them, and contribute to the development of common interests and concerns. Even if certain states are dominant in one or another international organization, NGOs have gained access to such international organizations contributing at least to increased transparency. Specialized international organizations have the potential to absorb the knowledge and input of epistemic communities, providing stronger input in favour of environmental concerns than is possible at the national level. Also, international institutions can co-ordinate and supervise the implementation of international environmental agreements and, in particular, can contribute to compliance control and compliance assistance at the international level.

Although private non-state actors play a more ambivalent role than international organizations, they enjoy certain comparative advantages within a multilevel system of environmental governance. While NGOs, in principle, represent only their constituencies, they manage to place issues of common environmental concern on the international agenda. The record of business entities is mixed in this regard. They have at times, even sought to keep issues off the international agenda.

V. CONCLUSION

Statehood must be evaluated as an element of a larger system of international environmental governance. Although the role of states as authors and guardians of the law has changed in a number of respects, states have remained central to international

[78] Peter Haas, 'Introduction: Epistemic Communities and International Policy Coordination' *International Organisation*, 46/1 (1992): 1.

environmental law. Neither have they become obsolete nor has an effective international bureaucracy been established that is able to perform governmental functions adequately.

While international environmental governance does not necessarily depend on statehood, states do contribute in significant ways to effective environmental governance. Since international organizations lack the authority and capacity to implement international norms directly, national implementation is essential, and it may be argued that states are a necessary intermediate level for the implementation of international environmental standards. Only states have sufficient legislative means at hand, and only states can provide the indispensable administrative infrastructure. In other words, states continue to play a crucial role as addressees of international environmental law. States, however, do not act in isolation. They are networked with other states and, increasingly, act under the supervision of international compliance control procedures. In addition, cross-cutting networks of epistemic communities, of NGOs, and of other actors, have an impact on state behaviour.

States enjoy certain comparative advantages in international environmental governance. They are well-established actors, equipped with the necessary tools to participate both in international environmental law-making and in its implementation. States have the capacity to participate in cooperative law enforcement vis-à-vis each other as well as to implement and enforce standards vis-à-vis their own citizens and entities subject to their jurisdiction and control. The participation of states in international environmental governance, thus, is an asset that cannot be easily overlooked. However, states also suffer from certain deficiencies. Their activities are often guided by national interests rather than common interests or concerns. To make matters more complex, such national interests are subject not only to pressure from inside but also from outside. For example, sometimes states are less powerful than they perceive themselves to be, such as in relation to TNCs.[79]

As all different categories of actors in international environmental law enjoy certain comparative advantages, an important question is how to optimize[80] international environmental governance. In most cases there is a more, rather than a less, important role for the state to play within the increasingly overlapping networks of states, international organizations, and non-governmental actors. Roles are not only pre-defined but can also be attributed to actors on the basis of incentives agreed upon in multilateral treaties.[81] This is a matter that should be observed more closely in the future. Given the

[79] David Ong, 'The Impact of Environmental Law on Corporate Governance—International and Comparative Perspectives' *European Journal of International Law*, 12/4 (2001): 685.

[80] Daniel Esty, 'Toward Optimal Environmental Governance' *New York University Law Review*, 74/6 (1999): 1495.

[81] Thus, the CBD provides a utilitarian justification for the preservation of diversity, building on the direct and indirect usefulness of biological resources to humanity; see Rüdiger Wolfrum, 'The Convention on Biological Diversity: Using State Jurisdiction as a Means of Ensuring Compliance' in Rüdiger Wolfrum (ed), *Enforcing Environmental Standards: Economic Mechanisms as Viable Means?* (Springer 1996) 373.

strength of states as actors in international environmental relations, incentives should be developed and included in multilateral agreements to make use of their potential within multilevel international environmental governance. For example, the interest of states in an economic use of natural resources will stimulate their contribution to preserve such resources as a basis for development.

In the final analysis, the state still has a strong role to play in international environmental law—perhaps a stronger role than during the period of 'coexistence'. This growing role is due to the fact that new forms of governance have given the state much broader thematic scope to intervene and many more instruments to influence the behaviour of other actors. While it is true that some traditional mechanisms have been weakened, the overall assessment of the role of the state in international environmental law is positive. The law is not confronted with a paradigm shift but is experiencing a transformation of the role of the state that may—if properly used—be much to the benefit of international environmental law as a whole.

BIBLIOGRAPHY

Gerhard Loibl, 'The Role of International Organisations in International Law-Making International Environmental Negotiations' *Non-State Actors and International Law*, 1/1 (2001): 41

Joost Pauwelyn, Ramses Wessel, and Jan Wouters, 'When Structures Become Shackles: Stagnation and Dynamics in International Lawmaking' *European Journal of International Law*, 25/3 (2014): 734

Mark Pollack, 'Who Supports International Law, and Why? The United States, the European Union, and the International Legal Order' *International Journal of Constitutional Law*, 13/4 (2015): 873

Karen Scott, 'The Dynamic Evolution of International Environmental Law' *Victoria University of Wellington Law Review*, 49/4 (2018): 607

CHAPTER 36

INTERNATIONAL INSTITUTIONS

ELLEN HEY

I. INTRODUCTION

INTERNATIONAL institutions involved in the development of international environmental law ultimately aim to regulate human activity, even if the addressees of the rules and standards are states and the European Union (EU).[1] To take a few examples, by February 2019 the government of Argentina had signed agreements with seventeen of its twenty-four sub-national entities to implement the United Nations Sustainable Development Goals (SDGs), adopted by the United Nations General Assembly (UNGA) in 2015.[2] In this context, the Autonomous City of Buenos Aires is developing a sustainable mobility plan, which supports implementation of the 2015 Paris Agreement.[3] On 18 May 2018, the Global Environment Facility (GEF) took the first step towards the realization of a project on 'Agro-ecology, Ensuring Food Security and Sustainable Livelihoods while Mitigating Climate Change and Restoring Land in Dryland Regions' to be implemented in Burkina Faso, Brazil, Ethiopia, India, Morocco, Senegal, and South Africa, with the Food and Agriculture Organization (FAO) acting as implementing agency.[4] The project will support implementation of the 2015 Paris Agreement, the 1994 United Nations Convention to Combat Desertification (UNCCD), and the 1992 Convention on Biological Diversity (CBD). These projects seek to influence the choices we make regarding modes of transportation and land use.

1 EU is a party to most MEAs and participates in the work of international organizations; see Chapter 37, 'Regional Organizations: The European Union', in this volume.

2 See Chapter 39, 'Sub-National Actors', in this volume.

3 <https://www.odsargentina.gob.ar/Provincias> accessed 2 January 2020.

4 <https://www.thegef.org/project/avaclim-agro-ecology-ensuring-food-security-and-sustainable-livelihoods-while-mitigating> accessed 2 January 2020.

This chapter first maps the different roles of international institutions involved in the development of international environmental law by considering the initiating roles that some institutions play, the institutional structure of multilateral environmental agreements (MEAs) and the roles of scientific and financial institutions. It thereafter charts how MEAs link to each other substantively by focusing on the relationships between global and regional MEAs and the synergies and contestations between global MEAs. These mapping processes result in the identification of patterns that illustrate the different roles and types of links that exist between international institutions. Prior to engaging in this mapping exercise, a few remarks serve to delineate the topic of this chapter.

First, the origins and legal status of international institutions discussed in this chapter vary. They include the following:

- International organizations established by treaty, including the United Nations (UN) and UN specialized agencies,[5] such as the FAO, which have international legal personality.
- Conferences or meetings of the parties (COPs), such as the COP of the 1992 United Nations Framework Convention on Climate Change (UNFCCC). COPs are established by treaties or their protocols, known as MEAs, and do not have international legal personality.
- Institutions established by other international institutions, including the United Nations Environment Program (UNEP), founded by the UNGA,[6] and the GEF, founded by the International Bank for Reconstruction and Development (World Bank), itself a UN specialized agency, in cooperation with UNEP and the United Nations Development Program (UNDP). These institutions generally do not have international legal personality.

Second, this chapter focuses on institutions directly or indirectly established by states, even if relationships between these institutions and other actors are considered.

Third, the emphasis on the roles of and links between international institutions that develop international environmental law entails that specific institutions are referred to by way of example. This chapter, hence, does not seek to provide a complete overview of the institutions involved in the development of international environmental law.

Fourth, this chapter takes a broad approach to what constitutes international environmental law, including both legally binding and soft law instruments.[7] While MEAs and the treaties establishing international organizations are legally binding texts, most of the other instruments referred to in this chapter are not.

[5] A UN specialized agency is a formal international organization established by states through a treaty and linked to the UN through an agreement; see UN Charter, arts 57, 63.

[6] UNGA Res 2997/27, 'Institutional and financial arrangements for international environmental co-operation' (15 December 1972) UN Doc A/RES/2997(XXVII).

[7] See Chapter 25, 'Soft Law', in this volume.

II. ROLES: NO CENTRALIZED COORDINATION BUT A PATTERN

The activities of the institutions referred to in this chapter are not centrally coordinated, even if numerous coordinating efforts are ongoing. This situation can be attributed to the fragmented nature in which international law, including international environmental law, has developed,[8] and to lack of consensus among states on establishing a central coordinating institution.

While it has been suggested that UNEP, also known as UN Environment, be given this coordinating role and upgraded to a UN specialized agency,[9] UNEP remains a programme of the UNGA. This means that UNEP's budget largely depends on voluntary contributions from states and other partners, including the GEF, with most contributions earmarked for specific projects.[10] UNEP's position also means that it cannot formally establish subsidiary organs without the endorsement of the UNGA.[11] The manner in which the Intergovernmental Panel on Climate Change (IPCC) and the GEF were established reflect UNEP's position.[12]

In 2012, UNEP's previous governing body, the Governing Council—consisting of fifty-eight UN member states elected by the UNGA for four-year periods—was succeeded by the UN Environmental Assembly (UNEA), consisting of all UN member states.[13] This chapter illustrates that UNEP, despite being a programme of the UNGA, fulfils roles similar to those fulfilled by UN specialized agencies. One might also question whether transforming UNEP into an UN specialized agency would enable it to coordinate ongoing activities related to the environment. The well-established mandates of existing UN specialized agencies and COPs might also require amendment, steps which are unlikely to attract consensus among states.

Despite the lack of central coordination, a pattern illustrating the roles and interactions between the international institutions involved in the development of international environmental law is discernible. These interactions provide a measure of coherence for the development of international environmental law. The identified pattern is depicted in Figure 36.1 and informs the organization of the rest of this section. It consists of the following elements:

1. Initiatives resulting in the development of international environmental law, including the negotiation of MEAs, are adopted by the UNGA, the governing

[8] See Chapter 5, 'Fragmentation', in this volume.

[9] Frank Biermann *et al*, 'Navigating the Anthropocene: Improving Earth System Governance' *Science*, 335/6074 (2012): 1306; Bharat Desai, 'The Advent of the United Nations Environment Assembly' *ASIL Insight*, 19/2 (2015).

[10] UN Environment, 'Funding Facts' <https://www.unenvironment.org/about-un-environment/funding/funding-facts> accessed 2 January 2020.

[11] UNGA Res 29/3351, 'Pattern of conferences' (18 December 1974) UN Doc A/RES/3351(XXIX), para 5.

[12] See text at, and fns 41 and 46.

[13] UNGA Res 67/213, 'Report of the Governing Council of the United Nations Environment Programme on its twelfth special session and the implementation of section IV.C, entitled

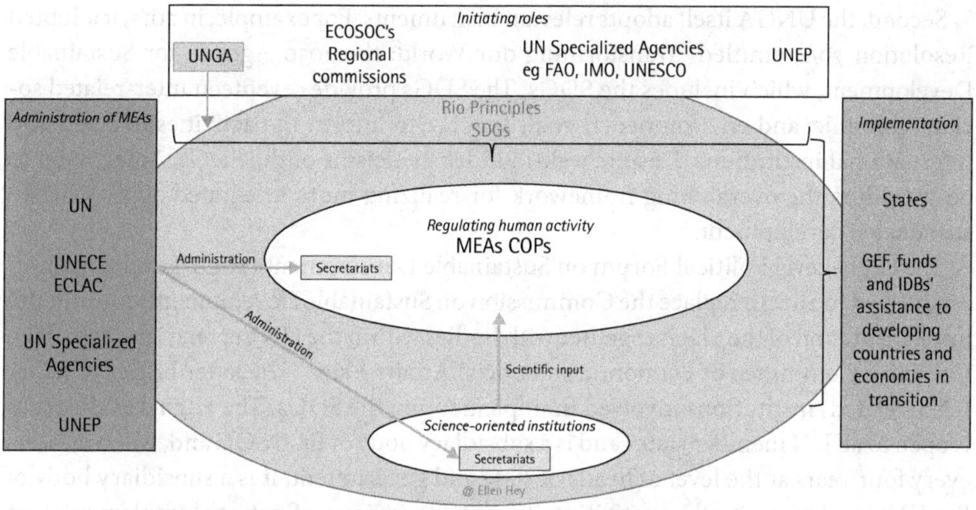

FIGURE 36.1 Main pattern in the roles of international institutions

bodies of UN specialized agencies, UNEP, and the regional commissions of the UN Economic and Social Council (ECOSOC). These same institutions also administer the secretariats of MEAs, even if not all MEA secretariats are administered by them.

2. Standards and rules aimed at regulating human activities, even if addressing states and the EU, are found in MEAs and further developed within the institutions established by MEAs or within UN bodies that administer the secretariats of MEAs.
3. International institutions focused on scientific research provide input for specific MEAs.
4. The implementation of MEAs in developing countries and economies in transition takes place with the assistance of the GEF, funds, and international development banks. The GEF cooperates with other international institutions, such as the FAO and UNEP, to realize projects it finances.

A. Initiating Roles

A number of UN-related institutions fulfil initiating roles in the development of international environmental law.

Prominent among these is the UNGA, which initiates the development of international environmental law in four main ways. First, it convenes global summits that develop international environmental law, such as the 1992 Conference on Environment and Development (Rio Conference) that adopted the Rio Principles. These principles, endorsed by the UNGA, are considered the main principles of international environmental law.[14]

"Environmental pillar in the context of sustainable development", of the outcome document of the United Nations Conference on Sustainable Development' (15 March 2013) UN Doc A/RES/67/213.

[14] UNGA Res 44/228, 'UN Conference on Environment and Development' (20 December 1988); UNGA Res 47/190, 'Report of the UN Conference on Environment and Development' (22 December 1992); see Chapter 3, 'Origin and History', in this volume.

Second, the UNGA itself adopts relevant instruments. For example, in 2015, it adopted Resolution 70/1, entitled 'Transforming our World: the 2030 Agenda for Sustainable Development', which includes the SDGs. The SDGs provide seventeen inter-related social, economic, and environmental goals that are to inform the activities of states and international institutions. Despite well-founded criticisms of the SDGs,[15] they seem to be providing the overarching framework for realizing more integrated approaches to sustainable development.

The High-Level Political Forum on Sustainable Development (High-Level Forum),[16] established in 2012 to replace the Commission on Sustainable Development, coordinates implementation of the SDGs together with bodies within the UN Secretariat, such as the Executive Committee of Economic and Social Affairs Plus.[17] The latter brings together UN (-related) institutions involved in implementing the SDGs. The High-Level Forum is open to all UN member states and is a subsidiary body of ECOSOC and, when it meets every four years at the level of heads of state and government, it is a subsidiary body of the UNGA. Amongst other activities, it conducts reviews of national implementation plans which states submit to it on a voluntary basis. In its 2017 plan to the High-Level Forum, Argentina mentioned the agreements it was in the process of concluding with its sub-national entities, referred to in the introduction to this chapter. Presumably, these agreements will be reported on when Argentina submits its 2020 plan.[18]

Third, the UNGA initiates the negotiation of MEAs, such as the UNFCCC,[19] the 1995 Fish Stocks Agreement,[20] and more recently the negotiations for an international legally binding instrument under the 1982 United Nations Convention on the Law of the Sea (UNCLOS) on the conservation and sustainable use of marine biological diversity of areas beyond national jurisdiction (BBNJ-negotiations).[21]

Fourth, the International Law Commission (ILC), a UNGA subsidiary body, develops and codifies international law relating to the environment. It developed the 1997 Convention on the Non-Navigational Uses of International Watercourses (UN Watercourses Convention).[22] Also relevant are the Draft Articles on the Prevention of Transboundary Damage from Hazardous Activities and the Draft Principles on the Allocation of Loss in the Case of Transboundary Harm Arising out of Hazardous

[15] Chapter 17, 'Sustainable Development', in this volume.

[16] UNGA Res 67/290, 'Format and organizational aspects of the high-level political forum on sustainable development' (9 July 2013); <https://sustainabledevelopment.un.org/hlpf> accessed 2 January 2020.

[17] <https://sustainabledevelopment.un.org/topics/sids/ecesaplus> accessed 2 January 2020.

[18] <https://sustainabledevelopment.un.org/memberstates/argentina> accessed 2 January 2020.

[19] UNGA Res 45/212, 'Protection of Global Climate for Present and Future Generations of Mankind' (21 December 1990).

[20] UNGA Res 47/192, 'UN Conference on straddling fish stocks and highly migratory fish stocks' (22 December 1992).

[21] UNGA Res 72/249, 'International legally binding instrument under the United Nations Convention on the Law of the Sea on the conservation and sustainable use of marine biological diversity of areas beyond national jurisdiction' (24 December 2017).

[22] See Chapter 30, 'Freshwater Resources', in this volume.

Activities.[23] Currently, the ILC agenda includes two environmental topics: the protection of the environment in relation to armed conflicts and the protection of the atmosphere. The ILC agenda also includes topics of a broader scope that relate to the environment. These topics include peremptory norms, general principles of law, and crimes against humanity.[24] ILC treaties provide general principles, but differ from other MEAs because they do not establish institutions which further develop the regime.

The negotiation of MEAs also has been initiated within the governing bodies of UN specialized agencies, UNEP, and ECOSOC's regional commissions. For example, the 1973/78 International Convention for the Prevention of Pollution from Ships (MARPOL) was negotiated within the International Maritime Organization (IMO), the 1993 Agreement to Promote Compliance with International Conservation and Management Measures by Fishing Vessels on the High Seas (Compliance Agreement) within the FAO and the CBD within UNEP. The International Union for the Conservation of Nature (IUCN),[25] took on a similar role with respect to the 1973 Convention on Trade in Endangered Species of Fauna and Flora (CITES), which originated in a 1963 IUCN resolution.[26] Also noteworthy is UNEP's Regional Seas Program, established in 1974, which has fostered the negotiation of fourteen regional seas conventions.[27]

ECOSOC's five regional commissions all address environmental issues. In particular, the Economic Commission for Europe (ECE) and, more recently, the Economic Commission for Latin America and the Caribbean (ECLAC), have fostered the development of MEAs. The following MEAs were negotiated within the ECE: the 1979 Convention on Long-range Transboundary Air Pollution, the 1991 Convention on Environmental Impact Assessment in a Transboundary Context (Espoo Convention), the 1992 Convention on the Protection and Use of Transboundary Watercourses and International Lakes (ECE Watercourses Convention), the 1992 Convention on the Transboundary Effects of Industrial Accidents, and the 1998 Convention on Access to Information, Public Participation in Decision-making and Access to Justice in Environmental Matters (Aarhus Convention). The 2018 Regional Agreement on Access to Information, Public Participation and Justice in Environmental Matters in Latin America and the Caribbean (Escazú Convention) was negotiated within ECLAC.

The Espoo, Aarhus, and Escazú Conventions, contrary to most MEAs, provide cross-cutting norms. These norms, within the remit of the MEA in question, apply to all human activities instead of to human activities in relation to a particular component of the environment (eg human activities that harm biodiversity) or a particular human activity (eg trade in endangered species of wildlife).

[23] See Chapter 16, 'Harm Prevention', in this volume.

[24] ILC, 'Analytical Guide to the Work of the International Law Commission' <https://legal.un.org/ilc/guide/gfra.shtml> accessed 2 January 2020; see also Chapter 31, 'Marine Environment: Pollution and Fisheries', in this volume.

[25] IUCN is a hybrid organization. Its membership consists of NGOs and sub-national actors; see Chapter 39, 'Sub-National Actors', in this volume.

[26] IUCN, 'Resolution on illegal traffic in wildlife species' GA 1963 Res 005.

[27] For information on regional seas conventions see Chapter 31, 'The Protection of the Marine Environment: Pollution and Fisheries', in this volume.

B. The Institutional Structure of MEAs

Most MEAs provide the principles that are to guide decision-making and the institutional structure for further decision-making.[28] Relevant principles are, for example, the principle of 'common but differentiated responsibilities' (CBDR), explicitly included in the UNFCCC and the Paris Agreement but which also informs other MEAs[29] and the principle of 'wise use', which informs the 1971 Convention on Wetlands of International Importance especially as Waterfowl Habitat (Ramsar Convention).[30] The institutional structure of most MEAs includes a COP, in which all states parties to the MEA are represented, and subsidiary bodies, often including a compliance mechanism.[31] It is within these MEA-based institutions that decisions are taken to develop the regime with the aim of regulating human activities.

The institutional and decision-making structures established by MEAs and their protocols have been found to operate in ways similar to international organizations.[32] The role of the FAO's Committee on Fisheries (COFI) vis-à-vis the Compliance Agreement and the role of the CBD-COP vis-à-vis the CBD illustrate this similarity. All member states of the FAO and all parties to the CBD are represented on these bodies. Examples of relevant decisions include the 2001 'International Plan of Action to Prevent, Deter and Eliminate Illegal, Unreported and Unregulated Fishing' adopted by COFI,[33] and the 2018 decision on 'Mainstreaming of Biodiversity in the Energy and Mining, Infrastructure, Manufacturing and Processing Sectors' adopted by the CBD-COP.[34] Within the FAO and the CBD these decisions also serve to implement broader strategies, respectively the 1995 Code of Conduct for Responsible Fisheries,[35] and the Strategic Plan for Biodiversity 2011–20, including the Aichi Biodiversity Targets.[36]

C. Science-Oriented Institutions

Most MEAs establish subsidiary bodies that provide scientific input for decision-making. The Scientific Council established by the 1979 Convention on the Conservation of Migratory Species of Wild Animals (CMS) provides an example.[37] International institutions specifically focused on science and scientific advice have also been established.[38]

[28] See Chapter 24, 'Multilateral Environmental Treaty Making', in this volume.
[29] See Chapter 19, 'Differentiation', in this volume.
[30] See Chapter 32, 'Wildlife', in this volume.
[31] See Chapter 56, 'Non-Compliance Procedures', in this volume.
[32] Robin Churchill and Geir Ulfstein, 'Autonomous Institutional Arrangements in Multilateral Environmental Agreements: A Little-Noticed Phenomenon in International Law' *AJIL*, 94/4 (2000): 623.
[33] <http://www.fao.org/fishery/ipoa-iuu/about/en> accessed 2 January 2020.
[34] 'Report of the COP to the CBD on its fourteenth meeting' (20 March 2019) UN Doc CBD/COP/14/14.
[35] <http://www.fao.org/fishery/code/en> accessed 2 January 2020.
[36] <https://www.cbd.int/sp/> accessed 2 January 2020.
[37] <https://www.cms.int/meetings/scientific-council> accessed 2 January 2020.
[38] See Chapter 15, 'Role of Science', in this volume.

The oldest of these institutions is a regional institution established in 1902, the International Council for the Exploration of the Sea (ICES). ICES was established by states, and provides scientific advice on ocean-related issues. It advises its member states in Europe and North America, the EU, the regional seas commissions for the North-East Atlantic (OSPAR Commission) and the Baltic Sea (HELCOM), as well as regional fisheries management organizations in the North Atlantic, such as the North-East Atlantic Fisheries Commission (NEAFC).[39]

The global institution that provides scientific advice on marine environmental issues is the Joint Group of Experts on the Scientific Aspects of Marine Pollution (GESAMP). It was established in 1968 by the IMO, FAO, World Metrological Organization (WMO), and the Intergovernmental Oceanographic Commission of the UN Educational, Scientific and Cultural Organization and is now sponsored by ten international organizations, which use its services. GESAMP currently has seventeen individual experts as members, works through a network of scientists, and the IMO administers its secretariat.[40]

The IPCC is probably the most renowned of the scientific institutions. It was established, in 1988, by the WMO and UNEP and endorsed by the UNGA.[41] Its main outputs are the authoritative scientific assessments of the state of climate change, its consequences, and mitigation and adaptation options. These assessments provide input for the development of climate change policy and law. The IPCC does not itself engage in research; instead it constitutes a cooperative network of thousands of scientists who assess 'the state of scientific, technical and socio-economic knowledge on climate change' and in cooperation with governments develop the IPCC reports.[42]

The Intergovernmental Science-Policy Platform on Biodiversity and Ecosystem Services (IPBES), established by states in 2012,[43] uses working methods similar to those of the IPCC. It provides scientific input for the development of biodiversity policy and law and developed the global assessment of biodiversity and ecosystem services for the CBD, as input for the evaluation and renewal of the Strategic Plan for Biodiversity 2011–20.[44]

D. The GEF, Funds, and Multilateral Investment Banks

The GEF finances projects that aim to implement international environmental law in developing countries and economies in transition, and acts as the financial mechanism

[39] <http://www.ices.dk/Pages/default.aspx> accessed 2 January 2020.

[40] <http://www.gesamp.org/> accessed 2 January 2020.

[41] UNGA Res 43/53, 'Protection of Global Climate for Present and Future Generations of Mankind' (6 December 1988) UN Doc A/RES/43/53.

[42] <https://www.ipcc.ch/about/preparingreports/> accessed 2 January 2020.

[43] On the complexity of its establishment see Denis Pesche, Guillaume Futhazar, and Sandrine Maljean-Dubois, 'IPBES Mandate and Governance: The Intergovernmental platform on biodiversity and ecosystem service (IPBES): Challenges, knowledge and actors' (2016).

[44] <https://www.ipbes.net/> accessed 2 January 2020.

for several MEAs.[45] It was initially established in 1991 by the World Bank. However, when developing states, after the Rio Conference, demanded a more inclusive financial mechanism for the UNFCCC and the CBD, the GEF instrument was revised. In 1994, the restructured GEF was de facto established by the World Bank, UNEP, and UNDP, even if de jure by the World Bank, which also acts as its trustee.[46] Besides its own fund, the GEF Trust Fund, the GEF administers other funds, including the Special Climate Change Fund and the CBD's Nagoya Protocol Implementation Fund.[47]

Within the GEF a number of so-called GEF Agencies cooperate to design, develop, and implement GEF-funded projects. In early 2019, there were eighteen GEF Agencies, including seven regional development banks,[48] three UN specialized agencies,[49] two sub-states actors,[50] three NGOs,[51] and its three founders.

The GEF, GEF Agencies, and funds administered by the GEF develop their own rules and standards that apply to projects they support. The GEF has adopted policies and guidelines, for example, on environmental and social safeguard standards, gender equality, and Indigenous peoples.[52] These policies and guidelines apply to GEF-funded projects, such as a project to strengthen 'policies, laws, and criminal justice capacities to address poaching and illegal wildlife trade' in Gabon, Kenya, Malawi, Mozambique, and Zambia, with UNEP acting as implementing agency. The project aims to attain its goals, among others, by furthering gender equality and engaging Indigenous peoples, in line with GEF and UNEP policies.[53]

The World Bank also administers funds that are relevant to the protection of the environment, including a number of carbon-related funds.[54] Most of these funds are financed by states with some, such as the World Bank's Carbon Partnership Facility,[55] being co-funded by private sector actors. International development banks, such as the World Bank, and regional development banks, also directly finance projects that implement international environmental law in developing countries and economies in transition. Moreover, these institutions and other donors regularly co-finance a single project.

[45] See Chapter 54, 'Financial Assistance', in this volume.

[46] GEF, 'Instrument for the establishment of the Restructured GEF' <https://www.thegef.org/documents/instrument-establishment-restructured-gef> accessed 2 January 2020.

[47] GEF, 'Funding' <https://www.thegef.org/about/funding> accessed 2 January 2020.

[48] Asian Development Bank (ADB), African Development Bank, European Bank for Reconstruction and Development (EBRD), Inter-American Development Bank, Development Bank of Latin America, Development Bank of Southern Africa, and West African Development Bank.

[49] The FAO, the International Fund for Agricultural Development, and the United Nations Industrial Development Organization.

[50] The Foreign Economic Cooperation Office of the Ministry of Environmental Protection of China and the Brazilian Biodiversity Fund.

[51] Conservation International, IUCN, and the World Wild Life Fund.

[52] <https://www.thegef.org/documents/policies-guidelines> accessed 2 January 2020.

[53] GEF, 'Enhancing Legislative, Policy, and Criminal Justice Frameworks for Combating Poaching and Illegal Wildlife Trade in Africa' <https://www.thegef.org/project/enhancing-legislative-policy-and-criminal-justice-frameworks-combating-poaching-and-illegal> accessed 2 January 2020, Request for CEO Approval Document SN, 25.

[54] World Bank, 'Climate Finance & Initiatives' <http://www.worldbank.org/en/topic/climatechange/brief/world-bank-carbon-funds-facilities> accessed 2 January 2020.

[55] <https://cpf.wbcarbonfinance.org/content/what-cpf> accessed 2 January 2020.

For example, the ADB, EBRD, and the International Finance Corporation (IFC), in 2015, invested in a hydropower project in Georgia.[56]

As for the GEF, these funds and financial institutions develop their own policies and guidelines that apply to projects. Furthermore, many of these institutions have established bodies that assess complaints of non-compliance from members of the public in states where projects they finance are being implemented. Such bodies include the World Bank Inspection Panel (WBIP) and the Compliance Advisor Ombudsman of the IFC.[57] The standards against which these bodies assess compliance are the standards adopted by the institution in question.[58] In applying these standards, bodies such as the WBIP contribute to the development of international environmental law.

E. The Pattern and Coherence

Despite the lack of central coordination in the development of international environmental law, elements of the pattern can promote cohesion.

First, the initiating role of the UNGA has resulted in instruments that afford substantive cohesion to the system. Particularly relevant are the Rio Principles and the SDGs. The SDGs also come with an institutional structure that addresses their implementation by states and international institutions, which is likely to foster cohesion.

Second, the GEF and international financial institutions, such as the World Bank, at least to some extent, coordinate the implementation of international environmental law in developing countries and economies in transition. This mode of coordination, however, raises questions about the powers exercised by these institutions vis-à-vis developing countries and economies in transition, and the regulation of human activities in those states. While developed states themselves determine how they meet the requirements of different MEAs, international financial institutions co-determine how this happens in developing countries and economies in transition.

In addition to the above, substantive links also exist between MEAs. These links have the potential to enhance coherence in international environmental law and are discussed in the next section.

III. SUBSTANTIVE LINKS BETWEEN MEAS

Given the lack of central coordination and the number of MEAs, their mandates overlap and links exist between them. These links manifest themselves between global and

56 IFC, 'IFC, ADB, EBRD, Tata Power, and Clean Energy Help Georgia Achieve Energy Self-sufficiency' (19 March 2015).

57 <https://inspectionpanel.org/>; <http://www.cao-ombudsman.org/> accessed 2 January 2020.

58 Andria Naudé Fourie, *World Bank Accountability: In Theory and Practice* (Eleven International Publishing 2016).

regional MEAs that cover the same or related topics, and between global MEAs. This section first discusses the links between global and regional MEAs and thereafter between global MEAs.

A. Links between Global and Regional MEAs

Global MEAs regularly require regional cooperation. For example, the UN Watercourses Convention requires states sharing a watercourse to cooperate. Watercourse specific agreements, such as the 1999 Convention on the Protection of the Rhine and 2004 Agreement on the Establishment of the Zambezi Watercourse Commission, are MEAs in their own right and implement the UN Watercourses Convention. In addition, they may implement regional water related MEAs such as the UNECE Water Convention and 2000 Revised Protocol on Shared Watercourses adopted within the Southern African Development Community.

While there are clear substantive links between global, regional, and watercourse-specific agreements, these links are not hierarchical in the sense that the institutions established by the watercourse-specific agreements formally report to institutions at regional or global levels. This is because obligations stemming from MEAs rest on states and the EU and not on international institutions.

Regional fisheries management organizations relate to the Fish Stocks Agreement, the Compliance Agreement, and UNCLOS, and regional seas agreements to UNCLOS, in ways similar to how watercourse-specific agreements relate to regional watercourse treaties and the UN Watercourses Convention.

The CMS provides a different arrangement.[59] It requires its parties that are range states for a migratory species with 'an unfavourable conservation status' to 'endeavour to conclude' agreements that are legally binding instruments.[60] In practice, range states have concluded both legally non-binding Memoranda of Understanding (MoU) and agreements. An example of the former is the 2005 MoU Concerning Conservation Measures for the West African Populations of the African Elephant, signed by all thirteen range states, the CMS Secretariat, and IUCN's Species Survival Committee.[61] The 1996 Agreement on the Conservation of African-Eurasian Migratory Waterbirds (AEWA) provides an example of a CMS agreement. It has been ratified by states in Africa, Europe, the Middle East, and Central Asia, even if not by all range states. AEWA itself has the characteristics of a MEA, with its own COP and secretariat, administered by UNEP.[62]

Some MEAs, such as the Ramsar Convention and the 1972 Convention Concerning the Protection of the World Cultural and Natural Heritage (World Heritage Convention), operate on the basis of listed areas, including transboundary areas.

[59] Chapter 32, 'Wildlife', in this volume.

[60] CMS, art 4.

[61] <https://www.cms.int/west-african-elephants/en/meetings/meetings-of-signatories> accessed 2 January 2020.

[62] <https://www.unep-aewa.org/en/legalinstrument/aewa> accessed 2 January 2020.

These areas meet certain conditions in terms of their special significance as a wetland or natural heritage site and if accepted for listing, require special protection. Relevant areas may also be covered by regional MEAs or area- or species-specific MEAs. The Wadden Sea offers an example of how various MEAs may apply to a specific area.

The Wadden Sea is a listed Transboundary Ramsar Site, a listed natural world heritage site, and a particularly sensitive sea area recognized by the IMO. Other MEAs relevant for its protection include the CBD, the CMS, AEWA, and the 1990 CMS Agreement on the Conservation of Seals in the Wadden Sea, concluded by the three Wadden Sea states—Denmark, Germany, and the Netherlands.[63] It is also protected by the Trilateral Wadden Sea Cooperation, based on the 1982 Joint Declaration on the Protection of the Wadden Sea. This declaration of intent, adopted by the three Wadden Sea states, established the Common Wadden Sea Secretariat (CWSS).[64] CWSS has observer status with the OSPAR Commission. Building on the GEF-financed project, Wings over Wetlands,[65] the CWSS, national and international NGOs, sub-national actors, and AEWA, as well as other partners, implemented the Wadden Sea Flyway Initiative. It furthered the protection of habitats of migratory birds along the East Atlantic Flyway and fostered capacity building in Western African range states. The current CWSS agenda specifies that the Flyway Initiative will be continued and expanded to include the Arctic and that an integrated Wadden Sea management plan will be developed, as requested by the World Heritage Committee.[66]

B. Links between Global MEAs

Global MEAs develop synergetic relationships. However, when human activities are deemed to require additional or new regulation, there are often contestations because several MEAs might regulate the activity. This sub-section first discusses examples of synergetic relations between MEAs and thereafter examples of more contentious relations.

1. *Synergies*

Synergies between global MEAs are achieved by institutionalizing cooperation between MEAs. Examples include cooperation on land use within the Joint Liaison Group established by the UNFCCC, CBD, and UNCCD, and on biodiversity conservation in the Liaison Group of biodiversity-related Conventions. In addition, UNCLOS in a unique way links into IMO conventions, including MARPOL. The latter will be discussed first, followed by the former two examples.

63 <https://www.cms.int/en/legalinstrument/wadden-sea-seals> accessed 2 January 2020.

64 <http://www.waddensea-secretariat.org/> accessed 2 January 2020.

65 <https://www.unep-aewa.org/en/project/wings-over-wetlands-wow-unep-gef-african-eurasian-flyways-project> accessed 2 January 2020.

66 <https://www.waddensea-worldheritage.org/da/news/wadden-sea-ministers-discuss-trilateral-future-leeuwarden> accessed 14 January 2020.

UNCLOS links to MARPOL by way of so-called rules of reference. These rules refer to 'generally accepted international rules and standards established through the competent international organization or general diplomatic conference'. According to UNCLOS the referenced international rules and standards provide the minimum standards that a flag state must impose upon its ships[67] and, special circumstances excepted,[68] provide the maximum standards that a coastal or port state may impose on foreign ships.[69] It is generally accepted that MARPOL is among the instruments referenced. As a result, UNCLOS incorporates MARPOL as it evolves. The 2014/2015 International Code for Ships Operating in Polar Waters provides an example.[70] It amended IMO-instruments, including MARPOL, and by virtue of the rules of reference in UNCLOS has attained normative relevance for all parties to the latter whose ships operate in Polar Regions.

Land use relates to biodiversity, desertification, and climate change. In 2001, the CBD, UNCCD, and the UNFCCC (the Rio Conventions), established the Joint Liaison Group to coordinate their activities on, amongst other activities, land use. In collaboration with the GEF, this group organized the 2004 'Regional Workshop for Africa on synergy among the Rio Conventions and other Biodiversity-related conventions in implementing the programmes of work on dry and sub-humid lands and agricultural biodiversity'.[71] More recently, in 2017, the Executive Secretaries of the three MEAs called for the establishment of a Project Preparation Facility that would finance integrated, coherent, and multidisciplinary projects on land degradation, biodiversity loss, and global warming.[72] The GEF's 2018 'Food, Land Use and Restoration Impact Program' finances these types of projects[73] and the GEF project, mentioned in the introduction to this chapter, aims to realize such projects. This sequence of activities illustrate how MEAs may link to each other and to other international institutions and how together they may enhance substantive coherence.

Biodiversity-related MEAs have developed a network of MoUs. In particular the CBD has concluded MoUs with the CMS, CITES, the Ramsar Convention, the 2004 International Treaty on Plant Genetic Resources for Food and Agriculture, and the 1952 International Plant Protection Convention.[74] Many of these MEAs have also concluded MoUs among themselves. Together with the secretariats of other MEAs, including the World Heritage Convention and the 1946 International Convention for the Regulation of Whaling, they coordinate their work through the Liaison Group of biodiversity-related

[67] arts 211.5, 218.1, 220.

[68] arts 211.6, 234.

[69] art 211.5.

[70] International Code for Ships Operating in Polar Waters (adopted 15 May 2015, entered into force 1 January 2017) MEPC 68/21/Add.1, 3, annex 10 (Polar Code)—as in IMO Res MEPC.264(68); see Chapter 31, 'The Protection of the Marine Environment: Pollution and Fisheries', in this volume.

[71] CBD, 'Activities' <https://www.cbd.int/cooperation/activities.shtml> accessed 2 January 2020.

[72] CBD, 'Joint Liaison Group' <https://www.cbd.int/cooperation/liaison.shtml> accessed 2 January 2020.

[73] GEF, 'GEF introduces impact programs to upscale landscape restoration' <https://www.thegef.org/news/gef-introduces-impact-programs-upscale-landscape-restoration> accessed 2 January 2020.

[74] CBD, 'Mandates for Cooperation' <https://www.cbd.int/cooperation/related-conventions/mandates.shtml#jwp> accessed 2 January 2020.

Conventions.[75] Together with UNEP, the biodiversity-related MEAs seek to further harmonize their reporting requirements and most MEAs involved have embraced the CBD's Aichi Biodiversity Goals. CITES, for example, in 2016 amended its Strategic Visions 2008–20 to include the SDGs and mapped its own objectives against the Aichi Biodiversity Goals.[76] The Ramsar Convention's COP adopted, with Ramsar specific annotations, the guidance on environmental impact assessment (EIA) and strategic environmental impact assessment (SEA) developed within the CBD.[77] CITES and Ramsar thereby contribute to enhancing coherence amongst MEA-based norms.

2. *Contestation*

Contestation primarily arises when human activities require additional or new regulation. The regulation of ship dismantling, ship-generated wastes, CO_2 emissions from ships and aircraft, trade in endangered marine fish species, and accessing biodiversity in areas beyond national jurisdiction (ABNJ) provide examples.[78] This section discusses these examples, with the exception of the regulation of CO_2 emissions from ships and aircraft and trade in endangered marine fish species, both discussed in earlier chapters.[79]

a) *Ship dismantling and ship-generated wastes: IMO and Basel Convention*

Ship dismantling, or recycling, as well as the regulation of ship-generated wastes are topics that have concerned the IMO and the 1989 Basel Convention on the Control of Transboundary Movements of Hazardous Wastes and their Disposal (Basel Convention). The unease of their interactions can be traced to the distinct context and related narrative associated with each of the regimes.[80]

The IMO-based narrative is shaped by the 1948 IMO Convention which formulates the following aim for the organization: '[t]o encourage the removal of discriminatory action and unnecessary restrictions by Governments affecting shipping engaged in international trade so as to promote the availability of shipping services to the commerce of the world without discrimination'.[81] The IMO furthers this aim by developing universal regulation for the shipping sector, including for purposes of preventing and controlling marine pollution from ships, with the objective of attaining non-discrimination and no more favourable treatment in the sector.[82]

[75] CBD, 'Liaison Group of Biodiversity-related Conventions' <https://www.cbd.int/blg/> accessed 2 January 2020.

[76] <https://www.cites.org/eng/documents/Strategic_vision> accessed 2 January 2020.

[77] Ramsar Convention, Res VIII.9 'Guidelines for incorporating biodiversity-related issues into environmental impact assessment legislation and/or processes and in strategic environmental assessment' (2002); Res X.17, 'Environmental Impact Assessment and Strategic Environmental Assessment: updated scientific and technical guidance' (2008).

[78] See also Ellen Hey, 'Regime Interaction and Common Interests in Regulating Human Activities in ABNJ' in Seline Trevisanut *et al* (eds), *Regime Interaction in Ocean Governance: Problems, Theories and Methods* (Brill 2020) 85–123.

[79] See respectively Chapters 31 and 34, 'The Protection of the Marine Environment: Pollution and Fisheries' and 'Aviation and Maritime Transport', in this volume.

[80] Jeffrey Dunoff, 'A New Approach to Regime Interaction' in Margaret Young (ed), *Regime Interaction in International Law* (CUP 2012) 136–174.

[81] art 1(b).

[82] IMO Convention, art 1.

The Basel Convention was adopted in the 1980s when developing and Eastern European states found hazardous wastes dumped in their territories because developed states had adopted more stringent disposal regulations. It is rooted in the South-North divide, seeks to protect weaker states from often illegal waste dumping practices and entitles states to prohibit the import of hazardous and other wastes.[83] Moreover, the IMO has strong ties with the shipping industry, which has considerable influence within the IMO. Moving decision-making about ship dismantling or ship-generated wastes from the IMO to the Basel Convention implied that the sector would lose that position.

Concerns about ship dismantling/recycling arose around the turn of the century when reports emerged about the unsafe working conditions under which beached ships, containing hazardous wastes such as asbestos, were being dismantled in developing states. At the time, the question arose whether ships travelling to be dismantled qualified as wastes under the Basel Convention. On the one hand, these ships have value in terms of, for example, the scrap metals they generate. On the other hand, if the purpose of their voyage is their dismantling they might qualify as wastes under the Basel Convention.

These considerations resulted in the Basel-COP adopting the 2002 Technical Guidelines for the Environmentally Sound Management of the Full and Partial Dismantling of Ships and the IMO adopting the 2003 Guidelines on Ship Recycling.[84] In 2004, recognizing that ships may become wastes under the Basel Convention, its COP adopted a resolution inviting the IMO to continue work on what would become the 2009 Hong Kong International Convention for the Safe and Environmentally Sound Recycling of Ships (Hong Kong Convention), which has yet to enter into force.[85] The Hong Kong Convention sets out a cradle-to-grave approach to ship recycling and addresses both the shipbuilding and recycling sectors. In 2011, while encouraging parties to ratify the Hong Kong Convention, the parties to the Basel Convention could not achieve consensus on whether the Hong Kong Convention meets the equivalence requirement of Article 11 of the Basel Convention, which if it did, would exempt ship dismantling from the Basel Convention.[86] At present both institutions, as well as the International Labour Organization, cooperate to assist states in meeting the conditions of the Hong Kong Convention so that they may ratify it. The project on Safe and Environmentally Sound Ship Recycling in Bangladesh provides an example.[87]

Ship-generated wastes are another topic on which the IMO and the Basel Convention have interacted.[88] Within the IMO, MARPOL, based on uniform regulations for the

[83] Basel Convention, art 4.1; see Chapter 33, 'Hazardous Substances and Activities', in this volume.

[84] Basel Convention, 'Ship Dismantling' <http://www.basel.int/Implementation/ShipDismantling/Overview/tabid/2762/Default.aspx> accessed 2 January 2020; IMO, 'Recycling of Ships' <http://www.imo.org/en/OurWork/Environment/ShipRecycling/Pages/Default.aspx> accessed 2 January 2020.

[85] Decision VII/26, 'Environmentally sound management of ship dismantling' (25 January 2005) UN Doc UNEP/CHW.7/33, 63.

[86] Decision 10/17, 'Environmentally sound dismantling of ships' (1 November 2011) UN Doc UNEP/CHW.10/28, 53.

[87] IMO, 'Safe and Environmentally Sound Ship Recycling in Bangladesh—Phase I' <http://www.imo.org/en/OurWork/Environment/MajorProjects/Pages/Ship-recycling.aspx> accessed 2 January 2020.

[88] Gabriela Argüello Moncayo, 'Testing the Boundaries between the Basel and MARPOL Regime: Are They Complementary or Mutually Exclusive?' *Transportation Research Procedia*, 25 (2017): 233.

sector, regulates the reduction of ship generated wastes and requires port states to accept such wastes and provide adequate port reception facilities. MARPOL does not address the further treatment or disposal of the wastes, after they enter the port reception facility. The Basel Convention focuses on minimizing and regulating inter-state transport of wastes, hazardous wastes in particular, and entitles states to prohibit the import of wastes. Moreover, it focuses on the environmentally sound management of wastes once they enter a state of import. Since 2006, both MEAs have adopted measures to address ship-generated wastes. A 2017 Guidance Manual on how to improve the sea-land interface prepared by the Basel Secretariat, in cooperation with the IMO, illustrates the difficulties involved in aligning the two regimes.[89] For example, MARPOL does not distinguish between hazardous and non-hazardous wastes and the Basel Convention addresses states, but not in their flag state capacity.

b) *Accessing marine biological diversity in areas beyond national jurisdiction*

Accessing marine biodiversity in areas beyond national jurisdiction is not regulated by an MEA, which is why the UNGA initiated the BBNJ negotiations. The starting point for the negotiations was the 2017 final report of the Preparatory Committee (BBNJ PrepCom).[90] The report illustrates that the negotiations are likely to be difficult because in the BBNJ negotiations three global regimes interact.

The final report of the BNNJ PrepCom contains recommendations, and identifies a list of elements which generated convergence, and a list of elements on which views diverged. The former list includes issues such as the application of the ecosystem and precautionary approaches, the need to address access and benefit sharing, as well as more technical issues, including the need to develop area-based management measures. However, it also shows that difficult choices have not been made, for example, about which institution is to designate area-based management measures or regulate access and benefit sharing. The latter list indicates why these choices have not been made. It mentions that further discussion is required about, among other things, the principles of the common heritage of mankind and the freedom of the high seas as well as about the institutional arrangements to be adopted.

In the negotiations, three narratives about how to regulate access to genetic resource in areas beyond national jurisdiction meet, with each narrative presenting a different worldview about regulating access. The three narratives are grounded in three different principles linked to three regimes: the freedom of the high seas/fishing applicable to the high seas, the common heritage of mankind applicable to the Area, and the common concern of mankind applicable to the conservation of biodiversity.

[89] Basel Convention, 'Guidance' <http://www.basel.int/Implementation/LegalMatters/Ships/Guidance/tabid/7569/Default.aspx> accessed 2 January 2020.

[90] 'Report of the Preparatory Committee established by General Assembly resolution 69/292: Development of an international legally binding instrument under the United Nations Convention on the Law of the Sea on the conservation and sustainable use of marine biological diversity of areas beyond national jurisdiction' (31 July 2017) UN Doc A/AC.287/2017/PC.4/2; Kristine Dalaker Kraable, 'The BBNJ PrepCom and Institutional Arrangements: The Hype about the Hybrid Approach' in Myron Nordquist, John Moore, and Ronán Long (eds), *The Marine Environment and the United Nations Sustainable Development Goal 14* (Brill 2019) 137.

The high seas/fisheries regime implies freedom of access to the resources, subject to regulations of a technical nature, aiming to conserve the resource and marine ecosystems. These regulations would be adopted internationally but administered by states. Moreover, benefits would accrue to those who are able to access the resource. The regime for the Area suggests internationally regulated access to the resources based on technical regulations and on benefit and burden sharing. Such a regime would be administered by an international institution, possibly with the competence to license activities and oversee benefit and burden sharing, similar to the International Seabed Authority (ISA) for deep-sea mining. The CBD regime suggests a regime based on technical regulations and, based on the principle of CBDR, that developed states commit to facilitate access to BBNJ and the benefits obtained therefrom for developing states. The CBDR-related commitments would be guided by international standards, but otherwise left for states to agree amongst themselves.

Related to the BBNJ negotiations are also initiatives of regional seas commissions and regional fisheries management organizations adopting area-based management measure in areas beyond national jurisdiction. The OSPAR Commission and NEAFC, for example, based on a 2008 MoU and the 2014 Collective Arrangement are seeking to implement such measures in the North-East Atlantic.[91] Striking a balance between the various global regimes and determining the role of regional institutions are among the thorny tasks that the BBNJ negotiations have to address.

IV. CONCLUSION: MULTIFACETED GOVERNANCE

The analysis presented above shows that the origin and legal status of an international institution do not necessarily determine its roles. The similarity of the roles engaged in by UNEP and UN specialized agencies illustrates this point. NGOs also take on roles similar to those engaged in by institutions of a public nature. CITES originating in an IUCN resolution might be an exception; however, it is well known that IUCN has played a pivotal role in the development of other biodiversity conservation treaties, including the CBD. NGOs furthermore act as GEF agencies, thereby fulfilling roles that UNEP and UN specialized agencies also fulfil.

The analysis presented in this chapter also illustrates that international institutions, together with NGOs,[92] engage in two types of activities in developing international environmental law. First, they engage in normative development. That is the development of rules and standards that are to regulate human activity. Second, they engage in

[91] Stefán Ásmundsson (NEAFC) and Emily Corcoran (OSPAR), 'Information Paper—On the Process of Forming a Cooperative Mechanism Between NEAFC and OSPAR: From the First Contact to a Formal Collective Arrangement' *UNEP Regional Seas Reports and Studies No. 196* (2015); see also <https://www.ospar.org/about/international-cooperation/collective-arrangement> accessed 2 January 2020.

[92] See Chapter 38, 'Non-State Actors', in this volume.

implementing these rules and standards. Implementation generally is effected by states or the EU, for example when the World Heritage Convention's normative framework is applied to the Wadden Sea and the three Wadden Sea states cooperate through the CWSS to develop an integrated management plan. However, implementation in developing countries and economies in transition also takes place through the GEF, GEF agencies, funds, and international development banks. In so doing, these institutions apply the MEA-based rules, but also their own internal rules on, for example, gender equality.

While synergies between international institutions involved in the development of international environmental law have emerged, there is also contestation. Such contestation is intimately linked to law, as it is law that enables states to construct and maintain the various narratives underpinning different regimes. For instance, benefit sharing is central to the regime for the Area and the principle of CBDR is a basic tenant of the biodiversity regime, but neither of these principles are components of the freedom of fishing. A further example is the IMO seeking to attain the universal regulation of a sector, while the Basel Convention enables states to decide unilaterally on the import of wastes. Similarly, by allocating the regulation of CO_2 emissions from ships and aircraft to respectively the IMO and the International Civil Aviation Organization, developing states lost the principle of CBDR that is central to the climate change regime.[93] Ultimately, which regime addresses a human activity determines how it will be regulated and who benefits and bears burdens as a result of regulation. As a consequence, when human activities become candidates for additional or new regulation, contestation is likely to emerge and compromise is required. The ongoing BBNJ negotiations provide an example.

Finally, the multiple international institutions involved in the development of international environmental law together provide a complex network of regulations that is neither layered horizontally (suggesting a hierarchy between global and regional institutions) nor layered vertically (assuming functionally clearly defined pillars). Instead, the network reflects multiple facets that each aim to regulate human activity with a limited number of elements in place to secure a measure of coherence.

BIBLIOGRAPHY

Robin Churchill and Geir Ulfstein, 'Autonomous Institutional Arrangements in Multilateral Environmental Agreements: A Little-Noticed Phenomenon in International Law' *American Journal of International Law*, 94/4 (2000): 623

Ellen Hey, 'Regime Interaction and Common Interests in Regulating Human Activities in ABNJ' in Seline Trevisanut *et al* (eds), *Regime Interaction in Ocean Governance: Problems, Theories and Methods* (CUP 2020)

Kristine Kraable, 'The BBNJ PrepCom and Institutional Arrangements: The Hype about the Hybrid Approach' in Myron Nordquist, John Moore, and Ronán Long (eds), *The Marine Environment and the United Nations Sustainable Development Goal 14* (Brill 2019) 137

93 See Chapter 34, 'Aviation and Maritime Transport', in this volume.

CHAPTER 37

REGIONAL ORGANIZATIONS

The European Union

SANDRINE MALJEAN-DUBOIS*

I. INTRODUCTION

By nature, the European Union (EU) was created by agreements between states, and belongs to the category of intergovernmental regional organizations. However, by structure, functions, and powers, it is distinctive, and even regarded as a *sui generis* organization. Standing out from the model of traditional international organizations, it has been entrusted by member states with the adoption of legally binding acts which can have immediate and direct effects on national law. In its landmark decision, *Costa v ENEL* in 1964, the European Court of Justice (ECJ) clearly stated that 'the Member States have limited their sovereign rights, albeit within limited fields, and have thus created a body of law which binds both their nationals and themselves'.[1] EU law is thus regarded as an autonomous legal order.

The institutional structure of the EU (with the European Council, European Parliament, Council of Ministers, Commission, Court of Justice, European Central Bank, and Court of Auditors) comes closer to that of a state, but its functioning is different, especially as regards the distribution of executive, legislative, and judiciary

* I would like to warmly thank my friend and colleague Professor Rostane Mehdi for his helpful feedback on the first version of this chapter. Any error or omission lies with me.

[1] Case 6-64 *Flaminio Costa v ENEL* [1964] ECR 585, 593.

powers. Furthermore, unlike states, the EU is not sovereign and has only conferred powers, the legal bases for which are found in the treaties and mainly in the Treaty on the Functioning of EU (TFEU).[2] Its distinctive characteristics have been internationally recognized, since the EU is often the one-of-a-kind Regional Economic Integration Organization (REIO), allowed as such to be a member of some international organizations and to enter in agreements with third countries, alone or along with its twenty-seven member states.

Consolidating step by step its competences regarding environmental protection, the EU has gradually developed a comprehensive legally binding body of legislation in this field. At first, the European legislation mainly intended to avoid or limit distortions of competition rather than to protect the environment itself. However, from the precursory European Economic Community (1957 Treaty of Rome) to the European Union (1992 Treaty on European Union, Maastricht), the organization has progressively evolved towards a more preventive and comprehensive policy, including nature conservation. In this area as in others, the dynamic of European integration has benefitted from the interaction of political and judicial processes. Meanwhile, the Union has been developing an external environmental policy, and has become an influential international actor at the regional as well as the global level. It has indeed played a crucial role in different environmental negotiations, organizations, and treaty bodies. Some other regional organizations have also developed an environmental policy, albeit less broad and with much less interface with international environmental law than the EU.

This chapter discusses the EU as a preeminent example of a regional organization and its role in international environmental law. The chapter first examines the progressive affirmation of EU competence in the environmental field and its development of a distinctive environmental policy. The chapter then turns to the external dimension of EU environmental competence, discussing the EU's participation in and enforcement of international environmental law, as well as the general question of whether the EU can be said to have an external environmental policy. The chapter concludes with some brief reflections on other regional organizations and their distinctions from the largely *sui generis* EU example.

[2] Adopted in 2007 and entered into force in 2009, the Lisbon Treaty amended the Treaty of Rome (1957), known in its updated form as the Treaty on the Functioning of the European Union or TFEU, and the Maastricht Treaty (1992), known in its updated form as the Treaty on European Union (2007) or TEU. These two treaties form the constitutional basis of the European Union.

II. PROGRESSIVE AFFIRMATION OF EU COMPETENCE IN THE ENVIRONMENTAL FIELD

A. The Consecration of EU Competence

The EU does not have any autonomous source of authority, independently of its sovereign member states. According to the principle of conferral, the EU may act only within the limits of the powers conferred upon it by the member states in the treaties. And yet, its environmental competence was far from obvious in its early stages. There is no reference to the protection of the environment in the 1957 Treaty of Rome, written before the quality of the environment became a political concern. However, with the development of international environmental law, member states gradually developed legislation in this area that could threaten competition and the free movement of goods and services within the 'Common Market'. It became necessary to seek harmonization at the European level. At the same time, a landmark Meeting of the Heads of State or Government in Paris in 1972 recognized that economic development does not constitute an end in itself, but should serve to improve the quality of life.[3] By this declaration, a flexible interpretation of the Treaty of Rome was then legitimized. This led to the adoption of the First Community Environment Action Programme in 1973, followed by six other programmes over the years. Although these programmes are only guidance documents, they have played a fundamental role in the strategic orientation of the EU's environmental policy.

In the late 1970s, while the first Community legislative instruments were being adopted, the legal bases of the Community's competence were the subject of lengthy debate. The Community found them in Article 100 of the Treaty of Rome (now Article 115 TFEU), which allows for the adoption of directives for the approximation of laws, regulations, and administrative provisions that have a direct impact on the Common Market. This provision made it possible to regulate non-market barriers (eg product standards). The Community also used Article 235 (now Article 352 TFEU), which states that '[i]f action by the Community should prove necessary, … to attain one of the objectives set out in the Treaties, and the Treaties have not provided the necessary powers, the Council, acting unanimously on a proposal from the Commission and after obtaining the consent of the European Parliament, shall adopt the appropriate measures'. It is significant that these two legal bases required the unanimity of member states. This explains why, during this first period, Community environmental law was essentially based on the lowest common denominator.

[3] 'The First Summit Conference of the Enlarged Community' Bull. EC 10.1972, 'Declaration', 14, para 3.

Founded on fragile legal bases, the Community's competence remained limited until the adoption of the Single European Act in 1986. The latter added a new title on the 'Environment' to the Treaty of Rome, thus laying down the framework for an environmental 'action' of the Community.[4] From being implicit only, the Community competence became clear and explicit, operating therefore on firm legal bases. More changes were made by the Treaty of Maastricht (1992), the Treaty of Amsterdam (1997), and the Treaty of Lisbon (2007). The initial European Economic Community became a Union with competences broadened far beyond the economic field. Regarding environmental protection, the decision-making process gradually evolved from unanimity to a qualified majority of the Council in most cases, which facilitated legal development.

Meanwhile, the EU articulated the objectives of a comprehensive environmental policy. In addition to its internal environmental objectives, the Union aims at 'promoting measures at international level to deal with regional or worldwide environmental problems, and in particular combating climate change'.[5] Moreover, Article 3 of the TEU now states that 'The Union ... shall work for the sustainable development of Europe based on balanced economic growth and price stability, a highly competitive social market economy, aiming at full employment and social progress, and a high level of protection and improvement of the quality of the environment.' Sustainable development is thus an overriding objective of the EU. In practice, the legal bases of environmental measures are varied and go beyond Article 192 and the Environment Title. In particular, many measures were also adopted under Article 114 TFEU, which primarily aims at the establishment and functioning of the internal market. The choice of legal basis generates considerable discussion since it has practical implications on the legislative process and the residual freedom of member states.[6]

B. A Shared Competence between the Union and Its Member States

With the exception of the common commercial policy and the conservation of marine biological resources under the common fisheries policy, for which the EU has exclusive competence, competence is shared between member states and the EU in the field of the environment. Both the Union and member states may legislate and adopt legally binding acts. Member states have original competence: they can take measures as long as the EU itself has not already regulated the issue. Member states retain a residual—circumscribed—competence after the EU's intervention: they can then complete, strengthen, or derogate from EU legislation. However, they do not have the right to undertake obligations which would affect the EU's rules.

[4] [1987] OJ L169/1, Title VII, arts 130r–130t, now TFEU, arts 191–193.

[5] TFEU, art 191.1.

[6] David Langlet and Said Mahmoudi, *EU Environmental Law and Policy* (OUP 2016) 97.

The much-discussed sharing of legislative power between the EU and its member states is governed by different principles.

The 1986 Single European Act first introduced the subsidiarity principle. It was initially applicable only to environmental measures. It has since become a general principle and is now formulated in Article 5.3 TEU. In accordance with this principle, the Union 'shall act only if and in so far as the objectives of the proposed action cannot be sufficiently achieved by the Member States, either at central level or at regional and local level, but can rather, by reason of the scale or effects of the proposed action, be better achieved at Union level'. By nature, due to their transboundary dimension, environmental actions are generally better achieved at the EU level. It remains, however, difficult to assess whether a measure's objective can be better achieved at the EU level. This gives rise to considerable debates between the EU and member states.

The principle of proportionality is also of particular significance here. According to Article 5.4 TEU, '[u]nder the principle of proportionality, the content and form of Union action shall not exceed what is necessary to achieve the objectives of the Treaties'. It applies to both the choice of legal instruments—between a directive or framework-directive, which provides greater flexibility to member states, or a regulation—and the content of legislative acts that could restrict, more or less, the freedom of action of individual member states.[7]

The principle of sincere cooperation between the EU and member states (sometimes called loyal or fair cooperation) is also worth referring to.[8] This is a far-reaching obligation that has significant implications for member states. The Court of Justice has, for instance, derived from this a requirement for member states' authorities to redress the unlawful consequences of a breach of EU law and a requirement that enforcement shall be effective, proportionate, and dissuasive.[9]

Regarding EU external action, it is noteworthy that according to the implicit powers theory, competence in external matters derives from explicit internal competence. This is the principle of parallelism between internal and external powers. In other words, where the treaties assign explicit powers to the EU in a particular area, it must also have similar powers to conclude agreements with non-EU countries in the same field.[10]

The issue of the distribution of competence between the Union and its member states is a complex and evolving one. It has long been a matter of discussion between the European Commission and EU member states, regularly arbitrated by the ECJ.

[7] On this principle see Case C-414/16 *Vera Egenberger v Evangelisches Werk für Diakonie und Entwicklung e.V.* (ECJ, 17 April 2018).

[8] See TEU, art 4.3.

[9] See Case C-201/02 *The Queen, on the application of Delena Wells v Secretary of State for Transport, Local Government and the Regions* [2004] ECR 723 [64]–[65]; Case 68/88 *Commission of the European Communities v Hellenic Republic* [1989] ECR 2965 [23]–[24].

[10] See the landmark judgement in Case 22-70 *Commission of the European Communities v Council of the European Communities* [1971] ECR 263.

Indeed, 'the exact definition of competences is not set at the constitutional level, but rather in the implementation of policy . . . and in the substance of fairly technical pieces of legislation.'[11]

C. EU Environmental Policy

EU environmental law has experienced a high inflation rate, with about 250 main acts, mainly directives, but also hundreds of soft law instruments. The environmental policy framework is now relatively comprehensive. In addition to extensive sectoral instruments—covering pollution of water, air and soil, noise, waste, chemicals, biotechnology, nature conservation, landscape, etc—the EU has adopted some cross-cutting texts on assessment of the effects of certain public and private projects, access to environmental information, public participation in environmental decision-making, and liability for environmental damage. For several years now, the emphasis has been on improving the implementation of existing instruments, called the 'environmental acquis', rather than on adopting new acts.

EU environmental law has had very significant effects on the domestic legislation of member states. In most of the member states, the environmental legal framework is simply equivalent to EU environmental law.[12] EU policy has largely contributed to the diffusion and strengthening of environmental law, and has allowed its harmonization at a relatively high standard among the member states. The EU has also disseminated its rules far beyond its borders, in countries which are members of the European Economic Area,[13] or by setting them as conditions that external actors must meet in order to obtain rewards or avoid sanctions in trade agreements or accession treaties or, even more indirectly, by convincing others of their appropriateness.[14]

EU environmental law is also in constant interaction with international environmental law. Large parts of EU environmental law are being developed under international influence. This is the case in the areas, for example, of trade in endangered wildlife species, protection of the ozone layer, transportation of hazardous waste, acid rain, or climate change. EU environmental law is, in some respects, a communitization of the contents of international environmental law. Conversely, because it often goes further, EU law has had an impact on international environmental law, and has pushed it forward in its turn. The issue of access to environmental

[11] Hans Vedder, 'The Formalities and Substance of EU External Environmental Competence: Stuck between Climate Change and Competitiveness' in Elisa Morgera (ed), *The External Environmental Policy of the European Union: EU and International Law Perspectives* (CUP 2012) 11.

[12] Ludwig Kramer, *EU Environmental Law* (Sweet & Maxwell 2011).

[13] The European Economic Area has been ratified by the European Union, Iceland, Liechtenstein, and Norway.

[14] Frank Schimmelfennig, 'EU External Governance and Europeanization Beyond the EU' in David Levi-Faur (ed), *The Oxford Handbook of Governance* (OUP 2012) 659.

information is a good illustration of the dynamic interactions between international and EU law.[15]

It is first of all up to member states to finance and implement Community environmental legislation in their respective national systems. To that end, they must monitor the application of EU law and report on it to the Commission. The Commission for its part is often referred to as the 'Guardian of the Treaty'; it 'shall ensure the application of the Treaties, and of measures adopted by the institutions pursuant to them'.[16] It has the possibility of triggering infringement proceedings whenever it believes that a member state has breached EU law. If necessary, the Commission can then refer the case to the ECJ. Some of the latter's judgements have played an important role in improving the application of EU environmental law. Moreover, if a member state does not comply with the Court's judgement within a reasonable timeframe, the Commission may trigger new infringement proceedings with, this time, the eventuality of (deterrent) pecuniary sanctions. The monitoring of the implementation of European environmental law is more sophisticated and elaborated than the monitoring of international environmental law.[17]

The EU is widely seen[18] as the best guarantor of the correct application of EU environmental laws.[19] In addition to the cases brought on the Commission's own-initiative, EU citizens' complaints are the main source of information on the implementation of EU law; the Commission receives 600 or so complaints per annum. The highest number of new Commission enforcement actions in 2016 was related to the environmental 'acquis' (19%) whereas only 10% of the registered complaints concerned environmental legislation.[20] The Commission has significantly increased the number of initiatives in order to ensure greater effectiveness of environmental law.[21]

D. Recent Developments and Prospects

At the domestic, regional, and international levels, the early years of environmental law—from the 1970s to 1990s—were characterized by normative frenzy. Emphasis was primarily placed on the development of a body of regulations aimed at environmental protection. As this body of regulations reached critical mass, academics and

[15] Marc Pallemaerts (ed), *The Aarhus Convention at Ten: Interactions and Tensions between Conventional International Law and EU Environmental Law* (Europa Law 2011); see also Chapter 21, 'Public Participation', in this volume.

[16] TEU, art 17.1.

[17] See also Chapters 51 and 52, 'Compliance Theory' and 'Transparency Procedures', in this volume.

[18] By 83% of EU citizens.

[19] Environment Commission, 'Environment poll: citizens trust the EU, but expect more' (25 January 2018).

[20] EU, 'Monitoring the implementation of EU Law, Tools and Challenges—Study' (2017) 7.

[21] See eg Commission, 'EU actions to improve environmental compliance and governance' COM (2018) 10 final.

practitioners highlighted the causes of the relative ineffectiveness of many adopted instruments and the means to remedy it. Because environmental threats are worsening, strengthening the effectiveness of environmental law is a major challenge for the future.[22]

The EU Commission has followed this trend and has developed a strategy since its 1996 Communication.[23] Since then it has adopted several complementary documents aimed at providing member states with tools to improve implementation on the ground and clarifying the Commission's enforcement strategy to tackle breaches of EU environmental law.[24] The strategy articulates preventive and corrective measures and is based on a combination of means. It fits within a wider Commission's strategy for improving implementation of EU law.[25] Following this strategic approach, the Commission published, on 3 February 2017, the Environmental Implementation Review package, which includes a Communication that proposes specific actions in order to improve the situation, and an annex that suggests priorities for action aiming at a better environmental implementation by each of the EU member states.[26]

Deliberation on the choice of instruments has led to experimentation with market-based tools—emissions trading schemes, ecolabelling[27]– in addition to more classical command-and-control approaches. Several instruments aim at supporting the implementation and enforcement of EU environmental legislation, such as the directive on environmental liability,[28] the recommendation providing for minimum criteria for environmental inspections,[29] or the directive on the protection of the environment through criminal law.[30] An informal network of environmental authorities of the EU member states was set up in 1992. Called IMPEL—for European Union Network for the Implementation and Enforcement of Environmental Law—it brings together acceding and candidate countries of the EU, European Economic Area, and European Free Trade Association countries. It promotes a more efficient implementation of EU environmental legislation by information and experience sharing, or joint projects.

In the last few years, the European Commission has focused on its REFIT programme (Regulatory Fitness and Performance Programme) set up by the 2015 'Better Regulation

[22] See Chapter 57, 'Effectiveness', in this volume.

[23] Commission, 'Implementing Community environmental law' COM (96) 500 final.

[24] For instance Commission, 'Improving the delivery of benefits from EU environment measures: building confidence through better knowledge and responsiveness' COM/2012/095 final.

[25] See Commission, 'A Europe of Results—Applying Community Law' COM/2007/0502 final.

[26] Commission, 'The EU Environmental Implementation Review: Common challenges and how to combine efforts to deliver better results' COM (2017) 63 final.

[27] See Chapters 6 and 53, 'Instrument Choice' and 'Market Mechanisms', in this volume.

[28] Directive 2004/35/CE of the European Parliament and of the Council of 21 April 2004 on environmental liability with regard to the prevention and remedying of environmental damage [2004] OJ L143/56.

[29] Recommendation of the European Parliament and of the Council of 4 April 2001 providing for minimum criteria for environmental inspections in the Member States [2001] OJ L118/41.

[30] Directive 2008/99/EC of the European Parliament and of the Council of 19 November 2008 on the protection of the environment through criminal law [2008] OJ L328/28.

Communication' to determine 'how to make EU regulation more efficient and effective while reducing burden and without undermining policy objectives'.[31] Under this programme, the Commission is screening the entire stockpile of EU legislation on an ongoing and systematic basis to identify burdens, inconsistencies, ineffective measures, and determine corrective actions. The Commission started its systematic review of existing legislation on environmental policy with the legislation on water, waste, environmental liability, protection of birds and habitats, and on chemicals legislation outside of REACH.[32] It acknowledges that this is a complex exercise.[33] As yet, REFIT has not produced very concrete consequences, but it carries the risk of deregulation and, in the end, of a lower level of environmental protection. Indeed, a better or smart regulation agenda is easily hijacked by those seeking less regulation for their own narrow interests.[34] Furthermore, even if simplification is actually a challenge, '[g]iven the complexity and breadth of the whole environmental problem, the ideal of a clear, transparent, and easy to understand legislative package is illusionary'.[35]

III. EXTERNAL DIMENSION OF ENVIRONMENTAL COMPETENCE—THE EU AS A GLOBAL ACTOR?

The EU participates in environmental international agreements. It contributes to the enforcement of international environmental law in the EU legal order. But can we speak of an external environmental policy?

A. Participation in Environmental International Agreements: A Shared Competence

The EU has an international legal personality and thus the capacity to enter into agreements with states and international organizations, if accepted as a contracting party. Its external competence was originally developed through case law, and then by

[31] Commission, 'Better regulation for better results—An EU agenda' COM (2015) 215 final.

[32] REACH is the Regulation (EC) No 1907/2006 of the European Parliament and of the Council of 18 December 2006 concerning the Registration, Evaluation, Authorisation and Restriction of Chemicals, establishing a European Chemicals Agency [2006] OJ L396/1.

[33] 'Monitoring the implementation' (n 20) 23.

[34] Andrew Farmer, 'Better Regulation and the Future of EU Environmental Policy' *Institute for European Environmental Policy* (20 July 2017).

[35] 'Concluding Observations' in Marjan Peeters and Rosa Uylenburg (eds), *EU Environmental Legislation: Legal Perspectives on Regulatory Strategies (New Horizons in Environmental and Energy Law Series)* (Edward Elgar 2014) 235.

the Lisbon Treaty.[36] The EU's external competence is clear and explicit in the field of the environment. According to Article 191.4 TFEU:

> Within their respective spheres of competence, the Union and the Member States shall cooperate with third countries and with the competent international organisations. The arrangements for Union cooperation may be the subject of agreements between the Union and the third parties concerned. The previous subparagraph shall be without prejudice to Member States' competence to negotiate in international bodies and to conclude international agreements.

In practice, the EU has had an aggressive strategy and is now a party to about forty environmental treaties, including the 1976 Barcelona Convention for the Protection of the Mediterranean Sea against Pollution and almost all its protocols, the 1998 Aarhus Convention on Access to Information, Public Participation in Decision-making and Access to Justice in Environmental Matters, the 1991 Espoo Convention on Environment Impact Assessment in a Transboundary Context, the 2001 Stockholm Convention on Persistent Organic Pollutants, the 1989 Basel Convention on the Control of Transboundary Movements of Hazardous Wastes and their Disposal, the 1992 Convention for the Protection of the Marine Environment of the North-East Atlantic, the 1992 Convention on Biological Diversity, the 1987 Montreal Protocol on Substances that Deplete the Ozone Layer, the 1992 United Nations Framework Convention on Climate Change (UNFCCC), its 1997 Kyoto Protocol and the 2015 Paris Agreement, and the 1973 Convention on International Trade in Endangered Species of Wild Fauna and Flora (CITES).

Most environmental treaties allow the EU's participation as an REIO—the only organization belonging to this category—but it was not the case as regards the oldest treaties, at least initially. Some of these have been amended for this purpose. For instance, CITES did not originally authorize membership of international organizations despite covering matters such as environmental protection and trade, which fall under the competence of the Union. Decisions taken by the Conference of the Parties like the amendments to the CITES Appendices also affect EU legislation. The Convention was modified upon EU request in 1983 by the 'Gaborone Amendment' which allows a REIO to accede to CITES. The amendment only entered into force in 2013, after ratification by two-thirds of the eighty states that were party to the CITES in 1983. The EU, which was until then given an observer status, finally became a full party in 2015.[37] When an agreement affects the EU competence, member states that are a party are obliged to act in the Union's interest in its context.

The EU appears as a distinctive player in multilateral environmental negotiations. Its unity in external representation, which no other group of countries has achieved, makes

36 TFEU, Title V.

37 See CITES, art XXI(2).

'the Union together with its members one of the most influential players in multilateral environmental affairs'.[38]

In the environmental field, as a matter of shared competence, the Union accedes along with the member states. This creates complex internal and external problems. It can cause confusion on the sharing of competence and responsibility between the EU and its member states. Third parties need to know and understand what is within the remit of the Union. In the CITES example, its Article XXI(3) specifies that in their instruments of accession, such organizations 'shall declare the extent of their competence with respect to the matters governed by the Convention'. Then, '[i]n matters within their competence, such regional economic integration organisations shall exercise the rights and fulfil the obligations which this Convention attributes to their Member States, which are Parties to the Convention. In such cases the Member States of the organisations shall not be entitled to exercise such rights individually'.[39] The same rule applies to the right to vote.[40]

Most environmental treaties which allow the EU's accession alongside that of its member states use the same wording. But what seems to be clear in theory is not so clear in practice. The distribution is frequently discussed within the EU and evolves over time, with external consequences. Indeed, the mixed nature of most international environmental agreements generates peculiar difficulties regarding their negotiation and adoption as well as their implementation. The process for concluding a new convention is now, after the Lisbon Treaty, detailed by Article 218, except for the common commercial policy covered by Article 207. Since Lisbon, the Commission is explicitly mandated to represent the EU externally.[41] Within the framework of multilateral environmental agreements' (MEAs) treaty bodies, the Commission's officials represent the Union as well. However, some member states are reluctant since it reduces their leeway. The continuing power struggle between institutions (Council and Commission) and between institutions and member states does not facilitate the role of the EU. In the end, it hampers the effectiveness and visibility of the European policy. Once the treaty is adopted and in force, speaking with one voice on the international scene within treaty bodies requires considerable preparatory work at the European level. Because of its internal contradictions, the EU is not always able to perform, beyond its member states, as a powerful negotiator and can be weaker than the collection of its individual member states even if, as already mentioned, the EU and its member states are bound by the principle of loyal cooperation.[42]

[38] Matthias Buck, 'The EU's Representation in Multilateral Environmental Negotiations After Lisbon' in Morgera (n 11) 76.

[39] CITES, art XXI(4).

[40] CITES, art XXI(5).

[41] Except for matters falling under the Common Foreign and Security Policy (CFSP) which is not the case of environmental policy.

[42] TEU, art 4.3.

B. Enforcement of International Environmental Law in the EU Legal Order

According to the TFEU, 'Agreements concluded by the Union are binding upon the institutions of the Union and on its Member States'.[43] The ECJ has confirmed on several occasions that the Union is bound by international rules, including customary rules, which are an integral part of the Union legal order.[44] The treaties binding upon the Union are fully formal legal sources. The ECJ has recognized the primacy of international law on Union secondary legislation.[45] From this point of view, mixed agreements have the same status as purely Union agreements, insofar as their provisions fall within the scope of Community competence. In the hierarchy of norms, treaties are between primary and secondary legislation. All EU international agreements, once incorporated in the EU legal order, become the *law of the land*.[46] According to the Court,

> In ensuring compliance with commitments arising from an agreement concluded by the Community institutions, the Member States therefore fulfil, within the Community system, an obligation in relation to the Community, which has assumed responsibility for the due performance of the agreement.[47]

Hence, the ECJ has the jurisdiction to interpret and appraise the compatibility of national law with international treaties, as long as the Union is committed, alone or alongside its member states. This also applies to customary law.

The Court has recognized the direct application, or at least the justiciability of international agreements when their provisions are sufficiently clear and detailed and do not need to be completed by subsequent legislation.[48] It is not automatic, however; a balance is to be found between the obligation to comply with international law and the integrity of the EU legal order.[49] Due to the special nature of the EU, it has to ensure compliance with international obligations not only by its own institutions, but also by member states which sometimes are not even contracting parties to EU agreements. By contrast, the

[43] TFUE, art 216.2.

[44] Case C-366/10 *Air Transport Association of America and Others v Secretary of State for Energy and Climate Change* [2011] ECR I-13755 [101].

[45] Cf. Joined cases 21-24/72 *International Fruit Company NV and others v Produktschap voor Groenten en Fruit* [1972] ECR 1219; Case 181/73 *R. & V. Haegeman v Belgian State* [1974] ECR 449.

[46] Francesca Martines, 'Direct Effect of International Agreements of the European Union' *European Journal of International Law*, 25/1 (2014): 129, 130.

[47] Case C-239/03 *Commission of the European Communities v French Republic ('Étang de Berre')* [2004] ECR I-9325 [25]–[26], [31]; see also Case 12/86 *Meryem Demirel v Stadt Schwäbisch Gmünd* [1987] ECR 3719 [9]; Case C-13/00 *Commission of the European Communities v Ireland* [2002] ECR I-2943 [14].

[48] Case C-344/04 *The Queen, on the application of International Air Transport Association and European Low Fares Airline Association v Department for Transport* [2006] ECR I-403; Case C-612/13 *ClientEarth v European Commission* (ECJ, 16 July 2015) [33]–[37].

[49] Martines (n 46) 147.

EU order is much less permeable as regards the international law obligations assumed only by member states, in situations in which the EU is not a contracting party.[50]

Notwithstanding this observation, international environmental agreements concluded by the EU benefit from the European monitoring mechanism.[51] Even if it is not perfect, it remains quite sophisticated and effective compared to other international mechanisms.

From an external point of view, this mixed participation raises specific issues regarding responsibility in case of a breach of an international obligation.[52] In this case, is/are the EU or/and member states liable? The Court of Justice of the EU (CJEU) has suggested that the non-performance of obligations under environmental mixed agreements by the EU and/or member states can result in joint responsibility.[53] In the case of a dispute between EU countries, the *MOX Plant* case has shown that, bound by the principle of loyal cooperation, a member state cannot institute proceedings against another member state on the basis of an MEA without previously being cleared by Union institutions.[54]

It is also important to consider non-contentious international control mechanisms. Indeed, most MEAs are now equipped with institutionalized multilateral control procedures known as compliance or non-compliance mechanisms.[55] Member states and/or the Union can be involved with such procedures. From this point of view, interesting interactions between the European control mechanism and the Kyoto Protocol compliance procedure have been identified, contributing to ensure the very credibility of the Protocol and the reliability of the international and European economic tools to reduce greenhouse gas emissions.[56] In another field, several cases were

[50] Ibid, 135; see Case C-308/06 *The Queen, on the application of International Association of Independent Tanker Owners (Intertanko) and Others v Secretary of State for Transport* [2008] ECR I-4057 [50]; see also Judgement, CJEU, 8 March 2011, Case C-240/09, *Lesoochranárske zoskupenie VLK c/ Ministerstvo životného prostredia Slovenskej republiky* [2011] ECR I-1255, where the Court finds that art 9.3 of the Aarhus Convention has no direct effect in Union Law; see Allan Rosas, 'The Status in EU Law of International Agreements Concluded by EU Member States' *Fordham International Law Journal*, 34/5 (2011): 1304.

[51] Ami Barav, *Judicial Enforcement and Implementation of European Union Law* (Bruylant 2017).

[52] See Chapter 58, 'International Environmental Responsibility and Liability', in this volume.

[53] Case C-316/91 *European Parliament v Council of the European Union* [1994] ECR I-625 [29]; Case C-239/03 *Commission of the European Communities v French Republic* [2004] ECR I-9325 (*Etang de Berre II*), quoted by André Nollkaemper, 'Joint Responsibility between the EU and Member States for Non-Performance of Obligations Under Multilateral Environmental Agreements' in Morgera (n 11) 305.

[54] The Court has recently recalled its exclusive jurisdiction regarding disputes related to the interpretation and application of the treaties in Case C-284/16 *Slowakische Republik contre Achmea BV* (ECJ, 6 March 2018).

[55] Tullio Treves *et al* (eds), *Non-Compliance Procedures and Mechanisms and the Effectiveness of International Environmental Agreements* (TMC Asser 2009); see also Chapter 56, 'Non-Compliance Procedures', in this volume.

[56] Anne-Sophie Tabau and Sandrine Maljean-Dubois, 'Non-Compliance Mechanisms: Interaction between the Kyoto Protocol System and the European Union' *European Journal of International Law*, 21/3 (2010): 749.

brought before the Aarhus Convention Compliance Committee that raised delicate issues concerning the participation of the EU and its member states: the joint/shared responsibility of the EU and its member states vis-à-vis MEAs; the Union's responsibility with regard to the implementation of MEAs at EU and national levels; the effects of MEAs on the jurisdiction of the ECJ; the responsibility of the EU for the actions of member states that are not party to a MEA.[57]

C. Is There an EU External Environmental Policy?

The EU has now a long-standing practice and a growing role on the international environmental scene. But the organization—more precisely the Commission or the Commission jointly with member states—remains torn between its aspiration to international leadership, an aspiration well-reflected in the Lisbon Treaty, and the hurdles to becoming a truly global actor. The EU's capacity to be a global actor has varied over time. In that respect, the Lisbon Treaty established a new constitutional—legal and institutional—framework, with new treaty rules on EU external representation. It is now under a general obligation to 'promote multilateral solutions to common problems, in particular in the framework of the United Nations'.[58]

The EU increasingly exercises its external action through different instruments—unilateral, bilateral, inter-regional, and multilateral—to support actively the development and implementation of international environmental law.[59] It has demonstrated its role as a promoter of environmental protection standards. For instance, EU incentives motivate third states to ratify environmental treaties.[60] In particular, the EU is the world's largest provider of development assistance. It has, at least in quantitative terms, the potential to support environmental protection objectives and processes.

The channels of influence vary over time, depending on the progress of multilateral cooperation. But the EU performance varies according to the areas involved as well. For instance, in the field of climate change, it has high aspirations to leadership and has been successful—at least at times—in playing an active role. Indeed, climate change has been prioritized and is the most prominent of the areas of EU external action. In addition to its action within the UNFCCC, the EU has increasingly sought to use its political and

[57] Antonio Ali, 'The EU and the Compliance Mechanisms of Multilateral Environmental Agreements: The Case of the Aarhus Convention' in Morgera (n 11) 288.

[58] TEU, art 21.1; see also arts 3.5, 21.2.

[59] Elisa Morgera, 'The Trajectory of EU Biodiversity Cooperation: Supporting Environmental Multilateralism through EU External Action' in Morgera (n 11) 235.

[60] Kai Schulze and Jale Tosun, 'External Dimensions of European Environmental Policy: An Analysis of Environmental Treaty Ratification by Third States' *European Journal of Political Research* 52/5 (2013): 581.

economic influence to advance climate change objectives through its bilateral and inter-regional external relations.[61]

Although the EU has acquired new and more convincing means, and progressively gained external recognition, according to Kramer the EU is 'not equipped to assume a permanent global leadership function'.[62] Despite the new provisions of the Lisbon Treaty,[63] ensuring coherence between environmental protection and other conflicting priorities at the European level (horizontal coherence), and between the external action of the Union and of its member states (vertical coherence) remains a major issue.[64] Furthermore, in the meantime, the EU has been through successive enlargements, making internal cohesion harder. It remains a complex issue as regards the 'unique and evolving nature of the Union as a global actor'.[65]

IV. OTHER REGIONAL ORGANIZATIONS

Other regional organizations have developed environmental policies and actions, although environmental protection is generally not their exclusive task. However, some regional organizations have contributed to the development of international environmental law by adopting secondary legislation, or encouraging the adoption and implementation of new treaties. Grouping fewer and closer states favours consensus-building and may permit more ambitious action than at the global level. Although not exhaustive, examples include the action of the Council of Europe (for instance, with the 1979 Bern Convention on the conservation of wildlife and natural habitats), the African Union (with the 2003 Maputo revised African convention on the conservation of nature and natural resources), the Pacific Regional Environment Programme (eg with the 1995 Convention of Waigani to ban the importation into forum island countries of hazardous and radioactive wastes and to control the transboundary movement and management of hazardous wastes within the South Pacific Region), or the UN regional commissions (for instance, with the 1998 Aarhus Convention on access to information, public participation in decision-making, and access to justice in environmental matters for Europe, or the 2018 Escazú Regional Agreement on access to information, public participation, and justice in environmental matters in Latin America and the Caribbean). Other regional organizations serve more of a policy role, such as the Organisation for Economic Co-operation and Development (OECD).

61 Kati Kulovesi, 'Climate Change in EU External Relations: Please Follow My Example (or I Might Force You To)' in Morgera (n 11) 139.

62 Kramer (n 12) 443.

63 TFEU, art 7; TEU, art 21.3.

64 Marise Cremona, 'Coherence and EU Environmental Policy' in Morgera (n 11) 34.

65 'Introduction' in Morgera (n 11) 1.

V. CONCLUSION

The EU is a distinctive regional organization that has played a major role in the development of demanding domestic environmental laws in EU countries, the application of which it monitors and non-compliance with which it sanctions. This is well illustrated by the concerns raised by the impact of Brexit on environmental protection in the United Kingdom.[66]

The EU internal environmental policy expands on the international stage. Even if it lacks the internal structures and resources fully and effectively to assume a role as a global environmental leader,[67] the EU participates in environmental negotiations, concludes and implements international treaties, and exercises its 'soft power' to promote the development and implementation of international environmental law. It contributes to improving the effectiveness of international environmental treaties and principles.

The content of EU environmental law, being itself the result of an international negotiation, has improved in terms of legitimacy and appropriateness. It is able to inspire international environmental rules and domestic legislation of third countries. Legal transplants of EU law into the domestic laws of non-EU countries are frequent.[68]

The Lisbon Treaty offers new opportunities and challenges as regards the consistency and effectiveness of the EU external policy.[69] But there still are uncertainties and thus room for experimentation. The EU has to consolidate its role as a global actor, and to adapt its structures to this end. European integration is a unique adventure and it takes time to overcome understandable resistance. From this point of view, the challenges presented by the last enlargement, as well as the consequences of Brexit, deserve special attention.

BIBLIOGRAPHY

Nicolas de Sadeleer, *EU Environmental Law and the Internal Market* (OUP 2014)

Suzanne Kingston, *European Environmental Law* (CUPs 2017)

David Langlet and Said Mahmoudi, *EU Environmental Law and Policy* (OUP 2016)

Elisa Morgera (ed), *The External Environmental Policy of the European Union: EU and International Law Perspectives* (CUP 2012)

Patrick Thieffry, *Handbook of European Environmental Law* (Bruylant 2018)

66 Colin Reid, 'Brexit and the Future of UK Environmental Law' *Journal of Energy & Natural Resources Law*, 34/4 (2016): 407.

67 Kramer (n 12) 444.

68 Sean Whittaker, 'The Right of Access to Environmental Information and Legal Transplant Theory: Lessons from London and Beijing' *Transnational Environmental Law*, 6/3 (2017): 509.

69 'Introduction' in Morgera (n 11) 3.

CHAPTER 38

NON-STATE ACTORS

J MICHAEL ANGSTADT AND MICHELE BETSILL

I. INTRODUCTION

NON-STATE actors (NSAs) encompass a range of entities that collectively extend international environmental law beyond traditional state authority in numerous regimes. Characterized by considerable breadth and diversity, NSAs exist within the traditional, state-centric treaty architecture while simultaneously contesting its structure. Several individual sub-classes of NSAs appear elsewhere in this volume, including epistemic communities[1] and business and industry.[2] Collectively, however, NSAs perform key roles that advance international environmental law; indeed, some suggest that, 'with the exception of human rights, no other area has experienced such a strong participation from civil society'.[3]

Because diverse institutional actors can satisfy the definition of 'non-state actor', this chapter analyses a subset of NSAs: non-governmental organizations (NGOs). However, it is necessary to further delimit analysis for two reasons. First, NGOs are broadly and variously defined by scholars, who lack consensus on how best to delineate them.[4] Moreover, NGOs, like NSAs more broadly, may include actors bearing diverse motivations. Some definitions include criminal syndicates and drug cartels, emphasizing that entities need not possess a social welfare motivation to qualify broadly as NGOs.[5]

[1] See Chapter 40, 'Epistemic Communities', in this volume.

[2] See Chapter 41, 'Business and Industry', in this volume.

[3] Jorge Viñuales and Pierre-Marie Dupuy, *International Environmental Law* (CUP 2015) 32.

[4] See eg Kerstin Martens, 'Mission impossible? Defining nongovernmental organizations' *Voluntas*, 13/3 (2002): 271, 272.

[5] Rodney Hall and Thomas Biersteker (eds), *The Emergence of Private Authority in Global Governance* (CUP 2002).

Therefore, this chapter will constrain analysis to non-profit and non-violent entities that promote the public good.[6]

Second, international environmental law is expansive, and alongside treaties, NGOs may engage with soft law,[7] private standard-setting efforts,[8] and domestic implementation of international regulations.[9] There are numerous opportunities for NGOs to influence international environmental law and diverse roles that NGOs may perform to advance its development. Similarly, an extensive existing literature characterizes NGOs, and this chapter does not attempt an exhaustive review. Instead, it characterizes contemporary environmental NGOs and the nature of their contributions to international environmental law.

To do so, this chapter first defines NGOs, identifying some common characteristics that influence their ability to advance international environmental law, and noting fundamental criteria used to distinguish among NGOs. It then discusses three key functions that NGOs perform in contemporary international environmental law: serving as activists engaged in agenda-setting functions; performing diplomacy to shape and facilitate international rule-making processes; and contributing to rule-making, implementation, and enforcement in contemporary global governance. The chapter concludes by forecasting strong continued NGO participation in developing non-treaty international environmental law.

II. NGO ATTRIBUTES

This chapter emphasizes NGOs' considerable diversity by underscoring their multiple contributions in international environmental law. However, it also builds upon a rich scholarly foundation which seeks to define NGOs collectively, notes several possible bases for sub-categorization, and identifies attributes that distinguish NGOs from other actors.

First, international environmental law scholars have offered foundational definitions of NGOs. Some such attempts characterize NGOs expansively, including all actors within 'that slice of collective life that takes place above the individual yet below the state',[10] and encapsulating essentially all non-state actors. The United Nations (UN) has employed a similarly broad definition, characterizing NGOs as 'any international organization which is not established by inter-governmental agreement'.[11] This approach

[6] See eg Bas Arts, 'Non-State Actors in Global Environmental Governance: New Arrangements Beyond the State' in Mathias Koenig-Archibugi and Michael Zurn (eds), *New Modes of Governance in the Global System: Exploring Publicness, Delegation and Inclusiveness* (Palgrave Macmillan 2006) 177.

[7] See Chapter 25, 'Soft Law', in this volume.

[8] See Chapter 26, 'Private and Quasi-Private Standards', in this volume.

[9] See Chapter 59, 'National Implementation', in this volume.

[10] Paul Wapner, *Environmental Activism and World Civic Politics* (SUNY Press 1996) 158.

[11] Shamima Ahmed and David Potter, *NGOs in International Politics* (Kumarian Press 2006) 8.

provides some sense of the scope of NGOs engaged in international environmental law; for example, the UN Environment Programme (UNEP) documents nearly 500 accredited NGOs,[12] and, as discussed in Section IV, other environmental regimes enjoy similarly expansive civil society engagement.

However, other international law and international relations scholars define NGOs more narrowly. For instance, Martens characterizes NGOs as 'formal (professionalized) independent societal organizations whose primary aim is to promote common goals at the national or the international level'.[13] This narrower definition permits researchers to emphasize NGOs' orientation towards promoting public goods, considerable dependence upon memberships and private donations (rather than public funding), and organizational structures that promote continuity.[14] Charnovitz, similarly, defines NGOs within international law as 'groups of persons or of societies, freely created by private initiative, that pursue an interest in matters that cross or transcend national borders and are not profit seeking'.[15] Beyond excluding for-profit entities, Charnovitz's approach focuses upon organizations that source members from across national political boundaries.[16] Together, these definitions emphasize two criteria adopted by this chapter: NGOs' non-profit and public interest orientation. Both factors help to distinguish NGOs and their contributions from other international environmental law actors.

While NGOs in international environmental law share numerous traits, researchers also identify several distinguishing features, including the character of their membership, the scope of activities that they undertake, and their primary aims.[17] In terms of membership characteristics, researchers variously highlight the contributions of expert NGOs, general membership NGOs,[18] and NGOs that 'bridge the lay-expert, activist-professional and local-global divides' that traditionally complicate international environmental law.[19] Second, researchers distinguish NGOs by the scope of their activities. For instance, domestic NGOs that engage with international environmental law within

[12] See UN Environment, 'List of Accredited Organizations' (6 June 2018) <https://www.unenvironment.org/civil-society-engagement/accreditation/list-accredited-organizations> accessed 15 October 2018.

[13] Martens (n 4) 282.

[14] Ibid.

[15] Steve Charnovitz, 'Nongovernmental Organizations and International Law' *American Journal of International Law*, 100/2 (2006): 348, 350.

[16] Ibid.

[17] See eg Sebastian Oberthür *et al*, *Participation of Non-Governmental Organisations in International Environmental Governance: Legal Basis and Practical Experience* (Ecologic—Institute for International and European Environmental Policy 2002) 33–37.

[18] See eg Jiang Ru and Leonard Ortolano, 'Development of Citizen-Organized Environmental NGOs in China' *Voluntas*, 20/2 (2009): 141.

[19] Sheila Jasanoff, 'NGOs and the Environment: From Knowledge to Action' *Third World Quarterly*, 18/3 (1997): 579, 581.

countries perform valuable regime design and advocacy functions,[20] and they are complemented by similar organizations across domestic contexts and governmental settings.[21] At the same time, domestic NGOs are complemented by numerous international NGOs (INGOs) in diverse domestic contexts[22] that undertake consciousness-raising,[23] management and oversight, and that seek to influence regime design and negotiation.[24] Accordingly, contemporary international environmental law reflects the contributions of NGOs operating at both domestic and global scales. Finally, some distinguish NGOs by the activities that they undertake. Charnovitz suggests that NGOs perform a variety of functions, including assisting during regime development and negotiation, interpreting international law, participating during international adjudicative proceedings, and contributing to enforcement efforts.[25] Likewise, Oberthür *et al* note that environmental NGO (ENGO) functions can include knowledge enhancement, advocacy, participation, transparency, and support.[26]

While individual NGOs may be distinguished by numerous factors, they also share several attributes unique or distinctive among international environmental law actors. First, NGOs advance international environmental law development meaningfully within a state-centric conception of international law. The subject matter expertise, legal and technical competence, and focused environmental mission of many NGOs equips them ideally to operate 'within the system'. At the same time, global environmental regulation and legal governance increasingly rejects the primacy of formal, state-based sovereignty.[27] NGOs are also uniquely positioned to function 'outside the system' in a broader conception of international environmental law. Finally, the diversity of ENGOs renders them uniquely equipped to advance interdependencies between state-based actors and others.[28] Accordingly, the various capacities that equip NGOs to both support and supplement state-based regulation also enable NGOs to negotiate and mediate 'between the systems'.

[20] Kemi Fuentes-George, 'Neoliberalism, Environmental Justice, and the Convention on Biodiversity: How Problematizing the Commodification of Nature Affects Regime Effectiveness' *Global Environmental Politics*, 13/4 (2013): 144.

[21] See eg Tobias Böhmelt, 'Political Opportunity Structures in Dictatorships? Explaining ENGO Existence in Autocratic Regimes' *Journal of Environment and Development*, 23/4 (2014): 446.

[22] Dewan Ahsan, Angel DelValls, and Julian Blasco, 'The Relationship of National and International Environmental NGOs in Bangladesh and Their Role in Wetland Conservation' *International Journal of Environmental Research*, 3/1 (2009): 23.

[23] See eg Carol Farbotko and Heather Lazrus, 'The First Climate Refugees? Contesting Global Narratives of Climate Change in Tuvalu' *Global Environmental Change*, 22/2 (2012): 382.

[24] See eg Michele Betsill and Elisabeth Corell, 'NGO Influence in International Environmental Negotiations: A Framework for Analysis' *Global Environmental Politics*, 1/4 (2001): 65; see also Böhmelt (n 21).

[25] See eg Charnovitz (n 15) 352–355.

[26] Oberthür *et al* (n 17) 40–51.

[27] See Dan Tarlock, 'The Role of Non-Governmental Organisations in the Development of International Environmental Law' *Chicago-Kent Law Review*, 68/1 (1992): 61.

[28] See eg Farhana Yamin, 'NGOs and International Environmental Law: A Critical Evaluation of their Roles and Responsibilities' *Review of European, Comparative & International Environmental Law*, 10/2 (2001): 149.

III. NGOS AS ACTIVISTS

Within international environmental law, NGOs perform multiple activist functions. Collectively, they set agendas, elevate the prominence of issues not yet subject to international regulation, maintain issues' centrality within the collective consciousness, and use media and public attention to shape negotiation outcomes to favour NGOs' objectives. These functions facilitate international environmental law's development in key regimes, including maritime[29] and climate issues,[30] and they incorporate diverse perspectives into policy-making. NGOs pursue these contributions through various efforts including: direct action intended to raise awareness, lobbying within formal treaty architectures intended to provide information, and facilitation of conferences and dialogue intended to increase access.

A. Direct Action Advocacy

First, NGOs undertake direct action. These efforts frequently seek to generate public sentiment favouring a group's perspective. Thus, while advocacy NGOs may engage directly in the international negotiations and regulatory efforts discussed below, many remain focused on undertaking campaigns outside of formal policy-making that increase public awareness of international issues.

While NGO engagement tactics differ, many groups utilize activism surrounding conferences of parties (COPs), meetings of parties (MOPs), and other key gatherings, particularly when their ability to participate directly is limited.[31] NGOs introduce alternative perspectives into the narrow context of state-defined interests, and they use activism to insert science in decision-making.[32] However, this engagement may be conditioned by provisions limiting NGO participation in some formal settings.[33]

In addition to NGO activism surrounding intergovernmental negotiations, NGOs engage directly within contentious environmental regimes, where protest activities may raise awareness and alter outcomes. In recent years, NGOs have been particularly active in whaling[34] and energy development regimes,[35] seeking to give voice to citizen and non-human interests across scales and counterbalance powerful governmental and corporate

[29] See Chapter 31, 'The Protection of the Marine Environment: Pollution and Fisheries', in this volume.

[30] See Chapter 29, 'Climate Change', in this volume.

[31] Shannon Orr, 'Institutional Control and Climate Change Activism at COP 21 in Paris' *Global Environmental Politics*, 16/3 (2016): 23.

[32] See Betsill and Corell (n 24) (process tracing analysis of NGO influence).

[33] See eg Orr (n 31).

[34] See eg Anthony Moffa, 'Two Competing Models of Activism, One Goal: A Case Study of Anti-Whaling Campaigns in the Southern Ocean' *Yale Journal of International Law*, 37/1 (2012): 201.

[35] See eg Paul Bowles and Fiona MacPhail, 'The Town That Said "No" to the Enbridge Northern Gateway Pipeline: The Kitimat Plebiscite of 2014' *Extractive Industries and Society*, 4/1 (2017): 15.

interests. Similarly, NGOs have elevated critical perspectives in the proliferating climate justice movement, critiquing the treaty-based climate regime and emphasizing vulnerability among sensitive populations.[36] While the outcomes of direct advocacy efforts remain contested and uneven, they demonstrate NGO capacity to broaden participation within international environmental law regimes and negotiations.

B. NGO Lobbying and Engagement Efforts

In addition to undertaking direct action, NGOs frequently seek to influence formal international environmental law negotiations through lobbying and other indirect agenda-setting and engagement. While NGOs can formally engage in some international environmental law regimes and intergovernmental forums, as discussed in Section IV, NGOs can also influence decision-making without directly participating.

First, because states are the dominant actors in formal, treaty-based regimes, NGOs lobby state delegations before negotiations to promote their agendas. NGOs undertake efforts, both solicited and unsolicited, that seek to shape state engagement.[37] Such NGO efforts are well-documented and widely practised;[38] for example, a study of forestry initiatives found evidence of extensive NGO lobbying at national and higher governmental levels.[39]

NGOs also undertake lobbying directly within multilateral negotiations. Through 'corridor diplomacy', NGOs encourage diplomats to adopt positions that advance their interests.[40] At international levels, NGOs engage in environmental regimes both individually and through collective efforts reflecting common interests in particular issue regimes, including climate. In pursuing these objectives, NGOs embrace diverse tactics, including face-to-face lobbying and outreach to other delegates.[41]

NGOs also generate publications, prepare policy briefs, and author white papers that support decision-making.[42] In some regimes, these forms of written engagement are pervasive; one study estimated that NGOs furnish up to 80% of information received by the UN Center on Human Rights.[43] Similar levels of engagement are likely within

[36] See eg Michele Betsill, 'NGOs' in Karin Bäckstrand and Eva Lövbrand (eds), *Research Handbook on Climate Governance* (Edward Elgar 2016) 254.

[37] See Kal Raustiala, 'States, NGOs, and International Environmental Institutions' *International Studies Quarterly*, 41/4 (1997): 719, 724.

[38] See eg Yamin (n 31).

[39] See Clare Barnes and Frank van Laerhoven, 'Making It Last? Analysing the Role of NGO Interventions in the Development of Institutions for Durable Collective Action in Indian Community Forestry' *Environmental Science and Policy*, 53 (2015): 192, 201.

[40] Raustiala (n 37).

[41] Marcelo Varella, *The Role of Nongovernmental Organizations in International Environmental Law* (2013) <https://dx.doi.org/10.2139/ssrn.2237677> accessed 15 October 2018.

[42] See Joy Twemlow, 'Non-Governmental Organisations and International Environmental Law: The Search for Legitimacy' *Public Interest Law Journal of New Zealand*, 1 (2013): 39, 48.

[43] Varella (n 41) 67.

international environmental law regimes, where numerous groups provide technical information,[44] generate reports, and collaborate among public interest international lawyers.[45] While the cumulative effect of these direct NGO lobbying efforts is not always readily quantifiable,[46] NGO engagement is believed to be effective in influencing developing states and other actors in international environmental law regimes.[47]

C. NGO Conferences and Dialogue

Third, NGOs facilitate conferences and dialogue to promote evaluation and interpretation of international environmental law issues favouring their perspective. In some instances, these conferences provide a parallel forum for engagement alongside formal negotiations.[48] Elsewhere, NGOs organize independent conferences explicitly geared to non-state actors.[49] Altogether, the foregoing mechanisms represent NGOs' diverse approaches to advocacy in contemporary international environmental law.

IV. NGOS AS DIPLOMATS

While NGOs make substantial activist contributions to international environmental law, they also perform valuable diplomatic functions. Working alongside other actors, they shape and advance desired policies in international environmental regimes. Like state diplomats, NGOs exert formal agency in international negotiations to facilitate information exchange and shape the proposed content of legal agreements.

In formal terms, many international organizations, institutions, and conferences provide avenues for NGO participation.[50] Though the specific mechanisms differ, organizations frequently permit NGO engagement due to belief that NGOs offer

44 See eg World Wildlife Fund, 'Working for Strong International Laws and Agreements' (2017) <https://wwf.panda.org/our_work/governance/policy/conventions/> accessed 15 October 2018.

45 Earthjustice, 'Office: International Program' <https://earthjustice.org/about/offices/international> accessed 15 October 2018.

46 Betsill and Corell (n 24).

47 Jen Allan and Jennifer Hadden, 'Exploring the Framing Power of NGOs in Global Climate Politics' *Environmental Politics*, 26/4 (2017): 600, 614.

48 See Barbara Gemmill and Abimbola Bamidele-Izu, 'The Role of NGOs and Civil Society in Global Environmental Governance' in Daniel Esty and Maria Ivanova (eds), *Global Environmental Governance: Options and Opportunities* (Yale School of Forestry and Environmental Studies 2002) 5; see also Shannon Orr, 'Institutional Control and Climate Change Activism at COP 21 in Paris' *Global Environmental Politics*, 16/3 (2016): 23.

49 See eg NGO CoNGO, 'CoNGO Assembly adopts resolution on UN funding, raises alarm that decreased funding imperils NGO access at the UN' (2017) <https://www.ngocongo.org/> accessed 15 October 2018.

50 Betsill and Corell (n 24); Oberthür *et al* (n 17).

expertise and descriptively represent diverse and historically marginalized interests.[51] As the UN Economic and Social Council (ECOSOC) notes, NGO engagement enables the Council 'to avail itself of valuable and expert advice' that includes 'specialized competence, hands-on experience and flexibility that is of great benefit to the UN'. In exchange, NGOs gain 'the opportunity to be heard by a truly global audience and contribute to its agenda'.[52]

Within formal treaty regimes, foundational authorization for NGO engagement in international environmental law derives from Article 71 of the UN Charter. Its provisions permit formal consultation by NGOs possessing subject matter competence and permissively authorize ECOSOC to credential both international NGOs and domestic NGOs after consulting with relevant member states. In turn, ECOSOC outlines formal procedures for NGO engagement and repeatedly asserts that NGO participation can advance international law negotiation and development.[53]

Many other forums integral to international environmental law negotiation also provide for NGO engagement.[54] For instance, UNEP maintains a Civil Society Unit which seeks actively to promote 'transparency and inclusiveness in the intergovernmental decision-making process at UN Environment'.[55] This inclusive mandate has been repeatedly affirmed, including in the Rio+20 'The Future We Want' outcome document,[56] which exhorts the organ to 'explor[e] new mechanisms to promote transparency and the *effective engagement of civil society*'.[57] Additionally, many international environmental regimes enable civil society engagement. For instance, the 1992 UN Framework Convention on Climate Change (UNFCCC) has permitted NGO engagement in climate change negotiations since 1992, uses a formal process to admit qualified NGOs,[58] and currently grants observer status to diverse NGO entities.[59]

Permitting participation in international negotiations enables NGOs to contribute expert insight and perspectives in formal settings. For example, NGOs with consultative status in ECOSOC may attend meetings of ECOSOC and subsidiary bodies,[60] submit written statements concerning matters within their competence,[61] and make oral

[51] See Gemmill and Bamidele-Izu (n 48) 7.

[52] ECOSOC, 'Working with NGOs: An NGO's Guide to Consultative Status' (September 2011) UN Doc 11-42007, 7.

[53] Ibid.

[54] Oberthür *et al* (n 17).

[55] UN Environment Civil Society Unit, 'Why civil society matters' <https://www.unenvironment.org/civil-society-engagement/why-civil-society-matters> accessed 15 October 2018.

[56] UNGA Res 66/288, 'The Future We Want' (11 September 2012) UN Doc A/Res/66/288.

[57] Ibid, para 88(h), emphasis added.

[58] See eg 'UNFCCC standard admission procedure for non-governmental organizations (NGOs)' (2017) <https://unfccc.int/files/parties_and_observers/observer_organizations/application/pdf/unfccc_standard_admission_process_ngos.pdf> accessed 15 October 2018, 2.

[59] 'Admitted NGOs' (2018) <https://unfccc.int/process/parties-non-party-stakeholders/non-party-stakeholders/admitted-ngos/list-of-admitted-ngos> accessed 15 October 2018.

[60] ECOSOC Res 1996/31, 'Consultative relationship between the United Nations and non-governmental organizations', Supp No. 1, UN Doc E/1996/96, 56, para 29.

[61] Ibid, paras 30–31.

presentations in permitted instances.[62] Similarly, within meetings of the United Nations Environment Assembly, credentialed groups can review working documents and offer oral and written input to negotiations.[63]

However, within many formal international law negotiations, the terms by which NGO diplomacy may be conducted frequently reify fundamental power dynamics; UN member states themselves determine the ground rules of formal negotiations. In ECOSOC, these rules explicitly distinguish NGOs from other voting and non-voting participants. NGOs' formal consultative status ranks low on a participatory hierarchy, with ECOSOC stating that NGO engagement must not 'overburden the Council or transform it from a body for coordination of policy and action ... into a general forum for discussion'.[64] Furthermore, NGO access is conditioned by the discretionary nature of credentialing determinations. For example, candidate NGOs must show that their entity meets foundational criteria including two years' existence and a 'democratic decision making mechanism', and must furthermore demonstrate that their activities are 'relevant to the work of ECOSOC'.[65] Accordingly, while consultative status provides NGOs an exceptional engagement avenue, admissions criteria may constrain participation by nascent or fragmented NGOs, NGOs with views falling outside the policy mainstream, and NGOs lacking institutional expertise or resources to navigate accreditation. This concern is particularly relevant because such NGOs can give voice to Indigenous and global South interests that have historically been minimized in dialogue[66] regarding climate change and other pressing regimes.[67]

Moreover, NGO engagement in formal diplomacy is mutable and constrained in important respects. First, an NGO's participation, once formalized, is neither permanent nor guaranteed. Both ECOSOC and UNEP periodically review NGO credentialing and provide mechanisms to withdraw consultative status. Second, as emphasized above, NGO diplomatic engagement is often bounded. For instance, NGOs may only make one oral statement at each ECOSOC annual meeting. Similarly, ENGOs are often granted special, rather than general, consultative status; this designation limits the permitted length of written statements to ECOSOC to 500 words rather than 2,000 (and 1,500 rather than 2,000 within commissions and subsidiary bodies).[68] In practical terms, these

[62] Ibid, para 32.

[63] FCCC, 'Admitted NGOs' (n 59).

[64] ECOSOC, 'Resolutions and Decisions of the Economic and Social Council, Official Records of 1996,' Supp No. 1, UN Doc E/1996/96.

[65] United Nations Department of Economic and Social Affairs, 'How to Apply for Consultative Status' <https://csonet.org/?menu=83> accessed 15 October 2018.

[66] See eg Catherine Corson, Lisa Campbell, and Kenneth MacDonald, 'Capturing the Personal in Politics: Ethnographies of Global Environmental Governance' *Global Environmental Politics*, 14/3 (2014): 21.

[67] See eg Heike Schroeder, 'Agency in International Climate Negotiations: The Case of Indigenous Peoples and Avoided Deforestation' *International Environmental Agreements*, 10/4 (2010): 317.

[68] See eg ibid; see also ECOSOC Res 1996/31 (n 60).

restrictions can inhibit the incorporation of diverse viewpoints during late stages of formal negotiations.[69]

Finally, NGO diplomatic engagement is less formalized, severely constrained, or altogether absent in many settings beyond ECOSOC. For instance, the UN General Assembly limits direct engagement to member states and only invites participation by a limited suite of non-state actors.[70] Similarly, the International Court of Justice (ICJ), an essential venue for interpreting and contesting international environmental law norms and principles, affords only nominal mechanisms for formal NGO engagement. The ICJ limits standing in contentious cases exclusively to state parties and provides no formal mechanism for non-state *amicus* engagement.[71] Under court procedure, NGO statements and documents are 'not to be considered as part of the case file'.[72] Additionally, ICJ protocol specifies that NGO statements should be stored in a public location that receives no priority over other documents.[73] This effective exclusion of NGOs from formal participation at the ICJ[74] has received critique for its limiting effect,[75] and it further conditions NGO participation in international environmental law.

To augment their engagement in informal and formal official drafting committees,[76] NGO employees have also begun to appear as members of national delegations. The practice is common and widely-documented in many international environmental law regimes, including climate change.[77] There, NGOs provide specialized expertise and augment governmental policy-makers' perspectives.[78] These efforts shape state-to-state relationships by introducing expert insight and giving voice to citizens' views in international negotiations.[79]

In sum, NGOs contribute insight, expertise, and perspective to formal, high-level negotiations. At the same time, their ability to effect substantial change within these venues is limited, uneven, and frequently difficult to document.[80] Accordingly, NGOs and associated researchers have examined new forms of engagement.[81]

[69] See eg Lars Gulbrandsen and Steinar Andresen, 'NGO Influence in the Implementation of the Kyoto Protocol: Compliance, Flexibility Mechanisms, and Sinks' *Global Environmental Politics*, 4/4 (2004): 54.

[70] UNGA, 'Note by Secretariat—List of non-Member States, entities and organizations having received a standing invitation to participate as observers in the sessions and the work of the General Assembly' (19 October 2017) UN Doc A/INF/72/5.

[71] ICJ Statute, art 34.1.

[72] ICJ, 'Practice Directions (as amended on 20 January 2009 and 21 March 2013)' direction XII(1).

[73] Ibid, direction XII(3).

[74] See eg Ruth Mackenzie *et al*, *Manual on International Courts and Tribunals* (OUP 2010) 30.

[75] Cathrin Zengerling, *Greening International Jurisprudence: Environmental NGOs before International Courts, Tribunals, and Compliance Committees* (Marinus Nijhoff 2013) 190.

[76] Martens (n 4) 373.

[77] Tobias Böhmelt, Vally Koubi, and Thomas Bernauer, 'Civil Society Participation in Global Governance: Insights From Climate Politics' *European Journal of Political Research*, 53/1 (2014): 18.

[78] Jeffrey Dunoff, 'From Green to Global: Toward the Transformation of International Environmental Law' *Harvard Environmental Law Review*, 19 (2015): 241, 277.

[79] Lucy Smith and Katharina Klaas, 'Networks and NGOs Relevant to Fighting Environmental Crime' (2014).

[80] See generally Betsill and Corell (n 24) (difficulties of process tracing).

[81] See eg Eytan Gilboa, 'Searching for a Theory of Public Diplomacy' *Annals of the American Academy of Political and Social Science*, 616/1 (2008): 55.

V. NGOS AS GLOBAL GOVERNORS

Alongside advocacy and formal diplomatic efforts, NGOs have also made prolific and diverse contributions to global environmental governance. Global governance references 'governing without sovereign authority'[82] and encompasses governmental activity alongside many other channels by which obligations are transmitted. A manifestation of 'politics beyond the state',[83] global governance emphasizes the emergence of new, disaggregated regulatory power dynamics.[84] The global governance of environmental challenges has been well-documented[85] in diverse legal settings. Its emergence appears to mirror the fragmentation and diversification of international environmental law and associated non-state regulatory efforts. Within this context, researchers emphasize that civil society plays an important role[86] and that increasing consideration of human rights and access to justice demands regulatory mechanisms that complement the dominant, treaty-based framework.[87]

In this evolving international environmental law regulatory milieu, NGOs are uniquely positioned to function as global governors. The distinctions between NGO capacity and traditional state-centric approaches suggest that enhanced NGO engagement in international environmental law can address regulatory deficits and enhance international environmental law governance authority. At the same time, the capacity of NGOs to secure compliance in the absence of formal international environmental law is conditioned upon their ability to establish credibility by leveraging expertise, moral authority,[88] and other bases of legitimacy.[89] Whereas states enjoy broad police powers within their jurisdictions, NGOs must develop alternate implementation and enforcement mechanisms. Nevertheless, NGOs actively and effectively advance international

[82] Lawrence Finkelstein, 'What Is Global Governance ?' *Global Governance*, 1/3 (1995): 367.

[83] Klaus Dingwerth and Philipp Pattberg, 'Global Governance as a Perspective on World Politics' *Global Governance*, 12/2 (2006): 185, 188.

[84] James Rosenau, 'Governing the Ungovernable: The Challenge of a Global Disaggregation of Authority' *Regulation and Governance*, 1/1 (2007): 88, 89.

[85] See eg Oran Young (ed), *Global Governance: Drawing Insights from the Environmental Experience* (MIT Press 1997).

[86] Viñuales and Dupuy (n 3) 31.

[87] Patricia Birnie, Alan Boyle, and Catherine Redgwell, *International Law and the Environment* (3rd edn, OUP 2009) 334.

[88] Deborah Avant, Martha Finnemore, and Susan Sell, 'Who Governs the Globe?' in Deborah Avant, Martha Finnemore, and Susan Sell (eds), *Who Governs the Globe?* (CUP 2012).

[89] See eg Steven Bernstein and Benjamin Cashore, 'Can Non-State Global Governance Be Legitimate? An Analytical Framework?' *Regulation & Governance*, 1/4 (2007): 347; Benjamin Cashore, 'Legitimacy and the Privatization of Environmental Governance: How Non-State Market-Driven (NSMD) Governance Systems Gain Rule-Making Authority' *Governance*, 15/4 (2002): 503.

environmental law as global governors in three ways: rule-making, implementation, and enforcement.[90]

A. Rule-Making

Historically, international environmental law efforts have reflected state authority and traditional geo-political considerations.[91] However, the transboundary character of contemporary environmental challenges transcends state borders and political structures, as do many international environmental law actors and arenas, including corporations and markets.[92] Accordingly, NGOs have responded by actively contributing to rule-making beyond state authority.

First, NGOs have established various domestic and transnational certification schemes that support and enshrine international environmental law principles and norms. Certification schemes, ecolabels, and similar efforts voluntarily commit adherents to specified environmental standards in production, marketing, and other activities.[93] They can incentivize more environmentally-conscious production, offer cues to consumers regarding suppliers' environmental commitment,[94] and promote justice among traditionally disenfranchised populations through production and purchasing mechanisms.[95] Certification schemes complement state-based mechanisms and can expand participation in international environmental law rule-making[96] by affording new avenues for compliance and legitimacy.[97]

Certification schemes and ecolabels have proven a key rule-making source within certain international environmental regimes, including forestry. Efforts there, including those set forth by the Forestry Stewardship Council (FSC), have sought to articulate

[90] Graeme Auld, Michele Betsill, and Stacy VanDeveer, 'Transnational Governance for Mining and the Mineral Lifecycle' *Annual Review of Environment and Resources*, 43 (2018): 425.

[91] Viñuales and Dupuy (n 3).

[92] Jonas Ebbesson, 'The Rule of Law in Governance of Complex Socio-Ecological Changes' *Global Environmental Change*, 20/3 (2010): 414, 421.

[93] Maria Lemos and Arun Agrawal, 'Environmental Governance' *Annual Review of Environment and Resources*, 31/1 (2006): 297, 307; see also Benjamin Cashore, Graeme Auld, and Deanna Newsom, *Governing Through Markets: Forest Certification and the Emergence of Non-State Authority* (Yale University Press 2004); Magnus Boström and Kristina Hallström, 'NGO Power in Global Social and Environmental Standard-Setting' *Global Environmental Politics*, 10/4 (2010): 36; Marie-Laure Djelic and Kerstin Sahlin-Andersson (eds), *Transnational Governance: Institutional Dynamics of Regulation* (CUP 2006).

[94] Lemos and Agrawal, ibid, 307.

[95] See eg Kimberley Suiseeya and Susan Caplow, 'In Pursuit of Procedural Justice: Lessons from an Analysis of 56 Forest Carbon Project Designs' *Global Environmental Change*, 23/5 (2013): 968.

[96] Jolene Lin, 'The Emergence of Transnational Environmental Law in the Anthropocene' in Louis Kotzé (ed), *Reimagining Environmental Law and Governance for the Anthropocene* (Hart Publishing 2017) 1, 4.

[97] Ibid, 17.

certification standards,[98] secure compliance commitments from timber harvesters,[99] and provide regulatory guidance in the absence of a state-based forestry treaty.[100] Certification schemes address additional regimes, including biofuels,[101] fisheries,[102] and others.[103] In each instance, NGOs have proven integral to articulating certification schemes and ecolabels, whether acting singly or collaboratively. For instance, within the forestry regime, the Rainforest Alliance NGO established the SmartWood certification scheme,[104] while FSC certification was created by an alliance of various NGO, private, and individual stakeholders.[105] In addition to establishing rule-making systems, NGOs provide resources and capacity to maintain compliance across rule-making efforts; for example, the Climate, Community, and Biodiversity Alliance sought to standardize forest carbon offset projects.[106] In short, certification schemes, ecolabels, and other extra-legal international environmental law frameworks reflect active NGO engagement.[107]

Second, NGOs have made key contributions to public-private partnerships (PPPs). PPPs have gained widespread currency over the past two decades, spurred by their broader inclusion into the international human rights policy-making landscape[108] and the 2002 World Summit on Sustainable Development (WSSD).[109] There, the UN acknowledged that active engagement by the private sector 'can contribute to the achievement of sustainable development'[110] and emphasized its commitment to 'stable partnerships with all major groups, respecting the independent, important roles of each of them'.[111] Specifically, WSSD outcome documents advocated

[98] Errol Meidinger, 'The Administrative Law of Global Private-Public Regulation: The Case of Forestry' *European Journal of International Law*, 17/1 (2006): 47, 51.

[99] Steven Bernstein and Ben Cashore, 'Complex Global Governance and Domestic Policies: Four Pathways of Influence' *International Affairs*, 88/3 (2012): 585, 600.

[100] See eg David Vogel, 'Private Global Business Regulation' *Annual Review of Political Science*, 11/1 (2008): 261, 267.

[101] Lin (n 96).

[102] See eg Klaus Dingwerth and Philipp Pattberg, 'World Politics and Organizational Fields: The Case of Transnational Sustainability Governance' *European Journal of International Relations*, 15/4 (2009): 707, 726.

[103] Steven Bernstein, 'Legitimacy in Intergovernmental and Non-State Global Governance' *Review of International Political Economy*, 18/1 (2011): 17, 36.

[104] Meidinger (n 98) 51.

[105] Forestry Stewardship Council, 'What is FSC?' <https://ic.fsc.org/en/what-is-fsc> accessed 15 October 2018.

[106] Suiseeya and Caplow (n 95) 3.

[107] Ebbesson (n 92) 10; see also Harriet Bulkeley *et al*, *Transnational Climate Change Governance* (CUP 2014).

[108] Tanya Börzel and Thomas Risse, 'Public-Private Partnerships : Effective and Legitimate Tools of International Governance' in Edgar Grande and Louis Pauly (eds), *On the Reconstitution of Political Authority* (University of Toronto Press 2007).

[109] Viñuales and Dupuy (n 3) 381.

[110] UNGA Res 66/288 (n 56) para 46.

[111] *Report of World Summit on Sustainable Development* (UN 2002) ch I.1, annex—'Johannesburg Declaration on Sustainable Development', para 26.

the utility of PPPs for multiple objectives, including transferring agricultural and natural resources knowledge,[112] accelerating poverty eradication,[113] supporting sustainable energy,[114] promoting links between health and sustainable development,[115] and enhancing domestic implementation of sustainable development.[116] Collectively, PPPs provide a mechanism for inserting public interest into environmental efforts.[117]

Since the 2002 World Summit, PPPs have enjoyed broad embrace throughout the UN system, the World Bank,[118] and elsewhere. Similarly, they increasingly contribute to governance across diverse environmental regimes, including forestry, climate change, and biodiversity.[119] While the traditional PPP framework envisages collaboration between government and industry, NGOs can also contribute by providing resources to raise capital and fund initiatives,[120] offering relevant expertise,[121] and supporting the management of regulatory efforts initiatives.[122] In contemporary governance, PPPs can enable NGOs and states to leverage their comparative strengths and congruent interests for stronger governance.

B. Implementation

NGOs also actively contribute to international environmental law norm implementation by negotiating the interface between international environmental law principles and domestic legal contexts. NGOs operate both transnationally and multilaterally, facilitating information exchange, fostering mutual learning, helping domestic actors to secure expertise, and constructing actor coalitions that collectively promote international environmental law norms. This role has been formally institutionalized in the climate change regime where non-state actors may be engaged in monitoring and

112 Ibid, 6, 'Plan of Implementation', para 7(j).

113 Ibid, para 9(g).

114 Ibid, para 20(t).

115 Ibid, para 54(l).

116 Ibid, para 96.

117 Viñuales and Dupuy (n 3) 33; Philipp Pattberg, *Public-Private Partnerships for Sustainable Development. Emergence, Influence, and Legitimacy* (Edward Elgar 2012).

118 See eg World Bank, 'Infrastructure and Public-Private Partnerships' (2018) <https://www.worldbank.org/en/topic/publicprivatepartnerships> accessed 15 October 2018.

119 See UNGA Res 70/1, 'Transforming our World: The 2030 Agenda for Sustainable Development' (21 October 2015) UN Doc A/RES/70/1.

120 Bertrand Quelin, 'Are Public-Private Partnerships the Best Way to Provide Government Services?' *Yale Insights* (20 October 2015).

121 Lemos and Agrawal (n 93) 316.

122 See eg Erick Solana, 'Public Private Not-For-Profit Partnerships: Delivering Public Services to Developing Countries' *Procedia Engineering*, 78 (2014): 259. However, researchers have also noted limitations of PPPs in IEL governance; see eg Marco Schäferhoff, Sabine Campe, and Christopher Kaan, 'Transnational Public-Private Partnerships in International Relations: Making Sense of Concepts, Research Frameworks, and Results' *International Studies Review*, 11/3 (2009): 451.

implementing national commitments under the 2015 Paris Agreement, which also recognizes the contributions of non-state climate action to achieving global goals.[123]

Within a transnational setting, NGOs have effectively facilitated the transmission of key emergent norms. For instance, NGOs have been particularly active in spreading an access or participation norm and its tripartite obligations of access to information, public participation in decision-making, and access to justice.[124] These norms have manifested in domestic constitutional provisions codifying environmental rights;[125] the emergence of dedicated environmental ministries;[126] and the establishment of specialist environmental courts and tribunals.[127] Across diverse settings, NGOs have proven key to promoting both norm implementation[128] and spread.[129] Additionally, NGOs themselves have identified efforts to promote international environmental law norms. For instance, the World Wildlife Fund (WWF) documents information regarding rights-based environmental approaches and notes its efforts to enhance 'integration of human rights in conservation policy and practice'.[130] Similarly, the Conservation Initiative on Human Rights, an NGO consortium, works collectively to advance links between conservation and citizens' rights.

C. Enforcement

NGOs further serve as key actors in domestic efforts to secure compliance with, and bring enforcement actions in cases of derogations against, international environmental law norms. NGO diversity enables the organizations to perform three distinct functions: leveraging strong existing governmental frameworks, undertaking actions to supplement weak state authority, and supplanting or substituting for inadequate or absent state enforcement authority.

1. *Leveraging strong governmental frameworks*

First, NGOs have used existing governmental frameworks to secure enforcement of environmental rights. These efforts are especially manifest in the context of the climate regime, where NGOs' resources, competence, and membership have been leveraged in several unique ways to secure redress and attach liability to adaptation and mitigation

[123] Karin Bäckstrand *et al*, 'Non-State Actors in Global Climate Governance: From Copenhagen to Paris and Beyond' *Environmental Politics*, 26/4 (2017): 561.

[124] See Chapter 21, 'Public Participation', in this volume.

[125] See eg Joshua Gellers, *The Global Emergence of Constitutional Environmental Rights* (Routledge 2017).

[126] David Boyd, *The Rights of Nature: A Legal Revolution That Could Save the World* (ECW Press 2017).

[127] See UNEP, *Environmental Courts & Tribunals: A Guide for Policy Makers* (2016).

[128] Oberthür *et al* (n 17) 16.

[129] See eg Gemmill and Bamidele-Izu (n 48).

[130] See eg WWF Global Project, 'Human Rights and Conservation' (2017) <https://wwf.panda.org/our_work/people/people_and_conservation/our_work/human_rights/> accessed 15 October 2018.

failures at the domestic level. For instance, NGOs use their diverse memberships to overcome the procedural barrier of standing and, where permitted, bring claims for injuries directly on behalf of the public interest.[131] Likewise, many expert NGOs possess specialized competence and resources that enable them to pursue or enhance litigation that domestically addresses key international environmental law tenets.[132]

2. *Supplementing weak or insufficient state resources*

Second, NGOs supplement enforcement capacity among states lacking adequate resources. This approach has become particularly manifest within the area of biodiversity conservation. There, the IUCN's 1973 Convention on International Trade in Endangered Species of Wild Fauna and Flora (CITES) outlines a comprehensive framework for preserving imperilled species[133] that benefits from explicit NGO engagement across varied domestic settings. Under this cooperative approach, parties to the Convention commit to seek enforcement funding, information, and expertise from relevant NGOs in ways that complement, rather than conflict with, state authority.

NGOs have actively promoted CITES enforcement for at least thirty years. For instance, CITES' MIKE (Monitoring the Illegal Killing of Elephants) programme pursues more robust and uniform monitoring, enforcement, and management of elephant populations.[134] The MIKE programme recently emphasized NGOs' contributions to implementation and its hope that NGOs will collaborate with elephants' range states to 'help themselves, but hopefully in the spirit of a family rather than "empire carving"'.[135] In sum, NGOs provide institutional and financial resources that complement domestic enforcement efforts and promote compliance of multilateral environmental agreements.[136]

3. *Exercising enforcement capacity beyond state-treaty architecture*

Third, NGOs demonstrate the value of exercising enforcement capacity beyond the traditional treaty-state architecture. This approach is useful for supplementing state-centred enforcement capacity in regimes with weak enforcement capacity, such as the climate regime,[137] or in areas beyond national jurisdiction. Such efforts have proven particularly effective in the enforcement contexts of marine protected areas (MPAs). As researchers

[131] See eg *Kids v Global Warming* Petition to Massachusetts Department of Environmental Protection (2012) (seeking to compel agency rule-making to reduce greenhouse gas emissions).

[132] See Diane Stone, 'Non-Governmental Policy Transfer: The Strategies of Independent Policy Institutes' *Governance*, 13/1 (2000): 45.

[133] art II(1).

[134] CITES, 'Trade in Elephant Specimens', Conf 10.10 Rev CoP17 <https://stag.cites.org/sites/default/files/document/E-Res-10-10-R17.pdf> accessed 15 October 2018.

[135] CITES, 'Monitoring the Illegal Killing of Elephants (MIKE) Communiqué of the MIKE/NGO open day' (29 May 2002) <https://www.cites.org/eng/prog/mike/info/communique_0205.shtml> accessed 15 October 2018.

[136] Peter Haas, 'Addressing the Global Governance Deficit' *Global Environmental Politics*, 4/4 (2004): 1, 12.

[137] See Chapter 29, 'Climate Change', in this volume.

have suggested, MPAs, and particularly large MPAs, present enforcement challenges to coastal states in terms of their scale, governability, visibility, accessibility, and familiarity. As a result, there are unique opportunities for novel enforcement approaches to shape local decision-making and regulation. In addition to providing enforcement capacity, NGOs also contribute innovation by leveraging satellite and other emergent visualization technologies to monitor for illegal fishing and other incursions against MPA provisions.[138] In all, NGOs have demonstrated their capacity to advance international environmental law governance and enforcement actively by exerting authority beyond the traditional, state-centred treaty regime.

VI. CONCLUSION

As this chapter indicates, non-state actors, and specifically NGOs, have contributed to international environmental law governance, evolution, and development. While NGOs in international environmental law may be distinguished by their scope of action, memberships, and primary aims, they collectively perform three functions. First, NGOs advance critical activist functions in international environmental law, engaging in direct action campaigns and performing direct and indirect lobby functions. Second, NGOs serve as diplomats, collaborating with diverse actors to craft policies in key environmental regimes. Finally, and critically, NGOs serve as global governors, performing many roles in conjunction with, or in place of, state actors. Their actions support environmental rule-making, implementation of international environmental law agreements, and enforcement efforts.

Altogether, this chapter underscores the centrality of NGOs to an increasingly non-state international environmental law landscape. The complexity and multiscale nature of contemporary environmental challenges indicates that meaningful progress demands participation that promotes diverse actors and expertise. The range of NGO structures, competencies, and efforts may render them uniquely qualified to fulfil these functions.

BIBLIOGRAPHY

Michele Betsill and Elisabeth Corell (eds), *NGO Diplomacy: The Influence of Nongovernmental Organizations in International Environmental Negotiations* (MIT Press 2008)

Magnus Böstrom and Kristina Hallström, 'NGO Power in Global Social and Environmental Standard-Setting' *Global Environmental Politics*, 10/4 (2010): 36

[138] See eg Rebecca Gruby *et al*, 'Toward a Social Science Research Agenda for Large Marine Protected Areas' *Conservation Letters*, 9/3 (2016): 153.

Steve Charnovitz, 'Nongovernmental Organizations and International Law' *American Journal of International Law*, 100/2 (2006): 348
Kal Raustiala, 'States, NGOs, and International Environmental Institutions' *International Studies Quarterly*, 41/4 (1997): 719
Dan Tarlock, 'The Role of Non-Governmental Organisations in the Development of International Environmental Law' *Chicago-Kent Law Review*, 68/1 (1992): 61
Farhana Yamin, 'NGOs and International Environmental Law: A Critical Evaluation of their Roles and Responsibilities' *Review of European Community and International Environmental Law*, 10/2 (2001): 149

CHAPTER 39

SUB-NATIONAL ACTORS

HARI M OSOFSKY*

I. INTRODUCTION

This chapter focuses on the evolving role of sub-national actors in international environmental law. As a matter of formal law, international environmental law is formed among sovereign nation-states; sub-national actors are treated as sub-units of their nation-states.[1] However, sub-national actors, through transnational networks, are playing a growing role in international environmental governance. Rather than attempt to cover all forms of sub-national participation in international environmental law, this chapter uses the example of cities' participation in climate change networks to illustrate the complex ways in which sub-national actors participate in international law-making. It highlights how the nuanced geographies of local and international intersect to help form international law.

This chapter focuses on three aspects of sub-national actors' participation in international environmental law. First, it considers why including sub-national actors is crucial to solving international environmental problems. Second, it examines the emergence of networks interacting with international environmental law-making and each other at transnational, national, and sub-national scales. Third, it analyses how those networks interact directly with the formal processes of international environmental law-making and develop the parallel voluntary agreements in which sub-national actors pledge to uphold commitments made by nation-states.

* This chapter is an edited and updated excerpt from Hari Osofsky, 'Rethinking the Geography of Local Climate Action: Multi-Level Network Participation in Metropolitan Regions' *Utah Law Review* (2015): 173. As always, I am grateful for the love, support, and patience of Josh, Oz, and Scarlet Gitelson.

[1] James Crawford, *Brownlie's Principles of International Law* (8th edn, OUP 2012) 5.

II. THE IMPORTANCE OF SUB-NATIONAL ACTORS TO SOLVING INTERNATIONAL ENVIRONMENTAL PROBLEMS

Although formal international environmental law processes largely occur among nation-states, the problems that they are addressing often have a multiscalar geography and require the involvement of sub-national entities. Local participation in climate change networks provides an important example of the role that sub-national actors increasingly play in international environmental law because urban action is critical to addressing climate change. Over half the world's population lives in cities.[2] Cities and their power plants are the largest human-created sources of greenhouse gas emissions, producing at least 70% of the world's fossil-fuel carbon dioxide emissions.[3] No effective strategy for controlling emissions or adapting to impacts can ignore such a substantial part of the population.

International-level entities and nation-states cannot develop effective solutions without involving cities in crafting them. Many important climate change policy decisions are made at a local level as part of urban land use planning. Moreover, in larger urban areas, cities are clustered together into metropolitan regions. Reducing emissions in those places depends not only on city centres taking action, but also on smaller suburban ones, ideally coordinated at county and metro-regional local scales.

Mayors, city and county officials, and members of metropolitan regional councils have recognized this need for local involvement in addressing climate change. As international climate change negotiations struggle, even after the conclusion of the 2015 Paris Agreement, to find a path that will reduce emissions at a rate needed to prevent the worst impacts, a growing number of cities around the world play increasingly critical roles in multilevel efforts to address climate change. As described in depth in the sections that follow, they influence the language in the climate change treaty negotiations, form their own transnational agreements, and use their local governmental power to make commitments that often exceed those of their nation-states. Multilevel networks—at local, state, regional, national, and international levels—help foster local action. These networks provide models and frameworks for cities to use in developing their policies and opportunities for local climate change leaders to connect with one another.[4]

These networks face limitations that constrain their impacts, as the US example highlights. First, not enough cities participate in them, especially in the suburbs. For

[2] See US Central Intelligence Agency, 'Urbanization—The World Factbook' <https://www.cia.gov/library/publications/the-world-factbook/fields/349.html> accessed 6 February 2020.

[3] California Institute of Technology—NASA Jet Propulsion Lab, 'Megacities Carbon Project, Why Are Cities Important?' <http://perma.cc/TX86-HE57> accessed 6 February 2020.

[4] For examples of these networks and a discussion of their development, see Section II.

example, the 1,066 US mayors that have joined the US Mayors Climate Protection Agreement (Mayors Agreement) represent only a small percentage of US cities.[5] Second, the networks often have an insufficient connection with one another. Many networks offer overlapping, but uncoordinated, resources that create inefficiencies for cities joining multiple networks. While the Mayors Agreement cities made parallel commitments in the Copenhagen City Climate Catalogue,[6] this type of interlinking is rare. Even leader cities—which take early action on climate change and collaborate with other cities in doing so—will join some transnational local agreements, but not others, and participate unevenly in international, national, regional, and state networks.[7] Third, many networks differentiate among types of cities insufficiently. While some networks will highlight small versus large cities, they generally do not consider the diversity of cities within a metropolitan region or how to align climate change policies with cities' varying needs; city centres, stressed inner suburbs, affluent and developed job-centre suburbs, and outer-ring and often rapidly growing developing job centres and bedroom communities vary in multiple ways that affect their mitigation and adaptation possibilities and trajectories.[8]

With most of the global population living in cities and a low percentage of cities actively participating in climate change networks, more local action is clearly needed. Fostering local action, however, requires first understanding what 'local' is. Answering this question is complicated for two primary reasons. First, the category of local includes a diverse set of entities. Cities, counties, and metropolitan councils are all local government units, and the larger scale of them have other local government units within them. Moreover, these local governments vary greatly in physical size, population, and demographic characteristics. Understanding how these local structures intersect and the particular needs of each type of entity and its people is critical to effective mitigation and adaptation planning.[9]

Second, local decisions are not made purely within that locality. Localities have to balance their local autonomous control and the constraints that other levels put upon them. For example, the law varies from state to state on whether cities can mandate energy efficiency standards that exceed state ones. Local entities also participate in local,

[5] The US Conference of Mayors, 'Mayors Climate Protection Center' <https://www.usmayors.org/mayors-climate-protection-center/> accessed 1 February 2020. The US Census Bureau indicated that as of 2010, there were 19,540 incorporated places in the US; US Census Bureau, '28—Incorporated Places by Population Size' <https://www.census.gov/library/publications/2011/compendia/statab/131ed/population.html> accessed 8 February 2020.

[6] See Hari Osofsky, 'Suburban Climate Change Efforts: Possibilities for Small and Nimble Cities Participating in State, Regional, National, and International Networks' *Cornell Journal of Law and Public Policy*, 22/2 (2012): 395, 439–440; see also n 54.

[7] See Section III.

[8] See Osofsky (n 6); see also Section II.

[9] Gerald Frug and David Barron describe cities 'as simultaneously subordinate domestic governments and independent international actors'; see Gerald Frug and David Barron, 'International Local Government Law' *Urban Law*, 38/1 (2006): 1, 2; see also Keith Aoki *et al*, '(In)visible Cities: Three Local Government Models and Immigration Regulation' *Oregon Review International Law*, 10 (2008): 453, 47–78 (analyzing Frug and Barron's ideas' applicability to immigration).

state, regional, national, and international networks—the subject of this chapter—some of which focus on topics relevant to climate change. Those interactions among localities fundamentally shape decision-making, even if agreements made through such networks tend to be voluntary.[10]

Effective strategies for fostering local climate change action need to consider these complexities of scale. Each local entity has core local-scale powers relevant to climate change and particularized local needs tied to socio-economics, culture, and geography. Understanding these powers and needs can help shape strategies for motivating climate action. At the same time, these local entities make choices through interactions with governmental and non-governmental actors at other levels, including climate networks. Increasing conscious interconnectivity of and synergy among networks maximizes their impact.

III. THE EMERGENCE OF MULTILEVEL NETWORKS OF SUB-NATIONAL GOVERNMENTS

Sub-national governments have built multiscalar networks that serve as key vehicles by which they participate in international environmental law-making. This section explores some of the climate change networks that have developed at international, national, state, and local scales as examples of the types of networks that have emerged and how they interact with formal international law processes. This detailing of networks is not intended to be comprehensive, but rather aims to provide a sense of the types of networks that exist at each scale and some of their major activities.

Although the networks described in this section operate at different levels and have diverse core activities, they share in common a focus on assisting localities in efforts to do more to address climate change. Much of that 'more' takes place at a local scale. The networks provide tool-kits, examples, and recognition for local leaders who want to take additional steps, as well as a supportive network of similarly committed leaders. Participating leaders in some of these programmes have indicated that these mechanisms provide a helpful framework for their activities.[11]

As becomes clear in this section's descriptions, however, many of these voluntary local networks—even smaller-scale ones—also interact significantly with the international climate negotiations between nation-states. Some networks were formed in

[10] I have explored some of these dynamics in the sources cited above in Osofsky (n 6); see also Judith Resnik *et al*, 'Ratifying Kyoto at the Local Level: Sovereigntism, Federalism, and Translocal Organizations of Government Actors (TOGAs)' *Arizona Law Review*, 50/3 (2008): 709, 726–733, 764 (analyzing the many TOGAs working on climate change and their current and potential roles in shaping federal policy).

[11] Osofsky (n 6) 447.

reaction to failures by nation-states generally, and the United States in particular, to commit to action in the international negotiations. In fact, many of the international-scale agreements among cities are made in parallel with annual Conference of the Party (COP) negotiations among nation-state parties to the 1992 United Nations Framework Convention on Climate Change (UNFCCC). This interactivity helps reinforce the polycentric nature of climate change governance in general and the multiscalar character of local action in particular.[12]

A. International-Level Climate Change Networks

International-level networks of localities focus on changing behaviour at multiple scales. A big part of their efforts involves trying to influence nation-state behaviour and the course of international negotiations among them. Intertwined with that large-scale goal are local-level commitments made in international contexts by participating localities using their governmental powers. This sub-section highlights five of the most significant international networks of sub-national governments working on climate change to give a sense of the details of these interactions.

The International Council for Local Environmental Initiatives (ICLEI) is a longstanding active international network working on climate change.[13] ICLEI emerged from the first World Congress of Local Governments for a Sustainable Future in 1990 in New York, where it was founded by 200 local governments from forty-three countries.[14] It has grown in the three decades since to include over 1,750 local governments of different sizes in 124 countries, representing over 20% of the global population and over 25% of the global urban population.[15] Although ICLEI's overall focus is more broadly on sustainability,[16] its climate change efforts include a wide range of programmes that influence international treaty negotiations, create agreements among localities, and guide activities within localities. ICLEI's first programme, Cities for Climate Protection (CCP) Campaign, eliminated more than sixty million tons of carbon-dioxide-equivalent emissions annually.[17] From the start, its

[12] Kevin Cox, 'Spaces of Dependence, Spaces of Engagement and the Politics of Scale, or: Looking for Local Politics' *Political Geography*, 17/1 (1998): 1, 4–21.

[13] 'About Us' <https://www.iclei.org/en/About_ICLEI_2.html> accessed 26 January 2020.

[14] ICLEI, 'Three Decades of Global Sustainability' <http://icleiusa.org/iclei-at-30/> accessed 26 January 2020.

[15] See ICLEI, 'Local and Regional Governments and ICLEI' <https://www.iclei.org/en/our_network.html> accessed 26 January 2020.

[16] 'ICLEI works at multiple scales, building connections across local, regional, national and global actors and policies. We create systems change, developing integrated solutions along five interconnected development pathways that transform urban areas'; see ICLEI, 'What We Do' <https://www.iclei.org/en/what_we_do.html> accessed 26 January 2020.

[17] ICLEI, 'Who We Are' <https://icleiusa.org/about-us/who-we-are/> accessed 26 January 2020.

programmes have often paralleled international-level efforts by nation-states. For example, two of ICLEI's earliest initiatives were Local Agenda 21, 'a program promoting participatory governance and local sustainable development planning', and CCP, 'the world's first and largest program supporting cities in climate action planning using a five milestone process including greenhouse gas emissions inventories to systematically reduce emissions'.[18] Its sustainability focus and tool-kit approach have since been used in different variations by many other organizations, including much smaller-scale initiatives such as Minnesota's Greenstep Cities programme.

The World Mayors Council on Climate Change (WMCCC) was founded in 2005 by the mayor of Kyoto just after the international-scale 1997 Kyoto Protocol came into force in parallel with the Montreal Conference of the Parties.[19] WMCCC's goals include (1) 'strengthening political leadership on global sustainability by building a group of committed local sustainability leaders'; and (2) 'being the prime political advocacy force of cities and local governments on global sustainability matters'.[20] WMCCC implements this mission by (1) 'showcasing local leaders' climate and sustainability actions that contribute to policy change at local and global levels'; (2) 'supporting its members to enhance their climate and sustainability leadership capacities'; (3) 'addressing global climate and sustainability policy makers as a global body of leaders from diverse local governments'; and (4) 'politically steering the development and implementation of mechanisms that support local climate and sustainability action'.[21] Although the Council was constituted separately from ICLEI and functions independently, ICLEI provides technical and strategic support and often collaborates with it.[22]

The C40 Cities Climate Leadership Group was established in 2005 when the mayor of London convened representatives from eighteen major cities. It has since grown to ninety-four cities representing over 700 million people and a quarter of the global economy and has extensive requirements for its member cities.[23] C40 cities have set emissions reductions goals in parallel to international negotiations. In 2016, C40 established its Deadline 2020 Initiative, in which every member city was required to establish 'a robust plan for how they will deliver climate action consistent with constraining global heating to no more than 1.5°C by 2020' and more than 100 cities had made commitments and begun implementation by 2019.[24] The group is focused on establishing a 'Global Green New Deal—a series of essential steps to

[18] Ibid.

[19] WMCCC, 'History' <https://perma.cc/K86P-WSSF> accessed 6 February 2020.

[20] WMCCC, 'Mission and Method' <https://perma.cc/ZUB6-S4JB> accessed 6 February 2020.

[21] Ibid.

[22] Ibid.

[23] C40 Cities, 'City Action to Address Climate Emergency' <https://www.c40.org/other/city-commitments> accessed 26 January 2020.

[24] C40 Cities, 'About C40' <https://www.c40.org/about> accessed 26 January 2020.

reduce temperatures, cut emissions, invest in clean energy, protect our natural resources, and ensure a just transition for workers impacted by rapid changes in our economy'.[25]

United Cities and Local Governments (UCLG) has a broader focus on serving as 'the united voice and world advocate of democratic local self-government, promoting its values, objectives and interests, through cooperation between local governments, and within the wider international community'.[26] However, it is relevant to this chapter's analysis because of its active participation in the international climate change negotiations and its partnership with the other networks highlighted in this section. It formed the UCLG Climate Negotiation Group at its 2009 World Council, and that group has been actively participating in the climate change negotiations and in developing the transnational agreements among localities since then.[27] For example, the UCLG spokesperson played a leadership role in creating the 2013 Nantes Declaration of Mayors and Subnational Leaders on Climate Change discussed below.[28]

The Global Covenant of Mayors for Climate and Energy represents the maturing and intertwining of the above-described and other efforts. It launched in 2016 and brought together the Compact of Mayors—a 2014 initiative launched by UN General Secretary Ban Ki-moon and former New York City Mayor Michael Bloomberg—with the European Union (EU)'s Covenant of Mayors.[29] It is 'the largest global alliance for city climate leadership, built upon the commitment of over 10,000 cities and local governments. These cities hail from 6 continents and 138 countries. In total, they represent more than 800 million people'.[30] It is supported by an alliance of twelve partners, which include among them ICLEI, C40 Cities, and UCLG.[31]

Together, these and other networks provide an opportunity for sub-national governments to coordinate, learn from each other, and scale up their voice. As the networks build additional collaborative networks, such as the Global Covenant of Mayors for Climate and Energy, they involve a growing number of sub-national governments around the world and continue to increase their impact. Section IV explores that influence in more depth.

[25] Ibid.

[26] UCLG, 'Who We Are' <https://www.uclg.org/en/organisation/about> accessed 6 February 2020.

[27] UCLG, 'Climate Change' <http://www.uclg.org/en/issues/climate-change> accessed 6 February 2020.

[28] UCLG, 'Mayors and Subnational Leaders Meet in Nantes and Renew Commitment to Upscale Climate Change Actions' (10 October 2013) <https://www.uclg.org/en/node/20653> accessed 6 February 2020.

[29] Nicole Orttung, 'Why Cities are Forming a Global Alliance to Fight Climate Change' *Christian Science Monitor* (24 June 2016).

[30] Global Covenant of Mayors for Climate and Energy, 'Who We Are' <https://www.globalcovenantofmayors.org/about/> accessed 1 February 2020.

[31] Ibid.

B. National-level and Sub-National Climate Change Networks

These transnational climate change networks interact with smaller-scale networks as they shape and are shaped by international climate change negotiations. For example, the United States contains numerous national-level and sub-national level networks that bring local officials together and interact with the transnational networks described above. These networks have played an important role in bringing US cities together to make commitments in line with the original US Paris Agreement Nationally Determined Contribution in the aftermath of President Trump's withdrawal from the Paris Agreement.

The most long-standing US domestic climate-focused network is the Mayors Agreement in which mayors pledge to meet the commitments the United States would have had under the Kyoto Protocol—reducing emissions to 7% below 1990 levels by 2012—and to encourage larger-scale governments to do the same.[32] It focuses specifically on climate change and is highly inclusive; any city can join that takes its pledge and as of 2020, 1,066 have done so.[33] Seattle Mayor Greg Nickels launched this network in 2005 in response to the US decision not to participate in the Kyoto Protocol. He worked with other mayors to organize an initial group of 141 mayors to pledge to meet the Kyoto Protocol targets. The US Conference of Mayors unanimously endorsed the Mayors Agreement and has encouraged cities to sign on since then.[34] In 2007, Douglas Palmer, then-Mayor of Trenton and President of the US Conference of Mayors, in collaboration with Conference Executive Director Tom Cochran, launched the US Conference of Mayors Climate Protection Center 'in recognition of an increasingly urgent need to provide mayors with the guidance and assistance they need to lead their cities' efforts to reduce the greenhouse gas emissions that are linked to climate change'.[35] The Center provides best practices models[36] and gives awards to leader cities in large and small categories.[37]

Climate Mayors—'a bipartisan, peer-to-peer network of U.S. mayors working together to demonstrate leadership on climate change through meaningful actions in their communities, and to express and build political will for effective federal and global policy action'[38]—was launched in 2014 with one million dollars in start-up funding

[32] Mayors Climate Protection Center (n 5).

[33] Ibid.

[34] Ibid; see also The United States Conference of Mayors—Mayors Climate Protection Center, 'About the Mayors Climate Protection Center' <https://perma.cc/5ZZC-98KL> accessed 6 February 2020.

[35] The United States Conference of Mayors (n 34).

[36] The United States Conference of Mayors—Mayors Climate Protection Center, 'Taking Local Action—Mayors and Climate Protection: Best Practices' <https://www.usmayors.org/wp-content/uploads/2019/06/climateawards2019.pdf> accessed 6 February 2020.

[37] The United States Conference of Mayors—Mayors Climate Protection Center, 'Awards' <https://perma.cc/6EU9-8FZQ> accessed 6 February 2020.

[38] Climate Mayors <https://climatemayors.org/> accessed 6 February 2020.

from the Clinton Global Initiative.[39] It describes itself as 'a key voice and demonstration of the ongoing commitment of U.S. cities to accelerate climate progress'.[40] When President Trump withdrew from the Paris Agreement, the Climate Mayors issued a statement committing to US goals under that Agreement. As President Biden pledged to rejoin the Agreement, they have committed to partnership.[41]

In addition, many US states, cities, and regions have developed complementary smaller-scale networks. For example, the Environmental Protection Agency (EPA) Region 5—which includes Illinois, Indiana, Michigan, Minnesota, Ohio, Wisconsin, and thirty-five tribes[42]—has a climate action plan and a network providing resources to local governments.[43] The Atlanta Regional Commission Certified Green Communities provides voluntary sustainability certifications for local governments in the ten-county Atlanta metropolitan region.[44] The Colorado Climate Network aims to support mitigation and adaptation efforts by local governments and allied organizations in the state.[45] New York's Climate Smart Communities is a 'state-local partnership'[46] that provides various services to local governments, including community coordinators, a communities listserv, webinars, and a local-action guide.[47] GreenStep Cities is a statewide Minnesota sustainability programme targeting local governments that includes categories relevant to climate change.[48]

Because some of these smaller-scale networks achieve greater participation than the larger-scale networks in particular metropolitan regions, they become an important gateway for encouraging local mitigation and adaptation that connect to global goals. These networks vary in their focus and geographic scale. Some of these networks focus directly on climate change, while others have a broader focus, such as sustainability, but do substantial work related to climate change. The networks range from inter-state

[39] Clinton Global Initiative, 'Mayors' National Climate Action Agenda' <https://www.clintonfoundation.org/clinton-global-initiative/commitments/mayors-national-climate-action-agenda> accessed 6 February 2020.

[40] Climate Mayors (n 38).

[41] Climate Mayors, 'Paris Climate Agreement' <https://climatemayors.org/actions/paris-climate-agreement/> accessed 6 February 2020. Climate Mayors, 'Climate Mayors Statement on President Biden's Executive Order to Rejoin Paris Agreement' <https://climatemayors.org/climate-mayors-statement-on-rejoining-paris-agreement/> accessed 4 April 2021.

[42] See US EPA, 'Region 5 Climate Change' <https://perma.cc/7SKU-CA8U> accessed 6 February 2020. The other EPA regions are also involved in various forms of climate change action, but this chapter focuses on Region 5 as an exemplar.

[43] See US EPA, 'Municipalities' <https://perma.cc/NDA9-MM2F> accessed 6 February 2020.

[44] <https://www.atlantaregional.com/environment/green-communities> accessed 6 February 2020. The stated benefits of certification are that it '[f]osters civic pride[,] [c]reates a positive image of a place to live or conduct business[,] [s]ets an example for businesses and organizations seeking to reduce their environmental impact[, and] [l]eads to a greater quality of life'.

[45] Colorado Climate Network, 'Local resilience project' <https://perma.cc/QAP4-LAYU> accessed 6 February 2020.

[46] New York State Department of Environmental Conservation, 'Community Sustainability' <https://perma.cc/R6MZ-FTRL> accessed 6 February 2020.

[47] Ibid.

[48] Minnesota GreenStep Cities, 'Welcome to GreenStep Cities' <https://greenstep.pca.state.mn.us/index.cfm> accessed 6 February 2020.

regional to state-wide to metro-regional, and many of them have linkages to other levels of government or key public and private actors. In their strategic approaches, many employ variations on the toolkit approach described above with respect to ICLEI.

IV. THE ROLE OF SUB-NATIONAL NETWORKS IN INTERNATIONAL ENVIRONMENTAL LAWMAKING

Sub-national networks interact directly with international treaty negotiations and form parallel agreements in which they make commitments related to the goals of those treated. The role these networks play in international climate change negotiations exemplifies the role sub-national networks play more generally in international environmental law-making.

The annual COPs have provided a primary site for networks of localities to gather and attempt to push nation-states both to do more and to recognize the local role in the treaties being negotiated.[49] These efforts have been organized since the 2007 COP in Bali under the auspices of a Local Government Climate Roadmap by ICLEI and UCLG. This effort was originally supposed to finish by the Copenhagen COP, but has continued through the more recent COPs.[50] At each COP negotiation, this coalition has made progress in getting more language on cities, localities, and sub-national government into the international agreements and initiatives taking place under them. With the adoption of the Nantes Declaration of Mayors and Sub-national Leaders on Climate Change in fall 2013, the climate roadmap entered a new phase.[51] The gathered localities created the Friends of the Cities group to bring together 'national governments who wish to collaborate with local and subnational governments'.[52]

ICLE and UCLG influence text at the COP negotiations by using their status as observers, mobilizing within countries, and participating in bilateral meetings.[53] Side meetings among localities and other sub-national government, often taking place parallel to the COPs, augment these efforts. The participating governments create agreements in which they voluntarily commit to taking steps within their local control. These agreements have become more detailed over time, and have evolved from an initial focus primarily on mitigation to increasingly including adaptation. However, the

[49] ICLEI, 'Press Release Durban Outcomes: Nations Invest in Time, World Must Invest in Cities' (12 December 2011) <https://perma.cc/GQ8N-FVAR> accessed 6 February 2020.

[50] See Local Government Climate Roadmap, 'From Copenhagen to Cancún to South Africa: COP15—COP16—COP17' (2010) <https://perma.cc/GMA3-VMUY> accessed 6 February 2020.

[51] Gino Begin, 'Comment: Look to Cities for Genuine Low Carbon Progress' *Responding to Climate Change* (11 October 2013) <https://perma.cc/P86N-LK9F> accessed 6 February 2020.

[52] Ibid.

[53] See Local Government Climate Roadmap (n 50).

participation rate of cities in key US metropolitan regions has been low other than in the Copenhagen City Climate Catalogue.

A sampling of agreements made from 2009 to the present exemplifies these trends. The 2,903 localities registered with the Copenhagen City Climate Catalogue—created in conjunction with the 2009 negotiations—made climate change commitments, often a percentage reduction in CO_2 equivalents by a certain date.[54] The 2010 Mexico City Pact, which ICLEI facilitated, built on the types of commitments localities made at Copenhagen, adding more substance to them. The 250 signatories to the pact—substantially fewer than those making commitments in the Catalogue—'voluntarily commit to 10 action points to advance local climate action, including the reduction of emissions, adaptation to the impacts of climate change and fostering city-to-city co-operation',[55] with an emphasis on 'globally measurable, reportable, and verifiable (MRV) local climate action'.[56] Signatories were encouraged to report their climate actions on the 'carbon*n* Cities Climate Registry' (cCCR).[57]

The Durban Adaptation Charter, an agreement among localities parallel to the 2011 Durban negotiations, moved the focus to adaptation.[58] The original 107 mayors and elected officials representing 950 local governments have grown to 341 mayors and elected official representing 1,069 organizations. These leaders have committed to various initiatives around adaptation—including integrating it into their local planning, preparing adaptation strategies, aligning adaptation and mitigation goals, and promoting multilevel, integrated governance and partnerships.[59] In addition, the Charter 'offers cities a channel of opportunity to leverage funding sources and partnerships, an ever growing need in cities in emerging economies'.[60] Ninety-four per

[54] ICLEI, 'City Climate Catalogue: Over 1700 Communities Making a Point' (30 October 2009) <https://perma.cc/UA5V-FQ2K> accessed 6 February 2020; The City Climate Catalogue, 'How Does the Catalogue Work?' <https://perma.cc/A4M8-84TH> accessed 6 February 2020. As of the website's most recent update, 2,903 communities have listed 3,251 targets; see The City Climate Catalogue, 'List of Commitments' <https://perma.cc/ES88-N6EM> accessed 6 February 2020.

[55] ICLEI, 'Low-carbon City' <https://perma.cc/7RKR-TT9X> accessed 6 February 2020; see also International Secretariat, 'Global Cities Covenant on Climate: The Mexico City Pact, Second Annual Report' (2012) <https://perma.cc/RU7A-XADW> accessed 6 February 2020.

[56] World Mayors Council on Climate Change, 'Global Cities Covenant on Climate Change—The Mexico City Pact' <https://perma.cc/B6A4-5CYQ> accessed 6 February 2020.

[57] Ibid.

[58] See Durban Local Government Convention, 'Durban Adaptation Charter for Local Governments as Adopted on the 4th December 2011 of the Occasion of the "Durban Local Government Convention: Adapting to a Changing Climate"—Towards COP17/CMP7 and Beyond' (2011) 2–3 <https://unfccc.int/files/meetings/durban_nov_2011/statements/application/pdf/111209_cop17_hls_iclei_charter.pdf> accessed 4 February 2020; eThekwini Municipality, 'Implementation of the Durban Adaptation Charter' <https://www.durban.gov.za/City_Services/development_planning_management/environmental_planning_climate_protection/Projects/Pages/11.Implementation-of-the-Durban-Adaptation-Charter.aspx> accessed 6 February 2020.

[59] See eThekwini Municipality (n 58).

[60] ICLEI, 'Global Climate Change Adaptation Charter Gains Momentum with 11 New Signatories' (6 June 2013) <https://perma.cc/YB6R-UQSB> accessed 6 February 2020; see Durban Adaptation Charter (n 58).

cent of those who had signed by 31 July 2012 were located in developing nations—with the majority coming from the southern hemisphere[61]—a point of concern—though recent signatories include, among others, Bonn, Germany; Fort Lauderdale, Florida; North Vancouver, Canada; Linkping, Sweden; and Seferihisar, Turkey.[62]

Although not in conjunction with a COP, the 2013 Nantes Declaration of Mayors and Subnational Leaders on Climate Change[63] is interesting because of its focus on the multiscalar dimensions of local action. Adopted 'with the support of over 50 mayors from 30 countries, and more than 20 regional and global networks of local and subnational governments,'[64] the Nantes Declaration aims to increase connections between the local and global levels. It emphasizes scaling up local climate action and engaging with government and members of the private and financial sectors at multiple levels.[65]

Since the 2015 Paris Agreement, cities have become even more integrated with nation-state efforts. For example, the Marrakech Partnership for Global Climate Action, which was launched as a complementary agreement at the December 2016 COP, 'supports implementation of the Paris Agreement by enabling collaboration between governments and the cities, regions, businesses and investors that must act on climate change'.[66] The partnership focuses on seven inter-related thematic areas: land use, oceans and coastal zones, water, human settlements, transport, energy, industry, and climate finance.[67] In the lead-up to the 2019 COP in Madrid, it released a 'Yearbook of Climate Action 2019—Climate Action Pathways', and an Executive Summary for each of the Thematic Groups that updates the collaborative progress.[68]

Sub-national commitments to nation-state goals under the international treaty regime also continue to grow. As described above, members in the international-level C40 network are making commitments to plans that put them in line with limiting temperature rise to 1.5°C.[69] The national-level Climate Mayors similarly pledged to meet

[61] eThekwini Municipality, 'Durban Adaptation Charter' (2012) 3 <https://www.durban.gov.za/City_Services/development_planning_management/environmental_planning_climate_protection/Projects/Documents/DAC__Pamphlet.pdf> accessed 6 February 2020.

[62] See ICLEI, 'Global Climate Change' (n 60). According to the Adaptation Charter's website, two localities from the US are signatories; Durban Adaptation Charter, 'Signatories of the Durban Adaptation Charter' <https://www.durbanadaptationcharter.org/signatories> accessed 6 February 2020.

[63] See ICLEI, 'Nantes Declaration of Mayors and Subnational Leaders on Climate Change Local Government Climate Roadmap' (2013–15) 1.

[64] ICLEI, Local Government Climate Roadmap, 'Nantes: World Mayors Summit on Climate Change 2013' <https://perma.cc/S9ZV-VCML> accessed 6 February 2020.

[65] See Nantes Declaration (n 63) 2–3; Begin (n 51).

[66] UNFCCC, 'Marrakech Partnership for Global Climate Action' <https://unfccc.int/climate-action/marrakech-partnership-for-global-climate-action> accessed 1 February 2020.

[67] UNFCCC, 'Yearbook of Climate Action 2019—Marrakech Partnership for Global Climate Action' (2019) <https://unfccc.int/sites/default/files/resource/GCA_Yearbook2019.pdf> accessed 6 February 2020.

[68] ICLEI, 'Marrakech Partnership for Global Climate Action' <https://iclei.org/en/COP25.html> accessed 4 February 2020.

[69] See n 23 and accompanying text.

what US goals would have been had it not withdrawn from the Paris Agreement under President Trump, and have committed to partnership as President Biden has rejoined the agreement.[70]

The on-the-ground impact of these networks on needed local action could be enhanced by (1) creating differentiated tool-kits and models, (2) increasing multiscalar network collaboration and coordination, and (3) reducing participation costs.[71] First, divergent needs and opportunities in different city types made it critical to create more differentiated models and toolkits.[72] Second, the models, tool-kits, and recognition provided by numerous networks at different levels address many similar steps that cities could take, but are framed in various ways. This variation means that a city participating in more than one network would need to spend time reframing similar actions multiple times. If networks collaborated to create more consistency in what they ask of cities, they might increase their individual impact and the ability to measure across networks their impact on what their members are doing.[73] Finally, an important question moving forward is the extent to which the cost of joining a network influences participation rates. Networks vary significantly in whether and how much they charge member cities, and some local government representatives have indicated that some fees are cost prohibitive.[74]

V. CONCLUSION: THE EVOLVING ROLE OF SUB-NATIONAL ACTORS IN INTERNATIONAL ENVIRONMENTAL LAW

Cities' involvement in international and transnational efforts on climate change provides an important example of the evolving role of sub-national actors in international environmental law. Although the formal structures of international law have not changed—the treaties still take place only among nation-states—sub-national actors are forming networks at multiple scales that interact with each other and with emerging international environmental law. The multiscalar networks of cities, and the ways in which they partner and intersect, illustrate this trend.[75]

As a consequence of these networks' efforts, the formal processes of international environmental law-making increasingly acknowledge the role of sub-national actors and

[70] See n 41 and accompanying text.

[71] See Osofsky (n 6) 45–57.

[72] See ibid.

[73] See Section II.

[74] 'Join UCLG' <https://www.uclg.org/en/join-uclg> accessed 6 February 2020; ICLEI US, 'Membership Dues' <https://perma.cc/5N4N-DX9H> accessed 6 February 2020; World Mayors Council on Climate Change, 'Registration Form' <https://perma.cc/V6B5-RAD8> accessed 6 February 2020; 'Confidential Meeting with Local Leaders' (7 February 2014) (notes on file with author).

[75] See Sections II and III.

find ways to include them. The Marrakech Partnership for Global Climate Action, for example, emerged from a COP, but included sub-national actors.[76] Moreover, this growing inclusion of sub-national actors in international environmental law-making processes is complemented by them creating parallel agreements to uphold commitments made by nation-states. The cities making pledges in line with—and in the case of C40 cities exceeding—the Paris Agreement illustrate this trend.[77]

This growing role for sub-national actors in international environmental law-making represents a significant evolution from a view of international law centred on sovereign nation-states. However, as the example of their role in addressing climate change illustrates, this evolution is much needed. Many important problems in international environmental law, such as climate change, require active involvement at multiple scales to make progress.

BIBLIOGRAPHY

Kevin Cox, 'Spaces of Dependence, Spaces of Engagement and the Politics of Scale, or: Looking for Local Politics' *Political Geography*, 17/1 (1998): 1

James Crawford, *Brownlie's Principles of International Law* (8th edn, OUP 2012)

Gerald Frug and David Barron, 'International Local Government Law' *Urban Law*, 38/1 (2006): 1

Hari Osofsky, 'Suburban Climate Change Efforts: Possibilities for Small and Nimble Cities Participating in State, Regional, National, and International Networks' *Cornell Journal of Law and Public Policy*, 22/2 (2012): 395

Judith Resnik *et al*, 'Ratifying Kyoto at the Local Level: Sovereigntism, Federalism, and Translocal Organizations of Government Actors (TOGAs)' *Arizona Law Review*, 50/3 (2008): 709

[76] Marrakech Partnership for Global Climate Action (n 66).

[77] C40 Cities (n 24).

CHAPTER 40

EPISTEMIC COMMUNITIES

PETER M HAAS*

I. INTRODUCTION

As the world becomes more globalized, decision-makers grow uncertain about what their interests are and how best to achieve them. Ideas become increasingly important as maps or frames for decision-makers in an unfamiliar setting, as they cannot rely on geo-political doctrines for a guide to various areas of foreign policy and international practice.

The environment provides a telling issue area in which to address the role of ideas in an increasingly uncertain global policy context. This chapter looks at the concept of 'epistemic communities' and the role of epistemic communities in institutionalizing ideas in international relations. In particular, it examines the role played by ecological ideas in the development of international environmental law and the role played by sympathetic international environmental lawyers in converting such rules of nature to rules for humans.

This chapter begins with a definition and intellectual history of epistemic communities. It then applies this definition to the study of international environmental law and discusses whether or not international lawyers constitute an epistemic community. It concludes with discussion of some of the recent challenges to the influence of epistemic communities in world politics more broadly, and thus the future of international environmental law.

* A number of international lawyers educated me about their craft for the first edition of the handbook. I still thank Cesare Romano, Peter Sand, Edith Brown Weiss, Kal Raustiala, Dan Esty, Laurence Boisson de Chazournes, Alexandre Kiss, and Naomi Roht-Arriaza, as well as Lavanya Rajamani and Jacqueline Peel.

II. EPISTEMIC COMMUNITIES

A. The Concept of Epistemic Communities

'Epistemic communities' is a concept developed by 'soft' constructivist scholars of international relations concerned with agency. Soft constructivists in general focus on the role of various types of norms, principled beliefs, causal beliefs, and discourses in establishing roles and rules in international relations: that is determining the identities, interests, and practices that shape the identification of actors in international relations.[1]

The concept helps international relations scholars to describe the actors associated with the formulation of causal beliefs, and the circumstances, resources, and mechanisms by which new ideas or policy doctrines get developed and influence the political process. It also aids in understanding and explaining the broader process by which their ideas shape politics. Epistemic communities are important actors that are responsible for developing and circulating causal ideas and associated normative beliefs. They thus help to identify state interests and preferences, as well as to identify legitimate participants in the policy process, and influence the form and content of negotiated outcomes by shaping how conflicts of interest will be resolved. Attention to epistemic communities provides a way to understand agency in politics and policy formation. Under conditions of complexity, decision-makers are uncertain of their goals or how to achieve them. Ideas may play important roles in framing the policy debate, and in predisposing outcomes highlighted by each perspective.

Epistemic communities are networks—often transnational—of knowledge-based experts with an authoritative claim to policy relevant knowledge within their domain of expertise. Their members share knowledge about the causation of social or physical phenomena in an area for which they have a reputation for competence, and a common set of normative beliefs about what actions will benefit human welfare in such a domain. Members are experts with professional training who enjoy social authority based on their reputation for impartial expertise. In the environmental realm they are primarily scientists and engineers, and in economic matters they are economists. Such individuals may hold positions in multiple locations over their careers: academia, think tanks, governments, and even within firms. Few are

[1] See Chapter 9, 'International Relations Theory', in this volume; Emanuel Adler, 'Seizing the Middle Ground: Constructivism in World Politics' *European Journal of International Relations*, 3/3 (1997): 319; Peter Katzenstein, Robert Keohane, and Stephen Krasner, 'International Organization and the Study of World Politics' *International Organisation*, 52/4 (1998): 645; Stephen Walt, 'International Relations: One World, Many Theories' *Foreign Policy*, 110 (1998): 29; Stefano Guzzini, 'A Reconstruction of Constructivism in International Relations' *European Journal of International Relations* 6/2 (2000): 147; Jack Snyder, 'One World, Rival Theories' *Foreign Policy*, 145 (2004): 52; Peter Haas, *Epistemic Communities, Constructivism and International Environmental Politics* (Routledge 2015); Emanuel Adler, *World Ordering: A Social Theory of Cognitive Evolution* (CUP 2019).

drawn to non-governmental organizations (NGOs), because most NGOs value principled beliefs over causal beliefs in formulating and justifying their policy discourses.[2] Their beliefs are an analytic level below those of Dryzek's 'discourses', although their political involvement can contribute in a causal way to the institutionalization of such broader discourses.[3] In particular, they are a group of professionals, often from a number of different disciplines, who share all of the following characteristics:

1. *Shared consummatory values or principled beliefs*: Such beliefs provide a value-based rationale for social action by the members of the community.
2. *Shared causal beliefs or professional judgement*: Such beliefs provide analytic reasons and explanations of behaviour, offering causal explanations for the multiple linkages between possible policy actions and desired outcomes. While they need not agree on every element—in fact they are likely to disagree vehemently about some elements—they do agree both about the core assumptions and causal forces from which their models of the world derive, as well as about the means by which such differences can potentially be reconciled.
3. *Common notions of validity*: Intersubjective, internally defined criteria for validating knowledge.
4. *A common policy enterprise*: A set of practices associated with a central set of problems that have to be tackled, presumably out of a conviction that human welfare will be enhanced as a consequence.

This combination of factors—especially the socialized truth tests and common causal beliefs—distinguish epistemic communities from other types of policy networks and groups active in politics and policy-making. Unlike other organized interest groups active in politics and policy-making, epistemic communities are bound by the truth tests to which they were socialized. They thus are more likely to provide information that is politically untainted and 'workable' in the political sense that it will be embraced and followed by political authorities concerned about the need for appearing impartial. Their advice is also more likely to be technically effective, in the sense of obtaining the desired goals, than would be policies derived by political compromise. Politically their reputation for expertise and impartiality provides a social provenance, in the sense of the pedigree imparted, for example, by antiques appraisers, that confers confidence in their advice by potential consumers.

[2] See Chapter 38, 'Non-State Actors', in this volume.
[3] See Chapter 2, 'Discourses', in this volume.

B. Intellectual History of Scholarship About Epistemic Communities

Constructivism has achieved the intellectual status as one of the dominant approaches in international relations.[4] The ideational focus was absorbed into the broader constructivist programme developed in international relations and comparative politics that looked at the role of beliefs and ideas in shaping state interests and practices. Epistemic communities provide a mechanism by which new ideas are developed and circulated, and a means for focusing on agency when studying international cooperation and governance. Consequently, the role of causal ideas and epistemic communities in explaining international cooperation has received increased attention.[5] Causal ideas and epistemic communities are now generally regarded as significant sources of state interests under conditions of complexity and uncertainty, as a main source in the origins and forms of multilateral regimes, and as important actors in the broader processes of social learning, reflexive governance, and identity formation.[6] That is, constructivists have demonstrated that globalization makes actors uncertain about their interests and policies, and that various forms of social constructs (ideas) play a significant role in helping actors plot their course in uncertain conditions.

The focus on causal ideas and their transmission mechanisms has been largely eclipsed since the late 1990s by greater attention to the role of norms and principled beliefs. A variety of critiques have been offered of the epistemic communities' research programme.[7] Some of these challenges include the following:

- Epistemic communities' knowledge base is itself socially constructed, and represents the potential systematic bias of those responsible for articulating research agendas.
- It is difficult to isolate the influence of the causal beliefs of epistemic communities from the institutional influence of the formal institutions with which they are associated.
- Epistemic communities' scholarship lacked a compelling theory of the state and did not pay sufficient attention to the domestic politics of the countries in which epistemic communities exercised a potential influence.
- Better appreciation is needed for which ideas are likely to prove attractive to decision-makers in response to uncertainty.

[4] See Chapter 9, 'International Relations Theory', in this volume.

[5] See n 1.

[6] Ibid.

[7] For an overview of these critiques and some trenchant rejoinders see Claire Dunlop, 'Epistemic Communities: A Reply to Toke' *Politics*, 20/3 (2000): 137; Haas (n 1).

These critiques have led to increased analytic clarification and to stronger theoretical foundations and refinements for the constructivist epistemic communities' research programme. While states are key juridical actors, and act wilfully, they vary in their administrative and political ability to formulate environmental (and other) policy, to absorb ideas domestically and from abroad, and to enforce policies at home. States are functionally differentiated, and vary widely according to their state/society relations and their technical capacity to formulate and enforce public policies in technical domains. State capacity in this sense is issue-specific: that is, regulatory potential varies by issue because the nature of the state's institutions, their resources, and policy networks vary by issue. Consequently, governance varies depending on the issue area.

Epistemic communities are most likely to emerge initially under circumstances affected both by issue and state characteristics. They are likely to be found working on substantive issues where scientific disciplines have been applied to policy-oriented work such as environmental protection, economic development, and energy policy. Thus, epistemic communities arise in disciplines associated with natural science, engineering, ecology, and even economics. They usually emerge around specific topics whose research support is relatively inexpensive and not directly related to the explicit mission of the sponsoring research body. For instance, the discipline of ecology—relatively cheap and distanced from funding agencies—enjoyed more legitimacy in the United States than nuclear physics during the Cold War when physics was closely tied to the Manhattan Project and the US nuclear programme. Oceanographers during the Cold War enjoyed generous funding from the US Office of Naval Research due to its utility for seafloor mapping which could be used for hiding US nuclear submarines and finding Soviet ones, while retaining autonomy for conducting research on currents and water quality.[8] Consequently, the research and policy guidance of the epistemic community will be relatively independent of the explicit agenda of the research sponsor. Epistemic communities will thus enjoy broader political influence on issues such as the environment and ecology, rather than nuclear energy, because their findings are seen as being impartial or independent of explicit political influence. Environmental research is relatively inexpensive, compared to that of nuclear energy, and is conducted through networks of researchers who are not directly associated with the government or government laboratories. Epistemic communities are also most likely to emerge in countries with well-established research capacity and where scientists enjoy some autonomy from the state. In such social settings, the knowledge base will be relatively untainted and as a result enjoy a stronger political authority and legitimacy.

[8] Chandra Mukerji, *A Fragile Power: Scientists and the State* (Princeton University Press 1989); Virginia Walsh, *Global Institutions and Social Knowledge: Generating Research at the Scripps Institution and the Inter-American Tropical Tuna Commission, 1900s–1990s* (MIT Press 2004); Elena Aronova, Karen Baker, and Naomi Oreskes, 'Big Science and Big Data in Biology' *Historical Studies in the Natural Sciences*, 40/2 (2010): 183.

States will look for new ideas after highly publicized crises. Such crises, potential or actual environmental disasters, or economic crises will prompt decision-makers to take action to ameliorate pressure from domestic constituencies and from abroad.

The empirical experience with the global reception of environmental ideas does not directly engage the question of which ideas will matter at such points, other than saying that new ideas must have some affinity with existing beliefs or discourses, and that there is a strong path-dependent element to the dynamics of causal ideas. In the early 1970s, when international institutions were founded to address global environmental threats under the influence of the United Nations (UN) Conference on the Human Environment (Stockholm Conference), there were few contending epistemic communities. In fact, there were only three major intellectual approaches to international environmental management. Traditional Resource managerial approaches were widely discredited by the 'Limits to Growth' study and the 1973 Oil Crisis.[9] Market-based approaches to environmental management were weakly advanced by economists, the World Bank, and the General Agreement on Tariffs and Trade (GATT) at the Stockholm Conference but they, and their institutional backers, generally paid little heed to the conference. Market-based approaches did receive more attention in the 1990s, particularly in the drafting of the Kyoto Protocol.[10] Access to information—a form of economic instrument that confers information and improves the prospects for informed consent and contracting—also became more prominent, especially in the 1998 Aarhus Convention on Access to Information, Public Participation in Decision-Making and Access to Justice in Environmental Matters,[11] and the 1998 Rotterdam Convention on Prior Informed Consent (PIC) in Hazardous Chemicals Management.[12] What is striking analytically, however, is the relative infrequency with which the negotiated outcomes that correspond to the dominant expertise paradigm—economics—have been adopted. Even in the climate change regime, for example, market mechanisms are instrumentally applied to achieve the substantive goals, identified by scientists, of ensuring that anthropogenic greenhouse gas emissions do not exceed the carrying capacity of the atmosphere.[13] Market mechanisms are primarily concerned with means rather than ends. They seek to provide mechanisms that improve environmental quality, but they are agnostic about the desirable level of environmental quality to be pursued. Conversely, epistemic communities specify the desirable environmental target and work backwards to get to the policy instruments. Even with the popularity of market-based discourses in the 1990s, negotiated outcomes—including the 2001 Stockholm Convention on POPs—the command-and-control approach of the ecological epistemic

[9] Stephen Macekura, *Of Limits and Growth: The Rise of Global Sustainable Development in the Twentieth Century* (CUP 2015).

[10] See Chapters 6 and 53, 'Instrument Choice' and 'Market Mechanisms', in this volume.

[11] See Chapter 21, 'Public Participation', in this volume.

[12] See Chapter 33, 'Hazardous Substances and Activities', in this volume.

[13] See Chapter 29, 'Climate Change', in this volume.

community,[14] which derives environmental standards from the causal beliefs of the community, has persisted.

The nascent ecological epistemic community remained the only game in town to assert a technical claim to expertise for addressing the new agenda of issues. Subsequently, this approach has retained its dominance as the presumptive approach to environmental management. At the time of its inception and institutionalization into international law, as well as the operating routines of international organizations and national environmental agencies, the ecological beliefs of the epistemic community at least corresponded loosely to the overarching policy paradigm and political imperatives of the time. It asserted the role of the state in promoting environmental protection.[15]

More generally, some hypotheses were offered about which ideas are likely to be favoured in response to uncertainty and crises. Thus, analysts suggested that it is not the accuracy of objective truth that matters, but rather the political function that potential ideas serve. In either case, truth alone is insufficient, politicians must believe that these ideas serve some political utility in order to apply them. Judith Goldstein suggested that ideas that have been regarded as successful in the past are likely to enjoy favour,[16] such as trade liberalization; while John Odell suggested that simple ideas will enjoy an edge over more complicated ones.[17] Moreover, Jeffrey Garrett and Barry Weingast suggested that ideas that are favourable to cementing political coalitions, either internationally or domestically, will prevail.[18] In general, if there is only one candidate it is likely to prevail. The political factors associated with selection are only salient if there exist a large number of competing ideas. In practice, the universe of available causal policy ideas is not very large, and there may not be a vast opportunity for political competition at moments of selection following crises.

More attention also has been paid to the broader dynamics by which ideas are transferred internationally. While they may initially be developed and consolidated in advanced democracies, they will be emulated and borrowed in other countries with sufficient domestic scientific capacities. International institutions are also likely to play an influential role in the broader transmission pattern.[19] Major formal international institutions that can play a role are those that enjoy strong organizational resources and some autonomy from their member governments, through a combination of secretariat skills, porous organizational boundaries, and executive leadership. Such institutions are most likely to be immediately responsive to recognizing changes in the policy environment and to absorbing new ideas about their underlying missions.

[14] See Chapter 6, 'Instrument Choice', in this volume.

[15] See Chapter 35, 'The State', in this volume.

[16] Judith Goldstein, *Ideas, Interests and American Trade Policy* (Cornell University Press 1993).

[17] John Odell, 'Understanding International Trade Policies: An Emerging Synthesis' *World Politics*, 43/1 (1990): 139.

[18] Geoffrey Garrett and Barry Weingast, 'Ideas, Interests and Institutions: Constructing the European Community's Internal Market' in Judith Goldstein and Robert Keohane (eds), *Ideas and Foreign Policy* (Cornell University Press 1993) 173.

[19] See Chapter 36, 'International Institutions', in this volume.

In the environmental realm, these institutions include United Nations Environment Programme (UNEP), the World Bank, and the UN Economic Commission for Europe (UNECE). Subsequently, organizations may transmit the new ideas to member states through training programmes and the demonstration effect, as well as to other international organizations through joint activities.

There are partial overlaps of epistemic communities and international institutions, as some institutions are intimately intertwined with science policy advisory bodies, such as in the climate change regime. It is possible analytically to disentangle the causal effects of ideas from the institutions associated with them by controlling for the influence of the institution, and by looking at the same institution's behaviour over time, subject to the ideas that enjoy popularity within it. For instance, the World Bank encouraged much stronger environmental policies after the 1987 reforms that had the effect of lodging more ecological ideas within the Bank.[20] Thus, epistemic communities and causal ideas have played a determinative role in influencing the ends to which institutional resources will be deployed in practice.

More generally, studies have separated two distinct mechanisms by which ideas disseminate internationally.[21] One is active social learning, in which individual decision-makers are persuaded of the virtue of new ideas through direct exposure to epistemic community members or international institutions acting on their behalf. Such social learning is most likely to lead to robust changes in national practices as a consequence of profound long-term shifts in the appreciation of the national interest and how countries' prospects for material welfare are influenced by ecological stability. An example of this pattern is the European acid rain regime (LRTAP),[22] in which the concept of critical loads was developed by UNECE and the Institute for Applied Systems Analysis (IIASA) and disseminated through key countries to inform international treaties on sulphur and nitrogen oxide emissions, as well as national policies and legislation adopted to implement treaty obligations.[23]

A second pattern of dissemination lacks the social element of direct contact that social learning entails. This second pattern is one of policy borrowing, or emulation of patterns of behaviour and policies from salient countries and organizations. While policy borrowing is a major pattern by which ideas diffuse internationally and lead

20 Robert Wade, 'The World Bank and the Environment' in Morten Boas and Desmond McNeill (eds), *Global Institutions and Development: Framing the World?* (Routledge 2004) 72; Tamar Gutner, 'World Bank Environmental Reform' International Organisation, 59/3 (2005): 773–83; Susan Park, 'Socialization, the World Bank Group and global environmental governance' in Frank Biermann, Bernd Siebenhuner, and Anna Schreyogg (eds), *International Organizations in Global Environmental Governance* (Routledge 2009) 91.

21 Richard Rose, *Lesson Drawing in Public Policy* (Chatham House 1993); Claire Dunlop and Claudio Radaelli, 'Systematising Policy Learning: From Monolith to Dimensions' *Political Studies*, 61/3 (2012): 599, Peter Haas, 'Ideas, Experts and Governance' in Monika Ambrus *et al* (eds), *The Role of 'Experts' in International Decision-Making: Advisors, Decision-Makers or Irrelevant?* (CUP 2014) 193.

22 1989 Convention on Long-Range Transboundary Air Pollution.

23 See Chapter 28, 'Transboundary Air Pollution', in this volume.

to policy harmonization, it lacks the resilience of social learning, as without deeper institutionalized socialization borrowed lessons may not enjoy the same degree of persistence as policies developed and diffused through social learning. Instances of this have to do with adoptions of economic incentives for environmental protection in Europe, and the widespread application of toxic chemical standards developed by the United States or the World Health Organization (WHO), which are widely adopted but selectively enforced.[24]

Social learning is better understood now as a path-dependent process of collective social change. New ideas are solicited by uncertain policy-makers in the aftermath of well-publicized disasters or shocks, which encourage decision-makers to seek guidance for responding to new and uncertain issues. Such conditions are more frequent under conditions of globalization and complexity. Through the steps described above, new ideas imparted to decision-makers by epistemic community members have the effect of changing state understandings of the policy environment and of their own national interests and lead eventually to changes in state practices as well. These beliefs become institutionalized through the redeployment of state resources and through the consolidation of administrative practices and laws.

C. The Ecological Epistemic Community and Multilateral Environmental Governance

A new environmental management doctrine based on ecological principles emerged in the 1960s. Since 1972, the ecological epistemic community has increasingly institutionalized this new management doctrine in state policies and practices, in the programmatic activities of international institutions, and in international regimes. As a consequence of the international institutionalization of ideas held by the ecological epistemic community, states have undertaken more comprehensive styles of environmental management for transboundary and global environmental threats, leading to selective improvements in environmental quality. Members of the ecological epistemic community subscribed to holistic ecological beliefs about the need for policy coordination subject to ecosystemic laws, as compared to more philosophical or normative approaches to governance.[25] Their ideas about ecological management were based on a systems perspective of environmental and social systems. Ecological management proposals favour setting comprehensive environmental standards based on conservative estimates of the ability of ecosystems to sustain stress, subject to the epistemic community's technical understanding of the behaviour of particular

[24] See Chapter 33, 'Hazardous Substances and Activities', in this volume; Per-Olof Busch, Helge Jorgens, and Kerstin Tews, 'The Global Diffusion of Regulatory Instruments: The Making of a New International Environmental Regime' *The Annals of the American Academy of Political and Social Science*, 598/1 (2005): 146–167.

[25] See Chapters 2 and 14, 'Discourses' and 'Earth Jurisprudence', in this volume.

ecosystems. They promoted international environmental regimes that are grounded on policies that offered coherent plans for the management of entire ecosystems, sensitive to interactions between environmental media (such as air and water), sources of pollution, and contending uses of common property resources. Rather than limiting themselves to more traditional policies for managing discrete state activities or governing geographic areas, within fairly short-term time horizons through uniform commitments, they proposed treaties, in which bans and emissions limits were set for multiple contaminants, with environmental standards for each contaminant set according to scientific understanding about its environmental impact and its interactive effects with other contaminants.

Over time, the ecological epistemic community added a broader social component regarding the need for widespread stakeholder participation in research and negotiations, out of the belief that such non-state actors, and particularly Indigenous peoples, would have access to vital ecological knowledge outside the traditional domain of ecological sciences.[26] Moreover, such non-state actors, it was felt, would prove powerful political forces for compliance once management efforts were designed.

Thousands of multilateral environmental agreements have been concluded since the Second World War, according to Ron Mitchell's careful count.[27] The most intensive periods of treaty adoption were the 1970s through the 1990s, although treaties continue to be adopted, at a slightly slower pace.[28] Despite profound geo-political realignments, countries continue to adopt environmental treaties and to comply with their obligations.

Four ideal types of MEAs stand out: social learning, institutional bargaining, least common denominator outcomes, and parallel play. Each has a distinctive political process associated with it, as well as characteristic forms of governance and effectiveness.

1. *Social learning*

When regimes are negotiated with the involvement of epistemic communities and strong international institutions, they develop through a process of 'social learning'. Treaties concluded with epistemic community input reflect causal beliefs about environmental management. These treaties are based on environmental standards that reflect the epistemic community's technical understanding of the ability of specific environments to sustain stress. Negotiations occur within a scientific discourse, in which political debate and compromise reflect expert consensus on the behaviour of ecosystems and their ability to sustain stress. The substance of regimes reflects scientific

[26] See Chapter 42, 'Indigenous Peoples', in this volume.

[27] Ronald Mitchell, 'International Environmental Agreements: A Survey of their Features, Formation, and Effects' *Annual Review of Environment and Resources*, 28 (2003): 429; Ronald Mitchell et al,'What We Know (and Could Know) about International Environmental Agreements' *Global Environmental Politics*, 20/1 (2020): 103–121.

[28] Daniel Bodansky, *The Art and Craft of International Environmental Law* (Harvard University Press 2010); Philippe Sands and Jacqueline Peel, *Principles of International Environmental Law* (4th edn, CUP 2018); see Chapter 24, 'Multilateral Environmental Treaty Making', in this volume.

consensus about the most important environmental threats, and negotiated standards reflect consensus about the degree of environmental stress the target environment can sustain. Social learning generates treaties with differentiated national obligations and substantive commitments, based on expert consensus on causes and environmental effects. Agenda setting is responsive to scientific advice and publicized crises. States' interests may be altered as a consequence of being exposed to new ideas, and negotiated treaties will reflect an increased willingness to sacrifice short-term economic gains for longer term collective environmental protection.

Examples of social learning treaties include the 1987 Montreal Ozone Protocol, the application of the 'critical loads' approach to the 1994 Oslo Protocol to LRTAP on Further Reduction of Sulphur Emissions, the Mediterranean pollution control regime, the Stockholm Treaty on Persistent Organic Pollutants (POPs), the brief Revised Management Procedures for the international whaling regime, and the 1959 Antarctic Treaty System, in particular, the 1980 Convention on the Conservation of Antarctic Marine Living Resources (CCAMLR).

2. *Institutional bargaining*

Patterns of institutional bargaining embrace universal standards that are based on political compromise but have no clear relationship to environmental quality, such as the arbitrary, across-the-board cuts in pollution contained in early European air pollution agreements or North Sea emission controls. In the absence of technical consensus on the behaviour of the North Sea and the impact of individual pollutants on the overall health of the ecosystem, North Sea diplomats adopted 30% and 50% reductions in the emissions of a wide array of chemicals. Such standards, while politically attractive, lack any clear connection to overall environmental quality, and thus may impose economic costs without any offsetting environmental benefit.

3. *Least common denominator*

Treaties negotiated in the absence of strong institutions or epistemic communities are likely to generate least common denominator outcomes, comprising weak negotiated outcomes, which reflect the preferences of the most outspoken oppositional party. Examples include most fisheries treaties for Regional Marine Fishery Organizations.

4. *Parallel play*

Epistemic communities without strong institutions will lack any compelling foundation for their cognitive influence. Responsiveness to epistemic advice may still vary at the national level, leading to treaty and regimes which have mixed national behaviour. Countries with epistemic influence will follow epistemic advice, whereas others will not, leading to relatively incoherent regimes with disparate national policies and practices. Examples include the 2015 Paris Agreement on Climate Change, and the Sustainable Development Goals.

5. *Epistemic communities and multilateral environmental agreements*

Since the 1970s, an increasing number of regimes have been developed through the process of social learning. Only regimes negotiated in the shadow of epistemic communities and strong international institutions have yielded patterns of comprehensive environmental management through a process of social learning. Ecological epistemic community members, often working with UNEP, helped draft comprehensive international environmental regimes governing marine pollution, acid rain, stratospheric ozone protection, wetlands protection, protection of migratory species, polar bear protection, and the preservation of Antarctica. An increasing proportion of all environmental regimes are now based on the comprehensive ecological approach promoted by the ecological epistemic community as the epistemic community has increased in vigour and influence, and countries have institutionalized their ideas. In 1973, three out of eleven international environmental regimes were based on ecological management styles, in 1985, seven out of twenty-two, and in 1995, nine out of twenty-five, or ten, if the climate change regime's commitment to stabilizing atmospheric concentrations at safe levels is interpreted as an ecological frame. The frequency of environmental treaty signings has declined since 1973,[29] although states continue to adopt comprehensive treaties with epistemic community participation (such as the 2001 Stockholm POPs Contention, the 2010 Nagoya Protocol, the 2016 Kigali Amendment on Stratospheric Ozone, and the 2013 Minamata Convention on Mercury) and arrangements with formally associated science advisory bodies continue to persist (see Table 40.1). The application of ecological management ideas to environmental regimes spanning a number of geographic areas and functional activities means that most states have accepted ecological obligations for governing a wide variety of human activities.

The following illustrative table (Table 40.1) indicates the variety of negotiated outcomes that characterize the environmental regimes that were established since the Stockholm Conference. Social learning yielded comprehensive ecological efforts, with the combination of epistemic community involvement and strong international institutions. Such comprehensive efforts entail differentiated national obligations, substantive commitments, based on experts' consensus on the causes of environmental degradation. Institutional bargaining results from strong institutions that encourage states to compromise in the absence of epistemic consensus. Such treaties and regimes tend to involve disjointed treaties with uniform national regulatory obligations chosen for their political and emotional appeal. Finally, least common denominator results of weak collective obligations result from negotiations undertaken in the absence of strong institutions or strong scientific consensus, such as with most fisheries agreements, where the institutional context for treaty negotiation and

[29] Steinar Andresen, Elin Lerum Boasson, and Geir Hønneland, *International Environmental Agreements* (Routledge 2012).

national enforcement is extremely weak, and where fisheries biologists, although able to demonstrate that over-fishing is occurring, cannot convincingly identify sustainable fishery yields.

Table 40.1 Major environmental MEAs and their negotiated form

	Strong institutions	Weak institutions
	Social Learning	**Parallel Play**
EPISTEMIC COMMUNITIES	• 1987 Montreal Ozone Protocol and Amendments • Long Range Transport of Air Pollution • Persian Gulf Regional Seas Programme (pre-1980) • South Pacific Regional Seas Programme • South East Pacific Regional Seas Programme • 1959 Antarctic Treaty System • 1979 Convention on the Conservation of Migratory Species • 1973 Agreement on the Preservation of Polar Bears • 1971 Ramsar Treaty on Wetlands • 2001 Stockholm Convention on POPs • 2010 Nagoya Biodiversity Protocol • 1998 Rotterdam Convention (PIC) • 2013 Minamata Mercury	• 2015 Paris Agreement on Climate Change • 1987 Kyoto Protocol • 2015 Sustainable Development Goals
	Institutional Bargaining	**Least Common Denominator**
NO EPISTEMIC COMMUNITIES	• Red Sea Regional Seas Programme • Convention and Protocols on the Protection of the Black Sea • 1974 Convention on the Protection of the Baltic Sea • Protocols on the Protection of the North Sea (1987–) • 1972 London Dumping Convention/ marine dumping agreements under IMO • MARPOL 73–78/operational oil pollution • 1946 International Whaling Convention • 1989 Basel Convention of Transboundary Movements of Hazardous Wastes	• Caribbean Regional Seas Programme • West Africa Regional Seas Programme • East Africa Regional Seas Programme • Protocols on the Protection of the North Sea (1972–87) • Fisheries management conventions • Persian Gulf Regional Seas Programme (1980–)

The climate change and biodiversity regimes shed light on the nature of the consensual knowledge shared by the epistemic community. While in each case there exists a cohort of like-minded environmental specialists who believe that action is necessary in order to prevent calamitous climate change or loss of biodiversity, the knowledge base is insufficiently mature (or 'useable') in each instance to provide meaningful targets and deadlines for decision-makers to apply.

III. EPISTEMIC COMMUNITIES AND INTERNATIONAL ENVIRONMENTAL LAWYERS

International environmental lawyers do not themselves constitute an epistemic community.[30] However, they have played a key role in institutionalizing the ideas and actual participation of the ecological epistemic community in the formation of international environmental law and regimes.

A. International Environmental Lawyers Are Not an Epistemic Community

While there is now an active community of international environmental lawyers involved in the development and interpretation of international environmental law, they remain a policy community and not an epistemic community. Their shared beliefs take a different form from that of the ecological epistemic community discussed above, and they lack the social authority enjoyed by the ecological epistemic community.

International law as a field lacks the social authority or legitimacy of the technical authority commanded by epistemic communities. Legitimacy in the ecological epistemic community rests on the internally consistent substantive nature of the ideas put forth for policy-makers by experts, and the transparent way in which such ideas are developed and gain consensus. International environmental law, and international law more generally, is philosophically and epistemologically different from the social domain of ecological science. Whereas ecology and the technical domains in which epistemic communities operate are the realms of hybrid and brute facts, where claims about physical phenomena may be evaluated by recourse to mechanisms independent of the subject of study, law is a different activity. Law operates in the domain of social facts. The substantive domain of law is not subject to the type of shared tangible understandings that characterize the political domain in which ecological facts are identified for public policy. While international environmental law as a corpus may provide a presumptive backdrop against which negotiations and treaty drafting occurs,[31] international lawyers lack the authority in environmental policy circles that scientists and engineers enjoy.

[30] See Chapter 7, 'Scholarship', in this volume.

[31] Ian Johnstone, 'The Power of Interpretive Communities' in Michael Barnett and Raymond Duvall (eds), *Power in Global Governance* (CUP 2005) 185.

International environmental law also lacks epistemic status for sociological reasons. International lawyers lack the public respect for impartial views about the world to which their advice is deployed, for the reasons mentioned above. In addition, the professional knowledge base of international environmental law is insufficiently institutionalized to generate common truth tests and a tight sociological network. Law school curricula tend to offer only one elective course on international environmental law, and there are few professional career path opportunities for international environmental lawyers in the absence of litigation opportunities in the realm of international environmental law. The array of professional niches for international environmental lawyers remain fairly narrow, limited to submitting *amicus curiae* briefs and policy analysis, from law firms, legal NGOs (such as the Center for International Environmental Law), policy analysts, and law school professors.

International environmental law texts now exist, but they are largely collections of treaties rather than resting on a deductive set of propositions from which conclusions about institutional design and appropriate behaviour may derive. Most law texts summarize the variety of often competing legal principles which may be applied to environmental governance, as well as list of the relevant treaties.[32] For Daniel Bodansky and Jutta Brunnée,[33] for instance, international law is a process as much as the application of precedents and established principles and practices.[34] Thus, international environmental law lacks the core causal beliefs and truth tests that define an epistemic community.

B. International Environmental Lawyers and the Translation of Epistemic Communities' Ideas into International Environmental Law

International environmental lawyers have played an active role in the development of international environmental law, and of converting the causal ideas of epistemic communities into treaties for the management of environmental threats by institutionalizing scientists' involvement in collective decision-making and in drafting treaties based on the scientists' insights. Since the Stockholm Conference, a core network of individuals has been involved in the formulation of much of the

[32] Alan Boyle and Catherine Redgwell, *International Law and the Environment* (4th edn, OUP 2021); Bodansky (n 28); Sands and Peel (n 28).

[33] Bodansky (n 28); Jutta Brunnée and Stephen Toope, 'Interactional International Law and the Practice of Legality' in Emanuel Adler and Vincent Pouliot (eds), *International Practices* (CUP 2011) 108; Jutta Brunnée and Stephen Toope, 'Constructivism and International Law' in Jeffrey Dunoff and Mark Pollack (eds), *Interdisciplinary Perspectives on International Law and International Relations: The State of the Art* (CUP 2012) 119.

[34] Bodansky (n 28).

corpus of international environmental law. A small clique of lawyers initially worked for the Stockholm secretariat and cut their teeth drafting the 1972 London Dumping Convention. Subsequently, their rules of thumb were reproduced and acquired the status of precedent amongst the broader community of international lawyers. The cadre of sympathetic lawyers grew, with their foundations and institutional memories residing in UNEP's legal office (now called the Division of Environmental Law and Conventions), in the World Bank's legal office, and in some government offices. Some central figures included Patrick Szell (United Kingdom), Johann Lammers (Netherlands), Winfried Lang (Austria), Susan Biniaz (United States), and Peter Sand (Food and Agriculture Organization, UNEP, UNECE, and World Bank).

These lawyers developed a kernel of procedural techniques by which ecological principles of environmental management would be applied to environmental law. These techniques include the following:

- The umbrella convention-protocol sequence was developed in the 1976 Barcelona Convention for the Protection of the Mediterranean and Protocols on Marine Dumping and Emergency Co-operation. Initially, in the regional seas' treaties, this technique required states to commit not only to broad amorphous principles but also to more specific binding commitments as well, since states in most cases had to ratify at least one protocol. But this no longer seems to be true for current MEAs, which allow a state to become a party to the main treaty only, without ratifying the subsequently adopted protocol. The climate change and the Biodiversity regimes are both relevant examples.[35]
- COPs and treaty amendments: COPs (Conference of the Parties), through their decisions, develop the MEA-based regimes, thereby circumventing the problem of having to amend the treaty. In addition, by provisions such as those developed under the auspices of the Montreal Protocol, diplomats can approve environmental standards by amending an Annex to the Protocol without having to go through time consuming domestic ratification processes.[36]
- Lists of banned or regulated substances: The 1972 London Convention differentiates between banned substances (black list) and regulated substances (grey list). As of March 2006, for those states that are parties to the 1996 Protocol, this system was replaced by a ban on all dumping of wastes at sea, except for those substances listed (the so-called reverse listing approach).[37] Both systems require the identification of substances and setting appropriate standards and thus the involvement of environmental specialists.
- Standing expert committees and panels: Most international environmental regimes have been designed to have standing scientific panels associated with them for

[35] See Chapter 24, 'Multilateral Environmental Treaty Making', in this volume.

[36] Ibid.

[37] See Chapter 31, 'The Protection of the Marine Environment: Pollution and Fisheries', in this volume.

the provision of timely environmental monitoring and policy information. Such arrangements provide the regularized mechanism by which individual scientists and epistemic community members may be recruited and involved in international environmental treaty making.
- The establishment of dedicated voluntary trust funds so that regimes may be self-supporting. These funds have the effect of making the conventions financially self-supporting as well as creating more resources for programmatic activities.[38]

More broadly, international environmental lawyers have come to appreciate international environmental negotiations as an exercise in communication and learning, where individual parties develop new ways of understanding the world, others, and themselves as a consequence of being exposed to the causal ideas articulated by epistemic communities. Such a reflexive approach also provides the means by which international law development can accelerate past a snail's pace dictated by the least enthusiastic party.

IV. Conclusion

Over the last fifty years, the environment has become firmly established on the international diplomatic agenda and, through regime formation, binding rules have been developed for most human activities affecting environmental quality. Epistemic communities' participation in multilateralism is now a social fact, and UNEP (or UN Environment as it is now known) is the presumptive international institution for facilitating environmental treaty negotiations. Substantively the focus on international environmental regimes has shifted from discrete environmental standards to ecosystem protection. Procedurally it has come to rely much more heavily on the expert advice of the ecological epistemic community.

Epistemic communities are one of the principal vehicles by which new ideas of ecological sustainability and governance have evolved. International environmental lawyers have helped provide the institutional mechanisms by which these ideas have reached and been disseminated to states and other actors. Constructivist theories of international relations help to provide the explanatory parameters by which these processes occur and their effects.

In the aggregate, experience with environmental governance has triggered social learning about the international agenda and national interests. Whereas issues had traditionally been addressed in isolation of one another, increasingly substantive links are being drawn between issues which call for their joint governance. Thus, environment and security, environment and development, environment and trade, and

[38] See Chapter 54, 'Financial Assistance', in this volume.

the Sustainable Development Goals have all become recent items on the international agenda for collective action, as well as informing national practices. New institutions have been created at the behest of ecological epistemic communities to capture the interlinkages between issues, moving from just environmental protection to a broader environment plus agenda.[39]

Such emergent properties of the international environmental governance system are due to the gradual institutionalization of epistemic communities, science panels, and deference to expertise by states. However, such political representation is currently under siege from climate denialists and those who seek to undermine the legitimacy of science and expertise in environmental governance, and global governance more generally.[40] Such disputation hangs on the broader legitimacy of science; a topic for which multiple dimensions of legitimacy are widely invoked to justify the utility of organized science, while surprisingly few dimensions are used by the critics, affording defenders of expert governance and of epistemic communities the continued moral high ground with a wider array of arguments to support scientific governance.[41]

BIBLIOGRAPHY

Steinar Andresen et al, *Science and Politics in International Environmental Regimes* (Manchester University Press 2000)

Paolo Contini and Peter Sand, 'Methods to Expedite Environmental Protection: International Ecostandards' *American Journal of International Law*, 66/1 (1972): 37

Peter Haas (ed), *Knowledge, Power and International Policy Coordination* (University of South Carolina Press 1997)

Peter Haas, 'Environment: Pollution' in P J Simmons and Chantal Oudraat (eds), *Managing Global Issues: Lessons Learned* (Carnegie Foundation 2001) 310

Peter Haas and Ernst Haas, 'Learning to Learn' *Global Governance*, 1/3 (1995): 255

Edward Miles et al, *Environmental Regime Effectiveness* (MIT Press 2002)

[39] Daniel Deudney and Elizabeth Mendenhall, 'Green Earth: The Emergence of Planetary Civilization' in Simon Nicholson and Sikina Jinnah (eds), *New Earth Politics* (MIT Press 2016) 43; Robert Falkner and Barry Buzan, 'The Emergence of Environmental Stewardship as a Primary Institution of Global International Society' *European Journal of International Relations*, 25/1 (2019): 131.

[40] Naomi Oreskes and Erik Conway, *Merchants of Doubt* (Bloomsbury Press 2010); Daniel Drezner, *The Ideas Industry* (OUP 2017); Tom Nichols, *The Death of Expertise* (OUP 2017); Michiko Kakutani, *The Death of Truth* (Tim Duggan Books 2018).

[41] Peter Haas, 'The Epistemic Authority of Solution Oriented Global Environmental Assessments' *Environmental Science and Policy*, 77 (2017): 221–224.

CHAPTER 41

BUSINESS AND INDUSTRY

BENJAMIN J RICHARDSON AND BEATE SJÅFJELL

I. ORIENTATION

In the study of international environmental law, business corporations are typically viewed as actors under the auspices of various regulatory regimes developed by nation-states, or recognized as having some tacit influence over the agenda setting and implementation of such regimes.[1] This perspective might also acknowledge the limited accountability of corporations under international law.[2] Another perspective, which this chapter includes, is the business sector's initiative in shaping its own environmental agenda, often in the name of 'corporate social responsibility' (CSR). The traditional conception of international environmental law as dominated by nation-states and intergovernmental organizations is at odds with the heterogeneous and pluralistic character of contemporary governance unleashed by economic globalization and market deregulation that have opened significant space for business in global environmental decision-making.

This chapter introduces this subject, focusing on four key themes: (1) the institutional characteristics of the business corporation and its marketplace that influence the environmental performance of the private sector; (2) the CSR movement, which responds to criticisms of the environmental performance of business; (3) corporate accountability and liability under international environmental law; and (4) governance regimes fostering collaborative, multi-stakeholder processes that involve the private sector. This chapter should be read in conjunction with several others in this handbook that touch directly or indirectly on the business sector, notably chapters on investment law[3] and non-state actors.[4]

[1] Ulrich Beyerlin and Thilo Marauhn, *International Environmental Law* (Bloomsbury 2011).
[2] Elisa Morgera, *Corporate Accountability in International Environmental Law* (OUP 2009).
[3] See Chapter 44, 'Investment', in this volume.
[4] See Chapter 38, 'Non-State Actors', in this volume.

The diversity of business structures, practices, and their impacts belie the impression given by a cursory read of the scholarly literature and popular press that the business sector is a ubiquitous impediment to sustainable development. There is no homogenous business 'community', even though business actors operate within an increasingly homogenous market due to global deregulation. Furthermore, some corporations are involved in intrinsically environmentally problematic activities, notably the coal and oil industries. Others are more aligned to sustainability, in sectors as renewable energy, organic agriculture, green buildings, and eco-tourism.[5] Many corporations are between these two ends of the spectrum: in a range of industries that could be made more environmentally friendly, such as textiles and electronics, but where the transition is made difficult because of industry's prevailing business models based on overconsumption.

The next section surveys the role of corporate law and corporate governance in shaping environmental performance, and thereafter introduces the goals, mechanisms, and actors of the global CSR movement. Section III examines the governance of business in international environmental law including corporate liability for wrongdoing. Section IV discusses examples of new forms of multi-stakeholder environmental collaboration involving the business sector, while Section V concludes with reflections on the need for more fundamental change.

II. BUSINESS AND THE ENVIRONMENT: MAPPING THE TERRITORY

A. Corporate Environmental Performance and Its Governance

The corporation is the world's most prevalent business form, far outstripping alternatives, such as the cooperative or partnership. Changing societal needs and expectations have helped shift the modern corporation from being just an economic actor to also playing an important role in environmental management and social affairs. Many business actors, like much of the public sector, now ostensibly endorse the philosophy of sustainable development, reinforced by the adoption of the United Nations (UN) Sustainable Development Goals (SDGs) in 2015.[6] The transnational scope of business activity, through global supply chains, trading, and multinational operations, has put the corporate sector's environmental impacts under growing international

[5] Oliver Williams, *Corporate Social Responsibility: The Role of Business in Sustainable Development* (Routledge 2014).

[6] Norichika Kanie and Frank Biermann (eds), *Governing through Goals: Sustainable Development Goals as Governance Innovation* (MIT Press 2017).

scrutiny and stimulated public debate about whether the governance challenges are inherent in the institutional fabric of corporations and markets or relate more to the quality of their regulation at national or international levels.[7]

The environmental performance of the business sector is a contentious issue. Some firms offer the means and resources to alleviate unsustainable practices, such as through green-tech innovations, catering to green consumerism and conveyance of price signals about pending resource scarcities. Scholars, including John Elkington and Michael Porter, believe 'win-win' gains for the environment and the economy are attainable, in which business profitability dovetails with sustainability.[8] Yet, the business sector also levies a major environmental burden, owing to myriad factors including its short-term time horizons, deficits in firms' environmental expertise, and the priority given to profit-making and economic growth, with business models based on overconsumption. A UN study estimated in 2008 the cost of environmental damage caused by the world's 3,000 largest publicly listed businesses to be USD 2.15 trillion.[9] While some companies allegedly attempt to 'offset' this collateral damage through philanthropy, the financial contributions are relatively modest.[10] Further, philanthropy serves as a deflection device away from the impact of business and the need for change, undermining the potential of the CSR movement.[11]

The legal context to business activity is germane to the foregoing issues. Corporations are legal artefacts, as too is the marketplace they operate in via corporate and securities law, and international trade and investment law. Whereas historically the creation of a business corporation was a privilege granted by government charter in order to promote a prescribed social purpose, such as to enhance public infrastructure, the contemporary company is open to virtually any entrepreneur for any lawful purpose.[12]

Although company law emanates from the domestic realm, considerable transnational dissemination of the Anglo-American corporate governance model has made it globally dominant.[13] There is therefore a tension between company law, which allows

[7] Beate Sjåfjell and Benjamin Richardson (eds), *Company Law and Sustainability: Barriers and Opportunities* (CUP 2015).

[8] John Elkington, 'Towards the Sustainable Corporation: Win-win-win Business Strategies for Sustainable Development' *California Management Review*, 36/2 (1994): 90; Michael Porter and Claas van der Linde, 'Green and Competitive: Ending the Stalemate' *Harvard Business Review*, 73/5 (1995): 120.

[9] United Nations Environment Programme—Finance Initiative (UNEP-FI), 'Universal Ownership: Why Environmental Externalities Matter to Institutional Investors' (2010) 2.

[10] Approximately USD 430 billion for the *entire* US philanthropic sector in 2014, compared to the 2015 market value of the Fortune 500. USD 17 trillion with profits of USD 945 billion, representing 67% of US GDP; National Philanthropic Trust, 'Charitable Giving Statistics' <https://www.nptrust.org/philanthropic-resources/charitable-giving-statistics> accessed 8 January 2020; Fortune, 'Fortune 500' (2015) <https://fortune.com/fortune500> accessed 8 January 2020.

[11] Beate Sjåfjell, 'Why Law Matters: Corporate Social Irresponsibility and the Futility of Voluntary Climate Change Mitigation' *European Company Law*, 8/2–3 (2011): 56–64.

[12] Janet Dine, *The Governance of Corporate Groups* (CUP 2006).

[13] Christopher Bruner, *Corporate Governance in the Common-Law World: The Political Foundations of Shareholder Power* (CUP 2013).

and to a certain extent encourages a shift towards more environmentally friendly companies, and the Anglo-American shareholder primacy drive.[14] The latter is a social norm, which has taken over much of the scope of the law across jurisdictions. It gives boards, and by extension managers, little incentive to shift the business onto a more sustainable path.[15]

In practice, company law enables deleterious conduct because the discretion to be socially minded is also the discretion to act otherwise. The latter prevails because of the competitive pressures of the market, especially for public companies subject to the shareholder primacy drive. While environmental and other sustainability reporting obligations on companies are becoming ever more frequent, there is still a lack of sufficiently comprehensive and stringent requirements, and environmental reporting need be neither relevant, reliable, nor comparable.[16] Furthermore, the possibilities corporate law and contract law give corporate actors to organize business across transnational corporate groups and global value chains, enable adverse environmental performance to be 'shifted' to entities least likely to be held accountable for their environmental performance.

Reforming corporate law to integrate environmental protection, and more broadly, sustainability, into the role and duties of the board, is therefore a crucial contribution to the necessary transition of corporations to sustainability. This would give a better grounding for, and should be combined with, stringent, verifiable, and enforceable reporting requirements that enable companies' environmental performance to be compared. Reforming corporate law alone is nevertheless insufficient. At stake are systemic and structural features of global capitalism, within which the legal frameworks of business are one piece. These systemic issues include the absence of any mechanism to restrict the overall size of the economy within planetary boundaries in the face of business models based on overconsumption, market imperfections in valuation of ecological goods and services, and global inequalities and poverty that can exacerbate environmental irresponsibility.[17] This underlines the inadequacy of current corporate law reforms, which have concentrated on giving business more flexibility to pursue socially responsible practices. One model is to allow businesses to be constituted as community benefit enterprises. Legislated for in a rising number of jurisdictions across the world, these may include obligations to promote a community benefit; restrictions on company assets and profits from being transferred to ensure

[14] Beate Sjåfjell *et al*, 'Shareholder Primacy: The Main Barrier to Sustainable Companies' in Sjåfjell and Richardson (n 7) 79; see also David Kershaw, *The Foundations of Anglo-American Corporate Fiduciary Law* (CUP 2018).

[15] This scope is in practice widened through the business judgement rule: Sjåfjell *et al* (n 14); Lyman Johnson, 'Corporate Officers and the Business Judgment Rule' *Business Lawyer*, 60 (2005): 439.

[16] Charlotte Villiers and Jukka Mähönen, 'Accounting, Auditing, and Reporting: Supporting or Obstructing the Sustainable Companies Objective?' in Sjåfjell and Richardson (n 7) 175.

[17] See Robin Hahnel, *Green Economics: Confronting the Ecological Crisis* (Routledge 2011); see also Chapter 14, 'Earth Jurisprudence', in this volume.

the company remains adequately funded and able to fulfil its community purpose; and disclosure obligations.[18] Such reforms leave untouched the mainstream corporate form, and actors in the 'benefit company' field are criticized for reinforcing the legal myth that corporations are obligated to maximize returns for shareholders to the detriment of, inter alia, the environment.[19]

The need for fundamental change is not just a message from activists, such as Naomi Klein,[20] or academic critics such as John McMurtry.[21] The Governor of the Bank of England, Mark Carney, has called for a shift from a model of pure market capitalism to one of 'social capitalism' in which individuals and business institutions assume broader responsibilities for social well-being.[22] The 2019 youth protests against climate change inaction, and the 'Extinction Rebellion' give hope that some of these systemic issues might be tackled by a new generation of environmentally concerned citizens.[23] The business sector has itself begun, to some extent, to accept the need for change, which the following section considers.

B. Mapping the Evolution of Corporate Environmental Standards in Their Global Context

A growing sphere of international environmental standard setting transpires through CSR regimes developed by or with the business sector. CSR has historically been perceived as referring to voluntary initiatives by which companies agree to adhere to social or environmental standards that purport to go beyond minimum legal requirements.[24] Given deficiencies in the robustness of domestic and international environmental laws, CSR standards can, in theory, help to close these governance gaps. A positive example of voluntary action is that of businesses and investors in the United States accepting more ambitious strategies to shift towards clean energy, to compensate for the announced retreat of the Trump Administration from the international

[18] Carol Liao, 'Social Enterprise Law: Friend or Foe to Corporate Sustainability?' in Beate Sjåfjell and Christopher Bruner (eds), *Cambridge Handbook of Corporate Law, Corporate Governance and Sustainability* (CUP 2019) 655.

[19] Victoria Baumfield, 'How Change Happens: The Benefit Corporation in the United States and Considerations for Australia' in Beate Sjåfjell and Irene Fannon (eds), *Creating Corporate Sustainability. Gender as an Agent for Change* (CUP 2018) 188; Carol Liao, 'A Critical Canadian Perspective on the Benefit Corporation' *Seattle University Law Review*, 40/2 (2017): 683.

[20] Naomi Klein, *This Changes Everything: Capitalism vs the Climate* (Simon and Schuster 2014).

[21] John McMurtry, *The Cancer Stage of Capitalism* (Pluto Press 1999).

[22] Mark Carney, 'Inclusive Capitalism: Creating a sense of the systemic' (27 May 2014) <https://www.bis.org/review/r140528b.pdf> accessed 8 January 2020.

[23] Mattha Busby, 'Extinction Rebellion and Momentum join forces on climate crisis' *The Guardian* (29 April 2019).

[24] Archie Carroll, 'Corporate Social Responsibility: Evolution of a Definitional Concept' *Business and Society*, 38/3 (1999): 268.

climate agreements.[25] Corporations sometimes draw on international environmental law standards in setting their own CSR standards, especially in countries lacking robust local regulation.[26]

Companies' motivations for raising their game have been extensively theorized, with three principal rationales of CSR being the business case, stakeholder relations, and ethical responsibility.[27] The business case, the most prevalent rationale, portrays social and environmental issues as financially material to corporate economic success (a problematic assumption), either as costly risks and liabilities to avoid or sources of potential profits. Stakeholder theory depicts companies as embedded within a network of interests in the wider society, and the purpose of a corporation is to create value not just for itself but for its stakeholders: its customers, suppliers, owners, employees, and local communities.[28] The third basis of CSR relates to the normative status of fundamental ethical precepts of corporate citizenship that transcend any specific stakeholder concerns or business advantage, such as evoked by major international human rights and environmental principles. Unethical corporate behaviour that violates such precepts may be construed on the basis of 'complicity' (eg behaviours that facilitate others to commit wrong, such as investing in the fossil-fuels industry) or having the 'leverage' to influence the behaviour of others (eg through a business supply chain).[29]

The aspirations of the CSR movement have been formalized into codes, standards, guidelines, and other instruments. At least 300 such codes have been developed by industry groups, governments, and other parties interested in CSR.[30] This number is in addition to the thousands of internal codes of conduct developed by individual companies for their own operations. Some codes espouse CSR standards broadly to have applicability across many industries, while others focus narrowly on specific economic sectors.[31] The former type includes the International Organization for Standardization's (ISO) Social Responsibility 26000 standard, while the latter type includes Responsible Care[32] (for the chemical industry) and the Extractive Industries

[25] We are Still In <https://www.wearestillin.com/businesses-investors> accessed 8 January 2020.

[26] Natasha Affolder, 'Looking for Law in Unusual Places: Cross-Border Diffusion of Environmental Norms' *Transnational Environmental Law*, 7/3 (2018): 425.

[27] Andrew Crane *et al*, *The Oxford Handbook of Corporate Social Responsibility* (OUP 2008); Elisabeth Garriga and Domenec Mele, 'Corporate Social Responsibility Theories: Mapping the Territory' *Journal of Business Ethics*, 53/1–2 (2004): 51.

[28] Domenec Mele, 'Corporate Social Responsibility Theories' in Crane (n 27) 19.

[29] Benjamin J. Richardson, 'SRI's Normative and Ethics-Based Rationales' in Deborah Poff and Alex Michalos (eds), *Encyclopedia of Business and Professional Ethics* (Springer 2017) 1.

[30] Wesley Cragg (ed), *Ethics Codes, Corporations and the Challenge of Globalization* (Edward Elgar 2005).

[31] Kevin McKague and Wesley Cragg, *A Compendium of Ethics Codes and Instruments of Corporate Responsibility* (York University 2007).

[32] See <https://www.icca-chem.org/responsible-care> accessed 8 January 2020.

Transparency Initiative.[33] New CSR codes continue to appear, such as the Climate Principles for Enterprises adopted in 2018.[34]

With the ascendancy of finance capitalism that now dominates the global economy, characterized by the influence of financial markets and institutional investors over the productive economy, has come increasing societal awareness of the environmental sequelae of the impact of financial flows, and the need for new standards tailored to this sector. The fossil fuels divestment movement, a governance phenomenon in its own right, targets financial actors because of its hope that coal, oil, and gas industries can be crippled by stigmatization or lack of funding.[35] The finance industry has developed numerous voluntary codes on climate change and other environmental issues, a development spawned by the long-standing movement for socially responsible investing (SRI), originating in faith-based investors screening their investment portfolios to avoid alcohol, tobacco, and gambling businesses.[36] The codes typically cover disclosure of environmental performance, due diligence, shareholder activism, and fiduciary responsibility.[37] Leading examples, with high support from investors, include the Principles for Responsible Investment (UNPRI)[38] and the UN Environment Programme's Finance Initiative (UNEP-FI).[39] Several codes now relate to climate change issues, such as the Montreal Pledge of 2014 in which investors 'pledge' to lower their carbon footprint.[40] These voluntary codes or standards, offered to financiers on a take-it-or-leave-it basis, furnish both normative goals and procedural standards that may help to fill the lacunae or weaknesses of international environmental law that largely ignores the financial sector.[41]

C. Governance Integrity in Corporate Environmental Standards

The robustness of corporate environmental standards depends on a variety of factors, relating to the design of CSR codes and standards as well as the economic, political,

[33] See <https://eiti.org> accessed 8 January 2020.

[34] See <https://climateprinciplesforenterprises.org> accessed 8 January 2020.

[35] Benjamin Richardson, 'Divesting from Climate Change: The Road to Influence' *Law and Policy*, 39/4 (2017): 325.

[36] Russell Sparkes, *Socially Responsible Investment: A Global Revolution* (Wiley 2002); Marcel Jeucken, *Sustainable Finance and Banking: The Financial Sector and the Future of the Planet* (Earthscan 2001).

[37] Benjamin Richardson, 'Socially Responsible Investing Through Voluntary Codes' in Pierre-Marie Dupuy and Jorge Viñuales (eds), *Harnessing Foreign Investment for Environmental Protection: Incentives and Safeguards* (CUP 2013) 383.

[38] See <https://www.unpri.org> accessed 8 January 2020.

[39] See <https://www.unepfi.org> accessed 8 January 2020.

[40] See <https://montrealpledge.org> accessed 8 January 2020.

[41] For further analysis see Oren Perez, 'The New Universe of Green Finance: From Self-regulation to Multi-polar Governance' in Olaf Dilling, Martin Herberg, and Gerd Winter (eds), *Responsible Business. Self-Governance and Law in Transnational Economic Transactions* (Hart Publishing 2008) 151.

and legal context in which business operates. Ideally, CSR mechanisms create an institutional milieu through which firms can deploy their business acumen, managerial skill, and technological wizardry to further sustainable development. Quite commonly, however, voluntary measures tinker with such challenges, and lack transparency and accountability to other stakeholders. They may even facilitate deliberate circumvention of official regulation and thereby forestall meaningful change. Indeed, corporate capture has held back the development of effective regulation and the recognition of CSR as both legal compliance and beyond.[42]

When CSR practices are subject only to insular, business self-regulation, they are highly vulnerable, at best, to perfunctory compliance without any tangible environmental benefits.[43] The open-ended nature of the concept of sustainable development, despite efforts such as the SDGs to provide more substance,[44] gives companies considerable discretion to interpret it in ways that may actually undermine environmental stewardship. Indeed, 'SDG washing' has become a danger, and the SDGs themselves are criticized for being internally inconsistent in their goals.[45] There are also considerable difficulties translating sustainability's meta-principles, such as the precautionary principle or the polluter pays principle, into workable business management.[46] Some CSR codes give signatories considerable discretion while others are more prescriptive. Some codes contain generic performance targets (eg to prevent or minimize adverse environmental impacts) while others are specific (eg to reduce greenhouse gas emissions by a set quantity and time-frame).

Crucial to the credibility of voluntary mechanisms are means of external verification of performance and sanctions for non-compliance. Self-verification involves a company assessing and determining its own compliance. By contrast, second-party verification entails compliance assessment by another party with a commercial interest in the subject company, as with many industry-sector codes such as Responsible Care. Potentially strongest of all, third-party verification involves an independent, impartial third-party evaluating compliant performance, such as by governments or NGOs.[47] Transparency standards are important for all these processes.[48]

42 Ernesto Bó, 'Regulatory Capture: A Review' *Oxford Review of Economic Policy*, 22/2 (2006): 203; Sjåfjell, 'Why Law Matters' (n 11).

43 See eg Robert Gibson (ed), *Voluntary Initiatives: The New Politics of Corporate Greening* (Broadview Press 1999); Stepan Wood, 'Voluntary Environmental Codes and Sustainability' in Benjamin Richardson and Stepan Wood (eds), *Environmental Law for Sustainability* (Hart Publishing 2006) 229.

44 See <https://www.un.org/sustainabledevelopment/sustainable-development-goals>.

45 Beate Sjåfjell, 'Redefining the Corporation for a Sustainable New Economy' *Journal of Law and Society*, 45/1 (2018): 29.

46 Eloise Scotford, *Environmental Principles and the Evolution of Environmental Law* (Hart Publishing 2016).

47 Ibid.

48 Ans Kolk, David Levy, and Jonatan Pinkse, 'Corporate Responses in an Emerging Climate Institutionalization and Commensuration of Carbon Disclosure' *European Accounting Review*, 17/4 (2008): 719.

The ostensible voluntariness of CSR codes does not mean they are devoid of legal significance. They may be legally binding by virtue of contracts among participating institutions; a bank could include in its contract with a borrower a covenant that the latter will adhere to a specific CSR standard. A code may also have consequences for regulatory compliance; companies reporting according to the European Union (EU)'s Non-Financial Reporting Directive of 2014,[49] the only regulatory initiative following up the EU's CSR Action Plan of 2011, may fulfil these requirements by reporting inter alia according to the UN Global Compact.[50] Pressure to heed voluntary standards may also arise from a threat of mandatory regulation.[51]

One of the ways states are shaping corporate environmental governance is through their own investing arms, notably sovereign wealth funds (SWFs). About sixty SWFs exist worldwide with assets over USD 8 trillion as of early 2018.[52] Sovereign wealth funds in France, New Zealand, Norway, and Sweden are subject to domestic legal mandates to invest ethically and responsibly, enabling them to favour leading CSR businesses. Their efforts, especially that of the Norwegian Government Pension Fund Global (the world's largest SWF), are shifting some investors towards a longer term approach to managing their portfolios aligned with sustainability, although tensions persist in reconciling this orientation with the economic profitability mindset within which SWFs function.[53] The Norwegian fund's legislative framework enables it, on the advice of an independent Council on Ethics, to exclude companies associated with 'severe environmental damage'.[54] Sovereign wealth funds participate in global markets and by practising SRI they are contributing to its legitimacy as an international aspiration for all.

The next section considers how the international legal system itself is becoming more responsive to the environmental practice of business.

[49] Directive 2014/95/EU of the European Parliament and of the Council of 22 October 2014 amending Directive 2013/34/EU as regards disclosure of non-financial and diversity information by certain large undertakings and groups [2014] OJ L/330.

[50] See text accompanying n 58.

[51] Monica Saha and Geoffrey Darnton, 'Green Companies or Green Con-panies: Are Companies Really Green, or Are They Pretending to Be?' *Business and Society Review*, 110/2 (2005): 117.

[52] Sovereign Wealth Fund Institute, *Fund Rankings* <http://www.swfinstitute.org/fund-rankings> accessed 8 January 2020.

[53] Beate Sjåfjell, Heidi Nilsen, and Benjamin Richardson, 'Investing in Sustainability or Feeding on Stranded Assets? The Norwegian Government Pension Fund Global' *Wake Forest Law Review*, 52/4 (2017): 949.

[54] Norwegian Ministry of Finance, 'Guidelines for Observation and Exclusion from the Government Pension Fund Global's Investment Universe' (2014), s 3(c). Although they are criticized for not realizing the potential of this rule; Sjåfjell, Nilsen, and Richardson (n 53).

III. BUSINESS AND INTERNATIONAL ENVIRONMENTAL LAW

A. Regulating Business Actors

The law of nations treats corporations as primarily the objects, rather than the subjects, of its rules, and thus shields them from direct *international* responsibility for their environmental conduct.[55] However, a variety of soft law codes sponsored by states, through forums such as the UN and World Bank, have delineated global expectations of environmental responsibility for corporations. These instruments are notionally voluntary in nature, but can have significant normative force owing to businesses' desire to maintain their social licence or to avoid the imposition of more stringent environmental regulation by states. The range of soft law codes is too numerous to consider here, but a few representative examples can be briefly identified.

One is the Organisation for Economic Co-operation and Development's (OECD) Guidelines for Multinational Enterprises, drafted in 1976 and since revised several times.[56] While the Guidelines are not obligatory for companies, they are unique in that OECD members must promote the Guidelines among companies operating within their borders. They provide standards in relation to, inter alia, human rights, anti-corruption, labour relations, environment, science and technology, and consumer protection. The text of the environmental chapter in the Guidelines broadly reflects the principles and objectives of the 1992 Agenda 21 of the Earth Summit.[57] The Guidelines also provide for a complaint and mediation process for alleged violations.

Another international instrument supported by states is the UN Global Compact (UNGC), adopted in 1999.[58] Its participants pledge adherence to ten principles distilled from key environmental, labour, and human rights agreements. The UNGC draws on key international instruments in these fields[59] and reframes them as corporate commitments. On the environment, the UNGC obliges businesses to take a precautionary approach and to develop environmentally friendly technologies.[60] While the

[55] Amanda Perry-Kessaris, 'Corporate Liability for Environmental Harm' in Malgosia Fitzmaurice, David Ong, and Panos Merkouris (eds), *Research Handbook of International Environmental Law* (Edward Elgar 2007) 361.

[56] See <https://www.oecd.org/investment/mne> accessed 8 January 2020.

[57] *Report of the United Nations Conference on Environment and Development* (UN 1993) vol I, annex II, 'Agenda 21'.

[58] See <https://www.unglobalcompact.org> accessed 8 January 2020.

[59] See eg UNGA Res 217(III), 'Universal Declaration of Human Rights' (10 December 1948) UN Doc A/RES/217(III); UNCED report (n 57) vol I, annex I—'Rio Declaration of Environment and Development'.

[60] Rio Declaration (n 59) principles 7, 8, 9.

UNGC enjoys the prestige of UN backing, as a non-binding instrument it is vulnerable to perfunctory implementation.[61] The Compact lacks formal auditing and certification mechanisms, and companies sign up merely by sending a letter of support to the UN Secretary-General and publicly pledging to adhere to the principles.

A third example is the Equator Principles, developed in 2003 by the International Finance Corporation (IFC), the private sector arm of the World Bank, for encouraging private banks to consider social and environmental issues when funding projects.[62] Aimed principally at project financing in developing countries, the ten principles establish requirements for prospective borrowers and lenders, including rigorous environmental and social assessments of their proposed projects, conforming to the IFC's social and environmental standards. Although the principles are voluntary, they can acquire binding legal status through inclusion in lending agreements, and over 90% of the global project lenders have endorsed them. Although compliance with the Equator Principles has been patchy, according to the NGO watchdog BankTrack,[63] it has occasionally helped leverage positive environmental action, such as when Australia's ANZ Bank declined to finance a proposed pulp mill, which contributed to the demise of the project.[64]

Since 2008, the UN Guiding Principles on Business and Human Rights (UNGPs) have emerged as an influential standard for articulating best practice for corporate social and related environmental behaviour around the world.[65] The UNGPs expect companies to avoid infringing the human rights of others (respect) and to create avenues for victims to receive redress for breaches (remedy), while the role of states is to safeguard people against human rights abuses by third parties (protect). The UNGPs were developed through a highly consultative process with business and other stakeholders, and thus enjoy considerable global legitimacy. However, they lack strong accountability mechanisms such as third-party oversight by business practice.

The value of international soft law instruments as transformative tools for improved corporate environmental performance remains highly uncertain and debatable. Given their voluntary nature and lack of specificity of their standards, these instruments are likely more to promote environmental responsibility at a very general level, such as expectations about promotion of sustainability, rather than in any specific regulatory context such as quantifiable reduction of greenhouse gas emissions. The codes may also create valuable 'discursive space' in which various non-corporate actors acquire legitimacy to judge corporate behaviour on environmental performance and other

[61] See Georg Kell, 'The Global Compact Selected Experiences and Reflections' *Journal of Business Ethics*, 59/1 (2005): 69.

[62] See <https://equator-principles.com> accessed 8 January 2020.

[63] See <https://www.banktrack.org> accessed 8 January 2020.

[64] Louise Crealy, 'ANZ Walks Away from Gunns Project' *ABC News* (30 May 2008).

[65] John Ruggie, 'Promotion and Protection of all Human Rights, Civil, Political, Economic, Social and Cultural Rights including the Rights to Development. Protect, Respect and Remedy: A Framework for Business and Human Rights' (2008) UN Doc A/HRC/8/5.

standards.[66] The scope of these instruments to make companies actually liable for environmental misconduct is considered in the next section.

B. Corporate Liability

Under the traditional conception of international environmental law that focuses on states as the bearers of environmental responsibilities, corporations have been able to operate without any significant obligations at the international level.[67] Compounding this deficit is the paucity of institutional machinery to enforce or adjudicate environmental responsibilities. International law, with rare exceptions, does not empower courts with global and compulsory jurisdiction, as many states are reluctant to be accountable to judicial oversight that they have little control over. In this permissive legal milieu, the continuing opening of borders to international trade and investment enables expansion of multinational corporate operations, which are further emboldened by the proliferation of foreign investor protection agreements that give companies privileged access to adjudicatory forums to challenge unreasonable host state regulations including environmental law.[68]

Several alternate means of making corporations accountable for their environmental activities are available, although with limitations. One opportunity is through international rules of civil liability 'that channel responsibility for an environmental wrong on the polluter rather than the state'.[69] Civil liability via multilateral environmental conventions is typically achieved by obliging the state parties to provide remedies in their legal systems for aggrieved persons against corporate or other private entities. For instance, the 1997 Convention on the Law of the Non-Navigational Uses of International Watercourses requires states to provide foreign nationals injured by activities that originated on their territory with 'access to judicial or other procedures, or a right to claim compensation or other relief'.[70] Similar provisions are found in several other environmental conventions including those concerned with nuclear energy[71] and transportation of nuclear materials,[72] and offshore oil pollution.[73]

Another avenue of corporate accountability is under national legislation that provides redress for international wrongs. The United Kingdom's Modern Slavery Act 2015, which

[66] Michael Barnett and Raymond Duvall, 'Power in International Politics' *International Organization*, 59 (2005): 39, 61.

[67] Elisa Morgera, *Corporate Accountability in International Environmental Law* (OUP 2009).

[68] Saverio Benedetto, *International Investment Law and the Environment* (Edward Elgar 2013).

[69] Lakshman Guruswamy, 'State Responsibility in Promoting Environmental Corporate Accountability' *Fordham Environmental Law Review*, 21/1 (2010): 209.

[70] art 32.

[71] 1963 Vienna Convention on Civil Liability for Nuclear Damage.

[72] 1971 Convention relating to Civil Liability in the field of Maritime Carriage of Nuclear Material.

[73] 1971 International Convention on the Establishment of an International Fund for Compensation for Oil Pollution Damage.

addresses global human trafficking, obliges companies to audit and report on their supply chains in an effort to reduce use of slave labour in foreign business operations. This reform has, however, been criticized for very low rates of compliance.[74] In 2017, France introduced a law requiring companies to be vigilant in respecting human rights in their global operations.[75] The US Alien Torts Statute 1789[76] potentially enables foreign nationals to sue for compensatory damages that ensue from breaches of international law outside the United States, which could pin liability on multinational companies for environmental degradation abroad. The 2013 decision of the US Supreme Court in the *Kiobel* case severely limited the Alien Torts Statute as a tool for corporate accountability abroad, by creating a presumption against extraterritoriality. The presumption can be displaced when claims 'touch and concern the territory of the United States ... with sufficient force'.[77] The latter is illustrated in a 2018 decision in the Ninth Circuit Court, allowing a claim against Nestlé for human rights violations in other countries, based on the reasoning that these were facilitated through decisions taken in US headquarters.[78] This may be seen as part of an international trend of a heterogonous mix of cases, which have in common that the courts are being asked to stop environmental harms and human rights violations across national borders.[79]

A third avenue of corporate accountability is through the proliferation of soft law international standards and private governance regimes. They bring accountability in two ways. First, by setting standards of best practice or due diligence for companies to achieve, which may then feed into the applicable national laws governing corporations such as statutory duties of care. Secondly, they may bring accountability by providing mechanisms for receiving complaints and engaging with offending companies. One such example is the complaint procedure for investigating alleged breaches of the OECD Guidelines for Multinational Enterprises. The designated 'national contact point' (NCP) of each OECD country has established a 'specific instance' procedure, to allow any person to raise a specific complaint about the conduct of a company.[80] The NCP must establish an advisory body representative to review the complaint, and if it feels the matter has some merit, it can consult with the enterprise concerned and other parties and facilitate mediation. To illustrate, in 2013 the Norwegian NCP upheld a complaint against the country's SWF for its investment in a Korean company's steel project

[74] Andrew Phillips and Alexander Trautrims, 'Agriculture and Modern Slavery Act Reporting: Poor Performance Despite High Risks' *Office of the Independent Anti-Slavery Commissioner* (2018).

[75] France: Loi no. 2017-399 du 27 Mars 2017 relative au devoir de vigilance des sociétés mères et des entreprises donneuses d'ordre (The French Law on Duty of Care of parent and subcontracting companies).

[76] 28 USC 1350 (2000).

[77] *Kiobel v Royal Dutch Petroleum Co.* (2013) 133 S Ct 1659, 1669.

[78] *Doe v Nestlé* (2018) No 17-55435, DC No 2:05-cv-05133-SVW-MRW.

[79] See eg John Schwartz, 'New York sues Exxon Mobil, saying it deceived shareholders on climate change' *New York Times* (24 October 2018).

[80] OECD, 'Guidelines for Multinational Enterprises: Ministerial Booklet' (2000) 32, 35–37.

in India.[81] The company, POSCO, acquired extensive rural lands for its environmentally controversial development, and allegedly violated local regulations. The decision led the Norwegian SWF to divest from POSCO.[82]

IV. NEW DIRECTIONS: CIVIL SOCIETY–BUSINESS COLLABORATIONS

Governance of the environmental behaviour of business is no longer a binary choice between corporate self-regulation and governmental regulation. Another approach to setting environmental standards is collaborative global rule-making whereby public authorities, civil society actors, and business create joint rule-making institutions and develop codes. Such approaches have similarities to the so-called 'corporatist' modes of interest group intermediation found in some western states in the 1970s and 1980s, as a supplement to polyarchal modes of political decision-making.[83] These collaborations have the potential to offer greater legitimacy and accountability than purely industry-controlled CSR processes, or government-determined regulation, and may help overcome deficits or gaps in international environmental law. The following paragraphs illustrate a few examples of global significance.

Collaborative governance is seen as the hallmark of the Marine Stewardship Council (MSC), an international non-profit entity established by WWF and the company Unilever in 1996 to help put the global seafood market on an ecologically sustainable footing.[84] The core of the MSC governance is its 'chain of custody' certification, a traceability programme that helps restaurants, fishmongers, and other intermediaries identify seafood from wild fisheries certified to the MSC standard.[85] The affiliated MSC's fishery certification programme recognizes and rewards sustainable fishing practices, and currently covers about 30,000 seafood products and 3,000 companies. While MSC may illustrate the benefits of collaborative, multi-stakeholder governance, potentially offering greater accountability than many CSR codes and standards, it has

[81] The Norwegian National Contact Point for the OECD Guidelines for Multinational Enterprises, 'Final Statement: Complaint from Lok Shakti Abhiyan, Korean Transnational Corporations Watch, Fair Green and Global Alliance and Forum for Environment and Development vs POSCO (South Korea), ABP/APG (Netherlands) and NBIM (Norway)—Final Statement' (27 May 2013) 6.

[82] However see also 'OECD watchdog calls for reform of failing complaint system' *OECD Watch* (15 June 2015) regarding the report 'Remedy Remains Rare'.

[83] Leo Panitch, 'The Development of Corporatism in Liberal Democracies' *Comparative Political Studies*, 10/1 (1977): 61.

[84] MSC <https://www.msc.org> available 8 January 2020.

[85] See Fred Gale and Marcus Haward, *Global Commodity Governance: State Responses to Sustainable Forests and Fisheries Certification* (Palgrave Macmillan 2011).

faced criticism for not being rigorous enough in its ecological standards even after two decades.[86]

A second example, relating to the finance sector, is the Geneva-based United Nations Environment Programme's Finance Initiative (UNEP-FI).[87] Established in 1991, UNEP-FI is a global partnership of investor, civil society, and government representatives to promote governance standards, education, and research on SRI,[88] although in practice financial institutions are its dominant stakeholders. In 1992 UNEP-FI released its first code, the Statement by Banks on Environment and Sustainable Development, to help lenders manage their environmental risks.[89] In 1995 UNEP-FI sponsored a similar statement for the insurance industry.[90] In 1997 UNEP-FI issued a more general code for all financiers, known as the Statement by Financial Institutions on the Environment and Sustainable Development, which had about 250 signatories as of September 2018.[91] In an effort to boost financiers' attention to climate change, in 2007 UNEP-FI issued a Declaration on Climate Change by the Financial Services Sector, which calls on financial institutions to integrate climate change considerations into their decision-making including to reduce their direct carbon footprint.[92] Paralleling the international growth of SRI in recent years, UNEP-FI has greatly expanded its own awareness-raising activities, including convening workshops, taskforce meetings, global and regional roundtables, and training events.[93]

However, the UNEP-FI does not audit or certify environmental practices, let alone apply sanctions for non-compliance with its governance standards. A 2007 survey by BankTrack of forty-five international banks, including thirty UNEP-FI signatories, alleged grounds for concern and concluded that 'voluntary standards and initiatives are no substitute for stringent policies developed by banks themselves'.[94] In the past decade UNEP-FI has gained more respect for its global leadership in promoting sustainability in the finance sector, especially on climate change. It has pushed for stronger carbon disclosure practices, assisted with the implementation of the G20 Task Force on Climate-Related Financial Disclosures (TCFD) with fourteen global banks, and has created the 'Portfolio Decarbonization Coalition' for

[86] See WWF Statement on Marine Stewardship Council Reforms (29 March 2018) <https://wwf.panda.org/wwf_news/press_releases/?325605/WWF-Statement-on-Marine-Stewardship-Council-Reforms> accessed 8 January 2020.

[87] UNEP-FI <http://www.unepfi.org> accessed 14 January 2020.

[88] See eg UNEP-FI, 'Managing Environmental Risks in Project Finance—Fact Sheet No 1' (1999).

[89] UNEP Advisory Committee on Banking and the Environment, 'Statement by Banks on Environment and Sustainable Development (1992).

[90] Carlos Joly, 'UNEP Insurance Industry Initiative on the Environment: Developments in 1996' *International Journal of Insurance Law*, 3 (1997): 171.

[91] See <https://www.unepfi.org/about/unep-fi-statement> accessed 8 January 2020.

[92] <https://www.unepfi.org/fileadmin/documents/cc_statement_jun2007.pdf> accessed 8 January 2020.

[93] See eg UNEP-FI, '2009 Overview' (2010).

[94] BankTrack, 'Mind the Gap: Benchmarking Credit Policies of International Banks' (2007) xi.

twenty-nine major institutions to reduce their climate risk exposure from fossil-fuels assets.[95]

V. CONCLUSION

Business is an increasingly influential stakeholder in global environmental affairs. State-centric international environmental law may formally and ostensibly be blind to the private sector, except as a subsidiary actor within states, but the reality in practice is rather different. Multinational corporations are increasingly being scrutinized and held accountable for their environmental performance, independently of any host states in which they operate. The global movement for CSR, and its offshoots such as SRI, has become a governance phenomenon in its own right, attempting to push the sustainability agenda into corporate boardrooms and shareholder meetings. Yet, the proliferation of CSR codes and standards to fill deficits in international environmental law has had mixed results, and faces countervailing pressures from the global marketplace and sometimes even the corporate governance frameworks that institutionalize business identity. The development of state-sponsored CSR codes, such as from the UN and OECD, along with collaborative governance regimes between civil society and business stakeholders, such as the MSC and UNEP-FI, are a further innovation that may help to inculcate global environmental responsibility. Some companies are also becoming de facto agents of implementation of international environmental law, such as by incorporating their standards into business contracts, supply chain agreements, financial loans, and other transactions. But the majority of businesses remain insouciantly tied to the status quo.

A persistent theme in these trends is that the promotion of sustainability cannot be left to corporate volunteerism alone, because the market contains too many countervailing forces including: incomplete or imperfect valuation of ecosystem services; collective action problems that undermine cooperation in addressing environmental problems; and the economy's lack of a mechanism to contain its overall scale within planetary boundaries.[96] The dominant 'business case' driver of CSR faces structural limitations when the economy continues to offer a business case, albeit in the short term, for unsustainable plundering of the biosphere. The long-term time horizons necessary for aligning business activity and sustainability are missing from the business plans and policies of many corporations.[97]

A sustainability economy, premised on respecting ecological limits, requires new rules of the game to make economic actors responsible for environmental degradation,

[95] See further UNEP-FI, 'Climate Change' <https://www.unepfi.org/climate-change/climate-change> accessed 8 January 2020.

[96] David Vogel, *The Limits of the Market for Virtue* (Brookings Institution 2005).

[97] See further Benjamin Richardson, *Time and Environmental Law: Telling Nature's Time* (CUP 2017).

prevent exhaustibility of natural resources, and achieve other indicia of environmental performance. The emerging recognition of the limits of our planet and the financial risks of continued unsustainability is illustrated by the EU's Sustainable Finance Initiative, aiming to integrate environmental concerns into the decision-making in financial markets—and in business more broadly.[98] However, the initiative also illustrates the difficulty of identifying sustainable investments, and the tendency to focus on the climate, to the detriment of equally pressing environmental (and social) issues.[99]

While the legal system, and governments more generally, suffer from well-known limitations including imperfect information, bureaucratic rigidities, and corruption, there is an urgent need to invest in better environmental governance, with a global perspective, given the transnational character of many business operations and their environmental impacts. This ranges from reforms to business law itself, especially company law and financial markets regulation, to meta-regulation at the global level itself in soft law and through collaborative governance regimes.

BIBLIOGRAPHY

Wesley Cragg (ed), *Ethics Codes, Corporations and the Challenge of Globalization* (Edward Elgar 2005)

Andrew Crane *et al*, *The Oxford Handbook of Corporate Social Responsibility* (OUP 2008)

Elisabeth Garriga and Domenec Mele, 'Corporate Social Responsibility Theories: Mapping the Territory' *Journal of Business Ethics*, 53/1–2 (2004): 51

Elisa Morgera, *Corporate Accountability in International Environmental Law* (OUP 2009)

Beate Sjåfjell and Benjamin Richardson (eds), *Company Law and Sustainability: Legal Barriers and Opportunities* (CUP 2015)

98 Commission, 'Action Plan: Financing Sustainable Growth' COM (2018) 97 final, 2.

99 As illustrated by the first proposals: 'Commission legislative proposals on sustainable finance' (24 May 2018) <https://ec.europa.eu/info/publications/180524-proposal-sustainable-finance_en> accessed 14 January 2020.

CHAPTER 42

INDIGENOUS PEOPLES

JACINTA RURU

I. INTRODUCTION

COMPLEX legal quandaries have been borne from intercontinental contact and assumptions by Europeans about Indigenous peoples and their nations. Significant tracts of lands, waters, and oceans throughout the world were known only to the Indigenous peoples. The expansion of the European empire into this 'new world' of old Indigenous autonomous homes has ignited violent conflict resonating from colonial beliefs of sovereignty and ownership of Indigenous states. Until recently, international law has done little to recognize the rights, interests, and responsibilities of Indigenous peoples. Now, many contemporary domestic courts, domestic legislatures, and, importantly for this chapter, international instruments, are attempting to find more palatable answers as to how best to reconcile with Indigenous peoples in the face of this onslaught of colonial contended control.[1]

This chapter is focused on Indigenous peoples and international environmental law. The expression 'Indigenous peoples' is often defined to include those who have been subjected to colonial settlement, have historical continuity with pre-invasion or pre-colonial societies, an identity that is distinct from the dominant society in which they are encased, and a concern with the preservation and replication of culture.[2] International law is important to all peoples, including Indigenous peoples, as a recourse to a higher

[1] See eg *Delgamuukw v British Columbia* [1997] 3 SCR 1010 (Supreme Court of Canada); *Mabo v Queensland No 2* (1992) 175 CLR (High Court of Australia); *A-G v Ngati Apa* [2003] 3 NZLR 643 (New Zealand Court of Appeal). These cases overruled early cases from their jurisdictions including: *Wi Parata v Bishop of Wellington* SC 1877 3 NZ Jur (NZ) 72; *St Catherines Milling & Lumber v The Queen* (1888) 14 AC 46 (Privy Council on appeal from Canada); *Cooper v Stuart* (1889) 14 AC 286 (Privy Council on appeal from Australia).

[2] Paul Keal, *European Conquest and the Rights of Indigenous Rights: The Moral Backwardness of International Society* (CUP 2003) 7; see also James Anaya, *Indigenous Peoples in International Law* (2nd edn, OUP 2004).

order of justice. There is a myriad of international instruments and commitments that presently incorporate some recognition of Indigenous peoples. It is not possible in this chapter to capture all of this activity.[3] The chapter intends to provide a broad overview of some of these milestones in international environmental law to demonstrate the general tenor of how these instruments are purporting to encompass (or not) Indigenous peoples' aspirations for self-determination in caring for the environment. Also, a brief insight into Indigenous peoples' law and their general critique of western law provides an understanding of the tenacity and vision of Indigenous peoples when confronted with the development of international environmental law.

This chapter, first, provides a brief discussion of Indigenous peoples' law. Second, the development of rights of Indigenous peoples at international law is considered with particular focus on the International Labour Organization's (ILO) 1989 Convention concerning Indigenous and Tribal Peoples in Independent Countries and the 2007 United Nations (UN) Declaration on the Rights of Indigenous Peoples. The third part of the chapter explores the significance of international environmental law for Indigenous peoples by drawing on some prominent Indigenous commentary that emphasizes the ongoing failures of international law to address Indigenous concerns. The chapter concludes that international environmental law is simply at the early stages of recognizing the aspirations of Indigenous peoples.

II. INDIGENOUS PEOPLES' LAW

Indigenous peoples all have their own languages, laws, and customs.[4] The intricacies of these distinct nations have their histories embedded in thousands of years of development and wisdom. While colonial forces have drastically changed Indigenous realities, through colonial violence, technological modernization, and globalization, Indigenous peoples remain committed to preserving their own identities, and adapting their ancestral knowledges to make sense of the modern world. For many Indigenous communities, self-determination, in whatever form it is defined, is the end goal.[5] For some Indigenous communities, this vision might simply mean knowing that their ways

[3] For an annual comprehensive insight into Indigenous peoples' activity on the international stage in relation to the environment, see *Yearbook of International Environmental Law*. The most recent update at the time of writing is: Stefania Errico, 'Indigenous Peoples' *Yearbook of International Environmental Law*, 26 (2015): 159 [note published in 2017].

[4] See eg James Henderson, *First Nations Jurisprudence and Aboriginal Rights: Defining the Just Society* (Native Law Centre, University of Saskatchewan 2006); John Borrows (Kegedonce), *Drawing Out Law: A Spirit's Guide* (University of Toronto Press 2010); Law Commission of Canada, 'Justice Within: Indigenous Legal Traditions' Discussion Paper (2006); Hirini Mead, *Tikanga Maori: Living by Maori Values* (Huia Publishers 2016); New Zealand Law Commission, 'Maori Custom and Values' Study Paper 9 (2001).

[5] For commentary see Felix Hoehn, *Reconciling Sovereignties: Aboriginal Nations and Canada* (Native Law Centre, University of Saskatchewan 2012); Roger Maaka and Augie Fleras, *The Politics of Indigeneity: Challenging the State in Canada and Aotearoa, New Zealand* (Otago University Press 2005);

of doing things are respected within a dominant colonial regime, and for others it might mean regaining total separate state control of their own destinies.

Indigenous peoples have forcefully challenged the mono-cultural nature of the western legal system, including international law, from the time it was first imposed upon them. In the legal journals, for example, the Cree legal academic and judge, Mary Ellen Turpel-Lafond began publishing about the cultural authority evident in the Canadian legal system in the 1980s by asserting that the rule of law is simply 'one particular cultural expression of social life',[6] and 'legal knowledge and processes are localized or contingent, both as matters of history and culture'.[7] James (Sakej) Youngblood Henderson, Director of the Native Law Centre in Canada, wrote in agreement early on by stating that the values inherent in the mainstream legal system simply represent 'the Anglocentric legal culture'[8] and that 'legal decisions are the normative visions that protect the colonizers' prosperity, their system of rights, and their institutions of government and adjudication'.[9] Prominently, the Anishinaabe law professor, John Borrows, warned: 'North Americans require different principles to judge Indigenous contributions because contemporary legal rules were developed within a cultural logic that erased prior Indigenous presence and ecological relationships'.[10]

Since then, with more Indigenous and allied law academics in the tertiary sector worldwide, the written critique of western colonial law has swelled.[11] These Indigenous legal scholars are now also disseminating significant works that specifically detail Indigenous laws. For example, Turpel herself set out the four principles of social interaction in some First Nations communities—trust, kindness, sharing, and strength. She stated, 'These are *responsibilities* which each person owes to others representing the larger function of social life'.[12] Henderson explains that the centre of the Mikmaq legal institutions and heritage is reflected in their verb-centred worldview, which 'emphasised the flux of the

Larissa Behrendt, Chris Cunneen, and Terri Libesman, *Indigenous Legal Relations in Australia* (OUP 2009); David Wilkins and Tsiaina Lomawaima, *Uneven Ground: American Indian Sovereignty and Federal Law* (University of Oklahoma Press 2001).

[6] Mary Turpel, 'Aboriginal Peoples and the Canadian Charter: Interpretive Monopolies, Cultural Difference' *Canadian Human Rights Yearbook*, 6 (1989–90): 3, 25.

[7] Ibid, 45.

[8] James (Sakej) Henderson, 'First Nations Legal Inheritances in Canada: The Mikmaq Model' *Manitoba Law Journal*, 23 (1996): 1, 11.

[9] Ibid, 12.

[10] John Borrows, *Recovering Canada: The Resurgence of Indigenous Law* (University of Toronto Press 2002) 34.

[11] See eg Gordon Christie, 'Law, Theory and Aboriginal Peoples' *Indigenous Law Journal* 2 (2003): 67; Ani Mikaere, *Colonising Myths Māori Realities He Rukuruku Whakaaro* (Huia Publishers 2011); Larissa Behrendt, *Achieving Social Justice: Indigenous Rights and Australia's Future* (The Federation Press 2003); Carwyn Jones, *New Treaty New Tradition: Reconciling New Zealand and Maori Law* (UBC Press 2017); Irene Watson, *Aboriginal Peoples, Colonialism and International Law: Raw Law* (Routledge 2015); Val Napoleon and Hadley Friedland, 'An Inside Job: Engaging with Indigenous Legal Traditions through Stories' *McGill Law Journal*, 61/4 (2016): 725; Hadley Friedland, *The Wetiko Legal Principles: Cree and Anishinbek Responses to Violence and Victimization* (Scholarly Publishing 2018).

[12] Turpel (n 6) 29 (emphasis added).

world, encouraging harmony in all relationships'.[13] They believe 'that the world was made according to an implicit design that could be at least partially apprehended and enforced by them, not simply as a matter of balancing rights and wrongs or of reducing conflict resolution to trial by battle'.[14] Borrows has written at length about Anishinabek law, telling the legal stories of, for example, *Nanabush v Duck, Mudhen and Geese*, and *Nanabush the Trickster v Deer, Wolf et al.*[15] According to Borrows, 'Indigenous law originates in the political, economic, spiritual, and social values expressed through the teachings and behaviour of knowledgeable and respected individuals and elders'.[16] In Aotearoa New Zealand, the Māori appeal court judge, Joe Williams, positions kinship as the glue that holds the Māori legal system together, expanding to regulate and inform human relationships with both the physical and spiritual worlds. For example, as he writes:

> Thus the story of what happened to Rata when he felled his totara tree without proper procedure confirms that good relations must be maintained with the forest itself as a related descent group in order to maintain the human right to be a user of forest resources.[17]

This fleeting insight emphasizes that Indigenous peoples have their own legal systems that operate within and across other nations. How contemporary international environmental law seeks to recognize and respect Indigenous peoples and their own laws and aspirations for the environment is now considered.

III. DEVELOPMENT OF INDIGENOUS PEOPLES' RIGHTS AT INTERNATIONAL LAW

A. The Evolving Context for International Law Recognition

Initial growth of international law in the early twentieth century fundamentally ignored Indigenous peoples, including their ongoing assertions in law as continuing sovereign entities with jurisdiction over their lands, territories, and resources.[18]

[13] Henderson (n 8) 13.
[14] Ibid.
[15] Borrows (n 10).
[16] Ibid, 13.
[17] Justice Williams, 'Lex Aotearoa: An Heroic Attempt to Map the Māori Dimension in Modern New Zealand Law' *Waikato Law Review*, 21 (2013): 1, 4.
[18] See eg Anaya (n 2); Claire Charters, 'A Self-Determination Approach to Justifying Indigenous Peoples' Participation in International Law and Policy Making' *International Journal on Minority*

Attempts to engage with the League of Nations were rebuffed. For example, Indigenous representatives in the 1920s were denied access to speak to the League about the rights of their people to live under their own laws, on their own land, and under their own faith.[19] It was not until the 1970s and 1980s that the UN and member states began taking small steps towards recognizing Indigenous peoples' rights.[20] Earlier views that Indigenous peoples should be simply assimilated or integrated began to become unacceptable, at least by some.[21]

In 1970, the UN Economic and Social Council authorized its Sub-Commission on Prevention of Discrimination and Protection of Minorities to prepare a study on the 'problem of discrimination against indigenous populations' and to suggest the necessary national and international measures for eliminating such discrimination.[22] The Sub-Commission was also authorized to establish a Working Group on Indigenous Populations to review developments pertaining to the protection of human rights and fundamental freedoms of Indigenous peoples and to give attention to the evolution of international standards for Indigenous rights.[23] Indigenous representatives from around the world became very active in this group and began working on a draft declaration on the rights of Indigenous peoples. In 2007, the Working Group was replaced by the Expert Mechanism on Rights of Indigenous Peoples to increase formally the ability to demand, for example, state reporting.[24]

Beyond the UN, other important entities also emerged at a more regional level. The continental Inter-American system, created by the Organization of American States in 1948 for regional solidarity, contains all thirty-five independent states of the Americas.[25] In 1979, the Inter-American Court of Human Rights was created. Early on, it heard a case concerning the rights of the Indigenous peoples in Nicaragua. The case, *Mayagna (Sumo) Awas Tingni Community v Nicaragua*,[26] has been noted as the

and Group Rights, 17/2 (2010): 215, 228; Joshua Castellino and Niamh Walsh (eds), *International Law and Indigenous Peoples* (Martinus Nijhoff 2005); Federico Lenzerini (ed), *Reparations for Indigenous Peoples: International & Comparative Perspectives* (OUP 2008).

[19] See eg Claire Charters, 'Indigenous Peoples and International Law and Policy' in Benjamin Richardson, Shin Imai, and Kent McNeil (eds), *Indigenous Peoples and the Law: Comparative and Critical Perspectives* (Hart Publishing 2009) 161.

[20] Mattias Åhrén, *Indigenous Peoples' Status in the International Legal System* (OUP 2016) 83.

[21] Sarah Pritchard, 'Working Group on Indigenous Populations: Mandate, Standard-Setting Activities and Future Perspectives' in Sarah Pritchard (ed), *Indigenous Peoples, the United Nations and Human Rights* (The Federation Press 1998) 40–41.

[22] ECOSOC Res 1589(L), 'The problem of indigenous populations' (21 May 1971) UN Doc E/5044 Supp No 1, 16, para 7.

[23] Pritchard (n 21).

[24] Ben Saul, *Indigenous Peoples and Human Rights: International and Regional Jurisprudence* (Hart Publishing 2016) 7.

[25] Ibid, 3.

[26] *Mayagna (Sumo) Awas Tingni Community v Nicaragua* (Judgement of 21 August 2001 on Merits, Reparations and Costs) IACtHR Series C No 79 (Mayagna case).

first of its kind before an international court.[27] An Indigenous community on the Atlantic Coast of Nicaragua lodged a petition against the Nicaraguan government's granting of a logging concession to Sol del Caribe SA on communal lands without the community's consent. The community lands were not demarcated or differentiated from state lands and partly overlapped with other Indigenous claimants. The court accepted that Indigenous groups, by the very fact of their existence, have the right to live freely in their own territory, and their close ties with the land must be recognized and understood as the fundamental basis of their cultures, their spiritual life, their integrity, and their economic survival.[28] Subsequently, this approach was affirmed by the Inter-American Commission on Human Rights, which confirmed that general international legal principles applicable to Indigenous human rights encompass a right for Indigenous peoples over territories traditionally used, and highlighted that Indigenous peoples must only be deprived of their ancestral lands with their consent.[29]

Numerous petitions by Indigenous peoples in the Americas have now been brought before the Inter-American Court of Human Rights. Many are centred on core environmental issues, especially concerning the mineral extraction industry. For example, a recent case concerned an Indigenous community in Guatemala relating to the environmental impact of mining on their traditional lands.[30] The Q'eqchi' Mayan community argued that Guatemala violated its collective property rights to land and natural resources and its right to self-determination and self-governance because existing state laws fail to recognize and enable the community's participation in the processes that adjudicate mineral exploration and decision-making to consent or not to mining projects. While several civil cases brought within Guatemala were unsuccessful, the reliance on this international court brought international attention to the issue. The Inter-American Court accepted Q'eqchi' Mayan community's petition.[31] However, success in this forum is not always forthcoming. In comparison, a high-profile failed petition was the Inuit petition

[27] Laurence Burgorgue-Larsen and Amaya Torres, *The Inter-American Court of Human Rights: Case Law and Commentary* (OUP 2011) 501.

[28] Mayagna case (n 26) [149].

[29] Åhrén (n 20) 83; *Mary and Carrie Dann v US* (Judgement of 27 December 2002 on merits) IACtHR Case No 11.140 Report No 75/02, 29–37.

[30] 'Report on Admissibility—Maya Q'eqchi' Agua Caliente Community (Guatemala)' No 30/17, Petition 1118-11, Doc 37, OEA/Ser.L/V/II.161 (18 March 2017).

[31] For further consideration of this court, see Monica Feria-Tinta and Simon Milnes, 'The Rise of Environmental Law in International Dispute Resolution: The Inter-American Court of Human Rights Issues a Landmark Advisory Opinion on the Environment and Human Rights' *Yearbook of International Environmental Law*, 27 (2016): 64; Joel Correia, 'Indigenous Rights at Crossroads: Territorial Struggles, the Inter-American Court Of Human Rights, and Legal Geographies of Liminality' *Geoforum*, 97 (2018): 73.

filed in 2005, claiming that the US climate change policy violated the rights of Inuit in the United States and Canada.[32]

B. ILO's 1989 Convention Concerning Indigenous and Tribal Peoples in Independent Countries (ILO 169)

The first international treaty focusing exclusively on Indigenous peoples was ILO Convention No 107 of 1957, however, its final goal was the assimilation of Indigenous groups into mainstream society. This document was revised, resulting in ILO 169. During negotiations for ILO 169, Indigenous participants insisted on references to 'peoples' and 'self-determination', which caused a political deadlock. The negotiating committee was under a deadline and agreed to the use of the term 'peoples', along with clarifying that it was not intended to convey any implications regarding rights that may attach to the term under international law.[33] ILO 169 entered into force in 1991 and has been ratified by twenty-three states.[34] Article 15 especially safeguards Indigenous peoples' rights to the natural resources pertaining to their lands, including the right to participate in the use, management, and conservation of these resources. Governments shall consult, 'in good faith … with the objective of achieving agreement or consent to the proposed measures' when considering legislative or administrative measures which may affect Indigenous peoples directly.[35] Special measures to safeguard persons, institutions, property, labour, cultures, and environment of the Indigenous peoples shall not be contrary to the freely-expressed wishes of the peoples concerned.[36] The Convention acknowledges Indigenous peoples to be distinct polities within states.[37]

Norway was the first country to ratify the Convention in 1990 and has since partially implemented it in its Finnmark Act 2005, which transferred land ownership in the northernmost municipality to its residents.[38]

[32] See Hari Osofsky, 'The Inuit Petition as a Bridge? Beyond Dialectics of Climate Change and Indigenous Peoples' Rights' *American Indian Law Review*, 31 (2007): 675; Rebecca Tsosie, 'Climate Change and Indigenous Peoples: Comparative Models of Sovereignty' *Tulane Environmental Law Journal*, 26 (2013): 239.

[33] Russel Barsh, 'Framework' in Lawrence Watters (ed), *Indigenous Peoples, the Environment and Law* (Carolina Academic Press 2004):15, 22–23; see ILO Convention No 169, art 1.3; Luis Rodriguez-Pinero, *Indigenous Peoples, Postcolonialism, and International Law: The ILO Regime (1919–1989)* (OUP 2005).

[34] ILO, 'Ratifications of C169—Indigenous and Tribal Peoples Convention, 1989 (No. 169)'. The countries to ratify it are: Argentina, Bolivia, Brazil, Central African Republic, Chile, Columbia, Costa Rica, Denmark, Dominica, Ecuador, Fiji, Guatemala, Honduras, Luxembourg, Mexico, Nepal, Netherlands, Nicaragua, Norway, Paraguay, Peru, Spain, and Venezuela.

[35] ILO Convention No 169, art 6.

[36] ILO Convention No 169, art 4.

[37] Barsh (n 33) 23.

[38] Nigel Bankes and Timo Koivurova (eds), *The Proposed Nordic Saami Convention: National and International Dimensions of Indigenous Property Rights* (Hart Publishing 2013); Christina Allard and Skogvang Susann (eds), *Autonomous Sami Law: Indigenous Rights in Scandinavia* (Ashgate 2015).

C. 2007 UN Declaration on the Rights of Indigenous Peoples

In September 2007, the UN General Assembly adopted the Declaration on the Rights of Indigenous Peoples following a 143:4 vote.[39] Those four countries in the minority (Aotearoa New Zealand, Australia, Canada, and the United States) later endorsed the Declaration in 2010/2011. This Declaration has been described as the 'most comprehensive statement to date of indigenous peoples' rights'.[40] The international instrument affirms the 'minimum standards for the survival, dignity and well-being of the Indigenous peoples of the world'[41] and has been celebrated globally as a symbol of triumph and hope.[42] It is to be utilized as a means to assist Indigenous peoples 'in combating discrimination and marginalisation'.[43] The Declaration 'emphasizes the rights of indigenous peoples to maintain and strengthen their own institutions, cultures and traditions and to pursue their development in keeping with their own needs and aspirations'.[44]

The Declaration consists of a preamble of twenty-four paragraphs and forty-six articles. Article 1 articulates the basic principle that Indigenous peoples hold the same 'human rights and fundamental freedoms as recognised in the Charter of the United Nations, the Universal Declaration of Human Rights and international human rights law'. The Declaration encapsulates many protective rights for Indigenous peoples, including the right to be free from discrimination,[45] the right to self-determination,[46] and the right to a nationality.[47] The Declaration states that Indigenous peoples 'shall not be forcibly removed from their lands or territories'[48] and that they have the right to 'practice and revitalise their cultural traditions and customs'.[49] States shall 'consult and co-operate in good faith with the indigenous peoples' and obtain their consent before implementing legislation that may affect

[39] Claire Charters and Rodolfo Stavenhagen (eds), *Making the Declaration Work: The United Nations Declaration on the Rights of Indigenous Peoples* (IWGIA 2009).

[40] UN Office of the High Commissioner for Human Rights in Nepal, Press Release, 'High Commissioner for Human Rights Hails Adoption of Declaration on Indigenous Rights' (13 September 2007).

[41] UNGA Res 61/295, 'United Nations Declaration on the Rights of Indigenous Peoples' (2 October 2007) UN Doc A/RES/61/295 (UNDRIP) art 43.

[42] See eg 'International Working Group for Indigenous Affairs' <https://www.iwgia.org/iwgia/what-we-do> accessed 9 January 2019.

[43] UN Permanent Forum on Indigenous Issues, 'FAQs: Declaration on the Rights of Indigenous Peoples' <https://www.un.org/esa/socdev/unpfii/documents/FAQsindigenousdeclaration.pdf> accessed 9 January 2019.

[44] Ibid.

[45] UNDRIP, art 2.

[46] art 3.

[47] art 6.

[48] art 10.

[49] art 11.

them.[50] The use of traditional health practices and employment of traditional medicines is protected.[51]

Universal support for the Declaration was not initially forthcoming. For example, Aotearoa New Zealand often tabled apprehension for the draft Declaration and uncertainty towards its influence and compatibility with the country's legal framework.[52] The four articles that proved the most contentious were articles: 19 (States shall consult with Indigenous peoples in order to obtain their free, prior, and informed consent); 26 (Indigenous peoples have the right to the lands, territories, and resources which they have traditionally owned or occupied); 28 (Indigenous peoples have the right to redress, by means that can include restitution or, when this is not possible, just, fair, and equitable compensation); and 32 (Indigenous peoples have the right to determine and develop priorities and strategies for the development or use of their lands or territories and other resources). These articles are important to Indigenous peoples and their continuing relationships with lands and waters, but because the articles expect a shift of some decision-making power from government states to Indigenous peoples, states dislike these articles. For example, Aotearoa New Zealand's Ambassador and representative to the UN at the time of the Assembly vote in 2007 remarked that these four articles are 'fundamentally incompatible with New Zealand's constitutional and legal arrangements' because they sought to provide a right of veto to Māori.[53] In 2010, Aotearoa New Zealand endorsed the Declaration but with caveats stipulating no support for these four articles.[54] The Declaration has now been referenced and supported in domestic courts, including in Aotearoa New Zealand.[55]

D. Other Relevant Environmental International Law Instruments

Several other significant international law instruments have been developed that are inclusive of Indigenous peoples and their environments. For example, in 1992, the World

[50] art 20.

[51] art 24.

[52] See Andrew Erueti (ed), *International Indigenous Rights in Aotearoa New Zealand* (Victoria University Press 2017); Sarah Stevenson, 'Comment, Indigenous Land Rights and the Declaration on the Rights of Indigenous Peoples: Implications for Maori Land Claims in New Zealand' *Fordham International Law Journal*, 32 (2008): 298, 312–313; Jacinta Ruru, 'Finding Support for a Changed Property Discourse for Aotearoa New Zealand in the United Nations Declaration on the Rights of Indigenous Peoples' *Lewis & Clark Law Review*, 15/4 (2011): 951.

[53] 'General Assembly adopts Declaration on Rights of Indigenous Peoples; 'Major step forward' towards human rights for all, says President' (13 September 2007) <https://www.un.org/press/en/2007/ga10612.doc.htm> accessed 22 January 2020.

[54] Hansard—Questions for Oral Answer, 'Questions to Ministers: UN Declaration on the Rights of Indigenous Peoples—Government Support' (20 April 2010) 662 New Zealand Parliamentary Debates 10238.

[55] See eg *Proprietors of Wakatū v Attorney-General* [2017] NZSC 17, [2017] 1 NZLR 423.

Heritage Convention became the first international legal instrument to recognize and protect cultural landscapes. The Tongariro National Park in Aotearoa New Zealand became the first property to be inscribed with this status because of the importance of the mountains in this park to Māori.[56] In 1992, the UN committed to the non-binding Agenda 21 action plan that includes a detailed programme area for recognizing and strengthening the role of Indigenous peoples and their communities with lands. For example, an objective is to recognize that sustainable harvest 'continues to be essential to the cultural, economic and physical wellbeing of indigenous people and their communities'.[57]

The 1992 Convention on Biological Diversity (CBD), in force since 1993, recognizes the value of Indigenous peoples' knowledge of and their dependence on biological resources. The preamble includes a statement that the contracting parties are:

> recognizing the close and traditional dependence of many indigenous and local communities embodying traditional lifestyles on biological resources, and the desirability of sharing equitably benefits arising from the use of traditional knowledge, innovations and practices relevant to the conservation of biological diversity and the sustainable use of its components.

Article 8(j) states that each contracting party shall, as far as possible and as appropriate:

> Subject to its national legislation, respect, preserve and maintain knowledge, innovations and practices of indigenous and local communities embodying traditional lifestyles relevant for the conservation and sustainable use of biological diversity and promote their wider application with the approval and involvement of the holders of such knowledge, innovations and practices and encourage the equitable sharing of the benefits arising from the utilization of such knowledge, innovations and practices.

In 2010, the Nagoya Protocol on Access to Genetic Resources and the Fair and Equitable Sharing of Benefits Arising from their Utilization was adopted as a supplementary agreement to the CBD. Several of its thirty-six articles are specifically relevant to Indigenous peoples. For example, the Nagoya Protocol requires each party to aim to ensure that 'traditional knowledge associated with genetic resources that is held by indigenous and local communities is accessed with the prior and informed consent or

[56] World Heritage Convention, 'Cultural landscapes' <https://whc.unesco.org/en/culturallandscape/> accessed 29 December 2018; Department of Conservation, *Tongariro National Park Management Plan 2006–2016* (2006).

[57] *Report of the United Nations Conference on Environment and Development* (UN 1993) vol I, annex II, 'Agenda 21', ch 26.3(a)(iv).

approval and involvement of these indigenous and local communities, and that mutually agreed terms have been established.'[58]

Importantly, in 2000, the World Commission on Protected Areas (WCPA), in conjunction with the International Union for Conservation of Nature (IUCN) and the World Wildlife Federation (WWF), accepted that 'the rights of indigenous ... peoples inhabiting protected areas must be respected by promoting and allowing full participation in co-management of resources' and 'governments and protected area managers should incorporate customary and indigenous tenure and resource use, and control systems, as a means of enhancing biodiversity conservation'. The instrument further stipulated that this should occur 'in a way that would not affect or undermine the objectives for the protected area as set out in its management plan'.[59]

The WWF and IUCN/WCPA have committed to several key principles regarding recognizing Indigenous peoples' relationship to land. The first principle reads:[60]

> Principle 1: Indigenous and other traditional peoples have long associations with nature and a deep understanding of it. Often they have made significant contributions to the maintenance of many of the earth's most fragile ecosystems, through their traditional sustainable resource use practices and culture-based respect for nature. Therefore, there should be no inherent conflict between the objectives of protected areas and the existence, within and around their borders, of indigenous and other traditional peoples. Moreover, they should be recognised as rightful, equal partners in the development and implementation of conservation strategies that affect their lands, territories, waters, coastal seas, and other resources, and in particular in the establishment and management of protected areas.

Other principles reinforce this strong commitment to equal partnership. Principle 2 demands that partnership agreements 'should be based on the full respect for the rights of indigenous and other traditional peoples' including their 'responsibility to conserve biodiversity'. Principle 3 emphasizes the importance of taking into account 'decentralisation, participation, transparency and accountability' in all matters. Principle 4 accepts that Indigenous peoples should be able to 'share fully and equitably in the benefits associated with protected areas'. Principle 5 recognizes Indigenous geographical tribal boundaries often a cross national state boundaries, and therefore, there is an important role and responsibility for international law and action.

More recently, the negotiation of REDD, and subsequently REDD+ (reducing emissions from deforestation, degradation, and enhanced conservation of forests in developing countries) as a climate change mitigation solution portrays a continuing typical frustration by Indigenous peoples to ensure their experiences, rights, and interests

[58] art 7; See Maria Teran, 'The Nagoya Protocol and Indigenous Peoples' *The International Indigenous Policy Journal*, 7/2 (2016).

[59] Javier Beltrán (ed), *Indigenous and Traditional Peoples and Protected Areas: Principles, Guidelines and Case Studies* (IUCN World Commission on Protected Areas 2000) ix.

[60] Ibid, ix–x.

are taken seriously at the international level. REDD, described blatantly as a violation of Indigenous rights by many,[61] and the more flexible REDD+, continue to pose significant challenges for Indigenous peoples. Apparently though, international discussions about REDD+ have had a greater focus on Indigenous peoples than other mitigation policy tools considered under the 1992 UN Framework Convention on Climate Change (UNFCCC).[62] One development has been the Amazon Indigenous REDD+ which operates in Peru, Columbia, Brazil, and Ecuador. This seeks to address more holistically equitable and culturally appropriate solutions according to Indigenous life plans. As described by an Indigenous leader:[63]

> We manage governance, the empowerment of the territory and the adaptation of public policies to our context.

The 2015 climate change treaty, the Paris Agreement to the UNFCCC, explicitly recognizes the rights of Indigenous peoples and that adaptation action should be based on and guided by the best available science including the 'knowledge of indigenous peoples'.[64]

A further example of international law-making with relevance for Indigenous peoples is the work of the governments of Norway, Sweden, Finland, and the Saami parliaments of these countries who have developed a Nordic Saami Convention. A draft text was agreed to in 2005 and signed in 2017.[65] The aspiration for the Convention is to define the Saami people's rights as Indigenous peoples. The Convention consists of a preambular section and forty-six articles. The preamble is divided into two parts to provide a place for the voice of the governments *and* the Saami parliaments. This is rather unique for an international document. The rationale is to commit to, and bring alive, the concept of partnership whereby each party to the Convention has an opportunity to express how they perceive the Convention to be important. The articles are grouped into seven chapters dealing with: the general rights of the Saami people, Saami governance, Saami language and culture, Saami rights to land and water, Saami livelihoods, implementation and development of the Convention, and final provisions. The draft Nordic Saami

[61] See Randall Abate and Elizabeth Kronk, 'Commonality Among Unique Indigenous Communities: An Introduction to Climate Change and Its Impacts on Indigenous Peoples' in Randall Abate and Elizabeth Ann (eds), *Climate Change and Indigenous Peoples: The Search for Legal Remedies* (Edward Elgar 2013) 10; Stephanie Baez, 'The 'Right' REDD Framework: National Laws that Best Protect Indigenous Rights in a Global REDD Regime' *Fordham Law Review*, 80 (2011): 821.

[62] Donna Craig, 'Legal Strategies to Expand Indigenous Governance in Climate Change Adaptation' in Paul Martien *et al* (eds), *The Search for Environmental Justice* (Edward Elgar 2015) 309, 322–323; see also Linda Wallbott, 'Indigenous Peoples in UN REDD+ Negotiations: "Importing Power" and Lobbying for Rights through Discursive Interplay Management' *Ecology and Society*, 19/1 (2014): 21.

[63] As quoted in an article by Eliana Garzon, 'Amazon Indigenous REDD+: An Innovative Approach to Conserve Colombian Forests?' *Mongabay* (6 January 2017).

[64] art 7.5; see also preamble.

[65] Atle Staalesen, 'Historic Sami agreement starts long way towards ratification' *The Barents Observer* (16 January 2017).

Convention was described as 'a considerable and imaginative achievement',[66] and as 'an innovative and progressive way to advance the rights of transnational indigenous peoples'.[67] The Convention is now being implemented in national legislation.

Considerably more instruments exist that seek to accommodate Indigenous peoples' traditional practices across various activities. In some circumstances, these permit the traditional take of whales,[68] seals,[69] and polar bears.[70] Other instruments seek to protect Indigenous peoples' interests in the environment within the contexts of, for example, mining.[71]

Indigenous peoples often join forces with others to seek international environmental justice. For example, the Swedish Saami Youth Association is working with families from countries worldwide to bring their *Peoples' Climate* case. They seek stronger European Union (EU) climate targets to protect their fundamental rights of life, health, occupation, and property. In May 2019, the European General Court dismissed the case on procedural grounds.[72] At the time of writing, the case is being appealed to the European Court of Justice.

A notable office, rather than an instrument per se, has been creating the Special Rapporteur on the rights of Indigenous peoples by the UN Commission on Human Rights in 2001. The Rapporteur has the mandate to promote good practices and laws, and often reports on selected countries. The Rapporteur has also issued several thematic reports including on climate change and conservation.[73]

66 Bankes and Koivurova (n 38) 399.

67 Ibid, 404.

68 See International Whaling Commission, 'Aboriginal Subsistence Whaling' <https://iwc.int/aboriginal> accessed 9 January 2019.

69 1957 Interim Convention between the US, Canada, Japan and the USSR on Conservation of North Pacific Fur Seals, art VII.

70 1973 Agreement on the Conservation of Polar Bears, art 3(d); see Robert Miller, 'Exercising Cultural Self-Determination: The Makah Indian Tribe Goes Whaling' *American Indian Law Review*, 25 (2000–01): 165; Leena Heinamaki, 'Protecting the Rights of Indigenous Peoples—Promoting the Sustainability of the Global Environment?' *International Community Law Review*, 11 (2009): 3; Nigel Bankes, 'The Conservation and Utilization of Marine Mammals in the Arctic Region' in Erik Molenaar, Alex Elferink, and Donald Rothwell (eds), *The Law of the Sea and the Polar Regions: Interactions between Global and Regional Regimes* (Martinus Nijhoff 2013) 293; Jerry Firestone, Jonathan Lily, and Isable Noronha, 'Cultural Diversity, Human Rights and the Emergence of Indigenous Peoples in International and Comparative Environmental Law' *American University International Law* Review, 20/2 (2005): 219.

71 See Andrew Erueti, Sarah Down, and Jacinta Ruru, 'International Indigenous Rights, investment and sustainability in the mining sector' in Shawkat Alam, Jahid Bhuiyan, and Jona Razzaque (eds), *International Natural Resources Law, Investment and Sustainability* (Routledge 2017) 310; Sarah Morales, 'Canary in a Coal Mine: Indigenous Women and Extractive Industries in Canada' in Aimee Craft *et al*, *UNDRIP Implementation: More Reflections on the Braiding of International, Domestic and Indigenous Laws* (Centre for International Governance Innovation and Wiyasiwewin Mikiwahp Native Law Centre 2018) 73.

72 For all details, including links to the court orders, see 'The Peoples Climate case' website at: <https://peoplesclimatecase.caneurope.org> accessed 3 January 2020.

73 See eg Human Rights Council, 'Report of the Special Rapporteur on the rights of indigenous peoples' (15 September 2017) UN Doc HRC/36/46 (15 Sep 2017).

IV. SIGNIFICANCE OF INTERNATIONAL ENVIRONMENTAL LAW FOR INDIGNEOUS PEOPLES

James Anaya (a former UN Special Rapporteur on the rights of Indigenous peoples) has characterized two dominant but complementary strands of argument made by Indigenous peoples about what international law can, or should, provide:[74]

- The state-centred framework, which characterizes Indigenous groups as nations, with attributes of sovereignty that predate, and in some circumstances, should trump the sovereignty of states that now assert power over them.
- The human rights framework deriving from the modern human rights movement with the welfare of human beings as its subject. Indigenous peoples in this framework are viewed as a group of human beings, with fundamental human rights concerns that deserve attention.

Anaya posits that, more generally, the human rights-based argument has gained most traction whereby there has been an increasing global awareness of, and involvement in, human rights and moral considerations.[75] The failure of international law to recognize Indigenous nations is a perpetrated ongoing tragedy of colonialism. Indigenous critique of modern international law remains, including of the much more broadly celebrated UNDRIP. For example, as Irene Watson writes:[76]

> Our hope was that [UNDRIP] might provide a reprieve from the genocidal impact of colonialism. However, it has been a disappointment.... [I]t is a bit like states having their cake and eating it too in its approach to the recognition of First Nations.... [O] n the one hand it recognises the right of First Nations to self-determination and, on the other hand, it limits self-determination to being exercised in accord with state power.

This lack of acknowledgement of Indigenous peoples' inherent rights to self-determination matters immensely in the journey of disrupting colonialism to find ways

[74] 'Introduction' in James Anaya (ed), *International Law and Indigenous Peoples* (Ashgate 2003) xiii; see also some early work by Cherie Metcalf where she positions two models as underlying the relationship between Indigenous peoples' rights in international law and international environmental law: 'Cultural integrity' vs 'self-determination' in Cherie Metcalf, 'Indigenous Rights and the Environment: Evolving International Law' *Ottawa Law Review,* 35/1 (2003): 101.

[75] Anaya, ibid, xiii.

[76] Irene Watson, 'First Nations, Indigenous Peoples: Our Laws Have Always Been Here' in Irene Watson (ed), *Indigenous Peoples as Subjects of International Law* (Routledge 2018) 96, 98.

to enable Indigenous laws and knowledges to have the primacy required to care for lands and waters. As Borrows writes:[77]

> Indigenous laws flow from specific landscapes, ecosystems and peoples . . . Indigenous laws should be recognized for what they are, without necessarily altering them to fit international or national law sensibilities.

But, arguably, international law has not yet contributed to enabling this significant shift. For example, Maria Teran has captured several powerful quotes from Indigenous peoples specific to the Nagoya Protocol. Despite the Protocol stating that, for instance, 'Parties shall in accordance with domestic law take into consideration indigenous and local communities' customary laws',[78] Indigenous persons have recorded experiences in their own words in different terms:[79]

> In our vision the plants, animals, rivers, everything is related and interconnected. We believe that the resources from Mother Earth are for the well-being of humanity. Consequently, it was very painful for us to understand these initial discussions on the commercialization of our resources and to put a price on genetic resources and traditional knowledge. (N Reyes, personal communication, 25 January 2006)
>
> For six years we defended with love and passion the sustainability of our Mother Earth to ensure our life and the survival of the coming generations. Indigenous Peoples will continue to be the guardians and protectors of Mother Earth, Pachamama, and all her beings in the same way that our ancestors did. (F Lopez, personal communication, 29 October 2010)
>
> Since ancestral times, Mother Earth has been cared for, protected, and respected by Indigenous Peoples as a living being and life giver. She is the basis for human and cultural development. Since our childhoods, we have learned how to treat the plants, the animals, and all resources that are forming the ecosystems. We were taught how to talk to the plants and how to ask permission before using them either as medicine or protection. In that regard, our grandparents shared with us that the resources are for the benefit of all humanity free of charge in accordance with our ancestral values of sharing and caring for one another, reciprocity and protecting our sacred land, Pachamama. Indigenous Peoples have land, territories, and waters surrounded by medicinal plants and herbs that we use only whenever necessary. They grow freely for our collective well-being. We never put a price on a plant. We never have the idea that outside our communities there are people and organizations that are making a profit from the use and commercialization of our plants. (A M Guacho, personal communication, 16 March 2015)

[77] John Borrows, 'Introduction: Challenging Law' in Aimée Craft *et al*, 'UNDRIP Implementation: More Reflections on the Braiding of International, Domestic and Indigenous Laws' *Centre for International Governance Innovation Special Report* (30 October 2018) 2.

[78] art 12.

[79] Maria Teran, 'The Nagoya Protocol and Indigenous Peoples' *International Indigenous Policy Journal*, 7/2 (2016): 9, 14–15.

V. CONCLUSION

International environmental law is an essential tool for disrupting systemic colonization to encourage domestic nations to better recognize the enormous value of Indigenous peoples and their laws for knowing and caring for the environment. These instruments demonstrate that we are globally still in the early stages of transitioning to a more respectful and inclusive environmental regime. More inter-cultural sophisticated dialogue and action is required to value the knowledge and experience that Indigenous peoples can bring to addressing complex global environmental issues.

BIBLIOGRAPHY

Randall Abate and Elizabeth Ann (eds), *Climate Change and Indigenous Peoples: The Search for Legal Remedies* (Edward Elgar 2013)

Mattias Åhrén, *Indigenous Peoples' Status in the International Legal System* (OUP 2016)

James Anaya, *Indigenous Peoples in International Law* (2nd edn, OUP 2004)

Nigel Bankes and Timo Koivurova (eds), *The Proposed Nordic Saami Convention: National and International Dimensions of Indigenous Property Rights* (Hart Publishing 2013)

Claire Charters and Rodolfo Stavenhagen (eds), *Making the Declaration Work: The United Nations Declaration on the Rights of Indigenous Peoples* (IWGIA 2009)

Aimée Craft *et al*, 'UNDRIP Implementation: More Reflections on the Braiding of International, Domestic and Indigenous Laws' *Centre for International Governance Innovation Special Report* (30 October 2018)

Ben Saul, *Indigenous Peoples and Human Rights: International and Regional Jurisprudence* (Hart Publishing 2016)

Irene Watson (ed), *Indigenous Peoples as Subjects of International Law* (1st edn, Routledge 2018)

PART VII

INTER-LINKAGES WITH OTHER REGIMES

CHAPTER 43

TRADE

HARRO VAN ASSELT

I. INTRODUCTION

CAN a country adopt a regulation banning imports of illegally logged timber? Is it legal to require genetically modified food from another country to be labelled as such before giving it access to the domestic market? And what if a party to the 2015 Paris Agreement on climate change wants to achieve emission reductions by imposing a border tax on carbon-intensive goods from non-parties? These are just some of the many questions that arise at the interface of trade and international environmental law.

The relationship between trade and the environment is multifaceted and fiercely debated. Trade can be an engine for sustainable development by opening up the exchange of environmentally friendly goods and services. Yet trade and environmental protection are often seen to be at loggerheads. International trade law may have a 'chilling effect' on the adoption or effective implementation of international environmental agreements.[1] Conversely, environmental policies employing trade restrictions can become 'green protectionism'[2] and even 'eco-imperialism.'[3] Aided by a growing number of disputes brought before the international trade regime, these arguments have become part of a long-standing debate on trade and the environment. At its core, this debate is about balancing competing values and objectives.

This chapter aims to disentangle the interactions between international trade law and environmental protection. The chapter begins by explaining how trade and

[1] Robyn Eckersley, 'The Big Chill: The WTO and Multilateral Environmental Agreements' *Global Environmental Politics*, 4/2 (2004): 24.

[2] Walden Bello, 'The Threat of Green Protectionism' *International Centre for Trade and Sustainable Development* (1 July 1997).

[3] See Daniel Esty, *Greening the GATT: Trade, Environment, and the Future* (Peterson Institute for International Economics 1994) 185–188.

environmental protection are physically interlinked (Section II), before offering an account of the evolution of the trade and environment debate (Section III). Next, the chapter examines the relationship between multilateral environmental agreements (MEAs) and trade (Section IV), followed by an analysis of questions that have arisen in assessing the compatibility of environmental measures with trade law (Section V). The chapter then explores two emerging developments of relevance for the trade and environment debate, including the rise of regional trade agreements and the growing importance of climate change-related disputes (Section VI). The chapter ends with a critical assessment of the prospects for strengthening coherence between international environmental and trade law (Section VII).

II. ENVIRONMENTAL IMPACTS OF TRADE

The impacts of free trade on the environment have been heavily debated by economists. The theory of international trade underpinning the multilateral trading system suggests that if each country focuses on producing and exporting goods in which they have a comparative advantage, this will leave everyone better off. The resulting economic growth, neoclassical economists argue, frees up resources for environmental protection.[4] Ecological economists, however, question the assumptions behind the relationships between international trade and economic growth, and economic growth and environmental protection.[5] To establish whether free trade helps or harms the environment, these relationships require testing in the real world.[6]

A distinction can be made between trade's direct and indirect effects on the environment. An example of a direct effect is the introduction of invasive alien species: an increase in trade volumes leads to more (and more frequent) introductions of non-indigenous species, with attendant socio-ecological consequences.[7] Another direct effect is the pollution resulting from international transport, such as shipping and aviation.[8]

[4] See eg Jagdish Bhagwati, 'The Case for Free Trade' *Scientific American*, 269/5 (1993): 42.

[5] See eg Herman Daly, 'The Perils of Free Trade' *Scientific American*, 269/5 (1993): 50.

[6] Paul Ekins *et al*, 'Trade, Environment and Development: The Issues in Perspective' *Ecological Economics*, 9/1 (2004): 1, 8.

[7] Peter Jenkins, 'Free Trade and Exotic Species Introductions' *Conservation Biology*, 10/1 (1996): 300; Charles Perrings *et al*, 'International Cooperation in the Solution to Trade-Related Invasive Species Risks' *Annals of the New York Academy of Science*, 1195/1 (2010): 198.

[8] See Chapter 34, 'Aviation and Maritime Transport', in this volume.

Indirect effects can be further divided into *scale*, *technique*, and *composition* effects.[9] The impacts of free trade on the environment depend primarily on whether the positive composition and technique effects outweigh the negative direct, scale, and composition effects.

Scale effects refer to the growing environmental impacts due to an increase in economic activity. Composition effects concern the environmental impacts resulting from the sectoral specialization in the area in which a country has a comparative advantage. If such an area includes pollution-intensive industries, the environmental impacts will be negative. Conversely, if a country has a comparative advantage in cleaner industries, then free trade will lead to less pollution.

The composition effect may be related to differences in the stringency of environmental policy. Trade liberalization between one country with stringent regulation and another with lax environmental standards may increase pollution-intensive activity in the latter.[10] This would happen through the 'pollution haven effect', which suggests that firms would relocate to countries with weak environmental regulation.[11] This, in turn, could lead to a 'race to the bottom' in which countries compete to attract trade and investment by lowering environmental standards.[12] Evidence supporting the pollution haven hypothesis is limited, mainly because firms' decisions on where to locate depend on much more than just the stringency of environmental regulation.[13] In the climate change context, the pollution haven hypothesis has resurfaced under the guise of 'carbon leakage', which refers to the relocation of carbon-intensive production to countries with lower carbon constraints. However, like the pollution haven hypothesis, there is limited proof of carbon leakage.[14]

Technique effects refer to reduced environmental impacts in the production process of goods, which may take place through the transfer of environmental technologies or the diffusion of environmental standards. The latter may be driven through a 'California effect' of 'upward ratcheting of regulatory standards in competing political jurisdictions'.[15] For instance, there is evidence that the trade in automobiles and their components between countries with low and high emissions standards has led to an overall increase in stringency of standards.[16]

9 Gene Grossman and Alan Krueger, 'Environmental Impacts of a North American Free Trade Agreement' in Peter Garber (ed), *The Mexico–U.S. Free Trade Agreement* (MIT Press 1993) 13.

10 Kevin Gallagher, 'Introduction: International Trade and the Environment' in Kevin Gallagher (ed), *Handbook of Trade and the Environment* (Edward Elgar 2008) 1, 4.

11 Brian Copeland and M Scott Taylor, 'Trade, Growth, and the Environment' *Journal of Economic Literature*, 42/1 (2004): 7.

12 Gareth Porter, 'Trade Competition and Pollution Standards: "Race to the Bottom" or "Stuck at the Bottom"?' *Journal of Environment and Development*, 8/2 (1999): 133.

13 Brian Copeland, 'The Pollution Haven Hypothesis' in Gallagher (n 10) 60, 66.

14 John Ward *et al*, *Carbon Leakage: Theory, Evidence and Policy Design* (World Bank Group 2015) 2.

15 David Vogel, 'Trading Up and Governing Across: Transnational Governance and Environmental Protection' *Journal of European Public Policy*, 4/4 (1997): 556, 561.

16 Richard Perkins and Eric Neumayer, 'Does the 'California Effect' Operate across Borders? Trading- and Investing-Up in Automobile Emission Standards' *Journal of European Public Policy*, 19/2 (2012): 217.

III. A SHORT HISTORY OF THE TRADE AND ENVIRONMENT DEBATE

A. The Early Days

Even some of the earliest environmental and trade treaties reflected awareness of the linkages between trade and the environment. For instance, import prohibitions were used in the 1902 Convention for the Protection of Birds Useful to Agriculture.[17] One of the first trade agreements, the 1927 International Convention for the Abolition of Import and Export Prohibitions and Restrictions, included an early form of environmental exception.[18] This example was followed in the 1947 General Agreement on Tariffs and Trade (GATT), which also provided regulatory space for environmental measures through two exceptions (see Section V.C).[19]

As environmental concerns began appearing on the international political agenda, the interlinkages with trade also started to garner attention. In the run-up to the 1972 Stockholm Conference, the GATT Secretariat released a study on trade measures for environmental protection.[20] Around the same time, the GATT Council established the unfortunately named 'Environmental Measures and International Trade' (EMIT) group, which was mandated to consider, upon request, 'matters relevant to the trade policy aspects of measures to control pollution and protect the human environment'.[21] However, the group remained inactive for almost twenty years.

B. Signs of Conflict

The rise of environmental disputes under the GATT in the early 1990s increased the political salience of trade and environment interlinkages. Most prominent among these were the *Tuna-Dolphin* cases, in which two GATT panels issued controversial rulings about the legality of trade measures to protect the environment.[22] The cases concerned measures taken by the United States under its Marine Mammal Protection Act, which were challenged by Mexico and the European Community. In response to concerns about the bycatch of dolphins when fishermen caught yellowfin tuna with purse seine

[17] arts 2, 5.

[18] art 4.

[19] art XX(b) and (g).

[20] GATT Secretariat, 'Industrial Pollution Control and International Trade' (9 June 1971) L/3538.

[21] GATT Council, 'Minutes of Meeting Held in the Palais des Nations, Geneva on 9 November 1971' (17 November 1971) C/M/74, 4.

[22] *US—Restrictions on Imports of Tuna* (Panel Report) [3 September 1991] 30 ILM 1594 (unadopted) (Tuna-Dolphin I); *US—Restrictions on Imports of Tuna* (Panel Report) [16 June 1994] 33 ILM 839 (unadopted) (Tuna-Dolphin II).

nets, the Act banned imports of tuna not caught using methods that prevented incidental kills.

The GATT panels ruled that the United States could not distinguish between tuna products based on the way they were produced.[23] Moreover, the panels were reluctant to accept a unilateral measure that sought to protect resources in another country's territory.[24] The *Tuna-Dolphin* panel reports were never adopted, diminishing their legal significance. Moreover, in hindsight, the decisions can be considered an 'outlier' in trade law jurisprudence.[25] Nevertheless, they sparked an outcry by environmentalists, who perceived the rulings as confirmation that trade law undermines environmental protection.[26]

In parallel to the GATT rulings, the 1992 Rio Conference addressed the use of unilateral trade measures for environmental protection, with Principle 12 of the Rio Declaration providing that '[u]nilateral actions to deal with environmental challenges outside the jurisdiction of the importing country should be avoided'.[27] Some countries used the Rio Conference as an opportunity to activate the EMIT group, which from 1991 to 1994 discussed trade measures in MEAs, transparency of environmental regulations, and trade impacts of environmental packaging and labelling.[28]

Environmental protection also began to emerge on the agenda of trade negotiations. This included the Uruguay Round of multilateral trade negotiations, which were to lead to the creation of the World Trade Organization (WTO). In addition, environmental concerns surfaced in regional trade talks. Driven by non-governmental organizations in the United States, the North American Free Trade Agreement came to include environmental provisions in several of its chapters, and was followed by an environmental 'side-agreement'.[29]

C. The World Trade Organization

The creation of a permanent international organization for trade in 1995 marked a turning point in the trade and environment debate. The WTO was established to further

[23] Tuna-Dolphin I (n 22) [5.14]–[5.15].

[24] Ibid [5.27], [5.32]; Tuna-Dolphin II (n 22) [5.26].

[25] Aaron Cosbey and Petros Mavroidis, 'Heavy Fuel: Trade and Environment in the GATT/WTO Case Law' *Review of European, Comparative and International Environmental Law*, 23/3 (2014): 288, 289.

[26] See eg Matthew Hurlock, 'The GATT, U.S. Law and the Environment: A Proposal to Amend the GATT in Light of the Tuna/Dolphin Decision' *Columbia Law Review*, 92/8 (1992): 2098.

[27] *Report of the United Nations Conference on Environment and Development* (UN 1993) vol I, annex I—'Rio Declaration on Environment and Development', principle 12.

[28] GATT Council, 'Minutes of Meeting Held in the Centre William Rappard on 8 October 1991' (4 November 1991) C/M/252, 24.

[29] 1992 North American Free Trade Agreement; 1993 North American Agreement on Environmental Co-operation; see Richard Steinberg, 'Trade-Environment Negotiations in the EU, NAFTA, and WTO: Regional Trajectories of Rule Development' *American Journal of International Law*, 91/2 (1997): 231, 245–248.

the implementation, administration, and operation of multilateral trade agreements concluded under its auspices. In addition, the organization also serves as a forum for further trade negotiations and offers a mechanism to resolve disputes between its members.[30]

The 1994 GATT, which largely incorporates the 1947 version, is the main agreement dealing with the trade in goods. Its core rules revolve around non-discrimination. It provides that a country should not discriminate between producers from other countries and domestic producers ('national treatment'), and should treat 'like' imported and domestic products as such.[31] The other main rule is that a country should not discriminate between its trading partners ('most-favoured nation' treatment).[32] The purpose of this rule is to ensure that like products are treated alike, irrespective of their origins or destination. Like its predecessor, the 1994 GATT contains two environmental exceptions (see Section V.C).

Several other new agreements were concluded with relevance to trade and the environment, including agreements dealing with the trade in services[33] and intellectual property rights.[34] Other WTO agreements concerned with reducing trade barriers for goods include the 1994 Agreement on Technical Barriers to Trade, which deals with the international harmonization of technical regulations and standards; the 1994 Agreement on Sanitary and Phytosanitary Measures, which seeks to ensure that health and safety measures are not used to protect domestic producers;[35] and the 1994 Agreement on Subsidies and Countervailing Measures, aimed at disciplining the use of subsidies.

Environmental protection is not listed as a main objective of the organization. Still, the preamble to the Marrakesh Agreement suggests that achieving its trade-related goals should allow 'for the optimal use of the world's resources in accordance with the objective of sustainable development, seeking both to protect and preserve the environment and to enhance the means for doing so in a manner consistent with [Parties'] respective needs and concerns at different levels of economic development'.[36] Offering a further signal that environmental concerns were becoming prominent, the creation of the WTO was accompanied by a Ministerial Decision on Trade and Environment, which established a dedicated Committee on Trade and Environment (CTE).[37] The Committee discusses trade-environment linkages, and can issue recommendations on possible modifications to trade rules.[38] While it has not recommended any changes thus

[30] 1994 Marrakesh Agreement establishing the World Trade Organization (Marrakesh Agreement), art III.

[31] 1994 General Agreement on Tariffs and Trade (GATT 1994), art III.

[32] Ibid, art I.

[33] 1994 General Agreement on Trade in Services.

[34] 1994 Agreement on Trade-Related Aspects of Intellectual Property Rights (TRIPS); see also Chapter 48, 'Intellectual Property', in this volume.

[35] See also Chapter 18, 'Precaution', in this volume.

[36] Marrakesh Agreement, preamble, recital 1.

[37] WTO, 'Decision on Trade and Environment' (15 April 1994) LT/UR/D-6/2.

[38] Ibid.

far, the Committee's discussions have led to further negotiations in other WTO forums, for instance on fisheries subsidies.

The launch of the Doha Round of trade negotiations in 2001 brought further attention to environmental issues. The Doha Ministerial Declaration called on the CTE to focus on eco-labelling, intellectual property rights, and the effects of environmental measures on market access, especially for developing countries.[39] The declaration also called for new negotiations, taking place in special sessions of the CTE, on the relationship between trade obligations under MEAs and trade rules, procedures for information exchange between MEA secretariats and the WTO, and the reduction of trade barriers for environmental goods and services.[40] The prospects for these negotiations are dismal, however, as the entire Doha Round ground to an almost complete halt in 2008.

Notwithstanding this general lack of progress, some steps have been taken on specific issues such as fisheries subsidies. Initial talks on these environmentally harmful subsidies in the late 2000s did not yield results, but the adoption of the 2015 Sustainable Development Goals gave new impetus to the talks. WTO members have since agreed to work towards rules prohibiting subsidies that contribute to overfishing, as well as illegal, unregulated, and unreported fishing.[41]

IV. MULTILATERAL ENVIRONMENTAL AGREEMENTS AND TRADE

Whilst environmental concerns have moved up the trade agenda, trade measures have become part of MEAs on issues as diverse as wildlife protection, ozone depletion, genetically modified organisms, and hazardous waste and chemicals.[42]

The form of trade measures in MEAs depends on a treaty's purpose. Trade regulation is at the heart of the 1973 Convention on International Trade in Endangered Species (CITES), which stipulates the conditions for the trade in species listed in its appendices, using a system of import/export permits and certificates.[43] Likewise, trade controls are central to the 1989 Basel Convention on the transboundary movement of hazardous waste,[44] the 1998 Rotterdam Convention on trade in hazardous chemicals and pesticides,[45] and the 2000 Cartagena Protocol on Biosafety.[46] These treaties use

[39] WTO, 'Doha Ministerial Declaration' (20 November 2001) WT/MIN(01)/DEC/1, para 32.

[40] Ibid, para 31.

[41] WTO, 'Fisheries Subsidies, Ministerial Decision' (13 December 2017) WT/MIN(17)/64, WT/L/1031, para 1.

[42] See WTO, 'Matrix Trade-Related Measures Pursuant to Selected Multilateral Environmental Agreements' (9 October 2017) WT/CTE/W/160/Rev.8, TN/TE/S/5/Rev.6.

[43] See Chapter 32, 'Wildlife', in this volume.

[44] See Chapter 33, 'Hazardous Substances and Activities', in this volume.

[45] Ibid.

[46] See Chapter 32, 'Wildlife', in this volume.

a variety of techniques to regulate trade, including requiring prior consent by the importing party,[47] establishing an advance informed agreement procedure that allows the importing party to carry out its own risk assessment of potentially hazardous substances,[48] or banning trade altogether.[49]

Environmental treaties also use trade measures as one means to achieve their goals. Some MEAs restrict trade with non-parties to prevent undermining the integrity of a treaty by shifting the production or consumption of regulated substances. An example is the 1987 Montreal Protocol on ozone-depleting substances, which bans trade in controlled substances with non-parties, unless these countries comply with the provisions of the Protocol.[50] Along with financial support to developing countries, these measures have helped secure universal participation.[51]

Another set of measures targets non-compliance. CITES parties, for instance, have developed a system of collective trade sanctions. Specifically, the CITES Standing Committee can 'recommend the suspension of commercial or all trade in specimens of one or more CITES-listed species' for non-complying parties.[52] Due to their significant economic impact, the use—or even the threat—of these trade sanctions has been remarkably successful.[53] Similarly, the Montreal Protocol's non-compliance procedure allows for the adoption of trade measures.[54]

Trade-restrictive measures may also be adopted pursuant to MEAs that are silent about their use. This is the case for MEAs on climate change, which do not specify the measures parties should take to achieve their emission reduction targets. These types of trade measures raise serious questions of compatibility with trade law. By contrast, trade measures explicitly provided for in MEAs have yet to be challenged in a trade dispute.

MEAs could be used in three different ways in WTO dispute settlement: (1) as applicable law in a dispute, (2) to interpret ambiguous WTO terms, or (3) as factual evidence.[55] Considering MEAs as applicable law would mean they could be used as an independent defence of a violation of WTO norms,[56] but this possibility remains contested.[57] The

[47] See Chapter 33, 'Hazardous Substances and Activities', in this volume.

[48] Cartagena Protocol, arts 7–12.

[49] Although unconditional trade bans in MEAs are rare, the Basel Convention's 'ban amendment' seeks to ban all trade in hazardous wastes from OECD to non-OECD countries; see Chapter 34, 'Hazardous Substances and Activities', in this volume.

[50] See Chapter 28, 'Transboundary Air Pollution', in this volume.

[51] Scott Barrett, *Environment and Statecraft* (OUP 2003) 325.

[52] CITES Res Conf 14.3, 'CITES Compliance Procedures' (2007) annex, para 30.

[53] Rosalind Reeve, 'Wildlife Trade, Sanctions and Compliance: Lessons from the CITES Regime' *International Affairs*, 82/5 (2006): 881, 895; Peter Sand, 'Enforcing CITES: The Rise and Fall of Trade Sanctions' *Review of European Community and International Environmental Law*, 22/3 (2013): 251, 255.

[54] See also Chapter 56, 'Non-Compliance Procedures', in this volume.

[55] Margaret Young, *Trading Fish, Saving Fish: The Interaction between Regimes in International Law* (CUP 2011) 195–206.

[56] Ibid, 196.

[57] See eg Gabrielle Marceau, 'Conflicts of Norms and Conflicts of Jurisdictions: The Relationship between the WTO Agreement and MEAs and other Treaties' *Journal of World Trade*, 35/6 (2001): 1081, 1116.

use of MEAs as interpretive devices is less controversial. Notably, the WTO Appellate Body referred to the 1982 Law of the Sea Convention, the 1992 Convention on Biological Diversity (CBD), and the 1979 Convention on Migratory Species to support its evolutionary interpretation of the term 'natural resources' in GATT Article XX(g) in its well-known *Shrimp-Turtle* ruling.[58] However, in the later *Biotech* dispute, the WTO Panel did not seek recourse to the CBD or the Cartagena Protocol, despite their obvious relevance to the dispute, effectively laying down the nearly impossible requirement of parallel membership of the WTO and the MEA in question.[59] *Shrimp-Turtle* also showed how the WTO adjudicators could use MEAs as relevant facts (or evidence of such facts). The Appellate Body used the fact that sea turtles were listed in CITES as evidence of the fact that they were threatened with extinction.[60]

V. ENVIRONMENTAL MEASURES UNDER TRADE LAW

States can adopt various trade-related measures to pursue environmental ends, such as taxes, border taxes, tradeable permits, subsidies, product or process standards, and eco-labels. The design and implementation of these measures can raise trade concerns. This section explores some of the main questions and legal considerations arising from these measures, including the use of unilateral trade measures and questions of extraterritoriality, discrimination between products based on processes and production methods (PPMs), and the interpretation of the environmental exceptions of GATT Article XX.

A. Unilateral Trade Measures and Extraterritoriality

Principle 12 of the Rio Declaration privileges cooperative approaches over unilateral action by states. However, unilateral trade measures that go beyond multilaterally agreed rules are not prohibited, and some MEAs explicitly allow them. Indeed, unilateral action in the face of multilateral inaction can help advance environmental protection.[61] Nevertheless, unilateral trade measures raise several concerns. They may be

[58] *United States—Import Prohibition of Certain Shrimp and Shrimp Products* (Appellate Body Report) [12 October 1998] WTO Doc WT/DS58/AB/R (Shrimp/Turtle case) [130].

[59] *European Communities—Measures Affecting the Approval and Marketing of Biotech Products* (Panel Report) [29 September 2006] WTO Docs WT/DS291/R, WT/DS292/R, WT/DS293/R [7.74]–[7.75], [7.95]; see Margaret Young, 'The WTO's Use of Relevant Rules of International Law: An Analysis of the Biotech Case' *International and Comparative Law Quarterly*, 56/4 (2007): 907.

[60] Shrimp/Turtle case (n 58) [132].

[61] Daniel Bodansky, 'What's So Bad about Unilateral Action to Protect the Environment?' *European Journal of International Law*, 11/2 (2000): 339, 339.

viewed as protectionism in disguise,[62] and, to the extent such measures are imposed by developed countries on countries in the global South, they give rise to charges of 'eco-imperialism'.[63] Moreover, the measures can be seen as extraterritorial, impinging on the sovereignty of other states.

Extraterritoriality refers to the exercise of jurisdiction beyond a state's borders. Unilateral trade measures that target, for instance, the environmental impacts of production methods in another country could be considered extraterritorial. However, a requirement that all shrimp (including imports) is caught using a 'turtle excluder device'—the main measure at stake in *Shrimp-Turtle*—does not *regulate* activities outside a state's territory. After all, countries are still free to export their products elsewhere. Nonetheless, such measures have an extraterritorial effect.[64] They are examples not of extraterritoriality, but of 'territorial extension', meaning that the 'application of a measure is triggered by a territorial connection but in applying the measure the regulator is required, as a matter of law, to take into account conduct or circumstances abroad'.[65]

Measures with extraterritorial effects have been contested in several trade disputes, including *Tuna-Dolphin*, *Shrimp-Turtle*, and the more recent *Seal Products* case.[66] In *Shrimp-Turtle*, the Appellate Body refused to rule on whether there were any jurisdictional limitations implied by GATT Article XX(g), but found that there was a 'sufficient nexus between the migratory and endangered marine populations involved and the United States'.[67] In *Seal Products*, the Appellate Body likewise declined to rule on the jurisdictional limitation question.[68]

Drawing on Charnovitz's distinction between inward- and outward-looking measures,[69] Cooreman suggests the key lies in the location of environmental concerns.[70] Inward-looking measures are concerned with protecting the environment and public health within the country imposing a measure (eg through banning imports containing

[62] Margaret Young, 'Trade Measures to Address Environmental Concerns in Faraway Places: Jurisdictional Issues' *Review of European, Comparative and International Environmental Law*, 23/3 (2014): 302, 304.

[63] Carmen Gonzalez, 'Beyond Eco-Imperialism: An Environmental Justice Critique of Free Trade' *Denver University Law Review*, 78/4 (2001): 979.

[64] See Natalie Dobson, 'The EU's Conditioning of the 'Extraterritorial' Carbon Footprint: A Call for an Integrated Approach in Trade Law Discourse' *Review of European, Comparative and International Environmental Law*, 27/1 (2018): 75, 78–79.

[65] Joanne Scott, 'Extraterritoriality and Territorial Extension in EU Law' *American Journal of Comparative Law*, 62/1 (2014): 87, 90.

[66] *European Communities—Measures Prohibiting the Importation and Marketing of Seal Products* (Appellate Body Report) [22 May 2014] WTO Docs WT/DS400/AB/R, WT/DS401/AB/R (Seal Products case).

[67] Shrimp/Turtle case (n 58) [133].

[68] Seal Products case (n 66) [5.173].

[69] Steve Charnovitz, 'The Moral Exception in Trade Policy' *Virginia Journal of International Law*, 38/4 (1998): 689.

[70] Barbara Cooreman, *Global Environmental Protection through Trade: A Systematic Approach to Extraterritoriality* (Edward Elgar 2017) 131ff.

asbestos). Outward-looking measures target environmental harm caused elsewhere, for instance, by restricting imports of products made from species threatened with extinction that can solely be found in another country. In between are environmental concerns that are by their very nature transboundary, including the conservation of migratory animals and global commons problems such as climate change and ozone depletion. While inward-looking measures generally can be justified under GATT Article XX, this is more challenging for outward-looking concerns, unless a country can demonstrate that its concerns are based on the public morals exception of the GATT.[71] However, in addition to the location of the environmental problem, the nature of the concern may justify a measure with extraterritorial effect. For example, a measure can be justified more easily if it relates to a treaty that parties to a dispute have adopted than a measure without support in international law. This once again underlines the importance of pursuing multilateral environmental cooperation even if a country adopts a unilateral trade measure.

B. Processes and Production Methods

Some of the major disputes on trade and the environment, including *Tuna-Dolphin* and *Shrimp-Turtle*, have revolved around the question of whether products made using different processes and production methods are 'like' under the GATT's national treatment provision.[72] Regulation may target PPMs to address the environmental impacts of how a product has been made. A common distinction in this regard is between product-related PPMs that are physically traceable in the final product (eg the use of pesticides in fruit farming), and non-product-related PPMs that do not leave a discernible trace (eg the use of renewable energy in aluminium production).[73]

Whereas measures discriminating against products based on product-related PPMs are generally uncontroversial,[74] the status of non-product-related PPMs is less settled. The *Tuna-Dolphin* rulings led to an academic debate in which some argued that measures targeting non-product-related PPMs are not allowed.[75] To others, however, the product/process distinction was an 'illusory' one,[76] based on the false 'assumption

71 Which is what the EU sought to do in Seal Products case (n 66).

72 See Christiane Conrad, *Processes and Production Methods (PPMs) in WTO Law: Interfacing Trade and Social Goals* (CUP 2011) 13–20.

73 OECD, *Processes and Production Methods (PPMs): Conceptual Framework and Considerations on Use of PPM-Based Trade Measures* (OECD 1997) 10–11.

74 See eg Cooreman (n 70) 25.

75 See eg Thomas Schoenbaum, 'Free International Trade and the Environment: Irreconcilable Conflict?' *American Journal of International Law*, 86/4 (1992): 700, 722.

76 Robert Howse and Donald Regan, 'The Product/Process Distinction: An Illusory Basis for Disciplining 'Unilateralism' in Trade Policy' *European Journal of International Law*, 11/2 (2000): 249.

that consumer preferences can be neatly divided between the physical characteristics of the product and a bundle of other ecological or moral concerns'.[77]

Notwithstanding this scholarly disagreement, WTO jurisprudence has moved away from the strict distinction applied in *Tuna-Dolphin*. To determine 'likeness', dispute settlement bodies carry out an economic assessment of the competitive relationship between two products, focusing on: (1) the properties, nature, and quality of the products, (2) their end-uses, (3) consumers' tastes and habits, and (4) the products' tariff classification.[78] As the Appellate Body pointed out in the *Asbestos* case, the health risks of a product (ie risks associated with asbestos fibres) should be assessed under the first criterion.[79] For other products, the determination of likeness depends primarily on how consumers' tastes and habits are constructed.[80] However, even if measures targeted at non-product-related PPMs are found to violate the non-discrimination rules of the WTO, they may be saved by recourse to the GATT's environmental exceptions.

C. Environmental Exceptions

The environmental exceptions of GATT Article XX have played a central role in WTO jurisprudence on trade and the environment. These exceptions can uphold measures deemed to violate the GATT's core disciplines but taken for legitimate public policy reasons.

The GATT offers exceptions for measures that are 'necessary to protect human, animal or plant life or health',[81] or 'relating to the conservation of exhaustible natural resources'.[82] Although environmental protection is not explicitly mentioned, the exceptions have been interpreted broadly to encompass environmental concerns. The Appellate Body in *Shrimp-Turtle* interpreted the term 'natural resources' to include 'living resources',[83] and in *Reformulated Gasoline*, the Panel considered clean air a resource that is both 'exhaustible' and 'natural' under Article XX(g).[84]

[77] Steve Charnovitz, 'The Law of Environmental PPMs in the WTO: Debunking the Myth of Illegality' *Yale Journal of International Law*, 27/1 (2002): 59, 66.

[78] See eg *European Communities—Measures Affecting Asbestos and Products Containing Asbestos* (Appellate Body Report) [12 March 2001] WTO Doc WT/DS135/AB/R [101].

[79] Ibid [116].

[80] Emily Lydgate, 'Consumer Preferences and the National Treatment Principle: Emerging Environmental Regulations Prompt a New Look at an Old Problem' *World Trade Review*, 10/2 (2011): 165.

[81] GATT 1994, art XX(b).

[82] Ibid, art XX(g).

[83] Shrimp/Turtle case (n 58) [131].

[84] *United States—Standards for Reformulated and Conventional Gasoline* (Panel Report) [29 April 1996] WTO Doc WT/DS2/R [6.37]. Linking the impacts of climate change to human health, another Panel found that reducing carbon dioxide emissions would be covered by Article XX(b); see *Brazil—Certain Measures Concerning Taxation and Charges* (Panel Report) [30 August 2017] WTO Docs WT/DS472/R, WT/DS497/R [7.880].

The more difficult question under these sub-paragraphs concerns the link between a trade measure and its environmental goal. Under Article XX(b), the necessity test requires 'weighing and balancing'[85] a series of factors, including whether there is a 'a genuine relationship of ends and means',[86] the proportionality of a measure related to the interests at stake, and the availability of less trade-restrictive alternatives.[87] In comparison, the 'relating to' test under Article XX(g) has been easier to meet.[88]

Measures that are provisionally justified through these exceptions must also satisfy the requirements of the *chapeau* of Article XX, which specifies that a measure may not be applied in a manner that would constitute: (1) arbitrary discrimination between countries where the same conditions prevail, (2) unjustifiable discrimination between countries where the same conditions prevail, or (3) a disguised restriction on international trade. In its jurisprudence on the *chapeau*, the Appellate Body has emphasized the importance of 'basic fairness and due process' in applying environmental measures.[89] 'Serious, across-the-board negotiations' with a view to concluding environmental agreements are another important precondition.[90] Likewise, flexibility in the regulation is important: the country imposing a measure cannot require other countries to essentially adopt the same regulation, though it is possible to demand that such regulation is 'comparable in effectiveness'.[91]

Through Article XX, the WTO dispute settlement bodies have been able to accommodate some environmental concerns over time. However, the fact that most of the relevant jurisprudence revolves around *exceptions* shows that environmental considerations are not on equal footing with the WTO's core goals of trade liberalization.

VI. EMERGING ISSUES IN THE TRADE AND ENVIRONMENT DEBATE

Whereas the relationship between trade and the environment has largely been shaped by the disputes and questions surveyed so far, two trends are changing the dynamics of trade-environment interactions. First, regional trade agreements are assuming greater importance in advancing environmental goals. Second, responses to climate change are

85 *Brazil—Measures Affecting Imports of Retreaded Tyres* (Appellate Body Report) [3 December 2007] WTO Doc WT/DS332/AB/R [182].

86 Ibid [145], [210].

87 Ibid [156].

88 See eg Shrimp/Turtle case (n 58) [141].

89 Ibid [180]–[181].

90 Ibid [166].

91 *United States—Import Prohibition of Certain Shrimp and Shrimp Products (Recourse to Article 21.5 by Malaysia)* (Appellate Body Report) [22 October 2001] WTO Doc WT/DS58/AB/RW [144].

testing the fragile relationship between the multilateral trading system and environmental protection.

A. The Rise of Regionalism

The growing importance of regional trade agreements should be seen against the backdrop of a stalemate in multilateral negotiations, with WTO members agreeing to disagree on the way forward.[92] The formation of trade blocs in the Americas and Europe in the late 1980s and early 1990s meant that countries were induced to join or craft trade agreements.[93] The number of regional trade agreements has increased dramatically since, and by 2021, 342 regional agreements were in force.[94] This increase has been accompanied by a growing use of environmental provisions. While some of these provisions reflect WTO rules (eg environmental exceptions), others comprise legal innovations,[95] such as the inclusion of a reference to precaution,[96] the creation of institutional arrangements for environmental cooperation,[97] or requiring compliance with MEA obligations.[98]

A more recent trend is the conclusion of 'mega-regional' trade agreements involving nations responsible for a substantial share of world trade. These agreements have also introduced novel environmental provisions. For example, the 2018 Comprehensive and Progressive Agreement for Trans-Pacific Partnership, a trade agreement between eleven Pacific nations (excluding the United States), contains detailed provisions on fisheries subsidies.[99]

In addition, limited sets of WTO Members have negotiated new 'plurilateral' agreements, including on services and information technology. Following the adoption of an agreement by the Asia-Pacific Economic Cooperation group on environmental goods, several major trading powers (including China, the EU, and the United States)

[92] WTO, 'Nairobi Ministerial Declaration' (21 December 2015) WT/MIN(15)/DEC, para 30.

[93] Richard Baldwin, 'The Causes of Regionalism' *The World Economy*, 20/7 (1997): 865.

[94] WTO, 'Regional Trade Agreements Database' <https://rtais.wto.org/UI/PublicMaintainRTAHome.aspx> accessed 30 July 2019.

[95] Jean-Frédéric Morin *et al*, 'The Trade Regime as a Complex Adaptive System: Exploration and Exploitation of Environmental Norms in Trade Agreements' *Journal of International Economic Law*, 20/2 (2017): 365.

[96] See eg Trade Agreement between the European Union and its member states, of the one part, and Colombia and Peru, of the other part [2012] OJ L354/3, art 278.

[97] For example the EU provides for a 'Committee on Trade and Sustainable Development' in several of its trade agreements.

[98] See eg 2006 US-Peru Trade Promotion Agreement, art 18.2, annex 18.2 <https://ustr.gov/trade-agreements/free-trade-agreements/peru-tpa/final-text> accessed 30 July 2019; see Sikina Jinnah and Elisa Morgera, 'Environmental Provisions in American and EU Free Trade Agreements: A Preliminary Comparison and Research Agenda' *Review of European Community and International Environmental Law*, 22/3 (2013): 324.

[99] art 20.16.

have similarly launched negotiations on an Environmental Goods Agreement in 2014, aiming to liberalize trade in environmental goods such as solar panels or recycling equipment.[100] However, the talks have stalled over disagreement on the definition of 'environmental goods'.[101] Nonetheless, these negotiations underscore the potential of a mutually supportive approach to trade and the environment.

B. Climate Change and Trade

The gradual ramping up of climate action has uncovered a new frontier in the trade and environment relationship. Although an outright clash between trade law and multilateral climate treaties has yet to materialize, a new generation of trade disputes has emerged, centred around governmental efforts to boost low-carbon industries.[102]

In a first dispute, the Appellate Body found that renewable energy support measures by the government of the Canadian province Ontario contravened multilateral trade rules.[103] A subsequent complaint by the United States concerning India's National Solar Mission also led to a ruling striking down a renewable energy support measure.[104] Although neither measure was deemed a 'subsidy' under the Agreement on Subsidies and Countervailing Measures, the dispute settlement bodies found the use of discriminatory local content requirements unlawful. Such requirements may help garner domestic support for building a green economy, but their effectiveness remains in question.[105]

Are these disputes just the tip of the iceberg?[106] The discretion granted to countries under the bottom-up architecture of the Paris Agreement[107] seemingly reduces the chances of a direct clash with multilateral trade rules. Yet countries' varying levels of ambition may lead to calls for trade measures to prevent carbon leakage or level the

[100] WTO, 'Environmental Goods Agreement' <https://www.wto.org/english/tratop_e/envir_e/ega_e.htm> accessed 30 July 2019.

[101] Mark Wu, 'Why Developing Countries Won't Negotiate: The Case of the WTO Environmental Goods Agreement' *Trade Law and Development*, 6/1 (2014): 93, 102–103.

[102] Mark Wu and James Salzman, 'The Next Generation of Trade and Environment Conflicts: The Rise of Green Industrial Policy' *Northwestern University Law Review*, 108/2 (2014): 401.

[103] *Canada—Certain Measures Affecting the Renewable Energy Generation Sector* and *Canada—Measures Relating to the Feed-In Tariff Program* (Appellate Body Report) [6 May 2013] WTO Docs WT/DS412/AB/R and WT/DS426/AB/R.

[104] *India—Certain Measures Relating to Solar Cells and Solar Modules* (Appellate Body Report) [16 September 2016] WTO Doc WT/DS456/AB/R. India later successfully challenged support measures by US states. *United States—Certain Measures Relating to the Renewable Energy Sector* (Panel Report) [27 June 2019] WTO Doc WT/DS510/R.

[105] Jan-Christoph Kuntze and Tom Moerenhout, 'Local Content Requirements and the Renewable Energy Industry—A Good Match?' *International Centre for Trade and Sustainable Development* (2013).

[106] Other climate-related cases deal with anti-dumping measures on imports of biodiesel; see eg *European Union—Anti-Dumping Measures on Biodiesel from Argentina* (Appellate Body Report) [6 October 2016] WTO Doc WT/DS473/AB/R.

[107] See Chapter 29, 'Climate Change', in this volume.

competitive playing field in countries that take more progressive climate action. The WTO compatibility of any such measure, should they be adopted, remains uncertain.[108] Furthermore, the widespread use of market-based mechanisms in climate change law, such as greenhouse gas emissions trading and carbon taxes,[109] raises new questions concerning the relationship with trade law.[110]

Notwithstanding these rising tensions, trade agreements can also support climate action.[111] An Environmental Goods Agreement could help facilitate the worldwide deployment of low-carbon technologies. Moreover, while most attention thus far has focused on how WTO rules constrain renewable energy support, trade rules can potentially also be used to discipline fossil-fuel subsidies.[112]

VII. CONCLUSION

The balancing of values and objectives embedded in trade and environmental policy remains a vexed issue. Thus far, this balance has been struck largely based on trade rules, and specifically their application and interpretation by the WTO's dispute settlement bodies. The environmental exceptions in GATT Article XX play a central role in this balancing exercise. As *Shrimp-Turtle* underscored, WTO jurisprudence has become more amenable to integrating environmental concerns over time. However, this accommodation has its limits, as the *Biotech* dispute underscores. Given the strength of the WTO dispute settlement mechanism compared to dispute resolution and compliance mechanisms in MEAs, the result is 'a particular *kind* of balance—which inevitably favours some interests and values over others'.[113]

This poses challenges not just for countries wishing to adopt trade-related environmental measures, but also for the legitimacy of the multilateral trading system and its dispute settlement bodies.[114] These concerns would be even greater if a measure taken pursuant to an MEA would be challenged in a dispute.

[108] Michael Mehling *et al*, 'Designing Border Carbon Adjustments for Enhanced Climate Action' *American Journal of International Law*, 113/3 (2019): 433.

[109] See Chapter 53, 'Market Mechanisms', in this volume.

[110] Jacob Werksman, 'Greenhouse Gas Emissions Trading and the WTO' *Review of European Community and International Environmental Law*, 8/3 (1999): 251.

[111] Kasturi Das *et al*, 'Making the International Trading System Work for Climate Change: Assessing the Options' *Environmental Law Reporter*, 49/6 (2019): 10553.

[112] Cleo Verkuijl *et al*, 'Tackling Fossil Fuel Subsidies through International Trade Agreements: Taking Stock, Looking Forward' *Virginia Journal of International Law*, 58/2 (2019): 309.

[113] Andrew Lang, 'Legal Regimes and Professional Knowledges: The Internal Politics of Regime Definition' in Margaret Young (ed), *Regime Interaction in International Law: Facing Fragmentation* (CUP 2012) 113.

[114] Kati Kulovesi, *The WTO Dispute Settlement System: Challenges of the Environment, Legitimacy and Fragmentation* (Kluwer Law International 2011).

So how might the principle of 'mutual supportiveness' be implemented in the trade and environment context?[115] The 2030 Agenda for Sustainable Development and its Sustainable Development Goals reiterate that trade should be a driver for sustainable development,[116] but this requires trade agreements fit for the twenty-first century. Within the WTO, reform efforts have been constrained by diverging positions on the trade-environment relationship and the broader political stalemate plaguing the Doha Round. Multilateral, negotiated solutions (eg amending the WTO Agreements) thus remain a distant prospect, notwithstanding a wealth of proposals. In the interim, it may be possible to pursue mutually supportive approaches in smaller settings, such as regional and plurilateral trade agreements. Moreover, procedural changes, such as granting observer status to MEA secretariats in WTO bodies, improved transparency of trade-related environmental measures, and strengthening the environmental expertise of the WTO dispute settlement bodies, though by no means a panacea for resolving normative conflicts, may offer a way forward.

BIBLIOGRAPHY

Barbara Cooreman, *Global Environmental Protection through Trade: A Systematic Approach to Extraterritoriality* (Edward Elgar 2017)

International Institute for Sustainable Development (IISD) and United Nations Environment Programme, *Trade and Green Economy: A Handbook* (2014)

Richard Steinberg, 'Trade-Environment Negotiations in the EU, NAFTA, and WTO: Regional Trajectories of Rule Development' *American Journal of International Law*, 91/2 (1997): 231

Mark Wu and James Salzman, 'The Next Generation of Trade and Environment Conflicts: The Rise of Green Industrial Policy' *Northwestern University Law Review*, 108/2 (2014): 401

115 Riccardo Pavoni, 'Mutual Supportiveness as a Principle of Interpretation and Law-Making: A Watershed for the 'WTO-and-Competing-Regimes' Debate?' *European Journal of International Law*, 21/3 (2010): 649.

116 UNGA Res 70/1, 'Transforming our World: The 2030 Agenda for Sustainable Development' (21 October 2015) UN Doc A/RES/70/1, para 68 and SDGs 17.10–17.12.

CHAPTER 44

INVESTMENT

KATE MILES

I. INTRODUCTION

THE relationship between foreign investment and the environment is multilayered and, at times, contradictory, involving the interaction, integration, impact, alignment of interests, mutual support, conflict, and the prioritizing of one field over the other. Essentially, there are both positive and negative aspects to the relationship. The 'environmental' component of this nexus encompasses environmental protection objectives, domestic environmental protection policies and regulation, international environmental law, and global environmental impacts. A consideration of 'foreign investment' includes the activities of multinational corporations, the drafting of international investment agreements, investor-state arbitration, institutional investment, and domestic programmes for development and economic growth. Complex areas in themselves, they are even more so when their paths cross—there is, in fact, a myriad of ways in which these two fields interact.

Each of those modes of interaction has, in their own way, become a high-profile international issue. Annual global foreign direct investment flows are in the realm of USD 1.5 trillion.[1] This level of global economic activity has been linked to increasing global rates of environmental degradation and depletion of resources,[2] as well as contributing

[1] United Nations Conference on Trade and Development (UNCTAD), *World Investment Report 2018: Investment and New Industrial Policies*, 14.

[2] See eg Nick Mabey and Richard McNally, 'Foreign Direct Investment and the Environment: From Pollution Havens to Sustainable Development' *WWF* (August 1999) 3, 13–17; Elisa Morgera, 'The UN and Corporate Environmental Responsibility: Between International Regulation and Partnerships' *Review of European Community and International Environmental Law*, 15/1 (2006): 93; Åsa Romson, *Environmental Policy Space and International Investment Law* (Acta Universitatis Stockholmiensis 2012) 22–26; K V Bhanu Murthy and Sakshi Gambhir, 'International Trade and Foreign Direct Investment: Empirical Testing of the Trade–Environment Triangle' *Transnational Corporations Review*, 9/2 (2017): 122.

to complex international environmental problems such as climate change, deforestation, desertification, and biodiversity loss.[3] The problematic side of foreign investment has also been illustrated in a series of individual catastrophic events resulting from the activities of multinational corporations—for example, the Union Carbide disaster in Bhopal, India,[4] the 'die-back' experienced downstream from the Broken Hill Proprietary Co (BHP) copper and gold mine at Ok Tedi, Papua New Guinea,[5] the conflict involving the Shell Oil Company in Nigeria,[6] and the leaching of crude oil into the Amazonian ecosystem by Chevron/Texaco.[7]

Another prominent manifestation of the environment/investment nexus is in the context of investor-state arbitration. In the late 1990s, investment disputes that implicated domestic environmental regulation and decision-making and measures taken by states to comply with international environmental agreements began to be filed with international tribunals.[8] These complaints were brought by foreign investors against the host states in which they operated and they sought compensation for state action implementing environmental policies that impacted on the value of their investments. Concerns were expressed that such claims interfered with a state's right to regulate in the public interest, that they conflicted with states' international obligations under environmental treaties, and that the spectre of large compensation awards would influence state decision-making and have a 'chilling' effect on the raising of environmental standards.[9]

At the same time, however, foreign investment has also been identified as a significant contributor to economic growth and as a particularly important factor in

[3] Mabey and McNally (n 2) 3.

[4] See the discussion in Simon Chesterman, 'Oil and Water: Regulating the Behaviour of Multinational Corporations Through Law' *New York University Journal of International Law and Politics*, 36 (2004): 307; Sukanya Pillay, 'Absence of Justice: Lessons from the Bhopal Union Carbide Disaster for Latin America' *Michigan State Journal of International Law*, 14 (2006): 479; see also NGO commentary of Bhopal.net: International Campaign for Justice in Bhopal <https://www.bhopal.net/> accessed 1 December 2018).

[5] Chesterman (n 4); see also NGO commentary on the environmental degradation from the mine tailings at Polly Ghazi, 'Ok Tedi Mine: Unearthing Controversy' *World Resources Institute* (July 2003) 188 <https://pdf.wri.org/wr2002_fullreport.pdf> accessed 27 January 2020.

[6] See eg the discussion in Edna Eguh Udobong, 'Multinational Corporations Facing the Long Arm of American Jurisdiction for Human Rights and Environmental Abuses: The Case of *Wiwa* v. *Royal Dutch Petroleum, Co.*' *Southeastern Environmental Law Journal*, 14 (2005): 89.

[7] See eg the discussion in Chesterman (n 4); see also NGO commentary of Amazon Defense Coalition, 'ChevronToxico: The Campaign for Justice in Ecuador' <https://chevrontoxico.com/> accessed 27 January 2020.

[8] See eg *Ethyl Corporation v Canada* (Jurisdiction Phase) 38 ILM 708 (1999); *S.D. Myers Inc. v Canada* (Partial Award) NAFTA Arbitration (UNCITRAL Rules) (13 November 2000) (Myers case); *Metalclad Corporation v The United Mexican States*, International Centre for Settlement of Investment Disputes Case No ARB(AF)/97/1 (Award of 25 August 2000) (2001) 40 ILM 36 (Metalclad case); *Compania del Desarrollo de Santa Elena S.A. v The Republic of Costa Rica* (2000) 39 ILM 1317 (Santa Elena case).

[9] See eg Kyla Tienhaara, *The Expropriation of Environmental Governance: Protecting Foreign Investors at the Expense of Public Policy* (CUP 2009).

supporting sustainable development programmes in developing states.[10] Research has explored the potential modalities in which foreign investment can be used to promote environmental protection and sustainability initiatives.[11] There have been important cultural shifts in the environment/investment relationship that have led to the development of voluntary codes of corporate conduct, the adoption of corporate social responsibility expectations, and the emergence of socially and environmentally responsible investment.[12] It is also now increasingly accepted that the early model bilateral investment treaties (BITs) signed from 1959 to the early 2000s,[13] which gave rise to the initial rounds of claims involving environmental measures, have the potential to constrain the policies and regulatory frameworks of host states.[14] Appreciation of this potential has seen a more nuanced mode of treaty-drafting introduced in the so-called 'New Generation' BITs and free trade agreements (FTAs) with investment provisions that include references to environmental protection and sustainable development.[15]

It will be clear from these introductory remarks that the environment/investment nexus is a complex relationship with various dimensions and a changing dynamic. This chapter gives a brief introduction to the international investment protection framework and its key instruments. It then focuses on one of the most contentious manifestations of the environment/investment relationship, being that of investor-state disputes, before examining recent trends that seek a more balanced approach to the environmental issues raised by investment disputes.

[10] UNCTAD, 'Making FDI Work for Sustainable Development' (2004) Doc No UNCTAD/DITC/TED/9.

[11] See eg Pierre-Marie Dupuy and Jorge Viñuales (eds), *Harnessing Foreign Investment to Promote Environmental Protection: Incentives and Safeguards* (CUP 2013).

[12] See the discussion in Benjamin Richardson, *Socially Responsible Investment Law: Regulating the Unseen Polluters* (OUP 2008); Doreen McBarnet, 'Corporate Social Responsibility Beyond Law, Through Law, For Law: The New Corporate Accountability' in Doreen McBarnet, Aurora Voiculescu, and Tom Campbell (eds), *The New Corporate Accountability: Corporate Social Responsibility and the Law* (CUP 2007) 9; Benjamin Richardson and Maziar Peihani, 'Universal Investors and Socially Responsible Finance: A Critique of a Premature Theory' *Banking and Finance Law Review*, 30 (2015): 405; see also Chapter 41, 'Business and Industry', in this volume.

[13] The first bilateral investment treaty was signed in 1959: Treaty Between the Federal Republic of Germany and Pakistan for the Promotion and Protection of Investments.

[14] See eg '"Improving ISDS to Prevent Abuse"—Statement by EU Trade Commissioner Karel De Gucht on the launch of a public consultation on investment protection in TTIP' (27 March 2014) <https://europa.eu/rapid/press-release_STATEMENT-14-85_en.htm> accessed 4 November 2018.

[15] See eg Agreement between Canada and the Federal Republic of Nigeria for the Promotion and Protection of Investments (signed 6 May 2014) <https://www.international.gc.ca/trade-commerce/trade-agreements-accords-commerciaux/agr-acc/nigeria/fipa-apie/index.aspx?lang=eng> accessed 27 January 2020; see eg Agreement Between Canada and the Czech Republic for the Promotion and Protection of Investments (adopted 6 May 2009, entered into force 22 January 2012) <https://www.treaty-accord.gc.ca/text-texte.aspx?id=105128&lang=eng> accessed 12 September 2018.

II. INTERNATIONAL INVESTMENT AGREEMENTS

Since 1959, states have signed a large number of international investment agreements containing what have now become standard protections for their investing nationals.[16] There are currently more than 3,000 BITs and FTAs with investment provisions,[17] including regional agreements such as the 1992 North American Free Trade Agreement (NAFTA), the 2009 Association of Southeast Asian Nations (ASEAN) Comprehensive Investment Agreement, the 2018 Comprehensive and Progressive Agreement for Trans-Pacific Partnership (CPTPP), and the 1994 Energy Charter Treaty. The terminology used to set out the investor protections varies from treaty to treaty, and to an even greater extent in the new generation BITs and FTAs, however, the core protections are essentially the same. They tend to consist of prohibitions on uncompensated expropriation and guarantees of fair and equitable treatment, national treatment, most-favoured-nation treatment, and full protection and security.[18]

A. Expropriation

Expropriation of foreign-owned property is permitted if it is carried out for a public purpose, is non-discriminatory and not arbitrary, and if compensation is paid.[19] Direct expropriation entails the seizure of physical assets;[20] indirect expropriation involves more subtle forms of taking that leave the ownership of the investment intact—such as changes to regulation or the cumulative effect of a series of actions—but result in a substantial or full deprivation in the value of the investment or of the use or enjoyment of the investment by the investor.[21]

B. National Treatment

Claims that national treatment guarantees have been breached centre on whether or not a foreign investor has been discriminated against, specifically, whether the foreign

[16] See n 13.

[17] UNCTAD, 'International Investment Agreements Navigator' <https://investmentpolicyhub.unctad.org/IIA> accessed 28 December 2018.

[18] Campbell McLachlan, Laurence Shore, and Matthew Weiniger, *International Investment Arbitration: Substantive Principles* (OUP 2007) 207.

[19] Peter Malanczuk (ed), *Akehurst's Modern International Law* (7th edn, Routledge 1997) 235–238.

[20] Muthucumaraswamy Sornarajah, *The International Law on Foreign Investment* (4th edn, CUP 2017) 430–445.

[21] Ibid; McLachlan, Shore, and Weiniger (n 18) 266–267.

investor has received less favourable treatment from the host state than it accorded its own domestic investors in 'like circumstances'.

C. Fair and Equitable Treatment

Arbitral tribunals have filled in the meaning of the fair and equitable treatment treaty standard so that it has been held to entail a requirement for a host state to act in accordance with the legitimate expectations of the investor, comply with due process obligations, and maintain a stable legal and business environment for investor operations.[22]

D. Most-Favoured-Nation Treatment

Most-favoured-nation clauses require states to accord investing nationals of a contracting party to a BIT treatment no less favourable than investing nationals of other states, again in 'like circumstances'.

E. Investor-State Dispute Settlement

Most international investment agreements contain recourse to a form of investor-state arbitration to resolve disputes that arise out of alleged breaches of their investor protection provisions. They tend to reference particular arbitral institutions or sets of procedural rules to govern the conduct of arbitrations such as the arbitral rules of the United Nations Commission on International Trade Law (UNCITRAL)[23] and the 1965 Convention on the Settlement of Investment Disputes between States and Nationals of other States (the ICSID Convention). Investor-state arbitrations can be conducted on an ad hoc basis or through one of several arbitral institutions, such as the International Centre for the Settlement of Investment Disputes (ICSID), the Permanent Court of Arbitration, or the Stockholm Centre for Arbitration. Procedural aspects of the investor-state dispute settlement system, known as ISDS, attracted criticism for its lack of transparency, restrictions on public participation, and absence of an appeals mechanism.[24] Reforms were introduced to both the ICSID and UNCITRAL investor-state rules of

[22] See eg *Tecnicas Medioambientales Tecmed, S.A. v United Mexican States* (2004) 43 ILM 133, 173 (Tecmed case).

[23] 'UNCITRAL Arbitration Rules' (as revised in 2010) <https://www.uncitral.org/pdf/english/texts/arbitration/arb-rules-revised/arb-rules-revised-2010-e.pdf> accessed 27 January 2020.

[24] Gus Van Harten, *Investment Treaty Arbitration and Public Law* (OUP 2007); International Institute for Sustainable Development (IISD), 'Revising the UNCITRAL Arbitration Rules to Address Investor-State Arbitrations' (2007).

procedure, improving the transparency of arbitral proceedings and opportunities for *amicus curiae* participation in investor-state disputes.[25]

III. ENVIRONMENTAL REGULATION AND DECISION-MAKING AS A TREATY VIOLATION

Since the late 1990s, there has been controversy surrounding the way in which the operation of international investment agreements can impact on environmental protection objectives. Environmental issues have been implicated in investment disputes in a wide range of contexts, including regulation and decision-making related to water resources, climate-related measures, nuclear energy phase-outs, pesticide prohibitions, and environmental impact assessments. This section examines several of those key disputes.

A. Early Cases: Investment and Environmental Protection as Competing Norms

Early investment cases in which environment-related matters arose were characterized by the pitching of investment protection and environmental protection as competing norms. The controversy generated by the approach embodied in these cases was grounded in their not taking adequate account of environmental matters, the prioritizing of investment protection over environmental protection even where obligations under multilateral environmental agreements (MEAs) were invoked as a defence to allegations of a BIT violation, and at the encroachment of private commercial interests into a state's legitimate public welfare policy space. In essence, the concerns centred around the loss of state control over matters impacting domestic health and environmental law and policy.

Cases such as *Metalclad Corporation v The United States of Mexico*[26] and *Tecnicas Medioambientales Tecmed, SA v United Mexican States* (*Tecmed*)[27] established expansive interpretations of investor protections that encompassed government measures taken on grounds of health, environmental protection, or land use designations.

[25] ICSID, 'Rules of Procedure for Arbitration Proceedings' (2006); UNCITRAL, 'Rules on Transparency in Treaty-based Investor-State Arbitration' (adopted 16 December 2013, entered into force 1 April 2014) <https://www.uncitral.org/pdf/english/texts/arbitration/rules-on-transparency/Rules-on-Transparency-E.pdf> accessed 8 December 2018; 2014 United Nations Convention on Transparency in Treaty-based Investor-State Arbitration.

[26] Metalclad case (n 8).

[27] Tecmed case (n 22) 173.

Compañía del Desarrollo de Santa Elena, S.A. v Costa Rica[28] and *S.D. Myers v Government of Canada*[29] were cases in which the requirements under MEAs such as the 1992 Convention on Biological Diversity (CBD) and the 1989 Convention on the Control of Transboundary Movement of Hazardous Wastes and their Disposal (Basel Convention) were effectively pitted against requirements to protect foreign investment. The international environmental obligations of states were viewed through a lens of international trade and investment protection rather than in their own right.

Even an award in which the state's right to regulate was upheld was one in which environmental and investment rules were framed as being in direct competition with each other.[30]

B. Recent Cases: More Balanced Approaches to Environmental Considerations

There has been a discernible shift in the way in which tribunals in investor-state arbitration discuss international environmental obligations and domestic environmental law and policy.[31] And in a series of significant cases that adopted more innovative lines of reasoning, this has resulted in outcomes that take better account of non-investment issues than the first wave of investor-state disputes mentioned above.

One approach has been to introduce alternative interpretations of investment protections, such as in *Glamis Gold Ltd v United States of America*,[32] which involved mining on lands of Indigenous cultural significance. The tribunal examined the requirements of the fair and equitable treatment standard in the context of the customary international law minimum standard, altering the threshold to be met before a treaty violation could be said to have occurred. In considering the criteria for 'like circumstances' in a claim based on an alleged breach of the national treatment standard, the tribunal in *Parkerings-Compagniet AS v Republic of Lithuania* considered the cultural heritage and environmental impacts of the two projects under consideration as a key component in determining whether or not the claimant and the competitor investor were in 'like circumstances', meaning that the environmental positives of one project could be a legitimate factor in treating the projects differently.[33]

In a turnaround for the accommodation of host state policy space and attitudes towards international environmental obligations, the tribunal in *Chemtura v Canada*[34]

[28] Santa Elena case (n 8).

[29] Myers case (n 8).

[30] *Methanex Corporation v United States of America* (2005) 44 ILM 1345.

[31] See the discussion in Jorge Viñuales, 'Foreign Investment and the Environment in International Law: Current Trends' in Kate Miles (ed), *Research Handbook on Environment and Investment* (Edward Elgar 2019) 12.

[32] *Glamis Gold Ltd v United States of America* (Award) NAFTA Arbitration (UNCITRAL Rules) (8 June 2009).

[33] *Parkerings-Compagniet AS v Republic of Lithuania* (Award) ICSID Case No ARB/05/8 (2007) [375], [392].

[34] *Chemtura Corporation v Government of Canada* (Award) NAFTA Arbitration (UNCITRAL Rules) (2 August 2010).

took account of widespread international practice on the prohibiting of a particular pesticide, lindane, and the state's obligations under MEAs to which it was a party.

A further angle to the investment/environment relationship has recently been added in the form of what can only be described as the active use of investor-state arbitration as an environmental protection mechanism. These examples include the filing of environmental counterclaims seen in *Perenco v Ecuador*[35] and *Burlington Resources v Ecuador*,[36] the filing of a claim based on non-enforcement of domestic environmental regulations in *Allard v Barbados*,[37] and the filing of claims based on the roll-back of environmentally motivated regulation such as the solar energy disputes against Spain and the Czech Republic.[38]

The case of *Allard v Barbados* was unusual for the way in which the claimant used investor-state arbitration. A key critique of the first-generation investor-state arbitral awards had been focused on the negative impact that international investment law could potentially have on the host state's environmental regulation and decision-making. However, in *Allard v Barbados*, the claimant was seeking to compel the state to implement its existing environmental standards. Allard alleged that Barbados had breached the Canada–Barbados BIT by allowing run-off from a sewerage treatment plant to pollute his eco-tourist site, failing to enforce its own environmental laws, and failing to abide by its international obligations under the CBD and the 1971 Ramsar Convention on Wetlands. The claim failed on the facts. However, the use of investor-state arbitration to seek to bring about improved environmental practices is itself an interesting development.

The linked cases of *Perenco*[39] and *Burlington Resources*[40] are significant for their innovative procedural approach. In addition to mounting a defence in each case, Ecuador also made an environmental counterclaim, alleging that the claimants had caused substantial environmental damage to the areas in which they operated.

The *Perenco* tribunal issued a ruling that it was likely that the claimant would be held liable for breaches of Ecuadorian environmental law in a future final decision. Given the way in which environmental matters had been treated in the first wave of investor-state arbitration, it is the tone of the tribunal's discussion that is particularly noteworthy. This included acknowledgements of the need for 'proper environmental stewardship' and the 'fundamental imperatives of the protection of the environment'.[41]

[35] *Perenco Ecuador Ltd. v The Republic of Ecuador and Empresa Estatal Petróleos del Ecuador* (Interim Decision on the Environmental Counterclaim) ICSID Case No ARB/08/6 (2015) (Perenco case).

[36] *Burlington Resources Inc. v Republic of Ecuador* (Decision on Counterclaims) ICSID Case No ARB/08/5 (2017) (Burlington case).

[37] *Peter A. Allard (Canada) v The Government of Barbados* (Final award of 27 June 2016) PCA Case no 2012-06.

[38] See eg *Charanne B.V. and Construction Investments S.A.R.L v The Kingdom of Spain* (Final award of 21 January 2016) SCC Case no 062/2012.

[39] Perenco case (n 35).

[40] Burlington case (n 36).

[41] Perenco case (n 35) [34]–[35].

Mechanisms such as an environmental counterclaim have potential to act as a restraint on investor conduct, but what is also of particular significance is the pitch of the language used in these awards. It is very different from the approach seen in the early environment/investment cases.[42] It not only indicates a more visible acknowledgement that the domestic environmental law of the host state is part of the law governing the relationship between the host state and the investor, but also that investment is not being viewed in isolation from other legitimate matters with which states necessarily have to concern themselves. This would suggest that a normalizing process is underway for the embedded consideration of social and environmental matters within investment disputes.

However, it cannot yet be said that environmental matters are consistently given a sophisticated treatment in recent investor-state awards. In particular, there are legitimate questions around the lack of specialist understanding of environmental law on arbitral panels in investment disputes, which can lead to decisions that still do not take adequate account of environmental concerns and that interpret administrative decision-making based on environmental norms as arbitrary. A case in point is that of *Clayton & Bilcon v Canada*.[43] This dispute arose out of a planned quarry and marine terminal in an ecologically sensitive area of Nova Scotia. Bilcon submitted an Environmental Impact Statement addressing the physical, biological, and social impacts of the project.[44] The Joint Review Panel found that Bilcon's Environmental Impact Statement was inadequate and recommended that the project be rejected. The Panel adopted an approach familiar to those working within environmental legal fields, including the wide-ranging scope generally given to such concepts as 'sustainable development' and 'environmental effects', and the expansive view of what is to be encompassed within environmental impact assessments.[45] Bilcon argued that the Panel's use of the term 'community core values' was a fundamentally novel term unknown to environmental assessment and that Bilcon had not been made aware that its proposal would be assessed against this criteria. The majority of the tribunal accepted Bilcon's arguments, deciding that the Panel had violated NAFTA in its use of the term 'community core values'.

Several scholars consider the award to be remarkable in its appreciative tone when discussing the environmental issues.[46] However, the majority decision reflects a misunderstanding of international environmental law, the relevant domestic environmental law and policy, and sustainability norms. The dissenting arbitrator, McRae, is a world-leading expert in environmental law and provided the tribunal with an invaluable

[42] Viñuales (n 31).

[43] *In the Matter of an Arbitration under Chapter Eleven of the North American Free Trade Agreement and the UNCITRAL Rules of 1976 between William Ralph Clayton et al v Government of Canada* (Award) (10 March 2015).

[44] Ibid [18].

[45] Ibid (Dissenting Opinion of Professor Donald McRae); David VanderZwaag and Jason May, 'Quarrels over a Proposed Quarry in Nova Scotia: Successful Application of Sustainability Principles in Environmental Impact Assessment but not a Perfect Ending' in Klaus Bosselmann *et al* (eds), 'Governance for Sustainability: Issues, Challenges, Successes' *IUCN Environmental Policy and Law Paper* 70 (2008): 111.

[46] See eg Viñuales (n 31).

perspective in analyzing such issues. It is, perhaps, surprising then that the majority did not take up the views of such an expert on the key environmental matters in dispute. It is, perhaps, also indicative of the need for greater appreciation within investment law circles that the perspective from which one comes to the investment/environment nexus is significant for the way in which these complex issues are understood. Experts from the different sides of that relationship may categorize state action quite differently, as legitimate environmental processes and decision-making on the one hand, and as arbitrary action violating international investment protections on the other.

In essence, it is a form of arguing at cross purposes in which the concerns raised, such as those by McRae in *Bilcon*, are answered by a re-framing of the issues, rather than addressing their substance. Without greater engagement and appreciation of the substantive content of the non-investment fields with which international investment law inevitably intersects, it can be expected that this type of misdirected *Bilcon* approach to domestic regulation and administrative decision-making in non-investment fields will continue to occur. On this front, although there is most certainly a cultural shift underway in navigating the environment/investment relationship, there are also still problematic aspects to the way in which that relationship manifests.

IV. NEW TRENDS IN TREATY-DRAFTING

The awards that were generated by the first wave of investor-state arbitration illustrated the potential that existed for an inadequate consideration of domestic environmental law and policy and a contest between rules of international investment law and international environmental law. As a result, attention turned to the way in which the drafting of investment treaties could address those conflicts. New trends in drafting emerged in what have been termed the 'New Generation' BITs and FTAs. It proved to be a significant development that pointed to a shift in the environment/investment relationship.

A. Model BITs

Recent Model BITs have introduced measures designed to limit the impact of the expansive interpretations seen in the early environment-related investor-state arbitral awards. One of the earliest examples was that of the 2004 United States' Model BIT, revised in 2012.[47] Right at the outset of that 2004 Model BIT, the instrument indicated

[47] United States State Department, Treaty between the Government of the United States of America and the Government of [Country] Concerning the Encouragement and Reciprocal Protection of Investments (2004) <https://ustr.gov/sites/default/files/U.S.%20model%20BIT.pdf> accessed 27 January

contemporary concerns at the interaction between investor activities and host state policy space with its preamble, stating:

> Desiring to achieve these objectives in a manner consistent with the protection of health, safety, and the environment, and the promotion of internationally recognized labor rights.

It introduced a provision tightening the scope of protections regarding expropriation:[48]

> Except in rare circumstances, non-discriminatory regulatory actions by a Party that are designed and applied to protect legitimate public welfare objectives, such as public health, safety, and the environment, do not constitute indirect expropriation.

It also made explicit references to the need for environmental sensitivity:[49]

> Nothing in this Treaty shall be construed to prevent a Party from adopting, maintaining, or enforcing any measure otherwise consistent with this Treaty that it considers appropriate to ensure that investment activity in its territory is undertaken in a manner sensitive to environmental concerns.

These innovations in drafting were significant for the discontent they symbolized, but, other than expropriation, they did not so much alter the substance of the rules on investment protection as change the context in which those protections were to be considered. However, a more substantively far-reaching example of new generation Model BITs is that of India's 2016 Model BIT.[50]

The drafting approach in India's Model BIT creates an overall impression of an instrument in which the investor protections are to be interpreted within an embedded framework of social and environmental responsibility, not as treaty protections separate from their domestic public welfare context.[51] Its key environment-related sections include directions to investors to incorporate standards of corporate social responsibility

2020; United States State Department, Treaty between the Government of the United States of America and the Government of [Country] Concerning the Encouragement and Reciprocal Protection of Investments (2012) <https://ustr.gov/sites/default/files/BIT%20text%20for%20ACIEP%20Meeting.pdf> accessed 27 January 2020.

48 Ibid, annex B, art 4(b).

49 Ibid, art 12.

50 Model Text for the Indian Bilateral Investment Treaty, Bilateral Investment Treaty between the Government of the Republic of India and [----] (Final Draft released 28 December 2015, adopted 14 January 2016) <https://www.dea.gov.in/sites/default/files/ModelBIT_Annex_0.pdf> accessed 27 December 2018.

51 See arts 5.5, 12, 26.3, 32.1; see for a detailed consideration of India's 2016 Model BIT, Romesh Weeramantry and Montse Ferrer, 'Going Green? The Evolution of Environmental Provisions in India's Investment Treaties' in Miles (n 31) 313.

into their practices and an environmental counterclaim mechanism similar to that seen in *Perenco* and *Burlington Resources*. It also includes the type of carve-outs typically seen in trade agreements, but which have only recently become an expected component in new BITs and the investment sections of FTAs. In a radical departure from standard investment protections, the Indian Model BIT omitted the guarantee of fair and equitable treatment, the expansive interpretation of which by arbitral tribunals has been the cause of such controversy, replacing it at Article 3.1 with the more specific terminology of protection against a violation of customary international law through: (i) denial of justice in any judicial or administrative proceedings; or (ii) fundamental breach of due process; or (iii) targeted discrimination on manifestly unjustified grounds, such as gender, race, or religious belief; or (iv) manifestly abusive treatment, such as coercion, duress, and harassment. The Model BIT also left out a most-favoured-nation clause, precluding the incorporation of more investor-favourable provisions at the expense of the public welfare orientation of the instrument.

Taken as a whole, the environment-related provisions in the Indian Model BIT point to a shifting culture in the consideration of investment protections, one in which the nature of the environment/investment discourse has changed significantly. The implicit message in such instruments is that states have not been satisfied with the effect of the first-generation BITs and their manifest encroachment into host state policy space. It is clear that one form of state response has been this attempt to remodel that relationship through treaty-drafting. Once disputes begin to arise under the treaties that have been based on these revised model agreements, it will be interesting to see the way in which this new, carefully refashioned, emphasis is given effect by arbitrators in the application of the investment protection provisions.

B. Environmentally Significant Investment Agreements

In addition to the Model BITs produced by states, there are also several key environmentally significant trade and investment treaties that should be noted. The 2016 Canada–EU Comprehensive Economic and Trade Agreement (CETA) is one such agreement. It contains numerous references to environmental protection and the promotion of sustainable development, including an entire chapter dedicated to 'Trade and the Environment', which sets a more environmentally-aware tone for the consideration of environment, trade, and investment interaction throughout the entirety of the agreement.[52]

The investment chapter of CETA certainly maintains traditional investor protections, but it also contains express references to environmental matters. Of particular note are the provisions aimed at preserving host state regulatory space through a positive reaffirmation of that right to regulate.[53] In an attempt to curb the more expansive

[52] CETA, ch 24.
[53] Ibid, arts 8.9(1)–(2).

interpretations of the fair and equitable treatment standard, CETA sets out detailed categories in which the protection could be activated, moving away from the vague, general formulations of the first-generation BITs.[54] The Agreement also adopts the increasingly standard approach of new generation BITs and FTAs to guarantees against expropriation, limiting its application so as not to encompass legitimate environmental regulation.[55]

A multilateral FTA that included particularly progressive environmental protection measures was the Trans-Pacific Partnership, which, following the withdrawal of the United States, was renegotiated to form the 2018 Comprehensive and Progressive Agreement for Trans-Pacific Partnership (CPTPP). In a similar structure to CETA, the CPTPP also contains a full chapter on the environment, setting out a series of positive obligations that apply to the state parties, including commitments to continue to improve their levels of environmental protection, to enforce environmental laws, to adhere to a system of environmental monitoring amongst the parties, to reaffirm the commitments state parties have also made under multilateral environmental agreements, and including non-compliance mechanisms for failures to implement satisfactorily the obligations in Chapter 20 of the agreement. It was disappointing, however, that specific climate-targeted provisions were not included, which is a surprising omission and somewhat detracts from the agreement's claims to environmental progressiveness.

Core investment protections still remain firmly in place in the CPTPP, but modifications have been made. Within the investment chapter itself (Chapter 9), the inclusion of provisions promoting environmentally responsible conduct on the part of both states and investors suggests a desire to influence the culture that pervaded the interaction of the late 1990s and early 2000s between environmental issues, investment activity, and arbitral decision-making. For example, Article 9.16 contains an 'environmental sensitivity' provision similar to that discussed above regarding the US Model BIT and Article 9.17 is a 'Corporate Social Responsibility' provision. The incorporation of principles of corporate social responsibility by investing entities operating within the domestic jurisdiction of state parties to the agreement remains a voluntary exercise. However, culturally, provisions such as Article 9.17 shift the expectations of investor behaviour, as well as the nature of the agreement as a whole, which one would expect to then translate into a more environmentally respectful emphasis in any investor-state awards arising out of the CPTPP.

Much as with CETA, there is very clearly in the CPTPP an attempt to limit the scope and impact of the first-generation approach to the fair and equitable treatment standard through express clarification of its intended application and exclusion of specific circumstances that have regularly been held in arbitral awards to fall within

[54] Ibid, art 8.10.

[55] Ibid, annex-8A(3).

that particular investment protection. To this end, the article explicitly refers to inconsistencies with the expectations of investors and the failure to maintain or renew subsidies in setting out that such state action without more does not constitute a breach of the fair and equitable standard.[56]

Agreements such as CETA and CPTPP are illustrations of one form of response to the contentious nature of the environment/investment nexus embodied in several early investor-state arbitral awards. Whilst every problematic aspect of that relationship has not been addressed through treaty-drafting to date, it is also likely that the process of producing more environmentally responsive trade and investment agreements will continue to evolve for some time as new types of mechanisms are designed and new provisions are drawn up to take account of changing circumstances. It is also likely that the advances that have already been made in the drafting of investment agreements such as CETA and CPTPP with respect to preserving environmental protection measures will become normalized and, culturally, it will become very difficult to roll-back those developments.

V. SYNERGIES BETWEEN FOREIGN INVESTMENT AND ENVIRONMENTAL PROTECTION

Although the contentious mode of interaction between environmental protection objectives, international environmental law, and protections in investment treaties is a particularly important aspect of the environment/investment nexus, it is not its only manifestation. There is a form of the relationship that exhibits shared objectives and mutually supportive arrangements, one in which the synergies between foreign investment activities and environmentally sound practices are enhanced and the role of foreign capital in achieving levels of sustainable development is emphasized. In particular, this can be seen in approaches that seek to harness foreign investment to promote economic growth in an environmentally responsible manner and to support domestic sustainable development programmes.[57] Culturally, there have also been shifts in the standards of expected corporate/investor behaviour that have led to the development of voluntary codes of corporate conduct, the normalization of adherence to corporate

[56] CPTPP, art 9.6(2).

[57] UNCTAD, 'Making FDI Work' (n 10); United Nations Environment Programme (UNEP), 'Towards a Green Economy: Pathways to Sustainable Development and Poverty Eradication' (2011); see also <https://www.unep.org/greeneconomy> accessed 1 December 2018; UNGA Res 69/313, 'Addis Ababa Action Agenda of the Third International Conference on Financing for Development' (17 August 2015) UN Doc A/RES/69/313, annex.

social responsibility principles, and the growth in 'sustainable finance' in the form of socially and environmentally responsible institutional investment.[58]

The connection between the encouraging of foreign capital inflows and the achieving of sustainability goals has been recognized for some time. It was regarded as an important part in the United Nations Millennium Development Goals in 2000[59] and it is still envisaged that foreign investment will play a role in realizing the Sustainable Development Goals set out in the United Nations sustainable development blueprint, 'Transforming Our World: The 2030 Agenda for Sustainable Development'.[60]

Investment features explicitly in the 2030 Agenda at Goal 17.3 in which the need to encourage the mobilization of 'additional financial resources for developing countries from multiple sources' is emphasized. Again specifically at Goal 17.5 there is reference to the need to adopt and implement 'investment promotion regimes for least developed countries'. With respect to achieving particular substantive sustainability goals on food security, energy, and inequality, the role of investment inputs is expressly identified as a component in fulfilling those aims.[61]

The prevalence of voluntary codes of environmental corporate conduct across local, national, and international levels and corporate social responsibility initiatives have normalized expectations of a more environmentally responsible standard of behaviour from foreign investors. In addition to high-profile examples of voluntary regimes, such as the United Nations Global Compact,[62] several codes have been aimed directly at the financing and investment sector, including the Equator Principles[63] and the Principles for Responsible Investment,[64] which have contributed to the sense of shifting expectations in the environment/investment nexus.[65]

These developments in sustainable finance have also been complemented by a further layer taking the form of socially and environmentally responsible institutional investment. As an approach, it integrates a consideration of the social and environmental consequences of investment decisions into the portfolio management of pension funds, mutual funds, managed funds at financial institutions, and insurance company funds.[66] Essentially, it seeks to influence corporate practices, encouraging more socially and

[58] See the discussion in Richardson, *Socially Responsible Investment Law* (n 12); McBarnet (n 12) 9; OECD (n 12); Richardson and Peihani (n 12).

[59] United Nations, 'United Nations Millennium Development Goals' (2000) <https://www.un.org/millenniumgoals/> accessed 27 January 2020.

[60] UNGA Res 70/1, 'Transforming our World: The 2030 Agenda for Sustainable Development' (21 October 2015) UN Doc A/RES/70/1.

[61] Ibid, Goals 2.a, 7.a, 10.b.

[62] United Nations Global Compact <https://www.unglobalcompact.org/> accessed 15 September 2018.

[63] Equator Principles (initially launched 4 June 2003) <https://equator-principles.com/> accessed 24 September 2018.

[64] Principles for Responsible Investment (2006) <https://www.unpri.org/> accessed 24 September 2018.

[65] See also Chapter 41, 'Business and Industry', in this volume.

[66] Richardson, *Socially Responsible Investment Law* (n 12).

environmentally responsible policies and conduct so as to attract the capital investment of ethical institutional investors.[67]

VI. CONCLUSION

It is clear that there are a multitude of ways in which international environmental law, environmental protection objectives more generally, and investment, intersect. And it is likely that the relationship will continue to evolve, producing new manifestations in the years to come. Although this chapter has referred to several aspects of their interaction, the focus has been on one particularly contentious mode, that of the environment and international investment law. The contestation between the fields that emerged in the context of investor-state arbitration was blunt and initially resulted in the rules of international investment law being prioritized over the obligations of states under MEAs, domestic environmental protection policies and decision-making, and the host state's public welfare regulatory space. Responding to that contest, the new generation BITs and FTAs reflect the desire of states to work within a more balanced version of the environment/investment nexus. It is not yet, however, at a point where it can be said to be equally balanced in the engagement of international environmental law and international investment law, and there is evidently still room for significant improvements in the way in which environmental issues are understood and interpreted by arbitrators in investor-state disputes. But the culture and context in which the environment and investment are meeting is most definitely shifting and it is hoped that the trajectory continues still further in that direction.

BIBLIOGRAPHY

Pierre-Marie Dupuy and Jorge Viñuales (eds), *Harnessing Foreign Investment to Promote Environmental Protection: Incentives and Safeguards* (CUP 2013)

Kate Miles (ed), *Research Handbook on Environment and Investment* (Edward Elgar 2019)

Kyla Tienhaara, *The Expropriation of Environmental Governance: Protecting Foreign Investors at the Expense of Public Policy* (CUP 2009)

Jorge Viñuales, *Foreign Investment and the Environment in International Law* (CUP 2012)

67 Ibid, 8; Russell Sparkes and Christopher Cowton, 'The Maturing of Socially Responsible Investment: A Review of the Developing Link with Corporate Social Responsibility' *Journal of Business Ethics*, 52 (2004): 45.

CHAPTER 45

HUMAN RIGHTS

JOHN H KNOX

I. INTRODUCTION

LINKAGES between environmental protection and human rights depend on two premises: (a) the full enjoyment of many human rights, including the rights to life, health, and an adequate standard of living, depends on an environment that is healthy for human beings; and (b) the exercise of human rights, including the rights to information, participation in governance, and access to justice, helps to ensure that individuals and communities can advocate for and achieve satisfactory levels of environmental protection.

In principle, this interdependent relationship between human rights and the environment could be recognized through inclusion of a right to a healthy environment in a global declaration or treaty. However, the 1948 Universal Declaration of Human Rights and the two International Covenants on human rights[1] preceded the modern environmental movement, and later efforts to persuade the United Nations (UN) to recognize the right have not been successful. Although Principle 1 of the 1972 Stockholm Declaration comes close to stating the right explicitly, the UN has declined to extend or even repeat its language.

The absence of a globally recognized human right to a healthy environment has not prevented the evolution of rights-based approaches to environmental protection, but it has meant that the evolution has occurred without the benefit of an overarching international legal framework or agreed normative touchstone. Instead, the relationship of human rights and the environment has developed through the adoption and interpretation of many different national constitutions and laws, human rights treaties, and

[1] 1966 International Covenant on Civil and Political Rights (ICCPR); 1966 International Covenant on Economic, Social and Cultural Rights (ICESCR).

multilateral environmental agreements. Remarkably, this disparate set of sources has produced a relatively consistent set of norms.

The development of what might be called 'environmental human rights law' has occurred in three main channels. First, efforts to achieve recognition of a human right to a healthy environment, while ineffective at the UN, have achieved widespread success at the national and regional levels. Second, some multilateral environmental instruments have incorporated human rights norms, especially rights of access to information, public participation, and remedy. Third, human rights tribunals and other monitoring bodies have 'greened' human rights law by applying a wide range of human rights to environmental harm.

The following sections explain each of these paths of development. A concluding section describes recent signs that the approaches are converging, and sketches potential lines of further development through recognition of the rights of nature and of future generations.[2]

II. RECOGNITION OF THE HUMAN RIGHT TO A HEALTHY ENVIRONMENT

That environmental degradation interferes with the full enjoyment of human rights is not a new insight. In 1968, when the UN General Assembly decided to convene the first international environmental conference, it expressed concern about the effects of 'the continuing and accelerating impairment of the quality of the human environment ... on the condition of man, his physical, mental and social well-being, his dignity and his enjoyment of basic human rights'.[3] Four years later, the nations participating in the conference stated, in the Stockholm Declaration, that the natural as well as the human-made environment is essential to human well-being 'and to the enjoyment of basic human rights—even the right to life itself'.[4]

The recognition that a healthy environment is necessary to human well-being leads naturally to the idea that humans have a human right to a healthy environment, as they have human rights to other interests of fundamental importance to human dignity, freedom, and equality. So it is unsurprising that the first principle of the Stockholm Declaration refers to the 'right to freedom, equality and adequate conditions of life, in an environment of a quality that permits a life of dignity and well-being'.[5]

[2] See Chapters 14 and 20, 'Earth Jurisprudence' and 'Equity', in this volume.

[3] UNGA Res 2398(XXIII), 'Problems of the human environment' (3 December 1968) UN Doc A/RES/2398(XXIII).

[4] UN, 'Report of the United Nations Conference on the Human Environment' (5-16 June 1972) UN Doc A/CONF.48/14/Rev.1, 3, ch 1—'Declaration of the United Nations Conference on the Human Environment'.

[5] Ibid, principle 1.

What may be more surprising is that the UN has never elaborated, or even repeated, this recognition, despite several opportunities to do so. The 1987 report of the World Commission on Environment and Development (the Brundtland Commission), which urged the international community to adopt sustainable development as a goal, presented legal principles drafted by an experts group, the first of which declared that 'all human beings have the fundamental right to an environment adequate for their health and well-being'.[6] However, the 1992 UN Conference on Environment and Development did not include this language in the Rio Declaration.[7] Neither did later conferences on sustainable development in Johannesburg in 2002 and Rio de Janeiro in 2012. Similarly, in 1994 an independent expert on the Sub-Commission on Prevention of Discrimination and Protection of Minorities, a subsidiary body to the UN Human Rights Commission, presented draft principles on human rights and the environment that included 'the right to a secure, healthy and ecologically sound environment', but the Commission did not adopt the draft declaration.[8]

In contrast, the right has been widely recognized at the regional and national levels. In 1981, the African Charter on Human and Peoples' Rights became the first human rights treaty to include an environmental right, stating that 'all peoples' have the right to 'a general satisfactory environment favourable to their development'.[9] The 1988 San Salvador Protocol to the 1969 American Convention on Human Rights includes the right of everyone 'to live in a healthy environment' in its list of economic, social, and cultural rights.[10] The Aarhus Convention, concluded ten years later under the auspices of the UN Economic Commission for Europe, states in its first article that parties shall guarantee rights of information, participation, and remedy in environmental matters '[i]n order to contribute to the protection of the right of every person of present and future generations to live in an environment adequate to his or her health and well-being'.[11]

Recognition of the right has progressed even more rapidly and extensively at the national level. Beginning in the 1970s and continuing steadily to the present, at least 100

[6] World Commission on Environment and Development, *Our Common Future* (OUP 1987).

[7] *Report of the United Nations Conference on Environment and Development* (UN 1993) vol I, annex I—'Rio Declaration on Environment and Development'.

[8] 'Human Rights and the Environment—Final report prepared by Mrs. Fatma Zohra Ksentini, Special Rapporteur' (6 July 1994) UN Doc E/CN.4/Sub.2/1994/9, 74, annex I—'Draft principles on human rights and the environment', principle 2. See Neil Popović, 'In Pursuit of Environmental Human Rights: Commentary on the Draft Declaration of Principles on Human Rights and the Environment' *Columbia Human Rights Law Review*, 27/2 (1996): 487.

[9] art 24.

[10] art 11.1.

[11] 1998 Convention on Access to Information, Public Participation in Decision-Making and Access to Justice in Environmental Matters, art 1. Two other regional instruments, the 2004 Arab Charter on Human Rights and the 2012 Association of Southeast Asian Nations (ASEAN) Human Rights Declaration (adopted 18 November 2012) <https://asean.org/asean-human-rights-declaration/> accessed 22 January 2020, each include the right to a 'healthy' (Arab Charter, art 38) or 'safe, clean and sustainable' (ASEAN Declaration, para 28(f)) environment as an element of the right to an adequate standard of living.

states have adopted explicit constitutional rights to a healthy environment.[12] Other countries have included the right in national legislation. In all, more than 150 countries have recognized the right in their constitutions or other national legislation, through judicial interpretation of other constitutional rights, or through ratification of regional agreements. Although some states have done little or nothing to implement it, courts in many countries apply the right as a basis for, among other things, reviewing government actions with environmental effects, protecting rights of information and participation, imposing substantive standards, and ordering legal remedies for environmental harm.[13]

III. INCORPORATION OF HUMAN RIGHTS NORMS IN MULTILATERAL ENVIRONMENTAL AGREEMENTS

Multilateral environmental agreements almost never refer to human rights explicitly. The principal exception is the Paris Agreement of 2015, whose preamble states that 'Parties should, when taking action to address climate change, respect, promote and consider their respective obligations on human rights, the right to health, the rights of Indigenous peoples, local communities, migrants, children, persons with disabilities and people in vulnerable situations and the right to development, as well as gender equality, empowerment of women and intergenerational equity'. Although the preambular language does not have operational effect, it may help to spur governments to pay greater attention to human rights in their responses to climate change.[14]

More often, environmental instruments include language that implicitly reflects and supports human rights norms, especially rights of access to information, public participation, and effective remedies.[15] The most important global instrument in this respect is the 1992 Rio Declaration, Principle 10 of which states:

> Environmental issues are best handled with participation of all concerned citizens, at the relevant level. At the national level, each individual shall have appropriate access to information concerning the environment that is held by public authorities,

[12] See David Boyd, 'Catalyst for Change: Evaluating Forty Years of Experience in Implementing the Right to a Healthy Environment' in John Knox and Ramin Pejan (eds), *The Human Right to a Healthy Environment* (CUP 2018) 17. About two-thirds of the constitutional provisions refer to health; alternative formulations include rights to a clean, safe, favourable, or wholesome environment.

[13] See generally David Boyd, *The Environmental Rights Revolution: A Global Study of Constitutions, Human Rights, and the Environment* (UBC Press 2012); James May and Erin Daly, *Global Environmental Constitutionalism* (CUP 2015).

[14] See Lavanya Rajamani, 'Human Rights in the Climate Regime: From Rio to Paris and Beyond' in Knox and Pejan (n 12) 236.

[15] See Chapter 21, 'Public Participation', in this volume.

> including information on hazardous materials and activities in their communities, and the opportunity to participate in decision-making processes. States shall facilitate and encourage public awareness and participation by making information widely available. Effective access to judicial and administrative proceedings, including redress and remedy, shall be provided.

Two regional agreements codify the Principle 10 access rights and define the obligations of states in more detail. The Aarhus Convention, which has forty-seven parties in Europe and central Asia, sets out detailed requirements that its parties: provide environmental information (defined broadly) on request; update and disseminate environmental information; provide for public participation in environmental decision-making; and ensure that members of the public have access to legal remedies for failures to provide environmental information and facilitate public participation.[16] Its compliance committee, composed of independent experts, receives communications from members of the public, issues findings, and makes recommendations.[17]

In 2018, Latin American and Caribbean countries adopted the Escazú Agreement, which also includes detailed provisions requiring that its parties: ensure the public's right of access to environmental information; collect and disseminate environmental information; provide for public participation in environmental decision-making, and ensure access to remedies in relation not only to information and public participation, but also to 'any other decision, action or omission that affects or could affect the environment adversely or violate laws and regulations related to the environment'.[18]

The Escazú Agreement also requires each party to guarantee a 'safe and enabling environment for persons, groups and organizations that promote and defend human rights in environmental matters'.[19] The Conference of the Parties, at its first meeting, will determine the rules of a committee to support implementation and compliance.[20]

Although there is no global equivalent to the regional agreements implementing Principle 10, many multilateral environmental agreements encourage or require their parties to provide access to information and/or promote public participation on specified topics within the scope of the agreements.[21] In addition, in 2010, the UN

[16] arts 4–9.

[17] The committee may make recommendations to the Meeting of the Parties and, with the permission of the party concerned, directly to the party; see Decision I/7, 'Review of Compliance' (2 April 2004) UN Doc ECE/MP.PP/2/Add.8, annex.

[18] Regional Agreement on Access to Information, Public Participation and Justice in Environmental Matters in Latin America and the Caribbean, arts 5–8. The agreement was opened for signature in September 2018, and it entered into force in April 2021.

[19] art 9.

[20] art 18.

[21] See eg 1992 UN Framework Convention on Climate Change (UNFCCC), art 6(a); Paris Agreement, art 12; 1994 Convention to Combat Desertification in Countries Experiencing Serious Drought and/or Desertification, Particularly in Africa, arts 3(a), 16; 1998 Rotterdam Convention on

Environment Programme (UNEP) Governing Council adopted guidelines for national legislation implementing access to information, public participation, and access to justice in environmental matters.[22]

The 1992 Convention on Biological Diversity (CBD) provides linkages to a different set of human rights norms, concerning the Indigenous and tribal rights described in the following section.[23] The CBD encourages its parties to respect, preserve, and maintain Indigenous and traditional knowledge, innovations, and practices relevant for the conservation and sustainable use of biological diversity, to promote their wider application with the approval and involvement of the holders, and to encourage the equitable sharing of the benefits arising from their utilization.[24] It also urges the parties to protect and encourage the customary use of biological resources in accordance with traditional cultural practices that are compatible with conservation or sustainable use requirements.[25] In 2010, the parties to the CBD adopted the Nagoya Protocol, which provides for 'the prior informed consent or approval and involvement of indigenous and local communities' in relation to access to traditional knowledge associated with genetic resources, and requires that its parties take steps to ensure that the benefits arising from utilization of genetic resources and traditional knowledge are shared in a fair and equitable way with the communities concerned.[26]

IV. APPLICATION OF HUMAN RIGHTS LAW TO ENVIRONMENTAL ISSUES

Much of the development of environmental human rights law has occurred through the application by human rights bodies of existing rights, such as rights to life and health, to environmental issues. Although the development has occurred in many different forums, construing different human rights sources, it has resulted in a coherent set of norms. In addition, international instruments set out Indigenous and tribal rights, many of which directly relate to the environment.

Prior Informed Consent Procedure for Certain Hazardous Chemicals and Pesticides in International Trade, art 15.2; 2001 Stockholm Convention on Persistent Organic Pollutants, arts 7.2, 10.1; 2013 Minamata Convention on Mercury, art 18.1.

22 UNEP, 'Guidelines for the Development of National Legislation on Access to Information, Public Participation and Access to Justice in Environmental Matters' (26 February 2010); see UNEP, *Putting Rio Principle 10 into Action: An Implementation Guide* (2015).

23 See Chapters 32 and 42, 'Wildlife' and 'Indigenous Peoples', in this volume.

24 art 8(j).

25 art 10(c).

26 Nagoya Protocol on Access to Genetic Resources and the Fair and Equitable Sharing of Benefits Arising from their Utilization, arts 5, 7.

A. Indigenous and Tribal Rights Relating To The Environment

The two most important sources of Indigenous and tribal rights relating to the environment are International Labour Organisation Convention (No 169) concerning Indigenous and Tribal Peoples in Independent Countries, and the UN Declaration on the Rights of Indigenous Peoples (UNDRIP).[27] The ILO Convention has twenty-three parties, most of which are in Latin America. While not legally binding in itself, UNDRIP has been generally accepted by states as setting benchmark standards in relation to Indigenous rights,[28] and has influenced human rights bodies in their application of other treaties to Indigenous and tribal peoples.[29]

Both ILO Convention No 169 and UNDRIP provide that states must recognize and protect the rights of Indigenous peoples to the lands, territories, and resources that they have traditionally owned, occupied, or used, including those to which they have had access for their subsistence and traditional activities.[30] The ILO Convention provides that states have obligations to consult with Indigenous and tribal peoples when considering measures that may affect them directly, before undertaking or permitting any programmes for the exploration or exploitation of resources pertaining to their lands or territories, and when considering their capacity to alienate their lands or territories or otherwise transfer their rights outside their own community.[31] UNDRIP takes an important further step, stating that the free, prior, and informed consent of Indigenous peoples is necessary before the adoption or implementation of any laws, policies, or measures that may affect them, and in particular before the approval of any project affecting their lands, territories, or resources, including the extraction or exploitation of mineral, water, or other resources, or the storage or disposal of hazardous materials.[32]

UNDRIP also states that Indigenous peoples have the right to the conservation and protection of the environment and the productive capacity of their lands, territories, and resources, and to receive assistance from states for such conservation and protection.[33]

[27] UNGA Res 61/295, 'United Nations Declaration on the Rights of Indigenous Peoples' (2 October 2007) UN Doc A/RES/61/295.

[28] The UNGA resolution adopting UNDRIP received only four negative votes, from Australia, Canada, New Zealand, and the United States, each of which later reversed its position and indicated support for the declaration.

[29] See eg *Kichwa Indigenous People of Sarayaku v Ecuador* (Judgement of 27 June 2012 on Merits, Reparations, Costs) IACtHR Ser C No 245 [187], [215] (Kichwa case); 'Report of the Committee on the Elimination of Racial Discrimination' (28 November 2010) UN Doc A/64/18 (country report on Guatemala) para 40(11); 'Report of the Special Rapporteur on the situation of human rights and fundamental freedoms of indigenous people' (4 September 2009) UN Doc A/64/338, para 48.

[30] ILO 169, arts 14–15; UNDRIP, arts 26–27.

[31] arts 6, 15, 17.

[32] arts 19, 29.2, 32.2.

[33] art 29.1.

ILO Convention No 169 requires states to safeguard the rights of the peoples concerned to the natural resources pertaining to their lands, including their right to participate in the use, management, and conservation of these resources.[34]

The ILO Convention provides that states must ensure that the peoples concerned shall, wherever possible, participate in the benefits of exploration or exploitation of mineral or sub-surface resources pertaining to their lands and shall receive fair compensation for any damages which they may sustain as a result of such activities.[35] More generally, UNDRIP indicates that states must provide for just and fair redress for harm resulting from any activities affecting their lands, territories, or resources, particularly in connection with the development, utilization, or exploitation of mineral, water, or other resources, and 'appropriate measures shall be taken to mitigate adverse environmental, economic, social, cultural or spiritual impact'.[36] They have the right to restitution or, if this is not possible, compensation for their lands, territories, and resources that have been taken, used, or damaged without their consent.[37]

B. 'Greening' Human Rights

1. *Regional human rights tribunals*

Several regional instruments recognize the human right to a healthy (or satisfactory) environment, as noted above, but only the African Charter makes the right reviewable by a tribunal or other monitoring body.[38] Instead, regional bodies in Africa, the Americas, and Europe have applied other human rights, including the rights to life, health, private and family life, and property, to environmental issues. The regional human rights systems include courts with the authority to issue decisions that legally bind the state parties, as well as commissions and other expert bodies able to review complaints but not issue binding decisions.

a) *African Commission and African Court on Human and Peoples' Rights*

The most important environmental decision in the African system is *Social and Economic Rights Action Centre v Nigeria*, a case involving massive oil pollution in the Niger delta region by a consortium of the Nigerian government and Royal Dutch Shell.[39] The African Commission on Human and Peoples' Rights (AComHPR) found that the

[34] art 15.1.

[35] art 15.2.

[36] art 32.3.

[37] art 28.

[38] Neither the Arab Charter nor the ASEAN Declaration creates an oversight body for any of its rights; the reference to most right in art 1 of the Aarhus Convention is not reviewable by its compliance committee; and the rights in the San Salvador Protocol are not subject to review by the Inter-American Commission or Court of Human Rights.

[39] *Social and Economic Rights Action Center (SERAC) and the Center for Economic and Social Rights (CESR) v Nigeria*, AComHPR (2001) Communication No 155/96.

exploitation violated the human rights of the Ogoni people living in the delta, including their rights to health and to a satisfactory environment, which are protected by Articles 16 and 24 of the African Charter. The Commission stated that Nigeria had duties to take 'reasonable and other measures to prevent pollution and ecological degradation, to promote conservation, and to secure an ecologically sustainable development and use of natural resources', and that compliance with the 'spirit' of Articles 16 and 24 'must also include ordering or at least permitting independent scientific monitoring of threatened environments, requiring and publicizing environmental and social impact studies prior to any major industrial development, undertaking appropriate monitoring and providing information to those communities exposed to hazardous materials and activities and providing meaningful opportunities for individuals to be heard and to participate in the development decisions affecting their communities'.[40]

Other important environmental decisions from the African system include *Centre for Minority Rights Development et al v Kenya*[41] and *African Commission on Human and Peoples' Rights v Kenya*,[42] in which the commission and the court (ACtHPR), respectively, held that the actions of a government concerning protected areas must respect and protect the rights of Indigenous peoples living there.[43]

b) *European Court of Human Rights*

The European Court of Human Rights (ECtHR) has developed an extensive environmental jurisprudence since 1994.[44] The pathbreaking decision was *López Ostra v Spain*, in which the court held that severe environmental pollution could violate the right to respect for private and family life protected by Article 8 of the 1950 European Convention on Human Rights. The court stated that even when pollution does not seriously endanger the health of a claimant, it may give rise to a positive duty on the state to take reasonable and appropriate measures to secure her rights.[45]

In subsequent cases under Article 8, the court has distinguished between substantive and procedural obligations. With respect to the former, it has emphasized that states have wide discretion (or 'margin of appreciation') and has given near-dispositive weight to whether they followed their own domestic standards.[46] However, the court has adopted more specific procedural requirements, which require states to assess the effects of proposed activities that cause environmental harm and infringe human rights,

[40] Ibid [52], [53].

[41] *Centre for Minority Rights Development (Kenya) and Minority Rights Group (on behalf of Endorois Welfare Council) v Kenya*, AComHPR (2009) Communication No 276/03.

[42] ACtHPR (26 May 2017) No 006/2012.

[43] See Lilian Chenwi, 'The Right to a Satisfactory, Healthy, and Sustainable Environment in the African Regional Human Rights System' in Knox and Pejan (n 12) 59.

[44] See Council of Europe, *Manual on Human Rights and the Environment* (2nd edn, 2012).

[45] (1994) 16798/90 [51].

[46] See eg *Hatton v UK* (Judgement) Grand Chamber ECtHR (8 July 2003) Application no 36022/97 [99]–[104].

to make environmental information public, and to allow the individuals concerned to have access to judicial remedies, especially if 'they consider that their interests or their comments have not been given sufficient weight in the decision-making process'.[47]

The court has also applied Article 2 of the European Convention, which protects the right to life, to environmental threats. The court has long held that Article 2 imposes positive as well as negative duties—that is, obligations on states to protect against threats to the right to life, not just to refrain from infringing the right directly. In the environmental context, the court has held that states must establish legislative and administrative frameworks that effectively deter threats to the right to life, including by regulating the licensing and supervision of hazardous and industrial activities and by providing the public information about such activities and natural disasters such as floods and mudslides.[48] If loss of life nevertheless results, states must conduct independent and impartial investigations and punish breaches as appropriate.[49]

The court may issue judgements for damages, but it may not invalidate laws. However, its decisions influence domestic courts that are able to apply the protections of the Convention more directly. A notable recent example is the 2019 decision of the Supreme Court of the Netherlands that Articles 2 and 8 impose a duty on the Dutch government to protect against the serious risk of loss of life and disruption of family life threatened by climate change, and that the government violated this duty by not striving to reduce greenhouse gas emissions at least 25% from 1990 levels by the end of 2020.[50]

c) *European Committee for Social Rights*

The European Committee for Social Rights oversees the 1961 European Social Charter, which sets out economic, social, and cultural rights. The committee has interpreted the right to health in the Charter to include the right to a healthy environment.[51] Among other things, the committee has held that states must take specific measures to prevent air pollution, including by informing and educating the public about environmental problems, introducing threshold values for emissions, measuring air quality, monitoring health risks, and enforcing standards once adopted.[52] In setting standards, states should take into account the norms and guidelines set by national and international bodies.[53]

47 *Taskin and Ors v Turkey* (2004) ECtHR, 46117/99 [119].

48 See *Öneryildiz v Turkey* (2004) ECtHR, 48939/99 (improper maintenance of municipal rubbish tip); *Brincat and others v Malta* (2014) ECtHR, 60908/11 (workplace exposure to asbestos); *Kolyadenko v Russia* (2012) ECtHR, 17423/05 (flash flood); *Budayeva v Russia* (2008) ECtHR, 15339/02 (mudslide).

49 See Manual on Human Rights and the Environment (n 44) 38–39 (summarizing jurisprudence).

50 *The State of the Netherlands (Ministry of Economic Affairs and Climate Policy) v Stichting Urgenda* (Judgement of 20 December 2019) No 19/00135, ECLI:NL:HR:2019:2007 (Supreme Court of the Netherlands) (Urgenda Foundation case).

51 *Marangopoulos Foundation for Human Rights v Greece* (2006) No 30/2005 [200] (Marangopoulos case); *International Federation for Human Rights (FIDH) v Greece* (2013) No 72/2011 [49] (FIDH case).

52 Marangopoulos case (n 51) [203].

53 FIDH case (n 51) [148].

d) *Inter-American Commission and Court of Human Rights*

Many of the important decisions in the Inter-American human rights system have involved Indigenous and tribal peoples. The Inter-American Court has stated that their right to property under the American Declaration and American Convention[54] includes the lands that they have traditionally occupied and the natural resources that they have traditionally used, because the lands and resources are necessary for their physical and cultural survival.[55] Drawing on ILO Convention No 169 and UNDRIP, the court has held that states have obligations to delimit and title the ownership of the lands traditionally occupied by Indigenous and tribal peoples, consult with them regarding any proposed concessions or other activities that may affect their lands and natural resources, ensure that no concession will be issued without a prior environmental and social impact assessment, and guarantee that they receive a 'reasonable benefit' from any such plan if approved.[56] Regarding large-scale development or investment projects that would have a major impact within the territory of Indigenous or tribal peoples, the state may only proceed if it obtains 'their free, prior, and informed consent, according to their customs and traditions'.[57]

More recently, in response to a request by Columbia seeking clarification of the application of the American Convention to environmental harm, the Inter-American Court issued a far-reaching Advisory Opinion on human rights and the environment.[58] Among other things, the opinion indicates that the responsibility of states under the American Convention extends to actions within their territory or control that cause transboundary environmental harm, and that the rights to information, public participation, and access to justice are integral to the rights of life and personal integrity in the environmental context.[59]

2. *UN human rights bodies*

UN treaty bodies have applied human rights to environmental issues in the course of their oversight of states' compliance with the major human rights treaties, including the 1966 International Covenant on Economic, Social and Cultural Rights (ICESCR)

[54] American Declaration of the Rights and Duties of Man (adopted 2 May 1948), art XXIII; 1969 American Convention on Human Rights, art 21.

[55] See eg Kichwa case (n 29); *Case of the Saramaka People v Suriname* (Judgement of 28 November 2007 on Merits, Reparations and Costs) IACtHR Ser C No 172 [121]–[122] (Saramaka People case); *Indigenous Community Yakye Axa v Paraguay* (Judgement of 17 June 2005 on Merits, Reparations and Costs) IACtHR Ser C No 142 [143]; *Mayagna (Sumo) Awas Tingni Community v Nicaragua* (Judgement of 31 August 2001 on Merits, Reparations and Costs) IACtHR Ser C No 79 [148]-[149].

[56] Saramaka People case (n 55) [129].

[57] Ibid [134].

[58] *State Obligations in Relation to the Environment* (Advisory Opinion) IACtHR (2017) OC-23/17 (State Obligations in Relation to the Environment case); see Maria Banda, 'Inter-American Court of Human Rights' Advisory Opinion on the Environment and Human Rights' *American Society of International Law Insights*, 22/6 (2018).

[59] State Obligations in Relation to the Environment case (n 58) [101], [211]–[241]; see also Chapter 27, 'Judicial Development', in this volume.

and the International Covenant on Civil and Political Rights (ICCPR).[60] Treaty bodies do not have the authority to issue binding decisions, but through their general comments, assessments of country reports, and decisions in response to individual communications, they have indicated that environmental harm interferes with the enjoyment of human rights and that states have obligations to protect against such harm.[61]

The Human Rights Council (HRC), the main UN intergovernmental human rights body, has also examined environmental issues, including through its Universal Periodic Review programme, in which it reviews the human rights records of every UN member state, and in a series of resolutions calling attention to the effects of climate change on human rights.[62] In addition, the Council has appointed independent experts, often called special rapporteurs, with mandates to examine human rights in particular areas. Many of these experts, including the special rapporteurs on Indigenous peoples, human rights defenders, toxic substances, and the right to food, have issued reports applying human rights norms to specific environmental issues.[63]

In 2012, the Human Rights Council appointed an independent expert with a mandate to study the human rights obligations relating to the enjoyment of a safe, clean, healthy, and sustainable environment.[64] The present author received the mandate and prepared a series of reports mapping how human rights bodies have applied human rights norms to environmental issues.[65] In 2015, the Council renewed the mandate for another three years, changed the title of the mandate-holder to special rapporteur, and requested that he promote the realization of the obligations.[66] To that end, he prepared 'Framework

[60] Unusually among UN human rights treaties, the 1989 Convention on the Rights of the Child includes an explicit reference to the environment: it requires its parties to pursue full implementation of children's right to health by taking measures, among others, to combat disease and malnutrition through 'the provision of adequate nutritious foods and clean drinking-water, taking into consideration the dangers and risks of environmental pollution' (art 24.2(c)).

[61] See eg Human Rights Committee, 'General Comment No 36 [on the right to life]' (30 October 2018) UN Doc CCPR/C/GC/36, paras 26, 62; Committee on Economic, Social and Cultural Rights (CESCR), 'General Comment No. 15: The right to water' (20 January 2003) UN Doc E/C.12/2002/11, paras 10, 21, 23; CESCR, 'General Comment No. 14: The right to the highest attainable standard of health' (11 August 2000) UN Doc E/C.12/2000/4, paras 4, 11, 15, 34.

[62] See eg HRC Res on 'Human rights and climate change': 10/4 (25 March 2009); 18/22 (30 September 2011); 29/15 (2 July 2015); 38/4 (5 July 2018).

[63] See eg James Anaya, 'Report of the Special Rapporteur on the rights of indigenous peoples: Extractive industries operating within or near indigenous territories' (11 July 2011) UN Doc A/HRC/18/35; Michel Forst, 'Report of the Special Rapporteur on the situation of human rights defenders' (3 August 2016) UN Doc A/71/281 (environmental human rights defenders); Baskut Tuncak, 'Report of the Special Rapporteur on the implications for human rights of the environmentally sound management and disposal of hazardous substances and wastes' (2 August 2016) UN Doc A/HRC/33/41 (effect of pollution and toxics on children); Hilal Elver, 'Report of the Special Rapporteur on the right to food' (24 January 2017) UN Doc A/HRC/34/48 (pesticides).

[64] HRC Res 19/10, 'Human Rights and the Environment' (12 March 2012).

[65] See John Knox, 'Report of the Independent Expert on the issue of human rights obligations relating to the enjoyment of a safe, clean, healthy and sustainable environment: Mapping Report' (30 December 2013) UN Doc A/HRC/25/53.

[66] HRC Res 28/11, 'Human Rights and the Environment' (26 March 2015).

Principles on Human Rights and the Environment' that summarize the human rights obligations relating to the environment.[67] In 2018, the Council took note with appreciation of the report presenting the Framework Principles and renewed the mandate for another three years.[68]

C. The Framework Principles on Human Rights and the Environment

The Framework Principles and their accompanying commentary do not purport to create new obligations under human rights law; rather, they reflect the application of existing obligations in the environmental context, as stated in international instruments and by the tribunals and other human rights bodies described above. The report presenting the Principles states that while not all governments have formally accepted all of these norms, their coherence is 'strong evidence of the converging trends towards greater uniformity and certainty in the understanding of human rights obligations relating to the environment'.[69]

The Framework Principles describe procedural obligations of states, including: to respect and protect the rights to freedom of expression, association, and peaceful assembly in relation to environmental matters; to provide for environmental education and public awareness; to provide public access to environmental information; to require the prior assessment of the possible environmental and human rights impacts of proposed projects and policies; to provide for and facilitate public participation in decision-making related to the environment; and to provide for access to effective remedies for violations of human rights and domestic laws relating to the environment.[70]

The Framework Principles also outline human rights obligations relating to substantive standards. As noted above, human rights bodies have held that states have discretion in determining the appropriate levels of environmental protection, taking into account the need to balance the goal of preventing all environmental harm with other social goals. However, the establishment and implementation of appropriate levels of environmental protection must always comply with obligations of non-discrimination, and there is a strong presumption against retrogressive measures in relation to the progressive realization of economic, social, and cultural rights. Other factors that human rights bodies have taken into account in assessing substantive environmental standards include whether the government has taken into account relevant international standards, such as those promulgated by the World Health Organization.[71] Once adopted, states

[67] John Knox, 'Report of the Special Rapporteur on the issue of human rights obligations relating to the enjoyment of a safe, clean, healthy and sustainable environment' (24 January 2018) UN Doc A/HRC/37/59, annex (Framework Principles).

[68] David Boyd succeeded to the mandate on 1 August 2018.

[69] Framework Principles (n 67) para 9.

[70] Ibid, principles 5–10, paras 10–30.

[71] Ibid, principle 11, paras 31–32.

must monitor and effectively enforce compliance with the standards by private actors as well as governmental authorities.[72] With respect to global or transboundary environmental harm that adversely affects human rights, states have obligations of international cooperation.[73]

The obligations of states under human rights law to prohibit discrimination and to ensure equal and effective protection against discrimination apply to the equal enjoyment of human rights relating to the environment. States therefore have obligations, among others, to protect against environmental harm that results from or contributes to discrimination, to provide for equal access to environmental benefits and to ensure that their actions relating to the environment do not themselves discriminate.[74] In addition, states must take additional steps to protect the rights of those who are particularly vulnerable to or at risk from environmental harm, including environmental human rights defenders and Indigenous peoples.[75]

V. CONCLUSION

As the three strands of the law of human rights and the environment mature, they increasingly take note of and converge with one another. As noted above, in 2015, the Paris Agreement became the first global environmental agreement to refer explicitly to human rights. The Conference of the Parties to the CBD has adopted guidelines on environmental and social assessment and on consultation with Indigenous peoples and local communities.[76] The Escazú Agreement on procedural access rights, adopted in 2018, provides that 'each Party shall guarantee the right of every person to live in a healthy environment and any other universally-recognized human right related to the present Agreement'.[77] And in 2018, UNEP announced a new 'environmental rights initiative' to support realization of human rights related to the environment.[78]

Conversely, human rights bodies are increasingly referring to international environmental norms. In its 2017 Advisory Opinion, the Inter-American Court of Human Rights indicated that the duties of states in relation to the rights of life and personal integrity must take into account international environmental principles, including the duty to prevent significant environmental harm, the precautionary principle, and the duty of international cooperation.[79] Similarly, the Human Rights Committee, the

[72] Ibid, principle 12, paras 34–35.

[73] Ibid, principle 13, paras 36–39.

[74] Ibid, principle 3, paras 7–9.

[75] Ibid, principles 4, 14–15, paras 10–11, 40–53.

[76] See Elisa Morgera, 'Dawn of a New Day? The Evolving Relationship between the Convention on Biological Diversity and International Human Rights Law' *Wake Forest Law Review*, 53/1 (2018): 101.

[77] Escazú Agreement, art 4.1.

[78] UNEP, 'UN Launches Environmental Rights Initiative', *UN News* (6 March 2018).

[79] State Obligations in Relation to the Environment case (n 58) [127]–[210].

treaty body overseeing the ICCPR, stated in 2018 that 'Obligations of States parties under international environmental law should ... inform the contents of article 6 of the Covenant [on the right to life], and the obligation of States parties to respect and ensure the right to life should also inform their relevant obligations under international environmental law'.[80]

Efforts are again underway to convince the UN to recognize the human right to a healthy environment. In 2017, France proposed a Global Pact for the Environment whose first article would recognize the right of every person 'to live in an ecologically sound environment adequate for their health, well-being, dignity, culture and fulfilment'.[81] The UNGA responded to the proposal by creating an ad hoc open-ended working group to discuss possible gaps in international environmental law.[82] In 2018, the outgoing and incoming UN special rapporteurs on human rights and the environment urged the UNGA to recognize the right through a resolution or a treaty such as the Global Pact.[83]

Finally, two potential further lines of development of rights-based approaches to environmental protection should be noted: rights of nature, and rights of future generations.

Legal recognition of rights of nature has long been proposed as a way to protect the intrinsic value of the environment and its components,[84] which an approach focused only on *human* rights may ignore.[85] In recent years, some states have incorporated natural rights in national constitutions, laws, and judicial decisions.[86] At the international level, no treaty explicitly protects rights of nature, and the ECtHR has refused to derive such rights from the European Convention.[87] However, the Inter-American Court recently stated that the American Convention includes an implicit right to a healthy environment that protects environmental components such as forests and rivers, even in the absence of evidence of harm to human life and health.[88] It seems likely that as more

80 General Comment No 36 (n 61) para 62.

81 Le Club des Juristes, 'Toward a Global Pact for the Environment' (White Paper, September 2017) 45.

82 UNGA Res 72/277 'Towards a Global Pact for the Environment' (14 May 2018) UN Doc A/RES/72/277.

83 UNGA, 'Human rights obligations relating to the enjoyment of a safe, clean, healthy and sustainable environment' (19 July 2018) UN Doc A/73/188, paras 46–48.

84 Christopher Stone, 'Should Trees Have Standing? Toward Legal Rights for Natural Objects' *Southern California Law Review*, 45/2 (1972): 450.

85 Günther Handl, 'Human Rights and Protection of the Environment: A Mildly 'Revisionist' View' in Antônio Trindade (ed), *Derechos Humanos, Desarrollo Sustentable y Medio Ambiente* (Instituto Interamericano de derechos 1995) 117, 138.

86 See eg *Constitución de la República del Ecuador* (2008), art 71; *Ley Marco de la Madre Tierra y Desarrollo Integral para Vivir Bien* (Framework Law of Mother Earth and Integral Development for Living Well), Law No 300 (2012) (Bolivia); Te Urewera Act 51 of 2014 (New Zealand); *Mohd. Salim v State of Uttarakhand & Others* (20 March 2017) Uttarakhand High Court (India) PIL 126/2014.

87 *Kyrtatos v Greece* (22 May 2003) ECtHR, 41666/98, para 52.

88 State Obligations in Relation to the Environment case (n 58) [62].

facets of the human dependence on healthy ecosystems become clearer, advocates will increase their efforts to employ human rights norms to protect biodiversity.[89]

International environmental agreements and declarations on sustainable development often emphasize the importance of protecting future generations,[90] in accordance with the Brundtland Commission's famous definition of sustainable development as 'development that meets the needs of the present without compromising the ability of future generations to meet their own needs'.[91] However, international law has done little to define the rights of future generations or the obligations of states to them. One potential avenue for further development in this respect may be to clarify the current human rights of children and youth in relation to the long-term but foreseeable future effects of climate change.[92]

BIBLIOGRAPHY

Sumudu Atapattu, *Human Rights Approaches to Climate Change* (Routledge 2016)

David Boyd, *The Environmental Rights Revolution: A Global Study of Constitutions, Human Rights, and the Environment* (UBC Press 2012)

John Knox and Ramin Pejan (eds), *The Human Right to a Healthy Environment* (CUP 2018)

James May and Erin Daly, *Global Environmental Constitutionalism* (CUP 2015)

[89] See John Knox, 'Report of the Special Rapporteur on the issue of human rights obligations relating to the enjoyment of a safe, clean, healthy and sustainable environment' (19 January 2017) UN Doc A/HRC/34/49.

[90] See eg Rio Declaration (n 7) principle 3; UNFCCC, art 3.1; CBD, preamble.

[91] *Our Common Future* (n 6) ch 2, para 1.

[92] See Urgenda Foundation case (n 50) [37]; *Future Generations v Ministry of the Environment* (2018) Colombia Supreme Court; *Juliana v United States* (2016) District Court of Oregon, 217 F.Supp.3d 1224, reversed and remanded (2020) 9th Circuit Court of Appeals, 947 F.3d 1159.

CHAPTER 46

MIGRATION

WALTER KÄLIN

I. INTRODUCTION

TRADITIONALLY, environmental law and migration law have had little in common and rarely interacted. However, their respective subject matters are increasingly reflected as integrated issues in international instruments alongside the growing recognition that environmental factors are important drivers of forced migration (hereinafter displacement) as well as predominantly voluntary migration[1] (hereinafter migration).

This chapter argues that environmental law has a relevant role to play in addressing these challenges despite the fact that they are primarily within the purview of migration and human rights law. In particular, as discussed in Section II, it can contribute to addressing environmental drivers of migration and mitigate displacement risks by reducing natural hazards and enhancing the resilience of populations at risk as well as dealing with the environmental consequence of such human mobility. On the negative side, environmental law may contribute to forcing people out of conservation areas, unless it provides for measures mitigating such effects of environmental protection, a topic discussed in Section III.

[1] Particularly in the context of slow-onset events, many movements will fall somewhere in the middle between the two poles of compulsion and voluntariness.

II. ADDRESSING ENVIRONMENTAL FACTORS AS DRIVERS OF DISPLACEMENT AND MIGRATION

A. Scenarios

Between 2008 and 2017, an average 24.6 million people were newly displaced each year in the context of sudden-onset disasters, particularly those linked to floods and tropical storms but also earthquakes in some years.[2] An unknown number of people had to move to escape the effects of slow-onset events such as drought, desertification, and the effects of sea level rise, as well as other forms of environmental degradation. The combined impacts of sudden- and slow-onset hazards may also trigger population movements. For example, low-lying atoll islands risk becoming uninhabitable due to coastal erosion, the salinization of groundwater and infertile soil due to storm tides, or the destruction of housing and infrastructure wrought by tropical storms. Finally, environmental deterioration may exacerbate violent conflicts between communities over diminishing resources, which in turn trigger displacement.[3]

The vast majority of people affected by disasters and environmental factors remain within their own country as internally displaced persons (IDPs) or internal migrants. Some people cross international borders, usually into neighbouring countries or within their region, to find protection and assistance or, in the case of predominantly voluntary migration, better livelihoods. Dynamics vary from region to region. For instance, drought and flooding are the key drivers of population movement in Africa, with hurricanes, flooding, and earthquakes most prominent in the Americas and the Caribbean.[4] While some instances of cross-border displacement are well documented,[5] the overall number of people moving across borders in disaster contexts is unknown.

2 Internal Displacement Monitoring Centre (IDMC), 'GRID 2018: Global Report on Internal Displacement' (June 2018) 2.

3 For these and other scenarios see Walter Kälin, 'Conceptualising Climate-Induced Displacement' in Jane McAdam (ed), *Climate Change and Displacement: Multidisciplinary Perspectives* (Hart Publishing 2010) 81, 84–86.

4 See Dina Ionesco, Daria Mokhnacheva, and François Gemenne, *The Atlas of Environmental Migration* (Routledge 2017); The Nansen Initiative, 'Agenda for the Protection of Cross-Border Displaced Persons in the Context of Disasters and Climate Change—Volume 2' (2015) 8–34.

5 Eg in the Greater Horn of Africa and Central Africa regions see, The Nansen Initiative, 'Volume 2' (n 4) 9–11.

According to the Intergovernmental Panel on Climate Change (IPCC), climate change is likely to increase the number of people moving as a consequence of the adverse effects of global warming,[6] citing extreme weather events, among others, in particular. Much, however, will depend on what measures to mitigate climate change and increase resilience of affected communities will be taken. While not quantifying its predictions, the IPCC concluded in 2018 that while 'at 1.5°C there will be *increased* incidents of internal migration and displacement',[7] the tropics would experience '*significant* (population) displacement' in a 2°C world.[8] The World Bank estimates that, without any mitigation and adaptation measures, over 143 million people in sub-Saharan Africa, South Asia, and Latin America alone will migrate within their own countries by 2050, whereas robust action could reduce this number to fifty million.[9]

B. Conceptualizing Human Mobility in the Context of Disasters and Adverse Effects of Climate Change

People are forced to move when they are: (i) exposed or expect to be exposed to (ii) a sudden-onset natural hazard or slow-onset process of environmental change and (iii) lack the resilience to withstand the resulting impacts. People exposed to hazards and environmental degradation may lack resilience for a multitude of socio-economic and political reasons, including poverty, social and economic marginalization, poor urban planning, expansion of settlements into risk-prone areas, population growth, weak governance regarding disaster risk reduction and management, and in some situations, violence or armed conflict.[10] As compared to the impacts of the natural hazard itself, these factors contribute as much as, and sometimes even more, to whether affected people will be able to stay or have to move.[11]

Thus, as highlighted by the non-binding Nansen Initiative Protection Agenda,[12] it is the combination of factors that lead to disasters—understood as serious disruptions of the functioning of a community or society due to the interaction of hazardous events with conditions of exposure, vulnerability, and capacity[13]—that

[6] IPCC, *Climate Change 2014: Impacts, Adaptation and Vulnerability*, Summary for Policymakers, 20.

[7] IPCC, *Global warming of 1.5°C—Special Report* (2018) 235 (emphasis added).

[8] Ibid, 245 (emphasis added).

[9] Kanta Rigaud *et al*, *Groundswell: Preparing for Internal Climate Migration* (World Bank 2018) 110.

[10] See The Nansen Initiative, 'Agenda for the Protection of Cross-Border Displaced Persons in the Context of Disasters and Climate Change—Volume 1' (2015) 16. IPCC acknowledges that 'social, economic and environmental factors underlying migration are complex . . . ; therefore, detecting the effect of observed climate change . . . with any degree of confidence is challenging'; see IPCC, *Global Warming of 1.5°C* (n 7) 244.

[11] IDMC, 'Disaster-related Displacement Risk: Measuring the Risk and Addressing its Drivers' (2015) 27.

[12] See The Nansen Initiative, 'Volume 1' (n 10). It was endorsed in October 2015 by 109 states. On the background, structure, and process of The Nansen Initiative see Walter Kälin, 'Disaster Displaced Persons in the Age of Climate Change: The Nansen Initiative's Protection Agenda' in Flavia Giustiniani *et al* (eds), *Human Rights in Times of Disaster: International Law Put to the Test* (Routledge 2018) 349.

[13] UN Office for Disaster Risk Reduction (UNDRR) defines disaster as '[A] serious disruption of the functioning of a community or a society at any scale due to hazardous events interacting with

ultimately compel people to leave their homes, rather than the presence of natural hazards as such.[14]

Similarly, migration as the predominantly voluntary movement of persons 'is often used as a coping mechanism' or as an option to 'avoid anticipated disasters triggering displacement in the future'.[15] The ability to migrate indicates a person's ability to respond to disaster risk by taking steps to avoid exposure or cope with the impacts of a natural hazard, such as by sending money to family members to enable structural home improvements.

The 2018 Global Compact for Safe, Orderly and Regular Migration (GCM)[16] explicitly recognizes and provides for measures in line with this understanding. Under Objective 2 on minimizing adverse drivers of migration, states commit to create conditions allowing people to lead satisfactory lives in their countries and ensure that 'deteriorating environments do not compel them to seek livelihoods elsewhere through irregular migration'.[17] Possible preventive actions are clustered under the document's only thematic sub-title, 'Natural disasters, the adverse effects of climate change and environmental degradation'.[18] Actions include: i) enhancing data and knowledge on migration that may result from sudden- or slow-onset environmental events;[19] ii) helping people at risk to stay in their countries through adaptation and resilience strategies;[20] iii) integrating displacement considerations into disaster preparedness strategies and cooperative arrangements with neighbouring and other relevant countries to prepare, inter alia, 'evacuation planning, reception and assistance';[21] iv) harmonizing and developing regional and sub-regional mechanisms to ensure access to humanitarian assistance for persons affected by sudden- or slow-onset disasters in line with their rights;[22] and v) developing 'coherent approaches to address the challenges of migration movements in the context of sudden- and slow-onset disasters', and in doing so, considering recommendations by the Nansen Initiative Protection Agenda.

conditions of exposure, vulnerability and capacity, leading to one or more of the following: human, material, economic and environmental losses and impacts'; see UNDRR, 'Terminology on Disaster Risk Reduction'—'Disaster' <https://www.unisdr.org/we/inform/terminology#letter-d> accessed 18 May 2019.

[14] The Nansen Initiative, 'Volume 1' (n 10) 16.

[15] Ibid, 17, with reference to Jon Barnett and Michael Webber, 'Migration as Adaptation: Opportunities and Limits' in McAdam (n 3) 37.

[16] UNGA, 'Intergovernmental Conference to Adopt the Global Compact for Safe, Orderly and Regular Migration—Draft outcome document of the Conference' (30 July 2018) UN Doc A/CONF.231/3, annex—'Global Compact for Safe, Orderly and Regular Migration'.

[17] Ibid, para 18.

[18] The sub-title inserted between GCM, ibid, paras 18(g) and 18(h) reads: 'Natural disasters, the adverse effects of climate change, and environmental degradation'.

[19] Ibid, para 18(h).

[20] Ibid, para 18(i).

[21] Ibid, para 18(j).

[22] Ibid, para 18(k). The wording of this sub-paragraph is somewhat convoluted but reference to affected persons 'wherever they are' suggests that it is intended to cover displaced persons too.

C. The Role of Environmental Law to Reduce Displacement Risk

1. *Reducing hazards*

It is possible to reduce hazards associated with climate change to prevent conditions that force people to move away from their homes. The full implementation of the 2015 Paris Agreement's commitment to 'holding the increase in the global average temperature to well below 2°C above pre-industrial levels' would be most effective by limiting the temperature increase to 1.5°C[23] through a significant reduction of greenhouse gas emissions.[24] Consequently, the Task Force on Displacement set up under the Warsaw Mechanism on Loss and Damage[25] recommends that states '[i]ntegrate human mobility challenges and opportunities into national planning processes, including nationally determined contributions'.[26]

2. *Reducing vulnerability and increasing resilience*

Disaster risk reduction and climate change adaptation measures that integrate displacement risk can significantly reduce vulnerability to the impacts of hazards and thus help people to stay in their homes.

While the Sendai Framework for Disaster Risk Reduction[27] promotes specific measures to reduce displacement risks through resilience-building measures,[28] climate change law is less explicit. Nevertheless, the so-called Cancun Climate Change Adaptation Framework adopted by the 2010 Conference of the Parties (COP) to the 1992 United Nations Framework Convention on Climate Change (UNFCCC) in Cancun invites states to enhance their action on adaptation, including through '[m]easures to enhance understanding, coordination and cooperation with regard to climate change induced displacement, migration and planned relocation'.[29] In 2019, the Task Force on

[23] art 2(a).

[24] See Daniel Bodansky, Jutta Brunnée, and Lavanya Rajamani, *International Climate Change Law* (OUP 2017) 131–136.

[25] Decision 1/CP.21, 'Adoption of the Paris Agreement' (12 December 2015) UN Doc FCCC/CP/2015/L.9/Rev.1, para 49.

[26] Decision 10/CP.24, 'Report of the Executive Committee of the Warsaw International Mechanism for Loss and Damage associated with Climate Change Impacts' (19 March 2019) UN Doc FCCC/CP/2018/10/Add.1, 40.

[27] UNGA Res 69/283, 'Sendai Framework for Disaster Risk Reduction 2015–2030' (23 June 2015) UN Doc A/RES/69/283, annex II.

[28] See ibid, in particular paras 28(d), 30(l); UNDRR, 'Disaster Displacement: How to Reduce Risk, Address Impacts and Strengthen Resilience—Words into Action' (2019) provides practical guidance on how to integrate disaster displacement and related forms of human mobility into disaster risk reduction strategies.

[29] Decision 1/CP.16, 'The Cancun Agreements: Outcome of the work of the Ad Hoc Working Group on Long-term Cooperative Action under the Convention' (15 March 2011) UN Doc FCCC/CP/2010/7/Add.1, para 14(f); see also Decision 3/CP.18, 'Approaches to address loss and damage associated with climate change impacts in developing countries that are particularly vulnerable

Displacement recommended integrating human mobility challenges into national climate change adaptation plans.[30]

While Article 7 of the Paris Agreement does not mention human mobility, its paragraph 9(e) obliges states to build resilience not only through economic diversification, but also as part of the 'sustainable management of natural resources'. In this regard, the 1992 Convention on Biodiversity (CBD) is particularly relevant. Ecosystems can, as was highlighted by the United Nations Environment Programme (UNEP), 'play a crucial role in climate change mitigation, for example through carbon sequestration and the reduction of greenhouse gas emissions'.[31] Furthermore, they may buffer 'societies from the impacts of climate change', such as when flood plains and mangrove forests 'provide natural protection against extreme weather events and rising sea levels'.[32] Consequently, the effects of both intact and restored ecosystems provide important contributions to reducing displacement risk. The 1994 UN Convention to Combat Desertification (UNCCD), with its aim to prevent land degradation in arid, semi-arid, and dry sub-humid areas and mitigate drought,[33] is another important instrument to address key drivers of displacement and migration. The UNCCD 2018–2030 Strategic Framework explicitly recognizes UNCCD's potential to reduce substantially migration forced by desertification and land degradation as a consequence of a broader objective to 'improve the living conditions of affected populations'.[34]

3. *Reducing exposure by helping people to move out of harm's way*

Reducing exposure to natural hazards to avoid displacement is also possible. Measures that allow people to move out of harm's way before disasters strike or to cope with the impacts in the aftermath of sudden- and slow-onset disasters include providing pathways for regular migration and facilitating planned relocation processes.

As stressed by the IPCC, '[e]xpanding opportunities for mobility can reduce vulnerability' for populations at risk.[35] Thus, '[c]hanges in migration patterns can be responses to both extreme weather events and long-term climate variability and change, and migration can also be an effective adaptation strategy'.[36] However, if circular, temporary, or

to the adverse effects of climate change to enhance adaptive capacity' (28 February 2013) UN Doc FCCC/CP/2012/8/Add.1, para 7(vi).

[30] Decision 10/CP.24 (n 26) annex, para 1(g)(iv).

[31] UNEP and World Conservation Monitoring Centre, 'Addressing climate change: Why biodiversity matters' (2014) 2.

[32] Ibid.

[33] arts 1, 2; National (art 10) and sub-regional or regional (art 11) action programmes are the main instruments to achieve these goals.

[34] Decision 7/COP.13 'The future strategic framework of the Convention' (23 October 2017) UN Doc ICCD/COP(13)/21/Add.1, annex—'UNCCD 2018–2030 Strategic Framework', para 5.

[35] IPCC, *Climate Change 2014* (n 6) 20.

[36] Ibid.

permanent migration is irregular and not properly supported, people may be exposed to exploitation and discrimination and thus become even more vulnerable.[37]

International instruments rarely address how to use migration to reduce exposure to natural hazards. The legally non-binding GCM is an exception, with its commitment under Objective 5 to enhance *pathways for regular migration* in order to, inter alia, 'respond to the needs of migrants in a situation of vulnerability'.[38] Such pathways are particularly relevant for persons who seek temporary opportunities abroad as migrants to cope with the impacts of natural hazards, climate change, and environmental degradation and thus can profit from measures such as labour mobility schemes or free movement of persons regimes.

Planned relocation as a process in which communities 'are settled in a new location, and are provided with the conditions for rebuilding their lives' in order 'to protect persons from risks and impacts related to disasters and environmental change' is another measure to reduce exposure. It is usually undertaken within countries, for instance to move villages away from eroding coastlines.[39] The Sendai Framework calls for the development of planned relocation policies for human settlements located in disaster risk-prone zones (para 27(k)) and the 'identification of areas that are safe for human settlement' (para 30(g)). The GCM envisages planned relocation across international borders for people compelled to move as a consequence of slow-onset disasters, provided that 'adaptation in or return to their country of origin is not possible'.[40] Such relocation may become relevant in the future when the territory of low-lying atoll island states has become uninhabitable due to sea level rise. Planned relocation is a measure of last resort that must be undertaken with the consent of affected communities and with full respect for relevant human rights of relocated persons.[41]

D. Protecting Displaced Persons

Reducing hazards and exposure, and increasing the resilience of people at risk of displacement, are important measures to manage displacement risk. At the same time,

37 Koko Warner *et al*, 'Where the Rain Falls: Climate Change, Food and Livelihood Security and Migration: Global Policy Report' (UNU-EHS 2012) 17.

38 GCM (n 16) para 21.

39 See Government of Fiji, 'Planned Relocation Guidelines—A framework to undertake climate change related relocation' (2018) <https://www.refworld.org/docid/5c3c92204.html> accessed 18 May 2019.

40 GCM (n 16) para 21(h).

41 Res 6/2018, Committee on International Law and Sea Level Rise, 78th Conference of the International Law Association, held in Sydney, Australia, 19–24 August 2018, annex—'Sydney Declaration of Principles on the Protection of Persons Displaced in the Context of Sea Level Rise', principle 6. On this and other requirements stemming from international human rights law see Bruce Burson *et al*, 'The Duty to Move People Out of Harm's Way in the Context of Climate Change and Disasters' *Refugee Survey Quarterly*, 37/4 (2018): 379, 398–401.

displacement cannot always be avoided and may even be a lifesaving measure. In these circumstances, displaced people need specific protection.[42]

As mentioned above, the vast majority of people displaced in the context of disasters and climate change become 'internally displaced persons' (IDPs). At the normative level, their protection is relatively well developed.[43] The legally non-binding 1998 UN Guiding Principles on Internal Displacement[44] have been recognized by the international community as an 'important international framework for the protection of internally displaced persons'.[45] Their personal scope of application includes persons forced to flee or leave their homes for reasons of human-made or natural disasters. At the African regional level, the same is true for the binding 2006 Great Lakes IDP Protocol[46] and the 2009 Kampala Convention. In addition to disaster IDPs, the latter also refers to persons displaced by climate change.[47] However, without proper incorporation into the domestic legal order, all these normative frameworks are difficult to implement. In 2018, Vanuatu set a good example with the adoption of a policy specifically addressing climate change and disaster-induced internal displacement.[48]

People *displaced across borders* in the context of disasters and climate change legally qualify as refugees in only rare cases.[49] At the centre of this branch of law lies the notion of persecution or similar harm emanating from *human actors in the country of origin*,[50]

[42] On the protection needs of disaster-displaced persons see Walter Kälin and Hannah Chapuisat, 'Displacement in the Context of Disasters And Adverse Effects of Climate Change' in Susan Breau and Katja Samuel (eds), *Research Handbook on Disasters and International Law* (Edward Elgar 2016) 358.

[43] See Elizabeth Ferris, 'The Relevance of the Guiding Principles on Internal Displacement for the Climate-Migration Nexus' in Benoît Mayer and François Crépeau (eds), *Climate Change, Migration and the Law* (Edward Elgar 2017) 108–130; Ademola Jegede, 'Indigenous Peoples, Climate Migration and International Human Rights Law in Africa, with Reflections on the Relevance of the Kampala Convention' in ibid, 169–189.

[44] UN Human Rights Commission, 'Report of the Representative of the Secretary-General, Mr. Francis M. Deng, submitted pursuant to Commission resolution 1997/39 – Addendum: Guiding Principles on Internal Displacement' (11 February 1998) UN Doc E/CN.4/1998/53/Add.2 (1998).

[45] UNGA Res 60/01, '2005 World Summit Outcome' (24 October 2005) UN Doc A/RES/60/1, para 132 and many subsequent resolutions by the UN General Assembly and Human Rights Council.

[46] International Conference on the Great Lakes Region, 'Protocol on the Protection and Assistance to Internally Displaced Persons' (30 November 2006) <https://www.refworld.org/docid/52384fe44.html> accessed 18 May 2019.

[47] 2009 African Union Convention for the Protection and Assistance of Internally Displaced Persons in Africa (Kampala Convention), art 5.4.

[48] Vanuatu National Disaster Management Office, 'National Policy on Climate Change and Disaster-Induced Displacement 2018'. The Policy identifies twelve strategic areas at institutional and operational levels, delineating time-bound actions for each.

[49] See Sanjula Weerasinghe, 'In Harm's Way—International Protection in the Context of Nexus Dynamics between Conflict or Violence and Disaster or Climate Change' *Legal and Protection Policy Series, UNHCR* (December 2018) PPLA/2018/05.

[50] See the New Zealand cases *AF (Kiribati)* (25 June 2013) NZIPT 800413 [54], upheld on appeal, including in *Teitiota v The Chief Executive of the Ministry of Business, Innovation and Employment* (20 July 2015) NZSC 107; see also *AC (Tuvalu)* (2014) NZIPT 800517-520. For a more general discussion see Jane McAdam, *Climate Change, Forced Migration, and International Law* (OUP 2012) 39–51; Hélène Ragheboom, *The International Legal Status and Protection of Environmentally-Displaced Persons: A European Perspective* (Brill 2017) 293–357.

which is not the case even with regard to man-made global warming. To address this protection gap, some authors promote the idea of elaborating conventions creating a specific protection status for 'climate change refugees' or 'environmentally-displaced persons'.[51] These endeavours have not found much traction in the international community,[52] not only because of the present political unwillingness to expand refugee protection to new categories but also for other, more conceptual reasons.[53]

Another approach invokes concepts of 'climate justice' to justify expansion of the refugee definition and builds upon the fact that most people displaced by the adverse effects of climate change are not responsible for global warming, and therefore deserve special protection, to justify the creation of a legal status for such persons.[54] From a human rights perspective it is difficult to justify the exclusion of individuals displaced by disasters linked to geo-physical hazards and weather events not attributable to climate change who might have the same protection needs.[55] Even more importantly, the concept of 'climate refugee' presupposes that persons applying for such status would have to show that their displacement has been caused by the effects of global warming. However, despite progress in climate science,[56] most 'climate asylum seekers' would be unable to make a credible case that the specific weather event they were escaping was attributable to global warming. Such claims would also risk being rejected due to the multi-causality[57] of such displacement.

Presently, the international community is taking a different approach. Instead of creating new legal obligations, it has sought to build on effective practices found in the domestic migration law of some countries.

The Global Compact on Migration, Objective 5 envisages actions such as the provision of humanitarian visas or temporary work permits for people displaced across borders in the context of sudden-onset disasters 'while adaptation in or return to their country of origin is not possible', and permanent admission when, for instance due to sea level rise, such adaptation is impossible in the long run.[58] Under Objective 21 states

[51] See in particular Bonnie Docherty and Tyler Giannini, 'Confronting a Rising Tide: A Proposal for a Convention on Climate Change Refugees' *Harvard Environmental Law Review*, 33/2 (2009): 349; Michel Prieur, 'Draft Convention on the International Status of Environmentally-Displaced Persons' *The Urban Lawyer*, 42/43 (2011): 247.

[52] See, however, the decision by Heads of Government from the Polynesian Leaders Group to 'support Tuvalu's efforts to seek legal protection for people displaced by climate change through a UN General Assembly resolution'—'Amatuku Declaration on Climate Change and Oceans by the Polynesian Leaders Group' (adopted on 29 June 2018), para 9.

[53] See Jane McAdam, 'Swimming against the Tide: Why a Climate Change Displacement Treaty is Not the Answer' *International Journal of Refugee Law*, 23/1 (2011): 2.

[54] For a discussion of such approaches see Peter Penz, 'International Ethical Responsibilities to "Climate Change Refugees"' in McAdam (n 3) 151.

[55] Kälin (n 12) 352.

[56] See eg the studies cited in Hannah Parker *et al*, 'Using a Game to Engage Stakeholders in Extreme Event Attribution' *International Journal of Disaster Risk Science*, 7/4 (2016): 353, 355; see also Rachel James *et al*, 'Attribution: How Is It Relevant for Loss and Damage Policy and Practice?' in Reinhard Mechler *et al*, *Loss and Damage from Climate Change* (Springer 2019) 113.

[57] See Section II.B.

[58] GCM (n 16) para 21(g).

commit to '[c]ooperate in facilitating safe and dignified return and readmission, as well as sustainable reintegration', which is important to ending temporary protection measures and finding durable solutions for displaced persons upon return.[59]

The GCM also envisages, as an effective practice, 'visa options' for the permanent admission of persons:

> compelled to leave their countries of origin due to slow-onset natural disasters, the adverse effects of climate change, and environmental degradation, such as desertification, land degradation, drought and sea level rise in cases where adaptation in or return to their country of origin is not possible.[60]

People displaced temporarily or permanently across borders may also invoke states' commitment in Objective 21, which upholds the prohibition of forcing migrants to return to their countries of origin when they face a foreseeable risk of 'other irreparable harm' in addition to 'death, torture, and other cruel, inhuman, and degrading treatment'.

The Global Compact for Refugees (GCR) addresses the issue in a very limited way, in particular by mentioning that relevant stakeholders may provide guidance on 'measures to assist those forcibly displaced by natural disasters, taking into account national laws and regional instruments as applicable, as well as practices such as temporary protection and humanitarian stay arrangements, where appropriate'.[61] This not only reflects the reluctance of states to deal with cross-border disaster-displacement in the context of refugee law and policy, but also suggests that the GCM rather than the GCR will be the centre of gravity for future discussions and actions on cross-border disaster- and climate change-related human mobility.

Regional organizations and processes are increasingly recognizing the challenges of cross-border movements in the context of disasters. One example is the Regional Conference on Migration (RCM) in Central America, the Caribbean, and North America, which adopted 'A Guide to Effective Practices for RCM Member Countries: Protection for persons moving across borders in the context of disasters' in November 2016.[62] This is in line with the GCM, paragraph 21(g)'s suggestion to '[d]evelop and build on existing national and regional practices for admission and stay of appropriate duration based on compassionate, humanitarian or other considerations for migrants compelled to leave their countries of origin, due to sudden-onset natural disasters and other precarious situations', and sets an example for other regions.

Environmental law cannot directly contribute to the protection of displaced persons. However, the Task Force on Displacement working under the auspices of the Warsaw International Mechanism for Loss and Damage[63] has presented a first set of, albeit very

[59] See ibid, para 37(e), (h).

[60] Ibid, para 21(h).

[61] 'Report of the United Nations High Commissioner for Refugees—Part II—Global compact on refugees' (2018) UN Doc A/73/12(Part II) para 63.

[62] <https://www.preventionweb.net/publications/view/58189> accessed 18 May 2019.

[63] Decision 1/CP.21 (n 25) para 49.

general, recommendations on this topic. They were endorsed in 2018[64] and represent a first (limited) attempt to look at displacement from a loss and damage perspective.

Environmental law may be relevant for addressing the harmful impact of large numbers of refugees and other displaced persons on the environment as, for instance, in the case of large refugee[65] or IDP camps and settlements. In such situations, the principle of precautionary action suggests that refugee hosting countries have the primary responsibility to take 'cost-effective measures to prevent environmental degradation'[66] and proactively seek support from the international community. In this regard, UN member states strive 'to support environmental ... rehabilitation in areas affected by large movements of refugees'.[67]

The principle of precaution also applies to situations where voluntary migration risks having serious impacts on the environment. Rural to urban migration, for instance, and the ensuing appearance of irregular settlements may, if not well managed, lead to land degradation, contamination of ground water, and other negative environmental impacts.[68]

III. MITIGATING CONSERVATION-INDUCED RELOCATION AND DISPLACEMENT

A. A Dilemma

Environmental protection may call for the prohibition of human settlements in vulnerable ecosystems or wildlife areas designated as protected areas in accordance with the CBD, Article 8 and thus necessitate the relocation of people living there. This creates specific dilemmas as the environmental gains may be offset by the loss of access to livelihoods and cultural traditions.[69] To mitigate this dilemma, international law requires that relocations and prohibitions to return to one's former home be in accordance with

[64] Decision 10/CP.24 (n 26) annex, paras 1(g)(v)–(vi).

[65] See eg UN Development Programme, 'Report on Environmental Impact of Rohingya Influx' (March 2018).

[66] *Report of the United Nations Conference on Environment and Development* (UN 1993) vol I, annex I—'Rio Declaration on Environment and Development', principle 15; see Chapter 18, 'Precaution', in this volume.

[67] UNGA Res 71/1, 'New York Declaration for Refugees and Migrants' (3 October 2016) UN Doc A/RES/71/1, para 85.

[68] See eg Ionesco, Mokhnacheva, and Gemenne (n 4) 80.

[69] Asmita Kabra, 'Dilemmas of Conservation Displacement from Protected Areas' in Michael Cernea and Julie Maldonado (eds), *Challenging the Prevailing Paradigm of Displacement and Resettlement* (Routledge 2018) 88. On the negative impacts of climate mitigation projects under the REDD+ framework on Indigenous communities in Africa see Jegede (n 43) 174–176.

relevant provisions of human rights law to avoid prohibited arbitrary displacement or forced eviction. This is mandatory, as the CBD does not affect the obligations of states parties under other international agreements.[70] The Guiding Principles on Internal Displacement list the conditions for lawful relocation. According to Principle 7(3), which synthesizes relevant treaty and soft law norms, decisions to relocate must be taken by an authority empowered by law to order such a measure; those to be moved must be given 'full information on the reasons and procedures for their displacement and, where applicable, on compensation and relocation'; people's free and informed consent must be sought; all those affected should be involved in the planning and management; any law enforcement measures must be executed by competent legal authorities; and the right to an effective remedy (including judicial review) must be respected.[71] Guarantees regarding the relocation of Indigenous peoples enshrined in the 1989 ILO Convention No 169,[72] and the UNDRIP,[73] are even stricter.[74]

At the regional level, two important African cases illustrate the relevance of human rights law for Indigenous peoples, as well as the limits such law imposes on states creating protected areas. In 2009, the African Commission on Human and Peoples' Rights found that Kenya violated the rights of the Endorois Indigenous people to use and enjoy the natural resources it traditionally owned as well as the rights to development and to a satisfactory environment under the 1981 African Convention on Human and Peoples' Rights (ACHPR) when, in order to make space for a game park, they were displaced from their lands without adequate compensation and redress.[75] In 2017, the African Court on Human and Peoples' Rights recognized that the right to property (ACHPR, Article 14) applies not only to individuals but also to groups or communities

[70] art 22.1.

[71] These duties derive inter alia from the 1966 International Covenant on Economic, Social and Cultural Rights (ICESCR), arts 4, 11; 1966 International Covenant on Civil and Political Rights (ICCPR), arts 2.3, 12.3, 25(a); 1989 ILO Convention No 169 Concerning Indigenous and Tribal Peoples in Independent Countries, art 16; UNGA Res 61/295, 'United Nations Declaration on the Rights of Indigenous Peoples' (2 October 2007) UN Doc A/RES/61/295 (UNDRIP) art 10; see also UN Human Rights Council, 'Report of the Special Rapporteur on adequate housing as a component of the right to an adequate standard of living' (5 February 2007) UN Doc A/HRC/4/18, annex I—'Basic principles and guidelines on development-based evictions and displacement', para 37. For more details see Burson *et al* (n 41) 398–401; see also World Bank, 'Operational Manual: OP 4.12—Involuntary Resettlement' (2014) para 6(a); African Development Bank & African Development Fund, 'Involuntary Resettlement Policy' (November 2003); Asian Development Bank, 'ADB Policy Paper: Safeguard Policy Statement' (June 2009) <https://www.adb.org/sites/default/files/institutional-document/32056/safeguard-policy-statement-june2009.pdf> accessed 19 January 2020; Practical guidance on planned relocation can be found in Brookings Institution, Georgetown University, and United Nations High Commissioner for Refugees (UNHCR), 'Guidance on Protecting People from Disasters and Environmental Change Through Planned Relocation' (7 October 2015).

[72] art 16.

[73] arts 10, 28.1.

[74] See Chapters 42 and 45, 'Indigenous Peoples' and 'Human Rights', in this volume.

[75] *Centre for Minority Rights Development (Kenya) and Minority Rights Group (on behalf of Endorois Welfare Council) v Kenya*, AComHPR (2009) Communication No 276/03, in particular [147] ff and [251] ff referring to ACHPR, arts 21, 22, 24.

as a collective right[76] and found a violation with regard to the Ogiek people who were evicted from the Kenyan Mau Forest although the government had been unable to show that their continued presence would have jeopardized the envisaged preservation of the natural ecosystem in question.[77]

B. Emerging Standards

Conservation efforts have been heavily criticized with the argument that the creation of protected areas has led to the unjustified 'displacement of tens of millions of people who formerly lived, hunted, fished, and farmed in areas now protected for wildlife, watersheds, reefs, forests, or rare ecosystems'.[78] While there are still no universal legal standards specifically addressing conservation-induced displacement, some important steps can be identified.

At the global level, safeguards established by World Bank and other financial institutions are particularly important. The World Bank's Environmental and Social Standard 5 (ESS5),[79] which must be met by borrowers receiving Bank financing and also applies to conservation measures,[80] serves to 'avoid involuntary resettlement' as well as 'forced eviction'. The Standard stipulates that when resettlement is unavoidable, borrowers must 'minimize involuntary resettlement by exploring project design alternatives' as well as 'mitigate unavoidable adverse social and economic impacts from land acquisition or restrictions on land use'.[81] ESS5 contains very detailed requirements for borrowers, including with regard to community engagement,[82] grievance mechanisms,[83] and the many aspects of actual displacement[84] as well as the details of resettlement plans.[85] It covers not only physical displacement of persons forced to leave a specific area, but also 'economic displacement',[86] defined as 'loss of land, assets or access to assets, including those that lead to loss of income sources or other means of livelihood'[87] of persons who live outside protected areas.

[76] *African Commission on Human and Peoples' Rights v Republic of Kenya*, ACtHPR (2017) Application No 006/2012, reprinted in 56 ILM 730 (2017) [123].

[77] Ibid [129] ff. Furthermore, the prohibition to access religious sites in the Mau Forest violated the freedom of religion, ibid [162].

[78] Arun Agrawal and Kent Redford, 'Conservation and Displacement: An Overview' *Conservation and Displacement: An Overview*, 7/1 (2009): 1, 5–6; Kabra (n 69) 88–92, both with numerous references.

[79] World Bank, 'The World Bank Environmental and Social Framework' (2017) 53—'Environmental and Social Standard 5: Land Acquisition, Restrictions on Land Use and Involuntary Resettlement'.

[80] See the general scope of application and explicit reference to protected areas in ibid, paras 4, 21.

[81] Ibid, para 2.

[82] Ibid, paras 17, 18.

[83] Ibid, para 19.

[84] Ibid, paras 26–36.

[85] Ibid, annex 1—'Involuntary resettlement instruments'.

[86] Ibid, 104.

[87] Ibid, paras 33–36.

These requirements are also reflected in the standards of the Global Environment Facility (GEF)[88] that seek to avoid or at least minimize involuntary resettlement,[89] and the 'Policy on Conservation and Human Rights for Sustainable Development' adopted in 2012 by the International Union for Conservation of Nature (IUCN).[90] The adoption of a rights-based approach to conservation by an influential organization such as the IUCN is an important step forward.

Regional conventions such as the 1940 Western Hemisphere Convention[91] and the 1985 ASEAN Agreement on the Conservation of Nature and Natural Resources[92] follow the traditional approach of excluding human settlements from protected areas without reference to the rights of affected people and communities. In contrast, the revised African Convention on the Conservation of Nature and Natural Resources[93] of 2003 offers an approach to reconciling conservation with the rights of communities unwilling to relocate. While calling for the establishment of conservation areas, it does not provide for relocation. Rather, it obliges parties to 'promote the establishment by local communities of areas managed by them primarily for the conservation and sustainable use of natural resources'[94] and 'to enable active participation by the local communities in the process of planning and management of natural resources upon which such communities depend'.[95] The Convention thus opts for participatory and community-based, rather than exclusionary, conservation approaches.[96] These developments suggest that the following standards are emerging in the realm of environmental law and policy:

(i) Conservation measures such as the creation of protected areas do not necessarily require the displacement or relocation of people and communities. Therefore, alternatives to displacement, such as community-based conservation arrangements should be prioritized.

88 The Global Environment Facility is the financial mechanism for the CBD, UNFCCC, UNCCD, and related international agreements.

89 The Global Environment Facility, 'Policy on Environmental and Social Safeguards' Policy: SD/PL/03 (last updated on 13 June 2019) para 9: 'Minimum Standard 4: Restrictions on Land Use and Involuntary Resettlement' contains detailed guidance on how to achieve this goal. The GEF 'does not finance involuntary resettlement of Indigenous Peoples'; see GEF, *Principles and Guidelines for Engagement with Indigenous Peoples* (2012) 21.

90 IUCN, 'Policy on Conservation and Human Rights for Sustainable Development' WCC-2012-Res-099-EN, annex.

91 Convention on Nature Protection and Wildlife Preservation in the Western Hemisphere.

92 art 13.2 even provides that 'Contracting Parties shall, wherever possible, prohibit within such protected areas activities which are inconsistent with such objectives' which can be read as, at least in some situations, to displace people living there.

93 African Convention on the Conservation of Nature and Natural Resources (Revised Version) (adopted 11 July 2003, entered into force 23 July 2016) <https://au.int/en/treaties/african-convention-conservation-nature-and-natural-resources-revised-version> accessed 19 January 2020.

94 art XII(3).

95 art XVII.

96 On the shift to community-based conservation in general and its limitations see Kabra (n 69) 98–100.

(ii) Information for, consultation with, and the participation of affected people and communities are essential. Their free, prior, and informed consent to being removed from protected areas should be sought in all cases. In the case of Indigenous communities dependent on their ancestral lands, relocation without such consent is not permissible.

(iii) Where displacement cannot be avoided or is undertaken without the consent of affected people and communities, it must be implemented with full respect for their rights.

IV. CONCLUSION

For a long time, environmental and migration law were separate branches of international law with little, if any, interaction. This is changing, particularly as the climate change negotiations under the UNFCCC increasingly focus on the need to adapt to the human consequences of global warming, and deal with loss and damage posed by climate change, which includes forced displacement and the permanent loss of habitable land. Human mobility is, thus, becoming part of emerging rules of climate change law. At the same time, the humanitarian consequences of large-scale displacement in the context of sudden-onset disasters and environmental degradation, as well as climate change's economic consequences as drivers of migration, have motived states to address disaster- and climate change-related displacement and migration in several instruments including, in particular, the GCM and the Sendai Framework. Although they largely constitute soft rather than hard law, these instruments, together with conventions in the area of environmental law that are relevant for the prevention of displacement, such as the Paris Agreement, the CBD, and the UNCCD, as well as recent standards on planned relocation from protected conservation areas, are pertinent for the field of environmental law insofar as they increasingly converge towards what could be called the law of environmental migration.

BIBLIOGRAPHY

Robert McLeman and François Gemenne (eds), *Routledge Handbook of Environmental Displacement and Migration* (Routledge 2018)

Benoît Mayer and François Crépeau (eds), *Climate Change, Migration and the Law* (Edward Elgar 2017)

Jane McAdam (ed), *Climate Change and Displacement: Multidisciplinary Perspectives* (Hart Publishing 2010)

Jane McAdam, *Climate Change, Forced Migration, and International Law* (OUP 2012)

Hélène Ragheboom, *The International Legal Status and Protection of Environmentally-Displaced Persons: A European Perspective* (Brill 2017)

The Nansen Initiative, 'Agenda for the Protection of Cross-Border Displaced Persons in the Context of Disasters and Climate Change—Volume 1' (2015)

CHAPTER 47

DISASTER

ROBERT R M VERCHICK AND PAUL RINK*

I. INTRODUCTION

A handbook on environmental protection would be incomplete without an examination of disaster law and policy. This is so for two reasons. First, environmental disturbances—along with armed conflict[1]—cause or contribute to most of the world's catastrophic events. To understand the environment's role in affecting human well-being, one must appreciate the special characteristics of disaster risk and the strategies used to address that risk. Second, disasters (by definition) have profound effects on the surrounding environment: human and non-human, biological, geo-physical, chemical, economic, political, and social. How well we approach disaster risk helps determine how functional our surrounding environment will be.

This chapter examines a range of international laws and policies used to manage disaster risk, focusing on those that are particularly relevant to environmental issues. It begins with a brief look at global disaster risk in the twenty-first century, placing it in the context of natural systems, human activities, and, of course, climate change. It then examines the United Nations' (UN) major frameworks on reducing disaster risk (the Hyogo and Sendai Frameworks), along with the international strategy to implement framework goals (the UN Plan of Action). Finally, this chapter turns to other areas of international law that have strong overlapping interests in disaster risk, particularly ecosystem management and rules pertaining to transboundary harm.

First, a few words on terminology and social context. The UN Office of Disaster Risk Reduction (UNDRR, formerly UNISDR) defines disaster as 'a serious disruption of the functioning of a community or a society involving widespread human, material, economic or environmental losses and impacts, which exceeds the ability of the affected

* The authors are grateful to Kaitlin Brockett, who provided excellent research assistance.

[1] See Chapter 50, 'Armed Conflict', in this volume.

community or society to cope using its own resources'.[2] A disaster's impact is thus a function of an external *force* of disruption and an internal ability to *cope*. Much of the law in this area focuses on disruptions triggered by natural forces like cyclones, tsunamis, or wildfires. Such events are often called 'natural disasters', although the truth is that nearly all disasters betray some human failing, whether it be poor planning, faulty infrastructure, or inadequate emergency response. Add climate change, and our fingerprints are everywhere. For this reason, the main disaster regimes tend to avoid sharp distinctions between natural and human-caused events. One important exception, discussed later in the chapter, involves disasters in which one party is liable for harming another party, as in an oil spill or industrial explosion.

Disasters are sometimes divided into those that are 'sudden-onset' (a volcanic eruption, a chemical leak) and those that are 'slow-onset' (desertification, sea level rise). The main disaster regimes address both, with the exception of liability law which, because of the need to trace a causative link, tends to concentrate on more straight-forward events that occur suddenly.

When studying disaster law, it is helpful to think of a 'Circle of Risk Management' which can be visualized as points on a clock face (see Figure 47.1).[3] Beginning at twelve o'clock—before disaster strikes—we have the planning, or 'risk-reduction' stage. The goal here is to minimize the potential for damage when the big one hits. At two o'clock, disaster strikes. Just afterward, at three o'clock, comes the emergency response. Six o'clock represents compensatory efforts to get people back on their feet and restore vital ecosystems. Nine o'clock begins the long road to recovery, which, ideally, feeds into a thoughtful process of risk-reduction planning. Some of these stages take longer than others, and they will often overlap.

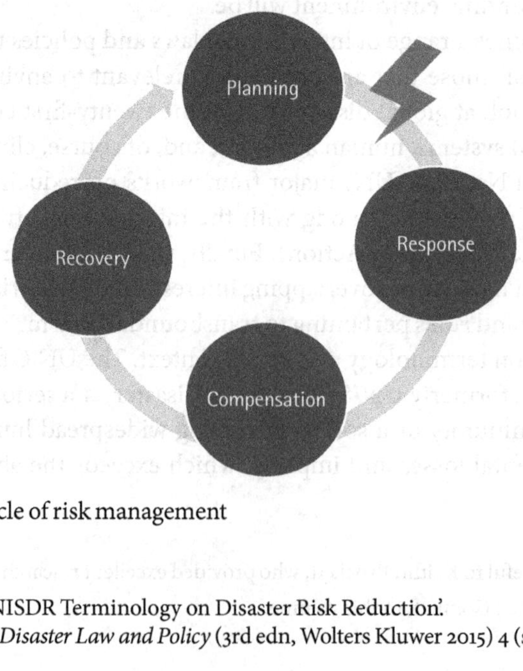

FIGURE 47.1 The circle of risk management

[2] UNDRR, '2009 UNISDR Terminology on Disaster Risk Reduction'.

[3] Daniel Farber *et al*, *Disaster Law and Policy* (3rd edn, Wolters Kluwer 2015) 4 (suggesting this image).

A community's *social* vulnerability is, in part, determined during the planning stage of the Circle of Risk Management and has an enormous impact on all the other stages. Social vulnerability is an essential aspect of a community's ability to survive a disruption, respond to the threat, and build back in a way that is safer and more resilient. Across the globe, social vulnerability amplifies risk on every point of the risk management circle.[4] The poor and marginalized live in cheaper, more disaster-prone areas; and they are less prepared for extreme events. When disaster hits, engrained patterns of discrimination make it harder for them to access the services, supplies, and shelter they need.[5] Recovery comes more slowly too. In the disaster context, unequal treatment and outcomes based on income, race, ethnicity, religion, caste, and disability have all been documented.[6] In many countries, women and children are at a special disadvantage, lacking money, transport, or even the ability to swim.[7] And in oppressive, authoritarian regimes all of this can get much worse, leading to epic human and environmental tragedy.[8]

These facts explain why the ability to *cope* is highlighted in the UN's definition of disaster. To be effective, risk management strategies must necessarily address *social* vulnerabilities, in addition to the more obvious *geo-physical* ones.

With this in mind, one can conceptualize international disaster law as the combination of treaties, principles, and customs that protect human and environmental well-being along with all points of the Circle of Risk Management. Some international laws are designed to address specific geo-physical risks like drought and desertification.[9] Other initiatives, such as the Hyogo and Sendai Frameworks and the UN Plan of Action on Disaster Risk Reduction, attack the problem holistically. In addition, many international mechanisms work indirectly to help manage and reduce catastrophic risk in important ways by establishing liability rules and other protections for ecosystems and human rights.

II. THE WORLD IS A DANGEROUS PLACE

Every year, natural disasters cause thousands of deaths and cost billions of dollars in disaster aid, disruption of commerce, and destruction of homes and critical infrastructure. In 2013, Typhoon Haiyan tore across the central Philippines, killing more than 6,000

[4] See Robert Verchick, *Facing Catastrophe: Environmental Action for a Post Katrina World* (Harvard University Press 2010) 107–116.

[5] Ibid, 110–111.

[6] Ibid, 111–116.

[7] Ibid, 112.

[8] Ibid, 113.

[9] 1994 Convention to Combat Desertification in those Countries Experiencing Serious Drought and/or Desertification, particularly in Africa.

people and costing USD 13 billion in economic damage.[10] In 2018, Hurricane Maria crashed through the Antilles and into the US territory of Puerto Rico.[11] In Puerto Rico, alone, nearly 3,000 people are thought to have died.[12] At the time, the island's government put the cost of immediate recovery needs at USD 94 billion.[13] But disaster is about more than wind and rain. The European heatwave of 2003 was the worst natural disaster to strike the developed world in modern history. 70,000 people lost their lives in what was the hottest European summer in 500 years.[14] In 2012, a record heat wave in the Moscow region, along with related wildfires, claimed 56,000 lives.[15] One-third of Russia's grain was lost, driving up food prices worldwide.[16]

A UN survey of disaster loss from 2005 to 2015 shows the big picture. During that time, some 700,000 people were killed, more than 1.4 million people were injured, and roughly 23 million were left homeless.[17] In those ten years, disasters are thought to have affected more than 1.5 billion people in various ways, with women and children being disproportionately burdened.[18] Economic loss totalled more than USD 1.3 trillion.[19] Studies show that disaster fatalities in the global South dwarf those in the global North, while the quantum of economic loss goes the other way around.[20] Of course, the practical effects of economic damage in the South are unquestionably higher: even comparatively small losses in a poor country can represent a significant share of its gross domestic product (GDP).[21]

Several factors explain such high loss. The human population is growing and expanding into areas that are more prone to natural hazards, such as coastlines, flood

[10] 'Typhoon Haiyan and the Philippines—Stress Test: Responding to this disaster is essential, but so is preparing for the next' *The Economist* (16 November 2013) (noting fatalities); Aon Benfield, 'Annual Global Climate and Catastrophe Report: Impact Forecasting—2013', 4, exhibit 1.

[11] Sarah Almukhtar *et al*, 'Maps: Hurricane Maria's Path Across Puerto Rico' *New York Times* (18 September 2017).

[12] Sheri Fink, 'Nearly a Year After Hurricane Maria, Puerto Rico Revises Death Toll to 2,975' *New York Times* (28 August 2018).

[13] Erik Wassan, 'Trump $44 Billion Aid Request Puts Off Puerto Rico Demands' *Bloomberg News* (17 November 2017) (Puerto Rico's estimate also factored in damage from Hurricane Irma, which had skirted the island earlier the same month).

[14] Anastasia Telesetsky, 'Insurance as a Mitigation Mechanism: Managing International Greenhouse Gas Emissions through Nationwide Mandatory Climate Change Catastrophe Insurance' *Pace Environmental Law Review*, 27/3 (2010): 691, 692.

[15] Patrick Reichenmiller *et al*, 'Weathering Climate Change: Insurance Solutions For More Resilient Communities' *Swiss Re* (2010) 1 <https://media.swissre.com/documents/A10485_Climate_adaption_Publication_A4.pdf> accessed 22 January 2020.

[16] Ibid, 13.

[17] UN General Assembly (UNGA) Res 69/283, 'Sendai Framework for Disaster Risk Reduction 2015–2030' (23 June 2015) UN Doc A/RES/69/283.

[18] Ibid.

[19] Ibid.

[20] See generally UNDRR, 'Risk and poverty in a changing climate' in 'Summary and Recommendations: 2009 Global Assessment Report on Disaster Risk Reduction' <https://www.preventionweb.net/files/9414_GARsummary.pdf> accessed 11 November 2018.

[21] Ibid.

plains, and precarious hillsides. Zoning and building codes are scant or non-existent in many countries, particularly in congested mega-cities. A lot of people lack the resources—information, transportation, social networks, money—to protect their assets and evacuate safely.

Climate change tightens the screws—cooking the landscape, raising the seas, upsetting rain patterns, and amplifying other 'climate-related extremes'.[22] According to the UN Intergovernmental Panel on Climate Change (IPCC), climate change impacts are now occurring 'on all continents and across the oceans'.[23] The effect of climate change on natural disaster is contentious and notoriously hard to pin down. It is very difficult, if not impossible, to establish a causal connection between climate change and a single extreme event, although our ability to make such assessments is likely to improve.[24] Regardless, the IPCC made clear the effect is there in a 2012 report on disasters and climate change.[25] The IPCC found it likely that 'the frequency of heavy precipitation or the proportion of total rainfall from heavy rainstorms will increase in the twenty-first century over many areas of the globe'.[26] Such downpours, it reported, will affect landslides in some areas and probably increase flooding in catchment areas. The IPCC found it likely that tropical cyclone speeds will increase and will pose particular threats to small island states.[27] It predicted that droughts will 'intensify . . . in some seasons and areas, due to reduced precipitation and/or increased evapotranspiration'.[28] Susceptible areas include, among others, southern Europe, Central America, and southern Africa.[29] In its most recent 2018 report, the IPCC reaffirmed these causative links and warned that some disaster risks could soar if global temperatures are allowed to rise much more than 1.5°C beyond pre-industrial levels.[30]

While natural disasters cause the most damage, man-made disasters can also inflict staggering harm. In 1984, for instance, an industrial accident at a Union Carbide

[22] Ibid.

[23] IPCC, *Climate Change 2014: The Synthesis Report* (2014) Summary for Policymakers, 6.

[24] See generally Mike Hulme, 'Attributing Weather Extremes to "Climate Change"' *Progress in Physical Geography*, 38/4 (2014): 499 (noting technical as well as conceptual challenges with cause-and-effect attribution); Thomas Knutson *et al*, 'Detection and Attribution of Climate Change' in Donald Wuebbles *et al* (eds), *Climate Science Special Report: Fourth National Climate Assessment* (US Global Change Research Program 2017) 1 (noting trend towards improvement).

[25] Sonia Seneviratne *et al*, 'Chapter 3—Changes in Climate Extremes and Their Impacts on the Natural Physical Environment' in Christopher Field *et al* (eds), *Managing the Risks of Extreme Events and Disasters to Advance Climate Change Adaption* (CUP 2012) 109.

[26] Ibid, 13.

[27] Ibid, 13, 15.

[28] Ibid.

[29] Ibid.

[30] IPCC, *Global warming of 1.5°C—Special Report* (2018) 3:6–3:13 (noting increased risks from heavy precipitation, flooding, and sea level rise with warming beyond 1.5°C, and a substantial increase in risks from heatwaves, drought, and water scarcity in such a scenario); see also Robert Verchick, 'Can "Loss and Damage" Carry the Load?' *Philosophical Transactions of the Royal Society A: Mathematical, Physical, and Engineering Sciences*, 376/2119 (2018) (examining the implications for addressing 'loss and damage' in scenarios where global warming exceeds 1.5°C).

plant in central India released tons of methyl isocyanate into the air above Bhopal. The gas—a toxic chemical used in making pesticides—killed an estimated 15,000 people and poisoned the landscape for generations.[31] The event is considered the worst industrial disaster in history. In 2010, a blowout on the Deepwater Horizon oil rig off the shore of Louisiana killed eleven workers and sent millions of barrels of petroleum billowing into the Gulf of Mexico for nearly three months.[32] Sometimes such technological disasters can be caused or aggravated by natural disasters. For example, the 2011 Great East Japan Earthquake and resulting tsunami triggered a chain of runaway events at Japan's Fukushima Daiichi Nuclear Power Plant, leading to three nuclear meltdowns, hydrogen-air explosions, and the release of dangerous amounts of radioactive material.[33] The long-term effects of that exposure on human populations and terrestrial and marine ecosystems remain uncertain.[34]

III. THE UNITED NATIONS AND DISASTER RISK REDUCTION

A. The Hyogo and Sendai Frameworks

The most significant and far-reaching international agreements on disaster are the Hyogo Framework for Action 2005–2015 and its successor—the Sendai Framework for Disaster Risk Reduction 2015–2030.[35] Adopted in January 2005, the Hyogo Framework established and extended a set of disaster initiatives through 2015 and charged the UN International Strategy for Disaster Reduction with overseeing their implementation.[36]

[31] Alan Taylor, 'Bhopal: The World's Worst Industrial Disaster, 30 Years Later' *The Atlantic* (2 December 2014).

[32] See National Commission on the BP Deepwater Horizon Oil Spill and Offshore Drilling, 'Deep Water: The Gulf Oil Disaster and the Future of Offshore Drilling: Report to the President' (January 2011).

[33] See International Atomic Energy Agency (IAEA), 'The Fukushima Daiichi Accident— Report by the Director General' (2015).

[34] Fred Pearce, 'What was the fallout from Fukushima?' *The Guardian* (3 June 2018); See Per Strand *et al*, 'On the Divergences in Assessment of Environmental Impacts from Ionising Radiation Following the Fukushima Accident' *Journal of Environmental Radioactivity*, 169–170 (2017): 159.

[35] Earlier, but less comprehensive efforts, include those of the World Conference on Natural Disaster Reduction at Yokohama, Japan from 23 to 27 May 1994; see International Decade for Natural Disaster Reduction (IDNDR) 1990–2000, 'Yokohama Strategy for a Safer World: Guidelines for Natural Disaster Prevention, Preparedness and Mitigation and its Plan of Action' (UN 1994) <https://www.unisdr.org/files/8241_doc6841contenido1.pdf> accessed 15 November 2018. (This established many of the principles expanded upon in Hyogo, and the Agenda for Humanitarian Action adopted by the International Conference of the Red Cross and Red Crescent in December 2003.) Note that many human rights treaties under the UN are also relevant to disaster management. For further discussion on international human rights law, see Chapter 45, 'Human Rights', in this volume.

[36] See UNDRR World Conference on Disaster Reduction, 'Hyogo Framework for Action 2005–2015: Building the Resilience of Nations and Communities to Disasters, extract from the Final Report of

The Hyogo Framework called upon governments to reduce disaster risk by developing 'national platforms' based on a series of goals that would guide regulatory and development decisions. The framework encouraged a multisector approach, paying special attention to issues of poverty, land use, and education. It promoted a strategy in which countries would incorporate risk reduction polices into more general initiatives dealing with economic development, environmental protection, scientific research, and other concerns. The framework urged wealthy countries to offer financial and technical assistance to poorer countries and to provide 'adequate voluntary financial contributions' to the UN's own disaster management fund.

Today more than eighty countries, from Afghanistan to the United Kingdom, have national platforms;[37] and more than 100 countries are monitoring progress towards framework goals. In earthquake-prone Kazakhstan, the UN Development Programme (UNDP) is helping to incorporate disaster response information in grade school curricula as a way of building resilience in poorer communities.[38] Nigeria, whose people suffer heavy rains and dangerous floods, has integrated risk reduction into its regional planning budgets and anti-poverty initiatives.[39] In Vietnam, a special partnership of government offices, private donors, and NGOs is promoting disaster management for the country's storm-swept jungles and shores; the project includes strategies for lifting villagers out of poverty as well as protecting river basins from environmental damage.[40] These efforts, combined with many others, appear to be working. For instance, since the Hyogo Framework took effect, the number of people in Asia who have been directly affected by natural disasters has fallen by almost one billion.[41]

Hyogo's successor agreement, the Sendai Framework for Disaster Risk Reduction, builds on the strategies of its predecessor but places greater emphasis on building technical capacity to understand global and regional risks in all of their dimensions. Like the Hyogo Framework, the Sendai Framework underlines the need for good governance, strong financial commitments, and recovery plans committed to 'building back better' in the aftermath of a disaster.[42] The Sendai Framework sets some ambitious goals over the next ten years, ranging from substantial reductions in damage to critical infrastructure and in disaster mortality, as well as more modest reductions in economic

the World Conference on Disaster Risk Reduction (A/CONF.206/6)' (2005) UN/ISDR-07-2007-Geneva <https://www.unisdr.org/files/1037_hyogoframeworkforactionenglish.pdf> accessed 11 November 2018.

[37] UNDRR, 'National Platforms' <https://www.preventionweb.net/english/hyogo/national/list/?pid:23&pih:2> accessed 11 November 2018.

[38] Alexandr Kravchuk, 'Republic of Kazakhstan—Disaster Risk Reduction Review' (July 2009) 8 <https://www.preventionweb.net/files/10481_DRRReviewKaz.pdf> accessed 15 November 2018.

[39] International Monetary Fund, 'Nigeria: Poverty Reduction Strategy Paper—National Economic Empowerment and Development Strategy' (2004) 33.

[40] Socialist Republic of Vietnam, 'Implementation of Sustainable Development: National Report at the United Nations Conference on Sustainable Development (RIO+20)' (Hanoi—May 2012) <https://sustainabledevelopment.un.org/content/documents/995vietnam.pdf≥ accessed 5 February 2020.

[41] 'Sendai: UN conference adopts new, people-centred disaster risk reduction strategy' *UN News* (18 March 2015).

[42] Sendai Framework (n 17) para 19(k).

losses from disaster damages.[43] While important in an aspirational sense, experts have already questioned whether some of the goals, such as the reduction of economic loss, are obtainable.[44]

B. Operationalizing Disaster Risk Reduction

The UN Plan of Action on Disaster Risk Reduction (UN Plan of Action) breathes life into the goals envisioned in Hyogo and Sendai. Released in 2013, the plan aims to strengthen communities most likely to be harmed by forces of nature—typically through sustainable, adaptive development.[45] Specifically, the plan provides 'the UN system with a common framework to strengthen system-wide coherence; build UN system capacity to deliver coordinated, high-quality support to countries on disaster risk reduction; and . . . ensure that disaster risk reduction remains a priority for UN organizations'.[46]

The UN Plan of Action sets guidelines and targets to facilitate progress towards its goals. For example, in order to achieve more coherent system-wide support of the Sendai Framework, the UN Plan of Action describes how disaster and climate risk reduction efforts should be incorporated into already existing sustainable development initiatives.[47] In order to develop support capacity within the UN, the Plan of Action seeks to build disaster risk information into country assessments, development assistance frameworks, and recovery programmes.[48] To ensure disaster risk reduction remains a top priority throughout the UN system, the Action Plan prescribes coherent stakeholder engagement as well as a 2020 monitoring and reporting target for installing disaster risk reduction into organizational strategic plans.[49]

The UN has also considered how disaster risk reduction can work best in the era of climate change. The 2007 Bali Action Plan implicitly recognized the interconnection between disaster risk reduction policies and existing climate change adaptation programmes.[50] There are many advantages to combining efforts within the two frameworks, not the least of which is consolidating work to save time and money.[51]

[43] Ibid, para 18.

[44] See 'New Study Shows Little Prospect of Reducing Economic Losses from Disasters' *UNDRR* (18 March 2015) <https://www.undrr.org/news/new-study-shows-little-prospect-reducing-economic-losses-disasters> accessed 5 February 2020.

[45] John Hay, *Disaster Risk Reduction & Climate Change Adaptation in the Pacific—An Institutional and Policy Analysis* (UNISDR and UNDP 2012) ii.

[46] International Organization for Migration (IOM) and UN Migration Agency, 'Taking Sendai Forward: IOM Strategic Work Plan on Disaster Risk Reduction & Resilience 2017–2020' (2013).

[47] UNDRR, 'United Nations Plan of Action on Disaster Risk Reduction for Resilience: Towards a Risk-informed and Integrated Approach to Sustainable Development' (2017) 1, 8.

[48] Ibid, 9.

[49] Ibid, 10.

[50] Decision 1/CP.13, 'Bali Action Plan' (14 March 2008) UN Doc FCCC/CP/2007/6/Add.1, para 1(c).

[51] Ibid, para 1(c)(iv); But see Mohammad Shamsuddoha *et al*, 'Establishing Links between Disaster Risk Reduction and Climate Change Adaptation in the Context of Loss and Damage: Policies and Approaches in Bangladesh' (June 2013).

Thus, there has been a recent emphasis on integrating disaster risk reduction and climate change adaptation efforts so as to foster global resiliency against climate-related impacts.[52]

Even so, leaders continue to debate how to address particular kinds of disaster risk. Nowhere is this more apparent than in considerations of 'loss and damage', a phrase used to describe the negative impacts of climate change that cannot be avoided through emissions reductions or adaptive behaviour. There is no consensus on where the costs of such harms should fall. Some scholars focus on the fact that poorer countries, many of which will suffer the most loss and damage, have typically contributed the least to anthropogenic climate change. Arguably fairness requires that richer countries—which have historically contributed more to this ongoing catastrophe—compensate the poorer ones who suffer the most.[53]

Other scholars contend that surely every nation bears some responsibility for minimizing risk and protecting its own inhabitants. Disaster risk is at least partly a product of social and economic choices, such as where to develop, what infrastructure to build, and so on.[54] If suffering nations could completely escape the cost of loss and damage, they would have little incentive to exercise caution in the future. In addition, scholars point to the difficulty in ascertaining how, and how much, developed countries should compensate disaster-impacted countries (as well as how to enforce such compensation).[55]

Although conversations about loss and damage are contentious, the UN system exhibits far more unified agreement around the idea that disaster risk reduction can complement efforts to achieve the 2015 UN Sustainable Development Goals (SDGs). The Plan of Action acknowledges that severe disasters represent a significant threat to SDG achievement around the world: '[i]ndeed, ten of the seventeen SDGs have targets related to disaster risk, firmly establishing the role of disaster risk reduction in realizing the 2030 Agenda for Sustainable Development'.[56]

52 See eg Walid Ali, 'Integrating Climate Change Adaptation and Disaster Risk Reduction' *UNDP* (5 May 2017) (focusing on DRR and CCA response integration in the Arab world); Blaž Kurnik *et al*, *Climate Change Adaptation and Disaster Risk Reduction in Europe* (European Environment Agency 2017) 15; Giuseppe Forino *et al*, 'Climate Change Adaptation and Disaster Risk reduction integration: Strategies, Policies, and Plans in three Australian Local Governments' *International Journal of Disaster Risk Reduction*, 24 (2017): 100.

53 Sam Edelman, 'Climate Justice, Loss and Damage and Compensation for Small Island Developing States' *Journal of Human Rights and Environment*, 7/1 (2016): 32, 35.

54 Andrew Crabtree, 'Capabilities, Ethics and Disasters' in Donal O'Mathúna *et al* (eds), *Disasters: Core Concepts and Ethical Theories* (Springer International Publishing 2018) ch 12, 183 ('[T]here are two necessary causes of a disaster, namely a hazard and a society. Hence there are two sets of responsibility').

55 Alexis Durand *et al*, 'Financing Options for Loss and Damage: A Review and Roadmap' (Brown University Climate Development Lab and International Centre for Climate Change and Development 2016) <https://unfccc.int/files/adaptation/groups_committees/loss_and_damage_executive_committee/application/pdf/browncdl-icccadfinancinglossanddamagepaperdraft.pdf> accessed 13 November 2018.

56 UNDRR, 'Plan of Action' (n 47) 7.

In fact, the UN has recognized the impact of disasters on international development for over twenty-five years (well before the 2015 SDGs).[57] Back in 1992, the UN General Assembly (UNGA), christened the 1990s 'the International Decade for Natural Disaster Reduction' in the hopes of lowering social disruption and loss of life and property from natural disasters.[58] As decades have passed, the UN has maintained many of the same prescriptions related to better disaster preparedness and increased human resource capacity building.

What can be said of this remarkable consistency? Maybe the best practice guidelines are the finest that practical wisdom has to offer. Or maybe the UN is caught in a rut. Assuming the truth is somewhere in the middle, we think it imperative that lessons and insights of the past be recalibrated to take into account the accelerating disaster trends of the new century.

One immediate area for improvement concerns slow-onset disasters. Historically, the UN's disaster reduction efforts have focused on sudden-onset disasters (although the UN Plan of Action in particular could be interpreted to apply broadly to either type of disaster). The UN has not yet established clear guidelines on the best way to prepare for and respond to significant but slow-moving natural disasters like rising sea levels or disappearing glacial melt. In some ways these types of disasters will be harder to address because of their relative permanence and their comparative inability to capture heightened sympathy from the global community. It is likely that the UN will have to rethink a lot of historic methods for addressing disasters when contemplating best responses to slow-onset disasters in the future.[59]

IV. DISASTER AND ECOSYSTEM MANAGEMENT

Since the Indian Ocean Tsunami in 2004, policy-makers have been looking more at the role ecosystems play in shaping disaster risk. This trend, which further accelerated after the Great East Japan Earthquake in 2011, cast new light on some existing environmental agreements and gave rise to a new movement called ecosystem-based disaster risk reduction, or 'Eco-DRR'.[60] The idea is that ecosystems, when they are healthy, do

[57] United Nations Office for Disaster Risk Reduction, 'Disaster Risk Reduction in Sustainable Development Outcome Documents' <https://www.unisdr.org/files/42613_drrinsustainabledevelopmentoutcomed.pdf> accessed 5 February 2020; *Report of the United Nations Conference on Environment and Development* (UN 1993) vol I, annex II—'Agenda 21', para 7.58 (setting the objective 'to mitigate the negative impact of natural and man-made disasters on human settlements, national economies and the environment').

[58] UNGA Res 44/236, 'International Decade for Natural Disaster Reduction' (22 December 1989) UN Doc A/RES/44/236, annex, para A.1.

[59] Such rethinking will be especially crucial in the context of disaster-induced human migration. For more on this topic, see Chapter 46, 'Migration', in this volume.

[60] Furuta Naoya, 'Ecosystem-Based Disaster Risk Reduction: A Review of Recent Progress and Remaining Gaps' *Disaster and Biodiversity: Biology International*, 36 (2017): 154.

a lot of 'free work' in managing and reducing disaster risk. Healthy insect and wildlife populations, for instance, can help ecosystems rebound after a wildfire or an industrial accident. Sturdy forests and wetlands protect human settlements from landslides and storm surge. Genetic diversity in crops can help a community feed its members in times of blight or drought.

Recognizing these connections, in 2015, the parties to the 1971 Ramsar Convention on Wetlands adopted a decision encouraging nations to integrate wetland management plans into their national disaster risk reduction and climate change adaptation strategies.[61] In 2016, the parties to the 1992 Convention on Biological Diversity (CBD) similarly called on nations and other relevant institutions to fold ecosystem-based approaches into such strategies.[62] Additionally, the International Union for Conservation of Nature has been particularly active in advocating for disaster resilience through biodiversity protections.[63] Examples of Eco-DRR initiatives can be found around the world. Japan, for instance, has long managed its forests to control landslides and diminish wind-borne sand in coastal areas.[64] In addition to its storied dike system, the Netherlands now maintains a national river work programme called 'Room for the River' that is intended to manage flood waters by restoring natural inlets and repairing frayed wetlands.[65] In the United States, 'green infrastructure' initiatives were woven into several parts of the 2013 Hurricane Sandy Rebuilding Strategy.[66] President Obama further issued an executive order encouraging green infrastructure in disaster mitigation projects of all kinds, although it was later rescinded by President Trump.[67]

V. DISASTER AND OBLIGATIONS TO OTHER STATES

Although completely preventing natural disasters is impossible, far too many disasters are the direct result of avoidable human activity. These 'man-made' disasters typically happen unpredictably and without regard to political boundaries. International law

[61] Draft Resolution XII.13, 'Wetlands and disaster risk reduction' (27 February 2015) Ramsar COP12 DR13.

[62] Decision XIII/4, 'Biodiversity and climate change' (10 December 2016) UN Doc CBD/COP/DEC/XIII/4, para 10.

[63] Naoya (n 60) 159–160.

[64] Ibid, 157.

[65] Ibid, 157–158.

[66] Ibid, 158.

[67] Executive Order 13693, 'Planning for Federal Sustainability in the Next Decade' *Federal Register*, 80/57 (19 March 2015): 15871 <https://www.govinfo.gov/content/pkg/FR-2015-03-25/pdf/2015-07016.pdf> accessed 15 November 2018, rescinded by Executive Order 13834, 'Efficient Federal Operations' (21 May 2018) <https://www.govinfo.gov/content/pkg/DCPD-201800342/pdf/DCPD-201800342.pdf> accessed 15 November 2018.

imposes obligations on the state where such a disaster originates if the disaster impacts or threatens to impact another state—that is, if it is a 'transfrontier disaster'.[68]

Transfrontier disasters exhibit one of the two following characteristics: (1) two or more states experience environmental harm or (2) one state experiences environmental harm that has significant implications for another state or states. A well-known example of the first type of transfrontier disaster is the explosion at the Chernobyl nuclear plant in which clouds of radioactive contamination spread over several countries. A well-known example of the second type of transfrontier disaster is the 1984 explosion of a Union Carbide plant in Bhopal, India which had transboundary implications for the United States on account of the potential liability of the US-headquartered Union Carbide company.[69]

Transfrontier disaster management involves three primary components: disaster prevention, damage minimization, and damage compensation.

A. The Disaster Prevention Duty

The disaster prevention duty is simultaneously the most cost-effective and the most commonly overlooked aspect of transfrontier disaster management in international law.[70] Although a duty to prevent transfrontier harm can be found in international legal documents and is often considered to be a fundamental aspect of international relations, it is often outlined in general terms with few or no specific requirements, standards, or consequences for non-compliance.[71] When states do articulate specific standards (often in agreements related to the shipment of hazardous substances) these standards typically remain limited to (1) adopting safety rules, (2) maintaining compliance with safety rules, (3) monitoring facilities and workers, and (4) training workers to follow safety rules.[72] Sometimes the language is couched so as to soften the preventative duty. For

[68] Edith Weiss *et al*, *International Law for the Environment* (1st edn, West Academic Publishing 2015) 288 (referring to environmental disasters with a 'transfrontier' character).

[69] Daniel Magraw, 'The Bhopal Disaster: Structuring a Solution' *University of Colorado Law Review*, 57/5 (1986): 835, 840.

[70] Note that disaster risk reduction efforts under the UN (discussed previously in this chapter) and the transfrontier disaster prevention duty are distinct. The former refers to a given state's efforts to mitigate the impacts of disasters on populations within that state, whereas the latter refers to a state's efforts to avert man-made disasters that might lead to transfrontier impacts.

[71] See eg UN, 'Report of the United Nations Conference on the Human Environment' (5-16 June 1972) UN Doc A/CONF.48/14/Rev.1, 3, ch 1—'Declaration of the United Nations Conference on the Human Environment', principle 21 ('States have ... the responsibility to ensure that activities within their jurisdiction or control do not cause damage to the environment of other states or of areas beyond the limits of national jurisdiction'); see Chapter 16, 'Harm Prevention', in this volume.

[72] Weiss *et al* (n 68); see eg Directive 2012/18/EU of the European Parliament and of the Council of 4 July 2012 on the control of major-accident hazards involving dangerous substances, amending and subsequently repealing Council Directive 96/82/EC Text with EEA relevance [2012] OJ L 197/1, arts 14–16 (requiring, inter alia, information exchange, safety reports, and emergency plans).

example, the 1987 US Restatement of Foreign Relations Law requires states to take necessary measures to prevent transfrontier environmental harm, but only 'to the extent practicable under the circumstances'.[73]

B. The Damage Compensation Duty

In direct contrast to the disaster prevention duty, the damage compensation duty is simultaneously the least effective and the most common aspect of international agreements related to transfrontier disaster.[74] International law surrounding liability for transfrontier damage from environmental disasters broadly adheres to the 'polluter pays' principle.[75] At the same time, the *extent* of liability seems to hinge on whether a state breached its duty to prevent or minimize damage from transfrontier disasters. Scholarly debate still has not settled whether transfrontier damage resulting from ultrahazardous activities or the use of very dangerous substances even in the absence of a breach of duty should result in strict liability for a state.[76] In practice, states have often turned to domestic legal processes (eg litigation or legislation) to compensate citizens injured by transfrontier pollution when international law imposes no liability.[77]

C. The Damage Minimization Duty

The obligation to minimize damage from a transfrontier disaster can be broken down into several duties many of which are contained in international agreements but only some of which have become customary international law. The obligation to minimize damage extends both to the state in which the disaster occurs and to other states potentially impacted by the disaster. Although different international legal documents emphasize different obligations, five recur regularly (see Table 47.1).

International legal documents address these duties differently. For example, Article 9 of the Montreal Rules emphasizes the obligations of the state of origin to warn potentially affected states (Category 2), to provide them with pertinent information (Category

[73] US Restatement Foreign Relations Law (Third), §601(1); but see Directive 2012/18/EU, ibid, art 12 (noting that private operators within Member States 'should have a general obligation *to take all necessary measures* to prevent major accidents') (emphasis added).

[74] Weiss *et al* (n 68) 304.

[75] See Chapter 58, 'International Environmental Responsibility and Liability', in this volume.

[76] Weiss *et al* (n 68); see eg 'Report of the International Law Commission on the work of its fifty-eighth session' (2006) UN Doc A/61/10, ch V.E—'Draft principles on the allocation of loss in the case of transboundary harm arising out of hazardous activities', principle 6.2 (stating that '[v]ictims of transboundary damage should have access to remedies in the state of origin that are no less prompt, adequate and effective than those available to victims that suffer damage, from the same incident, within the territory of that state').

[77] Weiss *et al* (n 68) 313–314.

Table 47.1 Recurring Duties under the Obligation to Minimize Harm from Transfrontier Disasters

	Duty prior to disaster	Duty following disaster			
	Category 1	Category 2	Category 3	Category 4	Category 5
	Develop Joint Contingency Plan with other states	Notify other states promptly	Provide information to other states	Take individual action to abate damage	Cooperate with other states to abate damage
State in which disaster occurs	X	X	X	X	X
State potentially impacted by the disaster	X				X

Note: Category titles adapted from Weiss *et al* (n 68) 309–310.

3), and to inform them about steps taken to abate the cause of the transfrontier pollution (Category 3).[78] In contrast, the CBD explicitly mentions all five duty categories. Article 14(c) mandates the 'exchange of information' regarding activities 'which are likely to significantly affect adversely the biological diversity of other States' (Category 3). Article 14(d) similarly requires the state of origin to 'notify immediately the potentially affected States' (Category 2) and to 'initiate action to prevent or minimize ... damage' (Category 4). Article 14(e) further requires states to 'encourage international cooperation to supplement ... national [arrangements for emergency responses]' (Category 5), and 'to establish joint contingency plans' (Category 1). As a final example, Article 28 of the 1997 United Nations Convention on the Law of the Non-Navigational Uses of International Watercourses obligates states to 'notify other potentially affected States' (Category 2), 'take all practicable measures ... to prevent, mitigate and eliminate harmful effects (Category 4) and to jointly develop contingency plans ... in cooperation, where appropriate, with other potentially affected States' (Categories 1 and 5).

Outside of formal international agreements, some of these duties have established themselves as customary international law. The Category 4 duty to act to prevent or reduce transfrontier damage simply represents an extension of the international legal principle to do 'no harm' which was first established in the Trail Smelter Arbitration.[79]

[78] International Law Association, 'Report of the Sixtieth Conference held at Montreal from 29 August–4 September 1982', 158—'Rules of International Law Applicable to Transfrontier Pollution', 176, art 9—'Emergency situations' (Montreal Rules).

[79] *Trail Smelter Arbitration (United States/Canada)* (1938 and 1941) 3 RIAA 1905, 1911.

Category 2 and 3 duties to notify and provide information to potentially affected states are also well established in customary international law. Many treaties and cases have articulated these requirements in relation to risky domestic activities.[80] Indeed, the World Commission on Environment and Development has even proposed the development of an international agreement that would require a state to provide information and establish mutually agreed criteria *before* installing a hazardous facility with the potential to affect a neighbouring state.[81] In addition, many treaties have incorporated the Category 2 requirement to notify other states specifically in the context of transfrontier disasters.[82]

In contrast, Categories 1 and 5, requiring cooperation with the impacted state, are not yet fully incorporated into customary international law, but they arguably represent emerging duties under international law. The Category 5 duty to cooperate with other states in minimizing damage from transfrontier disasters is becoming increasingly common in bilateral and multilateral agreements.[83] The Category 1 duty to develop joint contingency plans is arguably already a part of customary international law specifically in the context of marine pollution disasters.[84] At the same time, this Category 1 duty is not yet customary international law in relation to other types of transfrontier disasters such as nuclear fallout and forest fires (although some treaties broadly incorporate this duty).[85]

VI. CONCLUSION

Incorporating disaster law into the larger realm of international environmental law is not easy. Although the two legal regimes are related and share significant overlap, they have largely developed separately. This independent development is particularly apparent when discerning the relationship between disaster law and broader principles

[80] *Corfu Channel case (UK/Albania)* (Judgement) [1949] ICJ Rep 4, 22; 'Report of the International Law Commission on the work of its fifty-third session' (2001) UN Doc A/56/10, ch V.E—'Draft articles on prevention of transboundary harm from hazardous activities', art 8.1; World Commission on Environment and Development, *Our Common Future* (OUP 1987) para 83.

[81] Weiss *et al* (n 68) 307. Note that this proposal would require states to delegate aspects of their national sovereignty to help reduce the mere risk of transfrontier disaster. Based on past precedent, this would likely be a difficult agreement to achieve; see eg Ragnar Löfstedt, 'Fairness Across Borders: The Barsebäck Nuclear Power Plant' *RISK: Health, Safety & Environment*, 13/1 (1996): 7 (detailing Sweden's pushback against Danish objection to a Swedish nuclear power plant built less than 20 km from Copenhagen).

[82] See eg Montreal Rules (n 78); US Restatement Foreign Relations Law (Third) (n 73) §601(1), comment e.

[83] Weiss *et al* (n 68) 310.

[84] Ibid; see also US Restatement Foreign Relations Law (Third) (n 73) §603, comment f.

[85] Weiss *et al* (n 68) 310; See eg 1986 Convention for the Protection of the Natural Resources and Environment of the South Pacific Region, art 15 (stating that '[p]arties shall develop and promote individual contingency plans and joint contingency plans for responding to incidents').

of international environmental law. While some principles (ie the principle of sovereign responsibility and the duty to compensate for harm) are largely reflected in disaster law, others (ie the principles of international cooperation and preventative action) are either works in progress or are blatantly de-emphasized. Still others (eg the precautionary principle) are excluded all together.[86] Better integrating these two legal regimes will become increasingly important during the twenty-first century as the impact of disasters on the global environment grows.

Yet, disaster law itself is not a single, easily codified regime. Rather, it is a patchwork quilt of international agreements, frameworks, and customary duties, defined by their relevance to points on the circle of disaster risk management: planning, response, compensation, and recovery. As this chapter shows, some areas of disaster law (disaster risk reduction obligations, for example) are widely agreed upon. Others (liability for loss and damage) are hotly contested. Yet even in areas of relative agreement, impacts from climate change threaten to turn historically agreed upon best practices on their head. Previously unconsidered slow-onset disasters, as well as a predicted increase in the intensity and frequency of sudden-onset disasters, suggest that a re-evaluation of widely held disaster law in the coming years will be necessary. Indeed, the rising Eco-DRR movement, as well as debates around the proper international response to disaster migrants, both suggest important developments-to-come in international disaster law.[87]

BIBLIOGRAPHY

Daniel Farber *et al*, *Disaster Law and Policy* (3rd edn, Wolters Kluwer 2015)

IPCC, *Climate Change 2014: The Synthesis Report* (2014)

Furuta Naoya, 'Ecosystem-Based Disaster Risk Reduction: A Review of Recent Progress and Remaining Gaps' *Disaster and Biodiversity: Biology International*, 36 (2017): 154

Robert Verchick, *Facing Catastrophe: Environmental Action for a Post Katrina World* (Harvard University Press 2010)

Edith Weiss *et al*, *International Law for the Environment* (1st edn, West Academic Publishing 2015)

[86] Max Soto, 'General Principles of International Environmental Law' *International Law Students Association Journal of International & Comparative Law*, 3/1 (1996): 192.

[87] See Chapter 46, 'Migration', in this volume.

CHAPTER 48

INTELLECTUAL PROPERTY

LISA BENJAMIN

I. INTRODUCTION

INTELLECTUAL property law aims to reward investments in labour and creativity and incentivize innovation.[1] It does this by cordoning off intangible intellectual creations through the mechanism of private ownership, regulating the content, use, and exploitation of these creations.[2] The transition towards knowledge-based economies has elevated innovation to a primary economic virtue, and with it the protection of intellectual property rights (IPRs).[3] Intellectual property has a strong connection with environmental pollution through the protection of dirty and damaging technologies, but it can also drive innovation in clean technologies. IPRs such as patents are also closely associated with biotechnology developments, and so are highly relevant to efforts to preserve biological diversity, ensure food security, and implement sustainable development goals (SDGs).

The traditional mechanisms of intellectual property law privilege private rights and profitability. In the international environmental law field, this tendency has created significant tension between developed countries (where most owners of IPRs reside) and developing countries.[4] Developing countries often cite the need for technology transfer as a precondition for implementing environmental obligations.[5] Sustainable development instruments, and in particular Agenda 21, were the first to articulate clearly the

[1] Lionel Bently and Brad Sherman, *Intellectual Property Law* (4th edn, OUP 2014) 4–5.

[2] Ibid, 1.

[3] Peter Drahos and Imelda Maher, 'Innovation, Competition, Standards and Intellectual Property: Policy Perspectives from Economics and Law' *Information Economics and Policy*, 16/1 (2004): 1; Livia Ilie, 'Intellectual Property Rights: An Economic Approach' *Procedia Economics and Finance*, 16 (2014): 548.

[4] Michell Klein, 'Foreign Direct Investment and Collective IP Protection in Developing Countries' *Journal of Economic Behaviour and Organization*, 149/C (2018): 389.

[5] See Chapter 55, 'Technology Assistance and Transfers', in this volume.

relationship between implementation of environmental obligations by developing countries and access to environmental technologies.[6] Since the 1990s, the relationship between IPRs and international environmental law has become more complex and political.[7]

Issues relating to IPRs arise in three broad areas of international environmental law: 1) whether IPRs should be granted for potentially environmentally damaging technologies; 2) the extent to which IPRs protect Indigenous environmental knowledge; and 3) the extent to which IPRs may limit the transfer of environmentally sound technology.[8] Following an overview of IPRs under the 1994 Agreement on Trade-Related Aspects of Intellectual Property Rights (TRIPs) and their implications for sustainable development in developing countries in Section II, Section III discusses the first area of intersection, highlighting the example of biotechnology and patent protection in the context of food security and the 2001 International Treaty on Plant Genetic Resources for Food and Agriculture (ITPGFA). The chapter then turns to the second area of intersection in Section IV on IPRs and traditional knowledge as articulated under the 1992 Convention on Biological Diversity (CBD) and the 2010 Nagoya Protocol. Finally Section V touches on the third area, discussing technology transfer in the climate change context under the 1992 United Nations Framework Convention on Climate Change (UNFCCC) and the 2015 Paris Agreement. While there are numerous types of IPRs, it is patents which most closely intersect with international environmental law, and will hence be the main focus of this chapter.

II. SUSTAINABLE DEVELOPMENT, IPRS, AND THE TRIPS AGREEMENT

IPRs are national in scope, and therefore protection must be secured under distinct national systems. These jurisdictional restrictions can be problematic for multinational businesses whose works, inventions, and brands are traded transnationally. Knowledge-based industries in the United States exerted tremendous political clout in the 1990s, and were successful in tying IPRs to the World Trade Organization (WTO) regime through the TRIPs Agreement.[9] As a result of aggressive US trade

[6] *Report of the United Nations Conference on Environment and Development* (UN 1993) vol I, annex II, 'Agenda 21', para 34.

[7] Bently and Sherman (n 1) 4.

[8] Philippe Sands and Jacqueline Peel, *Principles of International Environmental Law* (4th edn, CUP 2018) 843.

[9] Susan Sell, *Private Power, Public Law: The Globalization of Intellectual Property Rights* (CUP 2003) 1–8.

sanction tactics, and in exchange for promises made to developing countries of greatly expanded access to markets for their agricultural products and textiles, the TRIPs Agreement was agreed in 1995, but has remained a source of tension between developed and developing countries ever since.[10] As the following sections will illustrate, IPRs are intimately connected with efforts to achieve sustainable development.

A. Sustainable Development and IPRs

A number of environmental issues that involve IPRs are inter-related. Climate change will negatively affect agricultural production, and will have the most devastating effects on poor and vulnerable populations in developing countries.[11] Agriculture is also one of the major contributors to anthropogenic greenhouse gas emissions.[12] Climate change adaptation technologies include bioengineered seeds such as drought and flood resistant crops which are often patent protected. Degradation and destruction of natural ecosystems has been identified as major threats to crop diversity and the stability of global food systems.[13] At the same time, the majority of biodiversity is located in developing countries, leaving the burden of protecting these resources on these states, whose populations still suffer from high levels of poverty, as well as energy and food insecurity.

Agenda 21, agreed in 1992, recognized the potential impediments that intellectual property (and patent protection in particular) posed to the achievement of sustainable development, and issues of access to and transfer of environmentally sound technologies (ESTs), particularly in developing countries.[14] The international community called for measures to mediate the negative impacts of IPRs, such as compulsory licensing provisions and payment of equitable and adequate compensation.[15] While some of these measures found their way into the TRIPs Agreement, the internationalization of IPRs has become closely intertwined with emerging environmental crises.

10 Ibid, 139–143.

11 Human Rights Council, 'Report of the Special Rapporteur on Extreme Poverty and Human Rights' (25 June 2019) UN Doc A/HRC/41/49.

12 Carmen Gonzalez, 'The Global Food System, Environmental Protection and Human Rights' *Natural Resources and Environment*, 26/3 (2012): 7.

13 Rafael Pérez-Escamilla, 'Food Security and the 2015–2030 Sustainable Development Goals: From Human to Planetary Health: Perspectives and Opinions' *Current Developments in Nutrition* 1/7 (2017): 1, 2.

14 Agenda 21 (n 6) paras 34.10, 34.18.

15 Subject to compliance with existing international conventions, ibid, para 34.18(e)(iv).

B. The TRIPs Agreement and Patent Protection

The TRIPs Agreement adopted minimum requirements for patent law which far exceeded those of the 1883 Paris Convention, both in subject matter and terms of protection. As with other WTO agreements, the TRIPs Agreement included principles of national treatment and most-favoured nation.[16] Section V contains requirements for the protection of patents, provided they are products or processes which are new, involve an inventive step, and are capable of industrial application.[17] Member states are allowed to incorporate provisions in their national laws necessary to exclude from patentability any invention to protect *ordre public* or morality, or to protect human, animal, or plant life or health, or to avoid serious prejudice to the environment.[18] Member states can exclude from patentability plants and animals (other than micro-organisms) and essentially biological processes for the production of plants and animals. Non-biological and microbiological processes, however, can be patented.[19] Member states must provide protection for plant varieties either by patent or an effective *sui generis* system.[20] The TRIPs Agreement contains some flexibilities for developing countries, such as transition periods, which have been extended for least developed countries to 1 July 2021.[21] There are also compulsory licensing provisions under Article 31 which can be applied in the case of a national emergency, other circumstances of extreme urgency, or for public non-commercial use.

C. TRIPs and Developing Countries

Patent protection often assumes importance only after a country has reached a certain threshold of indigenous innovation capacity.[22] Many developing countries have limited innovation capacity and so traditional economic incentives to protect intellectual property are less compelling.[23] As a result these countries historically have had weak or non-existent intellectual property regimes—it was not until the TRIPs regime kicked in that developing countries undertook significant intellectual property reform.[24] Despite these

[16] arts 3, 4 respectively; see Chapter 43, 'Trade', in this volume, which deals with these requirements (in a 1994 GATT context) in more depth.

[17] art 27.1.

[18] art 27.2. This provision as well as art 27.3 was included by the European Union (EU) and developing countries and was seen as a direct challenge to the US biotechnology industry; see Sell (n 9) 111.

[19] art 27.3(b).

[20] Ibid.

[21] Developing country transition periods under art 65.2 expired on 1 January 2000; see Michelle Balaklow, 'Helping Haiti: Incorporating NGO Technology Transfer into the TRIPS Agreement Framework to Aid LDCs in the Adoption of Clean Technologies' *Kentucky Journal of Equine, Agriculture, & Natural Resources Law*, 8/1 (2015): 137, 146. Negotiations under the 2001 Doha Round to reduce tariff and non-tariff barriers for environmental goods and services have not made much progress.

[22] Yee Kim *et al*, 'Appropriate Intellectual Property Protection and Economic Growth in Countries at Different Levels of Development' *Research Policy*, 41/2 (2012): 358, 359.

[23] Klein (n 4) 389.

[24] Ibid.

reforms, net sellers and exporters of intellectual property mainly remain developed countries, and net users and importers largely developing countries.[25]

Transnational corporations remain concerned that a lack of intellectual property protection in the global markets in which they operate will lead to piracy and infringement.[26] As patent laws create monopolies for at least twenty years, patent protection can lead to more expensive products, requirements to build and maintain expensive IPR infrastructure,[27] as well as barriers to entry, and restrictions to competition.[28] US insistence on intellectual property protection is often viewed as 'IP imperialism' by some developing countries.[29] This was well exampled during the HIV/AIDS crisis in the 1990s,[30] and continues in the area of biotechnology and agriculture.

III. PATENTS, SUSTAINABLE DEVELOPMENT, AND FOOD SECURITY

Food insecurity and limited access to nutritious food remain significant issues in the developing world, and climate change-induced droughts and extreme events directly and negatively affect agriculture.[31] The vast majority of the rural poor in developing countries are dependent on agriculture for their livelihoods.[32] Thus increased yields or decreased costs of production directly reduce poverty in those states.[33] As agriculture becomes increasingly feminized, the burden of adapting to or mitigating adverse yields under worsening climatic conditions will fall on women.[34] Innovations in

[25] Michael Smith, 'Bridging Developing Countries' Intellectual Property Laws to TRIPS Standards: Hurdles and Pitfalls Facing Vietnam's Efforts to Normalize Intellectual Property Regime' *Case Western Reserve Journal of Law*, 31/1 (1999): 211, 217–218.

[26] Ibid, 219.

[27] Balaklow (n 21) 145.

[28] Ilie (n 3) 551.

[29] Smith (n 25) 235.

[30] The lack of availability of medicines in developing and least developed countries, led to the WTO, 'Declaration on the TRIPS Agreement and Public Health' (20 November 2001) WT/MIN(01)/DEC/2 which limited obstacles for the compulsory licensing of medicines, although to date only Rwanda has filed a notification under the Declaration.

[31] John Ruane and Andrea Sonnino, 'Agricultural Biotechnologies in Developing Countries and Their Possible Contribution to Food Security' *Journal of Biotechnology*, 156 (2011): 356, 357; Anu Susan Sam, 'Linking Food Security with Household's Adaptive Capacity and Drought Risk: Implications for Sustainable Rural Development' *Social Indicators Research*, 142/1 (2019): 363, 364.

[32] Narayanan Lalitha, 'Diffusion of Agricultural Biotechnology and Intellectual Property Rights: Emerging Issues in India' *Ecological Economics*, 49/2 (2004): 187; Carmen Gonzalez, 'Genetically Modified Organisms and Justice: The International Environmental Justice Implications of Biotechnology' *Georgetown International Environmental Law Review*, 19/4 (2007): 583, 594.

[33] Lalitha (n 32).

[34] Bina Agarwal, 'Gender Equality, Food Security and the Sustainable Development Goals' *Current Opinion in Environmental Sustainability*, 34 (2018): 26, 28.

biotechnology and access to natural resources are key drivers of productivity, growth, and the sustainable use of resources.[35]

IPRs in biotechnology constitute both obstacles and opportunities for developing countries. Agricultural biotechnology can potentially contribute to sustainable agriculture, through the use of genetically modified organisms (GMOs) which can increase yields, develop drought and herbicide tolerant varieties, and lead to more efficient use of land.[36] However, GMO crop technology is expensive, and research and development in this area is dominated by private-sector firms primarily located in developed countries.[37] Approximately 80% of biotech patents in the cultivator category are attributed to but a few biotech multinationals (Monsanto, DuPont, and Syngenta).[38] The development of hybrid or high-yield plant varieties in developing countries often results from informal techniques used by farmers, such as seed saving or traditional cropping patterns.[39] Certain IPRs can prohibit the reuse of protected seeds, and can contribute to the loss of biodiversity by increased herbicide use, increased pest resistance, and negative impacts on wild gene pools.[40]

A. Patents and Biotechnology

Biotechnology is defined under the CBD as 'any technological application that uses biological systems, living organisms, or derivatives thereof, to make or modify products or processes for specific use'.[41] The approach to plant genetic resources changed dramatically in the twentieth century, from being considered a common resource to sovereign property, subject to private ownership through the use of IPRs.[42] This movement coincided with the rise of for-profit seed companies in the 1920s, leading to a global push for intellectual property protection of plant genetic resources.[43] Genetic resources are defined in CBD as genetic material (being 'any material of plant, animal, microbial, or other origin containing functional units of heredity') of actual or potential value.[44]

[35] Bogdan Bazgă, 'Food Security Component of Sustainable Development—Prospects and Challenges in the Next Decade' *Procedia Economics and Finance*, 32 (2015): 1075.

[36] Ademola Adenle *et al*, 'Analysis of Open Source Biotechnology in Developing Countries: An Emerging Framework for Sustainable Agriculture' *Technology in Society*, 34 (2012): 256, 256; Heather Leibowitz, 'Harmony with Nature and Genetically Modified Seeds: A Contradictory Concept in the United States and Brazil' *Pace Environmental Law Review*, 30/2 (2013): 558, 559.

[37] Adenle *et al* (n 36) 257.

[38] Ibid, 259.

[39] Lalitha (n 32) 187–188.

[40] Leibowitz (n 36) 561; Adenle *et al* (n 36) 261.

[41] art 2.

[42] Kal Raustiala and David Victor, 'The Regime Complex for Plant Genetic Resources' *International Organization*, 58/2 (2004): 277, 279.

[43] Ibid, 282.

[44] art 2.

Plant genetic resources are reproductive or propagating materials of plants that encode their unique characteristic genes that include functional units of heredity.[45]

Plant genetic diversity, uneven among states, is decreasing at alarming rates, and is a cause of conflict.[46] Disputes over IPRs dominate the debate over plant genetic resources, as IPRs provide incentives for biotech firms to isolate and adapt useful genetic information. They also create monopolies and restrict access to patented products and processes.[47] The legal regime for patents on biotechnology is complex, encompassing a number of agreements which take divergent approaches to the patenting of biotechnology, particularly plant varieties. These agreements include TRIPs, which strengthened rights of inventors, and the 1991 International Convention for the Protection of New Varieties of Plants (UPOV), which increased protection for seed producers.[48] The ITPGFA and the CBD instead focused on rights of farmers. In terms of national law, the United States and the EU developed the two major approaches to the patenting of biotechnology.

The United States adopted a product-oriented approach which assumes GMO processes and products pose no greater risks to human health than conventional plant breeding technologies.[49] The US Coordinated Framework for Regulation of Biotechnology states that biotechnology products are not fundamentally different than conventional products.[50] There is no federal regulation governing GMO products, and so the US system defaults to patent eligibility, while leaving subject matter exclusions to legislation.[51] The 1980 Bayh-Dole Act, which allowed universities and private entities to claim property rights on government-funded research, paired with the expansive definition of patentable subject matter under the 1980 *Diamond v Chakrabarty* decision of the US Supreme Court,[52] led to large investments in the biotechnology industry. In 1988, the US patent and trade mark office issued the world's first patent for a higher life form, the Harvard oncomouse, and legislation that attempted to impose a moratorium on patentability on animals such as these failed.[53]

[45] Gregory Rose, 'International Law of Sustainable Agriculture in the 21st Century: The International Treaty on Plant Genetic Resources for Food and Agriculture' *Georgetown International Environmental Law Review*, 15/4 (2003): 583, 584.

[46] Laurence Helfer, 'Intellectual Property Rights and the International Treaty on Plant Genetic Resources for Food and Agriculture' *American Society of International Law Proceedings*, 97 (2003): 33.

[47] Ibid.

[48] The 1978 UPOV allowed farmers to purchase protected seeds and reuse them without royalty, but the 1991 version removed this allowance, leaving it up to national law to provide exceptions for farmers.

[49] Gonzalez (n 32) 585.

[50] (26 June 1986) 51 Fed Reg 23, 302, 304.

[51] Margo Bagley, 'Patent First, Ask Questions Later: Morality and Biotechnology in Patent Law' *William & Mary Law Review*, 45/2 (2003): 469.

[52] 447 US 303 (1980) SCOTUS. The Supreme Court expansively interpreted the 1952 Patents Act to include patentable subject matter of any type of living or non-living matter as long as it was 'made by man'; see ibid, 339.

[53] Bagley (n 51) 498. The Harvard oncomouse patent was for a transgenic non-human mammal where an activated oncogene sequence had been inserted, making it more susceptible to the development of cancerous tumours. The patent was also approved by the Board of Appeal of the European Patent Office but rejected by the Supreme Court of Canada as not patentable.

The EU has taken a different approach to biotechnology in food and agriculture, adopting a more process-based analysis which incorporates the precautionary approach,[54] although the case law does not explicitly adopt this approach.[55] This more conservative approach is partly due to hostility and intolerance to GMOs on the part of certain governments and the public.[56] The Biotechnology Directive, designed to harmonize national legislation on biotechnology, was deeply controversial and took over ten years to negotiate.[57] Article 4 of the Directive stipulates that neither plant and animal varieties nor biological processes are patentable.[58]

All members of the EU are signatories to the 2000 European Patent Convention (EPC) administered by the European Patent Office (EPO).[59] Case law has established a high threshold for environmental considerations to qualify as exceptions to patentability under the *ordre public* exception.[60] While there is no general bar to the patenting of biotechnology material or inventions,[61] Article 53(b) of the EPC states that individual plant or animal varieties or essentially biological processes for the production of plants (including steps for breeding plant varieties) are generally non-patentable.[62] Until recently it was not clear whether Article 53(b) excluded from patentability product-by-process claims resulting from these excluded processes. The EPO considered provisions

[54] Gonzalez (n 32) 585; Robert Falkner and Aarti Gupta, 'The Limits of Regulatory Convergence: Globalization and GMO Politics in the South' *International Environmental Agreements: Politics, Law and Economics*, 9/2 (2009): 113, 114.

[55] Sands and Peel (n 8) 920.

[56] Laura Salvi, 'The EU Regulatory Framework on GMOs and the Shift of Power Towards Member States: An Easy Way Out of the Regulatory Impasse?' *European Food and Feed Law Review*, 11/3 (2016): 201. For example Directive 2001/18/EC ([2001] OJ L 106/1) and Regulation No 1829/2003 ([2003] OJ L 268/1) on the release of GMOs imposes marketing and labelling restrictions based on the precautionary approach. Directive 2015/412/EU ([2015] OJ L 68/1) conferred rights on member states to pass legislation which restricts or prohibits the cultivation of GMOs in their territory.

[57] Bagley (n 51) 526.

[58] A challenge by the Netherlands to provisions of the Directive being in violation of the access and benefit-sharing provisions of the 1992 CBD failed; see *Kingdom of the Netherlands v European Parliament and Council of the European Union* Case C-377/98, European Court Reports 2001 I-07079 [57]–[58].

[59] The 2000 EPC updated the 1973 EPC by incorporating provisions of TRIPs.

[60] art 53(a); *Greenpeace v Plant Genetic Systems* [1995] EPOR 357 involved Greenpeace's application to revoke a patent on transgenic plants resistant to herbicide under art 53(a) and was dismissed by the EPO Technical Board of Appeal. The test under art 53(a) has been established at a high level—that the public must consider the invention 'so abhorrent that the grant of the patent right would be inconceivable', *Howard Florey/Relaxin* T74/91 [1995] EPOR 541 (Op Div). *Harvard/Onco-mouse* [2003] OJ EPO 473 (Op Div) stated that while environmental considerations were part of art 53(a), the provision would only ever be applied in exceptional cases.

[61] Bently and Sherman (n 1) 499; Directive 98/44/EC of the European Parliament and of the Council on the Legal Protection of Biotechnological Inventions, art 3; see also *Harvard/Transgenic Animals*, T315/03 [2006] OJ EPO 15, 78.

[62] In *Novartis/Transgenic plant*, G1/98 [2000] EPOR 303, 319 the Enlarged Board of Appeal confirmed that 'a claim wherein specific plant varieties are not individually claimed is not excluded from patentability under Article 53(b), even though it may embrace plant varieties' so the exception only covers plant varieties per se which should be protected under 1991 UPOV; Bently and Sherman (n 1) 502.

of the Biotechnology Directive,[63] and two recent consolidated cases provided more expansive definitions of whether plant varieties can be patented.[64] One concerned a method of breeding tomatoes with reduced water content, and the other a method of selectively increasing *anticarcinogenic glucosinolates* in broccoli. In these two cases, the European Board of Appeal (EBA) of the EPO adopted a narrow interpretation of Article 53(b) as an exception to patentability, concluding that biotechnology inventions relating to plants are patentable if the technical feasibility of the invention is not confined to a particular plant variety, providing a favourable outcome to plant breeders and agro-chemical companies.[65] This narrow approach was dramatically reversed in 2020 when the EBA held that Rule 28(2) of the EPC provides a dynamic interpretation and new understanding of Article 53(b)—that the exclusion of patentability extends to any products exclusively obtained by means of an essentially biological process, or if the claimed process defines an essentially biological process.[66]

Developing countries display greater regulatory diversity on the issue of patenting biotechnology.[67] Whilst developing countries are faced with powerful external constraints such as trade imperatives, these pressures interact with domestic policies and priorities. The result is a combination of both policy restrictions and incentives in countries such as Mexico, China, and South Africa.[68] For example Mexico imposed a moratorium on GMOs until 2004, and NGOs in South Africa attempted to slow GM crop approvals.[69]

B. The 2001 ITPGRA

Colonization facilitated vast flows of agricultural species from the Americas to Europe, and from developing to developed countries.[70] This led to major asymmetries where raw materials were traded freely but materials protected by IPRs were not.[71] The

[63] art 4.2 of the Directive states that 'inventions which concern plants . . . shall be patentable if the technical feasibility of the invention is not confined to a particular plant . . . variety'.

[64] Decision of the Enlarged Board of Appeal 25 March 2015, G2/12 and G1/13.

[65] Timo Minssen and Ana Nordberg, 'The Impact of "Broccoli II" and "Tomatoes II" on European Patents in Conventional Breeding, GMOs, and Synthetic Biology: The Grand Finale of a Juicy Patents Tale?' *Biotechnology Law Report*, 34/3 (2015): 81, 82; Christine Godt, 'Experts and Politics in Patent Policy: The Final Report of the Expert Group on the Development and Implications of Patent Law in the Field of Biotechnology and Genetic Engineering of the European Commission, 17 May 2016' *International Review of Intellectual Property and Competition Law*, 47/8 (2016): 960, 965.

[66] Decision of the Enlarged Board of Appeal 14 May 2020, G3/19.

[67] Falkner and Gupta (n 54) 115.

[68] Ibid.

[69] Ibid, 125, although South Africa has undertaken intensive GM research efforts since then; Robert Paarlberg, 'GMO Food and Crops: Africa's Choice' *New Biotechnology*, 27/5 (2010): 609, 612.

[70] Ibid.

[71] Elsa Tsioumani, 'Beyond Access and Benefit-Sharing: Lessons from the Law and Governance of Agricultural Biodiversity' *The Journal of World Intellectual Property*, 21/3–4 (2018): 106, 110.

privatization of plant varieties led to justice concerns and the emergence of the principle of national sovereignty over natural and genetic resources.[72] IPRs in plant genetic resources are often critiqued as designed to suit the needs of developed countries, as farmers' varieties, popular in developing countries, are not sufficiently stable or novel to qualify for intellectual property protection.[73] In order to redress the balance, developing countries asserted national sovereignty over natural resources, including in plant genetic resources, and through benefit-sharing mechanisms under the CBD and at the Food and Agricultural Organization (FAO).

As part of this movement, the ITPGRA established a global network of seed banks under the auspices of the FAO which grants access to agricultural seeds for breeding purposes.[74] In reaction to TRIPs and UPOV, the ITPGRA incorporated the principle of national sovereignty over genetic resources with direct references to the CBD. Unlike TRIPs and UPOV, the ITPGRA also includes a benefit-sharing mechanism under the 2006 Standard Material Transfer Agreement (SMTA).[75] Under this multilateral system, parties can gain facilitated access to any of the sixty-four crops listed in Annex I of the treaty which are placed in the public domain, in exchange for a royalty payment of 1.1% to a joint fund under the multilateral system.[76] Article 9 explicitly recognizes the contribution of local and Indigenous communities and farmers to agriculture, and farmers' rights to save, use, exchange, and sell seeds (although implementation is left to national law).[77]

Article 12.3(d) on intellectual property became one of the most controversial points of the negotiation of the ITPGRA.[78] It prohibits recipients from claiming any intellectual property or other rights that limit facilitated access to the plant genetic resources or genetic parts of components in the form received from the multilateral system.[79] As of February 2017, over 3.3 million samples have been distributed, but no corresponding mandatory or voluntary payments have yet been contributed to the

[72] Ibid, 108.

[73] Ibid, 109.

[74] The treaty follows on from the International Understanding on Plant Genetic Resources adopted by the FAO in 1983 which ensured the exploration, preservation, evaluation, and availability of plant genetic resources.

[75] Intellectual property regimes have no benefit-sharing regimes based on the assumption that intellectual property protection benefits society as a whole by promoting innovation, see Tsioumani (n 71) 115.

[76] 30% is deducted making it a 0.77% payment for mandatory payments.

[77] eg the 2001 Protection of Plant Varieties and Farmers' Rights Act in India provides a unique *sui generis* system that provides for benefit sharing, protects rights of farmers to save, use and reuse, exchange, share or sell protected seed varieties, Lalitha (n 32) 193.

[78] David Cooper, 'The International Treaty on Plant Genetic Resources for Food and Agriculture' *Review of European, Comparative and International Environmental Law*, 11/1 (2002): 1, 8.

[79] Tabaro notes the rather cryptic language resulted from the combination of two proposals with developing countries' proposals constituting the first half, and the US' proposal constituting the second half; Edgar Tabaro, 'Negotiating a Standard Material Transfer Agreement under the International Treaty on Plant Genetic Resources for Food and Agriculture: Issues and Concerns for Africa' *The Comparative and International Law Journal of Southern Africa*, 39/2 (2006): 309, 313.

multilateral system.[80] Developments under the CBD and the conclusion of the 2010 Nagoya Protocol may also reduce the effectiveness of the ITPGRA, as parties may prefer more lucrative bilateral benefit-sharing arrangements under those agreements.

IV. THE 1992 CBD AND THE 2010 NAGOYA PROTOCOL

In reaction to the restrictions and omissions of TRIPs, developing countries engaged in regime-shifting through the introduction of biodiversity and traditional knowledge as new areas of IPRs.[81] The biodiversity arena has been used as a counter regime,[82] with the introduction of strategically inconsistent provisions on IPRs, making them subject to environmental protection imperatives.[83] The CBD and Nagoya Protocol were designed to combat biopiracy or appropriation without benefit sharing, and are strongly supported by mega-diverse developing countries.[84]

A. IPRs under the CBD

Both the CBD and the Nagoya Protocol specifically address IPRs. Article 16 of the CBD supports the transfer of technology, which includes biotechnology and associated IPRs. It states that each contracting party undertakes to provide and/or facilitate access for and transfer to other parties of technologies relevant to the conservation and sustainable use of biological diversity.[85] Such transfers to developing countries are to be made or facilitated under fair and most favourable terms, although where the technology is subject to patent or other IPRs, such transfers should be consistent with the adequate protection of IPRs.[86] Parties also have an obligation, recognizing that patents and other IPRs may influence the implementation of the Convention, to cooperate (subject to national and international law) to ensure that IPRs are supportive of and do not run counter to the objectives of the Convention.[87]

[80] Florian Rabitz, 'Access Without Benefit-Sharing: Design, Effectiveness and Reform of the FAO Seed Treaty' *International Journal of the Commons*, 11/2 (2017): 621, 628. This may be due to lack of commercialization of the distributed material or lack of clarity over when mandatory payments are due.

[81] Chidi Oguamanam, 'Regime Tension in the Intellectual Property Rights Arena: Farmers' Rights and Post-TRIPS Counter Regime Trends' *Dalhousie Law Journal*, 29 (2006): 413, 435.

[82] Ibid.

[83] Raustiala and Victor (n 42) 299–300.

[84] See Chapter 32, 'Wildlife', in this volume.

[85] art 16.1.

[86] art 16.2.

[87] art 16.5. The provisions on intellectual property contributed to the non-ratification of the treaty by the US.

B. IPRs under the Nagoya Protocol and Traditional Knowledge

The Nagoya Protocol filled critical gaps in the CBD. It supplemented the definition of genetic resources in the Convention by adding the concept of 'derivatives', as well as subjecting traditional knowledge to access and benefit-sharing obligations.[88] The Protocol imposes an obligation on parties to take measures to ensure that traditional knowledge held by Indigenous and local communities is accessed with their prior informed consent (PIC) or approval, their involvement, and on mutually agreed terms.[89] The Protocol also recognizes that genetic resources are imperative to the survival of most Indigenous groups, and that the sustainability of such resources often depends on the cultivation and preservation of skills of local communities.[90]

The amorphous and diffused nature of traditional knowledge makes attributing ownership of such knowledge to a community, or even a specific nation, difficult. Articles 5.5 and 7 of the Protocol do not explicitly prescribe Indigenous and local communities as rights-holders of traditional knowledge, but indirectly affirm these groups as such by identifying them as beneficiaries of access agreements and benefit-sharing.[91] In contrast, traditional intellectual property regimes such as TRIPs are too narrow to address adequately and protect traditional knowledge or expressions of folklore, as these types of knowledge and expressions are often passed down through generations and in the public domain.[92] As a result, they would not reach the thresholds of novelty and inventiveness required for patent protection.

Genetic resources used as inputs for patented works are also not protected by TRIPs, although Articles 22 and 29 require sufficiency of disclosure in a patent specification. A number of developing countries have submitted proposals to amend TRIPs to require origin-of-resource disclosures in patent applications to more easily enable the identification of genetic resources from provider nations.[93] Countries such as India, South

[88] CBD refers to traditional knowledge as 'knowledge, innovations and practices of indigenous and local communities embodying traditional lifestyles relevant for the conservation and sustainable use of biological diversity' (art 8(j)). Art 2 of the Protocol defines derivatives, although it is confined to anything naturally occurring, potentially ruling out anything treated chemically; see Simon Crompton, 'The Nagoya Protocol: A Disagreement Reduced to Writing' *Managing Intellectual Property* (2010): 1.

[89] art 7.

[90] Ibid; Kanchana Kariyawasam and Matthew Tsai, 'Access to Genetic Resources and Benefit Sharing: Implications of Nagoya Protocol on Providers and Users' *Journal of World Intellectual Property*, 21/5–6 (2018): 289, 295.

[91] Thomas Greiber *et al*, *An Explanatory Guide to the Nagoya Protocol on Access and Benefit-sharing* (IUCN 2012) 1, 109.

[92] Caroline Picart and Marlowe Fox, 'Beyond Unbridled Optimism and Fear: Indigenous Peoples, Intellectual Property, Human Rights and the Globalisation of Traditional Knowledge and Expressions of Folklore: Part II' *International Community Law Review*, 16/1 (2014): 3, 34.

[93] Wallace Feng, 'Appropriation without Benefit Sharing: Origin-of-Resource Disclosure Requirements and Enforcement under TRIPS and the Nagoya Protocol' *Chicago Journal of International Law*, 18/1 (2017): 245, 259.

Africa, and the Andean Community of Bolivia, Columbia, Ecuador, and Peru have implemented national legislations which require patent applicants to reveal the source of biological materials.[94] Disclosure obligations in patent offices in developed countries, where the majority of patents are filed, would be more effective, but countries such as the United States and Japan have proven resistant.[95]

C. The Nagoya Protocol and the TRIPs Agreement

The Protocol states it is not designed to create a hierarchy between it, and other international instruments (which would include TRIPs).[96] However, it also states that the Protocol shall not affect parties' rights and duties under other international agreements entered into prior to the Protocol, unless these rights and duties cause a serious threat to biodiversity.[97] The provision suggests that existing IPRs derived from TRIPs (for example) relating to innovations based on traditional knowledge are not affected by the Protocol provided those rights do not cause a serious threat to biodiversity.[98] In terms of future intellectual property agreements, the Protocol states that parties are free to enter into such agreements provided they do not cause a serious threat to biodiversity or run counter to the objectives of the CBD or the Nagoya Protocol.[99] Hence the Protocol limits parties from entering into future IPRs agreements that would affect their obligations under the Protocol.[100]

These innovative provisions aim to preserve existing IPRs yet prioritize biodiversity and the aims and objectives of the Convention and Protocol over IPRs. The Protocol allows states to create their own protective access and benefit-sharing mechanisms provided they adhere to the Protocol's principles. For example, Article 12 requires parties to take into consideration Indigenous and local communities' customary laws, community protocols and procedures with respect to traditional knowledge, and to establish checkpoints for monitoring and enforcement. While innovative, developing countries are struggling to implement the provisions of the Protocol due to lack of inventories of genetic resources, knowledge of their value, and limited capacity to negotiate mutually agreed terms and implement monitoring systems.[101] In addition, regulatory gaps still remain regarding the recognition and protection of Indigenous peoples' biocultural rights, rights to free prior informed consent, participation, and

[94] Ibid, 271.
[95] Picart and Fox (n 92) 23.
[96] art 4.1.
[97] Ibid.
[98] Greiber *et al* (n 91) 114.
[99] art 4.2.
[100] Ibid. This includes agreements under negotiation such as in the WIPO Intergovernmental Committee on Intellectual Property, Genetic Resources, Traditional Knowledge and Folklore.
[101] Kariyawasam and Tsai (n 90) 300–301.

self-governance in light of the 2007 United Nations Declaration on the Rights of Indigenous Peoples.[102]

V. IPRS, TECHNOLOGY TRANSFER, AND CLIMATE CHANGE

Technology transfer enabling access to environmentally sound technology (EST) is seen as an integral part of climate change resilience.[103] Technology transfer should enable recipients to access low carbon technology critical to reducing emissions as well as reduce energy poverty, and to build climate-resilient societies.[104] Access to technologies such as salt and drought-resistant plant varieties are also vital adaptation strategies for vulnerable countries. Developing countries often lack the technological, institutional, and financial capacity to carry out research and development, and to access and absorb technologies, although this is no longer the case for large developing countries such as China. Due to joint venture agreements and other arrangements, China has increased its endogenous innovation capacity and entered into South-South technology transfer arrangements.[105]

IPRs fuel innovation in ESTs so a careful balance needs to be struck between fair treatment for innovators, and mechanisms to ensure the fair diffusion of such technology.[106] Developed countries have argued that lack of intellectual property laws in developing countries are the main barrier to low carbon technology transfer, with concerns of loss of proprietary control, however this approach is often seen by developing countries as protectionism by western economies.[107] Technology transfer has always been an integral and often contentious part of the UNFCCC negotiations.

[102] UNGA Res 61/295, 'United Nations Declaration on the Rights of Indigenous Peoples' (2 October 2007) UN Doc A/RES/61/295; Claudio Chiarolla, 'Genetic Resources' in Elisa Morgera and Kati Kulovesi (eds), *Research Handbook on International Law and Natural Resources* (Edward Edgar 2016) 218, 239.

[103] See Chapter 55, 'Technology Assistance and Transfers', in this volume; Monirul Azam, 'Climate Change Resilience and Technology Transfer: The Role of Intellectual Property' *Nordic Journal of International Law*, 80/4 (2011): 485.

[104] Frauke Urban, 'China's Rise: Challenging the North-South Technology Transfer Paradigm for Climate Change Mitigation and Low Carbon Energy' *Energy Policy*, 113/C (2018): 320, 321.

[105] This is also due to climate change becoming a strategic national concern of China, although South-South technology transfer is not always effective, ibid, 320.

[106] Elizabeth Burleson, 'Energy Policy, Intellectual Property and Technology Transfer to Address Climate Change' *Transnational & Comparative Problems*, 18 (2009): 69, 86; Ahmed Abdel-Latif, 'Intellectual Property Rights and the Transfer of Climate Change Technologies: Issues, Challenges and Ways Forward' *Climate Policy*, 15/1 (2015): 103, 115, 121.

[107] David Ockwell *et al*, 'Intellectual Property Rights and Low Carbon Technology Transfer: Conflicting Discourses of Diffusion and Development' *Global Environmental Change*, 20/4 (2010): 729, 731.

A. IPRs under the UNFCCC

The UNFCCC is silent on IPRs, although Article 4.7 acknowledges that the ability of developing countries to fulfil their commitments under the Convention is conditional upon the provision of financial resources and technology transfer from developed countries. In the lead-up to the 2009 Copenhagen Conference of the Parties (COP), the Ad Hoc Working Group on Long-Term Cooperative Action identified five options to address intellectual property issues, including enhanced measures to promote the transfer of clean technology, measures to address barriers to technology transfer, exclusion and revocation of patents relating to ESTs, compulsory licensing of such technologies, and the creation of a Technology Mechanism.[108] Negotiations on intellectual property, however, became so contentious that only the Technology Mechanism survived.[109] The Mechanism consists of a Technology Executive Committee which acts as a policy body, and a Climate Technology Centre and Network which acts as the operational arm responding to requests from developing countries for assistance.

The Paris Agreement established a Technology Framework which provides an overarching framework to the Technology Mechanism, based on principles such as coherence, inclusiveness, and transparency.[110] Intellectual property issues have not appeared in recent COP decisions, leading some to argue that given that the Paris Agreement's provisions are vague on the role of intellectual property, parties may revert to business as usual under TRIPs.[111] While TRIPs contains some flexibilities and may provide an avenue for developing countries to pursue transfers of environmentally sound technologies, many developing countries either do not have local manufacturing and technological bases to take advantage of these flexibilities, or are under pressure not to use them and to agree to TRIPs-plus provisions in bilateral and regional trade arrangements.[112] Although some countries have recently declared climate emergencies,[113] no country has yet attempted to use climate change as a national emergency under the compulsory licensing provisions of TRIPs.

[108] 'Report of the Ad Hoc Working Group on Long-term Cooperative Action under the Convention on its seventh session' (20 November 2009) UN Doc FCCC/AWGLCA/2009/14.

[109] Navraj Ghaleigh, 'Barriers to Climate Technology Transfer – The Chimera of Intellectual Property Rights' *Carbon & Climate Law Review*, 5/2 (2011): 220, 230.

[110] art 6; art 10 covers technology development and transfer and ties the Technology Mechanism to the Financial Mechanism under the Convention.

[111] Chen Zhou, 'Can Intellectual Property Rights Within Climate Technology Transfer Work for the UNFCCC and the Paris Agreement?' *International Environmental Agreements*, 19/1 (2019): 107, 112. Tensions still remain—the Joint Report of the Technology Executive Committee and the Climate Technology Centre and Network was not adopted in 2013 due to disagreements on intellectual property rights, see Abdel-Latif (n 106) 106.

[112] Azam (n 103) 496.

[113] See 'UK Parliament declares climate change emergency' *BBC* (1 May 2019). A number of developing countries have made analogies between the 2001 Doha Declaration on TRIPs and climate change technology transfer, see Azam (n 103) 486.

B. Other Intellectual Property Arrangements

While the UNFCCC is silent on IPRs, certain countries have implemented their own procedures to encourage innovation in environmentally sound technologies in order to promote green growth. Established in 2009, the 'Green Channel' at the United Kingdom Patents Office is designed to accelerate patent applications relating to green or environmentally friendly technologies, and applicants can choose to accelerate the search, publication, and/or examination processes.[114] Japan, Australia, Canada, Brazil, and China have similar models.[115]

The Eco-Patents Commons was established by the World Business Council on Sustainable Development and makes available technology without royalties.[116] The World Intellectual Property Organization (WIPO) has developed an IP Green Inventory for green patents in order to facilitate the adaptation, adoption, and deployment of climate-friendly technology, particularly to developing countries.[117] Mission Innovation, a platform announced at the Paris Agreement negotiations, aims to drive investment in public research and development of climate-essential technologies, but is silent on IPRs.[118]

VI. CONCLUSION

Innovation in technologies is essential to combatting pressing global environmental and sustainable development issues such as loss of biological diversity, climate change, and energy and food insecurity. Tension over access to these technologies, through IPRs, has been a persistent source of conflict. International agreements reflect these tensions, with developing countries trying to balance the restrictions and omissions of TRIPs through biodiversity agreements. Attempts to amend TRIPs are unlikely to be successful in the near future, but increased use of existing TRIPs flexibilities may be imminent as environmental crises escalate. However, developments in biotechnology may outstrip the capacity of legal arrangements to manage them.[119]

[114] See UK IP Office, 'Published Green Channel Patent Applications' <https://www.ipo.gov.uk/p-gcp.htm> accessed 5 January 2020.

[115] Bingbin Lu, 'Expedited Patent Examination for Green Inventions: Developing Countries' Policy Choices' *Energy Policy*, 61/C (2013): 1529, 1534.

[116] See Jo Bowman, 'The Eco-Patent Commons: Caring through Sharing' *WIPO* (June 2009).

[117] See Anja von der Ropp, 'WIPO GREEN: Facilitating Dissemination of Green Technology' *WIPO* (June 2012).

[118] Brian Israel, 'International Cooperation, Intellectual Property and Climate-Essential Innovation' in Neil Craik *et al* (eds), *Global Environmental Change and Innovation in International Law* (CUP 2018) 223, 224.

[119] eg CRISPR (Clustered Regularly Interspaced Short Palindromic Repeats) tools to edit genomes and environmental or eDNA collected separately from material samples, see Michael Stramiello,

Existing levers, such as increased public investment in research and development, international cooperation in research and development,[120] and climate technology patent pools, could soften the private ordering strictures of existing intellectual property regimes,[121] and increase the availability and diffusion of existing and future technologies. Increased capacity in developing countries is also needed to create institutional, financial, and technological capacity to absorb emergent technologies and create and strengthen endogenous capacity to create and diffuse nationally appropriate technologies. At the same time, developing countries could create and strengthen their own regulatory structures to recognize and protect Indigenous and local knowledge and genetic resources, in order to secure benefits for the sustainable use of their resources.

BIBLIOGRAPHY

Robert Falkner and Aarti Gupta, 'The Limits of Regulatory Convergence: Globalization and GMO Politics in the South' *International Environmental Agreements: Politics, Law and Economics*, 9/2 (2009): 113

Carmen Gonzalez, 'Genetically Modified Organisms and Justice: The International Environmental Justice Implications of Biotechnology' *Georgetown International Environmental Law Review*, 19/4 (2007): 583

Susan Sell, *Private Power, Public Law: The Globalization of Intellectual Property Rights* (CUP 2003)

Elsa Tsioumani, 'Beyond Access and Benefit Sharing: Lessons from the Law and Governance of Agricultural Biodiversity' *The Journal of World Intellectual Property*, 21/3–4 (2018): 106

'CRISPR: The New Frontier of Biotechnology Innovation' *Landslide Digital Feature*, 10/3 (2018); Stephen Leahy, 'New eDNA Tool "changes everything in marine science"' *National Geographic* (2018).

120 eg the Indo-US Joint Clean Energy R&D Centre (JCERDC) was established in 2010.

121 Israel (n 118) 225, 235.

CHAPTER 49

ENERGY

CATHERINE REDGWELL

I. INTRODUCTION

It is incontrovertible that energy production and consumption[1] cause significant transboundary harm and are a major contributor to greenhouse gas (GHG) emissions. Although the 2015 Paris Agreement does not address energy directly,[2] achieving the Agreement's objectives will necessarily involve a fundamental transition in global energy systems. Hence, in setting forth decarbonization goals, nationally determined contributions (NDCs) have referred to energy policies and measures.[3] Whether energy constitutes conventional fossil-fuels or renewable energy sources, energy production and consumption can impact the environment,[4] for good or for ill. This 'Janus faced' characteristic of energy as both environmental threat and contributor to sustainable energy is reflected in the leading texts on international environmental law. These address (conventional) energy activities as part of the problem, viz, a source of environmental harm, and renewable energy and energy efficiency—that is, sustainable energy more broadly—as part of the solution.[5] That said, the adverse impact on habitat and

[1] See International Energy Agency (IEA), 'World Energy Outlook 2019' <https://www.iea.org/reports/world-energy-outlook-2019> accessed 27 December 2019.

[2] Its '[f]ailure to signal the phase-out of fossil fuels' is one of the limitations of the 'Paris Outcome' identified by Meinhard Doelle, 'Assessment of Strengths and Weaknesses' in Daniel Klein *et al* (eds), *The Paris Agreement on Climate Change: Analysis and Commentary* (OUP 2017) 384.

[3] See eg Panagiotis Fragkos *et al*, 'Energy System Impacts and Policy Implications of the European Intended Nationally Determined Contribution and Low-Carbon Pathway to 2050' *Energy Policy*, 100 (2017): 216; 'Background Note: Renewables and NDC Implementation Partnership' (9 October 2019) IRENA Doc C/18/BN/2; Chapter 29, 'Climate Change', in this volume.

[4] For early recognition see 'Recommendation on Reduction of Environmental Impacts from Energy Production and Use' (12 October 1976) Organisation for Economic Co-operation and Development (OECD) C (76)162 (Final).

[5] See eg Philippe Sands and Jacqueline Peel, *Principles of International Environmental Law* (4th edn, CUP 2018) 604–606, 886.

biodiversity of increased reliance on alternative fuel sources such as biofuels,[6] and of renewable energy projects on World Heritage properties,[7] illustrates that this dichotomy is too stark, and the reality is much more complex.

This 'Janus faced' characteristic of energy is reflected in the dominant narratives that emerge in discussion of energy and environment. One narrative is of energy activities as a pollution threat to be prevented, reduced, controlled,[8] and eliminated.[9] This framing is reflected, for example, in the definition of marine pollution in the 1982 United Nations Convention on the Law of the Sea (UNCLOS) as 'the introduction by man, directly or indirectly, of substances or energy into the marine environment'.[10] Such concerns are writ large where ultrahazardous energy activities are concerned, with the development, inter alia, of notification and assistance obligations, at treaty and customary law, reflecting concerns about the effects of such activities, heightened by the Chernobyl and Fukushima nuclear incidents.[11] Here there is a marked tendency to promote the economic activity first—for instance, transport of oil by sea, offshore petroleum operations, operation of nuclear power plants—followed by realization of the need to take further preventive and precautionary action to address risks and environmental harms. Legacy issues, such as large offshore platforms that cannot safely be entirely removed and radioactive waste requiring secure long-term disposal, are the result.[12]

Another aspect of the 'energy as environmental threat' narrative is that incompatible energy activities often undermine conservation and environmental protection objectives in habitat and biodiversity conservation treaties. In general, substantive treaty obligations such as the obligation to protect and preserve the marine environment,[13] to conserve biological diversity,[14] and to conserve natural and/or cultural heritage sites,[15] are not subject to express treaty exceptions permitting derogation for energy purposes. To the contrary: the 1992 Convention on Biological Diversity (CBD) requires

[6] See eg Decision XI/27, 'Biofuels and biodiversity' (5 December 2012) UNEP/CBD/COP/DEC/XI/27; Luciano Verdade, Carlos Piña, and Luís Rosalino, 'Biofuels and Biodiversity: Challenges and Opportunities' *Environmental Development*, 15 (2015): 64; see also Ramsar Resolution X.25, 'Wetlands and "biofuels"' (28 October 2008).

[7] See further text at n 107.

[8] The language eg of the UNCLOS, art 194.

[9] The more modern framing see eg 1992 Helsinki Water Convention on the Protection and Use of Transboundary Watercourses and International Lakes, art 3; 1996 London Protocol on the Prevention of Marine Pollution by Dumping of Wastes and Other Matter, art 2.

[10] art 1.4.

[11] International Atomic Energy Agency (IAEA) and OECD, 'International Nuclear Law in the Post-Chernobyl Period' (2006); Günther Handl, 'Preventing Transboundary Nuclear Pollution: A Post-Fukushima Legal Perspective' in Shunmugam Jayakumar *et al* (eds), *Transboundary Pollution: Evolving Issues of International Law and Policy* (Edward Elgar 2015) 190.

[12] Catherine Redgwell and Lavanya Rajamani, 'Energy Underground: What's International Law Got To Do With It?' in Donald Zillman *et al* (eds), *The Law of Energy Underground—Understanding New Developments in Subsurface Production, Transmission, and Storage* (OUP 2014) 101.

[13] UNCLOS, art 192.

[14] CBD, art 1.

[15] World Heritage Convention, art 4.

parties to regulate processes and categories which have significant adverse effect on biological diversity, and the 1972 World Heritage Convention expressly provides for a 'List of World Heritage in Danger' from, inter alia, 'large-scale public or private projects', each of which encompasses large-scale energy activities at the very least.[16] The very first site to be removed from the World Heritage List was in 2007 when the viability of an Arabian Oryx Sanctuary in Oman, with a dwindling population already under pressure from poaching and habitat degradation, was fatally undermined by a 90% reduction in the size of the protected area to facilitate hydrocarbon activities. This caused the loss of the outstanding universal value and integrity for which the site was first inscribed on the List in 1994.[17] The potential incompatibility of energy activities is also evident in Antarctica: the 1959 Antarctic Treaty established the first nuclear-free zone, prohibiting the disposal of radioactive waste there, while the 1991 Madrid Environmental Protocol prohibits all mining activities (including petroleum), both onshore and offshore, for fifty years.[18]

The other face of energy is reflected in another, more recent, narrative, where energy and environmental objectives are viewed more synergistically, and this is in the context of the role of energy—especially renewable energy and energy efficiency—in environmental protection and sustainable development.[19] It is in the sustainable energy context that we see some alignment, even convergence, of energy and environment. As will become evident, this convergence arises because environmental issues are increasingly drivers of energy law and policy, both nationally,[20] and internationally.[21] In turn, response to the adverse impacts of energy activities is a key stimulus for developing international environmental law, both substantively in fields such as nuclear energy and marine environmental protection, and procedurally, such as the duty to consult and to notify.

This chapter considers these narratives in the context of the applicable principles (Section II), and the procedural (Section III) and substantive norms (Section IV), governing the energy and environment interface. The concluding section of the chapter (Section V) considers whether the emerging picture is one of increasing, though still limited, convergence.

[16] CBD, art 8.1; World Heritage Convention, art 11.4; Catherine Redgwell, 'The International Law of Public Participation: Protected Areas, Endangered Species and Biological Diversity' in Donald Zillman *et al* (eds), *Human Rights in Natural Resources Development* (OUP 2002) 187.

[17] UNESCO Decision 31 COM 7B.11, 'State of conservation of World Heritage properties—Arabian Oryx Sanctuary' WHC-07/31.COM/24 (31 July 2007); see also <https://whc.unesco.org/en/soc/973> accessed 27 December 2019; see generally, Francesco Francioni, with Federico Lenzerini (eds), *The 1972 World Heritage Convention: A Commentary* (OUP 2008).

[18] Antarctic Treaty, art V(1); Madrid Environmental Protocol, art 7. Contrast with the Arctic (n 68).

[19] An example is Rosemary Lyster and Adrian Bradbrook, *Energy Law and the Environment* (CUP 2006).

[20] See eg Jody Freeman, 'The Uncomfortable Convergence of Energy and Environmental Law' *Harvard Environmental Law Review*, 41 (2017): 339, 342.

[21] See eg Lyster and Bradbrook (n 19); Catherine Redgwell, 'International Regulation of Energy Activities' in Martha Roggenkamp *et al* (eds), *Energy Law in Europe* (3rd edn, OUP 2016) 13.

II. KEY PRINCIPLES

Several principles of international environmental law and international law more generally are relevant, to differing degrees, for an understanding of the energy-environment interface. These include the principles of:

- Permanent sovereignty over natural resources (PSNR);
- Sustainable development;
- Due diligence;
- Prevention;
- Precaution; and
- Polluter pays

Certain principles can best (though not only) be explained by reference to concerns over energy resources, particularly the principle of permanent sovereignty over natural resources (PSNR).[22] However, PSNR is not an absolute principle, with limitations posed by environmental and sustainability concerns.[23] A dependable and sustainable energy future has been a core element of sustainable development policy since its emergence,[24] and is currently reflected in Sustainable Development Goal (SDG) 7 on 'affordable and cleaner energy'.[25] Sustainability imports requirements of fairness and equity when sharing among states, intra-generationally and inter-generationally, the benefits and burdens of energy resource exploration and exploitation.[26] It may be argued that many energy resource development decisions today are 'sustainability constrained',[27] with such constraints all the more urgent and important given the strong linkages between sustainable energy exploitation and consumption and combatting climate change,[28]

[22] United Nations General Assembly (UNGA) Res 1803/27, 'Permanent Sovereignty over Natural Resources' (14 December 1962) UN Doc A/RES/1803/XVII; *Armed Activities on the Territory of the Congo (Congo/Uganda)* (Judgement) [2005] ICJ Rep 168 (customary international law).

[23] Nico Schrijver, *Sovereignty over Natural Resources: Balancing Rights and Duties* (CUP 1997); Catherine Redgwell, 'Sustainable Development of National Energy Resources: What Has International Law Got To Do With It?' *Journal of Sustainable Development Law and Policy*, 8/1 (2017): 1.

[24] World Commission on Environment and Development, *Our Common Future* (OUP 1987) ch 7; Chapter 17, 'Sustainable Development', in this volume; on legal status see Vaughan Lowe, 'Sustainable Development and Unsustainable Arguments' in Alan Boyle and David Freestone (eds), *International Law and Sustainable Development* (OUP 1999) 19.

[25] 'Sustainable Energy for All' <https://www.se4all.org> accessed 27 December 2019; see further Section IV.B.2.

[26] Catherine Redgwell and Lavanya Rajamani, 'And Justice for All? Energy Justice in International Law' in Iñigo del Guayo *et al* (eds), *Energy Law and Distributional Justice* (OUP 2020) 48.

[27] Rosalyn Higgins, 'Natural Resources in the Case Law of the International Court' in Boyle and Freestone (n 24) 111.

[28] On the role of sustainable development in the 2015 Paris Agreement (preambular recital 8, arts 2.1, 4.1, 6.8) see María Carzo and Daniel Klein, 'Implications for Public International Law: Initial Considerations' in Klein (n 2) 408.

safeguarding food production, and ensuring access to secure energy supplies as part of sustainable development.[29]

Clearly, sustainability concerns foster increasing convergence between energy and environmental concerns—but only up to a point. In the international legal context, there is currently little foundation for arguing that the principle of sustainable development, and a duty of optimum or sustainable use, applies to (non-living) energy resources.[30] Moreover, while interconnected, 'sustainable' does not mean 'equitable': the principle of equitable use rests on the foundation of shared sovereignty and is of particular resonance for shared resources such as international watercourses—not energy resources.[31] In any case, 'sustainable use of natural resources' is highly contextualized and has no single fixed meaning.[32] This follows logically from the fact that the legal status of natural resources varies according to whether the resource is under the sovereignty of one state, shared by several states, or held in common for the benefit of all. Mainly, however, energy resources fall into the first category, with elements of the third only in respect of the common heritage of mankind principle applicable to deep seabed mineral resources.[33]

The pertinence of other key environmental principles, given the potential for significant transboundary harm caused by energy production and consumption, scarcely needs underscoring. Most notable is the obligation not to cause significant harm to the territory of other states or to areas beyond national jurisdiction and the allied principle of prevention and obligation of due diligence,[34] and the principle of cooperation, including the duty to notify and consult with other states regarding risks arising from hazardous activities, including accidents.[35] These principles are inextricably linked: 'If

[29] See IEA, 'Our Mission' <https://www.iea.org/about/mission> accessed 27 December 2019.

[30] Catherine Redgwell, 'Sustainable Use of Natural Resources' in Ludwig Krämer and Emanuela Orlando (eds), *Principles of Environmental Law: Elgar Encyclopedia of Environmental Law series* (Edward Elgar 2018) vol 6, 115; James Harrison and Elisa Morgera, 'Article 61' in Alexander Proelss (ed), *United Nations Convention on the Law of the Sea: A Commentary* (C.H. Beck/Hart/Nomos 2017) 482 (no equivalent conservation and management provision for non-living resources).

[31] See further Redgwell and Rajamani (n 12) 118–119; see Chapter 30, 'Freshwater Resources', in this volume.

[32] See further Redgwell, 'Sustainable Use' (n 30).

[33] Duncan French, 'From the Depths: Rich Pickings of Principles of Sustainable Development and General International Law on the Ocean Floor—The Seabed Disputes Chamber's 2011 Advisory Opinion' *International Journal of Marine and Coastal Law*, 26 (2011): 525.

[34] Chapter 16, 'Harm Prevention', in this volume; Leslie-Anne Duvic-Paoli and Jorge Viñuales, 'Principle 2: Prevention' in Jorge Viñuales (ed), *The Rio Declaration on Environment and Development* (OUP 2015) 107.

[35] Phoebe Okowa, 'Principle 18: Notification and Assistance in Case of Emergency' in Viñuales (n 34) 471; Laurence Chazournes and Komlan Sangbana, 'Principle 19: Notification and Consultation on Activities with Transboundary Impact' in ibid, 493. As Alan Boyle and Catherine Redgwell observe, 'even if notification and consultation in cases of transboundary risk are not independent customary rules, non-compliance with them is likely to be evidence of a failure to act diligently in protecting other states from harm under Rio Principle 2': Alan Boyle and Catherine Redgwell, *International Law and the Environment* (4th edn, OUP 2021) ch 3, 92.

due diligence is the first rule of transboundary environmental risk management, co-operation is the second'.[36]

The preventive and precautionary[37] principles are of vital importance in the energy context given that many energy activities may result in irreversible or irremediable environment harm, most notably, though not exclusively, in the context of ultrahazardous activities such as nuclear energy generation. While not part of general international law,[38] the polluter pays principle, which entails that the polluter should, in principle, bear the costs of pollution,[39] is reflected in a number of regional and global pollution treaties and civil liability regimes for example for nuclear and oil pollution damage.[40] However, since in practice these regimes channel and limit liability, the efficacy of the principle may be challenged both because it lacks a sufficiently preventive focus, and because 'the polluter' is not the only one that pays where there is a major oil spill (with responsibility shared by the ship's owner and the cargo owner) or widespread harm from a nuclear incident (where there is sharing of risk between the operator, state of operation, and state parties to the liability regime).[41]

III. PROCEDURAL NORMS

Several procedural norms of international environmental law, such as duties of cooperation, environmental impact assessment (EIA), and public participation, have particular resonance for energy activities. They serve as a means for integrating environmental considerations into energy development projects and, in turn, the energy context has served as a ground for testing and developing these norms.

[36] Boyle and Redgwell (n 35) ch 3, 89.

[37] See Chapter 18, 'Precaution', in this volume.

[38] See eg *Case concerning the audit of accounts between the Netherlands and France in application of the Protocol of 25 September 1991 Additional to the Convention for the Protection of the Rhine from Pollution by Chlorides of 3 December 1976* (2005) 25 RIAA 267 [103]; Boyle and Redgwell (n 35) ch 5, 69.

[39] *Report of the United Nations Conference on Environment and Development* (UN 1993) vol I, annex I—'Rio Declaration on Environment and Development', principle 16; Priscilla Schwartz, 'Principle 16: The Polluter-Pays Principle' in Viñuales (n 34) 429; defined in broadly similar terms in the 1994 Energy Charter Treaty, art 19.1.

[40] See eg 1960 Paris Convention on Third Party Liability in the Field of Nuclear Energy; 1997 Vienna Convention on Civil Liability for Nuclear Damage; 1969 International Convention on Civil Liability for Oil Pollution Damage (replaced by 1992 CLC); 1971 International Convention on the Establishment of an International Fund for Compensation for Oil Pollution Damage; Protocol of 1992 to amend the International Convention on Civil Liability for Oil Pollution Damage, 1969 (CLC); 2006 Small Tanker Oil Pollution Indemnification Agreement.

[41] Or, as in the case of Chernobyl, 'the victim pays': Boyle and Redgwell (n 35) ch 5, 72–73.

A. Cooperative Duties

Customary international law includes procedural obligations to cooperate, and to consult and to notify, in the context of shared resources and ultrahazardous activities in particular, both of which may be implicated in energy projects. Such obligations may also be embedded in specific treaties otherwise addressed to wider substantive issues. For example, in the provisional measures phase of the *MOX Nuclear Fuel Plant* arbitration before the International Tribunal for the Law of the Sea (ITLOS), the Tribunal recognized the duty to cooperate as a fundamental principle of marine pollution under Part XII of UNCLOS. ITLOS invoked this duty in ordering that Ireland and the United Kingdom were to exchange further information, monitor risks, and devise pollution prevention measures.[42]

B. Duty to Assess Environmental Impacts

The International Court of Justice (ICJ) has found an EIA[43] to be a necessary element of 'due diligence', which is interpreted so as to entail the 'adoption of appropriate rules and measures' as well as 'a certain level of vigilance in their enforcement and the exercise of administrative control applicable to public and private operators, such as the monitoring of activities undertaken by such operators'.[44] Although the specific content of the EIA is left to the state's discretion, international law requires that an EIA is conducted and that it bears a relation to the 'nature and magnitude of the proposed development and its likely adverse impact on the environment'.[45] The trigger for the requirement to conduct a transboundary EIA—for example, where a particular energy project may have wide-ranging environmental effects—is a high degree of probability of significant adverse transboundary impact from the proposed energy activities. Several MEAs also contain specific provisions requiring an EIA, where an EIA is an integral element of the environmental protection regime established.[46] International financial institutions with significant funding of the energy sector, such as the European Bank for

[42] *The MOX Plant case (Ireland/United Kingdom)* (Provisional Measures, Order of 3 December 2001) [2001] ITLOS Rep 95; on the obligation to consult and to notify in the nuclear context more generally, see Section IV.B.1.

[43] Neil Craik, 'Principle 17: Environmental Impact Assessment' in Viñuales (n 34) 107.

[44] *Pulp Mills on the River Uruguay (Argentina/Uruguay)* (Judgement) [2010] ICJ Rep 14 [197] (Pulp Mills case); see also *Responsibilities and obligations of States sponsoring persons and entities with respect to activities in the Area* (Advisory Opinion) [2011] ITLOS Rep 10 [145]–[148].

[45] Pulp Mills case (n 44) [205].

[46] See eg CBD, art 14; Madrid Environmental Protocol, art 8.1, annex 1; UNCLOS, art 206; 1998 Energy Protocol to the 1991 Alpine Convention, art 12; see also ECT, art 19.1(i) but subject to Understanding 13 in ECT which subordinates EIA to national determination of the methods and means of such assessment.

Reconstruction and Development (EBRD)[47] and the World Bank,[48] employ EIAs, and the tool is also included in the ISO 14000 standards.[49]

Further detailed provision for EIAs are found in the UN Economic Commission for Europe (ECE) 1991 Espoo Convention where the Annex I 'List of Activities' for which an EIA is required includes several energy-related activities, such as crude oil refineries, thermal power stations, nuclear installations, and large-diameter oil and gas pipelines. The likelihood of large-scale energy projects requiring an EIA is reinforced by the ECE's website which provides six illustrative case study fact sheets, four of which are energy-related projects.[50]

The Nord Stream gas pipeline project providing for the export of Russian gas to Western European markets via the Baltic sea was the first occasion a 'complex [energy] megaproject' was considered under the Espoo Convention.[51] An EIA was required not only as a matter of the domestic law of all five Baltic states, but also as a requirement under Espoo where the impacts on other littoral states, and of the project as a whole, were taken into account. One of the difficulties posed by the project was the implicitly limited transboundary notion at the heart of Espoo, ill-adapted to an offshore multi-jurisdictional project. An example is the requirement of consultation regarding project alternatives, including no action, which if applied in isolation at the national level would be highly impracticable where the pipeline route crosses multiple jurisdictions.[52] The parties chose to take a holistic, 'community' approach to the impacts across the region, and Nord Stream AG prepared an omnibus assessment covering all five jurisdictions with certain common elements—for example, water quality, seabed sediment, hydrography, and seabed topography, benthic flora and fauna, and cultural heritage impacts—as well as factors pertinent to only one or two states—for example, landscape impacts in Germany and Russia. Here the Espoo Convention appears to have acted as 'an efficient instrument for intergovernmental cooperation'; a joint report by the Swedish and Danish Ministries of Environment concluded that 'without Espoo, large transboundary pipeline projects would suffer from chaotic, uncoordinated public participation and unclear permitting processes'.[53]

[47] Oil and gas developments, large-scale pipelines, and minerals operations require compulsory EIA under World Bank, 'Environmental assessment sourcebook—Policies, procedures, and cross-sectoral issues' vol I (1992) appendix I—'Environmental Screening for Projects Requiring Environmental Assessment' <https://elibrary.worldbank.org/doi/pdf/10.1596/0-8213-1843-8> accessed 4 February 2020.

[48] Operational Manual, OP 4.01—Environmental Assessment (January 1999) <https://policies.worldbank.org/sites/ppf3/PPFDocuments/090224b0822f7384.pdfhttp:///> accessed 27 December 2019.

[49] 'International Organization for Standardization' <https://www.iso.org/home.html> accessed 27 December 2019.

[50] See <https://www.unece.org/env/eia/pubs/factsheets.html> accessed 27 December 2019.

[51] <https://www.nord-stream.com/> accessed 27 December 2019; Timo Koivurova and Ismo Pölönen, 'Transboundary Environmental Assessment in the Case of the Baltic Sea Gas Pipeline' *International Journal of Marine and Coastal Law*, 25 (2010): 151.

[52] art 5; Koivurova and Pölönen (n 51).

[53] Catherine Redgwell, 'Contractual and Treaty Arrangements Supporting Large European Transboundary Pipeline Projects' in Martha Roggenkamp *et al* (eds), *Energy Networks and the Law* (OUP 2012) 102, 115.

C. Public Participation

An integral part of the Espoo Convention is public participation in the EIA process. These provisions are amplified by another ECE instrument, the 1998 Aarhus Convention, which establishes international minimum standards in respect of its three pillars: access to environmental information; public participation in environmental decision-making; and access to environmental justice.[54] Both the Espoo and Aarhus Conventions establish compliance mechanisms, with the latter allowing submissions by members of the public, including NGOs, many of which have concerned energy projects.[55] Additionally, there are (non-binding) international instruments that recognize public participation in decision-making.[56] However, the ICJ in the *Pulp Mills* case did not find a general legal obligation to consult with the public.[57] The position, therefore, is weaker outside the ECE context. In relation to energy activities on Indigenous peoples' lands, however, the legal case for public participation is stronger. Indigenous peoples have the right to self-determination, and by extension, it is argued, to free, prior, and informed consent in relation to (energy) development projects within their lands, and which impact their resources.[58]

IV. SUBSTANTIVE NORMS

Substantive norms governing the interface of energy activities and the environment can be divided into two general categories, canvassed in the following sections. The first category concerns norms addressing the downstream environmental impacts of energy activities, such as marine or transboundary air pollution, or GHG emissions. The second category concerns the direct regulation of energy activities, such as nuclear energy and renewables, that have environmental impacts.

[54] arts 4, 6, 9 respectively. See further Chapter 21, 'Public Participation', in this volume.

[55] Leslie-Anne Duvic-Paoli, 'Public Participation in the Context of Energy Activities: The Role of the Aarhus Convention Compliance Committee' in Marc Ozawa *et al* (eds), *In Search of Good Energy Policy* (CUP 2019) 224.

[56] Jonas Ebbesson, 'Principle 10: Public Participation' in Viñuales (n 34) 288.

[57] Pulp Mills case (n 44) [215]–[219].

[58] See UN Human Rights Office of the High Commissioner, Indigenous Peoples – Annual Reports <https://www.ohchr.org/EN/Issues/IPeoples/SRIndigenousPeoples/Pages/AnnualReports.aspx> accessed 27 December 2019; UN Human Rights Council, 'Report of the Special Rapporteur on the rights of indigenous peoples, James Anaya—Extractive industries and indigenous peoples' (1 July 2013) UN Doc A/HRC/24/41; see further Chapter 42, 'Indigenous Peoples', in this volume.

A. Addressing the Environmental Impacts of Energy Activities

1. *Vessel source pollution*

Vessel source pollution,[59] though a relatively minor source of marine pollution, has been extensively regulated owing to the high visibility, and often high impact locally and transnationally, of oil tanker spills in particular, starting with the Torrey Canyon in 1967.[60] The 1973/78 MARPOL Convention[61] sets out the standards relating to operational and accidental pollution from ships. It is assumed that it establishes the 'global rules and standards' referred to in UNCLOS on pollution from vessels, as well as being one source of the 'generally accepted international rules and standards' applied and enforced by coastal and port states.[62]

MARPOL comprises a framework Convention and six Annexes, the first two of which (addressed to oil and noxious liquids in bulk, respectively) are obligatory to become a party to the Convention. Annex I reflects a particular preoccupation with vessel-source oil pollution, focusing on limiting discharges of oil as part of routine tanker operations. It sets forth oil discharge and tanker design criteria and requires coastal states to provide adequate reception facilities for oily residues. Some maritime areas have been designated as 'special areas' under MARPOL 73/78 in which no discharge is permitted, including areas such as the North-west Atlantic Ocean and Mediterranean Sea areas, and the Antarctic Southern ocean.

These preventive standard-setting and enforcement measures are buttressed by further measures on oil pollution preparedness and response and by substantial regulation of oil pollution liability, the regime for which has evolved to include recovery of the costs of preventive measures and for environmental damage.[63] There is no doubt that combined these measures have had some beneficial impact in reducing the number and adverse environmental impacts of maritime pollution incidents.[64]

[59] See Chapter 31, 'The Protection of the Marine Environment: Pollution and Fisheries', in this volume.

[60] See International Tanker Owners Pollution Federation, 'Oil Tanker Spill Statistics 2018' <https://www.itopf.org/fileadmin/data/Documents/Company_Lit/Oil_Spill_Stats_2019.pdf> accessed 27 December 2019.

[61] Malgosia Fitzmaurice, 'The International Convention For the Prevention of Pollution from Ships (MARPOL)' in Malgosia Fitzmaurice, Norman Gutiérrez, and Riyaz Hamza (eds), *The IMLI Manual on International Maritime Law Vol III: Marine Environmental Law and Maritime Security Law* (OUP 2016) 33.

[62] art 211.2; Catherine Redgwell, 'The Never Ending Story: The Role of GAIRS in UNCLOS Implementation in the Offshore Energy Sector' in Jill Barrett and Richard Barnes (eds), *Law of the Sea UNCLOS as a Living Treaty* (British Institute of International and Comparative Law 2016) 167.

[63] Måns Jacobsson, 'Liability and Compensation for Ship-Source Pollution' in Fitzmaurice, Gutiérrez, and Hamza (n 61) 285.

[64] Oil Tanker Spill Statistics 2018 (n 60).

2. *Offshore energy exploration and exploitation activities*

Environmental impacts from offshore energy activities may arise in many ways: the location of exploration and exploitation activities in areas of environmental sensitivity; deliberate disposal from offshore installations of domestic and industrial waste; operational discharges of oily or chemical drilling wastes; accidental blow-outs; collisions between installations and ships; and the rupture of pipelines from normal wear and tear or as a result of damage caused by trawling activities. In particular, major blow-outs in the Timor Sea (eg Montara, 2009) and Gulf of Mexico (eg Deepwater Horizon, 2010) focused renewed attention on the regulation of offshore petroleum installations.

Unlike in relation to vessel-source pollution, however, there is a notable gap in the international regulation of offshore energy activities, and in the general framework of UNCLOS which is criticized for failing adequately to protect the marine environment from the harmful effects of oil and gas activities.[65] Specific regional arrangements have more thoroughly addressed marine pollution arising from continental shelf exploration and exploitation, and can fill both substantive and procedural gaps in the implementation of UNCLOS in the offshore energy sector. One notable example is the 1994 Offshore Protocol to the Barcelona Convention[66] to which the European Union (EU) acceded as part of its response to Deepwater Horizon.[67] As new areas for petroleum exploration are opening up in fragile ecosystems such as the Arctic, these regulatory gaps may become all the more pressing. In 2013 the first legally binding instrument to be adopted by Arctic states was addressed to cooperation on marine oil pollution preparedness and response.[68]

In addition to new instruments, gap-filling in, and 'future proofing' of existing instruments is a common feature in the offshore energy sector given that certain technical developments could not be foreseen, such as: the extent of offshore renewables development and the need for related transmission infrastructure; the use of depleted offshore reservoirs for storage of CO_2 (carbon capture and storage (CCS)); and the exploitation of methane hydrates.[69] An example is amendments to the 1996 London

[65] Maria Gavouneli, 'Energy Installations in the Marine Environment' in Barrett and Barnes (n 62) 187, 188; Myron Nordquist *et al* (eds), *The Regulation of Continental Shelf Development: Rethinking International Standards* (Brill 2013).

[66] Protocol for the Protection of the Mediterranean Sea against Pollution Resulting from Exploration and Exploitation of the Continental Shelf and the Seabed and its Subsoil; see also the 1976 Protocol Concerning Cooperation In Combating Pollution Of The Mediterranean Sea By Oil And Other Harmful Substances In Cases Of Emergency and 1982 Protocol concerning Mediterranean Specially Protected Areas.

[67] See Commission, 'Facing the challenge of the safety of offshore oil and gas activities' COM(2010) 560 final.

[68] See also the (non-binding) 'Arctic Offshore Oil and Gas Guidelines: Systems Safety Management and Safety Culture—Avoiding Major Disasters in Offshore Oil and Gas Operations' (21 February 2014); supplementing existing IMO instruments, International Code for Ships Operating in Polar Waters (adopted 15 May 2015, entered into force 1 January 2017) MEPC 68/21/Add.1, 3, annex 10 (Polar Code)—IMO Res MEPC.264(68).

[69] See further Redgwell and Rajamani (n 12); Polar Code (n 68).

Protocol[70] in 2006 to allow disposal of CO_2 in sub-seabed geological formations,[71] and in 2013 to address marine geo-engineering,[72] both in response to proposed climate change measures.

3. *Transboundary air pollution*

A potentially wide range of energy activities may contribute to transboundary air pollution. For example, coal burning, particularly in coal-fired power stations, has been closely linked with acid rain.[73] The 1979 Convention on Long Range Transboundary Air Pollution (LRTAP)[74] was the first multilateral convention to regulate the transboundary environmental consequences of energy production at the regional level.[75] It is also the only major regional agreement addressed to air pollution, a reflection both of the severity of the problem in Europe (Canada and the United States are also parties)[76] and the difficulty in achieving international regulation of an activity impacting on sovereign energy and other choices.

The purpose of the Convention is to prevent, reduce, and control transboundary air pollution from both new and existing sources.[77] 'Air pollution' includes harm to living resources, ecosystems, and interference with amenities and legitimate uses of the environment.[78] The framework approach of the Convention has allowed a step-by-step approach by states allowing 'agreement' at the outset even where there is no consensus regarding the concrete steps to be taken to address a particular environmental problem. To date eight Protocols on monitoring and on specific air pollutants with specific reduction targets and timetables have been added to the initial framework convention, significantly expanding the scope of the parties' commitments and establishing an Implementation Committee to review compliance by parties with the reporting obligations of the Convention and any non-compliance with the Protocols.

4. *Climate change*

The global impact of human-induced climate change caused by the emission of GHGs is now widely recognized.[79] The chief GHGs are carbon dioxide, nitrous oxide, methane,

[70] Protocol to the (London) Convention on the Prevention of Marine Pollution by Dumping of Wastes and Other Matter.

[71] 'Carbon dioxide streams from carbon dioxide capture processes for sequestration' was added to annex I.

[72] art 6 bis, new annexes 4, 5.

[73] See Jutta Brunnée, *Acid Rain and Ozone Layer Depletion* (CUP 1988); UNDP *et al*, 'World Energy Assessment: Energy and the Challenge of Sustainability' (2000), ch 3; see eg the 1985 Protocol to the 1979 LRTAP on the Reduction of Sulphur Emissions or their Transboundary Fluxes by at Least 30 per cent, preamble.

[74] See Chapter 28, 'Transboundary Air Pollution', in this volume.

[75] The only global instrument is MARPOL Annex VI (Regulations for the Prevention of Air Pollution from Ships).

[76] But see Southeast Asian examples in Jayakumar *et al* (n 11) 295, 327.

[77] See eg 1994 Protocol to the 1979 LRTAP on Further Reduction of Sulphur Emissions, art 2.

[78] art 1(a).

[79] See Chapter 29, 'Climate Change', in this volume.

and tropospheric ozone. Of these sources it is the increasing release of carbon into the atmosphere which poses the greatest threat of increased global heating, to which conventional coal-fired power stations and the burning of fossil-fuels make a significant contribution. Unconventional sources likewise pose climate change challenges—the emission of methane from shale gas extraction for example.[80] In total, the energy sector accounts for around two-thirds of total GHG emissions, with more than 80% of global energy consumption based on fossil-fuels.[81]

Energy production and consumption are thus centre stage in climate change, both as a source of the problem and as part of solutions for mitigation and adaptation. There are clear synergies between the objectives and goals of the Paris Agreement 'which cannot be achieved without a significant increase of renewable energies and energy efficiency, and reduction of fossil fuel production, consumption and related subsidies' and (sustainable) energy production and consumption.[82] The energy sector is also vulnerable to climate change impacts, whether the immediate catastrophic effects of extreme weather events or the more long-term impacts of sea-level rise on coastal infrastructure and of changing patterns of heating and cooling on energy demand.[83]

B. Direct Regulation of Energy Production and Consumption

1. *Nuclear*

Given that nuclear energy activities are ultrahazardous in character with potentially devastating transboundary implications, the extent of international regulatory activity is unsurprising. Regional[84] and global[85] conventions have been adopted,[86] designed to elaborate and harmonize legislation relating to third party liability to ensure that compensation is paid for persons suffering nuclear damage, while at the same time ensuring that the development and use of nuclear energy remains commercially feasible. Channelling and limiting liability achieves both of these aims, with the nuclear

[80] See John Broderick *et al*, *Shale Gas: An Updated Assessment of Environmental and Climate Change Impacts* (Tyndall Centre for Climate Change Research 2011).

[81] IEA, 'Redrawing the Energy-Climate Map' (WEO Special Report 2013).

[82] Ibid, 409.

[83] eg in 2005 global refining capacity was affected by Hurricane Katrina's destruction of US Gulf coast refineries.

[84] The 1960 Paris Convention on Third Party Liability in the Field of Nuclear Energy and the 1963 Brussels Supplementary Convention were adopted under the auspices of the Nuclear Energy Agency of the OECD.

[85] The 1963 Vienna Convention on Civil Liability for Nuclear Damage. Both global and regional regimes remain untested by a major incident as neither applied to the Chernobyl and Fukushima accidents: Redgwell (n 21) 93.

[86] Linked by the 1988 Joint Protocol.

operator initially liable, then the state of operation and, finally, all contracting parties. Financial limits for liability, which is strict, are set for each level. The definition of nuclear damage includes not only personal injury and damage to property, but also economic losses such as the cost of preventive measures and of measures to reinstate an impaired environment, which may constitute the major portion of the damage caused by a nuclear incident. A Joint Protocol was concluded which links this regional system with the global regime,[87] with a further 1997 Supplemental Convention[88] increasing the amount of compensation available for nuclear damage.

Following the Chernobyl nuclear accident in 1986, the IAEA concluded two further international treaties addressed to early notification (1986 Notification Convention) and to assistance in the event of an international nuclear incident (1986 Assistance Convention). The former embraces in treaty form the customary law obligation to notify in the event of serious transboundary harm. In a more preventive vein, a further IAEA convention, the 1994 Convention on Nuclear Safety (CNS), is designed to ensure the safe design, operation, and decommissioning of land-based nuclear power plants. The main control element of the CNS, is the (non-binding) peer review of national reports on implementation,[89] which was identified as one of several key weaknesses following the Fukushima Daiichi nuclear plant incident in Japan in 2011. Procedural changes have since been instituted to strength peer review and transparency.[90]

Safety and security issues form an increasingly important area of the IAEA's activities with the object, inter alia, of protecting humans and the environment from harmful radiation exposure. In 1997 a further Joint Convention on the Safety of Spent Fuel and Radioactive Waste Management was concluded, modelled on the CNS, to ensure high safety standards and prevent accidents in the disposal of nuclear waste.[91] In many respects these recent developments of both the OECD and IAEA regimes demonstrate parallels with the regulation of oil pollution liability: preventive concern to ensure that the activity is carried out to minimize or avert pollution consequences; emergency response and notification systems; and a liability regime which increasingly acknowledges the environmental costs of prevention and of reinstatement. Despite the extent of legislative activity at the global and regional levels, a significant gap remains in the international legal regime for disposal of radioactive waste. However, as a matter of treaty and general international law, disposal of radioactive waste on or below the seabed, and in Antarctica, is prohibited.[92]

87 1988 Joint Protocol relating to the Application of the Vienna Convention and Paris Convention.

88 Convention on Supplementary Compensation for Nuclear Damage.

89 <https://www.iaea.org/topics/nuclear-safety-conventions/convention-nuclear-safety/documents> accessed 27 December 2019.

90 Handl (n 11) 190; Selma Kus, 'International Nuclear Law in the 25 years between Chernobyl to Fukushima and Beyond' *Nuclear Law Bulletin*, 87 (2011): 7; 'International Nuclear Law in the Post-Chernobyl Period' (n 11).

91 preambular recital (xiii), art 1.

92 Redgwell and Rajamani (n 12) 113.

2. *Energy efficiency and renewables*

Despite recognition of the importance of energy efficiency in reducing energy consumption and in combating climate change, there has been little law-making in this field at the international level. In part this is because such measures tend to be taken at the national and local levels and rarely have transboundary consequences.

An exception is the 1994 Energy Charter Treaty (ECT),[93] the only international treaty addressed to all sources of energy,[94] and which includes both an environmental provision and a Protocol on Energy Efficiency and Related Environmental Aspects (PEEREA). It is the first multilateral treaty instrument to address, inter alia, energy efficiency.[95] However, the obligations contained in the ECT and PEEREA are far from robust. Article 19 ECT is drafted in 'a non-binding and loose form'[96] and merely requires contracting parties to 'have particular regard to Improving Energy Efficiency, to developing and using renewable energy sources, to promoting the use of cleaner fuels and to employing technologies and technological means that reduce pollution'; to 'promote and co-operate in the research, development and application of energy efficiency and environmentally sound technologies'; and to 'encourage favourable conditions for their transfer and dissemination', consistent with intellectual property rights'.[97]

More detail is found in the PEEREA, the preamble to which acknowledges the energy consumption and environmental advantages of improved energy efficiency, as well as its contribution to energy security and in improving living standards. However, its provisions are likewise couched in largely hortatory terms, focusing on the three-fold objectives of promoting energy efficiency policies, creating framework conditions to induce energy efficiency by producers and consumers through efficient and transparent energy markets, and fostering cooperation in energy efficiency.[98] There is no enforcement mechanism in the PEEREA though states may volunteer for an 'In-depth Energy Efficiency Review', including review of renewable energy policy.[99] Unlike the ECT itself, which has been 'exported' beyond the European region, the PEEREA does not have

[93] Global participation in which was facilitated by the 2015 International Energy Charter, signatories to which can participate as observers to the Energy Charter Conference (the governing body of the ECT); see <https://www.energycharter.org/process/international-energy-charter-2015/overview/> accessed 4 February 2020.

[94] 'Energy Materials and Products' are defined in ECT, art 1.4 and listed in annex EM, and include nuclear energy, coal, natural gas, petroleum and petroleum products, electricity, fuel wood and charcoal.

[95] Adrian Bradbrook, 'The Development of Renewable Energy Technologies and Energy Efficiency Measures through Public International Law' in Donald Zillman *et al* (eds), *Beyond the Carbon Economy: Energy Law in Transition* (OUP 2008) 117.

[96] Lyster and Bradbrook (n 19) 59.

[97] ECT, arts 19.1(d), (g), (h); in identical terms, 2003 West African Energy Protocol, ECOWAS A/P4/1/03.

[98] art 1.

[99] <https://www.energycharter.org/> accessed 27 December 2019. Peer review is conducted by representatives of three or four other contracting parties and the ECT Secretariat, and the report is discussed by the Working Group on Energy Efficiency and Related Environmental Aspects and by the Energy Charter Conference.

global reach, nor are all the parties to the ECT also parties to the Protocol. Consequently, global consideration of energy efficiency has thus far been confined to the policy level, as an element of Sustainable Energy for All and SDG 7 setting the target of doubling the global rate of improvement in energy efficiency by 2030. However, at the sectoral level, mandatory energy efficiency measures have been adopted for ships, including for gas carriers, oil tankers, and liquefied natural gas carriers.[100]

Increasing the share of renewable energy in the global energy mix is also a target under SDG 7, but expressed in vaguer terms: by 2030 to 'increase substantially' the share of renewable energy in the global energy mix. The International Renewable Energy Agency (IRENA) established in 2009, is tasked with facilitating the achievement of this target, and the transformation of global energy systems to combat climate change.[101] IRENA was established to promote 'the widespread adoption and sustainable use of all forms of renewable energy, including bioenergy, geothermal, hydropower, ocean, solar and wind energy in the pursuit of sustainable development, energy access, energy security and low-carbon economic growth and prosperity'.[102] Renewable energy production is not entirely benign, however. International requirements exist, inter alia, for the protection of wildlife, especially migratory birds, from wind turbines and powerlines,[103] and for the regulation of noise generated in the construction and operation of marine renewable energy installations, especially to minimize the negative impact on cetaceans.[104]

V. CONCLUSION

As illustrated above, one persistent framing of energy activities in the environmental context, and a key catalyst for regulatory responses, is that of energy as a pollution threat to be prevented, reduced, controlled, and eliminated. In this framing, the environmental effects of energy activities are viewed largely as externalities, with the vast bulk of international energy regulation concerned with facilitating energy activities, and only secondarily with mitigating the negative transboundary effects of energy extraction and use through harmonized rules and procedures reliant on national implementation. In this narrative, it is claimed that the environmental risks, especially of fossil-fuel

[100] MARPOL 73/78, annex VI; IMO Res MEPC.203(62), 'Inclusion of regulations on energy efficiency for ships in MARPOL Annex VI' (15 July 2011) MEPC 62/24/Add.1, annex 19.

[101] Annual Report of the Director-General (October 2019) IRENA Doc C/18/1, para 2; see also IRENA, 'Transforming the energy system—and holding the line on rising global temperatures' (2019).

[102] <https://www.irena.org/> accessed 27 December 2019

[103] 1979 Convention on the Conservation of Migratory Species of Wild Animals (CMS) Res 7.5, 'Wind Turbines and Migratory Species' (2002); CMS Res 10.11, 'Power Lines and Migratory Birds' (2011).

[104] Agreement on the Conservation of Small Cetaceans of the Baltic, North East Atlantic, Irish and North Seas (ASCOBANS) Res 6.2, 'Adverse Effects of Underwater Noise on Marine Mammals during Offshore Construction Activities for Renewable Energy Production' (2009); OSPAR, 'Offshore renewables' <https://www.ospar.org/work-areas/eiha/offshore-renewables> accessed 27 December 2019.

use, 'remain essentially unregulated at the international level and beyond the scope of a concerted or coherent international regime' with only incidental regulation in consequence of rules addressed more broadly to areas such as atmospheric pollution and climate change.[105] Consequently the scope for convergence is slight.

Yet there is another strand to the narrative, where energy and environmental objectives are viewed more synergistically. For example, such synergies have been recognized, albeit cautiously, by the parties to the 1971 Ramsar,[106] and the 1972 World Heritage Conventions. An online guidance tool is currently being developed to address the impact of renewable energy transition projects, especially wind turbine projects, located within or near World Heritage properties 'and identify ways in which renewable energy initiatives and World Heritage protection could go hand in hand'.[107] A very modest attempt at reconciling environmental protection and energy activities is found in the ECT. However, it is principally addressed to energy trade and investment. It couples a robust iteration of the sovereign right of states to choose their own energy pathway with relatively weak environmental provisions, and does not make any reference to sustainable development, which might imply an obligation to utilize energy resources sustainably.[108] In sum, the ECT hardly represents the high water mark of convergence between energy and environment; ultimately the narrative of environment as an externality prevails.

Thus it is still principally general international law and MEAs that regulate, albeit incidentally, the environmental impacts of energy activities. The greatest pull to convergence will likely emerge in response to the climate emergency.

BIBLIOGRAPHY

Catherine Redgwell, 'International Regulation of Energy Activities' in Martha Roggenkamp *et al* (eds), *Energy Law in Europe* (3rd edn, OUP 2016) 13

Catherine Redgwell, 'Sustainable Development of National Energy Resources: What Has International Law Got To Do With It?' *Journal of Sustainable Development Law and Policy*, 8/1 (2017): 1

Catherine Redgwell and Lavanya Rajamani, 'Energy Underground: What's International Law got to do with it?' in Donald Zillman *et al* (eds), *The Law of Energy Underground—Understanding New Developments in Subsurface Production, Transmission, and Storage* (OUP 2014) 101

Nico Schrijver, *Sovereignty over Natural Resources: Balancing Rights and Duties* (CUP 1997)

105 Sands and Peel (n 5) 604.

106 Ramsar Res XI.10, 'Guidance for addressing the implications for wetlands of policies, plans and activities in the energy sector' (2012).

107 'Renewable Energy Transition and World Heritage' <https://whc.unesco.org/en/renewable-energy/> accessed 27 December 2019.

108 See text at n 27.

CHAPTER 50

ARMED CONFLICT AND THE ENVIRONMENT

CARL BRUCH, CYMIE R PAYNE, AND BRITTA SJÖSTEDT

I. INTRODUCTION

CONCERN for the environmental impacts of war goes back to the Old Testament, Babylon, and Ancient Greece.[1] In the modern era, the literature generally starts with the end of the Second World War, initially focusing on scorched earth tactics of the Nazi army and Cold War concerns about the implications of nuclear weapons.[2] The Vietnam War and the 1990–91 Gulf War further propelled the topic in public and policy discourse. In more recent conflicts, belligerents continue to target the environment and to weaponize it, as the Islamic State did in burning oil wells in northern Iraq.[3]

The concern for the environment in relation to armed conflict can be addressed from several bodies of international law. These diverse bodies of law emerged largely isolated from one another: international humanitarian law, international environmental law, international criminal law, international human rights law, the United Nations (UN) Charter, and so on. Hence, a fragmented and unclear legal framework protects the environment in times of armed conflict.

[1] Jay Austin and Carl Bruch (eds), *The Environmental Consequences of War: Legal, Economic, and Scientific Perspectives* (CUP 2000); Peter Gleick, 'Water and Conflict: Fresh Water Resources and International Security' *International Security*, 18/1 (1993): 79–112.

[2] Ken Conca and Geoffrey Dabelko (eds), *Environmental Peacemaking* (Johns Hopkins University Press 2002); Tom Deligiannis, 'The Evolution of Environment-Conflict Research, Toward a Livelihood Framework' *Global Environmental Politics*, 12/1 (2012): 78–100.

[3] Wim Zwijnenburg and Foeke Postma, 'Living under a Black Sky—Conflict Pollution and Health Concerns in Iraq' *PAX* (2017) <https://www.paxforpeace.nl/publications/all-publications/living-under-a-black-sky> accessed 28 January 2020.

Historically, protection of the environment in relation to armed conflict was viewed through the lens of *lex specialis*, often with the conclusion that international humanitarian law exclusively applied during armed conflict. This view has, however, been altered by courts' decisions and scholars over the years. For instance, the International Court of Justice (ICJ) has on several occasions concluded that human rights law continues to apply during armed conflict, albeit international humanitarian law being *lex specialis* prevails over human rights law in case of a conflict of norms.[4]

The International Law Commission (ILC) further modified that view in 2011, holding that treaties continue to apply during armed conflict to the extent that they do not directly conflict with international humanitarian law.[5] Moreover, recognizing the growing fragmentation of diverse bodies of international law, the ILC has emphasized the view that international law is to be conceptualized as a system and implemented in a coherent manner.[6]

Accordingly, this chapter focuses on the interlinkages between international environmental law and other bodies of international law to protect the environment in relation to armed conflict. Its thesis is that international environmental law norms are increasingly shaping the protection of the environment in relation to armed conflict, in contrast to the relative rigidity of international humanitarian law norms, which are traditionally the starting point for analyzing wartime environmental protection.

The chapter begins with a brief consideration of international law applicable during all temporal phases of armed conflict: before conflict (including conflict prevention); during conflict; and after conflict. It then explores the issues and relevant law particular to specific phases. It concludes with a brief look forward.

II. LAW APPLICABLE ACROSS THE CONFLICT LIFECYCLE

The ILC's work on the topic of 'Effects of Armed Conflicts on Treaties' has established a new starting point, presuming that environmental treaties continue to apply in relation to armed conflicts. Moreover, in regard to the topic on 'Protection of the Environment in Relation to Armed Conflicts', the ILC has provided a fresh approach on the topic, which has broadened the scope of applicable law.[7] The ILC has clearly shown that

[4] *Legal Consequences of the Construction of a Wall in the Occupied Palestinian Territory* (Advisory Opinion) [2004] ICJ Rep 136.

[5] 'Report of the International Law Commission on the work of its sixty-third session' (2011) UN Doc A/66/10, ch VI.E—'Text of the draft articles on the effects of armed conflicts on treaties'.

[6] 'Fragmentation of International Law: Difficulties Arising from the Diversification and Expansion of International Law—Report of the Study Group of the International Law Commission finalized by Martti Koskenniemi' (13 April 2006) UN Doc A/CN.4./L.682 and Corr.1.

[7] 'Report of the International Law Commission on the work of its seventy-first session' (2019) UN Doc A/74/10, ch VI.

environmental protection in relation to armed conflict goes well beyond international humanitarian law and—quite noteworthy for the normal routine of the Commission—also highlighted that non-binding (soft) law must be taken into account.

Even though it is clear that environmental treaties, also referred to as Multilateral Environmental Agreements (MEAs), can continue to apply during armed conflict, it remains unclear how they apply and, in particular, relate to norms under international humanitarian law. Furthermore, the legal status of the draft articles adopted by the ILC was undetermined, as the UN General Assembly merely took note of them, deferring the question as to what form may be given to the articles.[8] Nevertheless, MEAs have potential to set limitations on activities affecting the environment by balancing different interests, for instance the needs of the present and future generations, economic growth, and the maintenance of the ecosystems and their equilibrium, which may be of relevance in relation to armed conflict.[9]

International human rights law applies across all phases of armed conflict. As such, it complements international humanitarian law, as confirmed by the ICJ. Given that human rights and environmental protection are increasingly becoming intertwined,[10] human rights law has the potential to further enhance environmental protection across the conflict lifecycle.

III. INTERNATIONAL LAW PROTECTING THE ENVIRONMENT BEFORE ARMED CONFLICT

This section considers the environment as a potential contributing cause of armed conflict. It also examines the role of military manuals and training, and good governance as tools for conflict prevention, with beneficial consequences for the environment.

A. Environment as a Cause of Armed Conflict

People often fight to obtain valuable natural resources, including land, minerals, oil, gas, timber, water, and fish for profit and survival. However, since the end of the First World War, it has been illegal for states to initiate armed conflict to obtain territory or to settle

[8] See UNGA Res 66/99 and 72/121, 'Effects of armed conflicts on treaties' (27 February 2012) UN Doc A/RES/66/99 and (18 December 2017) UN Doc A/RES/72/121, paras 2 and 3.

[9] Britta Sjöstedt, *The Role of Multilateral Environmental Agreements: A Reconciliatory Approach to Environmental Protection in Armed Conflict* (Hart Publishing 2020).

[10] See eg *State Obligations in Relation to the Environment* (Advisory Opinion) IACtHR (2017) OC-23/17; see also Chapter 45, 'Human Rights', in this volume.

disputes, including such acts undertaken with the aim of acquiring natural resources.[11] The source of rules governing when states may legitimately initiate armed conflict, known as *jus ad bellum*, is both customary and treaty-based international law. The 1945 UN Charter in Article 2, requires parties to 'settle their international disputes by peaceful means' and to 'refrain in their international relations from the threat or use of force'. A breach of these obligations renders the belligerent subject to sanctions imposed by the doctrine of state responsibility, and to criminal sanctions. Non-international conflict over natural resources is subject to a more limited international law regime that addresses *jus ad bellum* only in light of the right of self-determination; whether a sovereign state's violation of this right could give rise to duties of state responsibility is untested.

Natural resource disputes and environmental problems have yet to be recognized as a legal justification for war. For example, the UN Security Council rejected Iraq's claims that its 1990 invasion of Kuwait was justified because Kuwait was allegedly slant drilling into Iraqi territory.[12] While some refer to the war in Darfur as the first climate change war, neither science nor law support this assertion. Climate change was a stressor, but most of the other Sahelian countries that experienced the same climatic stresses did not witness armed conflict.[13] Moreover, the argument that climate change caused the conflict in Darfur ignores the core issues of agency and the responsibility of those that decided to escalate the conflict. This analysis also applies to the ongoing Syrian civil war, in which drought played a substantial role.[14] The question of whether damage to the environment of another state could ever rise to an existential threat that could warrant an armed attack has yet to be settled—in the meantime, the obligation to resolve disputes peacefully remains the guiding principle of international law.

Where a belligerent state has breached its international legal obligations, either by instigating an illegal war or by violating the law of armed conflict, it will be liable under the doctrine of state responsibility.[15] This well-entrenched body of international law requires reparations to be provided to the injured state, usually in the form of financial compensation.[16] Where damage is to areas beyond national jurisdiction, such as the

[11] Quincy Wright, 'The Outlawry of War and the Law of War' *American Journal of International Law*, 47/3 (1953): 365.

[12] Ameber Pariona, 'Why Did Iraq Invade Kuwait in 1990?' *World Atlas* (1 April 2019); UN Security Council Res 660 (2 August 1990) UN Doc S/RES/660, 678 (29 November 1990) UN Doc S/RES/678, and 687 (3 April 1991) UN Doc S/RES/687.

[13] Michael Kevane and Leslie Gray, 'Darfur: Rainfall and Conflict' *Environmental Research Letters*, 3 (2008): 34006.

[14] Peter Gleick, 'Water, Drought, Climate Change, and Conflict in Syria' *Weather, Climate, and Society*, 6 (2014): 331; Jan Selby *et al*, 'Climate Change and the Syrian Civil War Revisited' *Political Geography*, 60 (2017): 232.

[15] 'Report of the International Law Commission on the work of its fifty-third session' (2001) UN Doc A/56/10, ch IV.E—'Draft Articles on Responsibility of States for Internationally Wrongful Acts', arts 31, 34–36; Ian Brownlie, *System of the Law of Nations: State Responsibility*, part 1 (OUP 1983) 23.

[16] Marjorie Whiteman, 'Damages in International Law' *American Journal of International Law*, 32/1 (1938): 191.

high seas or outer space, legal doctrine suggests that the harm is to the international community (*erga omnes*) and that the same rules apply, mutatis mutandis.[17]

B. Preparation: Military Manuals and Training

Preparing to protect the environment and natural resources during armed conflict can be carried out through four tools: legislation, military manuals and training, staffing, and reporting on compliance. Of these, international law can be of particular relevance to the content and use of military manuals, as they constitute a way to articulate clearly the environmental rules governing armed forces.

Military manuals establish policies governing military operations.[18] These policies include requirements from international and national law, as well as operational considerations. Thirty states have adopted national rules and legislation specifically addressing how their military forces must incorporate considerations of the environment.[19] For example, the Norwegian armed forces maintain an environmental database to which all units must continuously report all activities, products, and services that may have an impact on the environment.

North Atlantic Treaty Organization's (NATO) Military Principles and Policies for Environmental Protection encourage NATO and partner nations to adopt environmental standards.[20] NATO status-of-forces agreements also contain provisions relating to environmental protection. Additionally, NATO has six Standardization Agreements which address various areas of environmental protection.[21] The International Committee of the Red Cross (ICRC) Guidelines for Military Manuals and Instructions on the Protection of the Environment in Times of Armed Conflict summarize existing international rules and offer guidance to countries on how to address protection of the environment in their military manuals.[22]

In 2009, the UN Department of Peacekeeping Operations and the UN Department of Field Support adopted the Environmental Policy for UN Field Missions.[23] The Policy incorporates MEAs and other sources of international environmental law as binding standards for UN peacekeeping.

[17] ILC, 'Draft Articles on Responsibility' (n 15) art 48.

[18] Michael Reisman and William Leitzau, 'Moving International Law from Theory to Practice: The Role of Military Manuals in Effectuating the Law of Armed Conflict' *International Law Studies*, 64 (1991): 1.

[19] Marie Jacobsson, 'Second Report on the Protection of the Environment in Relation to Armed Conflicts' (28 May 2015) UN Doc A/CN.4/685.

[20] NATO/MC, MC 469—NATO Military Principles and Policies for Environmental Protection (EP) (NATO/MC, 27 June 2003). The most recent version of this document is: NATO/MC, MC 0469//1—NATO Military Principles and Policies for Environmental Protection (EP) (NATO/MC, 13 October 2011).

[21] See 'Environmental Protection: NATO Documents' <https://www.natolibguides.info/Environment/NATO-Documents> accessed 22 January 2020.

[22] <https://www.icrc.org/en/doc/resources/documents/article/other/57jn38.htm> accessed 29 January 2020.

[23] UN Department of Peacekeeping Operations (DPKO) and UN Department of Field Support (DFS), 'Environmental Policy for UN Field Missions' (2009). DPKO and DFS also developed draft

In addition, it is possible to designate certain environmentally important areas as protected zones that are to be avoided by all combatants. This may be done by belligerents entering agreements or otherwise designating such areas in accordance with the draft principles 4 and 17 of the ILC.[24] The International Union for Conservation of Nature (IUCN) has proposed a draft convention to support such designations.[25] However, the designation of an environmentally important area does not guarantee its protection during armed conflicts since neither the ILC draft principles nor the IUCN draft convention constitute binding law.

C. Good Environmental Governance as Conflict Prevention Within States

Growing attention is being paid to good environmental governance as a means to prevent violent conflict. While there are many elements of good environmental governance, most conflict prevention initiatives emphasize transparency, inclusion, rule of law, and benefit sharing.[26]

For example, the Extractive Industries Transparency Initiative (EITI) sets global standards for transparency in the management of oil, gas, and mining revenues and (since 2016) in transparency of concession agreements for those resources. EITI is designed to strengthen governance by improving transparency and accountability in the extractive sector through the full publication of company payments and government revenues from oil, gas, and mining.[27] When states join EITI, they are obligated to adopt implementing legislation and develop public reports on extractive industry payments and revenues. As of March 2019, fifty-one states implement EITI through implementing national legislation, and more than USD 2 trillion in government revenues have been published in open data formats.[28]

Environmental Guidelines for UN Field Missions, but these have yet to be adopted. Sophie Ravier *et al*, 'Environmental Experiences and Developments at United Nations Peacekeeping Operations' in Carl Bruch, Carroll Muffett, and Sandra Nichols (eds), *Governance, Natural Resources, and Post-Conflict Peacebuilding* (Routledge 2016) 195.

[24] ILC Report on its seventy-first session (n 7) 211, ch VI.C—'Text of the draft principles on protection of the environment in relation to armed conflicts'.

[25] See Richard Tarasofsky, 'Protecting Specially Important Areas during International Armed Conflict: A Critique of the IUCN Draft Convention on the Prohibition of Hostile Military Activities in Protected Areas' in Austin and Bruch (n 1) 567.

[26] See eg UNEP, 'Environmental Rule of Law: First Global Report' (2019); Michael Ross, Päivi Lujala, and Siri Rustad, 'Horizontal Inequality, Decentralizing the Distribution of Natural Resource Revenues, and Peace' in Päivi Lujala and Siri Rustad (eds), *High-Value Natural Resources and Post-Conflict Peacebuilding* (CRC Press 2011) 251; Achim Wennmann, 'Sharing Natural Resource Wealth during War-to-Peace Transitions' in Lujala and Rustad, ibid, 225.

[27] See eg Eddie Rich and Negbalee Warner, 'Addressing the Roots of Liberia's Conflict through the Extractive Industries Transparency Initiative' in Lujala and Rustad, ibid, 201; Levon Epremian, Päivi Lujala, and Carl Bruch, 'High-Value Natural Resources Revenues and Transparency: Accounting for Revenues and Peace' in *Oxford Research Encyclopedia of Politics* (OUP 2016) 1.

[28] <https://www.eiti.org> accessed 29 January 2020.

International certification, due diligence, and chain-of-custody systems seek to ensure that specific natural resources are harvested legally and do not contribute to conflict or human rights violations.[29] Examples include the Kimberley Process Certification Scheme (KPCS)[30] and the EU's Forest Law Enforcement, Governance and Trade (FLEGT) Action Plan and Regulation,[31] among others. While these (and EITI) are not generally considered international environmental law per se, they share many characteristics, require state implementing legislation, include periodic reviews for compliance, and can include penalties for non-compliance. Equally important, they tend to be developed by a group of like-minded countries and other actors, so the least common denominator is more ambitious than in most global environmental negotiations. As such, they represent a new form of international environmental governance that is both more ambitious and of comparable, if not better, enforceability than most MEAs.[32]

IV. International Law Protecting the Environment During Armed Conflict

During an armed conflict, emphasis is placed on international humanitarian law (also referred to as the law of armed conflict, or the law of war). This framework is specifically designed to deal with the conduct of warfare and protection of certain groups of persons not participating or no longer participating in the hostilities. The protection of the environment under international humanitarian law can be divided into direct protection of the environment and indirect protection of the environment to the extent it can be considered a civilian object. In general, the environment is granted a low level of protection under international humanitarian law, which has been criticized by international organizations,[33] as well as scholars,[34] for its vague, ambiguous, and inadequate rules.

[29] Harrison Mitchell, 'A More Formal Engagement: A Constructive Critique of Certification as a Means of Preventing Conflict and Building Peace' in Lujala and Rustad (n 26) 195.

[30] Andrew Grant, 'The Kimberley Process at Ten: Reflections on a Decade of Efforts to End the Trade in Conflict Diamonds' in Lujala and Rustad (n 26) 159; Andrew Bone, 'The Kimberley Process Certification Scheme: The Primary Safeguard for the Diamond Industry' in Lujala and Rustad (n 26) 189.

[31] Duncan Brack, 'Excluding Illegal Timber and Improving Forest Governance: The European Union's Forest Law Enforcement, Governance and Trade Initiative' in Lujala and Rustad (n 26) 211.

[32] Carl Bruch and John Broderick, 'International Law and Processes' in LeRoy Paddock, Robert Glicksman, and Nicholas Bryner (eds), *Decision Making in Environmental Law* (Edward Elgar 2017) 35.

[33] For further reading see ILC Report on its sixty-third session (n 5) 351, annex E—'Protection of the environment in relation to armed conflicts'.

[34] Dieter Fleck, 'The Protection of the Environment in Armed Conflict: Legal Obligations in the Absence of Specific Rules' *Nordic Journal of International Law*, 82/1 (2013): 7; Cordula Droege and Marie-Louse Tougas, 'The Protection of the Natural Environment in Armed Conflict–Existing Rules and Need for Further Legal Protection' *Nordic Journal of International Law*, 82/1 (2013): 21; Silja Vöneky,

A. Direct Environmental Protection Under International Humanitarian Law

In most cases, the environment is not the primary target for an attack, unless it becomes a military objective. This would be the case if it provides a military contribution, for example, a forest used as a hiding place for the enemy, a mountain used as a look-out point, or a river used for transport. Most environmental damage occurring as a result of hostilities is collateral damage.

Article 55 and Article 35 (discussed below) of Additional Protocol I (Protocol I) provide direct protection of the environment in times of armed conflict.[35] Article 55.1 obliges belligerents to protect the natural environment against widespread, long-term, and severe damage in order to protect civilians. The terms in the threshold are not defined in Protocol I and the provisions have not yet been subject to any court examination.[36] There seems, however, to be a common agreement among scholars that the provisions set an exceptionally high threshold because they require cumulatively 'widespread, long-term and severe damage' to the natural environment.[37]

Article 55.2 prohibits attacks against the natural environment by way of reprisals. A reprisal constitutes retaliation that is only lawful when used to enforce the rules of international humanitarian law. The ILC adopted, on first reading, draft principle 16 replicating Article 55.2 of Protocol I, affirming its customary law status. The prohibition against reprisals towards the environment demonstrates that environmental concerns are recognized under international humanitarian law.[38]

No corresponding treaty-based protection of the environment exists in non-international armed conflicts. However, the ILC study confirmed that draft principle 13.2 expressing a duty of care for belligerents to 'protect the environment against widespread, long-term and severe damage' applies in both international and non-international armed conflict. Thus, the inclusion of the prohibition to inflict widespread, long-term, and severe damage to the environment as included in Article 55 of Protocol I strengthens its status as customary international law, also reinforcing the inclusion of

'A New Shield for the Environment: Peacetime Treaties as Legal Restraints of Wartime Damage' *Review of European Community & International Environmental Law*, 9/1 (2000): 32; Michael Bothe *et al*, 'International Law Protecting the Environment During Armed Conflict: Gaps and Opportunities' *International Review of the Red Cross*, 92 (2010): 879.

[35] 1977 Protocol Additional to the Geneva Conventions of 12 August 1949, and relating to the protection of victims of international armed conflicts (Protocol I).

[36] See International Criminal Tribunal for the Former Yugoslavia, Final Report to the Prosecutor by the Committee Established to Review the NATO Bombing Campaign Against the Federal Republic of Yugoslavia (2000).

[37] See Karen Hulme, *War Torn Environment: Interpreting the Legal Threshold* (International Humanitarian Law Series) (Martinus Nijhoff 2004) 88–100.

[38] Bernard Schafer, 'The Relationship between the International Laws of Armed conflict and Environmental Protection: The Need to Reevaluate What Types of Conduct are Permissible During Hostilities' *California Western International Law Journal*, 19/2 (1988): 287, 312–313.

Rule 45 in the 2005 Customary Law Study by the ICRC which partly replicates Article 55 (and Article 35) in Protocol I.[39]

B. Indirect Environmental Protection Under International Humanitarian Law

The environment and its elements are granted general protection under international humanitarian law, by the rule of military necessity as well as by the principles of distinction, proportionality, and precaution.[40] The general rules have customary law status and apply to international as well as non-international armed conflict.[41] They are also codified in Protocol I.

When the environment and its components are regarded as civilian objects, excessive collateral damage is prohibited in accordance with the proportionality principle, as codified in Article 51.5(b) in Protocol I.[42] Protection is subject to a balancing test of the scale of the collateral damage compared to the direct military advantage anticipated of attacking a lawful military target.[43] The proportionality principle provides that the expected damage is assessed on the basis of the known risk at the time the attack is planned or launched. As the scientific knowledge on how the environment is affected constantly changes, the environmental damage is difficult to foresee. Acts that were tolerated as collateral environmental damage decades or a few years ago might now be unacceptable.[44] Consequently, the demands of the level of information on environmental risks that a reasonable commander should obtain prior an attack is difficult to establish.[45]

Finally, the Martens Clause, which is included in many major international humanitarian treaties, provides additional basic protections under 'the principles of humanity and the dictates of public conscience', even in cases where no express rules have been adopted.[46] As such, the Martens Clause may provide additional indirect protections for the environment.[47]

[39] The ICRC's Study on Customary Rules of International Humanitarian Law, as applicable in international and non-international armed conflicts, was published by Cambridge University Press in 2005 in a set of two volumes titled *Customary International Humanitarian Law*.

[40] Rule 43 in the ICRC Customary Law Study expands the application to include non-international armed conflict; See Jean-Marie Henckaerts and Louise Doswald-Beck (eds), *Customary International Humanitarian Law*, vol I—Rules (CUP 2005) 143; Droege and Tougas (n 34) 24.

[41] Rules 7–10 in the ICRC Customary Law Study expand the application to include non-international armed conflict; See Droege and Tougas (n 34) 25–35.

[42] See Droege and Tougas (n 34) 46–50.

[43] Bothe *et al* (n 34) 577.

[44] Richard Desgagné, 'The Prevention of Environmental Damage in Time of Armed Conflict: Proportionality and Precautionary Measures' *Yearbook of International Humanitarian Law*, 3 (2000): 116.

[45] Bothe *et al* (n 34) 578.

[46] Theodor Meron, 'The Martens Clause, Principles of Humanity, and Dictates of Public Conscience' *American Journal of International Law*, 94/1 (2000): 78.

[47] ILC, Draft Principles on Protection of Environment (n 24) 247, principle 12—'Martens Clause with respect to the protection of the environment in relation to armed conflict'.

C. Preventing and Minimizing Environmental Damage

Closely related to the proportionality principle is the principle of precaution[48] in international humanitarian law. This principle—which differs from the precautionary principle in international environmental law[49]—requires belligerents prior to an attack to adopt precautionary measures to avoid or minimize the adverse effects on civilians and civilian objects including the environment to the furthest extent possible based on the information available when planning or conducting an attack. The belligerents have different legal burdens of precaution based on the information, equipment, and ability that they have at a certain time and place.[50]

Similarly, Rule 44 of the 2005 Customary Law Study requires belligerents to take 'due regard' of the environment, by taking precautionary measures to avoid and minimize environmental damage.[51] Drawing from the international environmental law precautionary principle, Rule 44 states that lack of scientific certainty regarding the environmental effects of certain military operations does not absolve a belligerent from taking such precautions.[52] Finally, it recognizes the need to incorporate international environmental law to inform the application of the rules of international humanitarian law by obligating belligerents also to consider uncertain environmental risks at the time of attack. This is not a common feature in humanitarian law, which generally operates only on foreseeable risks.

D. Choice of Means and Methods of Warfare

The means of war are not unlimited, per treaty and customary international law.[53] The 2005 Customary Law Study asserted that customary international law prohibits the use of methods or means of warfare that are intended, or may be expected, to cause widespread, long-term, and severe damage to the environment.[54] Some major military powers have persistently objected to this general rule. Protocol I, Article 35, and the 1980 Conventional Weapons Convention use this threshold, but only restrict means and methods if the harm is intentional or foreseeable.[55] These standards are not waived by military necessity, nor is proportionality of the harm and military advantage a consideration.

48 Codified in Protocol I, arts 57–58.

49 See Chapter 18, 'Precaution', in this volume.

50 Yves Sandoz *et al* (eds), *Commentary on the Additional Protocols of 8 June 1977* (ICRC 1987).

51 Henckaerts and Doswald-Beck (n 40) 147; see also Droege and Tougas (n 34) 34.

52 For a lengthier discussion see Chapter 18, 'Precaution', in this volume.

53 1907 Hague Convention (IV) respecting the Laws and Customs of War on Land and its annex: Regulations concerning the Laws and Customs of War on Land, art 22.

54 Henckaerts and Doswald-Beck (n 40) 151, rule 45; cf. International Criminal Tribunal for the Former Yugoslavia (n 36) para 15.

55 1980 Convention on Prohibitions or Restrictions on the Use of Certain Conventional Weapons which may be deemed to be Excessively Injurious or to have Indiscriminate Effects (with Protocols I, II and III) (CCW), as amended in 2001, preamble; see also San Remo Manual on International Law

Treaties also restrict specific weapons. The Conventional Weapons Convention includes protocols limiting: mines, booby-traps, and other devices; incendiary devices; and explosive remnants of war.[56] Unconventional weapons—atomic, bacteriological, and chemical weapons—have the potential to cause widespread and indiscriminate environmental damage and are subject to relatively strict regulation. Use of chemical and biological weapons is banned by three treaties: the 1972 Biological Weapons Convention;[57] the 1925 Geneva Protocol;[58] and the 1992 Chemical Weapons Convention.[59] The legal regime for nuclear weapons development, testing, production, and use has slowed the expansion of atomic weapons without eliminating them. Nuclear weapons testing is restricted by the 1963 Nuclear Test Ban Treaty.[60] The 1968 Treaty on the Non-Proliferation of Nuclear Weapons is an agreement that non-nuclear states will not attempt to acquire nuclear weapons. A number of regional treaties establish nuclear-free zones, thus limiting the development and use of nuclear devices.[61] In addition, the 2017 Treaty on the Prohibition of Nuclear Weapons (TPNW) bans all types of activities regarding nuclear weapons. The convention entered into force in 2021 but only for its limited number of state parties (at present fifty-four states), which do not include the states that possess nuclear weapons. There is, at this time, no treaty addressing the use of depleted uranium (DU), although its use for tank-armouring and anti-tank munitions has raised questions of legality.[62]

Applicable to Armed Conflicts at Sea (12 June 1994) rules 44, 47 <https://www.jag.navy.mil/distrib/instructions/San_Remo_Manual%5b1%5d.pdf> accessed 4 February 2020.

56 1980 CCW Protocol II on Prohibitions or Restrictions on the use of Mines, Booby-Traps and other Devices, as amended 1996; 1980 CCW Protocol III on Prohibitions or Restrictions on the Use of Incendiary Weapons; 2003 CCW Protocol V on Explosive Remnants of War; see also 1997 Convention on the Prohibition of the Use, Stockpiling, Production and Transfer of Anti-Personnel Mines and on their Destruction.

57 1972 Convention on the Prohibition of the Development, Production and Stockpiling of Bacteriological (Biological) and Toxin Weapons and on their Destruction.

58 1925 Protocol for the Prohibition of the Use in War of Asphyxiating, Poisonous or Other Gases and of Bacteriological Methods of Warfare.

59 1992 Convention on the Prohibition of the Development, Production, Stockpiling and Use of Chemical Weapons and on their Destruction.

60 Treaty Banning Nuclear Weapon Tests in the Atmosphere, in Outer Space and Under Water.

61 1967 Tlatelolco Treaty for the Prohibition of Nuclear Weapons in Latin America and the Caribbean; 1985 Treaty of Rarotonga (South Pacific Nuclear Free Zone Treaty); 1995 Treaty of Bangkok on the Southeast Asia Nuclear Weapon-Free Zone; 1996 Treaty of Pelindaba for Africa; 2006 Treaty on a Nuclear-Weapon-Free Zone in Central Asia, and its Protocol; 1959 Antarctic Treaty, art 5.

62 UNGA Res 62/30 and 63/54, 'Effects of the use of armaments and ammunitions containing depleted uranium' (5 December 2007) and (2 December 2008); cf. Ambassador Robert Wood, United States Mission to the United Nations, Remarks at the Sixty-Ninth UNGA First Committee Cluster Five: Explanation of Vote Before the Vote on L.43, Agenda Item 96 (e) 'Effects of the Use of Armaments and Ammunitions Containing Depleted Uranium' (31 October 2014) <https://cd-geneve.delegfrance.org/69th-UNGA-Explanation-of-vote-on-resolution-L-43-Effects-of-the-use-of> accessed 5 February 2020.

A separate category of issues concerns the use of the environment as a weapon. The 1976 Convention on the Prohibition of Military or Any Other Hostile Use of Environmental Modification Techniques (ENMOD) prohibits deliberate manipulation of natural processes used as a weapon against other parties to the convention when such use has widespread, long-lasting, or severe environmental effects anywhere. The nature of the target is immaterial, but it must be another state party to ENMOD—whether hostile or neutral.[63] The treaty allows environmental modification techniques that only affect one's own territory, the territory of a non-party, or areas beyond national jurisdiction, as well as hostile uses that do not exceed any of the three thresholds: severe, widespread, or long-lasting.[64] Commentators consider that cyber weapons that damage 'works and installations containing dangerous forces' are governed by general international humanitarian law rules.[65] Cyber attacks would thus be subject to the requirements of distinction, necessity, and proportionality, and the special rules of Additional Protocol I and ENMOD for the parties to those conventions.[66]

E. Management of Waste and Other Toxic Substances

International legal requirements governing management of waste and other toxic substances during armed conflict are modest. If they are party to the relevant convention, belligerents may have obligations with respect to specific remnants of war, such as mines and explosive ordnance, covered by Protocols II and V to the Convention on Certain Conventional Weapons, the 2008 Cluster Munitions Convention, and the 1997 Ottawa Convention.[67] Moreover, principles of international environmental law prohibiting damage to other states, and calling for states to prevent environmental harm may apply, as well as the 1989 Basel Convention and the 1982 UN Convention on the Law of the Sea.[68]

[63] Yoram Dinstein, 'Protection of the Environment in International Armed Conflict' *Max Planck Yearbook of United Nations Law*, 5 (2000): 523, 529.

[64] Compliance is addressed in ENMOD, art V.

[65] Michael Schmitt, 'Wired Warfare: Computer Network Attack and Jus in Bello' *International Review of the Red Cross*, 84/846 (2002): 365, 374.

[66] Heather Dinniss, *Cyber War and Laws of War* (CUP 2012) 220–226.

[67] Convention on the Prohibition of the Use, Stockpiling, Production and Transfer of Anti-Personnel Mines and on their Destruction.

[68] See further Chapters 16, 31, and 33, 'Harm Prevention', 'Marine Environment: Pollution and Fisheries', and 'Hazardous Substances and Activities', in this volume.

F. Addressing Conflict Resources

Following the end of the Cold War, and the concomitant disappearance of funding for proxy wars, rebel groups sought other means of finance. The use of natural resources to finance conflict—that is, 'conflict resources'—flourished as rebel groups extracted, traded in, or informally taxed trade in natural resources. Between 1989 and 2018, at least thirty-six major armed conflicts were financed in part by natural resources ranging from gold and diamonds to timber to coca and cacao.[69]

Most conflict resources rely on international trade and access to markets, and a growing number of efforts to address conflict resources (and financing) focus on controlling international trade. These include, for example, the Kimberley Process and FLEGT (discussed above),[70] as well as a mandate from the UN Security Council for countries to adopt due diligence requirements,[71] which eventually led to provisions in the US Dodd-Frank Wall Street Reform Act and the EU Conflict Mineral Regulation.[72] The 1973 Convention on International Trade in Endangered Species of Fauna and Flora (CITES) provides another means for combatting trade in endangered species that may be financing armed conflict.

Recent years have also seen a revival of the ancient crime of pillage as a potential avenue to address conflict-related illegal natural resource exploitation. Prohibitions against pillage appear in the 1945 Charter of the International Military Tribunal (Nuremberg), the Hague Regulations, the Fourth Geneva Convention, and the Additional Protocol II to the Geneva Conventions (under Fundamental Guarantees),[73] and the prohibition against pillage is now accepted as a rule of customary international law.[74] As of 2015, similar prohibitions appear in forty-eight national military manuals, the national legislation of ninety-two countries, and the case law of twelve countries.[75] The ICJ has been the sole international tribunal to apply pillage directly to the exploitation of natural resources, in the *Congo v Uganda* case.[76]

[69] Carl Bruch *et al*, 'The Changing Nature of Conflict, Peacebuilding, and Environmental Cooperation' *Environmental Law Reporter*, 49/2 (2019): 10134.

[70] See Section III.C.

[71] UNSC Res 1896 (30 November 2009) UN Doc S/RES/1896, para 14.

[72] Dodd-Frank Wall Street Reform and Consumer Protection Act of 2010, s 1502; Regulation (EU) 2017/821 of the European Parliament and of the Council of 17 May 2017 laying down supply chain due diligence obligations for Union importers of tin, tantalum and tungsten, their ores, and gold originating from conflict-affected and high-risk areas [2017] OJ L 130/1.

[73] 1977 Protocol Additional to the Geneva Conventions of 12 August 1949 and relating to the protection of victims of non-international armed conflicts (Protocol II).

[74] James Stewart, *Corporate War Crimes: Prosecuting Pillage* (Open Society 2010).

[75] Olivia Radics and Carl Bruch, 'The Law of Pillage, Conflict Resources, and Jus Post Bellum' in Carsten Stahn, Jens Iverson, and Jennifer Easterday (eds), *Environmental Protection and Transitions from Conflict to Peace: Clarifying Norms, Principles and Practices* (OUP 2017) 143.

[76] *Armed Activities on the Territory of the Congo (Congo/Uganda)* (Judgement) [2005] ICJ Rep 168.

V. INTERNATIONAL LAW PROTECTING THE ENVIRONMENT AFTER ARMED CONFLICT

The post-conflict period offers a window of opportunity to address the causes of conflict, to reform inequitable laws and practices, and to lay a foundation for a sustained peace.[77] Post-conflict countries often review and reform environmental and natural resource laws, rebuild institutions governing natural resources and the environment, and change their practices to be more equitable, participatory, and sustainable.

A core post-conflict objective is to restore and strengthen rule of law, rather than the rule by gun. Considering the many ways that the environment affects and is affected by armed conflict, these rule of law efforts often become environmental rule of law efforts.[78] In many cases, armed conflict generates a power vacuum, and post-conflict peace can also see new power vacuums as rebel groups demobilize, disarm, and reintegrate. This was, for example, the reason that Colombia saw a rapid increase in illegal logging after the peace agreement with the FARC (Revolutionary Armed Forces of Colombia—People's Army).[79]

A. International Environmental Law as a Means to Assist Recovery

The environment is a prominent feature in the economic dimensions of post-conflict peacebuilding. Natural resources such as land, timber, minerals, and oil and gas are often the primary assets readily available to governments to generate revenues, build infrastructure, enhance livelihoods, and ensure food security.[80] The restoration and development of basic services can provide significant peace dividends by improving people's lives and showing the value of peace. The environment provides inputs and externalities to basic services, including water, sanitation, waste management, and energy. Common interests in natural resources—especially ones that cross boundaries—can be an entry point for dialogue, cooperation, and trust-building between divided groups.[81]

[77] Carl Bruch *et al*, 'Facilitating Peace or Fueling Conflict? Lessons in Post-Conflict Governance and Natural Resource Management' in Bruch, Muffett, and Nichols (n 23) 953.

[78] UNEP, 'Environmental Rule of Law' (n 26).

[79] Taran Volckhausen, 'Colombia Registers First Drop in Deforestation Since 2016 FARC Peace Deal' *Mongabay* (15 July 2019).

[80] Lujala and Rustad (n 26); Helen Young and Lisa Goldman (eds), *Livelihoods, Natural Resources, and Post-Conflict Peacebuilding* (Taylor & Francis 2015).

[81] Njeri Karuru and Louise Yeung, 'Integrating Gender into Post-Conflict Natural Resource Management' in Bruch, Muffett, and Nichols (n 23) 579.

Approached strategically, cooperation around shared environmental priorities can extend into other areas of collaborative action; for example, regional economic integration in both Europe and Central America was characterized by post-conflict cooperation around natural resources that laid the ground for broader political cooperation.[82]

International environmental law provides opportunities for countries emerging from conflict to re-engage with neighbours and the international community more broadly. For example, in 1999, the countries of Bosnia and Herzegovina, Croatia, Serbia and Montenegro, and Slovenia established the International Sava River Basin Commission to implement the Framework Agreement on the Sava River Basin, a cooperative river basin management programme.[83]

MEAs create opportunities for partnerships, projects, technical assistance, and capacity building (including seconding or embedding staff) in countries recovering from conflict.[84] Examples include projects funded by the Global Environment Facility (GEF) for implementation of key MEAs; efforts to establish peace parks and otherwise foster cooperation after conflict (eg in the Balkans and between Ecuador and Peru);[85] rebuilding livelihoods and the economy;[86] and reintegrating ex-combatants (eg as park rangers).[87]

Post-conflict efforts to strengthen environmental governance and management may support broader efforts to improve state governance and performance. There is often an emphasis, for example, on transparency, public participation, and accountability—the three 'Access Rights' of Principle 10 of the Rio Declaration.[88] This is generally in the environmental context, but it has implications well beyond the environmental sector. For example, the first time Liberia undertook notice-and-comment rule-making was for

[82] Matthew King *et al*, 'Environmental Governance and Peacebuilding in Post-Conflict Central America: Lessons from the Central American Commission for Environment and Development' in Bruch, Muffett, and Nichols (n 23) 777; Carl Bruch, Ross Wolfarth, and Vladislav Michalcik, 'Natural Resources, Post-Conflict Reconstruction, and Regional Integration: Lessons from the Marshall Plan and Other Reconstruction Efforts' in David Jensen and Steve Lonergan (eds), *Assessing and Restoring Natural Resources in Post-Conflict Peacebuilding* (Taylor & Francis 2012) 343.

[83] Amar Čolakhodžič *et al*, 'The Sava River: Transitioning to Peace in the Former Yugoslavia' in Erika Weinthal, Jessica Troell, and Mikiyasu Nakayama (eds), *Water and Post-Conflict Peacebuilding* (Taylor & Francis 2014) 271.

[84] See eg Belinda Bowling and Asif Zaidi, 'Developing Capacity for Natural Resource Management in Afghanistan: Process, Challenges, and Lessons Learned by UNEP' in Young and Goldman (n 80) 307.

[85] Carol Westrik, 'Transboundary Protected Areas: Opportunities and Challenges' in Young and Goldman (n 80) 145; Todd Walters, 'A Peace Park in the Balkans: Cross-Border Cooperation and Livelihood Creation through Coordinated Environmental Conservation' in Young and Goldman (n 80) 155.

[86] Lorena Castro and Adrienne Stork, 'Linking to Peace: Using BioTrade for Biodiversity Conservation and Peacebuilding in Colombia' in Young and Goldman (n 80) 253.

[87] Glaucia Boyer and Adrienne Stork, 'The Interface between Natural Resources and Disarmament, Demobilization, and Reintegration: Enhancing Human Security in Post-Conflict Situations' in Young and Goldman (n 80) 187.

[88] See Bruch (n 77).

regulations implementing the 2006 National Forest Reform Law; since then the practice has spread to other sectors.[89]

UN Security Council resolutions on women and peacebuilding (Resolution 1325), on youth and peacebuilding (Resolution 2250) and similar on-the-ground efforts emphasize participation and representation, protection, prevention (including economic opportunities), rights, and return and reintegration. Inclusion of marginalized groups in the development and implementation of natural resource governance systems can help to address these problems of equity; it is also an important mechanism for improving governmental legitimacy.[90]

B. Transitional Justice and Accountability

Transitional justice programmes increasingly consider environmental harm.[91] Legal processes provide accountability, reparations, and—in the context of international criminal law—sanctions for individual culpability. Damage claims can benefit the environment if they include the obligation to use awards for remediation and restoration. This contributes to post-conflict peacebuilding by restoring essential services such as water supply, habitable climate, and biodiversity.

The Charter of the Nuremberg Tribunal defined war crimes to include 'wanton destruction … not justified by military necessity' and convicted General Jodl for his 'scorched earth' tactics—effectively, attacks on the human environment.[92] The 1998 ICC Statute's Article VIII.2(b)(4)[93] provides that war crimes include 'intentionally launching an attack in the knowledge that such attack will cause incidental loss of life or injury to civilians or damage to civilian objects or widespread, long-term and severe damage to the natural environment which would be clearly excessive in relation to the concrete and direct overall military advantage anticipated'.

Violations of *jus ad bellum* (law governing going to war) or *jus in bello* (law governing the conduct of war) are subject to the sanctions of state responsibility: reparations that

[89] Sandra Nichols and Lisa Goldman, 'U.S. Bilateral Assistance to Liberia: Forestry as the Cornerstone to Peacebuilding' in Carl Bruch, Mikiyasu Nayakama, and Ilona Coyle (eds), *Harnessing Natural Resources for Peacebuilding: Lessons from U.S. and Japanese Assistance* (Environmental Law Institute 2011) 301.

[90] Karuru and Yeung (n 81); Juan Maldonado and Luisz Martínez, 'Indigenous Peoples, Natural Resources, and Peacebuilding in Colombia' in Bruch, Muffett, and Nichols (n 23) 605.

[91] Emily Harwell, 'Building Momentum and Constituencies for Peace: The Role of Natural Resources in Transitional Justice and Peacebuilding' in Bruch, Muffett, and Nichols (n 23) 633; Cymie Payne, 'Oversight of Environmental Awards and Regional Environmental Cooperation' in Cymie Payne and Peter Sand (eds), *Gulf War Reparations and the UN Compensation Commission: Environmental Liability* (OUP 2011) 105; UNCC Governing Council, 'Decision concerning follow-up programme for environmental claims awards' (8 December 2005) UN Doc S/AC.26/Dec.258.

[92] *Trial of the Major War Criminals before the International Military Tribunal*, vol 1 (International Military Tribunal 1947) 324–325.

[93] Rome Statute of the International Criminal Court.

include 'restitution, compensation and satisfaction, either singly or in combination'.[94] Courts and tribunals have expanded the traditional scope of harm subject to reparations from personal injury and property to include environmental harm.[95] The first to do so was the UN Compensation Commission (UNCC), established to provide war reparations for Iraq's 1990 invasion and occupation of Kuwait.[96] It provided reparations for environmental damage that included costs of monitoring and assessment, response measures, remediation and restoration, and public health monitoring.[97] Because the basis for liability was Iraq's breach of *jus ad bellum* and its UN Charter obligations,[98] UNCC claims were not subject to the limitations of international humanitarian law's threshold for legal liability. Claims for environmental damage resulting from armed conflict also featured in several other post-conflict proceedings where the legal basis for claims included violations of *jus ad bellum* and *jus in bello*.[99]

C. Use of Natural Resources and Their Revenues for Rebuilding

Natural resources and their revenues are often central to rebuilding efforts after conflict. They provide the inputs for livelihoods, infrastructure, and economic development. They also provide revenues necessary for the government to deliver basic services and security.

There are two key limitations on who can use these resources and for what purpose. The first is the Law of Occupation. The Law of Occupation is normally understood to be

[94] ILC, 'Draft Articles on Responsibility' (n 15) art 34; *Western Front, Aerial Bombardment and Related Claims—Eritrea's Claims 1, 3, 5, 9–13, 14, 21, 25 & 26* (Partial Award, Decision of 19 December 2005) 26 RIAA 291 [105] (finding that satisfaction constitutes reparation for a bombing that violated customary international humanitarian law but that did not cause damage); Paul Lewis, 'U.N. Helps Kuwait Recover Iraqi Loot' *New York Times* (30 July 1991); Hague Convention, art 3; Protocol I, art 91.

[95] Anne-Cecile Vialle *et al*, 'Peace through Justice: International Tribunals and Accountability for Wartime Environmental Damage' in Bruch, Muffett, and Nichols (n 23) 665.

[96] Payne and Sand (n 91).

[97] UNCC Governing Council Decision 7, 'Criteria for additional Categories of Claims' (17 March 1992) UN Doc S/AC.26/1991/7/Rev.1; UNCC, 'Report and Recommendations Made by the Panel of Commissioners Concerning the Fifth Instalment of "F4" Claims' (30 June 2005) UN Doc S/AC.26/2005/10, paras 777, 784, approved by UNCC Governing Council Decision 248, 'Decision concerning the fifth instalment of "F4" claims' (30 June 2005) UN Doc S/AC.26/Dec.248.

[98] UNSC Res 660 (2 August 1990) UN Doc S/RES/660; UNSC Res 687 (3 April 1991) UN Doc S/RES/687 (1991).

[99] Sean Murphy, Won Kidane, and Thomas Snider, *Litigating War: Arbitration of Civil Injury by the Eritrea-Ethiopia Claims Commission* (OUP 2013) 146, 227–228; 2000 Agreement between the Government of the State of Eritrea and the Government of the Federal Democratic Republic of Ethiopia for the resettlement of displaced persons, as well as rehabilitation and peacebuilding in both countries; International Criminal Tribunal for the Former Yugoslavia (n 36); *Certain Activities Carried Out by Nicaragua in the Border Area (Costa Rica/Nicaragua)* and *Construction of a Road in Costa Rica along the San Juan River (Nicaragua/Costa Rica)* (Judgement) [2015] ICJ Rep 665 [41].

part of *jus in bello*;[100] and applies when a territory is actually placed under the authority other than the sovereign.[101] In a growing number of circumstances, though, occupation continues long after there is a peace agreement or military victory, including for example in Iraq, Afghanistan, and Palestine. In the case of use of natural resources for rebuilding, it may continue to apply after hostilities have ceased but before a new government has been constituted. The Law of Occupation prevents the occupying power from exploiting natural resources for its benefit; rather decisions must be made in the best interest of the occupied territory and its inhabitants (not the occupier).[102]

VI. CONCLUSIONS

Thirty years ago, international environmental law did not pay much attention to armed conflict. The end of the Cold War brought about enhanced international cooperation to build peace and (separately) international cooperation around the environment.[103] In the ensuing decade, there were the 1990–91 Gulf War, the Rio Earth Summit, and the rapid expansion of international environmental law and institutions. Since then, there has been growing attention to the diverse ways that environment influences conflict and peace and to efforts by the UN and other actors to address environmental risks and pursue environmental opportunities—collectively, referred to as 'environmental peacebuilding'.[104]

Just as these diverse initiatives and approaches have started to integrate across sectors, actors, and peacebuilding objectives, there has been a growing trend to integrate the various bodies of applicable international law, both thematically and across the conflict lifecycle. The work of the ILC on protection of the environment in relation to armed conflict is a clarion call to this more integrated approach. It draws upon international humanitarian law, international human rights law, international criminal law, and international environmental law, among other bodies of international law. It looks at the issues across the conflict lifecycle, noting that some laws are more applicable at different phases (before, during, or after), but other legal norms apply across the conflict lifecycle. With this integration, the system of international law protecting the environment in relation to armed conflict is finally starting to resemble a functioning system.

[100] Carsten Stahn, '"Jus ad Bellum," "Jus in Bello"... "Jus post Bellum"?—Rethinking the Conception of the Law of Armed Conflict' *European Journal of International Law*, 17/5 (2006): 921.

[101] For a definition of occupation see the Hague Regulations, annex to 1907 Hague Convention (IV), art 42.

[102] ILC, 'Second report on protection of the environment in relation to armed conflicts by Marja Lehto, Special Rapporteur' (27 March 2019) UN Doc A/CN.4/728.

[103] Bruch *et al*, 'Changing Nature' (n 69).

[104] Carl Bruch, David Jensen, and Monica Emma, 'Defining Environmental Peacebuilding' in Richard Matthew and Crystal Murphy (eds), *The Routledge Handbook on Environmental Security* (forthcoming).

BIBLIOGRAPHY

'Report of the International Law Commission on the work of its seventy-first session' (2019) UN Doc A/74/10, ch VI.C—'Text of the draft principles on protection of the environment in relation to armed conflicts, adopted by the Commission on first reading'

Jay Austin and Carl Bruch (eds), *The Environmental Consequences of War: Legal, Economic, and Scientific Perspectives* (CUP 2000)

Daniëlla Jong, *International Law and Governance of Natural Resources in Conflict and Post-Conflict Situations* (CUP 2018)

Cymie Payne and Peter Sand (eds), *Gulf War Reparations and the UN Compensation Commission: Environmental Liability* (OUP 2011)

Carsten Stahn, Jens Iverson, and Jennifer Easterday (eds), *Environmental Protection and Transitions from Conflict to Peace: Clarifying Norms, Principles and Practices* (OUP 2017)

PART VIII

COMPLIANCE, IMPLEMENTATION, AND EFFECTIVENESS

CHAPTER 51

COMPLIANCE THEORY

RONALD B MITCHELL

I. INTRODUCTION

INTERNATIONAL environmental agreements (IEAs) to protect the natural environment and manage natural resources have a long history.[1] They provide considerable evidence on whether and when IEAs reduce human harm to the environment, how much they vary in compliance and effectiveness, and what factors foster their effectiveness. This chapter examines the conceptual and theoretical challenges raised by efforts to understand IEA compliance and effectiveness.

Scholars and practitioners often conflate two different questions when inquiring into compliance with international environmental law. A strictly legal approach asks whether state behaviours conform to relevant legal standards in IEAs. A political science approach more often compares state behaviours to counterfactuals of how those states would have behaved if the IEA did not exist. Scholars of both approaches often use the term 'compliance'. The present chapter seeks to clarify the distinction between compliance and effectiveness, as the latter is discussed in detail later in this volume.[2] Table 51.1 illustrates the key difference in terms of whether causation is obscured or highlighted. Both compliance and non-compliance can arise for reasons unrelated to an IEA's causal influence. Equating IEA compliance (comparing state behaviours to legal standards) with IEA influence can overstate the latter by conflating IEA-induced compliance and 'coincidental' compliance, in which state behaviours meet IEA standards for reasons unrelated to the IEA. States may negotiate IEA obligations that require no change in their behaviours, may comply because doing so is cheaper than violation, or may lack

[1] IEA Database, *International Environmental Agreements Database Project—Version 2020.1* (University of Oregon 2020); Ronald Mitchell *et al*, 'What We Know (and Could Know) About International Environmental Agreements' *Global Environmental Politics*, 20 (2020): 103; see Chapter 3, 'Origin and History', in this volume.

[2] See Chapter 57, 'Effectiveness', in this volume.

the capacity to violate IEA rules. Equating non-compliance with a lack of IEA influence also misleads because it ignores the fact that IEAs can lead states to take well-intended actions that fall short of legal standards, as when IEAs set ambitious obligations or exogenous changes put compliance out of reach. Indeed, IEAs with aggressive obligations may be highly effective despite having high non-compliance rates.

Table 51.1 Distinguishing the effectiveness of international law from compliance with international law

	Compliant behaviour	Non-compliant behaviour
IEA influenced behaviour	IEA-induced compliance	Good faith non-compliance
IEA did not influence behaviour	Coincidental compliance	Intentional non-compliance

In short, this chapter argues that investigations of compliance improve to the extent that scholars use them to identify the causal influence of IEAs rather than a causal assessment of rule-following. This chapter focuses on conceptual, theoretical, and methodological issues raised when assessing IEA compliance and IEA influence, thereby complementing the deeper insights into variation in the effectiveness of various IEAs detailed in Chapter 57 ('Effectiveness').

A. Identifying a 'Performance Indicator' of Compliance as IEA Influence

How should we evaluate compliance in a way that reflects an IEA's causal influence? Policy analysts often distinguish among policy outputs, behavioural outcomes, and environmental impacts. Outputs (laws and regulations) provide useful indicators of IEA influence because policy changes are necessary to most logics of such influence and because they can provide strong process-tracing evidence of an IEA's influence (eg language that replicates an IEA's). However, they are not sufficient conditions: we cannot assume that IEA-induced policy changes lead inexorably to behavioural change and environmental improvement. Environmental impacts (ie changes in environmental quality) offer different advantages and disadvantages. On the one hand, environmental improvement is what motivates states to create IEAs. On the other, arguments of IEA influence prove convincing only by overcoming numerous rival explanations of environmental improvements, including natural cycles and shocks and numerous non-IEA human influences.

Behavioural outcomes appear to offer a particularly useful indicator that reflects both the legal and social science perspectives on IEAs. First, behaviours are necessary causal links between IEAs and environmental improvement. If we observed environmental improvement after states established an IEA but no relevant behavioural change, we would readily dismiss claims that the IEA caused the environmental improvement. Second, although most behavioural changes we might observe have many non-IEA explanations, there are fewer such alternative explanations of behaviours than of environmental impacts. That said, we should avoid assuming that IEAs that dramatically alter behaviours necessarily lead to dramatic environmental improvements.

The choice of behaviours as indicators of compliance still poses several analytic challenges. First, data on many behaviours that IEAs target is incomplete, non-systematic, non-comparable, does not illuminate pre-IEA periods, or has never been collected. Second, discounting non-IEA influences on behaviours that IEAs target is analytically challenging. Third, although policy-makers often document whether they adopted new regulations in response to international treaties, governments and economic actors document what motivated new behaviours far less often. These are surmountable challenges but challenges nonetheless.

B. Selecting a Comparator of IEA Influence

To assess an IEA's influence also requires an appropriate comparator (reference point) for our observations of the performance indicator. We can compare observed behaviours to an IEA's explicit legal requirements, the estimated counterfactual of behaviours in the IEA's absence, or the IEA's behavioural goals, defined either by the IEA or an analyst.

1. *Legal requirements as comparators*

In its strict legal meaning, compliance is defined by comparing behaviours to legal standards and 'is agnostic about causality'.[3] But using those standards has several shortcomings. When IEAs have clear legal standards, such assessments are possible. However, many IEAs have vague or ambiguous standards and others have none at all. In these cases, an independent analyst cannot assess compliance. Nor can they rely on assessments by IEAs (and non-governmental organizations (NGOs)) of particular behaviours as compliant or not. Although such assessments of compliance are valuable *mechanisms* by which IEAs influence behaviour, the fact that they often reflect political considerations make them unreliable as systematic assessments of compliance. Finally, focusing on whether a behaviour met legal standards or not encourages the analyst to ignore important information embedded in whether the behaviour exceeded (or missed) those standards by a lot or a little.

2. *Goals as comparators*

Alternatively, we might compare behaviours to behavioural goals or objectives. Behavioural goals, whether defined in an IEA's text or by an analyst, can be intended as

[3] Kal Raustiala and Anne-Marie Slaughter, 'International Law, International Relations and Compliance' in Walter Carlsnaes, Thomas Risse, and Beth Simmons (eds), *Handbook of International Relations* (Sage 2002) 539.

realistic and achievable or ambitious and inspirational. Thus, using goals as comparators leads to assessments that vary as much based on the definition of the goal as the behaviour itself. Indeed, using goals as comparators could be expected to find that IEA goals were most likely to be achieved when those goals were set to be particularly unambitious.

3. *Counterfactuals as comparators*

Much political science argues that counterfactuals are the appropriate comparator for any assessment of international cooperation. Adopting legal standards or goals as comparators focuses our attention on correlation. Using counterfactuals, by contrast, focuses our attention on causation. A counterfactual is an analytically supported estimate of the behaviours that would have happened in the absence of the IEA, *ceteris paribus*. Good counterfactuals derive from efforts to estimate those behaviours as if all non-IEA influences had occurred as they did, but that the IEA had no influence on the state (eg because the IEA did not exist or the state never joined). Counterfactuals replace the dichotomizing question of 'did this IEA influence this behaviour or not?' by inquiring as to 'how much' influence an IEA had, allowing greater discrimination of whether and why state behaviour varies along a spectrum from significant over-compliance to significant shortfalls. Scholars can design counterfactuals that allow assessment of specific IEA provisions (vs IEAs as a whole) that can better inform IEA negotiations and re-negotiations. IEAs predicted to be influential but which fell short, can identify factors that inhibit IEA influence. And counterfactuals are particularly useful for assessing IEAs that lack or have unclear standards, in which strict legal compliance cannot be assessed.

C. Evaluating IEAs, IEA Provisions, or IEA Parties

The choice to compare across IEAs, across their provisions, or across parties requires aggregations that clarify some factors and obscure others. Research to clarify which IEAs have the most influence will obscure differences across diverse obligations and diverse parties. Research to clarify which types of parties are most influenced will obscure differences across obligations and across contextual conditions that foster or inhibit IEA influence. And research to clarify which types of provisions have the most influence will obscure differences in those contextual conditions and types of parties. The choices involved strongly influence any assessment of their influence precisely because IEAs vary in the number and type of member states and proscriptions and prescriptions as well as their background conditions.

An important but often overlooked issue here, flows from the fact that we can only assess the influence of IEAs through observational studies: neither provisions nor member states are randomly assigned to IEAs. The structure of the problem that states are seeking to address (including the power and interests of relevant states) influences how states *design* IEAs and the *membership* decisions of states about which IEAs to join. We must account for differences in underlying environmental problems before we can interpret differences across parties, IEAs, and IEA provisions as meaningful. Accurately assessing an IEA's influence requires disentangling the influence of problem structure from the independent effects of the IEA on parties. These issues pose methodological challenges that, although not insurmountable, threaten inaccurate conclusions if ignored.

II. UNDERSTANDING HOW AND WHY IEAS MAKE A DIFFERENCE WHEN THEY DO

The foregoing arguments suggest strategies for assessing how IEAs influence state behaviour. This section, therefore, reviews explanations of *how and why* IEAs have influence when they do.

A. Two Models of Actor Behaviour

International relations scholarship suggests that two distinct logics drive state behaviour: a logic of consequences and a logic of appropriateness.[4] The 'logic of consequences' model perceives states as choosing among behavioural options by comparing the costs and benefits of each on their material interests. In this view, IEAs influence decisions by making IEA-promoting behaviours more attractive to member states than IEA-degrading behaviours. The goals, preferences, resources, constraints, and values of states are viewed as largely impervious to international law's influence. In contrast, a 'logic of appropriateness' resonates with much international legal thinking and sees state behaviour being driven by the interplay of norms and identities. If states behave in ways that further their interests, they also behave in ways that reflect often-unquestioned assessments of 'legitimate' and 'appropriate' behaviours for actors who seek to promote a particular identity in particular situations.[5] In this view, new obligations in an IEA influence behaviour, at least in part, by transforming an undifferentiated spectrum of behaviours into compliant or non-compliant behaviours. That dichotomization, even without sanctions for violation, can lead states to adjust their behaviour towards the former, especially states that prefer to be seen as law-abiding, rule-of-law states. This can reflect broad meta-norms of *pacta sunt servanda* (agreements must be kept) or IEA-specific norms that link specific behaviours to a state's reputation as 'environmental'.

[4] James March and Johan Olsen, 'The Institutional Dynamics of International Political Orders' *International Organization*, 52/4 (1998): 943; Oona Hathaway, 'Do Human Rights Treaties Make a Difference?' *Yale Law Journal*, 111/8 (2002): 1935.

[5] Martha Finnemore and Kathryn Sikkink, 'International Norm Dynamics and Political Change' *International Organization*, 52/4 (1998): 887.

Indeed, when states adapt their behaviour quickly to comply with IEA rules, despite high costs or without considering those costs, it suggests that a logic of appropriateness is at work. For example, judges in many states regularly make rulings that defer to international law with little consideration of the economic costs.[6]

States acting within a logic of appropriateness may make the conscious calculations characteristic of a logic of consequences but assess costs to their reputation with others rather than material consequences. Indeed, states sometimes oppose IEA provisions during negotiations, object to them after adoption, or withdraw from an IEA altogether but nevertheless comply with those provisions.[7] Governments seeking to acquire 'green' identities are likely to feel a particularly strong compliance pull.[8]

The distinctions between these logics clarify how IEAs influence state behaviours but, in practice, are not mutually exclusive. They generate competing predictions about which, how, and when IEAs influence state behaviour. We can assess predictions from each logic against empirical evidence to distinguish IEAs that work mainly through one logic, mainly through the other, or where both logics are in play and reinforce or undercut each other.

B. Distinguishing State Compliance from IEA Influence

Isolating the influence of IEAs requires distinguishing coincidental compliance from behaviours that truly reflect such influence. The truth of Henkin's claim that states usually comply with their international obligations owes much to states negotiating IEAs that avoid 'obligations that might be harmful to them'.[9] In such cases, compliance is best understood as an expression of states' interests, not a result of IEA influence. One can more easily explain the absence of mining in Antarctica as reflecting prohibitive costs than IEA influence.[10] Similarly, international fisheries quotas are rarely exceeded when they are set to expected catch levels. Only when IEAs require behaviours that differ from business as usual can we equate high compliance with IEA influence.

Whether compliance reflects IEA influence depends considerably on the divergence between obligations and business-as-usual behaviour. Many IEAs include obligations that require little or no adjustment by the states advocating them, as those

[6] Harold Koh, 'Why Do Nations Obey International Law?' *Yale Law Journal*, 106/8 (1997): 2598; Raustiala and Slaughter (n 3) 538; Karen Alter, *The New Terrain of International Law: Courts, Politics, Rights* (Princeton University Press 2014).

[7] See eg 1946 International Convention on the Regulation of Whaling.

[8] Thomas Franck, *The Power of Legitimacy among Nations* (OUP 1990).

[9] Louis Henkin, *How Nations Behave: Law and Foreign Policy* (Columbia University Press 1979) 47; Hans Joachim Morgenthau, *Politics among Nations: The Struggle for Power and Peace* (McGraw-Hill 1993).

[10] Steven Chown *et al*, 'Challenges to the Future Conservation of the Antarctic' *Science*, 337/6091 (2012): 158.

states care about but do not contribute to the problem or have already acted unilaterally for domestic political reasons. To attract participation, these 'leader' states often accept obligations that require very little of other states.[11] When they adopt 'common obligations', the standards may be set so low that leaders have complied before the IEA is signed (as in early European acid rain agreements).[12] The increasing use of state-specific 'differentiated' obligations does not always overcome this problem.[13] Differentiated obligations that reflect scientific assessments may create standards that diverge significantly from business-as-usual trajectories, and in such cases compliance may well reflect IEA influence. But differentiated obligations that reflect political willingness to act (as under the 2015 Paris Climate Agreement) may simply be a codification of business-as-usual trajectories, with compliance providing little information on IEA influence. And compliance with initially-costly common or differentiated obligations becomes less compelling as evidence of IEA influence if economic or technological changes make compliance cheap or advantageous.

Scholars should thus *start* by assuming that states negotiate IEA obligations to reflect their short-term interests and subsequently comply because doing so remains in their interests. Yet, starting with that assumption does not require ending with it. IEAs can influence behaviour in several ways, resulting in either treaty-induced compliance or good faith non-compliance.

IEA influence may be passive, in the sense that institutional processes can alter state behaviour even without specific mechanisms of influence. Many international relations scholars assume that states start negotiations understanding the problem, knowing their interests, and supporting policy positions independent of the arguments and dynamics of negotiations.[14] Others have shown that negotiations are often forums for education about the causes and impacts of environmental harms and persuasion that alters what states consider to be in their interests.[15] Global environmental assessments

[11] Thomas Bernauer *et al*, 'Is There a 'Depth Versus Participation' Dilemma in International Cooperation?' *Review of International Organizations*, 8/4 (2013): 477.

[12] Arild Underdal, *The Politics of International Fisheries Management: The Case of the Northeast Atlantic* (Universitetsforlaget 1980); Jon Hovi and Detlef Sprinz, 'The Limits of the Law of the Least Ambitious Program' *Global Environmental Politics*, 6/3 (2006): 28; Marc Levy, 'European Acid Rain: The Power of Tote-Board Diplomacy' in Peter Haas, Robert Keohane, and Marc Levy (eds), *Institutions for the Earth: Sources of Effective International Environmental Protection* (MIT Press 1993) 75; James Murdoch and Todd Sandler, 'Voluntary Cutbacks and Pretreaty Behaviour: The Helsinki Protocol and Sulfur Emissions' *Public Finance Review*, 25/2 (1997): 139.

[13] See Chapter 19, 'Differentiation', in this volume.

[14] Michael Zürn and Jeffrey Checkel, 'Getting Socialized to Build Bridges: Constructivism and Rationalism, Europe and the Nation-State' *International Organization*, 59/4 (2005): 1045.

[15] Thomas Risse, '"Let's Argue": Communicative Action in World Politics' *International Organization*, 54/1 (2000): 1; Frank Schimmelfennig, 'The Community Trap: Liberal Norms, Rhetorical Action, and the Eastern Enlargement of the European Union' *International Organization*, 55/1 (2001): 47; Darren Hawkins, 'Explaining Costly International Institutions: Persuasion and Enforceable Human Rights Norms' *International Studies Quarterly*, 48/4 (2004): 779.

can clarify the benefits of action or costs of inaction, leading states to accept collective restraint or convincing them of the value of unilateral action, as when scientific evidence showed that acid rain from some European countries' factories was harming those countries' own lakes and forests.[16] Negotiations also allow early adopters to convince other states of the benefits of particular environmental policies and strategies for reducing their costs. Such dynamics can lead initially-opposed states to come to the view that significant behavioural change is in their interests. Even as this mode of influence is encouraging environmentally, it creates challenges for evaluating IEA influence, as it shows states complying with obligations that they considered to be in their interest when negotiations concluded (even if not when they began).

IEAs also create opportunities for states to engage in interdependent rather than independent decision-making. Fulfilling an IEA's obligations involves fewer risks than, say, with an arms control agreement and, therefore, states may be willing to take actions that generate benefits even if only a few states reciprocate. Negotiations may reassure states enough that they take interdependent actions they would not have taken otherwise. IEAs also benefit from a contextual reassurance that arises because the politics of environmental policy development makes such policies less susceptible to subsequent reversal than, for example, tariffs. This fosters dynamics in which positive actions by 'unilateralists' prompt similar actions by 'slightly-contingent' states that, in turn, prompt similar actions by 'strongly-contingent' states.

IEAs may also influence states through relatively passive processes involving a logic of appropriateness. When an IEA simply codifies existing norms, of course, we cannot attribute any norm-driven behaviour to that IEA's influence. Yet, IEAs sometimes serve to strengthen existing norms or to generate new ones. In such cases, the analyst must try to parse behaviour as prompted by an IEA's strengthening of a norm, the independent development of that norm, and other paths of influence. Yet, these analytic obstacles should not lead us to assume norms are not paths of IEA influence. The international meta-norm of *pacta sunt servanda* generates an expectation that states should comply with treaties and imposes a burden of proof on those urging non-compliance. Both the collective negotiation of treaty obligations and states' voluntary and public acceptance of them (through membership decisions) give IEAs a normative legitimacy that generates a 'compliance pull' on states.[17] Over time, processes of rhetorical entrapment reinforce this legitimacy both when states justify self-interested compliance in terms of meeting treaty obligations and when states adjust and justify non-compliance to fit within reservation, opt out, or escape clauses. As a norm gains strength, the discursive context shifts to make questions such as 'is fulfilling these obligations in our country's interest?' less legitimate. For example, consider the interest-based discussions of atmospheric nuclear testing likely during United States/Soviet negotiations of the 1963 Limited Test Ban

[16] See Chapter 28, 'Transboundary Air Pollution', in this volume.

[17] Franck (n 8).

Treaty, how they were discussed a decade later, and subsequent, more-normative, terms used to pressure France and China to end their atmospheric testing.

Norms can operate broadly or in identity-specific ways. The meta-norm of *pacta sunt servanda* presumably wields greater influence over rule-of-law and democratic states, making them systematically more likely to fulfil IEA obligations independent of costs and benefits.[18] International obligations offer these states the opportunity to reaffirm desired identities. Other states (eg the Scandinavian states) may desire to maintain self-perceptions and international reputations as environmental leaders, reputations that IEA-non-compliance undercuts. If compliance generates large domestic costs, normative pressures may not be determinative, as evident in Norway's ongoing commitment to commercial whaling; but, in less demanding cases, they may tip the balance in favour of fulfilling IEA commitments. In addition, conforming to an IEA's provisions reinforces their legitimacy and generates normative expectations among a state's citizens and other states that make it rhetorically difficult to claim, subsequently, that conformity is no longer in its interests. And if a state's executive assesses violation as in a state's interest, the legislative branch, judicial branch, or polity may point to the *normative* importance of meeting international commitments, as evident in civilian lawsuits calling on governments to adopt stronger climate policies to meet their obligations under the 1992 UNFCCC (United Nations Framework Convention on Climate Change) and Paris Agreement.[19]

Such normative forces may have particular force within corporations. Businesses promulgate and train personnel in corporate procedures that reflect domestic and international laws, even when violations are likely to go undetected. Corporations cannot flout domestic laws the way states can flout international law. They cannot (publicly) discuss compliance—whether international or not—in terms of interests. Indeed, multinational corporations sometimes conform to treaty obligations before their home government has implemented relevant domestic laws since, many corporations see themselves as—and benefit from—being law-abiding. They may adopt IEA-required behaviours in response to asking 'what is the law?' rather than in response to asking 'is complying with these laws in our interests?'

The processes by which states negotiate and join IEAs may change how states perceive and calculate their self-interest and the normative and discursive context in ways that favour bringing behaviours in line with IEA obligations. These processes involve passive, subtle dynamics that help explain that fraction of compliance and behaviour change, large in some IEAs and smaller in others, that emerges even before or in the absence of explicit, visible, and active compliance management.

[18] Eric Neumayer, 'Do Democracies Exhibit Stronger International Environmental Commitment?' *Journal of Peace Research*, 39/2 (2002): 139.

[19] See the special issue on climate litigation of *Carbon and Climate Law Review*, 5/1 (2011); see also Hari Osofsky, 'The Continuing Importance of Climate Change Litigation' *Climate Law*, 1/1 (2010): 29; Jolene Lin, 'Litigating Climate Change in Asia' *Climate Law*, 4/1–2 (2014): 140.

C. Explaining Why States Fail to Comply and Why IEAs May Not Have Influence

Explanations of non-conformance with IEA rules are not simply the inverse of the foregoing explanations of state compliance. To be sure, state non-conformance sometimes reflects a logic of consequences, with states engaging in intentional violations because the costs of compliance exceed its benefits. Likewise, IEA requirements that run counter to strongly-held norms will tend to have less influence than those aligned with such norms. However, three additional factors also explain why IEAs sometimes lack influence.

First, consider incapacity. States and sub-state actors sometimes fail to fulfil IEA commitments because they lack relevant resources. Financial, administrative, or technological incapacities can all inhibit behavioural change. Developing countries may even violate environmental commitments that would be in their interests, because of more pressing concerns or inadequate resources. Indeed, many IEAs' compliance procedures include facilitative strategies designed to address such sources of non-compliance.[20] Many IEAs obligate governments to regulate myriad sub-state actors, a challenging task for states with weak informational or regulatory infrastructures. Thus, developing countries may fail to induce peasant farmers to stop cutting timber or draining wetlands because the government lacks information on who engages in those activities or the abilities to communicate regulations to them. Marine pollution regulation proves difficult, in part, because an effective regulatory infrastructure is lacking: tankers registered in Liberia and Panama rarely enter their ports, making inspections by those states difficult. Some incapacities are less country-specific: cultural, social, legal, economic, and historical contexts can make compliance more difficult to elicit from companies and citizens of some countries than others and can favour certain governance styles and policy approaches over others that would be more effective or cheaper.

Inadvertence may also contribute to behavioural shortfalls. A tax sincerely designed to achieve a national pollution reduction target may fall short because of an unexpected economic boom. The effects of many policies, especially those granting actors flexibility, depend on numerous unpredictable factors and uncertainties that may mean even developed states' policies do not achieve their intended results.

Finally, normative and ideological factors can undercut, as well as reinforce, IEA influence. A state will tend to oppose negotiations that contradicts its values, either leading to the failure of negotiations or to that state rejecting membership, as exemplified by Malaysia's opposition to the 1992 Forest Agreement. But, at times, proponents may press states to join IEAs, or accept amendments to IEAs, that contradict their values, as occurred for Japan, Norway, and Iceland when other countries banned commercial whaling. States may oppose particular IEA obligations that run counter to strongly held views on rights to development, rights to equitable benefits from cooperation, or

[20] See Chapter 56, 'Non-Compliance Procedures', in this volume.

appropriate allocations of burdens and responsibilities. We should expect IEAs in such contexts to be less effective than they otherwise would be.

III. SYSTEMS AND STRATEGIES FOR INDUCING BEHAVIOURAL CHANGE

The foregoing has delineated general processes common to IEAs that may lead states and sub-state actors to fulfil their IEA commitments. But states also expend considerable effort designing, negotiating, and implementing policies that actively seek to promote compliance, behaviour change, and environmental improvement beyond a given baseline level. Variation in the influence of IEAs, across them and over time, helps scholars and practitioners better understand what makes some IEAs work better than others. National characteristics explain differences in the influence of IEAs across countries.[21] But some IEA designs also are systematically more influential than others.[22] Both national and institutional factors can help states design, and re-design, IEAs to increase their influence.

IEA design has been characterized as reflecting either an 'enforcement' or 'managerial' approach. Those committed to an enforcement view see states driven by a logic of consequences. States, therefore, typically negotiate 'shallow' obligations that require behaviours states would have undertaken anyway. If they somehow agree to 'deep' obligations, the IEA will lack influence unless it contains potent sanctions that make compliance, however costly, less costly than non-compliance.[23] By contrast, the managerial view posits various mechanisms that IEAs can deploy to induce more IEA-consistent behaviours.[24] In this view, state decision-making reflects both a logic of consequences and a logic of appropriateness, with compliance promoted when IEAs assess and redress the source of the problem, with sanctions effective in response to intentional violations but rewards or capacity-enhancements more effective in response to incapacity or inadvertence challenges. Despite its heuristic value, the enforcement/

[21] Edith Weiss and Harold Jacobson (eds), *Engaging Countries: Strengthening Compliance with International Environmental Accords* (MIT Press 1998); Oran Young (ed), *The Effectiveness of International Environmental Regimes: Causal Connections and Behavioural Mechanisms* (MIT Press 1999).

[22] Carsten Helm and Detlef Sprinz, 'Measuring the Effectiveness of International Environmental Regimes' *Journal of Conflict Resolution*, 44/5 (2000): 630; Edward Miles *et al* (eds), *Environmental Regime Effectiveness: Confronting Theory with Evidence* (MIT Press 2002); Ronald Mitchell, 'A Quantitative Approach to Evaluating International Environmental Regimes' *Global Environmental Politics*, 2/4 (2002): 58.

[23] George Downs, David Rocke, and Peter Barsoom, 'Is the Good News About Compliance Good News About Cooperation?' *International Organization*, 50/3 (1996): 379.

[24] Abram Chayes and Antonia Chayes, *The New Sovereignty: Compliance with International Regulatory Agreements* (Harvard University Press 1995).

management dichotomy obscures the range in and variation across the mechanisms IEAs use to influence state behaviour.

A. Types of IEAs

Oran Young[25] distinguishes four IEA governance approaches. *Regulatory* IEAs delineate proscriptions or prescriptions, for example the specific limits inscribed in many pollution IEAs. *Procedural* IEAs regularize collective decision-making to allow adaptive management, for example the many fisheries agreements that rely on scientific bodies for advice in setting catch quotas. *Programmatic* IEAs help states pool resources for collective projects, for example joint financing of environmental projects in developing countries under the Global Environment Facility. *Generative* IEAs foster development of new social practices, for example the requirement for 'wise use' of wetlands under the 1971 Ramsar Convention. We can expect different governance approaches to produce different effects on state behaviour. Programmatic IEAs should lead relatively immediately to projects that would not otherwise be undertaken but would have limited effects beyond such projects. The influence of generative regimes, by contrast, might take longer to appear and be more difficult to demonstrate convincingly. The distinction between regulatory and procedural categories nicely highlights the design endogeneity problem noted above. Thus, we might expect the precise, fixed rules of a regulatory IEA to be more effective than the changing annual quotas of a procedural IEA. But states will be more likely to adopt regulatory IEAs for pollution problems and procedural IEAs to foster the adaptive management needed for international fisheries management and the tendency to alter behaviours surely varies between these problem types.

We can make other distinctions among IEAs and the conditions under which states adopt them. States define environmental 'problems' and identify solutions through social and political processes that shape the material and perceived costs and benefits of an IEA. Those costs and benefits, in turn, determine support and opposition that make a problem more benign or malign (ie easier or harder to resolve) and the types of solutions that will be effective.[26] IEAs vary, inter alia, in the ambitiousness of their obligations, their specificity, their use of binding regulations or recommendations, the flexibility they grant states, and the degree to which they centralize institutional processes.[27] Such characteristics presumably shape an IEA's effectiveness, *ceteris paribus*, but also are likely to be adopted under systematically different circumstances. To accurately assess the contribution of specificity to IEA effectiveness, therefore, requires overcoming the

[25] Oran Young, *Governance in World Affairs* (Cornell University Press 1999).

[26] Arild Underdal, 'One Question, Two Answers' in Miles *et al* (n 22) 3.

[27] See eg Edith Weiss (ed), *International Compliance with Nonbinding Accords* (American Society of International Law 1997); Weiss and Jacobson (n 21); Barbara Koremenos, Charles Lipson, and Duncan Snidal, 'The Rational Design of International Institutions' *International Organization*, 55/4 (2001): 761.

analytic possibility that states accepted more specific rules for the easier-to-regulate problem and only vague rules for the more intractable problem.

B. Systems of Regulation

Regulatory IEAs typically provide more clarity than other IEA types about their obligations and nicely illustrate the three main sub-systems that contribute to an IEA's ability to effectively induce behaviour change.

An IEA's primary rule system consists of both core goals and specific proscriptions and prescriptions. Primary rule systems vary, inter alia, in whether their goals and rules are specific or vague; ambitious or limited; proscriptive or prescriptive; ban or limit behaviours; target few or many actors; or regulate acts of omission or commission. Deciding which activities to regulate and who will regulate dictate which actors with what interests and capacities must change their behaviour, the difficulty and cost of those changes, and whether other factors will reinforce or undercut compliance. Thus, specificity may foster behaviour change by clarifying expectations for those predisposed to comply while making it more difficult to claim inadvertence or misinterpretation by those predisposed to violate.[28] Primary rules tend to be most effective when they take account of the incentives, capacities, and other traits of the states the IEA targets.

Regulatory IEAs also require information systems to track how actors behave, as a basis both for fostering positive, and discouraging negative, behaviours and for assessing progress towards IEA goals. Research on transparency has documented the value of IEA systems that collect, verify, and distribute information about state behaviours in ways that reassure by clarifying how many states are fulfilling their obligations and warn states to protect their interests when some are not.[29] Many IEAs rely on self-reporting but develop programmes that incentivize, train, and build reporting capacity. Others review reports or verify performance independently, for example the 1973 CITES (Convention on International Trade in Endangered Species of Wild Fauna and Flora) reliance on TRAFFIC to monitor endangered species trade.[30] IEAs that incorporate NGOs in their information systems gain the benefits of NGOs often having greater incentives and capacities than states to monitor government and corporate behaviours.

Beyond primary rules and information, regulatory IEAs vary in how they respond to member states to foster IEA-consistent behaviour and discourage its opposite. The 'tit-for-tat' reciprocity that underpins many trade and arms treaties[31] can help resolve some symmetric externalities (eg overfishing) but proves less useful for many international

[28] Abram and Antonia Chayes (n 24).

[29] See Chapter 52, 'Transparency Procedures', in this volume.

[30] On systems of implementation review, see David Victor, Kal Raustiala, and Eugene Skolnikoff (eds), *The Implementation and Effectiveness of International Environmental Commitments: Theory and Practice* (MIT Press 1998).

[31] Robert Axelrod, *The Evolution of Cooperation* (Basic Books 1984).

environmental problems, such as pollution or habitat degradation, both because states supporting action will rarely degrade the environment to retaliate for degradation by others and because such retaliation would be unlikely to hold much power over those engaged in such degradation. More often, IEAs contain procedures to identify whether non-compliance arose from intention, incapacities, inadvertence, or other factors and then to decide collectively whether the best response is retaliation, deployment of economic sanctions, diplomatic 'naming and shaming', praising positive behaviours, or financial incentives and capacity enhancements.[32] These strategies can work either by increasing the material benefits of compliance, the material costs of non-compliance, or the normative pull of compliance.

C. Approaches to Regulation

We can conceptualize the approaches used by regulatory IEAs to shape behaviour as three pairs of two ideal types each: punitive and remunerative, preclusive and generative, and cognitive and normative.[33] First, IEAs often wield influence by distinguishing compliance from non-compliance and punishing or rewarding accordingly. Such punitive and remunerative approaches depend on information and response systems that effectively identify state behaviour and mobilize threatened or promised responses. Punitive approaches create incentives for states to hide non-compliant behaviours, often reducing information about the environmental problem; rewards, by contrast, can require compliance and its verification in advance. Both approaches are vulnerable to a lack of follow-through, however, as states imposing sanctions or providing rewards face significant costs but diffused and uncertain benefits.[34]

Second, beyond altering the costs and benefits of particular behaviours, IEAs can alter opportunities to engage in them. Preclusive approaches make it more difficult or costly *to engage in* proscribed behaviours, not *to have engaged* in them. The 1987 Montreal Protocol prohibited exports of ozone-depleting chemicals to prevent their consumption by non-member states and the 1973 International Convention for the Prevention of Pollution from Ships adopted standards that shipbuilders voluntarily accepted, which, in turn, precluded ship-owners from buying non-compliant ships.[35] These cases illustrate IEAs influencing non-member states whose behaviours they do not even regulate, cases that are not even captured by standard notions of compliance. Alternatively, IEAs can make it easier or less costly for actors to take IEA-conforming actions. Many regional

[32] Jørgen Wettestad, 'Science, Politics and Institutional Design: Some Initial Notes on the Long-Range Transboundary Air Pollution Regime' *Journal of Environment and Development*, 4/2 (1995): 165; Downs, Rocke, and Barsoom (n 23).

[33] Ronald Mitchell, *International Politics and the Environment* (Sage 2010).

[34] Robert Axelrod and Robert Keohane, 'Achieving Cooperation under Anarchy: Strategies and Institutions' in Kenneth Oye (ed), *Cooperation under Anarchy* (Princeton University Press 1986) 226.

[35] Ronald Mitchell, *Intentional Oil Pollution at Sea: Environmental Policy and Treaty Compliance* (MIT Press 1994).

agreements promote inspections to detect violations of various marine pollution IEAs by requiring states to submit inspection reports to a central database that inspectors use because it helps them target limited inspection resources more efficiently.[36] Neither approach requires post-hoc responses by other states, thereby avoiding the need to monitor compliance and non-compliance. Just as banks lock money in vaults and provide trashcans in their lobbies, states can structure IEAs to make violation harder and fulfilling their commitments easier.

Third, IEAs can alter states' cognitive and normative perspectives on their alternatives. Cognitive approaches clarify available alternatives and their consequences, hoping to alter state calculations of the best ways to further their interests. Such approaches assume IEA-inconsistent behaviour results from states lacking full and accurate knowledge of their choices. Thus, IEAs requiring prior informed consent depend on the assumption that states will reduce unsafe trade in pesticides and hazardous waste if given better information about its risks.[37] By contrast, normative approaches seek to induce states to prioritize certain values, norms, and goals in a given realm. They seek to change the ends actors pursue, their beliefs about legitimate means to pursue certain ends, or whether a logic of consequences is an appropriate basis for choice. Concepts such as 'the common heritage of mankind', 'sustainable development',[38] and the 'precautionary principle'[39] seek to influence how states perceive and discuss particular problems and, thereby, how they behave. Codifying these concepts in IEAs creates rhetorical standards that delegitimize certain still-available actions (extracting deep seabed resources or releasing genetically-modified organisms) as inappropriate ways to achieve their objectives.[40] Cognitive and normative approaches tend to rely on long-term, internalized shifts that promote broad behavioural changes with little need for monitoring or manipulation of incentives. Unfortunately, cognitive approaches only work when new information shows IEA-consistent behaviours to be in a state's interests and normative approaches tend not to work rapidly.

IV. OTHER CONSIDERATIONS

Before concluding, some final considerations deserve mention. First, a focus on compliance with binding international environmental law ignores the value of numerous forms of non-binding cooperation (eg declarations, joint policy statements, aid programmes)

[36] Alan Tan, *Vessel-Source Marine Pollution: The Law and Politics of International Regulation* (CUP 2006).

[37] See Chapter 33, 'Hazardous Substances and Activities', in this volume.

[38] See Chapter 17, 'Sustainable Development', in this volume.

[39] See Chapter 18, 'Precaution', in this volume.

[40] Nina Tannenwald, *The Nuclear Taboo: The United States and the Non-Use of Nuclear Weapons since 1945* (CUP 2007).

where issues of compliance, legally-defined, do not arise.[41] It also obscures the value of assessing IEAs against environmental, economic, social, and other criteria that an IEA fails to specify clearly enough to allow compliance to be assessed. Third, this chapter has glossed over the ways in which various forces inhibit or promote an IEA's influence including the nature of the problem being addressed and the solutions required (eg size and immediacy of problem; cost and availability of solutions; state of the science); the states involved (eg number, power, incentives, and traits); and the broader international context (eg trends in globalization and democratization; economic and security developments; levels of environmental concern). Such forces vary across problems, states, and contexts, and over time. And IEAs wield influence only when supportive governments, corporations, NGOs, and individuals 'breathe life into' them, tending to fail otherwise.

We understand compliance and IEA influence better when we focus on explaining variation in environmental behaviours rather than on whether and how IEAs influence those behaviours. The former approach foregrounds economic, political, and social influences on environmental behaviours that hinder or foster IEA influence. Identifying and controlling for these makes claims of IEA influence more convincing and allows assessment of whether IEAs wield more or less influence than other factors. New research can clarify when IEA influence is fast or slow and why it varies over time. Policymakers would benefit from research that compares the influence of IEAs to trade treaties that incorporate environmental considerations, private regulatory governance that sets environmental standards, public-private partnerships, and efforts by NGOs and civil society.

V. CONCLUSION

International environmental law scholarship and practice can be improved by recognizing that a focus on strictly-legal notions of compliance can overstate or understate IEA influence by erroneously crediting IEAs with coincidental compliance and ignoring behavioural changes that fall short of legal standards. An excessive focus on compliance precludes the study of IEAs with vague obligations that leave compliance indeterminate or that influence states that are not members. That said, a careful and causally-informed notion of compliance can focus scholarly attention on how to convincingly show the extent to which post-IEA compliance can be accurately attributed to an IEA and to carefully identify the conditions under which different regulatory approaches best foster an IEA's influence.

[41] Daniel Bodansky, 'Legally-Binding vs. Non-Legally-Binding Instruments' in Scott Barrett, Carlo Carraro, and Jaime Melo (eds), *Towards a Workable and Effective Climate Regime* (CEPR Press 2015) 155.

BIBLIOGRAPHY

Abram Chayes and Antonia Chayes, *The New Sovereignty: Compliance with International Regulatory Agreements* (Harvard University Press 1995)

Andrew Guzman, 'A Compliance Based Theory of International Law' *California Law Review*, 90/6 (2002): 1823

Edward Miles *et al* (eds), *Environmental Regime Effectiveness: Confronting Theory with Evidence* (MIT Press 2002)

Arild Underdal, 'Methodological Challenges in the Study of Regime Effectiveness' in Arild Underdal and Oran Young (eds), *Regime Consequences: Methodological Challenges and Research Strategies* (Kluwer Academic Publishers 2004) 27

David Victor, Kal Raustiala, and Eugene Skolnikoff (eds), *The Implementation and Effectiveness of International Environmental Commitments: Theory and Practice* (MIT Press 1998)

Oran Young (ed), *The Effectiveness of International Environmental Regimes: Causal Connections and Behavioural Mechanisms* (MIT Press 1999)

CHAPTER 52

TRANSPARENCY PROCEDURES

TOM SPARKS AND ANNE PETERS

I. INTRODUCTION

INFORMATION obligations on states—to collect, report, or publish—are an important aspect of most modern multilateral environmental agreements (MEAs). These have developed both alongside and as part of a wider 'turn to transparency'[1] in international law,[2] resulting in traditional forms of reporting, monitoring, and verification being incorporated into a more extensive set of transparency relationships.

This chapter will examine transparency as an increasingly important aspect of international environmental law, both as an end in itself and as a means of achieving other substantive goals. Section II will frame transparency in international environmental law within the wider transparency turn. Section III then examines the techniques that are employed in customary and conventional environmental law to realize transparency, focusing on the *compliance-centred*, *emancipatory*, and *advocative* functions it performs.

II. TURN TO TRANSPARENCY IN INTERNATIONAL (ENVIRONMENTAL) LAW

The concept of transparency is multifaceted and difficult to grasp. Even the most commonly used metaphor of transparency—the clear panes of a window—is, as

[1] The phrase is originally Gupta's; see Aarti Gupta, 'Transparency Under Scrutiny: Information Disclosure in Global Environmental Governance' *Global Environmental Politics*, 8/2 (2008): 1, 6.

[2] Anne Peters, 'The Transparency Turn of International Law' *Chinese Journal of Global Governance*, 1/1 (2015): 3; Andrea Bianchi and Anne Peters (eds), *Transparency in International Law* (CUP 2013).

Andrea Bianchi points out, somewhat opaque.[3] Transparency is more than the simple provision of information, but instead connotes openness as an end in itself. Besides this, transparency serves further objectives in international environmental law. These include the protection of states' sovereignty, supporting compliance with environmental law, 'emancipating' natural persons, and advocating environmental protection.

The last decade of the twentieth century saw a dramatic upsurge in domestic legislation on transparency and access to information,[4] mirrored later in international law. Before 1998, the majority of international environmental law conventions either contained minimal information provisions,[5] provided for exchanges of information only to directly affected states,[6] or required reporting of factual information concerning the state of the environment or actions taken.[7] By contrast, many post-1998 conventions emphasize public-facing transparency, and the 1998 Aarhus Convention and the 2015 Paris Agreement on Climate Change, in particular, seek to enable public participation in environmental decision-making.[8]

A similar progression can be seen in the relevant United Nations (UN) declarations. The 1972 Stockholm Declaration did not mention furnishing information,[9] although the attached Action Plan briefly referred to public information provision and to information exchanges. By contrast, the 1992 Rio Declaration and Agenda 21 contained a number of references both to information sharing between states and to public-facing measures,[10] including the recommendation that states 'facilitate and encourage public awareness and participation by making information widely available'.[11] The 2012 UN Conference on Sustainable Development (Rio+20), strengthened the formulation further, recognizing 'that opportunities for people to influence their lives and future,

[3] Andrea Bianchi, 'On Power and Illusion: The Concept of Transparency in International Law' in Bianchi and Peters (n 2) 6.

[4] Albert Meijer, 'Transparency' in Mark Bovens, Robert Goodin, and Thomas Schillemans (eds), *The Oxford Handbook of Public Accountability* (OUP 2014) 507, especially 508.

[5] See eg 1979 Convention on Long-Range Transboundary Air Pollution (LRTAP).

[6] See eg 1989 Basel Convention on the Control of Transboundary Movements of Hazardous Wastes and Their Disposal, in particular arts 6, 9, 13; 1991 Espoo Convention on Environmental Impact Assessment in a Transboundary Context, art 3; 1992 Helsinki Convention on the Protection and Use of Transboundary Watercourses and International Lakes, arts 4–6.

[7] See eg 1973 Convention on International Trade in Endangered Species of Wild Fauna and Flora, art 8.7; 1985 Vienna Convention for the Protection of the Ozone Layer, art 5.

[8] Convention on Access to Information, Public Participation in Decision-Making and Access to Justice in Environmental Matters (Aarhus Convention); Paris Agreement, art 12, see also arts 6.8(b), 7.12; see further 2001 Stockholm Convention on Persistent Organic Pollutants, arts 10, 11.2(e); 2003 Convention for the Strengthening of the Inter-American Tropical Tuna Commission established by the 1949 Convention between the United States of America and Costa Rica, art 16.

[9] United Nations, 'Report of the United Nations Conference on the Human Environment' (5–16 June 1972) UN Doc A/CONF.48/14/Rev.1, 3, ch 1—'Declaration of the United Nations Conference on the Human Environment'.

[10] *Report of the United Nations Conference on Environment and Development* (UN 1993) vol I, annex I—'Rio Declaration on Environment and Development'; ibid, annex II—'Agenda 21'.

[11] Rio Declaration (n 10), principle 10.

participate in decision-making and voice their concerns are fundamental for sustainable development'.[12]

The increasing importance given to information provisions in international environmental law instruments and declarations is also a response to the specific challenges facing the field. In this area of international law, the standard international law responses to breach and non-compliance, such as countermeasures and complaints before courts or arbitral tribunals, are rarely available; environmental harms often do not infringe the rights of specific states which would be motivated and entitled to take legal action. Transparency measures are thus employed as an alternative means to further compliance with international environmental law norms.[13] However, transparency obligations may also serve as a (weak) substitute to less politically palatable substantive obligations of results.

In parallel, the international environmental law framework of transparency towards individuals acknowledges that the importance of environmental standards for human welfare and the enjoyment of human rights requires individuals to be informed about them.[14]

In the following sections, transparency will be analysed and sub-divided according to the relationship in which it occurs (*who* is required to be transparent, for the benefit of *whom*?), and according to the functions a particular information rule is intended to perform.

III. TECHNIQUES AND FUNCTIONS OF TRANSPARENCY

A. Reporting and Verification

Reporting obligations require states to provide information about their activities to a designated recipient, often a specially affected state, or a treaty secretariat. These are among the tools most commonly used by international environmental law to monitor and encourage compliance, and are found in some of its earliest agreements.

[12] UNGA RES 66/288, 'The Future We Want' (11 September 2012) UN Doc A/Res/66/288.

[13] See eg Anne Peters, 'Towards Transparency as a Global Norm' in Bianchi and Peters (n 2) 568–570.

[14] UN Human Rights Council, 'Report of the Special Rapporteur on the issue of human rights obligations relating to the enjoyment of a safe, clean, healthy and sustainable environment' (24 January 2018) UN Doc A/HRC/37/59, annex—'Framework Principles on Human Rights and the Environment', principles 1–2; see further Chapter 45, 'Human Rights', in this volume.

Nevertheless, the modalities of reporting have developed over time, as have the purposes such rules are intended to serve.

1. *Reporting: compliance-centred transparency*

The model for the early MEAs was to require reporting of specific events. Of these, some agreements require that states report events which have implications for their implementation of a convention, thus recognizing the interest all states parties have in those developments. An early example is the 1933 London Convention on the Preservation of Fauna and Flora, which requires its parties to notify each other when they establish a natural reserve under Article 5.1.[15] Here, and in other MEAs following a similar pattern,[16] the transparency obligation is *erga omnes partes* in structure, and both enables and encourages compliance. The information rule serves a collectivizing function, enabling each of the parties to implement the convention without fearing a loss of competitiveness in other spheres,[17] as well as generating a 'soft' pressure towards compliance by making the actions of (non-)compliant states visible to their peers (and others), thus mobilizing praise and shame.[18]

The second type requires reporting of incidents which may impact *specific* other states. Here the obligation serves a different function—primarily protection of the other state's sovereignty—and is triggered by events which may impact on the latter's territory, for example a theft of nuclear material,[19] or an accident during the transboundary movement of hazardous waste.[20] A prospective variation of this principle requires that states conduct an environmental impact assessment (EIA), where a planned activity has the potential to cause (significant) environmental harm across borders,[21] and perhaps also where the harm would affect a common resource, such as the high seas.[22]

15 1933 Convention Relative to the Preservation of Fauna and Flora in their Natural State (London Convention), art 5.1.

16 See eg 1946 International Convention for the Regulation of Whaling (Whaling Convention), art VIII.1; 1958 Convention on the Continental Shelf, art 5.5.

17 Daniel Bodansky, Jutta Brunnée and Lavanya Rajamani, *International Climate Change Law* (OUP 2017) 151.

18 Gerhard Loibl, 'Reporting and Information Systems in International Environmental Agreements as a Means for Dispute Prevention—The Role of "International Institutions"' *Non State Actors and International Law*, 5/1 (2005): 1, 17.

19 1979 Convention on the Physical Protection of Nuclear Material, art 5.2(a).

20 1991 Bamako Convention on the Ban of the Import into Africa and the Control of Transboundary Movement and Management of Hazardous Wastes within Africa, art 13.1.

21 Espoo Convention (n 6).

22 *Responsibilities and obligations of States sponsoring persons and entities with respect to activities in the Area* (Advisory Opinion) [2011] ITLOS Rep 10 [148]-[150].

Both types of event-specific reporting requirements may be found in many modern MEAs, but an additional tool has now been added: most modern agreements require *regular* reporting by the parties.[23] Regular reporting seeks to track the compliance of the parties and thus enables the parties (and treaty bodies) both to assess the conduct of each party individually and to ascertain the overall effectiveness of the regime. The Vienna Convention on Ozone, for example, requires that parties submit to the Conference of the Parties (COP) information pertaining to the measures each has adopted to implement the Convention.[24] The 1992 UN Framework Convention on Climate Change (UNFCCC) is even more prescriptive in detailing which parties should submit reports, for what purpose, and when.[25] The obligation here is, as above, *compliance-centred*: intended to create pressure towards compliance and to build trust between the parties. Over and above ad hoc models of reporting, though, regular reporting allows other parties and treaty bodies to identify actual or potential non-compliance, and thus facilitates so-called *non-compliance procedures*—or pre-emptive, non-punitive processes which can be engaged to support the capacity of states in danger of missing commitments under MEAs.[26]

2. *Verification: state- and public-facing transparency for compliance*

Some MEA secretariats provide little more than a 'switchboard service', taking information submitted by a party and making it available to others.[27] However, some bodies assume a more active role in the form of *verification*. The kinds of procedures which exist under this heading vary widely. We use the term to denote a process beyond a purely formal review, in which the contents of a report are assessed in order to determine compliance or non-compliance; internal consistency; credibility; or whether the report corresponds with other sources of data, such as other states' reports, scientific information, and non-governmental organization (NGO) reports.[28]

The most extensive verification process is perhaps that of the climate regime (the UNFCCC, the 1997 Kyoto Protocol, and the Paris Agreement). Here the Annex

[23] Examples of conventions combining regular and situation-specific reporting include the 1972 Convention for the Conservation of Antarctic Seals, art 3.1, 4.2, 5.1–5.3, annex—para 6; Basel Convention, arts 3.1–3.2, 6, 11.2, 13.1, 13.3; 1973 International Convention for the Prevention of Pollution by Ships as amended by the Protocol of 1978 (MARPOL 73/78) arts 8, 11, 12.

[24] art 5.

[25] arts 4.1(j), 4.2(b), 12.1(b), 12.2–12.3, 12.5.

[26] See further Chapter 56, 'Non-Compliance Procedures', in this volume.

[27] Kamen Sachariew, 'Promoting Compliance with International Environmental Legal Standards: Reflections on Monitoring and Reporting Mechanisms' *Yearbook of International Environmental Law*, 2/1 (1992): 31, 45.

[28] Cf. UNEP, 'Guidelines on Compliance with and Enforcement of Multilateral Environmental Agreements' (2007) para 14(c)(iii); Patricia Birnie, Alan Boyle, and Catherine Redgwell, *International Law and the Environment* (3rd edn, OUP 2009) 369.

I parties are under extensive obligations to submit information to the COP concerning both the sources and sinks of emissions within their territories, and their activities in pursuit of their Convention obligations.[29] Article 7.2(e) of the UNFCCC requires the COP to '[a]ssess, on the basis of all information made available to it . . . the implementation of the Convention by the Parties'. It is supported in this pursuit by the Subsidiary Body for Implementation,[30] and (in relation to the parties to that Protocol) also by the Kyoto Protocol's Expert Review Teams.[31] Even where procedures of these kinds are lacking, however, a certain degree of verification can be achieved by requirements on convention secretariats simply to process the data they receive from parties.[32]

Verification procedures are an exercise in raising the stakes. The fact that the data submitted by states is subject to an assessment—of its adequacy, its accuracy, or of the underlying situation it discloses—creates an additional pressure on states to ensure that the information is complete and accurate, and that they are in a position to comply. Verification thus strengthens both the state- and public-facing elements of compliance-centred transparency.

B. Monitoring

Monitoring is similar to reporting under MEAs and serves similar purposes, but is focused on a treaty's objects rather than its parties. Here, states and others are required to collect scientific data on the species or environments that are the objects of the convention's protection.[33] Monitoring can be used 'to assess compliance with an agreement, identify compliance problems and indicate solutions'.[34] Other uses include: to build a scientific record of an environment or environmental problem; to assess whether a convention is having the intended effects, and to identify any adverse or unintended consequences; to identify changes to an environment which may require an altered response; and to generate understanding or insight into processes of environmental change.

[29] UNFCCC, arts 2.4(b)–2.4(d), 12; subsequent attempts to strengthen the transparency framework of the climate regime are discussed in Section III.B(2); see also Chapter 29, 'Climate Change', in this volume.

[30] art 10.

[31] Kyoto Protocol, art 8. The Paris Agreement refers to a 'technical expert review', which may serve in practice to extend the Kyoto Protocol's mechanism also to the Paris Agreement's signatories; see arts 13.11–13.12; Bodansky, Brunnée, and Rajamani (n 17) 152.

[32] Basel Convention, art 16.1(b); CITES, art XII.2(d); Rosalind Reeve, 'Verification Mechanisms in CITES' in Trevor Findlay and Oliver Meier (eds), *Verification Yearbook 2001* (Vertic 2001).

[33] See eg 1992 Convention for the Protection of the Marine Environment of the North-East Atlantic (OSPAR Convention) annex IV, arts 1.1(a)–(c).

[34] UNEP, 'Guidelines on Compliance' (n 28) para 14(c)(ii).

An early example of a monitoring provision is Article VIII of the 1946 Whaling Convention. Its section 3 requires each party to transmit annually 'scientific information available to that Government with respect to whales and whaling, including the results of research conducted pursuant to' the convention.[35] In Article VIII(4), the contracting parties recognize 'that continuous collection and analysis of biological data … are indispensable to sound and constructive management of the whale fisheries'. Similar requirements can be found in the 1992 Convention on Biological Diversity (CBD),[36] the LRTAP,[37] the UNFCCC,[38] and elsewhere. Unusually among MEAs pertaining to emergencies, minimal provisions on monitoring also appear in the Basel Convention on Hazardous Waste.[39]

Monitoring seeks to enhance compliance, albeit less directly than reporting. Perhaps more significantly, monitoring also promotes both emancipatory and advocative transparency, as will be examined in the next sections.

1. *Monitoring serving emancipatory transparency*

The term 'emancipatory transparency' was coined in 2010 by Arthur Mol, who described the promises and pitfalls associated with the use of 'information [by environmental defenders] as one of their main resources in struggles with the powers-that-be over environmental controversies'.[40] Transparency can function as a 'power-shifter', and 'break th[e] vicious circle' of 'political power combined with intransparency'.[41] The emergence of international transparency as a principle and practice is both a result and a promoter of shifts in power and perceptions of legitimacy.

International environmental law has begun to open up the preserve of secrecy available to states vis-à-vis their domestic and the international publics. Information is provided to the public as an end in itself and in support of two secondary aims, namely that the public (or specially affected groups) have the means actively to participate in environmental decision-making, and to facilitate access to remedies following environmental harm. Provisions on public access to information appear in many environmental agreements.[42] Preeminent is the Aarhus Convention, Article 1 of which requires that states 'guarantee the rights of access to information, public participation and decision-making, and access to justice in environmental matters in accordance with the provisions of this Convention'.

The Aarhus Convention represents the highest expression to date of the emancipatory form of transparency in international environmental law. Nevertheless, there remain

[35] art VIII(3).
[36] arts 7(b)–7(d).
[37] arts 6, 7(b), 8(a), 9.
[38] arts 4.1(a), 5.
[39] art 13.3(d). This may be as a result of its broader focus on monitoring *trade* in hazardous waste.
[40] Arthur Mol, 'The Future of Transparency: Power, Pitfalls and Promises' *Global Environmental Politics*, 10/3 (2010): 132, 135–136.
[41] Peters (n 13) 555.
[42] See eg UNFCCC, art 6(a)(ii)–(iii); Paris Agreement, art 12.

important gaps. First, the geographical scope of the Convention is limited.[43] Secondly, as Sand notes, to emancipate individuals it is not sufficient only to shift power to them from states, but also from other, notably private actors holding 'a huge mass of … environmental and health risk information that … is not covered by the Aarhus Convention at all'.[44] Finally, the Convention does not generally require states to take proactive efforts to educate or inform their citizens and does not create a right of citizens to be informed *ex officio*; rather it relies on an active citizenry that is in a position to request information.[45] That in itself presumes a certain level of knowledge and an ability to interact with state structures that may exclude some of those most in need from access to environmental information.

In short, transparency is no silver bullet that will unerringly shift power from the 'corrupt elites' to the 'common people'. Rather, it shifts power from those actors who know the right people to those who possess the know-how and resources to access, analyse, and interpret the data.[46] On average, the political actors of the First World (above all states, but also NGOs and businesses) can better exploit the opportunities for influence that are created by improving (international) transparency. Legal observers should not only acknowledge that 'the battle for transparency' is a 'struggle for power' but should also think about how to level the playing field of this battle.[47]

2. *Monitoring serving advocative transparency*

Advocative transparency, unlike the forms discussed above, does not exist in particular or paradigmatic relationships, but rather is employed in order to *build a narrative or community* in support of an actor, policy, or goal, and so is found in the relationship between the advocate and his or her audience.

Advocative transparency is perhaps primarily used in order to encourage greater ambition by actors (particularly states) towards environmental ends. For example, the Intergovernmental Panel on Climate Change (IPCC) and the Paris Agreement mobilize information in order to generate an appetite for more ambitious climate change action among states, civil society actors, and the general public. Through the personal authority of the scientists involved, the transparency of its processes, and publication of its data and conclusions, the IPCC has contributed to a stronger narrative on the need for action, and has provided information which can be used to press for enhanced ambition.

[43] As of December 2019, the Convention has forty-seven parties, all from Europe and Central Asia.

[44] Peter Sand, 'The Right to Know: Environmental Information Disclosure by Government and Industry' in Durwood Zaelke, Donald Kaniaru, and Eva Kruzíková (eds), *Making Law Work: Environmental Compliance & Sustainable Development*, II (Cameron May 2005) 25 (references omitted).

[45] The default position (under art 4.1) requires that public authorities provide information to the public on request. Proactive provision of information is required only under arts 5.3–5.7.

[46] Peters (n 13) 555.

[47] Ibid; citing 'Conclusions' in Ann Florini (ed), *The Right to Know: Transparency for an Open World* (Columbia University Press 2007) 348 (other references omitted).

A second stage to this strategy underpins the Paris Agreement. The Agreement sets no specific targets for reductions of greenhouse gas emissions. Rather, its parties are under the ostensibly weaker obligation to set national targets for emissions reductions, carbon sink enhancement, and other measures.[48] The Agreement explicitly prescribes that '[i]n communicating their nationally determined contributions, all Parties shall provide the information necessary for clarity, *transparency* and understanding'.[49] Here transparency not only serves a compliance-oriented purpose but also has an advocative element, seeking to press the parties towards greater ambition.[50]

Monitoring requirements engage emancipatory and advocative transparency through the simple device that states themselves are required to collect and to process the relevant data.[51] By requiring states to engage with data on changes in environments they are *forced to know*. This knowledge is in itself powerful. The fact that states must be aware of the damage which their activities cause to environments means that the choice *not* to protect must be actively taken. Beyond this, the requirement to collect and process the data has a capacity-building function at two levels. First, it requires state structures to receive, interpret, and (perhaps) act on environmental information. This may benefit, notably, developing country parties. Second, the corresponding (domestic) increase in the availability and quality of environmental information empowers individuals and civil society groups to campaign for adequate environmental protection. In parallel, the advocative potential of international actors (including international organizations and international NGOs) is enhanced by the availability of good-quality data.

However, advocative transparency can also be mobilized to support a narrative intended to 'excuse' the non-compliance of a state. Here the state involved may use the provision of environmental, economic, or other information to demonstrate to interested constituencies—other states, its population, or civil society—that it *could not* comply with its international environmental law obligations. Though there may be scenarios in which states (or other actors) cynically exploit such narratives, the implied requirement to explain non-compliance in this way perhaps serves as a bulwark against manipulation.

[48] art 4.2.

[49] art 4.8 (emphasis added). These requirements are further elaborated by the Paris Rulebook, discussed in Benoît Mayer, 'Transparency Under the Paris Rulebook: Is the Transparency Framework Truly Enhanced?' *Climate Law*, 9/1 (2019): 40.

[50] Anne-Sophie Tabau, 'Evaluation of the Paris Climate Agreement According to a Global Standard of Transparency' *Carbon and Climate Law Review*, 10/1 (2016): 23, 30; see further Chapter 29, 'Climate Change', in this volume.

[51] Fitzmaurice makes a similar observation with regard to reporting; see Malgosia Fitzmaurice, 'Environmental Compliance Control' in Anne Peters and Rüdiger Wolfrum (eds), *Max Planck Encyclopaedia of Public International Law* (online edn, OUP 2010) para 28.

C. Information Exchange

Obligations to provide or to exchange information are a near-ubiquitous feature of MEAs. These obligations are generally state-facing, and include both general and situation-specific requirements to provide information.[52]

1. *General information exchange*

The range of information required to be made available is as wide as the range of topics regulated. The UNFCCC, for example, requires 'full, open and prompt exchange of relevant scientific, technological, technical, socio-economic and legal information.'[53] The CBD requires that states 'facilitate the exchange of information, from all publicly available sources, relevant to the conservation and sustainable use of biological diversity';[54] and its 2000 Cartagena Protocol on Biosafety creates a detailed regime to '[f]acilitate the exchange of scientific, technical, environmental and legal information on, and experience with, living modified organisms.'[55]

The purpose of information exchange between states is twofold. First, it is intended to accelerate the development of environmentally favourable policies and technologies in states lacking the capacity for cutting-edge primary research on relevant questions.[56] Secondly, information sharing can contribute to 'emancipation' by addressing the power imbalances between states. By ensuring that information is shared, all parties are empowered to protect their environments, to develop in a sustainable way, and—where necessary—to complain of environmental harms.[57] This is particularly relevant in areas such as climate regulation or—as per Gupta's example—genetically modified organisms. In both areas, the potential harms predominantly affect developing states, while most of the institutions carrying out advanced monitoring, cutting-edge research, or development are based in the developed world.[58]

There are, however, significant concerns about whether such information exchange provisions can work, particularly where information has commercial value.[59] For example, the Cartagena Protocol regime does not function as designed: although 'the intended main beneficiaries [are] developing countries, the burden of disclosure has

[52] Only the former are information exchange obligations properly-so-called. Nevertheless, the latter will also be briefly discussed under this heading in order to highlight certain structural similarities; see Philippe Sands and Jacqueline Peel, *Principles of International Environmental Law* (4th edn, CUP 2018) 685, 686–689.

[53] art 4.1(h).

[54] art 17.1.

[55] art 20.1(a); Aarti Gupta, 'Transparency to What End? Governing by Disclosure through the Biosafety Clearing House' *Environment and Planning C: Government and Policy*, 28/1 (2010): 128.

[56] Rio Declaration (n 10) principle 9 on 'endogenous capacity building, . . . improving scientific understanding . . . and . . . enhancing the development, adaptation, diffusion and transfer of technologies, including new and innovative technologies'.

[57] Gupta (n 55) 131 et seq.

[58] Ibid, 134–135.

[59] Sands and Peel (n 52) 687–688.

shifted in practice onto such countries.'[60] The effect is, according to Gupta, that information exchange requirements are 'more likely to have *market-enabling* rather than the originally intended *market-regulating* effects'.[61] This 'turns on its head the originally intended aims of disclosure'.[62] Other areas of information sharing, especially in management regimes for shared resources, seem to function better, possibly because the rational self-interest of states is engaged.[63]

2. *Situation-specific information exchange*

Situation-specific information exchange requirements have already been mentioned in relation to inter-state reporting.[64] The label refers predominantly to the prior informed consent (PIC) procedure, and to notification of accidents causing (or threatening) transboundary harm.[65] In both cases, a number of MEAs give the affected state a right to receive information as a corollary of its sovereignty over territory.[66] Significantly, parallel obligations exist under customary law, at a minimum with regard to activities likely to cause 'significant' transboundary adverse impacts. First, states are obliged 'under general international law' to undertake an EIA 'where there is a risk that the proposed industrial activity may have a significant adverse impact in a transboundary context, in particular, on a shared resource', as the ICJ held in *Pulp Mills*.[67] As a second step, a state is under an obligation 'to notify, and consult with, the potentially affected State in good faith', where the EIA discloses a 'risk of significant transboundary harm'.[68]

The question of the threshold remains: the ICJ's double reference to a 'significant' impact and harm requires further definition. The term should be interpreted in the specific circumstances of the scenario, and it seems likely that the threshold is low. UNEP's Guidelines define 'significant effect' as referring 'to any appreciable effects on a shared natural resource, excluding "de minimis" effects'.[69]

60 Gupta (n 55) 140.

61 Ibid, 130.

62 Ibid, 140.

63 Gupta (n 55); Jonathan Chenoweth, 'International River Basin Management: Data and Information Exchange under International Law and the Case of the Mekong River Basin' *Energy and Natural Resources*, 18 (2000): 142.

64 See Section III.A.1.

65 See further Chapters 16, 23, and 27, 'Harm Prevention', 'Customary International Law and the Environment', and 'Judicial Development', in this volume.

66 See inter alia MARPOL, art 8; Convention on Physical Protection of Nuclear Material, art 5.2(a); Basel Convention, arts 6, 13.1; Espoo Convention (n 6); Bamako Convention, arts 4.3(s), 4.3(u), 6.1, 13; 1998 Rotterdam Convention on the Prior Informed Consent Procedure for Certain Hazardous Chemicals and Pesticides in International Trade; Cartagena Protocol, arts 8–11, 17.

67 The neglect of such an impact assessment violates 'due diligence, and the duty of vigilance and prevention', *Pulp Mills on the River Uruguay (Argentina/Uruguay)* (Judgement) [2010] ICJ Rep 14 (Pulp Mills case) [204].

68 *Certain Activities Carried Out by Nicaragua in the Border Area (Costa Rica/Nicaragua)* and *Construction of a Road in Costa Rica along the San Juan River (Nicaragua/Costa Rica)* (Judgement) [2015] ICJ Rep 665 [168].

69 UNEP, *Guidelines and Principles on Shared Natural Resources* (1978) 4.

Moreover, the obligation to notify affected states extends beyond planned activities and prospective harms—the focus of the EIA system—and applies also to environmental accidents and unforeseen events. This obligation is codified in a number of international treaties,[70] was included in the non-binding Rio declaration,[71] and was mentioned by the International Tribunal for the Law of the Sea (ITLOS) in a dictum in *MOX Plant*.[72] The strong connection between the obligation to inform and the sovereignty of potentially injured states, taken together with the many affirmations of obligations to exchange information in international documents and conventions, is at least suggestive of a customary norm.

D. Right to Information?

The ability of individuals and communities to access environmental information is the very essence of emancipatory transparency, and is vital for public-facing compliance-centred transparency. Absent reliable access to a source of good-quality information, individuals and communities cannot effectively mobilize to defend their environments, and cannot hold states and other actors to account for their actions. Increasingly, therefore, international environmental law moves beyond *inter partes* information rules ('the original reporting, consultation and notification obligations') towards a 'second generation' of rules, which serve, inter alia, 'to increase the public availability of information by enhancing access'.[73]

1. *Aarhus Convention*

The Aarhus Convention has acquired a totemic importance in this regard. It 'has become a symbol for environmental democracy, representing a set of ideas which transcend the detail of the actual obligations under the Convention'.[74] Despite some problems of compliance and implementation, the effectiveness of the regime is indicated by the 'impressive number of pieces of legislation that have been introduced, or strengthened, in order to meet the requirements of the Convention',[75] and the high level of compliance

[70] See inter alia Convention on Physical Protection of Nuclear Material, art 5.2(a); 1986 Convention on Early Notification of a Nuclear Accident, art 2; Basel Convention, art 13.1; Bamako Convention, art 13; Cartagena Protocol, art 17.

[71] Rio Declaration (n 10) principle 18.

[72] *The MOX Plant case (Ireland/United Kingdom)* (Provisional Measures, Order of 3 December 2001) [2001] ITLOS Rep 95 [84].

[73] Sands and Peel (n 52) 730–733; see further Chapter 21, 'Public Participation', in this volume.

[74] Jeremy Wates, 'The Future of the Aarhus Convention: Perspectives Arising from the Third Session of the Meeting of the Parties' in Marc Pallemaerts (ed), *The Aarhus Convention at Ten: Interactions and Tensions between Conventional International Law and EU Environmental Law* (Europa Law Publishing 2011) 389; see further Birnie, Boyle, and Redgwell (n 28) 291–292; Ulrich Beyerlin and Thilo Marauhn, *International Environmental Law* (Hart Publishing 2011) 236–237; Pierre-Marie Dupuy and Jorge Viñuales, *International Environmental Law* (CUP 2015) 76–77.

[75] Wates (n 74).

with reporting requirements.[76] As discussed above,[77] however, there remain significant structural obstacles to the global availability of environmental information, not least the Convention's limited geographical scope.[78] It is therefore necessary to look beyond the Aarhus Convention for the source of a more widely applicable right and obligation that could undergird the public-facing forms of transparency. The most promising source is human rights law.

2. *Human rights law*

International environmental law and international human rights law intersect,[79] for example, in a right of individuals to access environmental information. Philippe Sands and Jacqueline Peel note that this right is 'relatively recent, but now firmly entrenched' in international law.[80] A right to receive environmental information is established in at least certain circumstances under the 1950 European Convention for the Protection of Human Rights and Fundamental Freedoms (ECHR),[81] the 1969 American Convention on Human Rights (ACHR),[82] and the 1981 African Charter on Human and Peoples' Rights (ACHPR),[83] and in the communications and comments of the UN Human Rights Committee (UN HRC).[84]

The leading European case is *Taskin v Turkey*.[85] The procedural limb of the Article 8 right to respect of home and family life allows the court to consider not only whether an environmental harm actually caused an infringement, but also to 'scrutinise the decision-making process to ensure that due weight has been accorded to the interests of the individual'.[86] Three aspects are important. First, the state must have conducted 'appropriate investigations and studies' such that environmental harms

[76] Ibid, 392.

[77] See Section III.B.1.

[78] eg Russia, the US, Canada, and China remain non-parties to the Convention at time of writing. See <https://treaties.un.org/Pages/ViewDetails.aspx?src=TREATY&mtdsg_no=XXVII-13&chapter=27&clang=_en> accessed 23 January 2020.

[79] Framework Principles on Human Rights and the Environment (n 14) principles 1–2; for more detailed consideration of this point see Chapter 45, 'Human Rights', in this volume.

[80] Sands and Peel (n 52) 707.

[81] See eg *Taskin and Ors v Turkey* (10 November 2004) European Court of Human Rights (ECtHR), 46117/99 [115]–[119]; *Öneryildiz v Turkey* (30 November 2004) ECtHR, 48939/99; Alan Boyle, 'Environment and Human Rights' in Anne Peters and Rüdiger Wolfrum (eds), *Max Planck Encyclopaedia of Public International Law* (online edn, OUP 2009) paras 28–29.

[82] See eg *Maya Indigenous Communities of the Toledo District, Belize*, Inter-American Commission on Human Rights (12 October 2004) Report No 40/04, Case 12.053 [153]–[154]; *Claude Reyes et al v Chile* (Judgement of 19 September 2006) Inter-American Court of Human Rights Ser C No 151.

[83] *Social and Economic Rights Action Center (SERAC) and the Center for Economic and Social Rights (CESR) v Nigeria*, African Commission on Human and Peoples' Rights (2001) Communication No 155/96 (Ogoni case) [53].

[84] *Mahuika et al v New Zealand* (Decision of 27 October 2000) UN Human Rights Committee Communication No 547/1993, UN Doc CCPR/C/70/D/547/1993 [9.5]; UN Human Rights Committee, General Comment No 34, UN Doc CCPR/C/GC/34 [18].

[85] Taskin case (n 81) [115], [118].

[86] Ibid [115].

and consequent impacts on individual rights could be anticipated.[87] Secondly, the public must have access to the conclusions of such studies, in order that individuals can 'assess the danger to which they are exposed'.[88] Thirdly, adequate access to information is implied in the court's conclusion that 'the individuals concerned must also be able to appeal to the courts against' the decision.[89] This has rightly been described as 'a profound extension of the scope of Art. 8',[90] under which ancillary procedural obligations bring into being a de facto right to meaningful consultation where Article 8 is engaged. A similar right to consultation has also been recognized by the other regional human rights bodies,[91] and in the communications of the UN Human Rights Committee.[92]

The right to consultation remained dependent on the substantive right to private and family life, and the right to access information is in turn parasitic on the right to participate effectively in that consultation. The question posed, therefore, is whether a broader right to information of concerned citizens (or civil society groups) is recognized. Increasingly it appears that this question should be answered affirmatively. In the pioneering judgement of *Claude Reyes v Chile*, the Inter-American Court of Human Rights broadly defined the scope of the right to seek and to receive information under Article 13 of the ACHR as a 'right of all individuals to request access to state-held information', with the consequence that there is a 'right of the individual to receive such information and [a] *positive* obligation of the state to provide it'.[93] In recent years, the European Court of Human Rights has caught up with its Inter-American counterpart, and in so doing abandoned its previous narrow reading of Article 10 of the ECHR.[94] In a 2012 Grand Chamber judgement, the Court noted that a right 'to receive information in the form of access to the public documents concerned', is protected under Article 10 of the ECHR.[95]

In its General Comment of 2011 on the right to freedom of expression, the UN Human Rights Committee interpreted Article 19.2 of the 1966 International Covenant on Civil and Political Rights (ICCPR) as embracing 'a right of access to information held by public bodies'.[96] In order to give effect to this right, the General Comment further called upon parties to 'proactively put in the public domain Government information of public interest'.[97]

[87] Ibid [119].
[88] Ibid.
[89] Ibid.
[90] Boyle (n 81) [32].
[91] Maya Indigenous Community case (n 82) [153]–[154]; Ogoni case (n 83) [53], [55].
[92] Mahuika case (n 84) [9.5]; see also Chapter 45, 'Human Rights', in this volume.
[93] Claude Reyes case (n 82) [77] (emphasis added).
[94] See for the narrow reading *Sdružení Jihočeské Matky v Czech Republic* (10 July 2006) ECtHR, 19101/03, 9–10.
[95] *Gillberg v Sweden* (3 April 2012) ECtHR, 41723/06 [93].
[96] General Comment No 34 (n 84) para 18.
[97] Ibid, para 19.

Unsurprisingly, there remain shortcomings. Ebbesson notes that international law on public access to environmental information remains 'regionally asymmetric, quite fragmentary, and far from consistent',[98] and it seems likely that a customary right of access to information and to participate in environmental decision-making is yet to crystallize.[99] Nevertheless, Ebbesson rightly rejects as 'somewhat cynical' the conclusion that real progress towards a right to transparency in international environmental law exists only under the auspices of the Aarhus Convention, because 'normative fragments' also apply elsewhere.[100] Although a generally applicable right to public-facing transparency does not seem to exist *de lege lata*—and doubtless there will be cases that accordingly fall through the gaps—in an increasing number of instances individuals will, as a matter of (human rights) law, have a right to access information relating to environmental decision-making. And maybe as importantly, normative expectations are growing.

IV. CONCLUSION

This chapter has surveyed the functions that transparency plays in international environmental law, and has identified it as an increasingly central pillar of many international environmental law regimes. Whether as part of the Paris Agreement's 'enhanced transparency framework'—identified by Tabau as the *raison d'être* of the agreement[101]—or in the guise of the familiar tools of monitoring, reporting, and verification, transparency is employed in international environmental law both as a means of achieving various substantive ends, and as a substantive end in itself.

The increasing interest in transparency in environmental law is an aspect of a wider—and ongoing—'transparency turn' in international law. This is a foundational shift which could signal a paradigm change from international law as a private law-like legal order consisting of bilateral relations of rights and obligations among equally sovereign states imagined as sitting on a horizontal plane, towards a truly 'public' international legal order in which jointly established institutions and regimes work towards pursuing objectives in the interest of the entire community.[102] Nowhere is a shift of this kind more significant than in international regulation of environmental matters. The traditional bilateral structures and remedies of international law are an awkward fit when considering questions of international public interest such as the safeguarding of common resources, the prevention of transboundary harms, the protection of migratory species, and the

98 Jonas Ebbesson, 'Global or European Only?: International Law on Transparency in Environmental Matters for Members of the Public' in Bianchi and Peters (n 2) 55.

99 Certainly in 2010, the ICJ declared that '[t]he Court is of the view that no legal obligation to consult the affected populations arises for the Parties from the instruments invoked' in Pulp Mills case (n 67) [216].

100 Ebbesson (n 98) 73.

101 Tabau (n 50) 30.

102 Peters (n 13) 600–604.

problem of climate change. Transparency has played, and is increasingly playing, a central role in alternative processes which seek new and innovative ways to regulate state behaviour in this field, and to allow for scrutiny and contestation by affected or otherwise interested citizens, and members of a global public. Whether international environmental law will succeed in offering solutions to such problems as radiative forcing, ocean acidification, land degradation, and biodiversity loss, remains to be seen. But seen it will be.

BIBLIOGRAPHY

Jonas Ebbesson, 'Global or European Only?: International Law on Transparency in Environmental Matters for Members of the Public' in Andrea Bianchi and Anne Peters (eds), *Transparency in International Law* (CUP 2013) 55

Aarti Gupta, 'Transparency to What End? Governing by Disclosure through the Biosafety Clearing House' *Environment and Planning C: Government and Policy*, 28/1 (2010): 128

Gerhard Loibl, 'Reporting and Information Systems in International Environmental Agreements as a Means for Dispute Prevention—The Role of "International Institutions"' *Non State Actors and International Law*, 5/1 (2005): 1

Benoît Mayer, 'Transparency Under the Paris Rulebook: Is the Transparency Framework Truly Enhanced?' *Climate Law*, 9/1 (2019): 40

Anne Peters, 'Towards Transparency as a Global Norm' in Andrea Bianchi and Anne Peters (eds), *Transparency in International Law* (CUP 2013) 534

Anne-Sophie Tabau, 'Evaluation of the Paris Climate Agreement According to a Global Standard of Transparency' *Carbon and Climate Law Review*, 10/1 (2016): 23

CHAPTER 53

MARKET MECHANISMS

MICHAEL A MEHLING

I. INTRODUCTION

MARKET mechanisms have emerged as an instrument of environmental policy in recent decades, tracing an unparalleled trajectory from theoretical prescription to practised legal reality. Conceptually, these mechanisms reflect a departure from the conventional toolbox of environmental law, which has traditionally relied on instruments such as liability rules and sanctions to control environmental degradation and overuse.[1]

Environmental law has, of course, undergone major changes before. Different forms of administrative regulation, including building permits, operating licences, and technology standards,[2] have been added over time to limit the harmful effects of industrial activity. Yet as the frequency and scale of environmental threats proliferated, so did the density of regulatory constraints, stirring concern about their growing economic cost.[3]

Such preoccupation with cost, coupled with fiscal constraints and a broader trend towards deregulation and market liberalization in many jurisdictions, precipitated the eventual diffusion of concepts from economic theory into environmental law.[4] And while this process had its origins in a domestic context, markets have long since also become an established feature of international environmental law.

[1] David Schorr, 'Historical Analysis in Environmental Law' in Markus Dubber and Christopher Tomlins (eds), *The Oxford Handbook of Legal History* (OUP 2018) 1001.

[2] See Chapter 6, 'Instrument Choice', in this volume.

[3] See Bruce Ackerman and Richard Stewart, 'Reforming Environmental Law' *Stanford Law Review*, 37/5 (1985): 1333; Allen Kneese and Charles Schultze, *Pollution, Prices, and Public Policy* (Brookings Institution 1975); Robert Stavins (ed), *Harnessing Market Forces to Protect Our Environment* (Project 88 1988).

[4] Robyn Eckersley, 'Markets, the State and the Environment: An Overview' in Robyn Eckersley (ed), *Markets, the State and the Environment: Towards Integration* (Macmillan 1995) 7, 10.

In a relatively short period of time, scholars and practitioners of environmental law have come to embrace policy instruments that harness flexible market forces rather than legal coercion. Along the way, they have seen their professional vernacular evolve in line with the changing conceptual foundations of their field, while their discipline has ceded some of its former authority in environmental policy debates to the compelling empiricism and quantitative approaches of the social sciences.[5]

More than a mere recalibration of how different academic pursuits influence environmental policy formation, however, the ascent of market mechanisms has engendered new markets worth more than some traditional commodity markets.[6] Supporters argue that they have also helped meet environmental policy objectives at reduced cost, while fostering increased levels of innovation and participation. Critics, by contrast, have pointed to conceptual and normative limitations of market approaches—including tensions with entrenched legal doctrines—and drawn attention to implementation shortfalls in the real world. In short, academic debate about the merits of market mechanisms is far from over.

This chapter provides an overview of market mechanisms and their contemporary role in international environmental law. Section II sets out the conceptual foundations and theoretical rationale of market mechanisms when deployed for environmental ends, citing the main arguments levelled on different sides of the debate. As social constructs built on legal rights and obligations, moreover, markets rely on a sound regulatory framework for their efficient operation.[7] With environmental markets, this need for legal parameters is further accentuated by the fact that the article of trade is itself a regulatory artifice.[8] Section III, therefore, provides an overview of legal issues arising in the design and implementation of market mechanisms. Section IV surveys the most important environmental markets currently in place at the international level, and Section V concludes with an outlook on the future role of market mechanisms in international environmental law.

[5] Robert Hahn, 'The Impact of Economics on Environmental Policy' *Journal of Environmental Economics and Management*, 39/3 (2000): 375; Wallace Oates, 'From Research to Policy: The Case of Environmental Economics' *International Journal of Urban Sciences*, 4/1 (2000): 1.

[6] At its peak, for instance, the annual market value (including secondary markets) for Certified Emission Reductions (CERs) under the Clean Development Mechanism of the 1997 Kyoto Protocol was USD 32.8 billion, exceeding the size of global markets for commodities such as silver, nickel, or lead, see Karan Capoor and Philippe Ambrosi, 'State and Trends of the Carbon Market 2009' *World Bank Report 48998* (2009): 31 <https://documents.worldbank.org/curated/en/281731468336837686/State-and-trends-of-the-carbon-market-2009> accessed 14 February 2019.

[7] See already Max Weber, *Wirtschaft und Gesellschaft* (3rd edn, Mohr 1947) 347; Jens Beckert, 'The Social Order of Markets' *Theory and Society*, 38/3 (2009): 245.

[8] See eg Jonas Monast, Jon Anda, and Timothy Profeta, 'U.S. Carbon Market Design: Regulating Emission Allowances as Financial Instruments' *Nicholas Institute for Environmental Policy Solutions Working Paper CCPP 09-01* (2009): 15 <https://nicholasinstitute.duke.edu/climate/carbon-market-oversight/u.s.-carbon-market-design-regulating-emission-allowances-as-financial-instruments> accessed 12 February 2019.

II. CONCEPTUAL FOUNDATIONS

Understanding the theoretical rationale of market mechanisms necessarily requires engagement with fundamental concepts and terminology of standard economics. As discussed in Chapter 10, economic theory ascribes environmental challenges to different market failures, caused by, inter alia, positive or negative externalities.[9] For economists, such market failures denote an inefficient allocation of goods and services, justifying an intervention in the form of public policy.[10]

When seeking to correct a market failure, environmental policy-makers can take recourse to a broad portfolio of policy instruments.[11] Some of these policy instruments influence behaviour through explicit price signals, and are therefore commonly referred to as economic instruments.[12] While definitions vary, this category of instruments includes pricing[13] and quantity controls with trading,[14] both of which are widely credited with achieving environmental policy objectives at the lowest cost.[15]

Economic instruments that involve quantity rationing coupled with a defined, tradeable unit—such as a permit to emit a specified amount of a pollutant over a specified period of time—are often referred to as market mechanisms because they give rise to dynamics similar to those found in conventional markets for goods and services. Like economic instruments more generally, these market mechanisms promise various theoretical benefits relative to conventional regulation.[16]

[9] On the notion of externalities, see seminally James Buchanan and Craig Stubblebine, 'Externality' *Economica*, 29/116 (1962): 371.

[10] Francis Bator, 'The Anatomy of Market Failure' *Quarterly Journal of Economics*, 72/3 (1958): 351; see however the influential argument by Ronald Coase that government intervention becomes unnecessary if parties are able to engage in unobstructed bargaining, in Ronald Coase, 'The Problem of Social Cost' *The Journal of Law & Economics*, 3 (1960): 1; for discussion see Chapter 10, 'Economics', in this volume.

[11] For more detail see Chapter 6, 'Instrument Choice', in this volume.

[12] Johannes Opschoor and Hans Vos, *Economic Instruments for Environmental Protection* (OECD Publishing 1989); Robert Stavins, 'Market-Based Environmental Policies' in Paul Portney and Robert Stavins (eds), *Public Policies for Environmental Protection* (2nd edn, Routledge 2000) 31.

[13] As exemplified, most notably, by Pigouvian pricing set at the level of the social cost of externalities, see Arthur Pigou, *The Economics of Welfare* (Macmillan 1920).

[14] Thomas Crocker, 'The Structuring of Atmospheric Pollution Control Systems' in Harold Wolozin (ed), *The Economics of Air Pollution: A Symposium* (WW Norton 1966) 61; John Dales, *Pollution, Property & Prices: An Essay in Policymaking and Economics* (University of Toronto Press 1968); David Montgomery, 'Markets in Licenses and Efficient Pollution Control Programs' *Journal of Economic Theory*, 5/3 (1972): 395.

[15] William Baumol and Wallace Oates, 'The Use of Standards and Prices for Protection of the Environment' *Swedish Journal of Economics*, 73/1 (1971): 42; Carolyn Fischer and Richard Newell, 'Environmental and Technology Policies for Climate Mitigation' *Journal of Environmental Economics and Management*, 55/2 (2008): 142; Stavins (n 3) 15, 19.

[16] For discussion of the relative merits ascribed to these instruments, see Chapter 6, 'Instrument Choice', in this volume.

If the quantity control—such as an overall limit in pollutant emissions[17]—is adequately enforced, it guarantees the desired policy outcome, setting this policy option apart from pure pricing approaches, such as an environmental tax. Still, by incorporating tradeable units, market mechanisms also reveal an explicit price for environmental harm at the intersection of demand and supply, with the latter determined by the regulator. That price, in turn, internalizes some or all of the social cost of environmental harm in the private cost of underlying behaviour, thereby helping to operationalize the polluter pays principle.[18]

Market mechanisms often impose a declining quantity over time, progressively reducing the number of tradeable units in the market. As prices for units rise in response to growing scarcity, the demand for them should gradually decrease, creating a continuous incentive to reduce environmental harm. Entities with relatively lower compliance costs will sell unused units to entities with relatively higher compliance costs, ideally resulting in an equilibrium where marginal abatement costs are equalized across all regulated entities, and abatement of environmental harm occurs where it yields the largest net benefit to society.[19] In that optimal state—formally described as a 'Pareto equilibrium'[20]—a market mechanism will ensure that no compliance entity can contribute to the environmental policy objective at lower cost than any other.

In theory, thus, market mechanisms should lower the private and social cost of achieving environmental policy objectives relative to more rigid policy mandates.[21] Such cost reductions can, in turn, help increase environmental policy ambition by freeing up resources for additional abatement or reducing political resistance against more stringent policy commitments. In practice, however, a variety of factors can impede realization of these theoretical benefits; some detractors of markets have gone even further and challenged their very premise.[22]

Still, for better or for worse, markets have become firmly entrenched in the professional vocabulary of environmental lawyers, following a remarkable diffusion process that is traced in the next section.

[17] Aside from such an absolute limit, or 'cap', quantity rationing can also occur with a baseline (such as a business-as-usual projection or a defined performance standard) and crediting of environmental improvements relative to this baseline, be it at project, sectoral or economy-wide level, see Organisation for Economic Co-operation and Development (OECD), *Domestic Transferable Permits for Environmental Management: Design and Implementation* (2001) 19.

[18] Johannes Opschoor and Hans Vos, *Economic Instruments for Environmental Protection* (OECD Publishing 1989) 3. This principle has been enshrined in the domestic law of many jurisdictions as well as in international environmental documents, see eg *Report of the United Nations Conference on Environment and Development* (UN 1993) vol I, annex I—'Rio Declaration', principle 16.

[19] William Baumol and Wallace Oates, *The Theory of Environmental Policy* (2nd edn, CUP 1988) 177; Thomas Tietenberg, *Emissions Trading: Principles and Practice* (2nd edn, Resources for the Future 2006) 27.

[20] Based on the criteria described by Vilfredo Pareto in his seminal Alfred Bonnet (tr), *Manuel d'économie Politique* (Giard & Brière 1909) 354.

[21] Denny Ellerman *et al*, *Markets for Clean Air* (CUP 2000) 294; Tietenberg (n 19) 58–59.

[22] See Section IV.

III. LAWYERS AND THE ASCENDANCE OF MARKETS

Within thirty years of being first explored in the theoretical literature, market mechanisms had already been endorsed by the international community as an instrument of environmental policy.[23] This rise is inseparably linked to the sophistication of instrument choice theory, which, as outlined in Chapter 6, has been dominated by economic thought and its preoccupation with the costs and benefits of alternative policy options. Although other criteria for instrument choice are often mentioned, the academic literature has focused on the cost effectiveness of policy instruments.[24]

Given this preoccupation with cost effectiveness, economists have focused their efforts on identifying the perceived 'first-best' policy option, with much of their scholarly research devoted to narrow theoretical debates about relative merits—again expressed in economic terms—of different instrument designs.[25] Yet the mathematical formalization underlying such research extends authority to market mechanisms, legitimizing them in the eyes of the research community and helping to challenge 'the inertia of the status quo' that has otherwise favoured more traditional forms of regulation.[26]

More than merely engaging in a theoretical debate, economists have thus shaped the discourse about market mechanisms, with their discipline serving as a performative tool to advance policy choices in the real world.[27] By presenting a systematic and coherent framework for instrument choice and focusing research efforts on those instruments that best conform to self-defined criteria, they have helped narrow the range of options available for collective action, severing discussions about means from their intended ends, and shifting policy negotiations from public arenas to the confined world of policy experts.[28]

[23] Daniel Cole, 'Origins of Emissions Trading in Theory and Early Practice' in Stefan Weishaar (ed), *Research Handbook on Emissions Trading* (Edward Elgar 2016) 9, 25.

[24] See eg Lawrence Goulder and Ian Parry, 'Instrument Choice in Environmental Policy' *Review of Environmental Economics and Policy*, 2/2 (2008): 152; Nathaniel Keohane, Robert Stavins, and Richard Revesz, 'The Choice of Regulatory Instruments in Environmental Policy' *Harvard Environmental Law Review*, 22/2 (1998): 313.

[25] Perhaps most famous among these is the assessment of the relative merit of price- and quantity-based approaches under conditions of uncertainty by Martin Weitzman, 'Prices vs. Quantities' *Review of Economic Studies*, 41/4 (1974): 477, which spurred a voluminous discussion that continues to the present day.

[26] Tietenberg (n 19) 4–5, 48.

[27] Richard Lane, 'The Promiscuous History of Market Efficiency: The Development of Early Emissions Trading Systems' *Environmental Politics*, 21/4 (2012): 583; Oates (n 5) 146.

[28] Arno Simons and Jan-Peter Voß, 'Politics by Other Means: The Making of The Emissions Trading Instrument as a "Pre-History" of Carbon Trading' in Benjamin Stephan and Richard Lane (eds), *The Politics of Carbon Markets* (Routledge 2014) 51, 64.

It did not take long for these conceptual prescriptions to find their way into political discourse, bolstered by a broader shift in governance philosophy towards market liberalization and scepticism of government intervention.[29] At the domestic level, experimentation with market mechanisms began as early as 1974,[30] and its perceived success—once more affirmed through economic analysis[31]—prompted a surge in public interest and scholarly engagement across disciplines. Highly visible activities such as 'Project 88'[32] and endorsement by a wide range of actors including international organizations[33] imparted further credibility to the use of markets in environmental policy.

Invariably, the discussion also percolated through to environmental law scholarship. While by no means the earliest mention of market mechanisms by a legal scholar,[34] an influential article written by two pioneers of environmental law conveys the force with which supporters of regulatory innovation sought to reform traditional environmental controls, describing these as 'extraordinarily crude, costly, litigious and counterproductive'.[35] In support of market mechanisms, they saw not only a means of overcoming the perceived shortfalls of existing instruments, but also ways to 'make environmental law more democratically accountable and bureaucratically effective'.[36] Lawyers also played an instrumental role in operationalizing markets at the domestic level, acting both within government and as advocates in civil society.[37]

Because the central benefit ascribed to market mechanisms arises from differences in abatement cost, a larger market can leverage greater efficiency gains, arguing in favour of the broadest possible deployment. Unsurprisingly, therefore, market approaches were also soon considered for international environmental challenges. With its global

[29] David Driesen, 'Alternatives to Regulation? Market Mechanisms and the Environment' in Robert Baldwin, Martin Cave, and Martin Lodge (eds), *The Oxford Handbook of Regulation* (OUP 2010) 203, 205.

[30] Hugh Gorman and Barry Solomon, 'The Origins and Practice of Emissions Trading' *Journal of Policy History*, 14/3 (2002): 293.

[31] Ambivalent performance of the earliest experiments did not detract the economic community from praising market mechanisms as such, see Lane (n 27) 598. Later experience with the US Acid Rain programme provided a more favourable case study for economic analysis, see eg Ellerman *et al* (n 21).

[32] 'Project 88' was convened by two members of the US Senate, and helped prompt legislative action to create the US Acid Rain programme; see Stavins (n 3).

[33] In the early 1990s, the OECD and the United Nations Conference on Trade and Development (UNCTAD) issued reports endorsing the use of market mechanisms; see Simons and Voß (n 28) 62–63.

[34] See for instance the brief discussion by later Associate Justice of the US Supreme Court Stephen Breyer, 'Analyzing Regulatory Failure: Mismatches, Less Restrictive Alternatives, and Reform' *Harvard Law Review*, 92/3 (1979): 547, 582.

[35] Ackerman and Stewart (n 3) 1333.

[36] Ibid, 1365.

[37] Two lawyers—William Reilly, Administrator of the Environmental Protection Agency, and White House Counsel Boyden Gray—spearheaded efforts to introduce a national emissions trading system within the administration of President George HW Bush; another lawyer, Frederic Krupp, wielded his influence as president of the Environmental Defense Fund (EDF) to help overcome opposition against market approaches in the environmental community; see generally Eric Pooley, *The Climate War: True Believers, Power Brokers, and the Fight to Save the Earth* (Hyperion Books 2010) 69–79.

scale, high economic stakes, and unique physical features,[38] climate change attracted the most active discussion of markets as part of intergovernmental cooperation, and economists customarily led the charge.[39] Lawyers, however, were once again critical in seeing the idea through to implementation.

Perhaps the most pivotal moment for weaving markets into the fabric of international environmental governance occurred during the negotiations for the Kyoto Protocol, when the United States—represented by two influential lawyers[40]—insisted on inclusion of market mechanisms as a condition for their agreement.[41] As countries proceeded to render this framework operational, they were able to draw on prior work by legal scholars that 'borrowed'[42] insights from domestic experiences to recommend how market instruments could be implemented under international law.[43]

Just as the rise of market mechanisms at the domestic level was buoyed by a broader shift in regulatory culture and the preferred balance between governments and markets,[44] their diffusion to the international level coincided with broader trends in international law and diplomacy. For decades, the defining geo-political struggle had revolved around a deep ideological rift between central planning and market economies, with the latter emerging triumphant at the end of the Cold War.[45]

More recently, growing complexity and interdependence in international relations have occasioned calls for a shift away from the enforcement of binary rules in 'regulatory' treaties to a more 'managerial' style relying on transparency and facilitation through flexible cooperative arrangements.[46] Traditional intergovernmental cooperation has, in turn, ceded considerable terrain to a fragmented topography of informal networks and partnerships, in which varying constellations of state and non-state

[38] See Section V.

[39] Published in 1997, the 'Economists' Statement on Climate Change' was by then the largest public statement in the history of the profession, and endorsed an 'international emissions trading agreement' to address the climate challenge; see Stephen Decanio, *The Economics of Climate Change* (Redefining Progress 1997) 2.

[40] These lawyers were Ambassador Stuart Eizenstat, head of the US delegation, and Vice President Albert Gore Jr, who broke the deadlock in the final hours of negotiations by offering concessions in return for an international market framework; see Pooley (n 37) 92.

[41] Sebastian Oberthür and Hermann Ott, *The Kyoto Protocol: International Climate Policy for the 21st Century* (Springer 1999) 189.

[42] Jonathan Wiener, 'Something Borrowed for Something Blue: Legal Transplants and the Evolution of Global Environmental Law' *Ecology Law Quarterly*, 27/4 (2001): 1295.

[43] Richard Stewart and Jonathan Wiener, 'The Comprehensive Approach to Global Climate Policy: Issues of Design and Practicality' *Arizona Journal of International and Comparative Law*, 9/1 (1992): 83.

[44] Jason Czarnezki and Katherine Fiedler, 'The Neo-Liberal Turn in Environmental Regulation' *Utah Law Review*, 1 (2016): 1.

[45] John Williamson, 'Democracy and the "Washington Consensus"' *World Development*, 21/8 (1993): 1329.

[46] Abram Chayes and Antonia Chayes, *The New Sovereignty: Compliance with International Regulatory Agreements* (Harvard University Press 1998).

actors resort to public as well as private norms when addressing transboundary challenges.[47]

With their shared rejection of state-centric planning and regulation, these trends collectively provided a favourable context for the ascendance of market mechanisms in international environmental governance. Yet while economists continue to engage in a nuanced debate about the relative strengths and weaknesses of markets, the legal community seems more or less reconciled to their existence. With some notable exceptions, lawyers working on market mechanisms tend to examine these 'with the overall aim of promoting their use'.[48]

Perhaps because legal scholars generally lack quantitative skills, the majority of legal research has focused on regulatory design and structuring of market transactions rather than on the theoretical merits of different market approaches. As the next section highlights, however, that presents a missed opportunity: legal scholars can, and have, meaningfully contributed to the critical assessment of functional, conceptual, and normative aspects of market approaches.

IV. MARKETS AND THE CHALLENGES OF IMPLEMENTATION

Scholarship on the challenges of market mechanisms is substantial, and often as sophisticated as the economic literature advancing their deployment. A short overview of these challenges is presented here, focusing on three dimensions: design and implementation failures, theoretical and conceptual shortcomings, and normative or ideological flaws. Legal scholars have contributed to the literature on each of these dimensions, starting with some of the earliest analyses of the potential shortfalls of market mechanisms and other economic instruments in practice.[49]

Most challenges identified in the context of market mechanisms fall within the first category: functional deficiencies in the operation of markets that result from imperfect design and implementation. Market mechanisms place high demands on the institutional and regulatory architecture created for their implementation. Because they are premised on an artificially constrained supply of intangible and instantly transferable units, market mechanisms are particularly dependent on a robust governance framework that sets out clearly defined and enforceable rules.

[47] Kati Kulovesi, Michael Mehling, and Elisa Morgera, 'Global Environmental Law: Context and Theory, Challenge and Promise' *Transnational Environmental Law*, 8/3 (2019): 405.

[48] Sanja Bogojević, 'Trading Schemes' in Emma Lees and Jorge Viñuales (eds), *The Oxford Handbook of Comparative Environmental Law* (OUP 2019) 926, 936.

[49] Howard Latin, 'Ideal versus Real Regulatory Efficiency: Implementation of Uniform Standards and "Fine-Tuning" Regulatory Reforms' *Stanford Law Review*, 37/5 (1985): 1267.

At a minimum, they require a regulatory framework to ensure transparency, usually through measurement, reporting, and verification (MRV) of the environmental impacts of covered activities, as well as an infrastructure to track distribution and ownership of assigned and transacted units.[50] Establishing such structures is critical, yet frequently constrained by insufficient technical and administrative capacities, including resources and suitable personnel.[51] As market mechanisms move from theory to implementation, their elegant simplicity gives way to complex governance challenges.

Risks and shortcomings that follow from these challenges include, for instance, susceptibility to corruption and abuse,[52] or loopholes that incentivize pollution and reward routine behaviour.[53] At a conceptual level, markets have also been censored for undermining supplemental measures[54] and lowering costs in the near term at the expense of innovation in the long term.[55] Common to these criticisms is that they can be rectified at least partially with improved policy design, and the evolution of market approaches has indeed shown many valuable lessons put into practice.[56]

More fundamentally, however, critics also raise normative concerns, likening market mechanisms to a commodification of the environment through which monetary value is assigned to intangible goods.[57] This, in turn, creates the impression of a 'right to pollute' in violation of an established principle of environmental governance.[58] Also, the underlying rationale of market mechanisms has been censored for being fundamentally at odds with legal relations in the real world: while, in theory, the market should result in outcomes that increase overall welfare, there is no guarantee that its beneficiaries will compensate those who may see a loss of welfare.[59] By privatizing public discourse, moreover, complex decisions that affect society at large are devolved to the logic of market transactions, supplanting collective planning processes, and weakening democratic accountability.[60]

[50] Erik Haites and Geoffrey Bird, *An Emerging Market for the Environment: A Guide to Emissions Trading* (United Nations Environment Programme and UNCTAD 2002).

[51] See in the context of climate change, Thomas Brewer and Michael Mehling, 'Transparency of Climate Change Policies, Markets, and Corporate Practices' in Jens Forssbæck and Lars Oxelheim (eds), *The Oxford Handbook of Economic and Institutional Transparency* (OUP 2014) 179, 188.

[52] Ruth Bell, 'The Kyoto Placebo' *Issues in Science and Technology*, 22/2 (2006): 28.

[53] Michael Wara, 'Is the Global Carbon Market Working?' *Nature*, 445 (2007): 595.

[54] David Driesen, 'Emissions Trading versus Pollution Taxes: Playing "Nice" with Other Instruments' *Environmental Law*, 48/1 (2017): 29.

[55] David Driesen, 'Does Emissions Trading Encourage Innovation?' *Environmental Law Reporter*, 32/1 (2003): 10094.

[56] See for instance the essays collected in Jørgen Wettestad and Lars Gulbrandsen (eds), *The Evolution of Carbon Markets: Design and Diffusion* (Routledge 2018).

[57] Robert Goodin, 'Selling Environmental Indulgences' *Kyklos*, 47/4 (1994): 573.

[58] Jonathan Nash, 'Too Much Market: Conflict between Tradable Pollution Allowances and the Polluter Pays Principle' *Harvard Environmental Law Review*, 24/2 (2000): 465.

[59] David Driesen and Robin Malloy, 'Critiques of Law and Economics' in Francesco Parisi (ed), *The Oxford Handbook of Law and Economics* (OUP 2017) 300, 301.

[60] Alice Kaswan, 'Energy, Governance, and Market Mechanisms' *Miami Law Review*, 72/2 (2018): 476.

From the outset, the debate on markets has also included an ideological component, with opponents decrying them as a manifestation of capitalism[61] that conceals underlying power structures and exacerbates distributional biases.[62] Such censure of markets is often framed in terms of equity and justice, providing a fertile angle for contributions by lawyers.[63] For some commentators, for instance, international use of markets risks perpetuating colonial exploitation patterns by allowing wealthy countries to deplete affordable abatement opportunities in the developing world, causing poorer countries to forfeit space for economic growth.[64]

All these concerns are advanced in the negotiating processes for elaboration of market approaches at the international level. As will be shown in the next section, practical experiences with market mechanisms have been, at best, ambivalent, and securing consensus for their further advancement has become more challenging over time.

V. INTERNATIONAL EXPERIENCES WITH MARKET MECHANISMS

While market mechanisms have been discussed for various international environmental challenges, they have only seen meaningful deployment as a means to mitigate climate change. Although efforts are underway to leverage market approaches for the conservation of biological diversity and ecosystem services, relevant governance frameworks are still limited to the domestic plane or being operationalized through private and voluntary standards.[65] Similarly, despite attempts at regional cooperation, transferable fishing quota markets are so far mostly limited to the national level.[66] Consequently, this section will focus on the extensive—and revealing—lessons learned in applying market approaches under the climate regime.

Markets are particularly suited to address climate change because the anthropogenic greenhouse gases (GHGs) responsible for climate change are not in themselves toxic

[61] See for instance the essays collected in Steffen Böhm and Siddharta Dabhi (eds), *Upsetting the Offset: The Political Economy of Carbon Markets* (MayFly Books 2009).

[62] Robert Baldwin, 'Regulation Lite: The Rise of Emissions Trading' *Regulation & Governance*, 2/2 (2008): 193, 203.

[63] See eg the essays collected in Benjamin Richardson and Klaus Bosselmann, *Environmental Justice and Market Mechanisms: Key Challenges for Environmental Law and Policy* (Kluwer Law International 1999).

[64] Emily Richman, 'Emissions Trading and the Development Critique: Exposing the Threat to Developing Countries' *New York University Journal of International Law and Politics*, 36/1 (2003): 133.

[65] Jerneja Penca, 'Marketing the Market: The Ideology of Market Mechanisms for Biodiversity Conservation' *Transnational Environmental Law*, 2/2 (2013): 235.

[66] Anthony Cox, 'Quota Allocation in International Fisheries' *OECD Food, Agriculture and Fisheries Papers*, 22 (2009) <https://www.oecd-ilibrary.org/content/paper/218520326143> accessed 5 February 2020.

and the damage function of their accumulation in the atmosphere is shallow in the short run, which allows for spatial and temporal flexibility in the policy response.[67] Climate change is unique, moreover, in that the underlying causes are diffuse, widely heterogeneous, and virtually ubiquitous activities, necessitating policy solutions that are scalable and cost-effective. As the costs of climate change and its abatement rise over time—with cheap abatement options being, by design, exhausted first[68]—the cost-effectiveness of market-based instruments will become increasingly important to sustaining policy ambition over the long term.

Collectively referred to as 'carbon markets',[69] market mechanisms for climate change mitigation have in common a quantity limitation which generates demand for units, and an ability of market participants to purchase or sell units at the respective market price. At the international level, they have been introduced under the 1992 United Nations Framework Convention on Climate Change (UNFCCC) and subsequent treaties and decisions adopted within its regime architecture.

Under the Kyoto Protocol, developed country parties that entered quantified emission limitation and reduction obligations (QELROs) were able to meet these through a set of flexibility mechanisms: international emissions trading and two project mechanisms—Joint Implementation (JI) and the Clean Development Mechanism (CDM).[70] By leveraging the differences in abatement costs between developed and developing countries, these market approaches were aimed at lowering the economic cost of compliance with mitigation commitments. Parties also adopted a mandate to elaborate subsequent rules, modalities, procedures, and guidelines for the operationalization of these mechanisms, which were eventually agreed upon as part of the Marrakesh Accords, a series of decisions that govern the implementation of the Kyoto Protocol.[71]

Under these rules, use of the flexibility mechanisms has been voluntary, but subject to several eligibility requirements. To participate in international emissions trading, for instance, countries first have to calculate their assigned emission budgets pursuant to specified accounting modalities, establish a national system for the estimation of GHG emissions by sources and removals by sinks, and create the necessary infrastructure to account for the issuance, holding, transfer, cancellation, and retirement of tradeable

[67] Dieter Helm, 'Economic Instruments and Environmental Policy' *Economic & Social Review*, 36/3 (2005): 205, 223.

[68] Nicholas Stern, *The Economics of Climate Change: The Stern Review* (CUP 2007) 63, 191.

[69] Although other GHGs may be included, the term 'carbon market' is widely used because tradeable units are mostly denominated in terms of carbon dioxide equivalent (CO_2e); see Richard Newell, William Pizer, and Daniel Raimi, 'Carbon Markets 15 Years after Kyoto: Lessons Learned, New Challenges' *Journal of Economic Perspectives*, 27/1 (2013): 123, 124.

[70] See arts 6, 12, 17; for commentary see David Freestone, 'UNFCCC, the Kyoto Protocol, and the Kyoto Mechanisms' in David Freestone and Charlotte Streck (eds), *Legal Aspects of Implementing the Kyoto Protocol Mechanisms: Making Kyoto Work* (OUP 2005) 3.

[71] For analysis see Suraje Dessai and Emma Schipper, 'The Marrakech Accords to the Kyoto Protocol: Analysis and Future Prospects' *Global Environmental Change*, 13/2 (2003): 149.

units.[72] Annual submission of an accurate inventory is a key eligibility requirement,[73] as is maintenance of a 'commitment period reserve' limiting the share of tradeable units that parties may sell to 10% of their respective assigned amount.[74] Compliance with these requirements has been assessed through an independent review process, and failure to observe relevant obligations could result in sanctions, such as exclusion from the use of the flexibility mechanisms.[75]

Overall, however, activity under the emissions trading system has been fairly limited.[76] One explanation for this limited uptake is that sovereign states are not motivated by cost-minimization or profit-maximization to the same extent private actors are, and instead tend to be driven by geo-political and diplomatic considerations.[77] Much greater levels of market activity have been seen under JI and the CDM, which also allow for extensive involvement of the private sector.

Both are subject to a separate set of rules, reflecting their fundamentally different nature as project mechanisms that yield offset credits. Under both mechanisms, projects have to satisfy an 'additionality' test, demonstrating that the emission reductions would not have taken place without the project. Projects also have to result in emission reductions that go beyond a baseline scenario and result in real, measurable, and lasting climate benefits. Such reliance on a counterfactual baseline scenario has been highly contested, as it involves predicting future energy consumption patterns, fuel prices, and energy policies, all of which presuppose highly subjective assumptions.[78] With both parties to a mitigation project standing to benefit from its implementation, moreover, they share an incentive to overstate actual emission reductions.[79]

Particular concerns have been voiced against the CDM, which involves emission reduction projects in developing countries that do not have mitigation commitments under the Kyoto Protocol. Reflecting such concerns, the Marrakesh Accords set out a highly detailed procedure to determine the additionality of proposed mitigation projects. Under these rules, development and approval of CDM projects require

[72] See Kyoto Protocol, arts 3.7, 3.8, 5.1; Decision 18/CP.7, 'Modalities, Rules and Guidelines for Emissions Trading under Article 17 of the Kyoto Protocol' (21 January 2002) UN Doc FCCC/CP/2001/13/Add.2, 50.

[73] Kyoto Protocol, art 7.1; Decision 22/CP.7, 'Guidance for the Preparation of the Information Required under Article 7 of the Kyoto Protocol' (21 January 2002) UN Doc FCCC/CP/2001/13/Add.2, 14, annex, paras 3(a)–(f).

[74] Decision 5/CP.6, 'The Bonn Agreements on the Implementation of the Buenos Aires Plan of Action' (25 September 2001) FCCC/CP/2001/5, 15.

[75] Farhana Yamin, 'The International Rules on the Kyoto Mechanisms' in Farhana Yamin (ed), *Climate Change and Carbon Markets: A Handbook of Emissions Reduction Mechanisms* (Earthscan 2005) 1, 61–67.

[76] Igor Shishlov, Romain Morel, and Valentin Bellassen, 'Compliance of the Parties to the Kyoto Protocol in the First Commitment Period' *Climate Policy*, 16/6 (2016): 768, 778.

[77] Robert Hahn and Robert Stavins, *What Has the Kyoto Protocol Wrought?* (AEI Press 1999) 9.

[78] OECD, *Emission Baselines: Estimating the Unknown* (2000).

[79] Michael Wara and David Victor, 'A Realistic Policy on International Carbon Offsets' *Stanford University Working Paper*, 74 (2008): 23–24 <https://law.stanford.edu/publications/a-realistic-policy-on-international-carbon-offsets> accessed 5 February 2020.

evaluation and registration by the CDM Executive Board (EB), as well as independent project validation coupled with verification and certification of emission reductions by accredited Designated Operational Entities (DOEs).[80]

Transaction costs resulting from this elaborate process have been considerable, disproportionately impacting smaller emission reduction projects.[81] Despite more relaxed rules for the smaller projects prevalent in least developed countries, such transaction costs have influenced the geographic distribution of investment from poorer regions. Of the roughly 8,000 registered CDM projects to date, for instance, only about 3% are located in African countries,[82] where more diffuse emission patterns and generally challenging investment conditions have further exacerbated this uneven project distribution.

Coupled with a bias for large industrial projects,[83] the strong regional concentration of project activities in a small number of middle income countries has prevented the CDM from fully realizing its separate objective of promoting sustainable development.[84] Documented shortfalls in the quality of validation and certification functions performed by DOEs have also prompted scrutiny and resulted in the suspension of accreditations, while collusion between supposedly independent actors, such as project developers, national approval authorities, and even the supervisory CDM EB itself, has invited accusations of flawed governance and outright fraud.[85] Likewise, the design and operationalization of the CDM have evidenced susceptibility to regulatory capture by stakeholders.[86]

Soon after the entry into force of the Kyoto Protocol, moreover, several independent studies suggested that a considerable share of registered projects lacked additionality[87] or created perverse incentives, for instance spurring increased generation of industrial GHGs like HFC-23.[88] Such research quickly garnered attention in the mainstream

[80] See generally Decision 17/CP.7, 'Modalities and procedures for a clean development mechanism as defined in Article 12 of the Kyoto Protocol' (21 January 2002) UN Doc FCCC/CP/2001/13/Add.2, 20.

[81] Axel Michaelowa *et al*, 'Transaction Costs of the Kyoto Mechanisms' *Climate Policy*, 3/3 (2003): 261.

[82] UNFCCC, 'Annual Report of the Executive Board of the Clean Development Mechanism to the Conference of the Parties Serving as the Meeting of the Parties to the Kyoto Protocol' (7 October 2019) UN Doc FCCC/KP/CMP/2019/3, 5.

[83] Wara (n 53); Lambert Schneider, 'Perverse Incentives Under the CDM: An Evaluation of HFC-23 Destruction Projects' *Climate Policy*, 11/2 (2011): 851.

[84] Karen Olsen, 'The Clean Development Mechanism's Contribution to Sustainable Development: A Review of the Literature' *Climatic Change*, 84/1 (2007): 59.

[85] Florens Flues, Axel Michaelowa, and Katharina Michaelowa, 'What Determines UN Approval of Greenhouse Gas Emission Reduction Projects in Developing Countries?' *Public Choice*, 145/1 (2010): 1.

[86] Irja Vormedal, 'The Influence of Business and Industry NGOs in the Negotiation of the Kyoto Mechanisms: The Case of Carbon Capture and Storage in the CDM' *Global Environmental Politics*, 8/4 (2008): 36.

[87] See eg Lambert Schneider, 'Is the CDM Fulfilling Its Environmental and Sustainable Development Objectives? An Evaluation of the CDM and Options for Improvement' *Institute for Applied Ecology* (2007) <https://www.oeko.de/oekodoc/622/2007-162-en.pdf> accessed 12 March 2019; Michael Wara, 'Measuring the Clean Development Mechanism's Performance and Potential' *UCLA Law Review*, 55/6 (2008): 1759.

[88] Schneider (n 83).

media,[89] and undermined public support for the CDM, which in turn pressured governments into introducing restrictions on the acceptance of Certified Emission Reductions (CERs).[90] As a result, the global carbon market suffered a dramatic decline.

A landmark assessment of the CDM that concluded in 2012 found that the market had 'essentially collapsed',[91] with declining transaction volumes also causing a loss in institutional capacity as major market facilitators, including project developers, brokers, and other intermediaries, downsized their activities or ceased operations altogether. Numerous changes have been made to reform the CDM by closing regulatory loopholes, introducing greater standardization of methodologies and baselines, and streamlining the lengthy and bureaucratic approval process. Still, these reforms arguably come too late to undo the reputational damage and unilateral restrictions that have already been implemented in key jurisdictions as a response to the perceived shortcomings of the CDM.[92]

Given this cautionary experience, it is perhaps surprising that market mechanisms are also finding a place in the international climate regime beyond 2020.[93] At the 39th session of its Assembly, for instance, the International Civil Aviation Organization (ICAO) agreed on a global market mechanism—the 'Carbon Offsetting and Reduction Scheme for International Aviation' (CORSIA)—to stabilize global GHG emissions from international aviation from 2020 onwards.[94] Negotiations on the operationalization of CORSIA have been burdened by recurrent divisions, however, and concerns about regulatory shortfalls have already prompted several parties to consider alternative policy measures at the domestic level that would supersede the international market mechanism.[95]

Although the 2015 Paris Agreement does not make express reference to carbon markets, its Article 6 is widely held to be the 'latest incarnation of these approaches in

[89] See eg Elisabeth Rosenthal and Andrew Lehren, 'Incentive to Slow Climate Change Drives Output of Harmful Gases' *The New York Times* (2012): A1.

[90] See eg Commission Regulation (EU) No 550/2011 of 7 June 2011 on determining, pursuant to Directive 2003/87/EC of the European Parliament and of the Council, certain restrictions applicable to the use of international credits from projects involving industrial gases [2011] OJ L 149/1.

[91] Valli Moosa *et al*, 'Climate Change, Carbon Markets and the CDM: A Call to Action—Report of the High-Level Panel on the CDM Policy Dialogue' *CDM Policy Dialogue* (2012) 67 <https://www.cdmpolicydialogue.org/report/rpt110912.pdf> accessed 14 January 2020.

[92] Axel Michaelowa, 'A Call to Action: But Too Late, in Vain?' *Climate Policy*, 13/3 (2013): 408.

[93] Efforts to create an international legal framework for Reducing Emissions from Deforestation and Forest Degradation in Developing Countries (REDD) have resulted in a system of results-based payments rather than a market for tradeable units, see Danae Maniatis *et al*, 'Toward REDD+ Implementation' *Annual Review of Environment and Resources*, 44/1 (2019): 373. That could change in future, however, if a genuine market for forest-related carbon units were to emerge.

[94] ICAO Res A39-3, 'Consolidated Statement of Continuing ICAO Policies and Practices related to Environmental Protection—Global Market-based Measure (MBM) Scheme' (27 September–6 October 2016).

[95] Chris Lyle, 'Beyond the ICAO's CORSIA: Towards a More Climatically Effective Strategy for Mitigation of Civil-Aviation Emissions' *Climate Law*, 8/1–2 (2018): 104; see also Chapter 34, 'Aviation and Maritime Transport', in this volume.

an international climate treaty'[96] by allowing parties to cooperate on a voluntary basis in the pursuit of their pledged nationally determined contributions (NDCs). That market mechanisms would be included in the Paris Agreement was by no means always a given. Deep differences overshadowed the negotiations preceding adoption of the Paris Agreement, and some parties were altogether opposed to market-based approaches for climate change mitigation.[97]

Article 6 became the last article to be added to the final draft of the Paris Agreement before its release for adoption by the Conference of the Parties (COP).[98] It sets out two distinct channels of cooperation: the first is decentralized in nature, and allows parties to use internationally transferred mitigation outcomes (ITMOs) towards achievement of their NDCs,[99] whereas the second creates a centralized mechanism—under the supervision of an appointed body—that aims to contribute both to the mitigation of greenhouse gases and support sustainable development.[100]

Arguably, however, the tensions that characterized the negotiations on Article 6 remain enshrined in the ambiguous language on cooperative approaches in the Paris Agreement. Like other provisions of the Paris Agreement, Article 6 is sparsely worded and replete with undefined or vague concepts, reflecting a lack of consensus on more detailed language at the time of adoption. Acting upon mandates contained in the decision formally adopting the Paris Agreement and in Article 6 itself, parties have therefore been engaged in developing operational rules and guidance for the implementation of the Paris Agreement.[101]

Whereas all other operational elements for the Paris Agreement were successfully adopted in 2018, however, the guidance and rules, modalities, and procedures for Article 6 remained unresolved, evidencing the wide divergences of country positions and preferences on—including outright rejection of—market mechanisms in the international climate regime. Party statements and submissions to these negotiations reveal a spectrum of views between strong and weak prescriptiveness, oversight at the multilateral level and flexible self-determination at the national level, and a greater or lesser degree of centrally defined criteria related to ambition and environmental integrity. Particularly contentious issues included whether to recognize

[96] Andrew Howard, 'Incentivizing Mitigation: Using International Carbon Markets to Raise Ambition' *Koru Climate* (2018) 6 <https://www.carbon-mechanisms.de/en/publications/details/?jiko%5Bpubuid%5D=541> accessed 10 March 2019.

[97] Andrew Howard, 'Voluntary Cooperation (Article 6)' in Daniel Klein *et al* (eds), *The Paris Agreement on Climate Change: Analysis and Commentary* (OUP 2017) 178, 182; Benito Müller, 'Article 6: Market Approaches under the Paris Agreement' *European Capacity Building Initiative (ECBI) Policy Brief* (2018) 8 <https://ecbi.org/news/article-6-market-approaches-under-paris-agreement> accessed 10 March 2019.

[98] Howard (n 97) 183.

[99] art 6.2.

[100] art 6.4.

[101] See Decision 1/CMA.1, 'Matters Relating to the Implementation of the Paris Agreement' (31 January 2017) UN Doc FCCC/PA/CMA/2016/3/Add.1, paras 5–7.

legacy units generated under the Kyoto Protocol for compliance with the Paris Agreement, how to account for transfers of mitigation efforts so that they are not claimed by more than one party ('double counting'), whether to include reference to human rights, and how to operationalize additional safeguards as well as a share of proceeds from transactions earmarked towards climate finance.[102] If anything, the persistent disagreements along evolving faultlines raise serious questions about the future viability of market mechanisms as an instrument of international environmental governance, just as the growing scale and urgency of different global environmental challenges would benefit most from the ability of markets to lower the overall cost of our collective response.

VI. CONCLUSION

Following a remarkable trajectory from economic theory to practised reality, starting at the domestic level and soon extending to an international setting, market mechanisms have reached an inflection point in the evolution of environmental law. Experiences with their actual operation have been ambivalent to date, casting doubt on an earlier sense of inevitability and 'irrational exuberance'[103] about the ability of markets to effectively address environmental threats.

Still, market approaches have firmly entered the canon of international environmental law, finding many champions in the legal profession. Theoretical claims overshadow observed reality as institutional inertia continues to drive the perceived rationality of markets into new issue areas. Yet recent negotiating setbacks have shown that consensus about market approaches can no longer be taken for granted.

In the domestic sphere, vigorous policy learning and ceaseless reform have revived hope in the capacity of market approaches to achieve their intended objectives. If this trend can be replicated at the international level, market approaches might see a new dawn in environmental cooperation across borders. Given the urgency of the environmental crisis and its daunting economic implications, the ability to leverage the efficiency of markets would be eminently useful.

But for that promise to be realized, the performance of market mechanisms across all relevant—including normative—dimensions must be soberly assessed, with vigilance for unintended outcomes. And that is a process to which lawyers can, and must, contribute.

[102] See generally International Emissions Trading Association (IETA), 'COP25 Summary Report' (2019) <https://www.ieta.org/resources/Documents/IETA-COP25-Report_2019.pdf> accessed 24 January 2020.

[103] Lisa Heinzerling, 'The Environment' in Peter Cane and Mark Tushnet (eds), *The Oxford Handbook of Legal Studies* (OUP 2003) 701, 712–713.

BIBLIOGRAPHY

David Driesen, 'Alternatives to Regulation? Market Mechanisms and the Environment' in Robert Baldwin, Martin Cave, and Martin Lodge (eds), *The Oxford Handbook of Regulation* (OUP 2010) 203

Jody Freeman and Charles Kolstad (eds), *Moving to Markets in Environmental Regulation* (OUP 2006)

David Freestone and Charlotte Streck (eds), *Legal Aspects of Implementing the Kyoto Protocol Mechanisms: Making Kyoto Work* (OUP 2005)

Stefan Weishaar (ed), *Research Handbook on Emissions Trading* (Edward Elgar 2016)

Jonathan Wiener, 'Something Borrowed for Something Blue: Legal Transplants and the Evolution of Global Environmental Law' *Ecology Law Quarterly*, 27/4 (2001): 1295

CHAPTER 54

FINANCIAL ASSISTANCE

LAURENCE BOISSON DE CHAZOURNES

I. INTRODUCTION

FINANCIAL assistance plays an important role in furthering environmental protection.[1] It is composed of a complex mosaic of financial mechanisms and sources, which are linked to and affected by global conventions, multilateral institutions, bilateral aid, and private sector investment. Moreover, the principle of common but differentiated responsibilities has provided a specific rationale for the provision of financial assistance within multilateral environmental agreements (MEAs) and through various financial mechanisms. Through the provision of financial assistance, developed countries contribute to covering the incremental costs of protecting the global environment incurred by developing countries.

The functions of financial assistance include, inter alia, capacity-building, disaster relief, financing of pollution control equipment, and compliance assistance. Among these various targets, capacity-building has received an important political emphasis.[2] Effective environmental management by governments requires scientific and technical expertise, adequate infrastructure for environmental monitoring and management, and complex decision-making processes. These factors explain why the transfer of technology and provision of financial aid, including loans, credits, or grants, are all part of the broader issue of capacity-building.

This chapter will first set out the different types and sources of financial assistance, as well as its aim and nature. The legal structure of financial mechanisms will then be analysed. Finally, the multiplication of financial mechanisms, as well as the need for coherence of action in this context, will be appraised.

[1] See Chapters 17 and 19, 'Sustainable Development' and 'Differentiation', in this volume.

[2] *Report of the United Nations Conference on Environment and Development* (UN 1993) vol I, annex II—'Agenda 21', para 37.1.

II. THE DIFFERENT TYPES AND SOURCES OF FINANCIAL ASSISTANCE

The polymorphous character of financial assistance is reflected in the multiple channels through which it may be provided. Official development assistance (ODA), aimed at alleviating poverty, is provided through bilateral, regional, and multilateral channels and is one of the sources of public funds for developing countries. Specific environmental mechanisms, such as those based on MEAs, constitute another channel through which assistance flows. While specific environmental mechanisms and ODA may have different objectives and features, it is important to note that they may both feature in the activities of an institution. For example, the World Bank and the United Nations Development Programme (UNDP) are providers of financial assistance emanating both from ODA channels and environmental mechanisms.

A. The SDGs and Official Development Assistance

Although there has been a decline in the provision of ODA,[3] this form of assistance remains an essential means for financing development and for realizing the objectives of the international community, such as the Sustainable Development Goals (SDGs).[4] The SDGs comprise seventeen goals, are part of the UN's 2030 Agenda for Sustainable Development, and were adopted by states in 2015.[5] In order to achieve the SDGs by 2030, there are calls for new strategies to be developed. SDG 17 urges states to 'strengthen the means of implementation and revitalize the global partnership for sustainable development' by mobilizing domestic resources, meeting commitments on aid, and innovating to identify financial resources for development. In addition to ODA, green bonds, guarantee mechanisms, local currency financing, blended finance, and public-private partnerships are further examples of the emerging tools for development finance.[6] The Conference on Financing for Development held in Monterrey in 2002 and the Johannesburg Summit of the same year reaffirmed the commitment of developed

[3] See eg Donor Tracker, 'OECD's 2017 ODA figures show global decline in ODA for first time since 2012' (9 April 2018).

[4] UNGA Res 70/1, 'Transforming our World: The 2030 Agenda for Sustainable Development' (21 October 2015) UN Doc A/RES/70/1.

[5] UNDP, 'Sustainable Development Goals' <https://www.undp.org/content/undp/en/home/sustainable-development-goals.html> accessed 27 May 2019.

[6] UNDP and French Development Agency, 'Financing the SDGs in the Least Developed Countries (LDCs): Diversifying the Financing Tool-box and Managing Vulnerability' (2016); Pedro Conceição and Philippe Orliange, 'To leave no one behind, Least Developed Countries need new financing tools' *UNDP* (14 December 2016).

countries to the provision of ODA.[7] In particular, the Monterrey Conference adopted an ambitious resolution which reaffirms the target of dedicating 0.7% GDP of developed countries to ODA.[8]

B. The Greening of Development Aid Within International Institutions

While ODA does not generally aim at specific environmental objectives, increased concerns about the environment have led international finance institutions (IFIs) and other organizations to enlarge their 'green' activities. As strategic documents reflecting national development priorities over a period of three to five years, poverty reduction strategies have become one of the principal means by which multilateral funding is being allocated.[9]

Multilateral development banks such as the World Bank, and organizations like the Organisation for Economic Co-operation and Development (OECD) and the European Union (EU), have developed other strategies and tools for integrating environmental objectives into development aid.[10] Since the late 1980s, the World Bank has adopted a number of Operational Policies related to the environment.[11] Additionally, the World Bank has developed new programmatic lending instruments, supporting policy and institutional reforms that address links between poverty reduction and the environment. The World Bank has also adopted a stronger role in dealing with threats to global environmental goods. By way of example, the World Bank is one of the biggest financiers in the area of biodiversity conservation and sustainable use.[12]

[7] *Report of the International Conference on Financing for Development* (UN 2002) 9, para 42; see also *Report of World Summit on Sustainable Development* (UN 2002) para 85(a).

[8] Cf. UN, 'Monterrey Conference on Financing for Development Hears Statements by 28 Presidents, Prime Ministers' (22 March 2002) <https://www.un.org/press/en/2002/dev2385.doc.htm> accessed 13 January 2020.

[9] Fiona Nunan, *Understanding Poverty and the Environment: Analytical Frameworks and Approaches* (Routledge 2015).

[10] See eg World Bank, 'Toward a green, clean, and resilient world for all: a World Bank Group environment strategy 2012–2022' (2012); OECD, 'OECD Work on Sustainable Development (2011); European Commission, 'Increasing the impact of the EU Development Policy: An Agenda for Change' COM (2011) 637 final; European Council, 'The New European Consensus on Development: 'Our World, Our Dignity, Our Future'' (2017) OJ C 210/1.

[11] Laurence Boisson de Chazournes, 'Policy Guidance and Compliance Issues: The World Bank Operational Standards' in Dinah Shelton (ed), *Commitment and Compliance: The Role of Non-Binding Norms in the International Legal System* (OUP 2000) 281.

[12] It had a portfolio of 241 projects with a value of over USD 1.25 billion between 2006 and 2016; see World Bank Group and the Global Environment Facility, 'Innovation, Scale up, Transformation' (May 2018) <http://documents.worldbank.org/curated/en/390881529994815895/pdf/127590-25-6-2018-12-50-52-GEFProgramFINWEB.pdf> accessed 13 January 2020.

C. The Involvement of the Private and Non-Governmental Sectors

With the decline of the relative importance of ODA, non-state entities have emerged as significant actors in development aid. A major part of the discussion around the financing of the SDGs is the need to mobilize the private sector. More generally, the OECD reports that between 2012 and 2015, USD 81.1 billion was contributed by the private sector to ODA initiatives.[13] In that same period, USD 21.3 billion was climate-related finance.[14] These contributions have included guarantees, syndicated loans, shares in collective investment vehicles, credit lines, and direct investment in companies.

The 1992 Rio Conference and, more significantly, the Monterrey Conference and the Johannesburg Summit, paved the way for the 'privatization' of assistance.[15] The Johannesburg Summit, in particular, led to the establishment of a range of new 'partnership' arrangements between governments, the private sector, and civil society groups. The private sector and other actors have thus become increasingly involved in providing the necessary funds.

Examples of the increasing involvement of private actors in funding environmentally friendly projects are the Prototype Carbon Fund (PCF) established within the World Bank and the Clean Development Mechanism (CDM) created under the 1997 Kyoto Protocol. These mechanisms, through private resources, in addition to public resources, involved private actors in the development of what were hitherto considered to be public financing systems. As mechanisms intended to channel private sector investment towards climate friendly projects, the PCF and the CDM aimed to support the development of a new set of international arrangements for public/private partnerships, which will be discussed below. Under its Article 6.4, the 2015 Paris Agreement has established a new sustainable development mechanism aimed at promoting the mitigation of greenhouse gas emissions. It furthers sustainable development by incentivizing the mitigation of greenhouse gas emissions by actors in the public and private sectors.[16]

The International Finance Corporation (IFC) is another conduit for the involvement of the private sector. In order to be eligible for IFC funding, a project must meet a number of IFC criteria. It must be technically, environmentally, and socially sound with good prospects of being profitable for the local economy and must satisfy IFC environmental and social sustainability standards.[17]

[13] OECD, 'Amounts mobilised from the private sector for development' <http://www.oecd.org/development/stats/mobilisation.htm> accessed 27 May 2019.

[14] OECD, 'Results of the 2016 DAC Survey on mobilisation, 2012–2015, USD million' at 'Data visualisation on mounts mobilised' hyperlink (n 13); see also OECD, 'Private finance for climate action: Estimating the effects of public interventions' (November 2017).

[15] See Agenda 21 (n 2) para 33.16; WSSD report (n 7) paras 86(d)–(e), 87, 88.

[16] Paris Agreement, art 6.4.

[17] See IFC, 'Policy on Environmental and Social Sustainability' (1 January 2012).

The increasing involvement of non-state actors in the provision of financial assistance has been criticized as off-loading development issues to the private sector and there are concerns regarding the potential conflicts of interest and impartiality in the decision-making process. On the other hand, it is important to appreciate that, while large developing countries such as China or India may rely on private investments, for the poorest and smallest developing countries, ODA continues to be one of the most significant means for implementing development goals because of the difficulties they face in attracting private investment flows.[18] A significant current challenge is how ODA is being used to leverage and mobilise private investment for development. For example, ODA can help to finance activities in developing countries that create an enabling environment for private sector finance flows.[19]

III. NATURE AND AIM OF FINANCIAL ASSISTANCE

The aim of technical and financial assistance has evolved over time. It may involve both the more traditional aims of development aid, assisting developing countries in overcoming technical difficulties through providing emergency relief or setting up training programmes, and new types of projects such as the financing of investment projects that aim to benefit the global environment.

A. Traditional Nature and Aims

At the universal and regional levels, several conventions commit parties to respond to requests for assistance from states in specific instances of pollution or oil spills.[20] Financial assistance also serves as a significant tool to help developing countries in training national experts, as well as in providing at least part of the supporting capital for putting into place pollution control equipment or operational activities. For example, the General Trust Fund established by the 1984 Geneva Protocol on Long-term Financing of the Cooperative Programme for Monitoring and Evaluation of the Long-range Transmission of Air Pollutants in Europe (EMEP) to the 1979 LRTAP Convention

[18] See eg UN Economic Commission for Africa, 'The Increasing Importance of Quality Development Aid' (July 2016).

[19] Development Initiatives, 'The Enabling Environment for Private Sector Development: Donor Spending and Links to Other Catalytic Uses of Aid—Discussion Paper' (14 March 2018); see also the One Planet Coalition initiative <https://www.oneplanetsummit.fr/en> accessed 7 January 2020, which seeks to mobilize climate finance, particularly from the private sector.

[20] See eg 1982 UN Convention on the Law of the Sea, art 198; 1990 IMO Convention on Oil Pollution Preparedness, Response and Cooperation, art 9.

provides technical and financial assistance for the gathering of data and monitoring of air pollution by providing pollution control equipment and training on how to use the equipment. Helping countries put this equipment into place contributes to the implementation of, and compliance with, environmental agreements.

Financial assistance can also contribute to the development and implementation of national legislation. For instance, under the 1973 CITES Trust Fund, which is administered by UN Environment, the Secretariat provides assistance for supporting the development of CITES-related legislation and for conducting national wildlife trade policy reviews.[21] Other functions may include strengthening national capacities to submit reports providing data on the implementation of, and compliance with, the agreements concerned.

In its traditional form, financial assistance mostly addresses issues from a sectoral or specific viewpoint and its main aim is to help countries overcome technical obstacles in protecting the environment. Other emerging projects promote multisectoral approaches and proper environmental governance and their aim is to achieve global benefits. Financial assistance, relying on the principle of common but differentiated responsibilities, has become a means to address common concerns shared by developed and developing countries, moving from the concept of donors and recipients to one of partnership to solve global problems.

B. Changing Nature and Aims—Focus on Global Public Goods

Financial mechanisms such as the Montreal Multilateral Fund, the Global Environment Facility (GEF) and the Green Climate Fund (GCF) are means for promoting global benefits. Under the 1987 Montreal Protocol, the projects financed include institutional strengthening and technical assistance to meet the incremental costs incurred by developing countries when changing from ozone-depleting technologies to more ozone-friendly technologies and when phasing out the consumption of ozone-depleting substances. Within the GEF, the projects financed include those addressing GEF focal areas, which include biodiversity, international waters, land degradation, chemicals and waste, and climate change mitigation, as well as cross-cutting issues like sustainable forest management. The GEF mechanism has allowed for synergies among its focal areas and contributed to raising more resources than individual funds created for specific purposes. Projects in each of these areas address issues of environmental governance, thus assisting countries with integrating global concerns into their sustainable development policies. In so doing they rely on public participation, impact assessment techniques, and accountability mechanisms.[22]

[21] CITES, Decisions 13.74–13.75, 'National wildlife trade policy reviews' (2004); Decisions 14.21–14.24, 'National wildlife trade policy reviews' (2007).

[22] See Chapter 21, 'Public Participation', in this volume.

The broad scope of GEF activities requires a constant effort by donor countries to increase the level of their contributions. They commit money every four years through a process called the 'GEF Replenishment'. Over the years, donor countries have increased their commitments. As part of the most recent GEF Replenishment, countries have pledged USD 4.1 billion to the Fund.[23]

The Montreal Multilateral Fund and the GEF, as providers of global benefits, also play a role in inducing and restoring compliance with environmental agreements. For instance, the Montreal Protocol non-compliance procedure has been invoked on several occasions by parties that are encountering difficulties in implementing the Protocol.[24] Various measures have been recommended by the Meeting of the Parties (MOP) to the Montreal Protocol to deal with these problems of non-compliance, including the provision of financial assistance, notably through the GEF. In those situations, GEF financing was used as an incentive for compliance and contributed to the resolution of the issues through the Montreal Protocol non-compliance procedure.[25] The non-compliance procedures approved by the Conference of the Parties (COP) to the 1998 Aarhus Convention[26] provide an additional example of technical and financial assistance playing an important role in both avoiding non-compliance and restoring compliance with treaty obligations.

IV. FINANCIAL MECHANISMS

Since the Stockholm Conference, the creation of trust funds has become one of the most important techniques for transferring financial and technical resources aimed at the protection of the environment. Three main types of trust funds evolved over time. First-generation trust funds mostly focused on sectoral and technical approaches. Such trust funds have been established at the initiative of states, international organizations, or NGOs. In this case, the contributions made by developed countries were not conceived as aiming to benefit the international community as a whole. Instead, they were perceived as a means of offering technical assistance to developing countries and of facilitating the operations of the international institutions involved.

[23] See 'Fourth Meeting of the Seventh Replenishment of the GEF Trust Fund—Working Documents', GEF/R.7/18–22 <https://www.thegef.org/council-meetings/gef-7-replenishment-fourth-meeting> accessed 27 May 2019.

[24] See Chapter 56, 'Non-Compliance Procedures', in this volume.

[25] Laurence Boisson de Chazournes, 'The Global Environment Facility Galaxy: On Linkages among Institutions' *Max Planck Yearbook of United Nations Law*, 3 (1999): 254; Laurence Boisson de Chazournes, 'The Global Environment Facility (GEF): A Unique and Crucial Institution' *Review of European Community and International Environmental Law*, 14/3 (2005): 193.

[26] Aarhus Convention, 'Report of the First Meeting of the Parties' (17 December 2002) UN Doc ECE/MP.PP/2.

Due to the global nature and complexity of the problems to be tackled, international cooperation regarding financial assistance needed to be strengthened, which led to the establishment of a different type of trust fund, often referred to as second-generation trust funds. In particular, these financial mechanisms exhibit the following characteristics: they are essential means for implementing MEAs; the types of projects and activities financed through these mechanisms have been expanded; and the number of institutional partners involved in the running of these mechanisms has increased. They contribute to shaping the legal commitments in the area of financial assistance and in fostering global public goods.

Sui generis mechanisms have also emerged as a new means of achieving environmental aims. Established in the context of public/private partnerships, they exemplify the emphasis placed on the need for synergy between the public and private sectors.

A. First-Generation Mechanisms

Trust funds established on the basis of specific environmental agreements, such as the 1989 Basel Transboundary Wastes Convention, mainly aim to provide financial resources for supporting the costs of the activities of the secretariats charged with the administration of the conventions. Technical cooperation trust funds also may be used to enable representatives from developing countries to attend the meetings that take place within the framework of MEAs. Yet, some of these funds also promote technical cooperation activities in order to implement the agreements, notably through the financing of programmes for state capacity-building. For instance, the Basel Technical Cooperation Trust Fund covers a broad range of activities, including technical assistance in the implementation of the convention, as well as assistance in case of accidents and liability issues caused by transboundary movements of hazardous wastes.[27]

Trust funds may also be used to support general functions, such as the direction and coordination of environmental activities engaged in by an international institution. The UN Environment Programme (UNEP) Environment Fund is a prime example.[28] It is an important source of financing for the implementation of UNEP activities. Apart from a contribution from the UN Regular Budget, UNEP depends entirely on voluntary contributions to the Environmental Fund. In 2017, contributions to the Environment Fund reached USD 62.65 million.[29]

Although the first-generation financial mechanisms deal with a wide array of activities, the provision of financial assistance from developed to developing countries

[27] Decision V/32, 'Enlargement of the scope of the Technical Cooperation Trust Fund' (10 December 1999) UN Doc UNEP/CHW.5/29, elaborated/amended by Decisions VI/14, XI/14, and XII/11.

[28] UNGA Res 2997 (XXVII), 'Institutional and financial arrangements for international environmental cooperation' (15 December 1972) UN Doc A/RES/2997(XXVII).

[29] See 'Funding for UN Environment' <https://www.unenvironment.org/about-un-environment/funding/funding-facts/environment-fund> accessed 27 May 2019.

is perceived as a relationship between donor and recipient countries, which does not benefit the international community as a whole. Furthermore, the legal structure of the commitments in the provision of financial assistance is also different. Not relying on the principle of common but differentiated responsibilities, the contributions to the financial mechanisms of first-generation funds are often of a voluntary nature. These funds do not cover projects of investment and risk management, which play a significant role in the context of the second-generation financial mechanisms. Moreover, the amount of contributions made to first-generation funds is significantly lower than the financial resources administered by the financial mechanisms created in the wake of the 1992 Rio Conference and thereafter in the framework of the UN climate change regime.

B. Second-Generation Mechanisms

One of the prominent characteristics of the second-generation funds is the fact that, through their contributions, developed countries are providers of global public goods. The financing of the incremental costs incurred by developing countries, under financial mechanisms, benefits the international community and furthers the common interests of all states. These mechanisms are characterized by the involvement of several institutional partners. The GEF, for example, is managed by three institutions that act as implementing agencies, namely, the World Bank, UNDP, and UNEP.[30] While these organizations share some common responsibilities, they also have distinct roles. The World Bank, as the trustee of the GEF, is responsible for investment projects and the mobilization of private sector resources, while UNDP has the primary role of ensuring the development and management of capacity building programmes and technical assistance projects. For its part, UNEP is responsible for overseeing the development of scientific and technical analysis, as well as for promoting environmental management consistent with the purpose of the GEF. In addition, there are eighteen institutions that act as GEF Agencies.[31] These agencies conceive and implement projects, as well as supporting governments and NGOs to create and execute projects.

The GEF Secretariat has also endeavoured to enhance the involvement of the private sector in the GEF. The private sector is involved in the GEF via the implementing agencies. The World Bank, for its part, draws upon the investment expertise of the IFC. The projects financed by the IFC are channelled to the GEF through the World Bank. An open issue remains that, regardless of the potential profitability of most private investments, the GEF provides concessional funding in the form of grants and hence subsidies to recipients. Nevertheless, this type of funding can be seen as seed money or risk grants for initiating a process. It is in line with the concept of public/private

[30] The Montreal Multilateral Fund has four implementing agencies: World Bank, UNEP, UNDP, and UN Industrial Development Organization (UNIDO).

[31] See <https://www.thegef.org/partners/gef-agencies> accessed 27 May 2019.

partnerships as promoted at the Johannesburg meeting in 2002 and pursued under the SDGs.

The institutional framework in which second-generation financial mechanisms operate is also innovative, notably in the context of their relations with the bodies established by MEAs. The activities of these financial mechanisms are carried out in conjunction with guidelines and criteria forged by the COPs of the various MEAs. The COPs determine the eligibility criteria for the allocation of grants and concessional funding and decide on the policy and programme priorities. The executive bodies of the financial mechanisms, such as the GEF Council and the Executive Committee of the Montreal Multilateral Fund, act in conformity with the priorities established by the relevant COP. By placing the financial and technical activities to be undertaken within conventional legal frameworks, the MEAs offer a basis to assess the legitimacy of the actions undertaken by these financial mechanisms.[32]

The decision-making process in the second-generation financial mechanisms is also relevant. It indicates states' willingness to ensure that these funds are administered collectively, representing the interests of donor and recipient countries. Within the Montreal Multilateral Fund and GEF the governing principle in the decision-making process is that of consensus. If 'no consensus appears attainable' other procedures are provided for. In the Executive Committee of the Montreal Multilateral Fund, a two-thirds majority of the parties representing a majority of developed and developing countries is required.[33] In the GEF, the voting procedure provided for is characterized by the principle of a double-weighted majority, which requires a 60% majority of the total number of participating states, as well as a 60% majority of the total amount of contributions made to the Trust Fund of the GEF.[34]

Eligibility criteria in financial mechanisms mostly focus on state-driven projects. There are, however, vehicles favouring the provision of such assistance to actors other than states. In this context, an interesting model is the GEF's Small Grants Program, administered by UNDP. It provides grants of up to USD 50,000 to finance activities of NGOs and community-based organizations. With its grassroots approach, this programme has helped to develop innovative ways for promoting sustainable development and to increase the visibility of the GEF at the local level.[35] Also relevant is the GEF medium-sized grant programme (MSP), which is open to NGOs (albeit not exclusively)

[32] See eg Decision 12/CP.2, 'Memorandum of Understanding between the Conference of the Parties and the Council of the Global Environment Facility' (29 October 1996) UN Doc FCCC/CP/1996/15/Add.1, 55.

[33] 'Report of the Second Meeting of the Parties to the Montreal Protocol on Substances that Deplete the Ozone Layer' (29 June 1990) UN Doc UNEP/OzL.Pro.2/3, 45, appendix II—'Terms of reference of the Executive Committee'.

[34] Art 25(c), Instrument for the Establishment of the Restructured Global Environment Facility (GEF Instrument) (September 2019) <https://www.thegef.org/sites/default/files/publications/gef_instrument_establishment_restructured_2019.pdf> accessed 13 January 2020.

[35] See <https://sgp.undp.org/about-us-157.html> accessed 27 May 2019.

for grants below USD 2 million.[36] Expedited procedures were established to allow MSP grants to be processed in a simpler and quicker way than larger grants.

In the area of climate change, one issue is access by least developed countries to GEF funding. The parties noted that the largest share of the climate change resources of the GEF is assigned to mitigation projects. Thus, in 2008 the COP of the 1992 UN Framework Convention on Climate Change requested the GEF '[t]o continue to improve access for all developing countries, in particular least developed countries, small island developing States and countries in Africa, to Global Environment Facility resources'.[37] In Cancun, a decision aimed at improving access to financial resources from the Least Developed Countries Fund was adopted.[38]

During the 2001 Marrakesh Conference, a new fund named the Adaptation Fund was established.[39] Its purpose is to finance adaptation projects of developing countries that are particularly vulnerable to the adverse effects of climate change. The 2007 Bali Conference finalized and agreed upon its modalities of management,[40] and the Adaptation Fund began operating in 2010. It is to be noted that the eligibility criteria of the GEF are geared towards covering incremental costs related to projects having global environmental benefits. This was raised by developing countries as a matter of concern. They did not want these criteria to be applied to the Adaptation Fund as it would reduce their ability to access its funds, and some of these issues have been addressed in subsequent COPs.[41]

An Adaptation Fund Board supervises and manages the Adaptation Fund, under the authority and guidance of the COP/MOP of the Kyoto Protocol (and latterly the Paris Agreement) and is accountable to it. Eligible parties and implementing and executing agencies have direct access to the funding provided by the Adaptation Fund.[42] The Least Developed Countries Fund (LDCF) and the Special Climate Change Fund (SCCF) were also adopted as part of the 2001 Marrakesh Accords.[43] The LDCF is designed to support projects addressing the urgent and immediate adaptation needs of the least developed countries (LDCs) as identified by their National Adaptation Plans of Action (NAPAs).[44] The SCCF is designed to finance activities in areas such as renewable energy, forestry,

[36] See <https://www.thegef.org/about/funding/project-types> accessed 27 May 2019.

[37] Decision 4/CP.14, 'Additional Guidance to the Global Environment Facility' (18 March 2009) UN Doc FCCC/CP/2008/7/Add.1, 6.

[38] Decision 5/CP.16, 'Further guidance for the operation of the Least Developed Countries Fund' (15 March 2011) UN Doc FCCC/CP/2010/7/Add.2, 9.

[39] Decision 10/CP.7, 'Funding under the Kyoto Protocol' (21 January 2002) UN Doc FCCC/CP/2001/13/Add.1, 52.

[40] Decision 1/CMP.3, 'Adaptation Fund' (14 March 2008) UN Doc FCCC/KP/CMP/2007/9/Add.1, 3.

[41] Decision 5/CMP.2, 'Adaptation Fund' (2 March 2007) UN Doc FCCC/KP/CMP/2006/10/Add.1, 28.

[42] Decision 1/CMP.4, 'Adaptation Fund' (19 March 2009) UN Doc FCCC/KP/CMP/2008/11/Add.2, 1.

[43] The detailed rules for the implementation of the Kyoto Protocol were adopted at COP 7 in Marrakesh in 2001.

[44] Decision 5/CP.7, 'Implementation of Article 4, paragraphs 8 and 9, of the Convention (Decision 3/CP.3 and Article 2, paragraph 3, and Article 3, paragraph 14, of the Kyoto Protocol)' (21 January 2002) UN Doc FCCC/CP/2001/13/Add.1, 32.

and waste management. For both of these funds adaptation to climate change is the priority.

C. Green Climate Fund

The UNFCCC, the Kyoto Protocol, and other related instruments have given rise to a complex mosaic of financial mechanisms and funding sources.[45] Financial aid was indeed a highly contentious issue during the negotiations which led to the Paris Agreement. That said, some steps were taken towards the enhancement of financial flows, asking developed countries to ensure transparency and predictability on financial aid in both the context of mitigation and adaptation.[46]

Two types of financial aid are of particular importance: those that support adaptation projects and those that support mitigation projects in developing countries.[47] The need to balance the allocation of funds in these two areas has been a crucial element of the negotiations, especially with respect to actions taken by the GCF.[48]

In the context of the post-2012 negotiations, the Copenhagen Accord made quite a bold move with 'collective commitments'[49] to provide fast-start funding of USD 30 billion annually for 2010 to 2012, and a 2020 target of USD 100 billion annually.[50] It also provided for the establishment of a new fund, the GCF.[51] These funds are disproportional to the amounts managed by existing funds. Some of the envisaged sources are taxes on international aviation and shipping, financial transactions, and carbon taxes. A significant amount of the funds is intended to flow through the GCF.

The GCF was established as an operating entity of the financial mechanism of the UNFCCC.[52] Its governing instrument was approved in 2011 by the COP 17 held in

[45] Laurence Boisson de Chazournes, 'Climate Change and Financial Assistance: A Fragmented Unified or Coordinated Approach?' in Sharif Bhuiyan, Philippe Sands, and Nico Schrijver (eds), *International Law and Developing Countries: Essays in Honour of Kamal Hossain* (Martinus Nijhoff 2014) 126.

[46] See Decision 5/CP.20, 'Long-Term Climate Finance' (2 February 2015) UN Doc FCCC/CP/2014/10/Add.2, 9, paras 9–10.

[47] Decision 1/CP.13, 'Bali Action Plan' (14 March 2008) UN Doc FCCC/CP/2007/6/Add.1, 3. The Bali Action Plan endorsed both functions of financial aid.

[48] Decision 4/CP.19, 'Report of the Green Climate Fund to the Conference of the Parties and guidance to the Green Climate Fund' (31 January 2014) UN Doc FCCC/CP/2013/10/Add.1.

[49] Benito Müller, *Copenhagen 2009: Failure or Final Wake-Up Call for Our Leaders?* (Oxford Institute for Energy Studies 2010) 4.

[50] Decision 2/CP.15, 'Copenhagen Accord' (30 March 2010) UN Doc FCCC/CP/2009/11/Add.1, 4–9, art 8.

[51] Ibid, art 10.

[52] Decision 1/CP.16, 'The Cancun Agreements: Outcome of the work of the Ad Hoc Working Group on Long-term Cooperative Action under the Convention' (15 March 2011) UN Doc FCCC/CP/2010/7/Add.1, 2, para 102.

Durban.[53] During the pilot phase of the GCF (2012–13), the World Bank acted as an interim trustee, while the interim Secretariat of the Fund was jointly provided by the UNFCCC Secretariat and the GEF Secretariat. It has now gained autonomy. The GCF is governed by a Board of twenty-four members which has responsibility for funding decisions. Moreover, in 2013, a Private Sector Advisory Group was established to make recommendations to the Board. The Group includes representatives from the private sector and civil society groups.[54]

While the GCF received pledges from donor governments of over USD 10 billion in 2015, it is anticipated that it will subsequently only receive around USD 8 billion as the Trump administration announced they would not be donating the remaining USD 2 billion of the USD 3 billion pledged by President Obama.[55]

The COP to the UNFCCC provides guidance on funding priorities and the eligibility criteria to receive financial aid from the GCF.[56] The independent redress mechanism of the GCF reviews the funding decisions of the GCF.[57] It hears complaints from those who allege they have been negatively impacted by the activities of the GCF.[58] It also reviews funding decisions where a developing country requests that their rejected funding proposals are reconsidered. Moreover, the mechanism has an advisory function through which modification of operational policies and procedures can be suggested to the GCF Board.

D. *Sui Generis* Financial Mechanisms

New partnership arrangements between governments, the private sector, and other civil society actors, such as Indigenous, local communities and NGOs, are presently regarded as important instruments in order to further sustainable development. New vehicles for technical and financial assistance include *sui generis* mechanisms such as the PCF and the Rainforest Trust Fund. Both mechanisms were established within the World Bank and draw upon the experience of this institution in administering such mechanisms.

[53] 'Governing Instrument for the Green Climate Fund' <https://www.greenclimate.fund/documents/20182/1246728/Governing_Instrument.pdf/caa6ce45-cd54-4ab0-9e37-fb637a9c6235> accessed 20 January 2020.

[54] On 31 December 2017, the GCF was worth USD 5.44 billion, of which USD 5.434 billion was held in trust by the Green Climate Trust Fund administered by the World Bank and USD 6 million was held by the GCF in current accounts; GCF, 'Report on the execution of the 2017 administrative budget of the GCF and the 2017 unaudited financial statements', GCF/B.19/27 (9 February 2018).

[55] Megan Rowling, 'Green Climate Fund may ask donors for a refill in 2019: director' *Reuters* (3 May 2018).

[56] Decision 5/CP.19, 'Arrangements between the Conference of the Parties and the Green Climate Fund' (31 January 2014) UN Doc FCCC/CP/2013/10/Add.1, 13.

[57] The governing instrument of the GCF contains a section on accountability mechanisms: see GCF Governing Instrument (n 53) s XI, para 69.

[58] GCF, 'Independent Redress Mechanism' <https://www.greenclimate.fund/independent-redress-mechanism≥ accessed 27 May 2019.

The Rainforest Trust, which was originally established to support the Pilot Programme to Conserve the Brazilian Rain Forests,[59] was set up to buy and protect tropical forests that are under threat. It aims to help preserve wildlife and tropical ecosystems by establishing partnerships and engaging local communities.[60] The Rainforest Trust has served as a laboratory for experimenting with innovative strategies aimed at the protection and sustainable use of natural resources. Financial resources to the Fund are provided by individual donors (69.04%), foundations and institutions (24.38%), corporations (4.78%), and other sources (1.80%).[61]

The PCF is a rather elaborate institutional structure based on a public-private partnership between seventeen companies and six governments.[62] Managed by the World Bank, it uses private and public financial resources in support of climate-friendly projects and it involves the private sector in the development of a comprehensive and coherent financing system for the reduction of global concentrations of greenhouse gas emissions. The objective of PCF is the funding of projects, in developing countries and countries with economies in transition, that aim to reduce global concentrations of greenhouse gases, thereby contributing to compliance with the commitments under the climate regime.

The resolution establishing the PCF opens this mechanism both to public and private sector participants whose participation must be approved by the trustee, that is, the World Bank. It provides that 'each Public Sector Participant will be required to contribute USD 10 million to the Fund and each Private Sector Participant will be required to contribute USD 5 million to the Fund'.[63] These payments can be made at any time during the life of the Fund. Both public and private investors in the Fund participate in decision-making based on the size of their contribution to the Fund. The World Bank is also responsible for ensuring complementarity between GEF-financed projects and the projects financed by the PCF. Projects financed under this mechanism help leverage additional financial resources by involving the private sector. PCF leverages this provision by supporting the creation of 'carbon assets'—that is, verified and certified emission reductions—which are produced by PCF-funded projects.

The World Bank has also established two other carbon funds. The Forest Carbon Partnership Facility (FCPF),[64] aims to promote capacity-building and carbon finance in the context of REDD (Reducing Emissions from Deforestation and Forest

[59] Luiz Barbosa, *Guardians of the Brazilian Amazon Rainforest: Environmental Organizations and Development* (Routledge 2015) ch 8.

[60] See <https://www.rainforesttrust.org/about/what-we-do/> accessed 27 May 2019.

[61] Rainforest Trust, '2017 Annual Report', 37.

[62] See World Bank, 'Climate Finance and Initiatives' <https://www.worldbank.org/en/topic/climatechange/brief/world-bank-carbon-funds-facilities> accessed 22 January 2020.

[63] International Bank for Reconstruction and Development (IBRD), Res 99-1, 'Authorising Establishment of the Prototype Carbon Fund', art IV.

[64] See IBRD, 'Charter establishing the Forest Carbon Partnership Facility' (August 2010); see also Forest Carbon Partnership Facility, 'About the FCPF' <https://www.forestcarbonpartnership.org/about> accessed 21 January 2020.

Degradation).[65] It assists developing countries in reducing emissions from deforestation and degradation by recognizing the value in protecting existing forests. Borrowing countries that are located in a subtropical area or tropical area are eligible to be REDD participants.[66]

The FCPF includes two funds, namely the Readiness Fund and the Carbon Fund, for which the World Bank acts as trustee.[67] The minimum size of the Readiness Fund was set at USD 20 million, with contributions of at least USD 5 million per participant expected from governments, and other public and private entities. In 2017, the Readiness Fund had capital at just under USD 370 million.[68] The minimum operational size of the Carbon Fund was set at USD 40 million and its target size is USD 200 million.[69] The Carbon Fund had a capital of USD 740 million in 2017.[70] The principle of common but differentiated responsibilities is reflected in the FCPF's governance structure, which rests on cooperation between developing and developed countries.

E. Financial Mechanisms in the Legal Structure of Financial And Technical Assistance

In general, states may be reticent about characterizing their commitments to financial mechanisms as mandatory. That said, it has been noted that non-binding commitments, especially within a treaty framework, may create shared expectations among stakeholders and thus may have the same *de facto* weight as legal obligations.[71] Under the MEAs adopted in the wake of the 1992 Rio Conference, the whole legal regime is in fact built on shared responsibilities between groups of countries. The overall objectives of MEAs cannot be achieved without state parties acting collectively and in the common interest. The establishment of financial mechanisms and the way they operate are part of this collective endeavour. These financial mechanisms, whether within or outside the MEAs in question, constitute a powerful incentive to carry out all elements—whether fully binding or not—of these MEAs.

The evolution in the nature and aim of technical and financial assistance as one means of protecting global public goods has given rise to new features in the legal structure for the provision of technical and financial assistance. This legal structure relies on the principle of common but differentiated responsibilities, which in turn relies on technical

[65] Forest Carbon Partnership Facility, 'Annual Report 2014'.

[66] See for definitions of 'Subtropical Area' and 'Tropical Area': FCPF Charter (n 64) art 1, s 1.1, paras 71, 73.

[67] FCPF, 'Information Memorandum' (13 June 2008) 2.

[68] FCPF, 'Annual Report 2017'.

[69] Information Memorandum' (n 67). The targeted size was reached in 2012, see FCPF, 'Annual Report 2012', 53.

[70] FCPF Report 2017 (n 68).

[71] Michael Bothe, 'Legal and Non-Legal Norms-A Meaningful Distinction in International Relations?' *Netherlands Yearbook of International Law*, 11 (1980): 65, 85.

and financial assistance as an implementing tool[72] in order to achieve global benefits and protect global public goods.

The principle of common but differentiated responsibility serves as a defence for developing countries in the event they are not able to comply with a particular treaty. In case developed countries do not provide technical and financial assistance through the agreed channels, developing countries may invoke this situation in defence of their non-compliance with the commitments under the relevant agreements. Compliance by developing states in this context is therefore assessed from the angle of developed countries' behaviour, developing states having been given the power to pressure developed states to ensure that they have the necessary means to meet their commitments.

In contrast to other MEAs, the 1994 Convention to Combat Desertification contains provisions that weaken the concept of shared responsibilities between developed and developing countries in the implementation of the Convention. In particular, the Convention states that implementation by developing countries 'will be greatly assisted by the fulfilment of ... obligations ... in particular those regarding financial resources and transfer of technologies'.[73] This approach probably is due to the fact that combating desertification was not regarded as beneficial to the international community and thus as not involving a global public good. However, the inclusion of land degradation as one of the focal areas of the GEF has changed this perception. Supporting the incremental costs of projects related to the prevention and control of land degradation is now directly linked to the provision of global environmental benefits, as manifested in destroyed forests and degraded water resources, repercussions on biodiversity and the hydrological cycle, as well as climate change.

V. MULTIPLICATION OF CLIMATE-RELATED FINANCIAL MECHANISMS AND THE RISK OF FRAGMENTATION

Since the 1990s, the answer to requests for financial assistance for climate change purposes has mainly been through the creation of new financial funds and, as a result, climate finance is currently characterized by a great number of funds. Most of these funds were created to address specific objectives, each having its own governance structure. The climate change funding regime thus consists of many separate mechanisms and is characterized by complexity in its overall functioning.[74] While this is a welcome

72 UNFCCC, art 3.1; 1992 Biodiversity Convention, arts 18.2, 19.2; Desertification Convention, arts 5(a), 6(b); Kyoto Protocol, art 10; 2001 Stockholm Convention on Persistent Organic Pollutants, art 13.

73 art 20.7.

74 'Climate finance for Limiting Emissions and Promoting Green Development: Mechanisms, Regulation, and Governance' in Richard Stewart, Benedict Kingsbury and Bryce Rudyk, *Climate*

sign of commitment, interest, and the willingness of many actors to get involved in climate change-related activities,[75] the multiplication of financing mechanisms also runs the risk of fragmentation. An important challenge is to ensure coherence among these various mechanisms.

More specifically, fragmentation can threaten the effectiveness of climate finance, increasing transaction costs, reducing the amount the recipient country actually receives, and making it more difficult to align investments with country development objectives. In addition to the augmented transaction costs, inefficiencies in allocation, and limitations on scaling up become more likely with proliferation. Further still, fragmentation renders the need for monitoring, reporting, and verification more acute.

In this context, it is particularly important that complementarity and coherence is facilitated given the increasing number of funds that are concerned with carbon reduction and the amelioration of the climate-negative effects in the pursuit of development. Particularly where there exists a scarcity of resources, it is preferable to avoid the duplication of efforts or overlaps in funding.

Coordination is required internally under the UNFCCC and externally with other funds, with a view to enhancing complementarity and coherence. Under the UNFCCC, the GCF operates alongside the GEF, as well as the specialized funds described earlier such as the LDCF, Special Climate Change, and Adaptation Fund.

The GCF presently engages with bodies and funds under the UNFCCC, as well as external climate funds. The GCF has, moreover, endeavoured to learn from the experience of other institutions in the development of its own practices. In turn, the GCF also shares its experience with other funds. In addition to information exchange in this manner, the GCF has invited other funds to take up observer status with the GCF. The representatives of the GEF, Adaptation Fund, Montreal Multilateral Fund, and Climate Investment Fund attend meetings of the GCF Board. Similarly, GCF representatives attend meetings of the GEF and the Adaptation Fund.[76]

In the context of a complementarity and coherence framework, greater coordination at the activity, national programming, and climate finance delivery levels, is also sought.[77]

Mutual support and coherence are crucial for the fight against climate change, a 'common concern' of both developed and developing countries. There is a need to prevent policy conflicts that may be caused by competitive stances to attract funding. Coordination should not be conceived as equating to a centralized approach to climate finance as it is clear that the political will is to resort to a variety of funding mechanisms.

Finance: Regulatory and Funding Strategies for Climate Change and Global Development (New York University Press 2009) 8–9.

[75] Luis Gomez-Echeverri and Benito Müller, *The Reformed Financial Mechanism of the UNFCCC* (Oxford Institute for Energy Studies 2009) 168.

[76] GCF, 'Consideration of Accreditation Proposals' (22 February 2016) B.12/07.

[77] Ibid.

There is thus a need to forge an alliance between plurality and coordination so as to ensure coherence.

Each fund having its own governing structure, their functioning and accountability should be reassessed so as to ensure coherence through synergies and avoid detrimental competition and duplication of efforts. Their policy and oversight need to be compatible with a multi-actor and a multi-layered approach as developed so far in the area of climate financial assistance. They would also have to take into account the increasing use of, and reliance on, innovative sources of funding, in which the private sector is called upon to play a key role. This challenge is intrinsically linked to the legitimacy and effectiveness of the climate change regime. Inclusiveness, participation, and accountability[78] are key parameters in this endeavour.

VI. CONCLUSIONS

Financial assistance has become a key tool for promoting environmental governance through the adoption by states of policies and actions aimed at participation, impact assessment, and accountability mechanisms. Another important development is the establishment of new types of legal and institutional mechanisms through which financial assistance is provided. The establishment of financial mechanisms, moreover, has encouraged alternative ways of cooperation among a wide array of actors.

Through the financing of environmental projects, the private sector has increasingly played a role in the furtherance of common interest issues. Yet, this trend towards the 'privatization' of assistance requires that the allocation of responsibilities is clearly set so as to avoid conflicts of interest. In this context, financial mechanisms such as the GEF and the GCF, or other trust-based institutions, are a particularly appropriate means of avoiding both bias and indeed, allegations of bias.[79]

In the area of climate change, states and other actors have, so far, privileged diversifying the mechanisms rather than adopting a unified approach. However, the multiplication of these mechanisms runs the risk of inducing dysfunctional competition, which would be detrimental to dealing effectively with these challenges. Ultimately, it should be asked whether there is room for coherence. Overall, plurality, complementarity, and mutual support appear to be the best driving features for coherence in the area of climate financial assistance.

[78] Benedict Kingsbury and Lorenzo Casini, 'Global Administrative Law in the Operations of International Organizations' *International Organizations Law Review*, 6 (2009): 319.

[79] Antonella Angelini, 'A Trouble Shared is a Trouble Halved: How the Structure of Cooperation Matters for the Engagement of Responsibility in the World Bank Partnership Programmes' *International Organizations Law Review*, 13/1 (2016): 171.

BIBLIOGRAPHY

Laurence Boisson de Chazournes, 'The Global Environment Facility Galaxy: On Linkages among Institutions' *Max Planck Yearbook of United Nations Law*, 3 (1999): 243

Laurence Boisson de Chazournes, 'Is There Room for Coherence in Climate Financial Assistance?' *Laws* (2015): 541

Nele Matz, 'Environmental Financing: Function and Coherence of Financial Mechanisms in International Environmental Agreements' *Max Planck Yearbook of United Nations Law*, 6 (2003): 473

Alexander Zahar, *Climate Change Finance and International Law* (Routledge 2017)

CHAPTER 55

TECHNOLOGY ASSISTANCE AND TRANSFERS

SHAWKAT ALAM

I. INTRODUCTION: TECHNOLOGY TRANSFERS—PRINCIPLES AND CONTENTS

SOME of today's sustainable development challenges can be effectively addressed through the application of technically-based solutions, governed by international law. Accordingly, the transfer of environmentally sound technology from advanced economies to developing and least-developed countries (LDCs) plays an important role within international environmental law. Developing countries and LDCs are exposed to higher risks associated with environmental problems, such as climate change, and stand to benefit the most from a diffusion of new technology.[1] However, without the effective cross-pollination of new technology and ideas, developing countries and LDCs face a false dichotomy of needing to adopt conventional economic policies on the one hand, and to further environmental conservation objectives on the other.

The idea of technology transfers has generated several working definitions across the literature. According to Vac and Fitiu, technology transfer refers to 'the range of strategies that promote the transfer of new innovation, knowledge, technology, practices and/or skills from one setting to another'.[2] Technology transfers can come via a range of different modalities. Licensing, importation through goods and services, copying, joint

[1] OECD, 'Green Growth and Developing Countries: A Summary for Policy Makers' (June 2012).

[2] Calin Vac and Avram Fitiu, 'Building Sustainable Development through Technology Transfer in a Romanian University' *Sustainability*, 9/11 (2017): 2042; see also Bert Metz *et al*, *Methodological and Technological Issues in Technology Transfer: A Special Report of the Intergovernmental Report on Climate Change* (CUP 2000) 15.

ventures, mergers and acquisitions, are all different types of methods to transfer technology effectively.[3] 'Technology', in this sense, not only covers the use of 'hard' infrastructure, but also includes practices and know-how. Transfers can also occur through a range of different actors, including the private sector, universities, public research institutions, and government.

Technology transfer stands as its own separate concept that is distinct from other related activities such as technical assistance and foreign aid.[4] Although many states provide technical assistance as part of foreign aid projects, technology transfers focus on the effective dissemination of technology beyond the lifecycle of particular projects. Capacity-building, training, and professional human resource development are all elements of technology transfers into recipient countries that take place on longer timescales, so that developing countries and LDCs can possess the capabilities to pursue sustainable development.

At its heart, technology transfers aim to address the inequitable distribution of costs and benefits that have occurred between developed and developing countries under conventional patterns of economic growth.[5] As this chapter will consider in Section II, this has been reflected through a range of international environmental law instruments. However, despite the prevalence of technology provisions in international environmental law, there remains a lack of effective implementation. This can be attributed, in part, to the tension between technology transfers and the protection of intellectual property rights, discussed in Section III of this chapter. As Section IV will consider, direct confrontation between the intellectual property and technology transfer regimes has been side-stepped, but there remains a strong need to seek complementarity between the two systems.

II. THE EVOLUTION OF TECHNOLOGY TRANSFERS: FROM DEPENDENCY AND DIFFERENTIAL TREATMENT TO NORTH-SOUTH COLLABORATION

International environmental law has long recognized the importance of technology transfers through a range of mechanisms, from declaratory statements to specific treaty commitments, calling on parties to transfer technology on a fair and equitable basis. This can be attributed in part to the mutual recognition that a collective technological response to the challenges of sustainable development and environmental degradation

[3] Michael Waibel and William Alford, 'Technology Transfer' in Rüdiger Wolfrum (ed), *Max Planck Encyclopedia of Public International Law* (OUP 2015).

[4] See Chapter 54, 'Financial Assistance', in this volume.

[5] OECD (n 1).

is needed from the global community. This has been reflected through the progressive development of international environmental law and other key legal instruments.

A. Code of Conduct for Technology Transfers

One of the earliest soft law instruments that recognized the need to promote technology transfers was the Draft International Code of Conduct on the Transfer of Technology ('the Code of Conduct'), drafted under the auspices of the United Nations Conference on Trade and Development (UNCTAD). One of the basic principles of the Code of Conduct is to utilize emerging industrial technology to promote and facilitate economic growth in developing countries.[6] Although the Code of Conduct was negotiated before concepts such as sustainable development became mainstream within development discourse, the Code of Conduct did recognize that technology transfers play a central role in 'international peace and security, promoting international economic stability and progress, [and] for the general welfare of nations'.[7] Importantly, the Code of Conduct focuses on justifying technology transfers as a matter of justice, both to address past colonialism and systemic economic exploitation.[8]

The Code of Conduct contains several obligations requiring members to create national regulations to promote technology transfers. Article 3.4 specifies four main groups of regulatory reforms that are earmarked for action by signatories: financial reform, such as promoting conditions for domestic credit and financing; regulations allowing the renegotiation of transfer agreements; regulations governing technical aspects of transfers, such as providing analysis of technology transfer needs to assist negotiating parties; and regulations to support institutions charged with promoting technology transfers, such as information exchange mechanisms and enforcement provisions.[9]

The Code of Conduct also recognizes the special needs of developing countries by addressing issues of economic inequality. Chapter 6 of the Code of Conduct contains several obligations for developed countries to facilitate access to data, create facilities to encourage research and development, and promote developing country expertise.[10] Special treatment accorded to LDCs must also recognize their specific social and economic conditions.[11]

The Code of Conduct emerged from the power imbalance experienced by developing countries from the technological power held by large transnational corporations

[6] 'Draft International Code of Conduct on the Transfer of Technology as at the close of the 6th session of the Conference on 5 June 1985' (20 June 1985) UN Doc TD/CODE TOT/47, art 2.2(iv).

[7] Ibid, art 2.2 (iv).

[8] Waibel and Adford (n 3) para 28.

[9] Code of Conduct (n 6) art 4.4.

[10] Ibid, art 6.1.

[11] Ibid, art 6.4.

(TNCs) and developed countries. During negotiations, several developing countries signalled their intention to create instruments promoting the adaptation of new technology to their domestic economies. Latin America countries implemented several regulations addressing the loss of technology that occurred when large firms left their domestic markets to move to less regulated economies.[12] The Code of Conduct was negotiated in contemplation of this context, and was created primarily to serve the interests of developing countries in a bid to overcome the inherent hegemony enjoyed by developed economies with technological superiority.

In contrast, developed economies expressed their intention to continue to use the market as the best form of allocating technological resources, even though developing countries were unable to address inherent inequalities and market failures experienced as a result of this approach. The G77 and Nation Groups B and D of the Code of Conduct contested the adopted scope of an 'international transfer' of technology.[13] G77 and Group D argued that a transfer of technology within a multinational group of companies could constitute an international transfer and therefore encompass these transfers within the Code of Conduct. Group B, consisting of Western European nations and other advanced economies, disagreed by submitting that such transfers could not fall within the scope of the Code of Conduct. This submission presented a problem for developing countries: by carving out domestic multinational corporations from the Code, the Code would lose its significance as these bodies could simply establish a local subsidiary to bypass obligations.[14]

The failure of the Code of Conduct can also be attributed to fundamental philosophical differences between negotiating groups. To this extent, developed nations advocated the importance of free market principles and the 'freedom to contract' between parties. The mandatory nature of the Code of Conduct, reflected in the commitment that developed countries 'shall' transfer technology, was a clear affront to the free market approach advocated by developed countries.[15] Conversely, developing countries pointed to the fact that the purpose of the Code of Conduct was to address the structural inequalities and market failures that had resulted from attempting to liberalize economies and adopt a free market approach. What is clear is that since initial negotiations between the Global North and South, the Code of Conduct has failed to achieve a 'quantum leap' forward due to the political environment between negotiating countries at the time.[16]

[12] Debra Miller, 'Panacea or Problem? The Proposed International Code of Conduct for Technology Transfer' *Technology and the New International Order*, 33/1 (1979): 43.

[13] Ton Zuijdwijk, 'The UNCTAD Code of Conduct on the Transfer of Technology' *McGill Law Journal*, 24/4 (1978): 562; Padmashree Sampath and Pedro Roffe, 'Unpacking the International Technology Transfer Debate: Fifty Years and Beyond' *International Centre for Trade and Sustainable Development Issue Paper* 36 (June 2012).

[14] Zuijdwijk (n 13).

[15] Ibid.

[16] Sampath and Roffe (n 13).

B. Technology Transfers Under International Environmental Law Instruments

Technology transfers have been an important mechanism to achieve the objects and aims of several key international environmental legal instruments. The following sections discuss several prominent examples, tracing a shift from an early focus on technical assistance to a more comprehensive and collaborative approach.

1. *Barcelona Convention for the Protection of the Mediterranean Sea Against Pollution*

The technical capacity-building needs of states, and using transfer mechanisms to address constraints, were recognized within the 1976 Convention for the Protection of the Mediterranean Sea Against Pollution (the Barcelona Convention), which regulates the discharge of hazardous substances into the Mediterranean by contracting parties and restricts the dumping of waste from ships and aircraft into the marine ecosystem. Since its entry into force in 1978, the Barcelona Convention has expanded with the introduction of seven additional Protocols that restrict offshore pollution and biodiversity loss, and call on contracting parties to implement Integrated Coastal Zone Management (ICZM) in their coastal management plans.[17]

Initially, the Barcelona Convention required contracting parties to foster further scientific and technological cooperation. Article 11 required parties to coordinate their national research programmes relating to marine pollution, and for them to exchange data and other scientific information. This included the requirement, imposed by Article 11.3, to provide 'technical and other possible assistance ... with priority to be given to the special needs of developing countries in the Mediterranean region'. However, the Convention has since been amended in order to make the language consistent with other instruments regulating the marine environment, specifically the 1982 United Nations Convention on the Law of the Sea (UNCLOS).[18] Under the amended Article 11 of the Barcelona Convention, parties undertake a commitment to promote 'research on, access to, and transfer environmentally sound technology, including clean production technologies and to cooperate in the formulation, establishment and implementation of clean production processes'. The technology transfer mechanisms contained therein focus on creating partnerships to address technological inequality within the marine research arena.

[17] See eg 1995 Protocol Concerning Specially Protected Areas and Biological Diversity of the Mediterranean; 1996 Protocol on the Prevention of Pollution of the Mediterranean Sea by Transboundary Movements of Hazardous Waste and their Disposal.

[18] 1995 Amendments to the Convention for the Protection of the Mediterranean Sea Against Pollution. The Amending Instrument also renamed it the 'Convention for the Protection of the Marine Environment and the Coastal Region of the Mediterranean'.

2. *Cartagena Convention and Noumea Convention*

Echoing the original approach outlined above in the Barcelona Convention, further operationalization of an obligation to provide developing countries with technological assistance is provided by both the 1983 Cartagena Convention for the Protection and Development of the Marine Environment in the Wider Caribbean Region and the 1986 Noumea Convention which applies in the South-Pacific Region.[19] Article 13.3 of the Cartagena Convention provides that parties will cooperate with each other and international organizations to provide 'technical and other assistance', and, similar to the original approach of the Barcelona Convention above, 'tak[e] into account the special needs of the smaller island developing countries and territories'. The Noumea Convention imposes obligations for technological assistance in almost identical terms, contained in Article 18. The above three international agreements in the marine area illustrate early forms of differential treatment and technological assistance in international environmental law. There is a clear focus on cooperation and considering the different needs of developing nations. Although both the 1983 Cartagena Convention and the 1986 Noumea Convention only provided for technical assistance and subsequent multilateral environmental agreements (MEAs) provided more comprehensive transfer obligations, as discussed below, these earlier agreements marked a shift by placing a burden on developed countries to assist in disseminating new environmentally sound technology and recognize the special needs and technical capacity constraints that plagued developing countries.

3. *United Nations Convention on the Law of the Sea*

The primary purpose of UNCLOS is to outline the jurisdictional limits of coastal states, manage how states can use the world's marine resources, and create obligations concerning the protection and preservation of the marine environment.[20] Technology transfer is an important mechanism within UNCLOS, creating mutual obligations for developed and developing countries to build capacity with a view to effectively manage marine resources. As reflected in Article 150 of UNCLOS, the overall policy objective for technology transfers is to 'foster a healthy environment' and to promote 'cooperation for the overall development of all countries, especially developing States'.

UNCLOS arguably places a greater onus on developed countries to facilitate technology transfers to developing countries and LDCs than comparable instruments such as the Barcelona Convention, discussed above. Under Article 144.1(b), authorities are required to 'promote and encourage the transfer to developing States of [such] technology and scientific knowledge so that all State Parties benefit therefrom'. In addition, Article 144.2(a) requires states to ensure that all technology be provided under 'fair and reasonable terms and conditions'. Part XIV of UNCLOS also contains several provisions relating to technology transfers. Under Article 266, states have an 'active' obligation to

[19] Convention for the Protection of Natural Resources and Environment of the South Pacific Region.

[20] See further Chapter 31, 'The Protection of the Marine Environment: Pollution and Fisheries', in this volume.

ensure that they transfer marine science and technology on fair and reasonable terms,[21] and foster favourable economic and legal conditions to facilitate transfers.[22]

UNCLOS does not clarify what 'fair and reasonable terms' means. However, the technology transfer obligations under the regime are further supported by the work of the Intergovernmental Oceanographic Commission (IOC), which creates guidance material on key terms under the Convention.[23] The 'IOC Criteria and Guidelines on the Transfer of Marine Technology' (the IOC Guidelines) have provided a broad definition of 'marine technology'[24] and call for the establishment of a clearing-house mechanism to transfer marine technology.[25] Despite this effort, implementation is lacking to date. This can be attributed to the fact that a significant proportion of marine technology remains dispersed through a wide range of actors, such as private firms or universities.[26] In conjunction with this, there exists a lack of awareness in developing countries and LDCs of the potential for this mechanism to transfer marine technology.[27]

4. *Convention on Biological Diversity*

The 1992 Convention on Biological Diversity (CBD) contains important provisions concerning technology transfers. According to Waibel *et al*, the objective of the CBD is twofold: developed countries receive access to genetic material from developing countries, in return for a rules-based system to facilitate technology transfers and a share in the profits that result from the exploitation of genetic material.[28] Much like UNCLOS, Article 16.2 of the CBD states that developing countries are to be provided with technology on fair and the most favourable terms, including through concessional and preferential conditions. Importantly, however, the CBD goes further to clarify the relationship concerning intellectual property rights. Under Article 16.2, technology that is subject to intellectual property rights can also be subject to favourable access, whilst acknowledging that such access must be facilitated in a manner that is consistent with intellectual property rights.

The CBD recognizes that effective technological dissemination is operationalized through capacity-building projects with developing countries and LDCs.[29] Under Annex II of the CBD, parties must be sensitive to 'the capacity needs of recipients' when pre-assessing the adaptability of prospective technology to be transferred.[30] This is

[21] art 266.1.

[22] art 266.3.

[23] art 271.

[24] IOC Advisory Body of Experts on the Law of the Sea, 'IOC Criteria and Guidelines on the Transfer of Marine Technology' (UNESCO 2005) guideline A2.

[25] Ibid, guideline C1.

[26] Stephen Minas, 'Marine Technology Transfer Under a BBNJ Treaty: A Case for Transnational Network Cooperation' *American Journal of International Law*, 112 (2018): 144–145.

[27] See ibid, 148.

[28] Waibel and Adford (n 3) para 54.

[29] Decision IX/14, 'Technology Transfer and Cooperation' (9 October 2008) UN Doc UNEP/CBD/COP/DEC/IX/14, annex, para IV(19).

[30] Ibid, annex, para II(4).

consistent with the broader commitments under Article 18 of the CBD, which imposes an obligation to provide special attention 'to the development and strengthening of national capabilities, by means of human resource development and institution building'. This approach serves as an important function, as it requires developing countries also to examine their specific technological needs in order to improve the opportunity for effective integration into the local marketplace.

The obligation to provide access to technology on fair and the most favourable terms that are mutually agreed upon by parties promotes a collaborative approach. This approach is further elucidated by Article 20 of the Convention, calling for developed countries to provide financial and technical assistance to developing countries and LDCs in support of their capacity-building initiatives. Encouraging mutually agreed terms between developed and developing countries, and LDCs, thus disrupts patterns of creating long-term dependency on advanced economies to supply technological innovation, and of entrenched inequitable development.

5. *United Nations Framework Convention on Climate Change*

The international climate change regime contains a significant number of provisions concerning the diffusion of environmentally sound technology, and advances relevant institutional responses. Under Article 4.5 of the 1992 United Nations Framework Convention on Climate Change (UNFCCC), Annex II Parties (ie developed countries) shall 'take all practicable steps to promote, facilitate, and finance, as appropriate, the transfer of, or access to, environmentally sound technologies to other Parties, particularly developing country Parties'. This general commitment is reinforced by Articles 3.14, 10(c), and 11 of the 1997 Kyoto Protocol whereby parties commit to the 'promotion of effective modalities for the development and diffusion of ... environmentally sound technologies, know-how, practices and processes pertinent to climate change'. Articles 10 and 11 of the Kyoto Protocol also present a synthesis of technology transfer obligations with key ideas present in sustainable development discourse by framing transfers as a common but differentiated responsibility held by developed countries.[31]

The Kyoto Protocol also enabled the creation of the Clean Development Mechanism (CDM),[32] a framework which allows developed countries to obtain Certified Emission Reduction credits (CERs) in return for implementing clean technology within developing countries and LDCs. Subject to the requirement that a project provides support that is genuinely additional (ie CDM projects that are subject to CER credits would not occur but for CDM assistance), the CDM was anticipated to provide genuine opportunities for technology transfers and for developing countries to improve their ability to access environmentally sound technology. The CDM thus presented a landmark mechanism as it utilized market-based forces (in the form of CERs), rather than a general commitment, in order to drive innovation. However, to date, the performance

[31] Ibid, arts 10, 11.

[32] art 12.

of the CDM to generate technology transfers effectively has been poor, with only 0.6% of CDM projects eventually resulting in full technology transfers with the recipient country.[33]

The UNFCCC has since reached political consensus to establish a 'Technology Mechanism'.[34] The Technology Mechanism consists of a Technology Executive Committee (TEC) and the Climate Technology Centre and Network (CTCN) as established under the Cancun Agreement.[35] Under the Technology Mechanism, the TEC provides policy advice and recommendations on how to enhance the transfer of environmentally sound technologies. The TEC is further supported by a number of task forces to provide specialized policy advice on systemic issues concerning transfers of environmentally sound technology such as innovation financing, adaptation, research and development, mitigation, and endogenous capacity of recipient countries. Conversely, the CTCN is charged with implementation by providing technical assistance to developing countries and LDCs, fostering access to information and knowledge on climate technologies, and encouraging collaboration between developed and developing country partners.[36]

The 2015 Paris Agreement has since revitalized institutional responses to promote technology transfers to combat climate change through the establishment of the 'Technology Framework'.[37] At the 2018 Katowice Conference of the Parties, a preliminary determination was delivered to keep both the TEC and CTCN as part of the Technology Framework,[38] but in keeping with commitments from the Paris Agreement, also necessitating stronger collaboration with the Financial Mechanism of the Convention to develop more collaborative approaches to technology transfers. In particular, parties acknowledged that further action is required at the earlier stages of innovation (eg research and development, and improving endogenous capacity)[39] under the new Technology Framework.

6. *Technology transfers and sustainable development law*

Although the concept of sustainable development, more generally, is traceable in a number of texts pre-dating the 1972 UN Conference on the Human Environment

[33] Kasturi Das, 'Technology Transfer Under the Clean Development Mechanism: An Empirical Study of 1000 CDM Projects' *The Governance of Clean Development*, Working Paper Series No 14 (July 2011).

[34] Decision 2/CP.15, 'Copenhagen Accord' (30 March 2010) UN Doc FCCC/CP/2009/11/Add.1, 4, para 11.

[35] Decision 1/CP.16 'The Cancun Agreements: Outcome of the work of the Ad Hoc Working Group on Long-term Cooperative Action under the Convention' (15 March 2011) UN Doc FCCC/CP/2010/7/Add.1, para 117.

[36] See UNFCCC, 'Technology mechanism' <https://unfccc.int/ttclear/support/technology-mechanism.html> accessed 22 January 2020.

[37] art 10.4.

[38] UNFCCC, 'Preparations for the implementation of the Paris Agreement and the first session of the Conference of the Parties serving as the meeting of the Parties to the Paris Agreement' (14 December 2018) UN Doc FCCC/CP/2018/L.7, Draft Decision _/CMA.1, 'Technology framework under Article 10, paragraph 4, of the Paris Agreement', para 2.

[39] Paris Agreement, arts 10.5, 10.6.

(the Stockholm Conference),[40] the Stockholm Conference saw the initial emergence of technocratic responses to tackle global inequality and environmental damage. Principle 9 of the Report of the UN Conference on the Human Environment called for the 'transfer of substantial quantities of financial and technological assistance as a supplement to the domestic effort of the developing countries' in order to address environmental deficiencies.[41]

Subsequently, technology transfer to developing countries was reinforced under the 1992 UN Conference on Environment and Development and its Rio Declaration.[42] Principle 34 of the Rio Declaration called for developing countries to be assisted by gaining increased access to technology and know-how in the public domain, including technology and processes protected by intellectual property rights.[43] Although the Rio Declaration anticipated the creation of the Code of Conduct for Technology Transfers at the time of negotiation,[44] increased access to technology would be facilitated through the formation of a network of laboratories to examine new environmentally sound technology.[45] Principle 35 further supported this commitment, calling for states to measure the environmental performance of new technology.

However, the most significant issue arising from both the Stockholm and Rio Conferences was 'not an absence of ideas', but rather disagreement concerning how technology transfers could be effectively implemented.[46] In this context, the subsequent Johannesburg Conference in 2002 emphasized the need to develop partnerships and 'work together' in order to side-step the political impasse between the Global North and South.[47] However, the deep disagreement on how to create systematic transfers of technology, much like the debate over the UNFCCC Technology Mechanism, divided developed and developing countries during the negotiation process. In the outcome document of the Rio+20 summit, 'The Future We Want',[48] states merely affirmed 'the importance of technology transfers to developing countries'[49] and recommended that 'relevant UN agencies identify options for a facilitation mechanism that promotes the

[40] See eg Rachel Carson, *Silent Spring* (Houghton Mifflin Company 1962) which examined the collective impact of pesticide use on animal species and the ecosystem.

[41] United Nations, 'Report of the United Nations Conference on the Human Environment' (5–16 June 1972) UN Doc A/CONF.48/14/Rev.1, 3, ch 1—'Declaration of the United Nations Conference on the Human Environment', principle 9.

[42] See eg World Commission on Environment and Development, *Our Common Future* (OUP 1987).

[43] *Report of the United Nations Conference on Environment and Development* (UN 1993) vol I, annex I—'Rio Declaration', principle 34.

[44] Ibid.

[45] Ibid.

[46] Luc Hens and Bashutush Nath, 'The Johannesburg Conference' *Environment, Development and Sustainability*, 5/1 (2003): 7, 20.

[47] *Report of World Summit on Sustainable Development* (UN 2002) ch I.1, annex—'Johannesburg Declaration on Sustainable Development', para 18.

[48] See UNGA Res 66/288, 'The Future We Want' (11 September 2012) UN Doc A/Res/66/288, annex, paras 58(f), 269–276.

[49] See Matthew Rimmer, 'Rio+20: Who owns the green economy?' *The Conversation* (25 June 2012).

development, transfer and dissemination of clean and environmentally sound technology'.[50] The Rio+20 summit did not present tangible action on the ground to facilitate technology transfers to developing countries.

Since the Rio+20 summit, there has been a renewed impetus to establish a systematic approach to technology transfers as part of sustainable development. Building upon further negotiations since Rio+20,[51] the UN Secretary-General recommended several plans for reform, namely, capacity-building exercises, voluntary actions that can be undertaken by states (such as performing peer review of the specific technology needs of developing countries), and institutional reform, including the creation of a Technology Facilitation Mechanism (TFM).[52] The President of the General Assembly also noted a number of future deliverables, including the launch of an online platform to map existing technology facilitation mechanisms, improve coordination within the UN system of existing technology transfer mechanisms, analyse gaps that can create a barrier to effective diffusion and promote further discussions concerning collaborative intellectual property rights and public-private partnerships (PPPs).[53] The UN Secretary-General's Synthesis Report issued in 2014 also highlighted a need to create a Technology Bank and a Science, Technology and Innovation (STI) Capacity Building Mechanism for LDCs,[54] together with efforts to accelerate the innovation-to-market process of new technology.[55]

Calls to create a TFM came to fruition in the Addis Ababa Action Agenda.[56] Under paragraph 123 of the Agenda, the TFM is tasked with promoting coordination and coherence within the UN system, establishing an outline platform to promote open access for scientific publications, know-how, best practices and dissemination of other scientific knowledge to developing countries, and creation of a forum for stakeholder engagement between developed and developing countries. At the time of writing, the TFM had announced plans to develop

[50] 'Future We Want' (n 48) para 273.

[51] See 'Options for a facilitation mechanism that promotes the development, transfer and dissemination of clean and environmentally sound technologies—Report of the Secretary General' (4 September 2012) UN Doc A/67/348.

[52] 'Options for facilitating the development, transfer and dissemination of clean and environmentally sound technologies' (12 August 2013) UN Doc A/68/310, 21–24.

[53] 'General Assembly Structured Dialogues on: Possible arrangements for a facilitation mechanism to promote the development, transfer and dissemination of clean and environmentally sound technologies—Report' (13 August 2014) 6–7 <https://sustainabledevelopment.un.org/content/documents/4673techreport.pdf> accessed 2 May 2019.

[54] 'The road to dignity by 2030: Ending poverty, transformation of all lives and protecting the planet—Synthesis report of the Secretary-General on the post-2015 sustainable development goals' (4 December 2014) UN Doc A/69/700, para 126.

[55] Ibid.

[56] UNGA Res 69/313, 'Addis Ababa Action Agenda of the Third International Conference on Financing for Development (Addis Ababa Action Agenda)' (17 August 2015) UN Doc A/RES/69/313, para 123; see also UNGA Res 70/1, 'Transforming our World: The 2030 Agenda for Sustainable Development' (21 October 2015) UN Doc A/RES/70/1, para 70 which officially launched the TFM.

roadmaps and action plans to track and measure the transfer of technology into developing countries.[57]

C. Synthesis: Technology Transfers in International Environmental Law

Technology transfers are an important mechanism in international environmental law to fulfil the goals and objectives of several treaties and crosscutting environmental instruments.[58] From the analysis of technology transfer provisions above, it is evident that there has been an evolution towards a more collaborative approach to foster higher technological dissemination. A requirement to transfer has given way to strategies that emphasize collaboration through PPPs, technology assessments, and capacity-building exercises. More generally, this is consistent with how development discourse has progressed, with a movement away from the differential treatment of developing countries and LDCs, towards improved dialogue concerning sustainable development discourse that emphasizes capacity- and governance-building.[59] This approach directly tackles long-term trends of entrenched dependency to allow developing countries to become more self-sufficient in pursuing their own sustainable development aspirations.

Yet despite this objective, developed countries have abrogated their responsibility to build the capacity of developing countries and LDC partners. To date, technology transfer provisions within international environmental law have remained largely under-utilized, and there has been no clear action to translate obligations into tangible outcomes for developing countries.

It is worth noting that new dynamic relationships between developing countries and LDCs, or South–South transfers, are playing an ever increasingly important role in technology transfer. Developing countries are transferring technology within this bloc that is disrupting traditional North–South conceptions of technology inequity. However,

[57] See 'Technology Facilitation Mechanism—Online information repository for the STI roadmaps work' <https://sustainabledevelopment.un.org/tfm#roadmaps> accessed 1 May 2019.

[58] Technology transfers are also used as a mechanism in several other international environmental instruments and mirror similar commitments as outlined in this Chapter. These instruments include the 1992 Convention on the Transboundary Effects of Industrial Accidents; 1999 Protocol to Abate Acidification, Eutrophication and Ground Level Ozone; 1998 Aarhus Protocol on Persistent Organic Pollutants; 1998 Aarhus Protocol on Heavy Metals to the 1979 Convention on Long Range Transboundary Air Pollution; 1992 Convention on the Protection and Use of Transboundary Watercourses and International Lakes; 1989 Basel Convention on the Control of Transboundary Movements of Hazardous Wastes and their Disposal; 1994 Convention on Nuclear Safety; 1985 Vienna Convention for the Protection of the Ozone Layer, art 4.2; 1987 Montreal Protocol, art 10(A); 1994 United Nations Convention to Combat Desertification in those Countries Experiencing Serious Drought and/or Desertification, Particularly in Africa, arts 12, 16 and 18; 2001 International Treaty on Plant Genetic Resources for Food and Agriculture.

[59] Lavanya Rajamani, 'The Changing Fortunes of Differential Treatment in the Evolution of International Environmental Law' *International Affairs*, 88/3 (2012): 605.

such transfers are still experiencing the same issues of insensitivity to the capacity needs of recipient countries and insensitivity to their local political, social, and economic climates.[60] Transition economies such as China are also leveraging their market access to force technology transfers from developed countries. For instance, unscrupulous firms are requiring foreign investors to utilize joint ventures to obtain market access but are illegitimately copying sensitive intellectual property in the process.[61]

Underlying all of this, in part, is the role that intellectual property plays and how that shapes state, institutional, and individual firm responses to technology transfers for developing countries. In the lead-up to the Addis Ababa Action Agenda discussed above, negotiating parties were split along G77 and developed countries lines that predominately reflected whether their respective economies are net producers or recipients of technology transfers.[62] Since the failure of the Code of Conduct, developed countries have continued to resist efforts to trade technology and innovation freely, including environmentally sound technology, on the basis that it may harm competition and impede the encouragement of innovation by removing incentives from innovative firms.

However, to dismiss the system of intellectual property rights as a general roadblock for technological diffusion ignores the nuances present within the intellectual property rights regime which seeks complementarity with sustainable development objectives.[63] As Section III will highlight, both the technology transfer and intellectual property rights regimes have pursued coordination and complementarity, rather than conflict, to provide a consistent system governing innovation.

III. TECHNOLOGY TRANSFERS AND INTELLECTUAL PROPERTY: CHALLENGES AND SYNERGIES

The World Trade Organization (WTO) and its 1994 Agreement on Trade-Related Aspects of Intellectual Property Rights (TRIPs Agreement) govern the global system of intellectual property rights protection. For developed countries the core purpose of the TRIPs Agreement is to protect intellectual property rights for rights-holders. Conversely, developing countries advocate that the TRIPs Agreement must correct market failures and inequality arising from the protection of intellectual property

[60] See Oliver Hensengerth, 'South-South Technology Transfer: Who Benefits? A Case Study of the Chinese Built Bui Dam in Ghana' *Energy Policy*, 114 (2018): 499, 506–507.

[61] See Lee Bransetter, 'What is the Problem of Forced Technology Transfer in China?' *Econofact* (3 August 2018).

[62] See Nathalie Risse, 'The Technology Facilitation Mechanism: Conceived in Rio, Born in Addis' *IISD* (10 September 2015).

[63] See also Chapter 48, 'Intellectual Property', in this volume.

rights, including a denial of access to environmentally sound technologies that can benefit humankind.[64] In its final form, developed countries were successful in asserting their dominance within the TRIPs Agreement, with TRIPs providing strong protections for intellectual property rights. The issues developing countries face, such as the equitable transfer of technology, conversely failed to appear in the Agreement's preamble.[65] Although Article 7 of the TRIPs Agreement does provide solace to developing countries by recognizing the need to effect technology transfers, its non-binding language reflects the continued dominance of developed country interests in this debate.

TRIPs contains a range of protections for intellectual property such as patents, copyrights, trademarks, and industrial designs.[66] Notwithstanding these protections, TRIPs also provide caveats to these rights in order to pursue shared, public goals. Article 27.2 allows exceptions from intellectual property protections based on the need to preserve 'human, animal or plant life or health' or 'to avoid serious prejudice to the environment'. However, this provision prevents the commercial exploitation of the innovation within the member's jurisdiction and use of this caveat must be found to be necessary to achieve environmental protection. Article 31 also allows states to give 'compulsory licences' in certain circumstances where voluntary efforts to obtain licences have failed, subject to the requirement that the initial rights-holder is paid adequate remuneration and the licence is predominantly used to serve the domestic market.[67]

TRIPs also contains specific provisions to enable technology transfers to developing countries. Under Article 66.2, developed countries 'shall provide incentives to enterprises and institutions in their territories for the purpose of promoting and encouraging technology transfer to least developed country Members in order to enable them to create a sound and viable technological base'. This provision is further supported by Article 67, which requires developed countries to create the conditions in which technology can diffuse into developing countries and LDCs, including a favourable regulatory environment. These provisions are silent on whether developed countries are mandated to hand over technological development to developing countries, rather, Article 67 particularly points to the need to promote governance reform and institutional capacity-building as methods to foster technological dissemination.

International environmental law has also turned to focus on governance reform to promote a legislative environment favourable to new innovation and technological diffusion. For instance, under the CBD, states must create legislation that mutually supports both technological transfers and the protection of intellectual property rights.[68] Although this requirement has softened to a general commitment for

[64] Carlos Correa, 'Can the TRIPS Agreement Foster Technology Transfer to Developing Countries?' in Keith Maskus and Jerome Reichman (eds), *International Public Goods and Transfer of Technology Under a Globalized Intellectual Property Regime* (CUP 2005) 227.

[65] Ibid.

[66] Part II.

[67] arts 31, 31(h).

[68] art 16.5.

legislative reform regarding developing countries under the 2010 Nagoya Protocol,[69] these provisions mirror the TRIPs requirement to create marketplaces that are conducive to new innovation.

Although a range of international environmental instruments calls for technology transfers as discussed earlier, these are limited by the regime of intellectual property rights protected by TRIPs. Under Article 16.2 of the CBD, for instance, states must ensure that any technology transfers are consistent with the rights of rights-holders, with UNCLOS also containing similar provisions in relation to marine technology.[70] Principle 34 of Agenda 21 likewise recognizes the importance of intellectual property rights protection, noting that 'consideration must be given to the role of patent protection and intellectual property rights before recommending action such as creating technology clearing houses and performing technology assessments of developing countries'.[71]

These provisions provide cogent evidence of a push for further complementarity between the intellectual property rights and environmental technology transfer regimes. In the current era of Rio+20 and the 2030 Sustainable Development Agenda, the United Nations (UN) has earmarked this as a primary issue and area of focus for the future, so that states, intellectual property rights-holders, and communities in need are presented with a logically consistent system to facilitate long lasting technology transfers.

IV. CONCLUSION

Technology transfers are an important mechanism to implement the goals and objectives of several international environmental instruments. We have witnessed how understandings of this concept have evolved, from initially addressing structural inequality resulting from colonialism and economic exploitation of the South by the North, to an important mechanism to address and prevent environmental calamities and realize sustainable development.

Nevertheless, the rights of innovators are a central consideration complicating the realization of transfer provisions in environmental laws. Developed countries and advanced economies have continued to undermine the relevant provisions of international environmental law and other instruments by failing to comply with their transfer obligations and weakening their commitments during negotiations. Moving forward, transfer mechanisms that are present in instruments such as the UNFCCC and Addis Ababa Action Agenda will need to reconcile these competing interests.

[69] Nagoya Protocol on Access to Genetic Resources and the Fair and Equitable Sharing of Benefits Arising from their Utilization to the Convention on Biological Diversity, art 23.

[70] art 267.

[71] *Report of the United Nations Conference on Environment and Development* (UN 1993) vol I, annex II—'Agenda 21', para 34.7.

Current actions such as capacity-building and technology assessments have been effective in side-stepping this issue by focusing on commitments by developed countries. Accordingly, this will become a live issue in making mechanisms such as technology clearing houses an effective tool when there is a lack of political will to bring about change.

Finally, the WTO system and TRIPs will play an important role in implementing technological change. The use of compulsory licences and the application of Article 7 of the TRIPs by WTO judiciary bodies will play a key role in supplementing further action to address technological imbalances. To date, action on technology transfers by developed countries has been limited. However, as we have witnessed with new mechanisms in the Addis Ababa Action Agenda and UNFCCC, there is a slow shift towards many of the ideas envisioned by the Code of Conduct almost fifty years ago. Only time will tell whether developing countries and LDCs will benefit from the realization of obligations of fair and equitable technology transfers to address many of their pressing development and environmental issues.

BIBLIOGRAPHY

Shawkat Alam *et al* (eds), *International Environmental Law and the Global South* (CUP 2015)

Carlos Correa, 'Can the TRIPS Agreement Foster Technology Transfer to Developing Countries?' in Keith Maskus and Jerome Reichman (eds), *International Public Goods and Transfer of Technology Under a Globalized Intellectual Property Regime* (CUP 2005) 227

Debra Miller, 'Panacea or Problem? The Proposed International Code of Conduct for Technology Transfer' *Technology and the New International Order*, 33/1 (1979): 43

Lavanya Rajamani, 'The Changing Fortunes of Differential Treatment in the Evolution of International Environmental Law' *International Affairs*, 88/3 (2012): 605

UNFCCC, 'Technology mechanism' <https://unfccc.int/ttclear/support/technology-mechanism.html> accessed 22 January 2020

CHAPTER 56

NON-COMPLIANCE PROCEDURES

MEINHARD DOELLE

I. INTRODUCTION

Non-compliance procedures have emerged in multilateral environmental agreements (MEAs) as they have in other areas of international law. While the focus of international treaty negotiation may, at one point, have been the substantive issues, the scope has, over time, shifted to include efforts to ensure the effective implementation of the commitments and obligations negotiated.[1] Along with other elements, such as dispute settlement procedures, education, and capacity-building, non-compliance procedures have become a key element of the overall effort to ensure the effective implementation of MEAs.

The main part of this chapter proceeds in three sections. Section II considers the role of compliance systems in MEAs, with a brief survey of the debate over the respective roles of facilitation and enforcement, followed by an exploration of the relationship between the primary rule system and elements of the compliance system. This is followed with an overview in Section III of the key elements of compliance systems. Section IV then contains a high-level discussion of a selection of MEA compliance systems.

[1] See Chapter 57, 'Effectiveness', in this volume.

II. THE ROLE OF NON-COMPLIANCE PROCEDURES IN MEAS

A. Facilitative Versus Enforcement Approaches

There has been a long-standing debate in the academic literature about the relative effectiveness of facilitative approaches through managerial and norm-building efforts on the one hand, and enforcement approaches through deterrence and incentives on the other hand.[2] The debate was brought to the forefront in the mid-1990s with a book by Antonia and Abraham Chayes entitled *The New Sovereignty*, in which the authors advocate for a managerial approach. It still provides the most detailed rationale for a managerial approach to compliance to date.[3] The Chayes challenge the basic assumption of the rational choice theory of compliance that states only comply with international obligations when it is in their interest to do so. They instead argue that states have a general propensity to comply based on a number of observations.[4]

First, once a state ratifies a treaty or otherwise accepts an obligation, and directs its bureaucracy to undertake implementation, it takes effort to reach a decision not to comply. Compliance is therefore seen as the norm, and effort is needed to deviate from that norm. Secondly, the authors point to the fact that the obligations are assumed voluntarily, in that the agreements are negotiated on a consensus basis. This results in a presumption within a state that has accepted an obligation that the fulfilment of that obligation is in the state's best interest. Third, the process of negotiating the agreement results in those involved developing a sense of ownership in the agreement and its objectives. Finally, the authors argue that there is a norm among states, similar to a norm among individuals in a domestic context, that laws are to be obeyed. This norm results in international obligations being fulfilled unless there is a strong 'countervailing circumstance'.

These observations lead the Chayes to a discussion of sources of non-compliance.[5] The authors acknowledge that there are circumstances where the decision not to comply with an international obligation is a deliberate choice made by a given state. The more common sources of non-compliance offered by the authors are the following:

- Ambiguity and indeterminacy of treaty language;[6]
- Limitations in the capacity of parties to carry out their undertakings;[7] and

[2] See Chapter 51, 'Compliance Theory', in this volume.

[3] Abram Chayes and Antonia Chayes, *The New Sovereignty: Compliance with International Regulatory Agreements* (Harvard University Press 1998).

[4] Ibid, 3.

[5] Ibid, 9.

[6] Ibid, 10.

[7] Ibid, 13.

- The temporal dimension of the social, economic, and political changes contemplated by regulatory treaties.[8]

The basic argument put forward in *The New Sovereignty* is that compliance problems in international law are rarely a result of a deliberate choice not to comply with an obligation. Instead, non-compliance can be traced in most cases to ambiguity in the nature and extent of the obligation, lack of capacity, and unexpected intervening events that influence compliance with an obligation. The focus for compliance systems proposed by the authors is therefore to ensure transparency, settle disputes, build capacity, and to use of persuasion to achieve compliance.

Perhaps the sharpest critique of the managerial approach to compliance has come from George W Downs. Downs rejects the managerial approach based on his conclusion that it only works when the obligation in question is a minor or modest deviation from what a state would have done without the agreement. In his view, as the level of effort or deviation from business as usual increases, the managerial approach fails, and strong, deterrence-based enforcement is needed to ensure states meet their obligations.[9]

At the heart of the critique is that *The New Sovereignty* ignores the level of cooperation needed to meet the obligation in assessing the level of compliance achieved with respect to a given international agreement. Downs argues that managerialists are only able to show that compliance is high when the effort needed to meet obligations is modest or low. Downs argues that there are an ever-increasing number of challenges facing the international community that will require more than modest efforts by states. He refers to this higher level of cooperation as 'deep cooperation'.[10] Examples of areas where deep cooperation will be needed include human rights, arms control, and global environmental challenges such as climate change, biological diversity, and natural resource depletion. The fundamental argument Downs makes is that deep cooperation cannot be achieved without strong enforcement with effective sanctions and incentives.

Intuitively, Downs' view may be compelling. It seems reasonable to expect that as the level of effort and the level of cooperation required goes up, so does the likelihood that the propensity to comply will be overshadowed by a decision that the cost of compliance is too high and not in the interest of a given state. Without empirical evidence to support this view, it is difficult to predict under what circumstances and at what point this transition might take place. It is reasonable, however, to assume that under some circumstances, for some states, that point does arise. In fact, some of the examples provided in *The New Sovereignty* illustrate that states do get to a point where a deliberate choice is made not to comply. The question of what motivates such a deliberate choice,

[8] Ibid, 15.

[9] For a detailed review of deterrence based enforcement see George Downs, David Rocke, and Peter Barsoom, 'Is the Good News about Compliance Good News about Cooperation?' *International Organization*, 50/3 (1996): 379.

[10] For a detailed discussion of the definition of deep cooperation and how it might be measured see ibid, 382–383.

and whether it is possible to predict the circumstances under which such a deliberate choice may be made is not resolved by either 'New Sovereignty' or by Downs in his critique. In other words, both sides assume a clear, one-sided answer to the most basic question: what is the relative influence of self-interest and a desire to conform to international norms on state behaviour?

In the end, both offer valuable insights into compliance, but both lack the empirical evidence needed to resolve key questions about their relative importance in understanding specific cases of non-compliance, and both are incomplete in their analysis in dismissing the influence of the other.[11] The challenge for an effective compliance system design is to develop an overall compliance system that takes into account as many influences for compliance and non-compliance as possible and develops a range of compliance mechanisms and tools that allow the system to anticipate and respond to a range of motivations and circumstances.

B. Primary Rules, Compliance Information, and Non-Compliance Response

Whether based on a facilitative, enforcement, or combined approach, there are three basic elements to any compliance system: the primary rule system; the compliance information system; and the non-compliance response system.[12] The *primary rule system* refers to the substantive obligations, the rules established for meeting them, and the processes set up for the implementation of these rules. In other words, this part of the system is about setting the obligation and the process for meeting it. The *compliance information system* refers to the development, collection, analysis, and dissemination of information regarding the level of compliance with the obligation. Finally, the *non-compliance response system* deals with the question of how to respond to incidents of non-compliance. Much of the discussion on this last part of the compliance system complements the discussion above on inducements and sanctions.

From a compliance perspective, the consideration of the primary rules system is about understanding the relationship between the obligation and compliance. It considers the compliance implication of the nature of the obligations imposed, the actions expected from states in implementing the obligations, and the relationship between the expected actions of states and compliance. Is compliance an automatic result of states taking the expected action, or does compliance depend on the effectiveness of those actions, and on cooperation from other parties, non-parties, sub-national governments, or non-state actors?

[11] See Jutta Brunnée and Stephen Troope, 'Persuasion and Enforcement: Explaining Compliance with International Law' *Finnish Yearbook of International* Law, 13/1 (2002): 273.

[12] Ibid, 18–20.

The nature of the obligation is considered key to the compliance effort, including whether the expected change is technically or behaviourally difficult to implement, to monitor, or to enforce. Does it affect different states differently? Which non-state or sub-national actors does it affect and how? It is important to consider how clear the obligation itself is. The more open to interpretation the obligation is, the more likely there will be different levels of compliance, either due to self-interest in exploiting the uncertainty or through inadvertence. A related but distinct issue is to what extent the obligation itself is in the public eye and if the importance of the obligation is publicly recognized.[13] This is distinct from the issue of transparency of the compliance record of a party; the focus here is on whether the nature of the obligation is publicly understood and what level of public interest there is in the obligation and compliance with it.[14]

The compliance information system is largely about transparency of the level of compliance with the obligation. While we often think of transparency in terms of the general public or non-governmental organizations (NGOs), transparency is a crucial component of compliance regardless of whether the pressure to comply ultimately comes from another state, the public, an NGO, or an international institution.[15] It is furthermore important regardless of whether the predisposition to non-compliance results from lack of capacity, inadvertence, or preference. It is simply important for anyone in a position to influence the predisposition of a given state, to have access to information about the level of compliance and the causes of non-compliance in order to be able to exercise their role in the compliance system effectively. The most common form of information gathering in this context is self-reporting by parties, with some roles for NGOs, regime institutions, the public, and industries in generating information and verifying compliance.[16]

This leads to the third part of the compliance system, the non-compliance response system. As a starting point, in spite of its name, the compliance response system can address non-compliance in a preventative manner.[17] It can proactively seek to inform parties of their obligations to prevent inadvertent violations. It can seek to identify capacity gaps and work proactively to fill them. It can identify failure to make demonstrable progress and put pressure on parties to take measures to comply. Preventative measures can either be taken in response to early warning signs, or proactively to create additional motivation to comply.[18] The response to a specific incident of non-compliance

[13] See Henrik Eriksen and Franz Perrez, 'The Minamata Convention: A Comprehensive Response to a Global Problem' *Review of European, Comparative and International Environmental Law*, 23/2 (2014): 195 where the success of the 2013 Minamata Convention is attributed to mercury being a clear global risk that no country argued against the need to address it with global action.

[14] See Brown Weiss and Harold Jacobson, *Engaging Countries' Strengthening Compliance with International Environ*mental Accords (MIT Press 1998) 6–12.

[15] See Chapter 52, 'Transparency Procedures', in this volume.

[16] See discussion in Section II.

[17] Ronald Mitchell, 'Compliance Theory an Overview' in James Cameron, Jakob Werksman, and Peter Roderick (eds), *Improving Compliance with International Environmental Law* (Routledge 2014) 16–23.

[18] See Ronald Mitchell, 'Regime Design Matters: International Oil Pollution and Treaty Compliance' *International Organization*, 48/3 (1994): 425.

can originate from a compliance body, from some other international institution, from a party, or from a non-state actor. A preventative approach would include a focus on obligations that are suitable to effective enforcement action and on transparency of the obligations and efforts to comply with them. It then requires careful consideration and identification at the design stage of the non-compliance response system of opportunities to coerce or incentivize compliance and to eliminate or reduce opportunities to avoid compliance.[19]

The design of the response system to non-compliance in the narrower sense of the term is the element of the compliance system most closely linked to the theoretical debate about facilitation and enforcement, as it is here that key decisions are made about the role of capacity-building and education on the one hand, and the use of incentives and sanctions on the other hand.

Inducements tend to be expensive for the entity trying to influence a party's compliance, whereas sanctions are usually costly only if they do not work.[20] As a result, one would expect a tendency to rely on sanctions over inducements in motivating compliance.[21] While this may be the case generally within the context of enforcement, the overall focus in MEA compliance systems has been on facilitation and therefore on lack of capacity or inadvertent non-compliance. In many treaties, there has been an upfront recognition that developing countries and economies in transition lack the capacity, and sometimes the moral duty, to reach the same level of response to an environmental issue as wealthier nations. This has been addressed in part by placing different obligations on countries with less capacity and moral responsibility. It is understood that nature does not distinguish environmental effects of human activity on this basis, however, and that therefore environmental improvements have to be made in countries with less capacity or moral responsibility. This has resulted in a formal recognition that the way to achieve compliance in developing countries is through inducements, capacity-building, and other support, not through sanctions.

The roles of non-state actors, sub-national state actors, and international institutions have been among the most challenging issues in the context of the compliance response system. It is generally recognized that a party may be unwilling to impose sanctions on other parties for fear that this will make it more likely that sanctions will be imposed on it, should it fail to comply with its obligations at some point in the future. States have been similarly reluctant to design non-compliance procedures with effective non-party triggers. The effectiveness of leaving the imposition of sanctions in the hands of regime institutions or non-state actors, however, is dependent on the influence those actors will have over a non-complying party. Rationalists might conclude that compliance and the design of an effective compliance system will depend predominantly on the actions taken by, and motivation of, dominant states. As a result, an important test for the effectiveness of any compliance system may be whether it can demonstrate compliance

19 Mitchell (n 17) 16–23.

20 Ibid, 21.

21 Especially in cases of non-compliance by preference.

beyond, or independent of, the efforts of such dominant states, or whether it is merely facilitating efforts by those states to motivate others to comply.

III. APPROACHES TO DESIGN AND IMPLEMENTATION

An effectively designed compliance process has to consider many factors and will have to be tailored to the specific circumstances of the regime it is intended to serve.[22] Key elements in the design of any effective compliance system encompass: attention to the primary rules sought to be implemented, including the nature of the obligations and the effort needed to comply with them; the circumstances of the parties to the regime, including their capacity; the range of circumstances that can be expected to lead to non-compliance; the relationship between the compliance system and the willingness of parties to accept ambitious commitments and obligations; and the importance of full compliance.

The choice between a facilitative, deterrence-based, or a combined compliance system will be a fundamental choice resulting from the consideration of these and other factors. Having said this, it is important to recognize that the line between facilitation and deterrence is not as clear as the somewhat polarized theoretical debate discussed above might suggest. Many elements of a compliance system, such as the compliance information system, transparency, and even findings of non-compliance, are an important part of both facilitative and enforcement-based compliance systems. Furthermore, some so-called facilitative compliance systems include elements of deterrence and incentives that seem as much based on self-interest as norm and capacity-building. An example would be the sanction involving loss of regime privileges under the 1987 Montreal Protocol's compliance system.[23]

This section seeks to move beyond the debate between facilitation and enforcement to consider four key elements that are common to MEA compliance systems. These are: mechanisms for triggering or initiation of proceedings; the mandate or scope of the committee's work; the institutional design and process; and the measures or outcomes applied at the conclusion of the process. This discussion is followed by a brief overview of key MEA non-compliance procedures (NCPs) that illustrate different configurations of these elements.

[22] Jane Bulmer, 'Compliance Regimes in Multilateral Environmental Agreements' in Jutta Brunnée, Meinhard Doelle, and Lavanya Rajamani (eds), *Promoting Compliance in and Evolving Climate Regime* (CUP 2012) 55, 58.

[23] See Decision VII/18, 'Compliance with the Montreal Protocol by the Russian Federation' (27 December 1995) UN Doc UNEP/OzL.Pro.7/12, 33.

A. Initiation of Non-Compliance Procedures

The initiation of NCPs has been among the most contentious issues to resolve in MEA compliance negotiations. The least controversial trigger has been the self-trigger, which allows a party to bring itself before the committee seeking help with a particular issue of implementation or compliance. Experience has shown that this is not enough to bring important matters before a compliance committee. Similarly, the party-trigger, whereby a party can bring another party before the committee, has been shown at times to be a valuable trigger, but one that tends to play a limited role in the overall compliance effort. Allowing a group of parties to trigger a review of a party could offer a modest improvement to the party-trigger as it overcomes the barrier of a single party fearing retaliation for initiating non-compliance procedures against another party. Similarly, allowing the Conference of the Parties (COP) to initiate proceedings may be appropriate, but it is not on its own an adequate trigger.

Ultimately, therefore, the effectiveness of the compliance process will generally depend on an effective non-party trigger. The options available include: allowing the compliance committee to commence proceedings on its own initiative; providing for another institution within the regime to initiate; or allowing non-state actors outside the regime to initiate proceedings. The acceptability of each option will vary from regime to regime depending on the substantive obligations, the composition and design of the committee, and the parties involved.

Allowing the committee to initiate non-compliance proceedings can be an efficient way to trigger the process where there is clear and objective evidence of compliance issues that require the attention of the committee. As the decision to initiate proceedings moves from a technical assessment to a judgement call, resistance to granting compliance committees the power to initiate proceedings tends to grow.[24] Similarly, as the possible consequences of non-compliance become greater, the resistance to this type of trigger increases.[25] Where there is objective information available as the basis for the committee's decision to initiate proceedings, such as an expert review team's report on a party's performance of a particular set of commitments, there may be opportunities to overcome the resistance to clearly defined committee self-triggers.

[24] See Attila Tanzi and Cesare Pitea, 'Non-Compliance Mechanisms: Lessons Learned and the Way Forward' in Tullio Treves *et al* (eds), *Non-Compliance Procedures and Mechanisms and the Effectiveness of International Environmental Agreements* (TMC Asser Press 2009) 569.

[25] See the 1989 Basel Convention's Non-Compliance Procedures (NCP): Decision VI/12, 'Establishment of a mechanism for promoting implementation and compliance' (10 February 2003) UN Doc UNEP/CHW.6/40, 45 where the committee is only able to review information submitted to them partially to avoid risk of subjectivity; cf. Daniela Wehlend, 'Improving Compliance Mechanisms of the International Waste Trade Regime by Introducing Economic Compliance Incentives' in Armin Bogdandy, Rudiger Wolfrum, and Christiane Philipp (eds), *Max Planck Yearbook of United Nations Law*, 16/1 (2012): 397 where she discusses how this has not been helpful to the Basel Convention's inability to enforce its provisions.

An alternative to a committee trigger would be a trigger involving another institution within the regime. Options include expert review teams,[26] the secretariat,[27] or the COP itself.[28] Institutional triggers are sometimes tied to specific reports or similar sources of information in an effort to limit the discretion to initiate NCPs.[29] In the 1997 Kyoto Protocol compliance system, for example, the dominant trigger was the referral of issues of compliance by expert review teams tasked with reviewing reports and systems established by parties to comply with procedural and substantive obligations.

The most controversial trigger for the initiation of non-compliance proceedings is to allow civil society a role in the triggering process. Options vary from allowing specific actors a role,[30] to a general mechanism available to all non-state actors, including individuals and NGOs. The role of non-state actors in the triggering process can range from being able to initiate,[31] to being able to petition a regime institution to initiate proceedings.[32] Possible safeguards against abuse of a civil society trigger include the ability to reject applications that are frivolous or vexatious, and the inclusion of specific criteria that a petition or application has to meet in order to be considered.[33]

B. Scope and Mandate

The scope of NCPs and the related mandate of the compliance committee tends to be another contentious issue in compliance negotiations. The scope and mandate questions

[26] Decision 27/CMP.1, 'Procedures and mechanisms relating to compliance under the Kyoto Protocol' (30 March 2006) FCCC/KP/CMP/2005/8/Add.3, 92 (Kyoto Protocol NCP).

[27] See 1973 Convention on International Trade in Endangered Species of Wild Fauna and Flora (CITES) Res Conf.14.3, 'CITES compliance procedures' (2–15 June 2007) annex—'Guide to CITES compliance procedures' (CITES NCP); Decision IV/5, 'Non-compliance procedures' (25 November 1992) UN Doc UNEP/OzL.Pro.4/15, 16 amended by Decision X/10, 'Review of the non-compliance procedure' (3 December 1998) UN Doc UNEP/OzL.Pro.10/9, 25 (Montreal Protocol NCP).

[28] See 2013 Minamata Convention on Mercury.

[29] See ibid; the 2001 International Treaty on Plant Genetic Resources for Food and Agriculture (ITPGRFA) Res 2/2011, 'Procedures and operational mechanisms to promote compliance and address issues of non-compliance' (14–18 March 2011) (ITPGRFA NCP); Decision BS-I/7, 'Establishment of procedures and mechanisms on compliance under the Cartagena Protocol on Biosafety' (14 April 2004) UN Doc UNEP/CBD/BS/COP-MOP/1/15, 98, annex—'Procedures and mechanisms on compliance' (Cartagena Protocol NCP); Kyoto Protocol NCP (n 26); 'Compliance Procedures and Mechanisms pursuant to Article 11 of the 1996 Protocol to the London Convention 1972 (adopted in 2007: LC 29/17, annex 7)' <https://www.imo.org/en/OurWork/Environment/LCLP/Compliance/Documents/Compliance%20Procedures.pdf> accessed 14 January 2020; Basel Convention NCP (n 25); Montreal Protocol NCP (n 27).

[30] CITES NCP (n 27).

[31] Decision I/7, 'Review of compliance' (2 April 2004) UN Doc ECE/MP.PP/2/Add.8 (1998 Aarhus Convention NCP).

[32] CITES NCP (n 27); Decision III/2, 'Review of compliance' (4 June 2004) ECE/MP.EIA/6 as amended by Decision VI/2, 'Review of compliance with the Convention' (2014) ECE/MP.EIA/20/Add.1 (1991 Espoo Convention NCP).

[33] See the ability to reject applications within the Aarhus Convention NCP (n 31) para 18.

are often linked to the compliance systems' role in facilitating, incentivizing, and enforcing compliance, but also have a broader ambit. For instance, should the compliance system focus on selective primary rules, such as binding obligations, or consider all substantive provisions?[34] Similar differences exist over the extent to which a compliance system should look beyond instances involving individual parties to consider systemic issues or collective commitments and obligations.[35] Other issues that can arise include whether a committee deals with technical versus political determinations of compliance, and whether the committee treats different parties, or groups of parties differently, such as based on the principle of common but differentiated responsibilities (CBDR).[36]

C. Institutional Design and Process

Often less contentious but no less important or complex are the institutional arrangements and the process design. In the MEA experience, we see a range of institutional arrangements. The most common form uses a specialized committee, but there are instances of the compliance process being in the hands of a general standing committee or the COP. For those NCPs with specialized committees, membership is a key issue, in terms of regional distribution, independence, and expertise. Most committees have tended towards some formula of membership based on the five United Nations (UN) regions with some adjustments in light of the unique circumstances of the regime.[37] Most compliance systems have emphasized expertise and independence, while still allowing members to be nominated by parties and representing pre-determined regions.[38]

The internal structure of compliance committees ranges. Some operate as one committee,[39] while others are divided into branches with distinct tasks.[40] Some also include a bureau of co-chairs to take on specified tasks, such as screening applications, dismissing frivolous matters, allocating matters to appropriate branches or committees, or separating general or systemic compliance issues from more specific ones.[41]

[34] Contrast the Basel Convention NCP (n 25) and the Kyoto Protocol NCP (n 26) which are more restrictive than the Minamata Convention.

[35] See the Minamata Convention, art 15.2, where systemic issues are considered as well as individual ones.

[36] Contrast the London Convention NCP (n 29) where the circumstances of each country are considered, but on a more subjective basis than with the Montreal Protocol NCP (n 27) where each country has common, but differentiated responsibilities depending on an objective measurement.

[37] Basel Convention NCP (n 25); Kyoto Protocol NCP (n 26); Decision RC-3/4, 'Draft text of the procedures and mechanisms on compliance with the Rotterdam Convention' (10 November 2006) UNEP/FAO/RC/COP.3/26 (Rotterdam Convention Draft NCP); Minamata Convention.

[38] Earlier MEAs such as CITES NCP (n 27) and Montreal Protocol NCP (n 27) do not have independent experts but are representatives of the parties involved.

[39] See Basel Convention NCP (n 25); London Protocol NCP (n 29); Rotterdam Convention Draft NCP (n 37); Minamata Convention.

[40] Kyoto Protocol NCP (n 26).

[41] CITES NCP (n 27).

Compliance systems have taken a range of approaches to other institutional issues, such as the role of alternates, terms of appointments, liability, and decision-making. Most strive to make decisions by consensus and allow for some level of majority voting in cases where consensus is not possible.[42]

Key issues with respect to the design of the process include transparency, accountability, and due process. With respect to transparency, access to the information being considered by the committee and to the hearings are particularly important. A challenging issue is often the consideration of confidential information that is important for the work of the committee, including what information is considered confidential. Similarly, drawing an appropriate line between public hearings and private deliberations can be a challenge, as can be the use of electronic means to replace in-person meetings, and the implications for public access. Most importantly, there is often a tension between public access to the proceedings and the comfort of some of the parties with other elements of the compliance system, such as the scope, triggers, and consequences.[43]

With respect to accountability, in addition to transparency in terms of the process and information, the requirement to give detailed reasons for the decisions made in line with the mandate and direction under which the committee operates is critical. This is often complemented with requirements to report annually to the COPs on the committee's activities. These requirements to justify its decisions and actions, in combination with transparency of information and hearings, makes up the core of the accountability provisions of compliance systems under MEAs.[44] Some compliance systems have, in addition, experimented with opportunities to appeal decisions.[45] In the absence of an independent appeals tribunal similar to that of the WTO Appellate Body, there is little indication that opportunities to appeal decisions of the compliance committee have been utilized extensively, let alone that they have significantly contributed to the accountability of the compliance committee.[46]

Due process requirements tend to focus on the rights of accused parties to know the case against them, to have access to all information before the committee, and to have the opportunity to respond fully in writing and often also orally to the allegations made against parties. Due process can arise at the preliminary stage of deciding whether to take on a case, during the course of the proceedings, and at the decision-making and follow-up stages of the process.[47]

[42] This applies to most treaties discussed, other than ITPGRFA NCP (n 29) which is by consensus unless another way is decided by consensus; Montreal Protocol NCP (n 27) is consensus only; Aarhus Convention NCP (n 31) is if there are different views, all views must be reflected in the final report.

[43] Massimiliano Montini, 'Procedural Guarantees in Non-Compliance Mechanisms' in Treves (n 24) 389, 395.

[44] Ibid, 397.

[45] See Kyoto Protocol NCP (n 26).

[46] Meinhard Doelle, 'Experience with the Facilitative and Enforcement Branches of the Kyoto Compliance System' in Brunnée, Doelle, and Rajamani (n 22) 102, 117.

[47] Montini (n 43) 394.

D. Measures and Outcomes

The choice of measures and outcomes is, to a significant extent, informed by the choice between a facilitative, enforcement, or combined approach. Among the design options are the following:

1. What tools the committee has available to identify possible non-compliance or sub-optimal implementation before it becomes a non-compliance issue and to provide facilitation, capacity-building, finance, and other support to prevent non-compliance or encourage more effective implementation;
2. The committee's powers to make a formal declaration of compliance or non-compliance;
3. What tools are available to the committee to motivate compliance such as through the imposition of sanctions, provision of incentives, or a combination;
4. What tools the committee has to follow-up to ensure a non-complying party takes the measures necessary to come into compliance.

Other than the obvious choice between facilitation and enforcement of compliance, there are a few key issues that arise in the context of measures and outcomes. One is the concern that offering financial and other support can be an incentive, not only to self-report, but actually to fail to comply with obligations a party may be able to meet without the available support. Giving the committee the mandate to ensure that the non-compliance is inadvertent rather than calculated to gain access to resources would respond to this concern but might in turn raise concerns about the political nature of a compliance committee's decisions. A preferred approach, therefore, might be either to limit the access to resources to least developed countries,[48] or to separate the provision of support from the work of the compliance committee.[49]

The inclusion of a formal finding of non-compliance has been surprisingly contentious in some recent compliance negotiations.[50] While some negotiators have sought to characterize it as a measure appropriate only in an adversarial enforcement context, a factual finding of whether a given commitment has been complied with or not seems an important starting point for both facilitation and enforcement. It is not surprising, therefore, that a finding of non-compliance is a common element among most MEA

[48] See Montreal Protocol NCP (n 27) and discussion by Jacob Werksman, 'Compliance and Transition: Russia's Non-Compliance Tests the Ozone Regime' *ZaoRV*, 36 (1996): 750 on Russia's attempt to gain funding because of non-compliance.

[49] The Global Environment Fund is used in the Montreal Protocol and the Minamata convention. For further discussion see Francesca Jacur, 'The Non-Compliance Procedure of the 1987 Montreal Protocol to the 1985 Vienna Convention on Substances that Deplete the Ozone Layer' in Treves (n 24) 11, 30.

[50] Meinhard Doelle, 'Compliance in Transition: Facilitative Compliance Finding its Place in the Paris Climate Regime' *Carbon & Climate Law Review*, 12/3 (2018): 229.

compliance systems, whether they focus on facilitation or enforcement.[51] Where they differ, in the end, is with respect to the consequences imposed as a result of a finding of non-compliance.

The consequences utilized in MEA compliance systems tend to be more limited than other international regimes. Nevertheless, their range of possible approaches is quite wide. One approach is to focus on the provision of advice and reference to resources available outside the compliance system, either within the regime or outside it.[52] An alternative is to offer more direct support within the context of the compliance system, in terms of finance, technical expertise, education, capacity-building, or other form of direct support.[53] Moving from facilitation to enforcement, even some primarily facilitative compliance systems utilize sanctions (and incentives) to seek to encourage compliance.

IV. OVERVIEW OF MEA COMPLIANCE SYSTEMS

The four general elements of compliance systems discussed in the previous section feature prominently in existing MEA compliance systems. This section provides a high-level overview of compliance systems found across MEAs.

One of the earliest MEAs to include a non-compliance procedure was the CITES, though the process was not formalized until 2007. It operates through the CITES secretariat, a general standing committee, and the COP. Compliance issues are frequently identified by NGOs who submit information on suspected violations to the secretariat.[54] The secretariat has the power to receive such information, to investigate alleged violations, and to pass them on to the standing committee if they are deemed to warrant a formal response. The standing committee can make findings of non-compliance and recommendations both to the party being investigated and the COP. The standing committee has broad powers to investigate, to make findings, and to recommend specific actions, but its conclusions are non-binding. In addition to dealing with individual cases of non-compliance, the standing committee has also prepared general reports on general and systemic issues of non-compliance.[55]

[51] See CITES NCP (n 27); Montreal Protocol NCP (n 27); Basel Convention NCP (n 25); Kyoto Protocol NCP (n 26); Rotterdam Convention Draft NCP (n 37); Cartagena Protocol NCP (n 29); ITPGRFA NCP (n 29); Aarhus Convention NCP (n 31).

[52] See Basel Convention NCP (n 25); London Protocol NCP (n 29).

[53] See CITES NCP (n 27); Montreal Protocol NCP (n 27); Kyoto Protocol NCP (n 26).

[54] Barbara Gemmill and Abimbola Bamidele-Izu, 'The Role of NGOs and Civil Society in Global Environmental Governance' in Daniel Esty and Maria Ivanova (eds), *Global Environmental Governance: Options & Opportunities* (Yale School of Forestry & Environmental Studies 2002) 77, note that NGOs play a significant role; see also Peter Sand, 'Enforcing CITES: The Rise and Fall of Trade Sanctions' *Review of European, Comparative and International Environmental Law*, 22/3 (2013): 262.

[55] See CITES NCP (n 27).

The MEA considered by many to have been most effectively implemented to date is the Montreal Protocol on Ozone Depleting Substances. Given the success of the regime, it is not surprising that its compliance system is also highly regarded.[56] The process is generally considered facilitative, but it actually has a broad range of compliance tools at its disposal. It can require parties to submit reports, make binding decisions, issue warnings, make findings of non-compliance, impose some trade measures, and suspend some treaty privileges. The NCP operates under the direction of a ten-member committee with distributed geographical representation. The committee, in turn, operates under the supervision of the Meeting of the Parties (MOP) to the Montreal Protocol. Matters can come before the committee through self-reporting, party-to-party reporting, and on the initiative of the secretariat based on its review of implementation reports submitted by parties. A formal NGO trigger is not provided for. The Protocol incorporates a range of tools to support compliance by developing countries, including a fund to which developed countries are required to contribute. Decisions of the committee are made by consensus.[57]

The climate regime currently has two compliance systems, one under its 1997 Kyoto Protocol and one under the 2015 Paris Climate Agreement. The Kyoto compliance system has been operating since 2006, and will continue to do so for as long as the Kyoto Protocol still has a place in the regime. The NCP under the Kyoto Protocol has been the only compliance system to date to experiment with a combination of facilitation and enforcement through separate branches of the compliance committee.[58] Issues can be brought before the compliance committee through self-reporting, by another party, or by expert review teams tasked to review the performance of parties. The enforcement branch has the power to make findings of non-compliance, require the preparation of compliance plans, and suspend privileges under the Kyoto Protocol. In case of failure to reach emission reduction targets, the application of a penalty in the next commitment period is automatic.[59]

The compliance system under the Paris Climate Agreement was adopted in late 2018 and at the time of writing was just beginning its work. The compliance procedure under the Paris Agreement returns to the more traditional focus on facilitation, a cautious approach to triggering, and a somewhat limited scope. One of its potential innovations is its treatment of systemic issues. It is complemented by separate transparency and stocktake processes also designed to encourage the effective implementation of individual and collective goals of the Agreement.[60]

[56] See Marco Gonzalez, Kristen Taddonio, and Nancy Sherman, 'The Montreal Protocol: How Today's Successes Offer a Pathway to the Future' *Journal of Environmental Studies and Sciences*, 5/2 (2015): 122; Edith Weiss, 'The Five International Treaties: A Living History' in Edith Weiss and Harold Jacobson (eds), *Engaging Countries: Strengthening Compliance with International Environmental Accords* (MIT Press 1998) 89; Stephen Andersen, 'Lessons From the Stratospheric Ozone Layer Protection for Climate' *Journal of Environmental Studies and Sciences*, 5/2 (2015): 143.

[57] Montreal Protocol NCP (n 27).

[58] Kyoto Protocol NCP (n 26).

[59] Doelle (n 46).

[60] Gu Zihua, Christina Voigt, and Jacob Werksman, 'Facilitating Implementation and Promoting Compliance with the Paris Agreement Under Article 15: Conceptual Challenges and Pragmatic Choices' *Climate Law*, 9/1–2 (2019): 65.

The 2013 Minamata Convention on Mercury is one of the most recent, post-Kyoto MEAs to adopt and fully implement its NCPs. The process is facilitative, and the triggers are similar to those under the Montreal Protocol. An interesting innovation of the Minamata compliance system is that under Article 15.2 of the Convention, the compliance mandate specifically includes both individual cases and systemic issues. The Convention and its compliance procedures are fairly new, so there is not much experience to draw on to assess its effectiveness. Perhaps most significant is that it is largely based on the Montreal Protocol rather than the Kyoto Protocol, confirming a trend away from a separation of facilitative and enforcement approaches into distinct branches.

Finally, the Aarhus Convention was initially developed within Europe and while there have been efforts to broaden its membership, it is still largely a regional convention with a uniquely open and transparent non-compliance process. Perhaps its most notable innovation is its experiment with a formal citizen trigger.[61] In addition to the standard party and institutional triggers utilized in most regimes, the Aarhus Convention formally provides for private citizens to initiate non-compliance procedures. In practice, citizen petitions have resulted in the bulk of non-compliance proceedings under the Aarhus Convention.[62] The mandate of the compliance committee is quite broad. It permits the compliance committee to consider complaints connected to access to information, public participation in environmental decision-making, and access to justice. The measures available to the committee are similar to those under the Montreal Protocol.

There are, of course, a number of other MEAs that have non-compliance procedures. Some, such as the Basel Convention, have adopted procedures that have never been used. Others, such as the Rotterdam Convention, and the Stockholm Convention, have failed to conclude their compliance negotiations successfully. Others, particularly those negotiated before the Kyoto compliance system was adopted in 2005, have taken approaches similar to those described for the Montreal Protocol and the Minamata Convention.

V. CONCLUSION

This chapter's survey of experience with the design and implementation of compliance systems under MEAs suggests that the Montreal Protocol has emerged as the standard for MEA compliance systems. It is largely facilitative, but with some enforcement tools at its disposal. It is cautious in its approach to triggering, and offers some opportunities for differential treatment of parties according to CBDR. The Kyoto experience, on the

[61] Aarhus Convention NCP (n 31).

[62] Cesare Pitea, 'Procedures and Mechanisms for Review of Compliance under the 1998 Aarhus Convention on Access to Information, Public Participation and Access to Justice in Environmental Matters' in Treves (n 24) 221.

other hand, has shown that a compliance system with a dual function of facilitating and enforcing compliance can be effective. Nevertheless, to date, the Kyoto compliance system has been the outlier, with MEA regimes returning to the comfort of the Montreal approach, including the climate regime in the context of the Paris Agreement. It remains to be seen whether the compliance system under the Paris Agreement's approach to triggering will be effective, and whether its outcomes (including, in particular, its consideration of systemic issues) will improve compliance and implementation of the provisions of the agreement. Finally, the Aarhus Convention, particularly with respect to its approach to non-party triggers and transparency, continues to set a high bar for MEA compliance systems.

BIBLIOGRAPHY

Jutta Brunnée, Meinhard Doelle, and Lavanya Rajamani (eds), *Promoting Compliance in an Evolving Climate Change Regime* (CUP 2012)

Abram Chayes and Antonia Chayes, *The New Sovereignty: Compliance with International Regulatory Agreements* (Harvard University Press 1995)

George Downs, Kyle Danish, and Peter Barsoom, 'The Transformational Model of International Regime Design: Triumph of Hope or Experience?' *Columbia Journal of Transnational Law*, 38/3 (2000): 465

Tullio Treves et al (eds), *Non-compliance Procedures and Mechanisms and the Effectiveness of International Environmental Agreements* (TMC Asser Press 2009)

CHAPTER 57

EFFECTIVENESS

STEINAR ANDRESEN

I. INTRODUCTION

ESTABLISHING an international regime does not make much sense, unless it can be expected to have some effect. That realization motivated international relations (IR) scholars almost three decades ago to initiate a specific strand of research on regime effectiveness.[1] Many established regimes had 'matured', so it made sense to find out what practical significance they had in terms of solving the problems they had been intended to address. Most attention here has been paid to international *environmental* regimes.

Section II of this chapter introduces some key concepts: what international regimes are, how to measure their effectiveness (the dependent variable), how this can be explained (independent variable), and the severe methodological challenges associated with answering these questions. Two main explanatory perspectives are introduced: the nature of the problem dealt with by the regime and its problem-solving ability.[2] Section III then surveys some key general findings that have emerged from the study of the effectiveness of international environmental regimes. Perhaps the most important finding is that although most international regimes that have been studied have had some effect on the problems they address, they have very rarely been able—if at all—to solve them fully. Another important observation is the sizeable variation among regimes in their problem-solving ability. This section presents empirical examples to illustrate how effectiveness can be measured and explained in practice. Most attention is given to the global climate regime, given its prominence on the international agenda. Viewed from a problem-solving perspective, however, the climate regime emerges as a low-effectiveness regime. This is briefly contrasted with the highly successful international ozone regime, as well as a regime that is very hard to measure in terms of effectiveness

[1] Arild Underdal, 'The Concept of Regime Effectiveness' *Cooperation and Conflict*, 27/3 (1992): 227.

[2] Arild Underdal, 'Method of Analysis' in Edward Miles *et al* (eds), *Environmental Regime Effectiveness: Confronting Theory with Evidence* (MIT Press 2002) 47.

due to the deep and divisive conflicts over values, namely, the international whaling regime. Finally, Section IV offers some brief concluding remarks.

II. KEY CONCEPTS AND METHODOLOGICAL CHALLENGES

A. International Regimes

The study of international regimes concerns the significance of social institutions as determinants of interaction among actors in international politics, linked to the discussion of governance without government.[3] How is the concept of international regimes related to the concept of international institutions and organizations? Institutions are assemblages of rights, rules, and decision-making procedures that give rise to social practices, assigning rights to the participants in these practices and regulating interactions between them. International regimes differ from international organizations, as the latter are material entities with offices, budgets, and legal personalities. In empirical studies of international regimes—as in this chapter—the focus has been on multilateral environmental agreements (MEAs), which are usually equipped with secretariats, and with the same properties as international organizations.

A key premise in scholarship on international environmental regimes is that such regimes can make a difference. However, not everyone agrees. The 'realist' school, long dominant in IR studies, has held that international regimes are mere epiphenomena which reflect the interests of their most powerful members.[4] This perspective certainly has some merit and may be particularly applicable to international security regimes. Further, not all international regimes have made a difference: some are mere paper-tigers or 'dead-letter regimes'.[5] However, most of the international environmental regimes that have been studied have been shown to have had some effect on the actions and behaviour of their members.[6]

This chapter employs the approach taken by Steven Krasner (1983) in his classical definition of international regimes. Krasner defines international regimes as *intermediate* variables: although they may have an independent effect, they are rarely the main

[3] Oran Young, 'The Effectiveness of International Environmental Regimes: Existing Knowledge, Cutting-edge Themes and Research Strategies' *Proceedings of the National Academy of Sciences*, 108/50 (2011): 19853.

[4] John Mearsheimer, 'The False Promise of International Institutions' *International Security*, 19/3 (1995): 5.

[5] Marc Levy, Oran Young, and Michael Zurn, 'The Study of International Regimes' *European Journal of International Relations*, 1/3 (1995): 267.

[6] Miles *et al* (n 2); Helmut Breitmeier, Oran Young, and Michael Zürn, *Analyzing International Environmental Regimes: From Case Study to Database* (MIT Press 2006).

drivers in international politics. Other more basic forces, such as economic development, technological innovation, and population growth, tend to be more important. The challenge and key role of the international regimes is to channel and guide interaction in a 'positive' way within this broader framework.

B. Concept of Effectiveness

Effectiveness can be measured along three dimensions: output, outcome, and impact.[7] Output is the rules and regulation emanating from the regime, the formal requirements laid down for members to follow. As a point of departure, the stricter and more specific the rules, the higher their expected effectiveness. For example, a framework convention is usually less demanding or specific compared to its subsequent protocols. Also, legally binding conventions will normally have more regulatory bite than soft-law approaches, although this is not always the case due to variations among issue-areas under regulation.[8] Focusing on outputs and detailed studies of rules and regulation has been the traditional approach of international legal scholars.[9]

Political scientists and IR scholars cast the net wider by focusing also on the change(s) in behaviour caused by a regime, because regimes members do not always follow the rules. Seen from this perspective, output is not a 'true' indicator of the effectiveness of a regime: it can only indicate potential effectiveness. The advantage of using the output indicator is that it is fairly easy to measure and therefore scores high on reliability. However, as this indicator as such cannot show how effective the regime 'really' is, it scores lower on validity.

To study the effect of regimes in behavioural terms, the outcome variable is applied: how much of a (positive) change in behaviour among the relevant target groups follows from the regime in question? This is a key question for gauging the 'true' effectiveness of a regime. However, it is methodologically challenging to answer precisely, because of the difficulties establishing causality between the regime in question and behaviour on the ground. Other factors are often more important for changed behaviour than the regime. Causality, although difficult to establish, can be determined with a fairly high degree of precision, through careful process tracing, and detailed empirical studies.[10] This indicator, if successfully applied, has higher validity than the output indicator.

[7] Ronald Mitchell, *International Politics and the Environment* (Sage 2010); see also Chapter 51, 'Compliance Theory', in this volume.

[8] Jon Skjærseth, Olav Stokke, and Jørgen Wettestad, 'Soft Law, Hard Law and Effective Implementation of International Environmental Norms' *Global Environmental Politics*, 6/3 (2006): 104.

[9] Geir Ulfstein, with Thilo Marauhn and Andreas Zimmerman (eds), *Making Treaties Work: Human Rights, Environment and Arms Control* (CUP 2007).

[10] Olav Scram Stokke, *Disaggregating International Regime: A New Approach to Evaluation and Comparison* (MIT Press 2012).

The impact indicator—the actual problem-solving ability of a give regime—is really the ultimate question to be answered. However, due to the impact of a host of other regime-external factors on the actual level of problem-solving, there are huge methodological challenges entailed in using this indicator, as elaborated below.[11]

C. Methodological Challenges

Underdal in the Miles *et al* 2002 study used two distinct measurements of effectiveness: (1) performance obtained compared to the no-regime counterfactual, and (2) the actual state of affairs compared to the best solution that could be achieved (the collective optimum). The first dimension focuses on relative improvement caused by the regime; the second is designed to answer whether the problem has actually been solved (ie whether the regime had impact). Others have combined these two approaches into one comprehensive measure, 'arriving at a simple coefficient of regime effectiveness that falls into a standardized interval (0–1)'.[12] This would seem to give an elegant and scientifically clear answer to what has been achieved by various regimes—but is it possible in practice to provide such a score? As Young put it:

> How can we separate the signal of regime effects from the noise arising from the impacts of other sources that operate simultaneously in our efforts to understand regime effectiveness?[13]

In previous research, the present author has agreed with these points raised by Young.[14] However, there may be significant variations regarding how precisely effectiveness can be measured among regimes. In the climate regime, measurement is complicated by the 'noise' from so many other factors. Howsoever, a given regime leads to, say, a complete stop in the dumping of waste in the ocean, we can argue that the problem has been solved, and the proportional effect of the regime can be firmly determined.[15]

[11] Steinar Andresen, 'Effectiveness' in Philipp Pattberg and Fariborz Zelli (eds), *Encyclopedia of Global Environmental Governance and Politics* (Edward Elgar 2015) 441.

[12] Jon Hovi, Detlef Sprinz, and Arild Underdal, 'The Oslo–Potsdam Solution to Measuring Regime Effectiveness: Critique, Response and the Road Ahead' *Global Environmental Politics*, 3/3 (2003): 74.

[13] Oran Young, 'Inferences and Indices: Evaluating the Effectiveness of International Environmental Regimes' *Global Environmental Politics*, 1/1 (2001): 99.

[14] Steinar Andresen, 'International Regime Effectiveness' in Robert Falkner (ed), *The Handbook of Global Climate and Environment Policy* (Wiley-Blackwell 2013) 304; Andresen, 'Effectiveness' (n 11).

[15] Jon Birger Skjærseth, 'Toward the End of Dumping in the North Sea: The Case of the Oslo Commission' in Miles *et al* (n 2) 65.

D. Explaining Effectiveness

While there is broad consensus among regime scholars on how to measure effectiveness, (although not regarding the level of precision), there is no consensus on how to explain it. According to Mitchell, 'there is, arguably, an "embarrassment of riches" of variables, each with compelling logic and empirical support but which, collectively, lack logic'.[16] Edward Miles and colleagues, including the present author, used two explanatory perspectives: the nature of the problem, and the problem-solving ability of the regime in question.[17] A simplified account of this approach is presented below.

The focus on the nature of the problem sheds light on the character of the problem, whether it is 'malign' or 'benign', politically and/or intellectually. The more malign the problem, the more difficult it is to solve, therefore, less can be expected in terms of regime effectiveness. The degree of political 'malignancy' is particularly associated with the level of political conflict between the members of the regime, but various other dimensions are also relevant. For example, collective action problems are often associated with free-riding and strong differences between costs and benefits, over time as well as between regime members. Usually the problem is quite stable in nature, and difficult to change. It represents an important benchmark when comparing the effectiveness of various international regimes. As shown in Sections III.A and III.B, the main reason why the ozone regime has proven far more effective than the climate regime is the stark difference in problem malignancy. We cannot automatically conclude that the negotiators of the ozone regime did a better job than those negotiating the climate regime, as moving a knotty problem in the right direction may require more effort than solving a benign problem. This perspective is often neglected by policy-makers and media in comparing the performance of various diplomatic processes.

From an intellectual and policy perspective, the problem-solving perspective is more interesting as it can be more easily manipulated or changed. It can be conceived in terms of the configuration of power, leadership, and institutions. If powerful actors want a strong regime, that will increase the chances of a more effective regime, especially if those actors also exert leadership by generating followers. Conversely, if powerful actors are laggards, the chances of an effective regime are reduced. The discussion of the climate and ozone regimes in the following section illustrates what these differences mean in practice for the effectiveness of these regimes.

Regarding institutions, the general view is that the stronger and more sophisticated the institutions associated with the regime, the higher the chances of an effective regime, and vice versa. Important components are the strength of the associated secretariat and scientific input, and thereby the knowledge base of the decisions taken. Also, the existence of an epistemic community is expected to increase the effectiveness of a regime.[18]

16 Mitchell (n 7) 172.

17 Miles *et al* (n 2).

18 Peter Haas, 'Introduction: Epistemic Community and International Policy Coordination' *International Organization*, 1/1 (1992): 1; see also Chapter 40, 'Epistemic Communities', in this volume.

III. GENERAL FINDINGS AND EMPIRICAL EXAMPLES

Although there is a myriad of MEAs, relatively few of them have been studied empirically. Thus, generalization to the universe of all MEAs is not possible. The most important finding to date is that many MEAs have made a positive difference: without these regimes, the state of the global environment would have been worse. Still, the results achieved are not impressive. United Nations Environment Programme's (UNEP) 'Global Environmental Outlook—GEO 5'[19] stresses the significance of 'external noise' factors: economic globalization, population growth, hyper-consumerism, and the rise of emerging economies which all act to offset the positive effects of international environmental regimes. In a comprehensive account of ninety of the most important UN environmental goals, GEO 5 found that significant progress had been made on only four of them. There has been some progress in relation to forty goals, but little or no progress detected in forty-four. This is in line with the findings of empirical research.

MEAs vary considerably in their effectiveness. For example, among the thirty-seven units of analysis presented in the Miles *et al* study, the regime brought about significant improvement in more than half the cases.[20] On the other hand, in almost half the cases these regimes made little difference. As expected, MEAs dealing with malign problems tend to be less effective than those addressing benign ones. While there are examples of malign problems that have been dealt with effectively, that is more the exception than the rule. An important—and positive—finding is that most regimes tend to become more effective over time, usually from a moderate and general starting point. However, some of the overall improvements over time are due to 'fortunate circumstances' for which the regimes cannot take credit. Central factors here are the general demand from the public, and subsequent supply by governments—at least in the Organisation for Economic Co-operation and Development (OECD) region—of a more progressive environmental policy. Further, when there are economic downturns, like the global financial crisis, both demand and supply of environmental policy tend to fall.

As to the problem-solving perspective, power has been shown to be particularly important in dealing with malignant problems, as illustrated further below. Although some factors can be manipulated through careful institutional design and political engineering, this is a difficult exercise. Good institutional capacity is most important when it interacts with other positive forces like leadership and consensual science.[21] However,

[19] There was no similar overview in *Global Environment Outlook - GEO-6: Healthy Planet, Healthy People* (UNEP 2019).

[20] Miles *et al* (n 2); fifteen international regimes were studied, but they were split up into distinct time phases, yielding altogether thirty-seven units of analysis.

[21] Steinar Andresen *et al*, 'What Can be Learned from Experience with Scientific Advisory Committees in the Field of International Environmental Politics?' *Global Challenges*, 2/9 (2018): 1800055.

research has underlined the positive effect of MEA regimes in terms of facilitating transnational learning and contributing to strengthening the knowledge basis for decision-makers.[22]

This research will be fleshed out in the following empirical overview of the effectiveness of a few key international regimes.

A. The Climate-Change Regime—A Low-Effectiveness Regime

The challenge posed by climate change has been on the international political agenda for thirty years now. Formal negotiations within the UN started in 1991; the three main instruments (outputs) adopted are the 1992 United Nations Framework Convention on Climate Change (UNFCCC), the 1997 Kyoto Protocol, and the 2015 Paris Agreement.[23]

What characterizes the effectiveness of these instruments? The UNFCCC aims at stabilization of greenhouse gas (GHG) emissions at a level that would prevent dangerous anthropogenic interference with climate systems. The framework convention was described as a necessary start: process-oriented and focusing on the need to assemble more and better data domestically, and to introduce reporting requirements for the parties.[24] Most attention, however, was paid to the target and timetable approach, and whether the Convention should be legally binding. The result was a 'soft' obligation: the OECD (Annex 1) countries should aim for stabilization of their emissions by the year 2000. In the Kyoto Protocol it was decided that the Annex I countries should reduce their emissions by an average of 5% by 2018–12. Hence the Protocol, in terms of output, represented a strengthening of Annex 1 country obligations compared to the UNFCCC. That is, its effectiveness was *potentially* higher. However, a major weakness was soon demonstrated: it applied only to Annex I members despite the sharp increase in emissions in the global South.[25]

Policy-makers and analysts have hailed the Paris Agreement as a huge step in the right direction. Virtually all states have now accepted responsibility for taking measures to reduce emissions, as against a business-as-usual scenario. Moreover, it is argued that ambition will be increased subsequently. To this end, centralized collective appraisals—a global stocktake—are to be conducted regularly. The Agreement specifies the ambitious goal of holding the increase in global average temperatures to well below 2°C, and of pursuing efforts to limit this increase to 1.5°C.

22 Miles *et al* (n 2).

23 See further Chapter 29, 'Climate Change', in this volume.

24 Daniel Bodansky, 'The United Nations Framework Convention on Climate Change: A Commentary' *Yale Journal of International Law*, 18/2 (1993): 451.

25 Steinar Andresen, 'The Paris Agreement and its Rulebook in a Problem-Solving Perspective' *Climate Law*, 9 (2019): 122.

The price of getting everybody on board, however, has been the 'bottom-up' approach, which is the backbone of the treaty. The Paris Agreement obliges parties to submit pledges—termed nationally determined contributions (NDC)—on a regular basis. All states thus voluntarily decide their own goals and means of achieving them. While this is far more realistic than the top-down approach, it has been seen as weaker compared to a top-down, legally binding approach.[26] Moreover, the very fact that all members—with widely diverging interests and preferences—have hailed the Agreement as a success is indicative of its vagueness.[27] No doubt, the Paris Agreement contains some creative and positive elements but, as yet, we cannot know what it will mean in practical terms. Regarding emissions trajectories, it is expected that current NDCs will result in a global warming close to 3°C, rendering the 2°C target a distant dream—and the 1.5°C ambition even more so.

Where does this leave us in terms of overall problem-solving effectiveness after thirty years of intense diplomatic effort? The goal of the UNFCCC was to stabilize emissions—but CO_2 emissions have been rising sharply and are today more than 60% higher than when the Convention was adopted.[28] The adoption of these instruments (outputs) has not translated into the intended behavioural change among key target groups worldwide (outcome).

However, the process has undoubtedly stimulated learning and attention towards the necessity of a more sustainable and green development path. The issue is now very high on the international political agenda, and the public at large are more aware of the problem. The UN process probably also deserves some credit for positive developments regarding greater use of renewable energy, for example, but the market as well as domestic economic and political drivers are equally, if not more, important. Still, applying the counterfactual argument, emissions would probably have been higher without the UN regime.

How can we explain the inability of the climate regime to deal more effectively with this problem in light of the two explanatory perspectives outlined above? As to the nature of the problem, the challenge of climate change is exceedingly malign. Climate change is traditionally seen as an environmental problem and, in a sense, this is correct. However, it runs much deeper in international society, as virtually all types of human activity are intrinsically linked to this problem. Emissions involve virtually millions of individual micro-decisions. The main drivers of emissions are economic development (growth), population growth, and energy use. How, then, can we realistically expect a voluntary, broad, and essentially weak global environmental regime to affect these basic drivers, recalling that international regimes are intermediate variables? For all the talk of the necessity of environmental sustainability in various UN bodies and elsewhere,

[26] Robert Falkner, 'The Paris Agreement and the New Logic of International Climate Politics' *International Affairs*, 92/5 (2016): 1107.

[27] Steinar Andresen *et al*, 'The Paris Agreement: Consequences for the EU and Carbon Markets?' *Politics and Governance*, 4/ 3 (2016): 188.

[28] Andresen, 'Experience with Scientific Advisory Committees' (n 21).

economic growth is still the mantra for all states everywhere. Moreover, neither population growth nor international trade can realistically be controlled by the climate regime.

Other challenges associated with this collective-action problem are that the costs of reduction are concentrated, high, and up-front, while the benefits are distant and more diffuse. In addition, temptations for free-riding are strong, and the issue of fairness between the North and the South looms large. Today's developed countries industrialized and expanded their economies without considering GHG emissions. Understandably, then, developing countries argue that they too are entitled to prioritize economic development and poverty reduction over curbing their GHG emissions. This exacerbates the problem, as the strongest economic growth, increases in population and increases in emissions are taking place in the global South. Thus, a truly malign problem is a key factor in explaining why the climate regime has not managed to curb GHG emissions adequately.

Turning to our other explanatory factor, could more have been achieved if the problem-solving ability of the regime had been higher? Here the focus is on the combination of power and leadership. As noted, if powerful actors also stand forth as leaders, the chances of a more effective regime increase. However, this combination has rarely been seen in connection with negotiating the climate regime. Basically, the most powerful actor throughout most of this period has been the United States, but it has generally acted more as a laggard than as a leader. The most ambitious major actor has been the European Union (EU), but it has generally failed to generate a critical mass of followers.[29]

For example, in the UNFCCC negotiations, the United States managed to get acceptance for a 'soft' agreement regarding stabilization targets. The EU and other small progressive actors were not able to win through with their goal of a legally binding approach.[30] Also in the Kyoto negotiations, the United States was the most powerful actor, particularly in getting acceptance for the market mechanisms.[31] The significance of the Kyoto Protocol was sharply reduced, however, when the United States, the largest emitter at the time, refused to ratify the treaty in 2001.

The United States again played a key role in the making of the Paris Agreement. The crucial building block was the preceding bilateral agreement between the two most powerful actors, China and the United States (the G-2). Together they accounted for some 40% of global GHG emissions, rendering them very powerful in the negotiations. Some have argued that the United States served as leader in the process towards the Paris Agreement.[32] In this author's opinion, the United States acted primarily to secure

[29] Ibid.

[30] Bodansky (n 24).

[31] Michael Grubb, Christiaan Vrolijk, and Duncan Brack, *The Kyoto Protocol: A Guide and Assessment* (Royal Institute of International Affairs 1999).

[32] Charles Parker and Chrsiter Karlsson, 'The UN Climate Change Negotiations and the Role of the United States: Assessing American Leadership from Copenhagen to Paris' *Environmental Politics*, 27/ 3 (2018): 519.

its national interests through the adoption of the bottom–up approach, which the United States had favoured throughout much of the process. Moreover, the Agreement was shaped in a way that President Obama could sign it as an Executive Order: Senate ratification was not necessary. This was skilful diplomacy—but not leadership. We see that both the nature of the problem and the problem-solving ability of the regime explain why this regime scores low on effectiveness.

B. The Ozone Regime: A Rare Success Story

When policy-makers and analysts mention successful environmental diplomacy, they all usually refer to the ozone regime, the only global environmental regime with high effectiveness.[33]

In 1974 the theory was launched that a group of man-made chemicals called chlorofluorocarbons (CFCs) were destroying the ozone layer. During subsequent years the issue was discussed in scientific circles. Negotiations on a legally binding approach started in 1981. In 1985, the Vienna Convention on the Protection of the Ozone Layer was signed by twenty states and the EU. This was a traditional general framework convention. In contrast, the 1987 Montreal Protocol, adopted only two years later, represented a major step forward in terms of output in specificity and stringency. The Protocol included specific measures and timetables for reducing the production and consumption of ozone-depleting substances. Subsequent amendments have sped up and further specified these obligations through more ambitious timetables and the addition of new substances. The Montreal Protocol has evolved into a truly global agreement of universal state participation. Domestic implementation of commitments has varied somewhat, but it has been successful overall. By 2010, more than 95% of all production and use of chemicals controlled by the Montreal Protocol had been phased out.[34]

However, the nature of the challenge posed by emissions of CFC gases is benign compared to the challenge posed by GHG emissions. The number of consumers and producers is limited; nor it does not go to the heart of all economic activity—as the climate-change problem does. Moreover, it soon became clear that there were less harmful substitutes available that could replace CFC gases. Such a simple 'technological fix' has not been found for the climate regime. In terms of problem structure, the challenges posed by the CFC problem were modest compared to the climate-change problem.

There is also a strong contrast between the two regimes as to problem-solving ability. The start of the ozone process was rather slow, because of sharp political conflicts primarily between the United States and the EU, manifested in the weak Vienna

[33] Jon Birger Skjærseth, 'International Ozone Policies: Effective Environmental Cooperation' in Steinar Andresen, Elin Lerum Boasson, and Geir Hønneland (eds), *International Environmental Agreements: An Introduction* (Routledge 2012) 38.

[34] Ibid.

Convention. However, conflicts were gradually reduced, particularly when it became clear that alternative gases could be used. Here the United States was the main leader and pushed for a strong agreement—un doubtedly an important reason for the emergence of an effective agreement.

As to the institutional set-up, scientific uncertainty and disputes initially characterized the ozone process. However, gradually an elaborate scientific organization was established, forging subsequent scientific consensus. Also, in contrast to the climate regime, policy-makers closely followed the advice given by the various scientific bodies. However, this does not conclusively indicate that the science–policy nexus in the ozone regime was superior to that of the Intergovernmental Panel on Climate Change (IPCC). The economic costs of following scientific advice in the ozone regime were moderate compared to the climate regime.[35]

The ozone regime started out as a narrow regime in terms of geographic participation with only some developed countries taking part. From the perspective of effectiveness, as well as legitimacy, it was essential to bring the global South on board, and developing countries were offered clever incentives. First, due to their lower administrative capacity, they were given an extra decade to comply with commitments. Importantly, in 1990 a Multilateral Fund, financed by the developed states, was set up to support phase-outs in developing countries. This mechanism has proven very effective. Significant amounts have been channelled through the Fund, but less than for similar financial mechanisms within the climate regime. Again, that this Fund has been so notably effective illustrates the stark difference in terms of malignancy between the two regimes: the economic costs involved within the ozone regime are modest.

The negotiators of the ozone regime certainly deserve credit for their skilful diplomacy. However, we cannot automatically conclude that their problem-solving ability has been superior to that of the climate negotiators.

C. The Whaling Regime: Different Values Make Effectiveness Studies Difficult

The International Whaling Commission (IWC), established in 1948, is one of the oldest international organizations dealing with international environmental and resource cooperation.[36] It is also among those that have been transformed most dramatically in terms of institutional set-up, power, leadership, and values.[37]

The purpose of the 1946 Convention for the Regulation of Whaling (ICRW) is to provide for the proper conservation of whale stocks, thereby enabling the orderly

35 Andresen, 'Experience with Scientific Advisory Committees' (n 21).

36 See also Chapter 32, 'Wildlife', in this volume.

37 Steinar Andresen, 'Science and Policy in the International Whaling Commission' in M J Peterson (ed), *Contesting Global Environmental Knowledge, Norms and Governance* (Routledge 2019) 110.

development of the whaling industry. The history of the IWC may be split into different stages, because of the considerable variations in approach adopted, as well as in its effectiveness.[38]

The first stage goes from the late 1940s until the early 1960s. Briefly put, this period can be characterized by demonstrating neither conservation nor orderly development of the whaling industry. In those years the IWC was thus a failure in both economic and ecological terms. By the end of this period the whaling industry had been virtually wiped out, likewise most of the large Antarctica species like blue whales and fin whales. The next stage, until the late 1970s, scores markedly higher in terms of effectiveness, with several measures gradually introduced to secure better conservation.

The evaluation of effectiveness is fairly straightforward for these two phases. However, evaluating the third, protectionist, IWC phase—in the 1980s and 1990s—is far more difficult, due to the sharp polarization between pro- and anti-whaling forces. The milestone decision was the adoption of the moratorium in 1982, prohibiting commercial catches of the large whales under the purview of the IWC. Given the previous history of massive depletion, this can be regarded as a necessary step in terms of conservation. The large majority supporting the adoption of the moratorium no doubt saw it as greatly enhancing the effectiveness of the IWC. Unlike most decisions in international organizations, this decision was also effectively implemented: by the end of the 1980s, there was no more commercial whaling.[39] This yields a high effectiveness score in terms of outcome—*if* we accept this majority view as valid.

The minority of members, in favour of commercial whaling, have disagreed, claiming that the moratorium is ineffective from a biological as well as an economic perspective. These sharply diverging views were reflected in a questionnaire distributed to IWC members.[40] The pro-whalers bolstered their position by noting that the IWC Scientific Committee had *not* recommended a blanket moratorium, but that more selective conservation measures should be adopted.[41] They also pointed out that a moratorium was clearly counter to the official goal of the ICRW: to provide for the 'orderly development' of the whaling industry.

Where does this leave us in terms of assigning a score on effectiveness in this stage of the history of the IWC? Does it make sense to use a goal that was adopted more than fifty years ago, and under very different circumstances, as a valid measurement tool for effectiveness? The large majority, the anti-whaling nations, argued that the real goal of the IWC had changed, and that it would be a violation of the new spirit of the IWC not to protect the large whales from exploitation. Many members were also opposed

[38] Steinar Andresen, 'The International Whaling Commission (IWC): More Failure than Success?' in Miles *et al* (n 2) 47.

[39] Some commercial whaling resumed later, but this has not been accepted by the IWC majority, and the moratorium still stands.

[40] Jørgen Wettestad and Steinar Andresen, *The Effectiveness of International Environmental and Resource Regimes: Some Preliminary Findings* (The Fridtjof Nansen Institute 1991).

[41] Steinar Andresen, 'The Whaling Regime' in Steinar Andresen *et al*, *Science in International Environmental Regimes: Between Integrity and Involvement* (Manchester University Press 2000) 35.

to whaling as a matter of principle (it was morally wrong to kill these huge marine mammals). In contrast, the few remaining pro-whaling nations argued that the moratorium lacked scientific underpinning, and that continued (modest) harvesting was both rational and necessary. Given these strongly varying views, it makes most sense to argue that the score is undetermined, because of the difficulty of making value-free judgements; or that the score varies, depending on the indicator used.

Explaining the very poor performance of the IWC in its first phase is a straightforward matter. In terms of power, the Antarctica whaling nations were the dominant players, and the short-term economic interests of catching as many whales, as fast as possible, paved the way for the 'Whaling Olympics'.[42] Institutional deficiencies were also important: the scientific underpinning of decisions taken was extremely weak, and there was sharp disagreement in the scientific community.[43] The independent institutional basis was also very weak, as there was no IWC Secretariat in this period.

The next stage saw significant changes along all these dimensions. First, the scientific base improved significantly: there was considerable growth in the membership of the Scientific Committee, provisions were made for independent scientists to be brought in, and far more specific and consensual scientific advice was provided. This is one explanation for the more effective and conservation-oriented approach adopted by the Commission. Administrative capacity was also strengthened with the establishment of an IWC Secretariat in 1975.

However, the pivotal political development occurred outside the IWC. Whereas whaling in the 1950s and 1960s had proceeded without interference from external interests, this changed dramatically in the 1970s. The emerging environmental movement, particularly strong in the United States and parts of western Europe, adopted the whale as a symbol. At the UN Conference on the Human Environment in Stockholm in 1972, a ten-year moratorium on commercial whaling was called for. This shift in perceptions, and the significant growth in public opinion, strengthened the position of the non-whaling members of the IWC; the pro-whalers saw their position gradually reduced, and only a handful remained.

The United States emerged as the most powerful player. Solidly in favour of a more conservation-oriented approach, it was also at the forefront in strengthening the role of the IWC Scientific Committee. On the whole, then, the United States played a leadership role in changing the IWC.

In short, a combination of institutional strengthening of the IWC, as well as a shift in power and new leadership, helped to make it a more effective international organization. After decades of over-exploitation, the IWC finally seemed to be moving in the right direction.

[42] Alf Håkon Hoel, *The International Whaling Commission (1972–1984): New Members, New Concerns* (The Fridtjof Nansen Institute 1985).

[43] Tore Schweder, 'Distortion of Uncertainty in Science: Antarctic Fin Whales in the 1950s' *Journal of International Wildlife Law and Policy*, 3/1 (2000): 73.

How then can we explain the staunchly protectionist approach that was adopted, when the IWC had already become more conservation-oriented and scientists warned against a blanket moratorium? A complete shift of values explains why: 'saving the whales is for millions of people a crucial test of their political ability to halt environmental destruction'.[44] A large and powerful coalition of green NGOs, non-whaling nations with firm backing from the public, succeeded in changing the agenda—indeed, the very thinking about whales and whaling. Whaling was turned into a moral question: saving the whale was associated with a morally correct approach; catching (killing) whales was morally inferior or bad. It appeared that a new and almost-universal norm had been born.[45]

In this changed setting, the United States played a crucial role. The anti-whaling forces would no doubt argue that the United States played a leadership role in getting the moratorium adopted and even more so in getting it implemented. To get the moratorium adopted, new anti-whaling members would have to be recruited to join the IWC. Thanks to a creative and forceful strategy, particularly on the part of the United States, but also Greenpeace, this was achieved, and the IWC was packed with new (anti-whaling) members during the early 1980s.[46] At the adoption of the moratorium there were forty-two members; only a handful whaling nations objected to the moratorium. However, under the threat of US economic sanctions, all commercial whaling halted. Thus, the United States secured highly effective implementation of the moratorium. However, the pro-whaling nations Norway, Iceland, and Japan saw this not as leadership, but as traditional power politics, with Washington DC imposing its will on other states.

The whaling case illustrates the challenges involved in determining effectiveness and in choosing the labels to use in explaining it.

IV. CONCLUDING REMARKS

There is good news from extensive research on the effectiveness of international environmental regimes: such regimes generally do make a positive difference. That is, international environmental problems would have been more severe in the absence of these regimes. The not-so-good news is that these regimes are rarely, if ever, able to solve fully the problems they deal with. There are also noteworthy variations in their problem-solving effectiveness, due largely to differences in the problem-structure facing the decision-makers. This has been empirically illustrated by the cases of the climate and the ozone regimes, whereas the case of the international whaling regime illustrates the challenges of 'objective' scoring of effectiveness when there are deeply-held values

44 Sydney Holt, 'Whale Mining, Whale Saving' *Marine Policy*, 9/3 (1985): 92.

45 Jennifer Bailey, 'Arrested Development: The Prohibition of Commercial Whaling as a Case of Failed Norm Change' *European Journal of International Relations*, 14/2 (2008): 289.

46 Andresen, 'Whaling Regime' (n 41).

involved. Analysis of these regimes also illustrates that problem-solving ability makes a difference too and varies significantly. Having powerful actors as leaders who push for ambitious goals can significantly boost regime effectiveness.

However, there are serious methodological challenges entailed in determining the precise role played by international regimes in dealing with environmental problems. Usually they are intermediate variables, and the influence of more basic independent background variables is often very significant. Although this is a severe methodological challenge, it should not restrain us from further studies into the significance of international environmental regimes through continued refinement of method and approach, as well as detailed empirical studies. Global environmental challenges posed by, for example, climate change and loss of biodiversity are more severe than ever and research is one key element in boosting the ability of policy-makers to deal more effectively with them.

BIBLIOGRAPHY

Steinar Andresen, 'The Paris Agreement and its Rulebook in a Problem-Solving Perspective' *Climate Law*, 9 (2019): 122

Steinar Andresen, 'Science and Policy in the International Whaling Commission' in M J Peterson (ed), *Contesting Global Environmental Knowledge, Norms and Governance* (Routledge 2019) 110

CHAPTER 58

INTERNATIONAL ENVIRONMENTAL RESPONSIBILITY AND LIABILITY

CHRISTINA VOIGT

I. AN INTRODUCTION TO 'ENVIRONMENTAL ACCOUNTABILITY'

THE accountability of the subjects of international law for their acts and omissions, and the consequences thereof, is fundamental to the effectiveness and legitimacy of international law.[1] Yet, the international environmental accountability of states remains a difficult and controversial topic, for both doctrinal and political reasons. With few exceptions, states have not addressed this question in international environmental treaty law, neither have international courts been burdened with cases or requests for advisory opinions on questions of environmental responsibility or liability of states.[2]

For the purpose of this chapter, accountability is used as an 'umbrella term' and refers both to the responsibility of states and international organizations for internationally wrongful acts, as well as to their liability to make reparation for harm and damages resulting from their activities.

Accountability for internationally illegal acts, such as breach of a treaty or the violation of customary law rules, is relatively well developed in general international law under the concept of state responsibility, though not in a codified, treaty-based manner

[1] James Crawford and Jeremy Watkins, 'International Responsibility' in John Tasioulas and Samantha Besson (eds), *The Philosophy of International Law* (OUP 2010) 293; Ruth Grant and Robert Keohane, 'Accountability and Abuses of Power in World Politics' *American Political Science Review*, 99/1 (2005): 29, 35.

[2] Alan Boyle and James Harrison, 'Judicial Settlement of International Environmental Disputes: Current Problems' *Journal of International Dispute Settlement*, 4/2 (2013): 245.

and some uncertainties exist.[3] In general, 'state responsibility' refers to the accountability of a state for a violation of international law and is premised upon an internationally wrongful act which can be attributed to a state.[4] Such an internationally wrongful act can arise from the breach of an international legal obligation ('primary law'), established by treaty law (eg bilateral or multilateral environmental agreements) or by a customary norm of international law (eg the prohibition of environmental harm).[5] The consequences of international responsibility for a wrongful act are the obligation of the wrongdoer to cease that act, to offer assurances of non-repetition, and to make full reparation of the injury caused by the internationally wrongful act, including compensation for environmental damage.[6]

Rules for strict liability, however, for environmental harm resulting from lawful activities are not so well established, and remain singular and exceptional. In general, states have shown little interest in setting up a liability framework for environmental damage, and only very few international environmental regimes impose liability and compensation schemes on states. Some issue-specific international environmental treaties impose civil liability on private actors, but do not establish a compensation scheme for states. Those liability rules are not used to prevent pollution or damage, but serve as a 'backstop' to provide access to compensation when damage occurs despite the implementation of treaty rules that aim at preventing damage.[7]

Environmental damage can occur by accident or non-accidentally. In the latter case, compensation can be claimed where a state did not exercise proper care so as not to cause adverse environmental harm to other states or areas beyond national jurisdiction or to prevent others on its territory from causing such harm. This standard is captured by the concept of 'due diligence' which has been defined to require what a responsible government can be reasonably expected to do under normal conditions in a similar situation; applying its best practicable and available means to prevent environmental harm. Due diligence does not only refer to unlawful omissions by a state, but also predominantly to the obligation of conduct to show proper care by exercising good government, management and control, for example, through enacting necessary legislation, effective law enforcement to prevent or terminate illegal activities.

This chapter will provide an analysis of the relationship between international environmental law and state responsibility,[8] including a discussion of primary obligations, environmental harm, and the standard of care/due diligence.

[3] See 'Report of the International Law Commission on the work of its fifty-third session' (2001) UN Doc A/56/10, ch IV.E—'Draft Articles on Responsibility of States for Internationally Wrongful Acts'.

[4] James Crawford, *State Responsibility: The General Part* (CUP 2013) ch 1, 'Historical Development'.

[5] See generally James Crawford, *The ILC's Articles on State Responsibility: Introduction, Text and Commentaries* (CUP 2002); James Crawford, Alain Pellet, and Simon Olleson (eds), *The Law of International Responsibility* (OUP 2010).

[6] ILC, 'Draft Articles on Responsibility' (n 3) arts 30, 31.

[7] Daniel Bodansky, *The Art and Craft of International Environmental Law* (Harvard University Press 2010) 83.

[8] This chapter will not address civil liability of private actors, for which see Chapter 10, 'Economics', in this volume.

II. 'ENVIRONMENTAL ACCOUNTABILITY': SOME CHALLENGES

There are several challenges to establishing accountability for environmental harm: First, international environmental harm is, in many cases, not caused by state activity per se, but mostly by acts or omissions of private actors. In order to establish state responsibility, such acts or omissions need to be attributable to the state, or the state must have violated the obligation to apply reasonable care in its exercise of government functions (due diligence). The foundational obligation to avoid significant transboundary harm is not strict and absolute, but requires that adequate and appropriate efforts are made to prevent harm.[9] There are significant difficulties in establishing a lack of diligence on the part of a state. As states differ widely in their capacities to protect the environment and to avoid international environmental harm, the definition of a generally reasonable standard of conduct is difficult to establish.[10]

Second, environmental harm is often caused by the complex interplay of various factors. It is sometimes caused by a single event, but more often by the accumulated impacts of different actions (often by different actors, and over a long time). Proving causation can therefore be immensely challenging.[11] In addition, those affected by environmental harm can range from single individuals to particular groups, single states, whole regions, or the community of states.[12] Apart from the fact that it is not conducive to promoting the necessary cooperative steps, the multiplicity of polluters and victims would likely pose insurmountable evidentiary difficulties.[13] This raises questions of standing, invocation of state responsibility, and of who is the 'injured state'.

Third, the activities that give rise to harm are often lawful, at least in the state of origin, and may even be considered beneficial to (parts of the) society. As a total prohibition seems rarely feasible, the question turns then to allowable thresholds and appropriate standards of conduct, which are often difficult to define.[14]

Fourth, most transnational environmental concerns are resolved through negotiation or adoption of an agreement that regulates the issue at hand.[15] Obligations contained in

[9] See Chapter 16, 'Harm Prevention', in this volume.

[10] Jutta Brunnée, 'Of Sense And Sensibility: Reflections On International Liability Regimes As Tools For Environmental Protection' *International and Comparative Law Quarterly*, 53/2 (2004): 351.

[11] Caroline Foster, *Science and the Precautionary Principle in International Courts and Tribunals: Expert Evidence, Burden of Proof and Finality* (CUP 2011).

[12] Bruno Simma, 'From Bilateralism to Community Interest in International Law' *Recueil des Cours*, 250 (1994): 9.

[13] Brunnée (n 10).

[14] Bodansky (n 7) 83.

[15] Xue Hanquin, *Transboundary Damage in International Law* (CUP 2003) 286.

those Multilateral Environmental Agreements (MEAs) are owed inter se to the parties to the agreement. In some circumstances it is unclear to what extent states are entitled to invoke the responsibility of another state when it violates obligations that are owed towards everyone within a group of states (*erga omnes partes*).[16] It may be difficult to identify an injured state, particularly if the environmental damage is dispersed, global and/or felt in areas beyond national jurisdiction ('global commons').[17]

Fifth, determining environmental damage, how much ought to be compensated, and how the amount of compensation is to be calculated, raises complicated economic, political, and philosophical questions.[18]

Sixth, importantly, in environmental matters it might be more opportune to prevent damage, rather than seek reparations ex post, for example, in situations of irreversible damage.[19] In this situation, it seems unlikely that a state responsibility approach could or even should play a role in addressing global environmental problems.[20]

Seventh, recourse to state accountability could, potentially, adversely affect the success of cooperative efforts to address environmental problems. The potential benefits of relying on state accountability must be balanced against the potential disruptions an adjudicative approach could cause to the multilateral effort in designing a treaty-based, diplomatic solution. With respect to seeking an advisory opinion on the question of responsibility for climate change, it has been warned that 'the potential benefits of an advisory opinion do not justify risks of a ruling that complicates efforts to reach a political solution. Such a ruling could distract from international negotiations, make them more difficult, or lessen pressure on states to change their behaviour by letting them off the hook legally.'[21]

It is against this backdrop of challenges applying to responsibility for environmental harm that the following analysis of state responsibility needs to be seen, and its possibilities and shortfalls understood.

[16] See Jacqueline Peel, 'New State Responsibility Rules and Compliance with Multilateral Environmental Obligations: Some Case Studies of How the New Rules Might Apply in the International Environmental Context' *Review of European Community and International Environmental Law*, 10/2 (2001): 87.

[17] Hanquin (n 15).

[18] See more detail below in Section IV.A.2(b); see also Chapter 27, 'Judicial Development', in this volume; see also Alan Boyle 'Reparation for Environmental Damage in International Law: Some Preliminary Problems' in Michael Bowman and Alan Boyle (eds), *Environmental Damage in International and Comparative Law* (OUP 2002) 17.

[19] See for an overview Edith Brown-Weiss, 'Invoking State Responsibility in the 21st Century' *American Journal of International Law*, 96/4 (2002): 798.

[20] Daniel Bodansky, 'Ask the experts: Climate change and international law' (10 August 2012) <https://www.pbs.org/wnet/need-to-know/uncategorized/ask-the-experts/14420> accessed 22 January 2020; see also Tullio Scovazzi, 'State Responsibility for Environmental Harm' *Yearbook of International Environment Law*, 12/1 (2001): 43, 51.

[21] Bodansky (n 20).

III. INITIATIVES BY THE INTERNATIONAL LAW COMMISSION

The International Law Commission (ILC) has for a long time worked on the environmental responsibility and liability of states. Three projects are relevant: the 2001 Articles on Responsibility of States for Internationally Wrongful Acts[22] (Articles on State Responsibility); the 2001 Articles on the Prevention of Transboundary Harm from Hazardous Activities (Articles on Transboundary Harm);[23] and the 2006 Principles on the Allocation of Loss in the case of Transboundary Harm Arising out of Hazardous Activities (Principles on Allocation of Loss).[24]

The latter two works resulted from the topic of 'Responsibility for injurious consequences arising out of acts not prohibited by international law' which was included in the ILC's agenda in the late 1970s. The item 'Consideration of prevention of transboundary harm from hazardous activities and allocation of loss in the case of such harm' continues to be under consideration of the United Nations General Assembly (UNGA). By several resolutions since 2010,[25] the UNGA commended the articles and the principles to the attention of governments, without prejudice to any future action, as recommended by the ILC. The UNGA also requested the Secretary-General to submit a compilation of decisions of international courts, tribunals, and other bodies referring to the articles and the principles and decided to include the item in the provisional agenda of its seventy-fourth session in 2019.[26]

IV. INTERNATIONAL ENVIRONMENTAL LAW AND STATE RESPONSIBILITY

Despite the difficulties mentioned in Section II, state responsibility remains a legitimate and viable means to address environmental challenges; either by seeking to hold states

22 See ILC, 'Draft Articles on Responsibility' (n 3).

23 See 'Report of the International Law Commission on the work of its fifty-third session' (2001) UN Doc A/56/10, ch V.E—'Draft articles on prevention of transboundary harm from hazardous activities'.

24 Report of the International Law Commission on the work of its fifty-eighth session' (2006) UN Doc A/61/10, ch V.E—'Draft principles on the allocation of loss in the case of transboundary harm arising out of hazardous activities'.

25 UNGA Res 65/28, 68/114, and 71/143, 'Consideration of prevention of transboundary harm from hazardous activities and allocation of loss in the case of such harm' (10 January 2011, 18 December 2013, and 20 December 2016).

26 See website of the Sixth Committee of the UNGA <https://www.un.org/en/ga/sixth/71/prevention_of_harm.shtml> accessed 22 January 2020.

accountable to their prevention duties or by seeking reparation, where damage has occurred.

The ILC Articles on State Responsibility set out that '[e]very internationally wrongful act of a state entails the international responsibility of that state'.[27] It is a clear requirement that in order for a state to be legally responsible for an internationally wrongful act (or omission) and to incur the legal consequences of such responsibility, the act or omission must constitute a breach of an international obligation of that state, and be attributable to it.[28]

A. Breach of an International Obligation

The primary international obligation can only arise from the recognized sources of international law.[29]

1. *Treaties*

The most prominent source are individual, legally binding provisions, in multilateral, regional, or bilateral treaties which are in force and to which the state concerned is a party. Within international environmental law, hundreds of such treaties have come into existence, most of them over the last three to four decades.[30] There has been a remarkable development of states' primary obligations, and with it, the multiplication and the increasing precision of treaty obligations.[31]

International treaties contain different rights and obligations in relation to various environmental problems. They differ in their object and purpose, and spatial and/or temporal scope with respect to environmental aspects. Some address issues of global concern, such as the 1992 UN Framework Convention on Climate Change (UNFCCC) and the 2015 Paris Agreement or the 1992 Biodiversity Convention (CBD), while others apply to specific issues or address environmental challenges within certain regions only.[32] The legally binding provisions can be of different character; some establish legal obligations of result, which can be substantive in relation to implementing, for example, an environmental standard or pollution threshold. Others set out obligations of procedural character in terms of keeping with certain reporting requirements, measurements, governance structures, the duty to inform and to give access to information, the duty to

[27] ILC, 'Draft Articles on Responsibility' (n 3) art 1.

[28] Ibid, art 2.

[29] Statute of the International Court of Justice, art 38.1, which lists treaties, international custom, general principles of law and subsidiary sources (decisions of courts and tribunals and the writings of jurists).

[30] See Chapter 24, 'Multilateral Environmental Treaty Making', in this volume.

[31] See eg Sandrine Maljean-Dubois, 'International Litigation and State Liability for Environmental Damages: Recent Evolutions and Perspectives' in Jiunn-Rong Yeh (ed), *Climate Change Liability and Beyond* (National Taiwan University Press 2017) 27.

[32] See eg 'Ecolex' <https://www.ecolex.org> accessed 22 January 2020.

consult or cooperate, the duty to carry out an environmental impact assessment (EIA), etc.[33] There are also treaties that set up legal obligations of conduct; a certain standard of care, without requiring a particular outcome.

Few MEAs contain strict legal obligations to prevent environmental harm or adverse impacts or adopt a strict liability if such harm occurs.[34] The only Convention that contains a clear provision of objective international liability is the 1972 Convention on International Liability for Damage Caused by Space Objects.[35] Other treaties deal with liability in different ways.

The 1982 UN Convention on the Law of the Sea (UNCLOS) contains two provisions on damage liability of states. Article 235 sets out that states are 'responsible for the fulfilment of their international obligations concerning the protection and preservation of the marine environment. They shall be liable in accordance with international law.' This provision is generally recognized as incorporating the existing rules of state responsibility into UNCLOS and does not create a new liability rule for marine environmental damages.[36]

Article 139 states that '[w]ithout prejudice to the rules of international law ... damage caused by the failure of a State Party or international organization to carry out its responsibilities under this Part shall entail liability.... A State Party shall not however be liable for damage caused by any failure to comply with this Part by a person whom it has sponsored under article 152, paragraph 2(b), if the State Party has taken all necessary and appropriate measures to secure effective compliance under article 153, paragraph 4, and Annex III, article 4, paragraph 4.'[37] These provisions are subject to ongoing discussions about the extent of liability of states as well as the necessary and appropriate measures that a sponsoring state must take. The Seabed Disputes Chamber of the International Tribunal for the Law of the Sea (ITLOS) in its 2011 Advisory Opinion on *Responsibilities and Obligations in the Area* elaborated on these issues.[38]

The Chamber found first that the phrase 'activities in the area' covered some, but not all of the potentially threatening activities associated with seabed exploration and mining. On the primary question of legal responsibilities and obligations of a state sponsoring such activities, the Chamber pointed out that this is an obligation of conduct rather than of result, and is analogous to the obligation of due diligence and respective conduct that the International Court of Justice (ICJ) found in its *Pulp Mills* case.[39]

[33] See eg the Paris Agreement, or CBD.

[34] See Chapter 16, 'Harm Prevention', in this volume, on the duty to prevent environmental harm.

[35] art II.

[36] Philippe Sands and Jacqueline Peel, *Principles of International Environmental Law* (4th edn, CUP 2018) 764.

[37] See UNCLOS, art 139.1; see also arts 139.2, 139.3, annex III—art 4.4, for the full scope of liability provisions.

[38] *Responsibilities and obligations of States sponsoring persons and entities with respect to activities in the Area* (Advisory Opinion) [2011] ITLOS Rep 10 (Responsibilities in the Area case).

[39] See Section IV.B.2; *Pulp Mills on the River Uruguay (Argentina/Uruguay)* (Provisional Measures, Order of 13 July 2006) [2006] ICJ Rep 113.

Similarly to Article 139 of UNCLOS, the 1988 Convention on the Regulation of Antarctic Mineral Resource Activities (CRAMRA) provides that a sponsoring state will be liable, in accordance with international law, if damage under Article 8.2 would not have occurred if it had 'carried out its obligations under [the] Convention' with respect to the operator.[40] CRAMRA has, however, effectively been replaced by the 1991 Madrid Environment Protocol to the Antarctic Treaty, which establishes a seemingly less stringent liability regime,[41] where liability is mainly placed on operators, rather than states. State liability is now similar to Article 139 of UNCLOS where a state party would only be liable in the situation of insufficient implementation of its obligation, that is, if it has not taken all appropriate measures within its competence.[42]

On the one hand, in relation to certain activities, such as dangerous goods transportation, especially of hydrocarbons, nuclear energy, or genetically modified organisms, there are international treaties that place objective liability on operators (managers and owners), and shift responsibility from states. States are, however, reluctant to accept such strict legal obligations to prevent harm,[43] as illustrated by the lack of ratifications to the 1993 Lugano Convention on Civil Liability for Damage resulting from Activities Dangerous to the Environment, adopted by the Council of Europe.[44]

On the other hand, there are international treaties, which explicitly exclude liability and/or compensation. The 1979 Convention on Long-Range Transboundary Air Pollution (LRTAP) contains a footnote which states that the Convention 'does not contain a rule on state liability as to damage'. Similarly, the 2015 Paris Agreement although it contains in Article 8 a provision on 'loss and damage associated with the adverse effects of climate change', the decision adopting the Paris Agreement notes that this provision 'does not involve or provide a basis for any liability or compensation'.[45]

However, these do not prevent the application of general rules of international law on state responsibility and liability for damage resulting from the breach of other treaties and/or customary norms.

2. *Customary prohibition of transboundary harm*

With respect to customary norms, the most pertinent environmental obligation is the one that requires states to prevent significant environmental harm to other states or to areas beyond national jurisdiction, or to refrain from carrying out or permitting activities that could lead to such harm.[46]

[40] art 8.3(a).

[41] It is worth noting that CRAMRA is not likely to enter into force because of the mining ban under the Madrid Protocol; see for a discussion Alan Hemmings, 'Liability Postponed: The Failure to Bring Annex VI of the Madrid Protocol into Force' *The Polar Journal*, 8/2 (2018): 315.

[42] art 10.

[43] See Maljean-Dubois (n 31).

[44] As of January 2020 only three states have ratified the Lugano Convention.

[45] Decision 1/CP.21, 'Adoption of the Paris Agreement' (29 January 2016) UN Doc FCCC/CP/2015/10/Add.1, para 51.

[46] See for more detail Chapter 23, 'Customary International Law and the Environment', in this volume.

Under customary international law, states are under the obligation to not inflict damage on or violate the rights of other states. In international environmental law, this obligation has been translated into the obligation not to cause environmental harm ('no-harm rule') mentioned above.[47]

In order to establish an internationally wrongful act with respect to the obligation not to cause environmental harm, several requirements need to be fulfilled. These include (i) that environmental harm has occurred and that such harm is considered 'significant';[48] and (ii) that legally relevant state behaviour can be identified.[49]

a) *Environmental harm*

Defining damage, let alone environmental damage, in international law is difficult and controversial. Different definitions and approaches exist in treaty law and in the legal literature.[50]

'Damage' denotes loss, *damnum*, whether it is material or moral damages. 'Material damage' refers to damage to property, or to other interests that are assessable in financial terms. Damage can also be of an intangible, immaterial nature, usually referred to as 'moral damage'. The ILC's Articles on State Responsibility clarify that a state must make full reparation for injury caused, 'whether material or moral', which are 'financially assessable and may be subject of a claim for compensation' rather than satisfaction or restitution, or *a fortiori* punitive damages.[51] 'Financially assessable' is a damage, which is capable of being evaluated in financial terms.

Environmental damages often combine material and non-material aspects, such as ecological disruptions or social impacts on individuals and communities. Compensation for personal injury has also been dealt with by human rights bodies, in particular the European and Inter-American Court of Human Rights (IACtHR). Awards of compensation encompass material losses (loss of earnings, pensions, medical expenses, etc) as well as non-material damage (pain, suffering, mental angst, loss of enjoyment of life, etc). The latter category is often quantified on the basis of an equitable assessment.[52]

The only treaty-based definition of damage in respect of state liability is provided by the CRAMRA defining damage to the Antarctic environment as to include 'any impact on the living or non-living components of that environment or those ecosystems, including harm to atmospheric, marine or terrestrial life, beyond which is negligible or

[47] See Chapter 16, 'Harm Prevention', in this volume.

[48] The occurrence of damages is a central requirement of an internationally wrongful act with respect to a violation of the 'no-harm rule' (as part of the primary obligation), while for other obligations, eg to carry out an EIA or certain reporting obligations, that do contain harm prevention duties any question of damages would arise as a consequence once an internationally wrongful act has been established ('secondary law').

[49] See Robert Jennings and Arthur Watts (eds), *Oppenheim's International Law* (OUP 1992).

[50] Sands and Peel (n 36) 735.

[51] See ILC, 'Draft Articles on Responsibility' (n 3) arts 31, 34–37.

[52] Crawford (n 5) 224.

which has been assessed and judged to be acceptable pursuant to [the] convention'.[53] While this treaty has not entered into force (and most likely never will) the formulation of a liability rule is a helpful example of what states could agree to in other contexts if they wished.

The commentaries to the ILC Articles on Prevention of Transboundary Harm from Hazardous Activities (2001) understand environmental harm as effects on 'human health, industry, property, environment or agriculture in other States'. A more expansive understanding includes landscape and amenity values[54] or 'adverse effects on the conservation and sustainable use of biological diversity, taking into account risks to human health'.[55] Pollution prevention treaties[56] are only helpful to some extent. Pollution cannot generally be equated with environmental damage. Usually, environmental damage refers to additional adverse effects as a consequence of pollution above certain, agreed thresholds.[57] While the terms 'pollution' and 'adverse effects' might help in determining the threshold between legal and illegal pollution, they do not define environmental damage.

Environmental damage, such as the destruction of coral reefs, ecosystem changes, or destruction of biological diversity or ecosystems integrity will often extend beyond that which can be readily quantified in terms of clean-up costs or property devaluation.[58] Yet, damage to 'wider' environmental values is, 'as a matter of principle, no less real and compensable than damage to property, though it may be difficult to quantify'.[59] It has been argued that the 'intrinsic value of the environment' is covered by the contemporary concept of harm, including both whole ecosystems and individual components.[60]

b) *Compensation for environmental harm*

In cases where compensation has been awarded or agreed following an internationally wrongful act that causes or threatens environmental damage, payments have been directed to reimbursing the injured state for expenses incurred in preventing or remedying pollution, or to providing compensation for a reduction in the value of polluted property.[61] For example, in *Lake Lanoux*, a possibility of environmental harm

[53] art 1.15.

[54] See eg ILC, 'Draft articles on prevention of transboundary harm' (n 23) art 36; see also 1993 Lugano Convention.

[55] 2010 Nagoya-Kuala Lumpur Supplementary Protocol on Liability and Redress to the Cartagena Protocol on Biosafety, art 2.2(b).

[56] See eg 1979 LRTAP Convention, 1982 UNCLOS, 2013 Minamata Convention on Mercury.

[57] See eg 1993 Lugano Convention, 1985 Vienna Convention on the Protection of the Ozone Layer, 1992 UNFCCC, and Nagoya-Kuala Lumpur Supplementary Liability Protocol.

[58] See Michael Bowman and Alan Boyle (eds), *Environmental Damage in International and Comparative Law* (OUP 2002).

[59] Patricia Birnie, Alan Boyle, and Catherine Redgwell, *International Law and the Environment* (3rd edn, OUP 2009).

[60] Malgosia Fitzmaurice, 'International Responsibility and Liability' in Daniel Bodansky, Jutta Brunnée, and Ellen Hey (eds), *The Oxford Handbook of International Environmental Law* (1st edn, OUP 2008) 1014.

[61] Crawford (n 5) 223.

in the pure sense was indirectly recognized, as the court referred to changes in, for example, composition and temperature of the waters, which allegedly injured Spanish interests.[62]

International jurisprudence seems to support the approach that environmental damage also encompasses damage to the intrinsic value of the environment, beyond resources of a direct economic value. Claims regarding damage to the environment were put forward in the *Nuclear Tests* cases and in the case concerning *Certain Phosphate Lands in Nauru*.[63] None of these cases were judged on the merits but the ICJ, in its dismissal order of the second *Nuclear Test* case, recognized 'obligations of States to respect and protect the natural environment'.[64] In the subsequent Advisory Opinion on the *Legality of Nuclear Weapons*, the ICJ referred explicitly to a responsibility of states to control damage to the environment, which was reaffirmed in the *Pulp Mills* and *Gabčíkovo-Nagymaros* cases.[65]

Support for the obligation to compensate for environmental damage was also provided by the UN Security Council when it affirmed Iraq's liability under international law for any 'direct loss, damage, including environmental damage and the depletion of natural resources' occurring as a result of its unlawful invasion and occupation of Kuwait.[66] The work and the decisions of the UN Compensation Claims Commission between 1991 and 2011 provide further guidance in defining environmental damages.[67] Pursuant to the commission's decisions, compensation includes: precautionary monitoring to identify and assess long-term risks of environmental damage; assistance costs in environmental emergencies; continuing obligations to protect the environment as well as the obligations of the affected state to mitigate and contain damages; application of valuation methods for ecological harm, such as the 'habitat equivalency analysis'; and the requirement that compensation awards need to be spent on environmental remediation and restoration measures.[68]

---

[62] *The Gabčíkovo-Nagymaros Project (Hungary/Slovakia)* (Judgement) [1997] ICJ Rep 7 (Gabčíkovo-Nagymaros case) [41]; *Lake Lanoux Arbitration (Spain/France)* (1957) 12 RIAA.

[63] *Nuclear Tests (Australia/France)* (Judgement) [1974] ICJ Rep 253; *Nuclear Tests (New Zealand/France)* (Judgement) [1974] ICJ Rep 457 (Nuclear Tests I and II cases); *Request for an Examination of the Situation in Accordance with Paragraph 63 of the Court's Judgment of 20 December 1974 in the Nuclear Tests (New Zealand/France) Case* (Order) [1995] ICJ Rep 288 (Request for an Examination case); *Certain Phosphate Lands in Nauru, Preliminary Objections (Nauru/Australia)* (Judgement) [1992] ICJ Rep 240; see Chapter 11, 'Global South Approaches', in this volume.

[64] Request for an Examination case (n 63).

[65] *Legality of the Threat or Use of Nuclear Weapons* (Advisory Opinion) [1996] ICJ Rep 226; *Pulp Mills on the River Uruguay (Argentina/Uruguay)* (Judgement) [2010] ICJ Rep 14 (Pulp Mills case); Gabčíkovo-Nagymaros case (n 62).

[66] UN Security Council Res 687 (8 April 1991); see Chapter 27, 'Judicial Development', in this volume.

[67] For information on the UN Compensation Commission see <https://uncc.ch/home> accessed 22 January 2020.

[68] See Peter Sand, 'Compensation for Environmental Damage from the 1991 Gulf War' *Environmental Policy and Law*, 35/6 (2005): 244–249; see also Sands and Peel (n 36) 755–760.

Recently, several ground-breaking environmental decisions were rendered by international courts with respect to compensation for environmental damage. In 2017, the International Centre for the Settlement of Investment Disputes (ICSID) tribunal decided to award USD 39 million in damages to Ecuador for environmental remediation costs.[69] In 2018, the ICJ decided an environmental compensation case which marks a clear affirmation that environmental damage includes ecosystem services. The ICJ in the *Costa Rica v Nicaragua/Nicaragua v Costa Rica* cases ordered Nicaragua to pay compensation to Costa Rica for environmental damage.[70] However, the ICJ did not indicate how it calculated the value of the impairment or losses to the environmental services provided. The ICJ's way of quantifying environmental damages was criticized as an '"incrementalist" approach to quantification ... a methodologically ambiguous and context-sensitive approach which is not easily replicable for future environmental cases, given the complex nature of environmental damages in any given dispute'.[71]

Although the final compensation fell short of what Costa Rica had sought, the case is an important precedent in that the court noted that 'damage to the environment, and the consequent impairment or loss of the ability of the environment to provide goods and services, is compensable under international law',[72] which may include indemnification for such impairment or loss or payment for restoration of the damaged environment.[73]

c) *Threshold*

Not all environmental damage constitutes a breach of the 'no-harm rule' or is compensable under international law for other breaches.[74] The ILC in its 2006 Principles on the Allocation of Loss for Transboundary Harm requires 'significant damage', which is characterized as something more than 'detectable' but need not to be at the level of 'serious' or 'substantial'. The harm must lead to detrimental effect on, for example, human health, industry, property, environment, or agriculture in other states and must be susceptible of being measured by factual and objective standards.[75] The appropriate threshold will depend on the facts of each case, and may vary according to local and

[69] *Burlington Resources Inc. v Republic of Ecuador* (Decision on Counterclaims) ICSID Case No ARB/08/5 (2017).

[70] *Certain Activities Carried Out by Nicaragua in the Border Area (Costa Rica/Nicaragua)* (Judgement of 2 February 2018 on Compensation owed by Nicaragua to Costa Rica) ICJ (Certain activities case (Compensation Owed)); see Chapters 27 and 60, 'Judicial Development' and 'International Environmental Law Disputes before International Courts and Tribunals', in this volume.

[71] Diane Desierto, 'Environmental Damages, Environmental Reparations, and the Right to a Healthy Environment: The ICJ Compensation Judgment in Costa Rica v. Nicaragua and the IACtHR Advisory Opinion on Marine Protection for the Greater Caribbean' *EJIL Talk!* (14 February 2018).

[72] Certain activities case (Compensation Owed) (n 70).

[73] Nilufer Oral, 'ICJ Renders First Environmental Compensation Decision: A Summary of the Judgment' (9 April 2018) <https://www.iucn.org/news/world-commission-environmental-law/201804/icj-renders-it-first-environmental-compensation-decision-summary-judgment> accessed 3 March 2019.

[74] See UNGA Res 2995/(XXVII), 'Cooperation between States in the field of the environment' (15 December 1972) UN Doc A/RES/2995(XXVII) prohibits 'significant harmful effects' on other states when states utilize their natural resources.

[75] ILC, 'Draft principles on the allocation of loss' (n 24) principle 2, 65.

regional circumstances.[76] Given the absence of an agreed standard, it appears that the threshold for establishing international responsibility for environmental damage may still be relatively high.

B. Relevant State Behaviour and Attributability

1. *General*

In order for international responsibility of a state to arise, a legally relevant state behaviour needs to be identified. States can only act by and through their agents and representatives. The conduct of organs or officials of the state are thus attributable to the state. Acts by persons, entities, and individual groups may be imputable to the state if they are empowered (eg employed by the state) to exercise elements of governmental authority, and they act in that capacity in the particular instance. Acts by persons or entities not performing public functions may also be imputable to the state, if they in fact acted under the direction or control of the state.

If a treaty sets out a legally binding obligation, non-compliance with that obligation by a state party to the treaty is a violation of the general duty of that state and a failure to carry out its international obligation.[77] Where the primary obligation is the duty of a state to prevent, control, and reduce international environmental harm, the conduct of state officials or organs may not be directly relevant. More often, the damage is caused by activities of private actors, which raises the question of the standard of care a state must exercise over private actors, such as individuals, companies, or multinational corporations operating on its territory.

2. *Standard of conduct: acting with due diligence*

A state is accountable for acts or omissions conducted on its territory—including by private actors—if it can be established that it did not take proper care in exercising its governmental functions to manage and control activities carried out on its territory.[78] The due diligence standard of care assumes importance in this context.[79] Due diligence was identified by the ICJ in the *Pulp Mills* case as the applicable standard in respect of 'obligations of conduct' imposed under international environmental treaties. It has been described as the conduct that can *reasonably* be expected of a good government in the same situation.[80] This includes taking all appropriate measures to address private behaviour, including the regulatory aspects

[76] Ibid.

[77] ILC, 'Draft Articles on Responsibility' (n 3) art 2.

[78] Rosalyn Higgins and Baroness Higgins, *Problems and Process: International Law and How We Use It* (OUP 1994) 155; see Chapter 16, 'Harm Prevention', in this volume.

[79] This principle was applied in the Nauru case (n 63).

[80] See generally Alwyn Freeman, 'Responsibility of States for Unlawful Acts of their Armed Forces' *Recueil des Cours de l'Académie de Droit International de La Haye*, 88 (1955): 263, 277–278.

of adoption and implementation of laws and regulations, monitoring and as well as their enforcement.[81]

The term due diligence amounts to a framework concept, which has legal bearing in the context of specific activities and risks. The ILC in its commentary to the 2001 'Draft articles on Prevention of Transboundary Harm From Hazardous Activities' noted that acting with due diligence requires a state:

> to take unilateral measures to prevent significant transboundary harm or at any event minimize the risk thereof... Such measures include, first, formulating policies designed to prevent significant transboundary harm or to minimize the risk thereof and, secondly implementing those policies.[82]

It also implies that a due diligence standard requires governments to act in proportion to the risk to which they might be exposed.[83] In the *Pulp Mills* case the ICJ pointed out 'that the principle of prevention, as a customary rule, has its origins in the due diligence that is required of a State in its territory'.[84] The Seabed Disputes Chamber of ITLOS, in its *Responsibilities in the Area* Advisory Opinion, emphasized that precaution is, in effect, part of due diligence[85] and recognized that 'due diligence' may impose more rigorous requirements for riskier activities.

This may be particularly opportune in the context of global environmental challenges such as climate change. Each party to the Paris Agreement has committed to adopting successive nationally determined contributions (NDCs) which will reflect its 'highest possible level ambition'.[86] This is a treaty-based expression of due diligence, where each party has committed to taking all appropriate and adequate climate change mitigation measures according to its responsibility and its best capabilities in order to achieve the long-term temperature goals of the Agreement, as expressed in its Article 2.1.[87]

Other examples of treaty-based due diligence obligations are those provisions in CBD, which contain the formulation "Each Contracting Party shall, as far as possible and as appropriate", such as in Articles 6-11 and 14. The phrase "as far as possible and appropriate" indicates a standard of conduct, rather than of result, in relation to the obligation set out in those provisions. Both the ITLOS Chamber as well as the ICJ have identified further due diligence elements, including 'best environmental practices' and the requirements for an EIA ex ante; not ex post after construction has already started.[88]

81 Pulp Mills case (n 65) [187]; Responsibilities in the Area case (n 38).

82 ILC 'Report of its fifty-third session' (n 3) 154, art 3 commentary, para 10.

83 ILC, 'Draft articles on prevention of transboundary harm' (n 23) art 3.

84 Pulp Mills case (n 65) [101].

85 Responsibilities in the Area case (n 38).

86 art 4.3.

87 See Christina Voigt, 'The Paris Agreement: What is the Standard of Conduct for Parties?' *Questions of International Law* 26 (2016): 17; see also Christina Voigt and Felipe Ferreira, 'Dynamic Differentiation: The Principles of CBDR-RC, Progression and Highest Possible Ambition in the Paris Agreement' *Transnational Environmental Law*, 5/2 (2016): 285.

88 Pulp Mills case (n 65); *Certain Activities Carried Out by Nicaragua in the Border Area (Costa Rica/Nicaragua) and Construction of a Road in Costa Rica along the San Juan River (Nicaragua/Costa Rica)* (Judgement) [2015] ICJ Rep 665.

Where the EIA confirms a risk of significant transboundary harm, due diligence requires the state planning to undertake the activity to notify and consult in good faith with the affected state where this is necessary to determine the appropriate measures to prevent or mitigate that risk.[89] The procedural obligation to undertake an EIA is distinct from the substantive obligation not to cause transboundary harm.[90] However, the distinction between procedural and substantive obligations is not always easy to draw.[91]

ITLOS further expanded on the concept of due diligence in its 2015 *Sub-Regional Fisheries Commission* Advisory Opinion.[92] It found that "taking all necessary measures" included the adoption of enforcement mechanisms to monitor and secure compliance with laws and regulations and the application of sufficient sanctions to deter violations and to deprive offenders from benefits accruing from illegal activities.[93] Furthermore it observed that due diligence is a standard that varies according to context.[94] It is understood that the degree of care expected of a state with a well-developed economy and human and material resources and with highly evolved systems and structures of government is different from states which are not so well placed. However, the economic level of a state cannot entirely relieve the state from its obligations.[95]

Another aspect concerns the geographical extent of due diligence (and other) international obligations. It was long unclear whether a state is obliged to require multinational companies domiciled in its territory to adopt, at the headquarters level, policies and frameworks to ensure that subsidiaries or supply chain partners in other countries do not infringe human rights or the environment in their places of operation. A recent Advisory Opinion of the IACtHR supports such extraterritorial extension of obligation at a general level.[96]

In 2017, the IACtHR released an Advisory Opinion on state obligations on environment and human rights. The court focused on state obligations under international environmental law and human rights law in a transboundary context, in particular regarding the construction and operation of infrastructure mega-projects, petroleum exploration and exploitation, maritime transportation of hydrocarbons, and construction and enlargement of ports and shipping canals.[97] This is the first-ever ruling to have opened the door 'to cross-border human rights claims arising from

[89] Ibid.

[90] Duncan French and Tim Stephens, 'ILA Study Group on Due Diligence in International Law—Second Report' (July 2016) 5.

[91] Jutta Brunnée, 'Procedure and Substance in International Environmental Law: Confused at a Higher Level' *European Society of International Law Reflections*, 5/6 (2016).

[92] *Request for an advisory opinion submitted by the Sub-Regional Fisheries Commission (SRFC)* (Advisory Opinion) [2015] ITLOS Rep 4.

[93] Ibid [138].

[94] Ibid [117].

[95] Timo Koivurova, 'Due Diligence' in Rüdiger Wolfrum (ed), *Max Planck Encyclopedia of Public International Law* (OUP 2010).

[96] *State Obligations in Relation to the Environment* (Advisory Opinion) IACtHR (2017) OC-23/17.

[97] Ibid.

transboundary environmental impacts'.[98] The court carefully balanced the fundamental nature of the right to a healthy environment as a necessary condition for enjoyment of human rights generally, and the transboundary nature of environmental harms, by treating extraterritorial obligations and claims as 'exceptional'.

Moreover, although the IACtHR does not address climate change, commentators have noted that some of the court's observations on states' duties are 'clearly pertinent', and that the court's reasoning on 'jurisdiction' could support an argument that a state's contribution to the stock of greenhouse gases in the atmosphere could result in responsibility for the climate impacts in other states.[99]

In sum, while the due diligence standard is not specific or precise, it is the conduct that can be reasonably expected and if not followed, gives rise to fault. It implies that every state ought to employ its highest possible and appropriate level of ambition or standard of protection and act according to its best capabilities, or 'to do as well as it can'. The standard of due care must be determined on a case-by-case basis with regard to a country's obligation to reduce the risk of environmental harm under national circumstances compared to the best conduct expected of a state in similar circumstances.

3. *Circumstances precluding wrongfulness*

The 2001 ILC Articles on State Responsibility list six circumstances precluding wrongfulness in relation to state responsibility: consent (Article 20), self-defence (Article 21), countermeasures (Article 22), *force majeure* (Article 23), distress (Article 24), and necessity (Article 25). These circumstances do not annul or terminate the obligation; rather they provide a justification or excuse for non-performance while the circumstances in question subsist.

With respect to environmental harm, Hungary relied on the state of 'ecological necessity' in the 1997 *Gabčíkovo-Nagymaros Project* case to justify the suspension on the bilateral treaty with Slovakia on the development of a system of dams in the Danube river. The court acknowledged that Hungary's environmental concerns related to its 'essential interest' within the meaning of 'necessity' under the law of state responsibility. It indicated that an essential interest could be affected by 'a grave danger to ... the ecological preservation of all or some of [the] territory'[100] and specified that 'safeguarding the ecological balance has come to be considered an "essential interest" of all States'.[101] While the court did not perceive such danger in this case, it nevertheless acknowledged the possibility of 'ecological necessity' in case where it can be

[98] Monica Feria-Tinta, 'The Rise of Environmental Law in International Dispute Resolution: Inter-American Court of Human Rights issues Landmark Advisory Opinion on Environment and Human Rights' *EJIL Talk!* (26 February 2018).

[99] Ibid; see also Desierto (n 71).

[100] Gabčíkovo-Nagymaros case (n 62) [53]–[54], referring to the *Yearbook of the International Law Commission*, vol II, part 2 (1980): 35–39.

[101] Ibid [14], [35].

proven that a real, 'grave', and 'imminent' peril exists and that the measures taken are the only possible response to it.[102]

4. *Consequences*

If a state is found responsible, three legal consequences follow. First, the primary obligation persists.[103] Second, the state is obliged to cease the wrongful act.[104] Third, the state is obliged to make full reparation for any injury caused.[105]

The Articles on State Responsibility envisage that reparation for the injury shall take the form of restitution, compensation, and satisfaction.[106] In cases involving irreversible damage, it might be impossible to restore the situation ex ante. A victim state will therefore seek financial compensation to cover the costs associated with material damage to environmental resources (pure environmental damage) and consequential damage to people and property (consequential environmental damage), including restoration.

In this context, particular challenges arise, such as: (i) assessment of environmental harm, and (ii) contribution to the injury. With regard to the assessment of environmental harm, Article 31 defines injury as 'including any damage whether material or moral', caused by the internationally wrongful act. Material damage includes all potential losses in infrastructure, property, and other clearly defined economic assets. In order to determine the appropriate amount of compensation, the assessment needs to be quantifiable. Such quantification will vary, depending on the content of the primary obligation, an evaluation of the respective behaviour of the parties, and, more generally, the need to reach an equitable and acceptable outcome.[107] In the context of environmental harm, material damages will be easier to define and to assess in financial rather than purely environmental or ecological damages.

In a number of cases, payments have thus been negotiated between the injured and the injuring states as the full and final settlement.[108]

With regard to the contribution to the injury, Article 39 states that where the claimant state has, through wilful or negligent behaviour or omission, contributed to the injury, the extent of the reparation must be adjusted accordingly. Contribution to the damage will therefore not lead to an exculpation of the wrongful act, but may limit the legal consequences.

[102] Ibid [41].

[103] ILC, 'Draft Articles on Responsibility' (n 3) art 29.

[104] Ibid, art 30.

[105] Ibid, art 31.

[106] Ibid, arts 31–35.

[107] Crawford (n 5).

[108] See eg the General Agreement between Iran and the United States on the Settlement of Certain ICJ and Tribunal cases of 9 February 1996, Award on Agreed Terms by order of the Iran-US Claims Tribunals (20 February 1996) 32 Iran-USCTR 207, 213.

V. FINAL REMARKS

An increasing number of environmental claims are being brought before the ICJ, the World Trade Organization (WTO) dispute settlement system (especially with regard to renewable energy), the ITLOS, regional human rights courts,[109] investment treaty arbitration, etc.[110] These cases are an example of a 'turn to courts', as they are a challenge and a chance for courts to strengthen their role in the global public order with respect to environmental protection.[111] As scientific accounts of the global state of the environment become increasingly dire and the human effects on the environment more grave and tangible, the prospect of 'international environmental litigation' to address those concerns and to seek redress for harm and damages is expected to rise. In this situation, the law of state responsibility and liability can be expected to be put to the test. Recourse to international courts in environmental matters might move from singular attempts and a 'niche issue' to one of the international judiciary's main preoccupations.[112]

In this context, clearer environmental obligations would help to determine when a breach occurs that gives rise to international accountability. However, in their absence, courts will need to rely on the notion of due diligence—that states are obliged to adopt all appropriate and adequate means at their disposal to avoid environmental harm to other states and areas beyond national jurisdiction might help addressing gaps; not as an obligation of result; but a legal *obligation of conduct*.

A suggested legal definition of this general approach is the following: 'At a minimum, states shall act with due diligence in avoiding environmental harm to other states or areas beyond national jurisdiction. Accordingly, each state shall apply its best efforts and take all appropriate and adequate measures in proportion to the risk of environmental harm.'

This principle approach expresses the standard of care, which already is part of the general corpus of international law and contains a universal obligation. It captures all states' individual responsibilities and requires them to 'do the best they can'. A breach of this standard of care would give rise to state responsibility—and its legal consequences.

[109] Evadne Grant and Christina Voigt, 'The Legitimacy of Human Rights Courts in Environmental Disputes—Editorial' *Journal of Human Rights and the Environment*, 6/2 (2015): 131.

[110] Daniel Behn and Ole Fauchald, 'Governments under Cross-Fire?' *Manchester Journal of International Economic Law*, 12/2 (2015): 117.

[111] See Chapters 27 and 60, 'Judicial Development' and 'International Environmental Law Disputes before International Courts and Tribunals', in this volume; Tim Stephens, *International Courts and Environmental Protection* (CUP 2009); Christina Voigt (ed), *International Judicial Practice on the Environment—Questions of Legitimacy* (CUP 2019).

[112] See Voigt (n 111); Stephens (n 111).

BIBLIOGRAPHY

Julio Barboza, *The Environment, Risk and Liability in International Law* (Martinus Nijhoff 2001)

Daniel Bodansky, *The Art and Craft of International Environmental Law* (Harvard University Press 2010)

Alan Boyle and James Harrison, 'Judicial Settlement of International Environmental Disputes: Current Problems' *Journal of International Dispute Settlement*, 4/2 (2013): 245

Jutta Brunnée, 'Of Sense And Sensibility: Reflections On International Liability Regimes As Tools For Environmental Protection' *International and Comparative Law Quarterly*, 53/2 (2004): 351

Xue Hanquin, *Transboundary Damage in International Law* (CUP 2003)

Philippe Sands and Jacqueline Peel, *Principles of International Environmental Law* (4th edn, CUP 2018)

Tullio Scovazzi, 'State Responsibility for Environmental Harm' *Yearbook of International Environment Law*, 12/1 (2001): 43

CHAPTER 59

NATIONAL IMPLEMENTATION

ALICE PALMER

I. INTRODUCTION

NATIONAL implementation is a fundamental feature of international environmental law. The global nature of harmful environmental impacts requires an 'all for one, one for all' approach and domestic management of the environment in all states is essential to give effect to international protections. International environmental laws are recognized in national legal systems in accordance with the rules of each state and the resulting variables are many. The extensive reach of international environmental law into the domestic sphere limits state autonomy and local norms, further complicating national implementation.[1]

The concept of 'implementation' is understood in different ways. It can refer to measures taken by states working together to give effect to their international commitments.[2] It can also mean the application of international law in domestic legal systems.[3] This meaning can be distinguished from 'compliance', 'non-compliance', and 'enforcement', with still further distinctions made between treaties and customary international law.[4] Scholars also differentiate between implementation and 'effectiveness'.[5] The distinctions can, however, be difficult to maintain: forms of implementation can constitute compliance, and measures taken to address non-compliance might resemble

[1] Frank Jotzo, Joanna Depledge, and Harald Winkler, 'US and International Climate Policy under President Trump' *Climate Policy*, 18/7 (2018): 813; Rafiqul Islam, 'History of the North-South Divide in International Law: Colonial Discourses, Sovereignty, and Self-Determination' in Shawkat Alam *et al* (eds), *International Environmental Law and the Global South* (CUP 2015) 23, 48.

[2] Pierre-Marie Dupuy and Jorge Viñuales, *International Environmental Law: A Modern Introduction* (2nd edn, CUP 2018) 294.

[3] Philippe Sands and Jacqueline Peel, *Principles of International Environmental Law* (4th edn, CUP 2018) 147.

[4] See Chapter 51, 'Compliance Theory', in this volume.

[5] See Chapter 57, 'Effectiveness', in this volume.

enforcement and facilitate implementation. To speak of 'effective implementation' should be a tautology. Ultimately, the differences are possibly more a matter of perspective than substance.

This chapter is organized around three themes: contexts, means, and principles. 'Contexts' for implementation contemplates the different sources and forms of international law, the plurality of legal traditions, and the range of domestic structures for making law. 'Means' of national implementation addresses the roles of executive, legislative, and judicial organs in a state's adherence, recognition, and interpretation of international law. Examples of 'international environmental principles' that support implementation are examined in the final section before the conclusion.

The focus of this chapter is implementation through law at the national or 'domestic' level, with some consideration given to international facilitation of domestic implementation. The implementation of treaties and customary international law is highlighted although matters relevant to so-called soft law are also noted. The chapter recognizes the role of national enforcement in the implementation of international environmental law but it defers to Chapter 62 for a more comprehensive survey of judicial interventions.[6]

II. CONTEXTS FOR IMPLEMENTATION

The contexts in which international environmental law is implemented concern: the sources and forms of international commitments; the domestic structures for making and giving effect to international law; as well as the political, economic, and ecological landscapes of a given state.

A. Sources and Forms of International Environmental Law

International laws that are binding on a state—including international treaties and customary international law—are required under international and domestic law to be implemented in the domestic sphere.[7] However, the undertakings of states in treaties can range from the broad to the specific, with significant discretion afforded to states in their implementation of those undertakings. A requirement to introduce 'policies and measures' to reduce greenhouse gas emissions,[8] for example, gives states extensive

[6] Alice Palmer and Cairo Robb (eds), *International Environmental Reports, Volume 4: International Environmental Law in National Courts* (CUP 2004).

[7] For state responsibility for breaching customary international law see Chapter 58, 'International Environmental Responsibility and Liability', in this volume; for treaties, see Anthony Aust, 'Treaties and Domestic Law' in *Modern Treaty Law and Practice* (CUP 2013) 159, 160.

[8] 1992 United Nations Framework Convention on Climate Change (UNFCCC), art 4.2(a).

scope in their implementation choices compared with a commitment to ban trade in endangered animals and plants.[9] Some treaties guide parties in their conduct—for example requiring states parties to develop a national strategy on the protection of biodiversity.[10] Others anticipate a specific outcome or result,[11] such as a percentage decrease in carbon emissions.[12] The use of 'framework' treaties in international environmental law allows a wide range of approaches to implementation which can be limited by later, more specific, 'protocol' agreements.[13]

States must abide by customary international law but it is a source of law that can be problematic for implementation.[14] What is for some states 'customary international law' might not be so for others. Even where it is recognized in the domestic sphere, custom can be so broadly conceived that it leaves states much room for interpretation in crafting national laws to accommodate those international principles.[15] There is, for example, support for the principle of public access to environmental information having attained the status of customary international law.[16] However, the details of that principle can differ substantially, with any number of exceptions apparent in domestic freedom of information laws.[17]

So-called soft law in the domain of international environmental law is also a matter for implementation of international environmental law.[18] Whether contained in a treaty or an international instrument with no binding effect, the principles that populate international environmental law can be a significant element of national laws and policies. The precautionary principle, for example, has different manifestations in many domestic jurisdictions.[19] The articulation of soft laws of international environmental law

[9] 1973 Convention on International Trade in Endangered Species of Wild Fauna and Flora (CITES), art VIII(1).

[10] 1992 Convention on Biological Diversity (CBD); see Elisa Morgera and Elsa Tsioumani, 'Yesterday, Today, and Tomorrow: Looking Afresh at the Convention on Biological Diversity' *Yearbook of International Environmental Law*, 21/1 (2010): 3.

[11] See Pierre-Marie Dupuy, 'Reviewing the Difficulties of Codification on Ago's Classification of Obligations of Means and Obligations of Result in Relation to State Responsibility' *European Journal of International Environmental Law*, 10 (1999): 371.

[12] 1997 Kyoto Protocol; see Michael Rodi *et al*, 'Implementing the Kyoto Protocol in a Multidimensional Legal System: Lessons from a Comparative Assessment' *Yearbook of International Environmental Law*, 16/1 (2006): 3.

[13] Edith Weiss, 'The Evolution of International Environmental Law' *Japanese Yearbook of International Law* 54 (2011): 1, 7.

[14] See Chapter 58, 'International Environmental Responsibility and Liability', in this volume.

[15] See Chapter 23, 'Customary International Law and the Environment', in this volume.

[16] Svitlana Kravchenko, 'Is Access to Environmental Information a Fundamental Human Right?' *Oregon Review of International Law*, 11/2 (2009): 227.

[17] Ibid; see also Uzuazo Etemire, 'Public Access to Environmental Information: A Comparative Analysis of Nigerian Legislation with International Best Practice' *Transnational Environmental Law*, 3/1 (2014): 149.

[18] See Chapter 25, 'Soft Law', in this volume; see also Riccardo Pavoni and Dario Piselli, 'The Sustainable Development Goals and International Environmental Law: Normative Value and Challenges for Implementation' *Veredas do Direito* 13/26 (2016): 13.

[19] See Nicolas de Sadeleer (ed), *Implementing the Precautionary Principle: Approaches from the Nordic Countries, EU and USA* (Earthscan 2007); Jonas Ebbesson, 'The Notion of Public Participation in

in domestic spheres can constitute state practice and contribute to the development of international environmental law in treaties or as custom.[20]

B. Domestic Structures for Making and Giving Effect to International Law

A disparate array of domestic jurisdictions are charged with implementing the international environmental commitments made between states.[21] The foundations of legal governance in states can be grouped in terms of their common, civil, religious, or customary law histories. Yet there are possibly as many different methods for implementing international law as there are states. International law is implemented, for example, in a variety of ways in Antigua and Barbuda, Australia, Bangladesh, India, South Africa, Uganda, and the United States. Legal governance in those states differs, in turn, from that of the United Kingdom, the jurisdiction that informed the legal structures in those countries.[22]

Despite the plurality of domestic systems, legal theories distinguishing between monist states incorporating international law directly into domestic law, and dualist states requiring domestic action to give effect to international law, have been influential in fostering a binary conception of national regimes for the implementation of international law.[23] The distinction has, however, been described as misleading for its failure to acknowledge the many combinations and permutations for implementing international laws in different nations.[24] Factors in the implementation of international environmental law for a given country include: whether and how powers of governance

International Environmental Law' *Yearbook of International Environmental Law*, 8/1 (1998): 51; Patrícia Ferreira, '"Common but Differentiated Responsibilities" in the National Courts: Lessons from *Urgenda v. The Netherlands*' *Transnational Environmental Law*, 5/2 (2016): 329.

[20] See Chapter 25, 'Soft Law', in this volume.

[21] See eg Ben Boer, Ross Ramsay, and Donald Rothwell, *International Environmental Law in the Asia Pacific* (Kluwer Law International 1998); Wilbert Kaahwa, 'Improving Implementation of International Environmental Law: A View from the East African Community' *Thesaurus Acroasium* 31 (2002): 601; Wiek Schrage, Keith Bull, and Albena Karadjova, 'Environmental Legal Instruments in the UNECE Region' *Yearbook of International Environmental Law*, 18/1 (2007): 3; Tao Zhengua and Rüdiger Wolfrum (eds), *Implementing International Environmental Law in Germany and China* (Kluwer Law International 2001).

[22] On Antigua and Barbuda, see Aust (n 7) 173; on Australia, Bangladesh, Malaysia, Uganda, US, and UK, see Dinah Shelton (ed), *International Law and Domestic Legal Systems: Incorporation, Transformation and Persuasion* (OUP 2011); on India, see K Thakore, 'India' in Duncan Hollis, Merritt Blakeslee, and Benjamin Ederington (eds), *National Treaty Law and Practice* (Martinus Nijhoff 2005) 349; for civil law examples see Shelton, ibid; see also Richard Oppong, 'Re-Imagining International Law: An Examination of Recent Trends in the Reception of International Law into National Legal Systems in Africa' *Fordham International Law Journal*, 30/2 (2006): 296.

[23] See David Sloss, 'Domestic Application of Treaties' in Duncan Hollis (ed), *The Oxford Guide to Treaties* (OUP 2012) 370.

[24] Dinah Shelton, 'Introduction' in Shelton (n 22) 1, 3–4.

are divided among the executive, legislature, and judiciary; the role of those organs in overseeing the making of treaties and recognizing customary international law, as well as their role in making international laws effective at the domestic level; and the place given to international law in the hierarchy of laws that is applied, with additional factors arising for federated states.[25] Specific examples are discussed later in Section III.

C. Political, Economic, and Ecological Landscapes

There are significant variances in national implementation that are a function of politics, economics, and ecology.[26] These are matters typically raised in discussions of the 'effectiveness' of international law.[27]

States might implement their international environmental commitments but then fail or decline to execute or enforce them because of political or economic exigencies. Democracy, 'rule of law', and public engagement are often promoted as being conducive to the implementation of international environmental commitments but undemocratic state structures can also be 'effective' in the implementation of international environmental law.[28] Neo-conservatism in a democratic state can be as much of an impediment to implementation of international environmental law as corruption in an autocracy.[29] Low-income states might be thwarted in their efforts to implement international environmental laws, or to give effect to those laws when they are in place, because of the technical or financial resources needed to support them.[30] All states, including high-income states, can be capricious in their implementation efforts, readily changing their laws and policies to suit powerful domestic constituencies.[31]

[25] Eileen Denza, 'The Relationship between International and National Law' in Malcom Evans (ed), *International Law* (4th edn, OUP 2014) 412, 425.

[26] Daniel Bodansky, 'How and Why Do States Implement their Commitments' in Daniel Bodansky, *The Art and Craft of International Environmental Law* (Harvard University Press 2010) 205.

[27] See eg Peter Sand, 'The Effectiveness of Multilateral Environmental Agreements: Theory and Practice' in Melissa Lewis, Tuula Honkonen, and Seita Romppanen (eds), *International Environmental Law-making and Diplomacy Review* (University of Eastern Finland 2016) 1; Alexander Gillespie, 'Implementation and Compliance Concerns in International Environmental Law: The State of the Art within Three International Regimes' *New Zealand Journal of Environmental Law*, 7 (2003): 53.

[28] Edith Weiss, 'Understanding Compliance with International Environmental Agreements: The Baker's Dozen Myths' *University of Richmond Law Review*, 32/5 (1999): 1555, 1579.

[29] See eg Jotzo, Depledge, and Winkler (n 1); Gregory Rose, 'Australian Approaches to International Environmental Law During the Howard Years' *Australian Year Book of International Law*, 27 (2008): 115.

[30] Manuel Ruiz Muller (Peruvian Society for Environmental Law (SPDA)), 'Implementation of Multilateral Environmental Agreements in Peru' (Foundation for International Environmental Law and Development (FIELD) 2001) <https://www.cbd.int/doc/nbsap/legislation/PERU(Legal).pdf> accessed 1 November 2018; note issues of participation in international environmental governance in Sharan Paudel, 'The Legislation and Implementation of International Environmental Law and the Third-World' *National Judicial Academy Law Journal*, 9 (2015): 127.

[31] See Weiss, 'Understanding Compliance' (n 28) 1562; Joel Eisen, 'From Stockholm to Kyoto and Back to the United States: International Environmental Law's Effect on Domestic Law' *University of Richmond Law Review*, 32/5 (1999): 1435.

A country's ecological profile might also be relevant to the implementation of international environmental law.[32] Countries with healthy, biodiverse natural environments might place greater importance on the implementation of international environmental law than those with less 'natural capital'. Conversely, having less biodiversity could mean a state has more to lose from non-implementation. Nations with highly vulnerable ecologies, where environmental impacts readily compromise food security or cause displacement from land, will likely have compelling incentives to implement international environmental law.[33] The proposed 'Multi-Partner Trust Fund' for conservation in the Yasuní national park is arguably an instance of a poor state rich in environmental assets asking wealthy states to determine the economic value of preserving an ecologically significant area; when the initiative failed to attract sufficient funds from donor countries, the Ecuadorian government opened the area up to oil exploration.[34]

III. MEANS OF IMPLEMENTATION

The 'implementation' of international law in national jurisdictions is closely aligned to the practices of states in their adherence, recognition, and interpretation of international law. As discussed in this section, nations might divide those responsibilities between a governing executive, a law-making legislature, and a law-enforcing judiciary, under the direction or otherwise of a written constitution.[35]

A. Adhering to International Treaties

In some states, the nation's executive branch is solely responsible for decisions to enter into international treaties.[36] The executive might have the power to sign and ratify or accede to agreements with other states, with or without notice, for example, to a

[32] See Jacqueline Peel and Tim Stephens, 'Australia and International Environmental Law' in Donald Rothwell and Emily Crawford (eds), *International Law in Australia* (3rd edn, Lawbook Co. 2017) 457, 458; see also David Hunter, James Salzman, and Durwood Zaelke, *International Environmental Law and Policy* (4th edn, Foundation Press 2011) 86.

[33] See Hunter *et al* (n 32) 14 ff.

[34] See Multi-Partner Trust Fund for Yasuní <https://mptf.undp.org/yasuni> and <https://www.sosyasuni.org/en/index.php> accessed 1 November 2018; see also Hans Morten Haugen, 'Financialization of Mother Earth: Do Offsets and Payments or Rights-Based Approaches Provide for Better Conservationist Approaches' *Law, Environment and Development Journal (LEAD Journal)*, 14/1 (2018): 1.

[35] Cheryl Saunders and Anna Dziedzic, 'Parliamentary Sovereignty and Written Constitutions in Comparative Perspective' in Asanga Welikala (ed), *The Sri Lankan Republic at 40: Reflections on Constitutional History, Theory and Practice* (Centre for Policy Alternatives 2012) 477; see also James May and Erin Daly, *Global Environmental Constitutionalism* (CUP 2014).

[36] See Aust (n 7).

parliamentary body. Some executive organs have developed practices that allow for a degree of scrutiny by the legislature or other body before the state submits documentation that would bind the state as a party to an international treaty it has signed. In countries such as Australia, Canada, Israel, India, and the United Kingdom, for example, the executive is empowered to enter into binding treaties on behalf of the nation but in practice some or all treaties are tabled in parliament prior to ratification.[37]

Some national legislatures, by contrast, have extensive powers of scrutiny over international agreements before the signing or ratification of a treaty by the executive on behalf of the state.[38] In the United States, one legislative arm, the Senate, must approve treaties before they can be ratified while in Argentina, Japan, and Venezuela, the approval of two houses of parliament must be obtained before a treaty can bind the state.[39] In other countries, such as Hungary, administrative levels of government and the judiciary are also involved in the scrutiny of treaties.[40]

The legal status of an international instrument can determine the extent of executive power to enter into international agreements. In some countries, executive orders can be made in respect of international instruments that are authorized by an international agreement to which the state is already a party.[41] This was a distinction that was central to the international negotiations of the 2015 Paris Agreement on climate change: for the US government of the day, the instrument had to be characterized as subject to the UNFCCC, a treaty to which the United States was already a party, so that the executive could adhere to the agreement without having to submit it as a new international treaty for approval by an opposition-led Senate.[42]

B. Recognizing International Law

National implementation of international law that is binding on a state is automatic in so-called monist states.[43] However, treaties and customary international law might be treated differently.[44] In some instances, treaties addressing a particular subject matter are identified as 'self-executing' in the domestic law. In Colombia, for example, human rights treaties are identified in the constitution as self-executing while international

[37] See Sloss (n 23); see also Peel and Stephens (n 32) 547.

[38] See Aust (n 7).

[39] See Dinah Shelton, 'Introduction' in Shelton (n 22) 8; Jutta Brunnée 'The United States and International Environmental Law: Living with an Elephant' *European Journal of International Law*, 15/4 (2004): 617.

[40] See Dinah Shelton, 'Introduction' in Shelton (n 22) 8.

[41] Argentina, Austria, Germany, Italy, Poland, and Venezuela also have different procedures for executive agreements; see Dinah Shelton, 'Introduction' in Shelton (n 22) 9.

[42] Eun Kim, 'Language and Design of the Paris Agreement: An International Deal Crafted to Avoid the Need for Senate's Approval' *Thurgood Marshall Law Review*, 42/1 (2016): 45.

[43] Sloss (n 23) identifies as monist states: Austria, Chile, China, Colombia, Egypt, France, Germany, Japan, Mexico, the Netherlands, Poland, Russia, South Africa, Switzerland, Thailand, and the US.

[44] Malcolm Shaw, *International Law* (8th edn, CUP 2017) 130–135.

environmental laws have been given effect by courts through a legal doctrine known as the 'block of constitutionality'.[45] This distinction was apparent in a case challenging domestic forestry laws as contrary to international human rights and environmental laws: the matter was resolved with reference to self-executing human rights treaties concerning the rights of Indigenous peoples.[46]

Where international law is directly applicable in national law, it might have the same status as constitutional law or be subordinated to the country's constitution in the domestic hierarchy of laws. In the Netherlands, for example, treaties are granted the same authority as the constitution while Austria, Egypt, Germany, and the United States consider treaties to be equivalent to statutes.[47] In the United States, it is unclear whether customary international law is equivalent to the national 'federal' law or the provincial 'state' law.[48]

Even where international law is directly applicable, legislation might still be necessary in specific circumstances. The US Alien Tort Claims Act of 1789, for example, implements international law in the domestic sphere for foreign nationals.[49] Initially revived in 1980 in respect of human rights, it has since been invoked in cases concerning environmental damage occurring outside the United States.[50] However, findings that international environmental principles are not the 'law of nations' have undermined claims. In *Beanal v Freeport-McMoran, Inc.*, for example, the polluter pays principle was among several international environmental principles rejected as a basis for making a claim under the statute.[51]

In so-called dualist states, international law is transformed by an act of the state into domestic law.[52] Again, distinctions might be made between treaties and customary international law. Treaties might, for example, be implemented through legislation, while customary international law is applied directly as the 'law of the land'.[53] Some states require that national legislation conforms to treaty commitments prior to the state submitting instruments of ratification.[54] In Australia, there is a 'legitimate expectation'

45 Alejandro Gómez-Velásquez, 'The "Constitutionalization" Process of the International Environmental Law in Colombia' *Revista de Derecho*, 45 (2016): 1; see also Dinah Shelton, 'Introduction' in Shelton (n 22) 5 on Argentina, Slovakia, and Venezuela.

46 Daniel Maldonado, 'International Law, Cultural Diversity, and the Environment: The Case of the General Forestry Law in Colombia' in Alam *et al* (n 1) 508.

47 Sloss (n 23) 374.

48 Gary Born, 'Customary International Law in United States Courts' *Washington Law Review*, 92/4 (2017): 1641.

49 Alien Tort Statute, 28 USC §1350.

50 Kathleen Jawger, 'Environmental Claims under the Alien Tort Statute' *Berkeley Journal of International Law*, 28/2 (2010): 519.

51 *Beanal v Freeport-McMoran, Inc.* 969 F. Supp. 362 (E.D. La. 1997) 384, aff'd, 197 F.3d. 161 (5th Cir. 1999).

52 Dualist states include British Commonwealth States as well as Israel and some Nordic states, Aust (n 7) 173.

53 Shaw (n 44) 106.

54 See eg Australia: Annemarie Devereux and Sarah McCosker 'International Law and Australian Law' in Rothwell and Crawford (n 32) 23, 28; see generally Jonas Ebbesson, *Compatibility of International and National Environmental Law* (Kluwer Law International 1996).

that ministers will act in accordance with a ratified international treaty before it has been formally enacted through domestic legislation.[55] Implementation of international agreements can be complicated by a further layer of governance in federal systems. In Malaysia, for example, where powers over 'land' are the exclusive domain of the provincial states, efforts to implement national access and benefit sharing laws under the CBD, and now the 2010 Nagoya Protocol on Access and Benefit Sharing, have been stymied by divisions between state and federal governments.[56]

The recognition of customary international law in a given country might also require transformation through legislation.[57] It is, however, often the role of the judiciary to recognize customary international law in domestic law.[58] Well-known cases such as *Minors Oposa v Secretary of the Department of Environmental and Natural Resources*[59] in the Philippines, and the Indian case of *Vellore Citizens' Welfare Forum v Union of India and Others*,[60] led the way for the many active judiciaries that have since given prominence to customary international law relevant to environmental protection.[61] Many notable decisions are discussed in Chapter 60 of this volume. These decisions can themselves be a supplementary source of international environmental law.[62] However, as discussed below, the very nature of custom—broad and contested—might mean it is more often cited in judicial settings as informing the interpretation of domestic laws rather than being a ground for a claim.

C. Interpreting International Law

The interpretation of international environmental law is performed in different domestic contexts, including in: the articulation of international commitments in domestic laws; the application of the laws by administrative functionaries; and the evaluation or enforcement of the laws by courts and tribunals. In addition to interpretations of international law recognized in domestic law, interpretations of domestic law might be informed or guided by international law—whether or not it is binding on the state.[63] The Colombian Supreme Court of Justice, for example, considered the relevance of several

[55] Devereux and McCosker (n 54) 44–45.

[56] Gurdial Nijar, 'An Asian Developing Country's View on the Implementation Challenges of the Nagoya Protocol' in Elisa Morgera, Matthias Buck, and Elsa Tsioumani (eds), *The 2010 Nagoya Protocol on Access and Benefit-sharing in Perspective* (Brill Online 2012) 247, 264.

[57] See eg Alice de Jonge, 'Australia' in Shelton (n 22) 34.

[58] Shaw (n 44) 106 (UK).

[59] *Minors Oposa et al v Secretary of the Environment and Natural Resources Fulgencio Factoran* (30 July 1993) GR No 101083.

[60] [1996] 5 SCC 647.

[61] Palmer and Robb (n 6).

[62] ICJ Statute, art 38.

[63] See Part IX, 'International Environmental Law in National/Regional Courts', in this volume.

international laws in a public law action concerning deforestation in the Amazon. The court held that international law—including the Stockholm and Rio Declarations[64]—constituted a 'global ecological public order' to guide national law and 'resolve citizen complaints about the destruction of our habitat'.[65]

National courts and tribunals with specific jurisdiction over environmental matters can facilitate the implementation of international environmental law. With specialized knowledge and training, judges and arbitrators in environmental courts and tribunals can be well placed to identify and apply international law relevant to environmental protection.[66] The environmental courts and tribunals in countries such as Bangladesh, Chile, China, India, and Kenya have played an important role in activating international environmental law in the domestic sphere.[67] Concerns that specialization might serve to frustrate integration of environmental matters in mainstream laws have not stopped the ongoing creation of environmental courts in states and provinces around the world.[68]

International courts and tribunals can be asked to decide whether international environmental law has been implemented at the national level. In the *India—Certain Measures Relating to Solar Cells and Solar Modules* dispute decided by the World Trade Organization (WTO),[69] for example, India's argument that the challenged measure implemented international commitments was rejected. India had relied on several international instruments to justify its domestic content requirements in the production of solar energy,[70] including the UNFCCC, the Rio Declaration, and Rio+20 'The Future We Want'.[71] However, the WTO dispute settlement body was not satisfied that 'the international instruments India identified are rules that form part of its domestic legal system'.[72]

[64] UN, 'Report of the United Nations Conference on the Human Environment' (5–16 June 1972) UN Doc A/CONF.48/14/Rev.1, 3, ch 1—'Declaration of the United Nations Conference on the Human Environment'; *Report of the United Nations Conference on Environment and Development* (UN 1993) vol I, annex I.

[65] *Andrea Lozano Barragán and others v The President of Colombia and others* STC4360-2018 de la Corte Suprema de Justicia, Sala de Casacion Civil, MP Luis Armando Tolosa Villabona (5 April 2018) 22; see unofficial translation <https://www.elaw.org/CO_Amazon> accessed 1 November 2018.

[66] Brian Preston, 'The Role of Environmental Courts and Tribunals in Promoting the Rule of Law and Ensuring Equal Access to Justice for All' *Environmental Law and Management Journal*, 29 (2017): 7.

[67] Lal Kurukulasuriya and Kristen Powell, 'History of Environmental Courts and UNEP's Role' *Journal of Court Innovation*, 3/1 (2010): 269; Caiphas Soyapi, 'Environmental Protection in Kenya's Environment and Land Court' *Journal of Environmental Law*, 31/1 (2019): 151.

[68] George Pring and Catherine Pring, *Environmental Courts & Tribunals: A Guide for Policy Makers* (UNEP 2016).

[69] *India—Certain Measures Relating to Solar Cells and Solar Modules* (Appellate Body Report) [16 September 2016] WTO Doc WT/DS456/AB/R.

[70] Ibid [5.149].

[71] UNGA 66/288, 'The Future We Want' (11 September 2012) UN Doc A/Res/66/288.

[72] *India—Solar Cells* (n 69) [5.148].

IV. PRINCIPLES SUPPORTING IMPLEMENTATION

Assessments and audits have identified significant gaps in national measures to implement international environmental treaties.[73] States continue to be challenged by others for their failure to adhere to customary international law concerning the environment.[74] As discussed in this section, many of the principles of international environmental law addressed in this volume—such as cooperation,[75] differentiated responsibilities,[76] and public participation[77]—aim to facilitate implementation.

A. Cooperation

States have recognized the importance of cooperating in their protection of the environment and the principle extends to international efforts to implement international environmental law in the domestic sphere.[78] Information gathering and monitoring of implementation,[79] as well as awareness raising, are important cooperative functions that can aid implementation of international environmental law.

Clearing-house mechanisms and reporting requirements under international environmental treaties generate information on the state of the environment and make predictions that can be important for the implementation of international environmental law.[80] National reporting cycles can ensure that state parties are regularly reviewing implementation and they provide a degree of accountability to other states parties—and the public—for the implementation of treaty commitments. Initiatives aimed at streamlining national reports to multiple institutions can aid implementation and reduce costs.[81]

Some international environmental treaties establish expert bodies, and work with independent organizations, to generate information important for implementation. Subsidiary bodies that provide scientific or technical advice relevant to the implementation of a treaty have been established, for example, under CITES, UNFCCC, CBD, the

[73] See eg *Global Environment Outlook—GEO 5: Environment for the Future We Want* (UNEP 2012).

[74] See Chapter 51, 'Compliance Theory', in this volume.

[75] See Chapters 22 and 23, 'Good Faith' and 'Customary International Law and the Environment', in this volume.

[76] See Chapter 19, 'Differentiation', in this volume.

[77] See Chapter 21, 'Public Participation', in this volume.

[78] Stockholm Declaration (n 64) principle 24.

[79] See Chapter 52, 'Transparency Procedures', in this volume.

[80] See Sands and Peel (n 3) 685 ff.

[81] See eg Australian Government and the Secretariat of the Pacific Regional Environment Programme (SPREP) 'Streamlined reporting by Pacific Island countries to the biodiversity-related multilateral environmental agreements' (July 2010) <https://www.cbd.int/doc/nr/finalreport.pdf> accessed 1 November 2018.

1987 Montreal Protocol, and the 1946 Whaling Convention. Expert information from international organizations (such as the International Union for the Conservation of Nature, the Intergovernmental Platform on Biodiversity and Ecosystem Services, and the Intergovernmental Panel on Climate Change (IPCC)) is also instrumental in the monitoring of implementation of international environmental law.[82] The reports are available to the public which, as discussed in Section IV.C, can play a further role in aiding implementation.

Across the United Nations (UN), meetings of the various bodies charged with environmental oversight can facilitate implementation of international environmental law. These bodies develop goals, and report on progress in meeting the goals at the national level. The Sustainable Development Goals (SDGs),[83] for example, include environmental issues that are reviewed by the UN Environment Programme (UNEP) through the Global Environment Outlook.[84] UN bodies also undertake audits of national implementation of international environmental agreements in an effort to facilitate implementation.[85]

Oversight by the governing and subsidiary bodies administering a treaty is also a cooperative approach to implementation of treaty commitments. It has been suggested that regular meetings of the states parties to an international environmental treaty are themselves essential to implementation.[86] Treaty institutions can have a range of oversight functions, including a relatively passive review of national reports on implementation that might be required under a treaty, or more active forms of monitoring from which recommendations for implementation might arise. Under the CBD, for example, the Conference of the Parties is required to 'keep under review' the implementation of the treaty, including by overseeing the submission of national reports and establishing subsidiary bodies to advise on implementation.[87] The Global Biodiversity Outlook is prepared on a regular basis to report to the Conference of the Parties on the state of biodiversity and national implementation.[88] The 1972 World Heritage Convention actively monitors the natural properties on the World Heritage List, with concerns about implementation discussed regularly by the World Heritage Committee.[89]

[82] See Chapter 15, 'The Role of Science', in this volume.

[83] UNGA Res 70/1, 'Transforming our World: The 2030 Agenda for Sustainable Development' (21 October 2015) UN Doc A/RES/70/1, Declaration.

[84] See UNEP, 'Environment under review' <https://www.unenvironment.org/explore-topics/environment-under-review> accessed 1 November 2018.

[85] See eg *Auditing the Implementation of Multilateral Environmental Agreements (MEAs): A Primer for Auditors* (Developed in cooperation with INTOSAI-WGEA) (UNEP 2010); see also Piret Kuldna et al, *Reviewing the Coherence and Effectiveness of Implementation of UNEP Multilateral Biodiversity Agreements in Estonia and Tanzania: Summary Report* (SEI Tallinn and SEI Africa Centre 2014).

[86] P van Heijnsbergen, *International Legal Protection of Wild Fauna and Flora* (IOS Press 1997) 232.

[87] CBD, art 23.4.

[88] Decision II/1, 'Report of the First Meeting of the Subsidiary Body on Scientific, Technical and Technological Advice' (30 November 1995) UN Doc UNEP/CBD/COP/2/19, 44.

[89] Gionata Buzzini and Luigi Conorelli, 'Art 11 List of World Heritage in Danger and Deletion of a Property from the World Heritage List' in Francesco Francioni (ed), *The 1972 World Heritage Convention: A Commentary* (OUP 2008) 175.

The oversight and monitoring processes can lead to recommendations and assistance with implementation to individual state parties or to decisions that apply to the parties as a whole. Treaty mechanisms to deal with non-compliance also form part of the cooperative efforts of states parties to facilitate the implementation of treaty commitments.[90]

UN bodies dealing with environmental issues and environmental treaty regimes also promote implementation of international environmental law through raising awareness of environmental values and harms. Targets established for implementation of the CBD, for example, include ensuring that 'people are aware of the values of biodiversity and the steps they can take to conserve and use it sustainably'.[91] UNEP is engaged in a range of public outreach activities including World Environment Day.[92] The UNEP Art for the Environment initiative and other art-based projects have been used as an important vehicle for raising awareness of environmental values and harms among the states representatives attending UN and treaty meetings.[93] In India, the Science Express—Biodiversity Special was a mobile exhibition to inform the public about biodiversity that coincided with India hosting a meeting of the Conference of the Parties to the CBD in 2012.[94]

B. Common But Differentiated Responsibilities

Despite shifts in its conception, the principle of common but differentiated responsibilities remains a vehicle for developing countries to procure different forms of assistance with the implementation of international environmental law.[95] Provisions for the transfer of technology, capacity-building, and financial assistance in international environmental agreements are typical measures aimed at enabling implementation of treaty commitments in the global South.[96]

The transfer of technology provisions in the Montreal Protocol, for example, require 'that the best available, environmentally safe substitutes and related technologies are expeditiously transferred' to developing countries 'under fair and most favourable

[90] See Chapter 56, 'Non-Compliance Procedures', in this volume.

[91] Decision X/2, 'The Strategic Plan for Biodiversity 2011–2020 and the Aichi Biodiversity Targets' (29 October 2010) UN Doc UNEP/CBD/COP/DEC/X/2, 1, annex: Aichi Target 1, 8.

[92] See <https://www.worldenvironmentday.global> accessed 27 December 2019; UNEP, '12 art installations to be unveiled across Asia-Pacific to mark World Environment Day' (30 May 2018) <https://www.unenvironment.org/news-and-stories/press-release/12-art-installations-be-unveiled-across-asia-pacific-mark-world> accessed 1 November 2018.

[93] See Alice Palmer, 'Legal Dimensions to Valuing Aesthetics in World Heritage Decisions' *Social & Legal Studies*, 26/5 (2017): 581.

[94] See <https://sciencexpress.in/ScienceExpressV/> accessed 1 November 2018.

[95] See Chapter 19, 'Differentiation', in this volume; cf. Mario Prost and Alejandra Camprubí, 'Against Fairness? International Environmental Law, Disciplinary Bias, and Pareto Justice' *Leiden Journal of International Law*, 25/2 (2012): 379.

[96] See Chapters 54 and 55, 'Financial Assistance' and 'Technology Assistance and Transfers', in this volume.

conditions'.[97] The transfer of this technology was necessary for the implementation of that treaty in developing countries.[98] Capacity-building requirements under international environmental agreements—such as contributing to hazardous waste management capacity in developing countries under the 1989 Basel Convention[99]—are also intended to assist implementation of the treaty. Financial assistance is another manifestation of the principle of common but differentiated responsibilities. Where treaties make developing country commitments conditional on financial assistance from developed countries, there is a direct link between implementation and differentiated responsibility.[100]

Issues arise when these technical and financial assistance provisions are themselves not implemented, or when they are implemented in a way that promotes the interests of the donor countries over those of developing states.[101] Initiatives aimed at capacity-building as between countries of the global South can address some of these concerns, although they place less emphasis on the responsibility of industrialized states to support developing countries in their implementation efforts.[102]

C. Public Participation

Public participation in international and national environmental governance is an international environmental principle that is important for the implementation of international environmental law.[103] It is a principle that has been extended to other areas of international law impacting on domestic environmental measures, such as the rules and institutions of the WTO.[104] The principle is reflected in the extensive involvement of civil society in international environmental conferences and meetings of multilateral environmental agreements. It refers to a range of non-state actors and different forms of

[97] art 10(A), as amended.

[98] Peter Lawrence, 'Technology Transfer Funds and the Law—Recent Amendments to the Montreal Protocol on Substances that Deplete the Ozone Layer' *Journal of Environmental Law*, 4/1 (1992): 15.

[99] See Basel Convention Secretariat, 'Environmentally sound management of priority waste streams: end-of-life ships' <https://www.basel.int/Implementation/TechnicalAssistance1/Dismantlingofships/tabid/3868/Default.aspx> accessed 1 November 2018.

[100] See Mark Drumbl, 'Northern Economic Obligation, Southern Moral Entitlement, and International Environmental Governance' *Columbia Journal of International Law*, 27 (2002): 363.

[101] See Karin Mickelson, 'South, North, International Environmental Law, and International Environmental Lawyers' *Yearbook of International Environmental Law*, 11/1 (2000): 52.

[102] See Koh Kheng-Lian and Nicholas Robinson, 'South-South Cooperation: Foundations for Sustainable Development' in Alam *et al* (n 1) 553.

[103] See Chapter 21, 'Public Participation', in this volume.

[104] See Alice Palmer, 'Civil Society Participation in WTO Disputes' in Luiz Baptista, Umberto Junior, and Alan Yanovich (eds), *10 anos de OMC—Uma análise do Sistema de Solução de Controvérsias e Perspectivas* (Aduaneiras 2007) 223–258; Alfred Rest, 'Enhanced Implementation of International Environmental Treaties By Judiciary—Access to Justice in International Environmental Law for Individuals and NGOs: Efficacious Enforcement by the Permanent Court of Arbitration' *Macquarie Journal of International and Comparative Environmental Law*, 1/1 (2004): 1.

participation—in the making and implementation of international environmental law as well as mechanisms of accountability.[105]

Public participation can be internal to the governance processes, such as the participation of non-governmental organizations (NGOs) in the compliance committee of the 1998 Aarhus Convention. It can also be external to the treaty regime, ranging from technical assistance with implementation to scrutiny and shaming.[106] Interventions from public interest organizations in national and international disputes also serve an important function in the implementation of international environmental law.[107]

V. CONCLUSION

The condition of the global environment, and dire projections for the health of the planet's ecosystems, justify critical reflection on the foundation and methods of international environmental law.[108] But the world's environmental crisis also warrants reliance on the laws and institutions that states have created over many decades to protect the environment. National 'implementation' is the final stage at which those international environmental laws must take effect.

However, the nature of international environmental law is always evolving. The conception of 'implementation' as a top-down imposition of the law of nations on states is too limited for international environmental law. As evidenced so keenly in the Paris Agreement,[109] states are overtly determining their international environmental commitments in light of non-environmental domestic concerns while non-state actors are assuming responsibility for environmental protection at the local level in light of global environmental effects.[110] Local laws, policies, and knowledge systems are emerging as international standards made and administered by networks of local communities, business organizations, and sub-national municipal governments.[111]

[105] Harro van Asselt, 'The Role of Non-State Actors in Reviewing Ambition, Implementation, and Compliance under the Paris Agreement' *Climate Law*, 6/1–2 (2016): 91.

[106] See Sebastian Oberthür *et al*, *Participation of Non-Governmental Organisations in International Environmental Cooperation: Legal Basis and Practical Experience* (Erich Schmidt Verlag 2002).

[107] Lavanya Rajamani, 'Public Interest Litigation in India: Exploring Issues of Access, Participation, Equity, Effectiveness and Sustainability' *Journal of Environmental Law*, 19/3 (2007): 293.

[108] See Usha Natarajan, 'Third World Approaches to International Law (TWAIL) and the Environment' in Andreas Philippopoulos-Mihalopoulos and Victoria Brooks (eds), *Research Methods in Environmental Law: A Handbook* (Edward Elgar 2017) 207.

[109] See Chapter 29, 'Climate Change', in this volume.

[110] See Penny Wong, 'From Copenhagen to Paris: Climate Change and the Limits of Rationality, Multilateralism, and Leadership' *Brown Journal of World Affairs*, 21/2 (2015): 267.

[111] See Jutta Brunnée, 'International Environmental Law and Community Interests: Procedural Aspects' in Eyal Benvenisti and Georg Nolte (eds), *Community Interests Across International Law* (OUP 2018) ch 9, 151; Bradley Karkkainen, 'Post-Sovereign Environmental Governance' *Global Environmental Politics*, 4/1 (2004): 72.

These developments set international environmental law apart from other fields of international law, requiring a different conception of global law-making and implementation as a function of the state and more as a product of community enterprise.[112]

BIBLIOGRAPHY

Daniel Bodansky, 'Implementation of International Environmental Law' *Japanese Yearbook of International Law*, 54 (2011): 62

Wilbert Kaahwa, 'Improving Implementation of International Environmental Law: A View from the East African Community' *Thesaurus Acroasium* 31 (2002): 601

Alice Palmer and Cairo Robb (eds), *International Environmental Reports, Volume 4: International Environmental Law in National Courts* (CUP 2004)

Catherine Redgwell, 'National Implementation' in Daniel Bodansky, Jutta Brunnée, and Ellen Hey (eds), *The Oxford Handbook of International Environmental Law* (1st edn, OUP 2008) 922

Karen Scott, 'Non-Compliance Procedures and the Implementation of Commitments Under Wildlife Treaties' in Michael Bowman, Peter Davies, and Edward Goodwin (eds), *Research Handbook on Biodiversity and Law* (Edward Elgar 2016) 414

Dinah Shelton (ed), *International Law and Domestic Legal Systems: Incorporation, Transformation and Persuasion* (OUP 2011)

[112] See Edith Weiss, 'Rule of Law for Nature in a Kaleidoscopic World' in Christina Voigt (ed), *Rule of Law for Nature: New Dimensions and Ideas in Environmental Law* (CUP 2013) 27; Kishan Khoday and Usha Natarajan, 'Fairness and International Environmental Law from Below: Social Movements and Legal Transformation in India' *Leiden Journal of International Law*, 25/2 (2012): 415.

CHAPTER 60

INTERNATIONAL ENVIRONMENTAL LAW DISPUTES BEFORE INTERNATIONAL COURTS AND TRIBUNALS

NATALIE KLEIN*

I. INTRODUCTION

In the incipient stages of international environmental law (IEL), any focus on the role of international courts and tribunals was limited to the contribution that a small number of cases had made to some key IEL principles.[1] Some scholars gave early consideration to the potential use of international courts and tribunals to resolve IEL disputes,[2] but the possibilities explored in this literature were largely not pursued in the practice of states during the twentieth century. When the corpus of IEL expanded in the final decades of the twentieth century, proposals for an international court for IEL disputes

* The author gratefully acknowledges the editorial assistance of Matthew Kingsland in the preparation of this chapter. Any remaining errors are of course my own.

[1] See *Trail Smelter Arbitration (United States/Canada)* (1938 and 1941) 3 RIAA 1905; *Lake Lanoux Arbitration (Spain/France)* (1957) 12 RIAA 281. For discussion of these cases, see Chapter 27, 'Judicial Development', in this volume.

[2] See eg Richard Bilder, 'The Settlement of Disputes in the Field of the International Law of the Environment' *Recueil des Cours*, 144/1 (1975): 139.

were mooted,[3] but never gained enough traction to proceed. Instead, to the extent that IEL disputes emerged, they were managed through negotiations or otherwise dispute avoidance (non-compliance) procedures.[4]

Moreover, a core difficulty has been identifying what constitutes an IEL dispute.[5] Questions relating to the performance of IEL obligations also frequently incorporate general questions of international law, such as the law of treaties, state responsibility, and sources of law. For the purposes of this chapter, I consider 'international environmental law' as the law enshrined in diverse treaties addressing issues pertaining to the environment, as well as key environmental principles discussed in preceding chapters of this handbook. As such, IEL disputes are those where a complainant (or complainants) challenge the adherence of a state to its treaty commitments or the consistency of a state's actions with those key environmental principles reflected in customary or general international law or where there are implications for the environment under international law because of state action.[6] The focus of this chapter is on how these disputes are resolved before international courts or tribunals, rather than on the substance of the disputes before these bodies.[7]

In considering how IEL disputes are resolved before international courts and tribunals, this chapter will address (in Section II) when parties will decide to litigate an IEL dispute as opposed to utilizing another form of dispute settlement. Assuming there is reason to pursue adjudication or arbitration, Section III addresses questions of jurisdiction. Section IV deals with preliminary matters that emerge in these cases, notably questions of standing and whether provisional measures are needed and may be secured before an international court or tribunal. Section V turns to substantive matters, but only in the context of presentation of the case in terms of evidence and use of experts. As mentioned at the outset, substantive IEL, as decided in international courts and tribunals, is addressed elsewhere in this handbook. Section VI assesses the available reparations in the resolution of IEL disputes before international courts and tribunals. In conclusion, considerable progress may be noted in respect of the use of international courts and tribunals for IEL disputes, but it is prudent to observe that in this area of international law, preventing the emergence of IEL disputes is ultimately more important than ex post facto responses to environmental damage.

[3] See eg Stuart Bruce, 'The Project for an International Environmental Court' in Christian Tomuschat *et al* (eds), *Conciliation in International Law* (Brill Nijhoff 2016) 133; Sean Murphy, 'Does the World Need a New International Environmental Court?' *George Washington International Law and Economics*, 32/3 (2000): 333.

[4] For discussion see Chapter 56, 'Non-Compliance Procedures', in this volume.

[5] Alan Boyle and James Harrison, 'Judicial Settlement of International Environmental Disputes: Current Problems' *Journal of International Dispute Settlement*, 4/2 (2013): 245, 247–250.

[6] In this chapter, I put to one side those disputes where it may be argued that non-state actors are directly bound by IEL and could be held responsible for IEL violations.

[7] The latter is addressed in Chapter 27, 'Judicial Development', in this volume.

II. WHEN TO LITIGATE

Any decision to pursue legal proceedings before an international court or tribunal will entail many considerations as to the potential advantages and possible risks of litigation.[8] Incentives to pursue international litigation may include achieving a legally binding outcome issued by an ostensibly neutral third party to stop the respondent state from pursuing a particular course of conduct perceived as harmful to the environment or to change the behaviour of the respondent state to align with expected requirements under international law. Litigation may also be preferred where negotiations have reached an impasse or the bargaining power between the states concerned is uneven and the less powerful state considers that litigation will equalize their positions from a legal perspective. This option may be particularly appealing in the context of an IEL dispute where economic or strategic imperatives may otherwise drive a state to pursue an environmentally-harmful course of conduct.[9] A binding judgement may also contribute to resolving one aspect of a wider dispute and provide an additional bargaining tool in seeking to restore relations between the disputant parties.

Yet entrusting a dispute to a third party to produce a legally binding decision necessarily involves risk, as a complainant state's firm view as to its legal position will be challenged by the respondent state and may not ultimately be vindicated. Litigation may not always create a zero-sum outcome, but elements of cases are won and lost across the many claims presented. For example, in *Pulp Mills*, the International Court of Justice (ICJ) concluded that Argentina had not established that Uruguay had breached substantive obligations set out in the 1975 Statute governing their use of the River Uruguay, but that Uruguay had violated procedural obligations required under that 1975 Statute.

When assessing the relative benefits and disadvantages of litigation before international courts and tribunals, the advantages and drawbacks of alternative dispute resolution avenues are also relevant. Notable in this regard, negotiation remains a key mode of dispute settlement in international law.[10] IEL disputes are no exception,[11] and negotiations are often anticipated prior to resorting to any third-party mechanism.[12] Negotiations may hold inherent advantages over the resolution of IEL disputes through

[8] See Shirley Scott, 'Litigation Versus Dispute Resolution through Political Processes' in Natalie Klein (ed), *Litigating International Law Disputes: Weighing the Balance* (CUP 2014) 24.

[9] An example of this dynamic may be seen in Australia and New Zealand's efforts to challenge French nuclear testing in the Pacific, which was considered an issue of significant national security for France; see *Nuclear Tests (Australia/France)* (Judgement) [1974] ICJ Rep 253; *Nuclear Tests (New Zealand/France)* (Judgement) [1974] ICJ Rep 457; *Request for an Examination of the Situation in Accordance with Paragraph 63 of the Court's Judgement of 20 December 1974 in the Nuclear Tests (New Zealand/France) Case* (Order) [1995] ICJ Rep 288.

[10] See eg Yoshifumi Tanaka, *The Peaceful Settlement of International Disputes* (CUP 2018) 28.

[11] Malgosia Fitzmaurice, 'International Protection of the Environment' *Recueil des Cours*, 293/6 (2001): 352.

[12] See eg 1979 Convention on Migratory Species (CMS), art XIII.

litigation because they allow for consideration of non-legal issues and may directly engage scientific and other experts more than is possible in the confines of a court or arbitral proceeding. The *Aerial Herbicide Spraying* case was ultimately resolved through negotiations before proceeding to oral hearings at the ICJ.[13] Negotiations may also be more conducive to a compromise outcome between the parties concerned, but that compromise may not be the ideal result for the environment.

Multilateral environmental agreements (MEAs) do not prioritize the use of international courts and tribunals as a primary mode of resolving disputes arising under those treaties. Earlier treaties, such as the 1946 International Convention for the Regulation of Whaling (ICRW) and the 1971 Ramsar Convention on Wetlands, do not contain a dispute settlement clause. Both the 1973 Convention on the International Trade in Endangered Species (CITES) and the CMS expect parties to negotiate and only turn to arbitration with the consent of the states concerned.[14] A different approach is seen in the 1992 United Nations Framework Convention on Climate Change (UNFCCC), the 1994 Convention to Combat Desertification (CCD), and the 1992 Convention on Biological Diversity (CBD). Each of these treaties anticipates that states will resort to negotiations or use the good offices or mediation of a third party before resorting to either arbitration, adjudication or, if there is no agreement on arbitration or adjudication, compulsory conciliation.[15] The 2006 International Tropical Timber Agreement only contains non-compliance procedures whereby any complaint or dispute relating to interpretation or application of the agreement are to be submitted to the International Tropical Timber Council established under the Agreement.[16]

Beyond the MEAs, other treaties that may raise IEL disputes or have implications for IEL may entail their own dispute settlement procedures. This is evident in disputes brought to the World Trade Organization (WTO) in the context of challenges to trade measures that have been imposed to protect endangered species and exhaustible resources.[17] Investment disputes have also prompted consideration of IEL; most commonly the environmental questions have arisen where a state's introduction of new regulatory requirements to protect the environment have prompted the investor to claim an impairment of their rights for investment protection.[18] The 1982 UN Convention on the Law of the Sea (UNCLOS) allows for compulsory arbitration or adjudication in relation to disputes over the interpretation or application of its provisions that protect and preserve the marine environment.[19] In each of these instances, an international court or

[13] *Case Concerning Aerial Herbicide Spraying (Ecuador/Colombia)* (Judgement) [2013] ICJ Rep 278 (order removing the case from the list).

[14] CMS, art XIII; CITES, art XVIII.

[15] UNFCCC, art 14; CCD, art 28; CBD, art 27.

[16] art 31.

[17] *United States—Import Prohibition of Certain Shrimp and Shrimp Products* (Appellate Body Report) [12 October 1998] WTO Doc WT/DS58/AB/R.

[18] See eg *Methanex Corporation v United States of America* (Final Award of the Tribunal on Jurisdiction and Merits, 3 August 2005) <https://www.italaw.com/cases/documents/696>.

[19] A key example being the *South China Sea* arbitration; *The South China Sea Arbitration (Philippines/China)* (Final award of 12 July 2016) PCA Case no 2013-19 (South China Sea case).

tribunal may be engaged in resolving questions of IEL, or that otherwise have a bearing on the protection of the environment.

International courts and tribunals may also be relevant for IEL disputes where an Advisory Opinion is sought for a non-binding articulation of legal responses to specific questions for advice. For example, the ICJ considered the relevance of environmental principles in its Opinion on the *Threat or Use of Nuclear Weapons*.[20] More recently, a proposal from the International Union for Conservation of Nature at its World Conservation Congress adopted a resolution seeking an Advisory Opinion on 'the legal status and content of the principle of sustainable development taking the needs of future generations into particular account'.[21] The Alliance of Small Island States previously sought an ICJ Advisory Opinion as to whether countries have a legal responsibility to ensure that any activities on their territory that emit greenhouse gases do not harm other states.[22] The Advisory Opinions from the International Tribunal for the Law of the Sea (ITLOS) and its Seabed Disputes Chamber have made important contributions to the development of IEL in the marine context.[23] While Advisory Opinions may clarify or elaborate on IEL, they are not strictly a mechanism for dispute settlement.[24] Moreover, the availability of this option is quite limited as not all international courts and tribunals have the power to issue Advisory Opinions,[25] and because it usually requires a coalition of states, rather than an individual actor, to access this procedure.

III. JURISDICTION OVER IEL DISPUTES

Even if an actor decides to litigate in an international court or tribunal, there remains a key hurdle of determining where jurisdiction is available. Consent to the exercise of jurisdiction is essential to the resolution of IEL disputes before international courts or

[20] *Legality of the Threat or Use of Nuclear Weapons* (Advisory Opinion) [1996] ICJ Rep 226.

[21] IUCN World Conservation Congress, 'Request for an Advisory Opinion of the International Court of Justice on the principle of sustainable development in view of the needs of future generations' (1–10 September 2016) WCC-2016-Res-079-EN.

[22] For discussion on this option, see Mariya Gromilova, 'Rescuing the People of Tuvalu: Towards an ICJ Advisory Opinion on the International Legal Obligations to Protect the Environment and Human Rights of Populations Affected by Climate Change' *Intercultural Human Rights Law Review*, 10 (2015): 233.

[23] See *Request for an advisory opinion submitted by the Sub-Regional Fisheries Commission (SRFC)* (Advisory Opinion) [2015] ITLOS Rep 4; *Responsibilities and obligations of States sponsoring persons and entities with respect to activities in the Area* (Advisory Opinion) [2011] ITLOS Rep 10.

[24] See Hugh Thirlway, 'Advisory Opinions' in Rüdiger Wolfrum (ed), *Max Planck Encyclopedia of Public International Law* (OUP 2006) para 2.

[25] Ibid, para 4—The power to provide an Advisory Opinion is not considered an inherent power but must be provided for in the constituent instrument of the relevant court or tribunal.

tribunals.[26] For the resolution of IEL disputes before the ICJ, states have relied on the 'optional clause' in Article 36.2 of the ICJ Statute whereby states may agree in advance to the compulsory jurisdiction of the court for the resolution of disputes consistent with any restrictions that may be set out in the unilateral declarations accepting such jurisdiction. For example, Australia instituted proceedings challenging Japan's scientific whaling programme in the Antarctica for its consistency with the ICRW based on each state's acceptance of compulsory jurisdiction under Article 36.2.[27] The availability of general jurisdiction before the ICJ may be advantageous where an IEL dispute extends to other violations of international law, including, for example, human rights. However, it is more likely that the available jurisdiction will be more limited.[28]

An alternative basis of jurisdiction before the ICJ arises under Article 36.1 of the ICJ Statute, whereby jurisdiction may exist based on a compromissory clause in an MEA or other international treaty, or on the basis of a special agreement between the states in dispute referring the case to the court. The *Pulp Mills* case, for example, was based on the compromissory clause in the 1975 Statute whereas Ecuador relied on the compromissory clauses of the Pact of Bogota and the 1988 UN Convention against Illicit Traffic in Narcotic Drugs and Psychotropic Substances in the *Aerial Herbicide Spraying* case.[29]

Aspects of IEL disputes may be presented in compulsory dispute settlement mechanisms through the WTO and potentially under investment or free trade agreements. In this instance, the available jurisdiction may not align precisely with the environmental issue that needs to be addressed. The subject matter of these disputes will concern, respectively, the nullification or impairment of trade rights or alleged violations of principles protecting investment. As such, any IEL violation must be addressed in these more limited settings.

By contrast, disputes concerning the marine environment are likely to fall within the jurisdictional scope of UNCLOS. The claims presented to an UNCLOS court or tribunal must concern the interpretation or application of that Convention,[30] rather than allowing for claims of other related MEAs.[31] Nonetheless, Article 293 of UNCLOS, which sets out the applicable law for resolving disputes under UNCLOS, allows for consideration of 'other rules of international law not incompatible with' UNCLOS. For example, the *South China Sea* tribunal utilized the CBD in setting forth a definition of

[26] 'One of the fundamental principles of the Court's Statute is that it cannot decide a dispute between states without the consent of those states to its jurisdiction'; *East Timor (Portugal/Australia)* [1995] ICJ Rep 90 [26].

[27] *Whaling in the Antarctic (Australia/ Japan, New Zealand intervening)* (Judgement) [2014] ICJ Rep 226 (Whaling in the Antarctic case).

[28] For a discussion of these problems, including the risks of 'cluster litigation', see Boyle and Harrison (n 5) 250–256.

[29] *Aerial Herbicide Spraying (Ecuador/Colombia)* (Application instituting Proceedings) [2008] ICJ.

[30] art 288.

[31] See Kate Parlett, 'Beyond the Four Corners of the Convention: Expanding the Scope of Jurisdiction of Law of the Sea Tribunals' *Ocean Development and International Law*, 48/3–4 (2017): 284.

'ecosystem',[32] and considered CITES in assessing the application of Article 194.5's reference to preserving 'the habitat of depleted, threatened or endangered species and other forms of marine life'.[33] There is thus significant potential to utilize the UNCLOS dispute settlement procedures for IEL disputes relating to the marine environment, and scholars have considered this possibility for disputes concerning climate change.[34]

IV. PRELIMINARY MATTERS

Beyond the need to establish jurisdiction for the resolution of an IEL dispute before an international court or tribunal, a potential litigant must consider any challenges to the admissibility of the dispute. These challenges may concern the standing of the parties, whether the dispute is moot, whether a 'dispute' exists, or whether the question before the court is political rather than legal.[35] A challenge to standing is the most likely admissibility argument to emerge in IEL disputes given the broad harm that may ensue from IEL violations and is discussed in the first section below. Another preliminary matter concerns the initial steps that may need to be taken to preserve the rights of the parties pending the resolution of the dispute before the international court or tribunal. The relevant mechanism that may be brought into action in this regard is a request for the prescription of provisional measures and is discussed in the second section below.

A. Standing Before International Courts or Tribunals for IEL Disputes

For a state to have standing before an international court or tribunal, it must demonstrate that it has a sufficient legal interest in the case.[36] From the *South West Africa* cases, this interest may be evidenced through the existence of a treaty binding the parties concerned.[37] It was on this basis that it was apparent that Australia could institute

[32] South China Sea case (n 19) [945].

[33] Ibid [956].

[34] See eg Daniel Bodansky, 'The Role of the International Court of Justice in Addressing Climate Change: Some Preliminary Reflections' *Arizona State Law Journal*, 49/1 (2017): 659; Alan Boyle, 'Law of the Sea Perspectives on Climate Change' *International Journal of Marine and Coastal Law*, 27/4 (2012): 831.

[35] See Tanaka (n 10) 167–170.

[36] See *South West Africa, Second Phase (Ethiopia/South Africa; Liberia/South Africa)* (Judgement) [1966] ICJ Rep 6 (South West Africa cases); see further Natalie Klein and Tim Stephens, 'Enforcing Rights in Areas beyond National Jurisdiction through International Litigation' in Clive Schofield, Seokwoo Lee, and Moon-Sang Kwon (eds), *The Limits of Maritime Jurisdiction* (Martinus Nijhoff 2014) 525.

[37] South West Africa cases (n 36) 51.

proceedings against Japan challenging the legality of its scientific whaling programme in Antarctica under the ICRW.[38] Australia did not have to establish that it had suffered harm by dint of Japan's actions.[39]

Similarly, in the *South China Sea* arbitration where there was contested territorial sovereignty over features in the Spratly Island group and the tribunal was not addressing these competing claims, the Philippines was still able to allege that China was in violation of its obligations under Part XII of UNCLOS concerning land reclamation and harmful fishing activities.[40] It did not matter what maritime zone was at issue in resolving claims relating to the protection and preservation of the marine environment, as the Tribunal considered these obligations existed throughout the oceans and applied to all state parties.[41]

This approach is sensible in that it underlines the *erga omnes* (towards all) nature of key IEL principles.[42] Although the position from these cases is clear and was not contested in each of these cases, the question of standing has been a pertinent consideration in relation to any possible case at the ICJ challenging a state's failure to mitigate climate change.[43] Compensating one injured party when there is an *erga omnes* obligation is also potentially problematic, as is addressed in Section VI.

B. Provisional Measures

Another preliminary matter that concerns IEL disputes before international courts and tribunals is the availability of provisional measures. Provisional measures are important because they derive from the 'elementary juridical principle that the judgement of a court should be effective and that to ensure this it may, while a case is before the Court, be essential to restrain either party, or both, from disrupting the situation, or attempting to present its adversary with a fait accompli'.[44] The very existence of this tool may be an incentive to litigate on the basis that it provides a faster response to stop activities that may be prejudicial to the claimant state.

There is, however, a mixed record on the utility of provisional measures. Where it might be expected that provisional measures will be most useful for environmental protection is in the marine context, as UNCLOS anticipates that provisional measures will be prescribed when 'appropriate under the circumstances to preserve the respective

[38] Whaling in the Antarctic case (n 27).

[39] This argument was not ultimately raised by Japan, which only challenged the jurisdiction of the court in relation to a reservation in Australia's acceptance of compulsory jurisdiction; Whaling in the Antarctic case (n 27) [30]–[41].

[40] South China Sea case (n 19) [894]–[911].

[41] Ibid [927].

[42] See Boyle and Harrison (n 5) 258–260.

[43] Philippe Sands, 'Climate Change and the Rule of Law: Adjudicating the Future in International Law' *Journal of Environmental Law*, 28/1 (2016): 19, 28.

[44] John Merrills, *International Dispute Settlement* (3rd edn, CUP 1998) 129.

rights of the parties to the dispute *or to prevent serious harm to the marine environment*, pending the final decision'.[45] In the *Southern Bluefin Tuna* cases, ITLOS considered that the conservation of marine living resources was part of the protection and preservation of the marine environment and ordered that all parties refrain from harvesting southern bluefin tuna in excess of their national allocations pending the arbitration.[46] ITLOS was willing to take this step even in the face of uncertain scientific evidence.[47] By contrast, at the provisional measures stage of *MOX Plant*, ITLOS ordered the parties to consult on matters relating to monitoring the risks or effects of the MOX plant's operation on the Irish Sea and devise appropriate measures to prevent pollution of the marine environment.[48] This order placed the onus on the parties to reach decisions rather than specific measures being imposed by the tribunal and the environmental benefits of the order may be questioned as a result.

Consideration of the environment arose more recently in UNCLOS dispute settlement in the provisional measures stage of *Ghana—Côte d'Ivoire*.[49] The ITLOS Special Chamber considered environmental concerns in response to Côte d'Ivoire's request that Ghana suspend all ongoing oil exploration and exploitation activities and refrain from any new permits in the disputed area prior to their maritime boundary being delimited. Although it found there was no imminent risk of serious harm to the marine environment,[50] the Special Chamber still took into account key environmental principles, including the obligation not to cause transboundary harm[51] and the need to act with 'prudence and caution'.[52] Ghana was therefore required to carry out 'strict and continuous monitoring of all activities' in the disputed area to prevent serious harm to the marine environment.[53] As a result, this process 'place[d] [on Ghana] a procedural onus and third-party oversight of its actions' in relation to Ghana's adherence to environmental norms.[54]

The experience at the ICJ reflects that parties before the court view the availability of provisional measures as an important mechanism to halt potentially deleterious conduct pending the final resolution of IEL disputes. One of the earliest cases concerning

45 art 290.1 (emphasis added).

46 *Southern Bluefin Tuna Cases (New Zealand/Japan; Australia/Japan) (Provisional Measures, Order of 27 August 1999)* [1999] ITLOS Rep 280 [81], [90].

47 Ibid [80].

48 *The MOX Plant case (Ireland/United Kingdom)* (Provisional Measures, Order of 3 December 2001) [2001] ITLOS Rep 95 [89.1].

49 *Dispute Concerning Delimitation of the Maritime Boundary between Ghana and Côte d'Ivoire in the Atlantic Ocean* (Provisional Measures, Order of 25 April 2015) [2015] ITLOS Rep 146 (Ghana/Côte d'Ivoire case).

50 Ibid [67].

51 Ibid [71].

52 Ibid [72].

53 Ibid [108], Operative [1(b)]; the Special Chamber further noted that both parties were to take all necessary steps to prevent serious harm to the marine environment; see ibid [108], Operative [1(c)].

54 Natalie Klein, 'Provisional Measures and Provisional Arrangements' in Alex Elferink, Tore Henriksen, and Signe Busch (eds), *Maritime Boundary Delimitation—The Case Law* (CUP 2018) 117.

the environment at the ICJ, the *Nuclear Tests* cases, involved a request for provisional measures.[55] Argentina also sought provisional measures in the more recent *Pulp Mills* case, including that Uruguay suspend its authorization to construct the pulp mills and the actual construction works. The court did not indicate provisional measures to this effect, however, on the basis that there was no imminent harm established in the circumstances of the case.[56]

Costa Rica sought provisional measures at the ICJ in *Certain Activities carried out by Nicaragua in the Border Area* requiring inter alia that Nicaragua cease canal (caño) construction and associated activities because of potential damage caused by Nicaragua's construction works to rainforests and internationally-protected wetlands located in the disputed area. At the time, Nicaragua had already ended its work on one of the caño and to the extent it intended to proceed with further construction, the court followed a similar approach to ITLOS in setting up a procedural mechanism to minimize harm to the environment. In this regard, the court anticipated steps such as the dispatch of civilian personnel from Costa Rica to inspect the area, consultation with the Secretariat of the Ramsar Convention, and cooperation between Nicaragua and Costa Rica to find solutions.[57] The court also rejected a request from Costa Rica that Nicaragua suspend its dredging programme in the River San Juan because the evidence did not show a risk of irreparable prejudice to Costa Rica's environment or to the flow of the Colorado River nor was there an imminent risk of Costa Rica's rights being prejudiced.[58]

Despite the parties' perceptions of the importance of provisional measures to protect their rights, and the environment, the experience at the ICJ thus far demonstrates that such orders will not be easily obtained. Partly these results can be explained by the evidence and facts before the court on each occasion, as well as the substantive principles that were also at stake in these cases. Nonetheless, it is notable that the ICJ has not required suspension of construction work, and it may thus appear that development or economic imperatives implicitly weigh against environmental protection.

V. SUBSTANTIVE DETERMINATION

If an international court or tribunal is to discuss the merits of the case, the interpretation of IEL principles as enshrined in treaties or customary international law and the

[55] *Nuclear Tests Case (Australia/France)* (Order) [1973] ICJ Rep 99; *Nuclear Tests Case (New Zealand/France)* (Order) [1973] ICJ Rep 135.

[56] *Pulp Mills on the River Uruguay (Argentina/Uruguay)* (Provisional Measures, Order of 13 July 2006) [2006] ICJ Rep 113.

[57] *Certain Activities Carried Out by Nicaragua in the Border Area (Costa Rica/Nicaragua)* (Provisional Measures, Order of 8 March 2011) [2011] ICJ Rep 6 [80].

[58] Ibid [82].

application of these principles to the facts presented is critical. Also relevant in this regard is the nature of the IEL obligations, and the extent to which it allows for flexibility in assessing state conduct and decision-making (as may be seen with consideration of due diligence standards and in the distinctions drawn between procedural and substantive obligations).[59] These dimensions are discussed in detail in Chapter 16 of this handbook.[60] What is relevant for the purposes of this chapter are the evidentiary requirements to establish a breach of IEL, which may include the involvement of experts and witnesses, as discussed below.

A. Standard of Proof and Causation

A critical aspect of any IEL dispute before an international court or tribunal is producing evidence sufficient to establish facts that demonstrate a violation of an IEL obligation. This core process was described by the ICJ in *Pulp Mills* as follows: 'in keeping with its practice, the Court will make its own determination of the facts, on the basis of the evidence presented to it, and then it will apply the relevant rules of international law to those facts which it has found to have existed'.[61] As a general matter, the standard of proof is one of preponderance of evidence, although a higher standard may be applied for exceptionally grave international law violations.[62] A balance of probabilities may be a more appropriate standard for IEL disputes, especially when it is a risk of harm that is to be demonstrated rather than actual harm.[63]

In *Pulp Mills*, the ICJ further noted 'it is the duty of the party which asserts certain facts to establish the existence of such facts'.[64] Although Argentina argued this burden should be reversed in relation to the application of the precautionary approach or that there was an equal burden imposed on the parties by the 1975 Statute, the court rejected this view.[65] Causation may be problematic in terms of directly linking a state's activities to an IEL violation, and this concern has been highlighted in the context of climate change litigation where the actions of more than one state may cause an adverse environmental outcome.

[59] See Natalie Klein, 'Settlement of International Environmental Law Disputes' in Malgosia Fitzmaurice, David Ong, and Panos Merkouris (eds), *Research Handbook on International Environmental Law* (Edward Elgar 2010) 379, 381–383.

[60] Chapter 16, 'Harm Prevention', in this volume.

[61] *Pulp Mills on the River Uruguay (Argentina/Uruguay)* (Judgement) [2010] ICJ Rep 14 (Pulp Mills case) [168].

[62] Rüdiger Wolfrum and Mirka Möldner, 'International Courts and Tribunals, Evidence' in Rüdiger Wolfrum (ed), *Max Planck Encyclopedia of Public International Law* (OUP 2013) para 77.

[63] Boyle and Harrison (n 5) 269.

[64] Pulp Mills case (n 61) [162].

[65] Ibid [164].

B. Use of Experts and Witnesses

An important means of establishing facts and meeting any burden of proof before an international court or tribunal is through the use of experts and witnesses. In the context of IEL disputes, scientific experts may be particularly important to explain the reasons for and/or the consequences of actions that have been taken (or equally the reasons for and/or consequences of omissions).

Parties to a dispute may nominate witnesses or experts,[66] or the international court or tribunal may have powers to seek out expert opinion where necessary.[67] The *South China Sea* tribunal used this latter power in seeking to understand the extent of harm caused to the marine environment through China's land reclamation activities.[68] In assessing evidence from party-appointed experts, the ICJ has indicated a strong preference that they be presented as expert witnesses so they may be questioned directly by the opposing party, rather than serving as counsel in the presentation of the case.[69] This preference was heeded by the parties in the *Whaling* case.

There may be instances where non-state actors that are not connected to the state parties seek to provide evidence to the international court or tribunal, but there are limited opportunities to do so.[70] It then falls to the individual members of international courts and tribunals to grapple with the evidence presented, ensuring they have a full understanding of the material so as to be able to reach well-substantiated conclusions on whether any IEL principle has been violated or not.[71]

VI. REPARATIONS

In any calculation of whether to litigate an IEL dispute before an international court or tribunal, there must be careful consideration of what remedies may be sought and awarded by that court or tribunal. Related to this assessment will be considerations as to the likelihood of compliance with any reparations ordered by a court or tribunal and the availability of enforcement mechanisms to secure compliance if needed.

What remedy is awarded to resolve an IEL dispute will depend on what primary obligation has been breached and what the injured party seeks by way of reparations. The

66 See 1978 ICJ Rules, arts 63, 65; 1997 ITLOS Rules, arts 78, 80; for discussion, see Wolfrum and Möldner (n 62) paras 34–48.

67 ICJ Statute, art 50; ICJ Rules, arts 62.2, 67, 68; ITLOS Rules, arts 77.2 and 82.

68 See South China Sea case (n 19) [131], [136].

69 Pulp Mills case (n 61) [167].

70 The main possibilities are *amicus* briefs being submitted by non-governmental organizations (NGOs) before a WTO panel or in an Advisory Opinion derived from UNCLOS; for discussion see Boyle and Harrison (n 5) 264–266.

71 See Caroline Foster, *Science and the Precautionary Principle in International Courts and Tribunals* (CUP 2011) 80.

purposes of reparations are to remove the consequences of an unlawful act and restore the situation that existed prior to the commission of that unlawful act.[72] The reparations that may have critical importance in resolving IEL disputes most typically comprise of *restitutio in integrum*, compensation, and satisfaction.[73] In addition, an international court or tribunal may also make an order of cessation if there is a continuing unlawful act.[74] There is a further possibility of a complainant state asking for guarantees of non-repetition,[75] but an international court or tribunal will more typically assume that once a violation of international law has been identified in legal proceedings, the state concerned will act in good faith to align its conduct with its international obligations.[76]

Where IEL disputes have resulted in decisions on the merits, declarations have commonly been made as a form of satisfaction for reparations. In the *Pulp Mills* judgement, the court found that Uruguay was in breach of procedural obligations set out in the 1975 Statute and that a declaration to this effect was enough for a remedy of satisfaction. Argentina had requested the dismantling of the Orion (Botnia) mill on the basis of the close connection between the substantive and procedural obligations at issue.[77] However, the court did not consider this remedy to be appropriate in the absence of any violation of a substantive obligation.[78] The judgement therefore leaves open the possibility that a state may need to deconstruct infrastructure or buildings as a possible remedy if it is determined that the state is in violation of substantive IEL obligations.

Restitutio in integrum may seem an obvious option to respond to an IEL violation as the state that acted wrongfully would need to take steps to restore the environment to the position it was in prior to the commission of the wrongful act. However, such an order for restitution will not be made where it is 'materially impossible' or involves 'a burden out of all proportion to the benefit deriving from restitution instead of compensation'.[79] It was notable that in the *South China Sea* arbitration Philippines did not seek any order that would have required China to take action to restore the environment. Instead, the Tribunal issued declarations only noting the wrongfulness of China's conduct under the terms of the UNCLOS requirements on the protection and preservation of the marine environment and not requiring any future conduct.[80] It is questionable if the environment has suffered because of this approach.[81]

72 *The Factory at Chorzów (Germany/Poland)* (Judgement) [1928] PCIJ (ser A) 51–52 [124].

73 'Report of the International Law Commission on the work of its fifty-third session' (2001) UN Doc A/56/10, ch IV.E—'Draft Articles on Responsibility of States for Internationally Wrongful Acts', art 34.

74 Ibid, art 30(a).

75 Ibid, art 30(b).

76 See eg *Dispute regarding Navigational and Related Rights (Costa Rica/Nicaragua)* (Judgement) [2009] ICJ Rep 213 [150].

77 Pulp Mills case (n 61) [270].

78 Ibid [275].

79 ILC articles on responsibility (n 73) art 35.

80 South China Sea case (n 19) [1182]–[1201].

81 See Joshua Paine, 'Environmental Aspects of the South China Sea Award' *EJIL Talk!* (21 July 2016); but see Bernard Oxman, 'The South China Sea Arbitration Award' *University of Miami—Legal Studies Research Paper No 16-41* (29 August 2016).

Compensation was awarded for environmental harm in *Costa Rica v Nicaragua*.[82] This decision is important because it was the first time the ICJ addressed the principles of compensation in addressing IEL violations. In determining the amount of compensation payable by Nicaragua to Costa Rica, the ICJ articulated key principles relevant to determining compensation for environmental harm. These principles include that compensation was appropriate where restitution is materially impossible or unduly burdensome;[83] that an award of compensation should not have a punitive or exemplary character;[84] and that the valuation of damage does not require perfect evidence for compensation. Instead, 'absence of adequate evidence as to the extent of material damage will not in all situations preclude an award of compensation for damage'.[85]

The methodology to be applied in ascertaining the amount of compensation to be paid in an assessment of the environmental harm caused proved particularly challenging. The ICJ preferred not to prescribe any specific method of valuation but instead considered various elements viewed as a reasonable basis for valuation.[86] The court insisted that regard must be had to the circumstances of each case.[87] In valuing an ecosystem, the court stated:

> that it is appropriate to approach the valuation of environmental damage from the perspective of the ecosystem as a whole, by adopting an overall assessment of the impairment or loss of environmental goods and services prior to recovery, rather than attributing values to specific categories of environmental goods and services and estimating recovery periods for each of them.[88]

This overall valuation approach entailed considering the removal of trees and resultant environmental harm; the fact the area was a wetland that fell under the protection of the Ramsar Convention; and the capacity for natural regeneration.[89] The court concluded by awarding Costa Rica USD 120,000 for 'the impairment or loss of the environmental goods and services of the impacted area in the period prior to recovery'.[90]

This decision is an important benchmark for future decisions on reparations in the resolution of IEL disputes before international courts or tribunals. Notably, several of the judges reflected on the ramifications for climate change litigation even though the court did not address the question in its majority judgement.[91] In this regard, Judge

[82] *Certain Activities Carried Out by Nicaragua in the Border Area (Costa Rica/Nicaragua)* (Judgement of 2 February 2018 on Compensation owed by Nicaragua to Costa Rica) ICJ.

[83] Ibid [31].

[84] Ibid.

[85] Ibid [35].

[86] Ibid [52].

[87] Ibid.

[88] Ibid [78].

[89] Ibid [79]–[81].

[90] Ibid [86].

[91] Judge ad hoc Dugard considered this failure to be a lost opportunity for the Court; ibid [36].

Donoghue commented that Costa Rica could not claim for the entire amount of loss of carbon sequestration capacity because this harm is global damage.[92] Judge Gevorgian similarly questioned whether one single state should be compensated for an injury *erga omnes* caused by another state.[93] It remains to be seen whether such a view is ultimately endorsed by the court as a whole in any future case.

VII. CONCLUDING REMARKS

As identified in this chapter, there are many reasons that may prevent IEL disputes from going before an international court or tribunal or possible barriers and disincentives to pursuing this form of dispute settlement. Nonetheless, we have come a long way since the early decisions of *Trail Smelter* and *Lake Lanoux*. The role of international courts and tribunals for affirming the status of IEL principles and defining more clearly the standards and expectations associated with the application of those principles has been important in the development of this body of law. This phenomenon is reflected in different chapters in this volume.[94] Court decisions have thus had an important role in affirming many dimensions of IEL, reflecting its mature status as a body of international law. IEL disputes before international courts and tribunals have also contributed to jurisprudence of international law more broadly on questions of state responsibility and the law of treaties, as well as the principles associated with the peaceful settlement of international disputes.

While this progress is commendable, it is evident that international courts and tribunals still need to do more. Approaches to provisional measures as well as articulating the standard of proof and establishing causation in IEL disputes need further refinement where the substantive principles of IEL are analysed closely in relation to these dispute settlement dimensions. In this regard, there should be an appreciation that the judges are not just resolving the dispute before them and developing the law but also signalling to a broader audience the consequences of breaching IEL. Stronger messages are needed to this end, especially for an area of law where prevention should be a greater focus than the cure.

BIBLIOGRAPHY

Richard Bilder, 'The Settlement of Disputes in the Field of the International Law of the Environment' *Recueil des Cours*, 144/1 (1975): 139

[92] Ibid (Separate Opinion of Judge Donoghue) [18].

[93] Ibid (Separate Opinion of Judge Gevorgian) [9].

[94] See Chapters 27 and 23, 'Judicial Development' and 'Customary International Law and the Environment', in this volume.

Alan Boyle and James Harrison, 'Judicial Settlement of International Environmental Disputes: Current Problems' *Journal of International Dispute Settlement*, 4/2 (2013): 245

Natalie Klein, 'Settlement of International Environmental Law Disputes' in Malgosia Fitzmaurice, David Ong, and Panos Merkouris (eds), *Research Handbook on International Environmental Law* (Edward Elgar 2010) 379

Tim Stephens, *International Courts and Environmental Protection* (CUP 2009)

PART IX

INTERNATIONAL ENVIRONMENTAL LAW IN NATIONAL/ REGIONAL COURTS

CHAPTER 61

AFRICA

LOUIS J KOTZÉ

I. INTRODUCTION

THE relationship between international environmental law (IEL) and domestic legal systems is an intimate but complex one that should be understood within a specific context. First, states as the main actors in and subjects of IEL exist because of elaborate domestic constitutional and other laws that are also being shaped by IEL. IEL therefore governs relations between states and impacts to a greater or lesser extent a state's internal legal architecture and governance. Second, in a converse way, legal developments at the domestic level have the potential to influence IEL, although this occurs less frequently. Courts play an important role in facilitating the foregoing processes. This chapter offers a brief reflection on examples where some domestic and regional African courts have engaged directly and indirectly with IEL.

II. DIRECT APPLICATION OF IEL

One of the earliest examples of the direct application of IEL by a South African court, is *Director: Mineral Development Gauteng Region v Save the Vaal Environment*. The Supreme Court of Appeal directly invoked the Brundtland Report's definition of sustainable development in an effort to justify the application of the *audi alteram partem* (hear the other side) rule to ensure representative and inclusive administrative decision-making. The court also linked sustainable development with the right to a healthy environment, stating that '[O]ur Constitution, by including environmental rights as fundamental, justiciable human rights, by necessary implication requires that environmental considerations be accorded appropriate recognition and respect in the administrative processes in our country'.[1]

In a constitutional petition before Kenya's Environment and Land Court,[2] the petitioner challenged the erection of a telephone mast which was allegedly in contravention of the Kenyan Constitution's environmental right provisions.[3] The court relied on Principle 10 of the 1992 Rio Declaration on Environment and Development and Guidelines 8-14 of the 2010 Bali Guidelines for the Development of National Legislation on Access to Information, Public Participation and Access to Justice in Environmental Matters to conclude that: '[I]t is apparent … that the State, through its relevant organs, has the duty to ensure that the persons most affected by the project are consulted'.[4]

Similarly, in *Friends of Lake Turkana Trust v Attorney General & Two Others*,[5] the Kenyan Land and Environment Court reverted to Principle 10 of the Rio Declaration and to Chapter 8 of Agenda 21 to consider the alleged lack of public participation in developing a hydropower scheme, but this time innovatively connected the duty to ensure public participation with the right to access to information, which it believed was related to the principle of sustainable development. The court further held that Lake Turkana is classified as a world heritage site in terms of the 1972 Convention Concerning the Protection of the World Cultural Natural Heritage, and that Kenya was thus obliged to 'do all it can to protect, conserve and transmit to the future generation the cultural and natural heritage sites'.[6] The state had a duty to ensure that the resources of Lake Turkana are 'sustainably managed, utilized and conserved, and to exercise the necessary precautions in preventing environmental harm that may arise'.[7]

African courts have also directly relied on IEL in climate change disputes. One example is the South African High Court's decision in *Earthlife Africa v Minister of Environmental Affairs and Others*; the country's first climate change case. While South Africa's environmental framework law does not explicitly require a climate impact assessment, the court believed that domestic law 'must also be interpreted consistently with international law. Article 4.1(f) of the UN Framework Convention imposes an obligation on all states parties to take climate change considerations into account in their relevant environmental policies and actions.'[8]

A second example is the pending Ugandan climate case of *Mbabazi and Others v The Attorney General and National Environmental Management Authority*.[9] In this case, four minors and a non-governmental organization (NGO) approached the High

[1] (1996) 1 All SA 2004 (T) [20].

[2] *Ken Kasinga'a v Daniel Kiplagat Kirui and Others*, Petition No 50/2013 (Kasinga'a case).

[3] Specifically arts 42 and 70 of the 2010 Constitution of Kenya.

[4] Kasinga'a case (n 2) [67].

[5] Environment and Land Court Suit No 825/2012.

[6] Ibid, 16.

[7] Ibid, 17.

[8] (8 March 2017) Gauteng High Court Pretoria, Case No 65662/16 [83].

[9] *Mbabazi and Others v The Attorney General and National Environmental Management Authority* Civil Suit No 283/2012.

Court arguing that climate change significantly impacts people and the environment. As a signatory to the 1992 United Nations Framework Convention on Climate Change (UNFCCC) and its 1987 Kyoto Protocol, the government has a duty, so it is argued, to address climate change and its impacts, but has failed to do so. The plaintiffs are seeking an order, among others, 'directing government to implement international conventions, treaties and protocols on climate change'.[10] In all the foregoing cases, courts have directly applied IEL through the innovative use of instruments and principles of IEL as persuasive authority in domestic decisions.

III. INDIRECT APPLICATION OF IEL

African courts have also indirectly applied IEL. The South African Constitutional Court in *Government of the Republic of South Africa and Others v Grootboom and Others*,[11] indirectly relied on international law when it was tasked to interpret the nature of the state's duty to progressively realize the right of access to housing, which also has environmental dimensions.[12] With reference to the 1966 International Covenant on Economic, Social and Cultural Rights, the court noted in particular: '[T]he relevant international law can be a guide to interpretation but the weight to be attached to any particular principle or rule of international law will vary'.[13] Similarly, in *Mazibuko v City of Johannesburg*, the Constitutional Court indirectly relied on the Covenant to shed light on the meaning of the nature of the state's duty to progressively realize the right to access to water, as well as to clarify what a minimum core obligation might entail under this right.[14]

Also at a regional level, the African Commission on Human and Peoples' Rights (AComHPR) extensively relied on the foregoing Covenants to guide its interpretation of the right to a healthy environment contained in the 1981 African Charter on Human and Peoples Rights. The Commission clarified, in the well-known *Social and Economic Rights Action Center v Nigeria* (SERAC) Communication that: '[I]nternationally accepted ideas of the various obligations engendered by human rights indicate that all rights, both civil and political rights and social and economic [rights], generate at least four levels of duties for a State that undertakes to adhere to a rights regime, namely the duty to respect, protect, promote, and fulfil these rights'.[15]

[10] See the plaint <https://blogs2.law.columbia.edu/climate-change-litigation/wp-content/uploads/sites/16/non-us-case-documents/2012/20120920_Civil-Suit-No.-283-of-2012_complaint-1.pdf> accessed 5 January 2020.

[11] (CCT 11/00) [2000] ZACC 19.

[12] 1996 Constitution of the Republic of South Africa, s 26.

[13] Grootboom case (n 11) [26].

[14] (CCT 39/09) [2009] ZACC 28 [40]–[41], [52].

[15] *Social and Economic Rights Action Center (SERAC) and the Center for Economic and Social Rights (CESR) v Nigeria*, AComHPR (2001) Communication No 155/96 [44].

The South African High Court in *BP Southern Africa (Pty) Ltd v MEC for Agriculture, Conservation, Environment and Land Affairs*,[16] indicated its receptivity to IEL when it invoked Philippe Sands' understanding of 'ecological sustainable development' as being 'the fundamental building block around which environmental legal norms have been fashioned, both internationally and in South Africa'.[17] The South African Constitutional Court in *Fuel Retailers Association of Southern Africa v Director-General: Environmental Management Mpumalanga and Others*,[18] again relied on sustainable development to elaborate the need for conducting an environmental impact assessment (EIA) prior to developments. Referring with approval to the International Court of Justice (ICJ)'s finding in *Gabčíkovo-Nagymaros Project (Hungary/Slovakia)*, that the 'need to reconcile economic development with protection of the environment is aptly expressed in the concept of sustainable development',[19] the court believed it is entirely appropriate under the circumstances that an EIA be conducted.

In *Centre for Minority Rights Development and Minority Rights Group v Kenya*,[20] the AComHPR drew parallels throughout between international law provisions and the applicable regional law framework, including, among others, provisions of the 2007 UN Declaration on the Rights of Indigenous Peoples, the 1986 UN Declaration on the Right to Development, the 1966 International Covenants, and the work of the UN Special Rapporteur on the Rights and Fundamental Freedoms of Indigenous People. More recently in 2017, the African Court of Human and Peoples' Rights had occasion to adjudicate the alleged violation of several rights in the African Charter as a result of the arbitrary and forced eviction by the Kenyan government of the Ogiek people from their ancestral land without compensation or consultation.[21] The African Court stipulated there are criteria that 'generally reflect the current normative standards to identify indigenous populations in international law'; which 'allows it to draw inspiration from other human rights instruments to apply these criteria to this Application'.[22]

IV. CONCLUSION: CHALLENGES, BARRIERS, AND OPPORTUNITIES

Generally speaking, African states have had and continue to have a tenuous and/or superficial relationship with IEL. There are several reasons for this state of affairs. One

[16] (03/16337) [2004] ZAGPHC 18 (31 March 2004).

[17] Philippe Sands, *Principles of International Environmental Law* (1st edn, CUP 1995) 24–25.

[18] (CCT67/06) [2007] ZACC 13.

[19] *The Gabčíkovo-Nagymaros Project (Hungary/Slovakia)* (Judgement) [1997] ICJ Rep 7 [140].

[20] *Centre for Minority Rights Development (Kenya) and Minority Rights Group (on behalf of Endorois Welfare Council) v Kenya*, AComHPR (2009) Communication No 276/03.

[21] *African Commission on Human and Peoples Rights v Kenya* (26 May 2017) Application No 006/2012.

[22] Ibid [108].

is ideological: international law's genesis is systemically embedded in inter-Western European state relations, while African states have not historically been considered part of these relations. Such perceptions gave rise to critical counter-narratives such as Third World Approaches to International Law.[23] Significant tensions also remain between what is perceived as western-imposed obligations and the willingness of African states to subject themselves to these obligations. The debate on Africa's common but differentiated responsibilities and respective capabilities in respect of climate change is an example.[24] More worryingly though, while some African states have been engaging in human rights violations, many African states remain unable to subject themselves to IEL and its obligations.[25] Some states are suppressing community participation in environmental decision-making, and preventing potential litigants from accessing judicial recourse, as some of the cases above suggest, thus weakening grassroots level environmental governance efforts that seek to hold governments to account.[26]

Having said this, Africa is also a site for innovation and progressive development in the area of IEL, especially through the work of the courts. Regional judicial institutions are pioneering the innovative jurisprudential development of environmental norms, while domestic African courts are increasingly, either directly or indirectly, interpreting, applying, and further refining IEL. Collectively, while one must be wary of the challenges and barriers to the implementation of IEL, such innovation bodes well for the potential and gradual development of a more amicable and constructive relationship between IEL and Africa.

BIBLIOGRAPHY

Mirna Adjami, 'African Courts, International Law, and Comparative Case Law: Chimera or Emerging Human Rights Jurisprudence?' *Michigan Journal of International Law*, 24/1 (2002): 103

Lisa Chamberlain and Tumai Murombo 'International Environmental Law in South Africa' in Erika de Wet, Holger Hestermeyer, and Rüdiger Wolfrum (eds), *The Implementation of International Law in Germany and South Africa* (Pretoria University Law Press 2015) 277, 298–302

Louis J Kotzé and Alexander Paterson (eds), *The Role of the Judiciary in Environmental Governance: Comparative Perspectives* (Wolters Kluwer 2009)

[23] See Chapter 11, 'Global South Approaches', in this volume.

[24] Duncan French, 'Developing States and International Environmental Law: The Importance of Differentiated Responsibilities' *International and Comparative Law Quarterly*, 49/1 (2000): 35.

[25] John Ntambirweki, 'The Developing Countries in the Evolution of an International Environmental Law' *Hastings International and Comparative Law Review*, 14/4 (1991): 905.

[26] Carl Bruch, 'African Environmental Governance: Opportunities at the Regional, Subregional and National Levels' in Beatrice Chaytor and Kevin Gray (eds), *International Environmental Law and Policy in Africa* (Kluwer 2003) 217.

Richard Oppong, 'Re-imagining International Law: An Examination of Recent Trends in the Reception of International Law into National Legal Systems in Africa' *Fordham International Law Journal*, 30/2 (2006): 296

Francis Situma 'Africa's Potential Contribution to the Implementation of International Environmental Law' *Transnational Law and Contemporary Problems*, 10/2 (2000): 385

Frans Viljoen, *International Human Rights Law in Africa* (2nd edn, OUP 2012)

CHAPTER 62

CHINA

JOLENE LIN*

I. INTRODUCTION

INTERNATIONAL law was introduced by western missionaries to China in the late nineteenth century.[1] On 1 October 1949, a socialist domestic legal system was established with the founding of the People's Republic of China (PRC). The legal system reflected significant Soviet Union influence.[2] It was only after the 'open door policy' and economic reforms were adopted in the 1970s that China began to participate actively in international law-making.[3]

It is noteworthy that the first international conference that the PRC participated in after it was formally recognized by the United Nations (UN) in 1971, was the 1972 UN Conference on the Human Environment (Stockholm).[4] It is widely recognized that this conference brought environmental protection onto the Chinese government's radar and led to the promulgation of the Environmental Protection Law in 1979.[5] Since then, China has signed or ratified most multilateral environmental agreements including the 1985 Vienna Convention for the Protection of the Ozone Layer (and the 1987 Montreal Protocol on Substances that Deplete the Ozone Layer), the 1992 UN Framework

* I am grateful to Dr Fang Meng, Eric Bea, and Carol Yuen for superb research assistance. I also like to thank Dr Zhao Yue, Research Associate, Sichuan University Law School, for valuable comments on an earlier draft.

[1] Rune Svarverud, *International Law as World Order in Late Imperial China: Translation, Reception and Discourse, 1847–1911* (Brill 2007) 70.

[2] Keyuan Zou, 'International Law in the Chinese Domestic Context' *Valparaiso University Law Review*, 44/3 (2010): 935.

[3] For discussion see Zonglai Wang and Bin Hu, 'China's Reform and Opening-Up and International Law' *Chinese Journal of International Law*, 9/1 (2010): 193.

[4] For discussion see Shouqiu Cai and Mark Voights, 'The Development of China's Environmental Diplomacy' *Pacific Rim Law & Policy Journal*, 3/1 (1993): S-17, S-21–22.

[5] Zhilin Mu, Shuchun Bu, and Bing Xue, 'Environmental Legislation in China: Achievements, Challenges and Trends' *Sustainability*, 6/1 (2014): 8967, 8969.

Convention on Climate Change (UNFCCC) and its 2015 Paris Agreement, and the 1989 Basel Convention on the Control of Transboundary Movement of Hazardous Wastes and their Disposal (Basel Convention).[6]

A. Overview of the Chinese Legal System

The Chinese Constitution states that the National People's Congress (NPC) has the 'highest power' in the country. As such, the State Council, Supreme People's Court (SPC), and the Supreme People's Procuratorate are all responsible to the NPC. There are four levels of courts in China: the SPC at the apex, the High People's Courts at the provincial level, and the Intermediate and Basic People's Courts at the local levels.[7] In addition, nearly 1,000 environmental tribunals have been established in the past decade.[8]

There is no principle akin to *stare decisis* (precedent) in the Chinese legal system. Lower courts are not bound by the decisions of higher courts, and there is no comprehensive case law system. However, in practice, cases are often cited for their persuasive authority.[9] Directives issued by the SPC also play a significant role in guiding lower courts in the interpretation and application of laws. A recent development involves the use of 'guiding cases' to provide lower courts with what are effectively binding decisions to achieve adjudicative consistency across the judicial system.[10] At the time of writing, there are 112 guiding cases, of which four raise environmental law issues.[11] Of these four cases, only one indirectly refers to international environmental law (IEL), namely the 1992

[6] For a full list of multilateral treaties which China has signed or ratified see <https://www.china-un.org/eng/zghlhg/flsw/t28583.htm> accessed 10 January 2020.

[7] Albert Chen, *Introduction to the Legal System of the People's Republic of China* (LexisNexis 2011).

[8] Bixin Jiang, 'Environmental Tribunals (White Paper) and Environmental Justice Progress Report Release' *Supreme People's Court* (13 July 2017) <https://www.court.gov.cn/zixun-xiangqing-50682.html> accessed 10 January 2020.

[9] Yue Zhao, Shuang Lyu, and Zhu Wang, 'Prospects for Climate Change Litigation in China' *Transnational Environmental Law*, 8/2 (2019): 349.

[10] For discussion see Mark Jia, 'Chinese Common Law? Guiding Cases and Judicial Reform' *Harvard Law Review*, 129/8 (2016): 2213.

[11] The Supreme People's Court, 'Guiding Cases' <https://www.court.gov.cn/fabu-gengduo-77.html> accessed 10 January 2020; see also Stanford Law School's 'China Guiding Cases Project' <https://cgc.law.stanford.edu> accessed 10 January 2020. These four cases are: Guiding Case No 20 '*Siruiman Fine Chemical LTD in Shenzhen Suing Kengzi Water LTD in Shenzhen and Kangtailan Water Processing Equipment LTD for Infringing Invention Patent Right*' <https://www.court.gov.cn/fabu-xiangqing-6004.html>; Guiding Case No 75 '*China Biodiversity Protection and Green Sustainable Development Fund Suing Ruitai Technology LTD in Ningxia for Environmental Pollution*' <https://www.court.gov.cn/fabu-xiangqing-34322.html>; Guiding Case No 92 '*Jinhaizhongye LTD in Laizhou Suing Fukai Agricultural Technology LTD in Zhangye for Infringement of Rights to a New Plant Variety*' <https://www.court.gov.cn/fabu-xiangqing-74142.html>; Guiding Case No 100 '*A Dispute Litigated by Shandong Denghai Pioneering LTD against Shanxi Nongfengzhongye LTD and Shanxi Dafengzhongye LTD over Infringement of Rights to a New Plant Variety*' <https://www.court.gov.cn/fabu-xiangqing-136391.html> all accessed 10 January 2020.

Convention on Biological Diversity (CBD).[12] In addition, in March 2017, the SPC issued ten model environmental public interest litigation (EPIL) cases.[13] These model cases are issued to provide guidance to the lower courts in deciding EPIL cases and signals the apex court's desire to promote EPIL. All ten model cases concern interpretation of domestic environmental laws and do not interpret or rely on IEL. Finally, it is worth mentioning that another recent development to promote adjudicative consistency is that judges are now required to prepare a report on 'similar case analysis' before trial.[14]

Most Chinese scholars reject the monistic and dualistic views that are typically used to describe the relationship between domestic law and international law.[15] Instead, they favour a 'dialectical' model that is borrowed largely from Soviet legal philosophy.[16] According to this model, domestic law and international law are two distinct but closely related systems because the laws are made by states, collectively or individually. The Chinese Constitution and laws do not stipulate whether treaties are automatically incorporated into domestic law (a monistic approach) or have to be transformed into domestic legislation before having legal effect domestically (a dualistic approach). In practice, mixed approaches are adopted, including (1) direct implementation by the administrative departments concerned, (2) transformation of the treaty obligations by promulgating new legislation, and (3) amending existing laws.

For example, China has not introduced any laws to implement its international climate change legal obligations. Instead, it seeks to fulfil its Paris Agreement Nationally Determined Contribution (NDC) through a package of domestic policies and administrative regulations.[17] Another example is the Basel Convention, which is implemented in China via the Law of the People's Republic of China on Prevention of Environmental Pollution Caused by Solid Waste (Solid Waste law), administrative measures, and regulations promulgated by the environmental ministry and the State Council.[18] Article 90

[12] See Section III.

[13] Ziru Yu and Jingyi Fan, 'Supreme Court Issues Ten Guiding Cases for Environmental Public Interest Litigation' *Xinhua* (7 March 2017) <https://www.xinhuanet.com/legal/2017-03/07/c_129503245.htm> accessed 10 January 2020.

[14] See Central Committee of the Communist Party of China (CCCPC), 'Decision of the CCCPC on Some Major Issues Concerning Comprehensively Deepening the Reform' *China.org.cn* (17 January 2014) <https://www.china.org.cn/chinese/2014-01/17/content_31226494.htm> accessed 10 January 2020; see also Communist Party of China, 'Framework Opinions on Several Issues Concerning the Pilot Reform of the Judicial System' (2016); Supreme People's Court, 'Opinions on the Trial Implementation of the Judicial Responsibility System' (1 August 2017).

[15] Cf. Zou (n 2) 937–938.

[16] Ibid.

[17] For discussion see Alex Wang, 'Climate Change Policy and Law in China' in Cinnamon Carlarne, Kevin Gray, and Richard Tarasofsky (eds), *The Oxford Handbook of International Climate Change Law* (OUP 2016) 636.

[18] Qiuru Ye, 'Report on China's Implementation of Multilateral Environmental Agreements' *China Council for International Cooperation on Environment and Development* (23 September 1996) <https://www.cciced.net/dxhd/nh/1996nh/nhxw/201210/t20121019_84459.html> accessed 10 January 2020; Secretariat of the Basel Convention, 'Country Fact Sheets' (October 2011) ≤https://www.basel.int/Countries/Countryfactsheets/tabid/1293/Default.aspx> accessed 10 January 2020.

of the Solid Waste law provides that in cases of conflict between the international treaty to which China is a party, and the environmental law, 'the provisions of the international treaty shall prevail', except in relation to provisions to which the PRC has entered reservations.[19] Similar provisions are found in most Chinese environmental laws, although it has been noted that there is a trend of deleting this provision in recent legislative amendments.[20]

II. CASES DIRECTLY APPLYING INTERNATIONAL ENVIRONMENTAL LAW

To the best of my knowledge, there are no reported cases that directly apply IEL. This is not surprising for two reasons. First, China has many environmental laws, most of which have not been the subject of litigation before. Judges are not inclined to refer to IEL in lieu of domestic law particularly when the NPC has not explicitly stated that IEL is a domestic legal source.[21] Secondly, Chinese judges seek to avoid controversy in light of the political context in which they operate. When they do innovate, they 'tend to bypass the bold rhetoric of landmark decisions in favour of understated innovation at the margins'.[22] Arguably, this attitude also applies to the use of IEL and foreign case law interpreting IEL.

Despite this paucity of cases, at the time of writing, there were two cases concerning the 1973 Convention on International Trade in Endangered Species (CITES). China enacted the 'Regulation on Management of Import and Export of Endangered Wild Fauna and Flora' in September 2006 to implement its CITES obligations.[23] In 2016, China revised its Wildlife Protection Law.[24] Pursuant to this law, the State Council in 1989 approved the promulgation of two lists of wildlife that receive national-level protection because they are endangered or rare (Annexes to the Wildlife Protection Law).[25]

[19] An English translation of this law can be found at <https://www.npc.gov.cn/englishnpc/Law/2007-12/12/content_1383723.htm> accessed 10 January 2020.

[20] eg the current Environmental Protection Law (which came into force in 2015) no longer contains what was previously art 46, which was similarly worded to art 90 of the Solid Waste Law. An unofficial translation of the Environmental Protection Law produced by the European Union-China Governance Programme is available at <https://www.chinadialogue.net/Environmental-Protection-Law-2014-eversion.pdf> accessed 10 January 2020.

[21] Interviews on file with author.

[22] Rachel Stern, *Environmental Litigation in China: A Study in Political Ambivalence* (CUP 2013) 144.

[23] Dezhan Gao, 'Explanation on the Law of the People's Republic of China on Wild Animals (Draft)' *The National People's Congress on the People's Republic of China* (29 August 1988) <https://www.npc.gov.cn/npc/lfzt/rlyw/2015-12/27/content_1957119.htm> accessed 10 January 2020.

[24] An unofficial English translation of the law is available at <https://www.chinalawtranslate.com/2016wildlifeprotection/?lang=en> accessed 10 January 2020.

[25] State Forestry Administration of China, *China in Action: Protecting Wildlife and Combating Illegal Trade* (2014) 5.

A. The *Wild Cymbidium Orchids* Case

In January 2017, a farmer was charged with violating Article 344 of the Criminal Law (illegally cutting or damaging nationally protected plants) for harvesting wild cymbidium orchids. Although the cymbidium orchid is not listed in the Annexes to the Wildlife Protection Law, it is included in CITES Appendix II and the trial court decided that it therefore ought to be regarded as a protected species at the provincial level.[26] The defendant farmer was sentenced to three years' imprisonment and a fine of 3,000 renminbi. He appealed to the Lushi County Court, arguing, inter alia, that the trial judge erred by making direct reference to an international treaty (CITES) that has not been transposed into domestic law and therefore does not have any domestic legal validity. The appellate court ruled in favour of the defendant farmer, deciding that he had not violated Article 344. The appellate court held that the cymbidium orchid does not benefit from national legal protection, even though it is listed on CITES Appendix II, because it is not listed in the Wildlife Protection Law annexes.[27]

B. The *Shenzhen Parrots* Case

The SPC has issued an interpretation directive on the meaning of 'rare and endangered wildlife' in Article 341.1 of the Criminal Law which criminalizes the sale of endangered species. This interpretation sets out that 'rare and endangered wildlife' includes (1) species listed on the Annexes to the Wildlife Protection Law, (2) species listed on CITES Appendices I and II, and (3) domesticated and bred specimens of these listed species.[28] In the *Shenzhen Parrots* case, the defendant Wang Peng was charged pursuant to Article 341.1 of the Criminal Law for selling six parrots (two of which were sun parrots that are listed on both CITES appendices and Wildlife Protection Law annexes). Wang was found guilty and after serving two years in prison and paying a fine, he filed an appeal that has raised questions about the SPC's interpretation (namely whether the inclusion of CITES-listed species was correct). The decision of the Sub-Committee of Legislative Affairs of the NPC's Standing Committee on this appeal is not publicly available at the time of writing.[29]

[26] Convention on International Trade in Endangered Species of Wild Flora and Fauna, 'Cymbidium sinense' <https://cites.org/eng/node/31348> accessed 10 January 2020.

[27] People's Court of Lushi Country, Henan Province, 'The Verdict on Qin Yunhuan's Illegal Logging and Destruction of Highly State-Protected Flora' *China Judgements Online* (5 January 2017) <https://wenshu.court.gov.cn/content/content?DocID=dd1077a6-c869-4ae4-8cf7-1199ece28954&KeyWord> accessed 10 January 2020; details of the appellate decision can be found at <https://www.thepaper.cn/newsDetail_forward_2613969> accessed 10 January 2020.

[28] The Supreme Court's Interpretation on Several Issues Concerning the Application of Laws in Criminal Cases Involving Sabotaging Wide Life Resources (17 November 2000).

[29] Liao Zhou, 'The Supreme People's Court Accepts the "Parrot Case" and Sentences the Defendant to Two Years in Prison' *Xinhua News* (2 May 2018) <https://www.court.gov.cn/zixun-xiangqing-93752.html> accessed 10 January 2020.

III. CASES INDIRECTLY APPLYING INTERNATIONAL ENVIRONMENTAL LAW

In *Guiding Case Number 75: China Biodiversity Conservation and Green Development Foundation v Ningxia Ruitai Technology Co Ltd*, a 'social organization' sought to sue the defendant company for causing water pollution in the Tengger desert.[30] The Intermediate People's Court and High Court refused to accept the suit on the basis that the Green Development Foundation lacked standing. In deciding that the organization had standing to satisfy Article 58 of the Environmental Protection Law, the SPC used the CBD's definition of biological diversity to determine that the organization's charter included nature conservation.[31]

IV. CHALLENGES FOR THE GREATER APPLICATION OF INTERNATIONAL ENVIRONMENTAL LAW IN NATIONAL COURTS

While case law has grown rapidly, particularly after the Environmental Protection Law was amended in 2015 to promote EPIL, litigation remains secondary to government-led environmental governance.[32] Litigation is widely viewed as a last resort because litigants face many obstacles in a complex system that is prone to local government influence, and ambivalent about environmental litigation which borders on being a politically sensitive issue area that the courts should not venture into.[33] While some commentators have pointed to the non-litigious Confucian culture in Chinese society as an important factor explaining the paucity of environmental litigation in China, I would argue that institutional factors and political economy are more influential factors. In the area of company law, for example, China has had a robust level of derivative litigation for more

[30] *Guiding Case No 75: China Biodiversity Conservation and Green Development Foundation v Ningxia Ruitai Technology Co Ltd: A Case of Public Interest Litigation over Environmental Pollution* <https://cgc.law.stanford.edu/guiding-cases/guiding-case-75/> accessed 10 January 2020.

[31] Ibid.

[32] For discussion see eg Mingde Cao and Fengyuan Wang, 'Environmental Public Interest Litigation in China' *Asia Pacific Law Review*, 19/2 (2016): 217; Gu Gong and Ran An, 'Progress and Obstacles in Environmental Public Interest Litigation under China's Environmental Law: An Analysis of Cases Accepted and Heard in 2015' *Climate Law*, 7/2–3 (2017): 185.

[33] Cf. Stern (n 22).

than a decade despite not having a derivative action in its Company Law until 2006.[34] However, derivative litigation involving large government-linked Chinese companies does not exist because of the political constraints placed on such actions.[35]

V. ASSESSMENT

China has signed or ratified nearly all multilateral environmental agreements and is an active participant in global environmental diplomacy. However, Chinese courts do not play a significant role in interpreting or developing IEL. Even if environmental litigation were to flourish due to the steps taken to encourage EPIL, it is unlikely that IEL will feature prominently in the jurisprudence.

BIBLIOGRAPHY

Rachel Stern, *Environmental Litigation in China: A Study in Political Ambivalence* (CUP 2013)

Keyuan Zou, 'International Law in the Chinese Domestic Context' *Valparaiso University Law Review*, 44/3 (2010): 935

[34] Donald Clarke and Nicholas Howson, 'Pathway to Minority Shareholder Protection: Derivative Action in the People's Republic of China' in Dan Puchniak *et al* (eds), *The Derivative Action In Asia: A Comparative And Functional Approach* (CUP 2012) 243–244.

[35] Ibid, 275-278.

CHAPTER 63

EUROPEAN UNION/ UNITED KINGDOM

ELOISE SCOTFORD

I. INTRODUCTION

THIS chapter considers international environmental law (IEL) in the courts of the European Union (EU) and the United Kingdom. This topic potentially covers many different kinds of courts, considering that the EU comprises many member states, each with its own court system, and the United Kingdom itself is a system of devolved government with different court systems. To draw out some key themes, the chapter focuses on decisions of the EU courts; decisions of the UK courts in England and Wales; and notable decisions of other EU member state courts (available in English). The different experiences of IEL in these three sets of courts demonstrate that the doctrines of different legal systems and their legal cultures are critical to the experiences of their courts in implementing IEL.

An added dimension to the different courts covered in this chapter is their interaction. Since EU law has primacy in EU member states, any EU implementation of IEL obligations strengthens their implementation at the domestic member state level. In a dualist system such as that of the United Kingdom, this effectively bypasses any limits on the extent to which national courts can otherwise rely on international environmental treaties without specific domestic implementation. EU law can thus 'turbo boost' IEL in some domestic courts, acting as an implementation mechanism for IEL that bypasses national legal traditions. However, with the United Kingdom having left the EU,[1] the reverse effect may also be seen, at least in the United Kingdom.

This chapter examines the reception and application of IEL in these different courts in two steps. It first considers cases in which IEL has been directly applied by courts,

[1] European Union (Withdrawal Agreement) Act 2020.

considering the complex EU law in this area, and the EU's special role in implementing IEL in member states. The chapter then addresses cases where IEL applies indirectly in judicial reasoning. It concludes with an overall assessment of IEL in UK and EU courts.

II. CASES DIRECTLY APPLYING IEL

In both EU courts and UK courts, IEL is applied directly in different ways. In EU law, IEL can theoretically apply directly due to the part-monist nature of the EU legal order in giving effect to international law obligations, although the legal reality is more complicated. In UK law, a dualist system, there is no 'direct' applicability of IEL, but EU law has played a role as a conduit for implementing IEL directly. Beyond these direct applicability mechanisms, IEL is most often applied, and sometimes enhanced, in courts through the interpretation and application of domestic legislative measures that incorporate multilateral environmental agreements (MEAs) explicitly.

As the EU has matured as a legal order, it has transformed from being an institutional product of public international law (PIL) (an 'international organisation') to being an actor on the international plane, which is subject to customary international law and enters into international treaties, including MEAs. For the environmental sphere, this EU competence is generally shared,[2] meaning that the EU most often enters into MEAs as 'mixed agreements' alongside member states.[3] The impact of this IEL in EU law is partly provided for in the treaties,[4] with the Court of Justice of the European Union (CJEU) otherwise developing the law in this respect. PIL is an 'integral part' of the EU legal order.[5] In particular, IEL—whether customary international law or treaty-based—can have 'direct effect' in EU law.[6] However, this direct effect is circumscribed by legal criteria.[7] In relation to treaties specifically, these will have direct effect in EU law where (1) the EU is bound by the treaty; (2) the relevant treaty provision is sufficiently 'clear, precise and unconditional'; and (3) direct effect is not precluded by the 'nature and structure' or 'broad logic' of the treaty.[8] Two key environmental law decisions have shown that these criteria are to be applied strictly, promoting a vision of EU law as

[2] Treaty on the Functioning of the EU (TFEU), art 191.2.

[3] See further Chapter 37, 'Regional Organizations—The European Union', in this volume.

[4] TFEU, art 216.2.

[5] Case 181/73 *Haegeman v Belgium* [1974] ECR 449; Case 104/81 *Kupferberg v Hauptzollamt Mainz* [1982] ECR 3641.

[6] ie IEL norms are directly applicable, without any act of transposition: ibid; Case C-162/96 *Racke v Hauptzollamt Mainz* [1998] ECR I-3633; Case C-213/03 *Syndicat Professionel Coordination des Pecheurs* [2004] I-7359.

[7] Opinion 2/13 of the Court (Full Court)—Opinion pursuant to Article 218(11) TFEU (ECJ, 18 December 2014).

[8] Case C-308/06 *Intertanko et al v Secretary of State for Transport* [2008] ECR I-4057 (Intertanko case).

supreme, often alongside asserting more ambitious environmental protection goals or regulatory efforts in light of the EU's constitutionalized promotion of a high level of environmental protection.[9]

First, in the *Intertanko* case, the European Court of Justice (ECJ) was required to decide whether Directive 2005/35/EC on ship-source pollution was legally valid and, in particular, whether it needed to be consistent with EU obligations under the 1973/78 International Convention for the Prevention of Pollution from Ships (MARPOL) and the 1982 UN Convention on the Law of the Sea (UNCLOS). Relevantly, it found that neither treaty was directly applicable as a basis for determining the validity of Directive 2005/35. In the case of MARPOL, this was because the European Community (as it then was) was not bound by the treaty even though all its member states were signatories. In the case of UNCLOS, this comprehensive 'legal order for the seas and oceans'[10] was found to have a 'nature and structure' that was incompatible with direct effect within EU law as it was primarily state-centred. In addition, the direct effect requirement of having a relevantly clear, precise, and unconditional treaty provision was supplemented, or supplanted, with a requirement that relevant *direct and immediate legal rights or freedoms for individuals* must be created. In this case, rights were created for ships, but not necessarily for individuals associated with them.[11] This represented a departure from previous ECJ case law concerning the relationship between international law and EU law, restricting the direct applicability of IEL in EU law.

This trend was developed in the *Air Transport Association of America* (ATAA) case,[12] which concerned the contentious issue of whether the EU emissions trading scheme (EUETS) could lawfully extend to cover international aviation including flights outside the EU's airspace. Through the 2008 Aviation Directive, the EU had sought to include all flights that landed at, or departed from, an EU airport within the EUETS,[13] which is a scheme of market-based regulation of commercial operators on environmental grounds (aiming to mitigate climate change), requiring operators to obtain and surrender allowances equivalent to the greenhouse gas (GHG) emissions of their full flight sectors. This scheme was introduced in light of a failure (at the time) to institute a global market-based mechanism for civil aviation.[14] The Aviation Directive was challenged in the UK courts as unlawfully conflicting with several international treaties and principles of customary international law.

[9] TFEU, art 191.

[10] Intertanko case (n 8) [56].

[11] Ibid [61]–[64].

[12] Case C-366/10 *Air Transport Association of America and Others v SS for Energy and Climate Change* [2011] ECR I-13755 (ATAA case).

[13] Directive 2008/101/EC of the European Parliament and of the Council of 19 November 2008 amending Directive 2003/87/EC so as to include aviation activities in the scheme for greenhouse gas emission allowance trading within the Community [2009] OJ L8/3 (Aviation Directive).

[14] Case C-366/10 *Air Transport Association of America and Others v SS for Energy and Climate Change* [2011] ECR I-13755, Opinion of AG Kokott [186]–[187].

The case was referred to the CJEU as raising new questions of EU law.[15] The CJEU held that, whilst an international treaty and customary international law principles were directly applicable for testing the validity of the Aviation Directive,[16] the ETS scheme was compatible with those international law obligations. The nature of the obligations under the market-based mechanism of the ETS meant that it did not infringe the EU-US 'Open Skies Agreement'—which contained sufficiently clear and precise international law provisions effectively preventing national fuel taxes and charges being imposed on EU-US flights—or directly applicable principles of customary international law (affording complete and exclusive sovereignty to states over national airspace and providing that no state may subject any part of the high seas to its sovereignty). For the CJEU, it was decisive that the EU was imposing *internal* environmental regulation on flights that actually landed or originated in an EU member state, and that the 'full applicability' of EU law to such flights was justified, particularly where this internal regulation sought to support EU environmental protection objectives for a 'high level of protection' that 'follow on' from IEL (here the 1992 UN Framework Convention on Climate Change (UNFCCC) and 1997 Kyoto Protocol).[17] In the result, EU law doctrine effectively privileged EU environmental regulation over international law,[18] partly relying on the specific doctrines and provisions of international law at issue but also on the court's construction of the EUETS and its purposes, which justified 'full application' of this internal environmental measure with extraterritorial application.[19]

Whilst this might suggest some legal tension between IEL and EU law, the environmentally ambitious approach of much EU environmental law and policy often enhances the implementation of IEL. Thus the EU has legislated to implement many IEL agreements, and to augment them in some cases (eg 1979 Bern Convention on the Conservation of European Wildlife and Natural Habitats and EU Habitats Directive,[20]

[15] Notably the CJEU found that it had jurisdiction to resolve the alleged conflicts of international and EU law on the basis that no agreement as to the 'effect the provisions of [any applicable international treaty] are to have in the internal legal order of the contracting parties' had been settled in international law; see ATAA case (n 12) [49].

[16] Notably the Kyoto Protocol and environmental provisions of the 1944 Convention on Civil Aviation (Chicago Convention) were not directly applicable in this case; the former because it did not create unconditional and sufficiently precise obligations relevant to the contested Aviation Directive, and the latter because the EU was not bound by it.

[17] ATAA case (n 12) [128].

[18] See Sanja Bogojevic, 'Legalising Environmental Leadership: A Comment on the CJEU'S Ruling in C-366/10 on the Inclusion of Aviation in the EU Emissions Trading Scheme' *Journal of Environmental Law*, 24/2 (2012): 345.

[19] See further Marise Cremona and Joanne Scott, *EU law beyond EU Borders: The Extraterritorial Reach of EU Law* (OUP 2019).

[20] Directive 92/43/EEC of 21 May 1992 on the conservation of natural habitats and of wild fauna and flora [1992] OJ L206/7; see Case C-75/01 *Commission of the European Communities v Grand Duchy of Luxemburg* [2003] ECR-I 1585 (confirming that Directive 92/43/EEC offers greater protection than the Bern Convention).

or the 1979 Convention on Long-Range Transboundary Air Pollution, with its various protocols and the National Emissions Ceilings Directive).[21] CJEU decisions enforcing these EU measures have been a powerful engine for implementing IEL, particularly where they enhance their protective impact through the interpretive influence of EU principles of environmental policy.[22] Furthermore, EU law doctrine has otherwise developed so that some IEL obligations have legal effect in EU law despite not being directly effective. This can be seen in relation to the 1998 Aarhus Convention (Convention on Access to Information, Public Participation in Decision-Making and Access to Justice in Environmental Matters) and its access to justice provisions for environmental organizations, supported by EU environmental regulation and the EU Charter of Fundamental Rights.[23]

In contrast to the EU law position, in European national legal systems following a dualist approach (such as UK law), direct application of IEL only happens once IEL is legislatively adopted or otherwise incorporated into the relevant body of domestic law, or when EU law applies. In such legal orders, the machinery of EU law has been a powerful transmission belt for the implementation of IEL in member states. There are many examples of EU law using its legislative and enforcement machinery to implement IEL in member states, for example, through the adoption of the EU Waste Shipments Regulation, which creates an internal market in waste shipments and ensures compliance of all member states with the 1989 Basel Convention.[24] A notable example of IEL applying directly in member state legal orders through EU legislation is the Aarhus Convention,[25] which (prior to the UK's EU exit) fundamentally changed environmental litigation in the United Kingdom through the Convention's Article 9 access to justice

[21] Directive (EU) 2016/2284 of the European Parliament and of the Council of 14 December 2016 on the reduction of national emissions of certain atmospheric pollutants, amending Directive 2003/35/EC and repealing Directive 2001/81/EC [2016] OJ L344/1; see Joined cases C-165-167/09 *Stichting Natuur en Milieu v College van Gedeputeerde Staten van Groningen and College van Gedeputeerde Staten van Zuid-Holland* [2011] ECR-1 4559, Opinion of AG Kokott (explaining that the requirements of the directive are stricter).

[22] See eg Case C-127/02 *Landelijke Vereniging tot Behoud van de Waddenzee v Staatssecretaris van Landbouw, Natuurbeheer en Visserij* [2004] ECR I-7405, where the requirement to undertake an appropriate assessment where there was likely to be a significant effect on a protected site was interpreted strictly in light of the precautionary principle.

[23] Case C-664/15 *Protect Natur-, Arten- und Landschaftsschutz Umweltorganisation v Bezirkshauptmannschaft Gmünd* [2017] ECLI:EU:C:2017:987.

[24] Regulation (EC) No 1013/2006 of the European Parliament and of the Council of 14 June 2006 on shipments of waste [2006] OJ L190/1.

[25] Key provisions of the Aarhus Convention's three pillars have been adopted in EU law: Directive 2003/4/EC of the European Parliament and of the Council of 28 January 2003 on public access to environmental information and repealing Council Directive 90/313/EEC [2003] OJ L/41; Directive 2003/35/EC of the European Parliament and of the Council of 26 May 2003 providing for public participation in respect of the drawing up of certain plans and programmes relating to the environment and amending with regard to public participation and access to justice Council Directives 85/337/EEC and 96/61/EC [2003] OJ L156/17.

provisions relating to costs in particular, which have been partly implemented through EU legislation.[26]

III. CASES INDIRECTLY APPLYING IEL

IEL also applies indirectly in EU and member state law, through techniques of consistent interpretation in judicial reasoning. In EU law, the principle of consistent interpretation is based on the customary principle of good faith, found in general international law, and Article 4.3 of the Treaty on European Union (TEU).[27] A good example is the case of *PreussenElektra*. In that case, German feed-in-tariffs for renewable energy that might otherwise have infringed EU internal market rules were found to come within an exception to those rules, partly based on the EU's commitments under the UNFCCC and the Kyoto Protocol.[28]

Similarly, in member state courts, IEL can have persuasive authority. The well-known *Urgenda* case, in which the Dutch government was found to have acted unlawfully under Dutch law for failing to be sufficiently ambitious in its national climate policy, was decided on the basis of a Dutch tort and human rights doctrines, which were influenced by the international climate regime.[29] At first instance, the District Court explained how international law obligations, even if not directly binding on the state vis-à-vis the non-governmental association Urgenda, had a 'reflex effect' in national law, informing the application of Dutch law to find that the state had an inadequate climate mitigation

[26] At the time of writing, the Civil Procedure Rules in England and Wales had thrice been amended to introduce fixed costs in environmental litigation in an effort to comply with EU-mandated Aarhus provisions, following infraction proceedings brought by the EU Commission (Case C-530/11 *European Commission v United Kingdom of Great Britain and Northern Ireland* (ECJ, 13 February 2014)) and a judicial review brought by UK-based NGOs (*The Royal Society for the Protection of Birds Friends of the Earth Ltd & ClientEarth v Secretary of State for Justice the Lord Chancellor* [2017] EWHC 2309 (Admin)) challenging the UK costs regime. There remains an ongoing debate about whether all types of UK environmental litigation procedures are compliant with the Aarhus Convention (particularly relating to environmental litigation not covered by retained EU law)—in light of Aarhus Convention, Decision VI/8k, 'Compliance by the United Kingdom of Great Britain and Northern Ireland with its obligations under the Convention' (10 January 2018) UN Doc ECE/MP.PP/2017/2/Add.1, 55 (finding the UK was still failing to comply with the Convention's costs requirements for access to justice in 2017).

[27] Intertanko case (n 8) [52].

[28] Case C-379/98 *PreussenElektra v Schhleswag* [2001] ECR I-2099 [73]–[81].

[29] At first instance, the court relied on Dutch tort law to find the government liable (*Urgenda Foundation v The Netherlands* (The Hague District Court) ECLI:NL:RBDHA:2015:7196); in the first appellate court, it reached a similar conclusion based on human rights law (*The Netherlands v Urgenda Foundation* (The Hague Court of Appeal) ECLI:NL:GHDHA:2018:2610), which was confirmed in the Supreme Court on final appeal. In all cases, international climate law was relied on (along with relevant science) to establish that there is a real threat of dangerous climate change, informing the relevant Dutch doctrine; see *The State of the Netherlands (Ministry of Economic Affairs and Climate Policy) v Stichting Urgenda* (Judgement of 20 December 2019) No 19/00135, ECLI:NL:HR:2019:2007 (Supreme Court of the Netherlands).

policy.[30] This IEL influence is unsurprising in a partly monist system, but even in the United Kingdom (as a dualist legal tradition), there is the potential for unincorporated IEL to have legal effects. The UK House of Lords previously indicated that regard may be had to international obligations in applying common law doctrine,[31] although later case law has confirmed that the persuasive legal effects of IEL in UK law are circumscribed.[32] Moreover, the potential domestic legal impacts of incorporated treaties may raise complex questions of UK public law and statutory interpretation, depending on the domestic legal issue to which any IEL obligations may be relevant.[33]

IV. CONCLUSION

This chapter has shown how doctrines of EU law and member state law can implement IEL both directly and indirectly, but that the legal mechanisms in both cases are nuanced, reflecting the development and nature of different legal cultures within the EU. EU law allows IEL to have direct effect in EU law, subject to strict criteria, and there can also be jurisdictional barriers to implementing IEL directly, as seen in the subtle interplay between IEL and EU law in the *Air Transport for America* case. EU law nonetheless provides a powerful driver for implementing IEL in member states through EU measures that implement, and often enhance, IEL obligations. This effectively bypasses any domestic limits on the direct effectiveness of IEL in dualist systems. IEL can also be applied indirectly through the principle of consistent interpretation in judicial reasoning, which applies most clearly in part-monist systems.

As a short postscript, in the United Kingdom, the relationship between IEL and domestic law has become more complicated since the United Kingdom legally withdrew from the EU. From 1 January 2021, the United Kingdom retains all pre-existing EU law but this retained law may be amended over time, and it also remains bound by its IEL obligations (assuming it adopts responsibilities under all 'mixed' EU/member state MEAs).[34] The United Kingdom is thus bound by IEL within the culture of a dualist system, whilst having inherited some enhanced implementation of IEL through its

30 *Urgenda Foundation v The Netherlands* [4.43].

31 *A(FC) v Secretary of State for the Home Department, A (FC) v Secretary of State for the Home Department (joined appeals)* [2005] UKHL 71.

32 See eg *Morgan v Hinton Organics (Wessex) Ltd* [2009] EWCA Civ 107 (costs principles of the Aarhus Convention not directly incorporated via EU law are 'at most a matter to which the court may have regard in exercising its discretion': [47]); see also generally *R (Miller) v Secretary of State for Exiting the European Union* [2017] UKSC 5 [55]–[57] (setting out that a dualist system means that PIL gives rise to 'no legal rights or obligations in domestic law').

33 *R (Friends of the Earth Ltd and others) v Heathrow Airport Ltd* [2020] UKSC 52 [120]–[134].

34 UKELA, 'Brexit and Environmental Law: The UK and International Environmental Law After Brexit' (September 2017) <https://www.ukela.org/UKELA/ReadingRoom/Brexit/UKELAsworkonbrexit.aspx> accessed 27 January 2020.

previous EU membership, and there is some potential for indirect implementation of IEL in the future. Going forward, the UK's implementation of IEL will be a complex legal picture to analyse.

BIBLIOGRAPHY

Ioanna Hadjiyianni, *The EU as a Global Regulator for Environmental Protection: A Legitimacy Perspective* (Hart Publishing 2019)

Richard Macrory and Joe Newbigin, 'Brexit and International Environmental Law' *Centre for International Governance Innovation*, Paper No 8 (December 2017)

CHAPTER 64

INDIA, BANGLADESH, AND PAKISTAN

SHIBANI GHOSH

I. INTRODUCTION

As one of the most densely populated regions in the world with low levels of development, South Asia experiences severe pressures on its limited environmental resources. Conflicts over allocation and use of scarce resources and demands for better environmental quality often reach the national courts in this region. This Chapter focuses on three of the most populous countries in South Asia—India, Bangladesh, and Pakistan.

Till 1947, the three countries were, in most part, governed by the English common law system. The legal systems that evolved after independence thus bear many similarities. Each country has a detailed Constitution[1] and statutorily codified laws passed by their federal and regional legislatures. However, the common law tradition of the judiciary playing a key interpretive role has continued. The higher judiciary in these countries enjoys powers of judicial review, which they exercise through their original and appellate jurisdiction.[2]

The Constitution of each of the three countries guarantees a set of fundamental rights, and any law which derogates from, or is inconsistent with, any of the rights enumerated as a fundamental right is considered to be void.[3] While none of the Constitutions include a specific right to environment, or environmental protection, the judiciary in all three jurisdictions has actively recognized such a right to be part of other enumerated

[1] The Constitution of India came into force in 1950. Bangladesh adopted its Constitution in 1972. The current Constitution of Pakistan was promulgated in 1973. Over time significant amendments have been introduced in the three Constitutions.

[2] See eg Constitution of India, arts 32, 136, 226; Constitution of Bangladesh, arts 101, 102; Constitution of Pakistan, arts 184, 185.

[3] Constitution of India, art 13; Constitution of Bangladesh, art 26; Constitution of Pakistan, art 8.

fundamental rights, such as the right to life and the right to human dignity, and has thus given environmental rights constitutional gravitas.[4] Over the years, the judiciary in these countries has evolved a tradition of public interest litigation (PIL), with India taking the lead in 1980.[5] The objective of this form of litigation is to ensure that access to justice is not denied to marginalized sections of society. It allows issues of social, environmental, economic, or political salience to be brought before the courts, without having to discharge a high procedural burden. Environmental issues, in particular, have often (though not always) been adjudicated through the PIL route.[6]

In terms of domestic application of international law, the three countries essentially follow the doctrine of dualism.[7] While the executive has the power to enter into treaties, and ratify them, international law does not take effect unless it has been formally incorporated into the municipal law.[8] In terms of the legislature's engagement with international law, the parliaments in India and in Pakistan have the exclusive jurisdiction to enact a law implementing any international treaty.[9] However, in Bangladesh, the role of parliament is less clear, as the Constitution requires the president to lay all treaties with foreign countries before parliament, but does not define its role any further.[10]

4 See eg *Subhash Kumar v State of Bihar* (1991) 1 SCC 598 (Supreme Court of India); *Ms Shehla Zia v WAPDA* PLD 1994 SC 693 (Supreme Court of Pakistan); *Dr Mohiuddin Farooque v Bangladesh* 48 DLR 1996 (Supreme Court of Bangladesh, High Court Division) 438; see also Jona Razzaque, 'India, Pakistan and Bangladesh—Human Rights and the Environment—National Experiences' *Environmental Policy and Law*, 32/2 (2002): 99; Md Saiful Karim *et al*, 'Legal Activism for Ensuring Environmental Justice' *Asian Journal of Comparative Law*, 7/1 (2012): 1; Lovleen Bhullar, 'The Judiciary and the Right to Environment in India: Past, Present and Future' in Shibani Ghosh (ed), *Indian Environmental Law: Key Principles and Concepts* (Orient BlackSwan 2019) 21.

5 Shyam Divan, 'Public Interest Litigation' in Sujit Choudhry, Madhav Khosla, and Pratap Bhanu Mehta (eds), *The Oxford Handbook of the Indian Constitution* (OUP 2016) 662; Ridwanul Hoque, 'Taking Justice Seriously: Judicial Public Interest and Constitutional Activism in Bangladesh' *Contemporary South Asia*, 15/4 (2006): 399; Maryam Khan, 'Genesis and Evolution of Public Interest Litigation in the Supreme Court of Pakistan: Toward A Dynamic Theory of Judicialization' *Temple International and Comparative Law Journal*, 28/2 (2014): 285.

6 D S Sengar, 'PIL to Ensure that Institutions Behave Lawfully: Public Access to Environmental Justice in India' *Journal of the Indian Law Institute*, 45/1 (2003): 62; Parvez Hassan and Azim Azfar, 'Securing Environmental Rights through Public Interest Litigation in South Asia' *Virginia Environmental Law Journal*, 22/3 (2004): 215; see generally Jona Razzaque, *Public Interest Environmental Litigation in India, Pakistan and Bangladesh* (Kluwer Law International 2004).

7 In practice, however, the executive in India often incorporates international law in domestic law without parliamentary approval; see Aparna Chandra, 'India and International Law: Formal Dualism, Functional Monism' *Indian Journal of International Law*, 57/1–2 (2017): 25.

8 Lavanya Rajamani, 'International Law and the Constitutional Schema' in Choudhry *et al* (n 5) 143; Maira Sheikh and Moghees Khan, 'International Law Benchbook for the Judiciary in Pakistan' *Research Society of International Law* (2017); Sumaiya Khair, 'Bringing International Human Rights Law Home: Trends and Practices of Bangladeshi Courts' *Asian Yearbook of International Law*, 17 (2011): 47.

9 Constitution of India, art 253; Constitution of Pakistan, art 97, read with items 3 and 32 of the Fourth Schedule, part I.

10 Constitution of Bangladesh, art 145A; see also Bianca Karim and Tirza Theunissen, 'Bangladesh' in Dinah Shelton (ed), *International Law and Domestic Legal Systems: Incorporation, Transformation and Persuasion* (OUP 2011) 98; Khair (n 8) 57–60.

The judiciary in the three countries have adopted different approaches to international law. The Indian judiciary has been more amenable as Indian courts, particularly the Supreme Court, often rely on, or incorporate, international treaty provisions and norms while interpreting statutory obligations, even in the absence of relevant municipal law.[11] The Supreme Court of India has held that if a municipal law conflicts with international law, the former will prevail.[12] But in the absence of such a conflict, Indian courts will endorse international law[13] and municipal law will have to be read in a manner which conforms to international conventions.[14]

Courts in Bangladesh and Pakistan have adopted a far more cautious approach to implementing international law, and have held that unless there is a municipal statute enforcing the international law, the latter will not be enforced by domestic courts.[15] However, courts in both countries are open to using international legal provisions as tools for interpretation as long as they do not conflict with municipal law, and particularly while considering fundamental rights issues.[16]

II. DIRECT APPLICATION OF INTERNATIONAL ENVIRONMENTAL LAW

The Supreme Court of India has directly applied international environmental law (IEL) in at least two cases. In the landmark *Vellore* case, the court, while considering the widespread discharge of untreated effluent by tanneries into agricultural fields, water bodies, open lands, etc, issued a series of directions, including closure of certain tanneries,

[11] Venkatachala Hegde, 'Indian Courts and International Law' *Leiden Journal of International Law*, 23/1 (2010): 53; see also *Vishaka v State of Rajasthan* (1997) 6 SCC 241—a landmark judgement of the Indian Supreme Court on sexual harassment at workplace that relied on international law, and discussed its relevance in promoting constitutional guarantees.

[12] *Gramophone Company of India Ltd v Birendra Bahadur Pandey* (1984) 2 SCC 534.

[13] Ibid.

[14] *Justice Puttaswamy (Retd) v Union of India* 2017 SCC OnLine SC 1462.

[15] See eg *Govt of Punjab v Aamir Zahoor-ul-Haq* PLD 2016 SC 421; *Societe Generale de Surveillance S.A. v Pakistan through Secretary, Ministry of Finance* 2002 SCMR 1694; *BNWLA v Bangladesh* 14 BLC (2009) 703 (BNWLA case); *Chaudhury and Kendra v Bangladesh* 29 BLD (HCD) (2009); *Bangladesh v Hasina* 60 DLR (AD) (2008) 90.

[16] See Sheikh and Khan (n 8) 46–47; see also BNWLA case (n 15); *Hussain Muhammad Ershad v Bangladesh* 21 BLD (AD) (2001) 69. See also Order of 4 September 2015 of the Lahore High Court in *Ashgar Leghari v Federation of Pakistan* WP 25501/2015 where the court, while deciding on the implementation of Pakistan's national climate policy, observed that the fundamental rights to life and human dignity included IEL principles like sustainable development, precaution, intra- and intergenerational equity. However, the court did not analyse the relevance of, or contextualize, IEL any further.

installation of effluent treatment facilities, etc.[17] Significantly it observed that 'sustainable development' had been accepted as a part of the customary international law (CIL) though its salient features were yet to be finalized. It further observed that the precautionary principle and the polluter pays principle were essential features of sustainable development and declared the two principles to be part of Indian environmental law. Although relying on them in its final judgement, the Court did not delve into the definition, content, and status of these three principles in international law.

The three principles—sustainable development, precaution, and polluter pays—have since been frequently referred to and relied on by Indian courts, and are considered to be an integral part of Indian environmental jurisprudence. They have received statutory recognition (albeit without clear definitional guidance) through the 2010 National Green Tribunal Act. However, there has been limited judicial analysis by Indian courts of the status of these principles in international law before directly applying them in various cases.[18]

In the second case, the Supreme Court found the import of a leopard trophy to be illegal as the necessary approval under the 1973 Convention on International Trade in Endangered Species of Wild Fauna and Flora (CITES), ratified by India in 1976, had not been obtained.[19]

A third case that may be referred to is a judgement of the National Green Tribunal (NGT) which struck down parts of a government notification exempting construction projects from regulatory approvals. The Tribunal found various legal infirmities including violation of the principle of non-regression as there was considerable dilution of the existing environmental laws. The Tribunal did not discuss the origin or evolution of the principle of non-regression, and accepts it as a norm of international law applicable to Indian judicial decision-making.[20]

Courts in Bangladesh and Pakistan do not appear, for the most part, to have directly applied principles of IEL. However, in one instance, the reliance of the Supreme Court of Pakistan on the precautionary principle could arguably be viewed as direct application of the principle. In *Shehla Zia v WAPDA*, a landmark case on the right to life, and to human dignity, the issue before the court was whether a grid station should be constructed near a residential area as the electro-magnetic field created could pose a serious health hazard.[21] The court observed that in a situation of uncertainty, authorities should observe the rules of prudence and precaution. Despite clarifying that it was

[17] *Vellore Citizens' Welfare Forum v Union of India* (1996) 5 SCC 647; see Michael Anderson, 'International Environmental Law in Indian Courts' *Review of European, Comparative and International Environmental Law*, 7/1 (1998): 21.

[18] See Saptarishi Bandopadhyay, 'Sustainable Development and Indian Environmental Jurisprudence', Lovleen Bhullar, 'The Polluter Pays Principle: Scope and Limits of Judicial Decisions', and Lavanya Rajamani, 'The Precautionary Principle' in Ghosh (ed) (n 4).

[19] *Union of India v Zavaray S Poonawala* 2015 (7) SCC 347.

[20] *Society for Protection of Environment & Biodiversity v Union of India* 2017 SCC OnLine NGT 981.

[21] Shehla Zia (n 4).

invoking Principle 15 of the Rio Declaration for its persuasive value (as Pakistan had not ratified the Rio Declaration), the court seemed to implement the precautionary principle. The court held that the company could not wait for conclusive findings on the effect of electro-magnetic fields on human life before taking necessary measures.

III. INDIRECT APPLICATION OF INTERNATIONAL ENVIRONMENTAL LAW

The indirect application of IEL by courts in the three jurisdictions is more common. The courts invoke international legal instruments, of varying legal heft, while interpreting provisions of national laws, reviewing executive action, and in support of the final judicial outcome.

The Supreme Court of India has referred to the 1992 Convention on Biological Diversity (CBD) and the CITES while directing the government to protect sandalwood, an endangered plant species;[22] the Rio Declaration, Agenda 21, the Forestry Principles, and the CBD, along with International Labour Organization (ILO) conventions, to recognize customary rights of a tribal population;[23] the 1989 Basel Convention to give directions on management of hazardous waste, as well as regulate the ship-breaking industry;[24] and the 1971 Ramsar Convention to protect a critically vulnerable coastal area from illegal construction.[25]

One of the landmark environmental law judgements in Bangladesh, the *Flood Action Plan 20* Case decided by the Supreme Court,[26] triggered the beginning of PIL in the country. The case challenged certain activities planned under a Flood Action Plan which would cause environmental degradation. The Supreme Court's Appellate Division adopted a liberal definition for 'person aggrieved' under Article 102 of the Constitution while accepting the *locus standi* of the appellant organization. As part of his judicial reasoning, Chief Justice ATM Afzal found Principle 10 of the Rio Declaration to support the organization's standing in the case.

Other prominent instances of indirect application of IEL by Bangladesh courts include cases on ship-breaking. In a 2009 judgement, the Supreme Court of Bangladesh (High Court Division), while considering the legality of import of the ship *MT Enterprise* for dismantling, directed the government to frame rules for proper handling

22 *T.N. Godavarman v Union of India* (2012) 4 SCC 362.

23 *Orissa Mining Corporation v Ministry of Environment and Forests* (2013) 6 SCC 476.

24 *Research Foundation for Science Technology and Natural Resource Policy v Union of India* (2005) 10 SCC 510.

25 *Vaamika Island (Green Lagoon Resort) v Union of India* (2013) 8 SCC 760.

26 *Dr Mohiuddin Farooque v Bangladesh* 49 DLR 1997 (AD) 1.

and management of hazardous waste in accordance with the Basel Convention, which Bangladesh had ratified in 1993.[27]

In Pakistan, the indirect use of IEL is evident in a case challenging a road-widening project in Lahore. The Supreme Court of Pakistan considered whether inter alia the precautionary principle (as defined in the *Shehla Zia* case) and the principle of sustainable development (as defined by the Brundtland Commission) had been followed while designing and approving the project.[28] The court concluded that neither principle had been violated by the concerned agency.[29]

IV. ASSESSMENT AND CONCLUSION

Review of the case law reveals that Indian courts have led the adoption of the IEL principles in this region, with occasional references to IEL by Bangladeshi and Pakistani courts.[30] This appears to follow the trend of non-environmental cases, where the judiciaries of Bangladesh and Pakistan are also more reluctant than the Indian courts to turn to international law.

Although courts in the three countries have engaged with IEL, it has mostly been at a superficial level. Their reliance on IEL is not always accompanied by strong judicial reasoning, making it difficult to determine their content and scope, and even their relevance in particular scenarios. Given development imperatives in these countries, courts are often faced with the 'economy/development versus environment' question. In such situations, the courts rely on IEL in an instrumental fashion in support of the final outcome of the case, rather than engaging with the substantive content of the IEL principle.

BIBLIOGRAPHY

Shibani Ghosh (ed), *Indian Environmental Law: Key Principles and Concepts* (Orient BlackSwan 2019)

Bianca Karim and Tirza Theunissen, 'Bangladesh' in Dinah Shelton (ed), *International Law and Domestic Legal Systems: Incorporation, Transformation, and Persuasion* (OUP 2011) 98

[27] *Bangladesh Environmental Lawyers Association v Bangladesh* WP 7260/2008 (17 March 2009); see also Shawkat Alam and Abdullah Faruque, 'Legal Regulation of the Shipbreaking Industry in Bangladesh: The International Regulatory Framework and Domestic Implementation Challenges' *Marine Policy*, 47/1 (2014): 46.

[28] *Suo Moto Case No. 25 of 2009 (Cutting of Trees for Canal Widening Project Lahore)* (15 August 2011).

[29] See also judgement of the High Court of Lahore in *Imrana Tiwana v Province of Punjab* PLD 2015 Lahore 522.

[30] It should be noted that the text of judgements reviewed do not necessarily reflect the nature and extent of reliance on IEL by the parties before the courts.

Lavanya Rajamani, 'International Law and the Constitutional Schema' in Sujit Choudhry, Madhav Khosla, and Pratap Mehta (eds), *The Oxford Handbook of the Indian Constitution* (OUP 2016) 143

Jona Razzaque, *Public Interest Environmental Litigation in India, Pakistan and Bangladesh* (Kluwer Law International 2004)

Maira Sheikh and Moghees Khan, 'International Law Benchbook for the Judiciary in Pakistan' *Research Society of International Law Pakistan* (2017)

CHAPTER 65

NORTH AMERICA

NATASHA AFFOLDER

I. INTRODUCTION

UNCERTAINTY and unpredictability describe both the present and future of international environmental law (IEL) in North America. This manifests in at least three ways. First, the very utility of approaching North America as an analytical unit is open to debate. The 1992 North American Free Trade Agreement (NAFTA) was replaced in 2020 by a trade agreement that goes by three different names.[1] Second, the growing recognition of Indigenous law highlights the erasure inherent in thinking of North America through the lens of three federal states. And third, domestic courts in this region exhibit remarkable dexterity in dodging the IEL arguments that come before them. This means that any commentary emerges from a sparse and statistically insignificant record. Indeed, for some, particularly in the United States in recent years, the core challenge shifted from how to promote richer engagement with IEL, to how to prevent its repudiation.

This chapter explores the minimal engagement of US, Canadian, and Mexican courts with IEL. In so doing, it identifies signposts of a different course: one that contemplates a meaningful role for North American courts in advancing IEL. The exercise is not an imaginary one—signposts are there, albeit in some unusual forms, and in some unlikely places.

[1] The agreement is known as the United States-Mexico-Canada Agreement in the United States, as the Canada-United States-Mexico Agreement in Canada, and as the Tratado entre México, Estados Unidos y Canadá in Mexico.

II. APPLYING INTERNATIONAL ENVIRONMENTAL LAW

It is difficult to find cases, particularly recent ones, in the United States, Canada, or Mexico where IEL has served as a rule of decision or has been 'directly applied'. This observation applies across the three countries, despite the different approaches each takes to treaty incorporation and the recognition of customary international law.[2] Further, a sharp distinction in the degree of domestic court engagement with IEL between the common law jurisdictions of the United States and Canada and the civil law jurisdiction of Mexico (and the province of Quebec) also fails to manifest in practice. Andre Nollkaemper's observation that it is *judicial attitudes*, rather than formal features of the constitutional system, that explain the extent to which IEL enters the domestic sphere through the courts, aptly describes this region.[3]

In the United States, direct application cases are extremely infrequent, and often unsuccessful.[4] Cases where IEL has been relied upon as an 'interpretive aid' are equally hard to find. Easier to find are examples of US courts dismissing international law arguments as political questions,[5] or avoiding the international law arguments raised by litigants in environmental cases.[6] Even in climate change litigation, a site of significant activity in the United States, international law obligations fail to feature meaningfully in judicial decisions. This lack of explicit engagement with IEL by US courts is in line with the recent 'sluggish' record of US ratification of major multilateral environmental agreements.[7]

In the rare cases in which Canadian courts reference IEL, it is unclear whether these norms are invoked as rules, as part of an interpretive exercise, or to add, somehow, an additional layer of depth or legitimacy to principles, whose legal relevance emerges solely from their domestic incorporation.[8] In *Environmental Defence Canada v Canada*

[2] A detailed discussion of reception law is beyond the scope of this chapter. Moreover, recent scholarship on 'dubious dualism' and 'creeping monism' reveals the challenges of relying too heavily on formal and fixed categories to explain international law's domestic reception.

[3] Andre Nollkaemper, 'Judicial Application of International Environmental Law in the Netherlands' *Review of European, Comparative and International Environmental Law*, 7/1 (1998): 40, 45.

[4] A rare example is *Defenders of Wildlife Inc v Endangered Species Scientific Authority, et al* 65 F 2d 168 (DC Cir 1981).

[5] *Japan Whaling Association v American Cetacean Society* 478 US 221, 229 (1986).

[6] Ibid, 240–241.

[7] See Jutta Brunnée, 'The United States and International Environmental Law: Living with an Elephant' *European Journal of International Law*, 15/4 (2004): 617.

[8] See also Daniel Bodansky and Jutta Brunnée, 'Introduction: The Role of National Courts in the Field of International Environmental Law' in Michael Anderson and Paolo Galizzi (eds), *International Environmental Law in National Courts* (British Institute of International and Comparative Law 2002) 1.

(Minister of Fisheries and Oceans),[9] the court acknowledged Canada's obligation to apply the principles of the 1992 Biodiversity Convention. However, it failed to specify whether the Convention was being invoked as a binding obligation on Canada, as part of Canada's rebuttable presumption of conformity with international law, or as a source of interpretive principles. A wider review of Canadian case law reveals a pattern of courts avoiding explicit engagement with the *legal* relevance of IEL.[10] This is despite the fact that the Supreme Court of Canada has now taken steps to clarify Canada's approach to international law.[11]

A significant hurdle for litigants to overcome regarding the consideration of international law arguments in Canada and the United States is that of justiciability. On this issue, the *Friends of the Earth* case casts a long shadow in Canada. In that case, the Federal Court determined the question of Canada's violation of the 1997 Kyoto Protocol to be a 'political question' and thus non-justiciable. It thus held that it had '*no role to play* reviewing the reasonableness of the government's response to Canada's Kyoto commitments'.[12]

Like Canada and the United States, domestic courts in Mexico lack a robust record of applying IEL. The confluence of three separate legal developments suggests that this might change in the future.[13] First, Mexico has a Constitution that protects the right of every individual 'to live in a healthy environment for her development and welfare'.[14] Second, *amparo* actions allow individuals to pursue judicial relief in federal courts for acts of authorities that contravene the Constitution or individual rights. And third, the 2011 Human Rights Amendment to the Constitution obligates government to guarantee the protection of the human rights recognized in the Constitution *and* in the international treaties that Mexico ratifies.[15]

The fact that IEL arguments largely fail to feature as reasons for judgement does not mean that these arguments are not being heard, or are failing to exert influence. In emerging climate litigation, international norms may be influential within domestic dispute resolution contexts despite the lack of formal engagement with these norms.[16]

9 2009 FC 878.

10 Natasha Affolder, 'Domesticating the Exotic Species: International Biodiversity Law in Canada' *McGill Law Review*, 51/2 (2006): 217.

11 *R v Hape* [2007] 2 SCR 292; *Nevsun Resources Ltd v Araya* 2020 SCC 5.

12 *Friends of the Earth v Canada (Governor in Council)* 2008 FC 1183 (emphasis added).

13 Luis Avilés, 'Sustainable Development and Environmental Legal Protection in the European Union: A Model for Mexican Courts to Follow?' *Mexican Law Review* 6/2 (2014): 251, 254–255.

14 Constitución Política de los Estados Unidos Mexicanos (as amended), art 1, Diario Oficial de la Federación, 5 de febrero de 1917 (Mex).

15 Erika Cedillo, 'The Impact of Mexico's 2011 Human Rights Constitutional Amendment on Arbitral Practice: A View from Local Actors' in Ljiljana Biukovic and Pitman Potter (eds), *Local Engagement with International Economic Law and Human Rights* (Edward Elgar 2017) 109.

16 Andrew Long, 'International Consensus and U.S. Climate Change Litigation' *William and Mary Environmental Law and Policy Review*, 33/1 (2008): 177, 181.

III. ENGAGING WITH INTERNATIONAL ENVIRONMENTAL LAW

The normative influence of IEL is difficult to measure, but surely involves more than counting the raw number of domestic cases in which international law features. The *Juliana* case,[17] launched by youth plaintiffs in the United States, helped inspire a global movement of climate litigation even though it was dismissed.

In some jurisdictions, the influence of international law principles may be most often witnessed outside the jurisprudence of the highest courts. In Canada, it is the administrative tribunals and energy and utilities boards that are engaging with principles such as intergenerational equity,[18] and the precautionary principle.[19] Though courts are also referencing these principles, these references come across as further evidence in support of a decision already made. Thus, the Supreme Court of Canada in *Castonguay Blasting Ltd v Ontario (Environment)* affirmed a reading of Ontario's Environmental Protection Act that was 'also consistent with the precautionary principle'.[20] Much rarer are Canadian cases, such as *Spraytech*,[21] which use international law in a way that has been extensively cited, and relied upon, by courts in other countries.[22]

In Mexico, a small number of non-binding court precedents have emerged from the Collegiate Circuit Courts that directly engage with international sources to advance the principles of precaution and intergenerational equity. These precedents draw on international human rights instruments, notably the 1966 International Covenant of Cultural, Social and Economic Rights[23] and the 1969 American Convention on Human Rights.[24]

[17] *Juliana v United States* 217 F Supp 3d 1224 (D Or 2016), rev'd and remanded, 947 F.3d 1159 (9th Cir 2020).

[18] See eg *ATCO Pipelines, Re* [2007] AEUBD No 104 [39].

[19] *EnCana Corp, Re* [2009] AEUBD No 127 [200].

[20] *R v Castonguay Blasting Ltd* [2013] 3 SCR 323 [20].

[21] *114957 Canada Ltée (Spraytech, Société d'arrosage) v Hudson (Town)* 2001 SCC 40.

[22] Ironically, the case is often cited as judicial authority holding that the precautionary principle *is* customary international law. Madame Justice L'Heureux Dubé's exact words are (and she is quoting a scholarly article): 'there may be "currently sufficient state practice to allow a good argument that the precautionary principle is a principle of customary international law" '; ibid [32].

[23] Non-binding court precedent no 2011808, 'Derechos Humanos a la Salud y a un Medio Ambiente Sano. Procede Conceder la Suspensión Provisional Respecto de Omisiones de las Autoridades Responsables que conlleven una Afectación Directa de Aquéllos' Thesis Reg Num 2011808 [TA] III.20.A.66 A, 10th Epoch, Gaceta del Semanario Judicial de la Federación, Book 31, vol IV (June 2016) 2896.

[24] Non-binding court precedent no 2010877, 'Suspensión en el Amparo. Funcionalidad del Principio Precautorio en su Otorgamiento' Thesis Reg Num 2010877 [TA] XI.10.A.T.26 K, 10th Epoch, Gaceta del Semanario Judicial de la Federación, Book 26, vol IV (January 2016) 3487.

IV. CHALLENGES AND OPPORTUNITIES

While North America appears impoverished compared to other regions in terms of its formal record of domestic judicial engagement with IEL, there are some enticing developments in other areas of legal practice that hint at opportunities ahead. These lie at the intersection of IEL with Indigenous law, human rights law, and private international law.

A. Indigenous Law

Domestic implementation of international law in North America implicates more than federal-state relationships with treaties and customary international law. This is particularly the case now in Canada where the government has committed to implement the United Nations Declaration on the Rights of Indigenous Peoples (UNDRIP).[25] Domestic implementation of UNDRIP requires an unprecedented 'braiding together' of domestic, international, and Indigenous laws.[26] Indigenous litigants are drawing on international law to protect sacred places, arguing that culture, history, and spirituality are all deeply linked to the land of Indigenous people and worthy of legal protection.[27]

B. Human Rights Law

Human rights law serves as another possible port of entry for IEL in domestic cases. For example, Mexico's Human Rights Amendment paves the way for human rights treaties to advance IEL in Mexico. Also, regional bodies, such as the Inter-American Commission on Human Rights, offer a venue for advancing environmental claims through human rights complaints. While the Inuit Petition on Global Warming was formally declined, the Commission has before it another opportunity to consider similar human rights violations emerging from emissions of black carbon by Canada.[28]

[25] UNGA Res 61/295, 'United Nations Declaration on the Rights of Indigenous Peoples' (2 October 2007) UN Doc A/RES/61/295; see eg *R v Sayers* (2017) ONCJ 77 (where UNDRIP was invoked in a timber rights case).

[26] John Borrows *et al* (ed), *Braiding Legal Orders* (McGill-Queens Press 2019).

[27] *Ktunaxa Nation v British Columbia (Forests, Lands and Natural Resources Operations)* [2017] 2 SCR 386.

[28] Earth Justice, 'Petition to the Inter-American Commission on Human Rights Seeking Relief from Violations of the Rights of Arctic Athabaskan Peoples Resulting from Rapid Arctic Warming and Melting Caused by Emissions of Black Carbon by Canada' (23 April 2013) <https://earthjustice.org/sites/default/files/AAC_PETITION_13-04-23a.pdf> accessed 10 January 2020.

C. Private International Law

A final area to watch is private international law. In cases coming out of both Canada[29] and the United States,[30] courts have signalled that in the right circumstances, domestic environmental laws can be used against foreign companies for actions taking place within a foreign jurisdiction. Moreover, the 2020 decision of the Supreme Court of Canada's 2020[31] opens up the possibility of a radically expanded role for customary international law before national courts, and as applied to corporations.

V. ASSESSMENT

Environmental law cases in Canada, Mexico, and the United States are not immune to international law and international norms. But, as this review suggests, international environmental lawyers may be forced to look to some unlikely and unusual places to find IEL's normative influence. Environmental law cases in North America seem poised to engage most significantly with international law not in the 'bright lights' but rather on the sidelines, where environmental law norms interface with climate law, private international law, Indigenous law, and human rights law.

BIBLIOGRAPHY

Natasha Affolder, 'Domesticating the Exotic Species: International Biodiversity Law in Canada' *McGill Law Review*, 51/2 (2006): 217

Michael Anderson and Paolo Galizzi (eds), *International Environmental Law in National Courts* (British Institute of International and Comparative Law 2002)

29 *Edwards v DTE Energy Company*, Ontario Superior Court of Justice (16 January 2008) Doc No 298 (Southwest Region).

30 *Pakootas v Teck Cominco Metals, Ltd* 452 F.3d 1066 (9th Cir 2006).

31 *Nevsun Resources Ltd v Araya* 2020 SCC 5.

CHAPTER 66

OCEANIA

TIM STEPHENS*

I. INTRODUCTION

THE Oceania region stretches across Australasia, Melanesia, Micronesia, and Polynesia, embracing fourteen independent states,[1] two states in free association with New Zealand,[2] and offshore territories of three other states.[3] A range of topics of international environmental law (IEL) have been canvassed in Oceania courts from sustainable fisheries management to the protection of world heritage. Reflecting the major threat that global warming poses to Oceania, cases addressing climate issues represent a growing proportion of this region's environmental jurisprudence.

II. THE ROLE OF INTERNATIONAL LAW IN OCEANIA

The states of Oceania have generally been strong advocates for IEL[4] and have adopted notable regional environmental treaties such as the 1986 Convention for the Protection of the Natural Resources and Environment of the South Pacific Region (Noumea

* The author is grateful for research assistance provided by Jessica Horn.

[1] Australia, Papua New Guinea, New Zealand, Fiji, Solomon Islands, Vanuatu, Samoa, Kiribati, Tonga, Federated States of Micronesia, Marshall Islands, Palau, Tuvalu, and Nauru.

[2] The Cook Islands and Niue.

[3] France (New Caledonia, French Polynesia, Wallis and Futuna), the UK (Pitcairn Islands), and the US (American Samoa, Guam, Northern Mariana Islands).

[4] See Ben Boer, Ross Ramsay, and Donald Rothwell, *International Environmental Law in the Asia Pacific* (Kluwer 1998); see generally *Asia Pacific Journal of Environmental Law*.

Convention). Given the common law basis of most jurisdictions in Oceania, IEL can usually be given effect only by legislative implementation.[5]

III. STRUCTURE AND FUNCTION OF COURT SYSTEMS IN OCEANIA

All states in Oceania have legal systems in which courts have jurisdiction over various matters of planning and environmental law.[6] Unlike some other regions, there is no regional court, commission, or tribunal for Oceania. However, there is cooperation among the judiciary across the region, with judges from larger jurisdictions such as New Zealand serving on national appellate courts of smaller jurisdictions such as the Solomon Islands. In some jurisdictions there are specialist land or environment courts and tribunals, such as the Land and Environment Court in the Australian state of New South Wales (NSW LEC) and the Environment Court of New Zealand.

IV. CASES DIRECTLY APPLYING INTERNATIONAL ENVIRONMENTAL LAW IN OCEANIA

There have been a number of cases in Oceania directly applying IEL. In *Commonwealth v Tasmania* (*Tasmanian Dam* case)[7] the High Court of Australia found that Australia's federal parliament had constitutional authority to implement the 1972 World Heritage Convention. This decision has allowed Australia to implement a range of environmental treaties, including through the 1999 Environment Protection and Biodiversity Conservation Act 1999 (EPBC Act). There have been a large number of cases brought under the EPBC Act, several considering IEL. In *Booth v Bosworth*[8] the Federal Court of Australia granted an injunction to prevent the electrocution of spectacled flying foxes by farmers in Queensland as it impaired world heritage values. Another example is *Minister for the Environment & Heritage v Greentree (No 2)*[9] which concerned land clearing in a wetland listed under the 1971 Ramsar Convention.

[5] See eg *Environmental Defence Society (Incorporated) v Auckland Regional Council* (2002) NZEnvC 315 [22].

[6] Jennifer Corrin and Don Paterson, *Introduction to South Pacific Law* (4th edn, Intersentia 2017) ch 11, 'State Courts'.

[7] (1983) 158 CLR 1; see also *Richardson v Forestry Commission* (1988) 164 CLR 261; *Queensland v Commonwealth* (1989) 167 CLR 232.

[8] (2001) FCA 1453.

[9] (2004) FCA 741.

A number of other cases in Oceania have involved the application of national law implementing international obligations, as in *State v Kim Bentley & United Airco Ltd* in the High Court of Fiji which concerned regulations for ozone depleting substances.[10] The Environment Court of New Zealand referred to the 1987 Montreal Protocol on Substances that Deplete the Ozone Layer in *Envirofume Limited v Bay of Plenty Regional Council*[11] in a case concerning the discharge of methyl bromide from ships. In *Sustainability Council of New Zealand Trust v Environmental Protection Authority*[12] the High Court of New Zealand considered and applied legislation implementing New Zealand's obligations under the 2000 Cartagena Protocol on Biosafety.

Other cases have ranged more broadly, considering core principles of IEL such as environmental impact assessment (EIA), the precautionary principle, and sustainable development. A substantial body of jurisprudence on environmental principles has been developed in several Australian jurisdictions. In *Telstra v Hornsby Shire Council*[13] the NSW LEC considered the concept of ecologically sustainable development and the principles of integration, precaution, and intergenerational equity. Subsequent decisions have concluded that principles of ecologically sustainable development are 'plainly an element of the public interest'.[14] Several other courts in Oceania have also applied these principles. Precaution was considered by the New Zealand Supreme Court in *Sustain our Sounds Incorporated v New Zealand King Salmon Company Limited*[15] in finding that a decision-maker could legitimately take an adaptive approach in managing salmon farming.

In *Framhein v Attorney General* the High Court of the Cook Islands considered that customary international law required the government to undertake environmental impact assessment before approving purse seine fishing.[16] The Court referred to several treaties including the 1982 United Nations Convention on the Law of the Sea (UNCLOS) and specifically referenced *Pulp Mills on the River Uruguay (Argentina/Uruguay)*[17] and *Certain Activities Carried Out by Nicaragua in the Border Area (Costa Rica/Nicaragua) and Construction of a Road in Costa Rica along the San Juan River (Nicaragua/Costa Rica)*.[18]

In *Fiji Fish Marketing Group Ltd v Pacific Cement Ltd* the High Court of Fiji referred to the polluter pays principle as a supporting factor in granting an injunction to prevent the unloading of clinker (coal residue) on a jetty near the applicant's fish factory. The High Court also referred to the relevance of 'sustainable development with due regard to

[10] (2005) FJHC 713.

[11] (2017) NZEnvC 12.

[12] (2014) NZHC 1067.

[13] (2006) 146 LGERA 10.

[14] *Barrington—Gloucester—Stroud Preservation Alliance Inc v Minister for Planning and Infrastructure* (2012) NSWLEC 197.

[15] (2014) NZSC 40.

[16] (2017) CKHC 37 [47].

[17] [2010] ICJ Rep 14.

[18] [2015] ICJ Rep 665.

the environment'.[19] The polluter pays principle was also applied by the Supreme Court of the Federated States of Micronesia in *People of Rull ex rel Ruepong v MV Kyowa Violet*,[20] a nuisance and maritime tort case arising from an oil spill. Multilateral environmental agreements (MEAs) have also been directly considered and applied in a number of cases relating to fisheries management.[21]

V. CASES INDIRECTLY APPLYING INTERNATIONAL ENVIRONMENTAL LAW IN OCEANIA

International environmental law has arisen indirectly in human rights cases in Oceania. In *Bernard v Duban*[22] the National Court of Papua New Guinea referred to the impacts of a petroleum project on the culture and tradition of customary owners of land as infringing their right to life under the Papua New Guinea constitution.[23]

In administrative law proceedings plaintiffs have frequently invoked IEL as a relevant consideration for decision-makers, with success dependent upon the relevant legislation. For instance in *Greenpeace v Minister of Energy and Resources*, which concerned a challenge to a decision granting petroleum exploration rights within New Zealand's exclusive economic zone, the High Court concluded that the relevant statutory provision did not impose a mandatory obligation to take account of environmental obligations.[24]

There is a growing body of climate change-related cases in Oceania, with most being administrative law proceedings. *Gray v Minister for Planning*[25] was a key early decision in which the NSW LEC referred to the intergenerational equity and precautionary principles in finding that combustion emissions from mined coal needed to be considered when approving a coal mine. Several subsequent decisions in Australia have taken a similar approach to *Gray*,[26] while others have been dismissive of climate change concerns.[27] A recent landmark decision was the *Rocky Hill Coal Mine* case[28] in which

[19] (2017) FJHC 252 [47].

[20] (2006) FMSC 53.

[21] See eg *Chuuk v Secretary of Department of Finance* (2000) FMSC 36, which referred to UNCLOS.

[22] (2016) PGNC 121.

[23] 1975 Constitution of the Independent State of Papua New Guinea, s 35.

[24] (2012) NZHC 1422 [118].

[25] (2006) NSWLEC 720.

[26] See eg *Australian Conservation Foundation v Latrobe City Council* (2004) 140 LGERA 100.

[27] See eg *Wildlife Preservation Society of Queensland Proserpine/Whitsunday Branch Inc v Minister for the Environment and Heritage* (2006) FCA 736; *Xstrata Coal Queensland Pty Ltd v Friends of the Earth—Brisbane Co-Op Ltd* (2012) QLC 13; *Adani Mining Pty Ltd v Land Services of Coast and Country Inc* (2015) QLC 48; *Australian Conservation Foundation Inc v Minister for the Environment and Energy* (2017) FCAFC 134 [61].

[28] *Gloucester Resources Limited v Minister for Planning* (2019) NSWLEC 7.

NSW LEC refused consent for a coal mine on the basis of climate change, holding that a 'rapid and deep decrease' in greenhouse gas emissions is needed.[29]

There have also been a string of climate change cases in New Zealand. In *New Zealand Carbon Farming v Mighty River Power Limited* the New Zealand High Court referred to the threat of climate change and to the 1992 United Nations Framework Convention on Climate Change (UNFCCC) and noted that '[t]he reduction of emissions of greenhouse gases has been accepted by governments worldwide as being necessary to manage and limit the impact of climate change on society, the economy and the environment'.[30] New Zealand climate cases with broader legal implications have been those that have considered whether climate change is a relevant consideration for administrative decision-makers. In *Environmental Defence Society (Incorporated) v Auckland Regional Council*,[31] the New Zealand Environment Court recognized the seriousness of climate change and New Zealand's obligations under the UNFCCC and the 1997 Kyoto Protocol, but found it unreasonable to impose a condition on a development consent requiring an energy company to plant trees to offset emissions from a gas-fired power station.

The most significant New Zealand climate change case is *Thomson v Minister for Climate Change Issues*, in which a New Zealand law student sought judicial review of decisions adopting national emissions reduction targets. The New Zealand High Court found that the statutory power to set emissions reduction targets by regulation under the 2002 Climate Change Act must be interpreted consistently with New Zealand's international obligations under the UNFCCC and Kyoto Protocol, and the publication of a new IPCC (Intergovernmental Panel on Climate Change) report requires the Minister to consider whether a target should be reviewed. Significantly, the court held that the matter was justiciable and that 'it may be appropriate for domestic courts to play a role in Government decision making about climate change'.[32] However, on the facts, it could not be concluded that the target was irrational or unreasonable.

Another category of climate change cases has considered whether affected individuals may seek protection under the 1951 Convention Relating to the Status of Refugees (Refugees Convention). Most of these have been New Zealand cases and concern 'environmental refugees' from Fiji,[33] Kiribati,[34] and Tuvalu.[35] In *Teitiota v Ministry* the Supreme Court of New Zealand confirmed a series of lower tribunal and court decisions that an applicant from Kiribati was not a refugee under the Refugees

[29] Ibid [699].

[30] (2015) NZHC 1274 [1]; see also *The Outstanding Landscape Protection Society Inc v Hastings District Council* (2007) NZEnvC 87.

[31] (2002) NZEnvC 315.

[32] (2017) NZHC 733 [133].

[33] *BG (Fiji)* (2012) NZIPT 800091.

[34] *Ioane Teitiota v Chief Executive of the Ministry of Business Innovation and Employment* (2015) NZSC 107 (Teitiota case).

[35] *AC (Tuvalu)* (2014) NZIPT 800517–520; *AD (Tuvalu)* (2014) NZIPT 501370–371; *Vaisua* (2014) NZIPT 501465; *AF (Tuvalu)* (2015) NZIPT 800859; *AI (Tuvalu)* (2017) NZIPT 801093; *AJ (Tuvalu)* (2017) NZIPT 801120.

Convention as he would not, if returned, face 'serious harm' and there was no evidence that Kiribati was failing to protect its citizens from climate change.[36] However, the Supreme Court did note that its decision did not rule out the possibility that 'environmental degradation resulting from climate change or other natural disasters could never create a pathway into the Refugees Convention or protected person jurisdiction'.[37]

VI. BARRIERS TO GREATER APPLICATION OF INTERNATIONAL ENVIRONMENTAL LAW IN OCEANIA COURTS

The primary barrier to greater application of IEL in Oceania courts is the incomplete implementation of environmental treaty commitments in domestic law. Absent such incorporation courts in the region are rarely able to apply rules of IEL directly in disputes before them. The main avenue for raising international environmental obligations in Oceania courts therefore remains administrative law proceedings challenging government decisions on environmental matters, where it can often, but not always,[38] be argued that environmental treaties and customary norms of IEL are relevant considerations. The judiciary in Oceania has significant capacity to continue the development of a body of jurisprudence addressing IEL incrementally, on a case by case basis, and this process can be strengthened by greater dialogue and engagement between courts regionally and globally.

BIBLIOGRAPHY

Ben Boer, Ross Ramsay, and Donald Rothwell, *International Environmental Law in the Asia Pacific* (Kluwer 1998)

Jennifer Corrin and Don Paterson, *Introduction to South Pacific Law* (4th edn, Intersentia 2017)

Brian Preston, 'The Role of the Judiciary in Promoting Sustainable Development: The Experience of Asia and the Pacific' *Asia Pacific Journal of Environmental Law*, 9 (2005): 109

[36] Teitiota case (n 34) [12].

[37] Ibid [13].

[38] See eg *West Coast ENT Inc v Buller Coal* (2013) NZSC 87.

CHAPTER 67

SOUTH AMERICA

MARIA ANTONIA TIGRE

I. INTRODUCTION

SOUTH American countries, encompassing Argentina, Bolivia, Brazil, Chile, Colombia, Ecuador, Guyana, Paraguay, Peru, Suriname, Uruguay, and Venezuela, have undergone constitutional reforms in the last four decades, incorporating social and economic rights in their magna carta, including the right to a healthy environment.[1] With environmental parameters enshrined in the Constitution, environmental principles have flourished regionally. These often derive from multilateral environmental agreements (MEAs), which have inspired the proliferation of environmental norms at the national level.

MEAs have had a significant role in shaping domestic law in South America. Nonetheless, the hierarchy of laws, and the role of international law in particular, is traditionally inconsistent, with the changing interpretation within and among countries. For example, Argentina follows a monist theory,[2] while Chile follows a dualist theory,[3]

[1] David Boyd, *The Environmental Rights Revolution: A Global Study of Constitutions, Human Rights, and the Environment* (UBC Press 2012) 124.

[2] Constitución Política de La República Argentina, as amended, art 75 inc 22, 1 de Mayo de 1853; Sara Feldstein de Cárdenas, 'La Jurisprudencia Argentina en Materia de Fuentes del Derecho Internacional Privado: Ante Una Nueva Etapa a Partir del Codigo Civil y Comercial de la Nacion' (The Argentine Jurisprudence in Matters of Sources of Private International Law: Before a New Stage from the Civil and Commercial Code of the Nation) Urbe et Ius (2015) 30.

[3] Constitución Política (n 2) art 5; Diego Alonso Lillo Goffreri and Nelson Rodrigo Pérez Aravena, 'Tratados Internacionales Ambientales: Un Analisis de Eficacia en el Derecho Interno' (International Environmental Treaties: An Analysis of Effectiveness in Internal Law) *Universidad de Chile, Departamento de Derecho Internacional* (January 2012) 22–26.

and Colombia a moderate monism.[4] In most countries, human rights treaties are parallel to constitutional provisions, as part of the 'constitutional block'.[5] However, there is still no general agreement on the relationship between international and national law, even within courts. Brazil's Supremo Tribunal Federal (STF) still disagrees on the weight of treaties within the hierarchy of laws.[6]

Judiciaries in South American countries have undergone radical changes, undertaking new roles due to reforms in the last centuries.[7] Bolivia, Chile, Colombia, Ecuador, and Peru each have an independent national constitutional court, while Argentina, Brazil, and Uruguay each have a supreme court of justice. Brazil and Argentina rely on their supreme courts to decide matters of constitutional law and further legal questions, while countries such as Bolivia, Colombia, and Chile created separate courts exclusively for constitutional cases.[8] Paraguay and Venezuela each have a specialized constitutional chamber.[9] Brazil has both a constitutional and a higher court. The higher court (Superior Tribunal de Justiça (STJ)) is the authority on international law issues, and hears cases in which international and national law clash.

As civil law jurisdictions, South American countries apply laws created by the legislature or executive decree, and have traditionally not included jurisprudence as a source of law.[10] However, this traditional notion has been slowly shifting, and decisions of higher courts are considered binding (Bolivia, Venezuela), followed (Argentina, Brazil, Colombia, Peru), or orienting (Chile, Ecuador, Paraguay, Uruguay).[11] Often, courts hear similar cases repeatedly, sometimes reaching different conclusions. This often hampers the identification of trends and patterns. Due to the high number of courts and cases, this chapter provides an overview of important rulings applying international environmental law (IEL), highlighting, when applicable, general trends.

[4] Constitutional Court of Columbia (2 September 2009) Judgement C-615/09; Julián Huertas-Cárdenas, 'Monismo moderado colombiano: examen a la teoría oficial de la Corte Constitucional desde la obra de Alfred Verdross' (Colombian moderate monism: examination of the official theory of the Constitutional Court since the work of Alfred Verdross) *Vniversitas*, 132 (2016): 197.

[5] See Constituição da República Federativa do Brasil, 5 October 1988, as amended by the Constitutional Amendment No 45/04, 5 de outubre de 1998; *Recurso Extraordinário 349.703-1 Rio Grande do Sul* (12 April 2008) Brazil Supremo Tribunal Federal (Supreme Federal Court).

[6] Recurso Extraordinário case (n 5).

[7] Teresa Miguel-Stearns, 'Judicial Power in Latin America: A Short Survey' *Legal Information Management*, 15/2 (2015): 100.

[8] Ibid.

[9] Manuel Eduardo Góngora Mera, *Inter-American Judicial Constitutionalism: On the Constitutional Rank of Human Right Treaties in Latin America through National and Inter-American Adjudication* (Inter-American Institute of Human Rights 2011) 7.

[10] Miguel-Stearns (n 7) 100.

[11] Antonio Canova González, *El Modelo Iberoamericano de Justicia Constitucional: Característica y Originalidad* (The Ibero-American Model of Constitutional Justice: Characteristics and Originality) (Ediciones Paredes 2012) 140.

II. CASES DIRECTLY APPLYING INTERNATIONAL ENVIRONMENTAL LAW

International law is directly applied by South American courts on a limited scale. In general, treaties are used as the main norm when there is a gap in national law, when an international database such as CITES exists,[12] or when international cooperation is required, such as when transboundary damage occurs.[13] There is a general lack of knowledge about international law, and this is often not highlighted by plaintiffs. If there is a specific national law promoting the same rules, this is directly applied, making it unnecessary to engage international law. Exceptionally, international law is used to advance innovative legal theories.

Courts in Colombia have recently acted as trailblazers, with rulings based on IEL providing innovative views on nature rights and climate change. In 2017, the Constitutional Court recognized the rights of nature, declaring the Atrato River an entity in its own right.[14] To inform this decision, the court invoked international instruments such as the Convention on Biological Diversity (CBD) and the UN Declaration on the Rights of Indigenous People. This approach was demanded by the constitutional precautionary principle.[15] In 2018, the Supreme Court applied this jurisprudence to the protection of the Amazon rainforest.[16] The case was brought by a group of children who argued that their health would be impacted by climate change.[17] The claimants maintained that the government had committed to reduce deforestation through national law and international commitments, and sought a court order requiring the government to prevent deforestation of Amazonia.[18] The Court canvassed international and domestic environmental commitments, and found that authorities had violated domestic and international obligations by failing to combat deforestation.[19] It recognized the Amazon

[12] See *Fallo de la Corte Suprema, N.N. s/ infracción ley 22.421* (23 February 2016) Argentina Corte Suprema de Justicia de la Nación (Supreme Court of Justice of the Nation); *Club de Caza de Tandil s/ infracción ley 22.421 (art 25)* (23 February 2016) (applying the 1973 Convention on International Trade in Endangered Species of Wild Fauna and Flora).

[13] See *Fallo de la Corte Suprema, Papel Prensa S.A. c/ Estado Nacional (Buenos Aires, Provincia de, citada 3°) s/Acción meramente declarative* (3 November 2015) Argentina Corte Suprema de Justicia de la Nación (applying the 1989 Basel Convention on the Control of Transboundary Movements of Hazardous Wastes and Their Disposal).

[14] Constitutional Court of Colombia (10 November 2016) Judgement T-622/16 [2.1], [5.9].

[15] Ibid [7.35]–[7.41].

[16] Supreme Court of Colombia (5 April 2018) STC4360-2018, radcación no 11001-22-03-000-2018-00319-01.

[17] Ibid [2.1].

[18] Ibid [2.2] The claimants specifically cited the 2015 Paris Agreement, as incorporated into Colombian law.

[19] Ibid, 22–25; 35–39.

rainforest as an entity in its own right, 'a holder of rights to protection, conservation, maintenance and restoration'.[20]

III. CASES INDIRECTLY APPLYING INTERNATIONAL ENVIRONMENTAL LAW

More often, IEL is indirectly applied by courts to strenghten specific arguments. Several cases reference the Stockholm and Rio principles.[21] In a case concerning the burning of sugarcane straw in Brazil, the Rio principles, in particular the precautionary principle, reinforced caution in preventing environmental degradation, even when there was no scientific data to prove environmental damage.[22] The decision also recalled the commitments made by Brazil as a signatory of the United Nations Framework Convention on Climate Change.

International law is often cited as a guiding norm in rulings particularly applying the precautionary principle, since it substantiates decisions that have limited backing in national laws. These include the International Convention on Civil Liability for Oil Pollution Damage, the Vienna Convention for the Protection of the Ozone Layer, and the Montreal Protocol. Brazil has a few notable cases, including a ruling by the federal court concerning the use of methyl bromide, a substance with high atmospheric persistence and harmful to the ozone layer.[23] The judge in that case emphasized that the conflict should be resolved in a precautionary manner, based on international commitments such as the Vienna Convention for the Protection of the Ozone Layer and the Montreal Protocol. There is interesting case law in Chilean courts[24] related to protected areas and natural parks.[25] In a notable case involving an oil spill in Mejilloes

[20] Ibid, 45.

[21] UN, 'Report of the United Nations Conference on the Human Environment' (5–16 June 1972) UN Doc A/CONF.48/14/Rev.1, 3, ch 1—'Declaration of the United Nations Conference on the Human Environment'; *Report of the United Nations Conference on Environment and Development* (UN 1993) vol I, annex I—'Rio Declaration on Environment and Development'.

[22] Brazil Supreme Tribunal de Justiça (Superior Court of Justice) REsp 1.285.463 SP/2011/ 0190433-2(f) (28 February 2012); see also Supreme Tribunal de Justiça, CC 124.356 PR 2012/0187772-7 (10 October 2012) (referencing the Basel Convention and their Deposit); Supreme Tribunal de Justica, REsp 840.918 DF 2006/008611-1 (14 October 2008) (referencing the 1972 Convention Concerning the Protection of World Cultural and Natural Heritage).

[23] *Agência Nacional de Vigilância Sanitária v Nikkey Descupinização Dedetização Com de Produtos Químicos Ltda* (31 January 2007) Apelação Cível n.° 2000.61.00.010798-1, Brazil Tribunal Regional Federal (3ª Região) (Regional Federal Court of the 3rd Region).

[24] Chile Sentencia de la Corte de Apelaciones de Puerto Montt (16 August 1999), confirmada por la Corte Suprema (directly applying the CBD).

[25] Chile Fallo de la Corte Suprema, de fecha en recurso de protección caratulado, Rol N° 19.824-1985, 'Palza Corvacho, Humberto con Director de Riego de la Primera Región y otros' (19 December 1985); Chile Fallo de la Corte Suprema, de fecha recurso de protección, Rol N° 6.397-2008, 'contra la COREMA

Bay, the International Convention on Civil Liability for Oil Pollution Damage was directly applied.[26]

IV. CHALLENGES/BARRIERS FOR THE GREATER APPLICATION OF INTERNATIONAL ENVIRONMENTAL LAW IN NATIONAL COURTS

In theory, the majority of South American courts consider treaties to have the same value as domestic laws, with limited cases regarding them as mere recommendations. Nonetheless, treaties are still applied on a limited scale, reducing their practical value. For example, instead of applying general norms of environmental preservation, cases are brought based on property values. A study on the application of international environmental principles in judicial arguments and decisions at the highest Latin American national courts showed that despite wide support for MEAs at the diplomatic level, countries still find barriers to translating these obligations nationally.[27]

In Chile, even when judges refer to treaties, they fail to include these in the reasoning.[28] International norms are often disregarded, even when they have been incorporated into the national system.[29] This mostly occurs when international rules conflict with domestic norms.

Often treaties are ratified at the international level, but it takes years, sometimes decades, to properly integrate them at the national level.[30] Consequently, there is a lack of knowledge about commitments assumed by countries and treaty objectives.[31] Because of the perceived ineffectiveness of the judiciary, litigation can be discouraged.

de la Región de Los Lagos' (8 January 2009); Chile Fallo de la Corte Suprema, recurso de protección, Rol N° 2.262-2011, 'Municipalidad de Putre con COREMA de Arica y Parinacota' (16 June 2011); Chile Fallo de la Corte Suprema, recourse de protección, Rol N° 10.220-2011, 'Antonio Horvath Kiss y otros con Comisión de Evaluación Ambiental de la Región de Aysén' (4 April 2012, applying the 1933 Convention Relative to the Preservation of Fauna and Flora in their Natural State.

26 Chile Sentencia Corte Suprema, Considerando Decimo, Rol N°14.209-2013, 'Estado-Fisco de Chile con Minimal Enterprises Company' (2 June 2014).

27 Virginia Torresan Sanfelice *et al*, 'The Application of International Environmental Law Principles in Latin America. Compilation of a database of superior courts case-law, and initial findings' (2016) <https://ssrn.com/abstract=2746804> accessed 15 December 2018.

28 Goffreri and Aravena (n 4) 38–39.

29 Ibid, 5.

30 Rodrigo d'Araujo Gabsch, *Aprovação Interna de Tratados Internacionais pelo Brasil, Possíveis Opções para Acelerar seu Processo* (Internal Approval of International Treaties by Brazil, Possible Options to Speed Up Its Process) (Ministério das Relações Exteriores 2010).

31 Brazil, Supremo Tribunal Federal Med. Caut. em Arguição de Descumprimento de Preceito Fundamental 172-2 RJ, Ellen Gracie (10 June 2009).

International law, in particular, is rarely used as a source of law, and parties rely heavily on domestic law as a result.[32] Another challenge is the dismissal of suits on formal grounds, before environmental principles can be fully voiced in court and their merits analysed.[33] Finally, implementation of court decisions can be a challenge, rendering decisions pointless.[34]

V. ASSESSMENT

Courts in South America have applied IEL on a limited scale. MEAs are usually cited in higher courts to reinforce environmental principles or general norms already incorporated in national law. Whenever applicable, national law is preferred, reducing reliance on international law. Treaties are more likely used as an additional argument to advance theories with lower acceptance at the national level. For example, MEAs are often cited when decisions apply the precautionary principle and favour environmental protection in the absence of scientific certainty about environmental damage. More recently, international law has also been cited in pushing forward innovative theories without national legal support, such as the rights of nature. The recent decisions in Colombia have shifted the paradigm, as these directly use international law to justify environmental protection on a broader level. In light of the growth of climate cases filed in national courts, it is likely that international law will be directly applied in other national courts as well, as has happened in Colombia.

BIBLIOGRAPHY

David Boyd, *The Environmental Rights Revolution: A Global Study of Constitutions, Human Rights, and the Environment* (UBC Press 2012)

Maria Antonia Tigre, *Regional Cooperation in Amazonia: A Comparative Environmental Law Analysis* (Brill 2017)

Virginia Torresan Sanfelice *et al*, 'The Application of International Environmental Law Principles in Latin America: Compilation of a database of superior courts case-law, and initial findings' (2016) <https://ssrn.com/abstract=2746804> accessed 15 December 2018

32 Goffreri and Aravena (n 4) 36.

33 Sanfelice *et al* (n 27) 8.

34 See Maria Antonia Tigre, 'Environment Law of Ecuador' in Elizabeth Burleson *et al* (eds), *Comparative Environmental Law and Regulation* vol 1 (West Law 2013) ch 18A; Maria Antonia Tigre, 'Implementing Constitutional Environmental Rights in the Amazon Rainforest' in Erin Daly and Jim May (eds), *Implementing Environmental Constitutionalism: Current Global Challenges* (CUP 2018) ch 3.

Index

Tables are indicated by *t* following the page number

D

U